Pro ASP.NET 4 in C# 2010

Fourth Edition

Matthew MacDonald, Adam Freeman,
and Mario Szpuszta

Apress®

Pro ASP.NET in C# 2010, Fourth Edition

ISBN-13 (pbk): 978-1-4302-2529-4

ISBN-13 (electronic): 978-1-4302-2530-0

Printed and bound in the United States of America 9 8 7 6 5 4

President and Publisher: Paul Manning
Lead Editor: Ewan Buckingham
Technical Reviewer: Fabio Claudio Ferracchiati and Todd Meister
Editorial Board: Steve Anglin, Ewan Buckingham, Gary Cornell, Louise Corrigan, Morgan Ertel, Jonathan Gennick, Jonathan Hassell, Robert Hutchinson, Michelle Lowman, James Markham, Matthew Moodie, Jeff Olson, Jeffrey Pepper, Douglas Pundick, Ben Renow-Clarke, Dominic Shakeshaft, Gwenan Spearing, Matt Wade, Tom Welsh
Coordinating Editor: Anne Collett
Copy Editor: Ralph Moore, Katie Stence, Kim Wimpsett
Compositor: Mary Sudul
Indexer: BIM Indexing & Proofreading Services
Artist: April Milne
Cover Designer: Anna Ishchenko

Distributed to the book trade worldwide by Springer Science+Business Media New York, 233 Spring Street, 6th Floor, New York, NY 10013. Phone 1-800-SPRINGER, fax (201) 348-4505, e-mail `orders-ny@springer-sbm.com`, or visit `www.springeronline.com`.

For information on translations, please e-mail `rights@apress.com`, or visit `www.apress.com`.

Apress and friends of ED books may be purchased in bulk for academic, corporate, or promotional use. eBook versions and licenses are also available for most titles. For more information, reference our Special Bulk Sales–eBook Licensing web page at `www.apress.com/bulk-sales`.

Any source code or other supplementary materials referenced by the author in this text is available to readers at `www.apress.com`. For detailed information about how to locate your book's source code, go to `www.apress.com/source-code/`.

Contents at a Glance

Contents

About the Authors

Matthew MacDonald is an author, educator, and Microsoft MVP. He's the author of more than a dozen books about .NET programming, including *Pro Silverlight 3 in C#* (Apress, 2009), *Pro WPF in C# 2010* (Apress, 2010), and *Beginning ASP.NET 4 in C# 2010* (Apress, 2010). He lives in Toronto with his wife and two daughters.

Adam Freeman is an experienced IT professional who has held senior positions in a range of companies, most recently chief technology officer and chief operating officer of a global bank. He has written several of books on Java and .NET and has a long-term interest in all things parallel.

Mario Szpuszta works as an architect in the Developer and Platform group of Microsoft Austria and helps software architects of top enterprise and web customers with establishing new Microsoft technologies. For several years he has been focusing on secure software development, web services and interoperability, and the integration of Microsoft Office clients and servers in custom applications. Mario speaks regularly at local and international conferences such as DevDays and TechEd Europe Developers, and he has been a technical content owner of TechEd Europe Developers in the past two years.

About the Technical Reviewers

■ **Fabio Claudio Ferracchiati** is a prolific writer on cutting-edge technologies. Fabio has contributed to more than a dozen books on .NET, C#, Visual Basic, and ASP.NET. He is a .NET Microsoft Certified Solution Developer (MCSD) and lives in Rome, Italy. You can read his blog at `http://www.ferracchiati.com`.

■ **Todd Meister** has been using Microsoft technologies for more than ten years. He's been a technical editor on more than 50 books on topics ranging from SQL Server to the .NET Framework. Besides technical editing, he is an assistant director for computing services at Ball State University in Muncie, Indiana. He lives in central Indiana with his wife, Kimberly, and their four outstanding children.

Introduction

When .NET first appeared, it introduced a small avalanche of new technologies. There was a whole new way to write web applications (ASP.NET), a whole new way to connect to databases (ADO.NET), new typesafe languages (C# and VB .NET), and a managed runtime (the CLR). Not least among these new technologies was Windows Forms, a library of classes for building Windows applications.

As you no doubt already know, ASP.NET is Microsoft's next-generation technology for creating server-side web applications. It's built on the Microsoft .NET Framework, which is a cluster of closely related technologies that revolutionize everything from database access to distributed applications. ASP.NET is one of the most important components of the .NET Framework—it's the part that enables you to develop high-performance web applications.

It's not hard to get developers interested in ASP.NET. Without exaggeration, ASP.NET is the most complete platform for web development that's ever been put together. It far outclasses its predecessor, ASP, which was designed as a quick-and-dirty set of tools for inserting dynamic content into ordinary web pages. By contrast, ASP.NET is a full-blown platform for developing comprehensive, blisteringly fast *web applications*.

In this book, you'll learn everything you need to master ASP.NET 4. If you've programmed with a previous version of ASP.NET, you can focus on new features such as ASP.NET MVC (Chapter 32), ASP.NET Dynamic Data (Chapter 33), and Silverlight (Chapter 34). If you've never programmed with ASP.NET, you'll find that this book provides a well-paced tour that leads you through all the fundamentals, along with a backstage pass that lets you see how the ASP.NET internals *really* work. The only requirement for this book is that you have a solid understanding of the C# language and the basics of .NET. If you're a seasoned Java or C++ developer but you're new to C#, you may find it easier to start with a book about .NET fundamentals, such as *Pro C# 2010 and the .NET 4 Platform* by Andrew Troelsen (Apress, 2010).

What Does This Book Cover?

Here is a quick breakdown of what you'll find in this book:

Part 1: Core Concepts: You'll begin in Chapter 1 with a look at the overall ASP.NET platform, the .NET Framework, and an overview of the changes that have taken place in ASP.NET 4. In Chapter 2 you'll branch out to learn the tools of the trade—namely, Visual Studio 2008. In Chapters 3, 4, 5, and 6 you'll learn the key parts of the ASP.NET infrastructure, such as the web-page model, application configuration, and state management. As you learn these core concepts, you'll also take a low-level look at how ASP.NET processes requests and manages the lifetime of your web applications. You'll even learn how to extend the ASP.NET architecture.

Part 2: Data Access: This part tackles one of the core problem domains for all software development—accessing and manipulating data. In Chapters 7 and 8 you'll consider the fundamentals of ADO.NET as they apply to web applications and learn how to design data access components. In Chapters 9 and 10 you'll learn about ASP.NET's set of innovative data-bound controls that let you format and present data without writing pages of code. Chapter 11 branches out into advanced caching strategies that ensure first-class performance. Finally, Chapters 12, 13, and 14 move beyond the world of ADO.NET to show you how to work with files, LINQ, and XML content.

Part 3: Building ASP.NET Websites: In this part you'll learn about essential techniques and features for managing groups of web pages. You'll start simply with user controls in Chapter 15, which allow you to reuse segments of the user interface. In Chapter 16 you'll consider themes (for styling controls automatically) and master pages (for reusing a layout template across multiple pages). Chapter 17 shows how you can use ASP.NET's navigation model to let visitors surf from one page to another. Finally, Chapter 18 describes deployment and the IIS web server software.

Part 4: Security: In this part, you'll look at ASP.NET's rich complement of security features. You'll start with a high-level overview of security concepts in Chapter 19 and then learn the ins and outs of forms authentication (Chapter 20) and the membership feature that works with it (Chapter 21). In Chapter 22 you'll tackle Windows authentication, and in Chapter 23 you'll learn how to restrict authenticated users with sophisticated authorization rules and use role-based security. In Chapter 24 you'll explore the profiles feature—a prebuilt solution for storing user-specific information; in Chapter 25 you'll go one step further and learn how to protect the data you store in a database as well as the information you send in a URL with encryption. Finally, Chapter 26 shows how you can plug into the ASP.NET security model by designing a custom membership provider.

Part 5: Advanced User Interface: This part shows how you can extend web pages with advanced techniques. In Chapters 27 you'll get an introduction to custom controls. In Chapter 28 you'll branch out to use GDI+ for handcrafted graphics. In Chapters 29 and 30, you'll consider how to use JavaScript and Ajax techniques to make web pages more dynamic (by incorporating effects such as text autocompletion and drag-and-drop) and more responsive (by reacting to client-side events and seamlessly refreshing the web page). Finally, Chapter 31 explores ASP.NET's Web Parts feature, which allows you to easily create web portals.

Part 6: New Directions: In this part, you'll consider some of the most exciting innovations in modern web development. In Chapter 32 you'll explore ASP.NET MVC, a new alternative to the classic web forms model that gives developers complete control over HTML rendering and URL structure. In Chapter 33 you'll consider ASP.NET Dynamic Data, which is the perfect solution for quickly building applications that revolve around viewing and editing the information in a database. Finally, in Chapter 34 you'll dive into the world of Silverlight, a Microsoft-built browser plug-in that gives you the ability to bring rich graphics, animation, sound, and video to ordinary web pages on a variety of browsers and operating systems.

Who Is This Book For?

This book is intended as a primer for professional developers who have a reasonable knowledge of server-side web development. This book doesn't provide an exhaustive look at every ingredient in the .NET Framework—in fact, such a book would require twice as many pages. Instead, this book aims to provide an intelligent introduction to ASP.NET for professional programmers who don't want to rehash the basics. Along the way, you'll focus on other corners of the .NET Framework that you'll need in order to build professional web applications, including data access and XML. Using these features, you'll be able to create next-generation websites with the best tools on hand today.

This book is also relentlessly practical. You won't learn just about *features*; you'll also learn about the real-world *techniques* that can take your website to the next level. Later chapters are dedicated to cutting-edge topics such as custom controls, dynamic graphics, advanced security, and high-performance data access, all with the goal of giving you everything you need to build professional web applications.

To get the most from this book, you should be familiar with the syntax of the C# language and with object-oriented concepts. You don't need to have experience with a previous version of ASP.NET, because all the fundamentals are covered in this book. If you're an experienced Java or C++ developer with no .NET experience, you should consider supplementing this book with an introduction to .NET, such as *Pro C# 2010 and the .NET 4 Platform* by Andrew Troelsen (Apress, 2010).

What Do You Need to Use This Book?

To develop and test ASP.NET web applications, you need Visual Studio 2010. Although you could theoretically write code by hand, the sheer tedium and the likelihood of error mean this approach is never used in a professional environment. Additionally, if you plan to host ASP.NET websites, you'll need to use a server-based version of Windows, such as Windows Server 2003 or Windows Server 2008. You'll also need to install IIS (Internet Information Services), the web hosting software that's part of the Windows operating system. IIS is described in Chapter 18.

This book includes several examples that use sample databases that are included with SQL Server to demonstrate data access code, security techniques, and other features. You can use any version of SQL Server to try these examples, including SQL Server Express, which is included with some versions of Visual Studio (and freely downloadable at `http://www.microsoft.com/express/database`). If you use other relational database engines, the same concepts will apply, but you will need to modify the example code.

Customer Support

We always value hearing from our readers, and we want to know what you think about this book—what you liked, what you didn't like, and what you think we can do better next time. You can send your comments by e-mail to `feedback@apress.com`. Please be sure to mention the book title in your message.

Sample Code

To download the sample code, visit the Apress website at `http://www.apress.com`, and search for this book. You can then download the sample code, which is compressed into a single ZIP file. Before you use the code, you'll need to uncompress it using a utility such as WinZip. Code is arranged into separate directories by chapter. Before using the code, refer to the accompanying readme.txt file for information about other prerequisites and considerations.

Bonus Chapters

The Apress website also includes several additional chapters that you can download as PDFs. These chapters include content that couldn't be included in this book because of space limitations and isn't considered as important to ASP.NET web development. Here's what you'll find:

Bonus Chapter 1, "Resources and Localization": This chapter describes how to use resources and localization in ASP.NET websites. It's an essential chapter for developers who need to create websites that can be viewed in multiple languages.

Bonus Chapter 2, "Design-Time Support": This chapter describes how to add design-time support to your own custom controls so that they behave nicely in the Visual Studio environment, take charge of their own property serialization, and support advanced designer features such as smart tags.

■ **Note** The bonus chapters are reprinted from the previous edition of this book. The information in these chapters still applies to ASP.NET 4, because these features haven't changed.

Errata

We've made every effort to make sure the text and the code contain no errors. However, no one is perfect, and therefore mistakes do occur. If you find an error in the book, such as a spelling mistake or a faulty piece of code, we would be grateful to hear about it. By sending in errata, you may save another reader hours of frustration, and you'll be helping us provide higher-quality information. Simply e-mail the problem to `support@apress.com`, where your information will be checked and posted on the errata page or used in subsequent editions of the book. You can view errata from the book's detail page.

PART 1

Core Concepts

Before you can code an ASP.NET website, you need to master a small set of fundamental skills. In this part, you'll consider the .NET Framework, which supports every .NET application (Chapter 1), the Visual Studio design tool that helps you build and test websites (Chapter 2), and the ASP.NET infrastructure that makes websites work (Chapters 3, 4, 5, and 6).

Although these topics may seem like straightforward review for a professional ASP.NET developer, there are some critically important finer points. Every serious ASP.NET developer needs to thoroughly understand details such as the life cycle of web pages and web applications, the ASP.NET request processing pipeline, state management, and the ASP.NET configuration model. Not only is this understanding a key requirement for creating high-performance web applications, it's also a necessary skill if you want to extend the ASP.NET infrastructure—a topic you'll consider throughout the chapters in this part.

CHAPTER 1

■ ■ ■

Introducing ASP.NET

When the first version of the .NET Framework was released nearly a decade ago, it was the start of a radical new direction in software design. Inspired by the best of Java, COM, and the Web, and informed by the mistakes and limitations of previous technologies, Microsoft set out to "hit the reset button" on their development platform. The result was a set of surprisingly mature technologies that developers could use to do everything from building a Windows application to executing a database query, and a web-site-building tool known as ASP.NET.

Today, ASP.NET is as popular as ever, but it's no longer quite as revolutionary. And, although the basic functionality that sits at the heart of ASP.NET is—suprisingly—virtually the same as it was ten years ago, Microsoft has added layers of new features and higher-level coding abstractions. It has also introduced at least one new direction that competes with traditional ASP.NET programming, which is called ASP.NET MVC.

In this introduction, you'll get a quick outline of the fundamentals of the ASP.NET platform and an overview that explains how it has evolved into version 4. If you're new to ASP.NET, this chapter will quickly get you up to speed. On the other hand, if you're a seasoned .NET developer, you have two choices. Your first option is to read this chapter for a brisk review of where we are today. Alternatively, you can skip to the section "The Evolution of ASP.NET" to preview what ASP.NET 4 has in store.

The Seven Pillars of ASP.NET

When ASP.NET was first released, there were seven key facts that differentiated it from previous Microsoft products and competing platforms. If you're coming to ASP.NET from another web development platform, or you're an old-hand .NET coder who has yet to try programming for the Web, these sections will quickly give you a bit of ASP.NET insight.

#1: ASP.NET Is Integrated with the .NET Framework

The .NET Framework is divided into an almost painstaking collection of functional parts, with tens of thousands of *types* (the .NET term for classes, structures, interfaces, and other core programming ingredients). Before you can program any sort of .NET application, you need a basic understanding of those parts—and an understanding of why things are organized the way they are.

The massive collection of functionality that the .NET Framework provides is organized in a way that traditional Windows programmers will see as a happy improvement. Each one of the thousands of classes in the .NET Framework is grouped into a logical, hierarchical container called a *namespace*. Different namespaces provide different features. Taken together, the .NET namespaces offer functionality for nearly every aspect of distributed development from message queuing to security. This massive toolkit is called the *class library*.

Interestingly, the way you use the .NET Framework classes in ASP.NET is the same as the way you use them in any other type of .NET application (including a stand-alone Windows application, a Windows service, a command-line utility, and so on). Although there are Windows-specific and web-specific classes for building user interfaces, the vast majority of the .NET Framework (including everything from database access to multithreaded programming) is usable in any type of application. In other words, .NET gives the same tools to web developers that it gives to rich client developers.

■ **Tip** One of the best resources for learning about new corners of the .NET Framework is the .NET Framework class library reference, which is part of the MSDN Help library reference. If you have Visual Studio 2008 installed, you can view the MSDN Help library by clicking the Start button and choosing Programs ➤ Microsoft Visual Studio 2010 ➤ Microsoft Visual Studio 2010 Documentation (the exact shortcut depends on your version of Visual Studio). Or, you can find the most recent version of the class library reference online at http://tinyurl.com/2d42w5e.

#2: ASP.NET Is Compiled, Not Interpreted

ASP.NET applications, like all .NET applications, are always compiled. In fact, it's impossible to execute C# or Visual Basic code without it being compiled first.

.NET applications actually go through two stages of compilation. In the first stage, the C# code you write is compiled into an intermediate language called Microsoft Intermediate Language (MSIL), or just IL. This first step is the fundamental reason that .NET can be language-interdependent. Essentially, all .NET languages (including C#, Visual Basic, and many more) are compiled into virtually identical IL code. This first compilation step may happen automatically when the page is first requested, or you can perform it in advance (a process known as *precompiling*). The compiled file with IL code is an *assembly*.

The second level of compilation happens just before the page is actually executed. At this point, the IL code is compiled into low-level native machine code. This stage is known as *just-in-time* (JIT) compilation, and it takes place in the same way for all .NET applications (including Windows applications, for example). Figure 1-1 shows this two-step compilation process.

.NET compilation is decoupled into two steps in order to offer developers the most convenience and the best portability. Before a compiler can create low-level machine code, it needs to know what type of operating system and hardware platform the application will run on (for example, 32-bit or 64-bit Windows). By having two compile stages, you can create a compiled assembly with .NET code and still distribute this to more than one platform.

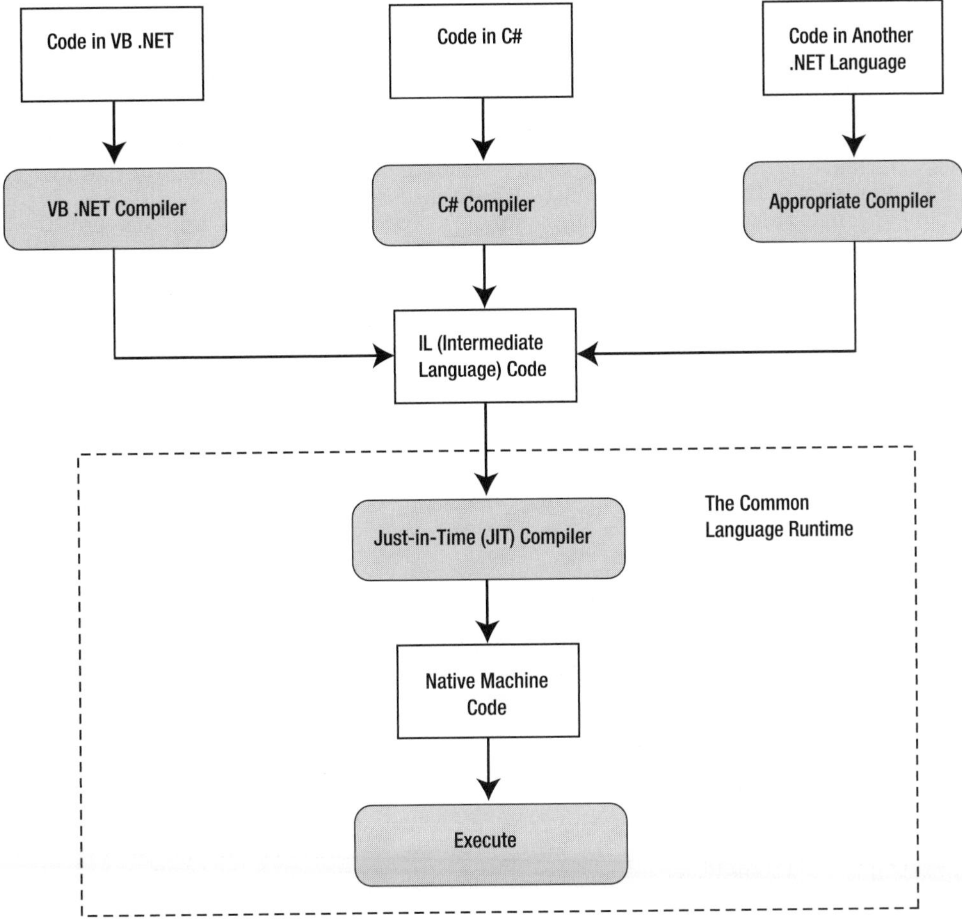

***Figure 1-1.** Compilation in an ASP.NET web page*

Of course, JIT compilation probably wouldn't be that useful if it needed to be performed every time a user requested a web page from your site. Fortunately, ASP.NET applications don't need to be compiled every time a web page is requested. Instead, the IL code is created once and regenerated only when the source is modified. Similarly, the native machine code files are cached in a system directory that has a path like c:\Windows\Microsoft.NET\Framework\[Version]\Temporary ASP.NET Files.

As you'll learn in Chapter 2, the actual point where your code is compiled to IL depends on how you're creating and deploying your web application. If you're building a web project in Visual Studio, the code is compiled to IL when you compile your project. But if you're building a lighter-weight projectless website, the code for each page is compiled the first time you request that page. Either way, the code goes through its second compilation step (from IL to machine code) the first time it's executed.

ASP.NET also includes precompilation tools that you can use to compile your application right down to machine code once you've deployed it to the production web server. This allows you to avoid the overhead of first-time compilation when you deploy a finished application (and prevent other people from tampering with your code). Precompilation is described in Chapter 18.

#3: ASP.NET Is Multilanguage

Though you'll probably opt to use one language over another when you develop an application, that choice won't determine what you can accomplish with your web applications. That's because no matter what language you use, the code is compiled into IL.

IL is a stepping stone for every managed application. (A *managed application* is any application that's written for .NET and executes inside the managed environment of the CLR.) In a sense, IL is the language of .NET, and it's the only language that the CLR recognizes.

To understand IL, it helps to consider a simple example. Take a look at this code written in C#:

```
using System;

namespace HelloWorld
{
    public class TestClass
    {
        static void Main(string[] args)
        {
            Console.WriteLine("Hello World");
        }
    }
}
```

This code shows the most basic application that's possible in .NET—a simple command-line utility that displays a single, predictable message on the console window.

Now look at it from a different perspective. Here's the IL code for the Main() method:

```
.method private hidebysig static void  Main(string[] args) cil managed
{
    .entrypoint
    // Code size       13 (0xd)
    .maxstack  8
    IL_0000:  nop
    IL_0001:  ldstr      "Hello World"
    IL_0006:  call       void [mscorlib]System.Console::WriteLine(string)
    IL_000b:  nop
    IL_000c:  ret
} // end of method TestClass::Main
```

It's easy enough to look at the IL for any compiled .NET application. You simply need to run the IL Disassembler, which is installed with Visual Studio and the .NET SDK (software development kit). Look for the file ildasm.exe in a directory like c:\Program Files\Microsoft SDKs\Windows\v7.0A\bin. Run ildasm.exe, and then use the File ➤ Open command, and select any DLL or EXE that was created with .NET.

■ **Tip** For even more disassembling power, check out the remarkable (and free) Reflector tool at `http://www.red-gate.com/products/reflector`. With the help of community-created add-ins, you can use Reflector to diagram, analyze, and decompile the IL code in any assembly.

If you're patient and a little logical, you can deconstruct the IL code fairly easily and figure out what's happening. The fact that IL is so easy to disassemble can raise privacy and code control issues, but these issues usually aren't of any concern to ASP.NET developers. That's because all ASP.NET code is stored and executed on the server. Because the client never receives the compiled code file, the client has no opportunity to decompile it. If it *is* a concern, consider using an obfuscator that scrambles code to try to make it more difficult to understand. (For example, an obfuscator might rename all variables to have generic, meaningless names such as f__a__234.) Visual Studio includes a scaled-down version of one popular obfuscator, called Dotfuscator.

The following code shows the same console application in Visual Basic code:

```
Imports System

Namespace HelloWorld
    Public Class TestClass
        Shared Sub Main(args() As String)
            Console.WriteLine("Hello World")
        End Sub
    End Class
End Namespace
```

If you compile this application and look at the IL code, you'll find that it's nearly identical to the IL code generated from the C# version. Although different compilers can sometimes introduce their own optimizations, as a general rule of thumb no .NET language outperforms any other .NET language, because they all share the same common infrastructure. This infrastructure is formalized in the CLS (Common Language Specification), which is described in the following sidebar, entitled "The Common Language Specification."

It's worth noting that IL has been adopted as an Ecma and ISO standard. This adoption allows the adoption of other common language frameworks on other platforms. The Mono project at `http://www.mono-project.com` is the best example of such a project.

The Common Language Specification

The CLR expects all objects to adhere to a specific set of rules so that they can interact. The CLS is this set of rules.

The CLS defines many laws that all languages must follow, such as primitive types, method overloading, and so on. Any compiler that generates IL code to be executed in the CLR must adhere to all rules governed within the CLS. The CLS gives developers, vendors, and software manufacturers the opportunity to work within a common set of specifications for languages, compilers, and data types. You can find a list of a large number of CLS-compliant languages at `http://dotnetpowered.com/languages.aspx`.

Given these criteria, the creation of a language compiler that generates true CLR-compliant code can be complex. Nevertheless, compilers can exist for virtually any language, and chances are that there may eventually be one for just about every language you'd ever want to use. Imagine—mainframe programmers who loved COBOL in its heyday can now use their knowledge base to create web applications!

#4: ASP.NET Is Hosted by the Common Language Runtime

Perhaps the most important aspect of the ASP.NET engine is that it runs inside the runtime environment of the CLR. The whole of the .NET Framework—that is, all namespaces, applications, and classes—is referred to as *managed* code. Though a full-blown investigation of the CLR is beyond the scope of this chapter, some of the benefits are as follows:

Automatic memory management and garbage collection: Every time your application instantiates a reference-type object, the CLR allocates space on the managed heap for that object. However, you never need to clear this memory manually. As soon as your reference to an object goes out of scope (or your application ends), the object becomes available for garbage collection. The garbage collector runs periodically inside the CLR, automatically reclaiming unused memory for inaccessible objects. This model saves you from the low-level complexities of C++ memory handling and from the quirkiness of COM reference counting.

Type safety: When you compile an application, .NET adds information to your assembly that indicates details such as the available classes, their members, their data types, and so on. As a result, other applications can use them without requiring additional support files, and the compiler can verify that every call is valid at runtime. This extra layer of safety completely obliterates whole categories of low-level errors.

Extensible metadata: The information about classes and members is only one of the types of metadata that .NET stores in a compiled assembly. *Metadata* describes your code and allows you to provide additional information to the runtime or other services. For example, this metadata might tell a debugger how to trace your code, or it might tell Visual Studio how to display a custom control at design time. You could also use metadata to enable other runtime services, such as transactions or object pooling.

Structured error handling: .NET languages offer structured exception handling, which allows you to organize your error-handling code logically and concisely. You can create separate blocks to deal with different types of errors. You can also nest exception handlers multiple layers deep.

Multithreading: The CLR provides a pool of threads that various classes can use. For example, you can call methods, read files, or communicate with web services asynchronously, without needing to explicitly create new threads.

Figure 1-2 shows a high-level look at the CLR and the .NET Framework.

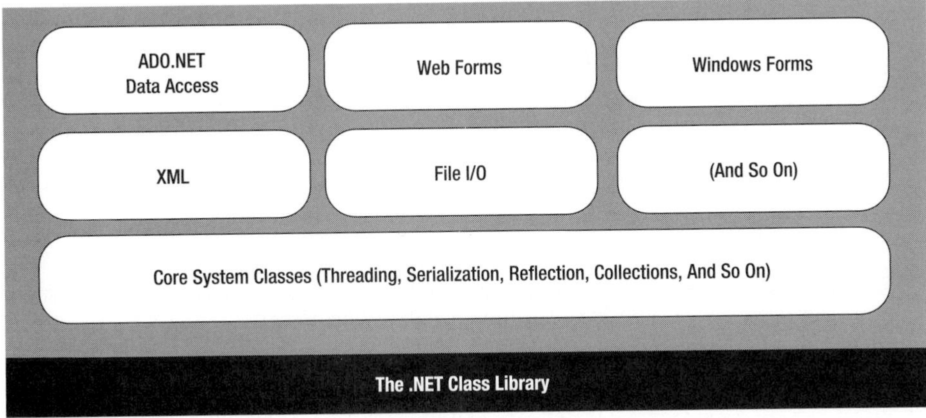

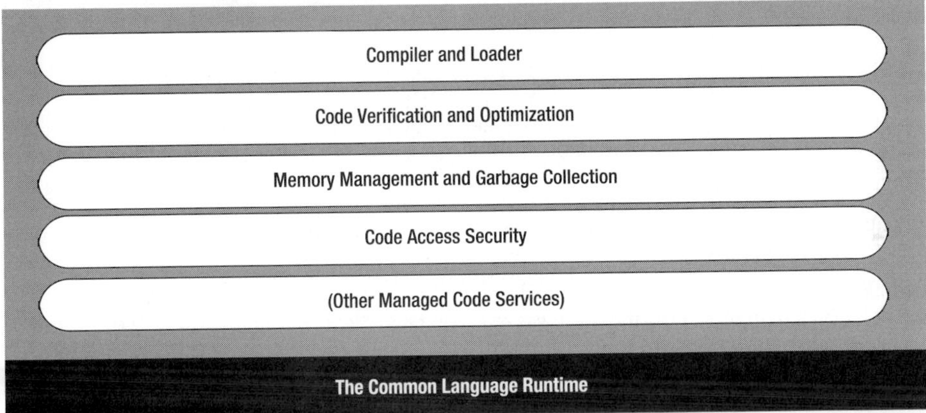

Figure 1-2. *The CLR and the .NET Framework*

#5: ASP.NET Is Object-Oriented

ASP provides a relatively feeble object model. It provides a small set of objects; these objects are really just a thin layer over the raw details of HTTP and HTML. On the other hand, ASP.NET is truly object-oriented. Not only does your code have full access to all objects in the .NET Framework, but you can also exploit all the conventions of an OOP (object-oriented programming) environment. For example, you can create reusable classes, standardize code with interfaces, extend existing classes with inheritance, and bundle useful functionality in a distributable, compiled component.

One of the best examples of object-oriented thinking in ASP.NET is found in server-based controls. Server-based controls are the epitome of encapsulation. Developers can manipulate control objects programmatically using code to customize their appearance, provide data to display, and even react to events. The low-level HTML markup that these controls render is hidden away behind the scenes. Instead of forcing the developer to write raw HTML manually, the control objects render themselves to HTML just before the web server sends the page to the client. In this way, ASP.NET offers server controls as a way to abstract the low-level details of HTML and HTTP programming.

Here's a quick example with a standard HTML text box that you can define in an ASP.NET web page:

```
<input type="text" id="myText" runat="server" />
```

With the addition of the runat="server" attribute, this static piece of HTML becomes a fully functional server-side control that you can manipulate in C# code. You can now work with events that it generates, set attributes, and bind it to a data source.

For example, you can set the text of this box when the page first loads using the following C# code:

```
void Page_Load(object sender, EventArgs e)
{
    myText.Value = "Hello World!";
}
```

Technically, this code sets the Value property of an HtmlInputText object. The end result is that a string of text appears in a text box on the HTML page that's rendered and sent to the client.

HTML Controls VS. Web Controls

When ASP.NET was first created, two schools of thought existed. Some ASP.NET developers were most interested in server-side controls that matched the existing set of HTML controls exactly. This approach allows you to create ASP.NET web-page interfaces in dedicated HTML editors, and it provides a quick migration path for existing ASP pages. However, another set of ASP.NET developers saw the promise of something more—rich server-side controls that didn't just emulate individual HTML tags. These controls might render their interface from dozens of distinct HTML elements while still providing a simple object-based interface to the programmer. Using this model, developers could work with programmable menus, calendars, data lists, validators, and so on.

After some deliberation, Microsoft decided to provide both models. You've already seen an example of HTML server controls, which map directly to the basic set of HTML tags. Along with these are ASP.NET web controls, which provide a higher level of abstraction and more functionality. In most cases, you'll use HTML server-side controls for backward compatibility and quick migration, and use web controls for new projects.

ASP.NET web control tags always start with the prefix *asp:* followed by the class name. For example, the following snippet creates a text box and a check box:

```
<asp:TextBox id="myASPText" Text="Hello ASP.NET TextBox" runat="server" />
<asp:CheckBox id="myASPCheck" Text="My CheckBox" runat="server" />
```

Again, you can interact with these controls in your code, as follows:

```
myASPText.Text = "New text";
myASPCheck.Text = "Check me!";
```

Notice that the Value property you saw with the HTML control has been replaced with a Text property. The HtmlInputText.Value property was named to match the underlying value attribute in the HTML <input> tag. However, web controls don't place the same emphasis on correlating with HTML syntax, so the more descriptive property name Text is used instead.

The ASP.NET family of web controls includes complex rendered controls (such as the Calendar and TreeView), along with more streamlined controls (such as TextBox, Label, and Button), which map closely to existing HTML tags. In the latter case, the HTML server-side control and the ASP.NET web control variants provide similar functionality, although the web controls tend to expose a more standardized, streamlined interface. This makes the web controls easy to learn, and it also means they're a natural fit for Windows developers moving to the world of the Web, because many of the property names are similar to the corresponding Windows controls.

#6: ASP.NET Supports all Browsers

One of the greatest challenges web developers face is the wide variety of browsers they need to support. Different browsers, versions, and configurations differ in their support of XHTML, CSS, and JavaScript. Web developers need to choose whether they should render their content according to the lowest common denominator, and whether they should add ugly hacks to deal with well-known quirks on popular browsers.

ASP.NET addresses this problem in a remarkably intelligent way. Although you can retrieve information about the client browser and its capabilities in an ASP.NET page, ASP.NET actually encourages developers to ignore these considerations and use a rich suite of web server controls. These server controls render their markup adaptively by taking the client's capabilities into account. One example is ASP.NET's validation controls, which use JavaScript and DHTML (Dynamic HTML) to enhance their behavior if the client supports it. Another example is the set of Ajax-enabled controls, which uses complex JavaScript routines that test browser versions and use carefully tested workarounds to ensure consistent behavior. These features are optional, but they demonstrate how intelligent controls can make the most of cutting-edge browsers without shutting out other clients. Best of all, you don't need any extra coding work to support both types of client.

#7: ASP.NET Is Easy to Deploy and Configure

One of the biggest headaches a web developer faces during a development cycle is deploying a completed application to a production server. Not only do the web-page files, databases, and components need to be transferred, but components need to be registered and a slew of configuration settings need to be re-created. ASP.NET simplifies this process considerably.

Every installation of the .NET Framework provides the same core classes. As a result, deploying an ASP.NET application is relatively simple. For no-frills deployment, you simply need to copy all the files to a virtual directory on a production server (using an FTP program or even a command-line command like XCOPY). As long as the host machine has the .NET Framework, there are no time-consuming registration steps. Chapter 18 covers deployment in detail.

Distributing the components your application uses is just as easy. All you need to do is copy the component assemblies along with your website files when you deploy your web application. Because all the information about your component is stored directly in the assembly file metadata, there's no need to launch a registration program or modify the Windows registry. As long as you place these components in the correct place (the Bin subdirectory of the web application directory), the ASP.NET engine automatically detects them and makes them available to your web-page code. Try that with a traditional COM component!

Configuration is another challenge with application deployment, particularly if you need to transfer security information such as user accounts and user privileges. ASP.NET makes this deployment process easier by minimizing the dependence on settings in IIS (Internet Information Services). Instead, most ASP.NET settings are stored in a dedicated web.config file. The web.config file is placed in the same directory as your web pages. It contains a hierarchical grouping of application settings stored in an easily readable XML format that you can edit using nothing more than a text editor such as Notepad. When you modify an application setting, ASP.NET notices that change and smoothly restarts the application in a new application domain (keeping the existing application domain alive long enough to finish processing any outstanding requests). The web.config file is never locked, so it can be updated at any time.

The Evolution of ASP.NET

When Microsoft released ASP.NET 1.0, even it didn't anticipate how enthusiastically the technology would be adopted. ASP.NET quickly became the standard for developing web applications with Microsoft technologies and a heavy-hitting competitor against all other web development platforms. Since that time, ASP.NET has had several updates. The following sections explain how ASP.NET has evolved over the years.

ASP.NET 1.0 and 1.1

When ASP.NET 1.0 first hit the scene, its core idea was a model of web page design called *web forms*. As you'll see in the early chapters in this book, the web form model is simply an abstraction that models your page as a combination of objects. When a browser requests a specific page, ASP.NET instantiates the page object, and then creates objects for all the ASP.NET controls inside that page. The page and its control go through a sequence of life-cycle events, and then—when the page processing is finished—they render the final HTML and are released from memory. The bulk of ASP.NET programming is filling in what happens in between.

ASP.NET 2.0

It's a testament to the good design of ASP.NET 1.0 and 1.1 that few of the changes introduced in ASP.NET 2.0 were fixes for existing features. Instead, ASP.NET 2.0 kept the same core abstraction (the web form model) and concentrated on adding new, higher-level features. Some of the highlights include:

- **Master pages:** Master pages are reusable page templates. For example, you can use a master page to ensure that every web page in your application has the same header, footer, and navigation controls.
- **Themes:** Themes allow you to define a standardized set of appearance characteristics for web controls. Once defined, you can apply these formatting presets across your website for a consistent look.
- **Navigation.** ASP.NET's navigation framework includes a mechanism for defining site maps that describe the logical arrangement of pages in a website. It also includes navigation controls (such as trees and breadcrumb-style links) that use this information to let users move through the site.
- **Security and membership:** ASP.NET 2.0 added a slew of security-related features, including automatic support for storing user credentials, a role-based authorization feature, and prebuilt security controls for common tasks like logging in, registering, and retrieving a forgotten password.
- **Data source controls:** The data source control model allows you to define how your page interacts with a data source *declaratively* in your markup, rather than having to write the equivalent data access code by hand. Best of all, this feature doesn't force you to abandon good component-based design—you can bind to a custom data component just as easily as you bind directly to the database.
- **Web parts:** One common type of web application is the *portal*, which centralizes different information using separate panes on a single web page. Web parts provide a prebuilt portal framework complete with a flow-based layout, configurable views, and even drag-and-drop support.

- **Profiles:** Profiles allow you to store user-specific information in a database without writing any database code. Instead, ASP.NET takes care of the tedious work of retrieving the profile data when it's needed and saving the profile data when it changes.

The Provider Model

Many of the features introduced in ASP.NET 2.0 work through an abstraction called the *provider model*. The beauty of the provider model is that you can use the simple providers to build your page code. If your requirements change, you don't need to change a single page—instead, you simply need to create a custom provider and update your website configuration.

For example, most serious developers will quickly realize that the default implementation of profiles is a one-size-fits-all solution that probably won't suit their needs. It doesn't work if you need to use existing database tables, store encrypted information, or customize how large amounts of data are cached to improve performance. However, you can customize the profile feature to suit your needs by building your own profile provider. This allows you to use the convenient profile features but still control the low-level details. Of course, the drawback is that you're still responsible for some of the heavy lifting, but you gain the flexibility and consistency of the profile model.

You'll learn how to use provider-based features and create your own providers throughout this book.

ASP.NET 3.5

Developers who are facing ASP.NET 3.5 for the first time are likely to wonder what happened to ASP.NET 3.0. Oddly enough, it doesn't exist. Microsoft used the name .NET Framework 3.0 to release new technologies—most notably, WPF (Windows Presentation Foundation), a slick new user interface technology for building rich clients, WCF (Windows Communication Foundation), a technology for building message-oriented services, and WF (Windows Workflow Foundation), a technology that allows you to model a complex business process as a series of actions (optionally using a visual flowchart-like designer). However, the .NET Framework 3.0 doesn't include a new version of the CLR or ASP.NET. Instead, the next release of ASP.NET was rolled into the .NET Framework 3.5.

Compared to ASP.NET 2.0, ASP.NET 3.5 is a more gradual evolution. Its new features are concentrated in two areas: LINQ and Ajax, as described in the following sections.

LINQ

LINQ (Language Integrated Query) is a set of extensions for the C# and Visual Basic languages. It allows you to write C# or Visual Basic code that manipulates in-memory data in much the same way you query a database.

Technically, LINQ defines about 40 query operators, such as select, from, in, where, and orderby (in C#). These operators allow you to code your query. However, there are various types of data on which this query can be performed, and each type of data requires a separate flavor of LINQ.

The most fundamental LINQ flavor is LINQ to Objects, which allows you to take a collection of objects and perform a query that extracts some of the details from some of the objects. LINQ to Objects isn't ASP.NET-specific. In other words, you can use it in a web page in exactly the same way that you use it in any other type of .NET application.

Along with LINQ to Objects is LINQ to DataSet, which provides similar behavior for querying an in-memory DataSet object, and LINQ to XML, which works on XML data. But one of the most interesting flavors of LINQ is LINQ to Entities, which allows you to use the LINQ syntax to execute a query against a relational database. Essentially, LINQ to Entities creates a properly parameterized SQL query based on your code, and executes the query when you attempt to access the query results. You don't need to write any data access code or use the traditional ADO.NET objects.

LINQ to Objects, LINQ to DataSet, and LINQ to XML are features that complement ASP.NET, and aren't bound to it in any specific way. However, ASP.NET includes enhanced support for LINQ to Entities, including a data source control that lets you perform a query through LINQ to Entities and bind the results to a web control, with no extra code required. You'll take a look at LINQ to Objects, LINQ to DataSet, and LINQ to Entities in Chapter 13. You'll consider LINQ to XML in Chapter 14.

■ **Note** If you programmed with ASP.NET 3.5, you may have used another technique to access relational databases, called LINQ to SQL. Although LINQ to SQL is still supported (so you don't need to rewrite existing applications), it's been largely replaced by LINQ to Entities. LINQ to Entities is far more flexible and supports more types of data providers, while LINQ to SQL is limited to SQL Server only.

ASP.NET AJAX

Because traditional ASP.NET code does all its work on the web server, every time an action occurs in the page the browser needs to post some data to the server, get a new copy of the page, and refresh the display. This process, though fast, introduces a noticeable flicker. It also takes enough time that it isn't practical to respond to events that fire frequently, such as mouse movements or key presses.

Web developers work around these sorts of limitations using JavaScript, the only broadly supported client-side scripting language. In ASP.NET, many of the most powerful controls use a healthy bit of JavaScript. For example, the Menu control responds immediately as the user moves the mouse over different subheadings. When you use the Menu control, your page doesn't post back to the server until the user clicks an item.

In traditional ASP.NET pages, developers use server controls such as Menu and gain the benefit of the client-side script these controls emit. However, even with advanced controls, some postbacks are unavoidable. For example, if you need to update the information on a portion of the page, the only way to accomplish this in ordinary ASP.NET is to post the page back to the server and get an entirely new HTML document. The solution works, but it isn't seamless.

Restless web developers have responded to challenges like these by using more client-side code and applying it in more advanced ways. One of the most talked about examples today is Ajax (Asynchronous JavaScript and XML). Ajax is programming shorthand for a client-side technique that allows your page to call the server and update its content without triggering a complete postback. Typically, an Ajax page uses client-side script code to fire an asynchronous request behind the scenes. The server receives this request, runs some code, and then returns the data your page needs (often as a block of XML markup). Finally, the client-side code receives the new data and uses it to perform another action, such as refreshing part of the page. Although Ajax is conceptually quite simple, it allows you to create pages that work more like seamless, continuously running applications. Figure 1-3 illustrates the differences.

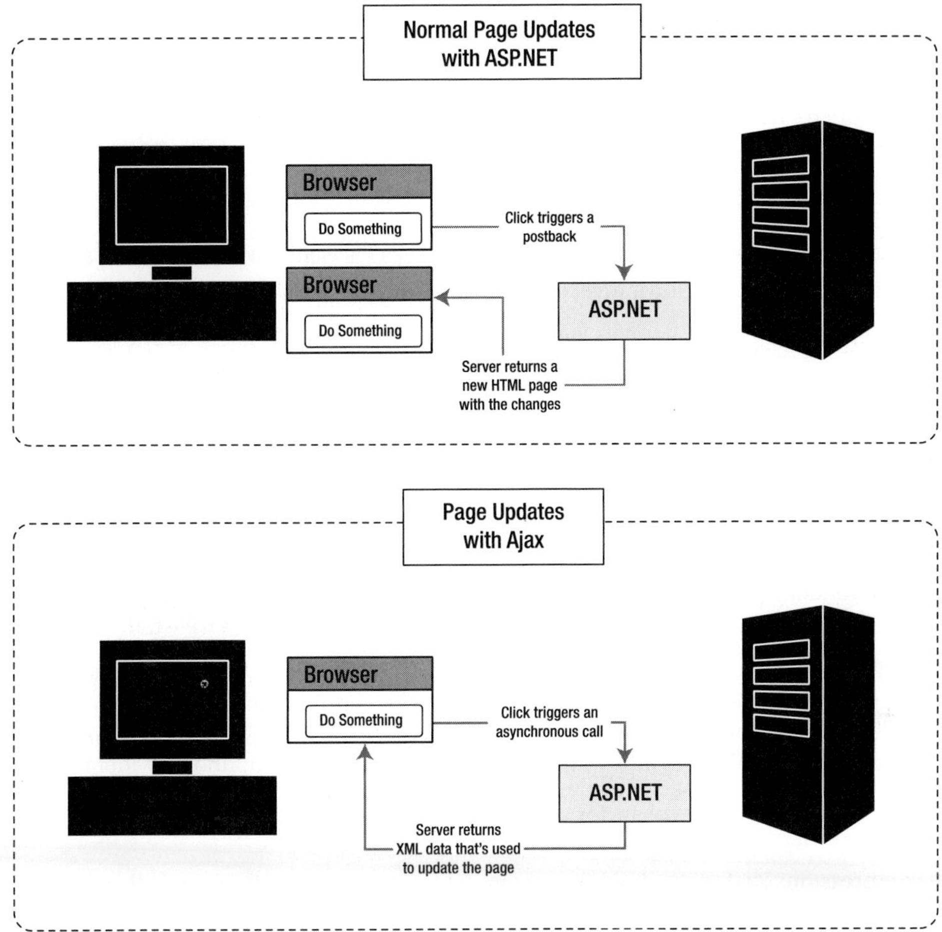

Figure 1-3. *Ordinary server-side pages vs. Ajax*

Ajax and similar client-side scripting techniques are nothing new, but in recent years they've begun to play an increasingly important role in web development. One of the reasons is that the XMLHttpRequest object—the plumbing that's required to support asynchronous client requests—is now present in the majority of modern browsers, including the following:

- Internet Explorer 5 and newer
- Netscape 7 and newer
- Opera 7.6 and newer
- Safari 1.2 and newer
- Firefox (any version)
- Google Chrome (any version)

However, writing the client-side script in such a way that it's compatible with all browsers and implementing all the required pieces (including the server-side code that handles the asynchronous requests) can be a bit tricky. As you'll see in Chapter 29, ASP.NET provides a client callback feature that handles some of the work. However, ASP.NET also includes a much more powerful abstraction layer named ASP.NET AJAX, which extends ASP.NET with impressive Ajax-style features. You'll explore ASP.NET AJAX in Chapter 30.

■ **Note** It's generally accepted that Ajax isn't written in all capitals, because the word is no longer treated as an acronym. However, Microsoft chose to capitalize it when naming ASP.NET AJAX. For that reason, you'll see two capitalizations of Ajax in this book—Ajax when talking in general terms about the technology and philosophy of Ajax, and AJAX when talking about ASP.NET AJAX, which is Microsoft's specific implementation of these concepts.

ASP.NET 4

In its latest version, ASP.NET continues to plug in new enhancements and refinements. The most significant ones include:

Consistent XHTML rendering; ASP.NET 3.5 made it possible to render ASP.NET web pages as XHTML documents, but there were still a few issues to trip up unsuspecting developers. (For example, you had to opt-in through a configuration file setting to get true, strict XHTML.) ASP.NET 4 smooths out the wrinkles and makes clean, quirk-free XHTML the standard. Chapter 3 covers the details.

Updated browser detection: ASP.NET 4 ships with updated browser definition files, which means its server-side rendering engine can recognize and provide properly targeted support to a wider range of browsers. Better-supported browsers include Google Chrome, Internet Explorer 8, Firefox 3.5, Opera 10, Safari 4, and the mobile browsers for the BlackBerry, IPhone, IPod, and Windows Mobile operating system. You'll learn more about browser definitions in Chapter 27.

Session state compression: Microsoft added the System.IO.Compression namespace with gzip support in .NET 2.0. Now, ASP.NET can use it to compress the data it passes to an out-of-processs session state service. This technique makes sense in a fairly narrow set of circumstances, but if it applies to you, the performance improvement is almost automatic. Chapter 6 explains how it works.

Opt-in view state. Rather than disabling view state selectively, per control, you can now turn it off for an entire page and then opt-in when necessary. This allows you to easily slim down your page size. Chapter 6 shows you how to use this feature.

Extensible caching: Caching is one of ASP.NET's premiere features, but with the exception of SQL Server cache dependencies, caching hasn't seen any new features since .NET 1.0. With ASP.NET 4, Microsoft finally begins exposing the caching extensibility points that will allow them (and other developers) to use new types of cache storage, including distributed caching solutions such as Windows Server AppFabric and memcached. Although these extra bits of infrastructure aren't all there yet, Chapter 11 shows how the model works.

The Chart control: For years, ASP.NET developers have been forced to master the GDI+ drawing model or purchase a third-party control to create a respectable graph. Now, ASP.NET includes an impressive Chart control that supports a range of beautifuly rendered two- and three-dimensional graphs (including line, bar, curve, area, pie, doughnut, and point charts, complete with features like error bars and Bollinger bands). You'll explore the Chart control in Chapter 28.

Revamped Visual Studio: Although the Visual Studio 2010 interface still follows the same basic design, it's been completely rebuilt using .NET and WPF (Windows Presentation Foundation). Along the way, Microsoft managed to introduce a few frills, like the enhanced IntelliSense you'll learn about in Chapter 2, and the new visual designer that makes designing Silverlight content a breeze (Chapter 34).

Routing: ASP.NET MVC includes support for meaningful, search-engine-friendly URLs. In ASP.NET 4, you can use the same routing technology to redirect web form requests. Chapter 17 demonstrates this technique.

Better deployment tools: Visual Studio now allows you to create *web packages*, compressed files that contain your application content and other details such as SQL Server database schemas and IIS settings. Web packages also work in conjunction with a new web.config transformation feature that allows you to cleanly separate the settings that apply to the test build of your application and the ones that apply to the deployed instance. Finally, you can load and precompile a newly deployed application more easily with the IIS application warm-up module. Chapter 18 has the details on all these features.

Although these features are undeniably useful, the most impressive new additions to ASP.NET development come from two separate add-ins: ASP.NET MVC and ASP.NET Dynamic Data. Both of these features invite you to abandon part of the traditional ASP.NET development model for a different approach, with a different set of benefits and drawbacks. In many ways, they represent the start of a new direction in web application programming. But if either one fits your needs, it has the potential to reduce your work dramatically.

ASP.NET MVC

ASP.NET MVC (which stands for Model-View-Controller) offers a dramatically different way to build web pages than the standard web forms model. The core idea is that your application is separated into three logical parts. The *model* includes the application-specific business code—for example, data-access logic and validation rules. The *view* creates a suitable representation of the model by rendering it to HTML pages. The *controller* coordinates the whole show, handling user interactions, updating the model, and passing the information to the view.

The MVC pattern sidelines several traditional ASP.NET concepts, including web forms, web controls, view state, postbacks, and session state. As a result, it forces developers to adopt a new way of thinking (and accept a temporary drop in productivity). To some, the MVC pattern is cleaner and more suited to the Web. To others, it's extra effort with no clear payoff. But if any of the following points are important to you, it's worth at least considering ASP.NET MVC:

Test-driven development: Thanks to the clean separation of parts in an ASP.NET MVC application, it's easy to create unit tests that exercise it. With web forms, automated testing is tedious and often impossible.

Control over HTML markup: With web forms, you program against a rich set of objects that take care of state management and HTML rendering. With ASP.NET MVC, you inject content in a way that's more like data binding. While this means that complex formatted pages may take more work to design, it also means that you have complete control over every markup detail. This control is useful if you plan to write client-side JavaScript or use a third-party JavaScript library like jQuery. (On the other hand, if you aren't comfortable or interested in mucking around with HTML, web forms is probably a better framework for your applications.)

Control over URLs: Although ASP.NET continues to give developers more control over URL routing, ASP.NET MVC has the concept built-in. Controllers handle the mapping between URLs and your application logic, which means it's easy to use URL configurations such as */Products/List/Beverages* instead of */Products/List.aspx?category=Beverages*. These clear, readable URLs make search-engine optimization easier and more effective.

On the other hand, if you prefer to have rapid application design, a high-level model that manages state for you, and a range of rich web controls, web forms will probably remain your first choice development model.

Most of this book focuses on web forms, ASP.NET's core model. You'll get an introduction to ASP.NET MVC in Chapter 32. For much more information, you can visit the official ASP.NET MVC website at `http://www.asp.net/mvc`, or refer to the excellent book *Pro ASP.NET MVC Framework* by Steven Sanderson (Apress, 2009).

ASP.NET Dynamic Data

ASP.NET Dynamic Data is a scaffolding framework that allows you to quickly build a data-driven application. When used in conjunction with LINQ to SQL or LINQ to Entities (as it almost always is), Dynamic Data gives you an end-to-end solution that takes you from database schema to a full-fledged web application with support for viewing, editing, inserting, and deleting records.

It's important to realize that Dyanmic Data isn't just a code and markup generation tool for developers who are too lazy to build their own custom applications. Instead, it's a template-based, componentized, and thoroughly customizable framework that's ideal for creating applications that are all about data. In fact, Dynamic Data can be seen as a logical extension of the rich data controls that ASP.NET already provides (like the GridView, DetailsView, and FormView). But instead of forcing you to modify many different data controls on many different pages to get the effect you want, Dynamic Data uses field-based templates that are defined once and shared everywhere. Combine this clean design with new features—such as validation that's based on the database schema and easier filtering based on foreign key relationships—and you can see why Dynamic Data is a compelling approach for web applications that focus on viewing and editing database records. You'll explore ASP.NET Dynamic Data in Chapter 33.

Silverlight

Recently, there's been a lot of excitement about Silverlight, a rapidly evolving Microsoft technology that allows a variety of browsers on a variety of operating systems to run true .NET code. Silverlight works through a browser plug-in, and provides a subset of the .NET Framework class library. This subset includes a slimmed-down version of WPF, the technology that developers use to craft next-generation Windows user interfaces.

So where does Silverlight fit into the ASP.NET world? Silverlight is all about client code—quite simply, it allows you to create richer pages than you could with HTML, DHTML, and JavaScript alone. In many ways, Silverlight duplicates the features and echoes the goals of Adobe Flash. By using Silverlight in a web page, you can draw sophisticated 2D graphics, animate a scene, and play video and other media files.

Silverlight is perfect for creating a mini-applet, like a browser-hosted game. It's also a good choice for adding interactive media and animation to a website. However, Silverlight obviously isn't a good choice for tasks that require server-side code, such as performing a secure checkout in an e-commerce shop, verifying user input, or interacting with a server-side database. And because Silverlight is still a new, emerging technology, it's too early to make assumptions about its rate of adoption. That means it's not a good choice to replace basic ingredients in a website with Silverlight content. For example, although you can use Silverlight to create an animated button, this is a risky strategy. Users without the Silverlight plug-in won't be able to see your button or interact with it. (Of course, you could create more than one front end for your web application, using Silverlight if it's available or falling back on regular ASP.NET controls if it's not. However, this approach requires a significant amount of work.)

In many respects, Silverlight is a complementary technology to ASP.NET. ASP.NET 4 doesn't include any features that use Silverlight, but you can freely mix ASP.NET pages and Silverlight pages on a website—or place Silverlight content in an ASP.NET page. It's also possible that developers will some day use ASP.NET web controls that render Silverlight content. Using these controls, you just might gain the best of both worlds—the server-side programming model of ASP.NET and the rich interactivity of client-side Silverlight. In Chapter 34, you'll get a thorough introduction to Silverlight. Or, for a comprehensive look that covers all the features of Silverlight consider *Pro Silverlight 3 in C#* (Apress, 2010).

Summary

So far, you've just scratched the surface of the features and frills that are provided in ASP.NET and the .NET Framework. You've taken a quick look at the high-level concepts you need to understand in order to be a competent ASP.NET programmer. You've also previewed the new features that ASP.NET 4 offers. As you continue through this book, you'll learn much more about the innovations and revolutions of ASP.NET 4 and the .NET Framework.

Summary

CHAPTER 2

■ ■ ■

Visual Studio

With ASP.NET, you have several choices for developing web applications. If you're inclined (and don't mind the work), you can code every web page and class by hand using a bare-bones text editor. This approach is appealingly straightforward but tedious and error-prone for anything other than a simple page. Professional ASP.NET developers rarely go this route.

Instead, almost all large-scale ASP.NET websites are built using Visual Studio. This professional development tool includes a rich set of design tools, including legendary debugging tools and IntelliSense, which catches errors and offers suggestions as you type. Visual Studio also supports the robust code-behind model, which separates the .NET code you write from the web-page markup tags. To seal the deal, Visual Studio adds a built-in test web server that makes debugging websites easy.

In this chapter, you'll tour the Visual Studio IDE (Integrated Development Environment) and consider the two ways you can create an ASP.NET web application in Visual Studio—either as a straightforward website or as a web project. You'll also learn about the code model used for ASP.NET web pages and the compilation process used for ASP.NET web applications. Finally, you'll take a quick look at the Web Development Helper, a browser-based debugging tool that you can use in conjunction with Visual Studio.

■ **What's New** Although Visual Studio 2010 follows the same basic model as earlier versions, it gets a significant facelift. In fact, Visual Studio 2010 has been completely rewritten using WPF (Microsoft's .NET-based user-interface technology), and the result is a cleaner, more modern interface. Most of the changes are in the details, such as reduced on-screen clutter and streamlined IntelliSense (as described in the "Visual Studio 2010 Improvements" section). But developers working with WPF or Silverlight (Chapter 34) get a long-awaited designer that lets them build user interfaces by dragging and dropping controls from the Toolbox, just like in an ASP.NET page.

Introducing Visual Studio

Writing and compiling code by hand would be a tedious task for any developer. But the Visual Studio IDE offers a slew of high-level features that go beyond basic code management. These are some of Visual Studio's advantages:

An integrated web server: To host an ASP.NET web application, you need web server software like IIS, which waits for web requests and serves the appropriate pages. Setting up your web server isn't difficult, but it can be inconvenient. Thanks to the integrated development web server in Visual Studio, you can run a website directly from the design environment. You also have the added security of knowing no external computer can run your test website, because the test server only accepts connections from the local computer.

Multilanguage development: Visual Studio allows you to code in your language or languages of choice using the same interface (IDE) at all times. Furthermore, Visual Studio allows you to create web pages in different languages, but include them all in the same web site. There are only two limitations: you can't use more than one language in the same web page (which would create obvious compilation problems), and you must use the projectless website model (not web projects).

Less code to write: Most applications require a fair bit of standard boilerplate code, and ASP.NET web pages are no exception. For example, when you add a web control, attach event handlers, and adjust formatting, a number of details need to be set in the page markup. With Visual Studio, these details are set automatically.

Intuitive coding style: By default, Visual Studio formats your code as you type, indenting automatically and using color-coding to distinguish elements such as comments. These minor differences make code much more readable and less prone to error. You can even configure what automatic formatting Visual Studio applies, which is great if you prefer different brace styles (such as K&R style, which always puts the opening brace on the same line as the preceding declaration).

■ **Tip** To change the formatting options in Visual Studio, select Tools ➤ Options, and then look at the groups under the Text Editor ➤ C# ➤ Formatting section. You'll see a slew of options that control where curly braces should be placed

---

Faster development time: Many of the features in Visual Studio are geared toward helping you get your work done faster. Convenience features allow you to work quickly and efficiently, such as IntelliSense (which flags errors and can suggest corrections), search-and-replace (which can hunt for keywords in one file or an entire project), and automatic comment and uncomment features (which can temporarily hide a block of code).

Debugging: The Visual Studio debugging tools are the best way to track down mysterious errors and diagnose strange behavior. You can execute your code one line at a time, set intelligent breakpoints that you can save for later use, and view current in-memory information at any time.

Visual Studio also has a wealth of features that you won't see in this chapter, including project management, integrated source code control, code refactoring, macros, and a rich extensibility model. Furthermore, if you're using Visual Studio 2010 Team System you'll gain advanced unit testing, collaboration, and code versioning support (which is far beyond that available in simpler tools such as Visual SourceSafe). Although Visual Studio Team System isn't discussed in this chapter, you can learn more from `http://msdn.microsoft.com/teamsystem`.

Websites and Web Projects

Somewhat confusingly, Visual Studio offers two ways to create an ASP.NET-powered web application:

- **Project-based development:** When you create a web project, Visual Studio generates a .csproj project file (assuming you're coding in C#) that records the files in your project and stores a few debugging settings. When you run a web project, Visual Studio compiles all your code into a single assembly before launching your web browser.

- **Projectless development:** An alternate approach is to create a simple website without any project file. In this case, Visual Studio assumes that every file in the website directory (and its subdirectories) is part of your web application. In this scenario, Visual Studio doesn't need to precompile your code. Instead, ASP.NET compiles your website the first time you request a page. (Of course, you can use precompilation to remove the first-request overhead for a deployed web application. Chapter 18 explains how.)

The first .NET version of Visual Studio used the project model. Visual Studio 2005 removed the project model in favor of projectless development. However, a small but significant group of developers revolted. Realizing that there were specific scenarios that worked better with project-based development, Microsoft released a download that added the project feature back to Visual Studio 2005. Now, both options are supported in Visual Studio 2010.

In this chapter, you'll begin by creating the standard projectless website, which is the simpler, more streamlined approach. Later in this chapter, you'll learn what scenarios work better with project-based development, and you'll see how to create web projects.

Creating a Projectless Website

To get right to work and create a new web application, choose File ➤ New ➤ Web Site. Visual Studio will show the New Web Site dialog box (see Figure 2-1).

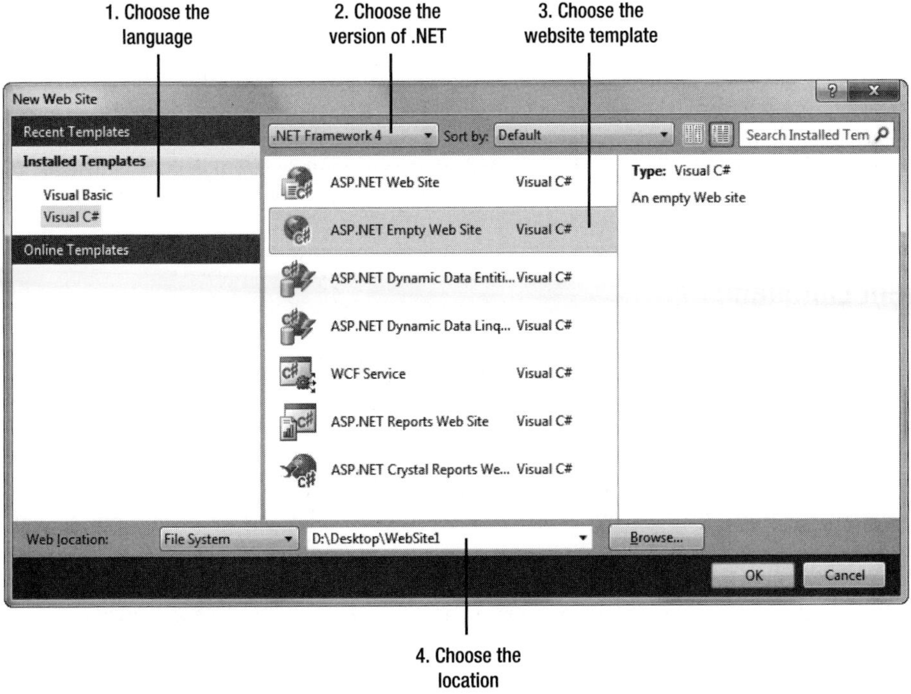

***Figure 2-1.** The New Web Site window*

To create a new website, you must choose the development language (at the left), the version of .NET (at the top of the middle section), the website template (in the middle), and the location (at the bottom). Then, once you've specified these details, click OK to create your website.

The following sections expand on each of these details.

The Hidden Solution File

Although projectless development simplifies life, the last vestiges of Visual Studio's solution-based system are still lurking behind the scenes.

When you create a web application, Visual Studio actually creates solution files (.sln and .suo) in a user-specific directory like c:\Users\[UserName]\Documents\Visual Studio 2010\Projects\[WebsiteFolderName]. The solution files provide a few Visual Studio-specific features that aren't directly related to ASP.NET, such as debugging settings. For example, if you add a breakpoint to the code in a web page (as discussed in the "Visual Studio Debugging" section later in this chapter), Visual Studio stores the breakpoint in the .suo file. The next time you open the website, Visual Studio locates the matching solution files automatically. Similarly, Visual Studio uses the solution files to keep track of the files that are currently open in the design environment so that it can restore your view when you return to the website. This approach to solution management is fragile—obviously, if you move the website from one location to another, you lose all this information. However, because this information isn't really all that important (think of it as a few project-specific preferences), losing it isn't a serious problem. The overall benefits of a projectless system are usually worth the trade-off.

If you want a more permanent solution, you can save your solution files explicitly in a location of your choosing. To do so, simply click the top item in the Solution Explorer (which represents your solution). For example, if you open a folder named MyWebSite, the top item is named Solution 'MyWebSite'. Then, choose File ➤ Save [SolutionName] As. This technique is handy if you've created a solution that combines multiple applications (for example, a projectless website and a class library component) and you want to edit and debug them at the same time.

The Development Language

The language identifies the .NET programming language you'll use to code your website. The language you choose is simply the default language for the project. This means you can explicitly add Visual Basic web pages to a C# website, and vice versa.

The Framework Version

Older versions of Visual Studio were tightly coupled to specific versions of .NET. You used Visual Studio .NET to create .NET 1.0 applications, Visual Studio .NET 2003 to create .NET 1.1 applications, and Visual Studio 2005 to create .NET 2.0 applications.

Visual Studio 2008 removed this restriction with multitargeting, and Visual Studio 2010 continues the trend. It allows you to create web applications that are designed to work with .NET 2.0, .NET 3.0, .NET 3.5, or .NET 4. Typically, you'll choose the latest version that your web server supports. Later versions give you access to more recent features, and all the samples that are included with this book target .NET 4.

■ **Note** Of course, there's no reason that you can't install multiple versions of .NET on the same web server and configure different IIS virtual directories to use different versions of ASP.NET (as described in Chapter 18).

To provide accurate multitargeting, Visual Studio 2010 includes *reference assemblies* for each version of .NET. These assemblies include the metadata of every type, but none of the code that's required to implement it. That means Visual Studio 2010 can use the reference assembly to tailor its Intellisense and error checking, ensuring that you aren't able to use controls, classes, or members that aren't available in the version of .NET that you're targeting. It also uses this metadata to determine what controls should appear in the toolbox, what members should appear in the Properties window and Object Browser, and so on, ensuring that the entire IDE is limited to the version you've chosen.

You can also change the version of .NET that you're targeting after you've created your website. To do that, follow these steps:

1. Choose Website ➤ Start Options.
2. In the list on the left, choose the Build category.
3. In the Target Framework list, choose the version of .NET you want to target.

■ **Note** This process is slightly different in a web project. In a web project, you begin by double-clicking the Properties node in the Solution Explorer. Then, choose the Application tab, which contains the Target Framework list in which you can choose the version of .NET you want to target.

When you change the .NET version, Visual Studio modifies your web.config file quite significantly. For example, the web.config file for a .NET 4 application is short and streamlined, because all of the plumbing it needs is set up in the computer's root web.config file. But the web.config file for a .NET 3.5 application needs a good deal of extra boilerplate to explicitly enable support for Ajax and C# 3.5 features. You'll dig deeper into the contents of the web.config file in Chapter 5.

The Template

Once you choose a language (in the list on the left), you'll see a list of all the templates that Visual Studio provides for that language (in the large box in the center). The template determines what files your website starts with.

Visual Studio supports several types of ASP.NET applications, but all of them are compiled and executed in the same way. The only difference is the files that Visual Studio creates by default. For example, if you create a WCF Service, Visual Studio generates a website that starts with a single WCF service in it, rather than an ASP.NET web page.

Here's a rundown of your template choices:

ASP.NET Web Site: This creates a full-featured ASP.NET website, with its basic infrastructure already in place. This website includes a master page that defines the overall layout (with a header, footer, and menu bar), and ready-made default.aspx and about.aspx pages. It also includes an Accounts folder with pages for registration, login, and password changing, and a Scripts folder with the jQuery library for client-side JavaScript.

ASP.NET Empty Web Site: This creates a nearly empty website. It includes a stripped-down web.config configuration file, and nothing else. Of course, it's easy to fill in the pieces you need as you start coding.

■ **Tip** If you're relatively new to ASP.NET, start with the ASP.NET Empty Web Site option. Once you've read the other chapters in this book and learned how to use such features as master pages and membership, you'll be ready to jump into the somewhat more convoluted ASP.NET Web Site template, if it suits your needs.

ASP.NET Dynamic Data Entites Web Site: This creates an ASP.NET website that uses the ASP.NET Dynamic Data feature described in Chapter 33. This website is designed to use the Entity Model to access the back-end database, while the similarly named ASP.NET Dynamic Data LINQ to SQL Web Site template uses the older LINQ to SQL approach.

WCF Service: This creates a WCF service—a library of server-side methods that remote clients (for example, Windows applications) can call. Although you won't examine the WCF model in detail in this book, you will create WCF services to provide server-side functionality for Silverlight pages in Chapter 34.

ASP.NET Reports Web Site: This creates an ASP.NET website that uses the ReportView control and SQL Server Reporting Services (a tool for generating database reports that can be viewed and managed over the Web). The ASP.NET Crystal Reports Web Site template provides a similar service, but it uses the competing Crystal Reports software.

Although most developers prefer to start with the ASP.NET Empty Web Site or ASP.NET Web Site template and begin coding, there are still more specialized templates for specific types of web applications. To view them, click the Online Templates heading on the far left of the New Web Site dialog box. There will be a short delay while Visual Studio contacts the Microsoft web servers, after which it will add a list of template subcategories, each with its own group of ready-made templates. For example, ASP.NET developers can download a template to create a DotNetNuke website (which uses the popular DotNetNuke portal framework) or an ASP.NET MVC website that uses OpenID for user authentication.

The Location

The location specifies where the website files will be stored. Typically, you'll choose File System and then use a folder on the local computer or a network path. However, you can also edit a website directly over HTTP or FTP (File Transfer Protocol). This is occasionally useful if you want to perform live website edits on a remote web server. However, it also introduces additional overhead. Of course, you should never edit a production web server directly because changes are automatic and irreversible. Instead, limit your changes to test servers.

If you simply want to create your project in a folder on the file system, you may decide to type it into the Location box by hand. But if you prefer to see all your options, and hunt for the right location, you can click the Browse button, which shows the Choose Location dialog box (Figure 2-2).

Along the left side of Choose Location dialog box, you'll see four buttons that let you connect to different types of locations:

File System: This is the easiest choice—you simply need to browse through a tree of drives and directories or through the shares provided by other computers on the network. If you want to create a new directory for your application, just click the Create New Folder icon above the top-right corner of the directory tree. (You can also coax Visual Studio into creating a directory by adding a new directory name to the end of your path.)

Local IIS: This choice allows you to browse the virtual directories made available through the IIS web hosting software, assuming it's running on the current computer. Chapter 18 describes virtual directories in detail and shows you how to create them with IIS Manager. Impressively, you can also create them without leaving Visual Studio. Just select the Default Web Site node and then click the Create New Web Application icon at the top-right corner of the virtual directory tree.

■ **Note** There are two significant limitations to the Local IIS location type, First, you must have IIS 6 Management Compatibility installed. (This is one of the optional subfeatures of IIS that you'll see when you install it from the Windows Features dialog box.) Second, you must choose to run Visual Studio as an administrator when you launch it. (To do this, right-click the Visual Studio shortcut and choose Run As Administrator.)

FTP Site: This option isn't quite as convenient as browsing for a directory—instead, you'll need to enter all the connection information, including the FTP site, the port, the directory, a user name, and a password before you can connect.

Remote Web Site: This option accesses a website at a specified URL (uniform resource locator) using HTTP. For this to work, the web server must have the FrontPage Extensions installed. When you connect, you'll be prompted for a user name and password.

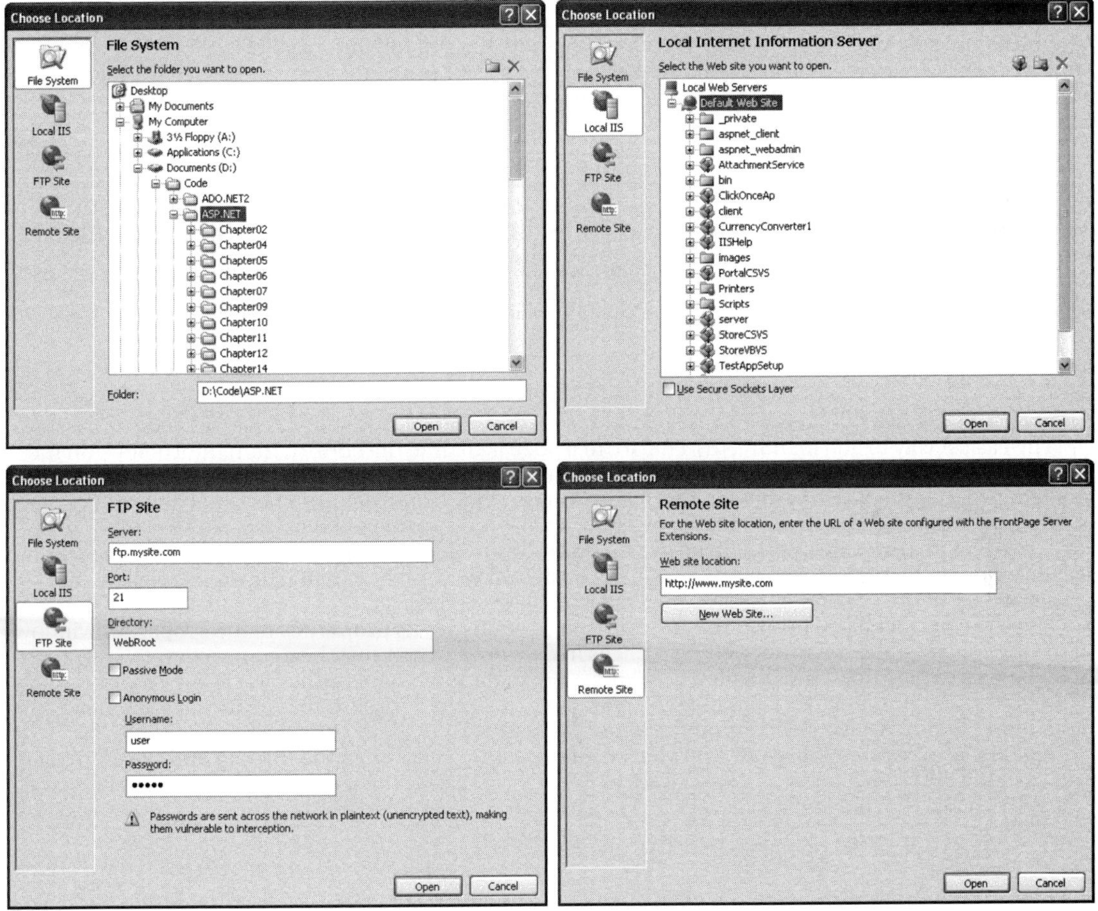

Figure 2-2. Browsing to a website location

Designing a Web Page

To start designing a web page, double-click the web page in the Solution Explorer. If you're using the ASP.NET Empty Web Site template, start by creating a new page (right-click the website in the Solution Explorer, choose Add New Item, and pick the Web Form template). A new page begins with the bare minimum markup that it needs, but has no visible content, so it will appear like a blank page in the designer.

Visual Studio gives you three ways to look at a web page: source view, design view, and split view. You can choose the view you want by clicking one of the three buttons at the bottom of the web page window (Source, Design, or Split). Source view shows the markup for your page (the HTML and ASP.NET control tags). Design view shows a formatted view of what your page looks like in the web browser. Split view combines the other two views so that you can see the markup for a page and a live preview at the same time.

■ **Note** Technically, most ASP.NET pages are made up of XHTML, and all ASP.NET controls emit valid XHTML unless configured otherwise. However, in this chapter we refer to web page markup as HTML, because it can use HTML or the similar but more stringent XHTML standard. Chapter 3 has more information about ASP.NET's support for XHTML.

The easiest way to add an ASP.NET control to a page is to drag the control from the Toolbox on the left. (The controls in the Toolbox are grouped in numerous categories based on their functions, but you'll find basic ingredients in the Standard tab.) You can drag a control onto the visual design surface of a page (using design view), or you can drop it in a specific position of your web page markup (using source view). Either way, the result is the same. Alternatively, you can type in the control tag that you need by hand in the source view. In this case, the design view won't be updated until you click in the design portion of the window or press Ctrl+S to save the web page.

Once you've added a control, you can resize it and configure its properties in the Properties window. Many developers prefer to lay out new web pages in design view, but switch to source view to rearrange their controls or perform more detailed tweaking. The exception is with ordinary HTML markup—although the Toolbox includes a tab of HTML elements, it's usually easiest to type the tags you need by hand, rather than dragging and dropping them one at a time.

Figure 2-3 shows a web page in split view, with the source markup in the top half and the graphical surface in the bottom half.

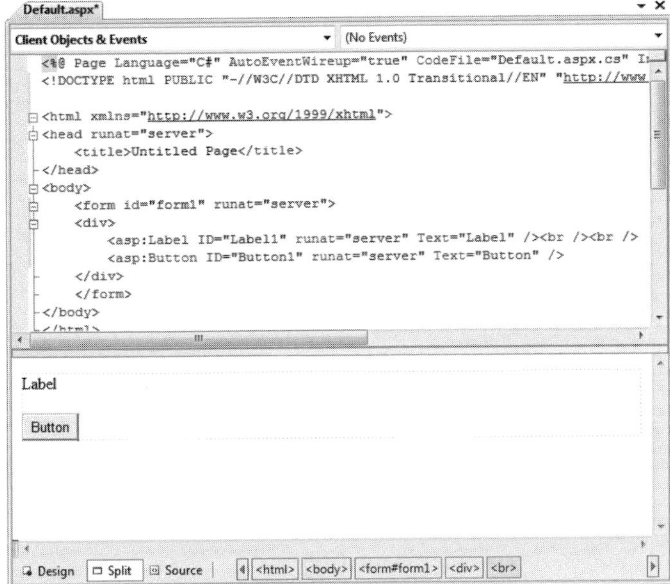
Default.aspx*
Client Objects & Events
(No Events)
<%@ Page Language="C#" AutoEventWireup="true" CodeFile="Default.aspx.cs" I
<!DOCTYPE html PUBLIC "-//W3C//DTD XHTML 1.0 Transitional//EN" "http://www
<html xmlns="http://www.w3.org/1999/xhtml">
<head runat="server">
<title>Untitled Page</title>
</head>
<body>
<form id="form1" runat="server">
<div>
<asp:Label ID="Label1" runat="server" Text="Label" />

<asp:Button ID="Button1" runat="server" Text="Button" />
</div>
</form>
</body>
Label
Button
Design
Split
Source
<html> <body> <form#form1> <div>

Figure 2-3. Editing a web page in split view

■ **Tip** If you have a widescreen monitor, you'll probably prefer to have the split view use two side-by-side regions (rather than a top and bottom region). Fortunately, it's easy to configure Visual Studio to do so. Just select Tools ➤ Options, and then head to the HTML Designer ➤General section in the tree of settings. Finally, select the Split Views Vertically option and click OK.

To configure a control, click once to select it, or choose it by name in the drop-down list at the top of the Properties window. Then, modify the appropriate properties in the window, such as Text, ID, and ForeColor. These settings are automatically translated to the corresponding ASP.NET control tag attributes and define the initial appearance of your control. Visual Studio even provides special "choosers" (technically known as UITypeEditors) that allow you to select extended properties. For example, you can select a color from a drop-down list that shows you the color, and you can configure the font from a standard font selection dialog box.

Absolute Positioning

To position a control on the page, you need to use all the usual tricks of HTML design, such as paragraphs, line breaks, tables, and styles. Visual Studio assumes you want to position your elements using flexible "flow" positioning, so content can grow and shrink dynamically without creating a layout problem. However, you can also use absolute positioning mode (also known as grid layout) with the help of the CSS standard. All you need to do is add an inline CSS style for your control that specifies absolute positioning. Here's an example that places a button exactly 100 pixels from the left edge of the page and 50 pixels from the top:

```
<asp:Button id="cmd" style="POSITION: absolute; left: 100px; top: 50px;"
 runat="server" ... />
```

Once you've made this change, you're free to drag the button around the window at will, and Visual Studio will update the coordinates in the style correspondingly.

It rarely makes sense to position individual controls using absolute positioning. It doesn't allow your layout to adapt to different web browser window sizes, and it causes problems if the content in one element expands, causing it to overlap another absolutely positioned element. It's also a recipe for inflexible layouts that are difficult to change in the future. However, you can use absolute positioning to place entire containers, and then use flow content inside your container. For example, you could use absolute positioning to keep a menu bar at the side, but use ordinary flow layout for the list of links inside. The <div> container is a good choice for this purpose, because it has no built-in appearance (although you can use style rules to apply a border, background color, and so on). The <div> is essentially a floating box. In this example, it's given a fixed 200 pixel width, and the height will expand to fit the content inside.

```
<div style="POSITION: absolute; left: 100px; top: 50px; width:200px">
 ...
</div>
```

You can find some common examples of multicolumn layout that use CSS at `http://www.glish.com/css`. You'll also learn more about styles in Chapter 16.

Smart Tags

Smart tags make it easier to configure complex controls. Smart tags aren't offered for all controls, but they are used for rich controls such as GridView, TreeView, and Calendar.

You'll know a smart tag is available if, when you select a control, you see a small arrow in the top-right corner. If you click this arrow, a window will appear with links (and other controls) that trigger higher-level tasks. For example, Figure 2-4 shows how you can use this technique to access Calendar autoformatting. (Smart tags can include many more features, but the Calendar smart tag provides only a single link.)

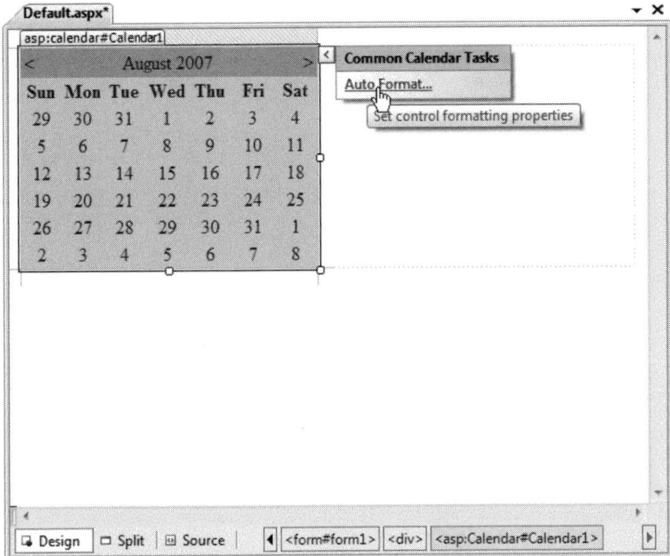

Figure 2-4. *A smart tag for the Calendar control*

Static HTML Tags

As you know, ASP.NET pages contain a mixture of ordinary HTML tags and ASP.NET controls. To add HTML tags, you simply type them in or drag them from the HTML tab of the Toolbox.

Visual Studio provides a valuable style builder for formatting any static HTML element with CSS style properties. To test it, add the <div> element from the HTML section of the Toolbox. The <div> will appear on your page as a borderless panel. Then click to select the panel, and click the Style box in the Properties window. An ellipsis (...) button will appear in the Style box. When you click it, the Modify Style dialog box (shown in Figure 2-5) will appear, with options for configuring the colors, font, layout, and border for the element.

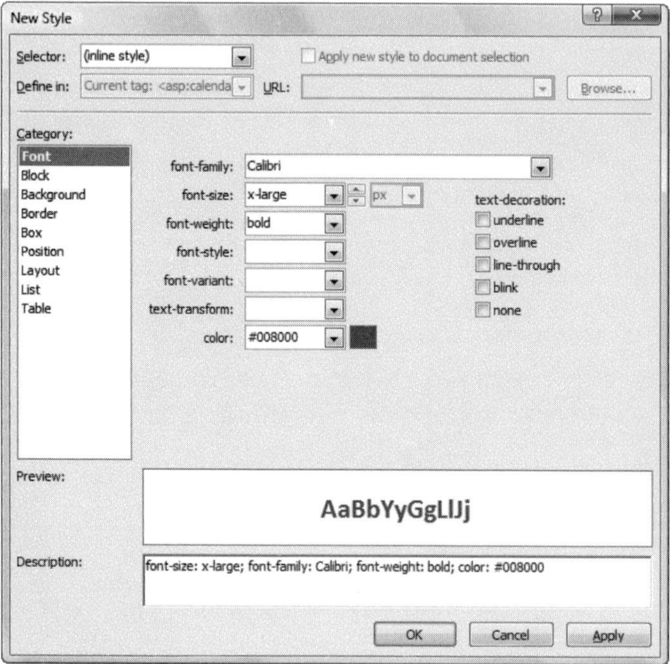

Figure 2-5. Building HTML styles

When you create a new style in this way, it will be stored as an inline style, and recorded in the style attribute of the element you're modifying. Alternatively, you can define a named style in the current page (the default) or in a separate stylesheet. You'll learn more about these techniques and Visual Studio's support for stylesheets in Chapter 16.

If you want to configure the HTML element as a server control so that you can handle events and interact with it in code, you need to switch to source view and add the required runat="server" attribute to the control tag.

HTML Tables

Visual Studio provides good design-time support for creating HTML tables. To try it, drag a table from the HTML tab of the Toolbox. You'll start with a standard 3×3 table, but you can quickly transform it using editing features that more closely resemble a word processor than a programming tool. Here are some of the tricks you'll want to use:

- To move from one cell to another in the table, press the Tab key or use the arrow keys. The current cell is highlighted with a blue border. Inside each cell you can type static HTML or drag and drop controls from the Toolbox. If you tab beyond the final cell, Visual Studio adds a new row.
- To add new rows and columns, right-click inside a cell, and choose from one of the many options in the Insert submenu to insert rows, columns, and individual cells.
- To resize a part of the table, just click one of the borders and drag.

- To format a cell, right-click inside it, click the Style box in the Properties window, and then click the ellipsis (...) button. This shows the same Modify Style dialog box you saw in Figure 2-5.
- To work with several cells at once, hold down Ctrl while you click each cell. You can then right-click to perform a batch formatting operation.
- To merge cells (for example, change two cells into one cell that spans two columns), just select the cells, right-click, and choose Modify ➤ Merge Cells.

With these conveniences, you might never need to resort to a design tool like Dreamweaver or Expression Web.

■ **Tip** Modern web design practices discourage using tables for layout. Instead, most professional developers favor CSS layout properties, which work equally well with Visual Studio. You'll learn more about Visual Studio's support for CSS in Chapter 16.

Structuring HTML Markup

There are endless ways to format the same chunk of HTML. Nested tags can be indented, and long tags are often broken over several lines for better readability. However, the exact amount of indentation and the preferred line length vary from person to person.

Because of these variations, Visual Studio doesn't enforce any formatting. Instead, it always preserves the capitalization and indenting you use. The drawback is that it's easy to be inconsistent and create web pages that use widely different formatting conventions or have messily misaligned tags.

To help sort this out, Visual Studio offers an innovative feature that lets you define the formatting rules you want to use and then apply them anywhere you want. To try this, switch to the source view for a page. Now, highlight some haphazard HTML, right-click the selection, and choose Format Selection. Visual Studio will automatically straighten out the selected HTML content, giving it the correct capitalization, indenting, and line wrapping.

Of course, this raises an excellent question—namely, who determines what the correct formatting settings are? Although Visual Studio starts with its own sensible defaults, you have the ability to fine-tune them extensively. To do so, right-click anywhere in the HTML source view, and choose Formatting and Validation. This shows the Options dialog box, positioned at the Text Editor ➤ HTML ➤ Formatting group of settings (see Figure 2-6).

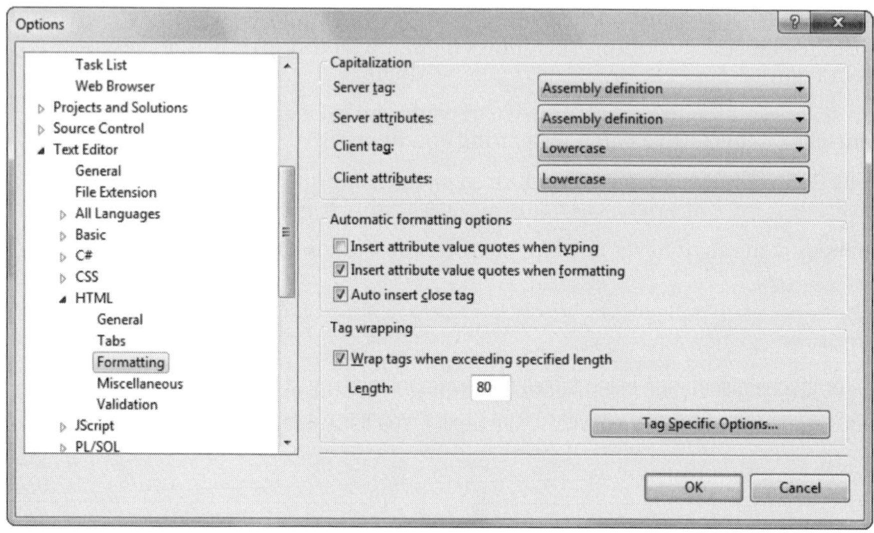

Figure 2-6. *Configuring HTML formatting settings*

This section lets you control what capitalization settings are used and how long lines can be before they have to wrap. By default, lines don't wrap until they hit an eye-straining 80 characters, so many developers choose to decrease this number. You can also control how attributes are quoted and set whether Visual Studio should automatically add the matching closing tag when you add an opening tag.

■ **Note** The formatting rules are applied whenever you use the Format Selection command and whenever you add HTML content by adding controls from the Toolbox in design view. If you type in your HTML by hand, Visual Studio won't apply the formatting to "correct" you.

If you're even more ambitious, you can click the Tag Specific Options button to set formatting rules that apply only to specific tags. For example, you can tell Visual Studio to add line breaks at the beginning and end of a <div> tag. Or, you can tell Visual Studio to use different colors to highlight specific tags, such as tags that you often need to locate in a hurry or tags you plan to avoid. (For example, developers who are planning to move to a CSS-based layout might try avoiding <table> tags and use color-coding to highlight them.)

Along with the formatting settings, the Options dialog box also has several useful settings in the subgroups of the HTML group:

General: Lets you configure Visual Studio's automatic statement completion, use automatic wrapping, and turn on line numbers to help you locate hard-to-remember places in your pages.

Tabs: Lets you choose the number of spaces to insert when you press Tab.

Miscellaneous: Includes the handy Format HTML on Paste option, which isn't enabled by default. Switch this on, and your formatting rules are applied whenever you paste new content into the source view.

Validation: Lets you set the browser or type of markup you're targeting (for example, HTML 4.01 or XHTML 1.1). Depending on your choices, Visual Studio will flag violations, such as the use of deprecated elements. (You can also change this option using the HTML Source Editing toolbar, where the option appears as a drop-down list.)

As these settings show, Visual Studio is a great partner when adding ordinary HTML content to ASP.NET pages.

The Visual Studio IDE

Now that you've created a basic website, it's a good time to take a tour of the different parts of the Visual Studio interface. Figure 2-7 identifies each part of the Visual Studio window, and Table 2-1 describes the most commonly used windows.

If you don't see a particular window, it's easy enough to summon it into view. You can pick the most common windows directly from the View window (for example, View→Solution Explorer) and you can find less common windows under the Other Windows submenu (for example, View→Other Windows→Macro Explorer). Finally, you'll find windows that are used for debugging under the Debug→Windows submenu.

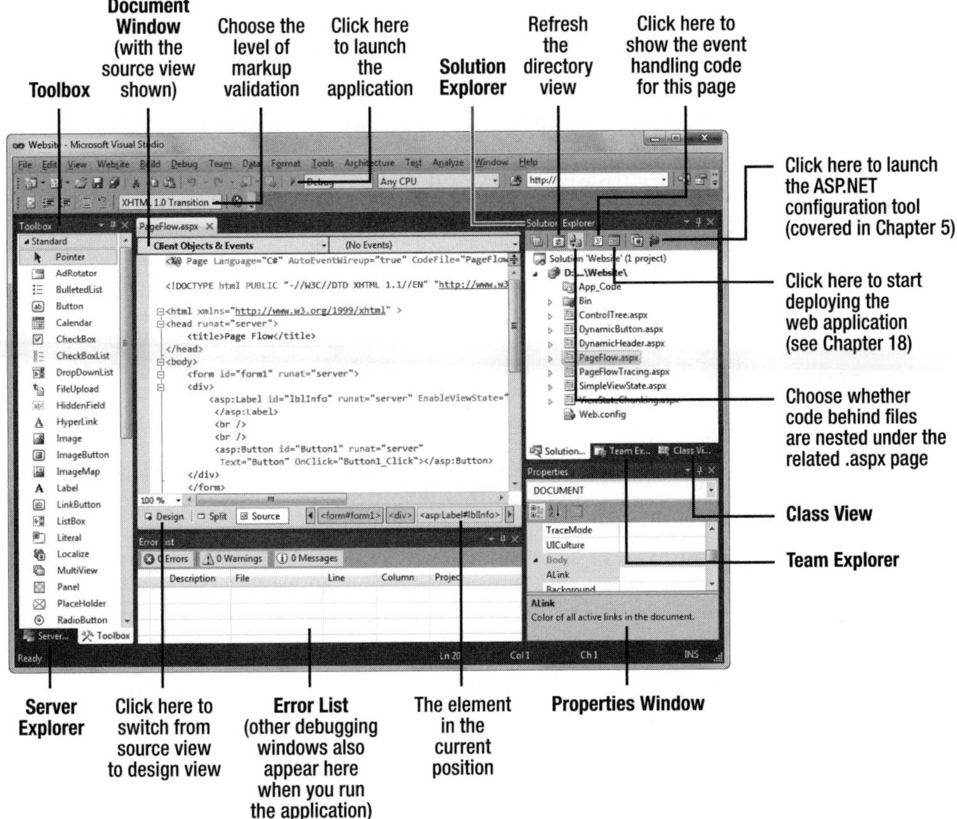

Figure 2-7. The Visual Studio interface

Table 2-1. Common Visual Studio Windows

Window	Description
Solution Explorer	Lists the files and subfolders that are in the web application folder.
Toolbox	Shows ASP.NET's built-in server controls and any third-party controls or custom controls that you build yourself and add to the Toolbox. Controls can be written in any language and used in any language.
Server Explorer	Allows access to databases, system services, message queues, and other server-side resources.
Properties	Allows you to configure the currently selected element, whether it's a file in the Solution Explorer or a control on the design surface of a web form.
Error List	Reports on errors that Visual Studio has detected in your code but that you haven't resolved yet.
Task List	Lists comments that start with a predefined moniker so that you can keep track of portions of code that you want to change and also jump to the appropriate position quickly. For example, you can flag areas that need attention by creating a comment that starts with // HACK or // TODO.
Document	Allows you to design a web page by dragging and dropping, and to edit the code files you have within your Solution Explorer. Also supports non-ASP.NET file types, such as static HTML and XML files.
Macro Explorer	Allows you to see all the macros you've created and execute them. Macros are an advanced Visual Studio feature; they allow you to automate tedious or time-consuming tasks, such as formatting code, creating backup copies of files, arranging document windows, changing debugging settings, and so on. Visual Studio exposes a rich extensibility model, and you can write a macro using pure .NET code.
Class View	Shows a different view of your application, which is organized to show all the classes you've created (and their methods, properties, and events).
Team Explorer	Shows team projects and allows you to check files out through source control so you can work on them. This window only appears if you've installed the Visual Studio Team Suite edition.
Manage Styles and Apply Styles	Allows you to modify styles in a linked stylesheet and apply them to the current web page. You'll see how these windows work in Chapter 16.

■ **Tip** The Visual Studio interface is highly configurable. You can drag the various windows and dock them to the sides of the main Visual Studio window. Also, some windows on the side automatically slide into and out of view as you move your mouse. If you want to freeze these windows in place, just click the thumbtack icon in the top-right corner of the appropriate window.

Solution Explorer

The Solution Explorer is, at its most basic, a visual filing system. It allows you to see the files that are in the web application directory.

Table 2-2 lists some of the file types you're likely to see in an ASP.NET web application.

In addition, your web application can contain other resources that aren't ASP.NET file types. For example, your web application directory can hold image files, HTML files, or CSS files. These resources might be used in one of your ASP.NET web pages, or they can be used independently.

Visual Studio distinguishes between different file types. When you right-click a file in the list, a context menu appears with the menu options that apply for that file type. For example, if you right-click a web page, you'll have the option of building it and launching it in a browser window.

Using the Solution Explorer, you can rename, rearrange, and add files. All these options are just a right-click away. To delete a file, just select it in the Solution Explorer and press the Delete key.

Table 2-2. *ASP.NET File Types*

File	Description
Ends with .aspx	These are ASP.NET web pages (the .NET equivalent of the .asp file in an ASP application). They contain the user interface and, optionally, the underlying application code. Users request or navigate directly to one of these pages to start your web application.
Ends with .ascx	These are ASP.NET user controls. User controls are similar to web pages, except that they can't be accessed directly. Instead, they must be hosted inside an ASP.NET web page. User controls allow you to develop an important piece of the user interface and reuse it in as many web forms as you want without repetitive code.
Ends with .asmx or .svc	These are ASP.NET web services. Web services work differently than web pages, but they still share the same application resources, configuration settings, and memory. However, ASP.NET web services are gradually being phased out in favor of WCF (Windows Communication Foundation) services, which were introduced with .NET 3.0 and have the extension .svc. You'll use web services with ASP.NET AJAX in Chapter 30.
web.config	This is the XML-based configuration file for your ASP.NET application. It includes settings for customizing security, state management, memory management, and much more. In a web project, you may have variations of this file that ar used in different deployment scenarios (like web.Debug.config, web.Release.config, and so on). This feature, called web.config transformation, only applies to setup packages and is explained in Chapter 18.

File	Description
global.asax	This is the global application file. You can use this file to define global variables and react to global events, such as when a web application first starts (see Chapter 5 for a detailed discussion). Visual Studio doesn't create a global.asax file by default—you need to add it if it's appropriate.
Ends with .cs	These are code-behind files that contain C# code. They allow you to separate the application from the user interface of a web page. The code-behind model is introduced in this chapter and used extensively in this book.

You can also add new files by right-clicking the Solution Explorer and selecting Add ➤ Add New Item. You can add various different types of files, including web forms, web services, and stand-alone classes. You can also copy files that already exist elsewhere on your computer (or an accessible network path) by selecting Add ➤ Add Existing Item. Use Add ➤ New Folder to create a new subdirectory inside your web application. You can then drag web pages and other files into or out of this directory. Use the Add ASP.NET Folder submenu to quickly insert one of the folders that has a specific meaning to ASP.NET (such as the App_LocalResources and App_GlobalResources folders for globalization, or the Theme folder for website-specific themes). ASP.NET recognizes these folders based on their names.

Visual Studio also checks for project management events such as when another process changes a file in a project you currently have open. When this occurs, Visual Studio will notify you and give you the option to refresh the file.

Document Window

The document window is the portion of Visual Studio that allows you to edit various types of files using different designers. Each file type has a default editor. To learn a file's default editor, simply right-click that file in the Solution Explorer, and then select Open With from the pop-up menu. The default editor will have the word Default alongside it.

Toolbox

The Toolbox works in conjunction with the document window. Its primary use is providing the controls that you can drag onto the design surface of a web form. However, it also allows you to store code and HTML snippets.

The content of the Toolbox depends on the current designer you're using as well as the project type. For example, when designing a web page, you'll see the set of tabs described in Table 2-3. Each tab contains a group of buttons. To view a tab, click the heading, and the buttons will slide into view.

Table 2-3. *Toolbox Tabs for an ASP.NET Project*

Tab	Description
Standard	This tab includes the rich web server controls that are the heart of ASP.NET's web form model.
Data	These components allow you to connect to a database. This tab includes nonvisual data source controls that you can drop onto a form and configure at design time (without using any code) and data display controls such as grids.

Tab	Description
Validation	These controls allow you to verify an associated input control against user-defined rules. For example, you can specify that the input can't be empty, that it must be a number, that it must be greater than a certain value, and so on. Chapter 4 has more details.
Navigation	These controls are designed to display site maps and allow the user to navigate from one page to another. You'll learn about the navigation controls in Chapter 17.
Login	These controls provide prebuilt security solutions, such as login boxes and a wizard for creating users. You'll learn about the login controls in Chapter 21.
WebParts	This set of controls supports web parts, an ASP.NET model for building componentized, highly configurable web portals. You'll learn about web parts in Chapter 31.
AJAX Extensions	These controls use ASP.NET AJAX techniques behind the scenes, allowing you to refresh parts of the page without a full postback. They're discussed in Chapter 30.
Dynamic Data	These controls are a part of ASP.NET Dynamic Data, an ASP.NET scaffolding system for building data-driven websites using intelligent templates. Chapter 33 explores Dynamic Data in detail.
Reporting	This tab includes the ReportViewer control, which allows you to generate reports from a database (much like the third-party package Crystal Reports). Although the ReportViewer isn't discussed in this book, you can learn more at `http://tinyurl.com/ycwyp6e`.
HTML	This tab allows you to drag and drop static HTML elements. If you want, you can also use this tab to create server-side HTML controls—just drop a static HTML element onto a page, switch to source view, and add the runat="server" attribute to the control tag.
General	This tab provides a repository for code snippets and control objects. Just drag and drop them here, and pull them off when you need to use them later.

You can customize both the tabs and the items in each tab. To modify the tab groups, right-click a tab heading, and select Rename Tab, Add Tab, or Delete Tab. To add an item to a tab, right-click the blank space on a Toolbox tab, and click Choose Items. You can also drag items from one tab group to another.

Error List and Task List

The Error List and Task List are two versions of the same window. The Error List catalogs error information that's generated by Visual Studio when it detects problematic code. The Task List shows a similar view with to-do tasks and other code annotations you're tracking. Each entry in the Error List and Task List consists of a text description and, optionally, a link that leads you to a specific line of code somewhere in your project.

With the default Visual Studio settings, the Error List appears automatically whenever you build a project that has errors (see Figure 2-8).

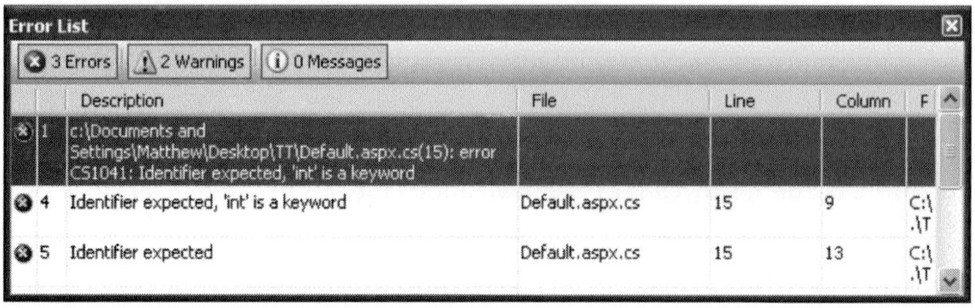

Figure 2-8. Viewing build errors in a project

To see the Task List, choose View ➤ Task List. Two types of tasks exist—user tasks and comments. You can choose which you want to see from the drop-down list at the top of the Task List. User tasks are entries you've specifically added to the Task List. You create these by clicking the Create User Task icon (which looks like a clipboard with a check mark) in the Task List. You can give your task a basic description, a priority, and a check mark to indicate when it's complete.

■ **Note** As with breakpoints, any custom tasks you add by hand are stored in the hidden solution files. This makes them fairly fragile—if you rename or move your project, these tasks will disappear without warning (or without even a notification the next time you open the website).

The comment entries are more interesting because they're added automatically and they link to a specific line in your code. To try the comment feature, move somewhere in your code, and enter the comment marker (//) followed by the word TODO (which is commonly referred to as a token tag). Now type in some descriptive text:

```
// TODO: Replace this hard-coded value with a configuration file setting.
string fileName = @"c:\myfile.txt"
```

Because your comment uses the recognized token tag TODO, Visual Studio recognizes it and automatically adds it to the Task List (as shown in Figure 2-9).

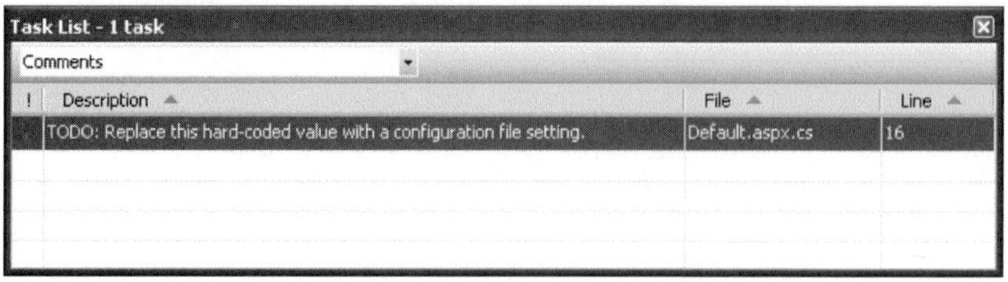

Figure 2-9. Keeping track of tasks

To move to the line of code, double-click the new task entry. Notice that if you remove the comment, the task entry is automatically removed as well.

Three token tags are built-in: HACK, TODO, and UNDONE. However, you can add more. Simply select Tools ➤ Options. In the Options dialog box, navigate to the Environment ➤ Task List tab. You'll see a list of comment tokens, which you can modify, remove, and add to. Figure 2-10 shows this window with a new ASP comment token that you could use to keep track of sections of code that have been migrated from classic ASP pages.

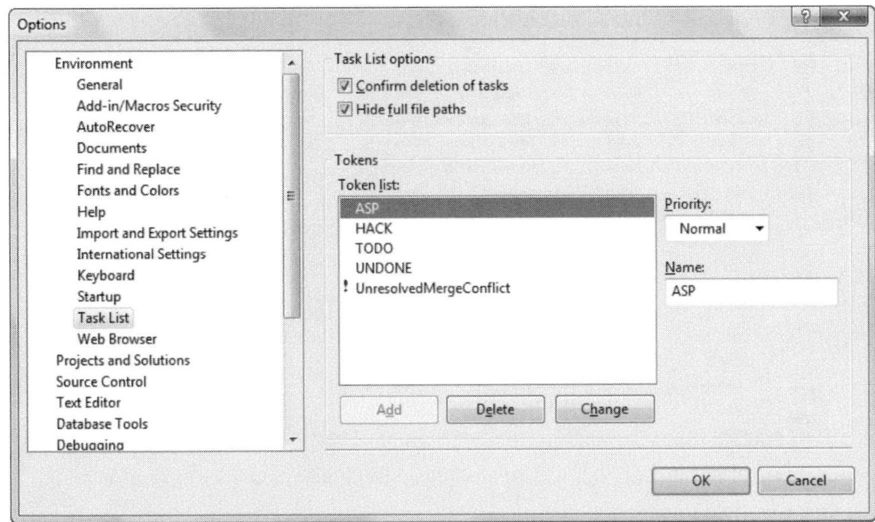

Figure 2-10. Adding a new comment token

■ **Tip** Comment tags are not case-sensitive. For example, you can use TODO and todo interchangeably.

Server Explorer

The Server Explorer provides a tree that allows you to explore various types of services on the current computer (and other servers on the network). It's similar to the Computer Management administrative tool. Typically, you'll use the Server Explorer to learn about available event logs, message queues, performance counters, system services, and SQL Server databases on your computer.

The Server Explorer is particularly noteworthy because it doesn't just provide a way for you to browse server resources; it also allows you to interact with them. For example, you can create databases, execute queries, and write stored procedures using the Server Explorer in much the same way that you would using SQL Server Management Studio, the administrative utility that's included with the full version of SQL Server. To find out what you can do with a given item, right-click it. Figure 2-11 shows the Server Explorer window listing the databases in a local SQL Server and allowing you to retrieve all the records in the selected table.

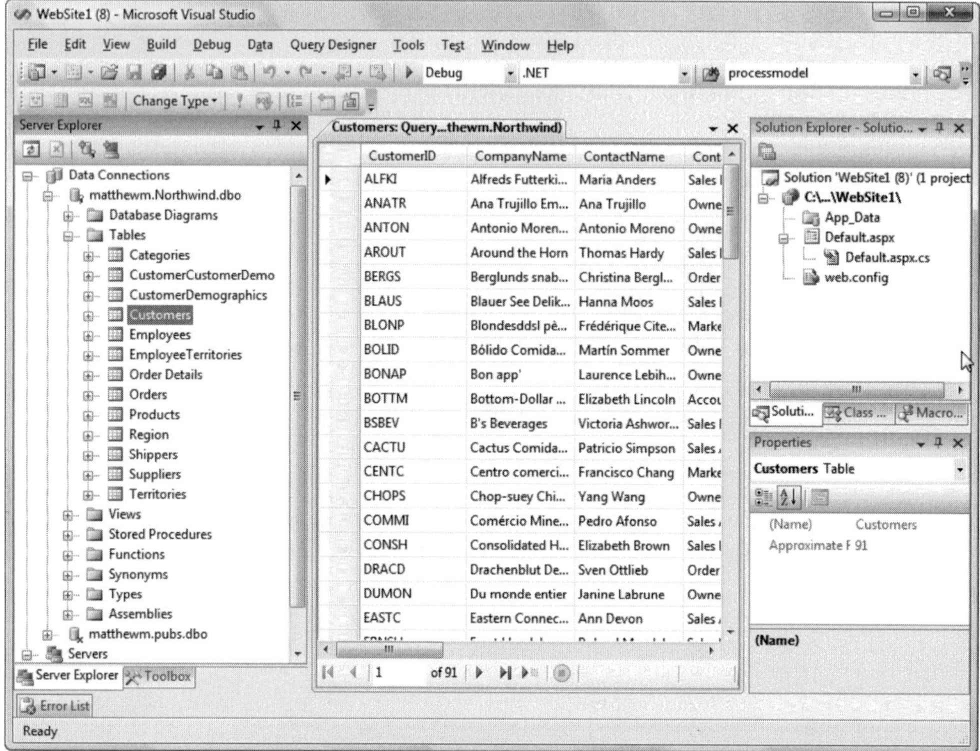

Figure 2-11. Querying data in a database table

The Code Editor

Many of Visual Studio's handiest features appear when you start to write the code that supports your user interface. To start coding, you need to switch to the code-behind view. To switch back and forth, you can use two buttons that are placed just above the Solution Explorer window. The tooltips identify these buttons as View Code and View Designer. When you switch to code view, you'll see the page class for your web page. You'll learn more about code-behind later in this chapter.

ASP.NET is event-driven, and everything in your web-page code takes place in response to an event. To create a simple event handler for the Button.Click event, double-click the button in design view. Here's a simple example that displays the current date and time in a label:

```
protected void Button1_Click(object sender, EventArgs e)
{
    Label1.Text = "Current time: " + DateTime.Now.ToLongTimeString();
}
```

To test this page, select Debug ➤ Start Debugging from the menu. Because this is the first time running any page in this application, Visual Studio will inform you that you need a configuration file that specifically enables debugging, and will offer to change your current web.config file accordingly (see Figure 2-12).

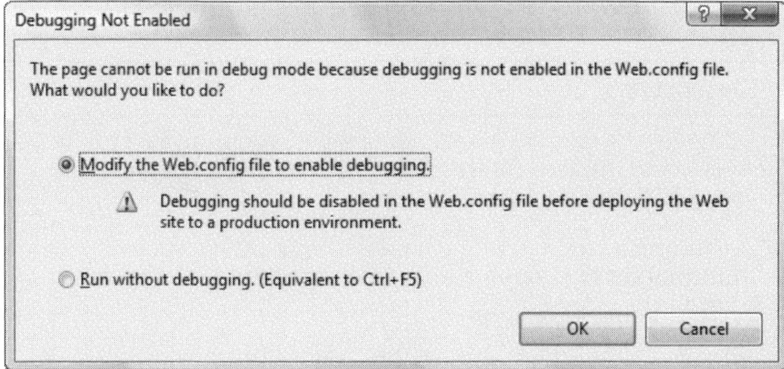

Figure 2-12. *Modifying a web.config file automatically*

Click OK to change the web.config configuration file. Visual Studio will then start the integrated test web server and launch your default browser with the URL set to the current page that's open in Visual Studio. At this point, your request will be passed to ASP.NET, which will compile the page and execute it.

To test your event-handling logic, click the button on the page. The page will then be submitted to ASP.NET, which will run your event-handling code and return a new HTML page with the data (as shown in Figure 2-13).

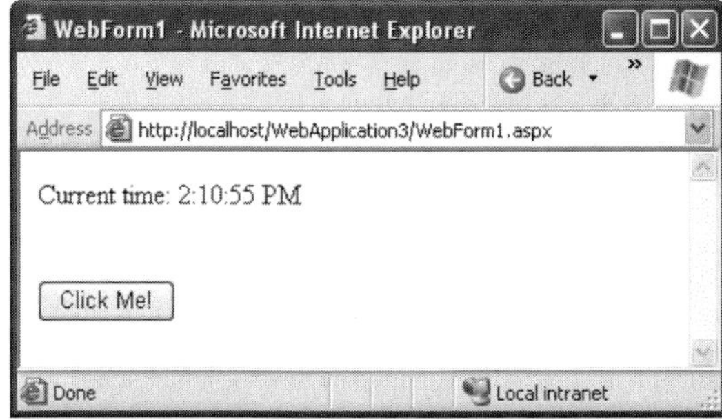

Figure 2-13. *Testing a simple web page*

Adding Assembly References

By default, ASP.NET makes a small set of commonly used .NET assemblies available to all web pages. These assemblies (listed in Table 2-4) are configured through a special machine-wide configuration file. You don't need to take any extra steps to use the classes in these assemblies.

Table 2-4. *Core Assemblies for ASP.NET Pages*

Assembly	Description
mscorlib.dll, Microsoft.CSharp.dll, and System.dll	Includes the core set of .NET data types, common exception types, and numerous other fundamental building blocks for .NET and the C# language.
System.Configuration.dll	Includes classes for reading and writing configuration information in the web.config file, including your custom settings.
System.Core.dll	Includes support for some of the core features that were introduced with .NET 3.5, such as LINQ.
System.Data.dll	Includes the data container classes for ADO.NET, along with the SQL Server data provider.
System.Data.DataSetExtensions.dll	Includes support for LINQ to DataSet.
System.Drawing.dll	Includes classes representing colors, fonts, and shapes. Also includes the GDI+ drawing logic you need to build graphics on the fly.
System.EnterpriseServices.dll	Includes .NET classes for COM+ services such as transactions. These are rarely used, as many of the classes have been superseded by newer platform features.
System.Web.dll	Includes the core ASP.NET classes, including classes for building web forms, managing state, handling security, and much more.
System.Web.ApplicationServices.dll	Includes some classes that were a part of the System.Web.dll assembly in previous releases, but were moved because they may also apply to desktop code. This allows developers to create rich client applications that target the slimmed-down .NET 4 Client Profile, which includes this assembly but not System.Web.dll.
System.Web.DynamicData.dll	Includes support for the ASP.NET Dynamic Data scaffolding system.
System.Web.Entity.dll	Includes the EntityDataSource control, which allows you to plug web forms into the LINQ to Entities feature.
System.Web.Extensions.dll	Includes ASP.NET-specific support for the features that were introduced with .NET 3.5, including LINQ and ASP.NET AJAX.
System.Web.Services.dll	Includes classes for building web services—units of code that can be remotely invoked over HTTP. This feature has largely been replaced by WCF (Windows Communication Foundation).
System.Xml.dll, System.Xml.Linq.dll	Includes .NET classes for reading, writing, searching, transforming, and validating XML, with or without LINQ to XML.

If you want to use additional features or a third-party component, you may need to import more assemblies. For example, if you want to use an Oracle database, you need to add a reference to the System.Data.OracleClient.dll assembly. To add a reference, select Website ➤ Add Reference (or Project ➤ Add Reference in a web project). The Add Reference dialog box will appear, with a list of registered .NET assemblies (see Figure 2-14).

■ **Note** Visual Studio 2010 has enhanced the Add Reference window to use asynchronous loading. As a result, it appears much quicker and doesn't freeze you out while it scans your system for assemblies. However, while these assemblies are being added to the list, you may find it difficult to select the item you want before it "jumps" to a new position.

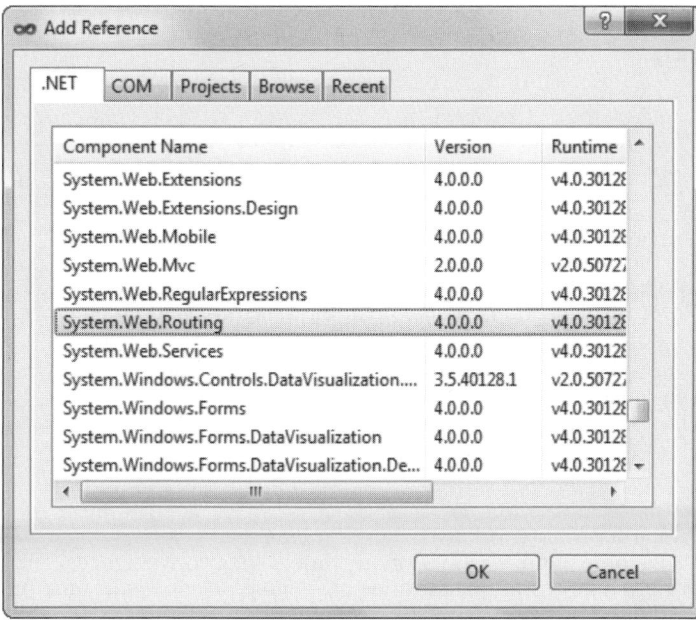

Figure 2-14. *Adding a reference*

In the Add Reference dialog box, select the component you want to use. If you want to use a component that isn't listed here, you'll need to click the Browse tab and select the DLL file from the appropriate directory (or from another project in the same solution, using the Projects tab).

If you're working with a projectless website and you add a reference to another assembly, Visual Studio modifies the web.config file to indicate the assembly you're using. Here's an example of what you might see after you add a reference to the System.Web.Routing.dll file:

```
<compilation debug="true" targetFramework="4.0">
  <assemblies>
    <add assembly=
"System.Web.Routing, Version=4.0.0.0, Culture=neutral,PublicKeyToken=31BF3856AD364E35" />
  </assemblies>
</compilation>
```

If you're working with a web project, and you add a reference to another assembly, Visual Studio doesn't need to change the web.config file. That's because Visual Studio is responsible for compiling the code in a web project, not ASP.NET. Instead, Visual Studio makes a note of this reference in the .csproj project file. The reference also appears in the Solution Explorer window under the References node. You can review your references here, and remove any one by right-clicking it and choosing Remove.

If you add a reference to an assembly that isn't stored in the GAC (global assembly cache), Visual Studio will create a Bin subdirectory in your web application and copy the DLL into that directory. (This happens regardless of whether you're using project-based or projectless development.) This step isn't required for assemblies in the GAC because they are shared with all the .NET applications on the computer.

If you look at the code for a web-page class, you'll notice that Visual Studio imports just a few core .NET namespaces. Here's the code you'll see:

```
using System;
using System.Collections.Generic;
using System.Linq;
using System.Web;
using System.Web.UI;
using System.Web.UI.WebControls;
```

Adding a reference isn't the same as importing the namespace with the using statement. The using statement allows you to use the classes in a namespace without typing the long, fully qualified class names. However, if you're missing a reference, it doesn't matter what using statements you include—the classes won't be available. For example, if you import the System.Web.UI namespace, you can write Page instead of System.Web.UI.Page in your code. But if you haven't added a reference to the System.Web.dll assembly that contains these classes, you still won't be able to access the classes in the System.Web.UI namespace.

IntelliSense and Outlining

As you program with Visual Studio, you'll become familiar with its many time-saving conveniences. The following sections outline the most important features you'll use (none of which is new in Visual Studio 2010).

Outlining

Outlining allows Visual Studio to "collapse" a subroutine, block structure, or region to a single line. It allows you to see the code that interests you, while hiding unimportant code. To collapse a portion of code, click the minus box next to the first line. Click the box again (which will now have a plus symbol) to expand it (see Figure 2-15).

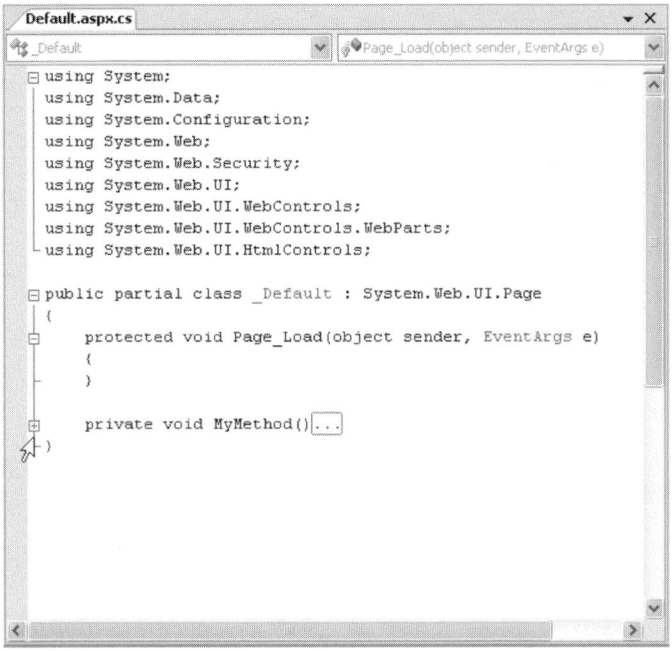

```
Default.aspx.cs
_Default    Page_Load(object sender, EventArgs e)
using System;
using System.Data;
using System.Configuration;
using System.Web;
using System.Web.Security;
using System.Web.UI;
using System.Web.UI.WebControls;
using System.Web.UI.WebControls.WebParts;
using System.Web.UI.HtmlControls;

public partial class _Default : System.Web.UI.Page
{
    protected void Page_Load(object sender, EventArgs e)
    {
    }

    private void MyMethod()...
}
```

Figure 2-15. Collapsing code

You can collapse an entire code file so that it only shows definitions (such as the namespace and class declarations, member variables and properties, method declarations, and so on), but hides all other details (such as the code inside your methods and your namespace imports). To get this top-level view of your code, right-click anywhere in the code window and choose Outlining ➤ Collapse to Definitions. To remove your outlining and expand all collapsed regions so you can see everything at once, right-click in the code window and choose Outlining ➤ Stop Outlining.

Member List

Visual Studio makes it easy for you to interact with controls and classes. When you type a period (.) after a class or object name, Visual Studio pops up a list of available properties and methods (see Figure 2-16). It uses a similar trick to provide a list of data types when you define a variable and to provide a list of valid values when you assign a value to an enumeration.

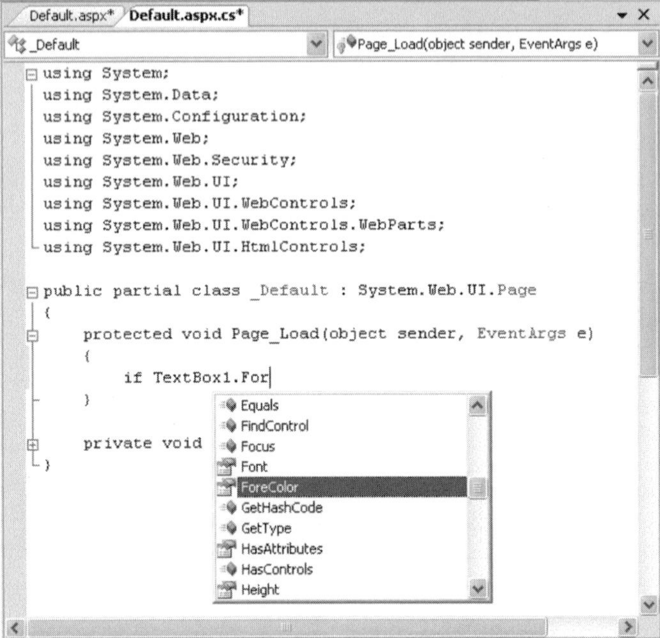

Figure 2-16. IntelliSense at work

Visual Studio also provides a list of parameters and their data types when you call a method or invoke a constructor. This information is presented in a tooltip below the code and is shown as you type. Because the .NET class library heavily uses function overloading, these methods may have multiple different versions. When they do, Visual Studio indicates the number of versions and allows you to see the method definitions for each one by clicking the small up and down arrows in the tooltip. Each time you click the arrow, the tooltip displays a different version of the overloaded method (see Figure 2-17).

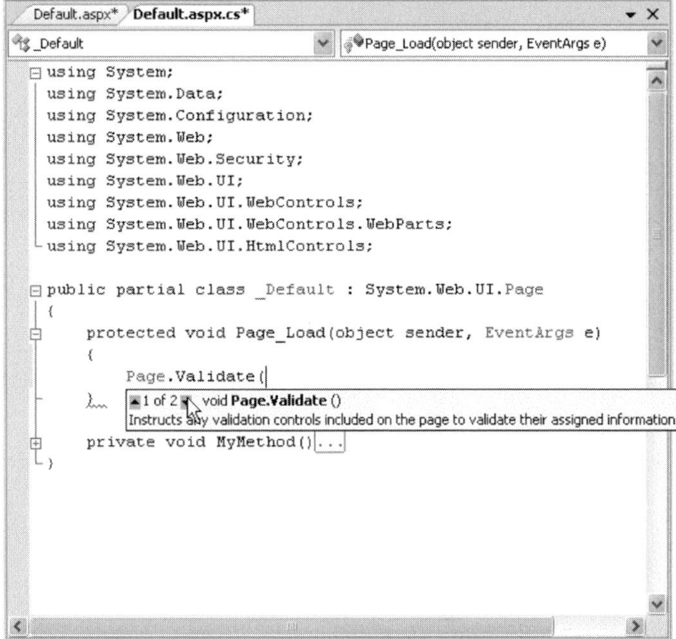

Figure 2-17. IntelliSense with overloaded method

Error Underlining

One of the code editor's most useful features is error underlining. Visual Studio is able to detect a variety of error conditions, such as undefined variables, properties, or methods; invalid data type conversions; and missing code elements. Rather than stopping you to alert you that a problem exists, the Visual Studio editor quietly underlines the offending code. You can hover your mouse over an underlined error to see a brief tooltip description of the problem (see Figure 2-18).

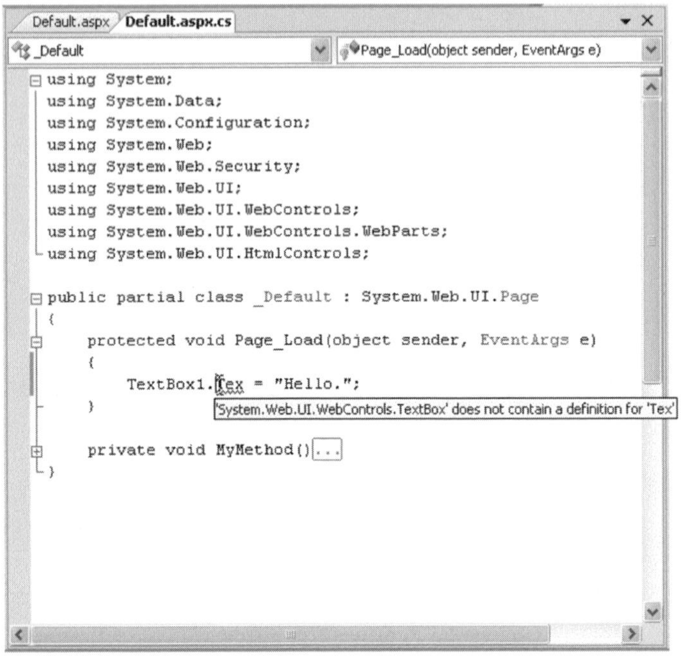

Figure 2-18. *Highlighting errors at design time*

Visual Studio won't flag your errors immediately. Instead, it will quickly scan through your code as soon as you try to compile it and mark all the errors it finds. If your code contains at least one error, Visual Studio will ask you whether it should continue. At this point, you'll almost always decide to cancel the operation and fix the problems Visual Studio has reported. (If you choose to continue, you'll actually wind up using the last compiled version of your application because the .NET compilers can't build an application that has errors.)

■ **Note** You may find that as you fix errors and rebuild your project you discover more problems. That's because Visual Studio doesn't check for all types of errors at once. When you try to compile your application, Visual Studio scans for basic problems such as unrecognized class names. If these problems exist, they can easily mask other errors. On the other hand, if your code passes this basic level of inspection, Visual Studio checks for more subtle problems such as trying to use an unassigned variable.

Visual Studio 2010 Improvements

The most remarkable change in Visual Studio 2010 is the behind-the-scenes architecture. In fact, despite being rebuilt with WPF, Visual Studio 2010 keeps most of the conventions of its predecessors.

Fortunately, Microsoft did take the time to slip in some welcome refinements. The following sections outline the most notable.

IntelliSense Gets More Intelligent

Every modern version of Visual Studio has had the ability to fill in class and member names as you type. For example, type the name of a text box, followed by a period and the letter "F" (as shown in Figure 2-16), and you'll get suggestions such as Font and ForeColor. But in Visual Studio 2010, these automatic suggestions become more helpful thanks to a new *filtering* feature.

Here's how it works. As soon as you've typed in at least two letters of a class or member name, Visual Studio filters the list of suggestions to show just those that match what you've entered so far. That means if you type "TextBox1.Fon", you'll see the Font property but not ForeColor. By comparison, the IntelliSense in previous versions of Visual Studio would show the entire member list, but simply move to the matching position (Font) and highlight that member.

This minor change seems obvious in retrospect, and many developers won't even realize that a shift has taken place. More useful is the way that filtering allows you to search inside a class or member name. For example, if you type "TextBox1.Fon", you'll match properties that start with "Fon" and properties that have the letters "Fon" in them. For example, if you type "GridView1.Sort", you'll see a list with the members Sort, *Sort*Direction, Allow*Sort*ing, Enable*Sort*ingAndPagingCallbacks, and so on, as shown in Figure 2-19.

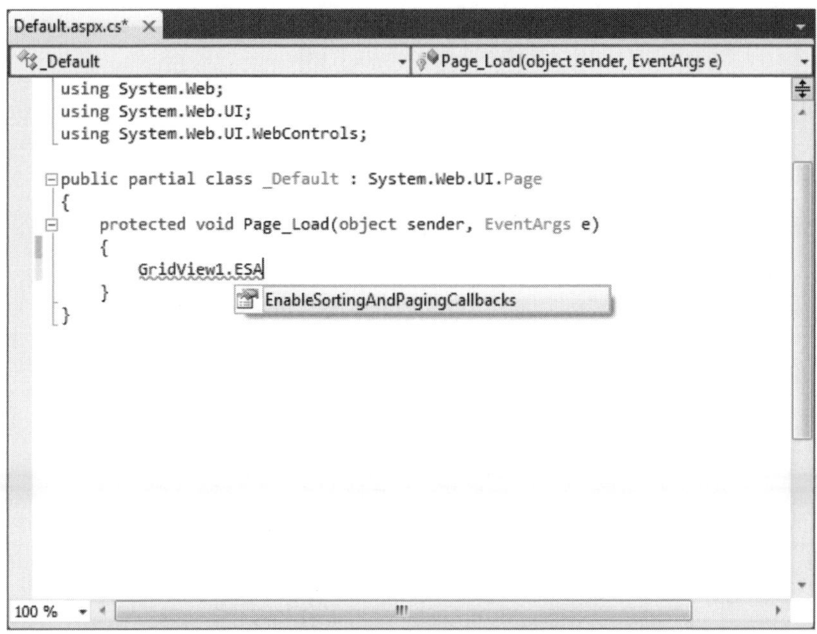

Figure 2-19. *IntelliSense Filtering*

This trick also works with class names. For example, if you type List when you begin declaring a new variable, you'll see class names such as List<T>, ListBox, LinkedList<T>, IList<T>, and so on.

Another IntelliSense filtering trick lets you use capitals to pick out long member names that are composed of several words. For example, type "GridView1.ES" to find all the members that incorporate a word starting with E and a word starting with S. This includes *E*ditRow*S*tyle and *E*nableView*S*tate. The Visual Studio designers call this feature "Pascal case filtering."

At first glance, this trick seems a bit too cute to be truly practical, but it can cut down on keystrokes when dealing with long member names. For example, you'll probably appreciate typing "GridView1.ESA" to bring up the *E*nable*S*orting*A*ndPagingCallbacks property, as shown in Figure 2-20.

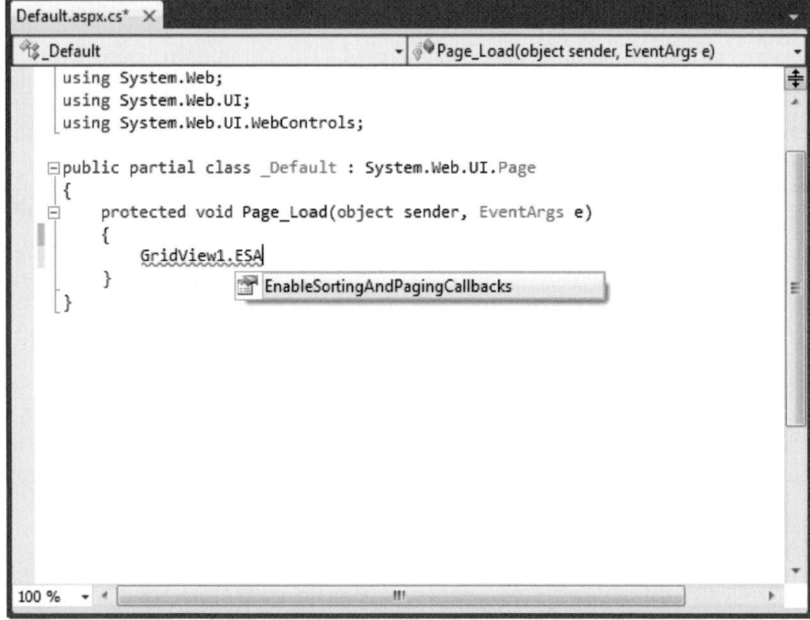

Figure 2-20. *Quick Matching with Capital Letters*

New Tools for Search and Navigation

One of the great challenges in a real-world project is navigating through tangled hierarchies of code. This is particularly true in mature applications that have their own business frameworks, data management components, and other libraries.

Visual Studio 2010 introduces several features that can help you find your way through the densest thickets of code. One of the nicest features is a tiny frill called variable highlighting. To use this feature, simply highlight a variable name. Visual Studio automatically highlights all occurences of that variable using a lighter shade of grey (Figure 2-21).

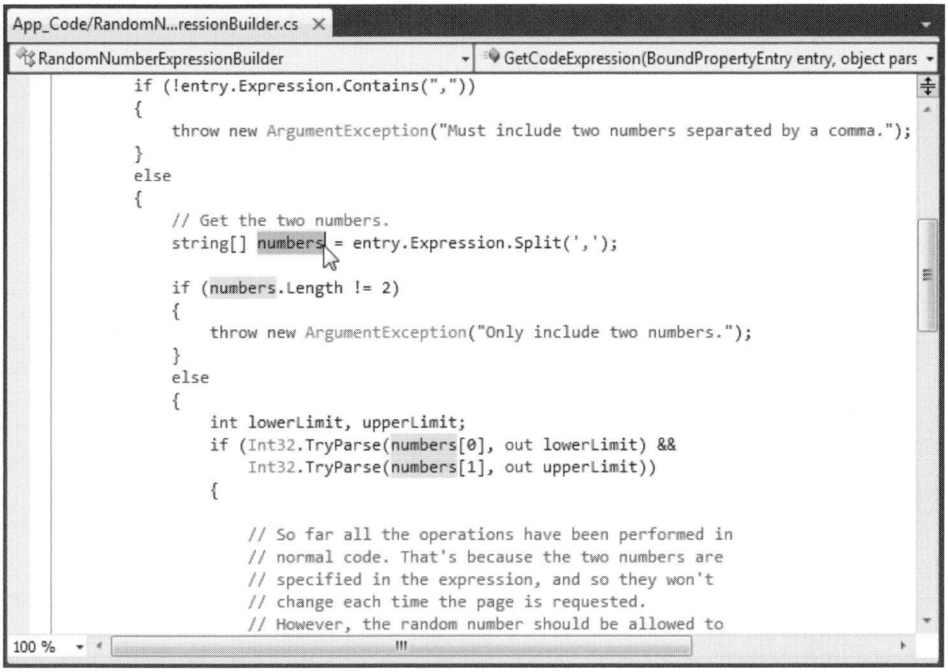

```
App_Code/RandomN...ressionBuilder.cs
RandomNumberExpressionBuilder | GetCodeExpression(BoundPropertyEntry entry, object pars
        if (!entry.Expression.Contains(","))
        {
            throw new ArgumentException("Must include two numbers separated by a comma.");
        }
        else
        {
            // Get the two numbers.
            string[] numbers = entry.Expression.Split(',');

            if (numbers.Length != 2)
            {
                throw new ArgumentException("Only include two numbers.");
            }
            else
            {
                int lowerLimit, upperLimit;
                if (Int32.TryParse(numbers[0], out lowerLimit) &&
                    Int32.TryParse(numbers[1], out upperLimit))
                {

                    // So far all the operations have been performed in
                    // normal code. That's because the two numbers are
                    // specified in the expression, and so they won't
                    // change each time the page is requested.
                    // However, the random number should be allowed to
100 %
```

Figure 2-21. *Highlighting a specific variable*

The highlighting disappears when you click somewhere else with the mouse or press a key. However, the highlighting doesn't disappear if you simply scroll through your document with the mouse, or if you use Ctrl+Shift+↓ to jump to the next highlighted match or Ctrl+Shift+↑ to jump to the previous one.

The next nifty navigation feature is a new call hierarchy explorer that lets you look at any method, quickly determine what methods call that method, and jump to their code. To access this feature, you simply right-click the name of the method that interests you and choose View Call Hierarchy. Visual Studio then opens a Call Hierarchy window that shows a tree of information (Figure 2-22). You can then expand the "Calls To" node to find the incoming method calls (the methods that call this method), or the "Calls From" node to find the outgoing method calls (the methods that this method calls). In Figure 2-22, you can see that the WriteEmployeeList() method in a web page calls the GetEmployees() method in a data component, which is currently being examined in the Call Hierarchy window. If you're viewing an overridden method, you'll also see an Overrides category that allows you to find methods that override or are overridden by this one.

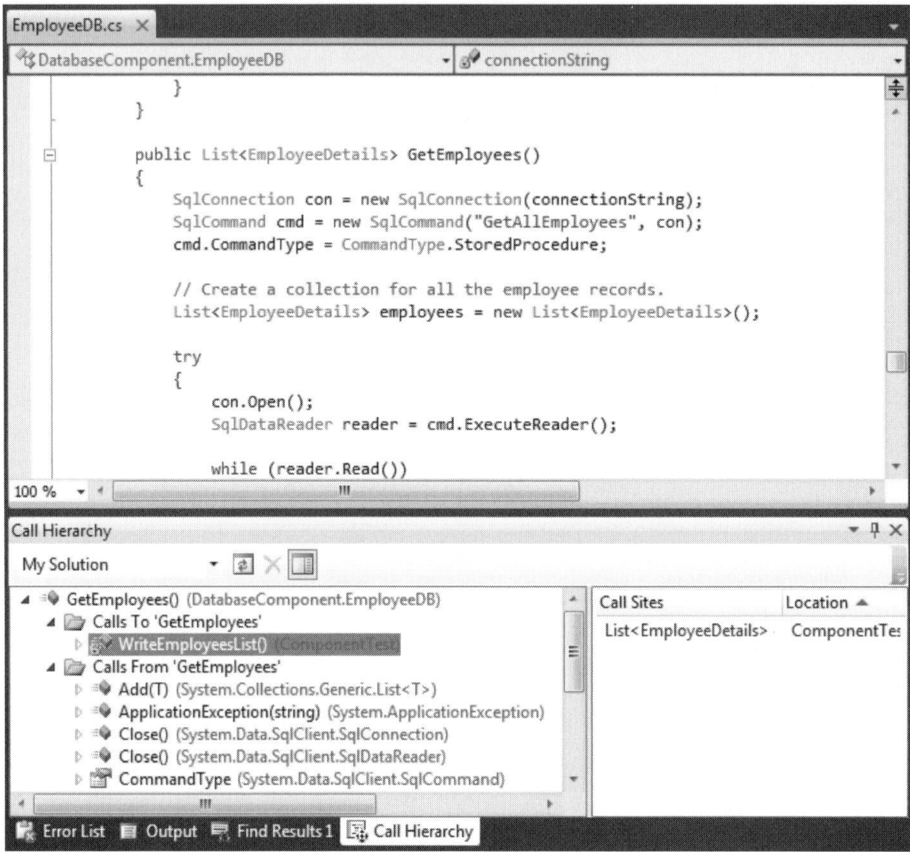

Figure 2-22. Navigating through the call hierarchy

Every time you right-click a method and choose View Call Hierarchy, it's added as a new item in the Call Hierarchy window. All the methods you add remain there until you explicitly remove them (by right-clicking it and choosing Remove Root).

■ **Note** Once you've expanded a node in the Call Hierarchy window, its method list won't be updated, even if you change the code. To force it to update itself to take new changes into account, you must right-click the method and choose Refresh.

You can jump to the code for any method by double-clicking it in the Call Hierarchy window. Or, you can expand it and continue the search another level. If you find yourself lost several levels deep in the call hierarchy, simply right-click the method that you're interested in and choose Add As New Root. Visual Studio will add it as a new top-level item in the Call Hierarchy window.

The last navigation feature is the new Navigation To window that acts as a sort of super-search feature. To access this window, press Ctrl+, (hold down Ctrl and press the comma key). Then, begin typing in the "Search terms" box.

The Navigate To searches asynchronously, so it begins adding matches as you type. To find its matches, it compares the text you supply with the names of types, variables, and members in your classes. It doesn't search the actual code or the comments in your methods, and it ignores the code-behind classes that sit behind your web pages altogether. For these reasons, the Navigate To window is best for searching through the object model of a complex system—for example, hunting down a piece of business logic in a multi-layered framework. Figure 2-23 shows how it can quickly find methods from a data access class.

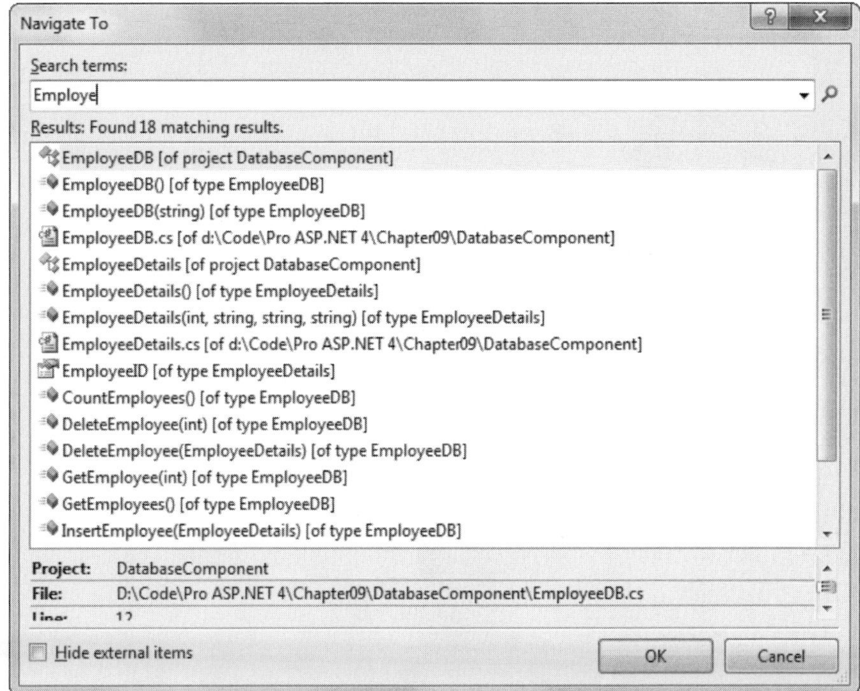

Figure 2-23. *Searching with the Navigate To window*

The Navigate To window has some clear advantages over ordinary searches. First, it ignores the messy code details, which would return thousands of hits in a large project and bury the members you're actually looking for. Second, it's blindingly fast. Third, it also uses some of the IntelliSense filtering tricks you learned about in the previous section. For example, when you type multiple search words separated by a space (such as "customer get"), you'll find results that incorporate both words in any combination (such as the members GetCustomers(), GetCustomerCount(), CustomerCommandGet, and so on). You can also use a sequence of capital letters to find matches with words that use those letters, in that order (so GCC matches the GetCustomerCount() and GetClientCache() methods). But the best way to get a feel for this intuitive searching feature is to try it out for yourself on a large project.

Draggable Document Windows

Visual Studio has always had a highly configurable user interface that supports a flexible (and sometimes confusing) docking system. But Visual Studio2010 is the first version that allows you to take a document window that shows your web page markup or code and drag it right out of the main window. In fact, a simple drag of the mouse is all you need to free any tab, or bring it back into the fold (Figure 2-23).

This feature gives developers complete control over the arrangement of their code windows. But the real purpose of it is to provide a better development experience on computers with multiple monitors. In this situation, it makes sense to drag a code window from the main Visual Studio user interface to another monitor.

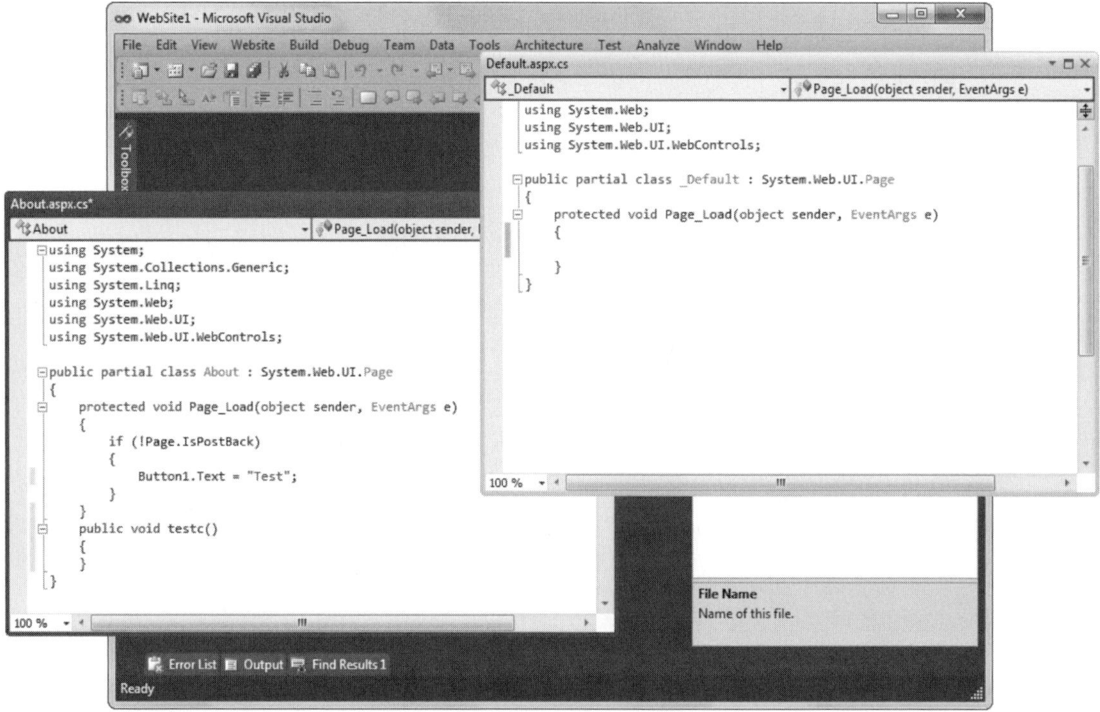

Figure 2-24. Dragging document windows out of Visual Studio

The Code Model

So far, you've learned how to design simple web pages, and you've taken a tour of the Visual Studio interface. But before you get to serious coding, it's important to understand a little more about the underpinnings of the ASP.NET code model. In this section, you'll learn about your options for using code to program a web page and how ASP.NET events wire up to your code.

Visual Studio supports two models for coding web pages:

Inline code: This model is the closest to traditional ASP. All the code and HTML markup is stored in a single .aspx file. The code is embedded in one or more script blocks. However, even though the code is in a script block, it doesn't lose IntelliSense or debugging support, and it doesn't need to be executed linearly from top to bottom (like classic ASP code). Instead, you'll still react to control events and use subroutines. This model is handy because it keeps everything in one neat package, and it's popular for coding simple web pages.

Code-behind: This model separates each ASP.NET web page into two files: an .aspx markup file with the HTML and control tags, and a .cs code file with the source code for the page (assuming you're using C# as your web page programming language). This model provides better organization, and separating the user interface from programmatic logic is keenly important when building complex pages.

In Visual Studio, you have the freedom to use both approaches. When you add a new web page to your website (using Website ➤ Add New Item), the Place Code in a Separate File check box lets you choose whether you want to use the code-behind model (see Figure 2-25). Visual Studio remembers your previous setting for the next time you add a new page, but it's completely valid (albeit potentially confusing) to mix both styles of pages in the same application.

This flexibility only applies to projectless development. If you've created a web project, you must use the code-behind model—there's no other choice. Furthermore, the code-behind model is subtly different for the code-behind model that's used in a projectless website, as you'll see shortly.

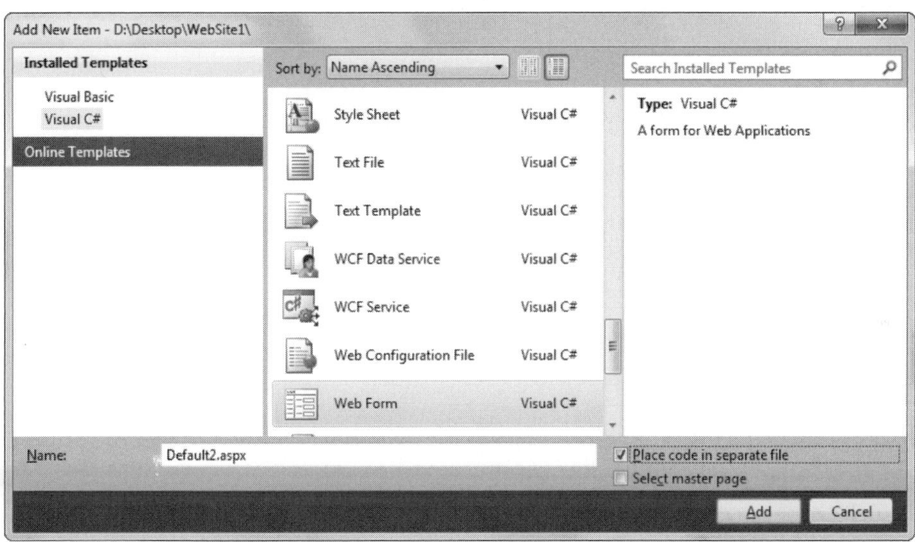

Figure 2-25. Choosing the code model

To better understand the difference between the inline code and code-behind models, it helps to consider a simple page. The following example shows the markup for a page named TestFormInline.aspx, which displays the current time in a label and refreshes it whenever a button is clicked. Here's how the page looks with inline code:

```
<%@ Page Language="C#" %>
<!DOCTYPE html PUBLIC "-//W3C//DTD XHTML 1.1//EN"
 "http://www.w3.org/TR/xhtml11/DTD/xhtml11.dtd">

<script runat="server">
    protected void Button1_Click(object sender, EventArgs e)
```

```
    {
        Label1.Text = "Current time: " + DateTime.Now.ToLongTimeString();
    }
</script>

<html xmlns="http://www.w3.org/1999/xhtml" >
<head runat="server">
    <title>Test Page</title>
</head>
<body>
    <form id="form1" runat="server">
    <div>
        <asp:Label ID="Label1" runat="server" Text="Click Me!" />
        <br /><br /><br />
        <asp:Button ID="Button1" runat="server" OnClick="Button1_Click"
         Text="Button" />
    </div>
    </form>
</body>
</html>
```

The following listings, TestFormCodeBehind.aspx and TestFormCodeBehind.aspx.cs, show how the page is broken up into two pieces using the code-behind model. This is TestFormCodeBehind.aspx:

```
<%@ Page Language="C#" AutoEventWireup="true" CodeFile="TestFormCodeBehind.aspx.cs"
 Inherits="TestFormCodeBehind"%>
<!DOCTYPE html PUBLIC "-//W3C//DTD XHTML 1.1//EN"
 "http://www.w3.org/TR/xhtml11/DTD/xhtml11.dtd">

<html xmlns="http://www.w3.org/1999/xhtml" >
<head runat="server">
    <title>Test Page</title>
</head>
<body>
    <form id="form1" runat="server">
    <div>
        <asp:Label ID="Label1" runat="server" Text="Click Me!"></asp:Label><br />
        <br />
        <br />
        <asp:Button ID="Button1" runat="server" OnClick="Button1_Click"
         Text="Button" />
    </div>
    </form>
</body>
</html>
```

This is TestFormCodeBehind.aspx.cs:

```
using System;
using System.Data;
using System.Configuration;
using System.Linq;
using System.Web;
```

```
using System.Web.Security;
using System.Web.UI;
using System.Web.UI.WebControls;
using System.Web.UI.WebControls.WebParts;
using System.Web.UI.HtmlControls;

public partial class TestFormCodeBehind : System.Web.UI.Page
{
    protected void Button1_Click(object sender, EventArgs e)
    {
        Label1.Text = "Current time: " + DateTime.Now.ToLongTimeString();
    }
}
```

The only real difference between the inline code example and the code-behind example is that the page class is no longer implicit in the latter—instead it's declared to contain all the page methods.

Overall, the code-behind model is preferred for complex pages. Although the inline code model is slightly more compact for small pages, as your code and HTML grows it becomes much easier to deal with both portions separately. The code-behind model is also conceptually cleaner, as it explicitly indicates the class you've created and the namespaces you've imported. Finally, the code-behind model introduces the possibility that a web designer may refine the markup in your pages without touching your code. This book uses the code-behind model for all examples.

How Code-Behind Files Are Connected to Pages

Every .aspx page starts with a Page directive
. This Page directive specifies the language for the page, and it also tells ASP.NET where to find the associated code (unless you're using inline code, in which case the code is contained in the same file).

You can specify where to find the associated code in several ways. In older versions of ASP.NET, it was common to use the Src attribute to point to the source code file or the Inherits attribute to indicate a compiled class name. However, both of these options have their idiosyncrasies. For example, with the Inherits attribute, you're forced to always precompile your code, which is tedious (and can cause problems in development teams, because the standard option is to compile every page into a single DLL assembly). But the real problem is that both approaches force you to declare every web control you want to use with a member variable. This adds a lot of boilerplate code.

You can solve the problem using a language feature called partial classes, which lets you split a single class into multiple source code files. Essentially, the model is the same as before, but the control declarations are shuffled into a separate file. You, the developer, never need to be distracted by this file—instead you can just access your web-page controls by name. Keen eyes will have spotted the word partial in the class declaration for your web-page code:

```
public partial class TestFormCodeBehind : System.Web.UI.Page
{ ... }
```

With this bit of infrastructure in place, the rest is easy. Your .aspx page uses the Inherits attribute to indicate the class you're using, and the CodeFile attribute to indicate the file that contains your code-behind, as shown here:

```
<%@ Page Language="C#" AutoEventWireup="true" CodeFile="TestFormCodeBehind.aspx.cs"
    Inherits="TestFormCodeBehind"%>
```

Notice that Visual Studio uses a slightly unusual naming syntax for the source code file. It has the full name of the corresponding web page, complete with the .aspx extension, followed by the .cs extension at the end. This is just a matter of convention, and it avoids a problem if you happen to create two different code-behind file types (for example, a web page and a web service) with the same name.

How Control Tags Are Connected to Page Variables

When you request your web page in a browser, ASP.NET starts by finding the associated code file. Then, it generates a variable declaration for each server control (each element that has the runat="server" attribute).

For example, imagine you have a text box named txtInput:

```
<asp:TextBox id="txtInput" runat="server"/>
```

ASP.NET generates the following member variable declaration and merges it with your page class using the magic of partial classes:

```
protected System.Web.UI.TextBox txtInput;
```

Of course, you won't see this declaration, because it's part of the automatically generated code that the .NET compiler creates. But you rely on it every time you write a line of code that refers to the txtInput object (either to read or to write a property):

```
txtInput.Text = "Hello.";
```

To make sure this system works, you must keep both the .aspx markup file (with the control tags) and the .cs file (with the source code) synchronized. If you edit control names in one piece using another tool (such as a text editor), you'll break the link, and your code won't compile.

Incidentally, you'll notice that control variables are always declared with the protected accessibility keyword. That's because of the way ASP.NET uses inheritance in the web-page model. The following layers are at work:

1. The Page class from the .NET class library defines the basic functionality that allows a web page to host other controls, render itself to HTML, and provide access to the traditional ASP-style objects such as Request, Response, and Session.

2. Your code-behind class (for example, TestFormCodeBehind) inherits from the Page class to acquire the basic set of ASP.NET web-page functionality.

3. When you compile your class, ASP.NET merges some extra code into your class (using the magic of partial classes). This automatically generated code defines all the controls on your page as protected variables so that you can access them in your code.

4. The ASP.NET compiler creates one more class to represents the actual .aspx page. This class inherits from your custom code-behind class (with the extra bit of merged code). To name this class, ASP.NET adds _aspx to the name of the code-behind class (for example, TestFormCodeBehind_aspx). This class contains the code needed to initialize the page and its controls and spits out the final rendered HTML. It's also the class that ASP.NET instantiates when it receives the page request.

Figure 2-26 diagrams this tangled relationship.

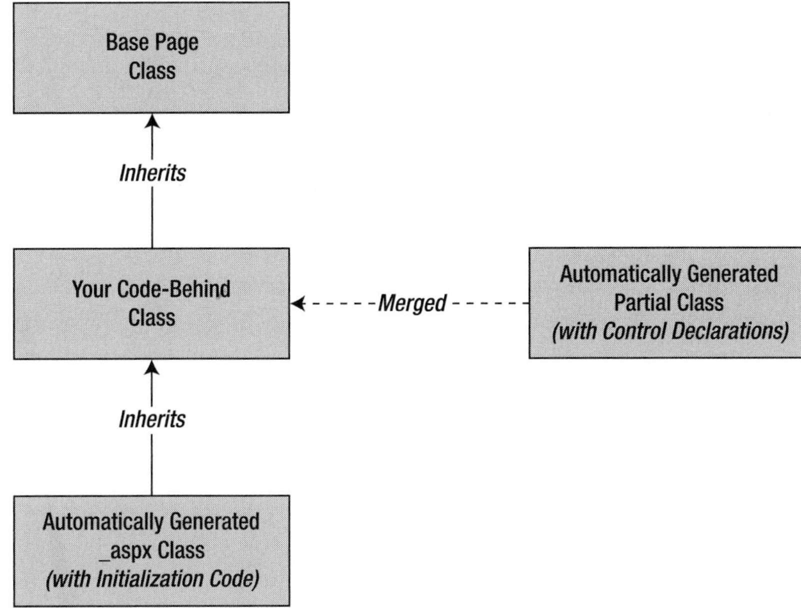

Figure 2-26. *How a page class is constructed*

So, why are all the control variables and methods declared as protected? It's because of the way inheritance is used in this series of layers. Protected variables act like private variables, with a key difference—they are accessible to derived classes. In other words, using protected variables in your code-behind class (for example, TestFormCodeBehind) ensures that the variables are accessible in the derived page class (TestFormCodeBehind_aspx). This allows ASP.NET to match your control variables to the control tags and attach event handlers at runtime.

How Events Are Connected to Event Handlers

Most of the code in an ASP.NET web page is placed inside event handlers that react to web control events. Using Visual Studio, you can add an event handler to your code in three ways:

Type it in by hand: In this case, you add the method directly to the page class. You must specify the appropriate parameters so that the signature of the event handler exactly matches the signature of the event you want to handle. You'll also need to edit the control tag so that it links the control to the appropriate event handler, by adding an OnEventName attribute. (Alternatively, you can use delegates to wire this up programmatically.)

Double-click a control in design view: In this case, Visual Studio will create an event handler for that control's default event (and adjust the control tag accordingly). For example, if you double-click the page, it will create a Page.Load event handler. If you double-click a Button control, Visual Studio will create an event handler for the Click event.

Choose the event from the Properties window: Just select the control, and click the lightning bolt in the Properties window. You'll see a list of all the events provided by that control. Double-click in the box next to the event you want to handle, and Visual Studio will automatically generate the event handler in your page class and adjust the control tag.

The second and third options are the most convenient. The third option is the most flexible, because it allows you to select a method in the page class that you've already created. Just select the event in the Properties window, and click the drop-down arrow at the right. You'll see a list that includes all the methods in your class that match the signature this event requires. You can then choose a method from the list to connect it. Figure 2-27 shows an example where the Button.Click event is connected to the Button_Click() method in your page class. The only limitation of this technique is that it works exclusively with web controls, not server-side HTML controls.

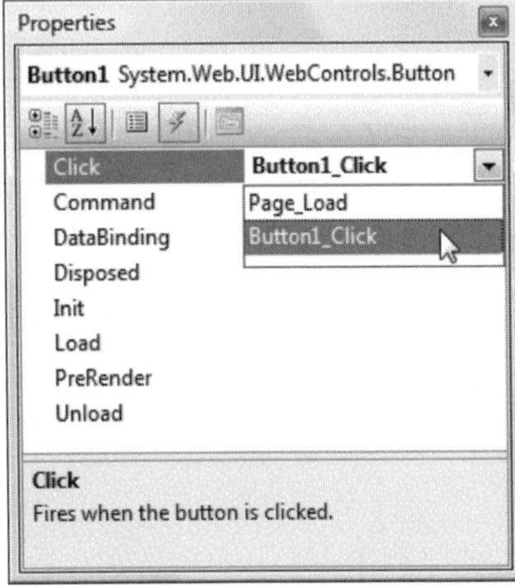

Figure 2-27. Attaching an event handler

Visual Studio uses automatic event wire-up, as indicated in the Page directive. Automatic event wire-up has two basic principles:

- All page event handlers are connected automatically based on the name of the event handler. In other words, the Page_Load() method is automatically called when the page loads.
- All control event handlers are connected using attributes in the control tag. The attribute has the same name as the event, prefixed by the word On.

For example, if you want to handle the Click event of the Button control, you simply need to set the OnClick attribute in the control tag with the name of the event handler you want to use. Here's the change you need:

```
<asp:Button id="cmdOK" OnClick="cmdOK_Click" runat="server">
```

ASP.NET controls always use this syntax. Remember, because ASP.NET must connect the event handlers, the derived page class must be able to access the code-behind class. This means your event handlers must be declared with the protected or public keyword. (Protected is preferred, because it prevents other classes from seeing this method.)

Of course, if you're familiar with .NET events, you know there's another approach to connect an event handler. You can do it dynamically through code using delegates. Here's an example:

```
cmdOK.Click += cmdOK_Click;
```

This approach is useful if you're creating controls on the fly. You'll see this technique in action in Chapter 3.

Web Projects

So far, you've seen how to create websites without any project files. The advantage of projectless development is that it's simple and straightforward. When you create a projectless website, you don't need to deploy any extra support files. Instead, every file in your web folder is automatically considered part of the web application. (This model makes sense because every web page in a virtual directory is independently accessible, whether or not you consider it an official part of your project.)

Projectless development remains popular for the following reasons:

Projectless development simplifies deployment: You simply need to copy all the files in the website directory to the web server—there aren't any project or debugging files to avoid.

Projectless development simplifies file management: If you want to remove a web page, you can simply delete the associated files using the file management tool of your choice. If you want to add a new page or move a page from one website to another, you simply need to copy the files—there's no need to go through Visual Studio or edit the project file. You can even author web pages with other tools, because there's no project file to maintain.

Projectless development simplifies team collaboration: Different people can work independently on different web pages, without needing to lock the project files.

Projectless development simplifies debugging: When creating a web project, you must recompile the entire application when you change a single page. With projectless development, each page is compiled separately, and the page is only compiled when you request it for the first time.

Projectless development allows you to mix languages: Because each web page is compiled separately, you're free to code your pages in different languages. In a web project, you'd be forced to create separate web projects (which is trickier to manage) or separate class library projects.

That said, there are some more specialized reasons that might lead you to adopt project-based development instead, or use web projects in specific scenarios. You'll consider these in the next section.

Project-Based Development

When you create a web project, Visual Studio generates a number of extra files, including the .csproj and .csproj.user project files and a .sln solution file. When you build your application, Visual Studio generates temporary files, which it places in the Obj subdirectory, and one or more .pdb files (in the Bin subdirectory) with debugging symbols. None of these files should be deployed to the web server when your web application is complete. Furthermore, none of the C# source code files (files with the extension .cs) should be deployed, because Visual Studio precompiles them into a DLL assembly.

■ **Note** At first glance, the precompilation of web projects seems like a big win—not only does it ensure pages don't need to be compiled the first time they're requested, but it also allows you to avoid deploying your source code to the web server. However, projectless websites can be compiled for deployment just as easily—you simply need to use the precompilation tool you'll learn about in Chapter 18.

Project-based development has a dedicated following. The most significant advantages to web projects are the following:

The project development system is stricter than projectless development: This is because the project file explicitly lists what files should be part of the project. This allows you to catch potential errors (such as missing files) and even deliberate acts of sabotage (such as unwanted files added by a malicious user).

Web projects allow for more flexible file management: One example is if you've created several separate projects and placed them in subdirectories of the same virtual directory. In this case, the projects are kept separate for development purposes but are in essence the same application for deployment. With projectless development, there's no way to keep the files in these subdirectories separate.

■ **Tip** For the same reason, web projects can be more efficient if you're creating a web application that uses a huge number of resource files—for example, a website that includes an Images subdirectory with thousands of pictures. With projectless development, Visual Studio examines these files and adds them to the Solution Explorer, because they're a part of your website directory. But a web project avoids this extra overhead because you won't explicitly add the images to the list of files in your project.

Web projects allow for a customizable deployment process: Visual Studio project files work with the web package feature, which gives you additional features for configuring the deployed version of your application (as described in Chapter 18).

Web projects work better in some migration scenarios: Any web application created with Visual Studio 2003 or earlier is a web project, because these versions of Visual Studio didn't include the projectless website feature. If you open one of these projects in Visual Studio 2010, Visual Studio runs the migration wizard to convert the application to a Visual Studio 2010 web project.

Both projectless and project-based development give you all the same ASP.NET features. Both approaches also offer the same performance. So which option is best when building a new ASP.NET website? There are advocates for both approaches. Officially, Microsoft suggests you use the simpler website model unless there's a specific reason to use a web project—for example, you've developed a custom MSBuild extension, you have a highly automated deployment process in place, you're migrating an older website created in Visual Studio 2003, or you want to create multiple projects in one directory.

■ **Note** The downloadable examples for this book use projectless websites.

Creating a Web Project

To create a web project, choose File ➤ New ➤ Project to show the New Project dialog box (which looks extremely similar to the New Web Site dialog box you considered earlier). In the Project Types tree, browse to Visual C# ➤ Web. Then choose ASP.NET Web Application.

When creating a web project, you supply a location, which can be a file path or a URL that points to a local or remote IIS web server. You can change the version of the .NET Framework that you're targeting using the list at the top of the window, as you can when creating a projectless website.

Although web projects and projectless websites have the same end result once they're deployed to the web server and compiled, there are some differences in the way they're structured at design time. These differences include the following:

- **Compilation:** As explained earlier, web projects are compiled by Visual Studio (not ASP.NET) when you run them. The web page classes are combined into a single assembly that has the name of the web project (like WebApplication1.dll), which is then placed in the Bin folder.
- **Code-behind:** The web pages in a web project always use the code-behind model. However, they include an extra file with the extension .aspx.designer.cs, which includes the declarations for all the controls on the web page. This means if you create a page named Default.aspx, you'll end up with a code-behind class in a file named Default.aspx.cs and control declarations in a file named Default.aspx.designer.cs (see Figure 2-28). At compile time, these two files will be merged. In a projectless website, you never see a file with the control declarations, because this part of the code is generated at compile time by ASP.NET.
- **The Page directive:** The web pages in a web project use a slightly different Page directive. Instead of using the CodeFile attribute to indicate the file that has the source code, they use the CodeBehind attribute. This difference is due to the fact that Visual Studio performs the compilation instead of ASP.NET. ASP.NET checks the CodeFile attribute, but Visual Studio uses the CodeBehind attribute.
- **Assembly references:** In a projectless website, all the assembly references are recorded in the web.config file, so ASP.NET can use them when resolving references at compile time. But the assembly references in a web project are stored in a project file, which Visual Studio uses when it compiles the code. The only exceptions are the references to the System.Core.dll and System.Web.Extensions.dll assemblies, which contain all the features that are specific to .NET 3.5. These references are defined in the web.config file because they include classes that you need to specify new configuration settings.

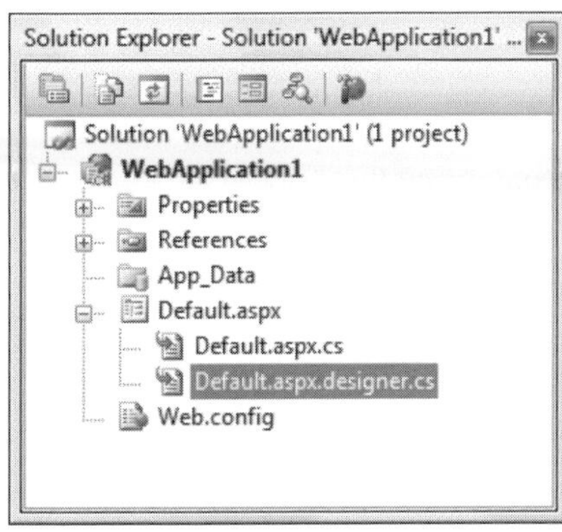

Figure 2-28. *The designer file with control declarations*

■ **Note** The code file with the control declarations isn't available in a projectless web application. Instead, it's generated behind the scenes the first time the application is compiled and executed. As a result, you never have the chance to view this code.

Migrating a Website from a Previous Version of Visual Studio

If you have an existing ASP.NET web application created with an earlier version Visual Studio, you can migrate it to the ASP.NET world with ease.

If you created a projectless website with an earlier version of Visual Studio, you use the File ➤ Open ➤ Web Site command, just as you would with a website created in Visual Studio 2010. The first time you open an old website in this way, you'll be asked if you want to adjust it to use ASP.NET 4 (see Figure 2-29). If you choose Yes, the web.config file will be modified to target .NET 4, as described in the "Multitargeting" section earlier in this chapter. If you choose No, your website will continue targeting the version of ASP.NET that it was designed for. You can modify this detail at any time by choosing Website ➤ Start Options. Either way, you won't be asked again, because your preference is recorded in the hidden solution file that's stored in a user-specific Visual Studio directory.

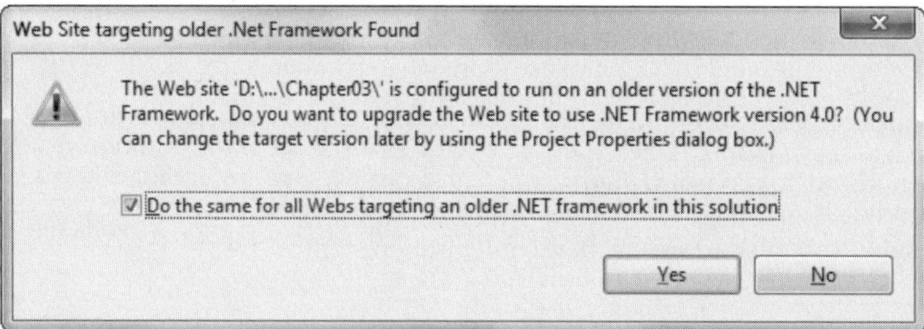

Figure 2-29. Opening a projectless website that was created with Visual Studio 2008

If you created a web project with an earlier version of Visual Studio, you need to use the File ➤ Open ➤ Project/Solution command. You also need to use this command if you created a solution that contains a website. (For example, you might take this step when designing and debugging a website along with a separately compiled component.) When you open an old project or solution, Visual Studio begins the Conversion Wizard (see Figure 2-30). The Conversion Wizard is exceedingly simple. It prompts you to choose whether to create a backup and, if so, where it should be placed. If this is your only copy of the application, a backup is a good idea in case some aspects of your application can't be converted successfully. Otherwise, you can skip this option.

Figure 2-30. *Importing a web project that was created with an older version of Visual Studio*

When you click Finish, Visual Studio performs an in-place conversion. Any errors and warnings are added to a conversion log, which you can display when the conversion is complete. If you're opening a solution that contains a website, Visual Studio will also show the same window you saw earlier (Figure 2-29), asking you if you want to update it.

When you update an ASP.NET 3.5 website, you end up with a modified web.config that contains some content you may not want. Here's the added content you're likely to find:

```
<?xml version="1.0"?>
<configuration>
  <system.web>
    <compilation debug="true" targetFramework="4.0">
    </compilation>
    <pages controlRenderingCompatibilityVersion="3.5" clientIDMode="AutoID" />
    ...
  </system.web>

  <system.codedom>
    <compilers>
      <compiler language="c#;cs;csharp" extension=".cs" ...>
        <providerOption name="CompilerVersion" value="v4.0"/>
      </compiler>
      <compiler language="vb;vbs;visualbasic;vbscript" extension=".vb" ...>
        <providerOption name="CompilerVersion" value="v4.0"/>
      </compiler>
    </compilers>
  </system.codedom>
</configuration>
```

The <pages> element tells ASP.NET to use the traditional page rendering (which has a few XHTML quirks), and the traditional method for assigning client-side control IDs (which creates huge, unpredictable names that are difficult to target with CSS rules or JavaScript). If you don't need this level of backward-compatibility, you can delete the <pages> element altogether. Chapter 3 has more information about these settings.

The <system.codedom> section registers the C# and VB language compilers. (ASP.NET 3.5 needed to take this step because it was deployed as an add-on to the core ASP.NET 2.0 engine rather than a completely new, separate release.) Although Visual Studio isn't intelligent enough to strip this information out, you can remove the <system.codedom> section yourself, unless you've modified it to register other, third-party language compilers.

Visual Studio Debugging

To debug a specific web page in Visual Studio, select that web page in the Solution Explorer, and click the Start Debugging button on the toolbar. (If you are currently editing the web page you want to test, you don't need to select it at all—just click Start Debugging to launch it directly.)

What happens next depends on the location of your project. If your project is stored on a remote web server or a local IIS virtual directory, Visual Studio simply launches your default browser and directs you to the appropriate URL. If you've used a file system application, Visual Studio starts its integrated web server on a dynamically selected port (which prevents it from conflicting with IIS, if it's installed). Then Visual Studio launches the default browser and passes it a URL that points to the local web server. Either way, the real work—compiling the page and creating the page objects—is passed along to the ASP.NET worker process.

The test server only runs while Visual Studio is running, and it only accepts requests from your computer. When Visual Studio starts the integrated web server, it adds an icon for it in the system tray. If you want to get a little bit of extra information about the test server, or you want to shut it down, simply double-click the system tray icon.

■ **Tip** Visual Studio's built-in web server allows you to retrieve a file listing. This means if you create a web application named MyApp, you can make a request in the form of http://localhost:port/MyApp to see a list of pages. Then, just click the page you want to test. This process assumes your web application doesn't have a default.aspx page—if it does, any requests for the website root automatically return this page.

The separation between Visual Studio, the web server, and ASP.NET allows for a few interesting tricks. For example, while your browser window is open, you can still make changes to the code and tags of your web pages. Once you've completed your changes, just save the page, and click the Refresh button in your browser to request it again. Although you'll always be forced to restart the entire page to see the results of any changes you make, it's still more convenient than rebuilding your whole project.

Fixing and restarting a web page is handy, but what about when you need to track down an elusive error? In these cases, you need Visual Studio's debugging smarts, which are described in the next few sections.

■ **Note** When you use the test web server, it runs all code using your user account. This is different from the much more limited behavior you'll see in IIS, which uses a less-privileged account to ensure security. It's important to understand the difference, because if your application accesses protected resources (such as the file system, a database, the registry, or an event log), you'll need to make sure you explicitly allow the IIS user. For more information about IIS and the hosting model, refer to Chapter 18.

Single-Step Debugging

Single-step debugging allows you to execute your code one line at a time. It's incredibly easy to use. Just follow these steps:

1. Find a location in your code where you want to pause execution, and start single-stepping (you can use any executable line of code but not a variable declaration, comment, or blank line). Click in the margin next to the line code, and a red breakpoint will appear (see Figure 2-31).

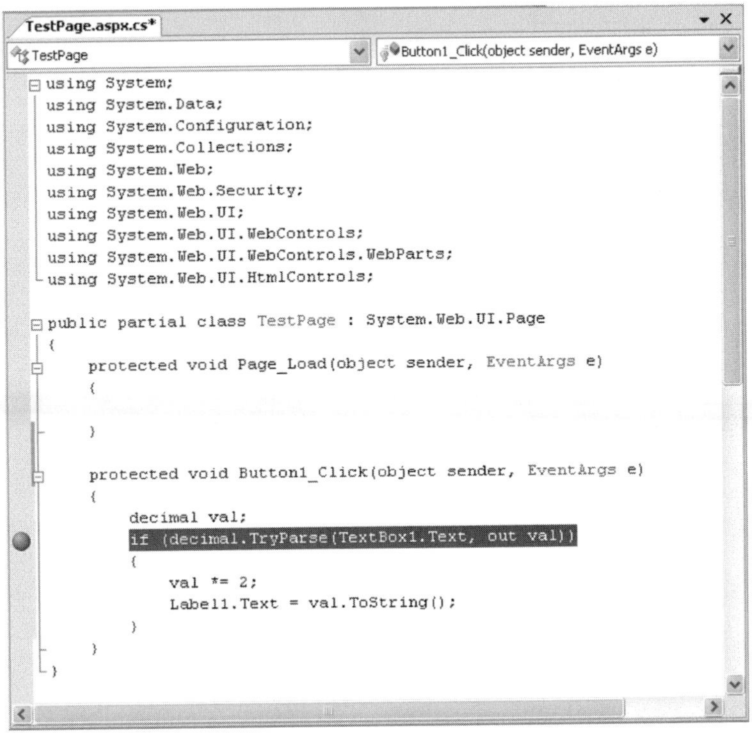

TestPage.aspx.cs*

TestPage | Button1_Click(object sender, EventArgs e)

```
using System;
using System.Data;
using System.Configuration;
using System.Collections;
using System.Web;
using System.Web.Security;
using System.Web.UI;
using System.Web.UI.WebControls;
using System.Web.UI.WebControls.WebParts;
using System.Web.UI.HtmlControls;

public partial class TestPage : System.Web.UI.Page
{
    protected void Page_Load(object sender, EventArgs e)
    {

    }

    protected void Button1_Click(object sender, EventArgs e)
    {
        decimal val;
        if (decimal.TryParse(TextBox1.Text, out val))
        {
            val *= 2;
            Label1.Text = val.ToString();
        }
    }
}
```

Figure 2-31. Setting a breakpoint

2. Now start your program as you would ordinarily. When the program reaches your breakpoint, execution will pause, and you'll be switched back to the Visual Studio code window. The breakpoint statement won't be executed.

3. At this point, you have several options. You can execute the current line by pressing F11. The following line in your code will be highlighted with a yellow arrow, indicating that this is the next line that will be executed. You can continue like this through your program, running one line at a time by pressing F11 and following the code's path of execution. Or, you can exit break mode and resume running your code by pressing F5.

■ **Note** Instead of using shortcut keys such as F11 and F5, you can use the buttons in the Visual Studio Debug toolbar. Alternatively, you can right-click the code window and choose an option from the context menu.

---

4. Whenever the code is in break mode, you can hover over variables to see their current contents. This allows you to verify that variables contain the values you expect (see Figure 2-32). If you hover over an object, you can drill down into all the individual properties by clicking the small plus symbol to expand it (see Figure 2-33).

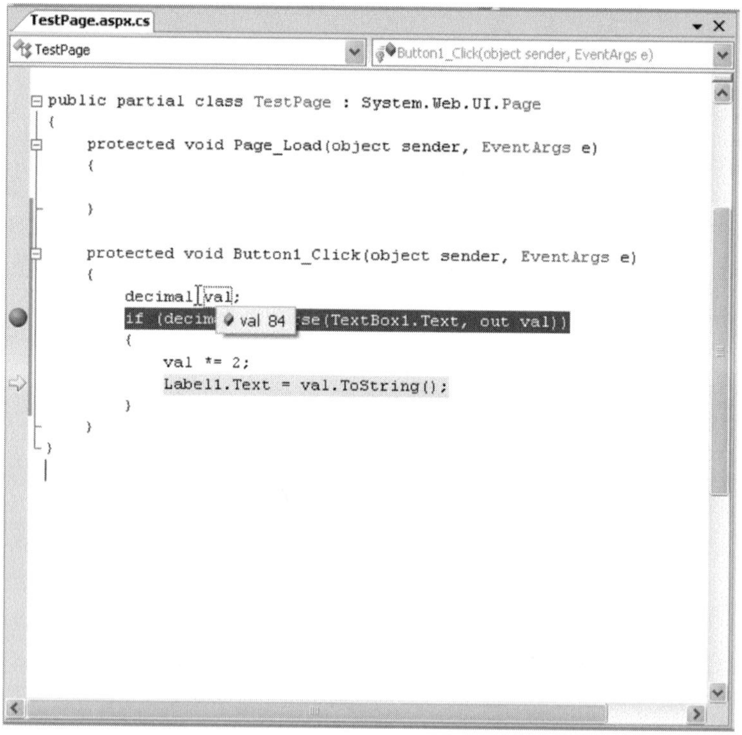
TestPage.aspx.cs
TestPage
Button1_Click(object sender, EventArgs e)
public partial class TestPage : System.Web.UI.Page
{
protected void Page_Load(object sender, EventArgs e)
{
}
protected void Button1_Click(object sender, EventArgs e)
{
decimal val;
if (decim
val 84
se(TextBox1.Text, out val))
{
val *= 2;
Label1.Text = val.ToString();
}
}
}

Figure 2-32. Viewing variable contents in break mode

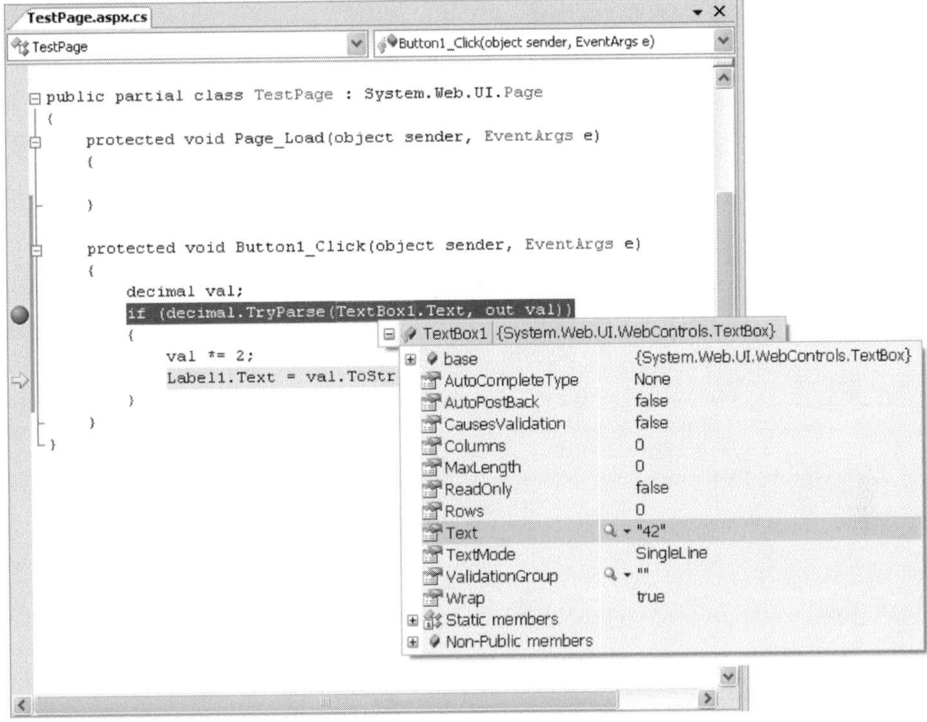

Figure 2-33. Viewing object properties in break mode

■ **Tip** You can even modify the values in a variable or property directly—just click inside the tooltip, and enter the new value. This allows you to simulate scenarios that are difficult or time-consuming to re-create manually or to test specific error conditions.

---

5. You can also use any of the commands listed in Table 2-5 while in break mode. These commands are available from the context menu by right-clicking the code window or by using the associated hot key.

You can switch your program into break mode at any point by clicking the pause button in the toolbar or by selecting Debug ➤ Break All.

Table 2-5. Commands Available in Break Mode

Command (Hot Key)	Description
Step Into (F11)	Executes the currently highlighted line and then pauses. If the currently highlighted line calls a method or property, execution will pause at the first executable line inside the method or property (which is why this feature is called stepping into).
Step Over (F10)	The same as Step Into, except that it runs methods (or properties) as though they are a single line. If you select the Step Over command while a method call is highlighted, the entire method will be executed. Execution will pause at the next executable statement in the current procedure.
Step Out (Shift+F11)	Executes all the code in the current procedure and then pauses at the statement that immediately follows the one that called this method or property. In other words, this allows you to step "out" of the current procedure in one large jump.
Continue (F5)	Resumes the program and continues to run it normally without pausing until another breakpoint is reached.
Run to Cursor	Allows you to run all the code up to a specific line (where your cursor is currently positioned). You can use this technique to skip a time-consuming loop.
Set Next Statement	Allows you to change your program's path of execution while debugging. It causes your program to mark the current line (where your cursor is positioned) as the current line for execution. When you resume execution, this line will be executed, and the program will continue from that point. You can use this technique to temporarily bypass troublemaking code, but it's easy to run into an error if you skip a required detail or leave your data in an inconsistent state.
Show Next Statement	Moves focus to the line of code that is marked for execution. This line is marked by a yellow arrow. The Show Next Statement command is useful if you lose your place while editing.

Variable Watches

In some cases, you might want to track the status of a variable without switching into break mode repeatedly. In this case, it's more useful to use the Locals, Autos, and Watch windows, which allow you to track variables across an entire application. Table 2-6 describes these windows.

Table 2-6. Variable Tracking Windows

Window	Description
Locals	Automatically displays all the variables that are in scope in the current procedure. This offers a quick summary of important variables.
Autos	Automatically displays variables that Visual Studio determines are important for the current code statement. For example, this might include variables that are accessed or changed in the previous line.
Watch	Displays variables you have added. Watches are saved with your project, so you can continue tracking a variable later. To add a watch, right-click a variable in your code, and select Add Watch; alternatively, double-click the last row in the Watch window, and type in the variable name.

Each row in the Locals, Autos, and Watch windows provides information about the type or class of the variable and its current value. If the variable holds an object instance, you can expand the variable and see its private members and properties. For example, in the Locals window you'll see the this variable, which is a reference to the current page object. If you click the plus symbol next to this, a full list will appear that describes many page properties (and some system values), as shown in Figure 2-34.

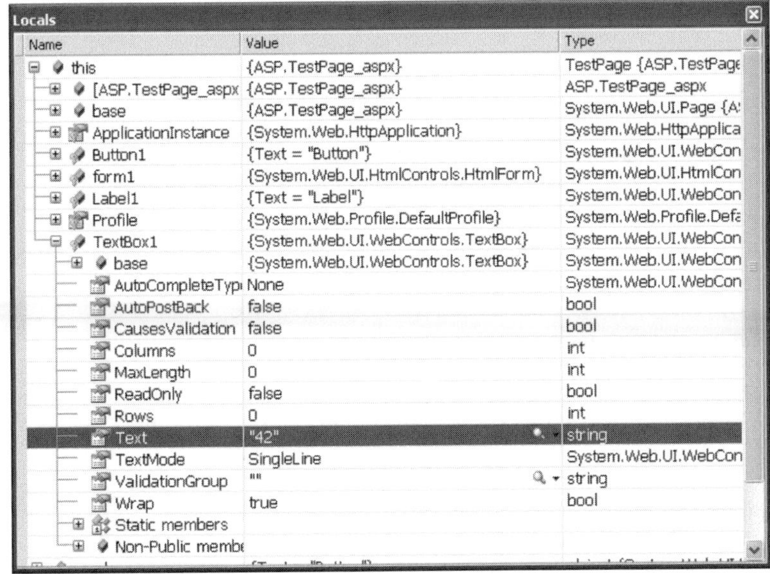

Figure 2-34. Viewing the current page object in the Locals window

The Locals, Autos, and Watch windows allow you to change variables or properties while your program is in break mode. Just double-click the current value in the Value column, and type in a new value. If you are missing one of the watch windows, you can show it manually by selecting it from the Debug ➤ Windows submenu.

Advanced Breakpoints

Choose Debug ➤ Windows ➤ Breakpoints to see a window that lists all the breakpoints in your current project. The Breakpoints window provides a hit count, showing you the number of times a breakpoint has been encountered (see Figure 2-35). You can jump to the corresponding location in code by double-clicking a breakpoint. You can also use the Breakpoints window to disable a breakpoint without removing it. That allows you to keep a breakpoint to use in testing later, without leaving it active. Breakpoints are automatically saved with the solution file described earlier.

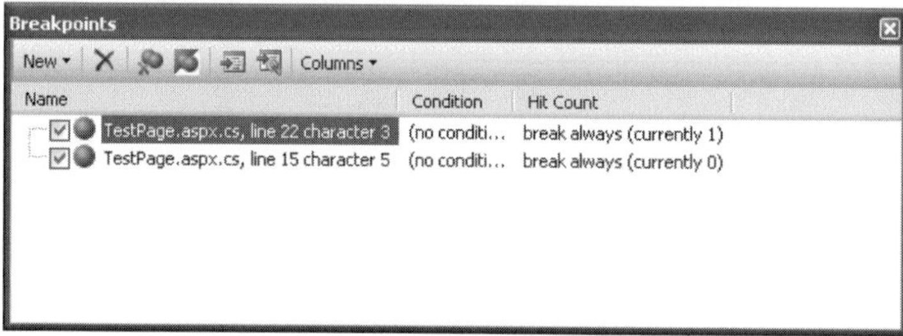

Figure 2-35. *The Breakpoints window*

Visual Studio allows you to customize breakpoints so that they occur only if certain conditions are true. To customize a breakpoint, right-click it, and choose one of the following options:

Location: Use this option to review the exact file and line where the breakpoint is placed.

Condition: Use this option to set an expression. You can choose to enable this breakpoint only when this expression is true or when it has changed since the last time the breakpoint was hit.

Hit Count: Use this option to create a breakpoint that pauses only after a breakpoint has been hit a certain number of times (for example, at least 20) or a specific multiple of times (for example, every fifth time).

Filter: Use this option to enable a breakpoint for certain processes or threads. You'll rarely use this option in ASP.NET, because all web page code is executed by the ASP.NET worker process, which uses a pool of threads.

When Hit: Use this option to set up an automatic action that will be performed every time the breakpoint is hit. You have two handy options. Your first option is to print a message in the Debug window, which allows you to monitor the progress of your code without cluttering it up with Debug.Write() statements. This feature is known as tracepoints. Your second option is to run a Visual Studio macro, which allows you to perform absolutely any action in the IDE.

The Web Development Helper

Another interesting tool that's not tied to Visual Studio is the Web Development Helper, a free tool created by Nikhil Kothari from the ASP.NET team. The central goal of the Web Development Helper is to improve the debugging experience for ASP.NET developers by enhancing the ability of the browser to participate in the debugging process. The Web Development Helper provides a few useful features:

- It can report whether a page is in debug or tracing mode.
- It can display the view state information for a page.

- It can display the trace information for a page (and hide it from the page, making sure your layout isn't cluttered).
- It can clear the cache or trigger an application restart.
- It allows you to browse the HTML DOM (document object model)—in other words, the tree of elements that make up the rendered HTML of the page.
- It can maintain a log of HTML requests, which information about what page was requested, how long it took to receive it, and how large the HTML document was.

Many of these work with ASP.NET features that we haven't covered yet. You'll use the Web Development Helper with ASP.NET's tracing feature in the next chapter.

The design of the Web Development Helper is quite interesting. Essentially, it's built out of two pieces:

- An HTTP module that runs on the web server and makes additional information available to the client browser. (You'll learn about HTTP modules in Chapter 5.)
- An unmanaged browser plug-in that communicates with the HTTP module and displays the important information in a side panel in the browser (see Figure 2-36). The browser plug-in is designed exclusively for Internet Explorer, but at least one other developer has already created a Firefox version that works with the same HTTP module.

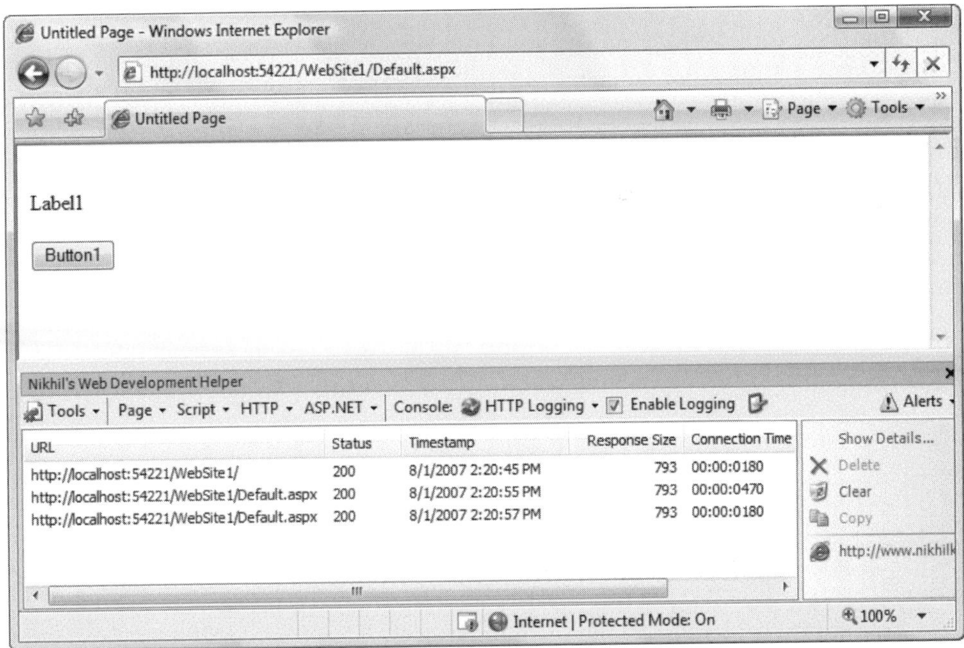

Figure 2-36. *The Web Development Helper*

To download the Web Development Helper, surf to `http://projects.nikhilk.net/Projects/WebDevHelper.aspx`. There you can download a setup program that installs two DLLs. One is a .NET assembly that provides the HTTP module (nStuff.WebDevHelper.Server.dll). The other is the browser plug-in (WebDevHelper.dll). The setup program copies both files to the c:\Program Files\nStuff\Web Development Helper directory, and it registers the browser plug-in with Internet Explorer. When the setup is finished, it gives you the option to open a PDF document that has a short but detailed overview of all the features of the Web Development Helper.

When you want to use this tool with a web application, you need to add a reference to the nStuff.WebDevHelper.Server.dll assembly. You also need to modify the web.config file so it loads the HTTP module, as shown here:

```
<configuration>
  <system.web>
    <httpModules>
      <add name="DevInfo" type="nStuff.WebDevHelper.Server.DevInfoModule,
nStuff.WebDevHelper.Server, Version=0.5.0.0, Culture=neutral,
PublicKeyToken=8fc0e3af5abcb6c4" />
    </httpModules>
    ...
  </system.web>
</configuration>
```

Now, run one of the pages from this application. To actually switch on the browser plug-in, you need to choose Tools ➤ Web Development Helper from the Internet Explorer menu. When you click this icon, a pane will appear at the bottom of the browser window. At the top of the pane are a series of drop-down menus with a variety of options for examining ASP.NET pages. You'll see one example that uses the Web Developer Helper in Chapter 3.

Summary

This chapter considered the role that Visual Studio can play in helping you develop your web applications. At the same time that you explored its rich design-time environment, you also learned about how it works behind the scenes with the code-behind model and how to extend it with time-saving features such as macros. In the next two chapters, you'll jump into full-fledged ASP.NET coding by examining web pages and server controls.

CHAPTER 3

■ ■ ■

Web Forms

ASP.NET pages (officially known as *web forms*) are a vital part of an ASP.NET application. They provide the actual output of a web application—the web pages that clients request and view in their browsers.

Essentially, web forms allow you to create a web application using the same control-based interface as a Windows application. To run an ASP.NET web form, the ASP.NET engine reads the entire .aspx file, generates the corresponding objects, and fires a series of events. You react to these events using thoroughly object-oriented code.

This chapter provides in-depth coverage of web forms. You'll learn how they work and how you can use them to build simple pages. You'll also get an in-depth first look at the page-processing life cycle and the ASP.NET server-side control model.

Web Forms Changes in ASP.NET 4

ASP.NET 4 introduces a few, mostly minor changes to the web forms model. Here they are, in the order you'll encounter them in this chapter:

- **Strict XHTML rendering:** Although you could configure ASP.NET 3.5 to get strict with XHTML, its default rendering had a few quirks. In ASP.NET 4, the last of these has finally been removed, which means your web form pages will be 100 percent XHTML-compliant (unless you break the rules of XHTML yourself). Read the "XHTML Compliance" section for the full details.
- **Predictable client IDs:** To ensure that every control gets a unique ID in the rendered HTML, ASP.NET uses a long-winded name generation system. Unfortunately, this complicates your life if you actually need to refer to one of these IDs, such as in client-side JavaScript. ASP.NET 4 improves this situation by allowing you to configure how the name generation system works in each page. You'll see how this works in the "Client-Side Control IDs" section.
- **New HtmlHead properties:** You can now set the description and keywords metatags through dedicated properties in the HtmlHead class. It's a minor change that you'll learn about in the section named "The Page Header."
- **Permanent redirects:** In its ongoing quest to provide better search engine optimization, ASP.NET now allows you to redirect requests with the HTTP status code 301, which signifies a permanent redirect. When search engine crawlers get this message, they know to update their catalogs. To see how it works, read the "Moving Between Pages" section.

Not included in this list is a far more significant change: the introduction of a whole new programming model, called ASP.NET MVC, that competes with traditional ASP.NET web forms. You'll explore ASP.NET MVC in detail in Chapter 32.

Page Processing

One of the key goals of ASP.NET is to create a model that lets web developers rapidly develop web forms in the same way that Windows developers can build made-to-measure windows in a desktop application. Of course, web applications are very different from traditional rich client applications. There are two key stumbling blocks:

Web applications execute on the server: For example, suppose you create a form that allows the user to select a product record and update its information. The user performs these tasks in the browser, but in order for you to perform the required operations (such as updating the database), your code needs to run on the web server. ASP.NET handles this divide with a technique called *postback*, which sends the page (and all user-supplied information) to the server when certain actions are performed. Once ASP.NET receives the page, it can then fire the corresponding server-side events to notify your code.

Web applications are stateless: In other words, once the page is rendered to HTML, your web-page objects are destroyed and all client-specific information is discarded. This model lends itself well to highly scalable, heavily trafficked applications, but it makes it difficult to create a seamless user experience. ASP.NET includes several tools to help you bridge this gap; most notable is a persistence mechanism called *view state*, which automatically embeds information about the page in a hidden field in the rendered HTML.

In the following sections, you'll learn about both the postback and the view state features. Together, these mechanisms help abstract the underlying HTML and HTTP details, allowing developers to work in terms of objects and events.

HTML Forms

If you're familiar with HTML, you know that the simplest way to send client-side data to the server is using a <form> tag. Inside the <form> tag, you can place other <input> tags to represent basic user interface ingredients such as buttons, text boxes, list boxes, check boxes, and radio buttons.

For example, here's an HTML page that contains two text boxes, two check boxes, and a submit button, for a total of five <input> tags:

```
<html xmlns="http://www.w3.org/1999/xhtml">
    <head>
        <title>Programmer Questionnaire</title>
    </head>
    <body>
        <form method="post" action="page.aspx">
            <div>
              Enter your first name: 
              <input type="text" name="FirstName" />
              <br />
              Enter your last name: 
              <input type="text" name="LastName" />
              <br /><br />
              You program with:
```

```
            <br />   
            <input type="checkbox" name="CS" />C#
            <br />   
            <input type="checkbox" name="VB" />VB .NET
            <br /><br />
            <input type="submit" value="Submit" id="OK" />
          </div>
      </form>
   </body>
</html>
```

Figure 3-1 shows what this basic page looks like in a web browser.

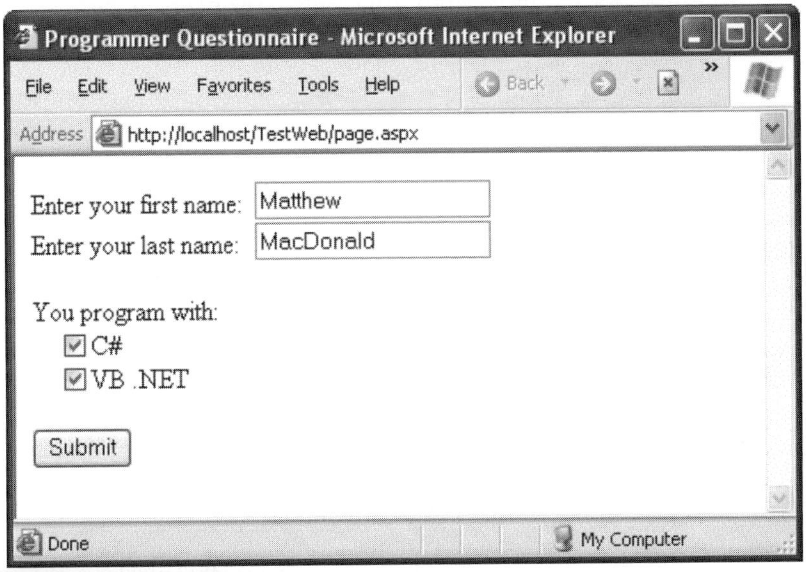

Figure 3-1. *A simple HTML form*

When the user clicks the submit button, the browser collects the current value of each control and pastes it together in a long string. This string is then sent back to the page indicated in the <form> tag (in this case, page.aspx) using an HTTP POST operation.

In this example, that means the web server might receive a request with this string of information:

```
FirstName=Matthew&LastName=MacDonald&CS=on&VB=on
```

The browser follows certain rules when constructing this string. Information is always sent as a series of name/value pairs separated by the ampersand (&) character. Each name/value pair is split with an equal (=) sign. Check boxes are left out unless they are checked, in which case the browser supplies the text *on* for the value. For the complete lowdown on the HTML forms standard, which is supported in every current browser, surf to `http://www.w3.org/TR/REC-html40/interact/forms.html`.

Virtually all server-side programming frameworks add a layer of abstraction over the raw form data. They parse this string and expose it in a more useful way. For example, JSP, ASP, and ASP.NET all allow you to retrieve the value of a form control using a thin object layer. In ASP and ASP.NET, you can look up values by name in the Request.Form collection. If you change the previous page into an ASP.NET web form, you can use this approach with code like this:

```
string firstName = Request.Form["FirstName"];
```

This thin veneer over the actual POST message is helpful, but it's still a long way from a true object-oriented framework. That's why ASP.NET goes another step further. When a page is posted back to ASP.NET, it extracts the values, populates the Form collection (for backward compatibility with ASP code), and then configures the corresponding control objects. This means you can use the following much more intuitive syntax to retrieve information in an ASP.NET web form:

```
string firstName = txtFirstName.Text;
```

This code also has the benefit of being typesafe. In other words, if you're retrieving the state of the check box, you'll receive a Boolean true or false value, instead of a string with the word on. In this way, developers are insulated from the quirks of HTML syntax.

■ **Note** In ASP.NET, all controls are placed inside a single <form> tag. This tag is marked with the runat="server" attribute, which allows it to work on the server side. ASP.NET does not allow you to create web forms that contain more than one server-side form tag, although it is possible to create a page that posts to another page using a technique called *cross-page posting*, which is discussed in Chapter 6.

Dynamic User Interface

Clearly, the control model makes life easier for retrieving form information. What's even more remarkable is how it simplifies your life when you need to *add* information to a page. Almost all web control properties are readable and writable. This means you can set the Text property of a text box just as easily as you can read it.

For example, consider what happens if you want to update a piece of text on a web page to reflect some information the user has entered earlier. In classic ASP, you would need to find a convenient place to insert a script block that would write the raw HTML. Here's a snippet of ASP.NET code that uses this technique to display a brightly colored welcome message:

```
string message = "<span style=\"color:Red\">Welcome " +
  FirstName + " " + LastName + "</span>";
Response.Write(message);
```

On the other hand, life is much neater when you define a Label control in ASP.NET:

```
<asp:Label id="lblWelcome" runat="server" />
```

Now you can simply set its properties:

```
lblWelcome.Text = "Welcome " +  FirstName + " " + LastName;
lblWelcome.ForeColor = Color.Red;
```

This code has several key advantages. First, it's much easier to write (and to write without errors). The savings seem fairly minor in this example, but it is much more dramatic when you consider a complete ASP.NET page that needs to dynamically render complex blocks of HTML that contain links, images, and styles.

Second, control-based code is also much easier to place inside a page. You can write your ASP.NET code wherever the corresponding action takes place. On the other hand, in classic ASP you need to worry about where the content appears on the page and arrange your script blocks code appropriately. If a page has several dynamic regions, it can quickly become a tangled mess of script blocks that don't show any clear relation or organization.

A subtler but equally dramatic advantage of the control model is the way it hides the low-level HTML details. Not only does this allow you to write code without learning all the idiosyncrasies of HTML, but it also allows your pages to support a wider range of browsers. Because the control renders itself, it has the ability to tailor its output to support different browsers or different flavors of HTML and XHTML. Essentially, your code is no longer tightly coupled to the HTML standard.

The ASP.NET Event Model

Classic ASP uses a linear processing model. That means code on the page is processed from start to finish and is executed in order. Because of this model, classic ASP developers need to write a considerable amount of code even for simple pages. A classic example is a web page that has three different submit buttons for three different operations. In this case, your script code has to carefully distinguish which button was clicked when the page is submitted and then execute the right action using conditional logic.

ASP.NET provides a refreshing change with its *event-driven* model. In this model, you add controls to a web form and then decide what events you want to respond to. Each event handler is a discrete method, which keeps the page code tidy and organized. This model is nothing new, but until the advent of ASP.NET it has been the exclusive domain of windowed UI programming in rich client applications.

So, how do ASP.NET events work? It's surprisingly straightforward. Here's a brief outline:

1. Your page runs for the first time. ASP.NET creates page and control objects, the initialization code executes, and then the page is rendered to HTML and returned to the client. The page objects are also released from server memory.
2. At some point, the user does something that triggers a postback, such as clicking a button. At this point, the page is submitted with all the form data.
3. ASP.NET intercepts the returned page and re-creates the page objects, taking care to return them to the state they were in the last time the page was sent to the client.
4. Next, ASP.NET checks what operation triggered the postback, and it raises the appropriate events (such as Button.Click), which your code can react to. Typically, at this point you'll perform some server-side operation (such as updating a database or reading data from a file) and then modify the control objects to display new information.
5. The modified page is rendered to HTML and returned to the client. The page objects are released from memory. If another postback occurs, ASP.NET repeats the process in steps 2 through 4.

In other words, ASP.NET doesn't just use the form data to configure the control objects for your page. It also uses it to decide what events to fire. For example, if it notices the text in a text box has changed since the last postback, it raises an event to notify your page. It's up to you whether you want to respond to this event.

■ **Note** Keep in mind that since HTTP is completely stateless, and all state made available by ASP.NET is reconstituted, the event-driven model is really an emulation. ASP.NET performs quite a few tasks in the background in order to support this model, as you'll see in the following sections. The beauty of this concept is that the beginner programmer doesn't need to be familiar with the underpinnings of the system to take advantage of server-side events.

Automatic Postbacks

Of course, one gap exists in the event system described so far. Windows developers have long been accustomed to a rich event model that lets your code react to mouse movements, key presses, and the minutest control interactions. But in ASP.NET, client actions happen on the client side, and server processing takes place on the web server. This means a certain amount of overhead is always involved in responding to an event. For this reason, events that fire rapidly (such as a mouse move event) are completely impractical in the world of ASP.NET.

■ **Note** If you want to accomplish a certain UI effect, you might handle rapid events such as mouse movements with client-side JavaScript. Or, better yet, you might use a custom ASP.NET control that already has these smarts built in, such as the ASP.NET AJAX controls you'll consider in Part 6. However, all your business code must execute in the secure, feature-rich server environment.

If you're familiar with HTML forms, you know there is one basic way to submit a page—by clicking a submit button. If you're using the standard HTML server controls in your .aspx web forms, this is still your only option. However, once the page is posted back, ASP.NET can fire other events at the same time (namely, events that indicate that the value in an input control has been changed).

Clearly, this isn't enough to build a rich web form. Fortunately, ASP.NET web controls extend this model with an automatic postback feature. With this feature, input controls can fire different events, and your server-side code can respond immediately. For example, you can trigger a postback when the user clicks a check box, changes the selection in a list, or changes the text in a text box and then moves to another field. These events still aren't as fine-grained as events in a Windows application, but they are a significant step up from the submit button.

Automatic Postbacks "Under the Hood"

To use automatic postback, you simply need to set the AutoPostBack property of a web control to true (the default is false, which ensures optimum performance if you don't need to react to a change event).

When you do, ASP.NET uses the client-side abilities of JavaScript to bridge the gap between client-side and server-side code.

Here's how it works: if you create a web page that includes one or more web controls that are configured to use AutoPostBack, ASP.NET adds a JavaScript function to the rendered HTML page named __doPostBack(). When called, it triggers a postback, posting the page back to the web server with all the form information.

ASP.NET also adds two hidden input fields that the __doPostBack() function uses to pass information back to the server. This information consists of the ID of the control that raised the event and any additional information that might be relevant. These fields are initially empty, as shown here:

```
<div class="aspNetHidden">
  <input type="hidden" name="__EVENTTARGET" id="__EVENTTARGET" value="" />
  <input type="hidden" name="__EVENTARGUMENT" id="__EVENTARGUMENT" value="" />
  ...
</div>
```

The __doPostBack() function has the responsibility for setting these values with the appropriate information about the event and then submitting the form. A sample __doPostBack() function is shown here:

```
<script type="text/javascript">
function __doPostBack(eventTarget, eventArgument) {
    if (!theForm.onsubmit || (theForm.onsubmit() != false)) {
        theForm.__EVENTTARGET.value = eventTarget;
        theForm.__EVENTARGUMENT.value = eventArgument;
        theForm.submit();
    }
  ...
}
</script>
```

Remember, ASP.NET generates the __doPostBack() function automatically. This code grows lengthier as you add more AutoPostBack controls to your page, because the event data must be set for each control.

Finally, any control that has its AutoPostBack property set to true is connected to the __doPostBack() function using the onclick or onchange attribute. These attributes indicate what action the browser should take in response to the client-side JavaScript events onclick and onchange.

The following example shows the rendered HTML for a list control named lstCountry, which posts back automatically. Whenever the user changes the selection in the list, the client-side onchange event fires. The browser then calls the __doPostBack() function, which sends the page back to the server.

```
<select name="lstCountry" onchange=
  "javascript:setTimeout(&#39;__doPostBack(\&#39;lstCountry\&#39;,\&#39;\&#39;)&#39;, 0)">
```

In other words, ASP.NET automatically changes a client-side JavaScript event into a server-side ASP.NET event, using the __doPostBack() function as an intermediary. If you're a seasoned ASP developer, you may have manually created a solution like this for traditional ASP web pages. ASP.NET handles these details for you automatically, simplifying life a great deal.

■ **Tip** Remember, ASP.NET includes two control models: the bare-bones HTML server controls and the more fully functional web controls. Automatic postback is available only with web controls.

View State

The final ingredient in the ASP.NET model is the view state mechanism. View state solves another problem that occurs because of the stateless nature of HTTP—lost changes.

Every time your page is posted back to the server, ASP.NET receives all the information that the user has entered in any <input> controls in the <form> tag. ASP.NET then loads the web page in its original state (based on the layout and defaults you've defined in the .aspx file) and tweaks the page according to this new information. The problem is that in a dynamic web form, your code might change a lot more. For example, you might programmatically change the color of a heading, modify a piece of static text, hide or show a panel of controls, or even bind a full table of data to a grid. All these actions change the page from its initial state. However, none of them is reflected in the form data that's posted back. That means this information will be lost after every postback. Traditionally, statelessness has been overcome with the use of simple cookies, session-based cookies, and various other workarounds. All of these mechanisms require homemade (and sometimes painstaking) measures.

To deal with this limitation, ASP.NET has devised its own integrated state serialization mechanism. Essentially, once your page code has finished running (and just before the final HTML is rendered and sent to the client), ASP.NET examines all the properties of all the controls on your page. If any of these properties has been changed from its initial state, ASP.NET makes a note of this information in a name/value collection. Finally, ASP.NET takes all the information it has amassed and then serializes it as a Base64 string. (A Base64 string ensures that there aren't any special characters that wouldn't be valid HTML.) The final string is inserted in the <form> section of the page as a new hidden field.

The next time the page is posted back, ASP.NET follows these steps:

1. ASP.NET re-creates the page and control objects based on its defaults (as defined in the .aspx file). Thus, the page has the same state that it had when it was first requested.

2. Next, ASP.NET deserializes the view state information and updates all the controls. This returns the page to the state it was in before it was sent to the client the last time.

3. Finally, ASP.NET adjusts the page according to the posted back form data. For example, if the client has entered new text in a text box or made a new selection in a list box, that information will be in the Form collection and ASP.NET will use it to tweak the corresponding controls. After this step, the page reflects the current state as it appears to the user.

4. Now your event-handling code can get involved. ASP.NET triggers the appropriate events, and your code can react to change the page, move to a new page, or perform a completely different operation.

Using view state is a great solution because server resources can be freed after each request, thereby allowing for scalability to support hundreds or thousands of requests without bogging the server down. However, it still comes with a price. Because view state is stored in the page, it results in a larger total page size. This affects the client doubly, because the client not only needs to receive a larger page, but the client also needs to send the hidden view state data back to the server with the next postback. Thus, it takes longer both to receive and post the page. For simple pages, this overhead is minimal, but if you configure complex, data-heavy controls such as the GridView, the view state information can grow to a size where it starts to exert a toll. In these cases, you can disable view state for a control by

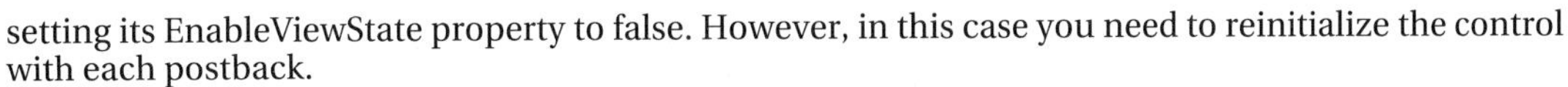

setting its EnableViewState property to false. However, in this case you need to reinitialize the control with each postback.

■ **Note** Even if you set EnableViewState to false, the control can still hold onto a smaller amount of view state information that it deems critical for proper functioning. This privileged view state information is known as control state, and it can never be disabled. However, in a well-designed control the size required for control state will be significantly smaller than the size of the entire view state. You'll see how it works when you design your own custom controls in Chapter 27.

ASP.NET uses view state only with page and control properties. ASP.NET doesn't take the same steps with member variables and other data you might use. However, as you'll learn later in this book (Chapter 6), you can place other types of data into view state and retrieve this information manually at a later time.

Figure 3-2 provides an end-to-end look at page requests that puts all these concepts together.

■ **Note** It is absolutely essential to your success as an ASP.NET programmer to remember that the web form is re-created with every round-trip. It does not persist or remain in memory longer than it takes to render a single request.

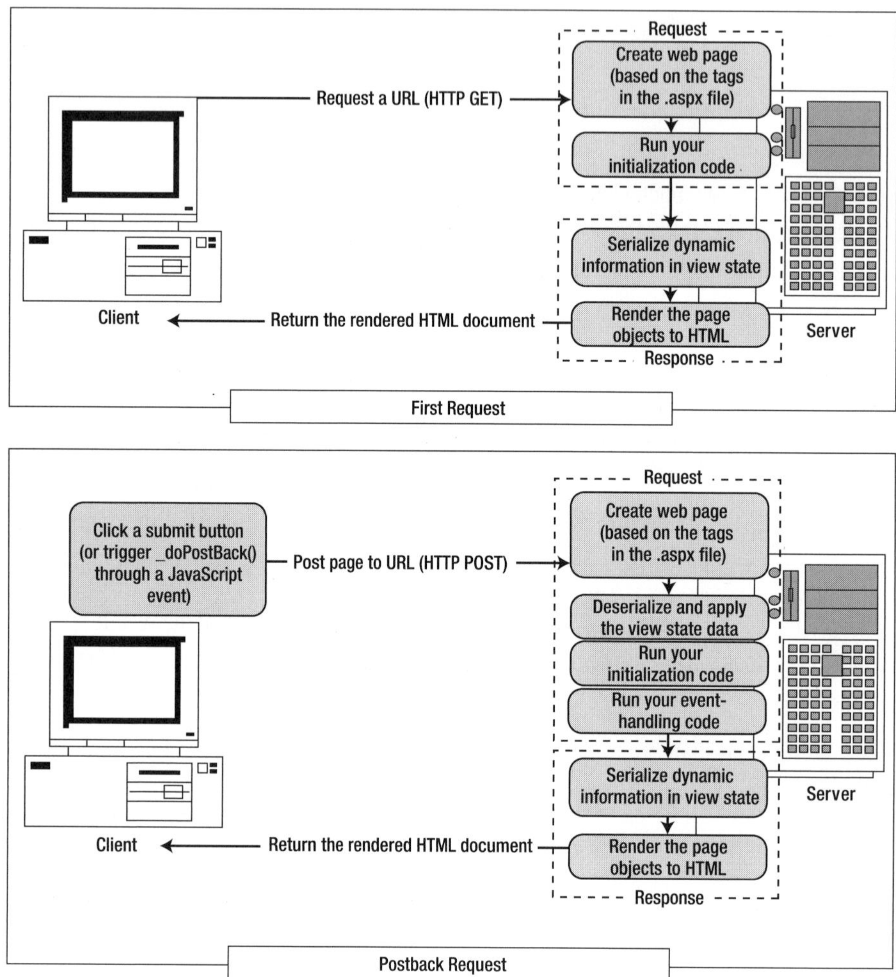

Figure 3-2. *ASP.NET page requests*

View State "Under the Hood"

If you look at the rendered HTML for an ASP.NET page, you can easily find the hidden input field with the view state information. The following example shows a page that uses a simple Label web control and sets it with a dynamic "Hello, world" message:

```
<html>
  <head>
    <title>Hello World Page</title>
  </head>
  <body>
    <form method="post" action="WebForm1.aspx" id="form1">
```

```
      <div class="aspNetHidden">
        <input type="hidden" name="__VIEWSTATE" id="__VIEWSTATE"
          value="/wEPDwUKLTE2MjY5MTY1NQ9kFgICAw9kFgICAQ8PFgIeBFRleHQFDEhlbGxv
IFdvcmxkIWRkZPsbiNOyNAufEt7OvNIbVYcGWHqf" />
        ...
      </div>
      <div>
        <input type="submit" name="Button1" value="Button" id="Button1" />
        <span id="lbl">Hello, world</span>
      </div>
    </form>
  </body>
</html>
```

The view state string isn't human readable—it just looks like a series of random characters. However, it's important to note that a user who is willing to go to a little work can interpret this data quite easily. Here's a snippet of .NET code that does the job and writes the decoded information to a web page:

```
// viewStateString contains the view state information.
// Convert the Base64 string to an ordinary array of bytes
// representing ASCII characters.
byte[] stringBytes = Convert.FromBase64String(viewStateString);

// Deserialize and display the string.
string decodedViewState = System.Text.Encoding.ASCII.GetString(stringBytes);
lbl.Text = decodedViewState;
```

In order to test this web page, you'll need to copy a view state string from an existing web page (using the View Source command in your web browser). Or, you can retrieve the view state string for the current web page using server-side code like this:

```
string viewStateString = Request["__VIEWSTATE"];
```

When you look at the decoded view state string, you'll see something like this:

```
? -162691655dd-Text Hello, worldddd????4 ?????U?Xz?
```

As you can see, the control text is clearly visible (along with some unprintable characters that render as blank boxes). This means that, in its default implementation, view state isn't a good place to store sensitive information that the client shouldn't be allowed to see—that sort of data should stay on the server. Additionally, you shouldn't make decisions based on view state that could compromise your application if the client tampers with the view state data.

■ **Tip** You can also decode the view state information for a page using the Web Development Helper utility that was introduced in Chapter 2.

Fortunately, it's possible to tighten up view state security quite a bit. You can enable automatic hash codes to prevent view state tampering, and you can even encrypt view state to prevent it from being decoded. These techniques raise hidden fields from a clumsy workaround to a much more robust and respectable piece of infrastructure. You'll learn about both of these techniques in Chapter 6.

View State Chunking

The size of the hidden view state field has no limit. However, some proxy servers, firewalls, and mobile browsers refuse to let pages through if they have hidden fields greater than a certain size. To circumvent this problem, you can use view state chunking, which automatically divides view state into multiple fields to ensure that no hidden field exceeds a size threshold you set.

To use view state, you simply need to set the maxPageStateFieldLength attribute of the <pages> element in the web.config file. This specifies the maximum view state size, in bytes. Here's an example that caps view state at 1 KB:

```
<configuration>
  <system.web>
    <pages maxPageStateFieldLength="1024" />
    ...
  </system.web>
</configuration>
```

When you request a page that generates a view state larger than this, several hidden input fields will be created:

```
<input type="hidden" name="__VIEWSTATEFIELDCOUNT" value="3" />
<input type="hidden" name="__VIEWSTATE" value="..." />
<input type="hidden" name="__VIEWSTATE1" value="..." />
<input type="hidden" name="__VIEWSTATE2" value="..." />
```

Remember, view state chunking is simply a mechanism for avoiding problems with certain proxies (which is a relatively rare occurrence). View state chunking does not improve performance (and adds a small amount of extra serialization overhead). As a matter of good design, you should strive to include as little information in view state as possible, which ensures the best performance.

XHTML Compliance

The web controls in ASP.NET are compliant with the XHTML 1.1 standard. However, it's still up to you to make sure the rest of your page behaves by the rules. ASP.NET doesn't take any steps to force XHTML compliance onto your page.

■ **Note** XHTML support doesn't add any functionality to your web pages that you wouldn't have with HTML 4.01. However, because XHTML is a stricter standard, it has a few benefits. For example, you can validate XHTML pages to catch minor errors that could trip up certain browsers. Most important, XHTML pages are also valid XML documents, which makes it easier for applications to read or analyze them programmatically and introduces the possibility of future extensibility. The current consensus is that XHTML will replace HTML in the future. You can learn more about XHTML by referring to the specification at `http://www.w3.org/TR/xhtml11`.

All the ASP.NET server controls render themselves using XHTML-compliant markup. That means this markup follows the rules of XHTML, which include the following:

- Tag and attribute names must be in lowercase.
- All elements must be closed, either with a dedicated closing tag (<p></p>) or using an empty tag that closes itself (<br />).
- All attribute values must be enclosed in single or double quotes (for example, runat="server").
- The id attribute must be used instead of the name attribute. (ASP.NET controls render both an id and name attribute.)

XHTML also removes support for certain features that were allowed in HTML, such as frames and formatting that doesn't use CSS. In most cases, a suitable XHTML alternative exists. However, one sticking point is the target attribute, which HTML developers can use to create links that open in new windows. The following ASP.NET controls allow you to use the target attribute:

- AdRotator
- TreeNode
- HyperLink
- HyperLinkColumn
- BulletedList

For example, if you set the HyperLink.Target property, the markup that ASP.NET generates will use the target attribute and so won't be XHTML-compliant.

Using the target attribute won't cause a problem in modern browsers. However, if you need to create a website that is completely XHTML-compliant, you must avoid using the target attribute.

■ **Note** You won't gain much immediate benefit by using XHTML. However, many companies and organizations mandate the use of XHTML, with a view to future standards. In the future, XHTML will make it easier to design web pages that are adaptable to a variety of different platforms, can be processed by other applications, and are extensible with new markup features. For example, you could use XSLT (XSL Transformations), another XML-based standard, to transform an XHTML document into another form. The same features won't be available to HTML pages.

Document Type Definitions

Every XHTML document should begin with a *doctype* (document type definition) that defines the type of XHTML it uses. In an ASP.NET web page, the doctype must be placed immediately after the Page directive in the markup portion of your web page. That way, the doctype will be rendered as the first line of your document, which is a requirement.

Here's an example that defines a web page that supports the full XHTML 1.1 standard, which is known as *XHTML 1.1 strict*:

```
<%@ Page Language="C#" AutoEventWireup="true"
 CodeFile="TestPage.aspx.cs" Inherits="TestPage" %>

<!DOCTYPE html PUBLIC "-//W3C//DTD XHTML 1.1//EN"
 "http://www.w3.org/TR/xhtml11/DTD/xhtml11.dtd">

<html xmlns="http://www.w3.org/1999/xhtml" >
<head>
    <title>Untitled Page</title>
</head>
<body>
    <form id="form1" runat="server">
      ...
    </form>
</body>
</html>
```

This page also defines the XML namespace for the <html> element. This is another detail that XHTML requires.

If you don't want to support the full XHTML 1.1 standard, you can make a few compromises. One other common choice for the doctype is *XHTML 1.0 transitional*, which enforces the structural rules of XHTML but allows HTML formatting features that have been replaced by stylesheets and are considered obsolete. Here's the doctype you need:

```
<!DOCTYPE html PUBLIC "-//W3C//DTD XHTML 1.0 Transitional//EN"
"http://www.w3.org/TR/xhtml1/DTD/xhtml1-transitional.dtd">
```

The XHTML transitional doctype is still too strict if your website uses HTML frames, which XHTML considers obsolete. If you need to use frames but still want to follow the other rules of XHTML transitional, you can use the XHTML 1.0 frameset doctype for your frames page, as shown here:

```
<!DOCTYPE html PUBLIC "-//W3C//DTD XHTML 1.0 Frameset//EN"
"http://www.w3.org/TR/xhtml1/DTD/xhtml1-frameset.dtd">
```

Remember, the ASP.NET server controls will work equally well with any doctype (and they will work with browsers that support only HTML as well). It's up to you to choose the level of standards compliance (and backward compatibility) you want in your web pages. It's always a good idea to include a doctype for your web pages to clearly indicate the markup standard they support. Without this detail, Internet Explorer renders pages using a legacy behavior known as "quirks" mode, which differs from the more standardized rendering found in other browsers like Firefox.

■ **Note** Most of the examples in this book use the XHTML 1.1 strict doctype. But to save space, the web page markup listings in this book don't include the lines that declare the doctype.

Configuring XHTML Rendering

The ASP.NET server controls automatically use strict XHTML 1.0 markup. Minor quirks that existed in previous versions have been eliminated.

ASP.NET's XHTML rendering is set through a configuration file attribute named controlRenderingCompatibilityVersion, which is applied on the <pages> element. By default, this attribute is set in the root web.config, so it applies to all ASP.NET 4 applications:

```
<configuration>
  <system.web>
    <pages controlRenderingCompatibilityVersion="4.0" />
    ...
  </system.web>
</configuration>
```

If you set controlRenderingCompatibility to 3.5 (the only other supported value at this time), web controls will use the same rendering that they did with ASP.NET 3.5.

■ **Note** When you use Visual Studio to upgrade a web application from an earlier version of ASP.NET to ASP.NET 4, Visual Studio sets the controlRenderingCompatibilityVersion attribute to 3.5. To get ASP.NET's stricter XHTML rendering, you simply need to remove this attribute.

Confusingly enough, when controlRenderingCompatibilityVersion is set to 3.5, ASP.NET's rendering behavior is controlled by another web.config setting, named <xhtmlConformance>:

```
<configuration>
  <system.web>
    <pages controlRenderingCompatibilityVersion="3.5" />
    <xhtmlConformance mode="Transitional" />
    ...
  </system.web>
</configuration>
```

The mode attribute in the <xhtmlConformance> element takes one of three values:

Strict: This produces XHTML-compliant rendering that's almost as clean as what you get when controlRenderingCompatibilityVersion is set to 4.0.

Transitional: This is the default value. It produces XHTML-compliant rendering with a small set of possible quirks. For example, ASP.NET adds the name attribute to the <form> element, some controls render border="0" to create invisible tables, and disabled controls sometimes use invalid styles. All of these details are forbidden by the rules of XHTML strict.

■ **Note** ASP.NET 3.5 rendering inconsistencies won't lead to errors. Browsers will still be able to process the page successfully, even if it uses the XHTML 1.1 strict doctype. However, any inconsistencies will be flagged as an error by an XHTML validation tool.

Legacy: This reverts to the rendering that was used in ASP.NET 1.1. When legacy rendering is enabled, ASP.NET controls do not use any of the XHTML refinements that aren't strictly compatible with HTML 4.01. For example, they render standard HTML elements such as <br> instead of the correct XHTML version, <br />. However, even if legacy rendering is enabled, ASP.NET won't strip out the namespace in the <html> tag or remove the doctype if these details are present in your page. To avoid confusion, you should make sure that your <xhtmlConformance> setting and your web page doctypes match. Ideally, you'll use the same doctype for all the web pages in your website, because ASP.NET doesn't allow you to configure XHTML rendering on a per-page basis.

■ **Note** ASP.NET makes no guarantee that the non-XHTML rendering will be supported in future versions of ASP.NET, so use it only if it's required for a specific scenario.

Most of the time, you should keep the default controlRenderingCompatibilityVersion of 4.0. You should set controlRenderingCompatibilityVersion to 3.5 and use the <xhtmlConformance> element only if you have older pages that need this level of backward compatibility. This might be the case if your pages contain client-side JavaScript code that expects one of these legacy details (for example, a script block that uses the name attribute from the <form> element). But most of the time, the latest and most modern XHTML rendering will give your web application the best standards compliance and compatibility with the widest range of browsers.

Visual Studio's Default Doctype

When you create a new web form in Visual Studio, it automatically adds a doctype for XHTML transitional. If this isn't what you want, it's up to you to modify the doctype in each new page. If you're using master pages (as described in Chapter 16), the solution is even easier. You can simply set the doctype in your master page, and all the child pages that use that master page will acquire it automatically.

It is technically possible to change Visual Studio's default web page template so that it uses a different doctype, but the process is a bit awkward. You need to first modify the templates, and then rebuild Visual Studio's template cache. Here's a quick rundown of the steps you need to follow:

1. You can find the Visual Studio templates in a series of ZIP files in various folders. You need to modify the WebForm.aspx and WebForm_cb.aspx files in the c:\Program Files\Microsoft Visual Studio 10.0\Common7\IDE\ItemTemplates\Web\CSharp\1033\WebForm.zip archive.

■ **Note** If you're running a 64-bit version of Windows, you'll find the Visual Studio templates in a directory that begins with c:\Program Files (x86)\Microsoft Visual Studio 10.0 rather than c:\Program Files\Microsoft Visual Studio 10.0.

---

2. When modifying the files, simply edit the doctype. You'll probably find it's easiest to copy the archive to another location, extract the appropriate files, edit them, add them back to the archive, and then copy the entire archive back to its original location. That's because you need administrator rights to edit these files, and most simple text editors (like Notepad) won't attempt to acquire these rights automatically. However, you'll be prompted through UAC (User Account Control) when you copy, delete, and replace the files in Windows Explorer.
3. Once you've updated the templates, delete the c:\Program Files\Microsoft Visual Studio 10.0\Common7\IDE\ItemTemplatesCache folder to clear out the template cache.
4. Run Visual Studio using the following command line to rebuild the template cache:

   ```
   devenv /InstallVSTemplates
   ```

   This step requires administrator privileges.
5. You can now run Visual Studio normally. Any new web form files you add to a web application should have the new doctype that you've set.

XHTML Validation

The core ASP.NET controls follow the rules of XHTML, but to make sure the finished page is XHTML-compliant, you need to make sure any static content you add also follows these rules. Visual Studio can help you with its own built-in validator. Just select the target standard from the drop-down list in the HTML Source Editing toolbar. For example, if you choose XHTML 1.1, Visual Studio flags structural errors, incorrect capitalization, improper or obsolete tags, and so on. For example, Figure 3-3 shows that <br> is not allowed in XHTML because it's a start tag without an end tag. Instead, you need to use the empty tag syntax, <br />.

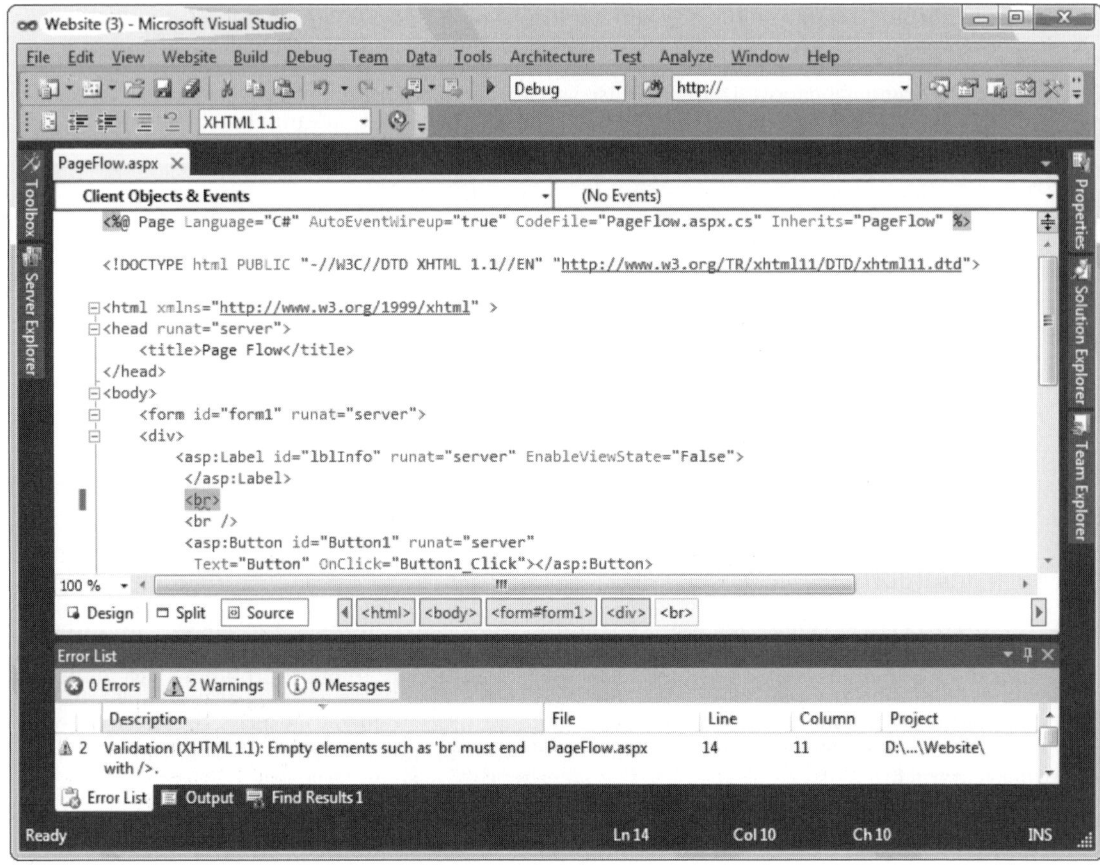

Figure 3-3. Validating for XHTML 1.1 in Visual Studio

It's still possible that an XHTML violation might slip through the cracks. For example, you could use a third-party control that emits noncompliant markup when it renders itself. Visual Studio won't be able to spot the problem, because it's examining the server-side web form markup, not the final rendered document that's sent to the client. Furthermore, your browser probably won't flag the error either.

To give your pages the acid test, you need use a third-party validator that can request your page and scan it for errors. One good resource is the free W3C validation service at `http://validator.w3.org`. Simply enter the URL to your web page, and click Check. You can also upload a file to check it, but in this case you must make sure you upload the final rendered page, not the .aspx source. You can see (and save) the rendered content for a page in Internet Explorer by choosing View ➤ Source.

Client-Side Control IDs

Certain parts of ASP.NET functionality require that the elements in the rendered HTML have unique IDs. (For example, ASP.NET needs to be able to uniquely determine what control has triggered a postback.) At first glance, this seems to be an easy challenge—after all, the controls also need to have unique server-side IDs in order for you to interact with them in code. So why not just use the server-side IDs for the client-side IDs?

First, a server-side control can exist without any server ID, even if it uses a client-side feature like automatic postback. Second, a single control can occur multiple times in the page in different containers. For example, this occurs if you have controls inside a user control, and you repeat the user control more than once on a page. It can also occur with master pages, and it's guaranteed to happen if you have a data-bound control such as the GridView, which repeats the same controls in every row. To deal with scenarios like these, ASP.NET fuses together the ID of the server control, all of its naming containers, and (if it's data bound) a numeric index. This leads to long and awkward client-side IDs like this:

```
ctl00_ContentPlaceHolder1_ParentPanel_NamingPanel_TextBox1
```

■ **Note** A *naming container* is a control that implements the INamingContainer interface. A control does this if it needs to provide a unique naming scope for its children to prevent ID conflicts. Examples of naming containers include Page, UserControl, and Content (a content region in a master page). Also, naming containers include all controls that can bind to a list of data, from basics such as HtmlSelect, ListBox, and CheckBoxList to rich data controls such as Details, FormView, and GridView. However, most simple containers aren't naming containers—think, for example, of the Panel class that wraps the <div> element.

Initially, ASP.NET developers didn't give much thought to client-side names, because they were a fully abstracted background detail. However, in modern web development you might find yourself needing to refer to a client-side element, either to format it with a CSS stylesheet or to manipulate it with a bit of client-side JavaScript. In both cases, having long, difficult-to-predict IDs makes your work more difficult.

ASP.NET 4 adds a ClientIDMode property that allows you to change the naming behavior for an entire page, a section of a page, or an individual control. Technically, the ClientIDMode property is a member of the base Control class from which all ASP.NET web controls derive. It supports four possible values, as listed in Table 3-1.

Table 3-1. *Values from the ClientIDMode Enumeration*

Value	Description
AutoID	ASP.NET generates the client-side ID by concatenating the IDs of the control with the IDs of its naming containers, separated by an underscore. A numeric index is added if the control is being bound in a data control. *Example:* `ctl00_ContentPlaceHolder1_ParentPanel_NamingPanel_TextBox1`
Static	ASP.NET uses the server-side ID to set the client-side ID. This is the simplest scenario, but it can run into issues if the control is repeated on the page in different naming containers. *Example:* `TextBox1`

Value	Description
Predictable	ASP.NET uses the same concatenating strategy as it does for the AutoID setting but simplifies it to create slightly cleaner names. First, the ID of the top-level page isn't included (which avoids having the client-side ID begin with an automatically generated page ID like ctl00). Second, ASP.NET uses the ClientIDRowSuffix property to generate unique values in a data-bound list control (which makes more sense than the standard numeric index). *Example:* `ContentPlaceHolder1_ParentPanel_NamingPanel_TextBox1`
Inherit	This control uses the naming strategy of its parent naming container. Or, if this is set in the Page, it uses the naming strategy that's specified in the <pages> element of the web.config file.

The default ClientIDMode setting is the same for every control: Inherit, which means the control takes the ClientIDMode of its parent naming container. Eventually, this inheritance bubbles up to the top-level page, which inherits its ClientIDMode setting from the <pages> element of the web.config file. In a newly created ASP.NET 4 website, the root web.config file sets the ClientIDMode to Predictable. But in a website that's been migrated to ASP.NET 4 from an earlier version of ASP.NET, Visual Studio adds the following web.config markup to set the default ClientIDMode to AutoID for backward compatibility:

```
<configuration>
  <system.web>
    <pages clientIDMode="AutoID" />
    ...
  </system.web>
</configuration>
```

You can remove or modify the clientIDMode property as needed.

To try the behavior of different ClientIDMode settings, you need to use master pages or data-bound controls, which are two topics we haven't covered yet. For a quick test, you can create a new ASP.NET website using the ASP.NET Web Site template (*not* the ASP.NET Empty Web Site template). Then, in the Default.aspx page, in the BodyContent region, add a simple named control like the TextBox shown here:

```
<%@ Page Title="Home Page" Language="C#" ... %>

<asp:Content ID="HeaderContent" runat="server" ContentPlaceHolderID="HeadContent">
</asp:Content>

<asp:Content ID="BodyContent" runat="server" ContentPlaceHolderID="MainContent">
    <asp:TextBox ID="txtNormal" runat="server"></asp:TextBox>
</asp:Content>
```

By default, the TextBox inherits the ClientIDMode of the Content control, which inherits it from the Page, which gets it from the web.config file. This value is Predictable, which means you end up with this rendered HTML for the text box:

```
<input name="ctl00$MainContent$txtNormal" type="text" id="MainContent_txtNormal" />
```

■ **Note** You'll notice that the ClientIDMode setting doesn't affect the value of the client-side name attribute. The name attribute is set with a string that looks almost identical to the ID when ClientIDMode is set to AutoID. The only difference is that dollar signs are used instead of underscores, so a typical name is `ctl00$ContentPlaceHolder1$ParentPanel$NamingPanel$TextBox1`.

Now you change this behavior by setting the ClientIDMode to Static, either for the entire page or for the specific TextBox control:

```
<asp:TextBox ID="txtNormal" ClientIDMode="Static" runat="server"></asp:TextBox>
```

This gives you the following rendered HTML:

```
<input name="ctl00$MainContent$txtNormal" type="text" id="txtNormal" />
```

It's important to realize that the ClientIDMode property could be set to several points in the hierarchy of a complex page. For example, you could have a container that uses static naming, which contains other controls that use predictable naming. In this situation, the controls with predictable naming get concatenated names that start with the static name of the parent control. Higher-level naming containers are ignored.

So now that you know how the ClientIDMode property works, how should you use it in a real-world application? Here are some guidelines:

- If you never need to refer to client-side elements, there's no need to think about this issue at all.
- If you rarely need to refer to a client-side element, than it's easiest to target just that element by setting its ClientIDMode property to Static.
- If you frequently use client-side IDs, you may want to evaluate whether you can use Static for entire pages. If these pages contain data-bound controls or repeated user controls, you can set the ClientIDMode of just these controls to Predictable.
- If you need to use client-side IDs in a data-bound control, it makes sense to make your life a bit easier by setting the control's ClientIDMode property to Predictable and using the ClientIDRowSuffix property, as described in Chapter 10.

Web Forms Processing Stages

On the server side, processing an ASP.NET web form takes place in stages. At each stage, various events are raised. This allows your page to plug into the processing flow at any stage and respond however you would like.

The following list shows the major stages in the process flow of an ASP.NET page:

- Page framework initialization
- User code initialization
- Validation
- Event handling
- Automatic data binding

- Cleanup

Remember, these stages occur independently for each web request. Figure 3-4 shows the order in which these stages unfold. More stages exist than are listed here, but those are typically used for programming your own ASP.NET controls and aren't handled directly by the page.

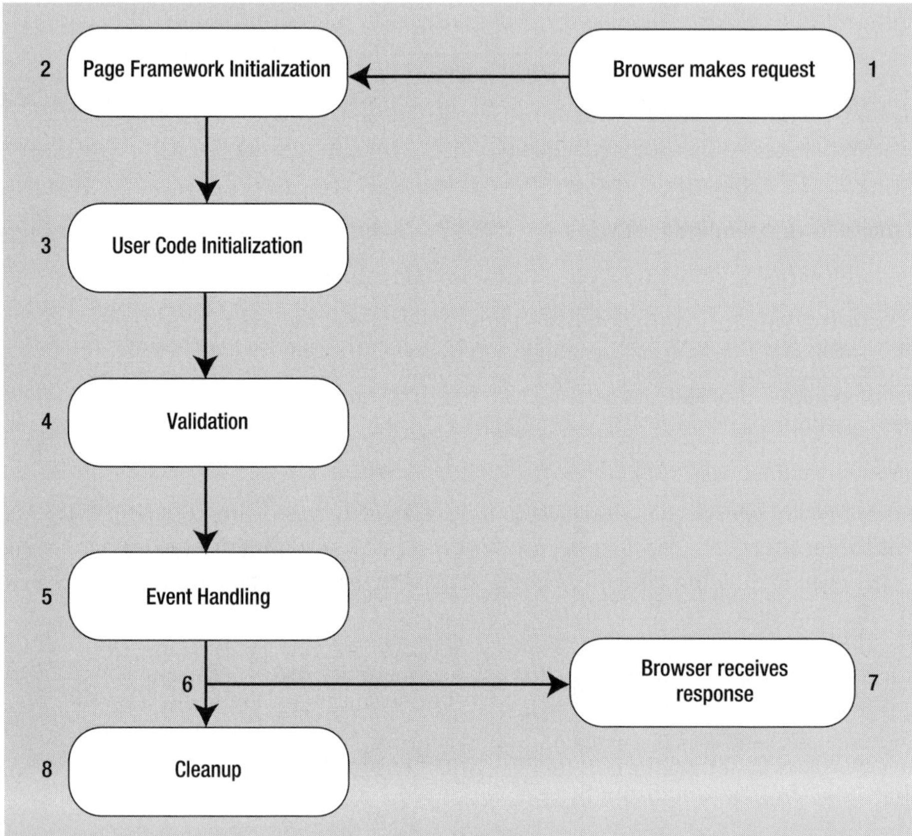

Figure 3-4. *ASP.NET page life cycle*

In the next few sections you'll learn about each stage and then examine a simple web page example.

Page Framework Initialization

This is the stage in which ASP.NET first creates the page. It generates all the controls you have defined with tags in the .aspx web page. In addition, if the page is not being requested for the first time (in other words, if it's a postback), ASP.NET deserializes the view state information and applies it to all the controls.

At this stage, the Page.Init event fires. However, this event is rarely handled by the web page, because it's still too early to perform page initialization. That's because the control objects may not be created yet and because the view state information isn't loaded.

User Code Initialization

At this stage of the processing, the Page.Load event is fired. Most web pages handle this event to perform any required initialization (such as filling in dynamic text or configuring controls).

The Page.Load event *always* fires, regardless of whether the page is being requested for the first time or whether it is being requested as part of a postback. Fortunately, ASP.NET provides a way to allow programmers to distinguish between the first time the page is loaded and all subsequent loads. Why is this important? First, since view state is maintained automatically, you have to fetch your data from a dynamic data source only on the first page load. On a postback, you can simply sit back, relax, and let ASP.NET restore the control properties for you from the view state. This can provide a dramatic performance boost if the information is expensive to re-create (for example, if you need to query it from a database). Second, there are also other scenarios, such as edit forms and drill-down pages, in which you need the ability to display one interface on a page's first use and a different interface on subsequent loads.

To determine the current state of the page, you can check the IsPostBack property of the page, which will be false the first time the page is requested. Here's an example:

```
if (!IsPostBack)
{
    // It's safe to initialize the controls for the first time.
    FirstName.Text = "Enter your name here";
}
```

■ **Note** It's a common convention to write Page.IsPostBack instead of just IsPostBack. This longer form works because all web pages are server controls, and all server controls include a Page property that exposes the current page. In other words, Page.IsPostBack is the same as IsPostBack—some developers simply think the first version is easier to read. Which approach you use is simply a matter of preference.

Remember, view state stores every *changed* property. Initializing the control in the Page.Load event counts as a change, so any control value you touch will be persisted in view state, needlessly enlarging the size of your page and slowing transmission times. To streamline your view state and keep page sizes small, avoid initializing controls in code. Instead, set the properties in the control tag (either by editing the tag by hand in source view or by using the Properties window). That way, these details won't be persisted in view state. In cases where it really is easier to initialize the control in code, consider disabling view state for the control by setting EnableViewState to false and initializing the control every time the Page.Load event fires, regardless of whether the current request is a postback.

Validation

ASP.NET includes validation controls that can automatically validate other user input controls and display error messages. These controls fire after the page is loaded but before any other events take place. However, the validation controls are for the most part self-sufficient, which means you don't need to respond to the validation events. Instead, you can just examine whether the page is valid (using the Page.IsValid property) in another event handler. Chapter 4 discusses the validation controls in more detail.

Event Handling

At this point, the page is fully loaded and validated. ASP.NET will now fire all the events that have taken place since the last postback. For the most part, ASP.NET events are of two types:

Immediate response events: These include clicking a submit button or clicking some other button, image region, or link in a rich web control that triggers a postback by calling the __doPostBack() JavaScript function.

Change events: These include changing the selection in a control or the text in a text box. These events fire immediately for web controls if AutoPostBack is set to true. Otherwise, they fire the next time the page is posted back.

As you can see, ASP.NET's event model is still quite different from a traditional Windows environment. In a Windows application, the form state is resident in memory, and the application runs continuously. That means you can respond to an event immediately. In ASP.NET, everything occurs in stages, and as a result events are sometimes batched together.

For example, imagine you have a page with a submit button and a text box that doesn't post back automatically. You change the text in the text box and then click the submit button. At this point, ASP.NET raises all of the following events (in this order):

- Page.Init
- Page.Load
- TextBox.TextChanged
- Button.Click
- Page.PreRender
- Page.Unload

Remembering this bit of information can be essential in making your life as an ASP.NET programmer easier. There is an upside and a downside to the event-driven model. The upside is that the event model provides a higher level of abstraction, which keeps your code clear of boilerplate code for maintaining state. The downside is that it's easy to forget that the event model is really just an emulation. This can lead you to make an assumption that doesn't hold true (such as expecting information to remain in member variables) or a design decision that won't perform well (such as storing vast amounts of information in view state).

Automatic Data Binding

In Chapter 9, you'll learn about the data source controls that automate the data binding process. When you use the data source controls, ASP.NET automatically performs updates and queries against your data source as part of the page life cycle.

Essentially, two types of data source operations exist. Any changes (inserts, deletes, or updates) are performed after all the control events have been handled but just before the Page.PreRender event fires. Then, after the Page.PreRender event fires, the data source controls perform their queries and insert the retrieved data into any linked controls. This model makes instinctive sense, because if queries were executed before updates, you could end up with stale data in your web page. However, this model also introduces a necessary limitation—none of your other event handlers will have access to the most recent data, because it hasn't been retrieved yet.

This is the last stop in the page life cycle. Historically, the Page.PreRender event is supposed to signify the last action before the page is rendered into HTML (although, as you've just learned, some data binding work can still occur after the prerender stage). During the prerender stage, the page and control objects are still available, so you can perform last-minute steps such as storing additional information in view state.

To learn much more about the ASP.NET data binding story, refer to Chapter 9.

Cleanup

At the end of its life cycle, the page is rendered to HTML. After the page has been rendered, the real cleanup begins, and the Page.Unload event is fired. At this point, the page objects are still available, but the final HTML is already rendered and can't be changed.

Remember, the .NET Framework has a garbage collection service that runs periodically to release memory tied to objects that are no longer referenced. If you have any unmanaged resources to release, you should make sure you do this explicitly in the cleanup stage or, even better, before. When the garbage collector collects the page, the Page.Disposed event fires. This is the end of the road for the web page.

A Page Flow Example

No matter how many times people explain how something works, it's always more satisfying to see it for yourself (or break it trying to learn how it works). To satisfy your curiosity, you can build a sample web form test that illustrates the flow of processing. The only thing this example won't illustrate is validation (which is discussed in the next chapter).

To try this, start by creating a new web form named PageFlow.aspx. In Visual Studio, you simply need to drag a label and a button onto the design surface of your web page. This places them inside the server-side <form> section. Next, select the Label control on the design surface. Using the Properties window, set the ID property to lblInfo and the EnableViewState property to false.

Here's the complete markup for the .aspx file, without any event handlers:

```
<%@ Page language="C#" CodeFile="PageFlow.aspx.cs"
    AutoEventWireup="true" Inherits="PageFlow" %>

<html xmlns="http://www.w3.org/1999/xhtml">
    <head runat="server">
        <title>Page Flow</title>
    </head>
    <body>
        <form id="form1" runat="server">
        <div>
            <asp:Label id="lblInfo" runat="server" EnableViewState="False">
            </asp:Label>
            <asp:Button id="Button1" runat="server" Text="Button">
            </asp:Button>
        </div>
        </form>
    </body>
</html>
```

The next step is to add your event handlers. When you're finished, the code-behind file will hold five event handlers that respond to different events, including Page.Init, Page.Load, Page.PreRender, Page.Unload, and Button.Click.

Page event handlers are a special case. Unlike other controls, you don't need to wire them up using attributes in your markup. Instead, page event handlers are automatically connected provided they use the correct method name (and assuming the Page directive sets AutoEventWireup to true, which is the default).

Here are the event handlers for various page events in the PageFlow example:

```
private void Page_Load(object sender, System.EventArgs e)
{
    lblInfo.Text += "Page.Load event handled.<br />";
    if (Page.IsPostBack)
    {
        lblInfo.Text +=
          "<b>This is not the first time you've seen this page.</b><br />";
    }
}

private void Page_Init(object sender, System.EventArgs e)
{
    lblInfo.Text += "Page.Init event handled.<br />";
}

private void Page_PreRender(object sender, System.EventArgs e)
{
    lblInfo.Text += "Page.PreRender event handled.<br />";
}

private void Page_Unload(object sender, System.EventArgs e)
{
    // This text never appears because the HTML is already
    // rendered for the page at this point.
    lblInfo.Text += "Page.Unload event handled.<br />";
}
```

Each event handler simply adds to the text in the Text property of the label. When the code adds this text, it also uses embedded HTML tags such as <b> (to bold the text) and
 (to insert a line break). Another option would be to create separate Label controls and configure the style-related properties of each one.

■ **Note** In this example, the EnableViewState property of the label is set to false. This ensures that the text is cleared every time the page is posted back and the text that's shown corresponds only to the most recent batch of processing. If you left EnableViewState set to true, the list would grow longer with each postback, showing you all the activity that has happened since you first requested the page.

Additionally, you need to add an event handler for the Button.Click event:

```
protected void Button1_Click(object sender, System.EventArgs e)
{
    lblInfo.Text += "Button1.Click event handled.<br />";
}
```

And you need to wire it up to the corresponding control:

```
<asp:Button id="Button1" runat="server" Text="Button" OnClick="Button1_Click">
</asp:Button>
```

The Button.Click event handler requires a different accessibility level than the page event handlers. The page event handlers are private, while all control event handlers are protected. To understand this difference, you need to reconsider the code model that was introduced in Chapter 2.

Page handlers are hooked up explicitly using delegates in a hidden portion of designer code. Because this designer code is still considered part of your class (thanks to the magic of partial classes), it can hook up any method, including a private method. Control event handlers are connected using a different mechanism—the control tag. They are bound at a later stage of processing, after the markup in the .aspx file and the code-behind class have been merged together. ASP.NET creates this merged class by deriving a new class from the code-behind class.

Here's where things get tricky. This derived class needs to be able to access the event handlers in the page so it can connect them to the appropriate controls. The derived class can access the event handlers only if they are public (in which case any class can access them) or protected (in which case any derived class can access them).

■ **Tip** Although it's acceptable for page event handlers to be private, it's a common convention in ASP.NET code to make all event handlers protected, just for consistency and simplicity.

Figure 3-5 shows the ASP.NET page after clicking the button, which triggers a postback and the Button1.Click event. Note that even though this event caused the postback, Page.Init and Page.Load were both raised first.

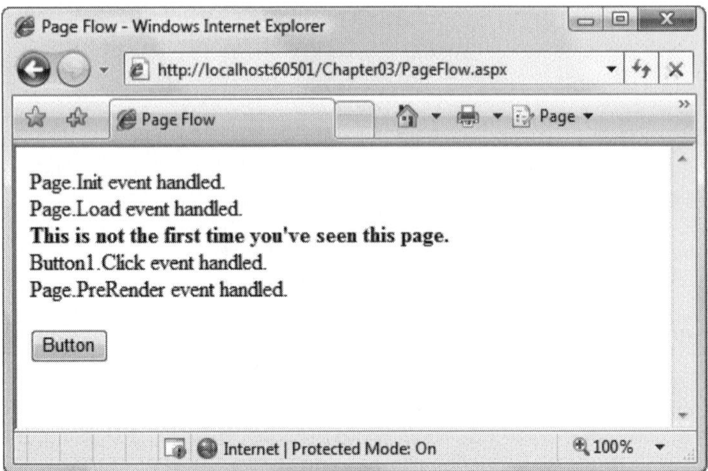

Figure 3-5. *ASP.NET order of operations*

The Page As a Control Container

Now that you've learned the stages of web forms processing, it's time to take a closer look at how the server control model plugs into this pipeline. To render a page, the web form needs to collaborate with all its constituent controls. Essentially, the web form renders itself and then asks all the controls on the page to render themselves. In turn, each of those controls can contain child controls; each is also responsible for their own rendering code. As these controls render themselves, the page assembles the generated HTML into a complete page. This process may seem a little complex at first, but it allows for an amazing amount of power and flexibility in creating rich web-page interfaces.

When ASP.NET first creates a page (in response to an HTTP request), it inspects the .aspx file. For each element it finds with the runat="server" attribute, it creates and configures a control object, and then it adds this control as a child control of the page. You can examine the Page.Controls collection to find all the child controls on the page.

Showing the Control Tree

Here's an example that looks for controls. Each time it finds a control, the code uses the Response.Write() command to write the control class type and control ID to the end of the rendered HTML page, as shown here:

```
// Every control derives from System.Web.UI.Control, so you can use
// that as a base class to examine all controls.
foreach (Control control in Page.Controls)
{
    Response.Write(control.GetType().ToString() + " - <b>" +
      control.ID + "</b><br />");
}
// Separate this content from the rest of the page with a horizontal line.
Response.Write("<hr />");
```

■ **Note** The Response.Write() method is a holdover from classic ASP, and you would almost never use it in a real-world ASP.NET web application. It effectively bypasses the web control model, which leads to disjointed interfaces, compromises ASP.NET's ability to create markup that adapts to the target device, and almost always breaks XHTML compatibility. However, in this test page Response.Write() allows you to write raw HTML without generating any additional controls—which is a perfect technique for analyzing the controls on the page without disturbing them.

To test this code, you can add it to the Page.Load event handler. In this case, the rendered content will be written at the top of the page before the controls. However, when you run it, you'll notice some unexpected behavior. For example, consider the web form shown in Figure 3-6, which contains several controls, some of which are organized into a box using the Panel web control. It also contains two lines of static HTML text.

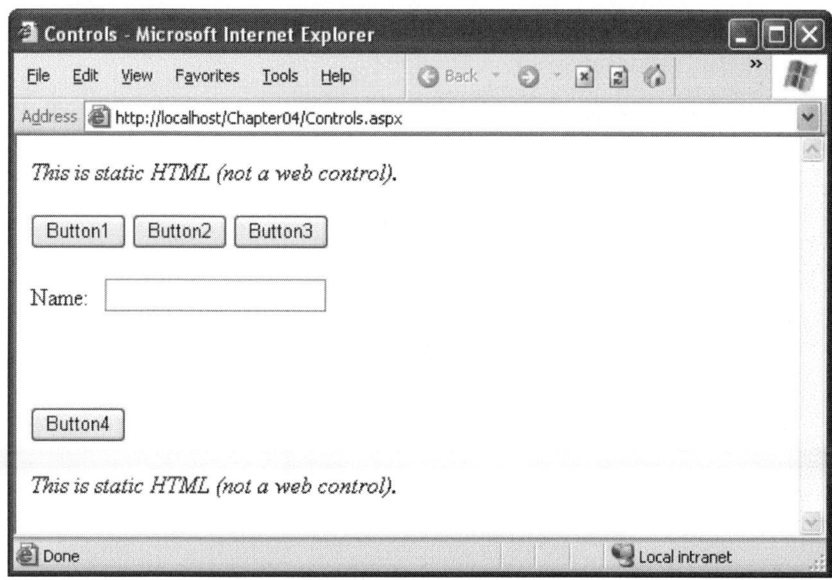

Figure 3-6. A sample web page with multiple controls

Here's the .aspx markup code for the page:

```
<%@ Page language="C#" CodeFile="ControlTree.aspx.cs" AutoEventWireup="true"
    Inherits="ControlTree" %>

<html xmlns="http://www.w3.org/1999/xhtml">
    <head>
        <title>Controls</title>
    </head>
```

```
    <body>
        <p><i>This is static HTML (not a web control).</i></p>
        <form id="Controls" method="post" runat="server">
        <div>
            <asp:panel id="MainPanel" runat="server" Height="112px">
            <p><asp:Button id="Button1" runat="server" Text="Button1"/>
            <asp:Button id="Button2" runat="server" Text="Button2"/>
            <asp:Button id="Button3" runat="server" Text="Button3"/></p>
            <p><asp:Label id="Label1" runat="server" Width="48px">
              Name:</asp:Label>
            <asp:TextBox id="TextBox1" runat="server"></asp:TextBox></p>
            </asp:panel>
            <p><asp:Button id="Button4" runat="server" Text="Button4"/></p>
        </div>
        </form>
        <p><i>This is static HTML (not a web control).</i></p>
    </body>
</html>
```

When you run this page, you won't see a full list of controls. Instead, you'll see the list shown in Figure 3-7.

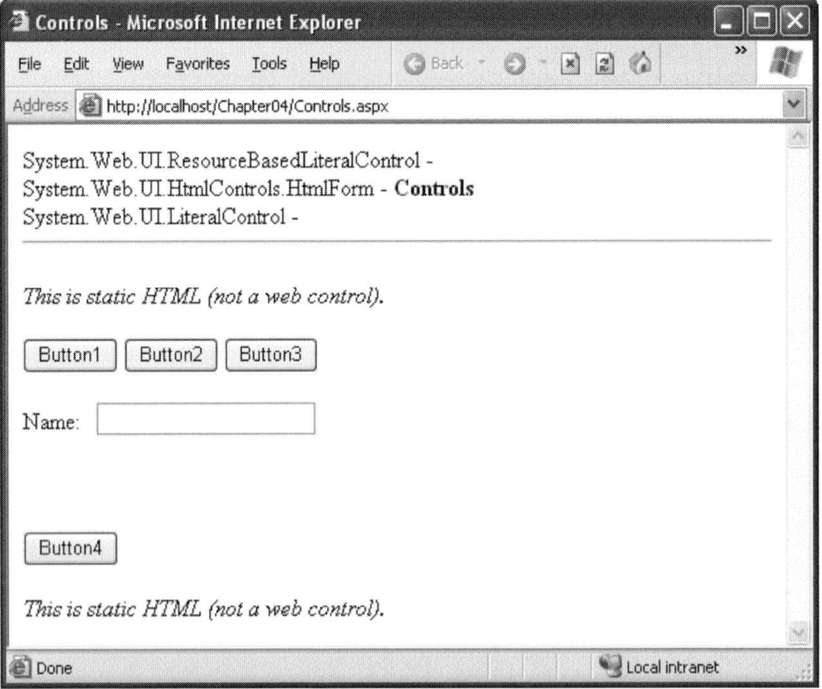

Figure 3-7. *Controls on the top layer of the page*

ASP.NET models the entire page using control objects, including elements that don't correspond to server-side content. For example, if you have one server control on a page, ASP.NET will create a LiteralControl that represents all the static content before the control and will create another LiteralControl that represents the content after it. Depending on how much static con- tent you have and how you break it up between other controls, you may end up with multiple LiteralControl objects.

LiteralControl objects don't provide much in the way of functionality. For example, you can't set style-related information such as colors and font. They also don't have a unique server-side ID. However, you can manipulate the content of a LiteralControl using its Text property. The following code rewrites the earlier example so that it checks for literal controls, and, if present, it casts the base Control object to the LiteralControl type so it can extract the associated text:

```
foreach (Control control in Page.Controls)
{
    Response.Write(control.GetType().ToString() + " - <b>" +
      control.ID + "</b><br />");

    if (control is LiteralControl)
    {
        // Display the literal content (whitespace and all).
        string text =((LiteralControl)control).Text;
        Response.Write("*** Text: "+ Server.HtmlEncode(text) + "<br />");
    }
}
Response.Write("<hr />");
```

The displayed text is HTML-encoded using the Server.HtmlEncode() method, which is discussed later in this chapter in the "HTML and URL Encoding" section. The result is that you don't see the formatted content—instead, you see the HTML markup that's used to create the content.

This example still suffers from a problem. You now understand the unexpected new content, but what about the missing content—namely, the other control objects on the page?

To answer this question, you need to understand that ASP.NET renders a page *hierarchically*. It directly renders only the top level of controls. If these controls contain other controls, they provide their own Controls properties, which provide access to their child controls. In the example page, as in all ASP.NET web forms, all the controls are nested inside the <form> tag. This means you need to inspect the Controls collection of the HtmlForm class to get information about the server controls on the page.

However, life isn't necessarily this straightforward. That's because there's no limit to how many layers of nested controls you can use. To really solve this problem and display all the controls on a page, you need to create a recursive routine that can tunnel through the entire control tree.

The following code shows the complete solution:

```
public partial class ControlTree : System.Web.UI.Page
{
    protected void Page_Load(object sender, System.EventArgs e)
    {
        // Start examining all the controls.
        DisplayControl(Page.Controls, 0);

        // Add the closing horizontal line.
        Response.Write("<hr />");
    }

    private void DisplayControl(ControlCollection controls, int depth)
    {
```

```
        foreach (Control control in controls)
        {
            // Use the depth parameter to indent the control tree.
            Response.Write(new String('-', depth * 4) + "> ");

            // Display this control.
            Response.Write(control.GetType().ToString() + " - <b>" +
              control.ID + "</b><br />");

            if (control.Controls != null)
            {
                DisplayControl(control.Controls, depth + 1);
            }
        }
    }
}
```

Figure 3-8 shows the new result—a hierarchical tree that shows all the controls on the page and their nesting.

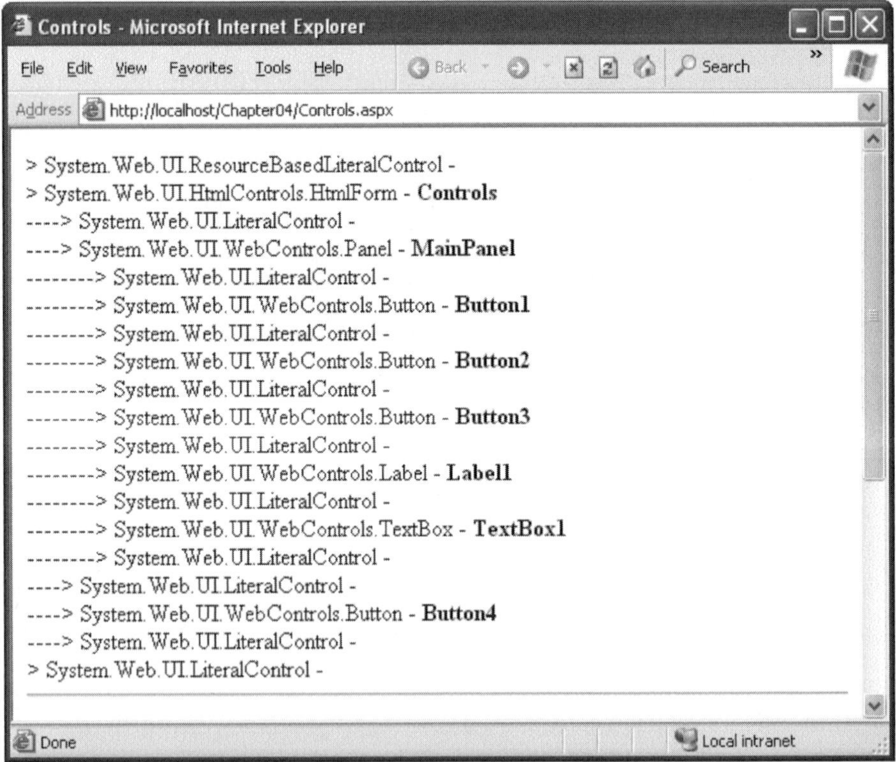

Figure 3-8. *A tree of controls on the page*

The Page Header

As you've seen, you can transform any HTML element into a server control with the runat="server" attribute, and a page can contain an unlimited number of HTML controls. In addition to the controls you add, a web form can also contain a single HtmlHead control, which provides server-side access to the <head> tag.

The control tree shown in the previous example doesn't include the HtmlHead control, because the runat="server" attribute isn't applied to the <head> tag in the page. However, the Visual Studio default is to always make the <head> tag into a server-side control, in contrast to previous versions of ASP.NET.

As with other server controls, you can use the HtmlHead control to programmatically change the content that's rendered in the <head> tag. The difference is that the <head> tag doesn't correspond to actual content you can see in the web page. Instead, it includes other details such as the title, metadata tags (useful for providing keywords to search engines), and stylesheet references. To change any of these details, you use one of a small set of members in the HtmlHead class, as described in Table 3-2).

Table 3-2. *Useful HtmlHead Properties*

Property	Description
Title	This is the title of the HTML page, which is usually displayed in the browser's title bar. You can modify this at runtime.
StyleSheet	This provides an IStyleSheet object that represents inline styles defined in the header. You can also use the IStyleSheet object to create new style rules dynamically by writing code that calls its CreateStyleRule() and RegisterStyle() methods.
Description	This is the text of the description metatag. This metatag is used to create the description of your website on search engines like Google.
Keywords	This is the text of the keywords metatag. Although search engines once used this information to determine search rankings for specific queries, almost all now ignore it.
Controls	You can add or remove metadata tags programmatically using this collection and the HtmlMeta control class. This is useful if you want to add metatags other than description and keywords.

Here's an example that sets title information and metadata tags dynamically:

```
Page.Header.Title = "Dynamically Titled Page";
Page.Header.Description = "A great website to learn .NET";
Page.Header.Keywords = ".NET, C#, ASP.NET";
```

And here's how you can add a different metatag to your header, such as the robots metatag that tells search engines not to index the current page:

```
// Define the robots metatag.
HtmlMeta metaTag = new HtmlMeta();
metaTag.Name = "robots";
metaTag.Content = "noindex";

// Add it.
Page.Header.Controls.Add(metaTag);
```

■ **Tip** The HtmlHead control is handy in pages that are extremely dynamic. For example, if you build a data-driven website that serves promotional content from a database, you might want to change the keywords and title of the page depending on the content you use when the page is requested.

Dynamic Control Creation

Using the Controls collection, you can create a control and add it to a page programmatically. Here's an example that generates a new button and adds it to a Panel control on the page:

```
protected void Page_Load(object sender, System.EventArgs e)
{
    // Create a new button object.
    Button newButton = new Button();

    // Assign some text and an ID so you can retrieve it later.
    newButton.Text = "* Dynamic Button *";
    newButton.ID = "newButton";

    // Add the button to a Panel.
    Panel1.Controls.Add(newButton);
}
```

You can execute this code in any event handler. However, because the page is already created, this code always adds the new control at the end of the collection. In this example, that means the new button will end up at the bottom of the Panel control.

To get more control over where a dynamically added control is positioned, you can use a PlaceHolder. A PlaceHolder is a control that has no purpose except to house other controls. If you don't add any controls to the Controls collection of the PlaceHolder, it won't render anything in the final web page. However, Visual Studio gives a default representation that looks like an ordinary label at design time, so you can position it exactly where you want. That way, you can add a dynamic control between other controls.

```
// Add the button to a PlaceHolder.
PlaceHolder1.Controls.Add(newButton);
```

When using dynamic controls, you must remember that they will exist only until the next postback. ASP.NET will not re-create a dynamically added control. If you need to re-create a control multiple times, you should perform the control creation in the Page.Load event handler. This has the additional benefit of allowing you to use view state with your dynamic control. Even though view state is normally restored *before* the Page.Load event, if you create a control in the handler for the Page.Load event, ASP.NET will apply any view state information that it has after the Page.Load event handler ends. This process is automatic.

If you want to interact with the control later, you should give it a unique ID. You can use this ID to retrieve the control from the Controls collection of its container. You can find the control using recursive searching logic, as demonstrated in the control tree example, or you can use the static Page.FindControl() method, which just searches the top-level Page.Controls collection for the control with the ID you specify. Here's an example that searches for the dynamically added control with the FindControl() method and then removes it:

```
protected void cmdRemove_Click(object sender, System.EventArgs e)
{
    // Search for the button in the Page.Controls collection.
    Button foundButton = (Button)Page.FindControl("newButton");

    // Remove the button.
    if (foundButton != null)
    {
        foundButton.Parent.Controls.Remove(foundButton);
    }
}
```

Dynamically added controls can handle events. All you need to do is attach an event handler using delegate code. You *must* perform this task in your Page.Load event handler. As you learned earlier, all control-specific events are fired after the Page.Load event. If you wait any longer, the event handler will be connected after the event has already fired, and you won't be able to react to it any longer.

```
// Attach an event handler to the Button.Click event.
newButton.Click += dynamicButton_Click;
```

Figure 3-9 demonstrates all these concepts. It generates a dynamic button. When you click this button, the text in a label is modified. Two other buttons allow you to dynamically remove or re-create the button.

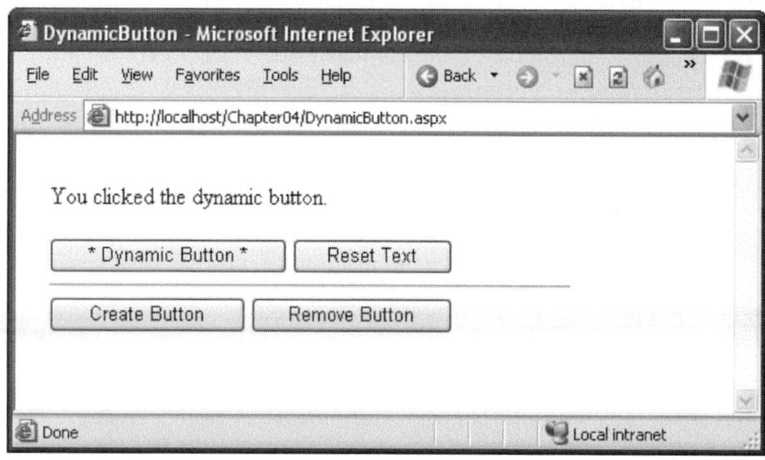

Figure 3-9. *Handling an event from a dynamically added control*

Dynamic control creation is particularly powerful when you combine it with user controls (reusable blocks of user interface that can combine a group of controls and HTML). You'll learn more about user controls in Chapter 15.

The Page Class

Now that you've explored the page life cycle and learned how a page contains controls, it's worth pointing out that the page itself is also instantiated as a type of control object. In fact, all web forms are actually instances of the ASP.NET Page class, which is found in the System.Web.UI namespace.

You may have already figured this out by noticing that every code-behind class explicitly derives from System.Web.UI.Page. This means that every web form you create is equipped with an enormous amount of out-of-the-box functionality. The FindControl() method and the IsPostBack property are two examples you've seen so far. In addition, deriving from the Page class gives your code the following extremely useful properties:

- Session
- Application
- Cache
- Request
- Response
- Server
- User
- Trace

Many of these properties correspond to intrinsic objects that you could use in classic ASP web pages. However, in classic ASP you accessed this functionality through built-in objects that were available at all times. In ASP.NET, each of these built-in objects actually corresponds to a Page property that exposes an instance of a full-featured class.

The following sections introduce these objects.

Session, Application, and Cache

The Session object is an instance of the System.Web.SessionState.HttpSessionState class. It's designed to store any type of user-specific data that needs to persist between web-page requests. The Session object provides dictionary-style access to a set of name/value pairs that represents the user's data for that session. Session state is often used to maintain things such as the user's name, the user's ID, a shopping cart, or various other elements that are discarded when a given user is no longer accessing pages on the website.

The Application object is an instance of the System.Web.HttpApplicationState class. Like the Session object, it's also a name/value dictionary of data. However, this data is global to the entire application.

Finally, the Cache object is an instance of the System.Web.Caching.Cache class. It also stores global information, but it provides a much more scalable storage mechanism because ASP.NET can remove objects if server memory becomes scarce. Like the other state collections, it's essentially a name/value collection of objects, but you can also set specialized expiration policies and dependencies for each item.

Deciding how to implement state management is one of the key challenges of programming a web application. You'll learn much more about all these types of state management in Chapter 6.

Request

The Request object is an instance of the System.Web.HttpRequest class. This object represents the values and properties of the HTTP request that caused your page to be loaded. It contains all the URL parameters and all other information sent by a client. Much of the information provided by the Request object is wrapped by higher-level abstractions (such as the ASP.NET web control model), so it isn't nearly as important as it was in classic ASP. However, you might still use the Request object to find out what browser the client is using or to set and examine cookies.

Table 3-3 describes some of the more common properties of the Request object.

Table 3-3. *HttpRequest Properties*

Property	Description
AnonymousID	This uniquely identifies the current user if you've enabled anonymous access. You'll learn how to use the anonymous access features in Chapter 24.
ApplicationPath and PhysicalApplicationPath	ApplicationPath gets the ASP.NET application's virtual directory (URL), while PhysicalApplicationPath gets the "real" directory.
Browser	This provides a link to an HttpBrowserCapabilities object, which contains properties describing various browser features, such as support for ActiveX controls, cookies, VBScript, and frames.
ClientCertificate	This is an HttpClientCertificate object that gets the security certificate for the current request, if there is one.
Cookies	This gets the collection of cookies sent with this request. Chapter 6 discusses cookies.
FilePath and CurrentExecutionFilePath	These return the real file path (relative to the server) for the currently executing page. FilePath gets the page that started the execution process. This is the same as CurrentExecutionFilePath, unless you've transferred the user to a new page without a redirect (for example, using the Server.Transfer() method), in which case CurrentExecutionFilePath reflects the new page and FilePath indicates the original page.
Form	This represents the collection of form variables that were posted back to the page. In almost all cases, you'll retrieve this information from control properties instead of using this collection.
Headers and ServerVariables	These provide a dictionary collection of HTTP headers and server variables, indexed by name. These collections are mostly made up of low-level information that's sent by the browser along with its web request (such as the browser type, its support for various features, its language settings, its authentication credentials, and so on). Usually, you can get this information more effectively from other properties of the HttpRequest object and higher-level ASP.NET classes.

Property	Description
IsAuthenticated and IsSecureConnection	These return true if the user has been successfully authenticated and if the user is connected over SSL (Secure Sockets Layer).
IsLocal	This returns true if the user is requesting the page from the local computer.
QueryString	This provides the parameters that were passed along with the query string. Chapter 6 shows how you can use the query string to transfer information between pages.
Url and UrlReferrer	These provide a Uri object that represents the current address for the page and the page where the user is coming from (the previous page that linked to this page).
UserAgent	This is a string representing the browser type. Internet Explorer provides the value "MSIE" for this property. ASP.NET uses this information to identify the browser and, ultimately, to determine the features the browser should support (such as cookies, JavaScript, and so on). This, in turn, can influence how web controls render themselves. For more information about ASP.NET's adaptive rendering model, refer to Chapter 27.
UserHostAddress and UserHostName	These get the IP address and the DNS name of the remote client. You could also access this information through the ServerVariables collection. However, this information may not always be meaningful due to network address translation (NAT). Depending on how clients connect to the Internet, multiple clients may share the same IP address (that of a gateway computer). The IP address may also change over the course of several requests.
UserLanguages	This provides a sorted string array that lists the client's language preferences. This can be useful if you need to create multilingual pages.

Response

The Response object is an instance of the System.Web.HttpResponse class, and it represents the web server's response to a client request. In classic ASP, the Response object was the only way to programmatically send HTML text to the client. Now server-side controls have nested, object-oriented methods for rendering themselves. All you have to do is set their properties. As a result, the Response object doesn't play nearly as central a role.

Table 3-4 lists the common HttpResponse members.

Table 3-4. HttpResponse Members

Member	Description
BufferOutput	When set to true (the default), the page isn't sent to the client until it's completely rendered and ready to be sent, as opposed to being sent piecemeal. In some specialized scenarios, it makes sense to set BufferOutput to false. The most obvious example is when a client is downloading a large file. If BufferOuput is false, the client will see the Save dialog box and be able to choose the file name before the file is fully downloaded.
Cache	This references an HttpCachePolicy object that allows you to configure output caching. Chapter 11 discusses caching.
Cookies	This is the collection of cookies sent with the response. You can use this property to add additional cookies.
Expires and ExpiresAbsolute	You can use these properties to cache the rendered HTML for the page, improving performance for subsequent requests. You'll learn about this type of caching (known as output caching) in Chapter 11.
IsClientConnected	This is a Boolean value indicating whether the client is still connected to the server. If it isn't, you might want to stop a time-consuming operation.
Redirect()	This method instructs the browser to request another URL, which can point to a new page in your web application or to a different website.
RedirectPermanent()	This method redirects the browser to a new URL, much like the Redirect() method. The difference is that it uses HTTP status code 301 (which indicates that the page has moved permanently) rather than HTTP status code 302 (which indicates that the page has moved temporarily).
RedirectToRoute() and RedirectToRoutePermanent ()	These methods parallel the Redirect() and RedirectPermanent() methods. The only difference is that they use a route (which is a registered URL pattern that doesn't map directly to a page). You'll learn much more about routing when you consider ASP.NET MVC in Chapter 32.
Transfer()	This method tells ASP.NET to abandon the current page and start to process a new web form page (which you specify). There's no round-trip required, and the web browser and web application user aren't notified of the change.
TransferRequest()	This method is similar to Transfer(), but it allows you to transfer the user to another type of page. For example, you can use it to send a user from an ASP.NET web form to an HTML page. When using the TransferRequest() method, the full IIS pipeline runs to handle the new resource, along with all the appropriate HTTP modules. But TransferRequest() also comes with a few sizable caveats. To use it, you must be using the IIS 7 web server in integrated mode. You must also release session state (if you've acquired it) to prevent a time-consuming delay.

Additionally, the HttpResponse class includes some members that you won't use in conjunction with ASP.NET's web control model. However, you might use these members when you create custom HTTP handlers (as described in Chapter 5) or return different types of content instead of HTML pages. Table 3-5 lists these members.

Table 3-5. *HttpResponse Members that Bypass the Control Model*

Member	Description
ContentType	When set to true (the default), the page isn't sent to the client until it's completely rendered and ready to be sent, as opposed to being sent piecemeal. In some specialized scenarios, it makes sense to set BufferOutput to false. The most obvious example is when a client is downloading a large file. If BufferOuput is false, the client will see the Save dialog box and be able to choose the file name before the file is fully downloaded.
OutputStream	This represents the data you're sending to the browser as a stream of raw bytes. You can use this property to plug into the .NET stream model (which is described in Chapter 12). For an example that demonstrates OutputStream, refer to Chapter 28, which uses it to return the image content from a dynamically generated graphic.
Write()	This method allows you to write text directly to the response stream. Usually, you'll use the control model instead and let controls output their own HTML. If you attempt to use Response.Write() and the control model, you won't be able to decide where the text is placed in the page. However, Response.Write() is important if you want to design controls that render their own HTML representation from scratch. You'll learn how to use Response.Write() in this context in Chapter 27.
BinaryWrite() and WriteFile()	These methods allow you to take binary content from a byte array or from a file and write it directly to the response stream. You won't use these methods in conjunction with server controls, but you might use them if you create a custom HTTP handler. For example, you could create an HTTP handler that reads the data for a PDF document from a record in a database and writes that data directly to the response stream using BinaryWrite(). On the client side, the end result is the same as if the user downloaded a static PDF file. (You'll see an example of WriteFile() with a custom HTTP handler that prevents image leeching in Chapter 5.) When writing non-HTML content, make sure you set the ContentType property accordingly.

Moving Between Pages

The most important function of the HttpResponse class is the small set of methods that allow you to leap from one page to another. The most versatile of these methods is Redirect(), which sends the user to another page. Here's an example:

```
// You can redirect to a file in the current directory.
Response.Redirect("newpage.aspx");

// You can redirect to another website.
Response.Redirect("http://www.prosetech.com");
```

The Redirect() method requires a round-trip. Essentially, it sends a message to the browser that instructs it to request a new page.

The Redirect() method has an overload that accepts a Boolean second parameter. This parameter indicates whether you want the page code to continue executing. By default, even though the Redirect() method redirects the user and closes the connection, any remaining code in the method will still run, along with other page events. This allows you to perform cleanup, if necessary. But if you supply the second parameter true, ASP.NET will stop processing the page immediately, potentially reducing the web server's workload.

If you want to transfer the user to another web form in the same web application, you can use a faster approach with the Server.Transfer() method. However, Server.Transfer has some quirks. Because the redirection happens on the server side, the original URL remains in the client's web browser. Effectively, the browser has no way of knowing that it's actually displaying a different page. This limitation leads to a problem if the client refreshes or bookmarks the page. Also, Server.Transfer() is unable to transfer execution to a non-ASP.NET page or a web page in another web application or on another web server.

■ **Tip** Another way also exists to get from one page to the next—*cross-page posting*. Using this technique, you can create a page that posts itself to another page, which allows you to effectively transfer all the view state information and the contents of any controls. You'll learn how to use this technique in Chapter 6.

ASP.NET 4 adds another redirection method to the HttpResponse class, called RedirectPermanent(). RedirectPermanent() has the same effect as Redirect()—it sends a redirect message to the browser, which asks it to request a new page. However, it uses the HTTP status 301 (which indicates a permanent redirect) rather than 302 (which indicates a temporary redirect). This distinction has no effect on web browsers, but it's important for search engines. If a search engine's web crawler is exploring your website and it receives the 301 status code, it will update the search catalog with the new URL information.

Thus, you use should Redirect() and RedirectPermanent() in very different ways. You use Redirect() for normal navigation and control of flow in an application (for example, as a user steps through a checkout process). You use RedirectPermanent() if an old URL is requested, which you supported in the past but no longer use. Typically, you'll call Redirect() somewhere in your web form code. However, you're more likely to call RedirectPermanent() in your application code—specifically, in the Application_BeginRequest() method in the global.asax file. That way, you can manage all of your permanent redirects in one place, without being forced to keep around stubs of your old pages. Here's an example:

```
protected void Application_BeginRequest(object sender, EventArgs e)
{
    // The web application no longer contains the about.aspx page.
    if (Request.FilePath == "/about.aspx")
    {
        Response.RedirectPermanent("/about/about-Us.aspx");
```

```
    }
    // (Add more redirects here.)
}
```

Chapter 5 has more about the Application_BeginRequest() method and other web application events.

Server

The Server object is an instance of the System.Web.HttpServerUtility class. It provides a handful of miscellaneous helper methods and properties, as listed in Table 3-6.

Table 3-6. *HttpServerUtility Members*

Member	Description
MachineName	A property representing the computer name of the computer on which the page is running. This is the name the web server computer uses to identify itself to the rest of the network.
GetLastError()	Retrieves the exception object for the most recently encountered error (or a null reference, if there isn't one). This error must have occurred while processing the current request, and it must not have been handled. This is most commonly used in an application event handler that checks for error conditions (an example of which you'll see in Chapter 5).
HtmlEncode() and HtmlDecode()	Changes an ordinary string into a string with legal HTML characters (and back again).
UrlEncode() and UrlDecode()	Changes an ordinary string into a string with legal URL characters (and back again).
MapPath()	Returns the physical file path that corresponds to a specified virtual file path on the web server. Calling MapPath() with / returns the physical path of the web application root. The MapPath() method also supports paths with the tilde (~) character, which represents the root of the web (for example, ~/homepage.aspx).
Transfer()	Transfers execution to another web page in the current application. This is similar to the Response.Redirect() method, but it's faster. It cannot be used to transfer the user to a site on another web server or to a non-ASP.NET page (such as an HTML page or an ASP page).

The Transfer() method is the quickest way to redirect the user to another page in your application. When you use this method, a round-trip is not involved. Instead, the ASP.NET engine simply loads the new page and begins processing it. As a result, the URL that's displayed in the client's browser won't change.

```
// You can transfer to a file in the current web application.
Server.Transfer("newpage.aspx");

// You can't redirect to another website
// (or another application pool on the same web server).
// This attempt will cause an error.
Server.Transfer("http://www.prosetech.com");
```

The MapPath() method is another useful method of the Server object. For example, imagine you want to load a file named info.txt from the current virtual directory. Instead of hard-coding the path, you can use Server.MapPath() to convert the relative path to your web application into a full physical path. Here's an example:

```
string physicalPath = Server.MapPath("info.txt");

// Now open the file.
StreamReader reader = new StreamReader(physicalPath);
// (Process the file here.)
reader.Close();
```

HTML and URL Encoding

The Server class also includes methods that change ordinary strings into a representation that can safely be used as part of a URL or displayed in a web page. For example, imagine you want to display this text on a web page:

```
To bold text use the <b> tag.
```

If you try to write this information to a page or place it inside a control, you would end up with this instead:

```
To bold text use the tag.
```

Not only will the text <b> not appear, but the browser will interpret it as an instruction to make the text that follows bold. To circumvent this automatic behavior, you need to convert potential problematic values to their special HTML equivalents. For example, < becomes < in your final HTML page, which the browser displays as the < character. Table 3-7 lists some special characters that need to be encoded.

***Table 3-7.** Common HTML Entities*

Result	Description	Encoded Entity
	Nonbreaking space	
<	Less-than symbol	<
>	Greater-than symbol	>
&	Ampersand	&
"	Quotation mark	"

Here's an example that circumvents the problem using the Server.HtmlEncode() method:

```
Label1.Text = Server.HtmlEncode("To bold text use the <b> tag.");
```

You also have the freedom to use HtmlEncode for some input, but not for all of it if you want to insert a combination of text that could be invalid and HTML tags. Here's an example:

```
Label1.Text = "To <b>bold</b> text use the ";
Label1.Text += Server.HtmlEncode("<b>") + " tag.";
```

■ **Note** Some controls circumvent this problem by automatically encoding tags. (The Label web control is not one of them. Instead, it gives you the freedom to insert HTML tags as you please.) For example, the basic set of HTML server controls include both an InnerText tag and an InnerHtml tag. When you set the contents of a control using InnerText, any special characters are automatically converted into their HTML equivalents. However, this won't help if you want to set a tag that contains a mix of embedded HTML tags and encoded characters.

The HtmlEncode() method is particularly useful if you're retrieving values from a database and you aren't sure if the text is valid HTML. You can use the HtmlDecode() method to revert the text to its normal form if you need to perform additional operations or comparisons with it in your code. Similarly, the UrlEncode() method changes text into a form that can be used in a URL, escaping spaces and other special characters. This step is usually performed with information you want to add to the query string.

It's worth noting that the HtmlEncode() method won't convert spaces to nonbreaking spaces. This means that if you have a series of space characters, the browser will display only a single space. Although this doesn't invalidate your HTML, it may not be the effect you want. To change this behavior, you can manually replace spaces with nonbreaking spaces using the String.Replace() method. Just make sure you perform this step after you encode the string, not before, or the nonbreaking space character sequence ( ) will be replaced with character entities and treated as ordinary text.

```
// Encode illegal characters.
line = Server.HtmlEncode(line);

// Replace spaces with nonbreaking spaces.
line = line. Replace(" ", " ");
```

Similarly, the HtmlEncode() method won't convert line breaks into <br> tag. This means that hard returns will be ignored unless you specifically insert <br> tags.

■ **Note** The issue of properly encoding input is important for more than just ensuring properly displayed data. If you try to display data that has embedded <script> tags, you could inadvertently end up executing a block of JavaScript code on the client. Chapter 29 has more about this danger and the ASP.NET request validation feature that prevents it.

User

The User object represents information about the user making the request of the web server, and it allows you to test that user's role membership.

The User object implements System.Security.Principal.IPrincipal. The specific class depends on the type of authentication you're using. For example, you can authenticate a user based on Windows account information using IIS or using a custom database and a dedicated login page. However, it's important to realize that the User object provides useful information only if your web application is performing some sort of authentication that restricts anonymous users.

Part 4 of this book deals with security in detail.

Trace

The Trace object is a general-purpose tracing tool (and an instance of the System.Web.TraceContext class). It allows you to write information to a log that is scoped at the page level. This log has detailed timing information so that not only can you use the Trace object for debugging but you can also use it for performance monitoring and timing. Additionally, the trace log shows a compilation of miscellaneous information, grouped into several sections. Table 3-8 describes all the information you'll see.

Table 3-8. *Trace Log Information*

Section	Description
Request Details	This section includes some basic information about the request context, including the current session ID, the time the web request was made, and the type of web request and encoding.
Trace Information	This section shows the different stages of processing the page went through before being sent to the client. Each section has additional information about how long it took to complete, as a measure from the start of the first stage (From First) and as a measure from the start of the previous stage (From Last). If you add your own trace messages (a technique described shortly), they will also appear in this section.
Control Tree	The control tree shows you all the controls on the page, indented to show their hierarchy, similar to the control tree example earlier in this chapter. One useful feature of this section is the Viewstate column, which tells you how many bytes of space are required to persist the current information in the control. This can help you gauge whether enabling control state could affect page transmission times.
Session State and Application State	These sections display every item that is in the current session or application state. Each item is listed with its name, type, and value. If you're storing simple pieces of string information, the value is straightforward. If you're storing an object, .NET calls the object's ToString() method to get an appropriate string representation. For complex objects, the result may just be the class name.

Section	Description
Cookies Collection	This section displays all the cookies that are sent with the request and response, as well as the content and size of each cookie in bytes. Even if you haven't explicitly created a cookie, you'll see the ASP.NET_SessionId cookie, which contains the current session ID. If you're using forms-based authentication, you'll also see the security cookie.
Headers Collection	This section lists all the HTTP headers associated with the request.
Forms Collection	This section lists the posted-back form information.
QueryString Collection	This section lists the variables and values submitted in the query string.
Server Variables	This section lists all the server variables and their contents.

■ **Tip** Tracing complements Visual Studio debugging. In many cases, debugging is the best approach for solving problems while you are coding a web application, while tracing gives you an easier option if you need to troubleshoot problems that appear while the application is running on a web server. However, tracing provides a few services that debugging doesn't (at least not as easily), such as showing you the amount of information in view state and the time taken to process the page on the server. Tracing also works regardless of whether you build your application in debug mode (with the debug symbols) or release mode.

You can enable tracing in two ways. You can set the Trace.IsEnabled property to true at any point in your code, as follows:

```
Trace.IsEnabled = true;
```

Usually, you'll do this in the Page.Load event handler. Another option is to use the Trace attribute in the Page directive:

```
<%@ Page Language="C#" CodeFile="PageFlow.aspx.cs" AutoEventWireup="true"
    Inherits="PageFlow" Trace="true" %>
```

By default, trace messages are listed in the order they were generated. Alternatively, you can specify that messages should be sorted by category, using the TraceMode attribute in the Page directive, as follows:

```
<%@ Page Language="C#" CodeFile="PageFlow.aspx.cs" AutoEventWireup="true"
    Inherits="PageFlow" Trace="true" TraceMode="SortByCategory" %>
```

or the TraceMode property of the Trace object in your code:

```
Trace.TraceMode = TraceMode.SortByCategory;
```

Figure 3-10 shows a partial listing of trace information with the PageFlow example demonstrated earlier.

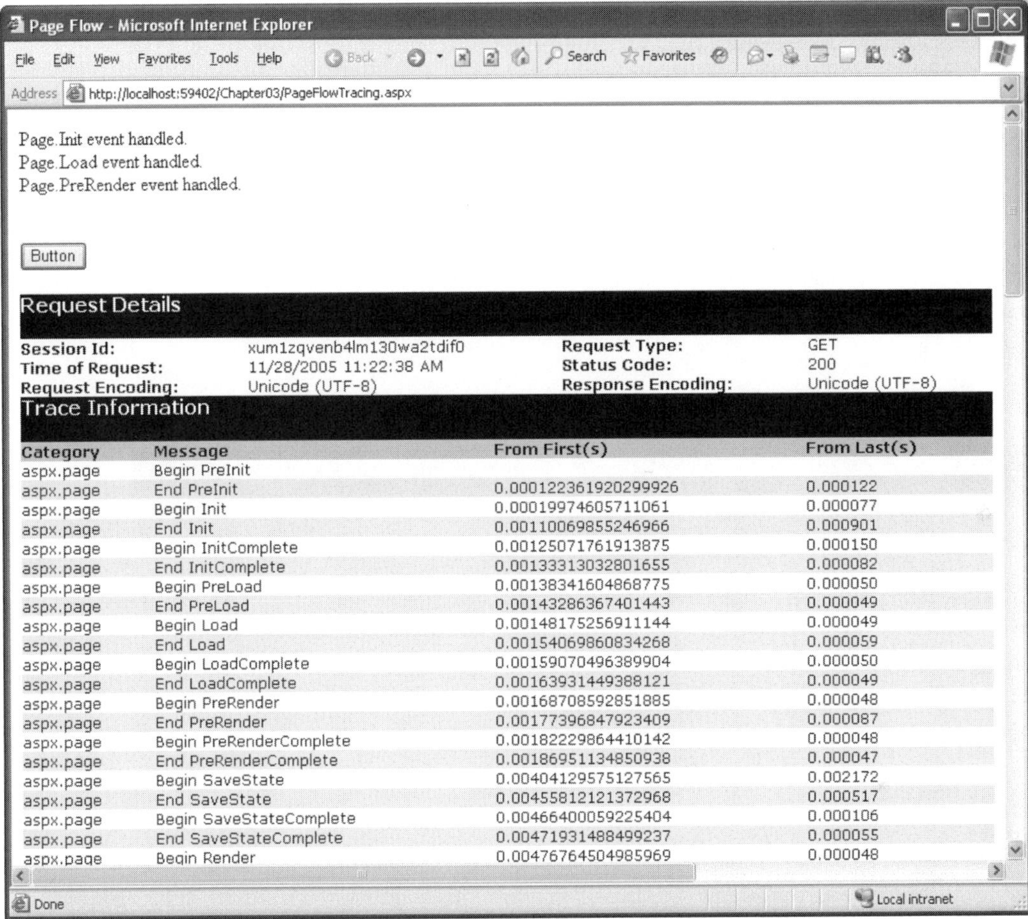

Figure 3-10. Basic trace information

You can also write your own information to the trace log (the portion of the trace log that appears in the Trace Information section) using the Trace.Write() or Trace.Warn() method. These methods are equivalent. The only difference is that Warn() displays the message in red lettering, which makes it easier to distinguish from other messages in the list.

Here's a code snippet that writes a trace message when the user clicks a button:

```
protected void Button1_Click(object sender, System.EventArgs e)
{
    // You can supply just a message, or include a category label,
    // as shown here.
    Trace.Write("Button1_Click", "About to update the label.");
    lblInfo.Text += "Button1.Click event handled.<br />";
    Trace.Write("Button1_Click", "Label updated.");
}
```

When you write trace messages, they are automatically sent to all trace listeners. However, if you've disabled tracing for the page, the messages are simply ignored. Tracing messages are automatically HTML-encoded. This means tags such as <br /> and <b> are displayed as text, not interpreted as HTML.

Figure 3-11 shows the new entries in the log.

■ **Tip** Not only can you send your own trace messages, but you can also create an event handler that receives every trace message. Although this is an uncommon and specialized technique, you could use it to filter out messages that are of particular interest to you during development and log them accordingly. All you need to do is handle the Trace.TraceFinished event, which provides you with a collection of TraceContext objects representing each trace message.

Trace Information

Category	Message	From First(s)	From Last(s)
aspx.page	Begin PreInit		
aspx.page	End PreInit	0.000139123827190327	0.000139
aspx.page	Begin Init	0.000217066694230691	0.000078
aspx.page	End Init	0.000311212737931776	0.000094
aspx.page	Begin InitComplete	0.000360380998143619	0.000049
aspx.page	End InitComplete	0.000416812751341302	0.000056
aspx.page	Begin LoadState	0.000465142916208624	0.000048
aspx.page	End LoadState	0.000799263593557282	0.000334
aspx.page	Begin ProcessPostData	0.000898438209325487	0.000099
aspx.page	End ProcessPostData	0.00102722552726673	0.000129
aspx.page	Begin PreLoad	0.00110349220361806	0.000076
aspx.page	End PreLoad	0.00115321919405958	0.000050
aspx.page	Begin Load	0.00119987316823786	0.000047
aspx.page	End Load	0.00125881920746911	0.000059
aspx.page	Begin ProcessPostData Second Try	0.00130575254676223	0.000047
aspx.page	End ProcessPostData Second Try	0.00135100969536631	0.000045
aspx.page	Begin Raise ChangedEvents	0.00139738430442975	0.000046
aspx.page	End Raise ChangedEvents	0.00144571446929708	0.000048
aspx.page	Begin Raise PostBackEvent	0.0014926478085902	0.000047
Button1_Click	About to update the label.	0.00488274347717377	0.003390
Button1_Click	Label updated.	0.00511154350622775	0.000229
aspx.page	End Raise PostBackEvent	0.00521826098009663	0.000107
aspx.page	Begin LoadComplete	0.00526882606588268	0.000051
aspx.page	End LoadComplete	0.00531715623075	0.000048
aspx.page	Begin PreRender	0.00536492766538764	0.000048
aspx.page	End PreRender	0.00543365148363828	0.000069
aspx.page	Begin PreRenderComplete	0.00548309910896497	0.000049
aspx.page	End PreRenderComplete	0.00552947371802841	0.000046
aspx.page	Begin SaveState	0.00672459767931399	0.001195
aspx.page	End SaveState	0.00711431201451581	0.000390
aspx.page	Begin SaveStateComplete	0.00719979773965686	0.000085
aspx.page	End SaveStateComplete	0.00725343584170614	0.000054
aspx.page	Begin Render	0.0073369660110433	0.000084
aspx.page	End Render	0.00856952489771745	0.001233

Figure 3-11. *Writing custom trace messages*

Application Tracing

By default, tracing is enabled on a page-by-page basis. This isn't always convenient. In some cases, you want to collect trace statistics for a page and then view them later. ASP.NET supports this approach with application-level tracing.

To enable application-level tracing, you need to modify the web.config configuration file. Look for the <trace> element and enable it as shown here:

```
<configuration>
  <system.web>
      <trace enabled="true" requestLimit="10" pageOutput="false"
       traceMode="SortByTime" localOnly="true" />
      ...
  </system.web>
</configuration>
```

This example turns on tracing (by setting enabled to true), stores a maximum of ten requests (by setting the requestLimit), and ensures that the trace information won't appear in the page (by setting the pageOutput to false). It also sorts traces by time (using the traceMode attribute), which means that the newest ten traces are kept, and it only allows local users to review the stored traces (using the localOnly attribute).

When you enable application-level tracing, you won't see the trace information on the page. Instead, to view tracing information you must request the trace.axd application extension in your web application's root directory. This extension doesn't correspond to an actual file—instead, ASP.NET automatically intercepts the request and lists the most recently collected trace requests (as shown in Figure 3-12), provided you're making the request from the local machine or have enabled remote tracing. You can see the detailed information for any request by clicking the View Details link.

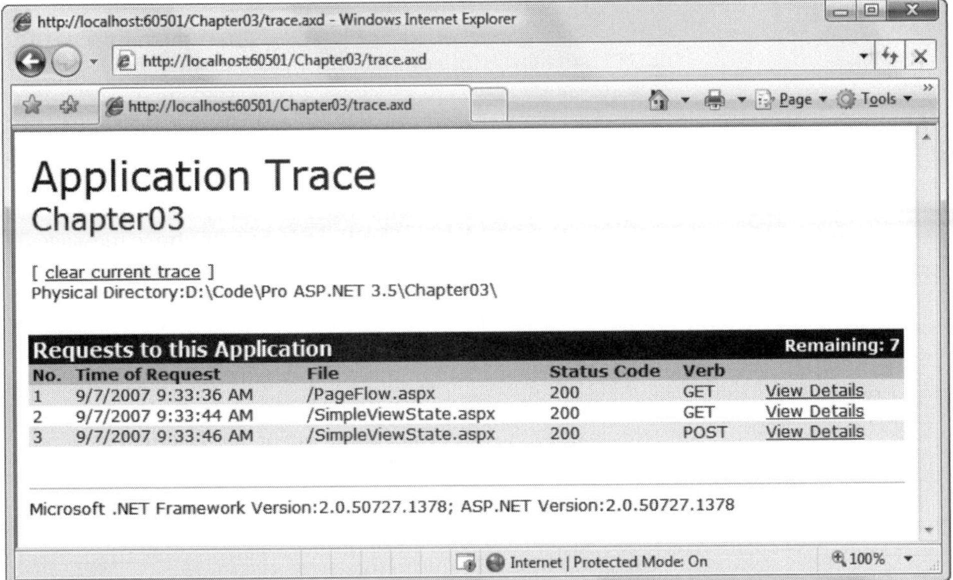

Figure 3-12. Traced application request

Table 3-9 describes the full list of tracing options in the web.config <trace> element.

Table 3-9. *Tracing Options*

Attribute	Values	Description
Enabled	true, false	This turns tracing on or off for all pages. This is the default setting for your web application—you can still override it on a page-by-page basis with the Page directive. Use the pageOutput setting to determine whether trace information is shown in the page or collected silently.
traceMode	SortByTime, SortByCategory	This determines the sort order of trace messages.
localOnly	true, false	This determines whether tracing information will be shown only to local clients (clients using the same computer) or can be shown to remote clients as well. By default, this is true and remote clients cannot see tracing information. In a production-level application, this should always be true to ensure security.
pageOutput	true, false	This determines whether tracing information will be displayed on the page (as it is with page-level tracing) or just stored on the server (application-level tracing). If you choose false to use application-level tracing, you'll still be able to view the collected information by requesting trace.axd from the virtual directory where your application is running.
requestLimit	Any integer	When using application-level tracing, this is the number of HTTP requests (for example, 10) for which tracing information will be stored. Unlike page-level tracing, this allows you to collect a batch of information from multiple requests. If you specify any value greater than 10,000, ASP.NET treats it as 10,000. When the maximum is reached, the behavior depends on the value of the mostRecent setting.
mostRecent	true, false	If true, ASP.NET keeps only the most recent trace messages. When the requestLimit maximum is reached, the information for the oldest request is abandoned every time a new request is received. If false (the default), ASP.NET stops collecting new trace messages when the limit is reached and ignores subsequent requests.
writeToDiagnostics Trace	true, false	If true, all trace messages are also forwarded to the System.Diagnostics tracing infrastructure and received by any trace listeners you've configured using that model. The default is false. The System.Diagnostics trace features are not ASP.NET-specific and can be used in a wide variety of .NET applications. They may be used in ASP.NET as a way to automatically capture trace messages and enter them in an event log.

Tracing with the Web Development Helper

If you've installed the Web Development Helper introduced in Chapter 2 (and available at `http://projects.nikhilk.net/Projects/WebDevHelper.aspx`), you have another option for looking at tracing information—viewing it in a separate window.

To try this out, follow the instructions in Chapter 2 to configure the module for the Web Development Helper in your web application, and then choose Tools ➤ Web Development Helper to switch it on in your browser.

When the Web Developer Helper is running, it automatically removes trace information from the page. To see the tracing information, you can either uncheck the Hide Trace option (choose Tools ➤ Options from the Web Development Helper and then click the ASP.NET tab) or you can open it in a separate window (choose ASP.NET ➤ Show Trace Information from the Web Development Helper).

Figure 3-13 shows this handy feature at work.

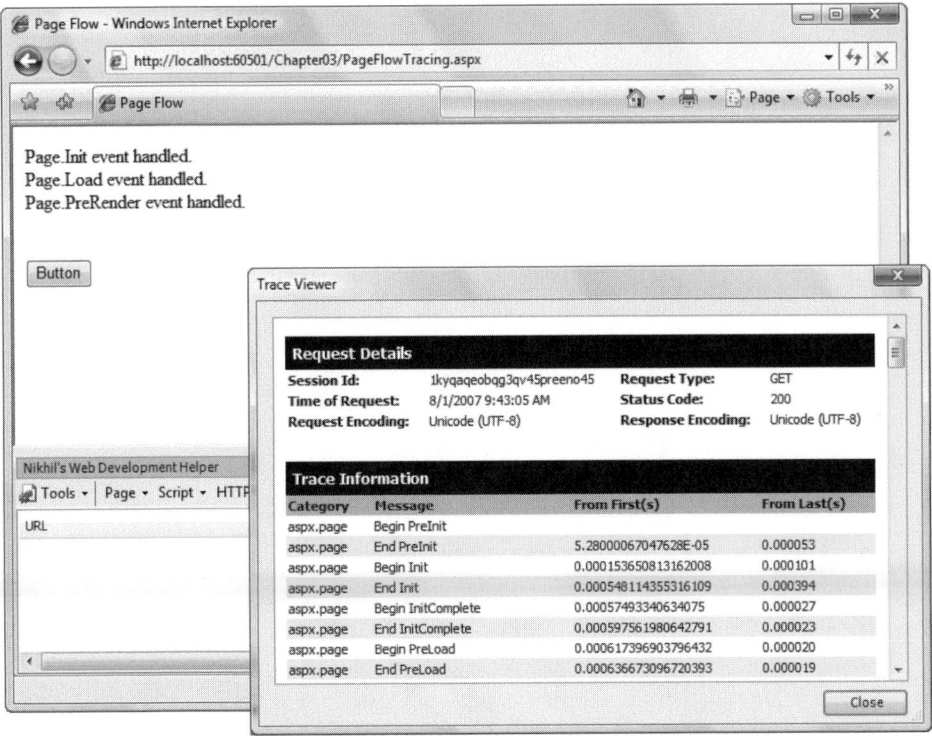

Figure 3-13. Managing trace information with the Web Development Helper

Accessing the HTTP Context in Another Class

Over the past several sections, you've seen how the Page class exposes a significant number of useful features that let you retrieve information about the current HTTP context. These details are available because they're provided as properties of the Page class. But what if you want to retrieve this information from inside another class, one that doesn't derive from Page?

Fortunately, another way exists to get access to all the HTTP context information. You can use the System.Web.HttpContext class. This class exposes a static property called Current, which returns an instance of the HttpContext class that represents all the information about the current request and response. It provides the same set of built-in ASP.NET objects as properties.

For example, here's how you would write a trace message from another component that doesn't derive from Page but is being used by a web page as part of a web request:

```
HttpContext.Current.Trace.Write("This message is from DB Component");
```

If you want to perform multiple operations, it may be slightly faster to retrieve a reference to the current context and then reuse it:

```
HttpContext current = HttpContext.Current;
current.Trace.Write("This is message 1");
current.Trace.Write("This is message 2");
```

Summary

In this chapter you walked through a detailed examination of the ASP.NET page. You learned what it is and how it really works behind the scenes with postbacks and view state. You also learned the basics of the server control model, examined the System.Web.UI.Page class, and learned how to use tracing. In the next chapter, you'll take a closer look at the web controls that ASP.NET gives you to build sophisticated pages.

CHAPTER 4

■ ■ ■

Server Controls

ASP.NET *server controls* are a fundamental part of the ASP.NET architecture. Essentially, server controls are classes in the .NET Framework that represent visual elements on a web form. Some of these classes are relatively straightforward and map closely to a specific HTML tag. Other controls are much more ambitious abstractions that render a more complex representation from multiple HTML elements.

In this chapter, you'll learn about the different types of ASP.NET server controls and how they're related. You'll also learn how to use validation controls to ensure that the user input matches specific rules before a web page is submitted to the server.

■ **What's New** ASP.NET 4 includes the same controls as earlier versions, with two notable exceptions. First, there's a new set of controls to deal with the ASP.NET Dynamic Data feature (Chapter 33). Second, there's a new Chart control for transforming data into richly detailed charts and graphs (Chapter 28). But this chapter concentrates on the standard set of controls that has been around since ASP.NET 2.0.

Types of Server Controls

ASP.NET offers many different server controls, which fall into several categories. This chapter explores the controls in the following categories:

HTML server controls: These are classes that wrap the standard HTML elements. Apart from this attribute, the declaration for an HTML server control remains the same. Two examples include HtmlAnchor (for the <a> tag) and HtmlSelect (for the <select> tag). However, you can turn any HTML tag into a server control. If there isn't a direct corresponding class, ASP.NET will simply use the HtmlGenericControl class. To change an ordinary HTML element into a server control, simply add the runat="server" attribute to the element tag.

Web controls: These classes duplicate the functionalities of the basic HTML elements but have a more consistent and meaningful set of properties and methods that make it easier for the developer to declare and access them. Some examples are the HyperLink, ListBox, and Button controls. In addition, several other types of ASP.NET controls (such as rich controls and validation controls) are commonly considered to be special types of web controls. In Visual Studio, you'll find the basic web forms controls in the Standard tab of the Toolbox.

Rich controls: These advanced controls have the ability to generate a large amount of HTML markup and even client-side JavaScript to create the interface. Examples include the Calendar, AdRotator, and TreeView controls. In Visual Studio, many rich controls are also found in the Standard tab of the Toolbox.

Validation controls: This set of controls allows you to easily validate an associated input control against several standard or user-defined rules. For example, you can specify that the input can't be empty, that it must be a number, that it must be greater than a certain value, and so on. If validation fails, you can prevent page processing or allow these controls to show inline error messages in the page. In Visual Studio, these controls are found in the Validation tab of the Toolbox.

Additionally, you'll examine several more specialized control groupings in other chapters. These include the following:

Data controls: These controls include sophisticated grids and lists that are designed to display large amounts of data, with support for advanced features such as templating, editing, sorting, and pagination. This set also includes the data source controls that allow you to bind to different data sources declaratively, without writing extra code. You'll learn about the data controls in Chapters 9 and 10.

Navigation controls: These controls are designed to display site maps and allow the user to navigate from one page to another. You'll learn about the navigation controls in Chapter 17.

Login controls: These controls support forms authentication, an ASP.NET model for authenticating users against a database and tracking their status. Rather than writing your own interfaces to work with forms authentication, you can use these controls to get prebuilt, customizable login pages, password recovery, and user-creation wizards. You'll learn about the login controls in Chapter 21.

Web parts controls: This set of controls supports WebParts, an ASP.NET model for building componentized, highly configurable web portals. You'll learn about WebParts in Chapter 31.

ASP.NET AJAX controls: These controls allow you to use Ajax techniques in your web pages without forcing you to write client-side code. Ajax-style pages can be more responsive because they bypass the regular postback-and-refresh page cycle. You'll learn much more in Chapter 30.

ASP.NET Dynamic Data controls: These controls support the ASP.NET Dynamic Data feature, which allows you to create a data-driven website by building flexible templates rather than writing tedious code. Chapter 33 explores this feature.

The Server Control Hierarchy

All server controls derive from the base Control class in the System.Web.UI namespace. This is true whether you're using HTML server controls, using web controls, or creating your own custom controls. It also applies to the Page class from which all web forms derive. Figure 4-1 illustrates the main branches of this inheritance chain.

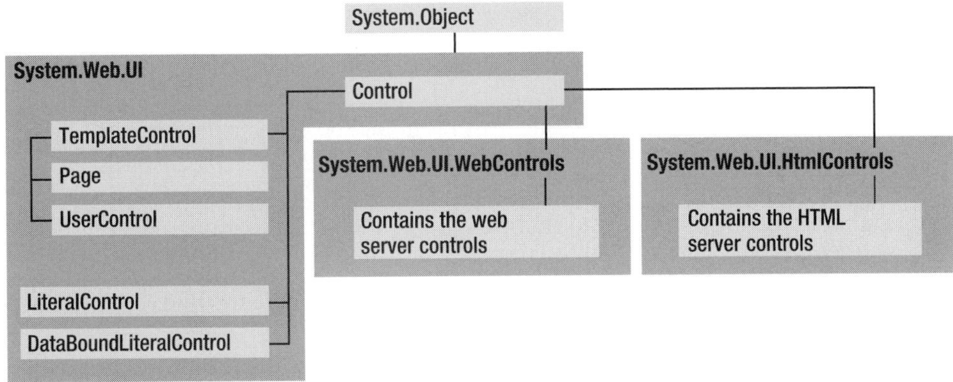

Figure 4-1. *Server control inheritance*

Because all controls derive from the base Control class, you have a basic common denominator that you can use to manipulate any control on the page, even if you don't know the specific control type. (For example, you could use this technique to loop through all the controls on the page and hide each one by setting the Visible property to false.) Tables 4-1 and 4-2 describe the most commonly used members of the Control class.

Table 4-1. *Control Class Properties*

Property	Description
ClientID	Returns the identifier of the control, which is a unique name created by ASP.NET at the time the page is instantiated.
Controls	Returns the collection of child controls. You can use the Page.Controls collection to get the top-level collection of controls on the page. Each control in the Controls collection may contain its own child controls, and those controls can hold still more controls of their own, and so on.
EnableViewState	Returns or sets a Boolean value indicating whether the control should maintain its state across postbacks of its parent page. This property is true by default.
ID	Returns or sets the identifier of the control. In practice, this is the name through which you can access the control from the server-side scripts or the code-behind class.
Page	Returns a reference to the page object that contains the control.
Parent	Returns a reference to the control's parent, which can be the page or another container control.
Visible	Returns or sets a Boolean value indicating whether the control should be rendered. If false, the control isn't just made invisible on the client—instead, the corresponding HTML tag is not generated.

Table 4-2. Control Class Methods

Method	Description
DataBind()	Binds the control and all of its child controls to the specified data source or expression. You'll learn about data binding in Part 2.
FindControl()	Searches for a child control with a specific name in the current control and all contained controls. If the child control is found, the method returns a reference of the general type Control. You can then cast this control to the proper type.
HasControls()	Returns a Boolean value indicating whether this control has any child controls. The control must be a container tag to have child controls (such as a <div> tag).
RenderControl()	Writes the HTML output for the control based on its current state. You don't call this method directly. Instead, ASP.NET calls it when the page is being rendered.

HTML Server Controls

In the following sections you'll learn about the HTML server controls, which are defined in the namespace System.Web.UI.HtmlControls. Overall, there are about 20 distinct HTML server control classes. They're split into separate categories based on whether they are input controls (in which case they derive from HtmlInputControl) or can contain other controls (in which case they derive from HtmlContainerControl). Figure 4-2 shows the inheritance hierarchy.

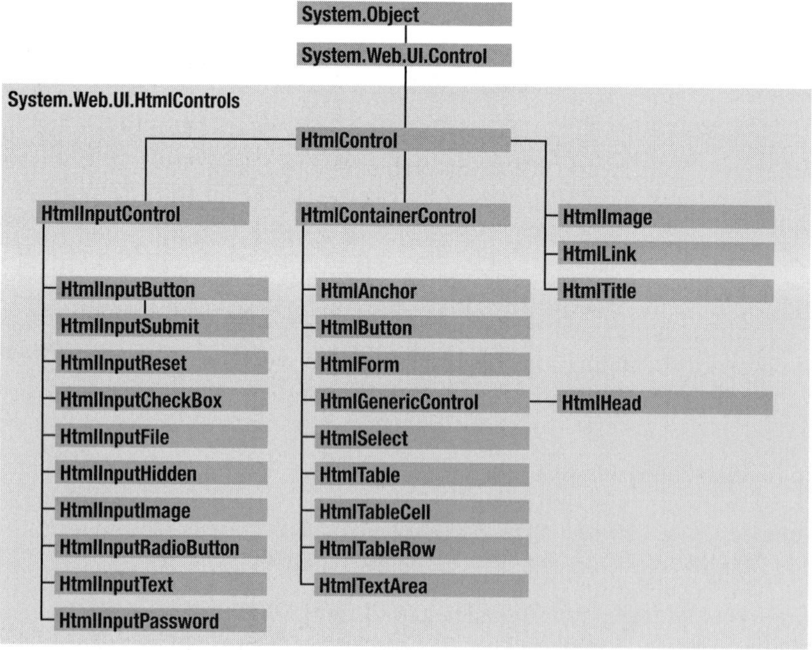

Figure 4-2. HTML server controls

The HtmlControl Class

All the HTML server controls derive from the base class HtmlControl. Table 4-3 shows the properties that the HtmlControl class adds to the base Control class.

Table 4-3. *HtmlControl Properties*

Property	Description
Attributes	Allows you to access or add attributes in the control tag. You can use this collection to add attributes that are not exposed by specific properties. (For example, you could add the onFocus attribute to a text box and specify some JavaScript code to configure what happens when the text box gets focus in the page.)
Disabled	Returns or sets the control's disabled state. If true, the control is usually rendered as a "grayed-out" control and is not usable.
Style	Returns a collection of CSS attributes that are applied to the control. In the web page you set this property as a semicolon-delimited list of style:value attributes. In Visual Studio, you can set this information using a designer by right-clicking the control and selecting New Style. Styles are discussed in more detail in Chapter 16.
TagName	Returns the control's tag name, such as a, img, and so on.

The HtmlContainerControl Class

Any HTML tag that has both an opening and a closing tag can contain other HTML content or controls. One example is the anchor tag, which usually wraps text or an image with the tags <a>...</a>. Many other HTML tags also work as containers, including everything from the <div> tag (which allows you to format a block of content) to the lowly <b> tag (which applies bold formatting). These tags don't map to specific HTML server control classes, but you can still use them with the runat="server" attribute. In this case, you interact with them using the HtmlGenericControl class, which itself derives from HtmlContainerControl.

To support containment, the HtmlContainerControl class adds the two properties shown in Table 4-4.

Table 4-4. *HtmlContainerControl Properties*

Property	Description
InnerHtml	Returns or sets the HTML text inside the opening and closing tags. When you use this property, all characters are left as is. This means you can embed HTML markup (bolding text, adding line breaks, and so on).
InnerText	Returns or sets the text inside the opening and closing tags. When you use this property, any characters that would be interpreted as special HTML syntax (such as <, the angle bracket) are automatically replaced with the HTML entity equivalents.

The HtmlInputControl Class

The HTML input controls allow for user interaction. These include the familiar graphical widgets, including check boxes, text boxes, buttons, and list boxes. All of these controls are generated with the <input> tag. The type attribute indicates the type of input control, as in <input type="text"> (a text box), <input type="submit"> (a submit button), and <input type="file"> (controls for uploading a file).

Server-side input controls derive from HtmlInputControl, which adds the properties shown in Table 4-5.

Table 4-5. *HtmlInputControl Properties*

Property	Description
Type	Gets the type of an HtmlInputControl. For example, if this property is set to text, the HtmlInputControl is a text box for data entry.
Value	Gets or sets the value associated with an input control. The value associated with a control depends on the type of control. For example, in a text box this property contains the text entered in the control. For buttons, this defines the text on the button.

The HTML Server Control Classes

Table 4-6 lists all the available HTML server controls and the specific properties and events that each one adds to the base class. As noted earlier, the declaration of HTML server controls on the page is the same as what you use for normal static HTML tags, with the addition of the runat="server" attribute. It is this attribute that allows ASP.NET to process them and translate them into instances of the corresponding .NET class. For this reason, the HTML server controls are a good option if you're converting your existing HTML or ASP page to an ASP.NET web form.

Table 4-6. *HTML Server Control Classes*

Tag Declaration	.NET Class	Specific Members
<a runat="server">	HtmlAnchor	HRef, Target, Title, Name, ServerClick event
<button runat="server">	HtmlButton	CausesValidation, ValidationGroup, ServerClick event
<form runat="server">	HtmlForm	Enctype, Method, Target, DefaultButton, DefaultFocus
<img runat="server">	HtmlImage	Align, Alt, Border, Height, Src, Width
<input type="button" runat="server">	HtmlInputButton	Type, Value, CausesValidation, ValidationGroup, ServerClick event
<input type="reset" runat="server">	HtmlInputReset	Type, Value

Tag Declaration	.NET Class	Specific Members
<input type="submit" runat="server">	HtmlInputSubmit	Type, Value, CausesValidation, ValidationGroup, ServerClick event
<input type="checkbox" runat="server">	HtmlInputCheckBox	Checked, Type, Value, ServerClick event
<input type="file" runat="server">	HtmlInputFile	Accept, MaxLength, PostedFile, Size, Type, Value
<input type="hidden" runat="server">	HtmlInputHidden	Type, Value, ServerChange event
<input type="image" runat="server">	HtmlInputImage	Align, Alt, Border, Src, Type, Value, CausesValidation, ValidationGroup, ServerClick event
<input type="radio" runat="server">	HtmlInputRadioButton	Checked, Type, Value, ServerChange event
<input type="text" runat="server">	HtmlInputText	MaxLength, Type, Value, ServerChange event
<input type="password" runat="server">	HtmlInputPassword	MaxLength, Type, Value, ServerChange event
<select runat="server">	HtmlSelect	Multiple, SelectedIndex, Size, Value, DataSource, DataTextField, DataValueField, Items (collection), ServerChange event
<table runat="server">, <td runat="server">	HtmlTable	Align, BgColor, Border, BorderColor, CellPadding, CellSpacing, Height, Width, Rows (collection)
<th runat="server">	HtmlTableCell	Align, BgColor, BorderColor, ColSpan, Height, NoWrap, RowSpan, VAlign, Width
<tr runat="server">	HtmlTableRow	Align, BgColor, BorderColor, Height, VAlign, Cells (collection)
<textarea runat="server">	HtmlTextArea	Cols, Rows, Value, ServerChange event
Any other HTML tag with the runat="server" attribute	HtmlGenericControl	None

---

■ **Note** Three specialized HTML controls aren't shown in Table 4-6. These are the HtmlHead, HtmlMeta, and HtmlTitle controls, which provide server-side access to the <head> portion of a web page. Using these controls, you can dynamically set the title, metadata, and linked stylesheets for the page. Chapter 3 shows an example.

The meaning of most of the HTML server control properties is quite obvious, because they match the underlying HTML tag attributes. This means there's no need to focus on each individual control. In the next few sections, you'll get an overview of some common techniques for using controls and dig a little deeper into their events and the common object model.

Setting Style Attributes and Other Properties

The following example shows how you can configure a standard HtmlInputText control (which represents the <input type="text"> tag). To read or set the current text in the text box, you use the Value property. If you want to configure the style information, you need to add new CSS style attributes using the Style collection. Finally, if you want to set other attributes that aren't exposed by any properties, you need to use the Attributes collection. This example uses the Attributes collection to associate some simple JavaScript code—showing an alert message box with the current value of the text box—to the client-side onfocus event of the control.

```
protected void Page_Load(object sender, System.EventArgs e)
{
    // Perform the initialization only the first time the page is requested.
    // After that, this information is tracked in view state.
    if (!Page.IsPostBack)
    {
        // Set the style attributes to configure appearance.
        Text1.Style["font-size"] = "20px";
        Text1.Style["color"] = "red";

        // Use a slightly different but equivalent syntax
        // for setting a style attribute.
        Text1.Style.Add("background-color", "lightyellow");

        // Set the default text.
        Text1.Value = "<Enter e-mail address here>";

        // Set other nonstandard attributes.
        Text1.Attributes["onfocus"] = "alert(Text1.value)";
    }
}
```

If you request the page, the following HTML code will be returned for the text box:

```
<input id="Text1" type="text"
 style="font-size:20px;color:red;background-color:lightyellow;"
 value="<Enter e-mail address here>"
 onfocus="alert(Text1.value)" />
```

The CSS style attribute may also include information that wasn't explicitly set in the code. For example, if you resize the input control in the Visual Studio designer, Visual Studio will add the height and width properties to the style it uses. These details will then also appear in the final HTML.

Figure 4-3 shows the resulting page when focus changes to the text box.

Figure 4-3. *Testing HTML server controls*

This process of control interaction is essentially the same for all HTML server controls. Style properties and attributes are always set in the same way. The only difference is that some controls expose additional properties that you can use. For example, the HtmlAnchor control exposes an HRef property that lets you set the target page for the link.

Programmatically Creating Server Controls

Sometimes you don't know in advance how many text boxes, radio buttons, table rows, or other controls you need because this might depend on other factors such as the number of records stored in a database or the user's input. With ASP.NET, the solution is easy—you can simply create instances of the HTML server controls you need, set their properties with the object-oriented approach used in the previous example, and then add them to the Controls collection of the containing page. This technique was introduced in the previous chapter, and it applies equally well to HTML server controls and web controls.

For example, the following code dynamically creates a table with five rows and four cells per row, sets their colors and text, and shows all this on the page. The interesting detail is that no control tags are declared in the .aspx file. Instead, everything is generated programmatically.

```
protected void Page_Load(object sender, System.EventArgs e)
{
    // Create a new HtmlTable object.
    HtmlTable table1 = new HtmlTable();
```

```
    // Set the table's formatting-related properties.
    table1.Border = 1;
    table1.CellPadding = 3;
    table1.CellSpacing = 3;
    table1.BorderColor = "red";

    // Start adding content to the table.
    HtmlTableRow row;
    HtmlTableCell cell;
    for (int i=1; i<=5; i++)
    {
        // Create a new row and set its background color.
        row = new HtmlTableRow();
        row.BgColor = (i%2==0 ? "lightyellow" : "lightcyan");

        for (int j=1; j<=4; j++)
        {
            // Create a cell and set its text.
            cell = new HtmlTableCell();
            cell.InnerHtml = "Row: " + i.ToString() +
              "<br />Cell: " + j.ToString();

            // Add the cell to the current row.
           row.Cells.Add(cell);
        }

        // Add the row to the table.
        table1.Rows.Add(row);
    }

    // Add the table to the page.
    this.Controls.Add(table1);
}
```

This example contains two nested loops. The outer loop creates the rows. The inner loop creates the individual cells for each row, and adds them to the Cells collection of the current row. When the inner loop ends, the code adds the entire row to the Rows collection of the table. The final step occurs when the outer loop is finished. At this point, the code adds the completed table to the Controls collection of the page.

Figure 4-4 shows the resulting page.

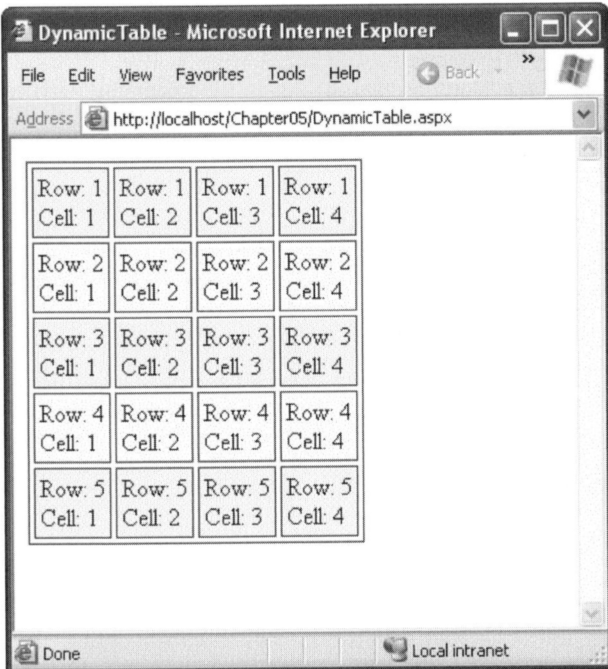

Figure 4-4. *A dynamically generated table*

This example used a table because it gave a good opportunity to show how child controls (cells and rows) are added to the Controls collection of the parent, but of course this mechanism works with any other server control.

Handling Server-Side Events

HTML server controls provide a sparse event model with two possible events: ServerClick and ServerChange. The ServerClick event is simply a click that is processed on the server side. It's provided by most button controls, and it allows your code to take immediate action. This action might override the expected behavior. For example, if you intercept the click event of a hyperlink control (the <a> element), the user won't be redirected to a new page unless you provide extra code to forward the request.

The ServerChange event responds when a change has been made to a text or selection control. This event doesn't occur until the page is posted back (for example, after the user clicks a submit button). At this point, the ServerChange event occurs for all changed controls, followed by the appropriate ServerClick.

Table 4-7 shows which controls provide a ServerClick event and which ones provide a ServerChange event.

Table 4-7. HTML Control Events

Event	Controls That Provide It
ServerClick	HtmlAnchor, HtmlButton, HtmlInputButton, HtmlInputSubmit, HtmlInputImage
ServerChange	HtmlInputText, HtmlInputCheckBox, HtmlInputRadioButton, HtmlInputHidden, HtmlSelect, HtmlTextArea

The ServerClick and ServerChange Events

The following example demonstrates the ServerClick and ServerChange events and shows you the order in which they unfold. To create this example, you need a text box, list box, and check box.

Here are the controls on the page:

```
<form runat="server">
  <div>
    <select runat="server" id="List1" size="5" multiple="true">
        <option>Option 1</option>
        <option>Option 2</option>
    </select>
    <br />
    <input type="text" runat="server" ID="Textbox1" Size="10" /><br />
    <input type="checkbox" runat="server" ID="Checkbox1" />
     Option text<br />
    <input type="submit" runat="server" ID="Submit1" value="Submit Query" />
  </div>
</form>
```

Note that this code declares two list items for the list box and includes the multiple attribute. This means that the user will be able to select multiple items by holding down the Ctrl key while clicking each entry.

The next step is to add event handlers for the ServerChange event. The text box and the check box are attached to the same event handler, while the list box uses a separate event handler with different code. Here's the event handling code that works with the text box and list box:

```
protected void Ctrl_ServerChange(object sender, System.EventArgs e)
{
    Response.Write("<ul><li>ServerChange detected for " +
      ((Control)sender).ID + "</li></ul>");
}
```

The actual event handler code is quite straightforward. It simply casts the sender object to a Control type, reads its ID property, and writes a message declaring that the event was detected (using the HTML <ul> element to create a bulleted list and <li> element to add a list item).

To attach the event handler to the appropriate server controls, you need to switch to the HTML source view, and add the OnServerChange attribute to the text box and check box tags, as shown here:

```
<input type="text" runat="server" ID="Textbox1" size="10"
 OnServerChange="Ctrl_ServerChange" /><br />
```

```
<input type="checkbox" runat="server" ID="Checkbox1"
 OnServerChange="Ctrl_ServerChange" />
```

■ **Note** Visual Studio provides a greater level of design-time support for events with web controls. When working with web controls, you can attach event handlers using a special event view in the Properties window—you just need to click the lightning bolt icon. With HTML server controls, this facility isn't available, so you need to wire up your event handlers manually, by editing the web page markup.

Next, you need to create the event handler for the list box. This event handler cycles through the control's Items collection and writes the value of all the selected items to the web page in a sublist, as follows:

```
protected void List1_ServerChange(object sender, System.EventArgs e)
{
    Response.Write("<ul><li>ServerChange detected for List1. " +
      "The selected items are:</li><ul>");
    foreach (ListItem li in List1.Items)
    {
        if (li.Selected)
            Response.Write("<li>" + li.Value + "</li>");
    }
    Response.Write("</ul></ul>");
}
```

You attach this event handler in the same way—by adding the OnServerChange attribute to the select element:

```
<select runat="server" OnServerChange="List1_ServerChange" ... >
```

Finally, the submit button handles the ServerClick event, as shown here:

```
protected void Submit1_ServerClick(object sender, System.EventArgs e)
{
    Response.Write("<ul><li>ServerClick detected for Submit1.</li></ul>");
}
```

You attach this event handler by adding the OnServerClick attribute:

```
<input type="submit" runat="server" OnServerClick="Submit1_ServerClick" ... />
```

As an added bonus, when the page is created, the event handler for the Page.Load event adds another three items to the list box, provided the page is being requested for the first time. This shows how easy it is to programmatically add list items.

```
protected void Page_Load(object sender, System.EventArgs e)
{
    if (!Page.IsPostBack)
    {
```

```
        List1.Items.Add("Option 3");
        List1.Items.Add("Option 4");
        List1.Items.Add("Option 5");
    }
}
```

To test this page, request it in the browser, select some items in the list box, type some characters in the text box, select the check box, and click the submit button to generate a postback. You should end up with something similar to what's shown in Figure 4-5.

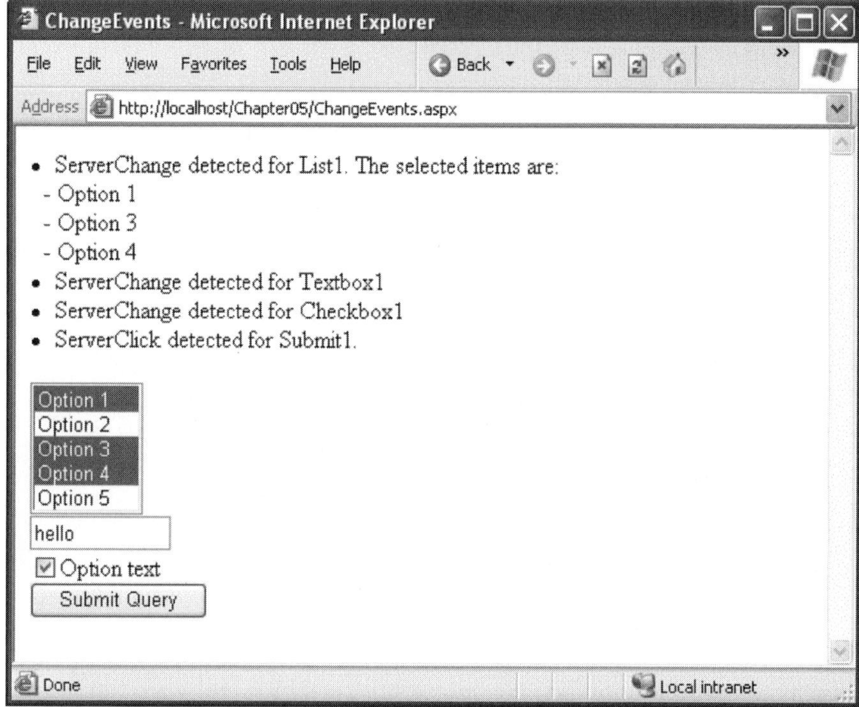

Figure 4-5. *Detecting change events*

Note that the order of change events is nondeterministic, and you shouldn't rely on these events occurring in any set order. However, you're likely to see events raised in the order in which the controls are declared. The only detail of which you're guaranteed is that all the change events fire before the ServerClick event that triggered the postback.

Web Controls

HTML server controls provide a relatively fast way to migrate to ASP.NET, but not necessarily the best way. For one thing, the names of HTML controls and their attributes are not always intuitive, and they don't have the same design-time support for attaching event handlers. The HTML controls also have certain limitations, such as that style properties must be set through CSS syntax (which is more difficult than setting a direct property) and that change events can't be raised until the page is posted back in response to another action. Finally, HTML server controls can't provide user interface elements that aren't already defined in the HTML standard. If you want to create some sort of aggregate control that uses a combination of HTML elements to render a complex interface, you're on your own.

To address these issues, ASP.NET provides a higher-level web control model. All web controls are defined in the System.Web.UI.WebControls namespace and derive from the WebControl base class, which provides a more abstract, consistent model than the HTML server controls. Web controls also enable additional features, such as automatic postback. But the really exciting part is that many extended controls don't just map a single HTML tag but instead generate more complex output made up of several HTML tags and JavaScript code. Examples include lists of check boxes, radio buttons, calendars, editable grids, and so on.

Figure 4-6 shows a portion of the inheritance hierarchy for web controls.

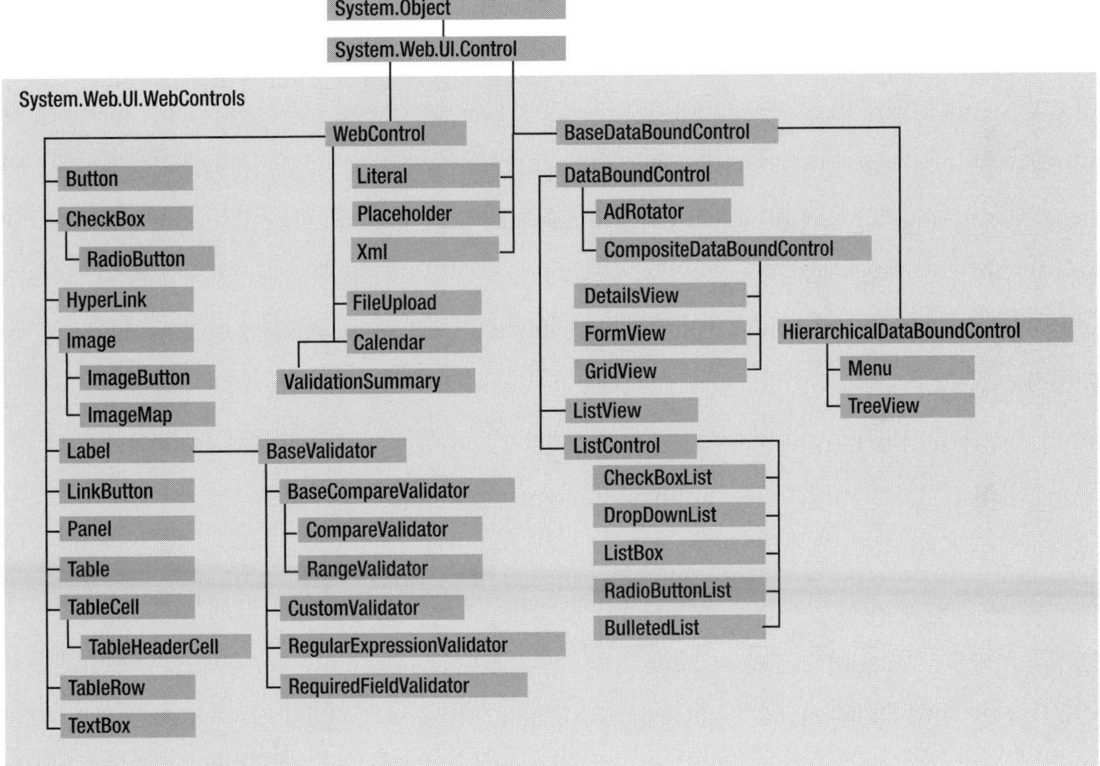

Figure 4-6. Web controls

The WebControl Base Class

All the web controls inherit from the WebControl class. The WebControl class also derives from Control. As a result, many of its properties and methods—such as Controls, Visible, and FindControl()—are similar to those of the HTML server controls. However, the WebControl class adds the properties shown in Table 4-8. Many of these properties wrap the CSS style attributes, such as the foreground or background color, the font, the height, the width, and so on. These properties allow you to configure the appearance of a web control much more easily (and with less chance of error).

Table 4-8. *WebControl Class Properties*

Property	Description
AccessKey	Returns or sets the keyboard shortcut that allows the user to quickly navigate to the control. For example, if set to A, the user can move the focus to this control by pressing Alt+A.
BackColor	Returns or sets the background color.
BorderColor	Returns or sets the border color.
BorderStyle	One of the values from the BorderStyle enumeration, including Dashed, Dotted, Double, Groove, Ridge, Inset, Outset, Solid, and None.
BorderWidth	Returns or sets the border width.
CssClass	Returns or sets the CSS style to associate with the control. The CSS style can be defined in a <style> section at the top of the page or in a separate CSS file referenced by the page.
Enabled	Returns or sets the control's enabled state. If false, the control is usually rendered grayed out and is not usable.
Font	Returns an object with all the style information of the font used for the control's text. This property includes subproperties that can be set with the object-walker syntax shown in this chapter.
ForeColor	Returns or sets the foreground color—for example, that of the text of the control.
Height	Returns or sets the control's height.
TabIndex	A number that allows you to control the tab order. The control with a TabIndex of 0 has the focus when the page first loads. Pressing Tab moves the user to the control with the next lowest TabIndex, provided it is enabled. This property is supported only in Internet Explorer 4.0 and higher.
Tooltip	Displays a text message when the user hovers the mouse above the control. Many older browsers don't support this property.
Width	Returns or sets the control's width.

Basic Web Control Classes

ASP.NET includes a web control that duplicates each HTML server control and provides the same functionality. These web controls inherit from WebControl and add their own properties and events. Table 4-9 summarizes these core controls and their specific members.

Table 4-9. *Basic Web Control Classes*

ASP.NET Tag Declaration	Generated HTML	Key Members
<asp:Button>	<input type="submit"/> or <input type="button"/>	Text, CausesValidation, PostBackUrl, ValidationGroup, Click event
<asp:CheckBox>	<input type="checkbox"/>	AutoPostBack, Checked, Text, TextAlign, CheckedChanged event
<asp:FileUpload>	<input type="file">	FileBytes, FileContent, FileName, HasFile, PostedFile, SaveAs()
<asp:HiddenField>	<input type="hidden">	Value
<asp:HyperLink>	<a>...</a>	ImageUrl, NavigateUrl, Target, Text
<asp:Image>	<img/>	AlternateText, ImageAlign, ImageUrl
<asp:ImageButton>	<input type="image"/>	CausesValidation, ValidationGroup, Click event
<asp:ImageMap>	<map>	HotSpotMode, HotSpots (collection), AlternateText, ImageAlign, ImageUrl
<asp:Label>	<span>...</span>	Text, AssociatedControlID
<asp:LinkButton>	<a><img/></a>	Text, CausesValidation, ValidationGroup, Click event
<asp:Panel>	<div>...</div>	BackImageUrl, DefaultButton, GroupingText, HorizontalAlign, Scrollbars, Wrap
<asp:RadioButton>	<input type="radio"/>	AutoPostBack, Checked, GroupName, Text, TextAlign, CheckedChanged event
<asp:Table>	<table>...	BackImageUrl, CellPadding, CellSpacing, GridLines, HorizontalAlign, Rows (collection)
<asp:TableCell>	<td>...	ColumnSpan, HorizontalAlign, RowSpan, Text, VerticalAlign, Wrap

ASP.NET Tag Declaration	Generated HTML	Key Members
<asp:TableRow>	<tr>...</tr>	Cells (collection), HorizontalAlign, VerticalAlign
<asp:TextBox>	<input type="text"/> or <textarea>...</textarea>	AutoPostBack, Columns, MaxLength, ReadOnly, Rows, Text, TextMode, Wrap, TextChanged event

The properties of web controls are all fairly intuitive. One of the goals of web controls is to make it easier to set a control's attributes through properties with consistent names, without having to worry about the details of how they translate to HTML code (although having a good knowledge of HTML certainly helps). For this reason, this chapter won't describe and show examples for every type of control. Instead, we'll provide a general discussion that's useful for every control.

To start highlighting some of the key differences between HTML server controls and web controls, consider the following web control tag:

```
<asp:TextBox runat="server" ID="TextBox1" Text="This is a test"
  ForeColor="red" BackColor="lightyellow" Width="250px"
  Font-Name="Verdana" Font-Bold="True" Font-Size="20" />
```

Web controls are always declared on the page with the syntax <asp:ControlName>, with the asp: prefix that makes them immediately recognizable as being different from the HTML controls. But this example also demonstrates a more dramatic difference—the way that style information is specified.

Essentially, this tag generates a text box control with a width of 250 pixels, a red foreground color, and a light yellow background. The text is displayed with the font Verdana, with a size of 20, and with bold formatting. The differences between the previous declaration and the respective declaration of a HTML tag are the following:

- The control is declared using its class name (TextBox) instead of the HTML tag name (input).
- The default content is set with the Text property, instead of a less obvious Value attribute.
- The style attributes (colors, width, and font) are set by direct properties, instead of being grouped together in a single style attribute.
- Web controls also have two special restrictions:
- Every control declaration must have a corresponding closing tag or use /> (the empty element syntax) at the end of the opening tag. In other words, ASP.NET tags follow the same rules as tags in XHTML. If you don't close the tag, you'll get a runtime error. Breaking this rule when working with HTML server controls has no adverse effect.
- All web controls must be declared within a server-side form tag (and there can be only one server-side form per page), even if they don't cause a postback. Otherwise, you'll get a run- time error. This rule is not necessary when working with HTML server controls, provided you don't need to handle postbacks.

If you request a page with this tag, you'll see that the control is translated into the following HTML tag when the page is rendered:

```
<input name="Textbox1" type="text" value="This is a test" id="Textbox1"
style="color:Red;background-color:LightYellow;font-family:Verdana;
font-size:20pt;font-weight:bold;width:250px;" />
```

■ **Note** The exact HTML that's rendered depends on the properties you've set and the browser that's making the request. You'll learn more about ASP.NET's rendering system (and how it differentiates between different types of browsers) when you consider custom controls in Chapter 27.

Units

All the control properties that use measurements, including BorderWidth, Height, and Width, require the Unit structure, which combines a numeric value with a type of measurement (pixels, percentage, and so on). This means that when you set these properties in a control tag, you must make sure to append px (for pixel) or % (for percentage) to the number to indicate the type of unit.

Here's an example with a Panel control that is 300 pixels tall and has a width equal to 50 percent of the current browser window:

```
<asp:Panel Height="300px" Width="50%" id="pnl" runat="server" />
```

If you're assigning a unit-based property through code, you need to use one of the static methods of the Unit type. Use Pixel() to supply a value in pixels, and use Percentage() to supply a percentage value.

```
// Convert the number 300 to a Unit object
// representing pixels, and assign it.
pnl.Height = Unit.Pixel(300);

// Convert the number 50 to a Unit object
// representing percent, and assign it.
pnl.Width = Unit.Percentage(50);
```

You could also manually create a Unit object and initialize it using one of the supplied constructors and the UnitType enumeration. This requires a few more steps but allows you to easily assign the same unit to several controls.

```
// Create a Unit object.
Unit myUnit = new Unit(300, UnitType.Pixel);
// Assign the Unit object to several controls or properties.
pnl.Height = myUnit;
pnl.Width = myUnit;
```

Enumerations

Enumerations are used heavily in the .NET class library to group a set of related constants. For example, when you set a control's BorderStyle property, you can choose one of several predefined values from the BorderStyle enumeration. In code, you set an enumeration using the dot syntax:

```
ctrl.BorderStyle = BorderStyle.Dashed;
```

In the .aspx file, you set an enumeration by specifying one of the allowed values as a string. You don't include the name of the enumeration type, which is assumed automatically.

```
<asp:TextBox BorderStyle="Dashed" Text="Border Test" id="txt"
 runat="server" />
```

Colors

The Color property refers to a Color object from the System.Drawing namespace. You can create Color objects in several ways:

- **Using an ARGB (alpha, red, green, blue) color value:** You specify each value as integer.
- **Using a predefined .NET color name:** You choose the correspondingly named read-only property from the Color class. These properties include all the HTML colors.
- **Using an HTML color name:** You specify this value as a string using the ColorTranslator class.

To use these any of techniques, you must import the System.Drawing namespace, as follows:

```
using System.Drawing;
```

The following code shows several ways to specify a color in code:

```
// Create a color from an ARGB value.
int alpha = 255, red = 0, green = 255, blue = 0;
ctrl.ForeColor = Color.FromArgb(alpha, red, green, blue);

// Create a color using a .NET name.
ctrl.ForeColor = Color.Crimson;

// Create a color from an HTML code.
ctrl.ForeColor = ColorTranslator.FromHtml("Blue");
```

When defining a color in the .aspx file, you can use any one of the known color names, as follows:

```
<asp:TextBox ForeColor="Red" Text="Test" id="txt" runat="server" />
```

Refer to the Visual Studio documentation for a full list of color names. Alternatively, you can use a hexadecimal color number (in the format #<red><green><blue>), as shown here:

```
<asp:TextBox ForeColor="#99FFFF" Text="Test"
     id="txt" runat="server" />
```

Fonts

The Font property actually references a full FontInfo object, which is defined in the System.Web.UI.WebControls namespace. Every FontInfo object has several properties that define a font's name, size, and style. Even though the WebControl.Font property is read-only, you can modify all the FontInfo properties (shown in Table 4-10).

Table 4-10. FontInfo Properties

Property	Description
Name	A string indicating the font name (such as Verdana).
Names	An array of strings with font names, which are ordered by preference.
Size	The size of the font as a FontUnit object. This can represent an absolute or relative size.
Bold, Italic, Strikeout, Underline, and Overline	Boolean properties that either apply the given style attribute or ignore it.

In code, you can assign values to the various font properties as shown here:

```
ctrl.Font.Name = "Verdana";
ctrl.Font.Bold = true;
```

You can also set the size using the FontUnit type:

```
// Specifies a relative size.
ctrl.Font.Size = FontUnit.Small;

// Specifies an absolute size of 14 points.
ctrl.Font.Size = FontUnit.Point(14);
```

In the .aspx file, you need to use a special object-walker syntax to specify object properties such as font. The object-walker syntax uses a hyphen (-) to separate properties. For example, you could set a control with a specific font (Tahoma) and font size (40 point) like this:

```
<asp:TextBox Font-Name="Tahoma" Font-Size="40" Text="Size Test" id="txt"
 runat="server" />
```

or with a relative size, as follows:

```
<asp:TextBox Font-Name="Tahoma" Font-Size="Large" Text="Size Test"
 id="txt" runat="server" />
```

Of course, in the world of the Internet, font names are just recommendations. If a given font isn't present on a client's computer, the browser attempts to substitute a similar font. (For more information on this font substitution process, refer to the CSS specification at `http://www.w3.org/TR/REC-CSS2/fonts.html`.)

If you want to provide a list of possible fonts, you can use the FontInfo.Names property instead of the FontInfo.Name property. The Names property accepts an array of names that will be rendered as an ordered list (with greatest preference given to the names at the top of the list). Here's an example:

```
<asp:TextBox Font-Names="Calibri, Times New Roman, Times"
 Font-Size="Large" Text="Size Test" id="txt" runat="server" />
```

■ **Tip** The Names and Name properties are kept synchronized, and setting either one affects the other. When you set the Names property, the Name property is automatically set to the first item in the array you used for the Names property. If you set the Name property, the Names property is automatically set with an array containing a single item. Therefore, you should use only the Name property or the Names property, but not both at once.

Focus

Unlike HTML server controls, every web control provides a Focus() method. The Focus() method has an effect only for input controls (controls that can accept keystrokes from the user). When the page is rendered in the client browser, the user starts in the focused control.

For example, if you have a form that allows the user to edit customer information, you might call the Focus() method on the first text box with customer address information. That way, the cursor appears in this text box immediately. Also, if the text box is partway down the form, the page scrolls to the correct position automatically. Once the page is rendered, the user can move from control to control using the time-honored Tab key.

Of course, if you're familiar with the HTML standard, you know there isn't any built-in way to give focus to an input control. Instead, you need to rely on JavaScript. This is the secret to ASP.NET's implementation. When your code is finished processing and the page is rendered, ASP.NET adds an extra block of JavaScript code to the end of your page. This JavaScript code simply sets the focus to the last control that had the Focus() method triggered. Here's the code that ASP.NET adds to your rendered web page to move the focus to a control named TextBox2:

```
<script type="text/javascript">
  WebForm_AutoFocus('TextBox2');
</script>
```

If you haven't called Focus() at all, this code isn't emitted. If you've called it for more than one control, the JavaScript code uses the more recently focused control.

Rather than call the Focus() method programmatically, you can set a control that should always be focused (unless you override it by calling the Focus() method). You do this by setting the Form.DefaultFocus property, like so:

```
<form id="Form1" DefaultFocus="TextBox2" runat="server">
```

Incidentally, the focusing code relies on a JavaScript method named WebForm_AutoFocus(), which ASP.NET generates automatically. Technically, the JavaScript method is provided through an ASP.NET extension named WebResource.axd. The resource is named Focus.js. If you dig through the rendered HTML of your page, you'll find an element that links to this JavaScript file that takes this form (where the d and t arguments are long):

```
<script src="WebResource.axd?d=...&t=..."></script>
```

You can type this request directly into your browser to download and examine the JavaScript document. It's quite lengthy, because it carefully deals with cases such as focusing on a nonfocusable control that contains a focusable child. However, the following code shows the heart of the focusing logic:

```
function WebForm_AutoFocus(focusId) {
    // Find the element based on the ID (code differs based on browser).
    var targetControl;
```

```
    if (__nonMSDOMBrowser) {
        targetControl = document.getElementById(focusId);
    }
    else {
        targetControl = document.all[focusId];
    }

    // Check if the control can accept focus or contains a child that can.
    var focused = targetControl;
    if (targetControl != null && (!WebForm_CanFocus(targetControl)) ) {
        focused = WebForm_FindFirstFocusableChild(targetControl);
    }
    // If there is a valid control, try to apply focus and scroll it into view.
    if (focused != null) {
        try {
            focused.focus();
            focused.scrollIntoView();
            if (window.__smartNav != null) {
                window.__smartNav.ae = focused.id;
            }
        }
        catch (e) {
        }
    }
}
```

As you can see, the first task this code performs is to test whether the current browser is an up-level version of Internet Explorer (and hence supports the Microsoft DOM). However, even if it isn't, the script code still performs the autofocusing, with only subtle differences.

Another way to manage focus is using access keys. For example, if you set the AccessKey property of a TextBox to A, then when the user presses Alt+A, focus will switch to the TextBox. Labels can also get into the game, even though they can't accept focus. The trick is to set the property Label.AssociatedControlID to specify a linked input control. That way, the label transfers focus to the control nearby.

For example, the following label gives focus to TextBox2 when the keystroke Alt+2 is pressed:

```
<asp:Label AccessKey="2" AssociatedControlID="TextBox2" runat="server">
 TextBox2:</asp:Label><asp:TextBox runat="server" ID="TextBox2" />
```

Access keys are also supported in non-Microsoft browsers, including Firefox.

The Default Button

Along with the idea of control focusing, ASP.NET includes a mechanism that allows you to designate a default button on a web page. The default button is the button that is "clicked" when the user presses the Enter key. For example, on a form you might want to turn the submit button into a default button. That way, if the user hits Enter at any time, the page is posted back and the Button.Click event is fired for that button.

To designate a default button, you must set the HtmlForm.DefaultButton property with the ID of the respective control, as shown here:

```
<form id="Form1" DefaultButton="cmdSubmit" runat="server">
```

The default button must be a control that implements the IButtonControl interface. The interface is implemented by the Button, LinkButton, and ImageButton web controls but not by any of the HTML server controls.

In some cases, it makes sense to have more than one default button. For example, you might create a web page with two groups of input controls. Both groups may need a different default button. You can handle this by placing the groups into separate panels. The Panel control also exposes the DefaultButton property, which works when any input control it contains gets the focus.

Scrollable Panels

The Panel control has the ability to scroll. This means you can fill your Panel controls with server controls or HTML, explicitly set the Height and Width properties of the panel so they won't be smaller than what's required, and then switch on scrolling by setting the ScrollBars property to Vertical, Horizontal, Both, or Auto (which shows scrollbars only when there's too much content to fit).

Here's an example:

```
<asp:Panel ID="Panel1" runat="server" Height="116px" Width="278px"
 BorderStyle="Solid" BorderWidth="1px" ScrollBars="Auto">
  This scrolls.
  <br /><br />
  <asp:Button ID="Button1" runat="server" Text="Button" />
  <asp:Button ID="Button2" runat="server" Text="Button" />
  <br />
  ...
</asp:Panel>
```

Figure 4-7 shows the result.

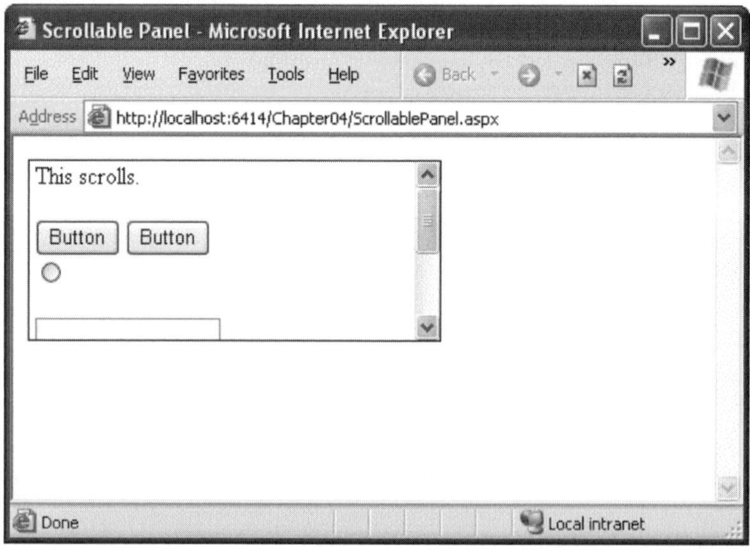

Figure 4-7. A scrollable panel

The panel is rendered as a <div> tag. The scrolling behavior is provided by setting the CSS overflow property.

Handling Web Control Events

Server-side events work in much the same way as the server events of the HTML server controls. Instead of the ServerClick events, there is a Click event, and instead of the generic ServerChange events there are specific events such as CheckedChanged (for the RadioButton and CheckButton) and TextChanged (for the TextBox), but the behavior remains the same.

The key difference is that web controls support the AutoPostBack feature described in the previous chapter, which uses JavaScript to capture a client-side event and trigger a postback. ASP.NET receives the posted-back page and raises the corresponding server-side event immediately.

To watch these events in action, it helps to create a simple event tracker application (see Figure 4-8). All this application does is add a new entry to a list control every time one of the events it's monitoring occurs. This allows you to see the order in which events are triggered and the effect of using automatic postback.

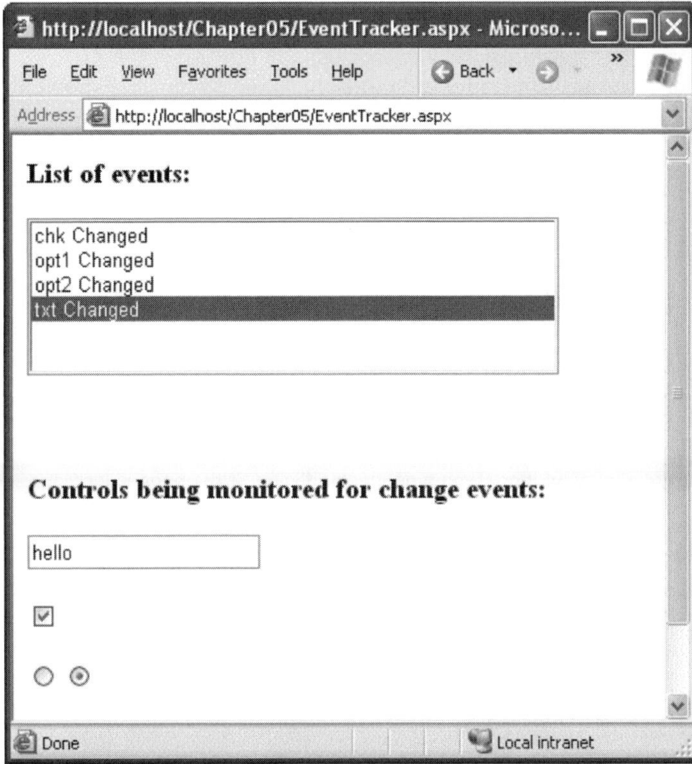

Figure 4-8. *The event tracker*

In this demonstration, all control change events are handled by the same event handler:

```
<form id="form1" runat="server">
  <div>
    <h3>List of events:</h3>
    <asp:ListBox id="lstEvents" runat="server" Height="107px" Width="355px"/>
    <br /><br />
    <h3>Controls being monitored for change events:</h3>
    <asp:TextBox id="txt" runat="server" AutoPostBack="true"
     OnTextChanged="CtrlChanged"/>
    <br /><br />
    <asp:CheckBox id="chk" runat="server" AutoPostBack="true"
     OnCheckedChanged="CtrlChanged"/>
    <br /><br />
    <asp:RadioButton id="opt1" runat="server" GroupName="Sample"
     AutoPostBack="true" OnCheckedChanged="CtrlChanged"/>
    <asp:RadioButton id="opt2" runat="server" GroupName="Sample"
     AutoPostBack="true" OnCheckedChanged="CtrlChanged"/>
  </div>
</form>
```

The event handler simply adds a new message to a list box and scrolls to the end:

```
protected void CtrlChanged(Object sender, EventArgs e)
{
    string ctrlName = ((Control)sender).ID;
    lstEvents.Items.Add(ctrlName + " Changed");

    // Select the last item to scroll the list so the most recent
    // entries are visible.
    lstEvents.SelectedIndex = lstEvents.Items.Count - 1;
}
```

■ **Note** Automatic postback isn't always a good thing. Posting the page back to the server interrupts the user for a brief amount of time. If the page is large, the delay may be more than a noticeable flicker. If the page is long and the user has scrolled to the bottom of the page, the user will lose the current position when the page is refreshed and the view is returned to the top of the page. Because of these idiosyncrasies, it's a good idea to evaluate whether you really need postback and to refrain from using it for minor cosmetic reasons. One possible alternative is to use the Ajax features described in Chapter 30.

The Click Event and the ImageButton Control

In the examples you've looked at so far, the second event parameter has always been used to pass an empty System.EventArgs object. This object doesn't contain any additional information—it's just a glorified placeholder.

One control that does send extra information is the ImageButton control. It sends a special ImageClickEventArgs object (from the System.Web.UI namespace) that provides X and Y properties representing the location where the image was clicked. Using this additional information, you can create a server-side image map. For example, here's the code that simply displays the location where the image was clicked and checks if it was over a predetermined region of the picture:

```
protected void ImageButton1_Click(object sender,
  System.Web.UI.ImageClickEventArgs e)
{
    lblResult.Text = "You clicked at (" + e.X.ToString() +
      ", " + e.Y.ToString() + "). ";

    // Check if the clicked point falls in the rectangle described
    // by the points (20,20) and (275,100), which is the button surface.
    if ((e.Y < 100) && (e.Y > 20) && (e.X > 20) && (e.X < 275))
    {
        lblResult.Text += "You clicked on the button surface.";
    }
    else
    {
        lblResult.Text += "You clicked the button border.";
    }
}
```

The sample web page shown in Figure 4-9 puts this feature to work with a simple graphical button. Depending on whether the user clicks the button border or the button surface, the web page displays a different message.

■ **Note** Another, more powerful approach to handling image clicks is to create a server-side image map using the ImageMap control. The ImageMap control is demonstrated in Chapter 28, which deals with dynamic graphics.

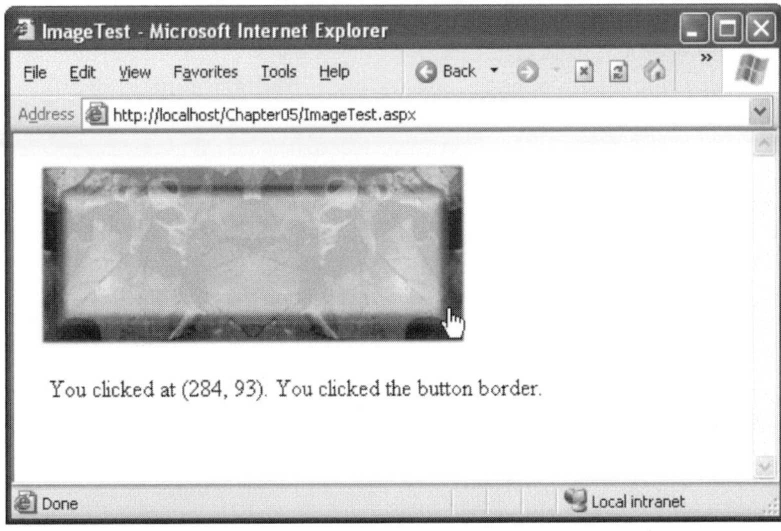

Figure 4-9. Using an ImageButton control

The List Controls

The list controls are specialized web controls that generate list boxes, drop-down lists, and other repeating controls that can be either bound to a data source (such as a database or a hard-coded collection of values) or programmatically filled with items. Most list controls allow the user to select one or more items, but the BulletedList is an exception—it displays a static bulleted or numbered list. Table 4-11 shows all the list controls.

***Table 4-11.** List Controls*

Control	Description
<asp:DropDownList>	A drop-down list populated by a collection of <asp:ListItem> objects. In HTML, it is rendered by a <select> tag with the size="1" attribute.
<asp:ListBox>	A list box list populated by a collection of <asp:ListItem> objects. In HTML, it is rendered by a <select> tag with the size="x" attribute, where x is the number of visible items.
<asp:CheckBoxList>	Its items are rendered as check boxes, aligned in a table with one or more columns.
<asp:RadioButtonList>	Like the <asp:CheckBoxList>, but the items are rendered as radio buttons.
<asp:BulletedList>	A static bulleted or numbered list. In HTML, it is rendered using the <ul> or <ol> tags. You can also use this control to create a list of hyperlinks.

All the list controls support the same base properties and methods as other web controls. In addition, they inherit from the System.Web.UI.WebControls.ListControl class, which exposes the properties described in Table 4-12 (among others). You can fill the lists automatically from a data source (as you'll learn in Part 2), or you can fill them programmatically or declaratively, as you'll see in the next section.

***Table 4-12.** ListControl Class Properties*

Member	Description
AutoPostBack	If true, the form is automatically posted back when the user changes the current selection.
Items	Returns a collection of ListItem items (the items can also be added declaratively by adding the <asp:ListItem> tag).
SelectedIndex	Returns or sets the index of the selected item. For lists with multiple selectable items, you should loop through the Items collection and check the Selected property of each ListItem instead.

Member	Description
SelectedItem	Returns a reference to the first selected ListItem. For lists with multiple selectable items, you should loop through the Items collection and check the Selected property of each ListItem instead.
DataSource	You can set this property to an object that contains the information you want to display (such as a DataSet, DataTable, or collection). When you call DataBind(), the list will be filled based on that object.
DataMember	Used in conjunction with data binding when the data source contains more than one table (such as when the source is a DataSet). The DataMember identifies which table you want to use.
DataTextField	Used in conjunction with data binding to indicate which property or field in the data source should be used for the text of each list item.
DataValueField	Used in conjunction with data binding to indicate which property or field in the data source should be used for the value attribute of each list item (which isn't displayed but can be read programmatically for future reference).
DataTextFormatString	Sets the formatting string used to render the text of the list item (according to the DataTextField property).

In addition, the ListControl control class also defines a SelectedIndexChanged event, which fires when the user changes the current selection.

■ **Note** The SelectedIndexChanged event and the SelectedIndex and SelectedItem properties are not used for the BulletedList control.

The Selectable List Controls

The selectable list controls include the DropDownList, ListBox, CheckBoxList, and RadioButtonList controls—all the list controls except the BulletedList. They allow users to select one or more of the contained items. When the page is posted back, you can check which items were chosen.

By default, the RadioButtonList and CheckBoxList render multiple option buttons or check boxes. Both of these classes add a few more properties that allow you to manage the layout of these repeated items, as described in Table 4-13.

Table 4-13. Added RadioButtonList and CheckBoxList Properties

Property	Description
RepeatLayout	This enumeration specifies whether the check boxes or radio buttons will be rendered in a table (Table), inline (Flow), in a <ul> element (UnorderedList), or in a <ol> elment (OrderedList).
RepeatDirection	This specifies whether the list of controls will be rendered horizontally or vertically.
RepeatColumns	This sets the number of columns, in case RepeatLayout is set to Table.
CellPadding, CellSpacing, TextAlign	If RepeatLayout is set to Table, then these properties configure the spacing and alignment of the cells of the layout table.

Here's an example page that declares an instance of every selectable list control, adds items to each of them declaratively, and sets a few other properties:

```
<form id="form1" runat="server">
  <div>
    <asp:ListBox runat="server" ID="Listbox1" SelectionMode="Multiple" Rows="5">
        <asp:ListItem Selected="true">Option 1</asp:ListItem>
        <asp:ListItem>Option 2</asp:ListItem>
    </asp:ListBox>
    <br /><br />
    <asp:DropDownList runat="server" ID="DropdownList1">
        <asp:ListItem Selected="true">Option 1</asp:ListItem>
        <asp:ListItem>Option 2</asp:ListItem>
    </asp:DropDownList>
    <br /><br />
    <asp:CheckBoxList runat="server" ID="CheckboxList1" RepeatColumns="3" >
        <asp:ListItem Selected="true">Option 1</asp:ListItem>
      <asp:ListItem>Option 2</asp:ListItem>
    </asp:CheckBoxList>
    <br />
    <asp:RadioButtonList runat="server" ID="RadiobuttonList1"
     RepeatDirection="Horizontal" RepeatColumns="2">
        <asp:ListItem Selected="true">Option 1</asp:ListItem>
        <asp:ListItem>Option 2</asp:ListItem>
    </asp:RadioButtonList>
    <asp:Button id="Button1" runat="server" Text="Submit"
     OnClick="Button1_Click"/>
  </div>
</form>
```

When the page is loaded for the first time, the event handler for the Page.Load event adds three more items to each list control programmatically, as shown here:

```
protected void Page_Load(object sender, System.EventArgs e)
{
    if (!Page.IsPostBack)
    {
        for (int i=3; i<=5; i++)
        {
            Listbox1.Items.Add("Option " + i.ToString());
            DropdownList1.Items.Add("Option " + i.ToString());
            CheckboxList1.Items.Add("Option " + i.ToString());
            RadiobuttonList1.Items.Add("Option " + i.ToString());
        }
    }
}
```

Finally, when the submit button is clicked, the selected items of each control are displayed on the page. For the controls with a single selection (DropDownList and RadioButtonList), this is just a matter of accessing the SelectedItem property. For the other controls that allow multiple selections, you must cycle through all the items in the Items collection and check whether the ListItem.Selected property is true. Here's the code that does both of these tasks:

```
protected void Button1_Click(object sender, System.EventArgs e)
{
    Response.Write("<b>Selected items for Listbox1:</b><br />");
    foreach (ListItem li in Listbox1.Items)
    {
        if (li.Selected) Response.Write("- " + li.Text + "<br />");
    }

    Response.Write("<b>Selected item for DropdownList1:</b><br />");
    Response.Write("- " + DropdownList1.SelectedItem.Text + "<br />");

    Response.Write("<b>Selected items for CheckboxList1:</b><br />");
    foreach (ListItem li in CheckboxList1.Items)
    {
        if (li.Selected) Response.Write("- " + li.Text + "<br />");
    }

    Response.Write("<b>Selected item for RadiobuttonList1:</b><br />");
    Response.Write("- " + RadiobuttonList1.SelectedItem.Text + "<br />");
}
```

To test the page, load it, select one or more items in each control, and then click the button. You should get something like what's shown in Figure 4-10.

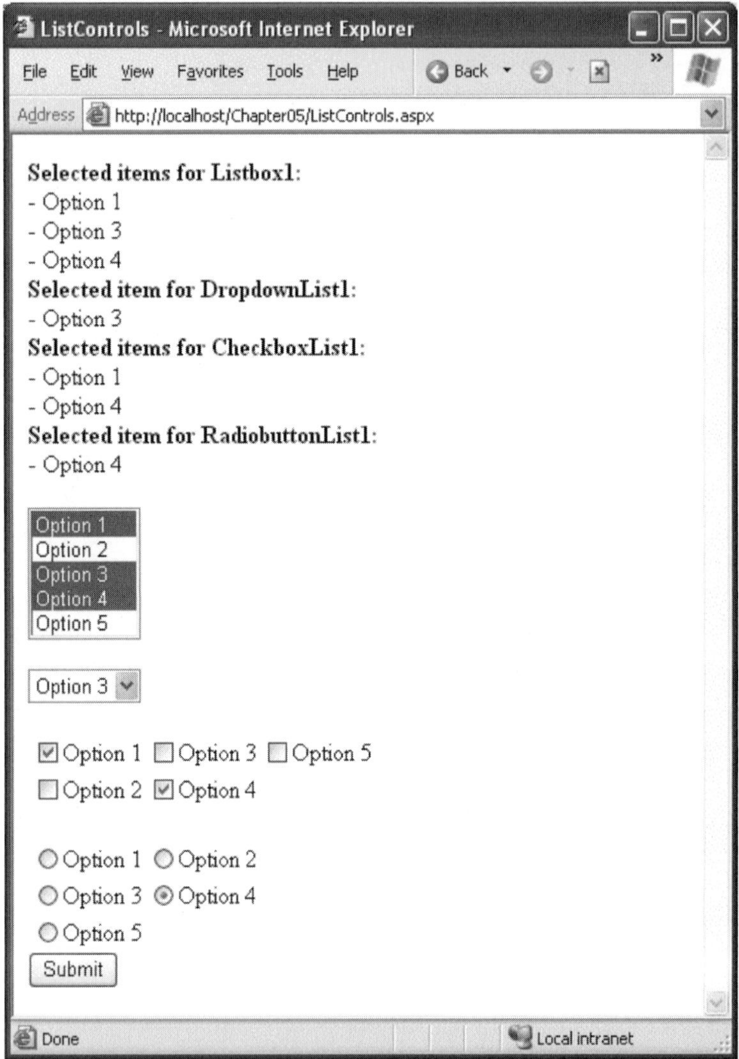

Figure 4-10. *Checking for selected items in the list controls*

■ **Tip** You can set the ListItem.Enabled property to false if you want an item in a RadioButtonList or CheckBoxList to be disabled. It will still appear in the page, but it will be grayed out and won't be selectable. The ListItem.Enabled property is ignored for ListBox and DropDownList controls.

The BulletedList Control

The BulletedList control is the server-side equivalent of the <ul> (unordered list) or <ol> (ordered list) elements. As with all list controls, you set the collection of items that should be displayed through the Items property. Additionally, you can use the properties in Table 4-14 to configure how the items are displayed.

Table 4-14. *Added BulletedList Properties*

Property	Description
BulletStyle	Determines the type of list. Choose from Numbered (1, 2, 3...), LowerAlpha (a, b, c...) and UpperAlpha (A, B, C...), LowerRoman (i, ii, iii...) and UpperRoman (I, II, III...), and the bullet symbols Disc, Circle, Square, or CustomImage (in which case you must set the BulletImageUrl property).
BulletImageUrl	If the BulletStyle is set to CustomImage, this points to the image that is placed to the left of each item as a bullet.
FirstBulletNumber	In an ordered list (using the Numbered, LowerAlpha, UpperAlpha, LowerRoman, or UpperRoman styles), this sets the first value. For example, if you set FirstBulletNumber to 3, the list might read 3, 4, 5 (for Numbered) or C, D, E (for UpperAlpha).
DisplayMode	Determines whether the text of each item is rendered as text (use Text, the default) or a hyperlink (use LinkButton or HyperLink). The difference between LinkButton and HyperLink is how they treat clicks. When you use LinkButton, the BulletedList fires a Click event that you can react to on the server to perform the navigation. When you use HyperLink, the BulletedList doesn't fire the Click event—instead, it treats the text of each list item as a relative or absolute URL, and renders them as ordinary HTML hyperlinks. When the user clicks an item, the browser attempts to navigate to that URL.

If you choose to set the DisplayMode to LinkButton, you can react to the Click event to determine which item was clicked. Here's an example:

```
protected void BulletedList1_Click(object sender, BulletedListEventArgs e)
{
    string itemText = BulletedList1.Items[e.Index].Text;
    Label1.Text = "You choose item" + itemText;
}
```

Figure 4-11 shows the different BulletStyle values. When you click one, the list is updated accordingly.

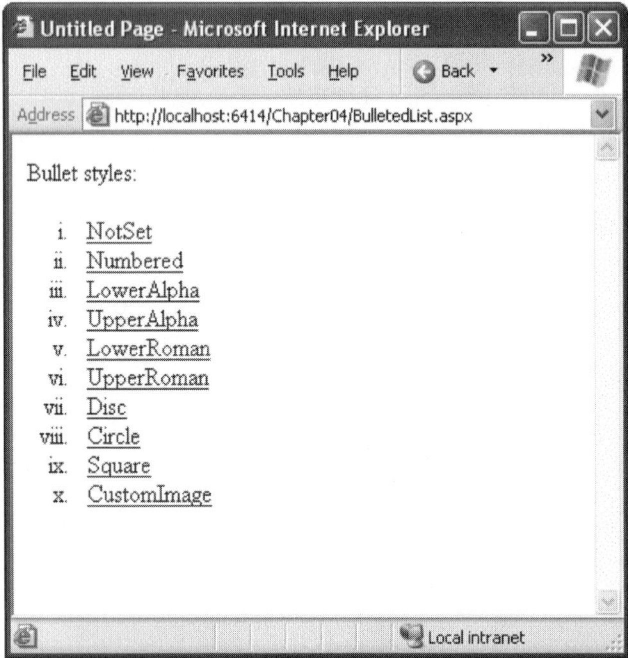

Figure 4-11. *Different BulletedList styles*

Input Validation Controls

One of the most common uses for web pages (and the reason that the HTML form tags were first created) is to collect data. Often, a web page will ask a user for some information and then store it in a back-end database. In almost every case, this data must be validated to ensure that you don't store useless, spurious, or contradictory information that might cause later problems.

Ideally, the validation of the user input should take place on the client side so that the user is immediately informed that there's something wrong with the input *before* the form is posted back to the server. If this pattern is implemented correctly, it saves server resources and gives the user faster feedback. However, regardless of whether client-side validation is performed, the form's data must also be validated on the server side. Otherwise, a shrewd attacker could hack the page by removing the client-side JavaScript that validates the input, saving the new page, and using it to submit bogus data.

Writing validation code by hand is a lengthy task, especially because the models for client-side programming (typically JavaScript) and server-side programming (in this case, ASP.NET) are quite different. The developers at Microsoft are well aware of this, so, in addition to the set of HTML and web controls, they also developed a set of validation controls. These controls can be declared on a web form and then bound to any other input control. Once bound to an input control, the validation control performs automatic client-side *and* server-side validation. If the corresponding control is empty, doesn't contain the correct data type, or doesn't adhere to the specified rules, the validator will prevent the page from being posted back altogether.

The Validation Controls

ASP.NET includes six validation controls. These controls all perform a good portion of the heavy lifting for you, thereby streamlining the validation process and saving you from having to write tedious code. Even better, the validation controls are flexible enough to work with the custom rules you define, which makes your code more reusable and modular. Table 4-15 briefly summarizes each validator.

Table 4-15. *The Validation Controls*

Validation Control	Description
<asp:RequiredFieldValidator>	Checks that the control it has to validate is not empty when the form is submitted.
<asp:RangeValidator>	Checks that the value of the associated control is within a specified range. The value and the range can be numerical—a date or a string.
<asp:CompareValidator>	Checks that the value of the associated control matches a specified comparison (less than, greater than, and so on) against another constant value or control.
<asp:RegularExpressionValidator>	Checks if the value of the control it has to validate matches the specified regular expression.
<asp:CustomValidator>	Allows you to specify any client-side JavaScript validation routine and its server-side counterpart to perform your own custom validation logic.
<asp:ValidationSummary>	Shows a summary with the error messages for each failed validator on the page (or in a pop-up message box).

It's important to note that you can use more than one validator for the same control. For example, you could use a validator to ensure that an input control is not empty and another to ensure that it contains data of a certain type. In fact, if you use the RangeValidator, CompareValidator, or RegularExpressionValidator, validation will automatically succeed if the input control is empty, because there is no value to validate. If this isn't the behavior you want, you should add a RequiredFieldValidator to the control. This ensures that two types of validation will be performed, effectively restricting blank values.

Although you can't validate RadioButton or CheckBox controls, you can validate the TextBox (the most common choice) and other controls such as ListBox, DropDownList, RadioButtonList, HtmlInputText, HtmlTextArea, and HtmlSelect. When validating a list control, the property that is being validated is the Value property of the selected ListItem object. Remember, the Value property is a hidden attribute that stores a piece of information in the HTML page for each list item, but it isn't displayed in the browser. If you don't use the Value attribute, you can't validate the control (validating the text of the selection isn't a supported option).

Technically, every control class has the option of designating one property that can be validated using the ValidationProperty attribute. For example, if you create your own control class named FancyTextBox, here's how you would designate the Text property as the property that supports validation:

```
[ValidationProperty("Text")]
public class FancyTextBox : WebControl
{...}
```

You'll learn more about how attributes work with custom controls in Chapter 27.

The Validation Process

You can use the validation controls to verify a page automatically when the user submits it or to verify it manually in your code. The first approach is the most common.

When using automatic validation, the user receives a normal page and begins to fill in the input controls. When finished, the user clicks a button to submit the page. Every button has a CausesValidation property, which can be set to true or false. What happens when the user clicks the button depends on the value of the CausesValidation property:

- **CausesValidation is false:** ASP.NET will ignore the validation controls, the page will be posted back, and your event-handling code will run normally.
- **CausesValidation is true (the default):** ASP.NET will automatically validate the page when the user clicks the button. It does this by performing the validation for each control on the page. If any control fails to validate, ASP.NET will return the page with some error information, depending on your settings. Your click event-handling code may or may not be executed—meaning you'll have to specifically check in the event handler whether the page is valid.

■ **Note** Many other button-like controls that can be used to submit the page also provide the CausesValidation property. Examples include the LinkButton, ImageButton, and BulletedList.

Based on this description, you'll realize that validation happens automatically when certain buttons are clicked. It doesn't happen when the page is posted back because of a change event (such as choosing a new value in an AutoPostBack list) or if the user clicks a button that has CausesValidation set to false. However, you can still validate one or more controls manually and then make a decision in your code based on the results.

In browsers that support it, ASP.NET will automatically add code for client-side validation. In this case, when the user clicks a CausesValidation button, the same error messages will appear without the page needing to be submitted and returned from the server. This increases the responsiveness of the application. However, if the page validates successfully on the client side, ASP.NET will still revalidate it when it's received at the server. By performing the validation at both ends, your application can be as responsive as possible but still remain secure. Best of all, the client-side validation works in most non-Microsoft web browsers.

Figure 4-12 shows a page that uses validation with several text boxes and ends with a validation summary. In the following section, you'll learn about how you can use the different validators in this example.

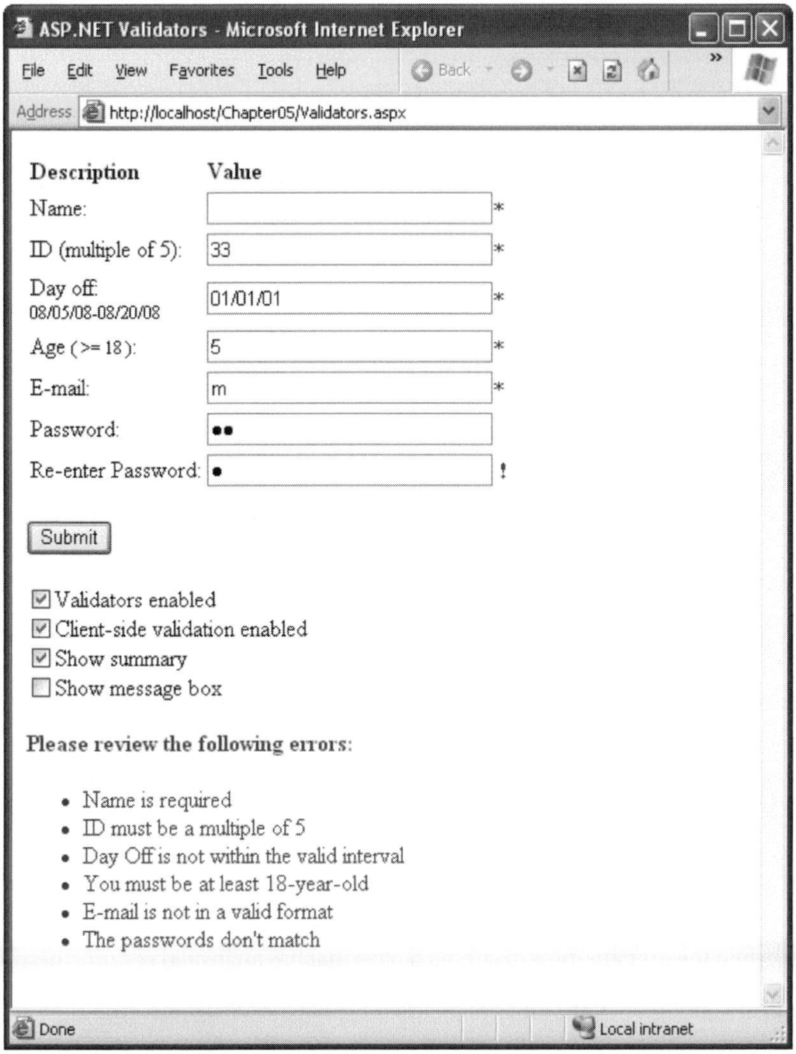

Figure 4-12. Validating a sample page

The BaseValidator Class

The validation control classes are found in the System.Web.UI.WebControls namespace and inherit from the BaseValidator class. This class defines the basic functionality for a validation control. Table 4-16 describes its key properties.

Table 4-16. BaseValidator Members

Member	Description
ControlToValidate	Indicates the input control to validate.
Display	Indicates how the error message will be shown. If Static, the space required to show the message will be calculated and added to the space layout in advance. If Dynamic, the page layout will dynamically change to show the error string. Be aware that although the dynamic style could seem useful, if your layout is heavily based on table structures, it could change quite a bit if multiple strings are dynamically added, and this could confuse the user.
EnableClientScript	A Boolean property that specifies whether the client-side validation will take place. It is true by default.
Enabled	A Boolean property that allows the user to enable or disable the validator. When the control is disabled, it does not validate anything. You can set this property programmatically if you want to create a page that dynamically decides what it should validate.
ErrorMessage	Error string that will be shown in the errors summary by the ValidationSummary control, if present.
Text	The error text that will be displayed in the validator control if the attached input control fails its validation.
IsValid	This property is also usually read or set only from script code (or the code-behind class) to determine whether the associated input control's value is valid. This property can be checked on the server after a postback, but if the client-side validation is active and supported by the client browser, the execution won't get to the server if the value isn't valid. (In other words, you check this property just in case the client-side validation did not run.) Remember that you can also read the Page.IsValid property to know in a single step if all the input controls are in a valid state. Page.IsValid returns true only if all the contained controls are valid.
SetFocusOnError	If true, when the user attempts to submit a page that has an invalid control, the browser switches focus to the input control so the value can be easily corrected. (If false, the button or control that was clicked to post the page retains focus.) This feature works for both client-side and server-side validation. If you have multiple validators with SetFocusOnError set to true, and all the input controls are invalid, the first input control in the tab sequence gets focus.
ValidationGroup	Allows you to group multiple validators into a logical group so that validation can be performed distinctly without involving other groups. This is particularly useful if you have several distinct panels on a web page, each with its own submit button.
Validate()	This method revalidates the control and updates the IsValid property accordingly. The web page calls this method when a page is posted back by a CausesValidation control. You can also call it programmatically (for example, if you programmatically set the content of an input control and you want to check its validity).

In addition, the BaseValidator class has other properties such as BackColor, Font, ForeColor, and others that are inherited (and in some case overridden) from the base class Label (and the classes it inherits from, such as WebControl and Control). Every derived validator adds its own specific properties, which you'll see in the following sections.

The RequiredFieldValidator Control

The simplest available control is RequiredFieldValidator, whose only work is to ensure that the associated control is not empty. For example, the control will fail validation if a linked text box doesn't contain any content (or just contains spaces). Alternatively, instead of checking for blank values you can specify a default value using the InitialValue property. In this case, validation fails if the content in the control matches this InitialValue (indicating that the user hasn't changed it in any way).

Here is an example of a typical RequiredFieldValidator:

```
<asp:TextBox runat="server" ID="Name" />
<asp:RequiredFieldValidator runat="server"
  ControlToValidate="Name" ErrorMessage="Name is required"
  Display="dynamic">*
</asp:RequiredFieldValidator>
```

The validator declared here will show an asterisk (*) character if the Name text box is empty. This error text appears when the user tries to submit the form by clicking a button that has CausesValidation set to true. It also occurs on the client side in Internet Explorer 5.0 or above as soon as the user tabs to a new control, thanks to the client-side JavaScript.

If you want to place a specific message next to the validated control, you should replace * with an error message. (You don't need to use the ErrorMessage property. The ErrorMessage is required only if you want to show the summary of all the errors on the page using the ValidationSummary control, which you'll see later in this chapter.) Alternatively, for a nicer result, you could use an HTML <img> tag to use a picture (such as the common ! sign inside a yellow triangle) with a tooltip for the error message. You'll see this approach later in this chapter as well.

The RangeValidator Control

The RangeValidator control verifies that an input value falls within a predetermined range. It has three specific properties: MinimumValue, MaximumValue, and Type. The MinimumValue and MaximumValue properties define an inclusive range of valid values. The Type property defines the type of the data that will be typed into the input control and validated. The supported values are Currency, Date, Double, Integer, and String.

The following example checks that the date entered falls within the range of August 5 to August 20 (encoded in the locale-independent form yyyy-mm-dd, so if your web server uses different regional settings, you'll have to change the date format):

```
<asp:TextBox runat="server" ID="DayOff" />
<asp:RangeValidator runat="server" Display="dynamic"
  ControlToValidate="DayOff" Type="Date"
  ErrorMessage="Day Off is not within the valid interval"
  MinimumValue="2008-08-05" MaximumValue="2008-08-20">*
</asp:RangeValidator>
```

The CompareValidator Control

The CompareValidator control compares a value in one control with a fixed value or, more commonly, a value in another control. For example, this allows you to check that two text boxes have the same data or that a value in one text box doesn't exceed a maximum value established in another.

Like the RangeValidator control, the CompareValidator provides a Type property that specifies the type of data you are comparing. It also exposes the ValueToCompare and ControlToCompare properties, which allow you to compare the value of the input control with a constant value or the value of another input control, respectively. You use only one of these two properties.

The Operator property allows you to specify the type of comparison you want to do. The available values are Equal, NotEqual, GreaterThan, GreaterThanEqual, LessThan, LessThanEqual, and DataTypeCheck. The DataTypeCheck value forces the validation control to check that the input has the required data type (specified through the Type property), without performing any additional comparison.

The following example compares an input with a constant value in order to ensure that the specified age is greater than or equal to 18:

```
<asp:TextBox runat="server" ID="Age" />
<asp:CompareValidator runat="server" Display="dynamic"
  ControlToValidate="Age" ValueToCompare="18"
  ErrorMessage="You must be at least 18 years old"
  Type="Integer" Operator="GreaterThanEqual">*
</asp:CompareValidator>
```

The next example compares the input values in two password text boxes to ensure that their value is the same:

```
<asp:TextBox runat="server" TextMode="Password" ID="Password" />
<asp:TextBox runat="server" TextMode="Password" ID="Password2" />
<asp:CompareValidator runat="server"
  ControlToValidate="Password2" ControlToCompare="Password"
  ErrorMessage="The passwords don't match"
  Type="String" Display="dynamic">
  <img src="imgError.gif" alt="The passwords don't match" />
</asp:CompareValidator>
```

This example also demonstrates another useful technique. The previous examples have used an asterisk (*) to indicate errors. However, this control tag uses an <img> tag to show a small image file of an exclamation mark instead.

The RegularExpressionValidator Control

The RegularExpressionValidator control is a powerful tool in the ASP.NET developer's toolbox. It allows you to validate text by matching against a pattern defined in a *regular expression*. You simply need to set the regular expression in the ValidationExpression property.

Regular expressions are also powerful tools—they allow you to specify complex rules that specify the characters, and in what sequence (position and number of occurrences) they are allowed, in the string. For example, the following control checks that the text input in the text box is a valid e-mail address:

```
<asp:TextBox runat="server" ID="Email" />
<asp:RegularExpressionValidator runat="server"
  ControlToValidate="Email" ValidationExpression=".*@.{2,}\..{2,}"
```

```
  ErrorMessage="E-mail is not in a valid format" Display="dynamic">*
</asp:RegularExpressionValidator>
```

The expression .*@.{2,}\..{2,} specifies that the string that it's validating must begin with a number of characters (.*) and must contain an @ character, at least two more characters (the domain name), a period (escaped as \.), and, finally, at least two more characters for the domain extension. For example, marco@apress.com is a valid e-mail address, while marco@apress or marco.apress.com would fail validation. The proposed expression is quite simple in reality. Using a more complex regular expression, you could check that the domain name is valid, that the extension is not made up (see `http://www.icann.org` for a list of allowed domain name extensions), and so on. However, regular expressions obviously don't provide any way to check that a domain actually exists or is online.

Table 4-17 summarizes the commonly used syntax constructs (modifiers) for regular expressions.

Table 4-17. *Metacharacters for Matching Single Characters*

Character Escapes	Description
Ordinary characters	Characters other than .$^{[(|)*+?\ match themselves.
\b	Matches a backspace.
\t	Matches a tab.
\r	Matches a carriage return.
\v	Matches a vertical tab.
\f	Matches a form feed.
\n	Matches a newline.
\	If followed by a special character (one of .$^{[(|)*+?\), this character escape matches that character literal. For example, \+ matches the + character.

In addition to single characters, you can specify a class or a range of characters that can be matched in the expression. For example, you could allow any digit or any vowel in any position and exclude all the other characters. The metacharacters in Table 4-18 accomplish this.

Table 4-18. *Metacharacters for Matching Types of Characters*

Character Class	Description
.	Matches any character except \n.
[aeiou]	Matches any single character specified in the set.
[^aeiou]	Matches any character not specified in the set.
[3-7a-dA-D]	Matches any character specified in the specified ranges (in the example the ranges are 3-7, a-d, A-D).

Character Class	Description
\w	Matches any word character; that is, any alphanumeric character or the underscore (_).
\W	Matches any nonword character.
\s	Matches any whitespace character (space, tab, form feed, newline, carriage return, or vertical feed).
\S	Matches any nonwhitespace character.
\d	Matches any decimal character.
\D	Matches any nondecimal character.

Using more advanced syntax, you can specify that a certain character or class of characters must be present at least once, or between two and six times, and so on. The quantifiers are placed just after a character or a range of characters and allow you to specify how many times the preceding character must be matched (see Table 4-19).

Table 4-19. *Quantifiers*

Quantifier	Description
*	Zero or more matches
+	One or more matches
?	Zero or one matches
{N}	N matches
{N,}	N or more matches
{N,M}	Between N and M matches (inclusive)

To demonstrate these rules with another easy example, consider the following regular expression:

```
[aeiou]{2,4}\+[1-5]*
```

A string that correctly matches this expression must start with two to four vowels, have a + sign, and terminate with zero or more digits between 1 and 5. The .NET Framework documentation details many more expression modifiers.

Table 4-20 describes a few common (and useful) regular expressions.

Table 4-20. *Commonly Used Regular Expressions*

Content	Regular Expression	Description
E-mail address[a]	\S+@\S+\.\S+	Defines an email address that requires an at symbol (@) and a dot (.), and only allows nonwhitespace characters.
Password	\w+	Defines a password that allows any sequence of word characters (letter, space, or underscore).
Specific-length password	\w{4,10}	Defines a password that must be at least four characters long but no longer than ten characters.
Advanced password	[a-zA-Z]\w{3,9}	Defines a password that allows four to ten total characters, as with the specific-length password. The twist is that the first character must fall in the range of a-z or A-Z (that is to say, it must start with a nonaccented ordinary letter).
Another advanced password	[a-zA-Z]\w*\d+\w*	Defines a password that starts with a letter character, followed by zero or more word characters, one or more digits, and then zero or more word characters. In short, it forces a password to contain a number somewhere inside it. You could use a similar pattern to require two numbers or any other special character.
Limited-length field	\S{4,10}	Defines a string of four to ten characters (like the password example), but it allows special characters (asterisks, ampersands, and so on).
Social Security number (US)	\d{3}-\d{2}-\d{4}	Defines a sequence of three, two, and then four digits, with each group separated by a hyphen. A similar pattern could be used when requiring a phone number.

[a]*Many different regular expressions of varying complexity can validate e-mail addresses. See* `http://www.4guysfromrolla.com/webtech/validateemail.shtml` *for a discussion of the subject and numerous examples.*

The CustomValidator Control

If the validation controls described so far are not flexible or powerful enough for you, and if you need more advanced or customized validation, then the CustomValidator control is what you need. The CustomValidator allows you to execute your custom client-side and server-side validation routines. You can associate these routines with the control so that validation is performed automatically. If the validation fails, the Page.IsValid property is set to false, as occurs with any other validation control.

The client-side and server-side validation routines for the CustomValidator are declared similarly. They both take two parameters: a reference to the validator and a custom argument object. The custom argument object provides a Value property that contains the current value of the associated input control (the value you have to validate) and an IsValid property through which you specify whether the input value is valid. If you want to check that a number is a multiple of five, for example, you could use a client-side JavaScript validation routine like this:

```
<script type="text/javascript">
  function EmpIDClientValidate(ctl, args)
  {

    // the value is a multiple of 5 if the modulus by 5 is 0
    args.IsValid=(args.Value%5 == 0);
  }
</script>
```

To associate this code with the control so that client-side validation is performed automatically, you simply need to set the ClientValidationFunction to the name of the function (in this case, EmpIDClientValidate).

Next, when the page is posted back, ASP.NET fires the CustomValidator.ServerValidate event. You handle this event to perform the same task using C# code. And although the JavaScript logic is optional, you must make sure you include a server-side validation routine to ensure the validation is performed even if the client is using a down-level browser (or tampers with the web-page HTML).

Here's the event handler for the ServerValidate event. It performs the C# equivalent of the client-side validation routine shown earlier:

```
protected void EmpIDServerValidate(object sender, ServerValidateEventArgs args)
{
    try
    {
        args.IsValid = (int.Parse(args.Value)%5 == 0);
    }
    catch
    {
        // An error is most likely caused by non-numeric data.
        args.IsValid = false;
    }
}
```

Finally, here's an example CustomValidator tag that uses these routines:

```
<asp:TextBox runat="server" ID="EmpID" />
<asp:CustomValidator runat="server" ControlToValidate="EmpID"
  ClientValidationFunction="EmpIDClientValidate" OnServerValidate="EmpIDServerValidate"
  ErrorMessage="ID must be a multiple of 5" Display="dynamic">*
</asp:CustomValidator>
```

The CustomValidator includes an additional property named ValidateEmptyText, which is false by default. However, it's quite possible you might create a client-side function that attempts to assess empty values. If so, set ValidateEmptyText to true to give the same behavior to your server-side event handler.

The ValidationSummary Control

The ValidationSummary control doesn't perform any validation. Instead, it allows you to show a summary of all the errors in the page. This summary displays the ErrorMessage value of each failed validator. The summary can be shown in a client-side JavaScript message box (if the ShowMessageBox property is true) or on the page (if the ShowSummary property is true). You can set both ShowMessageBox and ShowSummary to true to show both types of summaries, since they are not exclusive. If you choose to display the summary on the page, you can choose a style with the

DisplayMode property (possible values are SingleParagraph, List, and BulletList). Finally, you can set a title for the summary with the HeaderText property.

The control declaration is straightforward:

```
<asp:ValidationSummary runat="server" ID="Summary"
  ShowSummary="true" ShowMessageBox="true" DisplayMode="BulletList"
  HeaderText="<b>Please review the following errors:</b>"
/>
```

Figure 4-13 shows an example with a validation summary that displays a bulleted summary on the page and in a message box.

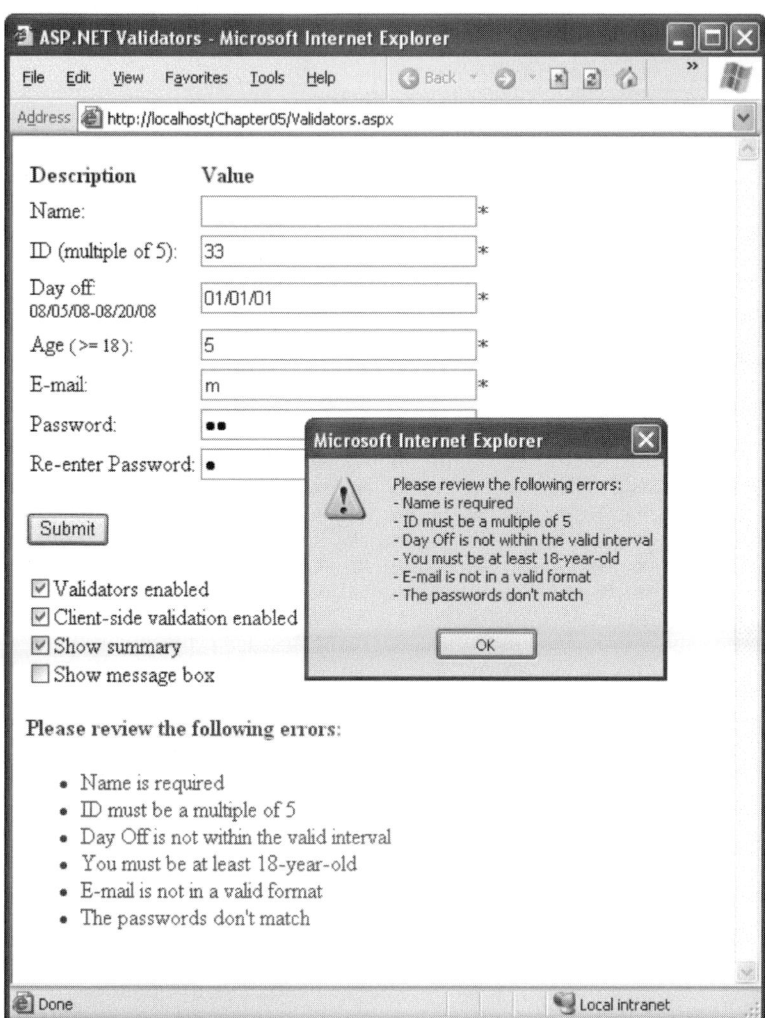

Figure 4-13. *The validation summary*

Using the Validators Programmatically

As with all other server controls, you can programmatically read and modify the properties of a validator. To access all the validators on the page, you can iterate over the Validators collection of the current page.

In fact, this technique was already demonstrated in the sample page shown in Figures 4-12 and 4-13. This page provides four check boxes that allow you to test the behavior of the validators with different options. When a check box is selected, it causes a postback. The event handler iterates over all the validators and updates them according to the new options, as shown here:

```
protected void Options_Changed(object sender, System.EventArgs e)
{
    // Examine all the validators on the back.
    foreach (BaseValidator validator in Page.Validators)
    {
        // Turn the validators on or off, depending on the value
        // of the "Validators enabled" check box (chkEnableValidators).
        validator.Enabled = chkEnableValidators.Checked;

        // Turn client-side validation on or off, depending on the value
        // of the "Client-side validation enabled" check box
        // (chkEnableClientSide).
        validator.EnableClientScript = chkEnableClientSide.Checked;
    }

    // Configure the validation summary based on the final two check boxes.
    Summary.ShowMessageBox = chkShowMsgBox.Checked;
    Summary.ShowSummary = chkShowSummary.Checked;
}
```

You can use a similar technique to perform custom validation. The basic idea is to add a button with CausesValidation set to false. When this button is clicked, manually validate the page or just specific validators using the Validate() method. Then examine the IsValid property and decide what to do.

The next example uses this technique. It examines all the validation controls on the page by looping through the Page.Validators collection. Every time it finds a control that hasn't validated successfully, it retrieves the invalid value from the input control and adds it to a string. At the end of this routine, it displays a message that describes which values were incorrect. This technique adds a feature that wouldn't be available with automatic validation, which uses the static ErrorMessage property. In that case, it isn't possible to include the actual incorrect values in the message.

```
protected void cmdOK_Click(Object sender, EventArgs e)
{
    // Validate the page.
    this.Validate();

    if (!this.IsValid)
    {
        string errorMessage = "<b>Mistakes found:</b><br />";

       // Create a variable to represent the input control.
       TextBox ctrlInput;

        // Search through the validation controls.
        foreach (BaseValidator ctrl in this.Validators)
```

```
        {
            if (!ctrl.IsValid)
            {
                errorMessage += ctrl.ErrorMessage + "<br />";
                ctrlInput = (TextBox)this.FindControl(ctrl.ControlToValidate);
                errorMessage += " * Problem is with this input: ";
                errorMessage += ctrlInput.Text + "<br />";
            }
        }
        lblMessage.Text = errorMessage;
    }
}
```

This example uses an advanced technique: the Page.FindControl() method. It's required because the ControlToValidate property is just a string with the name of a control, not a reference to the actual control object. To find the control that matches this name (and retrieve its Text property), you need to use the FindControl() method. Once the code has retrieved the matching text box, it can perform other tasks such as clearing the current value, tweaking a property, or even changing the text box color.

Validation Groups

In more complex pages, you might have several distinct groups of controls, possibly in separate panels. In these situations, you may want to perform validation separately. For example, you might create a form that includes a box with login controls and a box underneath it with the controls for registering a new user. Each box includes its own submit button, and depending on which button is clicked, you want to perform the validation just for that section of the page.

ASP.NET enables this scenario with a feature called *validation groups*. To create a validation group, you need to put the input controls and the CausesValidation button controls into the same logical group. You do this by setting the ValidationGroup property of every control with the same descriptive string (such as "Login" or "NewUser"). Every button control that provides a CauseValidation property also includes the ValidationGroup property. All validators acquire the ValidationGroup by inheriting from the BaseValidator class.

For example, the following page defines two validation groups, named Group1 and Group2:

```
<form id="form1" runat="server">
  <div>
    <asp:Panel ID="Panel1" runat="server">
        <asp:TextBox ID="TextBox1" ValidationGroup="Group1" runat="server" />
        <asp:RequiredFieldValidator ID="RequiredFieldValidator1"
         ErrorMessage="*Required" ValidationGroup="Group1"
         runat="server" ControlToValidate="TextBox1" />
        <asp:Button ID="Button1" Text="Validate Group1"
         ValidationGroup="Group1" runat="server" />
    </asp:Panel>
    <br />
    <asp:Panel ID="Panel2" runat="server">
        <asp:TextBox ID="TextBox2" ValidationGroup="Group2"
         runat="server" />
        <asp:RequiredFieldValidator ID="RequiredFieldValidator2"
         ErrorMessage="*Required" ValidationGroup="Group2"
         ControlToValidate="TextBox2" runat="server" />
        <asp:Button ID="Button2" Text="Validate Group2"
```

```
            ValidationGroup="Group2" runat="server" />
    </asp:Panel>
  </div>
</form>
```

Figure 4-14 shows the page. If you click the first button, only the first text box is validated. If you click the second button, only the second text box is validated.

An interesting scenario is if you add a new button that doesn't specify any validation group. In this case, the button validates every control that isn't explicitly assigned to a named validation group. In this case, no controls fit the requirement, so the page is posted back successfully and deemed to be valid. If you want to make sure a control is always validated, regardless of the validation group of the button that's clicked, you'll need to create multiple validators for the control, one for each group (and one with no validation group). Alternatively, you might choose to manage complex scenarios such as these using server-side code.

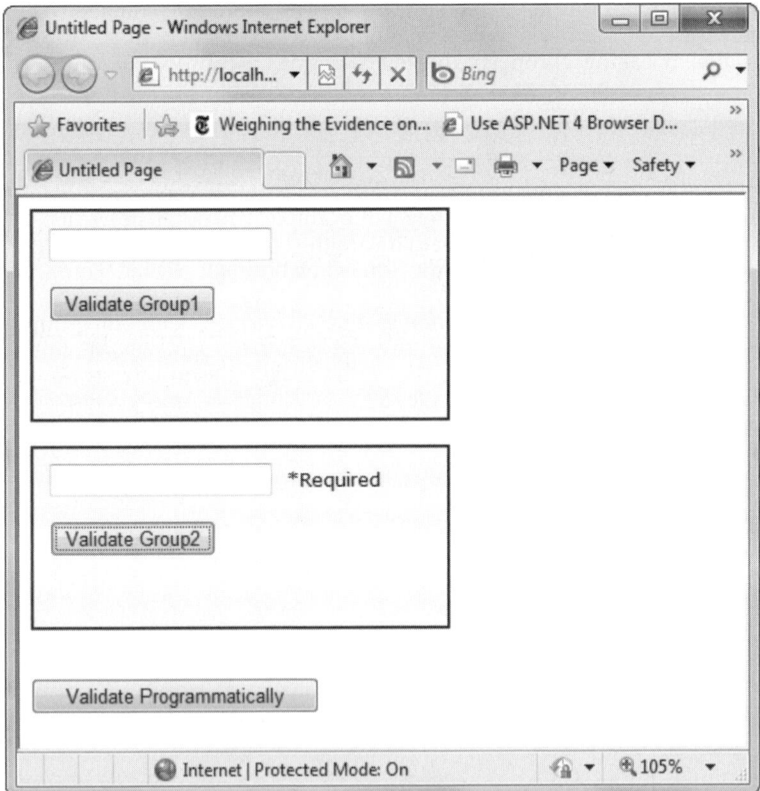

Figure 4-14. Grouping controls for validation

In your code, you can work with the validation groups programmatically. You can retrieve the controls in a given validator group using the Page.GetValidators() method. Just pass the name of the group as the first parameter. You can then loop through the items in this collection and choose which ones you want to validate, as shown in the previous section.

Another option is to use the Page.Validate() method and specify the name of the validation group. For example, using the previous page, you could create a button with no validation group assigned and respond to the Click event with this code:

```
protected void cmdValidateAll_Click(object sender, EventArgs e)
{
    Label1.Text = "Initial Page.IsValid State: " + Page.IsValid.ToString();
    Page.Validate("Group1");
    Label1.Text += "<br />Group1 Valid: " + Page.IsValid.ToString();
    Page.Validate("Group2");
    Label1.Text += "<br />Group1 and Group2 Valid: " + Page.IsValid.ToString();
}
```

The first Page.IsValid check will return true, because none of the validators were validated. After validating the first group, the Page.IsValid property will return true or false, depending on whether there is text in TextBox1. After you validate the second group, Page.IsValid will only return true if both groups passed the test.

Rich Controls

Rich controls are web controls that model complex user interface elements. Although there isn't a strict definition for rich controls, the term commonly describes web controls that provide an object model that is distinctly separate from the underlying HTML representation. A typical rich control can often be programmed as a single object (and defined with a single control tag), but renders itself with a complex sequence of HTML elements and may even use client-side JavaScript.

To understand the difference, consider the Table control and the Calendar control. When you program with the Table control, you use objects that provide a thin wrapper over HTML table elements such as <table>, <tr>, and <td>. The Table control isn't considered a rich control. On the other hand, when you program with the Calendar, you work in terms of days, months, and selection ranges—concepts that have no direct correlation to the HTML markup that the Calendar renders. For that reason, the Calendar is considered a rich control.

ASP.NET includes numerous rich controls that are discussed elsewhere in this book, including data-based list controls, navigation controls, security controls, and controls tailored for web portals. The following list identifies the rich controls that don't fall into any specialized category, and are found in the Standard section of the Toolbox in Visual Studio:

- **AdRotator:** This control is a banner ad that displays one out of a set of images based on a predefined schedule that's saved in an XML file.
- **Calendar:** This control is a calendar that displays and allows you to move through months and days and to select a date or a range of days.
- **MultiView, View, and Wizard:** You can think of these controls as more advanced panels that let you switch between groups of controls on a page. The Wizard control even includes built-in navigation logic. You'll learn about these controls in Chapter 17.
- **Substitution:** This control is really a placeholder that allows you to customize ASP.NET's output caching feature, which you'll tackle in Chapter 11.
- **Xml:** This control takes an XML file and an XSLT stylesheet file as input and displays the resulting HTML in a browser. You'll learn about the Xml control in Chapter 14.

The rich controls in this list all appear in the Standard tab of the Visual Studio Toolbox.

The AdRotator Control

The AdRotator randomly selects banner graphics from a list that's specified in an external XML schedule file.

Before creating the control, it makes sense to define the XML schedule file. Here's an example:

```
<Advertisements>
  <Ad>
    <ImageUrl>hdr_logo.gif</ImageUrl>
    <NavigateUrl>http://www.apress.com</NavigateUrl>
    <AlternateText>Apress - The Author's Press</AlternateText>
    <Impressions>20</Impressions>
    <Keyword>books</Keyword>
  </Ad>
  <Ad>
    <ImageUrl>techEd.jpg</ImageUrl>
    <NavigateUrl> http://www.microsoft.com/events/teched2008</NavigateUrl>
    <AlternateText>TechEd from Microsoft</AlternateText>
    <Impressions>20</Impressions>
    <Keyword>Java</Keyword>
  </Ad>
  <!-- More ads can go here. -->
</Advertisements>
```

Each <Ad> element has a number of other important properties that configure the link, the image, and the frequency, as described in Table 4-21.

Table 4-21. *Advertisement File Elements*

Element	Description
ImageUrl	The image that will be displayed. This can be a relative link (a file in the current directory) or a fully qualified Internet URL.
NavigateUrl	The link that will be followed if the user clicks the banner.
AlternateText	The text that will be displayed instead of the picture if it cannot be displayed. This text will also be used as a tooltip in some newer browsers.
Impressions	A number that sets how often an advertisement will appear. This number is relative to the numbers specified for other ads. For example, a banner with the value 10 will be shown twice as often as a banner with the value 5.
Keyword	A keyword that identifies a group of advertisements. This can be used for filtering. For example, you could create ten advertisements and give half of them the keyword *Retail* and the other half the keyword *Computer*. The web page can then choose to filter the possible advertisements to include only one of these groups.

The actual AdRotator class provides a limited set of properties. You specify both the appropriate advertisement file in the AdvertisementFile property and the type of window that the link should follow in the Target property. You can also set the KeywordFilter property so that the banner will be chosen from entries that have a specific keyword.

Here's an example that opens the link for an advertisement in a new window:

```
<asp:AdRotator runat="server" AdvertisementFile="Ads.xml" Target="_blank" />
```

Figure 4-15 shows the AdRotator control. Try refreshing the page. When you do, you'll see that a new advertisement is randomly selected each time.

Figure 4-15. *The AdRotator control*

Additionally, you can react to the AdRotator.AdCreated event. This occurs when the page is being created and an image is randomly chosen from the file. This event provides you with information about the image that you can use to customize the rest of your page.

The event-handling code for this example simply configures a HyperLink control so that it corresponds with the randomly selected advertisement in the AdRotator:

```
protected void Ads_AdCreated(Object sender, AdCreatedEventArgs e)
{
    // Synchronize a Hyperlink control elsewhere on the page.
    lnkBanner.NavigateUrl = e.NavigateUrl;

    // Synchronize the text of the link.
    lnkBanner.Text = "Click here for information about our sponsor: ";
    lnkBanner.Text += e.AlternateText;
}
```

The Calendar Control

This control creates a functionally rich and good-looking calendar box that shows one month at a time. The user can move from month to month, select a date, and even select a range of days (if multiple selection is allowed). The Calendar control has many properties that, taken together, allow you to change almost every part of this control. For example, you can fine-tune the foreground and background colors, the font, the title, the format of the date, the currently selected date, and so on. The Calendar also provides events that enable you to react when the user changes the current month (VisibleMonthChanged), when the user selects a date (SelectionChanged), and when the Calendar is about to render a day (DayRender).

The following Calendar tag sets a few basic properties:

```
<asp:Calendar runat="server" ID="Calendar1"
  ForeColor="red" BackColor="lightyellow" />
```

The most important Calendar event is SelectionChanged, which fires every time a user clicks a date. Here's a basic event handler that responds to the SelectionChanged event and displays the selected date:

```
protected void Calendar1_SelectionChanged(object sender, EventArgs e)
{
    lblDates.Text = "You selected: " + Calendar1.SelectedDate.ToLongDateString();
}
```

■ **Note** Every user interaction with the calendar triggers a postback. This allows you to react to the selection event immediately, and it allows the Calendar to rerender its interface, thereby showing a new month or newly selected dates. The Calendar does not use the AutoPostBack property.

You can also allow users to select entire weeks or months as well as single dates, or you can render the control as a static calendar that doesn't allow selection. The only fact you must remember is that if you allow month selection, the user can also select a single week or a day. Similarly, if you allow week selection, the user can also select a single day. The type of selection is set through the Calendar.SelectionMode property. You may also need to set the Calendar.FirstDayOfWeek property to configure how a week is selected. (For example, if you set FirstDayOfWeek to the enumerated value Monday, weeks will be selected from Monday to Sunday.)

When you allow multiple date selection (by setting Calendar.SelectionMode to something other than Day), you need to examine the SelectedDates property instead of the SelectedDate property. SelectedDates provides a collection of all the selected dates, which you can examine, as shown here:

```
protected void Calendar1_SelectionChanged(object sender, EventArgs e)
{
    lblDates.Text = "You selected these dates:<br />";
    foreach (DateTime dt in Calendar1.SelectedDates)
    {
        lblDates.Text += dt.ToLongDateString() + "<br />";
    }
}
```

The Calendar control exposes many more formatting-related properties, many of which map to the underlying HTML table representation (such as CellSpacing, CellPadding, Caption, and CaptionAlign). Additionally, you can individually tweak portions of the controls through grouped formatting settings called *styles* (which expose color, font, and alignment options). Example properties include DayHeaderStyle, DayStyle, NextPrevStyle, OtherMonthDayStyle, SelectedDayStyle, TitleStyle, TodayDayStyle, and WeekendDayStyle. You can change the subproperties for all of these styles using the Properties window.

Finally, by handling the DayRender event, you can completely change the appearance of the cell being rendered. The DayRender event is extremely powerful. Besides allowing you to tailor what dates are selectable, it also allows you to configure the cell where the date is located through the e.Cell property. (The Calendar control is really a sophisticated HTML table.) For example, you could highlight an important date or even add extra controls or HTML content in the cell. Here's an example that changes the background and foreground colors of the weekend days and also makes them nonclickable so that the user can't choose those days:

```
protected void Calendar1_DayRender(object sender, DayRenderEventArgs e)
{
    if (e.Day.IsWeekend)
    {
        e.Cell.BackColor = System.Drawing.Color.Green;
        e.Cell.ForeColor = System.Drawing.Color.Yellow;
        e.Day.IsSelectable = false;
    }
}
```

Figure 4-16 shows the result.

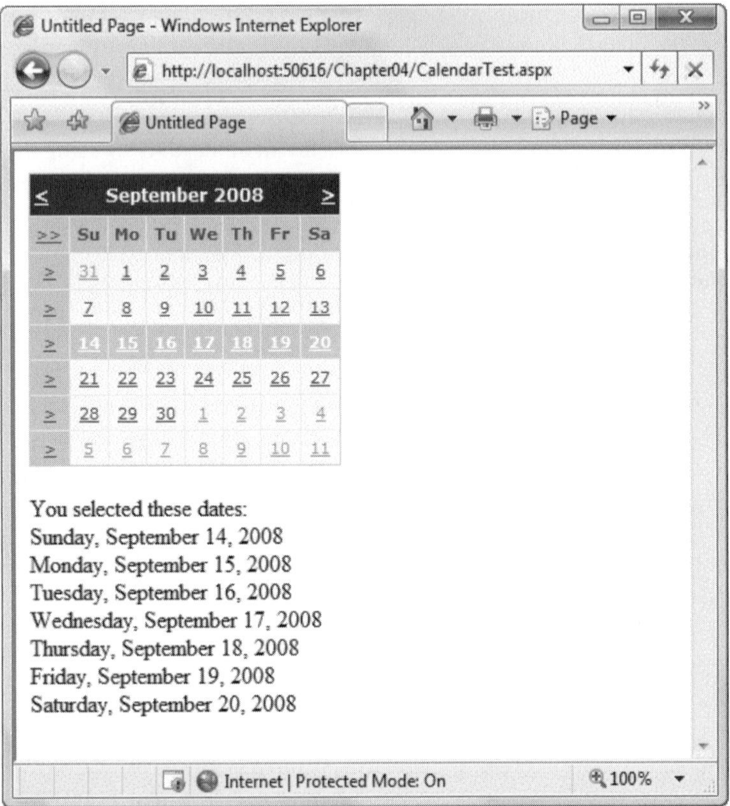

***Figure 4-16.** The Calendar control*

■ **Tip** If you're using a design tool such as Visual Studio, you can even set an entire related color scheme using the built-in designer. Simply select the Auto Format link in the smart tag. You'll be presented with a list of predefined formats that set various style properties.

Summary

In this chapter you learned the basics of the core server controls included with ASP.NET, such as HTML server controls, web controls, list controls, validation controls, and rich controls. You also learned how to use ASP.NET controls from your web-page code, access their properties, and handle their server-side events. Finally, you learned how to validate potentially problematic user input with the validation controls. In the next chapter, you'll learn how pages come together to form web applications.

CHAPTER 5

■ ■ ■

ASP.NET Applications

In traditional desktop programming, an *application* is an executable file with related support files. For example, a typical Windows application consists of a main executable file (EXE), supporting components (typically DLLs), and other resources such as databases and configuration files. An ASP.NET application follows a much different model.

On the most fundamental level, an ASP.NET application is a combination of files, pages, handlers, modules, and executable code that can be invoked from a virtual directory (and its subdirectories) on a web server. In this chapter, you'll learn why this distinction exists and take a closer look at how an ASP.NET application is configured and deployed. You'll also learn how to use components, HTTP handlers, and HTTP modules with an ASP.NET application.

Anatomy of an ASP.NET Application

The difference between ASP.NET applications and rich client applications makes a lot of sense when you consider the ASP.NET execution model. Unlike a Windows application, the end user never runs an ASP.NET application directly. Instead, a user launches a browser such as Internet Explorer and requests a specific URL (such as http://www.mysite.com/mypage.aspx) over HTTP. This request is received by a web server. When you're debugging the application in Visual Studio, you can use a local-only test server. When you deploy the application, you use the IIS web server, as described in Chapter 18.

The web server has no concept of separate applications—it simply passes the request to the ASP.NET worker process. However, the ASP.NET worker process carefully segregates code execution into different application domains based on the virtual directory. Web pages that are hosted in the same virtual directory (or one of its subdirectories) execute in the same *application domain*. Web pages in different virtual directories execute in separate application domains.

■ **Note** A *virtual directory* is simply a directory that's exposed through a web server. In Chapter 18, you'll learn how to create virtual directories. When using the test server in Visual Studio, your web project directory is treated like a virtual directory. The only exception is that the test server supports only local connections (requests initiated from the current computer).

The Application Domain

An application domain is a boundary enforced by the CLR that ensures that one application can't influence (or see the in-memory data) of another. The following characteristics are a direct result of the application domain model:

All the web pages in a single web application share the same in-memory resources, such as global application data, per-user session data, and cached data. This information isn't directly accessible to other ASP.NET or ASP applications.

All the web pages in a single web application share the same core configuration settings. However, you can customize some configuration settings in individual subdirectories of the same virtual directory. For example, you can set only one authentication mechanism for a web application, no matter how many subdirectories it has. However, you can set different authorization rules in each directory to fine-tune who is allowed to access different groups of pages.

All web applications raise global application events at various stages (when the application domain is first created, when it's destroyed, and so on). You can attach event handlers that react to these global application events using code in the global.asax file in your application's virtual directory.

In other words, the virtual directory is the basic grouping structure that delimits an ASP.NET application. You can create a legitimate ASP.NET application with a single web form (.aspx file). However, ASP.NET applications can include all of the following ingredients:

- **Web forms (.aspx files):** These are the cornerstones of any ASP.NET application.
- **Master pages (.master files):** These are templates that you can create and then use to build multiple web forms with the same structure. Chapter 16 describes master pages in detail.
- **Web services (.asmx files):** These allow you to share useful functions with applications on other computers and other platforms.

■ **Note** Web services have largely been replaced by WCF (Windows Communication Foundation) services, which support all the same protocols and more. You can host WCF services on an IIS web server as part of an ASP.NET web application. To learn more, refer to a dedicated book about WCF, such as the excellent *Programming WCF Services*, by Juval Lowy (O'Reilly Media, 2008). You'll use WCF web services with Silverlight in Chapter 34.

- **Code-behind files:** Depending on the code model you're using, you may also have separate source code files. If these files are coded in C#, they have the extension .cs.
- **A configuration file (web.config):** This file contains a slew of application-level settings that configure everything from security to debugging and state management.
- **global.asax:** This file contains event handlers that react to global application events (such as when the application is first being started).
- **Other components:** These are compiled assemblies that contain separate components you've developed or third-party components with useful functionality. Components allow you to separate business and data access logic and create custom controls.

Of course, a virtual directory can hold a great deal of additional resources that ASP.NET web applications will use, including stylesheets, images, XML files, and so on. In addition, you can extend the ASP.NET model by developing specialized components known as HTTP handlers and HTTP modules, which can plug into your application and take part in the processing of ASP.NET web requests.

■ **Note** It's possible to have file types that are owned by different handlers in the same virtual directory. One example is if you mingle .aspx and .asp files. A more complex example is if you configure ASP.NET 4 to process requests for.aspx files and configure ASP.NET 3.5 to process requests for another extension of your own devising (like .aspx35). You'll learn more about the configuration settings that map file types in the "Extending the HTTP Pipeline" section in this chapter, and you'll learn more about how the IIS web server implements this feature in Chapter 18.

Application Lifetime

ASP.NET uses a *lazy initialization* technique for creating application domains. This means that the application domain for a web application is created the first time a request is received for a page in that application.

An application domain can shut down for a variety of reasons, including if the web server itself shuts down. But, more commonly, applications restart themselves in new application domains in response to error conditions or configuration changes.

ASP.NET automatically recycles application domains when you change the application. One example is if you modify the web.config file. Another example is if you replace an existing web-page file or DLL assembly file. In both of these cases, ASP.NET starts a new application domain to handle all future requests and keeps the existing application domain alive long enough to finish handling any outstanding requests (including queued requests).

Application Domains vs. Application Pools

Although you won't get a formal introduction to IIS until Chapter 18, it's worth clearing up one point of possible confusion. In IIS, you configure the way web applications behave through *application pools*. Your application pool settings determine what version of .NET your application gets, how long it can remain idle before shutting down, whether it should restart itself automatically when facing certain errors, and so on. The application pool concept is similar to application domains, but slightly broader.

The difference is as follows. Each IIS application pool can configure one or more web applications. While running, each of these web applications typically consists of a single application domain. Technically, application pools are an IIS configuration feature, while application domains are a part of the .NET infrastructure.

Application Updates

One of the most remarkable features about the ASP.NET execution model is that you can update your web application without needing to restart the web server and without worrying about harming existing clients. This means you can add, replace, or delete files in the virtual directory at any time. ASP.NET then performs the same transition to a new application domain that it performs when you modify the web.config configuration file.

Being able to update any part of an application at any time without interrupting existing requests is a powerful feature. However, it's important to understand the architecture that makes it possible. Many developers make the mistake of assuming that it's a feature of the CLR that allows ASP.NET to seamlessly transition to a new application domain. But in reality, the CLR always locks assembly files when it executes them. To get around this limitation, ASP.NET doesn't actually use the ASP.NET files in the virtual directory. Instead, it uses another technique, called *shadow copy*, during the compilation process to create a copy of your files in c:\Windows\Microsoft.NET\Framework\[Version]\Temporary ASP.NET Files. The ASP.NET worker process loads the assemblies from this directory, which means these assemblies are locked.

The second part of the story is ASP.NET's ability to detect when you change the original files. This detail is fairly straightforward—it simply relies on the ability of the Windows operating system to track directories and files and send immediate change notifications. ASP.NET maintains an active list of all assemblies loaded within a particular application's application domain and uses monitoring code to watch for changes and acts accordingly.

■ **Note** ASP.NET can use files that are stored in the GAC (global assembly cache), a computer-wide repository of assemblies that includes staples such as the assemblies for the entire .NET Framework class library. You can also put your own assemblies into the GAC, but web applications are usually simpler to deploy and more straightforward to manage if you don't.

Application Directory Structure

Every web application should have a well-planned directory structure. Independently from the directory structure you design, ASP.NET defines a few directories with special meanings, as described in Table 5-1.

Table 5-1. *Special ASP.NET Directories*

Directory	Description
Bin	This directory contains all the precompiled .NET assemblies (usually DLLs) that the ASP.NET web application uses. These assemblies can include precompiled web-page classes, as well as other assemblies referenced by these classes. (If you're using the project model to develop your web application in Visual Studio, rather than the more common website model, the Bin directory will also contain an assembly that has the compiled code for your entire web application. This assembly is named after your application, as in WebApplication1.dll. To learn more about the difference between project and projectless development, refer to Chapter 2.)

Directory	Description
App_Code	This directory contains source code files that are dynamically compiled for use in your application. These code files are usually separate components, such as a logging component or a data access library. The compiled code never appears in the Bin directory, as ASP.NET places it in the temporary directories used for dynamic compilation. (If you're using the project model to develop your web application in Visual Studio, rather than the more common website model, you don't need to use the App_Code directory. Instead, all the code files in your project are automatically compiled into the assembly for your web application alongside your web pages.)
App_GlobalResources	This directory stores global resources that are accessible to every page in the web application.
App_LocalResources	This directory serves the same purpose as App_GlobalResources, except these resources are accessible for their dedicated page only.
App_WebReferences	This directory stores references to web services that the web application uses. This includes WSDL files and discovery documents.
App_Data	This directory is reserved for data storage, including SQL Server Express database files and XML files. Of course, you're free to store data files in other directories.
App_Browsers	This directory contains browser definitions stored in XML files. These XML files define the capabilities of client-side browsers for different rendering actions. Although ASP.NET does this globally (across the entire computer), the App_Browsers folder allows you to configure this behavior for separate web applications. See Chapter 27 for more information about how ASP.NET determines different browsers.
App_Themes	This directory stores the themes used by the web application. You'll learn more about themes in Chapter 16.

The global.asax Application File

The global.asax file allows you to write event handlers that react to global events. Users cannot request the global.asax file directly. Instead, the global.asax file executes its code automatically in response to certain application events. The global.asax file provides a similar service to the global.asa file in classic ASP applications.

You write the code in a global.asax file in a similar way to a web form. The difference is that the global.asax doesn't contain any HTML or ASP.NET tags. Instead, it contains methods with specific, predefined names. For example, the following global.asax file reacts to the HttpApplication.EndRequest event, which happens just before the page is sent to the user:

```
<%@ Application Language="C#" %>

<script language="C#" runat="server">
    protected void Application_OnEndRequest()
```

```
    {
        Response.Write("<hr />This page was served at " +
          DateTime.Now.ToString());
    }
</script>
```

Although it's not indicated in the global.asax file, every global.asax file defines the methods for a single class—the application class. The application class derives from HttpApplication, and as a result your code has access to all its public and protected members. This example uses the Response object, which is provided as a built-in property of the HttpApplication class, just like it's a built-in property of the Page class.

In the preceding example, the Application_OnEndRequest() event handler writes a footer at the bottom of the page with the date and time that the page was created. Because it reacts to the HttpApplication.EndRequest event, this method executes every time a page is requested, after all the event-handling code in that page has finished.

As with web forms, you can also separate the content of the global.asax file into two files, one that declares the file and another that contains the code. However, because there's no design surface for global.asax files, the division isn't required. Visual Studio doesn't give you the option to create a global.asax file with a separate code-behind class.

■ **Note** If you've created your web application as a web project, Visual Studio will use the code-behind approach and create both a global.asax file (which will be nearly empty) and a linked global.asax.cs (which contains the global application class that holds the event handlers). The end result is the same. For more information about the different between project-based and projectless development in Visual Studio, refer to Chapter 2.

The global.asax file is optional, but a web application can have no more than one global.asax file, and it must reside in the root directory of the application, not in a subdirectory. To add a global.asax file to a project, select Website ➤ Add New Item (or Project ➤ Add New Item if you're using the Visual Studio web project model) and choose the Global Application Class template. (This option doesn't appear if you already have a global.asax file in your project.) When Visual Studio adds a global.asax file, it includes empty event handlers for the most commonly used application events. You simply need to insert your code in the appropriate method.

It's worth noting that the application event handlers in the global.asax file aren't attached in the same way as the event handlers for ordinary control events. The usual way to attach an application event handler is just to use the recognized method name. For example, if you create a protected method named Application_OnEndRequest(), ASP.NET automatically calls this method when the HttpApplication.EndRequest event occurs. (This is really just a matter of convention. You can choose to attach an event handler to the HttpApplication.EndRequest event instead of supplying an Application_OnEndRequest() method. In fact, later in this chapter you'll see how HTTP modules handle application events using this technique.)

ASP.NET creates a pool of application objects when your application domain is first loaded and uses one to serve each request. This pool varies in size depending on the system and the number of available threads, but it typically ranges from 1 to 100 instances. Each request gets exclusive access to one of these application objects, and when the request ends, the object is reused. As different stages in application processing occur, ASP.NET calls the corresponding method, which triggers your code. Of course, if your methods have the wrong name, your implementation won't get called—instead, your code will simply be ignored.

■ **Note** The global application class that's used by the global.asax file should always be stateless. That's because application objects are reused for different requests as they become available. If you set a value in a member variable in one request, it might reappear in another request. However, there's no way to control how this happens or which request gets which instance of the application object. To circumvent this issue, don't use member variables unless they're static (as discussed in Chapter 6).

Application Events

You can handle two types of events in the global.asax file:

- Events that always occur for every request. These include request-related and response-related events.
- Events that occur only under certain conditions.

The required events unfold in this order:

1. **Application_BeginRequest():** This method is called at the start of every request.
2. **Application_AuthenticateRequest():** This method is called just before authentication is performed. This is a jumping-off point for creating your own authentication logic.
3. **Application_AuthorizeRequest():** After the user is authenticated (identified), it's time to determine the user's permissions. You can use this method to assign special privileges.
4. **Application_ResolveRequestCache():** This method is commonly used in conjunction with output caching. With output caching (described in Chapter 11), the rendered HTML of a web form is reused, without executing any of your code. However, this event handler still runs.
5. At this point, the request is handed off to the appropriate handler. For example, for a web form request, this is the point when the page is compiled (if necessary) and instantiated.
6. **Application_AcquireRequestState():** This method is called just before session-specific information is retrieved for the client and used to populate the Session collection. (Session state is covered in Chapter 6.)
7. **Application_PreRequestHandlerExecute():** This method is called before the appropriate HTTP handler executes the request.
8. At this point, the appropriate handler executes the request. For example, if it's a web form request, the event-handling code for the page is executed, and the page is rendered to HTML.
9. **Application_PostRequestHandlerExecute():** This method is called just after the request is handled.

10. **Application_ReleaseRequestState():** This method is called when the session-specific information is about to be serialized from the Session collection so that it's available for the next request.

11. **Application_UpdateRequestCache():** This method is called just before information is added to the output cache. For example, if you've enabled output caching for a web page, ASP.NET will insert the rendered HTML for the page into the cache at this point.

12. **Application_EndRequest():** This method is called at the end of the request, just before the objects are released and reclaimed. It's a suitable point for cleanup code.

Figure 5-1 shows the process of handling a single request.

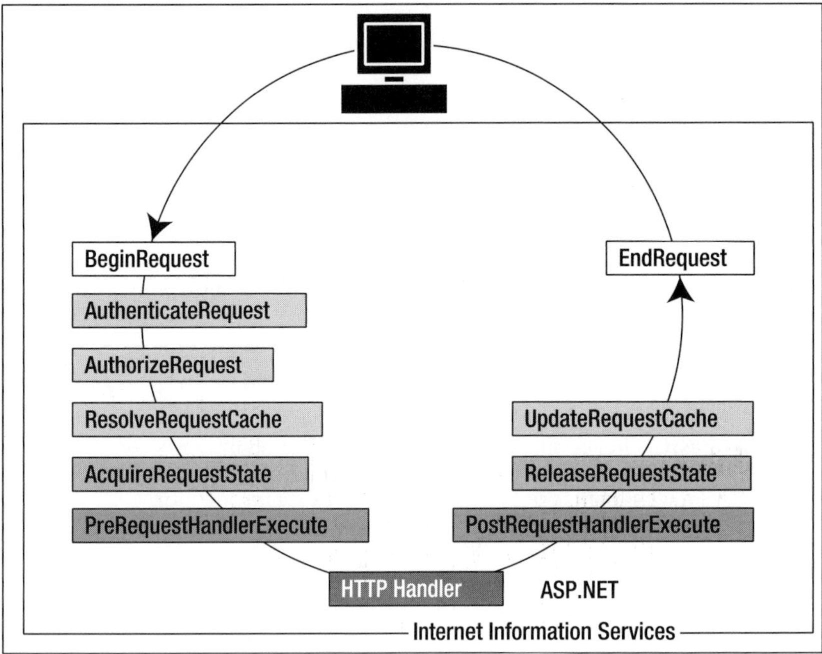

***Figure 5-1.** The application events*

Some events don't fire with every request:

Application_Start(): This method is invoked when the application first starts up and the application domain is created. This event handler is a useful place to provide application-wide initialization code. For example, at this point you might load and cache data that will not change throughout the lifetime of an application, such as navigation trees, static product catalogs, and so on.

Session_Start(): This method is invoked each time a new session begins. This is often used to initialize user-specific information. Chapter 6 discusses sessions with state management.

Application_Error(): This method is invoked whenever an unhandled exception occurs in the application.

Session_End(): This method is invoked whenever the user's session ends. A session ends when your code explicitly releases it or when it times out after there have been no more requests received within a given timeout period (typically 20 minutes). This method is typically used to clean up any related data. However, this method is only called if you are using in-process session state storage (the InProc mode, not the StateServer or SQLServer modes).

Application_End(): This method is invoked just before an application ends. The end of an application can occur because IIS is being restarted or because the application is transitioning to a new application domain in response to updated files or the process recycling settings.

Application_Disposed(): This method is invoked some time after the application has been shut down and the .NET garbage collector is about to reclaim the memory it occupies. This point is too late to perform critical cleanup, but you can use it as a last-ditch failsafe to verify that critical resources are released.

Application events are commonly used to perform application initialization, cleanup, usage logging, profiling, and troubleshooting. However, don't assume that your application will need to use global application events. Many ASP.NET applications don't use the global.asax file at all.

■ **Tip** The global.asax file isn't the only place where you can respond to global web application events. You can also create custom modules that participate in the processing of web requests, as discussed later in this chapter in the section "Extending the HTTP Pipeline."

Demonstrating Application Events

The following web application uses a global.asax file that responds to the HttpApplication.Error event. It intercepts the error and displays some information about it in a predefined format.

```
<script language="C#" runat="server">
    protected void Application_Error(Object sender, EventArgs e)
    {
        Response.Write("<b>");
        Response.Write("Oops! Looks like an error occurred!!</b><hr />");
        Response.Write(Server.GetLastError().Message.ToString());
        Response.Write("<hr />" + Server.GetLastError().ToString());
        Server.ClearError();
    }
</script>
```

To test this application event handler, you need to create another web page that causes an error. Here's an example that generates an error by attempting to divide by zero when a page loads:

```
protected void Page_Load(object sender, EventArgs e)
{
    int i = 0;
    int j = 1;
    int k = j/i;
}
```

If you request this page, you'll see the display shown in Figure 5-2.

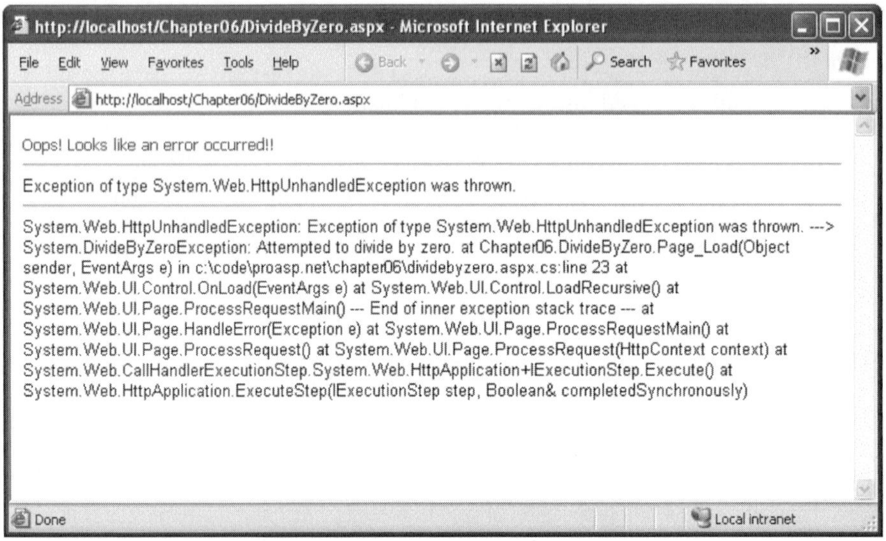

Figure 5-2. Catching an unhandled error

■ **Note** This technique only works when you're running your web application with IIS. When using the built-in web server, you'll get an ASP.NET error page instead.

Typically, you wouldn't use the Application_Error() method to control the appearance of a web page, because it doesn't give you enough flexibility to deal with different types of errors (without coding painstaking conditional logic). Instead, you would probably configure custom error pages using IIS. However, Application_Error() might be extremely useful if you want to log an error for future reference or even send an e-mail about it to a system administrator. In fact, in many events you'll need to use techniques such as these because the Response object won't be available. Two examples include the Application_Start() and Application_End() methods.

ASP.NET Configuration

Configuration in ASP.NET is managed with XML configuration files. All the information needed to configure an ASP.NET application's core settings, as well as the custom settings specific to your own application, is stored in these configuration files.

The ASP.NET configuration files have several advantages over traditional ASP configuration:

They are never locked: As described in the beginning of this chapter, you can update configuration settings at any point, and ASP.NET will smoothly transition to a new application domain.

They are easily accessed and replicated: Provided you have the appropriate network rights, you can modify a configuration file from a remote computer (or even replace it by uploading a new version via FTP). You can also copy a configuration file and use it to apply identical settings to another application or another web server that runs the same application in a web farm scenario.

They are easy to edit and understand: The settings in the configuration files are human-readable, which means they can be edited and understood without needing a special configuration tool.

The machine.config File

The configuration starts with a file named machine.config that resides in a directory like c:\Windows\Microsoft.NET\Framework\[Version]\Config. The machine.config file defines supported configuration file sections, configures the ASP.NET worker process, and registers providers that can be used for advanced features such as profiles, membership, and role-based security.

Compared with ASP.NET 1.x, the machine.config file in later versions of ASP.NET has been streamlined dramatically. To optimize the initialization process, many of the default settings that used to be in the machine.config file are now initialized programmatically. However, you can still look at the relevant settings by opening the new machine.config.comments file (which you can find in the same directory). It contains the full text for the standard settings along with descriptive comments (this is similar to the machine.config file in ASP.NET 1.x). Using the machine.config.comments file, you can learn about the default settings, and then you can add settings that override these values to machine.config.

Along with the machine.config file, ASP.NET uses a root web.config file (in the same directory) that contains additional settings. The settings register ASP.NET's core HTTP handlers and modules, set up rules for browser support, and define security policy.

All the web applications on the computer inherit the settings in these two files. However, most of the settings are essentially plumbing features that you never need to touch. Many of the settings don't apply when your application is deployed to an IIS web server, because they've been replaced by similar settings in IIS (which has its own configuration file, named ApplicationHost.config). The following section describes one exception—an important piece of information that still resides in the machine.config file.

<machineKey>

The <machineKey> section allows you to set the server-specific key used for encrypting data and creating digital signatures. You can use encryption in conjunction with several ASP.NET features. ASP.NET uses it automatically to protect the forms authentication cookie, and you can also apply it to protected view state data (as described in Chapter 6). The key is also used for authentication with out-of-process session state providers.

Ordinarily, the <machineKey> element takes this form:

```
<machineKey validationKey="AutoGenerate,IsolateApps"
  decryptionKey="AutoGenerate,IsolateApps" validation="SHA1" />
```

The AutoGenerate,IsolateApps value indicates that ASP.NET will create and store machine-specific, application-specific keys. In other words, each application uses a distinct, automatically generated key. This prevents potential cross-site attacks.

If you don't need application-specific keys, you can choose to use a single key for all applications on the current computer, like so:

```
<machineKey validationKey="AutoGenerate"
  decryptionKey="AutoGenerate" validation="SHA1" />
```

If you're using a web farm and running the same application on multiple computers, both of these approaches raise a problem. If you request a page and it's handled by one server, and then you post back the page and it's handled by another server, the second server won't be able to decrypt the view state and the forms cookie from the first server. This problem occurs because the two web servers use different keys.

To resolve this problem, you need to define the key explicitly in the machine.config file. Here's an example of a <machineKey> element with the two key attributes defined:

```
<machineKey
  validationKey="61EA54E005915332011232149A2EEB317586824B265326CCDB3AD9ABDBE9D
6F24B0625547769E835539AD3882D3DA88896EA531CC7AFE664866BD5242FC2B05D"
  decryptionKey="61EA54E005915332011232149A2EEB317586824B265337AF"
  validation="SHA1" />
```

■ **Tip** You can also hard-code application-specific keys by adding a hard-coded <machineKey> in the web.config file that you place in the application virtual directory. You'll need this approach if you're in a situation that combines the two scenarios described previously. (For example, you'll need this approach if you're running your application on multiple servers *and* these servers host multiple web applications that need individual keys.)

The validationKey value can be from 40 to 128 characters long. It is strongly recommended that you use the maximum length key available. The decryptionKey value can be either 16 or 48 characters long. If 16 characters are defined, standard DES (Data Encryption Standard) encryption is used. If 48 characters are defined, Triple DES (or 3DES) will be used. (This means DES is applied three times consecutively.) 3DES is much more difficult to break than DES, so it is recommended that you always use 48 characters for the decryptionKey. If the length of either of the keys is outside the allowed values, ASP.NET will return a page with an error message when requests are made to the application.

It doesn't make much sense to create the validation and decryption keys on your own. If you do, they're not likely to be sufficiently random, which makes them more subject to certain types of attacks. A better approach is to generate a strong random key using code and the .NET Framework cryptography classes (from the System.Security.Cryptography namespace).

The following is a generic code routine called CreateMachineKey() that creates a random series of bytes using a cryptographically strong random number generator. The CreateMachineKey() method accepts a single parameter that specifies the number of characters to use. The result is returned in hexadecimal format, which is required for the machine.config file.

```
public static string CreateMachineKey(int length)
{
    // Create a byte array.
    byte[] random = new byte[length/2];

    // Create a cryptographically strong random number generator.
    RNGCryptoServiceProvider rng = new RNGCryptoServiceProvider();

    // Fill the byte array with random bytes.
    rng.GetBytes(random);

    // Create a StringBuilder to hold the result once it is
    // converted to hexadecimal format.
```

```
    System.Text.StringBuilder machineKey = new
      System.Text.StringBuilder(length);

    // Loop through the random byte array and append each value
    // to the StringBuilder.
    for (int i = 0; i < random.Length; i++)
    {
        machineKey.Append(String.Format("{0:X2}", random[i]));
    }
    return machineKey.ToString();
}
```

You can use this function in a web form to create the keys you need. For example, the following snippet of code creates a 48-character decryption key and a 128-character validation key, and it displays the values in two separate text boxes:

```
txtDecryptionKey.Text = CreateMachineKey(48);
txtValidationKey.Text = CreateMachineKey(128);
```

You can then copy the information and paste it into the machine.config file for each computer in the web farm. This is a much more convenient and secure approach than creating keys by hand. You'll learn much more about the cryptography classes in the System.Security.Cryptography namespace described in Chapter 25.

Along with the validationKey and decryptionKey attributes described so far, you can also choose the algorithm that's used to create the view state hash code. The SHA1 algorithm is recommended for the best encryption strength, but you can alternately choose MD5 (Message Digest 5, which offers better performance), AES (Rijndael), or 3DES (TripleDES). In addition, you can add the validation attribute to specify what encryption method is used for the login ticket that's used with forms authentication. (Forms authentication is discussed in Chapter 20). Valid values are AES, DES, 3DES, and Auto (the default, which varies based on the form authentication settings you're using).

■ **Tip** The IIS Manager tool also allows you to change the machine key settings. To use this feature, you simply select the web server computer in the website tree and double-click the Machine Key icon. You can even create new, random validation and decryption keys at this point by clicking Generate Keys in the Actions column on the far right of the IIS Manager window.

The web.config File

Every web application inherits the settings from the machine.config file and the root web.config file. In addition, you can apply settings to individual web applications. For example, you might want to set a specific method for authentication, a type of debugging, a default language, or custom error pages. To do so, you supply a web.config file in the root virtual directory of your web application. To further configure individual subdirectories in your web application, you can place additional web.config files in these folders.

It's important to understand that the web.config file in a web application can't override all the settings in the machine.config file. Certain settings, such as the process model settings, can't be changed on a per-application basis. Other settings are application-specific. That means you can set them in the web.config file that's in the root virtual directory of your website, but you can't set them using a web.config file that's in a subdirectory.

The entire content of an ASP.NET configuration file is nested in a root <configuration> element. This element contains a <system.web> element, which is used for ASP.NET settings. Inside the <system.web> element are separate elements for each aspect of configuration. Along with <system.web> are the <appSettings> element%, which you can use to store custom settings, and the <connectionStrings> element, which you can use to store connection strings to databases that you use or that other ASP.NET features rely on.

Here is the absolute simplest web.config file, which is what you get when you create a blank ASP.NET website in Visual Studio:

```
<?xml version="1.0"?>
<configuration>
  <system.web>
    <compilation debug="true" targetFramework="4.0" />
  </system.web>
</configuration>
```

■ **Note** Like all XML documents, the web.config file is case-sensitive. Every setting uses camel case and starts with a lowercase letter. That means you cannot write <System.Web> instead of <system.web>.

The <system.web> section is the heart of ASP.NET configuration. Inside it are all the elements that configure ASP.NET features. Most ASP.NET applications also use the <appSettings> section to store miscellaneous configuration details that are application-specific, and the <connectionStrings> section to store connection strings for contacting a database. You can also use the <system.webServer> section to extend the ASP.NET pipeline with additional HTTP handlers and HTTP modules. Here's the basic skeletal structure of the web.config file with these details:

```
<?xml version="1.0"?>
<configuration>
  <appSettings />
  <connectionStrings />
  <system.web>
    <!-- ASP.NET configuration sections go here. -->
  </system.web>
  <system.webServer />
</configuration>
```

■ **Note** The configuration file for ASP.NET 3.5 applications was noticeably more convoluted, due to the way that ASP.NET 3.5 was released. Essentially, ASP.NET 3.5 fused together the core ASP.NET 2.0 model, with version 2.0 of the CLR, and a set of extensions. As a result, each application used the web.config file to opt into new features. However, ASP.NET 4 doesn't use this approach, and ASP.NET applications have simpler, more streamlined content. The additional settings have been moved into the machine.config and root web.config files, where they belong.

Configuration Inheritance

ASP.NET uses a multilayered configuration system that allows you to use different settings for different parts of your application. To use this technique, you need to create additional subdirectories inside your virtual directory. These subdirectories can contain their own web.config files with additional settings. ASP.NET uses *configuration inheritance* so that each subdirectory acquires the settings from the parent directory.

For example, consider the web request http://localhost/A/B/C/MyPage.aspx, where A is the root directory for the web application. In this case, multiple levels of settings come into play:

1. The default machine.config settings are applied first.
2. The web.config settings from the computer root are applied next. This web.config file is in the same Config directory as the machine.config file.
3. If there is a web.config file in the application root A, these settings are applied next.
4. If there is a web.config file in the subdirectory B, these settings are applied next.
5. If there is a web.config file in the subdirectory C, these settings are applied last.

In this sequence (shown in Figure 5-3), it's important to note that although you can have an unlimited number of subdirectories, the settings applied in step 1 and step 2 have special significance. That's because certain settings can be applied only at the machine.config level (such as the Windows account used to execute code), and other settings can be applied only at the application root level (such as the type of authentication your web application uses).

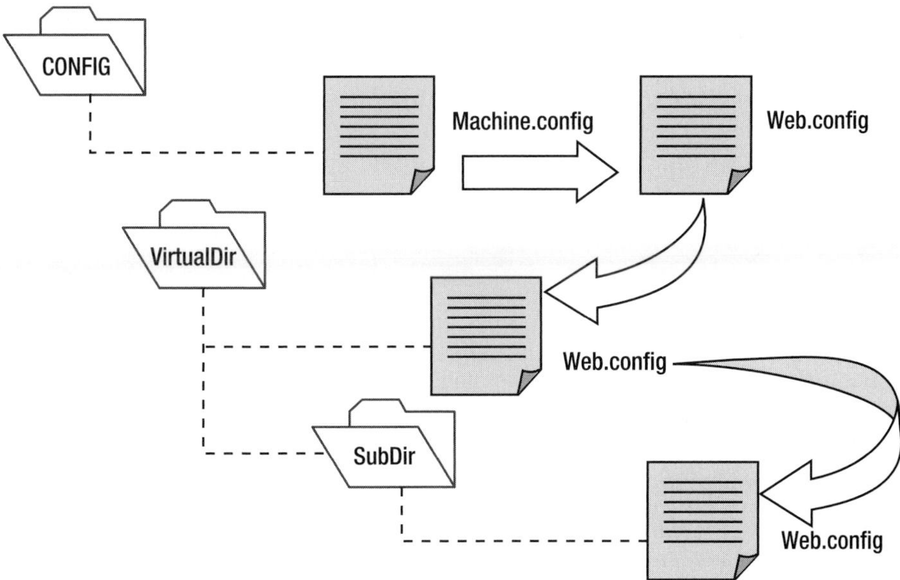

Figure 5-3. *Configuration inheritance*

In this way, subdirectories can specify just a small set of settings that differ from the rest of the web application. One reason you might want to use multiple directories in an application is to apply different security settings. Files that need to be secured would then be placed in a special directory with a web.config file that defines more stringent security settings than the root virtual directory.

If settings conflict, the settings from a web.config in a nested directory always override the settings inherited from the parent. However, one exception exists. You can designate specific locked sections that can't be changed. The next section describes this technique.

■ **Note** If you're developing a web project (as opposed to a projectless website), your project will also include the files web.Debug.config and web.Release.config. These files are designed to change between the settings you use when testing a web application and those you need when deploying it in a production environment. However, they have *no effect* when you run your application in Visual Studio—in fact, Visual Studio ignores them completely. Instead, they are only used when you build a deployment package, as described in Chapter 18.

Using <location> Elements

The <location> element is an extension that allows you to specify more than one group of settings in the same configuration file. You use the path attribute of the <location> element to specific the subdirectory or file to which the settings should be applied.

For example, the following web.config file uses the <location> element to create two groups of settings—one for the current directory and one that applies only to files in the subdirectory named Secure:

```
<configuration>
  <system.web>
    <!-- Basic configuration settings go here. -->
  </system.web>

  <location path="/Secure">
    <system.web>
      <!-- Configuration settings for the Secure subdirectory go here. -->
    </system.web>
  </location>
</configuration>
```

This web.config file essentially plays the role of two configuration files. It has the same result as if you had split the settings into two separate web.config files and placed one in the Secure subdirectory.

There's no limit to how many different location elements you can use in a single configuration file. However, the <location> element isn't used often, because it's usually easier to manage and update configuration settings when they are separated into distinct files. But there is one scenario where the <location> element gives you functionality you can't get any other way. This occurs when you want to lock specific settings so they can't be overridden.

To understand how this technique works, consider the next example. It defines two groups of settings and sets the allowOverride attribute of the <location> tag to false on one group, as shown here:

```
<configuration>
  <system.web>
    <!-- Unprotected configuration settings go here. -->
  </system.web>
```

```
  <location allowOverride="false">
    <system.web>
      <!-- Locked configuration settings go here. -->
    </system.web>
  </location>
</configuration>
```

In this case, you can't override any of the settings in the <location> section. If you try, ASP.NET will generate an unhandled exception when you request a page in the web application.

The allowOverride attribute of the <location> element is primarily useful for web hosting companies that want to make sure certain settings can't be changed. In this case, the administrator will modify the machine.config file on the web server and use the <location> element to lock specific sections.

■ **Tip** When you lock settings in the machine.config file, you have two choices. First, you can lock the settings for all applications by omitting the path attribute of the <location> tag. Second, you can lock settings for a specific application by setting the path attribute to the appropriate web application name.

<system.web>

The <system.web> element contains all the ASP.NET-specific configuration settings. These settings configure various aspects of your web application and enable services such as security, state management, and tracing. The schema of the <system.web> section is fixed—in other words, you can't change the structure or add your own custom elements here. However, you can include as few or as many configuration sections as you want.

Table 5-3 lists the basic child elements that the <system.web> element can contain and their purpose. This list is not complete and is intended only to give you a rough idea of the scope of ASP.NET configuration. Throughout this book, you'll consider different parts of the web.config file as you learn about the corresponding features.

Table 5-3. *Some Basic Configuration Sections*

Element	Description
authentication	This element configures your authorization system—in other words, it determines how you will verify a client's identity when the client requests a page.
authorization	This element controls which clients have access to the resources within the web application or current directory.
compilation	This element identifies the version of .NET that your web application is targeting (through the targetFramework attribute) and whether you want to generate debug symbols in .pdb files (through the debug attribute), so you can debug your application with a tool like Visual Studio. The compilation element can also contain the <assemblies> element, which lists additional assemblies that your web application uses. These assemblies are then made available to your code (as long as they can be found in the Bin directory or the GAC).

Element	Description
customErrors	This element allows you to set specific redirect URLs that should be used when specific (or default) errors occur. For example, this element could be used to redirect the user to a friendly replacement for the dreaded 404 (page not found) error. But although this setting still works with Visual Studio's built-in test web server, it's effectively been replaced by the <httpErrors> section in IIS 7.x.
membership	This element allows you to configure ASP.NET's membership feature, which manages user account information and provides a high-level API for security-related tasks such as user login and password resetting.
pages	This element defines default page settings (most of which you can override with the Page directive).
profile	This element allows you to configure ASP.NET's profile feature, which automatically stores and retrieves user-specific information (usually, profile settings). Typically, profile data is serialized to a database.
roleManager	This element allows you to configure ASP.NET's role-based security feature, which provides a way to store role information and a high-level API for role-based authorization.
sessionState	This element configures the various options for maintaining session state for the application, such as whether to maintain it at all and where to maintain it (SQL, a separate Windows service, and so on).
trace	This element configures tracing, an ASP.NET feature that lets you display diagnostic information in the page (or collect it for viewing separately).

■ **Note** The configuration file architecture is a .NET standard, and other types of applications (such as Windows applications) can also use configuration files. For that reason, the root <configuration> element isn't tailored to web application settings. Instead, web application settings are contained inside the dedicated <system.web> section.

<system.webServer>

This section contains settings that affect to the web server. You use the <handlers> element inside this section to register custom HTTP handlers. You use the <modules> section to register HTTP modules. Both tasks are demonstrated later in this chapter.

<appSettings>

You add custom settings to a web.config file in a special element called <appSettings>. Here's where the <appSettings> section fits into the web.config file:

```
<?xml version="1.0"?>
<configuration>
  <appSettings>
    <!-- Custom application data goes here. -->
  </appSettings>
  <system.web>...</system.web>
</configuration>
```

The custom settings that you add are written as simple string variables. You might want to use a special web.config setting for several reasons. Often, you'll want the ability to record hard-coded but changeable information for connecting to external resources, such as database query strings, file paths, and web service URLs. Because the configuration file can be modified at any time, this allows you to update the configuration of an application as its physical deployment characteristics change without needing to recompile it.

Custom settings are entered using an <add> element that identifies a unique variable name (the key) and the variable contents (the value). The following example adds two new custom configuration settings:

```
<?xml version="1.0" ?>
<configuration>
  <appSettings>
    <add key="websiteName" value="My New Website"/>
    <add key="welcomeMessage" value="Welcome to my new Website, friend!"/>
  </appSettings>
  <system.web>...</system.web>
</configuration>
```

Once you've added this information, .NET makes it extremely easy to retrieve it in your web-page code. You simply need to use the WebConfigurationSettings class from the System.Web.Configuration namespace. It exposes a static property called AppSettings, which contains a dynamically built collection of available application settings for the current directory. For example, if the ASP.NET page class referencing the AppSettings collection is at a location such as http://localhost/MyApp/MyDirectory/MySubDirectory, it is possible that the AppSettings collection contains settings from three different web.config files. The AppSettings collection makes that hierarchy seamless to the page that's using it.

To use the WebConfigurationSettings class, it helps to first import the System.Web.Configuration namespace so you can refer to the class without needing to use the long fully qualified name, as shown here:

```
using System.Web.Configuration;
```

Next, you simply need to retrieve the value by name. The following example fills two labels using the custom application information:

```
protected void Page_Load(object sender, EventArgs e)
{
    lblSiteName.Text =
      WebConfigurationManager.AppSettings["websiteName"];
    lblWelcome.Text =
```

```
        WebConfigurationManager.AppSettings["welcomeMessage"];
}
```

Figure 5-4 shows the test web page in action.

Figure 5-4. *Retrieving custom application settings*

An error won't occur if you try to retrieve a value that doesn't exist. If you suspect this could be a problem, make sure to test for a null reference before retrieving a value.

■ **Note** Values in the <appSettings> element of a configuration file are available to any class in your application or to any component that your application uses, whether it's a web form class, a business logic class, a data access class, or something else. In all these cases, you use the ConfigurationSettings class in the same way.

<connectionStrings>

This section allows you to define database connection strings that will be used elsewhere in your application. Seeing as connection strings need to be reused exactly to support connection pooling and may need to be modified without recompiling the web application, it makes perfect sense to store them in the web.config file.

You can add as many connection strings as you want. For each one, you need to specify the ADO.NET provider name (see Chapter 7 for more information).

Here's an example that defines a single connection string:

```
<configuration>
  <connectionStrings>
    <add name="NorthwindConnection"
         connectionString=
  "Data Source=localhost;Integrated Security=SSPI;Initial Catalog=Northwind;"
         providerName="System.Data.SqlClient" />
  </connectionStrings>
  <system.web>...</system.web>
</configuration>
```

You can retrieve connection strings in your code using the static WebConfigurationManager.ConnectionStrings property:

```
string connectionString =
  WebConfigurationManager.ConnectionStrings["NorthwindConnection"].Value;
```

The ConnectionStrings collection includes the connection strings that are defined directly in your web.config file and any that are defined in higher-level configuration files (namely, the root web.config file and the machine.config file). That means you'll automatically get a connection string named LocalSqlServer that points to a local instance of SQL Server Express (which is the scaled-down version of SQL Server that's included with Visual Studio). The connection string looks like this:

```
Data Source=.\SQLEXPRESS;Integrated Security=SSPI;AttachDBFilename=
|DataDirectory|aspnetdb.mdf;User Instance=true
```

The interesting thing about SQL Server Express is that it allows you to connect directly to a database file in your website. To learn more about SQL Server Express, refer to Chapter 15.

Reading and Writing Configuration Sections Programmatically

As you've already learned, ASP.NET provides the WebConfigurationManager class in the System.Web.Configuration namespace, which allows you to extract information from a configuration file at runtime. The WebConfigurationManager provides the members shown in Table 5-4.

Table 5-4. *WebConfigurationManager Members*

Member	Description
AppSettings	Provides access to any custom information you've added to the <appSettings> section of the application configuration file. Individual settings are provided through a collection that's indexed by name.
ConnectionStrings	Provides access to data in the <connectionStrings> section of the configuration file. Individual settings are provided through a collection that's indexed by name.
GetSection()	Returns an object that wraps the information from a specific section of the configuration file.
OpenWebConfiguration()	Returns an editable Configuration object that provides access to the configuration information for the specified web application.
OpenMachineConfiguration()	Returns an editable Configuration object that provides access to the configuration information that's defined for the web server (in the machine.config file).

The WebConfigurationManager class gives convenient access to two configuration sections: the <appSettings> section, where you can define custom settings, and the <connectionStrings> section, used to define how your application connects to the database. You can get this information using the AppSettings and ConnectionStrings properties.

Using the WebConfigurationManager.GetSection() method, you can retrieve information about any other configuration section.

However, you'll need to go to a little more work. The trick is that the GetSection() method returns a different type of object depending on the type of section. For example, if you're retrieving information from the <authentication> section, you'll receive an AuthenticationSection object, as shown here:

```
// Search for the <authentication> element inside the <system.web> element.
AuthenticationSection authSection =
  (AuthenticationSection)WebConfigurationManager.GetSection("system.web/authentication");
```

The search is performed using a pathlike syntax. You don't indicate the root <configuration> element, because all configuration sections are contained in that element.

Classes for every configuration section are defined in the class library in the System.Web.Configuration namespace (not the System.Configuration namespace, which includes only configuration classes that are generic to all .NET applications). All these classes inherit from the ConfigurationSection class.

Using a ConfigurationSection object allows you to retrieve a good deal of information about the current state of your application. Here's an example that displays information about the assemblies that are currently referenced:

```
CompilationSection compSection =
  (CompilationSection)WebConfigurationManager.GetSection("system.web/compilation");
foreach (AssemblyInfo assm in compSection.Assemblies)
{
    Response.Write(assm.Assembly + "<br /");
}
```

■ **Note** When you retrieve information using the GetSection() method (or the OpenWebConfiguration() method described next), it reflects the cumulative configuration for the current application. That means settings from the current web.config file are merged with those defined higher up the configuration hierarchy (for example, in the root web.config and the machine.config files).

You can also modify most configuration sections programmatically with the WebConfigurationManager—in fact, ASP.NET relies on this functionality for its administrative web pages. To use this approach, you need to call the OpenWebConfiguration() method first to get a Configuration object. You can then use the Configuration.GetSection() method to retrieve exactly the section you want to change, and the Configuration.Save() method to commit the change. When modifying a setting, ASP.NET handles the update safely, by using synchronization code to ensure that multiple clients can't commit a change simultaneously. As with any configuration change, ASP.NET creates a new application domain with the new settings, and uses this application domain to handle new requests while winding down the old application domain.

In your code, you're most likely to change settings in the <appSettings> section or the <connectionStrings> section. Here's an example that rewrites the application settings shown earlier so that it updates one of the settings after reading it:

```
protected void Page_Load(object sender, EventArgs e)
{
    Configuration config =
      WebConfigurationManager.OpenWebConfiguration(Request.ApplicationPath);

    lblSiteName.Text =
```

```
        config.AppSettings.Settings["websiteName"].Value;
      lblWelcome.Text =
        config.AppSettings.Settings["welcomeMessage"].Value;

      config.AppSettings.Settings["welcomeMessage"].Value = "Welcome, again.";
      config.Save();
}
```

■ **Tip** This example reflects the cumulative configuration in the root web application directory, because it uses the value Request.ApplicationPath when calling the OpenWebConfiguration() method. If you use the name of a subdirectory, you'll get the cumulative settings for that folder. If you use the path Request.CurrentExecutionFilePath, you'll get cumulative settings for the directory where the current web page is located.

Note that the web.config file is never a good solution for state management. Instead, it makes sense as a way to occasionally update a setting that, under normal circumstances, almost never changes. That's because changing a configuration setting has a significant cost. File access has never been known for blistering speed, and the required synchronization adds a certain amount of overhead. However, the real problem is that the cost of creating a new application domain (which happens every time a configuration setting changes) is significant. The next time you request the page, you'll see the effect—the request will complete much more slowly while the page is compiled to native machine code, cached, and loaded. Even worse, information in the Application and Caching collections will be lost, as well as any information in the Session collection if you're using the in-process session provider (see Chapter 6 for more information). Unfortunately, the new configuration model makes it all too easy to make the serious mistake of storing frequently changed values in a configuration file.

By default, the Configuration.Save() method persists only those changes you have made since creating the Configuration object. Settings are stored in the local web.config file, and one is created if needed. It's important to realize that if you change an inherited setting (for example, one that's stored in the machine.config file), then when you save the changes, you won't overwrite the existing value in the configuration file where it's defined. Instead, the new value will be saved in the local web.config file so that it overrides the inherited value for the current application only. You can also use the SaveAs() method to save configuration settings to another file.

When calling Configuration.Save(), you can use an overloaded version of the method that accepts a value from the ConfigurationSaveMode enumeration. Use Modified to save any value you changed, even if it doesn't differ from the inherited values. Use Full to save everything in the local web.config, which is useful if you're trying to duplicate configuration settings for testing or deployment. Finally, use Minimal to save only those changes that differ from the inherited levels—this is the default.

■ **Note** In order to successfully use the methods and properties of the WebConfigurationManager, the ASP.NET worker process needs certain permissions (such as read read access to the web application directory). If you are using the OpenWebConfiguration() method to change these settings programmatically, the worker process also requires write access. (The same limitation doesn't apply to the GetSection() method or the AppSettings and ConnectionStrings properties.) To protect against problems, you should always wrap your configuration calls in exception-handling code.

The Website Administration Tool (WAT)

You might wonder why the ASP.NET team went to all the trouble of creating a sophisticated tool like the WebConfigurationManager that performs too poorly to be used in a typical web application. The reason is because the WebConfigurationManager isn't really intended to be used in your web pages. Instead, it's designed to allow developers to build custom configuration tools that simplify the work of configuring web applications. ASP.NET even includes a graphical configuration tool that's entirely based on the WebConfigurationManager, although you'd never know it unless you dived into the code.

This tool is called the WAT, and it lets you configure various parts of the web.config file using a web-page interface. To run the WAT to configure the current web application in Visual Studio, select Website ➤ ASP.NET Configuration (or Project ➤ ASP.NET Configuration if you're using project-based development). Visual Studio will open an Internet Explorer window (see Figure 5-5), and Internet Explorer will authenticate you automatically under the current user account.

You can use the WAT to automate the web.config changes you made in the previous example. To try this, click the Application tab. Using this tab, you can edit or remove application settings (select the Manage Application Settings link) or create a new setting (click the Create Application Settings link). Figure 5-6 shows how you can edit an application setting.

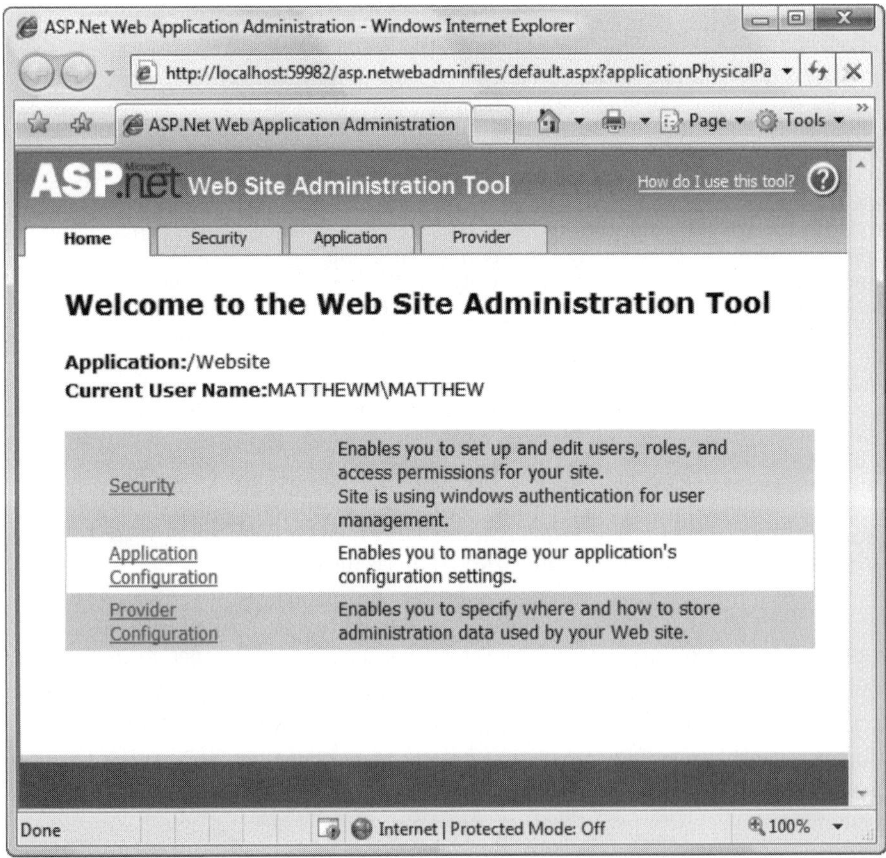

Figure 5-5. Running the WAT

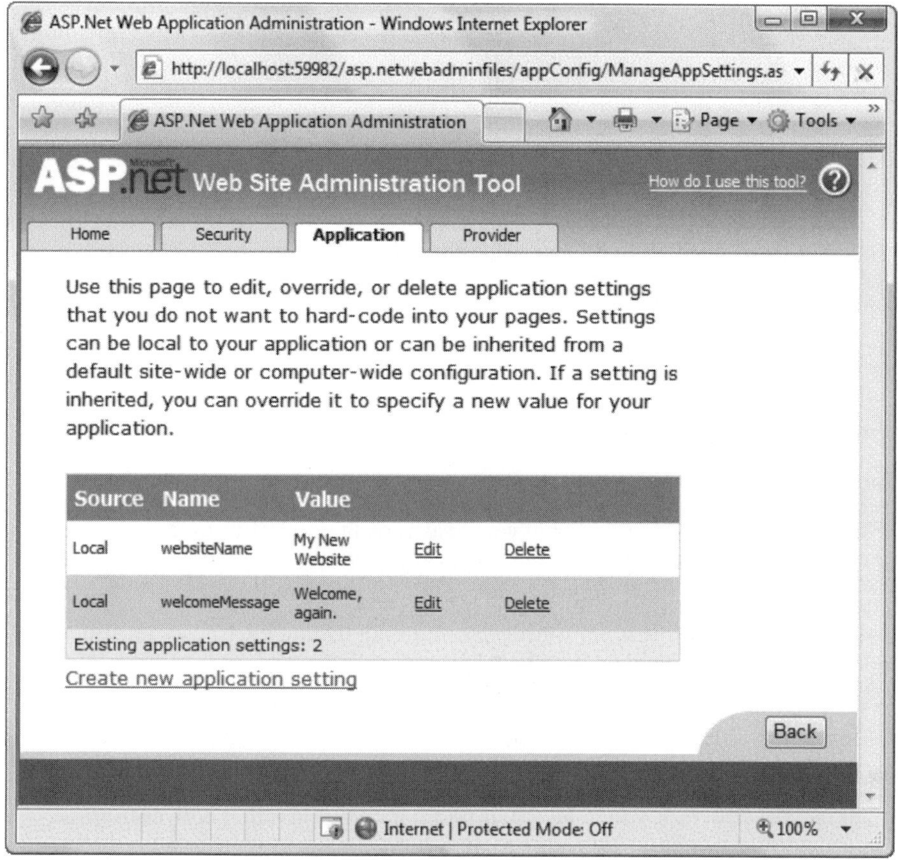

Figure 5-6. *Editing an application setting with the WAT*

This is the essential idea behind the WAT. You make your changes using a graphical interface (a web page), and the WAT generates the settings you need and adds them to the web.config file for your application behind the scenes. Of course, the WAT has a number of settings for configuring more complex ASP.NET settings, and you'll see it at work throughout this book.

Extending the Configuration File Structure

Earlier in this chapter, you learned how you can use the <appSettings> element to store custom information that your application uses. The <appSettings> element has two significant limitations. First, it doesn't provide a way to store structured information, such as lists or groups of related settings. Second, it doesn't give you the flexibility to deal with different types of data. Instead, the <appSettings> element is limited to single strings.

Fortunately, ASP.NET uses a modular, highly extensible configuration model that allows you to extend the structure of the web.config and machine.config configuration files with your own custom sections. To extend a configuration file, you need to take three basic steps:

1. Determine the information you want to store in the configuration file and how it will be organized into elements and attributes. Ideally, you'll have one element for each conceptually related group of settings. You'll use attributes to store each piece of information that's associated with the element.
2. For each new element, create a C# class that encapsulates its information. When you run your application, ASP.NET will read the information from the element in the configuration file and use it to create an instance of your class. You can then read the information from this object whenever you need it.
3. the new section in your configuration file. To do this, you need to use the <configSections> element. The <configSections> element identifies each new element and maps it to the associated class.

The easiest way to see how this works is to consider a basic example. The following sections show you how to create and register a new element in the web.config file.

Creating a Section Class

Imagine you want to store several related settings that, when taken together, tell your application how to contact a remote object. For example, these settings could indicate a port number, server location, URL, user authentication information, and so on. Using what you've already learned, you could enter this information using separate settings in the <appSettings> group. However, there wouldn't be anything to indicate what settings are logically related. Not only does that make the settings harder to read and interpret, it could lead to problems if one setting is updated but the other related settings aren't.

A better option would be to break free from the limited structure of the <appSettings> section and wrap the information in a single XML element. Here's an example that defines a custom <orderService> element:

```
<orderService available="true" pollTimeout="00:01:00"
 location="tcp://OrderComputer:8010/OrderService"/>
```

If you want to use this sort of structure, you need to define a matching class that derives from System.Configuration.ConfigurationSection. You can place this class in a separate DLL component, or you can add the source code to the App_Code folder so it will be automatically compiled as part of the current web application. (Or, if you're creating your web application using a web project, simply add the source code file to your project and it will be compiled as part of the web application assembly automatically.)

■ **Note** For information about component reuse, see the ".NET Components" section later in this chapter. For now, you can use the quicker App_Code approach rather than creating a full-fledged, separately compiled component.

The following OrderService class plays that role. It represents a single <orderService> element and provides access to the three attributes through strongly typed properties:

```
public class OrderService : ConfigurationSection
{
    [ConfigurationProperty("available",
     IsRequired = false, DefaultValue = true)]
    public bool Available
    {
```

```
        get { return (bool)base["available"]; }
        set { base["available"] = value; }
    }

    [ConfigurationProperty("pollTimeout",
     IsRequired = true)]
    public TimeSpan PollTimeout
    {
        get { return (TimeSpan)base["pollTimeout"]; }
        set { base["pollTimeout"] = value; }
    }

    [ConfigurationProperty("location",
     IsRequired = true)]
    public string Location
    {
        get { return (string)base["location"]; }
        set { base["location"] = value; }
    }
}
```

As you can see, each property is mapped to the corresponding attribute name using the ConfigurationProperty attribute. This part is critically important, because it defines the schema (the structure) of your custom section. If you add an attribute in your custom section but you don't include a matching ConfigurationProperty attribute, ASP.NET will throw an exception when you try to read that part of the web.config file.

The ConfigurationProperty attribute also gives you the opportunity to decide whether that piece of information is mandatory and what default value should be used if it isn't supplied.

In the actual property procedures, the code uses the dictionary of attributes that's provided by the base class. You can retrieve the attribute you want from this collection by name.

Registering a Section Class

Once you've created the section class, your coding work is complete. However, you still need to register your section class in the web.config file so that ASP.NET recognizes your custom settings. If you don't perform this step, you'll get an error when you attempt to run the application because ASP.NET will notice an unrecognized section in the web.config file.

To register your custom section, you simply add a <section> element to the <configSections> section of the web.config file. You need to indicate the name of the section (using the name attribute) and the name of the corresponding section class (using the type attribute). Here's the full web.config file you need:

```
<configuration>
  <configSections>
    ...
    <section name="orderService" type="OrderService" />
  </configSections>

  <orderService available="true" pollTimeout="00:01:00"
   location="tcp://OrderComputer:8010/OrderService"/>

  <system.web>...</system.web>
</configuration>
```

The final step is to retrieve the information from your custom section when you need it in your web page. All you need is the ConfigurationManager.GetSection() method:

```
OrderService custSection =
  (OrderService)ConfigurationManager.GetSection("orderService");

lblInfo.Text += "Retrieved service information...<br />" +
  "<b>Location:</b> " + custSection.Location +
  "<br /><b>Available:</b> " + custSection.Available.ToString() +
  "<br /><b>Timeout:</b> " + custSection.PollTimeout.ToString() + "<br /><br />";
```

Figure 5-7 shows the displayed data.

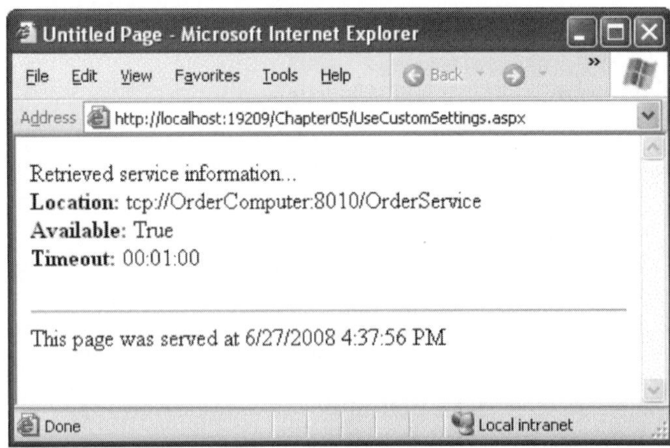

Figure 5-7. Retrieving custom configuration data

Custom section handlers can get a fair bit more sophisticated. For example, you might want to create a section that has nested subelements. Here's an example of a more complex <orderService> section that uses this design:

```
<orderService available="true" pollTimeout="00:01:00">
    <location computer="OrderComputer" port="8010" endpoint="OrderService" />
</orderService>
```

To work with this structure, you simply need to create a class that derives from ConfigurationElement to represent each nested element. Here's the class you need to repre- sent the <location> element:

```
public class Location : ConfigurationElement
{
    [ConfigurationProperty("computer",
    IsRequired = true)]
    public string Computer
    {
        get { return (string)base["computer"]; }
        set { base["computer"] = value; }
```

```
    }

    [ConfigurationProperty("port",
    IsRequired = true)]
    public int Port
    {
        get { return (int)base["port"]; }
        set { base["port"] = value; }
    }

    [ConfigurationProperty("endpoint",
    IsRequired = true)]
    public string Endpoint
    {
        get { return (string)base["endpoint"]; }
        set { base["endpoint"] = value; }
    }
}
```

And here's the revised Location property in the OrderService class:

```
[ConfigurationProperty("location",
 IsRequired = true)]
public Location Location
{
    get { return (Location)base["location"]; }
    set { base["location"] = value; }
}
```

Now you can write code like this:

```
lblInfo.Text = "<b>Server:</b> " + custSection.Location.Computer;
```

Using the techniques in this chapter, you can save changes to a custom configuration section, and you can encrypt it. You can also use additional attributes to validate configuration string values (look for the attributes that derive from ConfigurationValidatorAttribute), and you can create sections with nested elements and more complex structures. For more information about extending ASP.NET configuration files, refer to the MSDN Help.

Encrypting Configuration Sections

ASP.NET never serves requests for configuration files, because they often contain sensitive information. However, even with this basic restriction in place, you may want to increase security by encrypting sections of a configuration file. This is a recommended practice for data such as connections and user-specific details. (Of course, any passwords should also be encrypted, although ideally they won't be placed in a configuration file at all.)

ASP.NET supports two encryption options:

RSA: The RSA provider allows you to create a key pair that is then used to encrypt the configuration data. The advantage is that you can copy this key between computers (for example, if you want to use the same configuration file with all the servers in a web farm). The RSA provider is used by default.

DPAPI: The DPAPI (data protection API) provider uses a protection mechanism that's built into Windows. Configuration files are encrypted using a machine-specific key. The advantage is that you don't need to manage or maintain the key. The disadvantage is that you can't use a configuration file encrypted in this way on any other computer.

With both of these options, encryption is completely transparent. When you retrieve a setting from an encrypted section, ASP.NET automatically performs the decryption and returns the plain text to your code (provided the required key is available). Similarly, if you modify a value programmatically and save it, encryption is performed automatically. However, you won't be able to edit that section of the web.config file by hand. But you can still use the WAT, IIS Manager, or your own custom code. When you use the configuration API, the decryption and encryption steps are performed automatically when you read from or write to a protected section.

Programmatic Encryption

To enable encryption programmatically, you need to retrieve the corresponding ConfigurationSection.SectionInformation object and then call the ProtectSection() method. Any existing data is encrypted at this point, and any changes you make from this point on are automatically encrypted. If you want to switch off encryption, you simply use the corresponding UnprotectSection() method.

Here's an example that encrypts the application section if it's unencrypted or switches off encryption if it is:

```
Configuration config = WebConfigurationManager.OpenWebConfiguration("/");
ConfigurationSection appSettings = config.GetSection("appSettings");

if (appSettings.SectionInformation.IsProtected)
{
    appSettings.SectionInformation.UnprotectSection();
}
else
{
    appSettings.SectionInformation.ProtectSection(
      "DataProtectionConfigurationProvider");
}
config.Save();
```

Here's an excerpted version of what a protected <appSettings> section looks like:

```
<appSettings configProtectionProvider="DataProtectionConfigurationProvider">
  <EncryptedData>
    <CipherData>
      <CipherValue>AQAAANCMnd8BFdERjHoAwE/Cl+sBAAAAIEokx++BEOmpDaPjVrJ/jQQAAAA
CAAAAAAADZgAAqAAAABAAAAClK6Kt++FOJoJrMZs12KWdAAAAAASAAACgAAAAEAAAAFYA23iGZF1pe
FwDPTKM2/1IAQAAYG/Y4cmSlEVs/a4yK7KXoYbWtjDsQBnMAcndmK3q+ODw/8...</CipherValue>
    </CipherData>
  </EncryptedData>
</appSettings>
```

Note that you can't tell anything about the encrypted data, including the number of settings, the key names of settings, or their data types.

Command-Line Encryption

Currently, no graphical tool exists for encrypting and decrypting configuration file settings. However, if you don't want to write code, you can use the aspnet_regiis.exe command-line utility, which is found in the directory c:\Windows\Microsoft.NET\Framework\[Version]. To use this tool, you must have already created a virtual directory to set your application up in IIS (see Chapter 18 for more about that process).

When using aspnet_regiis to protect a portion of a configuration file, you need to specify these command-line arguments:

- The -pe switch specifies the configuration section to encrypt.
- The -app switch specifies your web application's virtual path.
- The -prov switch specifies the provider name.

Here's the command line that duplicates the earlier example for an application at http://localhost/TestApp:

```
aspnet_regiis -pe "appSettings" -app "/TestApp"
 -prov "DataProtectionConfigurationProvider"
```

.NET Components

A well-designed web application written for ASP.NET will include separate components that may be organized into distinct data and business tiers. Once you've created these components, you can use them from any ASP.NET web page seamlessly.

You can create a component in two ways:

Create a new .cs file in the App_Code subdirectory: ASP.NET automatically compiles any code files in this directory and makes the classes they contain available to the rest of your web application. When you add a new class in Visual Studio, you'll be prompted to create the App_Code directory (if it doesn't exist yet) and place the file there. (Web applications created using the Visual Studio web project model don't have an App_Code subdirectory. For web projects, you get the same result by simply adding the source code file to your project, so that Visual Studio compiles it as part of your web application assembly.)

Create a new class library project in Visual Studio: All the classes in this project will be compiled into a DLL assembly. Once you've compiled the assembly, you can use Visual Studio's Website ➤ Add Reference (or Project ➤ Add Reference) command to bring it into your web application. This step adds the assembly reference to your web.config file and copies the assembly to the Bin subdirectory of your application.

Both approaches have the same ultimate result. For example, if you code a database component, you'll access it in the same way regardless of whether it's a compiled assembly in the Bin directory or a source code file in the App_Code directory. Similarly, if you use ASP.NET's precompilation features (discussed in Chapter 18), both options will perform the same way. (If you don't, you'll find that the first request to your web application takes longer to execute when you use the App_Code approach, because an extra compilation step is involved.)

Although both approaches have essentially the same footprint, they aren't the same for code management. This is especially true in cases where you want to reuse the component in more than one web application (or even in different types of .NET applications). If you use the App_Code approach with multiple web applications, it's all too easy to make slight modifications and wind up with a mess of different versions of the same shared class. The second approach is also more practical for building large-scale applications with a team of developers, in which case you'll want the freedom to have different portions of the web application completed and compiled separately. For these reasons, the class library approach is always preferred for professional applications.

■ **Tip** The App_Code subdirectory should be used only for classes that are tightly coupled to your web application. Reusable units of functionality (such as business libraries, database components, validation routines, encryption utilities, and so on) should always be built as separate class libraries.

Creating a Component

The next example demonstrates a simple component that reads a random Sherlock Holmes quote from an XML file. (This XML file is available on the Internet and freely reusable via the GNU Public License—you can download it at `http://www.amk.ca/quotations/sherlock-holmes.xml` or with the samples for this chapter.) The component consists of two classes—a Quotation class that represents a single quote and a SherlockQuotes class that allows you to read a random quote. Both of these classes are placed in the SherlockLib namespace.

The first listing shows the SherlockQuotes class, which loads an XML file containing quotes in QEL (Quotation Exchange Language, an XML dialect) when it's instantiated. The SherlockQuotes class provides a public GetRandom() quote method that the web-page code can use.

```
using System;
using System.Xml;

namespace SherlockLib
{
    public class SherlockQuotes
    {
        private XmlDocument quoteDoc;
        private int quoteCount;
        public SherlockQuotes(string fileName)
        {
            quoteDoc = new XmlDocument();
            quoteDoc.Load(fileName);
            quoteCount = quoteDoc.DocumentElement.ChildNodes.Count;
        }

        public Quotation GetRandomQuote()
        {
            int i;
            Random x = new Random();
            i = x.Next(quoteCount-1);
            return new Quotation( quoteDoc.DocumentElement.ChildNodes[i] );
        }
    }
}
```

Each time a random quotation is obtained, it is stored in a Quotation object. The listing for the Quotation class is as follows:

```
using System;
using System.Xml;

namespace SherlockLib
{
    public class Quotation
    {
        private string qsource;
        public string Source
        {
            get {return qsource;}
            set {qsource = value;}
        }

        private string date;
        public string Date
        {
            get {return date;}
            set {date = value;}
        }

        private string quotation;
        public string QuotationText
        {
            get {return quotation;}
            set {quotation = value;}
        }

        public Quotation(XmlNode quoteNode)
        {
          if ( (quoteNode.SelectSingleNode("source")) != null)
            qsource = quoteNode.SelectSingleNode("source").InnerText;
          if ( (quoteNode.Attributes.GetNamedItem("date")) != null)
            date = quoteNode.Attributes.GetNamedItem("date").Value;
          quotation = quoteNode.FirstChild.InnerText;
        }
    }
}
```

Using a Component Through the App_Code Directory

The simplest way to quickly test this class is to copy the source code files to the App_Code subdirectory in a web application. You can take this step in Windows Explorer or use Visual Studio (Website ➤ Add Existing Item).

Now you might want to import the SherlockLib namespace into your web page to make its classes more readily available, as shown here:

```
using SherlockLib;
```

Finally, you can use the class in your web-page code just as you would use a class from the .NET Framework. Here's an example that displays the quotation information on a web page:

```
protected void Page_Load(object sender, System.EventArgs e)
{
    // Put user code to initialize the page here.
    SherlockQuotes quotes = new
      SherlockQuotes(Server.MapPath("./sherlock-holmes.xml"));
    Quotation quote = quotes.GetRandomQuote();
    Response.Write("<b>" + quote.Source + "</b> (<i>" + quote.Date + "</i>)");
    Response.Write("<blockquote>" + quote.QuotationText + "</blockquote>");
}
```

When you run this application, you'll see something like what's shown in Figure 5-8. Every time you refresh the page, you'll see a different quote.

■ **Note** When you use the App_Code directory, you face another limitation—you can use only one language. This limitation results from the way that ASP.NET performs its dynamic compilation. Essentially, all the classes in the App_Code directory are compiled into a single file, so you can't mix C# and VB.

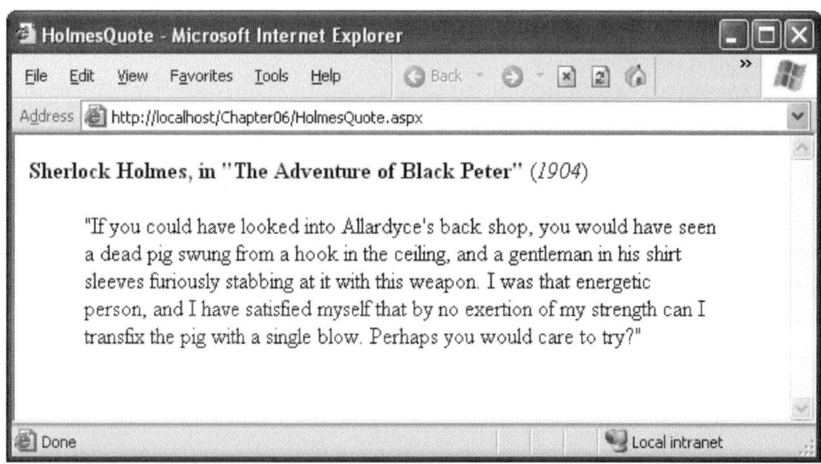

Figure 5-8. *Using the component in your web page*

Using a Component Through the Bin Directory

Assuming that your component provides a significant piece of functionality and that it may be reused in different applications, you'll probably want to create it using a separate project. This way, your component can be reused, tested, and versioned separately from the web application.

To create a separate component, you need to use Visual Studio to create a class library project. Although you can create this using a separate instance of Visual Studio, it's often easier to load both your class library project and your web application into a single Visual Studio solution to assist in debugging. This allows you to easily modify both the web application and the component code at the same time and single-step from a web-page event handler into a method in your component. To set this up, create your web application first. Then, select File ➤ Add ➤ New Project to open the Add New Project dialog box. In the list on the left, choose the Visual C# group of templates, and select the Class Library template (see Figure 5-9).

Figure 5-9. *Adding a class library project to a solution*

Once you've added the code to your class library project, you can compile your component by right-clicking the project in the Solution Explorer and choosing Build. This generates a DLL assembly that contains all the component classes.

To allow your web application to use this component, you need to add an assembly reference to the component. This allows Visual Studio to provide its usual syntax checking and IntelliSense. Otherwise, it will interpret your attempts to use the class as mistakes and refuse to compile your code.

To add a reference, choose Website ➤ Add Reference from your web application (or Project ➤ Add Reference if you're developing a web project). The Add Reference dialog box includes several tabs:

.NET: This allows you to add a reference to a .NET assembly. You can choose from the list of well-known assemblies that are stored in the registry. Typically, you'll use this tab to add a reference to an assembly that's included as part of the .NET Framework.

COM: This allows you to add a reference to a legacy COM component. You can choose from a list of shared components that are installed in the Windows system directory. When you add a reference to a COM component, .NET automatically creates an intermediary wrapper class known as an *interop assembly*. You use the interop assembly in your .NET code, and the interop assembly interacts with the legacy component.

Projects: This allows you to add a reference to a .NET class library project that's currently loaded in Visual Studio. Visual Studio automatically shows a list of eligible projects. This is often the easiest way to add a reference to one of your own custom components.

Browse: This allows you to hunt for a compiled .NET assembly file (or a COM component) on your computer. This is a good approach for testing custom components if you don't have the source project or you don't want to load it into Visual Studio where you might inadvertently modify it.

Recent: This allows you to add a reference to a compiled .NET assembly that you've used recently (rather than forcing you to browse for it all over again).

Figure 5-10 compares two ways to add a reference to the SherlockLib component—by adding a reference to a currently loaded project and by adding a reference to the compiled DLL file.

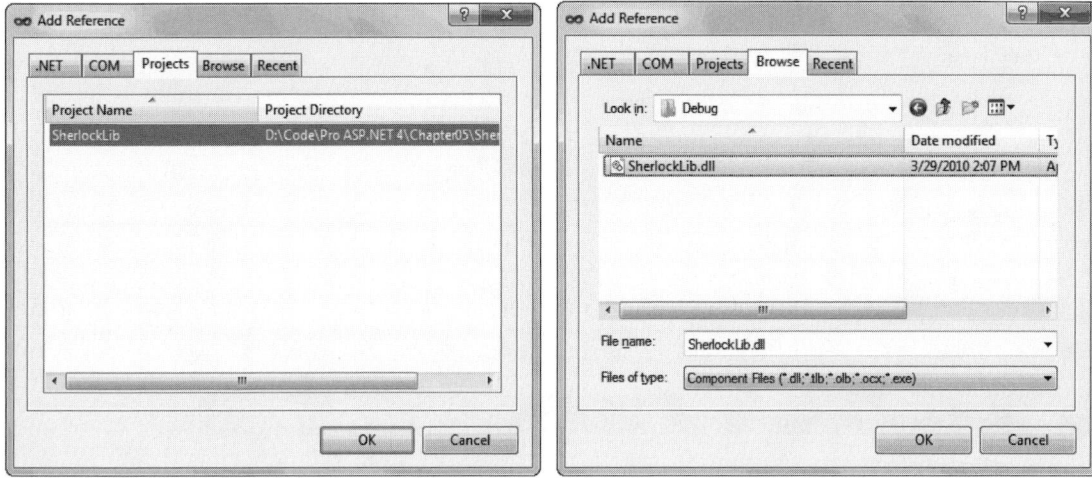

***Figure 5-10.** Adding a reference to SherlockLib.dll*

Once you add the reference, the corresponding DLL file will be automatically copied to the Bin directory of your current project. You can verify this by checking the Path property of the reference in the Properties window or just by browsing to the directory in Windows Explorer. The nice thing is that this file will automatically be overwritten with the most recent compiled version of the assembly every time you run the web application.

It really is that easy. To use another component—either from your own business tier, from a third-party developer, or from somewhere else—all you need to do is add a reference to that assembly.

■ **Tip** ASP.NET also allows you to use assemblies with custom controls just as easily as you use assemblies with custom components. This allows you to bundle reusable user interface output and functionality into self-contained packages so that they can be used over and over again within the same or multiple applications. Part 5 has more information about this technique.

Extending the HTTP Pipeline

The pipeline of application events isn't limited to requests for .aspx web forms. It also applies if you create your own handlers to deal with custom file types.

Why would you want to create your own handler? For the most part, you won't. However, sometimes it's convenient to use a lower-level interface that still provides access to useful objects such as Response and Request but doesn't use the full control-based web form model. One example is if you want to create a web resource that dynamically renders a custom graphic (a technique demonstrated in Chapter 28). In this situation, you simply need to receive a request, check the URL parameters, and then return raw image data as a JPEG or GIF file. By avoiding the full web control model, you save some overhead, because ASP.NET does not need to go through as many steps (such as creating the web-page objects, persisting view state, and so on).

ASP.NET makes scenarios like these remarkably easy through its pluggable architecture. You can "snap in" new handlers for specialized file types just by adding configuration settings. But first, you need to take a closer look at the HTTP pipeline.

HTTP Handlers

Every request into an ASP.NET application is handled by a specialized component known as an HTTP handler. The HTTP handler is the backbone of the ASP.NET request processing framework. ASP.NET uses different HTTP handlers to serve different file types. For example, the handler for web pages creates the page and control objects, runs your code, and renders the final HTML.

You can register HTTP handlers in two ways. First, if you're using Visual Studio's integrated web server, if you're running an old version of IIS, or if you're running IIS 7.x in classic mode, you need to add your HTTP handlers to the <httpHandlers> section in the <system.web> element of the web.config file. That's the location shown here:

```
<configuration>
  <system.web>
    <httpHandlers>
      ...
    </httpHanlders>
    ...
  </system.web>
</configuration>
```

Inside the <httpHandlers> section, you can place <add> elements that register new handlers and <remove> elements to unregister existing handlers. You can see the core set of HTTP handlers defined in this way in the root web.config file. Here's an excerpt of that file:

```
<httpHandlers>
    <add verb="*" path="trace.axd" validate="true"
     type="System.Web.Handlers.TraceHandler"/>
    <add verb="*" path="*.config" validate="true"
     type="System.Web.HttpForbiddenHandler"/>
    <add verb="*" path="*.cs" validate="true"
     type="System.Web.HttpForbiddenHandler"/>
    <add verb="*" path="*.aspx" validate="true"
     type="System.Web.UI.PageHandlerFactory"/>
    ...
</httpHandlers>
```

In this example, four classes are registered. All requests for trace.axd are handed to the TraceHandler, which renders an HTML page with a list of all the recently collected trace output (as described in Chapter 3). Requests for files that end in .config or .cs are handled by the HttpForbiddenHandler, which always generates an exception informing the user that these file types are never served. And files ending in .aspx are handled by the PageHandlerFactory. In this case, PageHandlerFactory isn't actually an HTTP handler. Instead, it's a factory class that will create the appropriate HTTP handler. This extra layer allows the factory to create a different handler or configure the handler differently depending on other information about the request.

This method of registering HTTP handlers doesn't work if you're using IIS 7.x in integrated mode (which is the default). In this situation, IIS reads the <system.webServer> section and uses the handlers defined in its <handlers> section:

```
<configuration>
  <system.web>
    ...
  </system.web>
  <system.webServer>
    <handlers>
      ...
    </hanlders>
  </system.webServer>
</configuration>
```

Just like the <httpHandlers> section, you register HTTP handlers by placing <add> elements inside the <handlers> section.

This minor change in the configuration file underlies a more significant shift in the way IIS works. In versions of IIS before IIS 7 (and when running IIS 7.x in classic mode), IIS deals with every request by first checking its file mappings. If a particular file type is mapped to ASP.NET, IIS passes the file to the ASP.NET engine, which then reads the handler information from the web.config file and decides how to deal with the request. The disadvantage of this approach is that the whole process relies on the initial file registration. If ASP.NET isn't registered for a specific file type, you can't run a custom HTTP handler or HTTP module when that file type is requested.

IIS 7.x is smarter. In integrated mode, it handles the task of sending the request to the appropriate HTTP handler, and it always reads the handler information from the <system.WebServer> section. If you attempt to register handlers in the <httpHandler> section, you'll receive an IIS error page when you run the application. This is to prevent the security risk of having a web application that appears to implement certain handlers, but doesn't actually use them. (Incidentally, you can disable this behavior so IIS 7.x simply ignores and accepts the <httpHandler> section by adding `<validation validateIntegratedModeConfiguration="false"/>` inside the <system.webServer> section, but it's not recommended.)

■ **Note** IIS 7.x doesn't use the root web.config to define its core set of handlers and modules. Instead, you'll find these in the Applicationhost.config file, which is a directory like c:\Windows\System32\inetsrv\config.

The examples in this chapter use the <httpHandlers> section, so that they work with the Visual Studio web server. The web.config file with the downloadable code for this chapter uses both types of registration.

■ **Note** IIS 7.0 is included with Windows Server 2008 and the Home, Premium, Business, Enterprise, and Ultimate editions of Windows Vista. IIS 7.5 is included with Windows Server 2008 R2 and Windows 7. For more information about IIS, including how to register an HTTP handler using the IIS Manager tool, refer to Chapter 18.

Creating a Custom HTTP Handler

If you want to work at a lower level than the web form model to support a specialized form of processing, you can implement your own HTTP handler.

To create a custom HTTP handler, you simply need to author a class that implements the IHttpHandler interface. You can place this class in the App_Code directory, or you can compile it as part of a stand-alone DLL assembly (in other words, a separate class library project) and add a reference to it in your web application.

The IHttpHandler requires your class to implement two members, which are shown in Table 5-5.

Table 5-5. *IHttpHandler Members*

Member	Description
ProcessRequest()	ASP.NET calls this method when a request is received. It's where the HTTP handlers perform all the processing. You can access the intrinsic ASP.NET objects (such as Request, Response, and Server) through the HttpContext object that's passed to this method.
IsReusable	After ProcessRequest() finishes its work, ASP.NET checks this property to determine whether a given instance of an HTTP handler can be reused. If it returns true, the HTTP handler object can be reused for another request of the same type current. If it returns false, the HTTP handler object will simply be discarded.

The following code shows one of the simplest possible HTTP handlers you can create. It simply returns a fixed block of HTML with a message.

```
using System;
using System.Web;

namespace HttpExtensions
{
    public class SimpleHandler : IHttpHandler
    {
        public void ProcessRequest(System.Web.HttpContext context)
        {
            HttpResponse response = context.Response;
            response.Write("<html><body><h1>Rendered by the SimpleHandler") ;
            response.Write("</body>") ;
        }

        public bool IsReusable
        {
```

```
            get {return true;}
        }
    }
}
```

■ **Note** If you create this extension as a class library project, you'll need to add a reference to the System.Web.dll assembly, which contains the bulk of the ASP.NET classes. Without this reference, you won't be able to use types such as IHttpHandler and HttpContext. (To add the reference, right-click the project name in the Solution Explorer, choose Add Reference, and find the assembly in the list in the .NET tab.)

Configuring a Custom HTTP Handler

Once you've created your HTTP handler class and made it available to your web application (either by placing it in the App_Code directory or by adding a reference), you're ready to use your extension. The next step is to alter the web.config file for the web application so that it registers your HTTP handler. Here's an example:

```
<configuration>
  <system.web>
    <httpHandlers>
      <add verb="*" path="test.simple"
           type="HttpExtensions.SimpleHandler,HttpExtensions" />
    </httpHandlers>
    ...
  <system.web>
</configuration>
```

When you register an HTTP handler, you specify three important details. The verb attribute indicates whether the request is an HTTP POST or HTTP GET request (use * for all request types). The path attribute indicates the file extension that will invoke the HTTP handler. In this example, the web.config section links the SimpleHandler class to the filename test.simple. Finally, the type attribute identifies the HTTP handler class. This identification consists of two portions. First is the fully qualified class name (in this example, HttpExtensions.SimpleHandler). That portion is followed by a comma and the name of the DLL assembly that contains the class (in this example, HttpExtensions.dll). Note that the .dll extension is always assumed, and you don't include it in the name.

If you're using the App_Code approach instead of a separately compiled assembly, you can omit the DLL name entirely, because ASP.NET generates it automatically.

```
<httpHandlers>
    <add verb="*" path="test.simple"
         type="HttpExtensions.SimpleHandler" />
</httpHandlers>
```

Visual Studio doesn't allow you to launch your HTTP handler directly. Instead, you need to run your web project and then type in a URL that includes test.simple. For example, if your web application URL is set to http://localhost:19209/Chapter05 in the local server, you need to manually change it to http://localhost:19209/Chapter05/test.simple. (If you don't remember the current web application URL, just run your application and then modify the URL in the browser.) You'll see the HTML shown in Figure 5-11.

Figure 5-11. Running a custom HTTP handler

Using Configuration-Free HTTP Handlers

ASP.NET provides an alternate approach that allows you to avoid registering HTTP handlers and worrying about configuration file settings—you can use the recognized extension .ashx. No matter what version of IIS you're using (or if you're using the integrated Visual Studio web server), requests that end in .ashx are automatically recognized as requests for a custom HTTP handler.

To create an .ashx file in Visual Studio, select Website ➤ Add New Item (or Project ➤ Add New Item for web projects) and choose Generic Handler. You can then fill in a suitable name and click Add to create the handler.

The .ashx file begins with a WebHandler directive. This WebHandler directive indicates the class that should be exposed through this file. Here's an example:

```
<%@ WebHandler Language="C#" Class="HttpExtensions.SimpleHandler" %>
```

The class name can correspond to a class in the App_Code directory or a class in a reference assembly. Alternatively, you can define the class directly in the .ashx file (underneath the WebHandler directive). Either way, when a client requests the .ashx file, the corresponding HTTP handler class is executed. If you save the previous example as the file simple.ashx, whenever the client requests simple.ashx your custom web handler will be executed. Best of all, the .ashx file type is registered in IIS, so you don't need to perform any IIS configuration when you deploy your application.

Whether you use a configuration file or an .ashx file is mostly a matter of preference. However, .ashx files are usually used for simpler extensions that are designed for a single web application. Configuration files also give you a little more flexibility. For example, you can register an HTTP handler to deal with all requests that end with a given extension, whereas an .ashx file only serves a request if it has a specific filename. Also, you can register an HTTP handler for multiple applications (by registering it in the web.config file and installing the assembly in the Global Assembly Cache). To achieve the same effect with an .ashx file, you need to copy the .ashx file to each virtual directory.

Creating an Advanced HTTP Handler

In the previous example, the HTTP handler simply returns a block of static HTML. However, you can create much more imaginative handlers. For example, you might read data that has been posted to the page or that has been supplied in the query string and use that to customize your rendered output.

Here's a more sophisticated example that displays the source code for a requested file. It uses the file I/O support that's found in the System.IO namespace.

```
using System;
using System.Web;
using System.IO;

namespace HttpExtensions
{
    public class SourceHandler : IHttpHandler
    {
        public void ProcessRequest(System.Web.HttpContext context)
        {
            // Make the HTTP context objects easily available.
            HttpResponse response = context.Response;
            HttpRequest request = context.Request;
            HttpServerUtility server = context.Server;

            response.Write("<html><body>");

            // Get the name of the requested file.
            string file = request.QueryString["file"];
            try
            {
                // Open the file and display its contents one line at a time.
                response.Write("<b>Listing " + file + "</b><br />");
                StreamReader r = File.OpenText(
                  server.MapPath(Path.Combine("./", file)));
                string line = "";
                while (line != null)
                {
                    line = r.ReadLine();

                    if (line != null)
                    {
                        // Make sure tags and other special characters are
                        // replaced by their corresponding HTML entities so that
                        // they can be displayed appropriately.
                        line = server.HtmlEncode(line);

                        // Replace spaces and tabs with nonbreaking spaces
                        // to preserve whitespace.
                        line = line.Replace(" ", " ");
                        line = line.Replace(
                          "\t", "     ");

                        // A more sophisticated source viewer might apply
                        // color coding.
                        response.Write(line + "<br />");
                    }
                }
                r.Close();
            }
            catch (Exception err)
```

```
            {
                response.Write(err.Message);
            }
            response.Write("</body>");
        }

        public bool IsReusable
        {
            get {return true;}
        }
    }
}
```

This code simply finds the requested file, reads its content, and uses a little string substitution (for example, replacing spaces with nonbreaking spaces and line breaks with the <br /> element) and HTML encoding to create a representation that can be safely displayed in a browser. You'll learn more about techniques for reading and manipulating files in Chapter 12.

Next, you can map the handler to a file extension, as follows:

```
<httpHandlers>
    <add verb="*" path="source.simple"
         type="HttpExtensions.SourceHandler,HttpExtensions"/>
</httpHandlers>
```

To test this handler, you can use a URL in this format:

```
http://localhost:[Port]/[Website]/source.simple?file=HolmesQuote.aspx.cs
```

The HTTP handler will then show the source code for the .cs file, as shown in Figure 5-12.

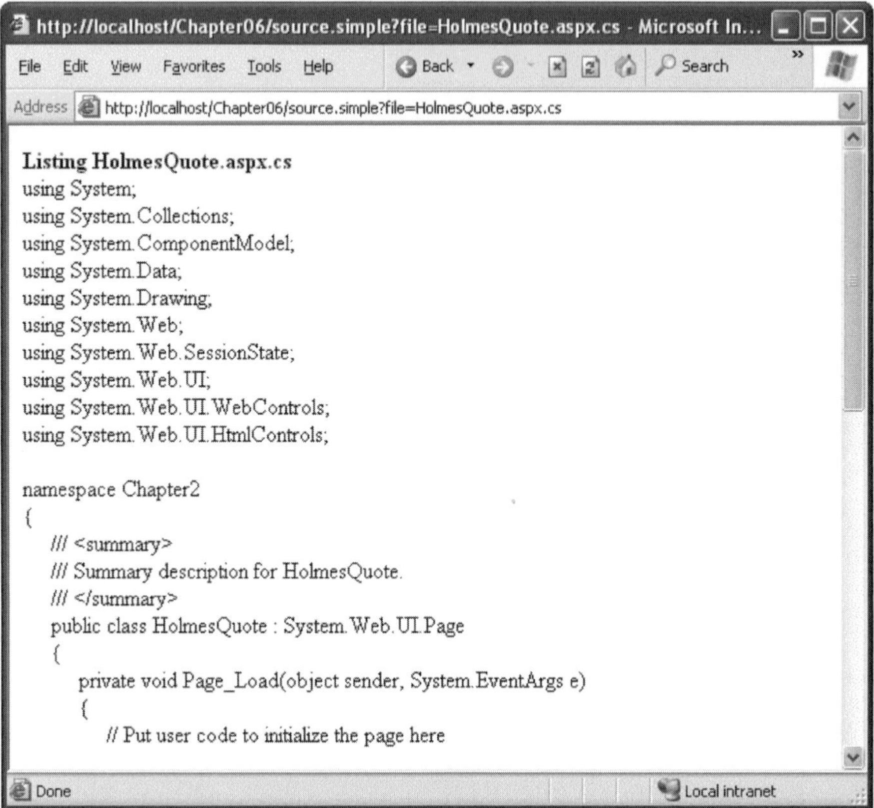

Figure 5-12. Using a more sophisticated HTTP handler

Creating an HTTP Handler for Non-HTML Content

Some of the most interesting HTTP handlers don't generate HTML. Instead, they render different types of content, such as images. This approach gives you the flexibility to retrieve or generate your content programmatically, rather than relying on fixed files. For example, you could read the content for a large ZIP file from a database record and use Response.BinaryWrite() to send it to the client. Or, you could get even more ambitious and use your HTTP handler to dynamically create a ZIP archive that combines several smaller files. Either way, to the client who is using your HTTP handler, it seems as though the browser is downloading an ordinary file. But in actuality, the content is being served using ASP.NET code.

The following example demonstrates an HTTP handler that deals with image files. This handler doesn't create the image content dynamically (for that trick, refer to Chapter 28), but it does use code to perform another important task. Whenever an image is requested, this HTTP handler checks the referrer header of the request. The referrer header provides the host name, which indicates whether the link to the image originates from one of the pages on your site, or whether it stems from a page on someone else's site. If the page that's using the image is on another site, you have a potential problem. Not only is this page stealing your image, it's also creating more work for your web server. That's because every time someone views the third-party site, the image is requested from your server. If the stolen image appears on a popular site, this could generate a significant amount of extra work and reduce the bandwidth you have available to serve your own pages.

This problem—sites that steal bandwidth by linking to resources on your server—is known informally as *leeching*. It's a common headache for popular websites that serve large amounts of non-HTML content (for example, photo-sharing sites such as Flickr). Many websites combat this problem using the same technique as the HTTP handler described previously—namely, they refuse to serve the image or they substitute a dummy image if the referrer header indicates that a request originates from another site.

Here's an HTTP handler that implements this solution in ASP.NET. In order for this code to work as written, you must import the System.Globalization namespace and the System.IO namespace.

```
public class ImageGuardHandler : IHttpHandler
{
    public void ProcessRequest(System.Web.HttpContext context)
    {
        HttpResponse response = context.Response;
        HttpRequest request = context.Request;
        string imagePath = null;

        // Check whether the page requesting the image is from your site.
        if (request.UrlReferrer != null)
        {
            // Perform a case-insensitive comparison of the referrer.
            if (String.Compare(request.Url.Host, request.UrlReferrer.Host,
                true, CultureInfo.InvariantCulture) == 0)
            {
                // The requesting host is correct.
                // Allow the image to be served (if it exists).
                imagePath = request.PhysicalPath;
                if (!File.Exists(imagePath))
                {
                    response.Status = "Image not found";
                    response.StatusCode = 404;
                    return;
                }
            }
        }

        if (imagePath == null)
        {
            // No valid image was allowed.
            // Return the warning image instead of the requested image.
            // Rather than hard-code this image, you could
            // retrieve it from the web.config file
            // (using the <appSettings> section or a custom
            // section).
            imagePath = context.Server.MapPath("./Images/notAllowed.gif");
        }

        // Set the content type to the appropriate image type.
        response.ContentType = "image/" +
          Path.GetExtension(imagePath).ToLower();

        // Serve the image.
```

```
        response.WriteFile(imagePath);
    }

    public bool IsReusable
    {
        get { return true; }
    }
}
```

For this handler to protect image files, you need to register it to deal with the appropriate file types. Here's the web.config settings that set this up for the .gif and .png file types (but not .jpg):

```
<httpHandlers>
    <add verb="*" path="*.gif"
         type="ImageGuardHandler"/>
    <add verb="*" path="*.png"
         type="ImageGuardHandler"/>
</httpHandlers>
```

■ **Note** This solution to leeching is far from perfect, but it serves to stop casual leechers. A programming-savvy user can easily circumvent it with a little JavaScript code. Some web developers create much more elaborate systems. For example, you can dynamically generate a timestamp code and append it to your image links whenever a page is requested. Your HTTP handler can then refuse to serve images if the timestamp is out of date, which suggests the link has been copied and is being reused on another page long after its creation time. However, none of these techniques can stop someone from creating a copy of the picture and serving it directly from their site.

Based on this example, you can probably imagine a variety of different ways you can use HTTP handlers. For example, you could render a custom image, perform an ad hoc database query, or return some binary data. These examples extend the ASP.NET architecture but bypass the web-page model. The result is a leaner, more efficient component.

You can also create HTTP handlers that work asynchronously. This means they create a new thread to do their work, instead of using one of the ASP.NET worker threads. This improves scalability in situations where you need to perform a task that takes a long time but isn't CPU-intensive. A classic example is waiting to read an extremely slow network resource. ASP.NET allows only a fixed number of worker threads (typically 25) to run at once. Once this limit is reached, additional requests will be queued, even if the computer has available CPU time.

With asynchronous handlers, additional requests can be accepted, because the handler creates a new thread to process each request rather than using the worker process. Of course, there is a risk with this approach. Namely, if you create too many threads for the computer to manage efficiently, or if you try to do too much CPU-intensive work at once, the performance of the entire web server will be adversely affected. Asynchronous HTTP handlers aren't covered in this book, but in Chapter 11 you'll learn how to use asynchronous pages, which use asynchronous HTTP handlers behind the scenes.

HTTP Handlers and Session State

By default, HTTP handlers do not have access to client-specific session state. That's because HTTP handlers are generally used for lower-level tasks, and skipping the steps needed to serialize and retrieve session state information achieves a minor increase in performance. However, if you do need access to session state information, you simply need to implement one of the following two interfaces:

- IRequiresSessionState
- IReadOnlySessionState

If you require just read-only access to session state, you should implement the IReadOnlySessionState interface. If you need to modify or add to session information, you should implement the IRequiresSessionState interface. You should never implement both at the same time.

These two interfaces are just marker interfaces and do not contain any methods. That means you don't need to write any extra code to enable session support. For example, if you want to use read-only session state with the SimpleHandler class, you would declare it in this way:

```
public class SimpleHandler : IHttpHandler, IReadOnlySessionState
{...}
```

To actually access the Session object, you'll need to work through the HttpContext object that's submitted to the ProcessRequest() method. It provides a Session property.

HTTP Modules

ASP.NET also uses another ingredient in page processing, called HTTP modules. HTTP modules participate in the processing of a request by handling application events, much like the global.asax file. ASP.NET uses a core set of HTTP modules to enable platform features such as caching, authentication, and error pages.

A given request can flow through multiple HTTP modules, but it always ends with a single HTTP handler. Figure 5-13 shows how the two interact.

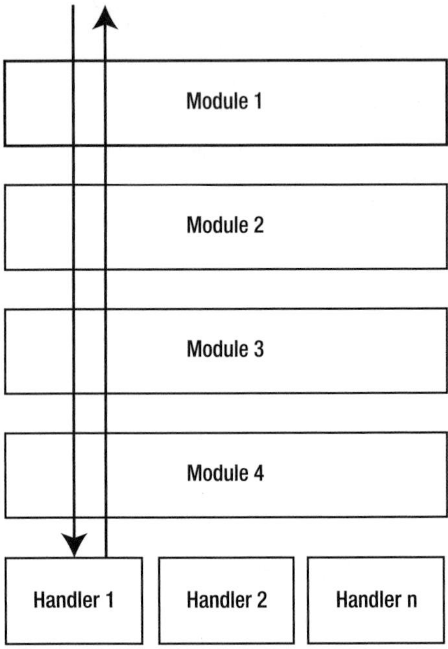

***Figure 5-13.** The ASP.NET request processing architecture*

If you're using Visual Studio's integrated web server, or if you're running an old version of IIS, or if you're running the IIS 7.x web server in classic mode, you need to add your HTTP modules to the <httpModules> section in the <system.web> element::

```
<configuration>
  <system.web>
    <httpModules>
      ...
    </httpModules>
    ...
  </system.web>
</configuration>
```

If you're running IIS 7.x in integrated mode, you use the <modules> section shown here instead:

```
<configuration>
  <system.web>
    ...
  </system.web>
  <system.webServer>
    <modules>
      ...
    </modules>
  </system.webServer>
</configuration>
```

Creating a Custom HTTP Module

It's just as easy to create custom HTTP modules as custom HTTP handlers. You simply need to author a class that implements the System.Web.IHttpModule interface. You can then register your module by adding it to the <httpModules> section of the web.config file. However, you don't need to configure IIS to use your HTTP modules. That's because modules are automatically used for every web request.

So, how does an HTTP module plug itself into the ASP.NET request processing pipeline? It does so in the same way as the global.asax file. Essentially, when an HTTP module is created, it registers to receive specific global application events. For example, if the module is concerned with authentication, it will register itself to receive the authentication events. Whenever those events occur, ASP.NET invokes all the interested HTTP modules. The HTTP module wires up its events with delegate code in the Init() method.

The IHttpModule interface defines the two methods shown in Table 5-6.

Table 5-6. *IHttpModule Members*

Member	Description
Init()	This method allows an HTTP module to register its event handlers to receive the events of the HttpApplication object. This method provides the current HttpApplication object for the request as a parameter.
Dispose()	This method gives an HTTP module an opportunity to perform any cleanup before the object gets garbage collected.

The following class is a custom HTTP module that handles the event HttpApplication.AuthenticateRequest and then logs the user information to a new entry in the Windows event log using the EventLog class from the System.Diagnostics namespace:

```
using System;
using System.Web;
using System.Diagnostics;

namespace HttpExtensions
{
    public class LogUserModule : IHttpModule
    {
        public void Init(HttpApplication httpApp)
        {
            // Attach application event handlers.
            httpApp.AuthenticateRequest += new EventHandler(OnAuthentication);
        }

        private void OnAuthentication(object sender, EventArgs a)
        {
            // Get the current user identity.
            string name = HttpContext.Current.User.Identity.Name;

            // Log the user name.
            EventLog log = new EventLog();
            log.Source = "Log User Module";
            log.WriteEntry(name + " was authenticated.");
```

```
        }

        public void Dispose()
        {}
    }
}
```

■ **Note** To use this example, the account used to run ASP.NET code must have permission to write to the event log. (More specifically, the account must have permission to modify the HKEY_Local_Machine\SYSTEM\CurrentControlSet\Services\EventLog registry key.) If you're using the Visual Studio test server, you'll need to explicitly run Visual Studio as an administrator (right-click the Visual Studio shortcut and choose Run As Administrator).

Now you can register the module with the following information in the web.config file. Here's an example that assumes it's compiled in a separate assembly named HttpExtensions.dll:

```
<configuration>
  <system.web>
    <httpModules>
      <add name="LogUserModule"
           type="HttpExtensions.LogUserModule,HttpExtensions" />
    </httpModules>
    ...
  </system.web>
</configuration>
```

To test this module, request any other page in the web application. Then check the entry in the Windows application event log. (To view the log, run the Event Viewer, which you find by searching the Start menu.

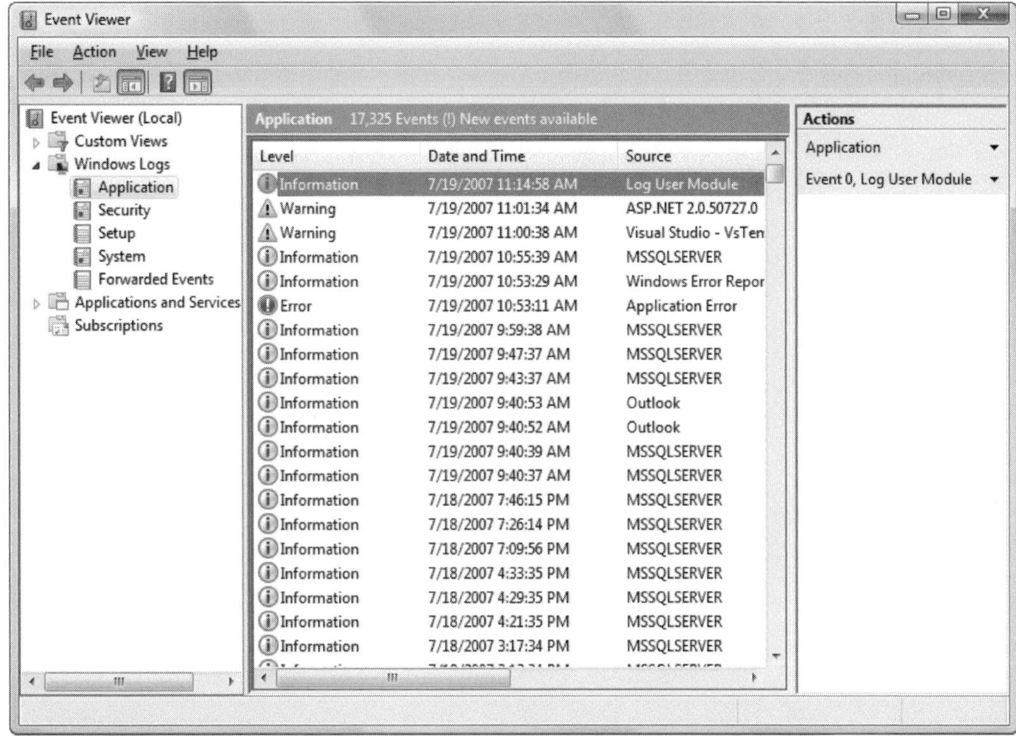

Figure 5-14. *Logging messages with an HTTP module*

Handling Events from Other Modules

The previous example shows how you can handle application events in a custom HTTP module. However, some global events aren't provided by the HttpApplication class but are still quite important. These include events raised by other HTTP modules, such as the events fired to start and end a session.

Fortunately, you can wire up to these events in the Init() event; you just need a slightly different approach. The HttpApplication class provides a collection of all the modules that are a part of the current HTTP pipeline through the Modules collection. You can retrieve a module by name and then use delegate code to connect an event handler.

For example, if you want to connect an event handler named OnSessionStart() to the SessionStateModule.Start event, you could use code like this for the Init() method in your HTTP module:

```
public void Init(HttpApplication httpApp)
{
    SessionStateModule sessionMod = (SessionStateModule)httpApp.Modules["Session"];
    sessionMod.Start += new EventHandler(OnSessionStart);
}
```

Summary

In this chapter, you took a closer look at what constitutes an ASP.NET application. After learning more about the life cycle of an application, you learned how to code global application event handlers with the global.asax file and how to set application configuration with the web.config file. Finally, you learned how to use separately compiled components in your web pages and how to extend the HTTP pipeline with your own handlers and modules.

CHAPTER 6

■ ■ ■

State Management

No web application framework, no matter how advanced, can change the fact that HTTP is a stateless protocol. After every web request, the client disconnects from the server, and the ASP.NET engine discards the objects that were created for the page. This architecture ensures that web applications can scale up to serve thousands of simultaneous requests without running out of server memory. The drawback is that your code needs to use other techniques to store information between web requests and retrieve it when needed.

In this chapter, you'll see how to tackle this challenge by maintaining information on the server and on the client using a variety of techniques. You'll also learn how to transfer information from one web page to another.

State Management Changes in ASP.NET 4

ASP.NET 4 adds a few refinements to its state management features:

Opt-in view state: ASP.NET 4 adds a ViewStateMode property that allows you to disable view state for a page but then selectively enable view state for those controls that absolutely require it. This opt-in model of view state is described in the "Selectively Disabling View State" section.

Session compression: ASP.NET 4 introduces a compression feature that reduces the size of data before it's sent to an out-of-process state provider. This feature is described in the "Compression" section.

Selectively enabling session state: ASP.NET 4 adds the HttpContext.SetSessionStateBehavior() method. You can create an HTTP module (as described in Chapter 5) that examines the current request and then calls SetSessionStateBehavior() to programmatically enable or disable session state. The idea here is to wring just a bit more performance out of your web application by disabling session state when it's not needed but still allowing it to work for some requests. However, this is a fairly specialized optimization technique that most developers won't use.

Partial session state: Session state now recognizes the concept of *partial* state storage and retrieval, which could theoretically allow you to pull just a single property out of a serialized object. As promising as this sounds, no current state providers support it, so you can't use this feature in your applications just yet. Microsoft may release session state providers that support this feature in future versions of ASP.NET or sooner—for example, with new products like Windows Server AppFabric (`http://tinyurl.com/yhds97y`).

ASP.NET State Management

ASP.NET includes a variety of options for state management. You choose the right option depending on the data you need to store, the length of time you want to store it, the scope of your data (whether it's limited to individual users or shared across multiple requests), and additional security and performance considerations. The different state management options in ASP.NET are complementary, which means you'll almost always use a combination of them in the same web application (and often the same page).

Table 6-1, Table 6-2, and Table 6-3 show an at-a-glance comparison of your state management options. You can review your options now, or you can use these tables as a reference after you work your way through the more detailed information in this chapter.

Table 6-1. *State Management Options Compared (Part 1)*

	View State	Query String	Custom Cookies
Allowed data types	All serializable .NET data types.	A limited amount of string data.	String data.
Storage location	A hidden field in the current web page.	The browser's URL string.	The client's computer (in memory or a small text file, depending on its lifetime settings).
Lifetime	Retained permanently for postbacks to a single page.	Lost when the user enters a new URL or closes the browser. However, can be stored and can persist between visits.	Set by the programmer. It can be used in multiple pages and it persists between visits.
Scope	Limited to the current page.	Limited to the target page.	The whole ASP.NET application.
Security	Tamper-proof by default but easy to read. You can use the Page directive to enforce encryption.	Clearly visible and easy for the user to modify.	Insecure and can be modified by the user.
Performance implications	Storing a large amount of information will slow transmission but will not affect server performance.	None, because the amount of data is trivial.	None, because the amount of data is trivial.
Typical use	Page-specific settings.	Sending a product ID from a catalog page to a details page.	Personalization preferences for a website.

Table 6-2. *State Management Options Compared (Part 2)*

	Session State	Application State
Allowed data types	All serializable .NET data types. Nonserializable types are supported if you are using the default in-process state service.	All .NET data types.
Storage location	Server memory (by default), or a dedicated database, depending on the mode you choose.	Server memory.
Lifetime	Times out after a predefined period (usually 20 minutes but can be altered globally or programmatically).	The lifetime of the application (typically, until the server is rebooted).
Scope	The whole ASP.NET application.	The whole ASP.NET application. Unlike most other types of methods, application data is global to all users.
Security	Secure, because data is never transmitted to the client. However, subject to session hijacking if you don't use SSL.	Very secure, because data is stored on the server.
Performance implications	Storing a large amount of information can slow down the server severely, especially if there are a large number of users at once, because each user will have a separate set of session data.	Storing a large amount of information can slow down the server, because this data will never time out and be removed.
Typical use	Store items in a shopping basket.	Storing any type of global data.

Table 6-3. *State Management Options Compared (Part 3)*

	Profiles	Caching
Allowed data types	All serializable .NET data types.	All .NET data types. Nonserializable types are supported if you create a custom profile.
Storage location	A back-end database.	Server memory.
Lifetime	Permanent.	Depends on the expiration policy you set, but may possibly be released early if server memory becomes scarce.

	Profiles	Caching
Scope	The whole ASP.NET application. May also be accessed by other applications.	The same as application state (global to all users and all pages).
Security	Fairly secure, because although data is never transmitted, it is stored without encryption in a database that could be compromised.	Very secure, because the cached data is stored on the server.
Performance implications	Large amounts of data can be stored easily, but there may be a nontrivial overhead in retrieving and writing the data for each request.	Storing a large amount of information may force out other, more useful cached information. However, ASP.NET has the ability to remove items early to ensure optimum performance.
Typical use	Store customer account information.	Storing data retrieved from a database.

Clearly, there's no shortage of choices for managing state in ASP.NET. Fortunately, most of these state management systems expose a similar collection-based programming interface. One notable exception is the *profiles* feature, which gives you a higher-level data model.

This chapter explores all the approaches to state management shown in Table 6-1 and Table 6-2, but not those in Table 6-3. Caching, an indispensable technique for optimizing access to limited resources such as databases, is covered in Chapter 11. Profiles, a higher-level model for storing user-specific information that works in conjunction with ASP.NET authentication, is covered in Chapter 24. However, before you can tackle either of these topics, you'll need to have a thorough understanding of state management basics.

In addition, you can write your own custom state management code and use server-side resources to store that information. The most common example of this technique is storing information in one or more tables in a database. The drawback with using server-side resources is that they tend to slow down performance and can hurt scalability. For example, opening a connection to a database or reading information from a file takes time. In many cases, you can reduce this overhead by supplementing your state management system with caching. You'll explore your options for using and enhancing database access code in Part 2.

View State

View state should be your first choice for storing information within the bounds of a single page. View state is used natively by the ASP.NET web controls. It allows them to retain their properties between postbacks. You can add your own data to the view state collection using a built-in page property called ViewState. The type of information you can store includes simple data types and your own custom objects.

Like most types of state management in ASP.NET, view state relies on a dictionary collection, where each item is indexed with a unique string name. For example, consider this code:

```
ViewState["Counter"] = 1;
```

This places the value 1 (or rather, an integer that contains the value 1) into the ViewState collection and gives it the descriptive name Counter. If there is currently no item with the name Counter, a new item will be added automatically. If there is already an item indexed under the name Counter, it will be replaced.

When retrieving a value, you use the key name. You also need to cast the retrieved value to the appropriate data type. This extra step is required because the ViewState collection casts all items to the base Object type, which allows it to handle any type of data.

Here's the code that retrieves the counter from view state and converts it to an integer:

```
int counter;
if (ViewState["Counter"] != null)
{
    counter = (int)ViewState["Counter"];
}
```

If you attempt to look up a value that isn't present in the collection, you'll receive a NullReferenceException. To defend against this possibility, you should check for a null value before you attempt to retrieve and cast data that may not be present.

■ **Note** ASP.NET provides many collections that use the same dictionary syntax. This includes the collections you'll use for session and application state as well as those used for caching and cookies. You'll see several of these collections in this chapter.

A View State Example

The following code demonstrates a page that uses view state. It allows the user to save a set of values (all the text that's displayed in all the text boxes of a table) and restore it later. This example uses recursive logic to dig through all child controls, and it uses the control ID for the view state key, because this is guaranteed to be unique in the page.

Here's the complete code:

```
public partial class ViewStateTest : System.Web.UI.Page
{
    protected void cmdSave_Click(object sender, System.EventArgs e)
    {
        // Save the current text.
        SaveAllText(Table1.Controls, true);
    }

    private void SaveAllText(ControlCollection controls, bool saveNested)
    {
        foreach (Control control in controls)
        {
            if (control is TextBox)
            {
                // Store the text using the unique control ID.
                ViewState[control.ID] = ((TextBox)control).Text;
            }

            if ((control.Controls != null) && saveNested)
            {
```

```
                SaveAllText(control.Controls, true);
            }
        }
    }

    protected void cmdRestore_Click(object sender, System.EventArgs e)
    {
        // Retrieve the last saved text.
        RestoreAllText(Table1.Controls, true);
    }

    private void RestoreAllText(ControlCollection controls, bool saveNested)
    {
        foreach (Control control in controls)
        {
            if (control is TextBox)
            {
                if (ViewState[control.ID] != null)
                  ((TextBox)control).Text = (string)ViewState[control.ID];
            }
            if ((control.Controls != null) && saveNested)
            {
                RestoreAllText(control.Controls, true);
            }
        }
    }
}
```

Figure 6-1 shows the page in action.

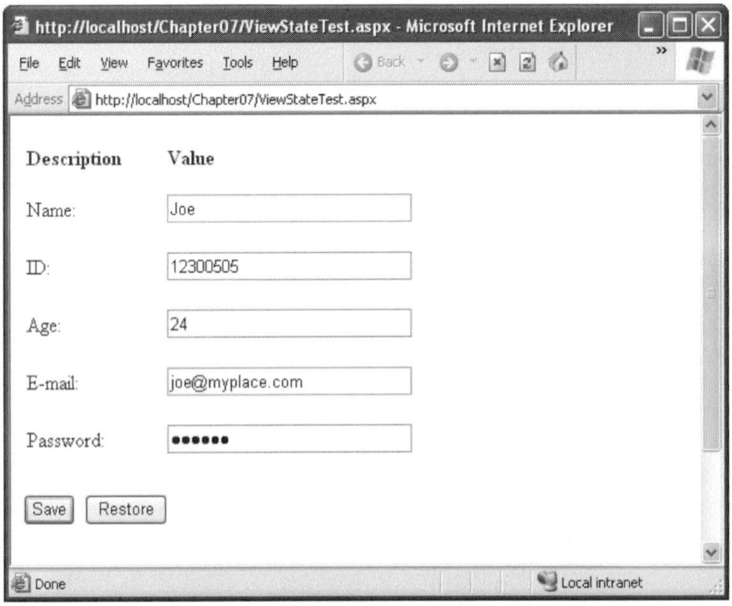

Figure 6-1. *Saving and restoring text using view state*

Storing Objects in View State

You can store your own objects in view state just as easily as you store numeric and string types. However, to store an item in view state, ASP.NET must be able to convert it into a stream of bytes so that it can be added to the hidden input field in the page. This process is called serialization. If your objects aren't serializable (and by default they aren't), you'll receive an error message when you attempt to place them in view state.

To make your objects serializable, you need to add the Serializable attribute before your class declaration. For example, here's an exceedingly simple Customer class:

```
[Serializable]
public class Customer
{
    public string FirstName;
    public string LastName;

    public Customer(string firstName, string lastName)
    {
        FirstName = firstName;
        LastName = lastName;
    }
}
```

Because the Customer class is marked as serializable, it can be stored in view state:

```
// Store a customer in view state.
Customer cust = new Customer("Marsala", "Simons");
ViewState["CurrentCustomer"] = cust;
```

Remember, when using custom objects, you'll need to cast your data when you retrieve it from view state.

```
// Retrieve a customer from view state.
Customer cust;
cust = (Customer)ViewState["CurrentCustomer"];
```

For your classes to be serializable, you must meet these requirements:

- Your class must have the Serializable attribute.
- Any classes it derives from must have the Serializable attribute.
- All the member variables of the class must use serializable data types. Any nonserializable data type must be decorated with the NonSerialized attribute (which means it is simply ignored during the serialization process).

Once you understand these principles, you'll also be able to determine what .NET objects can be placed in view state. You simply need to find the class information in the MSDN Help. Find the class you're interested in, and examine the documentation. If the class declaration is preceded with the Serializable attribute, the object can be placed in view state. If the Serializable attribute isn't present, the object isn't serializable, and you won't be able to store it in view state. However, you may still be able to use other types of state management, such as in-process session state, which is described later in the "Session State" section.

The following example rewrites the page shown earlier to use the generic Dictionary class. The Dictionary class is a serializable key-value collection that's provided in the System.Collections.Generic namespace. As long as you use the Dictionary to store serializable objects (and use a serializable data type for your keys), you can store a Dictionary object in view state without a hitch.

To demonstrate this technique, the following example stores all the control information for the page as a collection of strings in a Dictionary object, and it indexes each item by string using the control ID. The final Dictionary object is then stored in the view state for the page. When the user clicks the Display button, the dictionary is retrieved, and all the information it contains is displayed in a label.

```
public partial class ViewStateObjects : System.Web.UI.Page
{
    protected void cmdSave_Click(object sender, System.EventArgs e)
    {
        // Put the text in the Dictionary.
        Dictionary<string,string> textToSave = new Dictionary<string,string>();
        SaveAllText(Table1.Controls, textToSave, true);

        // Store the entire collection in view state.
        ViewState["ControlText"] = textToSave;
    }

    private void SaveAllText(ControlCollection controls,
      Dictionary<string, string> textToSave, bool saveNested)
    {
        foreach (Control control in controls)
        {
            if (control is TextBox)
            {
                // Add the text to the Dictionary.
                textToSave.Add(control.ID, ((TextBox)control).Text);
            }
            if ((control.Controls != null) && saveNested)
            {
                SaveAllText(control.Controls, textToSave, true);
            }
        }
    }

    protected void cmdDisplay_Click(object sender, System.EventArgs e)
    {
        if (ViewState["ControlText"] != null)
        {
            // Retrieve the Dictionary.
            Dictionary<string, string> savedText =
              (Dictionary<string, string>)ViewState["ControlText"];

            // Display all the text by looping through the Dictionary.
            lblResults.Text = "";
            foreach (KeyValuePair<string, string> item in savedText)
            {
                lblResults.Text += item.Key + " = " + item.Value + "<br />";
            }
        }
    }
}
```

Figure 6-2 shows the result of a simple test, after entering some data, saving it, and retrieving it.

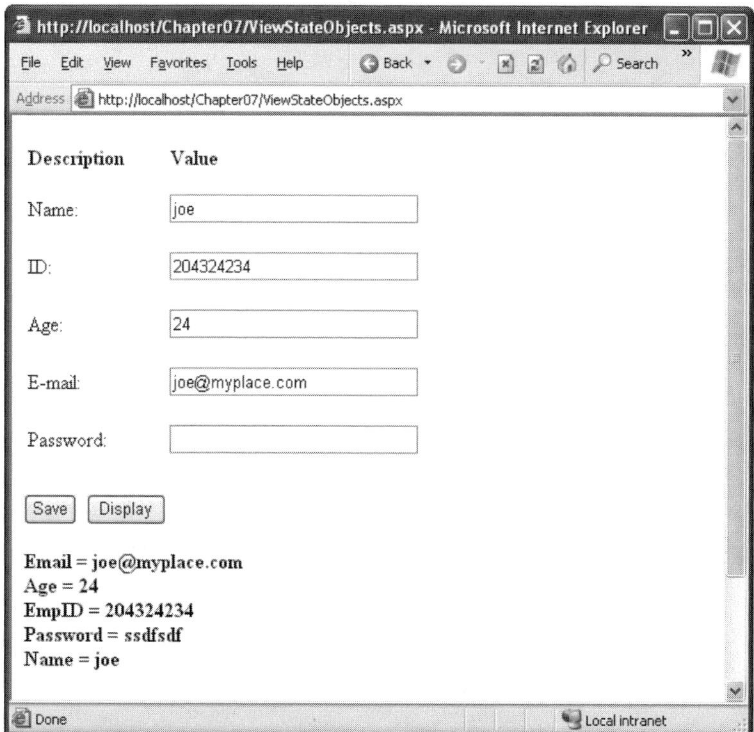

Figure 6-2. Retrieving an object from view state

Assessing View State

View state is ideal because it doesn't take up any memory on the server and doesn't impose any arbitrary usage limits (such as a time-out). So, what might force you to abandon view state for another type of state management? Here are three possible reasons:

- You need to store mission-critical data that the user cannot be allowed to tamper with. (An ingenious user could modify the view state information in a postback request.) In this case, consider session state. Alternatively, consider using the countermeasures described in the next section. They aren't bulletproof, but they will greatly increase the effort an attacker would need in order to read or modify view state data.
- You need to store information that will be used by multiple pages. In this case, consider session state, cookies, or the query string.
- You need to store an extremely large amount of information, and you don't want to slow down page transmission times. In this case, consider using a database, or possibly session state.

The amount of space used by view state depends on the number of controls, their complexity, and the amount of dynamic information. If you want to profile the view state usage of a page, just turn on tracing by adding the Trace attribute to the Page directive, as shown here:

```
<%@ Page Language="C#" Trace="true" ... %>
```

Look for the Control Tree section. Although it doesn't provide the total view state used by the page, it does indicate the view state used by each individual control in the Viewstate Size Bytes column (see Figure 6-3). Don't worry about the Render Size Bytes column, which simply reflects the size of the rendered HTML for the control.

■ **Tip** You can also examine the contents of the current view state of a page using the Web Development Helper described in Chapter 2.

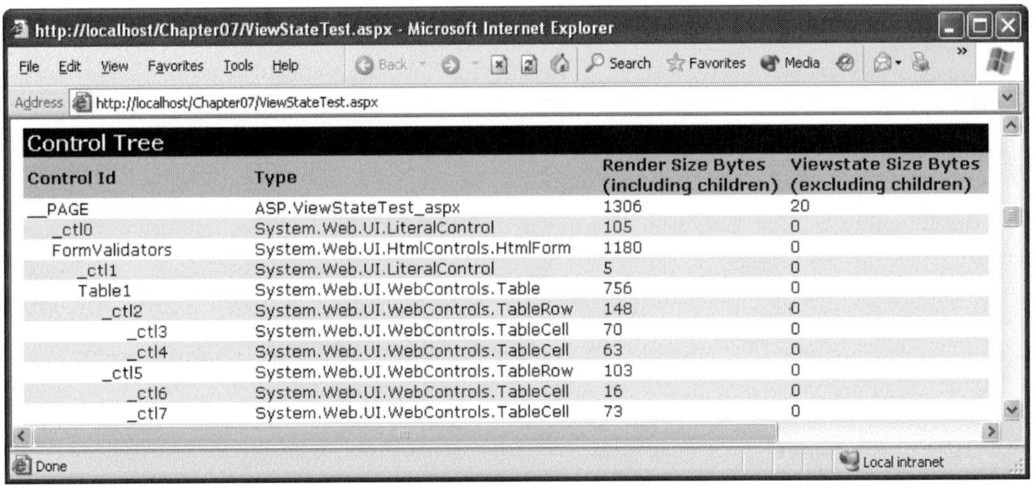

http://localhost/Chapter07/ViewStateTest.aspx - Microsoft Internet Explorer

Control Tree

Control Id	Type	Render Size Bytes (including children)	Viewstate Size Bytes (excluding children)
__PAGE	ASP.ViewStateTest_aspx	1306	20
_ctl0	System.Web.UI.LiteralControl	105	0
FormValidators	System.Web.UI.HtmlControls.HtmlForm	1180	0
_ctl1	System.Web.UI.LiteralControl	5	0
Table1	System.Web.UI.WebControls.Table	756	0
_ctl2	System.Web.UI.WebControls.TableRow	148	0
_ctl3	System.Web.UI.WebControls.TableCell	70	0
_ctl4	System.Web.UI.WebControls.TableCell	63	0
_ctl5	System.Web.UI.WebControls.TableRow	103	0
_ctl6	System.Web.UI.WebControls.TableCell	16	0
_ctl7	System.Web.UI.WebControls.TableCell	73	0

Figure 6-3. *Determining the view state used in a page*

Selectively Disabling View State

To improve the transmission times of your page, it's a good idea to eliminate view state when it's not needed. Although you can disable view state at the application and page level, it makes the most sense to disable it on a per-control basis. You won't need view state for a control in three instances:

- The control never changes. For example, a button with static text doesn't need view state.
- The control is repopulated in every postback. For example, if you have a label that shows the current time, and you set the current time in the Page.Load event handler, it doesn't need view state.

- The control is an input control, and it changes only because of user actions. After each postback, ASP.NET will populate your input controls using the submitted form values. This means the text in a text box or the selection in a list box won't be lost, even if you don't use view state.

■ **Tip** Remember that view state applies to *all* the values that change, not just the text displayed in the control. For example, if you dynamically change the colors used in a label, these changes are stored in view state, even if you don't dynamically set the text. (Technically, it's the control's responsibility to use view state. That means it is possible to create a server control that doesn't retain certain values, even if view state is enabled. However, the ASP.NET web controls always store changed values in view state.)

To turn off view state for a single control, set the EnableViewState property of the control to false. To turn off view state for an entire page and all its controls, set the EnableViewState property of the page to false, or use the EnableViewState attribute in the Page directive, as shown here:

```
<%@ Page Language="C#" EnableViewState="false" ... %>
```

Even when you disable view state for the entire page, you'll still see the hidden view state tag with a small amount of information in the rendered HTML. That's because ASP.NET always stores the control hierarchy for the page at a minimum. There's no way to remove this last little fragment of data.

You can turn view state off for all the web pages in your application by setting the enableViewState attribute of the <pages> element in the web.config file, as shown here:

```
<configuration>
  <system.web>
    <pages enableViewState="false" />
    ...
  </system.web>
</configuration>
```

Now, you'll need to set the EnableViewState attribute of the Page directive to true if you want to switch on view state for a particular page.

Finally, it's possible to switch of view state for a page (either through the Page directive or through the web.config file) but selectively override that setting by explicitly enabling view state for a particular control. This technique, which is new in ASP.NET 4, is popular with developers who are obsessed with paring down the view state of their pages to the smallest size possible. It allows you to switch on view state only when it's absolutely necessary—for example, with a data editing control such as the GridView (which uses view state to keep track of the currently selected item, among other details).

To use this approach, you need to use another property, called ViewStateMode. Like EnableViewState, the ViewStateMode property applies to all controls and page and can be set in a control tag or through an attribute in the page directive. ViewStateMode takes one of three values:

Enabled: View state will work, provided the EnableViewState property allows it.

Disabled: View state will not work for this control, although it may be allowed for child controls.

Inherit: This control will use the ViewStateMode property of its container. This is the default value.

To use opt-in state management, you set ViewStateMode of the page to Disabled. This turns off view state for the top-level page. By default, all the controls inside the page will have a ViewStateMode of Inherit, which means they also disable themselves.

```
<%@ Page Language="C#" ViewStateMode="Disabled" ... %>
```

Note that you do *not* set EnableViewState to false—if you do, ASP.NET completely shuts down view state for the page, and no control can opt in.

Now, to opt in for a particular control in the page, you simply set ViewStateMode to Enabled:

```
<asp:Label ViewStateMode="Enabled" ... />
```

This model is a bit awkward, but it's useful when view state size is an issue. The only drawback is that you need to remember to explicitly enable view state on controls that have dynamic values you want to persist or on controls that use view state for part of their functionality.

View State Security

As described in earlier chapters, view state information is stored in a single Base64-encoded string that looks like this:

```
<input type="hidden" name="__VIEWSTATE"
 id="__VIEWSTATE" value="dDw3NDg2NTI5MDg7Oz4="/>
```

Because this value isn't formatted as clear text, many ASP.NET programmers assume that their view state data is encrypted. It isn't. A malicious user could reverse-engineer this string and examine your view state data in a matter of seconds, as demonstrated in Chapter 3.

If you want to make view state secure, you have two choices. First, you can make sure that the view state information is tamper-proof by using a *hash code*.

A hash code is a cryptographically strong checksum. Essentially, ASP.NET calculates this checksum based on the current view state content and adds it to the hidden input field when it returns the page. When the page is posted back, ASP.NET recalculates the checksum and ensures that it matches. If a malicious user changes the view state data, ASP.NET will be able to detect the change, and it will reject the postback.

Hash codes are enabled by default, so if you want this functionality, you don't need to take any extra steps. Occasionally, developers choose to disable this feature to prevent problems in a web farm where different servers have different keys. (The problem occurs if the page is posted back and handled by a new server, which won't be able to verify the view state information.) To disable hash codes, you can use the EnableViewStateMAC property of the Page directive in your .aspx file:

```
<%@ Page EnableViewStateMac="false" ... %>
```

Alternatively, you can set the enableViewStateMac attribute of the <pages> element in the web.config file, as shown here:

```
<configuration>
  <system.web>
    <pages enableViewStateMac="false" />
    ...
  </system.web>
</configuration>
```

■ **Note** This step is strongly discouraged. It's much better to configure multiple servers to use the same key, thereby removing any problem. Chapter 5 describes how to do this.

Even when you use hash codes, the view state data will still be readable. To prevent users from getting any view state information, you can enable view state encryption. You can turn on encryption for an individual page using the ViewStateEncryptionMode property of the Page directive:

```
<%@Page ViewStateEncryptionMode="Always" ... %>
```

Or you can set the same attribute in the web.config configuration file:

```
<pages viewStateEncryptionMode="Always" />
```

Either way, this enforces encryption. You have three choices for your view state encryption setting—always encrypt (Always), never encrypt (Never), or encrypt only if a control specifically requests it (Auto). The default is Auto, which means that the page won't encrypt its view state unless a control on that page specifically requests it. To request encryption, a control must call the Page.RegisterRequiresViewStateEncryption() method at some point during its life cycle, before it's renders itself to HTML. If no control calls this method to indicate it has sensitive information, the view state is not encrypted, thereby saving the encryption overhead. However, the control doesn't have absolute power—if it calls Page.RegisterRequiresViewStateEncryption() and the encryption mode of the page is Never, the view state won't be encrypted.

When hashing or encrypting data, ASP.NET uses the computer-specific key defined in the <machineKey> section of the machine.config file, which is described in Chapter 5. By default, you won't actually see the definition for the <machineKey> because it's initialized programmatically. However, you can see the equivalent content in the machine.config.comments files, and you can explicitly add the <machineKey> element if you want to customize its settings.

■ **Tip** Don't encrypt view state data if you don't need to do so. The encryption will impose a performance penalty, because the web server needs to perform the encryption and decryption with each postback.

Transferring Information Between Pages

One of the most significant limitations with view state is that it's tightly bound to a specific page. If the user navigates to another page, this information is lost. This problem has several solutions, and the best approach depends on your requirements. In the following sections, you'll see how to pass information from one page to the next using the query string and cross-page posting. If neither of these techniques is right for your scenario, you'll need to use a form of state management that has a broader scope, such as cookies, session state, or application state, all of which are discussed later in this chapter.

The Query String

One common approach is to pass information using a query string in the URL. You will commonly find this approach in search engines. For example, if you perform a search on the Google website, you'll be redirected to a new URL that incorporates your search parameters. Here's an example:

```
http://www.google.ca/search?q=organic+gardening
```

The query string is the portion of the URL after the question mark. In this case, it defines a single variable named q, which contains the "organic+gardening" string.

The advantage of the query string is that it's lightweight and doesn't exert any kind of burden on the server. Unlike cross-page posting, the query string can easily transport the same information from page to page. It has some limitations, however:

- Information is limited to simple strings, which must contain URL-legal characters.
- Information is clearly visible to the user and to anyone else who cares to eavesdrop on the Internet.
- The enterprising user might decide to modify the query string and supply new values, which your program won't expect and can't protect against.
- Many browsers impose a limit on the length of a URL (usually from 1 to 2 KB). For that reason, you can't place a large amount of information in the query string and still be assured of compatibility with most browsers.

Adding information to the query string is still a useful technique. It's particularly well suited in database applications where you present the user with a list of items corresponding to records in a database, like products. The user can then select an item and be forwarded to another page with detailed information about the selected item. One easy way to implement this design is to have the first page send the item ID to the second page. The second page then looks that item up in the database and displays the detailed information. You'll notice this technique in e-commerce sites such as Amazon.com.

Using the Query String

To store information in the query string, you need to place it there yourself. Unfortunately, there is no collection-based way to do this. Typically, this means using a special HyperLink control, or you can use a Response.Redirect() statement like the one shown here:

```
// Go to newpage.aspx. Submit a single query string argument
// named recordID and set to 10.
int recordID = 10;
Response.Redirect("newpage.aspx?recordID=" + recordID.ToString());
```

You can send multiple parameters as long as you separate them with an ampersand (&), as shown here:

```
// Go to newpage.aspx. Submit two query string arguments:
// recordID (10) and mode (full).
Response.Redirect("newpage.aspx?recordID=10&mode=full");
```

The receiving page has an easier time working with the query string. It can receive the values from the QueryString dictionary collection exposed by the built-in Request object, as shown here:

```
string ID = Request.QueryString["recordID"];
```

If the query string doesn't contain the recordID parameter, or if the query string contains the recordID parameter but doesn't supply a value, the ID string will be set to null.

Note that information is always retrieved as a string, which can then be converted to another simple data type. Values in the QueryString collection are indexed by the variable name.

■ **Note** Unfortunately, ASP.NET does not expose any mechanism to automatically verify or encrypt query string data. This facility could work in almost the same way as the view state protection. Without these features, query string data is easily subject to tampering. In Chapter 25, you'll take a closer look at the .NET cryptography classes and learn how you can use them to build a truly secure query string.

URL Encoding

One potential problem with the query string is using characters that aren't allowed in a URL. The list of characters that are allowed in a URL is much shorter than the list of allowed characters in an HTML document. All characters must be alphanumeric or one of a small set of special characters (including *$-_.+!*'(),*). Some browsers tolerate certain additional special characters (Internet Explorer is notoriously lax), but many do not. Furthermore, some characters have special meaning. For example, the ampersand (&) is used to separate multiple query string parameters, the plus sign (+) is an alternate way to represent a space, and the number sign (#) is used to point to a specific bookmark in a web page. If you try to send query string values that include any of these characters, you'll lose some of your data.

If you're concerned that the data you want to store in the query string may not consist of URL-legal characters, you should use URL encoding. With URL encoding, special characters are replaced by escaped character sequences starting with the percent sign (%), followed by a two-digit hexadecimal representation. The only exception is the space character, which can be represented as the character sequence %20 or the + sign.

You can use the methods of the HttpServerUtility class to encode your data automatically. For example, the following shows how you would encode a string of arbitrary data for use in the query string. This replaces all the nonlegal characters with escaped character sequences.

```
string productName = "Flying Carpet";
Response.Redirect("newpage.aspx?productName=" + Server.UrlEncode(productName));
```

You can use the HttpServerUtility.UrlDecode() method to return a URL-encoded string to its initial value. However, you don't need to take this step with the query string because ASP.NET automatically decodes your values when you access them through the Request.QueryString collection. Usually, it's safe to call UrlDecode() a second time, because decoding data that's already decoded won't cause a problem. The only exception is if you have a value that legitimately includes the + sign. In this case, calling UrlDecode() will convert the + sign to a space.

Cross-Page Posting

You've already learned how ASP.NET pages post back to themselves. When a page is posted back, it sends the current content of all the controls in the form for that page (including the contents of the hidden view state field). To transfer information from one page to another, you can use the same postback mechanism, but send the information to a different page. This technique sounds conceptually straightforward, but it's a potential minefield. If you're not careful, it can lead you to create pages that are tightly coupled to one another and difficult to enhance and debug.

The infrastructure that supports cross-page postbacks is a property named PostBackUrl, which is defined by the IButtonControl interface and turns up in button controls such as ImageButton, LinkButton, and Button. To use cross-page posting, you simply set PostBackUrl to the name of another web form. When the user clicks the button, the page will be posted to that new URL with the values from all the input controls on the current page.

Here's an example that defines a form with two text boxes and a button that posts to a page named CrossPage2.aspx:

```
<%@ Page Language="C#" AutoEventWireup="true" CodeFile="CrossPage1.aspx.cs"
    Inherits="CrossPage1" %>
<html xmlns="http://www.w3.org/1999/xhtml">
<head runat="server">
    <title>CrossPage1</title>
</head>
<body>
    <form id="form1" runat="server" >
      <div>
        <asp:TextBox runat="server" ID="txtFirstName"></asp:TextBox>  
        <asp:TextBox runat="server" ID="txtLastName"></asp:TextBox>
        <asp:Button runat="server" ID="cmdSubmit"
         PostBackUrl="CrossPage2.aspx" Text="Submit" />
      </div>
    </form>
</body>
</html>
```

In CrossPage2.aspx, the page can interact with the CrossPage1.aspx objects using the Page.PreviousPage property. Here's an example:

```
protected void Page_Load(object sender, EventArgs e)
{
    if (PreviousPage != null)
    {
        lblInfo.Text = "You came from a page titled " +
          PreviousPage.Header.Title;
    }
}
```

Note that this page checks for a null reference before attempting to access the PreviousPage object. If there's no PreviousPage object, there's no cross-page postback.

ASP.NET uses some interesting sleight of hand to make this system work. The first time the second page accesses Page.PreviousPage, ASP.NET needs to create the previous page object. To do this, it actually starts the page processing life cycle, but interrupts it just before the PreRender stage. Along the way, a stand-in HttpResponse object is created to silently catch and ignore any Response.Write() commands from the previous page. However, there are still some interesting side effects. For example, all the page events of the previous page are fired, including Page.Load, Page.Init, and even the Button.Click event for the button that triggered the postback (if it's defined). Firing these events is mandatory, because they are required to properly initialize the page.

■ **Note** Trace messages aren't ignored like Response messages are, which means you may see tracing information from both pages in a cross-posting situation.

Getting Page-Specific Information

In the previous example, the information you can retrieve from the previous page is limited to the members of the Page class. If you want to get more specific details, such as control values, you need to cast the PreviousPage reference to the appropriate type.

Here's an example that handles this situation properly, by checking first if the PreviousPage object is an instance of the expected source (CrossPage1):

```
protected void Page_Load(object sender, EventArgs e)
{
    CrossPage1 prevPage = PreviousPage as CrossPage1;
    if (prevPage != null)
    {
        // (Read some information from the previous page.)
    }
}
```

■ **Note** In a projectless website, Visual Studio may flag this as an error, indicating that it does not have the type information for the source page class (in this example, that's CrossPage1). However, once you compile the website, the error will disappear.

You can solve this problem in another way. Rather than casting the reference manually, you can add the PreviousPageType control directive to your page, which indicates the expected type of the page initiating the cross-page postback. Here's an example:

```
<%@ PreviousPageType VirtualPath="CrossPage1.aspx" %>
```

However, this approach is more fragile because it limits you to a single type. You don't have the flexibility to deal with situations where more than one page might trigger a cross-page postback. For that reason, the casting approach is preferred.

■ **Tip** Seeing as the PostBackUrl property can point to only one page, it may seem that cross-page posting can accommodate a fixed relationship between just two pages. However, you can extend this relationship with various techniques. For example, you can modify the PostBackUrl property programmatically to choose a different target. Conversely, a cross-post target can test the PreviousPage property, checking if it is one of several different classes. You can then perform different tasks depending on what page initiated the cross-post.

Once you've cast the previous page to the appropriate page type, you still won't be able to directly access the control values. That's because the controls are declared as protected members. You can handle this by adding properties to the page class that wrap the control variables, like this:

```
public TextBox FirstNameTextBox
{
    get { return txtFirstName; }
}
public TextBox LastNameTextBox
{
    get { return txtLastName; }
}
```

However, this usually isn't the best approach. The problem is that it exposes too many details, giving the target page the freedom to read every control property. If you need to change the page later to use different input controls, it's difficult to maintain these properties. Instead, you'll probably be forced to rewrite code in both pages.

A better choice is to define specific, limited methods or properties that extract just the information you need. Here's an example:

```
public string FullName
{
    get { return txtFirstName.Text + " " + txtLastName.Text; }
}
```

This way, the relationship between the two pages is well documented and easily understood. If the controls in the source page are changed, you can probably still keep the same interface for the public methods or properties. For example, if you changed the name entry to use different controls in the previous example, you would still be forced to revise the FullName property. However, once your changes would be confined to CrossPage1.aspx, you wouldn't need to modify CrossPage2.aspx at all.

■ **Tip** In some cases, a better alternative to cross-page posting is to use some sort of control that simulates multiple pages or multiple steps, such as separate Panel controls or the MultiView or Wizard control. This offers much the same user experience and simplifies the coding model. You'll learn about these controls in Chapter 17.

Performing Cross-Page Posting in Any Event Handler

As you learned in the previous section, cross-page posting is available only with controls that implement the IButtonControl interface. However, there is a workaround. You can use an overloaded method of Server.Transfer() to switch to a new ASP.NET page with the view state information left intact. You simply need to include the Boolean preserveForm parameter and set it to true, as shown here:

```
Server.Transfer("CrossPage2.aspx", true);
```

This gives you the opportunity to use cross-page posting anywhere in your web-page code. As with any call to Server.Transfer(), this technique causes a server-side redirect. That means there is no extra roundtrip to redirect the client. As a disadvantage, the original page URL (from the source page) remains in the user's browser even though you've moved on to another page.

Interestingly, there is a way to distinguish between a cross-page post that's initiated directly through a button and the Server.Transfer() method. Although in both cases you can access Page.PreviousPage, if you use Server.Transfer(), the Page.PreviousPage.IsCrossPagePostBack property is false. Here's the code that demonstrates how this logic works:

```
if (PreviousPage == null)
{
    // The page was requested (or posted back) directly.
}
else if (PreviousPage.IsCrossPagePostBack)
{
    // A cross-page postback was triggered through a button.
}
else
{
    // A stateful transfer was triggered through Server.Transfer().
}
```

The IsPostBack and IsCrossPagePostBack Properties

It's important to understand how the Page.IsPostBack property works during a cross-page postback. For the source page (the one that triggered the cross-page postback), the IsPostBack property is true. For the destination page (the one that's receiving the postback), the IsPostBack property is false. One benefit of this system is that it means your initialization code will usually run when it should.

For example, imagine CrossPage1.aspx performs some time-consuming initialization the first time it's requested, using code like this:

```
protected void Page_Load(object sender, EventArgs e)
{
    if (!IsPostBack)
    {
        // (Retrieve some data from a database and display it on the page.)
    }
}
```

Now imagine the user moves from CrossPage1.aspx to CrossPage2.aspx through a cross-page postback. As soon as CrossPage2.aspx accesses the PreviousPage property, the page life cycle executes for CrossPage1.aspx. At this point, the Page.Load event fires for CrossPage1.aspx. However, on CrossPage1.aspx the Page.IsPostBack property is true, so your code skips the time-consuming initialization steps. Instead, the control values are restored from view state. On the other hand, the Page.IsPostBack property for CrossPage2.aspx is false, so this page performs the necessary first-time initialization.

In some situations, you might have code that you want to execute for the first request and all subsequent postbacks *except* when the page is the source of a cross-page postback. In this case, you can check the IsCrossPagePostBack property. This property is true if the current page triggered a cross-page postback.

That means you can use code like this in CrossPage1.aspx:

```
protected void Page_Load(object sender, EventArgs e)
{
    if (IsCrossPagePostBack)
    {
        // This page triggered a postback to CrossPage2.aspx.
```

```
        // Don't perform time-consuming initialization unless it affects
        // the properties that the target page will read.
    }
    else if (IsPostBack)
    {
        // This page was posted back normally.
        // Don't do the first-request initialization.
    }
    else
    {
        // This is the first request for the page.
        // Perform all the required initialization.
    }
}
```

There is a trick that allows you to avoid running the life cycle of the source page if you simply want to read one of its control values. You can get the control value directly from the Request collection using the control's ID. For example, Request["txtName"] gets the value of the text box named txtName, even though that text box is located on the previous page. However, retrieving Request["txtName"] *won't* cause ASP.NET to instantiate the source page and fire its events.

Before you use this approach, you should consider two serious caveats. First, you need to make sure you use the client-side control ID, which is slightly different from the server-side control ID if the control is nested inside a naming container such as a master page, data control, and so on (if in doubt, check the rendered HTML). The second, more serious consideration is that this approach violates good object-oriented practices; this approach is extremely fragile. If the source page is modified even slightly, this technique may fail, and you won't discover the problem until you run this code. As a rule, it's always better to restrict interaction between different classes to public properties and methods.

Cross-Page Posting and Validation

Cross-page posting introduces a few wrinkles when you use it in conjunction with the validator controls described in Chapter 4. As you learned in Chapter 4, when you use the validator controls, you need to check the Page.IsValid property to ensure that the data the user entered is correct. Although users are usually prevented from posting invalid pages back to the server (thanks to some slick client-side JavaScript), this isn't always the case. For example, the client browser might not support JavaScript, or a malicious user could deliberately circumvent the client-side validation checks.

When you use validation in a cross-page posting scenario, the potential for some trouble exists. Namely, what happens if you use a cross-page postback and the source page has validation controls? Figure 6-4 shows an example with a RequiredFieldValidator that requires input in a text box.

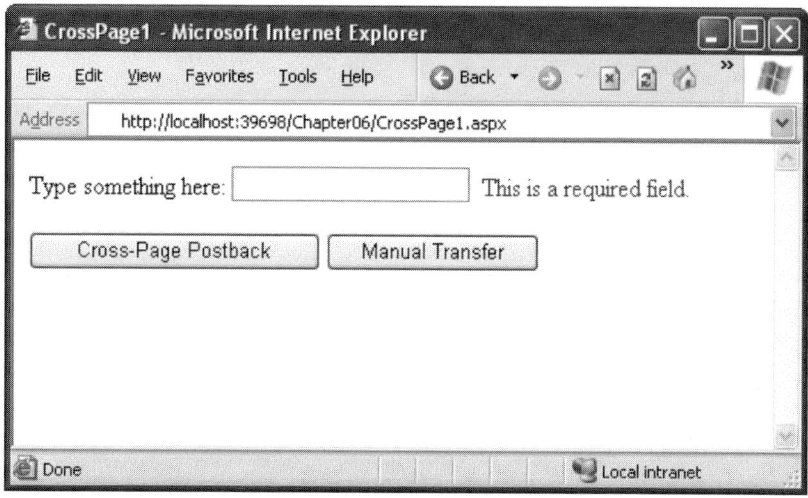

***Figure 6-4.** Using a validator in a page that cross-posts*

Both buttons have CausesValidation set to true. As a result, if you click the button to perform a cross-page postback, you'll be prevented by the browser's client-side checks. Instead, the error message will appear. However, you should also check what happens when client-side script isn't supported by setting the RequiredFieldValidator.EnableClientScript property to false. (You can change it back to true once you perfect your code.) Now when you click one of the buttons, the page is posted back, and the new page appears.

To prevent this from happening, you obviously need to check the validity of the source page in the target page by examining Page.IsValid before you perform any other action. This is the standard line of defense used in any web form that employs validation. The difference is that if the page isn't valid, it's not sufficient to do nothing. Instead, you need to take the extra step of returning the user to the original page. Here's the code you need in the destination page:

```
// This code is in the target page.
protected void Page_Load(object sender, EventArgs e)
{
    // Check the validity of the previous page.
    if (PreviousPage != null)
    {
        if (!PreviousPage.IsValid)
        {
            // Display an error message or just do nothing.
        }
        else
        { ... }
    }
}
```

It's still possible to improve on this code. Currently, when the user is returned to the original page, the error message won't appear, because the page is being re-requested (not posted back). To correct this issue, you can set a flag to let the source page know the page has been refused by the target page. Here's an example that adds this flag to the query string:

```
if (!PreviousPage.IsValid)
{
    Response.Redirect(Request.UrlReferrer.AbsolutePath + "?err=true");
}
```

Now the original page simply needs to check for the presence of this query string value and perform the validation accordingly. The validation causes error messages to appear for any invalid data.

```
// This code is in the source page.
protected void Page_Load(object sender, EventArgs e)
{
    if (Request.QueryString["err"] != null)
      Page.Validate();
}
```

You could do still more to try to improve the page. For example, if the user is in the midst of filling out a detailed form, re-requesting the page isn't a good idea, because it clears all the input controls and forces the user to start again from scratch. Instead, you might want to write a little bit of JavaScript code to the response stream, which could use the browser's back feature to return to the source page. Chapter 29 has more about JavaScript.

■ **Tip** This example demonstrates that cross-page postbacks are often trickier than developers first expect. If not handled carefully, cross-page postbacks can lead you to build tightly coupled pages that have subtle dependencies on one another, which makes it more difficult to change them in the future. As a result, think carefully before you decide to use cross-page postbacks as a method to transfer information.

Cookies

Custom cookies provide another way you can store information for later use. Cookies are small files that are created on the client's hard drive (or, if they're temporary, in the web browser's memory). One advantage of cookies is that they work transparently without the user being aware that information needs to be stored. They also can be easily used by any page in your application and even retained between visits, which allows for truly long-term storage. They suffer from some of the same drawbacks that affect query strings. Namely, they're limited to simple string information, and they're easily accessible and readable if the user finds and opens the corresponding file. These factors make them a poor choice for complex or private information or large amounts of data.

Some users disable cookies on their browsers, which will cause problems for web applications that require them. However, cookies are widely adopted because so many sites use them.

Cookies are fairly easy to use. Both the Request and Response objects (which are provided through Page properties) provide a Cookies collection. The important trick to remember is that you retrieve cookies from the Request object, and you set cookies using the Response object.

To set a cookie, just create a new System.Net.HttpCookie object. You can then fill it with string information (using the familiar dictionary pattern) and attach it to the current web response, as follows:

```
// Create the cookie object.
HttpCookie cookie = new HttpCookie("Preferences");

// Set a value in it.
cookie["LanguagePref"] = "English";

// Add another value.
cookie["Country"] = "US";

// Add it to the current web response.
Response.Cookies.Add(cookie);
```

A cookie added in this way will persist until the user closes the browser and will be sent with every request. To create a longer-lived cookie (which is stored with the temporary Internet files on the user's hard drive), you can set an expiration date, as shown here:

```
// This cookie lives for one year.
cookie.Expires = DateTime.Now.AddYears(1);
```

Cookies are retrieved by cookie name using the Request.Cookies collection, as shown here:

```
HttpCookie cookie = Request.Cookies["Preferences"];

// Check to see whether a cookie was found with this name.
// This is a good precaution to take,
// because the user could disable cookies,
// in which case the cookie would not exist.
string language;
if (cookie != null)
{
    language = cookie["LanguagePref"];
}
```

The only way to remove a cookie is by replacing it with a cookie that has an expiration date that has already passed. The following code demonstrates this technique:

```
HttpCookie cookie = new HttpCookie("LanguagePref");
cookie.Expires = DateTime.Now.AddDays(-1);
Response.Cookies.Add(cookie);
```

■ **Note** You'll find that some other ASP.NET features use cookies. Two examples are session state (which allows you to temporarily store user-specific information in server memory) and forms security (which allows you to restrict portions of a website and force users to access it through a login page).

Session State

Session state is the heavyweight of state management. It allows information to be stored in one page and accessed in another, and it supports any type of object, including your own custom data types. Best of all, session state uses the same collection syntax as view state. The only difference is the name of the built-in page property, which is Session.

Every client that accesses the application has a different session and a distinct collection of information. Session state is ideal for storing information such as the items in the current user's shopping basket when the user browses from one page to another. But session state doesn't come for free. Though it solves many of the problems associated with other forms of state management, it forces the web server to store additional information in memory. This extra memory requirement, even if it is small, can quickly grow to performance-destroying levels as thousands of clients access the site.

Session Architecture

Session management is not part of the HTTP standard. As a result, ASP.NET needs to do some extra work to track session information and bind it to the appropriate response.

ASP.NET tracks each session using a unique 120-bit identifier. ASP.NET uses a proprietary algorithm to generate this value, thereby guaranteeing (statistically speaking) that the number is unique and that it's random enough so a malicious user can't reverse-engineer or guess what session ID a given client will be using. This ID is the only piece of information that is transmitted between the web server and the client. When the client presents the session ID, ASP.NET looks up the corresponding session, retrieves the serialized data from the state server, converts it to live objects, and places these objects into a special collection so they can be accessed in code. This process takes place automatically.

■ **Note** Every time you make a new request, ASP.NET generates a new session ID until you actually use session state to store some information. This behavior achieves a slight performance enhancement—in short, why bother to save the session ID if it's not being used?

At this point you're probably wondering where ASP.NET stores session information and how it serializes and deserializes it. In classic ASP, the session state is implemented as a free-threaded COM object that's contained in the asp.dll library. In ASP.NET, the programming interface is nearly identical, but the underlying implementation is quite a bit different.

As you saw in Chapter 5, when ASP.NET handles an HTTP request, it flows through a pipeline of different modules that can react to application events. One of the modules in this chain is the SessionStateModule (in the System.Web.SessionState namespace). The SessionStateModule generates the session ID, retrieves the session data from external state providers, and binds the data to the call context of the request. It also saves the session state information when the page is finished processing. However, it's important to realize that the SessionStateModule doesn't actually *store* the session data. Instead, the session state is persisted in external components, which are named *state providers*. Figure 6-5 shows this interaction.

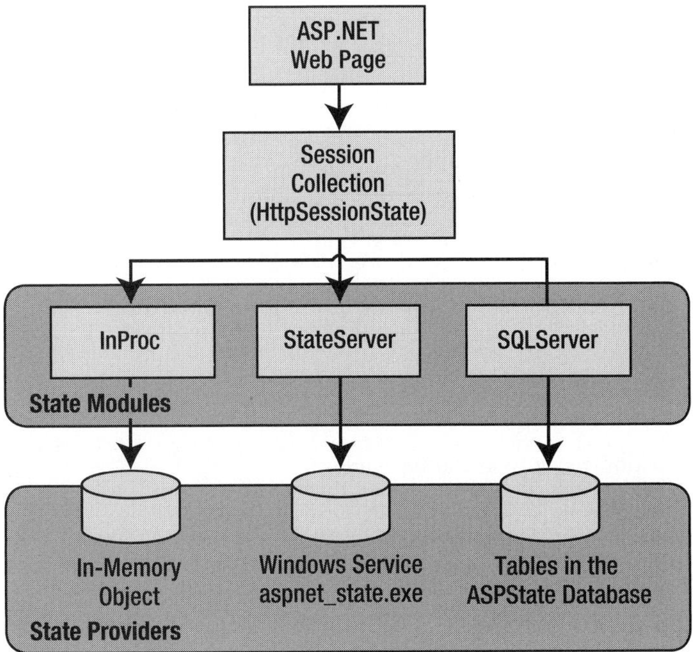

Figure 6-5. *ASP.NET session state architecture*

Session state is another example of ASP.NET's pluggable architecture. A state provider is any class that implements the IHttpSessionState interface, which means you can customize how session state works simply by building (or purchasing) a new .NET component. ASP.NET includes three prebuilt state providers, which allow you to store information in process, in a separate service, or in a SQL Server database.

For session state to work, the client needs to present the appropriate session ID with each request. The final ingredient in the puzzle is how the session ID is tracked from one request to the next. You can accomplish this in two ways:

Using cookies: In this case, the session ID is transmitted in a special cookie (named ASP.NET_SessionId), which ASP.NET creates automatically when the session collection is used. This is the default, and it's also the same approach that was used in earlier versions of ASP.

Using modified URLs: In this case, the session ID is transmitted in a specially modified (or "munged") URL. This allows you to create applications that use session state with clients that don't support cookies.

You'll learn more about how to configure cookieless sessions and different session state providers later in the "Configuring Session State" section.

Using Session State

You can interact with session state using the System.Web.SessionState.HttpSessionState class, which is provided in an ASP.NET web page as the built-in Session object. The syntax for adding items to the collection and retrieving them is basically the same as for adding items to the view state of a page.

For example, you might store a DataSet in session memory like this:

```
Session["ProductsDataSet"] = dsProducts;
```

You can then retrieve it with an appropriate conversion operation:

```
dsProducts = (DataSet)Session["ProductsDataSet"];
```

Session state is global to your entire application for the current user. Session state can be lost in several ways:

- If the user closes and restarts the browser.
- If the user accesses the same page through a different browser window, although the session will still exist if a web page is accessed through the original browser window. Browsers differ on how they handle this situation.
- If the session times out because of inactivity. By default, a session times out after 20 idle minutes.
- If the programmer ends the session by calling Session.Abandon().

In the first two cases, the session actually remains in memory on the server, because the web server has no idea that the client has closed the browser or changed windows. The session will linger in memory, remaining inaccessible, until it eventually expires.

In addition, session state will be lost when the application domain is re-created. This process happens transparently when you update your web application or change a configuration setting. The application domain may also be recycled periodically to ensure application health, as described in Chapter 18. If this behavior is causing a problem, you can store session state information out of process, as described in the next section. With out-of-process state storage, the session information is retained even when the application domain is shut down.

Table 6-4 describes the key methods and properties of the HttpSessionState class.

Table 6-4. *HttpSessionState Members*

Member	Description
Count	The number of items in the current session collection.
IsCookieless	Identifies whether this session is tracked with a cookie or with modified URLs.
IsNewSession	Identifies whether this session was just created for the current request. If there is currently no information in session state, ASP.NET won't bother to track the session or create a session cookie. Instead, the session will be re-created with every request.
Mode	Provides an enumerated value that explains how ASP.NET stores session state information. This storage mode is determined based on the web.config configuration settings discussed later in this chapter.
SessionID	Provides a string with the unique session identifier for the current client.
StaticObjects	Provides a collection of read-only session items that were declared by <object runat="server"> tags in the global.asax file. Generally, this technique isn't used and is a holdover from ASP programming that is included for backward compatibility.

Member	Description
Timeout	The current number of minutes that must elapse before the current session will be abandoned, provided that no more requests are received from the client. This value can be changed programmatically, giving you the chance to make the session collection longer term when required for more important operations.
Abandon()	Cancels the current session immediately and releases all the memory it occupied. This is a useful technique in a logoff page to ensure that server memory is reclaimed as quickly as possible.
Clear()	Removes all the session items but doesn't change the current session identifier.

Configuring Session State

You can configure session state through the <sessionState> element in the web.config file for your application. Here's a snapshot of all the available settings you can use:

```
<?xml version="1.0" encoding="utf-8" ?>
<configuration>
    <system.web>
        <!-- Other settings omitted. -->

        <sessionState
            mode="Off|InProc|StateServer|SQLServer|Custom"
            stateConnectionString="tcpip=127.0.0.1:42424"
            stateNetworkTimeout="10"
            sqlConnectionString="data source=127.0.0.1;Integrated Security=SSPI"
            sqlCommandTimeout="30" allowCustomSqlDatabase="false"
            useHostingIdentity="true|false"
            compressionEnabled="true|false"
            cookieless="UseCookies" cookieName="ASP.NET_SessionId"
            regenerateExpiredSessionId="true|false"
            timeout="20"
            customProvider=""
        />
    </system.web>
</configuration>
```

The session attributes are described in the following sections.

Mode

The mode session state settings allow you to configure what session state provider is used to store session state information between requests. The following sections explain your options.

Off

This setting disables session state management for every page in the application. This can provide a slight performance improvement for websites that are not using session state.

InProc

InProc is similar to how session state was stored in classic ASP. It instructs ASP.NET to store information in the current application domain. This provides the best performance but the least durability. If you restart your server, the state information will be lost.

InProc is the default option, and it makes sense for most small websites. In a web farm scenario, though, it won't work at all. To allow session state to be shared between servers, you must use the out-of-process or SQL Server state service. Another reason you might want to avoid InProc mode is because it makes for more fragile sessions. In ASP.NET, application domains are recycled in response to a variety of actions, including configuration changes, updated pages, and when certain thresholds are met (regardless of whether an error has occurred). If you find that your application domain is being restarted frequently and contributing to prematurely lost sessions, you can change to one of the more robust session state providers.

Before you use either the out-of-process or the SQL Server state service, keep in mind that more considerations will apply:

- When using the StateServer or SQLServer mode, the objects you store in session state must be serializable. Otherwise, ASP.NET will not be able to transmit the object to the state service or store it in the database.
- If you're hosting ASP.NET on a web farm, you'll also need to take some extra configuration steps to make sure all the web servers are in sync. Otherwise, one might encode information in session state differently than another, which will cause a problem if the user is routed from one server to another during a session. The solution is to modify the <machineKey> section of the machine.config file so it's consistent across all servers. For more information, refer to Chapter 5.
- If you aren't using the in-process state provider, the SessionStateModule.End event won't be fired, and any event handlers for this event in the global.asax file or an HTTP module will be ignored.

StateServer

With this setting, ASP.NET will use a separate Windows service for state management. Even if you run this service on the same web server, it will be loaded outside the main ASP.NET process, which gives it a basic level of protection if the ASP.NET process needs to be restarted. The cost is the increased time delay imposed when state information is transferred between two processes. If you frequently access and change state information, this can make for a fairly unwelcome slowdown.

When using the StateServer setting, you need to specify a value for the stateConnectionString setting. This string identifies the TCP/IP address of the computer that is running the StateServer service and its port number (which is defined by ASP.NET and doesn't usually need to be changed). This allows you to host the StateServer on another computer. If you don't change this setting, the local server will be used (set as address 127.0.0.1).

Of course, before your application can use the service, you need to start it. The easiest way to do this is to use the Microsoft Management Console. Select Start ➤ Programs ➤ Administrative Tools ➤ Computer Management (you can also access the Administrative Tools group through the Control Panel). Then, in the Computer Management tool, find the Services and Applications ➤ Services node. Find the service called ASP.NET State Service in the list, as shown in Figure 6-6.

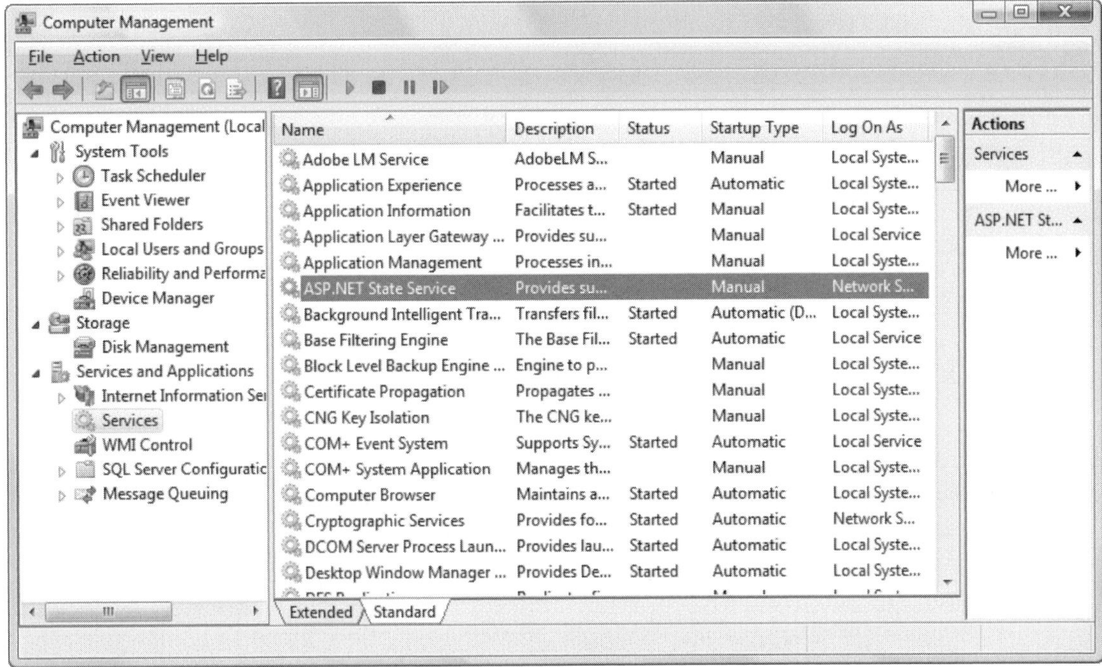

Figure 6-6. The ASP.NET state service

Once you find the service in the list, you can manually start and stop it by right-clicking it. Generally, you'll want to configure Windows to automatically start the service. Right-click it, select Properties, and modify the Startup Type setting to Automatic, as shown in Figure 6-7. Then click Start to start it immediately.

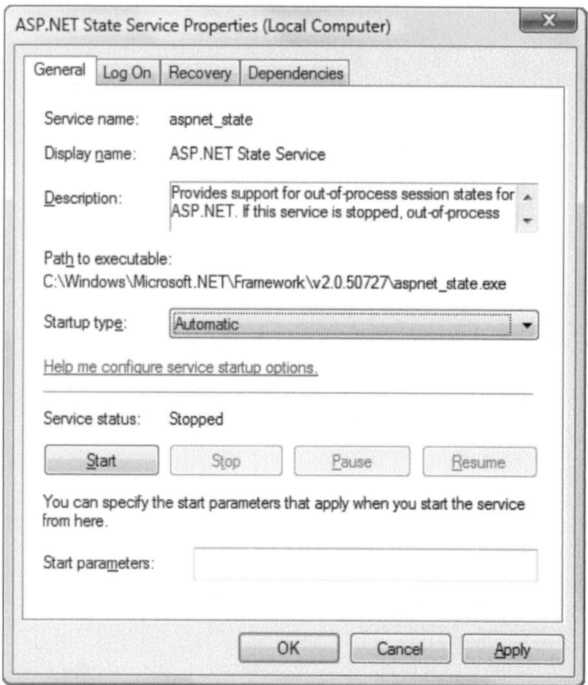

Figure 6-7. Service properties

■ **Note** When using StateServer mode, you can also set an optional stateNetworkTimeout attribute that specifies the maximum number of seconds to wait for the service to respond before canceling the request. The default is 10 seconds.

SQLServer

This setting instructs ASP.NET to use a SQL Server database to store session information, as identified by the sqlConnectionString attribute. This is the most resilient state store but also the slowest by far. To use this method of state management, you'll need to have a server with SQL Server installed.

When setting the sqlConnectionString, you follow the same sort of pattern you use with ADO.NET data access (which is described in Part 2). Generally, you'll need to specify a data source (the server address) and a user ID and password, unless you're using SQL integrated security.

In addition, you need to install the special stored procedures and temporary session databases. These stored procedures take care of storing and retrieving the session information. ASP.NET includes a command-line tool that does the work for you automatically, called aspnet_regsql.exe. It's found in the c:\Windows\Microsoft.NET\Framework\[Version] directory. The easiest way to run aspnet_regsql.exe is to start by launching the Visual Studio command prompt (open the Start menu and choose Programs ➤ Visual Studio 2010 ➤ Visual Studio Tools ➤ Visual Studio 2010 Command Prompt). You can then type in an aspnet_regsql.exe command, no matter what directory you're in.

You can use the aspnet_regsql.exe tool to perform several different database-related tasks. As you travel through this book, you'll see how to use aspnet_regsql.exe with ASP.NET features such as caching (Chapter 11), membership (Chapter 21), and profiles (Chapter 24). To use aspnet_regsql.exe to create a session storage database, you supply the -ssadd parameter. In addition, you use the -S parameter to indicate the database server name, and the -E parameter to log in to the database using the currently logged in Windows user account.

Here's a command that creates the session storage database on the current computer, using the default database name ASPState:

```
aspnet_regsql.exe -S localhost -E -ssadd
```

This command uses the alias localhost, which tells aspnet_regsql.exe to connect to the database server on the current computer. You can replace this detail with the computer name of your database server.

Once you've created your session state database, you need to tell ASP.NET to use it by modifying the <sessionState> section of the web.config file. If you're using a database named ASPState to store your session information (which is the default), you don't need to supply the database name. Instead, you simply need to indicate the location of the server and the type of authentication that ASP.NET should use to connect to it, as shown here:

```
<sessionState mode="SQLServer"
 sqlConnectionString="data source=localhost;Integrated Security=SSPI" ... />
```

This completes the setup procedure. However, you can alter these steps slightly if you want to use persistent sessions or use a custom database, as you'll see next.

■ **Tip** To remove the ASPState database, use the -ssremove parameter.

Ordinarily, the standard session state time-out still applies to SQL Server state management. That's because the aspnet_regsql.exe tool also creates a new SQL Server job named ASPState_Job_DeleteExpiredSessions. As long as the SQLServerAgent service is running, this job will be executed every minute.

Additionally, the state tables will be removed every time you restart SQL Server, no matter what the session time-out. That's because the state tables are created in the tempdb database, which is a temporary storage area. If this isn't the behavior you want, you can tell the aspnet_regsql.exe tool to install permanent state tables in the ASPState database. To do this, you use the -sstype p (for persisted) parameter. Here's the revised command line:

```
aspnet_regsql.exe -S localhost -E -ssadd -sstype p
```

Now session records will remain in the database, even if you restart SQL Server.

Your final option is to use aspnet_regsql.exe to create the state tables in a different database (not ASPState). To do so, you use the -sstype c (for custom) parameter, and then supply the database name with the -d parameter, as shown here:

```
aspnet_regsql.exe -S localhost -E -ssadd -sstype c -d MyCustomStateDb
```

When you use this approach, you'll create permanent session tables, so their records will remain even when SQL Server is restarted.

If you use a custom database, you'll also need to make two configuration tweaks to the <sessionState> element in your application's web.config file. First, you must set allowCustomSqlDatabase to true. Second, you must make sure the connection string includes the Initial Catalog setting, which indicates the name of the database you want to use. Here's the correctly adjusted element:

```
<sessionState Mode="SQLServer" allowCustomSqlDatabase="true" sqlConnectionString=
"data source=localhost;Integrated Security=SSPI;Initial Catalog=MyCustomStateDb"
... />
```

■ **Tip** When using the SqlServer mode, you can also set an optional sqlCommandTimeout attribute that specifies the maximum number of seconds to wait for the database to respond before canceling the request. The default is 30 seconds.

Custom

When using custom mode, you need to indicate what session state store provider to use by supplying the customProvider attribute. The customProvider attribute points to the name of a class that's part of your web application in the App_Code directory, or in a compiled assembly in the Bin directory or the GAC.

The most common reasons to use a custom session state provider are to store session information in a database other than SQL Server or to use an existing table in a database that has a specific schema. Creating a custom state provider is a low-level task that needs to be handled carefully to ensure security, stability, and scalability, so it's always best to use a prebuilt provider that has been designed and tested by a reliable third party rather than roll your own.

Custom state providers are also beyond the scope of this book. However, if you'd like to try creating your own, you can find an overview at `http://msdn2.microsoft.com/en-us/library/aa479034.aspx`.

Compression

ASP.NET includes a compression feature that allows you to reduce the size of serialized session data. When you set enableCompression to true, session data is compressed (using the System.IO.Compressio.GZipStream class) before it's passed out of process. The enableCompression setting has an effect only when you're using out-of-process session state storage, because it's only in this situation that the data is serialized.

To compress and decompress session data, the web server needs to perform additional work. However, this isn't usually a problem, because compression is used in scenarios where web servers have plenty of CPU time to spare but are limited by other factors. There are two key scenarios where session-state compression makes sense:

When storing huge amounts of session state data in memory: Web server memory is a precious resource. Ideally, session state is used for relatively small chunks of information, while a back-end database deals with the long-term storage of larger amounts of data. But if this isn't the case and if the out-of-process state server is hogging huge amounts of memory, compression is a potential solution.

When storing session state data on another computer: In some large-scale web applications, session state is stored out of process (usually in SQL Server) and on a separate computer. As a result, ASP.NET needs to pass the session information back and forth over a network connection. Clearly, this design reduces performance from the speeds you'll see when session state is stored on the web server computer. However, it's still the best compromise for some heavily trafficked web applications with huge session state storage needs.

In the first scenario, compression sacrifices CPU work for web server memory. In the second scenario, compression sacrifices CPU work for network bandwidth.

The actual amount of compression varies greatly depending on the type of data, but in testing Microsoft saw clients achieve 30 percent to 60 percent size reductions, which guarantees a significant performance benefit in these scenarios.

Cookieless

You can set the cookieless setting to one of the values defined by the HttpCookieMode enumeration, as described in Table 6-5. You can also set the name that's used for the cookie with the cookieName attribute. If you don't, the default value cookie name is ASP.NET_SessionId.

Table 6-5. *HttpCookieMode Values*

Value	Description
UseCookies	Cookies are always used, even if the browser or device doesn't support cookies or they are disabled. This is the default. If the device does not support cookies, session information will be lost over subsequent requests, because each request will get a new ID.
UseUri	Cookies are never used, regardless of the capabilities of the browser or device. Instead, the session ID is stored in the URL.
UseDeviceProfile	ASP.NET chooses whether to use cookieless sessions by examining the BrowserCapabilities object. The drawback is that this object indicates what the device should support—it doesn't take into account that the user may have disabled cookies in a browser that supports them. Chapter 27 has more information about how ASP.NET identifies different browsers and decides whether they support features such as cookies.
AutoDetect	ASP.NET attempts to determine whether the browser supports cookies by attempting to set and retrieve a cookie (a technique commonly used on the Web). This technique can correctly determine if a browser supports cookies but has them disabled, in which case cookieless mode is used instead.

Here's an example that forces cookieless mode (which is useful for testing):

```
<sessionState cookieless="UseUri" ... />
```

In cookieless mode, the session ID will automatically be inserted into the URL. When ASP.NET receives a request, it will remove the ID, retrieve the session collection, and forward the request to the appropriate directory. A munged URL is shown here:

```
http://localhost/WebApplication/(amfvyc55evojk455cffbq355)/Page1.aspx
```

Because the session ID is inserted in the current URL, relative links also automatically gain the session ID. In other words, if the user is currently stationed on Page1.aspx and clicks a relative link to Page2.aspx, the relative link includes the current session ID as part of the URL. The same is true if you call Response.Redirect() with a relative URL, as shown here:

```
Response.Redirect("Page2.aspx");
```

The only real limitation of cookieless state is that you cannot use absolute links, because they will not contain the session ID. For example, this statement causes the user to lose all session information:

```
Response.Redirect("http://localhost/WebApplication/Page2.aspx");
```

By default, ASP.NET allows you to reuse a session identifier. For example, if you make a request and your query string contains an expired session, ASP.NET creates a new session and uses that session ID. The problem is that a session ID might inadvertently appear in a public place—such as in a results page in a search engine. This could lead to multiple users accessing the server with the same session identifier and then all joining the same session with the same shared data.

To avoid this potential security risk, it's recommended that you include the optional regenerateExpiredSessionId attribute and set it to true whenever you use cookieless sessions. This way, a new session ID will be issued if a user connects with an expired session ID. The only drawback is that this process also forces the current page to lose all view state and form data, because ASP.NET performs a redirect to make sure the browser has a new session identifier.

■ **Note** You can test if a cookieless session is currently being used by checking the IsCookieless property of the Session object.

Timeout

Another important session state setting in the web.config file is the timeout. This specifies the number of minutes that ASP.NET will wait, without receiving a request, before it abandons the session.

```
<sessionState timeout="20" ... />
```

This setting represents one of the most important compromises of session state. A difference of minutes can have a dramatic effect on the load of your server and the performance of your application. Ideally, you will choose a time frame that is short enough to allow the server to reclaim valuable memory after a client stops using the application but long enough to allow a client to pause and continue a session without losing it.

You can also programmatically change the session time-out in code. For example, if you know a session contains an unusually large amount of information, you may need to limit the amount of time the session can be stored. You would then warn the user and change the timeout property. Here's a sample line of code that changes the time-out to ten minutes:

```
Session.Timeout = 10;
```

Securing Session State

The information in session state is very secure, because it is stored exclusively on the server. However, the cookie with the session ID can easily become compromised. This means an eavesdropper could steal the cookie and assume the session on another computer.

Several workarounds address this problem. One common approach is to use a custom session module that checks for changes in the client's IP address. However, the only truly secure approach is to restrict session cookies to portions of your website that use SSL. That way, the session cookie is encrypted and useless on other computers.

If you choose to use this approach, it also makes sense to mark the session cookie as a secure cookie so that it will be sent only over SSL connections. That prevents the user from changing the URL from `https://` to `http://`, which would send the cookie without SSL. Here's the code you need:

```
Request.Cookies["ASP.NET_SessionId"].Secure = true;
```

Typically, you'll use this code immediately after the user is authenticated. Make sure there is at least one piece of information in session state so the session isn't abandoned (and then re-created later).

Another related security risk exists with cookieless sessions. Even if the session ID is encrypted, a clever user could use a social engineering attack to trick a user into joining a specific session. All the malicious user needs to do is feed the user a URL with a valid session ID. When the user clicks the link, he joins that session. Although the session ID is protected from this point onward, the attacker now knows what session ID is in use and can hijack the session at a later time.

Taking certain steps can reduce the likelihood of this attack. First, when using cookieless sessions, always set regenerateExpiredSessionId to true. This prevents the attacker from supplying a session ID that's expired. Next, explicitly abandon the current session before logging in a new user.

Application State

Application state allows you to store global objects that can be accessed by any client. Application state is based on the System.Web.HttpApplicationState class, which is provided in all web pages through the built-in Application object.

Application state is similar to session state. It supports the same types of objects, retains information on the server, and uses the same dictionary-based syntax. A common example with application state is a global counter that tracks how many times an operation has been performed by all of the web application's clients.

For example, you could create a global.asax event handler that tracks how many sessions have been created or how many requests have been received into the application. Or you can use similar logic in the Page.Load event handler to track how many times a given page has been requested by various clients. Here's an example of the latter:

```
protected void Page_Load(Object sender, EventArgs e)
{
    int count = 0;
    if (Application["HitCounterForOrderPage"] != null)
        count = (int)Application["HitCounterForOrderPage"];

    count++;
    Application["HitCounterForOrderPage"] = count;
    lblCounter.Text = count.ToString();
}
```

Once again, application state items are stored as objects, so you need to cast them when you retrieve them from the collection. Items in application state never time out. They last until the application or server is restarted or until the application domain refreshes itself (because of automatic process-recycling settings or an update to one of the pages or components in the application).

Application state isn't often used, because it's generally inefficient. In the previous example, the counter would probably not keep an accurate count, particularly in times of heavy traffic. For example, if two clients requested the page at the same time, you could have a sequence of events like this:

1. User A retrieves the current count (432).
2. User B retrieves the current count (432).

3. User A sets the current count to 433.

4. User B sets the current count to 433.

In other words, one request isn't counted because two clients access the counter at the same time. To prevent this problem, you need to use the Lock() and UnLock() methods, which explicitly allow only one client to access the Application state collection at a time, as follows:

```
protected void Page_Load(Object sender, EventArgs e)
{
    // Acquire exclusive access.
    Application.Lock();

    int count = 0;
    if (Application["HitCounterForOrderPage"] != null)
        count = (int)Application["HitCounterForOrderPage"];

    count++;
    Application["HitCounterForOrderPage"] = count;

    // Release exclusive access.
    Application.UnLock();

    lblCounter.Text = count.ToString();
}
```

Unfortunately, all other clients requesting the page will now be stalled until the Application collection is released. This can drastically reduce performance. Generally, frequently modified values are poor candidates for application state. In fact, application state is rarely used in the .NET world because its two most common uses have been replaced by easier, more efficient methods:

- In the past, application state was used to store application-wide constants, such as a database connection string. As you saw in Chapter 5, this type of constant can now be stored in the web.config file, which is generally more flexible because you can change it easily without needing to hunt through web-page code or recompile your application.

- Application state can also be used to store frequently used information that is time-consuming to create, such as a full product catalog that requires a database lookup. However, using application state to store this kind of information raises all sorts of problems about how to check if the data is valid and how to replace it when needed. It can also hamper performance if the product catalog is too large. A similar but much more sensible approach is to store frequently used information in the ASP.NET cache. Many uses of application state can be replaced more efficiently with caching.

Application state information is always stored in process. This means you can use any .NET data types. However, it also introduces the same two limitations that affect in-process session state. Namely, you can't share application state between the servers in a web farm, and you will always lose your application state information when the application domain is restarted—an event that can occur as part of ASP.NET's normal housekeeping.

■ **Note** Application state is included primarily for backward compatibility with classic ASP. In new applications, it's almost always better to rely on other mechanisms for global data, such as using databases in conjunction with the Cache object.

Static Application Variables

You can store global application variables in one other way. You can add static member variables to the global.asax file (which was introduced in Chapter 5). These members are then compiled into the custom HttpApplication class for your web application and made available to all pages. Here's an example that declares a static array of strings:

```
public static string[] FileList;
```

The key detail that allows this to work is that the variable is static. That's because ASP.NET creates a pool of HttpApplication classes to serve multiple requests. As a result, each request might be served with a different HttpApplication object, and each HttpApplication object has its own instance data. However, there is only one copy of the static data, which is shared for all instances (on the same web server).

There's another requirement to make this strategy work. The rest of your code needs to be able to access the static members you've added to your custom application class. To make this possible, you need to specify the name that should be used for that class. To do this, you set the ClassName property of the Application directive, which is at the start of the global.asax file. Here's an example that gives the application class the name Global:

```
<%@ Application Language="C#" ClassName="Global" %>
```

Now you can write code like this in your web pages:

```
string firstEntry = Global.FileList[0];
```

To improve this example, and get better encapsulation (and more flexibility), you should use property procedures in your application class instead of public member variables. Here's the corrected code:

```
private static string[] fileList;
public static string[] FileList
{
    get { return fileList; }
}
```

When you add a member variable to the global.asax file, it has essentially the same characteristics as a value in the Application collection. In other words, you can use any .NET data type, the value is retained until the application domain is restarted, and state isn't shared across computers in a web farm. However, there's no automatic locking. Because multiple clients might try to access or modify a value at the same time, you should use the C# lock statement to temporarily restrict the variable to a single thread. Depending on how your data is accessed, you might perform the locking in the web page (in which case you could perform several tasks at once with the locked data) or in the property procedures or methods in the global.asax file (in which case the lock would be held for the shortest possible time).

Here's an example that uses two methods to manage access to a private dictionary of metadata. These methods ensure that the global collection is always accessed in a thread-safe manner:

```
private static Dictionary<string, string> metadata =
  new Dictionary<string, string>();

public void AddMetadata(string key, string value)
{
    lock (metadata)
    {
        metadata[key] = value;
    }
}

public string GetMetadata(string key)
{
    lock (metadata)
    {
        return metadata[key];
    }
}
```

Using static member variables instead of the Application collection has two advantages. First, it allows you to write custom code that runs automatically when the value is accessed or changed (by wrapping your data in property procedures or methods). You could use this code to log how many times a value is being accessed, to check if the data is still valid, or to re-create it. Here's an example that uses a lazy initialization pattern and creates the global object only when it's first requested:

```
private static string[] fileList;
public static string[] FileList
{
    get
    {
        if (fileList == null)
        {
            fileList = Directory.GetFiles(
              HttpContext.Current.Request.PhysicalApplicationPath);
        }
        return fileList;
    }
}
```

This example uses the file access classes described in Chapter 12 to retrieve a list of files in the web application. This approach wouldn't be possible with the Application collection.

The other benefit of using static member variables is that the code that consumes them can be typesafe. Here's an example that uses the FileList property:

```
protected void Page_Load(object sender, EventArgs e)
{
    StringBuilder builder = new StringBuilder();
    foreach (string file in Global.FileList)
    {
        builder.Append(file + "<br />");
    }
    lblInfo.Text = builder.ToString();
}
```

Notice that no casting step is required to gain access to the custom property you've added.

Summary

State management is the art of retaining information between requests. Usually, this information is user-specific (such as a list of items in a shopping cart, a user name, or an access level), but sometimes it's global to the whole application (such as usage statistics that track site activity). Because ASP.NET uses a disconnected architecture, you need to explicitly store and retrieve state information with each individual request. The approach you choose for storing this data can have a dramatic effect on the performance, scalability, and security of your application. To perfect your state management solution, you'll almost certainly want to consider adding caching into the mix, as described in Chapter 11.

PART 2

■ ■ ■

Data Access

The core data features of the .NET Framework remain in .NET 4, and are essentially unchanged. Developers can use the same ADO.NET data classes to interact with relational databases (Chapter 7), and other parts of the .NET Framework to interact with the file system (Chapter 12) and read XML documents (Chapter 14).

Similarly, the data binding features in ASP.NET remain unchanged, allowing you to pull information out of data classes and show it in a web page with as little code as possible (Chapter 9). The same rich data controls remain (Chapter 10), with their support for data display and data editing, and the same caching feature allows you to reduce the number of times you query the information (Chapter 11) to ensure optimum performance.

Developers in search of a higher-level model will appreciate ASP.NET's support for Language Integrated Query (LINQ). At its simplest, LINQ gives developers more powerful ways to manipulate in-memory data—for example, sorting, filtering, and grouping it to get key bits of information. But the most dramatic part of LINQ is the LINQ to Entities feature that's built on top of it, which allows you to pull information out of a database using little more than a LINQ query. That means there's no need to write lower-level ADO.NET data access code. LINQ to Entities isn't necessarily the best way to get your data or manipulate it—that depends on your exact requirements—but it is a compelling feature that should be in every developer's toolkit. You'll explore LINQ in Chapter 13.

Finally, it's important to remember that no matter what data access strategy you use—whether it relies on ADO.NET, LINQ to Entities, or a different set of classes—it shouldn't be a part of your main web application code. Instead, it makes much more sense to separate it into a dedicated component that can be coded, versioned, and refined separately. You'll learn more about this strategy in Chapter 8.

CHAPTER 7

■ ■ ■

ADO.NET Fundamentals

The .NET Framework includes its own data access technology: ADO.NET. ADO.NET consists of managed classes that allow .NET applications to connect to data sources (usually relational databases), execute commands, and manage disconnected data. The small miracle of ADO.NET is that it allows you to write more or less the same data access code in web applications that you write for client-server desktop applications, or even single-user applications that connect to a local database.

This chapter describes the architecture of ADO.NET and the ADO.NET data providers. You'll learn about ADO.NET basics such as opening a connection, executing a SQL statement or stored procedure, and retrieving the results of a query. You'll also learn how to prevent SQL injection attacks and how to use transactions.

Database Access Without ADO.NET

In ASP.NET, there are a few ways to get information out of a database without directly using the ADO.NET classes. Depending on your needs, you may be able to use one or more of these approaches to supplement your database code (or to avoid writing it altogether).

Your options for database access without ADO.NET include the following:

- **The SqlDataSource control:** The SqlDataSource control allows you to define queries declaratively. You can connect the SqlDataSource to rich controls such as the GridView, and give your pages the ability to edit and update data without requiring any ADO.NET code. Best of all, the SqlDataSource uses ADO.NET behind the scenes, and so it supports any database that has a full ADO.NET provider. However, the SqlDataSource is somewhat controversial, because it encourages you to place database logic in the markup portion of your page. Many developers prefer to use the ObjectDataSource instead, which gives similar data binding functionality but relies on a custom database component. When you use the ObjectDataSource, it's up to you to create the database component and write the back-end ADO.NET code. You'll learn more about data source controls in Chapter 9.
- **LINQ to Entities:** With LINQ to Entities, you generate a data model with the design support in Visual Studio. The appropriate database logic is generated automatically. LINQ to Entities supports updates, generates secure and well-written SQL statements, and provides wide ranging customizability. LINQ to Entites is also the preferred successor to the simpler LINQ to SQL model, which ASP.NET developers have used in the past. You'll get the full details in Chapter 13. LINQ to Entites also powers the new data scaffolding system called ASP.NET Dynamic Data, which you'll consider in Chapter 33.

None of these options is a replacement for ADO.NET, because none of them offers the full flexibility, customizability, and performance that hand-written database code offers. However, depending on your needs, it may be worth using one or more of these features simply to get better code-writing productivity.

Overall, most ASP.NET developers will need to write some ADO.NET code, even if it's only to optimize a performance-sensitive task or to perform a specific operation that wouldn't otherwise be possible. Also, every professional ASP.NET developer needs to understand how the ADO.NET plumbing works in order to evaluate when it's required and when another approach is just as effective.

The ADO.NET Architecture

ADO.NET uses a multilayered architecture that revolves around a few key concepts, such as Connection, Command, and DataSet objects.

One of the key differences between ADO.NET and some other database technologies is how it deals with the challenge of different data sources. In many previous database technologies, such as classic ADO, programmers use a generic set of objects no matter what the underlying data source is. For example, if you want to retrieve a record from an Oracle database using ADO code, you use the same Connection class you would use to tackle the task with SQL Server. This isn't the case in ADO.NET, which uses a data provider model.

ADO.NET Data Providers

A data provider is a set of ADO.NET classes that allows you to access a specific database, execute SQL commands, and retrieve data. Essentially, a data provider is a bridge between your application and a data source.

The classes that make up a data provider include the following:

- **Connection:** You use this object to establish a connection to a data source.
- **Command:** You use this object to execute SQL commands and stored procedures.
- **DataReader:** This object provides fast read-only, forward-only access to the data retrieved from a query.
- **DataAdapter:** This object performs two tasks. First, you can use it to fill a DataSet (a disconnected collection of tables and relationships) with information extracted from a data source. Second, you can use it to apply changes to a data source, according to the modifications you've made in a DataSet.

ADO.NET doesn't include generic data provider objects. Instead, it includes different data providers specifically designed for different types of data sources. Each data provider has a specific implementation of the Connection, Command, DataReader, and DataAdapter classes that's optimized for a specific RDBMS (relational database management system). For example, if you need to create a connection to a SQL Server database, you'll use a connection class named SqlConnection.

■ **Note** This book uses generic names for provider-specific classes. In other words, instead of discussing the SqlConnection and OracleConnection classes, you'll learn about all connection classes. Just keep in mind that there really isn't a generic Connection class—it's just convenient shorthand for referring to all the provider-specific connection classes, which work in a standardized fashion.

One of the key underlying ideas of the ADO.NET provider model is that it's extensible. In other words, developers can create their own providers for proprietary data sources. In fact, numerous proof-of-concept examples are available that show how you can easily create custom ADO.NET providers to wrap nonrelational data stores, such as the file system or a directory service. Some third-party vendors also sell custom providers for .NET.

The .NET Framework is bundled with a small set of four providers:

- **SQL Server provider:** Provides optimized access to a SQL Server database (version 7.0 or later).
- **OLE DB provider:** Provides access to any data source that has an OLE DB driver. This includes SQL Server databases prior to version 7.0.
- **Oracle provider:** Provides optimized access to an Oracle database (version 8i or later).
- **ODBC provider:** Provides access to any data source that has an ODBC driver.

■ **Tip** As of .NET 4, the Oracle provider is considered obsolete. Although it still works, Microsoft recommends using a third-party ADO.NET provider to access Oracle databases, such as Oracle's own ODP.NET (Oracle Data Provider for .NET), which is available at `http://www.oracle.com/technology/tech/windows/odpnet`. It provides richer support for specialized Oracle data types such as LOBs (large objects), timestamps, and XML data, along with a few additional features.

Figure 7-1 shows the layers of the ADO.NET provider model.

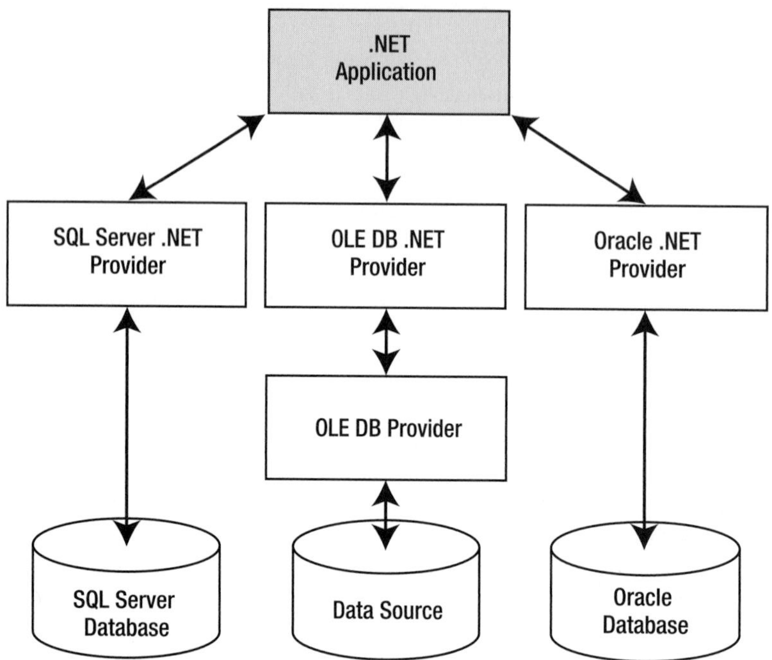

Figure 7-1. *The ADO.NET architecture*

When choosing a provider, you should first try to find a native .NET provider that's customized for your data source. If you can't find a native provider, you can use the OLE DB provider, as long as you have an OLE DB driver for your data source. The OLE DB technology has been around for many years as part of ADO, so most data sources provide an OLE DB driver (including SQL Server, Oracle, Access, MySQL, and many more). In the rare situation when you can't find a dedicated .NET provider or an OLE DB driver, you can fall back on the ODBC provider, which works in conjunction with an ODBC driver.

■ **Tip** Microsoft includes the OLE DB provider with ADO.NET so that you can use your existing OLE DB drivers. However, if you can find a provider that's customized specifically for your data source, you should use it instead. For example, you can connect to a SQL Server database using either the SQL Server provider or the OLE DB provider, but the SQL Server provider will always perform best.

Standardization in ADO.NET

At first glance, it might seem that ADO.NET offers a fragmented model, because it doesn't include a generic set of objects that can work with multiple types of databases. As a result, if you change from one RDBMS to another, you'll need to modify your data access code to use a different set of classes.

But even though different .NET data providers use different classes, all providers are *standardized* in the same way. More specifically, each provider is based on the same set of interfaces and base classes.

For example, every Connection object implements the IDbConnection interface, which defines core methods such as Open() and Close(). This standardization guarantees that every Connection class will work in the same way and expose the same set of core properties and methods.

Behind the scenes, different providers use completely different low-level calls and APIs. For example, the SQL Server provider uses the proprietary TDS (Tabular Data Stream) protocol to communicate with the server. The benefits of this model aren't immediately obvious, but they are significant:

- Because each provider uses the same interfaces and base classes, you can still write generic data access code (with a little more effort) by coding against the interfaces instead of the provider classes. You'll see this technique in action in the section "Provider-Agnostic Code."
- Because each provider is implemented separately, it can use proprietary optimizations. (This is different from the ADO model, where every database call needs to filter through a common layer before it reaches the underlying database driver.) In addition, custom providers can add nonstandard features that aren't included in other providers (such as SQL Server's ability to perform an XML query).

ADO.NET also has another layer of standardization: the DataSet. The DataSet is an all-purpose container for data that you've retrieved from one or more tables in a data source. The DataSet is completely generic—in other words, custom providers don't define their own custom versions of the DataSet class. No matter which data provider you use, you can extract your data and place it into a disconnected DataSet in the same way. That makes it easy to separate data retrieval code from data processing code. If you change the underlying database, you will need to change the data retrieval code, but if you use the DataSet and your information has the same structure, you won't need to modify the way you process that data.

Fundamental ADO.NET Classes

ADO.NET has two types of objects: *connection-based* and *content-based*.

Connection-based objects: These are the data provider objects such as Connection, Command, DataReader, and DataAdapter. They allow you to connect to a database, execute SQL statements, move through a read-only result set, and fill a DataSet. The connection-based objects are specific to the type of data source, and are found in a provider-specific namespace (such as System.Data.SqlClient for the SQL Server provider).

Content-based objects: These objects are really just "packages" for data. They include the DataSet, DataColumn, DataRow, DataRelation, and several others. They are completely independent of the type of data source and are found in the System.Data namespace.

In the rest of this chapter, you'll learn about the first level of ADO.NET—the connection-based objects, including Connection, Command, and DataReader. You won't learn about the higher-level DataAdapter yet, because the DataAdapter is designed for use with the DataSet and is discussed in Chapter 8. (Essentially, the DataAdapter is a group of related Command objects; these objects help you synchronize a DataSet with a data source.)

The ADO.NET classes are grouped into several namespaces. Each provider has its own namespace, and generic classes such as the DataSet are stored in the System.Data namespaces. Table 7-1 describes the most important namespaces for basic ADO.NET support.

Table 7-1. The ADO.NET Namespace

Namespace	Description
System.Data	Contains the key data container classes that model columns, relations, tables, datasets, rows, views, and constraints. In addition, contains the key interfaces that are implemented by the connection-based data objects.
System.Data.Common	Contains base, mostly abstract classes that implement some of the interfaces from System.Data and define the core ADO.NET functionality. Data providers inherit from these classes (such as DbConnection, DbCommand, and so on) to create their own specialized versions.
System.Data.OleDb	Contains the classes used to connect to an OLE DB provider, including OleDbCommand, OleDbConnection, OleDbDataReader, and OleDbDataAdapter. These classes support most OLE DB providers, but not those that require OLE DB version 2.5 interfaces.
System.Data.SqlClient	Contains the classes you use to connect to a Microsoft SQL Server database, including SqlCommand, SqlConnection, SqlDataReader, and SqlDataAdapter. These classes are optimized to use the TDS interface to SQL Server.
System.Data.OracleClient	Contains the classes required to connect to an Oracle database (version 8.1.7 or later), including OracleCommand, OracleConnection, OracleDataReader, and OracleDataAdapter. These classes are using the optimized Oracle Call Interface (OCI).
System.Data.Odbc	Contains the classes required to connect to most ODBC drivers. These classes include OdbcCommand, OdbcConnection, OdbcDataReader, and OdbcDataAdapter. ODBC drivers are included for all kinds of data sources and are configured through the Data Sources icon in the Control Panel.
System.Data.SqlTypes	Contains structures that match the native data types in SQL Server. These classes aren't required but provide an alternative to using standard .NET data types, which require automatic conversion.

■ **Note** An ADO.NET provider is simply a set of ADO.NET classes (with an implementation of Connection, Command, DataAdapter, and DataReader) that's distributed in a class library assembly. Usually, all the classes in the data provider use the same prefix. For example, the prefix OleDb is used for the ADO.NET OLE DB provider, and it provides an implementation of the Connection object named OleDbConnection.

The Connection Class

The Connection class allows you to establish a connection to the data source that you want to interact with. Before you can do anything else (including retrieving, deleting, inserting, or updating data), you need to establish a connection.

The core Connection properties and methods are specified by the IDbConnection interface, which all Connection classes implement.

Connection Strings

When you create a Connection object, you need to supply a *connection string*. The connection string is a series of name/value settings separated by semicolons (;). The order of these settings is unimportant, as is the capitalization. Taken together, they specify the basic information needed to create a connection.

Although connection strings vary based on the RDBMS and provider you are using, a few pieces of information are almost always required:

The server where the database is located: In the examples in this book, the database server is always located on the same computer as the ASP.NET application, so the loopback alias localhost is used instead of a computer name.

The database you want to use: Most of the examples in this book use the Northwind database, which is installed with older versions of SQL Server (and can be installed on newer versions using the SQL script that's included with the downloadable examples for this book).

How the database should authenticate you: The Oracle and SQL Server providers give you the choice of supplying authentication credentials or logging in as the current user. The latter choice is usually best, because you don't need to place password information in your code or configuration files.

For example, here's the connection string you would use to connect to the Northwind database on the current computer using integrated security (which uses the currently logged-in Windows user to access the database):

```
string connectionString = "Data Source=localhost; Initial Catalog=Northwind;" +
  "Integrated Security=SSPI";
```

If integrated security isn't supported, the connection must indicate a valid user and password combination. For a newly installed SQL Server database, the sa (system administrator) account is usually present. Here's a connection string that uses this account:

```
string connectionString = "Data Source=localhost; Initial Catalog=Northwind;" +
  "user id=sa; password=opensesame";
```

If you're using the OLE DB provider, your connection string will still be similar, with the addition of a provider setting that identifies the OLE DB driver. For example, you can use the following connection string to connect to an Oracle database through the MSDAORA OLE DB provider:

```
string connectionString = "Data Source=localhost; Initial Catalog=Sales;" +
  "user id=sa; password=da#ta_li#nk_43;Provider=MSDAORA";
```

Here's an example that connects to an Access database file:

```
string connectionString = "Provider=Microsoft.Jet.OLEDB.4.0;" +
  @"Data Source=C:\DataSources\Northwind.mdb";
```

■ **Tip** If you're using a database other than SQL Server, you might need to consult the data provider documentation (or the .NET Framework class library reference) to determine the supported connection string values. For example, most databases support the Connect Timeout setting, which sets the number of seconds to wait for a connection before throwing an exception. (The SQL Server default is 15 seconds.)

When you create a Connection object, you can pass the connection string as a constructor parameter. Alternatively, you can set the ConnectionString property by hand, as long as you do it before you attempt to open the connection.

There's no reason to hard-code a connection string. As discussed in Chapter 5, the <connectionStrings> section of the web.config file is a handy place to store your connection strings. Here's an example:

```
<configuration>
  <connectionStrings>
    <add name="Northwind" connectionString=
"Data Source=localhost; Initial Catalog=Northwind; Integrated Security=SSPI"/>
  </connectionStrings>
  ...
</configuration>
```

You can then retrieve your connection string by name from the WebConfigurationManager.ConnectionStrings collection. Assuming you've imported the System.Web.Configuration namespace, you can use a code statement like this:

```
string connectionString =
  WebConfigurationManager.ConnectionStrings["Northwind"].ConnectionString;
```

The following examples assume you've added this connection string to your web.config file.

User Instance Connections

Every database server stores a master catalog of all the databases that you've installed on it. This list includes the name of each database and the location of the files that hold the data. When you create a database (for example, by running a script or using a management tool), the information about that database is added to the master catalog. When you connect to the database, you specify the database name using the Initial Catalog value in the connection string.

Interestingly, SQL Server Express has a convenient feature that lets you bypass the master list and connect directly to any database file, even if it's not in the master catalog of databases. This feature is called *user instances*, and it isn't available in the full edition of SQL Server.

■ **Note** SQL Server Express is a scaled-down version of SQL Server 2008 that's free to distribute. SQL Server Express has certain limitations—for example, it can use only one CPU and a maximum of 1GB of RAM, and databases can't be larger than 4GB. However, it's still remarkably powerful and suitable for many midscale web sites. Even better, you can easily upgrade from SQL Server Express to a paid version of SQL Server if you need more features later. For more information about SQL Server Express or to download it with or without additional administrative tools, refer to `http://www.microsoft.com/express/database`.

To attach a user instance database, you need to set the User Instances value to True (in the connection string) and supply the file name of the database you want to connect to with the AttachDBFilename value. You don't supply an Initial Catalog value.

Here's an example connection string that uses this approach:

```
myConnection.ConnectionString = @"Data Source=localhost\SQLEXPRESS;" +
  "Integrated Security=SSPI;" +
  @"AttachDBFilename=|DataDirectory|\Northwind.mdf;User Instance=True";
```

There's another trick here. The file name starts with |DataDirectory|. This automatically points to the App_Data folder inside your web application directory. This way, you don't need to supply a full file path, which might not remain valid when you move the web application to a web server. Instead, ADO.NET will always look in the App_Data directory for a file named Northwind.mdf.

User instances is a handy feature if you have a web server that hosts many different web applications that use databases and these databases are frequently being added and removed. This feature also works well in conjunction with other, higher-level ASP.NET features like profiles and membership (see Part Four). By default, these features create file-based databases for SQL Server Express, which saves you the configuration work.

Visual Studio's Support for User Instance Databases

Visual Studio provides two handy features that make it easier to work with databases in the App_Data folder.

First, Visual Studio gives you a nearly effortless way to create new databases. Simply choose Website ➤ Add New Item. Then, pick SQL Server Database from the list of templates, choose a file name for your database, and click OK. The .mdf and .ldf files for the new database will be placed in the App_Data folder, and you'll see them in the Solution Explorer. Initially, they'll be blank, so you'll need to add the tables you want. (The easiest way to do this is to right-click the Tables group in the Server Explorer, and choose Add Table.)

Visual Studio also simplifies your life with its automatic Server Explorer support. When you open a web application, Visual Studio automatically adds a data connection to the Server Explorer window for each database that it finds in the App_Data folder. To jump to a specific data connection in a hurry, just double-click the .mdf file for the database in the Solution Explorer. Using the Server Explorer, you can create tables, edit data, and execute commands, all without leaving the comfort of Visual Studio.

Testing a Connection

Once you've chosen your connection string, managing the connection is easy—you simply use the Open() and Close() methods.

You can use the following code in the Page.Load event handler to test a connection and write its status to a label (as shown in Figure 7-2). To use this code as written, you must import the System.Data.SqlClient namespace.

```
// Create the Connection object.
string connectionString =
  WebConfigurationManager.ConnectionStrings["Northwind"].ConnectionString;
SqlConnection con = new SqlConnection(connectionString);

try
{
    // Try to open the connection.
    con.Open();
    lblInfo.Text = "<b>Server Version:</b> " + con.ServerVersion;
    lblInfo.Text += "<br /><b>Connection Is:</b> " + con.State.ToString();
}
catch (Exception err)
{
    // Handle an error by displaying the information.
    lblInfo.Text = "Error reading the database. " + err.Message;
}
finally
{
    // Either way, make sure the connection is properly closed.
    // Even if the connection wasn't opened successfully,
    // calling Close() won't cause an error.
    con.Close();
    lblInfo.Text += "<br /><b>Now Connection Is:</b> " +
      con.State.ToString();
}
```

Figure 7-2 shows the results of running this code.

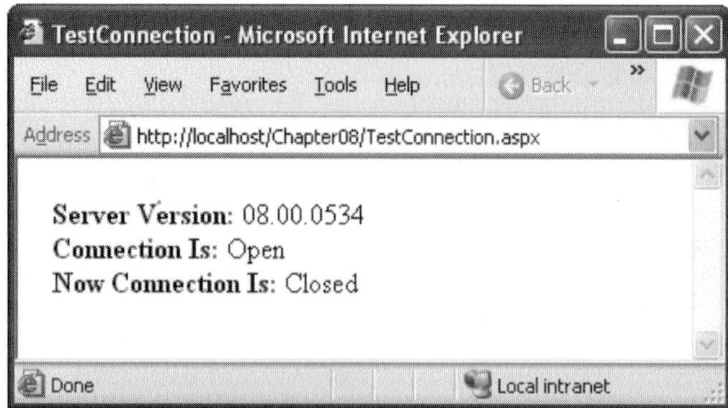

Figure 7-2. *Testing a connection*

■ **Note** When opening a connection, you face two possible exceptions. An InvalidOperationException occurs if your connection string is missing required information or the connection is already open. A SqlException occurs for just about any other type of problem, including an error contacting the database server, logging in, or accessing the specified database.

SqlException is a provider-specific class that's used for the SQL Server provider. Other database providers use different exception classes to serve the same role, such as OracleException, OleDbException, and OdbcException.

Connections are a limited server resource. This means it's imperative that you open the connection as late as possible and release it as quickly as possible. In the previous code sample, an exception handler is used to make sure that even if an unhandled error occurs, the connection will be closed in the finally block. If you don't use this design and an unhandled exception occurs, the connection will remain open until the garbage collector disposes of the SqlConnection object.

An alternate approach is to wrap your data access code in a using block. The using statement declares that you are using a disposable object for a short period of time. As soon as the using block ends, the CLR releases the corresponding object immediately by calling its Dispose() method. Interestingly, calling the Dispose() method of a Connection object is equivalent to calling Close(). That means you can rewrite the earlier example in the following, more compact, form:

```
string connectionString =
  WebConfigurationManager.ConnectionStrings["Northwind"].ConnectionString;
SqlConnection con = new SqlConnection(connectionString);

using (con)
{
    con.Open();
    lblInfo.Text = "<b>Server Version:</b> " + con.ServerVersion;
    lblInfo.Text += "<br /><b>Connection Is:</b> " + con.State.ToString();
}
lblInfo.Text += "<br /><b>Now Connection Is:</b> ";
lblInfo.Text +=  con.State.ToString();
```

The best part is that you don't need to write a finally block—the using statement releases the object you're using even if you exit the block as the result of an unhandled exception.

Connection Pooling

Acquiring a connection takes a short, but definite, amount of time. In a web application in which requests are being handled efficiently, connections will be opened and closed endlessly as new requests are processed. In this environment, the small overhead required to establish a connection can become significant and limit the scalability of the system.

One solution is connection pooling. Connection pooling is the practice of keeping a permanent set of open database connections to be shared by sessions that use the same data source. This avoids the need to create and destroy connections all the time. Connection pools in ADO.NET are completely transparent to the programmer, and your data access code doesn't need to be altered. When a client requests a connection by calling Open(), it's served directly from the available pool, rather than re-created. When a client releases a connection by calling Close() or Dispose(), it's not discarded but returned to the pool to serve the next request.

ADO.NET does not include a connection pooling mechanism. However, most ADO.NET providers implement some form of connection pooling. The SQL Server and Oracle data providers implement their own efficient connection pooling algorithms. These algorithms are implemented entirely in managed code and—in contrast to some popular misconceptions—do not use COM+ enterprises services. For a connection to be reused with SQL Server or Oracle, the connection string must match exactly. If it differs even slightly, a new connection will be created in a new pool.

■ **Tip** SQL Server and Oracle connection pooling use a full-text match algorithm. That means any minor change in the connection string will thwart connection pooling, even if the change is simply to reverse the order of parameters or add an extra blank space at the end. For this reason, it's imperative that you don't hard-code the connection string in different web pages. Instead, you should store the connection string in one place—preferably in the <connectionStrings> section of the web.config file.

With both the SQL Server and Oracle providers, connection pooling is enabled and used automatically. However, you can also use connection string parameters to configure pool size settings. Table 7-2 describes these parameters.

Table 7-2. *Connection Pooling Settings*

Setting	Description
Max Pool Size	The maximum number of connections allowed in the pool (defaults to 100). If the maximum pool size has been reached, any further attempts to open a connection are queued until a connection becomes available. (An error is raised if the Connection.Timeout value elapses before a connection becomes available.)
Min Pool Size	The minimum number of connections always retained in the pool (defaults to 0). This number of connections will be created when the first connection is opened, leading to a minor delay for the first request.
Pooling	When true (the default), the connection is drawn from the appropriate pool or, if necessary, is created and added to the appropriate pool.
Connection Lifetime	Specifies a time interval in seconds. If a connection is returned to the pool and its creation time is older than the specified lifetime, it will be destroyed. The default is 0, which disables this behavior. This feature is useful when you want to recycle a large number of connections at once.

Here's an example connection string that sets a minimum pool size:

```
string connectionString = "Data Source=localhost; Initial Catalog=Northwind;" +
  "Integrated Security=SSPI; Min Pool Size=10";
SqlConnection con = new SqlConnection(connectionString);

// Get the connection from the pool (if it exists)
// or create the pool with 10 connections (if it doesn't).
con.Open();

// Return the connection to the pool.
con.Close();
```

Some providers include methods for emptying out the connection pool. For example, with the SqlConnection you can call the static ClearPool() and ClearAllPools() methods. When calling ClearPool(), you supply a SqlConnection, and all the matching connections are removed. ClearAllPools() empties out every connection pool in the current application domain. (Technically, these methods don't close the connections. They just mark them as invalid so that they will time out and be closed during the regular connection cleanup a few minutes later.) This functionality is rarely used—typically, the only case in which it's useful is if you know the pool is full of invalid connections (for example, as a result of restarting SQL Server) and you want to avoid an error.

■ **Tip** SQL Server and Oracle connection pools are always maintained as part of the global resources in an application domain. As a result, connection pools can't be reused between separate web applications on the same web server or between web applications and other .NET applications. For the same reason, all the connections are lost if the application domain is restarted. (Application domains are restarted for a variety of reasons, including when you change a web page, assembly, or configuration file in the web application. Application domains are also restarted when certain thresholds are reached—for example, IIS may recycle an application domain that's using a large amount of memory or has a large number of requests in the queue. Both details may indicate that the performance of the application domain has degraded.)

The Command and DataReader Classes

The Command class allows you to execute any type of SQL statement. Although you can use a Command class to perform *data definition* tasks (such as creating and altering databases, tables, and indexes), you're much more likely to perform *data manipulation* tasks (such as retrieving and updating the records in a table).

The provider-specific Command classes implement standard functionality, just like the Connection classes. In this case, the IDbCommand interface defines a few key properties and the core set of methods that are used to execute a command over an open connection.

Command Basics

Before you can use a command, you need to choose the command type, set the command text, and bind the command to a connection. You can perform this work by setting the corresponding properties (CommandType, CommandText, and Connection), or you can pass the information you need as constructor arguments.

The command text can be a SQL statement, a stored procedure, or the name of a table. It all depends on the *type* of command you're using. Three types of commands exist, as listed in Table 7-3.

Table 7-3. *Values for the CommandType Enumeration*

Value	Description
CommandType.Text	The command will execute a direct SQL statement. The SQL statement is provided in the CommandText property. This is the default value.
CommandType.StoredProcedure	The command will execute a stored procedure in the data source. The CommandText property provides the name of the stored procedure.
CommandType.TableDirect	The command will query all the records in the table. The CommandText is the name of the table from which the command will retrieve the records. (This option is included for backward compatibility with certain OLE DB drivers only. It is not supported by the SQL Server data provider, and it won't perform as well as a carefully targeted query.)

For example, here's how you would create a Command object that represents a query:

```
SqlCommand cmd = new SqlCommand();
cmd.Connection = con;
cmd.CommandType = CommandType.Text;
cmd.CommandText = "SELECT * FROM Employees";
```

And here's a more efficient way using one of the Command constructors. Note that you don't need to specify the CommandType, because CommandType.Text is the default.

```
SqlCommand cmd = new SqlCommand("SELECT * FROM Employees", con);
```

Alternatively, to use a stored procedure, you would use code like this:

```
SqlCommand cmd = new SqlCommand("GetEmployees", con);
cmd.CommandType = CommandType.StoredProcedure;
```

These examples simply define a Command object; they don't actually execute it. The Command object provides three methods that you can use to perform the command, depending on whether you want to retrieve a full result set, retrieve a single value, or just execute a nonquery command. Table 7-4 lists these methods.

Table 7-4. Command Methods

Method	Description
ExecuteNonQuery()	Executes non-SELECT commands, such as SQL commands that insert, delete, or update records. The returned value indicates the number of rows affected by the command. You can also use ExecuteNonQuery() to execute data-definition commands that create, alter, or delete database objects (such as tables, indexes, constraints, and so on).
ExecuteScalar()	Executes a SELECT query and returns the value of the first field of the first row from the rowset generated by the command. This method is usually used when executing an aggregate SELECT command that uses functions such as COUNT() or SUM() to calculate a single value.
ExecuteReader()	Executes a SELECT query and returns a DataReader object that wraps a read-only, forward-only cursor.

The DataReader Class

A DataReader allows you to read the data returned by a SELECT command one record at a time, in a forward-only, read-only stream. This is sometimes called a firehose cursor. Using a DataReader is the simplest way to get to your data, but it lacks the sorting and relational abilities of the disconnected DataSet described in Chapter 8. However, the DataReader provides the quickest possible no-nonsense access to data.

Table 7-5 lists the core methods of the DataReader.

Table 7-5. DataReader Methods

Method	Description
Read()	Advances the row cursor to the next row in the stream. This method must also be called before reading the first row of data. (When the DataReader is first created, the row cursor is positioned just before the first row.) The Read() method returns true if there's another row to be read, or false if it's on the last row.
GetValue()	Returns the value stored in the field with the specified index, within the currently selected row. The type of the returned value is the closest .NET match to the native value stored in the data source. If you access the field by index and inadvertently pass an invalid index that refers to a nonexistent field, you will get an IndexOutOfRangeException exception. You can also access values by field name using the indexer for the DataReader. (In other words, myDataReader.GetValue(0) and myDataReader["NameOfFirstField"] are equivalent.) Name-based lookups are more readable, but slightly less efficient.

Method	Description
GetValues()	Saves the values of the current row into an array. The number of fields that are saved depends on the size of the array you pass to this method. You can use the DataReader.FieldCount property to determine the number of fields in a row, and you can use that information to create an array of the right size if you want to save all the fields.
GetInt32(),GetChar(), GtDateTime(), GetXxx()	These methods return the value of the field with the specified index in the current row, with the data type specified in the method name. Note that if you try to assign the returned value to a variable of the wrong type, you'll get an InvalidCastException exception. Also note that these methods don't support nullable data types. If a field might contain a null value, you need to check it before you call one of these methods. To test for a null value, compare the unconverted value (which you can retrieve by position using the GetValue() method or by name using the DataReader indexer) to the constant DBNull.Value.
NextResult()	If the command that generated the DataReader returned more than one rowset, this method moves the pointer to the next rowset (just before the first row).
Close()	Closes the reader. If the originator command ran a stored procedure that returned an output value, that value can be read only from the respective parameter after the reader has been closed.

The ExecuteReader() Method and the DataReader

The following example creates a simple query command to return all the records from the Employees table in the Northwind database. The command is created when the page is loaded.

```
protected void Page_Load(object sender, EventArgs e)
{
    // Create the Command and the Connection objects.
    string connectionString =
      WebConfigurationManager.ConnectionStrings["Northwind"].ConnectionString;
    SqlConnection con = new SqlConnection(connectionString);
    string sql = "SELECT * FROM Employees";
    SqlCommand cmd = new SqlCommand(sql, con);
    ...
```

■ **Note** This SELECT query uses the * wildcard to retrieve all the fields, but in real-world code you should retrieve only the fields you really need in order to avoid consuming time to retrieve data you'll never use. It's also a good idea to limit the records returned with a WHERE clause if you don't need all the records.

The connection is then opened, and the command is executed through the ExecuteReader() method, which returns a SqlDataReader, as follows:

```
...
// Open the Connection and get the DataReader.
con.Open();
SqlDataReader reader = cmd.ExecuteReader();
...
```

Once you have the DataReader, you can cycle through its records by calling the Read() method in a while loop. This moves the row cursor to the next record (which, for the first call, means to the first record). The Read() method also returns a Boolean value indicating whether there are more rows to read. In the following example the loop continues until Read() returns false, at which point the loop ends gracefully.

The information for each record is then joined into a single large string. To ensure that these string manipulations are performed quickly, a StringBuilder (from the System.Text namespace) is used instead of ordinary string objects.

```
...
// Cycle through the records, and build the HTML string.
StringBuilder htmlStr = new StringBuilder("");
while (reader.Read())
{
    htmlStr.Append("<li>");
    htmlStr.Append(reader["TitleOfCourtesy"]);
    htmlStr.Append(" <b>");
    htmlStr.Append(reader.GetString(1));
    htmlStr.Append("</b>, ");
    htmlStr.Append(reader.GetString(2));
    htmlStr.Append(" - employee from ");
    htmlStr.Append(reader.GetDateTime(6).ToString("d"));
    htmlStr.Append("</li>");
}
...
```

This code reads the value of the TitleOfCourtesy field by accessing the field by name through the Item indexer. Because the Item property is the default indexer, you don't need to explicitly include the Item property name when you retrieve a field value. Next, the code reads the LastName and FirstName fields by calling GetString() with the field index (1 and 2 in this case). Finally, the code accesses the HireDate field by calling GetDateTime() with a field index of 6. All these approaches are equivalent and included to show the supported variation.

■ **Note** In this example, the StringBuilder ensures a dramatic increase in performance. If you use the + operator to concatenate strings instead, this operation would discard the current string object and create a new one every time. This operation is noticeably slower, especially for large strings. The StringBuilder object avoids this problem by allocating a modifiable buffer of memory for characters.

The final step is to close the reader and the connection and show the generated text in a server control:

```
    ...
    reader.Close();
    con.Close();
    HtmlContent.Text = htmlStr.ToString();
}
```

If you run the page, you'll see the output shown in Figure 7-3.

In most ASP.NET pages, you won't take this labor-intensive approach to displaying data in a web page. Instead, you'll use the data controls described in later chapters. However, you're still likely to use the DataReader when writing data access code in a database component.

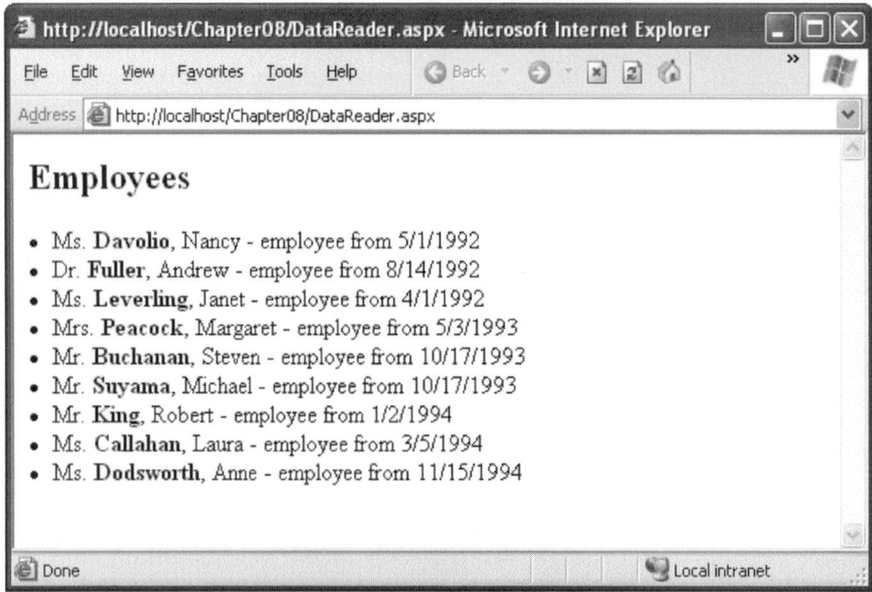

Figure 7-3. Retrieving results with a DataReader

Null Values

As you no doubt already know, databases use null values to represent missing or nonapplicable information. You can use the same concept in .NET with nullable data types, which can take a value and a null reference. Here's an example with a nullable integer:

```
// Nullable integer can contain any 32-bit integer or a null value.
int? nullableInteger = null;

// Test nullableInteger for a null value.
if (nullableInteger.HasValue)
{
    // Do something with nullableInteger.
    nullableInteger += 1;
}
```

Unfortunately, the DataReader isn't integrated with .NET nullable values. This discrepancy is due to historical reasons. The nullable data types were first introduced in .NET 2.0, at which point the DataReader model was already well established and difficult to change.

Instead, the DataReader returns the constant DBNull.Value when it comes across a null value in the database. Attempting to use this value or cast it to another data type will cause an exception. (Sadly, there's no way to cast between DBNull.Value and a nullable data type.) As a result, you need to test for DBNull.Value when it might occur, using code like this:

```
int? numberOfHires;

if (reader["NumberOfHires"] == DBNull.Value)
    numberOfHires = null;
else
    numberOfHires = (int?)reader["NumberOfHires"];
```

CommandBehavior

The ExecuteReader() method has an overloaded version that takes one of the values from the CommandBehavior enumeration as a parameter. One useful value is CommandBehavior.CloseConnection. When you pass this value to the ExecuteReader() method, the DataReader will close the associated connection as soon as you close the DataReader.

Using this technique, you could rewrite the code as follows:

```
SqlDataReader reader = cmd.ExecuteReader(CommandBehavior.CloseConnection);

// (Build the HTML string here.)

// No need to close the connection. You can simply close the reader.
reader.Close();
HtmlContent.Text = htmlStr.ToString();
```

This behavior is particularly useful if you retrieve a DataReader in one method and need to pass it to another method to process it. If you use the CommandBehavior.CloseConnection value, the connection will be automatically closed as soon as the second method closes the reader.

Another possible value is CommandBehavior.SingleRow, which can improve the performance of the query execution when you're retrieving only a single row. For example, if you are retrieving a single record using its unique primary key field (CustomerID, ProductID, and so on), you can use this optimization. You can also use CommandBehavior.SequentialAccess to read part of a binary field at a time, which reduces the memory overhead for large binary fields. You'll see this technique at work in Chapter 10.

The other values are less frequently used and aren't covered here. You can refer to the .NET documentation for a full list.

Processing Multiple Result Sets

The command you execute doesn't have to return a single result set. Instead, it can execute more than one query and return more than one result set as part of the same command. This is useful if you need to retrieve a large amount of related data, such as a list of products and product categories that, taken together, represent a product catalog.

A command can return more than one result set in two ways:

- If you're calling a stored procedure, it may use multiple SELECT statements.

- If you're using a straight text command, you may be able to batch multiple commands by separating commands with a semicolon (;). Not all providers support this technique, but the SQL Server database provider does.

Here's an example of a string that defines a batch of three SELECT statements:

```
string sql = "SELECT TOP 5 * FROM Employees;" +
  "SELECT TOP 5 * FROM Customers; SELECT TOP 5 * FROM Suppliers";
```

This string contains three queries. Together, they return the first five records from the Employees table, the first five from the Customers table, and the first five from the Suppliers table.

Processing these results is fairly straightforward. Initially, the DataReader will provide access to the results from the Employees table. Once you've finished using the Read() method to read all these records, you can call NextResult() to move to the next result set. When there are no more result sets, this method returns false.

You can even cycle through all the available result sets with a while loop, although in this case you must be careful not to call NextResult() until you finish reading the first result set. Here's an example of this more specialized technique:

```
// Cycle through the records and all the rowsets,
// and build the HTML string.
StringBuilder htmlStr = new StringBuilder("");
int i = 0;
do
{
    htmlStr.Append("<h2>Rowset: ");
    htmlStr.Append(i.ToString());
    htmlStr.Append("</h2>");

    while (reader.Read())
    {
        htmlStr.Append("<li>");
        // Get all the fields in this row.
        for (int field = 0; field < reader.FieldCount; field++)
        {
            htmlStr.Append(reader.GetName(field).ToString());
            htmlStr.Append(": ");
            htmlStr.Append(reader.GetValue(field).ToString());
            htmlStr.Append("   ");
        }
        htmlStr.Append("</li>");
    }
    htmlStr.Append("<br /><br />");
    i++;
} while (reader.NextResult());

// Close the DataReader and the Connection.
reader.Close();
con.Close();

// Show the generated HTML code on the page.
HtmlContent.Text = htmlStr.ToString();
```

Note that in this case all the fields are accessed using the generic GetValue() method, which takes the index of the field to read. That's because the code is designed generically to read all the fields of all the returned result sets, no matter what query you use. However, in a realistic database application, you would almost certainly know which tables to expect, as well as the corresponding table and field names.

Figure 7-4 shows the page output.

■ **Tip** There is one case where you might treat all result sets with the same code—if all your result sets contain data with the same structure. For example, you might call a stored procedure that returns three groups of employees in three distinct result sets, separated according the sales office where they work. You can then hardcode your field names instead of using GetValue(), because each result set will have the same fields.

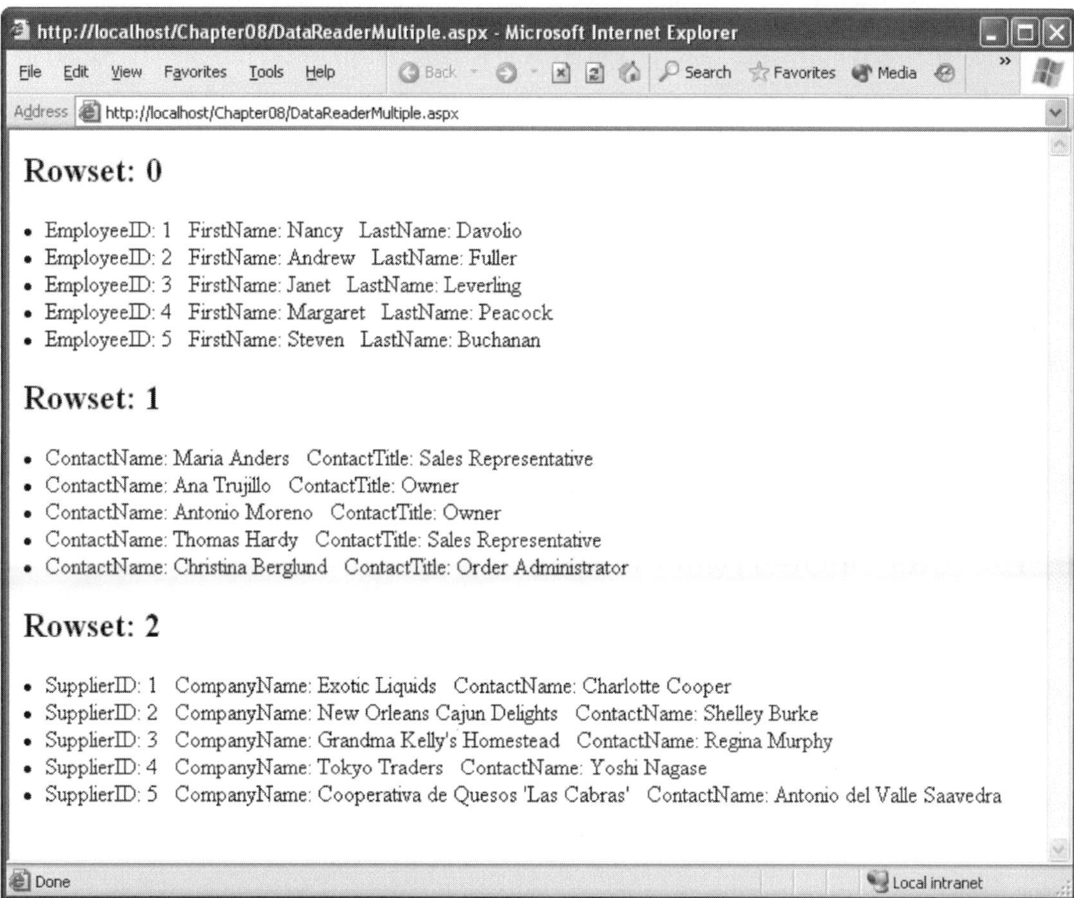

***Figure 7-4.** Retrieving multiple result sets*

You don't always need to step through each record. If you're willing to show the data exactly as it is, with no extra processing or formatting, you can add a GridView control to your page and bind the DataReader to the GridView control in a single line. Here is the code you would use:

```
// Specify the data source.
GridView1.DataSource = reader;

// Fill the GridView with all the records in the DataReader.
GridView1.DataBind();
```

You'll learn much more about data binding and how to customize it in Chapter 9 and Chapter 10.

The ExecuteScalar() Method

The ExecuteScalar() method returns the value stored in the first field of the first row of a result set generated by the command's SELECT query. This method is usually used to execute a query that retrieves only a single field, perhaps calculated by a SQL aggregate function such as COUNT() or SUM().

The following procedure shows how you can get (and write on the page) the number of records in the Employees table with this approach:

```
SqlConnection con = new SqlConnection(connectionString);
string sql = " SELECT COUNT(*) FROM Employees ";
SqlCommand cmd = new SqlCommand(sql, con);

// Open the Connection and get the COUNT(*) value.
con.Open();
int numEmployees = (int)cmd.ExecuteScalar();
con.Close();

// Display the information.
HtmlContent.Text += "<br />Total employees: <b>" +
  numEmployees.ToString() + "</b><br />";
```

The code is fairly straightforward, but it's worth noting that you must cast the returned value to the proper type because ExecuteScalar() returns an object.

The ExecuteNonQuery() Method

The ExecuteNonQuery() method executes commands that don't return a result set, such as INSERT, DELETE, and UPDATE. The ExecuteNonQuery() method returns a single piece of information—the number of affected records (or -1 if your command isn't an INSERT, DELETE, or UPDATE statement).

Here's an example that uses a DELETE command by dynamically building a SQL string:

```
SqlConnection con = new SqlConnection(connectionString);
string sql = "DELETE FROM Employees WHERE EmployeeID = " + empID.ToString();
SqlCommand cmd = new SqlCommand(sql, con);

try
{
    con.Open();
    int numAff = cmd.ExecuteNonQuery();
    HtmlContent.Text += string.Format(
```

```
        "<br />Deleted <b>{0}</b> record(s)<br />",  numAff);
}
catch (SqlException exc)
{
    HtmlContent.Text += string.Format(
      "<b>Error:</b> {0}<br /><br />", exc.Message);
}
finally
{
    con.Close();
}
```

This particular code won't actually delete the record, because foreign key constraints prevent you from removing an employee record if it's linked to other records in other tables.

SQL Injection Attacks

So far, all the examples you've seen have used hard-coded values. That makes the examples simple, straightforward, and relatively secure. It also means they aren't that realistic, and they don't demonstrate one of the most serious risks for web applications that interact with a database—*SQL injection* attacks.

In simple terms, SQL injection is the process of passing SQL code into an application, in a way that was not intended or anticipated by the application developer. This may be possible because of the poor design of the application, and it affects only applications that use SQL string building techniques to create a command with user-supplied values.

Consider the example shown in Figure 7-5. In this example, the user enters a customer ID, and the GridView shows all the rows for that customer. In a more realistic example the user would also need to supply some sort of authentication information such as a password. Or, the user ID might be based on a previous login screen, and the text box would allow the user to supply additional criteria such as a date range or the name of a product in the order.

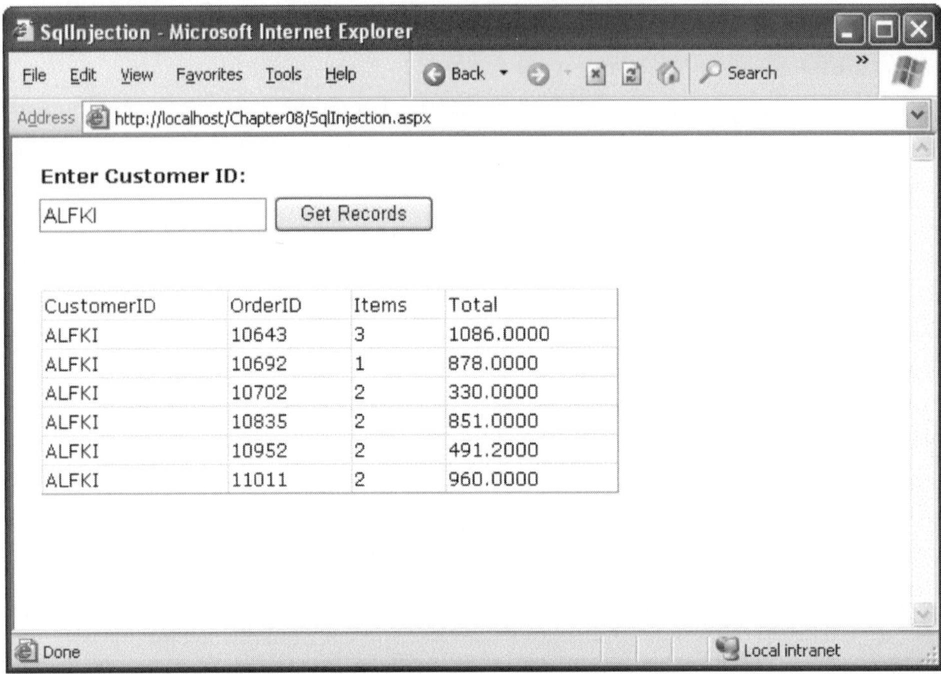

Figure 7-5. Retrieving orders for a single customer

The problem is how this command is executed. In this example, the SQL statement is built dynamically using a string building technique. The value from the txtID text box is simply pasted into the middle of the string. Here's the code:

```
string connectionString =
  WebConfigurationManager.ConnectionStrings["Northwind"].ConnectionString;
SqlConnection con = new SqlConnection(connectionString);
string sql =
  "SELECT Orders.CustomerID, Orders.OrderID, COUNT(UnitPrice) AS Items, " +
  "SUM(UnitPrice * Quantity) AS Total FROM Orders " +
  "INNER JOIN [Order Details] " +
  "ON Orders.OrderID = [Order Details].OrderID " +
  "WHERE Orders.CustomerID = '" + txtID.Text + "' " +
  "GROUP BY Orders.OrderID, Orders.CustomerID";
SqlCommand cmd = new SqlCommand(sql, con);

con.Open();
SqlDataReader reader = cmd.ExecuteReader();
GridView1.DataSource = reader;
GridView1.DataBind();
reader.Close();
con.Close();
```

In this example, a user might try to tamper with the SQL statement. Often, the first goal of such an attack is to receive an error message. If the error isn't handled properly and the low-level information is exposed to the attacker, that information can be used to launch a more sophisticated attack.

For example, imagine what happens if the user enters the following text into the text box:

```
ALFKI' OR '1'='1
```

Now consider the complete SQL statement that this creates:

```
SELECT Orders.CustomerID, Orders.OrderID, COUNT(UnitPrice) AS Items,
  SUM(UnitPrice * Quantity) AS Total FROM Orders
  INNER JOIN [Order Details]
  ON Orders.OrderID = [Order Details].OrderID
  WHERE Orders.CustomerID = 'ALFKI' OR '1'='1'
  GROUP BY Orders.OrderID, Orders.CustomerID
```

This statement returns all the order records. Even if the order wasn't created by ALFKI, it's still true that 1=1 for every row. The result is that instead of seeing the specific information for the current customer, all the information is exposed to the attacker, as shown in Figure 7-6. If the information shown on the screen is sensitive, such as Social Security numbers, dates of birth, or credit card information, this could be an enormous problem! In fact, simple SQL injection attacks exactly like this are often the source of problems that affect major e-commerce companies. Often, the vulnerability doesn't occur in a text box but appears in the query string (which can be used to pass a database value such as a unique ID from a list page to a details page).

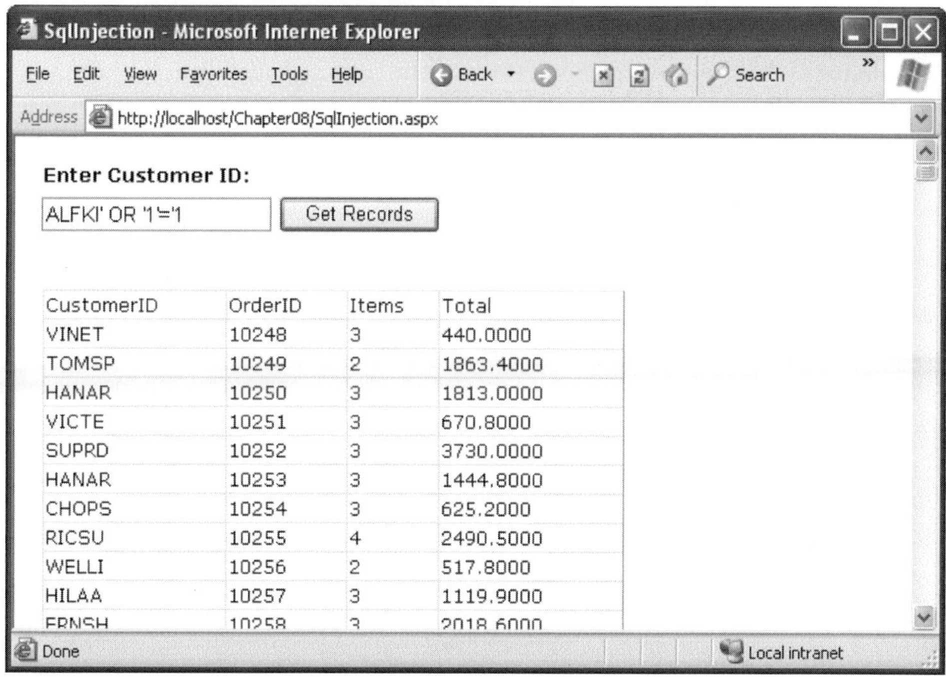

CustomerID	OrderID	Items	Total
VINET	10248	3	440.0000
TOMSP	10249	2	1863.4000
HANAR	10250	3	1813.0000
VICTE	10251	3	670.8000
SUPRD	10252	3	3730.0000
HANAR	10253	3	1444.8000
CHOPS	10254	3	625.2000
RICSU	10255	4	2490.5000
WELLI	10256	2	517.8000
HILAA	10257	3	1119.9000

Figure 7-6. *A SQL injection attack that shows all the orders*

More sophisticated attacks are possible. For example, the malicious user could simply comment out the rest of your SQL statement by adding two hyphens (—).This attack is specific to SQL Server, but equivalent exploits are possible in MySQL with the hash (#) symbol and in Oracle with the semicolon (;). Alternatively, the attacker could use a batch command to execute an arbitrary SQL command. With the SQL Server provider, the attacker simply needs to supply a semicolon followed by a new command. This exploit allows the user to delete the contents of another table, or even use the SQL Server xp_cmdshell system stored procedure to execute an arbitrary program at the command line.

Here's what the user would need to enter in the text box for a more sophisticated SQL injection attack to delete all the rows in the Customers table:

```
ALFKI'; DELETE * FROM Customers–
```

So, how can you defend against SQL injection attacks? You can keep a few good guidelines in mind. First, it's a good idea to use the TextBox.MaxLength property to prevent overly long entries if they aren't needed. That reduces the chance of a large block of script being pasted in where it doesn't belong. In addition, you can use the ASP.NET validator controls to lock out obviously incorrect data (such as text, spaces, or special characters in a numeric value). Furthermore, you should restrict the information that's given by your error messages. If you catch a database exception, you should report only a generic message such as "Data source error" rather than display the information in the Exception.Message property, which may provide more information about system vulnerabilities.

More important, you should take care to remove special characters. For example, you can convert all single quotation marks to two quotation marks, thereby ensuring that they won't be confused with the delimiters in your SQL statement:

```
string ID = txtID.Text().Replace("'", "''");
```

Of course, this introduces headaches if your text values really should contain apostrophes. It also suffers because some SQL injection attacks are still possible. Replacing apostrophes prevents a malicious user from closing a string value prematurely. However, if you're building a dynamic SQL statement that includes numeric values, a SQL injection attack just needs a single space. This vulnerability is often (and dangerously) ignored.

An even better approach is to use a parameterized command or a stored procedure that performs its own escaping and is impervious to SQL injection attacks. The following sections describe these techniques.

■ **Tip** Another good idea is to restrict the permissions of the account used to access the database so that it doesn't have the right to access other databases or execute extended system stored procedures. However, this can't remove the problem of SQL script injection, because the process you use to connect to the database will almost always require a broader set of privileges than the ones you would allocate to any single user. By restricting the account, you could prevent an attack that deletes a table, for example, but you probably can't prevent an attack that steals someone else's information.

Using Parameterized Commands

A parameterized command is simply a command that uses placeholders in the SQL text. The placeholders indicate dynamically supplied values, which are then sent through the Parameters collection of the Command object.

For example, take this SQL statement:

```
SELECT * FROM Customers WHERE CustomerID = 'ALFKI'
```

It would become something like this:

```
SELECT * FROM Customers WHERE CustomerID = @CustID
```

The placeholders are then added separately and automatically encoded.

The syntax for parameterized commands differs slightly for different providers. With the SQL Server provider, parameterized commands use named placeholders (with unique names). With the OLE DB provider, each hard-coded value is replaced with a question mark. In either case, you need to supply a Parameter object for each parameter, which you insert into the Command.Parameters collection. With the OLE DB provider, you must make sure you add the parameters in the same order that they appear in the SQL string. This isn't a requirement with the SQL Server provider, because the parameters are matched to the placeholders based on their names.

The following example rewrites the query to remove the possibility of a SQL injection attack:

```
string connectionString =
  WebConfigurationManager.ConnectionStrings["Northwind"].ConnectionString;
SqlConnection con = new SqlConnection(connectionString);
string sql =
  "SELECT Orders.CustomerID, Orders.OrderID, COUNT(UnitPrice) AS Items, " +
  "SUM(UnitPrice * Quantity) AS Total FROM Orders " +
  "INNER JOIN [Order Details] " +
  "ON Orders.OrderID = [Order Details].OrderID " +
  "WHERE Orders.CustomerID = @CustID " +
  "GROUP BY Orders.OrderID, Orders.CustomerID";
SqlCommand cmd = new SqlCommand(sql, con);
cmd.Parameters.AddWithValue("@CustID", txtID.Text);

con.Open();
SqlDataReader reader = cmd.ExecuteReader();
GridView1.DataSource = reader;
GridView1.DataBind();
reader.Close();
con.Close();
```

If you try to perform the SQL injection attack against this revised version of the page, you'll find it returns no records. That's because no order items contain a customer ID value that equals the text string ALFKI' OR '1'='1. This is exactly the behavior you want.

POST Injection Attacks

Savvy users might realize there's another potential avenue for attack with web controls. Although parameterized commands prevent SQL injection attacks, they don't prevent attackers from adding malicious values to the data that's posted back to the server. Left unchecked, this could allow attackers to submit control values that wouldn't otherwise be possible.

For example, imagine you have a list that shows orders made by the current user. A crafty attacker could save a local copy of the page, modify the HTML to add more entries to the list, and then select one of these "fake" entries. If this attack succeeds, the user will be able to see the orders made by another user, which is an obvious problem.

Fortunately, ASP.NET defends against this attack using a rarely discussed feature called *event validation*. Event validation checks the data that's posted back to the server and verifies that the values are legitimate. For example, if the POST data indicates the user chose a value that doesn't make sense (because it doesn't actually exist in the control), ASP.NET generates an error and stops processing.

You can disable event validation by setting the EnableEventValidation attribute of the Page directive to false. This step is sometimes necessary when you create pages that are dynamically modified using client-side script (as you'll see in Chapter 32). However, in these situations, be careful to check for potential POST injection attacks by validating selected values before you act on them.

Calling Stored Procedures

Parameterized commands are just a short step from commands that call full-fledged stored procedures.

As you probably know, a stored procedure is a batch of one or more SQL statements that are stored in the database. Stored procedures are similar to functions in that they are well-encapsulated blocks of logic that can accept data (through input parameters) and return data (through result sets and output parameters). Stored procedures have many benefits:

They are easier to maintain: For example, you can optimize the commands in a stored procedure without recompiling the application that uses it. They also standardize data access logic in one place—the database—making it easier for different applications to reuse that logic in a consistent way. (In object-oriented terms, stored procedures define the interface to your database.)

They allow you to implement more secure database usage: For example, you can allow the Windows account that runs your ASP.NET code to use certain stored procedures but restrict access to the underlying tables.

They can improve performance: Because a stored procedure batches together multiple statements, you can get a lot of work done with just one trip to the database server. If your database is on another computer, this reduces the total time to perform a complex task dramatically.

■ **Note** SQL Server precompiles all SQL commands, including off-the-cuff SQL statements. That means you gain the benefit of compilation regardless of whether you are using stored procedures. However, stored procedures still tend to increase the performance benefits, because systems that use stored procedures tend to have less variability. Systems that use ad hoc SQL statements tend to use slightly different commands to perform similar tasks, which means compiled execution plans can't be reused as effectively.

Here's the SQL code needed to create a stored procedure for inserting a single record into the Employees table. This stored procedure isn't in the Northwind database initially, so you'll need to add it to the database (using a tool such as SQL Server Management Studio) before you use it.

```
CREATE PROCEDURE InsertEmployee
  @TitleOfCourtesy varchar(25),
  @LastName        varchar(20),
  @FirstName       varchar(10),
  @EmployeeID      int OUTPUT
AS

INSERT INTO Employees
  (TitleOfCourtesy, LastName, FirstName, HireDate)
  VALUES (@TitleOfCourtesy, @LastName, @FirstName, GETDATE());

SET @EmployeeID = @@IDENTITY
```

This stored procedure takes three parameters for the employee's title of courtesy, last name, and first name. It returns the ID of the new record through the output parameter called @EmployeeID, which is retrieved after the INSERT statement using the @@IDENTITY function. This is one example of a simple task that a stored procedure can make much easier. Without using a stored procedure, it's quite awkward to try to determine the automatically generated identity value of a new record you've just inserted.

Next, you can create a SqlCommand to wrap the call to the stored procedure. This command takes the same three parameters as inputs and uses @@IDENTITY to get and then return the ID of the new record. Here is the first step, which creates the required objects and sets InsertEmployee as the command text:

```
string connectionString =
  WebConfigurationManager.ConnectionStrings["Northwind"].ConnectionString;
SqlConnection con = new SqlConnection(connectionString);

// Create the command for the InsertEmployee stored procedure.
SqlCommand cmd = new SqlCommand("InsertEmployee", con);
cmd.CommandType = CommandType.StoredProcedure;
```

Now you need to add the stored procedure's parameters to the Command.Parameters collection. When you do, you need to specify the exact data type and length of the parameter so that it matches the details in the database.

Here's how it works for a single parameter:

```
cmd.Parameters.Add(new SqlParameter(
  "@TitleOfCourtesy", SqlDbType.NVarChar, 25));
cmd.Parameters["@TitleOfCourtesy"].Value = title;
```

The first line creates a new SqlParameter object. It sets its name, type (using the SqlDbType enumeration), and size (as a number of characters) in the constructor. It then adds it to the Parameters collection. The second statement assigns the value for the parameter, which will be sent to the stored procedure when you execute the command.

Now you can add the next two parameters in a similar way:

```
cmd.Parameters.Add(new SqlParameter("@LastName", SqlDbType.NVarChar, 20));
cmd.Parameters["@LastName"].Value = lastName;
cmd.Parameters.Add(new SqlParameter("@FirstName", SqlDbType.NVarChar, 10));
cmd.Parameters["@FirstName"].Value = firstName;
```

The last parameter is an output parameter, which allows the stored procedure to return information to your code. Although this Parameter object is created in the same way, you must make sure you specify it is an output parameter by setting its Direction property to Output. You don't need to supply a value.

```
cmd.Parameters.Add(new SqlParameter("@EmployeeID", SqlDbType.Int, 4));
cmd.Parameters["@EmployeeID"].Direction = ParameterDirection.Output;
```

Finally, you can open the connection and execute the command with the ExecuteNonQuery() method. When the command is completed, you can read the output value, as shown here:

```
con.Open();
try
{
    int numAff = cmd.ExecuteNonQuery();
    HtmlContent.Text += String.Format(
      "Inserted <b>{0}</b> record(s)<br />", numAff);

    // Get the newly generated ID.
    int empID = (int)cmd.Parameters["@EmployeeID"].Value;
    HtmlContent.Text += "New ID: " + empID.ToString();
}
finally
{
    con.Close();
}
```

Adding Parameters with Implicit Data Types

One handy shortcut is the AddWithValue() method of the Parameters collection. This method takes the parameter name and the value but no data type information. Instead, it infers the data type from the supplied data. (Obviously, this works with input parameters but not output parameters, because you don't supply a value for output para- meters.) If you don't need to explicitly choose a nonstandard data type, you can streamline your code with this less-strict approach.

Here's an example:

```
cmd.Parameters.AddWithValue("@LastName", lastName);
cmd.Parameters.AddWithValue("@FirstName" firstName);
```

Assuming that lastName is a C# string with 12 letters, this creates a SqlParameter object with a Size of 12 (characters) and a SqlDbType of NVarChar. The database can convert this data as needed, provided you aren't trying to stuff it into a field with a smaller size or a completely different data type.

■ **Note** There's one catch—nullable fields. If you want to pass a null value to a stored procedure, you can't use a C# null reference, because that indicates an uninitialized reference, which is an error condition. Unfortunately, you can't use a nullable data type either (such as int?), because the SqlParameter class doesn't support nullable data types. To indicate null content in a field, you must pass the .NET constant DBNull.Value as a parameter value.

In the next chapter, you'll see a small but fully functional database component that does all its work through stored procedures.

Transactions

A transaction is a set of operations that must either succeed or fail as a unit. The goal of a transaction is to ensure that data is always in a valid, consistent state.

For example, consider a transaction that transfers $1,000 from account A to account B. Clearly there are two operations:

- It should deduct $1,000 from account A.
- It should add $1,000 to account B.

Suppose that an application successfully completes step 1, but because of some error, step 2 fails. This leads to inconsistent data, because the total amount of money in the system is no longer accurate. A full $1,000 has gone missing.

Transactions help avoid these types of problems by ensuring that changes are committed to a data source only if *all* the steps are successful. So, in this example, if step 2 fails, then the changes made by step 1 will not be committed to the database. This ensures that the system stays in one of its two valid states—the initial state (with no money transferred) and the final state (with money debited from one account and credited to another).

Transactions are characterized by four properties popularly called *ACID* properties. ACID is an acronym that represents the following concepts:

Atomic: All steps in the transaction should succeed or fail together. Unless all the steps from a transaction complete, a transaction is not considered complete.

Consistent: The transaction takes the underlying database from one stable state to another.

Isolated: Every transaction is an independent entity. One transaction should not affect any other transaction running at the same time.

Durable: Changes that occur during the transaction are permanently stored on some media, typically a hard disk, before the transaction is declared successful. Logs are maintained so that the database can be restored to a valid state even if a hardware or network failure occurs.

Note that even though these are ideal characteristics of a transaction, they aren't always absolutely attainable. One problem is that in order to ensure isolation, the RDBMS often needs to lock data so that other users can't access it while the transaction is in progress. The more locks you use, and the coarser these locks are, the greater the chance that a user won't be able to perform another task while the transactions are underway. In other words, there's often a trade-off between user concurrency and isolation.

Transactions and ASP.NET Applications

You can use three basic transaction types in an ASP.NET web application. They are as follows (from least to most overhead):

Stored procedure transactions: These transactions take place entirely in the database. Stored procedure transactions offer the best performance, because they need only a single round-trip to the database. The drawback is that you also need to write the transaction logic using SQL statements.

Client-initiated (ADO.NET) transactions: These transactions are controlled programmatically by your ASP.NET web-page code. Under the covers, they use the same commands as a stored procedure transaction, but your code uses some ADO.NET objects that wrap these details. The drawback is that extra round-trips are required to the database to start and commit the transaction.

COM+ transactions: These transactions are handled by the COM+ runtime, based on declarative attributes you add to your code. COM+ transactions use a two-stage commit protocol and always incur extra overhead. They also require that you create a separate serviced component class. COM+ components are generally a good choice only if your transaction spans multiple transaction-aware resource managers, because COM+ includes built-in support for distributed transactions. For example, a single COM+ transaction can span interactions in a SQL Server database and an Oracle database. COM+ transactions are not covered in this book.

Even though ADO.NET provides good support for transactions, you should not always use transactions. In fact, every time you use any kind of transaction, you automatically incur some overhead. Also, transactions involve some kind of locking of table rows. Thus, unnecessarily using transactions may harm the overall scalability of your application.

When implementing a transaction, you can follow these practices to achieve the best results:

- Keep transactions as short as possible.
- Avoid returning data with a SELECT query in the middle of a transaction. Ideally, you should return the data before the transaction starts. This reduces the amount of data your transaction will lock.
- If you do retrieve records, fetch only the rows that are required so as to reduce the number of locks.
- Wherever possible, write transactions within stored procedures instead of using ADO.NET transactions. This way, your transaction can be started and completed more quickly, because the database server doesn't need to communicate with the client (the web application).
- Avoid transactions that combine multiple independent batches of work. Put separate batches into separate transactions.
- Avoid updates that affect a large range of records if at all possible.

■ **Note** ADO.NET also supports a higher-level model of *promotable transactions*. However, a promotable transaction isn't a new type of transaction—it's just a way to create a client-initiated transaction that can automatically escalate itself into a COM+ transaction if needed. You don't need promotable transactions unless you need to perform operations with different data sources in the scope of the single transaction. You can learn more about promotable transactions in Pro ADO.NET 2.0 by Sahil Malik (Apress, 2005).

■ **Tip** As a rule of thumb, use a transaction only when your operation requires one. For example, if you are simply selecting records from a database, or firing a single query, you will not need a transaction. On the other hand, if you are inserting an Order record in conjunction with a series of related OrderItem records, you might want to use a transaction. In general, a transaction is never required for single-statement commands such as individual UPDATE, DELETE, or INSERT statements, because these are inherently transactional.

Stored Procedure Transactions

If possible, the best place to put a transaction is in stored procedure code. This ensures that the server-side code is always in control, which makes it impossible for a client to accidentally hold a transaction open too long and potentially cause problems for other client updates. It also ensures the best possible performance, because all actions can be executed at the data source without requiring any network communication. Generally, the shorter the span of a transaction, the better the concurrency of the database and the fewer the number of database requests that will be serialized (put on hold while a temporary record lock is in place).

Stored procedure code varies depending on the database you are using, but most RDBMSs support the SQL statement BEGIN TRANSACTION. Once you start a transaction, all subsequent statements are considered part of the transaction. You can end the transaction with the COMMIT or ROLLBACK statement. If you don't, the transaction will be automatically rolled back.

Here's a pseudocode example that performs a fund transfer between accounts. It's a simplified version that allows an account to be set to a negative balance.

```
CREATE Procedure TransferAmount
(
  @Amount Money,
  @ID_A int,
  @ID_B int
)
AS
  BEGIN TRANSACTION
  UPDATE Accounts SET Balance = Balance + @Amount WHERE AccountID = @ID_A
  IF (@@ERROR > 0)
      GOTO PROBLEM
  UPDATE Accounts SET Balance = Balance - @Amount WHERE AccountID = @ID_B
  IF (@@ERROR > 0)
      GOTO PROBLEM

  – No problem was encountered.
  COMMIT
  RETURN

  – Error handling code.
  PROBLEM:
      ROLLBACK
      RAISERROR('Could not update.', 16, 1)
```

The previous example uses the limited error handling features of Transact-SQL (the variant of SQL used by SQL Server). When using the @@ERROR value in Transact-SQL, you must be careful to check it immediately after each operation. That's because @@ERROR is reset to 0 when a successful SQL statement is completed. As a result, if the first update fails and the second update succeeds, @@ERROR returns to 0. It's therefore too late to check it at this point.

If you're using SQL Server 2005 or later, you have the benefit of a more modern try/catch structure that's similar to the structured error handling in C#. When you use this approach, any errors interrupt your code immediately, and execution passes to the subsequent error handling block. As a result, you can structure your transaction code more cleanly, like this:

```
CREATE Procedure TransferAmount
(
  @Amount Money,
  @ID_A int,
  @ID_B int
)
AS
  BEGIN TRY
    BEGIN TRANSACTION
      UPDATE Accounts SET Balance = Balance + @Amount WHERE AccountID = @ID_A
      UPDATE Accounts SET Balance = Balance - @Amount WHERE AccountID = @ID_B

      – If code reaches this point, all operations succeeded.
      COMMIT
  END TRY

  BEGIN CATCH
    – An error occurred somewhere in the try block.
    IF (@@TRANCOUNT > 0)
      ROLLBACK

    – Notify the client by raising an exception with the error details.
    DECLARE @ErrMsg nvarchar(4000), @ErrSeverity int
    SELECT @ErrMsg = ERROR_MESSAGE(), @ErrSeverity = ERROR_SEVERITY()
    RAISERROR(@ErrMsg, @ErrSeverity, 1)
  END CATCH
```

This example checks @@TRANCOUNT to determine if a transaction is underway. (The @@TRANCOUNT variable counts the number of active transactions for the current connection. The BEGIN TRANSACTION statement increments @@TRANCOUNT by one, while ROLLBACK or COMMIT decrements it by one.)

To prevent errors from being silently suppressed by the catch block, the RAISERROR statement is used. ADO.NET translates this message to a SqlException object, which you must catch in your .NET code.

■ **Note** In SQL Server, a stored procedure can also perform a distributed transaction (one that involves multiple data sources and is typically hosted on multiple servers). By default, every transaction begins as a local transaction, but if you access a database on another server, the transaction is automatically upgraded to a distributed transaction governed by the Windows DTC (Distributed Transaction Coordinator) service.

Client-Initiated ADO.NET Transactions

Most ADO.NET data providers include support for database transactions. Transactions are started through the Connection object by calling the BeginTransaction() method. This method returns a provider-specific Transaction object that's used to manage the transaction. All Transaction classes implement the IDbTransaction interface. Examples include SqlTransaction, OleDbTransaction, OracleTransaction, and so on.

The Transaction class provides two key methods:

Commit(): This method identifies that the transaction is complete and that the pending changes should be stored permanently in the data source.

Rollback(): This method indicates that a transaction was unsuccessful. Pending changes are discarded, and the database state remains unchanged.

Typically, you use Commit() at the end of your operation. However, if any exception is thrown along the way, you should call Rollback().

Here's an example that inserts two records into the Employees table:

```
string connectionString =
  WebConfigurationManager.ConnectionStrings["Northwind"].ConnectionString;
SqlConnection con = new SqlConnection(connectionString);

SqlCommand cmd1 = new SqlCommand(
  "INSERT INTO Employees (LastName, FirstName) VALUES ('Joe','Tester')",
  con);
SqlCommand cmd2 = new SqlCommand(
  "INSERT INTO Employees (LastName, FirstName) VALUES ('Harry','Sullivan')",
  con);
SqlTransaction tran = null;

try
{
    // Open the connection and create the transaction.
    con.Open();
    tran = con.BeginTransaction();

    // Enlist two commands in the transaction.
    cmd1.Transaction = tran;
    cmd2.Transaction = tran;

    // Execute both commands.
    cmd1.ExecuteNonQuery();
    cmd2.ExecuteNonQuery();

    // Commit the transaction.
    tran.Commit();
}
catch
{
    // In the case of error, roll back the transaction.
    tran.Rollback();
}
```

```
finally
{
    con.Close();
}
```

Note that it's not enough to create and commit a transaction. You also need to explicitly enlist each Command object to be part of the transaction by setting the Command.Transaction property to the Transaction object. If you try to execute a command that isn't a part of the current transaction while the transaction is underway, you'll receive an error. However, in the future this object model might allow providers to support more than one simultaneous transaction on the same connection.

■ **Tip** Instead of using separate command objects, you could also execute the same object twice and just modify its CommandText property in between (if it's a dynamic SQL statement) or the value of its parameters (if it's a parameterized command). For example, if your command inserts a new record, you could use this approach to insert two records in the same transaction.

To test the rollback features of a transaction, you can insert the following line just before the Commit() method is called in the previous example:

```
throw new ApplicationException();
```

This raises an exception, which will trigger a rollback and ensure that neither record is committed to the database.

Although an ADO.NET transaction revolves around the Connection and Transaction objects, the underlying commands aren't different from a stored procedure transaction. For example, when you call BeginTransaction() with the SQL Server provider, it sends a BEGIN TRANSACTION command to the database.

■ **Tip** A transaction should be completed as quickly as possible (started as late as possible and finished as soon as possible). Also, an active transaction puts locks on the various resources involved, so you should select only the rows you really require.

Isolation Levels

The *isolation level* determines how sensitive a transaction is to changes made by other in-progress transactions. For example, by default when two transactions are running independently of each other, records inserted by one transaction are not visible to the other transaction until the first transaction is committed.

The concept of isolation levels is closely related to the concept of locks, because by determining the isolation level for a given transaction you determine what types of locks are required. *Shared locks* are locks that are placed when a transaction wants to read data from the database. No other transactions can modify the data while shared locks exist on a table, row, or range. However, more than one user can use a shared lock to read the data simultaneously. *Exclusive locks* are the locks that prevent two or more transactions from modifying data simultaneously. An exclusive lock is issued when a transaction needs to update data and no other locks are already held. No other user can read or modify the data while an exclusive lock is in place.

■ **Note** SQL Server actually has several types of locks that work together to help prevent deadlocks and other situations. To learn more, refer to the information about locking in the SQL Server Books Online help, which is installed with SQL Server.

In a SQL Server stored procedure, you can set the isolation level using the SET TRANSACTION ISOLATION LEVEL command. In ADO.NET, you can pass a value from the IsolationLevel enumeration to the Connection.BeginTransaction() method. Table 7-6 lists possible values.

Table 7-6. *Values of the IsolationLevel Enumeration*

Value	Description
ReadUncommitted	No shared locks are placed, and no exclusive locks are honored. This type of isolation level is appropriate when you want to work with all the data matching certain conditions, irrespective of whether it's committed. Dirty reads are possible, but performance is increased.
ReadCommitted	Shared locks are held while the data is being read by the transaction. This avoids dirty reads, but the data can be changed before a transaction completes. This may result in nonrepeatable reads or phantom rows. This is the default isolation level used by SQL Server.
Snapshot	Stores a copy of the data your transaction accesses. As a result, the transaction won't see the changes made by other transactions. This approach reduces blocking, because even if other transactions are holding locks on the data, a transaction with snapshot isolation will still be able to read a copy of the data. This isolation level is supported in SQL Server 2005 and later, and it needs to be enabled through a database-level option.
RepeatableRead	In this case, shared locks are placed on all data that is used in a query. This prevents others from modifying the data, and it also prevents nonrepeatable reads. However, phantom rows are possible.
Serializable	A range lock is placed on the data you use, thereby preventing other users from updating or inserting rows that would fall in that range. This is the only isolation level that removes the possibility of phantom rows. However, it has an extremely negative effect on user concurrency and is rarely used in multiple user scenarios.

Table 7-6 introduces some database terminology that deserves a bit more explanation:

- **Dirty reads:** A dirty read is a read that sees a value from another, uncommitted transaction, which may be subsequently rolled back.
- **Nonrepeatable reads:** If nonrepeatable reads are allowed, it's possible to perform the query in the same transaction more than once and get different data. That's because merely reading data doesn't prevent other people from changing it while the transaction is underway. To prevent nonrepeatable reads, the database server needs to lock the rows that your transaction reads.
- **Phantom rows:** A phantom row is a row that doesn't appear in an initial read, but appears when the same data is read again during the same transaction. This can occur if another user inserts a record while the transaction is underway. To prevent phantom rows, when your transaction performs a query the database server needs to use a range lock based on its WHERE clause.

Whether these phenomena are harmless quirks or potential error conditions depends on your specific requirements. Most of the time, nonrepeatable reads and phantom rows are minor issues, and the concurrency cost of preventing them with locks is too high to be worthwhile. However, if you need to update a number of records at once, and these records have some interrelated data, you may need more stringent locking to prevent overlapping changes from causing inconsistencies.

The isolation levels in Table 7-6 are arranged from the least degree of locking to the highest degree of locking. The default, ReadCommitted, is a good compromise for most transactions. Table 7-7 summarizes the locking behavior for different isolation levels.

Table 7-7. *Isolation Levels Compared*

Isolation Level	Dirty Read	Nonrepeatable Read	Phantom Data	Concurrency
Read uncommitted	Yes	Yes	Yes	Best
Read committed	No	Yes	Yes	Good
Snapshot	No	No	No	Good
Repeatable read	No	No	Yes	Poor
Serializable	No	No	No	Very poor

Savepoints

Whenever you roll back a transaction, it nullifies the effect of every command you've executed since you started the transaction. But what happens if you want to roll back only part of an ongoing transaction? SQL Server handles this with a feature called *savepoints*.

Savepoints are markers that act like bookmarks. You mark a certain point in the flow of the transaction, and then you can roll back to that point. You set the savepoint using the Transaction.Save() method. Note that the Save() method is available only for the SqlTransaction class, because it's not part of the standard IDbTransaction interface.

Here's a conceptual look at how you use a savepoint:

```
// Start the transaction.
SqlTransaction tran = con.BeginTransaction();

// (Enlist and execute some commands inside the transaction.)

// Mark a savepoint.
tran.Save("CompletedInsert");

// (Enlist and execute some more commands inside the transaction.)

// If needed, roll back to the savepoint.
tran.Rollback("CompletedInsert");

// Commit or roll back the transaction.
tran.Commit();
```

Note how the Rollback() method is used with the savepoint name as a parameter. If you want to roll back the whole transaction, simply omit this parameter.

■ **Note** Once you roll back to a savepoint, all the savepoints defined after that savepoint are lost. You must set them again if they are needed.

Provider-Agnostic Code

For the most part, ADO.NET's provider model is an ideal solution for dealing with different data sources. It allows each database vendor to develop a native, optimized solution while enforcing a high level of consistency so that skilled developers don't need to relearn the basics.

However, the provider model isn't perfect. Although you can use standard interfaces to interact with Command and Connection objects, when you instantiate a Command or Connection object, you need to know the provider-specific, strongly typed class you want to use (such as SqlConnection). This limitation makes it difficult to build other tools or add-ins that use ADO.NET. For example, in Chapter 9 you'll consider the ASP.NET data source controls, which allow you to create data-bound pages without writing a line of code. To provide this functionality, you need a way for the data control to create the ADO.NET objects that it needs behind the scenes. This wasn't possible in .NET 1.x. However, .NET 2.0 introduced a new factory model that adds improved support for writing provider-agnostic code (code that can work with any database). This model remains unchanged in .NET 3.5.

■ **Note** Provider-agnostic code is useful when building specialized components. It may also make sense if you anticipate the need to move to a different database in the future or if you aren't sure what type of database you'll use in the final version of an application. However, it also has drawbacks. Provider-agnostic code can't take advantage of some provider-specific features (such as XML queries in SQL Server) and is more difficult to optimize. For those reasons, it's not commonly found in large-scale professional web applications.

Creating the Factory

The basic idea of the factory model is that you use a single factory object to create every other type of provider-specific object you need. You can then interact with these provider-specific objects in a completely generic way, through a set of common base classes.

The factory class is itself provider-specific—for example, the SQL Server provider includes a class named System.Data.SqlClient.SqlClientFactory. The Oracle provider uses System.Data.OracleClient.OracleClientFactory. At first glance, this might seem to stop you from writing provider-agnostic code. However, it turns out that there's a completely standardizedclass that's designed to dynamically find and create the factory you need. This class is System.Data.Common.DbProviderFactories. It provides a static GetFactory() method that returns the factory you need based on the provider name.

For example, here's the code that uses DbProviderFactories to get the SqlClientFactory:

```
string factory = "System.Data.SqlClient";
DbProviderFactory provider = DbProviderFactories.GetFactory(factory);
```

Even though the DbProviderFactories class returns a strongly typed SqlClientFactory object, you shouldn't treat it as such. Instead, your code should access it as a DbProviderFactory instance. That's because all factories inherit from DbProviderFactory. If you use only the DbProviderFactory members, you can write code that works with any factory.

The weak point in the code snippet shown previously is that you need to pass a string that identifies the provider to the DbProviderFactories.GetFactory() method. You would typically read this from an application setting in the web.config file. That way, you can write completely database-agnostic code and switch your application over to another provider simply by modifying a single setting.

■ **Tip** In practice, you'll need to store several provider-specific details in a configuration file. Not only do you need to retrieve the provider name, but you'll also need to get a connection string. You might also need to retrieve queries or stored procedure names if you want to avoid hard-coding them because they might change. It's up to you to determine the ideal trade-off between development complexity and flexibility.

For the DbProviderFactories class to work, your provider needs a registered factory in the machine.config or web.config configuration file. The machine.config file registers the four providers that are included with the .NET Framework:

```
<configuration>
  <system.data>
    <DbProviderFactories>
      <add name="Odbc Data Provider" invariant="System.Data.Odbc"
        type="System.Data.Odbc.OdbcFactory, ..." />
      <add name="OleDb Data Provider" invariant="System.Data.OleDb"
        type="System.Data.OleDb.OleDbFactory, ..." />
      <add name="OracleClient Data Provider"
        invariant="System.Data.OracleClient"
        type="System.Data.OracleClient.OracleClientFactory, ..." />
      <add name="SqlClient Data Provider" invariant="System.Data.SqlClient"
        type="System.Data.SqlClient.SqlClientFactory, ..." />
```

```
    </DbProviderFactories>
  </system.data>
  ...
</configuration>
```

This registration step identifies the factory class and assigns a unique name for the provider (which, by convention, is the same as the namespace for that provider). If you have a third-party provider that you want to use, you need to register it in the <DbProviders> section of the machine.config file (to access it across a specific computer) or a web.config file (to access it in a specific web application). It's likely that the person or company that developed the provider will include a setup program to automate this task or the explicit configuration syntax.

Create Objects with Factory

Once you have a factory, you can create other objects, such as Connection and Command instances, using the DbProviderFactory.CreateXxx() methods. For example, the CreateConnection() method returns the Connection object for your data provider. Once again, you must assume you don't know what provider you'll be using, so you can interact with the objects the factory creates only through a standard base class.

■ **Note** As explained earlier in this chapter, the provider-specific objects also implement certain interfaces (such as IDbConnection). However, because some objects use more than one ADO.NET interface (for example, a DataReader implements both IDataRecord and IDataReader), the base class model simplifies the model.

Table 7-8 gives a quick reference that shows what method you need in order to create each type of data access object and what base class you can use to manipulate it safely.

Table 7-8. *Interfaces for Standard ADO.NET Objects*

Type of Object	Base Class	Example	DbProviderFactory Method
Connection	DbConnection	SqlConnection	CreateConnection()
Command	DbCommand	SqlCommand	CreateCommand()
Parameter	DbParameter	SqlParameter	CreateParameter()
DataReader	DbDataReader	SqlDataReader	None (use IDbCommand.ExecuteReader() instead)
DataAdapter	DbDataAdapter	SqlDataAdapter	CreateDataAdapter()

A Query with Provider-Agnostic Code

To get a better understanding of how all these pieces fit together, it helps to consider a simple example. In this section, you'll see how to perform a query and display the results using provider-agnostic code. In fact, this example is an exact rewrite of the page shown earlier in Figure 7-3. The only difference is that it's no longer tightly bound to the SQL Server provider.

The first step is to set up the web.config file with the connection string, provider name, and query for this example:

```
<configuration>
  <connectionStrings>
    <add name="Northwind" connectionString=
"Data Source=localhost; Initial Catalog=Northwind; Integrated Security=SSPI"/>
  </connectionStrings>
  <appSettings>
    <add key="factory" value="System.Data.SqlClient" />
    <add key="employeeQuery" value="SELECT * FROM Employees" />
  </appSettings>
  ...
</configuration>
```

Next, here's the factory-based code:

```
// Get the factory.
string factory = WebConfigurationManager.AppSettings["factory"];
DbProviderFactory provider = DbProviderFactories.GetFactory(factory);

// Use this factory to create a connection.
DbConnection con = provider.CreateConnection();
con.ConnectionString =
  WebConfigurationManager.ConnectionStrings["Northwind"].ConnectionString;

// Create the command.
DbCommand cmd = provider.CreateCommand();
cmd.CommandText = WebConfigurationManager.AppSettings["employeeQuery"];
cmd.Connection = con;

// Open the Connection and get the DataReader.
con.Open();
DbDataReader reader = cmd.ExecuteReader();

// The code for navigating through the reader and displaying the records
// is identical from this point on.
```

To give this example a real test, try modifying the web.config file to use a different provider. For example, if you're using SQL Server 2005 or later, you can access the same database through the OLE DB provider by making this change:

```
<configuration>
  <connectionStrings>
    <add name="Northwind" connectionString="Provider=SQLNCLI; Data Source=
localhost; Initial Catalog=Northwind; Integrated Security=SSPI"/>
  </connectionStrings>
```

```
  <appSettings>
    <add key="factory" value="System.Data.OleDb" />
    <add key="employeeQuery" value="SELECT * FROM Employees" />
  </appSettings>
  ...
</configuration>
```

Now when you run the page, you'll see the same list of records. The difference is that the DbDataFactories class creates OLE DB objects to work with your code.

■ **Note** SQL Server 2005 introduced an OLE DB provider named SQLNCLI. Older versions of SQL Server use an OLE DB provider named SQLOLEDB. Either way, accessing SQL Server through OLE DB is discouraged for performance reasons. In this example, it's simply used to demonstrate how easily you can switch from one provider to another if you're using the factory model.

The challenges of provider-agnostic code aren't completely solved yet. Even with the provider factories, you still face a few problems. For example, there's no generic way to catch database exception objects (because different provider-specific exception objects don't inherit from a common base class). Also, different providers may have slightly different conventions with parameter names and may support specialized features that aren't available through the common base classes (in which case you need to write some thorny conditional logic).

Summary

In this chapter, you learned about the first level of database access with ADO.NET: connected access. In many cases, using simple commands and quick read-only cursors to retrieve results provides the easiest and most efficient way to write data access code for a web application. Along the way, you considered some advanced topics, including SQL injection attacks, transactions, and provider-agnostic code.
In the next chapter, you'll learn how to use these techniques to build your own data access classes and how to use ADO.NET's disconnected DataSet.

CHAPTER 8

Data Components and the DataSet

In the previous chapter, you had your first look at ADO.NET, and you examined connection-based data access. Now, it's time to bring your data access code into a well-designed application.

In a properly organized application, your data access code is never embedded directly in the code-behind for a page. Instead, it's separated into a dedicated database component. In this chapter, you'll see how to create a simple data access class of your own, adding a separate method for each data task you need to perform. Best of all, your database component won't be limited to code-only scenarios. In the next chapter, you'll see how to consume your database component with ASP.NET's new data binding infrastructure.

This chapter also tackles disconnected data—the ADO.NET features that revolve around the DataSet and allow you to interact with data long after you've closed the connection to the data source. The DataSet isn't required in ASP.NET pages. However, it gives you more flexibility for navigating, filtering, and sorting your data—topics you'll consider in this chapter.

Building a Data Access Component

In professional applications, database code is not embedded directly in the client but encapsulated in a dedicated class. To perform a database operation, the client creates an instance of this class and calls the appropriate method.

When creating a database component, you should follow the basic guidelines in this section. This will ensure that you create a well-encapsulated, optimized component that can be executed in a separate process, if needed, and even used in a load-balancing configuration with multiple servers.

Open and close connections quickly: Open the database connection in every method call, and close it before the method ends. Connections should never be held open between client requests, and the client should have no control over how connections are acquired or when they are released. If the client does have this ability, it introduces the possibility that a connection might not be closed as quickly as possible or might be inadvertently left open, which hampers scalability.

Implement error handling: Use error handling to make sure the connection is closed even if the SQL command generates an exception. Remember, connections are a finite resource, and using them for even a few extra seconds can have a major overall effect on performance.

Follow stateless design practices: Accept all the information needed for a method in its parameters, and return all the retrieved data through the return value. If you create a class that maintains state, it cannot be easily implemented as a web service or used in a load-balancing scenario. Also, if the database component is hosted out of the process, each method call has a measurable overhead, and using multiple calls to set properties will take much longer than invoking a single method with all the information as parameters.

Don't let the client use wide-open queries: Every query should judiciously select only the columns it needs. Also, you should restrict the results with a WHERE clause whenever possible. For example, when retrieving order records, you might impose a minimum date range (or a SQL clause such as TOP 1000). Without these safeguards, your application may work well at first but will slow down as the database grows and clients perform large queries, which can tax both the database and the network.

A good, straightforward design for a database component uses a separate class for every database table (or logically related group of tables). The common database access methods such as inserting, deleting, and modifying a record are all wrapped in separate stateless methods. Finally, every database call uses a dedicated stored procedure. Figure 8-1 shows this carefully layered design.

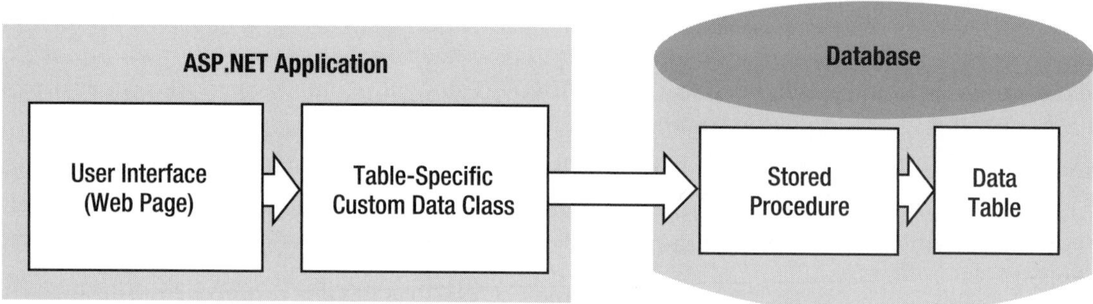

Figure 8-1. Layered design with a database class

The following example demonstrates a simple database component. Rather than placing the database code in the web page, it follows a much better design practice of separating the code into a distinct class that can be used in multiple pages. This class can then be compiled as part of a separate component if needed. Additionally, the connection string is retrieved from the <connectionStrings> section of the web.config file, rather than being hard-coded.

The database component actually consists of at least two classes—a data package class that wraps a single record of information (known as the *data class*) and a database utility class that performs the actual database operations with ADO.NET code (known as the *data access class*). In this chapter, we refer to the component that includes these ingredients as a database component. In the following sections, you'll consider an extremely simple database component that works with a single table.

■ **Note** Your database component doesn't need to use the ADO.NET classes to perform its work. In particular, you may be interested in using LINQ to Entities (as discussed in Chapter 13) to do some of the work. However, it's always a good idea to follow this essential design and create a separate, stateless component for your database logic.

The Data Package

To make it easier to shuffle information to the Northwind database and back, it makes sense to create an EmployeeDetails class that provides all the database fields as public properties. Here's the full code for this class:

```
public class EmployeeDetails
{
    private int employeeID;
    public int EmployeeID
    {
        get {return employeeID;}
        set {employeeID = value;}
    }

    private string firstName;
    public string FirstName
    {
        get {return firstName;}
        set {firstName = value;}
    }

    private string lastName;
    public string LastName
    {
        get {return lastName;}
        set {lastName = value;}
    }

    private string titleOfCourtesy;
    public string TitleOfCourtesy
    {
        get {return titleOfCourtesy;}
        set {titleOfCourtesy = value;}
    }

    public EmployeeDetails(int employeeID, string firstName, string lastName,
      string titleOfCourtesy)
    {
        EmployeeID = employeeID;
        FirstName = firstName;
        LastName = lastName;
        TitleOfCourtesy = titleOfCourtesy;
    }
}
```

Note that this class doesn't include all the information that's in the Employees table in order to make the example more concise.

When building a data class, you may choose to use *automatic properties*, a C# language feature that allows you to create a property wrapper and the underlying private variable with one code construct, like this:

```
public int EmployeeID
{ get; set; }
```

When using automatic properties, the private variable is generated automatically at compile time, so you won't know its name. In your code, you must always access the private variable through the property procedures. The C# compiler also adds the code that gets and sets the private variable, which is the same as the code you'd write yourself.

Automatic variables look similar to public member fields, but the implications of using them are dramatically different. Because automatic properties really are full-fledged properties, you can replace them with an explicit property at a later time (for example, if you need to add validation code) without changing the public interface of your data class or disturbing the other classes that use your data class. Similarly, automatic properties have all the metadata of explicit properties, so they work like properties in key coding scenarios. For example, unlike public member fields, automatic properties support the data binding techniques you'll learn about in Chapter 9.

The Stored Procedures

Before you can start coding the data access logic, you need to make sure you have the set of stored procedures you need in order to retrieve, insert, and update information. The following database script creates the five stored procedures that are needed:

```
CREATE PROCEDURE InsertEmployee
@EmployeeID      int OUTPUT,
@FirstName       varchar(10),
@LastName        varchar(20),
@TitleOfCourtesy varchar(25)
AS
INSERT INTO Employees
  (TitleOfCourtesy, LastName, FirstName, HireDate)
  VALUES (@TitleOfCourtesy, @LastName, @FirstName, GETDATE());
SET @EmployeeID = @@IDENTITY
GO

CREATE PROCEDURE DeleteEmployee
@EmployeeID      int
AS
DELETE FROM Employees WHERE EmployeeID = @EmployeeID
GO

CREATE PROCEDURE UpdateEmployee
@EmployeeID      int,
@TitleOfCourtesy varchar(25),
@LastName        varchar(20),
@FirstName       varchar(10)
AS

UPDATE Employees
    SET TitleOfCourtesy = @TitleOfCourtesy,
    LastName = @LastName,
    FirstName = @FirstName
    WHERE EmployeeID = @EmployeeID
GO

CREATE PROCEDURE GetAllEmployees
AS
```

```
SELECT EmployeeID, FirstName, LastName, TitleOfCourtesy FROM Employees
GO

CREATE PROCEDURE CountEmployees
AS
SELECT COUNT(EmployeeID) FROM Employees
GO

CREATE PROCEDURE GetEmployee
@EmployeeID      int
AS
SELECT EmployeeID, FirstName, LastName, TitleOfCourtesy FROM Employees
  WHERE EmployeeID = @EmployeeID
GO
```

The Data Utility Class

Finally, you need the utility class that performs the actual database operations. This class uses the stored procedures that were shown in the previous section.

In this example, the data utility class is named EmployeeDB. It encapsulates all the data access code and database-specific details. Here's the basic outline:

```
public class EmployeeDB
{
    private string connectionString;

    public EmployeeDB()
    {
        // Get default connection string.
        connectionString = WebConfigurationManager.ConnectionStrings[
          "Northwind"].ConnectionString;
    }
    public EmployeeDB(string connectionString)
    {
        // Set the specified connection string.
        this.connectionString = connectionString;
    }

    public int InsertEmployee(EmployeeDetails emp)
    { ... }
    public void DeleteEmployee(int employeeID)
    { ... }
    public void UpdateEmployee(EmployeeDetails emp)
    { ... }

    public EmployeeDetails GetEmployee(int employeeID)
    { ... }
    public List<EmployeeDetails> GetEmployees()
    { ... }
    public int CountEmployees()
    { ... }
}
```

■ **Note** You may have noticed that the EmployeeDB class uses instance methods, not static methods. That's because even though the EmployeeDB class doesn't store any state from the database, it does store the connection string as a private member variable. Because this is an instance class, the connection string can be retrieved every time the class is created, rather than every time a method is invoked. This approach makes the code a little clearer and allows it to be slightly faster (by avoiding the need to read the web.config file multiple times). However, the benefit is fairly small, so you can use static methods just as easily in your database components.

Each method uses the same careful approach, relying exclusively on a stored procedure to interact with the database. Here's the code for inserting a record, assuming you've imported the System.Data.SqlClient namespace:

```
public int InsertEmployee(EmployeeDetails emp)
{
    SqlConnection con = new SqlConnection(connectionString);
    SqlCommand cmd = new SqlCommand("InsertEmployee", con);
    cmd.CommandType = CommandType.StoredProcedure;
    cmd.Parameters.Add(new SqlParameter("@FirstName", SqlDbType.NVarChar, 10));
    cmd.Parameters["@FirstName"].Value = emp.FirstName;
    cmd.Parameters.Add(new SqlParameter("@LastName", SqlDbType.NVarChar, 20));
    cmd.Parameters["@LastName"].Value = emp.LastName;
    cmd.Parameters.Add(new SqlParameter("@TitleOfCourtesy",
      SqlDbType.NVarChar, 25));
    cmd.Parameters["@TitleOfCourtesy"].Value = emp.TitleOfCourtesy;
    cmd.Parameters.Add(new SqlParameter("@EmployeeID", SqlDbType.Int, 4));
    cmd.Parameters["@EmployeeID"].Direction = ParameterDirection.Output;

    try
    {
        con.Open();
        cmd.ExecuteNonQuery();
        return (int)cmd.Parameters["@EmployeeID"].Value;
    }
    catch (SqlException err)
    {
        // Replace the error with something less specific.
        // You could also log the error now.
        throw new ApplicationException("Data error.");
    }
    finally
    {
        con.Close();
    }
}
```

As you can see, the method accepts data as an EmployeeDetails data object. Any errors are caught, and the sensitive internal details are not returned to the web-page code. This prevents the web page from providing information that could lead to possible exploits. This would also be an ideal place to call another method in a logging component to report the full information in an event log or another database.

The GetEmployee() and GetEmployees() methods return the data using a single EmployeeDetails object or a list of EmployeeDetails objects, respectively:

```
public EmployeeDetails GetEmployee(int employeeID)
{
    SqlConnection con = new SqlConnection(connectionString);
    SqlCommand cmd = new SqlCommand("GetEmployee", con);
    cmd.CommandType = CommandType.StoredProcedure;
    cmd.Parameters.Add(new SqlParameter("@EmployeeID", SqlDbType.Int, 4));
    cmd.Parameters["@EmployeeID"].Value = employeeID;

    try
    {
        con.Open();
        SqlDataReader reader = cmd.ExecuteReader(CommandBehavior.SingleRow);

        // Check if the query returned a record.
        if (!reader.HasRows) return null;

        // Get the first row.
        reader.Read();
        EmployeeDetails emp = new EmployeeDetails(
         (int)reader["EmployeeID"], (string)reader["FirstName"],
         (string)reader["LastName"], (string)reader["TitleOfCourtesy"]);
        reader.Close();
        return emp;
    }
    catch (SqlException err)
    {
        throw new ApplicationException("Data error.");
    }
    finally
    {
        con.Close();
    }
}

public List<EmployeeDetails> GetEmployees()
{
    SqlConnection con = new SqlConnection(connectionString);
    SqlCommand cmd = new SqlCommand("GetAllEmployees", con);
    cmd.CommandType = CommandType.StoredProcedure;

    // Create a collection for all the employee records.
    List<EmployeeDetails> employees = new List<EmployeeDetails>();

    try
    {
        con.Open();
        SqlDataReader reader = cmd.ExecuteReader();
        while (reader.Read())
        {
```

```
            EmployeeDetails emp = new EmployeeDetails(
            (int)reader["EmployeeID"], (string)reader["FirstName"],
            (string)reader["LastName"], (string)reader["TitleOfCourtesy"]);
            employees.Add(emp);
        }
        reader.Close();
        return employees;
    }
    catch (SqlException err)
    {
        throw new ApplicationException("Data error.");
    }
    finally
    {
        con.Close();
    }
}
```

The UpdateEmployee() method plays a special role. It determines the concurrency strategy of your database component (see the next section, "Concurrency Strategies").

Here's the code:

```
public void UpdateEmployee(int EmployeeID, string firstName, string lastName,
  string titleOfCourtesy)
{
    SqlConnection con = new SqlConnection(connectionString);
    SqlCommand cmd = new SqlCommand("UpdateEmployee", con);
    cmd.CommandType = CommandType.StoredProcedure;

    cmd.Parameters.Add(new SqlParameter("@FirstName", SqlDbType.NVarChar, 10));
    cmd.Parameters["@FirstName"].Value = firstName;
    cmd.Parameters.Add(new SqlParameter("@LastName", SqlDbType.NVarChar, 20));
    cmd.Parameters["@LastName"].Value = lastName;
    cmd.Parameters.Add(new SqlParameter("@TitleOfCourtesy", SqlDbType.NVarChar,
      25));
    cmd.Parameters["@TitleOfCourtesy"].Value = titleOfCourtesy;
    cmd.Parameters.Add(new SqlParameter("@EmployeeID", SqlDbType.Int, 4));
    cmd.Parameters["@EmployeeID"].Value = EmployeeID;

    try
    {
        con.Open();
        cmd.ExecuteNonQuery();
    }
    catch (SqlException err)
    {
        throw new ApplicationException("Data error.");
    }
    finally
    {
        con.Close();
    }
}
```

Finally, the DeleteEmployee() and CountEmployees() methods fill in the last two ingredients:

```
public void DeleteEmployee(int employeeID)
{
    SqlConnection con = new SqlConnection(connectionString);
    SqlCommand cmd = new SqlCommand("DeleteEmployee", con);
    cmd.CommandType = CommandType.StoredProcedure;
    cmd.Parameters.Add(new SqlParameter("@EmployeeID", SqlDbType.Int, 4));
    cmd.Parameters["@EmployeeID"].Value = employeeID;

    try
    {
        con.Open();
        cmd.ExecuteNonQuery();
    }
    catch (SqlException err)
    {
        throw new ApplicationException("Data error.");

    }
    finally
    {
        con.Close();
    }
}

public int CountEmployees()
{
    SqlConnection con = new SqlConnection(connectionString);
    SqlCommand cmd = new SqlCommand("CountEmployees", con);
    cmd.CommandType = CommandType.StoredProcedure;

    try
    {
        con.Open();
        return (int)cmd.ExecuteScalar();
    }
    catch (SqlException err)
    {
        throw new ApplicationException("Data error.");
    }
    finally
    {
        con.Close();
    }
}
```

Concurrency Strategies

In any multiuser application, including web applications, there's the potential that more than one user will perform overlapping queries and updates. This can lead to a potentially confusing situation where two users, who are both in possession of the current state for a row, attempt to commit divergent updates. The first user's update will always succeed. The success or failure of the second update is determined by your *concurrency strategy*.

There are several broad approaches to concurrency management. The most important thing to understand is that you determine your concurrency strategy by the way you write your UPDATE and DELETE commands (particularly the way you shape the WHERE clause).

Here are the most common examples:

Last-in-wins updating: This is a less restrictive form of concurrency control that always commits the update (unless the original row has been deleted). Every time an update is committed, all the values are applied. Last-in-wins makes sense if data collisions are rare. For example, you can safely use this approach if there is only one person responsible for updating a given group of records. Usually, you implement a last-in-wins by writing a WHERE clause that matches the record to update based on its primary key. The UpdateEmployee() method in the previous example uses the last-in-wins approach.

```
UPDATE Employees SET ... WHERE EmployeeID=@EmployeeID
```

Match-all updating: To implement this strategy, your UPDATE command needs to use all the values you want to set, plus all the original values. You use all the original values to construct the WHERE clause that finds the original record. That way, if even a single field has been modified, the record won't be matched and the change will not succeed. One problem with this approach is that compatible changes are not allowed. For example, if two users are attempting to modify different parts of the same record, the second user's change will be rejected, even though it doesn't conflict. Another more significant problem with the match-all updating strategy is that it leads to large, inefficient SQL statements. You can implement the same strategy more effectively with timestamps (see the next point).

```
UPDATE Employees SET ... WHERE EmployeeID=@EmployeeID AND
  FirstName=@OriginalFirstName AND LastName=@OriginalLastName ...
```

Timestamp-based updating: Most database systems support a timestamp column, which the data source updates automatically every time a change is performed. You don't modify the timestamp column manually. However, if you retrieve it when you perform your SELECT statement, you can use it in the WHERE clause for your UPDATE statement. That way, you're guaranteed to update the record only if it hasn't been modified, just like with match-all updating. Unlike match-all updating, the WHERE clause is shorter and more efficient, because it only needs two pieces of information—the primary key and the timestamp.

```
UPDATE Employees SET ... WHERE EmployeeID=@EmployeeID AND TimeStamp=@TimeStamp
```

Changed-value updating: This approach attempts to apply just the changed values in an UPDATE command, thereby allowing two users to make changes at the same time if these changes are to different fields. The problem with this approach is it can be complex, because you need to keep track of what values have changed (in which case they should be incorporated in the WHERE clause) and what values haven't.

■ **Note** Last-in-wins is an example of database access with no concurrency control at all. Match-all updating, timestamp-based updating, and changed-value updating are examples of *optimistic concurrency*. With optimistic concurrency, your code doesn't hold locks on the data it's using—instead, your strategy is to hope that changes don't overlap and respond accordingly if they do. Later in this chapter you'll learn about transactions, which allow you to implement *pessimistic concurrency*. Pessimistic concurrency prevents concurrency conflicts by locking in-use records. The tradeoff is scalability, because other users who attempt to access the same data will be put on hold.

To get a better understanding of how this plays out, consider what happens if two users attempt to commit different updates to an employee record using a method such as UpdateEmployee(), which implements last-in-wins concurrency. The first user updates the mailing address. The second user changes the employee name and inadvertently reapplies the old mailing address at the same time. The problem is that the UpdateEmployee() method doesn't have any way to know what changes you are committing. This means that it pushes all the in-memory values back to the data source, even if these old values haven't been changed (and wind up overwriting someone else's update).

If you have large, complex records and you need to support different types of edits, the easiest way to solve a problem like this may be to create more-targeted methods. Instead of creating a generic UpdateEmployee() method, use more-targeted methods such as UpdateEmployeeAddress() or ChangeEmployeeStatus(). These methods can then execute more limited UPDATE statements that don't risk reapplying old values.

You might also want to consider allowing multiple levels of concurrency and giving the user the final say. For example, when a user commits an edit, you can attempt to apply the update using strict match-all or timestamp-based concurrency. If this fails, you can then show the user the data that's currently in the record and compare it with the data the user is trying to apply. At that point, you can give the user the option to make further edits or commit the change with last-in-wins concurrency, overwriting the current values. You'll see an example of this technique with ASP.NET's rich data controls in Chapter 10, in the section "Detecting Concurrency Conflicts."

Testing the Database Component

Now that you've created the database component, you just need a simple test page to try it out. As with any other component, you must begin by adding a reference to the component assembly. Then you can import the namespace it uses to make it easier to use the EmployeeDetails and EmployeeDB classes. The only step that remains is to write the code that interacts with the classes. In this example, the code takes place in the Page.Load event handler of a web page.

First, the code retrieves and writes the number and the list of employees by using a private WriteEmployeesList() method that translates the details to HTML and displays that HTML in a Literal control named HtmlContent. Next, the code adds a record and lists the table content again. Finally, the code deletes the added record and shows the content of the Employees table one more time.

Here's the complete page code:

```
public partial class ComponentTest : System.Web.UI.Page
{
    // Create the database component so it's available anywhere on the page.
    private EmployeeDB db = new EmployeeDB();

    protected void Page_Load(object sender, System.EventArgs e)
    {
```

```
        WriteEmployeesList();

        // The ID value is simply set to 0, because it's generated by the
        // database server and filled in automatically when you call
        // InsertEmployee().
        int empID = db.InsertEmployee(
          new EmployeeDetails(0, "Mr.", "Bellinaso", "Marco"));
          HtmlContent.Text += "<br />Inserted 1 employee.<br />";

        WriteEmployeesList();

        db.DeleteEmployee(empID);
        HtmlContent.Text += "<br />Deleted 1 employee.<br />";

        WriteEmployeesList();
    }

    private void WriteEmployeesList()
    {
        StringBuilder htmlStr = new StringBuilder("");

        int numEmployees = db.CountEmployees();
        htmlStr.Append("<br />Total employees: <b>");
        htmlStr.Append(numEmployees.ToString());
        htmlStr.Append("</b><br /><br />");

        List<EmployeeDetails> employees = db.GetEmployees();
        foreach (EmployeeDetails emp in employees)
        {
            htmlStr.Append("<li>");
            htmlStr.Append(emp.EmployeeID);
            htmlStr.Append(" ");
            htmlStr.Append(emp.TitleOfCourtesy);
            htmlStr.Append(" <b>");
            htmlStr.Append(emp.FirstName);
            htmlStr.Append("</b>, ");
            htmlStr.Append(emp.LastName);
            htmlStr.Append("</li>");
        }
        htmlStr.Append("<br />");
        HtmlContent.Text += htmlStr.ToString();
    }
}
```

Figure 8-2 shows the page output.

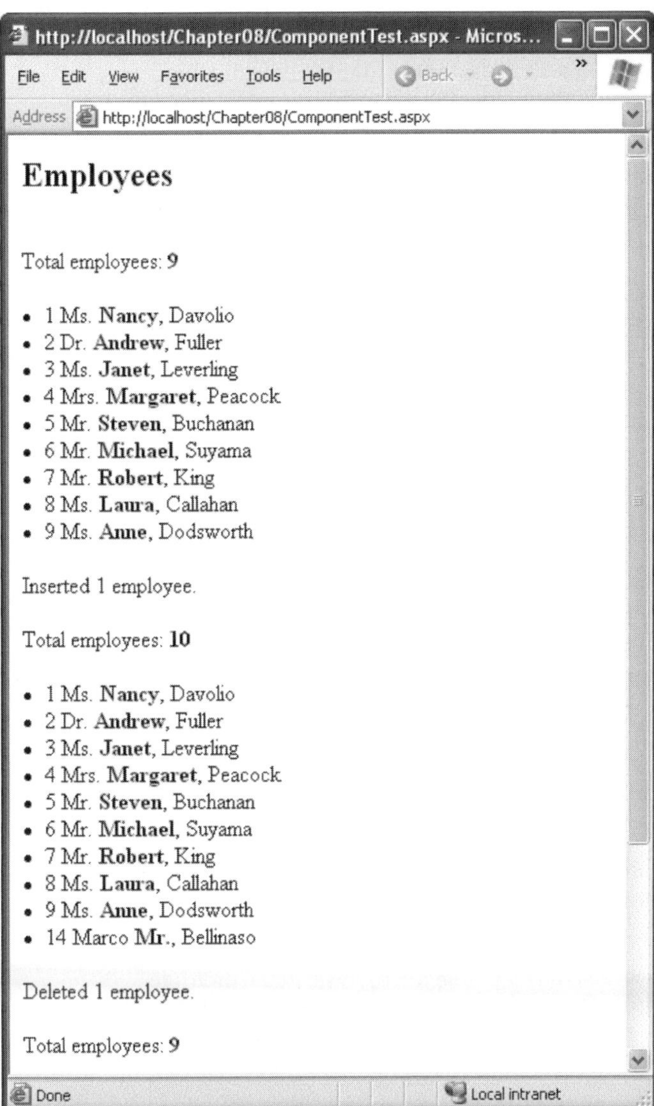

Figure 8-2. *Using a database component*

Disconnected Data

So far, all the examples you've seen have used ADO.NET's connection-based features. When using this approach, data ceases to have anything to do with the data source the moment it is retrieved. It's up to your code to track user actions, store information, and determine when a new command should be generated and executed.

ADO.NET emphasizes an entirely different philosophy with the DataSet object. When you connect to a database, you fill the DataSet with a copy of the information drawn from the database. If you change the information in the DataSet, the information in the corresponding table in the database isn't changed. That means you can easily process and manipulate the data without worry, because you aren't using a valuable database connection. If necessary, you can reconnect to the original data source and apply all your DataSet changes in a single batch operation.

Of course, this convenience isn't without drawbacks, such as concurrency issues. Depending on how your application is designed, an entire batch of changes may be submitted at once. A single error (such as trying to update a record that another user has updated in the meantime) can derail the entire update process. With studious coding you can protect your application from these problems—but it requires additional effort.

On the other hand, sometimes you might want to use ADO.NET's disconnected access model and the DataSet. Some of the scenarios in which a DataSet is easier to use than a DataReader include the following:

- When you need a convenient package to send the data to another component (for example, if you're sharing information with other components or distributing it to clients through a web service).
- When you need a convenient file format to serialize the data to disk (the DataSet includes built-in functionality that allows you to save it to an XML file).
- When you want to navigate backward and forward through a large amount of data. For example, you could use a DataSet to support a paged list control that shows a subset of information at a time. The DataReader, on the other hand, can move in only one direction: forward.
- When you want to navigate among several different tables. The DataSet can store all these tables, and information about the relations between them, thereby allowing you to create easy master-detail pages without needing to query the database more than once.
- When you want to use data binding with user interface controls. You can use a DataReader for data binding, but because the DataReader is a forward-only cursor, you can't bind your data to multiple controls. You also won't have the ability to apply custom sorting and filtering criteria, like you can with the DataSet.
- When you want to manipulate the data as XML.
- When you want to provide batch updates. For example, you might create a web service that allows a client to download a DataTable full of rows, make multiple changes, and then resubmit it later. At that point, the web service can apply all the changes in a single operation (assuming no conflicts occur).

In the remainder of this chapter, you'll learn about how to retrieve data into a DataSet. You'll also learn how to retrieve data from multiple tables, how to create relationships between these in-memory data tables, how to sort and filter data, and how to search for specific records. However, you won't consider the task of using the DataSet to perform updates. That's because the ASP.NET model lends itself more closely to direct commands, as discussed in the next section.

Web Applications and the DataSet

A common misconception is that the DataSet is required to ensure scalability in a web application. Now that you understand the ASP.NET request processing architecture, you can probably see that this isn't the case. A web application runs only for a matter of seconds (if that long). This means that even if your web application uses direct cursor-based access, the lifetime of the connection is so short that it won't significantly reduce scalability, except in the mostly highly trafficked web applications.

In fact, the DataSet makes much more sense with distributed applications that use a rich Windows client. In this scenario, the clients can retrieve a DataSet from the server (perhaps using a web service), work with their DataSet objects for a long period of time, and reconnect to the system only when they need to update the data source with the batch of changes they've made. This allows the system to handle a much larger number of concurrent users than it would be able to if each client maintained a direct, long-lasting connection. It also allows you to efficiently share resources by caching data on the server and pooling connections between client requests.

The DataSet also acts as a neat package of information for rich client applications that are only intermittently connected to your system. For example, consider a traveling sales associate who needs to enter order information or review information about sales contacts on a laptop. Using the DataSet, an application on the user's laptop can store disconnected data locally and serialize it to an XML file. This allows the sales associate to build new orders using the cached data, even when no Internet connection is available. The new data can be submitted later when the user reconnects to the system.

So, where does all this leave ASP.NET web applications? Essentially, you have two choices. You can use the DataSet, or you can use direct commands to bypass the DataSet altogether. Generally speaking, you'll bypass the DataSet when inserting, deleting, or updating records. However, you won't avoid the DataSet completely. In fact, when you retrieve records, you'll probably want to use the DataSet, because it supports a few indispensable features. In particular, the DataSet allows you to easily pass a block of data from a database component to a web page. The DataSet also supports data binding, which allows you to display your information in advanced data controls such as the GridView. For that reason, most web applications retrieve data into the DataSet but perform direct updates using straightforward commands.

■ **Note** Web services represent the only real web application scenario in which you might decide to perform batch updating through a DataSet. In this case, a rich client application downloads the data as a DataSet, edits it, and resubmits the DataSet later to commit its changes.

XML Integration

The DataSet also provides native XML serialization. You don't need to even be aware of this to enjoy its benefits, such as being able to easily serialize a DataSet to a file or transmit the DataSet to another application through a web service. At its best, this feature allows you to share your data with clients written in different programming languages and running on other operating systems. However, implementing such a solution isn't easy (and often the DataSet isn't the best approach) because you have little ability to customize the structure of the XML that the DataSet produces.

You'll learn more about the DataSet support for XML in Chapter 14.

The DataSet

The DataSet is the heart of disconnected data access. The DataSet contains two important ingredients: a collection of zero or more tables (exposed through the Tables property) and a collection of zero or more relationships that you can use to link tables together (exposed through the Relations property). Figure 8-3 shows the basic structure of the DataSet.

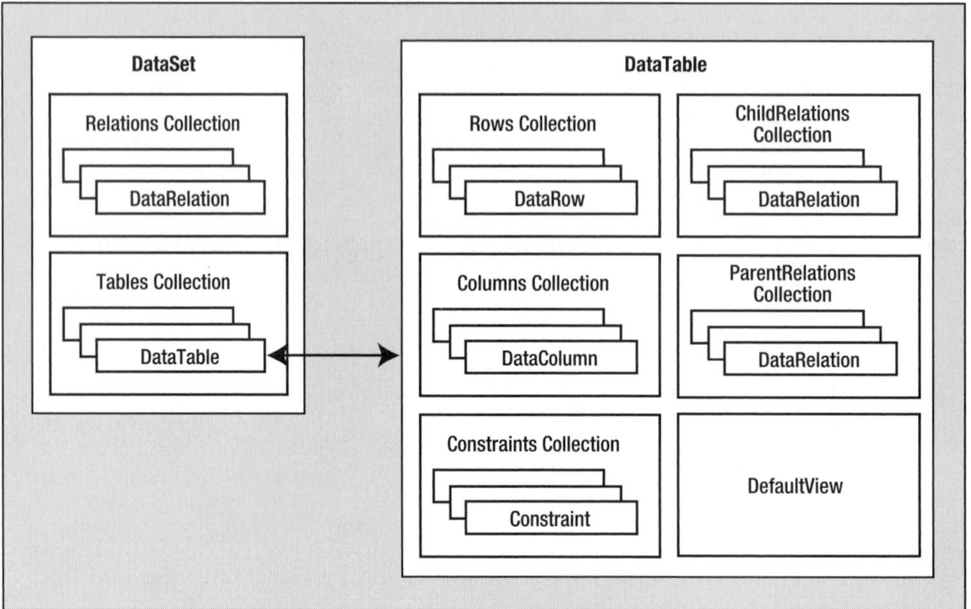

Figure 8-3. Dissecting the DataSet

■ **Note** Occasionally, novice ADO.NET developers make the mistake of assuming that the DataSet should contain all the information from a given table in the data source. This is not the case. For performance reasons, you will probably use the DataSet to work with a small subset of the total information in the data source. Also, the tables in the DataSet do not need to map directly to tables in the data source. A single table can hold the results of a query on one table, or it can hold the results of a JOIN query that combines data from more than one linked table.

As you can see in Figure 8-3, each item in the DataSet.Tables collection is a DataTable. The DataTable contains its own collections—the Columns collection of DataColumn objects (which describe the name and data type of each field) and the Rows collection of DataRow objects (which contain the actual data in each record).

Each record in a DataTable is represented by a DataRow object. Each DataRow object represents a single record in a table that has been retrieved from the data source. The DataRow is the container for the actual field values. You can access them by field name, as in myRow["FieldName"]. Always remember that the data in the data source is not touched at all when you work with the DataSet objects. Instead, all the changes are made locally to the DataSet in memory. The DataSet never retains any type of connection to a data source.

The DataSet also has methods that can write and read XML data and schemas and has methods you can use to quickly clear and duplicate data. Table 8-1 outlines these methods. You'll learn more about XML in Chapter 14.

Table 8-1. *DataSet XML and Miscellaneous Methods*

Method	Description
GetXml() and GetXmlSchema()	Returns a string with the data (in XML markup) or schema information for the DataSet. The schema information is the structural information such as the number of tables, their names, their columns, their data types, and their relationships.
WriteXml() and WriteXmlSchema()	Persists the data and schema represented by the DataSet to a file or a stream in XML format.
ReadXml() and ReadXmlSchema()	Creates the tables in a DataSet based on an existing XML document or XML schema document. The XML source can be a file or any other stream.
Clear()	Empties all the data from the tables. However, this method leaves the schema and relationship information intact.
Copy()	Returns an exact duplicate of the DataSet, with the same set of tables, relationships, and data.
Clone()	Returns a DataSet with the same structure (tables and relationships) but no data.
Merge()	Takes another DataSet, a DataTable, or a collection of DataRow objects as input and merges them into the current DataSet, adding any new tables and merging any existing tables.

The DataAdapter Class

To extract records from a database and use them to fill a table in a DataSet, you need to use another ADO.NET object: a DataAdapter. The DataAdapter comes in a provider-specific object, so there is a separate DataAdapter class for each provider (such as SqlDataAdapter, OracleDataAdapter, and so on).

The DataAdapter serves as a bridge between a single DataTable in the DataSet and the data source. It contains all the available commands for querying and updating the data source.

To enable the DataAdapter to edit, delete, and add rows, you need to specify Command objects for the UpdateCommand, DeleteCommand, and InsertCommand properties of the DataAdapter. To use the DataAdapter to fill a DataSet, you must set the SelectCommand.

The DataAdapter provides three key methods, as listed in Table 8-2.

Table 8-2. *DataAdapter Methods*

Method	Description
Fill()	Adds a DataTable to a DataSet by executing the query in the SelectCommand. If your query returns multiple result sets, this method will add multiple DataTable objects at once. You can also use this method to add data to an existing DataTable.
FillSchema()	Adds a DataTable to a DataSet by executing the query in the SelectCommand and retrieving schema information only. This method doesn't add any data to the DataTable. Instead, it simply preconfigures the DataTable with detailed information about column names, data types, primary keys, and unique constraints.

Method	Description
Update()	Examines all the changes in a single DataTable and applies this batch of changes to the data source by executing the appropriate InsertCommand, UpdateCommand, and DeleteCommand operations.

Figure 8-4 shows how a DataAdapter and its Command objects work together with the data source and the DataSet.

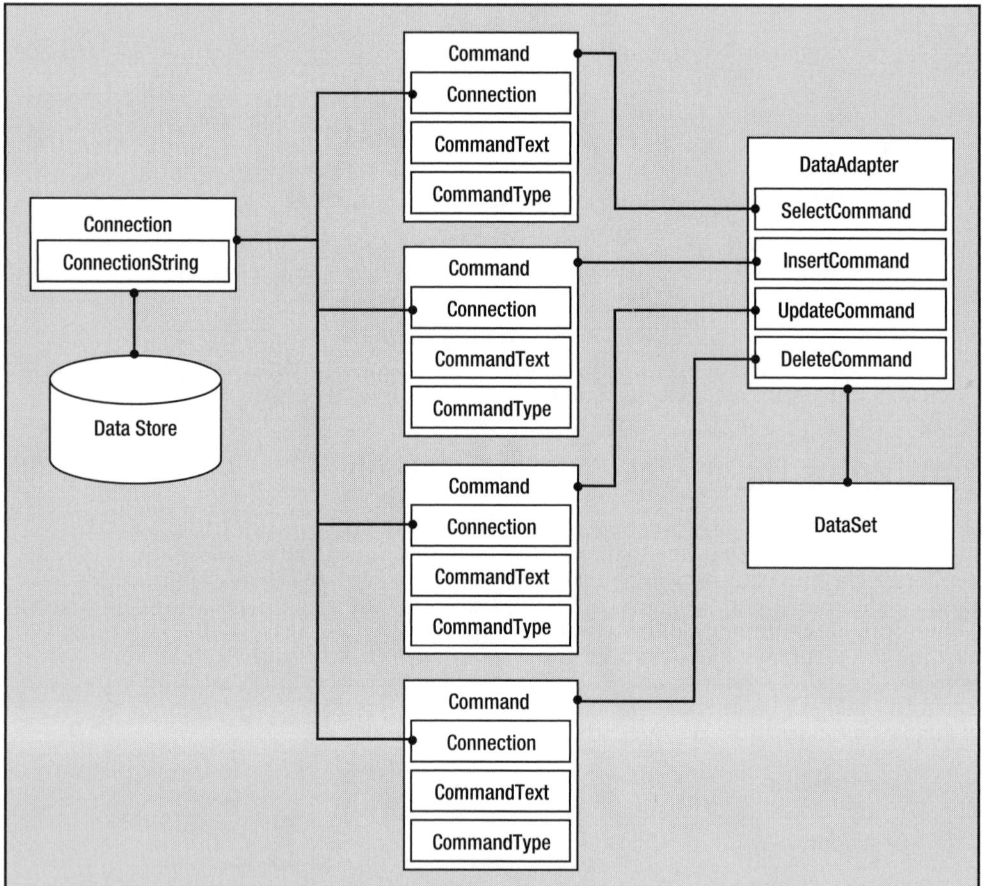

Figure 8-4. *How the DataAdapter interacts with the data source*

Filling a DataSet

In the following example, you'll see how to retrieve data from a SQL Server table and use it to fill a DataTable object in the DataSet. You'll also see how to display the data by programmatically cycling through the records and displaying them one by one. All the logic takes place in the event handler for the Page.Load event.

First, the code creates the connection and defines the text of the SQL query:

```
string connectionString =
  WebConfigurationManager.ConnectionStrings["Northwind"].ConnectionString;
SqlConnection con = new SqlConnection(connectionString);
string sql = "SELECT * FROM Employees";
```

The next step is to create a new instance of the SqlDataAdapter class that will retrieve the employee list. Although every DataAdapter supports four Command objects, only one of these (the SelectCommand) is required to fill a DataSet. To make life even easier, you can create the Command object you need and assign it to the DataAdapter.SelectCommand property in one step. You just need to supply a Connection object and query string in the DataAdapter constructor, as shown here:

```
SqlDataAdapter da = new SqlDataAdapter(sql, con);
```

Now you need to create a new, empty DataSet and use the DataAdapter.Fill() method to execute the query and place the results in a new DataTable in the DataSet. At this point, you can also specify the name for the table. If you don't, a default name (like Table) will be used automatically. In the following example, the table name corresponds to the name of the source table in the database, although this is not a requirement:

```
DataSet ds = new DataSet();
da.Fill(ds, "Employees");
```

Note that this code doesn't explicitly open the connection by calling Connection.Open(). Instead, the DataAdapter opens and closes the linked connection behind the scenes when you call the Fill() method. As a result, the only line of code you should consider placing in an exception-handling block is the call to DataAdapter.Fill(). Alternatively, you can also open and close the connection manually. If the connection is open when you call Fill(), the DataAdapter will use that connection and won't close it automatically. This approach is useful if you want to perform multiple operations with the data source in quick succession and you don't want to incur the additional overhead of repeatedly opening and closing the connection each time.

The last step is to display the contents of the DataSet. A quick approach is to use the same technique that was shown in the previous chapter and build an HTML string by examining each record. The following code cycles through all the DataRow objects in the DataTable and displays the field values of each record in a bulleted list:

```
StringBuilder htmlStr = new StringBuilder("");
foreach (DataRow dr in ds.Tables["Employees"].Rows)
{
    htmlStr.Append("<li>");
    htmlStr.Append(dr["TitleOfCourtesy"].ToString());
    htmlStr.Append(" <b>");
    htmlStr.Append(dr["LastName"].ToString());
    htmlStr.Append("</b>, ");
    htmlStr.Append(dr["FirstName"].ToString());
    htmlStr.Append("</li>");
}
HtmlContent.Text = htmlStr.ToString();
```

Of course, the ASP.NET model is designed to save you from coding raw HTML. A much better approach is to bind the data in the DataSet to a data-bound control, which automatically generates the HTML you need based on a single template. Chapter 9 describes the data-bound controls in detail.

■ **Note** When you bind a DataSet to a control, no data objects are stored in view state. The data control stores enough information to show only the data that's currently displayed. If you need to interact with a DataSet over multiple postbacks, you'll need to store it in the ViewState collection manually (which will greatly increase the size of the page) or the Session or Cache objects.

Working with Multiple Tables and Relationships

The next example shows a more advanced use of the DataSet that, in addition to providing disconnected data, uses table relationships. This example demonstrates how to retrieve some records from the Categories and Products tables of the Northwind database and how to create a relationship between them so that it's easy to navigate from a category record to all of its child products and create a simple report.

The first step is to initialize the ADO.NET objects and declare the two SQL queries (for retrieving categories and products), as shown here:

```
string connectionString =
  WebConfigurationManager.ConnectionStrings["Northwind"].ConnectionString;
SqlConnection con = new SqlConnection(connectionString);

string sqlCat = "SELECT CategoryID, CategoryName FROM Categories";
string sqlProd = "SELECT ProductName, CategoryID FROM Products";

SqlDataAdapter da = new SqlDataAdapter(sqlCat, con);
DataSet ds = new DataSet();
```

Next, the code executes both queries, adding two tables to the DataSet. Note that the connection is explicitly opened at the beginning and closed after the two operations, ensuring the best possible performance.

```
try
{
    con.Open();

    // Fill the DataSet with the Categories table.
    da.Fill(ds, "Categories");

    // Change the command text and retrieve the Products table.
    // You could also use another DataAdapter object for this task.
    da.SelectCommand.CommandText = sqlProd;
    da.Fill(ds, "Products");
}
finally
{
    con.Close();
}
```

In this example, the same DataAdapter is used to fill both tables. This technique is perfectly legitimate, and it makes sense in this scenario because you don't need to reuse the DataAdapter to update the data source. However, if you were using the DataAdapter both to query data and to commit changes, you probably wouldn't use this approach. Instead, you would use a separate DataAdapter for each table so that you could make sure each DataAdapter has the appropriate insert, update, and delete commands for the corresponding table.

At this point you have a DataSet with two tables. These two tables are linked in the Northwind database by a relationship against the CategoryID field. This field is the primary key for the Categories table and the foreign key in the Products table. Unfortunately, ADO.NET does not provide any way to read a relationship from the data source and apply it to your DataSet automatically. Instead, you need to manually create a DataRelation that represents the relationship.

A relationship is created by defining a DataRelation object and adding it to the DataSet.Relations collection. When you create the DataRelation, you typically specify three constructor arguments: the name of the relationship, the DataColumn for the primary key in the parent table, and the DataColumn for the foreign key in the child table.

Here's the code you need for this example:

```
// Define the relationship between Categories and Products.
DataRelation relat = new DataRelation("CatProds",
  ds.Tables["Categories"].Columns["CategoryID"],
  ds.Tables["Products"].Columns["CategoryID"]);

// Add the relationship to the DataSet.
ds.Relations.Add(relat);
```

Once you've retrieved all the data, you can loop through the records of the Categories table and add the name of each category to the HTML string:

```
StringBuilder htmlStr = new StringBuilder("");
// Loop through the category records and build the HTML string.
foreach (DataRow row in ds.Tables["Categories"].Rows)
{
    htmlStr.Append("<b>");
    htmlStr.Append(row["CategoryName"].ToString());
    htmlStr.Append("</b><ul>");
    ...
```

Here's the interesting part. Inside this block, you can access the related product records for the current category by calling the DataRow.GetChildRows() method. This method searches the in-memory data in the linked DataTable to find matching records. Once you have the array of product records, you can loop through it using a nested foreach loop. This is far simpler than the code you'd need in order to look up this information in a separate object or to execute multiple queries with traditional connection-based access.

The following piece of code demonstrates this approach, retrieving the child records and completing the outer foreach loop:

```
    ...
    // Get the children (products) for this parent (category).
    DataRow[] childRows = row.GetChildRows(relat);

    // Loop through all the products in this category.
    foreach (DataRow childRow in childRows)
    {
      htmlStr.Append("<li>");
      htmlStr.Append(childRow["ProductName"].ToString());
      htmlStr.Append("</li>");
    }
    htmlStr.Append("</ul>");
}
```

The last step is to display the HTML string on the page:

```
HtmlContent.Text = htmlStr.ToString();
```

The code for this example is now complete. If you run the page, you'll see the output shown in Figure 8-5.

■ **Tip** A common question new ADO.NET programmers have is, when do you use JOIN queries and when do you use DataRelation objects? The most important consideration is whether you plan to update the retrieved data. If you do, using separate tables and a DataRelation object always offers the most flexibility. If not, you could use either approach, although the JOIN query may be more efficient because it involves only a single round-trip across the network, while the DataRelation approach often requires two to fill the separate tables.

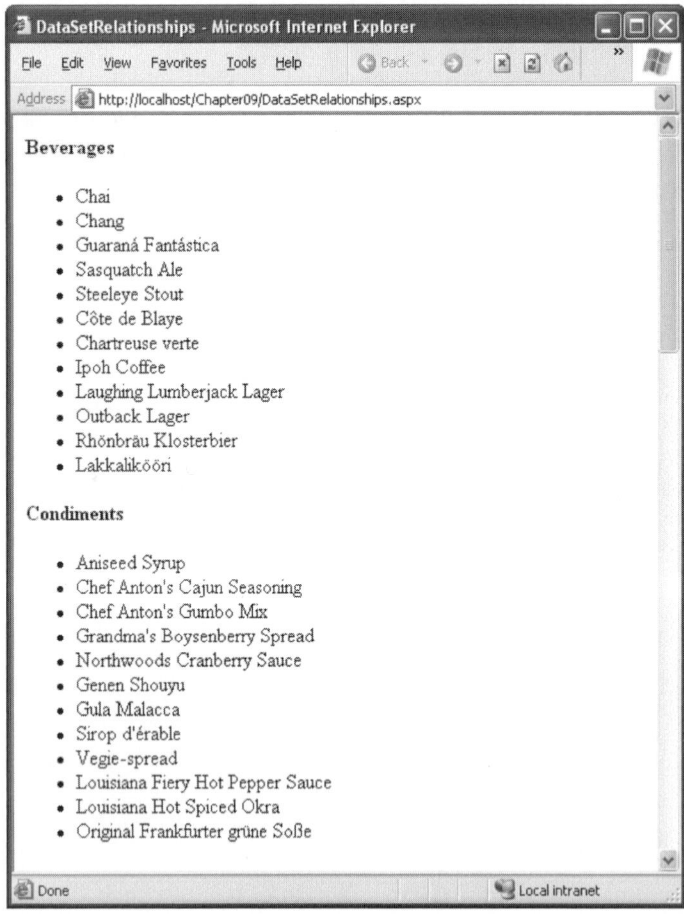

Figure 8-5. A list of products in each category

Referential Integrity

When you add a relationship to a DataSet, you are bound by the rules of referential integrity. For example, you can't delete a parent record if there are linked child rows, and you can't create a child record that references a nonexistent parent. This can cause a problem if your DataSet contains only partial data. For example, if you have a full list of customer orders, but only a partial list of customers, it could appear that an order refers to a customer who doesn't exist just because that customer record isn't in your DataSet. One way to get around this problem is to create a DataRelation without creating the corresponding constraints. To do so, use the DataRelation constructor that accepts the Boolean createConstraints parameter and set it to false, as shown here:

```
DataRelation relat = new DataRelation("CatProds",
  ds.Tables["Categories"].Columns["CategoryID"],
  ds.Tables["Products"].Columns["CategoryID"], false);
```

Another approach is to disable all types of constraint checking (including unique value checking) by setting the DataSet.EnforceConstraints property to false before you add the relationship.

Searching for Specific Rows

The DataTable provides a useful Select() method that allows you to search its rows using a SQL expression. The expression you use with the Select() method plays the same role as the WHERE clause in a SELECT statement, but it acts on the in-memory data that's already in the DataTable (so no database operation is performed).

For example, the following code retrieves all the products that are marked as discontinued:

```
// Get the children (products) for this parent (category).
DataRow[] matchRows = ds.Tables["Products"].Select("Discontinued = 0");

// Loop through all the discontinued products and generate a bulleted list.
htmlStr.Append("</b><ul>");
foreach (DataRow row in matchRows)
{
    htmlStr.Append("<li>");
    htmlStr.Append(row["ProductName"].ToString());
    htmlStr.Append("</li>");
}
htmlStr.Append("</ul>");
```

In this example, the Select() statement uses a fairly simple filter string. However, you're free to use more complex operators and a combination of different criteria. For more information, refer to the MSDN class library reference description for the DataColumn.Expression property, or refer to Table 8-3 and the discussion about filter strings in the "Filtering with a DataView" section.

■ **Note** The Select() method has one potential caveat—it doesn't support a parameterized condition. As a result, it's open to SQL injection attacks. Clearly, the SQL injection attacks that a malicious user could perform in this situation are fairly limited, because there's no way to get access to the actual data source or execute additional commands. However, a carefully written value could still trick your application into returning extra information from the table. If you create a filter expression with a user-supplied value, you might want to iterate over the DataTable manually to find the rows you want, instead of using the Select() method.

Using the DataSet in a Data Access Class

There's no reason you can't use the DataSet or DataTable as the return value from a method in your custom data access class. For example, you could rewrite the GetAllEmployees() method shown earlier with the following DataSet code:

```
public DataTable GetEmployees()
{
    SqlConnection con = new SqlConnection(connectionString);
    SqlCommand cmd = new SqlCommand("GetEmployees", con);
    cmd.CommandType = CommandType.StoredProcedure;


    SqlDataAdapter da = new SqlDataAdapter(cmd);
    DataSet ds = new DataSet();

    // Fill the DataSet.
    try
    {
        da.Fill(ds, "Employees");
        return ds.Tables["Employees"];

    }
    catch
    {
        throw new ApplicationException("Data error.");
    }
}
```

Interestingly, when you use this approach, you have exactly the same functionality at your fingertips. For example, in the next chapter you'll learn to use the ObjectDataSource to bind to custom classes. The ObjectDataSource understands custom classes and the DataSet object equally well (and they have essentially the same performance).

The DataSet approach has a couple of limitations. Although the DataSet makes the ideal container for disconnected data, you may find it easier to create methods that return individual DataTable objects and even distinct DataRow objects (for example, as a return value from a GetEmployee() method). However, these objects don't have the same level of data binding support as the DataSet, so you'll need to decide between a clearer coding model (using the various disconnected data objects) and more flexibility (always using the full DataSet, even when returning only a single record). Another limitation is that the DataSet is weakly typed. That means there's no compile-time syntax checking or IntelliSense to make sure you use the right field names (unlike with a custom data access class such as EmployeeDetails).

Data Binding

Although there's nothing stopping you from generating HTML by hand as you loop through disconnected data, in most cases ASP.NET data binding can simplify your life quite a bit. Chapter 9 discusses data binding in detail, but before continuing to the DataView examples in this chapter you need to know the basics.

The key idea behind data binding is that you associate a link between a data object and a control, and then the ASP.NET data binding infrastructure takes care of building the appropriate output.

One of the data-bound controls that's easiest to use is the GridVew. The GridView has the built-in smarts to create an HTML table with one row per record and with one column per field.

To bind data to a data-bound control such as the GridView, you first need to set the DataSource property. This property points to the object that contains the information you want to display. In this case, it's the DataSet:

```
GridView1.DataSource = ds;
```

Because data-bound controls can bind to only a single table (not the entire DataSet), you also need to explicitly specify what table you want to use. You can do that by setting the DataMember property to the appropriate table name, as shown here:

```
GridView1.DataMember = "Employees";
```

Alternatively, you could replace both of these statements with one statement that binds directly to the appropriate table:

```
GridView1.DataSource = ds.Tables["Employees"];
```

Finally, once you've defined where the data is, you need to call the control's DataBind() method to copy the information from the DataSet into the control. If you forget this step, the control will remain empty, and the information will not appear on the page.

```
GridView1.DataBind();
```

As a shortcut, you can call the DataBind() method of the current page, which walks over every control that supports data binding and calls the DataBind() method.

■ **Note** The following examples use data binding to demonstrate the filtering and sorting features of the GridView. You'll learn much more about data binding and the GridView control in Chapter 9 and Chapter 10.

The DataView Class

A DataView defines a view onto a DataTable object—in other words, a representation of the data in a DataTable that can include custom filtering and sorting settings. To allow you to configure these settings, the DataView has properties such as Sort and RowFilter. These properties allow you to choose what data you'll see through the view. However, they don't affect the actual data in the DataTable. For example, if you filter a table to hide certain rows, those rows will remain in the DataTable, but they won't be accessible through the DataView.

The DataView is particularly useful in data binding scenarios. It allows you to show just a subset of the total data in a table, without needing to process or alter that data if you need it for other tasks.

Every DataTable has a default DataView associated with it, although you can create multiple DataView objects to represent different views onto the same table. The default DataView is provided through the DataTable.DefaultView property.

In the following examples, you'll see how to create some grids that display records sorted by different fields and filtered against a given expression.

Sorting with a DataView

The next example uses a page with three GridView controls. When the page loads, it binds the same DataTable to each of the grids. However, it uses three different views, each of which sorts the results using a different field.

The code begins by retrieving the list of employees into a DataSet:

```
// Create the Connection, DataAdapter, and DataSet.
string connectionString =
  WebConfigurationManager.ConnectionStrings["Northwind"].ConnectionString;
SqlConnection con = new SqlConnection(connectionString);
string sql =
  "SELECT TOP 5 EmployeeID, TitleOfCourtesy, LastName, FirstName FROM Employees";

SqlDataAdapter da = new SqlDataAdapter(sql, con);
DataSet ds = new DataSet();

// Fill the DataSet.
da.Fill(ds, "Employees");
```

The next step is to fill the GridView controls through data binding. To bind the first grid, you can simply use the DataTable directly, which uses the default DataView and displays all the data. For the other two grids, you must create new DataView objects. You can then set its Sort property explicitly.

```
// Bind the original data to #1.
grid1.DataSource = ds.Tables["Employees"];

// Sort by last name and bind it to #2.
DataView view2 = new DataView(ds.Tables["Employees"]);
view2.Sort = "LastName";
grid2.DataSource = view2;

// Sort by first name and bind it to #3.
DataView view3 = new DataView(ds.Tables["Employees"]);
view3.Sort = "FirstName";
grid3.DataSource = view3;
```

Sorting a grid is simply a matter of setting the DataView.Sort property to a valid sorting expression. This example sorts by each view using a single field, but you could also sort by multiple fields, by specifying a comma-separated list. Here's an example:

```
view2.Sort = "LastName, FirstName";
```

■ **Note** The sort is according to the data type of the column. Numeric and date columns are ordered from smallest to largest. String columns are sorted alphanumerically without regard to case, assuming the DataTable.CaseSensitive property is false (the default). Columns that contain binary data cannot be sorted. You can also use the ASC and DESC attributes to sort in ascending or descending order. You'll use sorting again and learn about DataView filtering in Chapter 10.

Once you've bound the grids, you still need to trigger the data binding process that copies the values from the DataTable into the control. You can do this for each control separately or for the entire page by calling Page.DataBind(), as in this example:

```
Page.DataBind();
```

Figure 8-6 shows the resulting page.

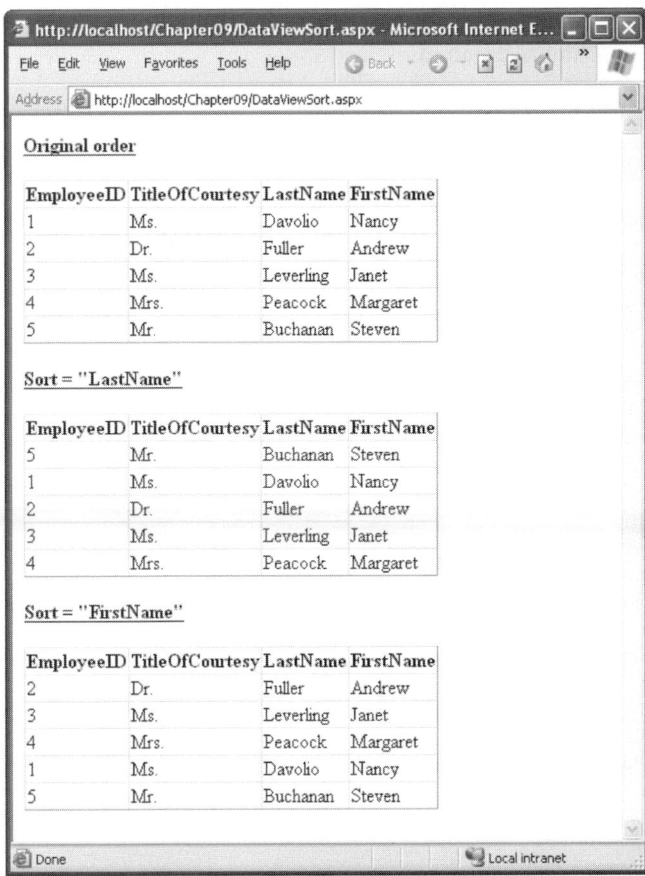

Original order

EmployeeID	TitleOfCourtesy	LastName	FirstName
1	Ms.	Davolio	Nancy
2	Dr.	Fuller	Andrew
3	Ms.	Leverling	Janet
4	Mrs.	Peacock	Margaret
5	Mr.	Buchanan	Steven

Sort = "LastName"

EmployeeID	TitleOfCourtesy	LastName	FirstName
5	Mr.	Buchanan	Steven
1	Ms.	Davolio	Nancy
2	Dr.	Fuller	Andrew
3	Ms.	Leverling	Janet
4	Mrs.	Peacock	Margaret

Sort = "FirstName"

EmployeeID	TitleOfCourtesy	LastName	FirstName
2	Dr.	Fuller	Andrew
3	Ms.	Leverling	Janet
4	Mrs.	Peacock	Margaret
1	Ms.	Davolio	Nancy
5	Mr.	Buchanan	Steven

Figure 8-6. *Grids sorted in different ways*

Filtering with a DataView

You can also use a DataView to apply custom filtering so that only certain rows are included in the display. To accomplish this feat, you use the RowFilter property. The RowFilter property acts like a WHERE clause in a SQL query. Using it, you can limit results using logical operators (such as <, >, and =) and a wide range of criteria. Table 8-3 lists the most common filter operators.

***Table 8-3.** Filter Operators*

Operator	Description
<, >, <=, and >=	Performs comparison of more than one value. These comparisons can be numeric (with number data types) or alphabetic dictionary comparisons (with string data types).
<> and =	Performs equality testing.
NOT	Reverses an expression. Can be used in conjunction with any other clause.
BETWEEN	Specifies an inclusive range. For example, "Units BETWEEN 5 AND 15" selects rows that have a value in the Units column from 5 to 15.
IS NULL	Tests the column for a null value.
IN(a,b,c)	A short form for using an OR clause with the same field. Tests for equality between a column and the specified values (a, b, and c).
LIKE	Performs pattern matching with string data types.
+	Adds two numeric values or concatenates a string.
-	Subtracts one numeric value from another.
*	Multiplies two numeric values.
/	Divides one numeric value by another.
%	Finds the modulus (the remainder after one number is divided by another).
AND	Combines more than one clause. Records must match all criteria to be displayed.
OR	Combines more than one clause. Records must match at least one of the filter expressions to be displayed.

The following example page includes three GridView controls. Each one is bound to the same DataTable but with different filter settings.

```
string connectionString =
  WebConfigurationManager.ConnectionStrings["Northwind"].ConnectionString;
SqlConnection con = new SqlConnection(connectionString);
string sql = "SELECT ProductID, ProductName, UnitsInStock, UnitsOnOrder, " +
  "Discontinued FROM Products";

SqlDataAdapter da = new SqlDataAdapter(sql, con);
DataSet ds = new DataSet();
```

```
da.Fill(ds, "Products");

// Filter for the Chocolade product.
DataView view1 = new DataView(ds.Tables["Products"]);
view1.RowFilter = "ProductName = 'Chocolade'";
grid1.DataSource = view1;

// Filter for products that aren't on order or in stock.
DataView view2 = new DataView(ds.Tables["Products"]);
view2.RowFilter = "UnitsInStock = 0 AND UnitsOnOrder = 0";
grid2.DataSource = view2;

// Filter for products starting with the letter P.
DataView view3 = new DataView(ds.Tables["Products"]);
view3.RowFilter = "ProductName LIKE 'P%'";
grid3.DataSource = view3;

Page.DataBind();
```

Running the page will fill the three grids, as shown in Figure 8-7.

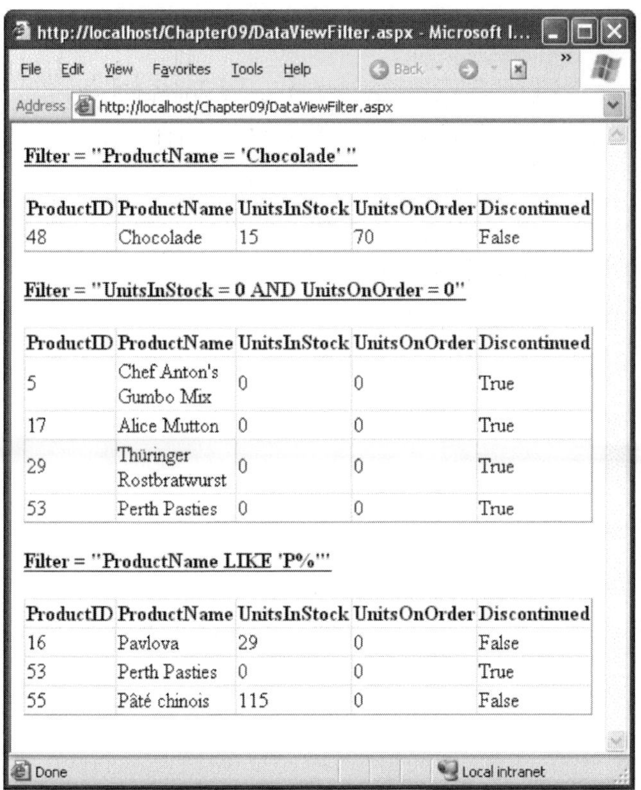

Filter = "ProductName = 'Chocolade' "

ProductID	ProductName	UnitsInStock	UnitsOnOrder	Discontinued
48	Chocolade	15	70	False

Filter = "UnitsInStock = 0 AND UnitsOnOrder = 0"

ProductID	ProductName	UnitsInStock	UnitsOnOrder	Discontinued
5	Chef Anton's Gumbo Mix	0	0	True
17	Alice Mutton	0	0	True
29	Thüringer Rostbratwurst	0	0	True
53	Perth Pasties	0	0	True

Filter = "ProductName LIKE 'P%'"

ProductID	ProductName	UnitsInStock	UnitsOnOrder	Discontinued
16	Pavlova	29	0	False
53	Perth Pasties	0	0	True
55	Pâté chinois	115	0	False

Figure 8-7. Grids filtered in different ways

Advanced Filtering with Relationships

The DataView allows for some surprisingly complex filter expressions. One of its little-known features is the ability to filter rows based on relationships. For example, you could display categories that contain more than 20 products, or you could display customers who have made a certain number of total purchases. In both of these examples, you need to filter one table based on the information in a related table.

To create this sort of filter string, you need to combine two ingredients:

- A table relationship that links two tables.
- An aggregate function such as AVG(), MAX(), MIN(), or COUNT(). This function acts on the data in the related records.

For example, suppose you've filled a DataSet with the Categories and Products tables and defined this relationship:

```
// Define the relationship between Categories and Products.
DataRelation relat = new DataRelation("CatProds",
  ds.Tables["Categories"].Columns["CategoryID"],
  ds.Tables["Products"].Columns["CategoryID"]);

// Add the relationship to the DataSet.
ds.Relations.Add(relat);
```

You can now filter the display of the Categories table using a filter expression based on the Products table. For example, imagine you want to show only category records that have at least one product worth more than $50. To accomplish this, you use the MAX() function, along with the name of the table relationships (CatProds). Here's the filter string you need:

```
MAX(Child(CatProds).UnitPrice) > 50
```

And here's the code that applies this filter string to the DataView:

```
DataView view1 = new DataView(ds.Tables["Categories"]);
view1.RowFilter = "MAX(Child(CatProds).UnitPrice) > 50";
GridView1.DataSource = view1;
```

The end result is that the GridView shows only the categories that have a product worth more than $50.

Calculated Columns

In addition to the fields retrieved from the data source, you can add calculated columns. Calculated columns are ignored when retrieving and updating data. Instead, they represent a value that's computed using a combination of existing values. To create a calculated column, you simply create a new DataColumn object (specifying its name and type) and set the Expression property. Finally, you add the DataColumn to the Columns collection of the DataTable using the Add() method.

As an example, here's a column that uses string concatenation to combine the first and last name into one field:

```
DataColumn fullName = new DataColumn(
  "FullName", typeof(string),
  "TitleOfCourtesy + ' ' + LastName + ', ' + FirstName");
ds.Tables["Employees"].Columns.Add(fullName);
```

■ **Tip** Of course, you can also execute a query that creates calculated columns. However, that approach makes it more difficult to update the data source later, and it creates more work for the data source. For that reason, it's often a better solution to create calculated columns in the DataSet.

You can also create a calculated column that incorporates information from related rows. For example, you might add a column in a Categories table that indicates the number of related product rows. In this case, you need to make sure you first define the relationship with a DataRelation object. You also need to use a SQL aggregate function such as AVG(), MAX(), MIN(), or COUNT().

Here's an example that creates three calculated columns, all of which use aggregate functions and table relationships:

```
string connectionString =
  WebConfigurationManager.ConnectionStrings["Northwind"].ConnectionString;
SqlConnection con = new SqlConnection(connectionString);
string sqlCat = "SELECT CategoryID, CategoryName FROM Categories";
string sqlProd = "SELECT ProductName, CategoryID, UnitPrice FROM Products";
SqlDataAdapter da = new SqlDataAdapter(sqlCat, con);
DataSet ds = new DataSet();

try
{
    con.Open();
    da.Fill(ds, "Categories");
    da.SelectCommand.CommandText = sqlProd;
    da.Fill(ds, "Products");
}
finally
{
    con.Close();
}

// Define the relationship between Categories and Products.
DataRelation relat = new DataRelation("CatProds",
  ds.Tables["Categories"].Columns["CategoryID"],
  ds.Tables["Products"].Columns["CategoryID"]);
// Add the relationship to the DataSet.
ds.Relations.Add(relat);

// Create the calculated columns.
DataColumn count = new DataColumn(
  "Products (#)", typeof(int), "COUNT(Child(CatProds).CategoryID)");
DataColumn max = new DataColumn(
  "Most Expensive Product", typeof(decimal), "MAX(Child(CatProds).UnitPrice)");
DataColumn min = new DataColumn(
```

```
    "Least Expensive Product", typeof(decimal), "MIN(Child(CatProds).UnitPrice)");

// Add the columns.
ds.Tables["Categories"].Columns.Add(count);
ds.Tables["Categories"].Columns.Add(max);
ds.Tables["Categories"].Columns.Add(min);

// Show the data.
grid1.DataSource = ds.Tables["Categories"];
grid1.DataBind();
```

Figure 8-8 shows the resulting page.

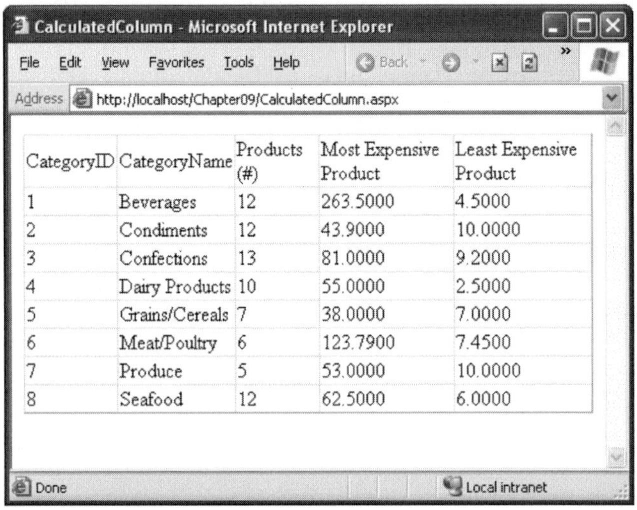

CategoryID	CategoryName	Products (#)	Most Expensive Product	Least Expensive Product
1	Beverages	12	263.5000	4.5000
2	Condiments	12	43.9000	10.0000
3	Confections	13	81.0000	9.2000
4	Dairy Products	10	55.0000	2.5000
5	Grains/Cereals	7	38.0000	7.0000
6	Meat/Poultry	6	123.7900	7.4500
7	Produce	5	53.0000	10.0000
8	Seafood	12	62.5000	6.0000

Figure 8-8. *Showing calculated columns*

■ **Note** Keep in mind that these examples simply demonstrate convenient ways to filter and aggregate data. These operations are only part of presenting your data properly. The other half of the equation is proper formatting. In Chapter 9 and Chapter 10, you'll learn a lot more about the GridView so that you can show currency values in the appropriate format and customize other details such as color, sizing, column order, and fonts. For example, by setting the format, you can change 4.5000 to the more reasonable display value, $4.50.

Summary

In this chapter, you learned how to create basic database components and took an in-depth look at the DataSet and DataView. In the next chapter, you'll continue working with the same database component and the DataSet—albeit through a new layer. You'll learn how the data source controls wrap the ADO.NET world with a higher-level abstraction and let you build rich data-bound pages with minimal code.

CHAPTER 9

■ ■ ■

Data Binding

Almost every web application has to deal with data, whether it's stored in a database, an XML file, a structured file, or something else. Retrieving this data is only part of the challenge—a modern application also needs a convenient, flexible, and attractive way to display the data in a web page.

Fortunately, ASP.NET includes a rich and full-featured model for *data binding*. Data binding allows you to bind the data objects you've retrieved to one or more web controls, which will then show the data automatically. That means you don't need to write time-consuming logic to loop through rows, read multiple fields, and manipulate individual controls.

To make your life even easier, you can use ASP.NET's *data source controls*. A data source control allows you to define a declarative link between your page and a data source (such as a database or a custom data access component). Data source controls are notable for the way they plug into the data binding infrastructure. Once you've configured a data source control, you can hook it up to your web controls at design time, and ASP.NET will take care of all the data binding details. In fact, by using a data source control, you can create a sophisticated page that allows you to query and update a database—all without writing a single line of code.

■ **Tip** Of course, in a professional application you probably *will* write code to customize various aspects of the data binding process, such as error handling. That's why you'll be happy to discover that the data binding model and data source controls are remarkably extensible. In the past, countless data binding models have failed because of a lack of flexibility.

In this chapter, you'll learn how data binding and the data source controls work. You'll learn a straightforward approach to using the data source controls and the best practices you'll need to make them truly practical. This distinction is important, because it's easy to use the data source controls to build pages that are difficult to maintain and impossible to optimize properly. When used correctly, data source controls don't need to prevent good design practices—in fact, informed developers can plug their own custom data access classes into the data binding framework without sacrificing a thing.

But before you can tackle the data source controls, you need to start at the beginning—with a description of ASP.NET data binding.

Basic Data Binding

Data binding is a feature that allows you to associate a data source with a control and have that control automatically display your data. The key characteristic of data binding is that it's *declarative*, not programmatic. That means data binding is defined outside your code, alongside the controls in the .aspx page. The advantage is that it helps you achieve a cleaner separation between your controls and your code in a web page.

In ASP.NET, most web controls (including TextBox, LinkButton, Image, and many more) support *single-value* data binding. With single-value binding, you can bind a control property to a data source, but the control can display only a single value. The property you bind doesn't need to represent something directly visible on the page. For example, not only can you bind the text of a hyperlink by setting the Hyperlink.Text property, but you can also bind the NavigateUrl property to specify the target destination of the link. To use single-value binding, you create *data binding expressions*.

Many web controls support *repeated-value* binding, which means they can render a set of items. Repeated-value controls often create lists and grids (the ListBox and GridView are two examples). If a control supports repeated-value binding, it always exposes a DataSource property, which accepts a data object. (Typically, the data object is some sort of collection, and each item in the collection represents a record of data.) When you set the DataSource property, you create the logical link from the server control to the data object that contains the data to render. However, this doesn't directly fill the control with that data. To accomplish that, you need the control's DataBind() method, which loops through the data source, extracts its data, and renders it to the page. Repeated-value binding is by far the more powerful type of data binding.

In the following sections, you'll consider both single-value binding and repeated-value binding.

Single-Value Binding

The controls that support single-value data binding allow you to bind some of their properties to a data binding expression. This expression is entered in the .aspx markup portion of the page (not the code-behind file) and enclosed between the <%# and %> delimiters. Here's an example:

```
<%# expression_goes_here %>
```

This may look like a script block, but it isn't. If you try to write any code inside this tag, you will receive an error. The only thing you can add is valid data binding expressions. For example, if you have a public, protected, or internal variable in your page class named EmployeeName, you could write the following:

```
<%# EmployeeName %>
```

To evaluate a data binding expression such as this, you must call the Page.DataBind() method in your code. When you call DataBind(), ASP.NET will examine all the expressions on your page and replace them with the corresponding value (in this case, the current value that's defined for the EmployeeName variable). If you forget to call the DataBind() method, the data binding expression won't be filled in—instead, it just gets tossed away when your page is rendered to HTML.

The source for single-value data binding can include the value of a property, member variable, or return value of a function (as long as the property, member variable, or function has an accessibility of protected, public, or internal). It can also be any other expression that can be evaluated at runtime, such as a reference to another control's property, a calculation using operators and literal values, and so on. The following data binding expressions are all valid:

```
<%# GetUserName() %>
<%# 1 + (2 * 20) %>
<%# "John " + "Smith" %>
<%# Request.Browser.Browser %>
```

You can place your data binding expressions just about anywhere on the page, but usually you'll assign a data binding expression to a property in the control tag. Here's an example page that uses several data binding expressions:

```
<html xmlns="http://www.w3.org/1999/xhtml">
  <body>
    <form method="post" runat="server">
      <asp:Image ID="image1" runat="server" ImageUrl='<%# FilePath %>' />
      <br />
      <asp:Label ID="label1" runat="server" Text='<%# FilePath %>' />
      <br />
      <asp:TextBox ID="textBox1" runat="server" Text='<%# GetFilePath() %>' />
      <br />
      <asp:HyperLink ID="hyperLink1" runat="server"
    NavigateUrl='<%# LogoPath.Value %>' Font-Bold="True" Text="Show logo" />
      <br />
      <input type="hidden" ID="LogoPath" runat="server" value="apress.gif">
      <b><%# FilePath %></b><br />
      <img src="<%# GetFilePath() %>">
    </form>
  </body>
</html>
```

As you can see, not only can you bind the Text property of a Label and a TextBox, but you can also use other properties such as the ImageUrl of an Image, the NavigateUrl property of a HyperLink, and even the src attribute of a static HTML <img> tag. You can also put the binding expression elsewhere in the page without binding to any property or attribute. For example, the previous web page has a binding expression between the <b> and </b> tags. When it's processed, the resulting text will be rendered on the page and rendered in bold type. You can even place the expression outside the <form> section, as long as you don't try to insert a server-side control there.

The expressions in this sample page refer to a FilePath property, a GetFilePath() function, and the Value property of a server-side hidden field that's declared on the same page. To complete this page, you need to define these ingredients in script blocks or in the code-behind class:

```
protected string GetFilePath()
{
    return "apress.gif";
}

protected string FilePath
{
    get { return "apress.gif"; }
}
```

In this example, the property and function return only a hard-coded string. However, you can also add just about any C# code to generate the value for the data binding expression dynamically.

It's important to remember that the data binding expression does not directly set the property to which it's bound. It simply defines a connection between the control's property and some other piece of information. To cause the page to evaluate the expression, run the appropriate code, and assign the appropriate value, you must call the DataBind() method of the containing page, as shown here:

```
protected void Page_Load(object sender, System.EventArgs e)
{
    this.DataBind();
}
```

Figure 9-1 shows what you'll see when you run this page.

You'll see data binding expressions again when you create templates for more advanced controls in Chapter 10.

■ **Tip** It's also common to see the command this.DataBind() written Page.DataBind(), or just DataBind(). All three statements are equivalent. Page.DataBind() works because all control classes (including pages) inherit the Control.Page property. When you write Page.DataBind(), you're actually using the Page property of the current page (which points to itself), and then calling DataBind() on the page object.

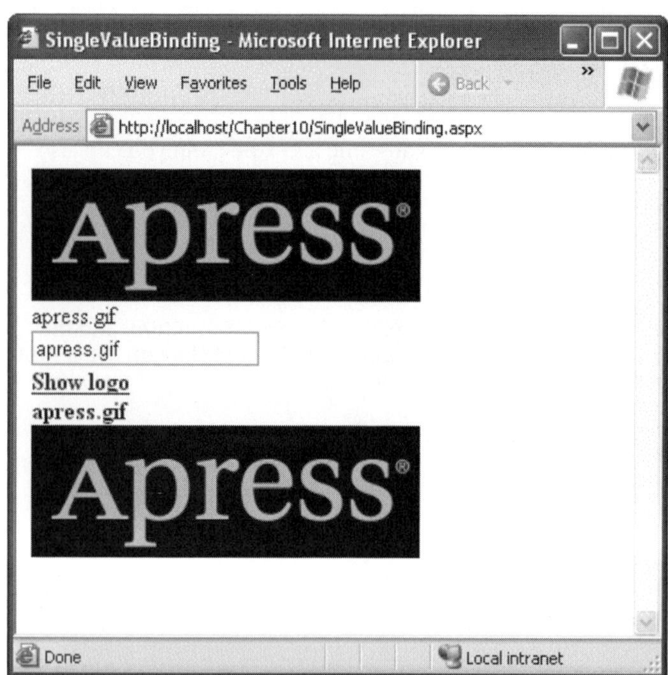

Figure 9-1. *Single-value data binding in various controls*

Other Types of Expressions

Data binding expressions are always wrapped in the <%# and %> characters. ASP.NET also has support for a different type of expression, commonly known as $ expressions because they incorporate the $ character. Technically, a $ expression is a code sequence that you can add to an .aspx page and that will be evaluated by an expression builder when the page is rendered. The expression builder processes the expression and replaces it with a string value in the final HTML.

ASP.NET includes a built-in expression builder that allows you to extract custom application settings and connection string information from the web.config file. For example, if you want to retrieve an application setting named appName from the <appSettings> portion of the web.config file, you can use the following expression:

```
<asp:Literal Runat="server" Text="<%$ AppSettings:appName %>" />
```

Several differences exist between $ expressions and data binding expressions:

- Data binding expressions start with the <%# character sequence, and $ expressions use <%$.
- Unlike data binding expressions, you don't need to call the DataBind() method to evaluate $ expressions. Instead, they're always evaluated when the page is rendered.
- Unlike data binding expressions, $ expressions can't be inserted anywhere in a page. Instead, you need to wrap them in a control tag and use the expression result to set a control property. That means if you just want to show the result of an expression as ordinary text, you need to wrap it in a Literal control (as shown in the previous example). (The Literal control outputs its text to plain, unformatted HTML.)

The first part of a $ expression indicates the name of the expression builder. For example, the AppSettings:appName expression works because a dedicated AppSettingsExpressionBuilder is registered to handle all expressions that begin with *AppSettings*. Similarly, ASP.NET includes a ResourceExpressionBuilder for inserting resources and a ConnectionStringsExpressionBuilder that retrieves connection information from the <connectionStrings> section of the web.config file. Here's an example that uses the ConnectionStringsExpressionBuilder:</EM>.

```
<asp:Literal Runat="server" Text="<%$ ConnectionStrings:Northwind %>" />
```

Displaying a connection string isn't that useful. But this technique becomes much more useful when you combine it with the SqlDataSource control you'll examine later in this chapter, in which case you can use it to quickly supply a connection string from the web.config file:

```
<asp:SqlDataSource ConnectionString="<%$ ConnectionStrings:Northwind %>" ... />
```

Technically, $ expressions don't involve data binding. But they work in a similar way to data binding expressions and have a similar syntax.

Custom Expression Builders

One of the most innovative features of $ expressions is that you can create your own expression builders that plug into this framework. This is a specialized technique that, while impressive, isn't always practical. As you'll see, custom $ expressions make the most sense if you're developing a feature that you want to use to extend more than one web application.

For example, imagine you want a way to create a custom expression builder that allows you to insert random numbers. You want to be able to write a tag such as this to show a random number between 1 and 6:

```
<asp:Literal Runat="server" Text="<%$ RandomNumber:1,6 %>" />
```

Unfortunately, creating a custom expression builder isn't quite as easy as you probably expect. The problem is how the code is compiled. When you compile a page that contains an expression, the expression evaluating the code also needs to be compiled with it. However, you don't want the expression to be evaluated at that point—instead, you want the expression to be reevaluated each time the page is requested. To make this possible, your expression builder needs to generate a segment of code that performs the appropriate task.

The technology that enables this is CodeDOM (Code Document Object Model)—a model for dynamically generating code constructs. Every expression builder includes a method named GetCodeExpression() that uses CodeDOM to generate the code needed for the expression. In other words, if you want to create a RandomNumberExpressionBuilder, you need to create a GetCodeExpression() method that uses CodeDOM to generate a segment of code for calculating random numbers. Clearly, it's not that straightforward—and for anything but trivial code, it's quite lengthy.

All expression builders must derive from the base ExpressionBuilder class (which is found in the System.Web.Compilation namespace). Here's how you might declare an expression builder for random number generation:

```
public class RandomNumberExpressionBuilder : ExpressionBuilder
{ ... }
```

To make the code more concise, you'll also need to import the following namespaces:

```
using System.Web.Compilation;
using System.CodeDom;
using System.ComponentModel;
```

The easiest way to build a simple expression builder is to begin by creating a static method that performs the task you need. In this case, the static method needs to generate a random number:

```
public static string GetRandomNumber(int lowerLimit, int upperLimit)
{
    Random rand = new Random();
    int randValue = rand.Next(lowerLimit, upperLimit + 1);
    return randValue.ToString();
}
```

The advantage of this approach is that when you use CodeDOM, you simply generate the single line of code needed to call the GetRandomNumber() method (rather than the code needed to generate the random number).

Now, you need to override the GetCodeExpression() method. This is the method that ASP.NET calls when it finds an expression that's mapped to your expression builder (while compiling the page). At this point, you need to examine the expression, verify no errors are present, and then generate the code for calculating the expression result. The code that you generate needs to be represented in a language-independent way, as a System.CodeDom.CodeExpression object that you construct. This dynamically generated piece of code will be executed every time the page is requested.

Here's the first part of the GetCodeExpression() method:

```
public override CodeExpression GetCodeExpression(BoundPropertyEntry entry,
  object parsedData, ExpressionBuilderContext context)
{
    // entry.Expression is the number string
    // without the prefix (for example "1,6").
    if (!entry.Expression.Contains(","))
    {
        throw new ArgumentException(
          "Must include two numbers separated by a comma.");
    }
```

```
else
{
    // Get the two numbers.
    string[] numbers = entry.Expression.Split(',');

    if (numbers.Length != 2)
    {
        throw new ArgumentException("Only include two numbers.");
    }
    else
    {
        int lowerLimit, upperLimit;
        if (Int32.TryParse(numbers[0], out lowerLimit) &&
          Int32.TryParse(numbers[1], out upperLimit))
        {
            ...
```

So far, all the operations have been performed in normal code. That's because the two numbers are specified as part of the expression. They won't change each time the page is requested, and so they don't need to be evaluated each time the page is requested. However, the random number should be recalculated each time, so now you need to switch to CodeDOM and create a dynamic segment of code that performs this task. The basic strategy is to construct a CodeExpression that calls the static GetRandomNumber() method.

First, the code needs to get a reference to the class that contains the GetRandomNumber() method. In this example, that's the expression builder class where the code is currently executing, which makes the process fairly straightforward:

```
            ...
            // Get a reference to the  class that has the
            // GetRandomNumber() method.
            // (It's the class where this code is executing.)
            CodeTypeReferenceExpression typeRef = new
              CodeTypeReferenceExpression(this.GetType());
            ...
```

Next, the code defines the parameters that need to be passed to the GetRandomNumber() method:

```
            ...
            CodeExpression[] methodParameters = new CodeExpression[2];
            methodParameters[0] = new CodePrimitiveExpression(lowerLimit);
            methodParameters[1] = new CodePrimitiveExpression(upperLimit);
            ...
```

With these details in place, the code can now create the CodeExpression that calls GetRandomNumber(). To do this, it creates an instance of the CodeMethodInvokeExpression class (which derives from CodeExpression):

```
            ...
            return new CodeMethodInvokeExpression(
              typeRef, "GetRandomNumber", methodParameters);
        }
        else
        {
```

```
                throw new ArgumentException("Use valid integers.");
            }
        }
    }
}
```

Now you can copy this expression builder to the App_Code folder (or compile it separately and place the DLL assembly in the Bin folder).

Finally, to use this expression builder in a web application, you need to register it in the web.config file and map it to the prefix you want to use:

```
<configuration>
  <system.web>
    <compilation debug="true">
      <expressionBuilders>
        <add expressionPrefix="RandomNumber"
             type="RandomNumberExpressionBuilder"/>
      </expressionBuilders>
    </compilation>
    ...
  </system.web>
</configuration>
```

Now you can use expressions such as <%$ RandomNumber:1,6 %> in the markup of a web form. These expressions will be automatically handled by your custom expression builder, which generates the code when the page is compiled. However, the code isn't executed until you request the page. As a result, you'll see a new random number (that falls in the desired range) each time you run the page.

The possibilities for expression builders are intriguing. They enable many extensibility scenarios, and third-party tools are sure to take advantage of this feature. However, if you intend to use an expression in a single web application or in a single web page, you'll find it easier to just use a data binding expression that calls a custom method in your page. For example, you could create a data binding expression like this:

```
<%# GetRandomNumber(1,6) %>
```

And add a matching public, protected, or internal method in your page, like this:

```
protected string GetRandomNumber(int lowerLimit, int upperLimit)
{ ... }
```

Just remember to call Page.DataBind() to evaluate your expression.

Repeated-Value Binding

Repeated-value binding allows you to bind an entire list of information to a control. This list of information is represented by a data object that wraps a collection of items. This could be a collection of custom objects (for example, in an ordinary ArrayList or Hashtable) or a collection of rows (for example, with a DataReader or DataSet).

ASP.NET includes several basic list controls that support repeated-value binding:

- All controls that render themselves using the <select> tag, including the HtmlSelect, ListBox, and DropDownList controls

- The CheckBoxList and RadioButtonList controls, which render each child item with a separate check box or radio button
- The BulletedList control, which creates a list of bulleted or numbered points

All these controls display a single-value field of a property from each data item. When performing data binding with one of these controls, you'll use the properties listed in Table 9-1.

Table 9-1. *Data Properties for List Controls*

Property	Description
DataSource	This is a data object that contains a collection of data items to display. This data object must implement one of the interfaces that ASP.NET data binding supports, typically ICollection.
DataSourceID	Instead of supplying the data object programmatically (using code), you can link your list control to a data source control by setting this property. The data source control will generate the required data object automatically. You can use either the DataSource property or the DataSourceID property, but not both.
DataTextField	Every data source represents a collection of data items. A list control can display only a single value from each list item. The DataTextField indicates the field (in the case of a row) or property (in the case of an object) of the data item that contains the value to display in the page.
DataTextFormatString	This property specifies an optional format string that the control will use to format each DataTextValue before displaying it. For example, you can specify that a number should be formatted as a currency value.
DataValueField	This property is similar to the DataTextField property, but the value from the data item isn't displayed in the page—instead, it's stored in the value attribute of the underlying HTML tag. This allows you to retrieve the value later in your code. The primary use of this field is to store a unique ID or primary key field so you can use it later to retrieve more data when the user selects a specific item.

All the list controls are essentially the same. The only differences are the way they render themselves in HTML and whether or not they support multiple selection.

Figure 9-2 shows a test page that uses all these list controls (except the BulletedList control, which doesn't support selection). In this example, the list controls are bound to the same data object—a hashtable. When the user clicks the Get Selection button, the page lists the currently selected items.

When the page loads for the first time, the code creates a data source and assigns it to all the list controls. In this example, the data object is a Hashtable object, which contains a series of strings (the values) indexed by name (the keys). Hashtable collections work in the same way as the ViewState, Session, Application, and Cache collections that you can use to store data.

Here's the code for creating and binding the hashtable:

```
protected void Page_Load(object sender, System.EventArgs e)
{
    if (!Page.IsPostBack)
    {
        // Create the data source.
```

```
        Hashtable ht = new Hashtable();
        ht.Add("Key1", "Lasagna");
        ht.Add("Key2", "Spaghetti");
        ht.Add("Key3", "Pizza");
        // Set the DataSource property for the controls.
        Select1.DataSource = ht;
        Select2.DataSource = ht;
        Listbox1.DataSource = ht;
        DropdownList1.DataSource = ht;
        CheckList1.DataSource = ht;
        OptionList1.DataSource = ht;

        // Bind the controls.
        this.DataBind();
}
```

■ **Note** Every control that supports repeated-value data binding includes a DataBind() method. You could call this method to bind a specific control. However, when you call the Page.DataBind() method, the page object calls DataBind() on every contained control, simplifying your life.

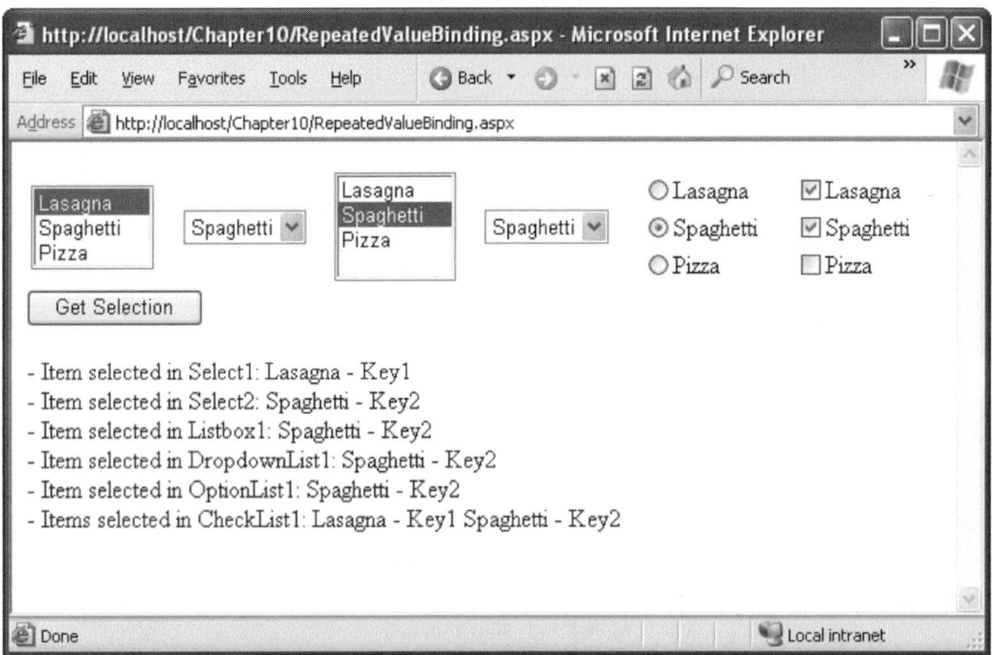

Figure 9-2. *Repeated-value data binding in list controls*

Each key-value pair in a hashtable is represented by an instance of the DictionaryStructure class. The DictionaryStructure class provides two properties: Value (the actual stored item, which is a string in this example) and Key (the unique name under which this item is indexed). When you bind a hashtable to a list control, you are actually binding a group of DictionaryStructure objects.

In this example, the bound controls display the Value property of each item, which contains the text. They also keep track of the Key property for later use. To accomplish this, you must set the DataTextField and DataValueField properties of the lists as follows:

```
<select runat="server" ID="Select1" size="3"
  DataTextField="Value" DataValueField="Key" />
<select runat="server" ID="Select2"
  DataTextField="Value" DataValueField="Key" />
<asp:ListBox runat="server" ID="Listbox1" Rows="3"
  DataTextField="Value" DataValueField="Key" />
<asp:DropDownList runat="server" ID="DropdownList1"
  DataTextField="Value" DataValueField="Key" />
<asp:RadioButtonList runat="server" ID="OptionList1"
  DataTextField="Value" DataValueField="Key" />
<asp:CheckBoxList runat="server" ID="CheckList1"
  DataTextField="Value" DataValueField="Key" />
```

When the user clicks Get Selection, the page adds the name and values of all the selected items to the label. Here's the code that accomplishes this task:

```
protected void cmdGetSelection_Click(object sender, EventArgs e)
{
    Result.Text += "- Item selected in Select1: " +
      Select1.Items[Select1.SelectedIndex].Text + " - " +
      Select1.Value + "<br />";
    Result.Text += "- Item selected in Select2: " +
      Select2.Items[Select2.SelectedIndex].Text + " - " +
      Select2.Value + "<br />";
    Result.Text += "- Item selected in Listbox1: " +
      Listbox1.SelectedItem.Text + " - " +
      Listbox1.SelectedItem.Value + "<br />";
    Result.Text += "- Item selected in DropdownList1: " +
      DropdownList1.SelectedItem.Text + " - " +
      DropdownList1.SelectedItem.Value + "<br />";
    Result.Text += "- Item selected in OptionList1: " +
      OptionList1.SelectedItem.Text + " - " +
      OptionList1.SelectedItem.Value + "<br />";
    Result.Text += "- Items selected in CheckList1: ";
    foreach (ListItem li in CheckList1.Items)
    {
        if (li.Selected)
            Result.Text += li.Text + " - " + li.Value + " ";
    }
}
```

Binding to a DataReader

The previous example used a hashtable as the data source. Basic collections certainly aren't the only kind of data source you can use with list data binding. Instead, you can bind any data structure that implements the ICollection interface or one of its derivatives. The following list summarizes many of these data classes:

- All in-memory collection classes, such as Collection, ArrayList, Hashtable, and Dictionary
- An ADO.NET DataReader object, which provides connection-based, forward-only, and read-only access to the database
- The ADO.NET DataView, which provides a view onto a single disconnected DataTable object
- Any other custom object that implements the ICollection interface

For example, imagine you want to fill a list box with the full names of all the employees contained in the Employees table of the Northwind database. Figure 9-3 shows the result you want to produce.

Figure 9-3. *Data binding with a DataReader*

The information in this example includes each person's title of courtesy, first name, and last name, which are stored in three separate fields. Unfortunately, the DataTextField property expects the name of only a single field. You cannot use data binding to concatenate these three pieces of data and create a value for the DataTextField. However, you can solve this issue with an easy but powerful trick—using a calculated column. You simply need to modify the SELECT query so that it creates a calculated column that consists of the information in the three fields. You can then use this column for the DataTextField. The SQL command that you need to accomplish this is as follows:

```
SELECT EmployeeID, TitleOfCourtesy + ' ' +
  FirstName + ' ' + LastName As FullName FROM Employees
```

The data-bound list box is declared on the page as follows:

```
<asp:ListBox runat="server" ID="lstNames" Rows="10" SelectionMode="Multiple"
  DataTextField="FullName" DataValueField="EmployeeID"/>
```

When the page loads, it retrieves the records from the database and binds them to the list control. This example uses a DataReader as the data source, as shown here:

```
protected void Page_Load(object sender, EventArgs e)
{
    if (!Page.IsPostBack)
    {
        // Create the Command and the Connection.
        string connectionString = WebConfigurationManager.ConnectionStrings[
          "Northwind"].ConnectionString;
        string sql = "SELECT EmployeeID, TitleOfCourtesy + ' ' + " +
          "FirstName + ' ' + LastName As FullName FROM Employees";

        SqlConnection con = new SqlConnection(connectionString);
        SqlCommand cmd = new SqlCommand(sql, con);

        try
        {
            // Open the connection and get the DataReader.
            con.Open();
            SqlDataReader reader = cmd.ExecuteReader();

            // Bind the DataReader to the list.
            lstNames.DataSource = reader;
            lstNames.DataBind();
            reader.Close();
        }
        finally
        {
            // Close the connection.
            con.Close();
        }
    }
}
```

The previous code sample creates a connection to the database, creates the command that will select the data, opens the connection, and executes the command that returns the DataReader. The returned DataReader is bound to the list box, and finally the DataReader and the connection are both closed. Note that the DataBind() method of the page or the control must be called before the connection is closed. It's not until you call this method that the actual data is extracted.

The last piece of this example is the code for determining the selected items. As in the previous example, this code is quite straightforward:

```
protected void cmdGetSelection_Click(object sender, System.EventArgs e)
{
    Result.Text += "<b>Selected employees:</b>";
    foreach (ListItem li in lstNames.Items)
    {
        if (li.Selected)
          Result.Text += String.Format("<li>({0}) {1}</li>", li.Value, li.Text);
    }
}
```

If you want to use a DropDownList, a CheckListBox, or a RadioButtonList instead of a ListBox, you need to change only the control declaration. The rest of the code that sets up the data binding remains the same.

The Rich Data Controls

In addition to the simple list controls, ASP.NET includes some rich data controls that support repeated-value binding. The rich data controls are quite a bit different from the simple list controls—for one thing, they are designed exclusively for data binding. They also have the ability to display several properties or fields from each data item, often in a table-based layout or according to a template you've defined; they support higher-level features such as editing; and they provide several events that allow you to plug into the control's inner workings at various points.

The rich data controls include the following:

GridView: The GridView is an all-purpose grid control for showing large tables of information. It supports selecting, editing, sorting, and paging. The GridView is the heavyweight of ASP.NET data controls. It's also the successor to the ASP.NET 1.*x* DataGrid.

DetailsView: The DetailsView is ideal for showing a single record at a time, in a table that has one row per field. The DetailsView supports editing and optional paging controls that allow you to browse through a sequence of records.

FormView: Like the DetailsView, the FormView shows a single record at a time, supports editing, and provides paging controls for moving through a series of records. The difference is that the FormView is based on templates, which allow you to combine fields in a much more flexible layout that doesn't need to be based on a table.

■ **Note** In addition to the controls in this list, some of ASP.NET's more specialized controls support data binding. These include the Menu and TreeView controls (see Chapter 17) and the AdRotator control (Chapter 4).

You'll explore the rich data controls in detail in Chapter 10. However, it's worth taking a look at a quick example now with the GridView, because you'll use it to work through a variety of examples in this chapter.

Like the list controls, the GridView provides a DataSource property for the data object and a DataBind() method that triggers it to read the data object and display each record. However, you don't need to use properties such as DataTextField and DataValueField, because the GridView automatically generates a column for every property (if you're binding to a custom object) or every field (if you're binding to a row). Here's all you need to get this basic representation:

```
<asp:GridView ID="grid" runat="server" AutoGenerateColumns="true" />
```

■ **Note** Technically, you don't even need to set the AutoGenerateColumns property, because true is the default value.

Now, define a query that selects several fields from the Employees table:

```
string sql = "SELECT EmployeeID, FirstName, LastName, Title, City " +
  "FROM Employees";
```

You can bind the GridView to a DataReader in the same way you bound the list control in the previous example. Only the name of the control changes:

```
grid.DataSource = reader;
grid.DataBind();
```

Figure 9-4 shows the GridView this code creates.

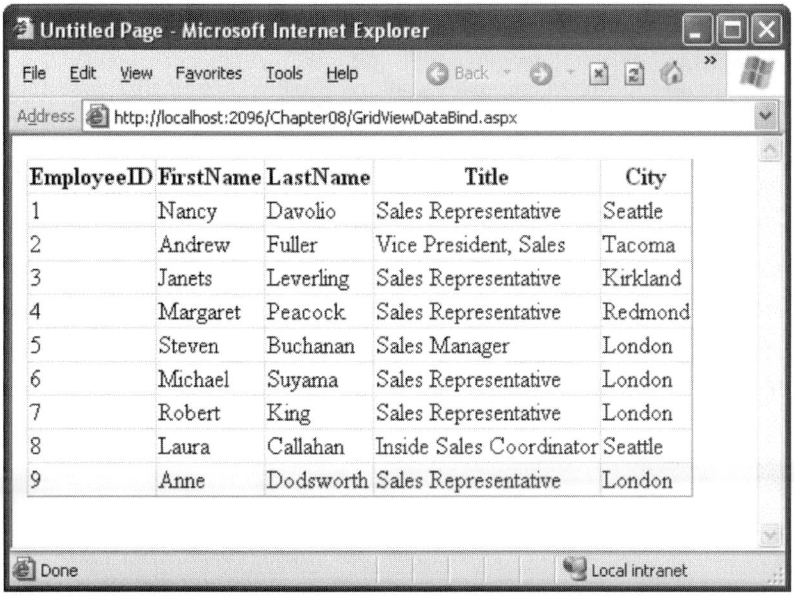

EmployeeID	FirstName	LastName	Title	City
1	Nancy	Davolio	Sales Representative	Seattle
2	Andrew	Fuller	Vice President, Sales	Tacoma
3	Janets	Leverling	Sales Representative	Kirkland
4	Margaret	Peacock	Sales Representative	Redmond
5	Steven	Buchanan	Sales Manager	London
6	Michael	Suyama	Sales Representative	London
7	Robert	King	Sales Representative	London
8	Laura	Callahan	Inside Sales Coordinator	Seattle
9	Anne	Dodsworth	Sales Representative	London

Figure 9-4. *The bare-bones GridView*

Of course, you can do a lot more to configure the appearance of the GridView. If you declare the columns explicitly (rather than relying on AutoGenerateColumns), you can fine-tune column order and formatting. You can also use advanced features such as sorting, paging, and editing. You'll learn about these features throughout this chapter and in the next chapter. You can also give your GridView a quick face-lift by choosing Auto Format from the GridView's smart tag.

Binding to a DataView

You will encounter a few limitations when you bind directly to a DataReader. Because the DataReader is a forward-only cursor, you can't bind your data to multiple controls. You also won't have the ability to apply custom sorting and filtering criteria on the fly. Finally, unless you take care to code your page using generic interfaces such as IDataReader, you lock your code into the data provider you're currently using, making it more difficult to modify or adapt your code in the future. To solve these problems, you can use the disconnected ADO.NET data objects.

If you fill a disconnected DataSet, you can bind it to one or more controls, and you can tailor the sorting and filtering criteria. The DataSet is also completely generic—no matter which data provider you use to fill your DataSet, the DataSet itself (and the data binding code) looks the same.

Technically, you never bind directly to a DataSet or DataTable object. Instead, you bind to a DataView object. A DataView represents a view of the data in a specific DataTable. That means the following:

```
grid.DataSource = dataTable;
grid.DataBind();
```

is equivalent to this:

```
grid.DataSource = dataTable.DefaultView;
grid.DataBind();
```

It's important to note that every DataTable includes a default DataView object that's provided through the DataTable.DefaultView property. This sleight of hand allows you bind directly to the DataTable. If you do, ASP.NET actually uses the default DataView automatically. The default DataView doesn't apply any sort order and doesn't filter out any rows. If you want to tweak these settings, you can either configure the default DataView or create your own and explicitly bind it. You can then use all the sorting and filtering techniques explained in Chapter 8.

Data Source Controls

In Chapter 7 and Chapter 8, you saw how you can directly connect to a database, execute a query, loop through the records in the result set, and display them on a page. In this chapter, you've already seen that you have a simpler option; with data binding, you can write your data access logic and then show the results in the page with no looping or control manipulation required. Now, it's time to introduce another convenience—data source controls. With data source controls, you can avoid writing any data access code.

■ **Note** As you'll soon see, there's often a gap between what you *can* do and what you *should* do. In most professional, large-scale applications, you'll still need to write and fine-tune your data access code for optimum performance, data aggregation, error handling, logging, and so on. Even if you do, you can still use the data source controls—just don't expect to escape without writing any code!

The data source controls include any control that implements the IDataSource interface. The .NET Framework includes the following data source controls:

SqlDataSource: This data source allows you to connect to any data source that has an ADO.NET data provider. This includes SQL Server, Oracle, and the OLE DB or ODBC data sources, as discussed in Chapter 7. When using this data source, you don't need to write the data access code.

ObjectDataSource: This data source allows you to connect to a custom data access class, such as the one you saw in Chapter 8. This is the preferred approach for large-scale professional web applications.

AccessDataSource: This data source allows you to read and write the data in an Access database file (.mdb). Access databases do not have a dedicated server engine (like SQL Server) that coordinates the actions of multiple people and ensures that data won't be lost or corrupted. For that reason, Access databases are best suited for very small websites, where few people need to manipulate data at the same time. A much better small-scale data solution is using the free SQL Server Express with the SqlDataSource control.

XmlDataSource: This data source allows you to connect to an XML file. You'll learn more in Chapter 14.

SiteMapDataSource: This data source allows you to connect to the Web.sitemap file that describes the navigational structure of your website. You'll learn more in Chapter 17.

You can find all the data source controls in the Data tab of the Toolbox in Visual Studio.

When you drop a data source control onto your web page, it shows up as a gray box in Visual Studio. However, this box won't appear when you run your web application and request the page.

The Page Life Cycle with Data Binding

Data source controls can perform two key tasks:

- They can retrieve data from a data source and supply it to linked controls.
- They can update the data source when edits take place in linked controls.

In order to understand how data controls work, you need to know how they fit into the page life cycle. This understanding is important when you run into situations where you need to work with or extend the data binding model. For example, you might want to add data or set a selected item in a control after it has been bound to the data source. Depending on the scenario, you might be able to respond to data source control events, but they aren't always fired at the point you need to perform your logic.

Essentially, data binding tasks take place in this order:

1. The page object is created (based on the .aspx file).
2. The page life cycle begins, and the Page.Init and Page.Load events fire.
3. All other control events fire.
4. The data source controls perform any updates. If a row is being updated, the Updating and Updated events fire. If a row is being inserted, the Inserting and Inserted events fire. If a row is being deleted, the Deleting and Deleted events fire.
5. The Page.PreRender event fires.
6. The data source controls perform any queries and insert the retrieved data in the linked controls. The Selecting and Selected events fire at this point.
7. The page is rendered and disposed.

In the rest of this chapter, you'll look in detail at the SqlDataSource and the ObjectDataSource and see how you can use both to enable a variety of data binding scenarios with the rich GridView control.

■ **Tip** Even if you plan to use the ObjectDataSource for binding your pages, you should begin by reading "The SqlDataSource" section, which will explain many of the basics about data source controls, including parameters, key fields, and two-way data binding.

The SqlDataSource

Data source controls turn up in the .aspx markup portion of your web page like ordinary controls. Here's an example:

```
<asp:SqlDataSource ID="SqlDataSource1" runat="server" ... />
```

The SqlDataSource represents a database connection that uses an ADO.NET provider. However, this has a catch. The SqlDataSource needs a generic way to create the Connection, Command, and DataReader objects it requires. The only way this is possible is if your data provider includes a data provider factory, as discussed in Chapter 7. The factory has the responsibility of creating the provider-specific objects that the SqlDataSource needs in order to access the data source.

As you know, .NET ships with these four provider factories:

- System.Data.SqlClient
- System.Data.OracleClient
- System.Data.OleDb
- System.Data.Odbc

These are registered in the machine.config file, and as a result you can use any of them with the SqlDataSource. You choose a data source by setting the provider name. Here's a SqlDataSource that connects to a SQL Server database:

```
<asp:SqlDataSource ProviderName="System.Data.SqlClient" ... />
```

The next step is to supply the required connection string—without it, you cannot make any connections. Although you can hard-code the connection string directly in the SqlDataSource tag, you should always place it in the <connectionStrings> section of the web.config file to guarantee greater flexibility and ensure you won't inadvertently change the connection string, which minimizes the effectiveness of connection pooling.

For example, if you create this connection string:

```
<configuration>
  <connectionStrings>
    <add name="Northwind"
connectionString="Data Source=localhost;Initial Catalog=Northwind;
Integrated Security=SSPI"/>
  </connectionStrings>
  ...
</configuration>
```

you would specify it in the SqlDataSource using a $ expression like this:

```
<asp:SqlDataSource ConnectionString="<%$ ConnectionStrings:Northwind %>" ... />
```

Once you've specified the provider name and connection string, the next step is to add the query logic that the SqlDataSource will use when it connects to the database.

Selecting Records

You can use each SqlDataSource control you create to retrieve a single query. Optionally, you can also add corresponding commands for deleting, inserting, and updating rows. For example, one SqlDataSource is enough to query and update the Customers table in the Northwind database. However, if you need to independently retrieve or update Customers and Orders information, you'll need two SqlDataSource controls.

The SqlDataSource command logic is supplied through four properties: SelectCommand, InsertCommand, UpdateCommand, and DeleteCommand, each of which takes a string. The string you supply can be inline SQL (in which case the corresponding SelectCommandType, InsertCommandType, UpdateCommandType, or DeleteCommandType property should be Text, the default) or the name of a stored procedure (in which case the command type is StoredProcedure). You need to define commands only for the types of actions you want to perform. In other words, if you're using a data source for read-only access to a set of records, you need to define only the SelectCommand property.

■ **Note** If you configure a command in the Properties window, you'll see a property named SelectQuery instead of SelectCommand. The SelectQuery is actually a virtual property that's displayed as a design-time convenience. When you edit the SelectQuery (by clicking the ellipsis next to the property name), you can use a special designer to write the command text (the SelectCommand) and add command parameters (the SelectParameters).

Here's a complete SqlDataSource that defines a SELECT command for retrieving records from the Employees table:

```
<asp:SqlDataSource ID="sourceEmployees" runat="server"
  ProviderName="System.Data.SqlClient"
  ConnectionString="<%$ ConnectionStrings:Northwind %>"  SelectCommand=
"SELECT EmployeeID, FirstName, LastName, Title, City FROM Employees"/>
```

■ **Tip** You can write the data source logic by hand or by using a design-time wizard that lets you create a connection and then create the command logic in a graphical query builder. To launch this tool, select the data source control, and choose Configure Data Source from the smart tag.

Once you've created the data source, you can reap the benefits—namely, the ability to bind your controls at design time, rather than writing logic in the event handler for the Page.Load event. Here's how it works:

1. Select the data source control, and click Refresh Schema in the smart tag. This step triggers the data source control to connect to the database and retrieve the column information for your query.

2. Add a ListBox to your form. Set the ListBox.DataSourceID property to the data source control. You can choose it from a drop-down list that shows all the data sources on the form (see Figure 9-5).

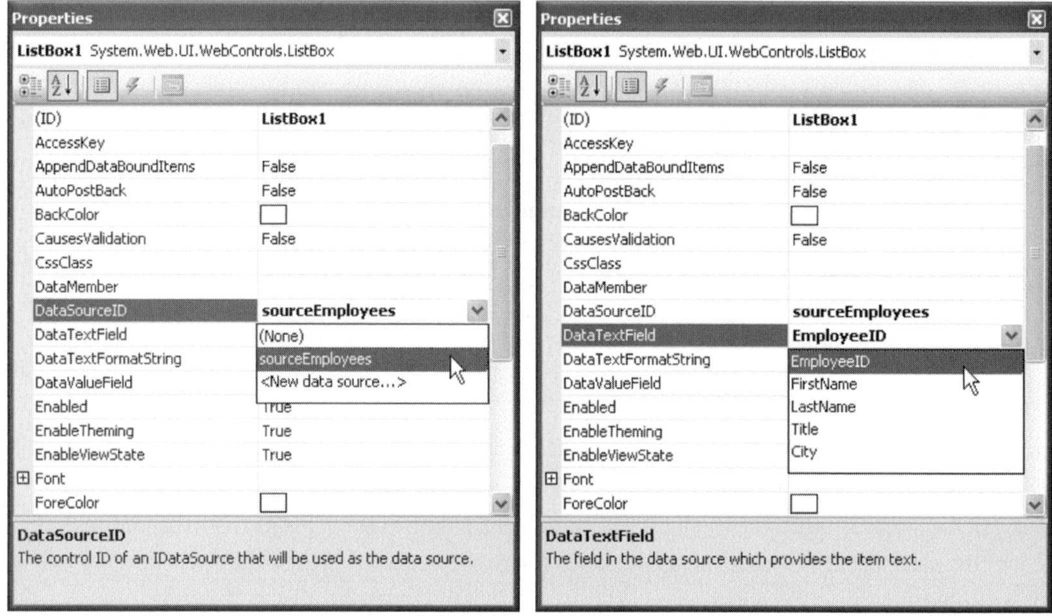

Figure 9-5. Binding a list control to a data source field

3. Set the ListBox.DataTextField to the column you want to display (in this case, choose EmployeeID). The list of fields should also be provided in a drop-down list (see Figure 9-5). If you didn't perform the first step (clicking Refresh Schema), you'd be forced to type the field names in by hand.

4. You can use the same steps to bind a rich data control. Add a GridView to your page, and set the GridView.DataSourceID property to the same data source. You don't need to set any field information, because the GridView can display multiple fields. You'll see the column headings from your query appear on the design surface of your page immediately.

5. Run your page. Don't worry about executing the command or calling DataBind() on the page—ASP.NET performs both of those tasks automatically. You'll see a data-bound page like the one in Figure 9-6.

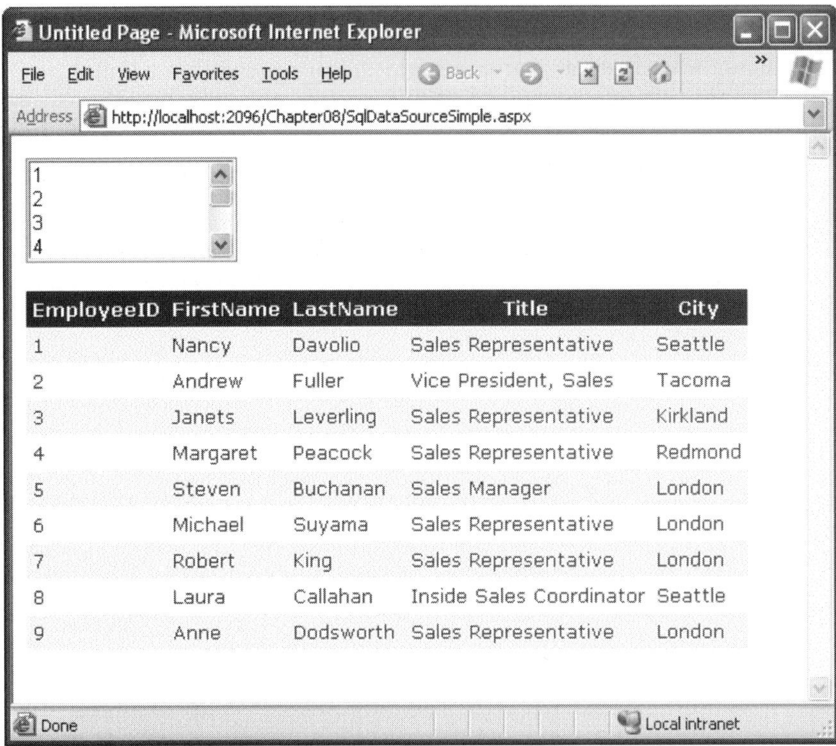

Figure 9-6. *A simple data-bound page with no code*

Clearly, the great advantage of the data source controls is that they allow you to configure data binding at design time, without writing tedious code. Even better, the results of your selections appear (to a limited degree) in the Visual Studio designer so you can get a better idea of what your form will look like.

Data Binding "Under the Hood"

As you learned earlier in this chapter, you can bind to a DataReader or a DataView. So, it's worth asking, which approach does the SqlDataSource control use? It's actually in your control, based on whether you set the DataSourceMode to SqlDataSourceMode.DataSet (the default) or to SqlDataSourceMode.DataReader. The DataSet mode is almost always better, because it supports advanced sorting, filtering, and caching settings that depend on the DataSet. All these features are disabled in the DataReader mode. However, you can use the DataReader mode with extremely large grids, as it's more memory-efficient. That's because the DataReader holds only one record in memory at a time—just long enough to copy the record's information to the linked control. Both modes support binding to multiple controls. To understand why this is possible, you need to take a closer look at how the selection is performed.

If you profile your database, you'll discover that by binding two controls to the same data source, you cause the query to be executed twice. On the other hand, if you bind the page manually, you have the ability to bind the same object to two different controls, which means you need to execute the query only once. Clearly, the SqlDataSource imposes a bit of unnecessary extra overhead here, but if you're aware of it you can design accordingly. First, you should consider caching, which the SqlDataSource supports natively through the EnableCaching, CacheExpirationPolicy, and CacheDuration properties (see Chapter 11 for a full discussion). Second, realize that most of the time you won't be binding more than one control to a data source. That's because the rich data controls—the GridView, DetailsView, and FormView—have the ability to present multiple pieces of data in a flexible layout. If you use these controls, you'll need to bind only one control, which allows you to avoid this limitation altogether.

It's also important to note that data binding is performed at the end of your web-page processing, just before the page is rendered. That means the Page.Load event will fire, followed by any control events, followed by the Page.PreRender event, and only then will the data binding take place. If you need to write code that springs into action after the data binding is complete, you can override the Page.OnPreRenderComplete() method. This method is called immediately after the PreRender stage but just before the view state is serialized and the actual HTML is rendered.

Parameterized Commands

In the previous example, the complete query was hard-coded. Often, you won't have this flexibility. Instead, you'll want to retrieve a subset of data, such as all the products in a given category or all the employees in a specific city.

The following example creates a master-details form using parameters. To create this example, you need two data sources. The first data source provides a list of cities (where various employees live). Here's the definition for this SqlDataSource:

```
<asp:SqlDataSource ID="sourceEmployeeCities" runat="server"
 ProviderName="System.Data.SqlClient"
 ConnectionString="<%$ ConnectionStrings:Northwind %>"
 SelectCommand="SELECT DISTINCT City FROM Employees">
</asp:SqlDataSource>
```

This data source fills a drop-down list with city values:

```
<asp:DropDownList ID="lstCities" runat="server"
  DataSourceID="sourceEmployeeCities" DataTextField="City" AutoPostBack="True">
</asp:DropDownList>
```

The list control has automatic postback enabled, which ensures that the page is posted back every time the list selection is changed, giving your page the chance to update the list of employees based on the current city selection. The other option is to create a dedicated button (such as Select) next to the list control for initiating the postback.

When you select a city, the second data source retrieves all the employees in that city. Here's the definition for the second data source:

```
<asp:SqlDataSource ID="sourceEmployees" runat="server"
 ProviderName="System.Data.SqlClient"
 ConnectionString="<%$ ConnectionStrings:Northwind %>"
 SelectCommand="SELECT EmployeeID, FirstName, LastName,
 Title, City FROM Employees WHERE City=@City">
  <SelectParameters>
    <asp:ControlParameter ControlID="lstCities" Name="City"
     PropertyName="SelectedValue" />
  </SelectParameters>
</asp:SqlDataSource>
```

The trick here is the query is written using a parameter. Parameters are always indicated with an @ symbol, as in @City. You can define as many symbols as you want, but you must map each parameter to a value. In this example, the value for the @City parameter is taken from the lstCities.SelectedValue property. However, you could just as easily modify the ControlParameter tag to bind to another property or control.

Here's the minimum required markup for the GridView that shows the employee list (without the formatting details):

```
<asp:GridView ID="GridView1" runat="server" DataSourceID="sourceEmployees">
</asp:GridView>
```

When you create a parameterized command in a SqlDataSource tag, the parameters are properly encoded and SQL injection attacks (as discussed in Chapter 7) aren't a problem.

■ **Note** If you look at the downloadable examples for this chapter, you'll find that the GridView markup is a fair bit more complex than what's shown here. That's because the GridView markup in these examples uses properties and styles to apply more attractive formatting. The markup also explicitly defines each column in the grid. You'll learn how to use these features when you take a closer look at the GridView in Chapter 10. For now, you'll focus on the plumbing of the ASP.NET data binding model and the data source controls.

Now when you run the page, you can view the employees in a specific city (see Figure 9-7).

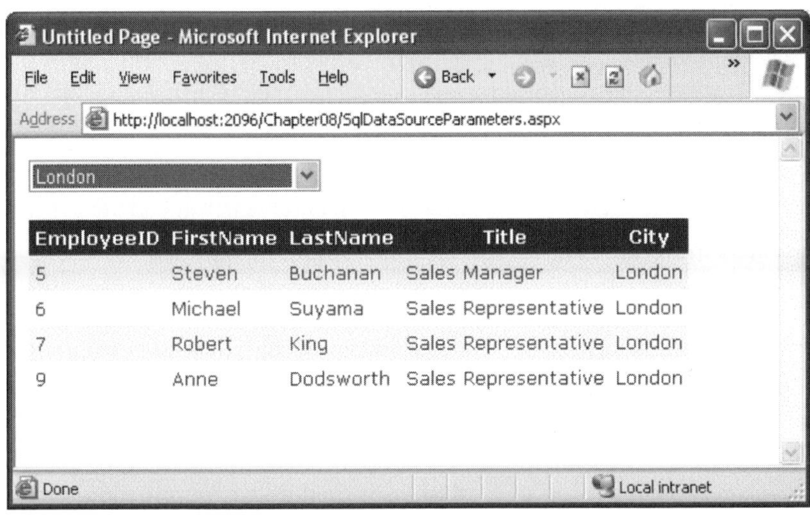

Figure 9-7. *Selecting records based on control selection*

Stored Procedures

You can adapt this example to work with a stored procedure just as easily. For example, if you have the following stored procedure in your database:

```
CREATE PROCEDURE GetEmployeesByCity
  @City varchar(15)
AS
  SELECT EmployeeID, FirstName, LastName, Title,
  City FROM Employees WHERE City=@City
```

you can change the sourceEmployees data source, as shown here:

```
<asp:SqlDataSource ID="sourceEmployees" runat="server"
 ProviderName="System.Data.SqlClient"
 ConnectionString="<%$ ConnectionStrings:Northwind %>"
 SelectCommand="GetEmployeesByCity" SelectCommandType="StoredProcedure">
  <SelectParameters>
    <asp:ControlParameter ControlID="lstCities" Name="City"
     PropertyName="SelectedValue" />
  </SelectParameters>
</asp:SqlDataSource>
```

Not only does this give you all the benefit of stored procedures, but it also streamlines the .aspx portion of your page by removing the actual SQL query, which can be quite lengthy in a real-world page.

More Parameter Types

Parameter values aren't necessarily drawn from other controls. You can map a parameter to any of the parameter types defined in Table 9-2.

Table 9-2. *Parameter Types*

Source	Control Tag	Description
Control property	<asp:ControlParameter>	A property from another control on the page.
Query string value	<asp:QueryStringParameter>	A value from the current query string.
Session state value	<asp:SessionParameter>	A value stored in the current user's session.
Cookie value	<asp:CookieParameter>	A value from any cookie attached to the current request.
Profile value	<asp:ProfileParameter>	A value from the current user's profile (see Chapter 24).
A form variable	<asp:FormParameter>	A value posted to the page from an input control. Usually, you'll use a control property instead, but you might need to grab a value straight from the Forms collection if you've disabled view state for the corresponding control.

Source	Control Tag	Description
A route value	<asp:RouteParameter>	A value from a routed URL. Routed URLs are described in the "URL Routing" section in Chapter 17.
Set programmatically	<asp:Parameter>	The base class from which all other parameters inherit. It's never set automatically, so it makes sense when you're using code to set a parameter value by hand.

You don't need to remember the different tag names, as Visual Studio provides a handy editor that lets you create your command and define your parameters (see Figure 9-8). To see this dialog box, click the ellipsis (...) next to the SelectQuery property in the Properties window. When you type a command that uses one or more parameters, click the Refresh Parameters button, and the list of parameters will appear. You can then choose the mapping for each parameter by making a choice in the Parameter Source box.

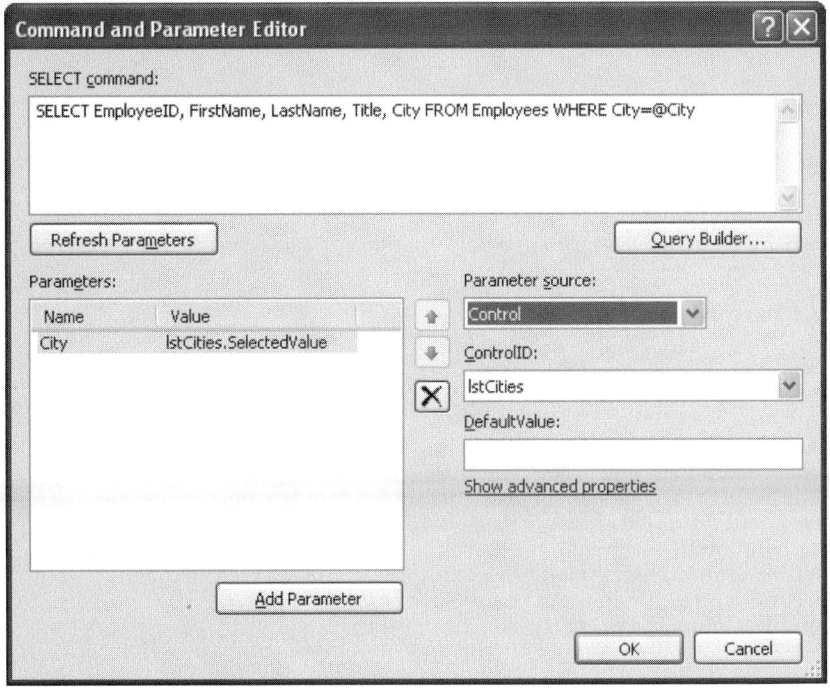

Figure 9-8. Configuring parameter binding at design time

For example, you could split the earlier example into two pages. In the first page, define a list control that shows all the available cities:

```
<asp:SqlDataSource ID="sourceEmployeeCities" runat="server"
 ProviderName="System.Data.SqlClient"
 ConnectionString="<%$ ConnectionStrings:Northwind %>"
 SelectCommand="SELECT DISTINCT City FROM Employees">
</asp:SqlDataSource>
<asp:ListBox ID="lstCities" runat="server" DataSourceID="sourceEmployeeCities"
 DataTextField="City"></asp:ListBox><br />
```

Now, you'll need a little extra code to copy the selected city to the query string and redirect the page. Here's a button that does just that:

```
protected void cmdGo_Click(object sender, EventArgs e)
{
    Response.Redirect("QueryParameter2.aspx?city=" + lstCities.SelectedValue);
}
```

Finally, the second page can bind the GridView according to the city value that's supplied in the query string:

```
<asp:SqlDataSource ID="sourceEmployees" runat="server"
 ProviderName="System.Data.SqlClient"
 ConnectionString="<%$ ConnectionStrings:Northwind %>"
 SelectCommand="GetEmployeesByCity" SelectCommandType="StoredProcedure">
  <SelectParameters>
    <asp:QueryStringParameter Name="City" QueryStringField="city" />
  </SelectParameters>
</asp:SqlDataSource>
```

Once again, the GridView markup is exceedingly straightforward:

```
<asp:GridView ID="GridView1" runat="server" DataSourceID="sourceEmployees">
</asp:GridView>
```

Sometimes you'll need to set a parameter with a value that isn't represented by any of the parameter classes in Table 9-2. Or, you might want to modify a parameter value before using it. In both of these scenarios, you need to use code to set the parameter value just before the database operation takes place.

The SqlDataSource has a number of events that are designed for this purpose. For example, you can fill in parameters for a select operation by reacting to the Selecting event. Similarly, you can use the Updating, Deleting, and Inserting events when updating, deleting, or inserting a record. In these event handlers, you can access the command that's about to be executed through the SqlDataSourceSelectingEventArgs.Command property, and modify its parameter values by hand. Here's an example:

```
protected void sourceEmployee_Selecting(object sender,
 SqlDataSourceSelectingEventArgs e)
{
    // Only keep the first three characters of the city name,
    e.Command.Parameters["@City"].Value ==
      Request.QueryString["city"].Substring(0, 3);
}
```

Note that when you look up a parameter in the Parameters collection, you need to add the @ character at the beginning of the parameter name.

Handling Errors

When you deal with an outside resource such as a database, you need to protect your code with a basic amount of error-handling logic. Even if you've avoided every possible coding mistake, you still need to defend against factors outside your control—for example, if the database server isn't running or the network connection is broken.

You can count on the SqlDataSource to properly release any resources (such as connections) if an error occurs. However, the underlying exception won't be handled. Instead, it will bubble up to the page and derail your processing. As with any other unhandled exception, the user will receive a cryptic error message or an error page. This design is unavoidable—if the SqlDataSource suppressed exceptions, it could hide potential problems and make debugging extremely difficult. However, it's a good idea to handle the problem in your web page and show a more suitable error message.

To do this, you need to handle the data source event that occurs immediately after the error. If you're performing a query, that's the Selected event. If you're performing an update, delete, or insert operation, you would handle the Updated, Deleted, or Inserted events instead. (If you don't want to offer customized error messages, you could handle all these events with the same event handler.)

In the event handler, you can access the exception object through the SqlDataSourceStatusEventArgs.Exception property. If you want to prevent the error from spreading any further, simply set the SqlDataSourceStatusEventArgs.ExceptionHandled property to true. Then, make sure you show an appropriate error message on your web page to inform the user that the command was not completed.

Here's an example:

```
protected void sourceEmployees_Selected(object sender,
 SqlDataSourceStatusEventArgs e)
{
    if (e.Exception != null)
    {
        // Mask the error with a generic message (for security purposes).
        lblError.Text = "An exception occurred performing the query.";

        // Consider the error handled.
        e.ExceptionHandled = true;
    }
}
```

Updating Records

Selecting data is only half of the equation. The SqlDataSource can also apply changes. The only catch is that not all controls support updating. For example, the humble ListBox doesn't provide any way for the user to edit values, delete existing items, or insert new ones. Fortunately, ASP.NET's rich data controls—including the GridView, DetailsView, and FormView—all have editing features that you can switch on.

The first step is to define suitable commands for the operations you want to perform, such as inserting (InsertCommand), deleting (DeleteCommand), and updating (UpdateCommand). If you know that you will allow the user to perform only certain operations (such as updates) but not others (such as insertions and deletions), you can safely omit the commands you don't need.

You define the InsertCommand, DeleteCommand, and UpdateCommand in the same way you define the command for the SelectCommand property—by using a parameterized query or stored procedure call. For example, here's a SqlDataSource that defines a basic update command that updates every field:

```
<asp:SqlDataSource ID="sourceEmployees" runat="server"
 ProviderName="System.Data.SqlClient"
 ConnectionString="<%$ ConnectionStrings:Northwind %>"
 SelectCommand="SELECT EmployeeID, FirstName, LastName, Title, City FROM Employees"
 UpdateCommand="UPDATE Employees SET FirstName=@FirstName, LastName=@LastName,
 Title=@Title, City=@City FROM Employees WHERE EmployeeID=@EmployeeID">
</asp:SqlDataSource>
```

In this example, the parameter names aren't chosen arbitrarily. As long as you give each parameter the same name as the field it affects and preface it with the @ symbol (so FirstName becomes @FirstName), you don't need to define the parameter. That's because the ASP.NET data controls automatically submit a collection of parameters with the new values before triggering the update. Each parameter in the collection uses this naming convention.

To try this, create a page with the SqlDataSource shown previously and a linked GridView control. To enable editing, set the GridView.AutoGenerateEditButton property to true. A new column appears at the left side of the grid. The GridView uses this column to show links for controlling the editing process.

When you run the page and the GridView is bound and displayed, the edit column shows a link named Edit next to every record. When clicked, this link switches the corresponding row into edit mode. All fields are changed to text boxes (with the exception of read-only fields), and the Edit link is replaced with an Update link and a Cancel link (see Figure 9-9).

The Cancel link returns the row to its initial state. The Update link passes the values to the SqlDataSource.UpdateParameters collection (using the field names) and then triggers the SqlDataSource.Update() method to apply the change to the database. Once again, you don't have to write any code.

■ **Note** The GridView is an extremely flexible control. Templates, one of its many features, allow you to define the controls and markup used when editing a record. This is handy if you want to enable editing through drop-down lists, add validation controls, or just fine-tune the appearance of a row in edit mode. You'll consider the GridView's support for templates in Chapter 10.

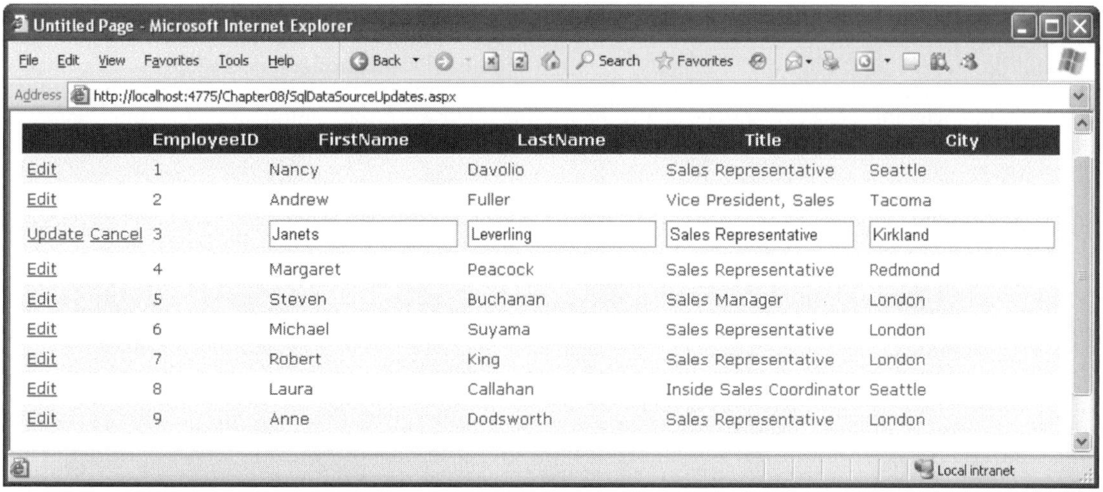

Figure 9-9. *Editing with the GridView*

Strict Concurrency Checking

The update command in the previous example matches the record based on its ID. The problem with this approach is that the update command updates every field indiscriminately—it has no way to distinguish between fields that are and aren't changed. As a result, you can end up obliterating the changes of another user, if they are made between the time the page is requested and the time the page is updated.

For example, imagine Chen and Lucy are viewing the same table of employee records. Lucy commits a change to the address of an employee. A few seconds later, Chen commits a name change to the same employee record. However, that update command not only applies the new name, but it also overwrites every field with the values in Chen's page—effectively replacing the address Lucy entered with the old address.

To defend against this sort of problem, you can enforce stricter concurrency checking. One way to do this is to create a command that performs the update only if every field matches, using a more stringent WHERE clause. Here's what that command would look like:

```
UpdateCommand="UPDATE Employees SET FirstName=@FirstName, LastName=@LastName,
Title=@Title, City=@City FROM Employees WHERE EmployeeID=@original_EmployeeID AND
FirstName=@original_FirstName AND LastName=@original_LastName AND
Title=@original_Title AND City=@original_City"
```

There's an important change in this command. The WHERE clause doesn't attempt to match the parameters named @FirstName, @LastName, and so on, because these parameters reflect the current values (which may not match the original values). Instead, it uses the parameter named @original_FirstName, @original_LastName, and so on. This raises an obvious question—where do these parameter values come from? In order to get access to these original values, you need to take first steps.

First, you need to tell the SqlDataSource that you need access to the original values by setting the SqlDataSource.ConflictDetection property to ConflictOptions.CompareAllValues instead of ConflictOptions.OverwriteChanges (the default).

The second step is to tell the SqlDataSource how to name the parameters that hold the original values. By default, the original values are given the same parameter names as the changed values. In fact, they overwrite the original parameter values. To prevent this behavior, you need to set the SqlDataSource.OldValuesParameterFormatString property. This property takes a string that has a {0} placeholder, where {0} indicates the original parameter name. For example, if you set OldValuesParameterFormatString to original_{0} (which is a common convention), the parameters that have the original values are given the prefix original_. For example, @FirstName becomes @original_FirstName and @LastName becomes @original_LastName, as in the update command shown previously.

Now that you understand these details, you can create a fully configured SqlDataSource that implements this technique:

```
<asp:SqlDataSource ID="sourceEmployees" runat="server"
  ProviderName="System.Data.SqlClient"
  ConnectionString="<%$ ConnectionStrings:Northwind %>"
  SelectCommand=
"SELECT EmployeeID, FirstName, LastName, Title, City FROM Employees"
  ConflictDetection="CompareAllValues"
  OldValuesParameterFormatString="original_{0}"
  UpdateCommand="UPDATE Employees SET FirstName=@FirstName, LastName=@LastName,
Title=@Title, City=@City FROM Employees WHERE EmployeeID=@original_EmployeeID
AND FirstName=@original_FirstName AND LastName=@original_LastName AND
Title=@original_Title AND City=@original_City">
</asp:SqlDataSource>
```

At the end of Chapter 10 you'll see an example that shows how you can implement a more sophisticated concurrency handling strategy that warns you when a change will conflict, and gives you the option of applying it or canceling it.

■ **Tip** Commands that compare values are often inefficient, because they require more data to be sent over the network and mean more comparison work for the database. A better solution is to use a timestamp field (which you can hide in your bound data control). If the row is unchanged, the timestamp will always match.

Incidentally, there's one other way to gain access to original values—by setting the DataKeyNames property of the bound control. For example, if you set GridView.DataKeyNames to EmployeeID, you'll have access to both the current and original value for EmployeeID (although you'll still need to use the OldValuesParameterFormatString if you want to distinguish between them). However, the DataKeyNames property is really meant to indicate the fields that compose the primary key, and it's used to gain access to other features in the bound data control, such as selection. If you want to keep track of old values for the purpose of concurrency checking, you should always use the SqlDataSource.ConflictDetection property. You'll see the DataKeyNames property in action in Chapter 10.

Updating with Stored Procedures

The update example works just as readily with stored procedures. In this case, you simply supply the stored procedure name for the UpdateCommand:

```
UpdateCommand="UpdateEmployee" UpdateCommandType="StoredProcedure"
```

However, this has a catch. As you've learned, the parameter names are based on the field names. If the stored procedure uses the same parameter names, the update works without a hitch. However, if the stored procedure parameter names are slightly different, the update will fail.

■ **Tip** The order of parameters is irrelevant. Only the names are important. The SqlDataSource does a case-insensitive comparison, so your parameters can have different capitalization.

For example, consider an UpdateEmployee stored procedure that takes parameters like this:

```
CREATE PROCEDURE UpdateEmployee
  @EmployeeID        int,
  @TitleOfCourtesy   varchar(25),
  @Last              varchar(20),
  @First             varchar(10)
AS
...
```

In this example, the FirstName and LastName fields map to parameters named @First and @Last. Unfortunately, there's no declarative way to correct this problem and map these parameters to their correct names. Instead, you need to define the new parameters and write a little custom code.

The first step is to add two parameters to the SqlDataSource.UpdateParameters collection. Unfortunately, you can't create these while the update is in progress. Instead, you need to add them to the SqlDataSource tag:

```
<asp:SqlDataSource ID="sourceEmployees" runat="server"
 ProviderName="System.Data.SqlClient"
 ConnectionString="<%$ ConnectionStrings:Northwind %>" SelectCommand=
 "SELECT EmployeeID, FirstName, LastName, TitleOfCourtesy FROM Employees"
 UpdateCommand="UpdateEmployee" UpdateCommandType="StoredProcedure"
 OnUpdating="sourceEmployees_Updating" >
  <UpdateParameters>
    <asp:Parameter Name="First" Type="String" />
    <asp:Parameter Name="Last" Type="String" />
  </UpdateParameters>
</asp:SqlDataSource>
```

Note that the parameter names don't include the @ symbol when you define them in the SqlDataSource tag.

The next step is to react to the SqlDataSource.Updating event, which fires immediately before the update is committed. You can then set the value for the @First and @Last parameters and remove the @FirstName and @LastName parameters from sight. Here's the code you need:

```
protected void sourceEmployees_Updating(object sender,
 SqlDataSourceCommandEventArgs e)
{
    e.Command.Parameters["@First"].Value = e.Command.Parameters["@FirstName"].Value;
    e.Command.Parameters["@Last"].Value = e.Command.Parameters["@LastName"].Value;
    e.Command.Parameters.Remove(e.Command.Parameters["@FirstName"]);
    e.Command.Parameters.Remove(e.Command.Parameters["@LastName"]);
}
```

This represents a fairly typical scenario in which the no-code data binding won't work. Overall, if you can design your stored procedures and classes to work with the data source controls, you'll avoid writing a great deal of code. On the other hand, if you introduce the data source controls to an existing application with a fixed database schema and database components, it may take a fair bit of extra code to fit these pieces together.

Deleting Records

Deleting a record is similar to updating it. You begin by creating a DeleteCommand that removes the record you want to delete. You can match the record using its primary key, or you can use the match-all-values approach described previously (in which case you must set the SqlDataSource.ConflictDetection property to ConflictOptions.CompareAllValues).

```
<asp:SqlDataSource ID="sourceEmployees" runat="server"
  ProviderName="System.Data.SqlClient"
  ConnectionString="<%$ ConnectionStrings:Northwind %>"
  SelectCommand=
"SELECT EmployeeID, FirstName, LastName, Title, City FROM Employees"
  DeleteCommand="DELETE Employees WHERE EmployeeID=@EmployeeID ">
</asp:SqlDataSource>
```

You also need to make minor adjustments to the GridView. First, set the GridView.AutoGenerateDeleteButton property to true to add a column that shows a link named Delete next to each record. (Alternatively, you can explicitly add a CommandField column to the GridView and set its ShowDeleteButton property to true, which accomplishes the same thing. You'll learn how to explicitly define GridView columns in Chapter 10.)

If you're using the standard ConflictDetection (ConflictOptions.OverwriteChanges), you also need to set the GridView.DataKeyNames with a comma-separated list of the field names that make up the primary key. If you don't remember to take this step, the GridView will not pass these parameters to the SqlDataSource, and the SqlDataSource won't be able to find the record it needs to delete.

Here's the minimum markup required to create a GridView that uses this SqlDataSource to allow record deletion:

```
<asp:GridView ID="GridView1" runat="server" DataSourceID="sourceEmployees"
 AutoGenerateDeleteButton="true" DataKeyNames="EmployeeID">
</asp:GridView>
```

Inserting Records

The GridView supports editing and deleting records, but it doesn't support insertion. However, the DetailsView and FormView do support insertion. The basic process is the same. Make sure you've defined the InsertCommand, as shown here:

```
<asp:SqlDataSource ID="sourceEmployees" runat="server"
  ProviderName="System.Data.SqlClient"
  ConnectionString="<%$ ConnectionStrings:Northwind %>"
  SelectCommand=
"SELECT EmployeeID, FirstName, LastName, Title, City FROM Employees"
  InsertCommand="INSERT INTO Employees (FirstName,LastName,Title,City)
VALUES (@FirstName,@LastName,@Title,@City)">
</asp:SqlDataSource>
```

You don't need to worry about the ConflictDetection and OldValuesParameterFormatString properties, because they have no effect when inserting records.

Next, you can configure the bound data control to support insertion. With the DetailsView, you simply need to set AutoGenerateInsertButton to true, as shown here:

```
<asp:DetailsView ID="DetailsView1" runat="server"
  DataSourceID="sourceEmployees" AutoGenerateInsertButton="true">
</asp:DetailsView>
```

Alternatively, you can add a CommandField to the DetailsView and set its ShowInsertButton to true. You can also define the fields in the DetailsView explicitly, which gives you the opportunity to set InsertVisible to false to hide fields that don't apply to insertion operations (like automatically generated identity values or timestamps). You'll also learn much more about the DetailsView in Chapter 10.

Additionally, you can set the DefaultMode property to Insert to start your DetailsView in insert mode, which is useful if you're combining a GridView and a DetailsView on one page, and using the GridView to show the current list of records and the DetailsView to allow the user to add new records. You'll see a page that uses this technique with the ObjectDataSource, shown later in Figure 9-12.

■ **Tip** When performing record insertions, it's a good idea to handle the SqlDataSource.Inserted event and check for errors by examining the SqlDataSourceStatusEventArgs.Exception property. Potential errors include inserting data that violates a database constraint or failing to supply a value for a required field.

Disadvantages of the SqlDataSource

As you've seen, when you use the SqlDataSource, you can often avoid writing any data access code. However, you also sacrifice a fair bit of flexibility. Here are the most significant disadvantages:

Data access logic embedded in the page: To create a SqlDataSource control, you need to hard-code the SQL statements in your web page. This means you can't fine-tune your query without modifying your web page. In an enterprise application, this limitation isn't acceptable, as it's common to revise the queries after the application is deployed in response to profiling, indexes, and expected loads.

■ **Tip** You can improve this situation a fair bit by restricting your use of the SqlDataSource to stored procedures. However, in a large-scale web application, the data access code will be maintained, tested, and refined separately from the business logic (and it may even be coded by different developers). The SqlDataSource just doesn't give you that level of flexibility.

Maintenance in large applications: Every page that accesses the database needs its own set of SqlDataSource controls. This can turn into a maintenance nightmare, particularly if you have several pages using the same query (each of which requires a duplicate instance of the SqlDataSource). In a component-based application, you'll use a higher-level model. The web pages will communicate with a data access library, which will contain all the database details.

Lack of flexibility: Every data access task requires a separate SqlDataSource. If you want to provide a user with multiple ways to view or query data, this can swamp your page with data source objects, one for each command variant. This can get complicated—fast.

Inapplicability to other data tasks: The SqlDataSource doesn't properly represent some types of tasks. The SqlDataSource is intended for data display and data editing scenarios. However, this model breaks down if you need to connect to the database and perform another task, such as placing a shipment request into an order pipeline or logging an event. In these situations, you'll need custom database code. It will simplify your application if you have a single database library that encapsulates these tasks along with data retrieval and updating operations.

■ **Note** In fact, in a well-abstracted three-tier application, your web page may call a method such as Business.PlaceOrder() without worrying about whether this operation involves saving an order record in a database, sending a message to a message queue, communicating with a remote component, or using a combination of all these tasks.

To get around these limitations, you should consider the ObjectDataSource. The ObjectDataSource allows you to bind your page to a custom data access component. Best of all, you get almost all the same frills, such as design-time data binding and no need to write code in your web page.

The ObjectDataSource

The ObjectDataSource allows you to create a declarative link between your web-page controls and a data access component that queries and updates data. The ObjectDataSource is remarkably flexible and can work with a variety of different components. However, to use it, your data access class must conform to a few rules:

- All the logic must be contained in a single class. (If you want to use different classes for selecting and updating your data, you'll need to wrap them in another higher-level class.)
- It must provide the query results when a single method is called.
- The query results are several records, which can be represented as a collection, an array, a DataSet, a DataTable, a DataView, or a list object that implements IEnumerable. Each record should be a custom object that exposes all its data through public properties.
- You can use instance methods or static methods. However, if you use instance methods the class must have a default, no-argument constructor so that the ObjectDataSource can create an instance when needed.
- It must be stateless. That's because the ObjectDataSource will create an instance only when needed and destroy it at the end of every request, if you're using instance methods. (And if you're using static methods, your class should always be stateless, just to avoid problems if more than one ASP.NET thread is using the same methods at the same time.)

You can work around many of these rules by handling ObjectDataSource events and writing custom code. However, if you want your data access class to plug into the data-binding model seamlessly without extra work, you should observe these guidelines.

Selecting Records

For example, consider the data-bound page shown earlier in Figure 9-6. You can create the same page using the custom data access component developed in Chapter 8. You can refer to Chapter 8 to see the full code, which has the following structure:

```
public class EmployeeDB
{
    public EmployeeDetails GetEmployee(int EmployeeID) { ... }
    public List<EmployeeDetails> GetEmployees() { ... }

    public int InsertEmployee(EmployeeDetails emp) { ... }
    public void DeleteEmployee(int employeeID) { ... }
    public void UpdateEmployee(int employeeID, string firstName,
      string lastName, string titleOfCourtesy) {... }

    public int CountEmployees() { ... }
}
```

The first step to use this class in your page is to define the ObjectDataSource and indicate the name of the class that contains the data access methods. You do this by specifying the fully qualified class name with the TypeName property:

```
<asp:ObjectDataSource ID="sourceEmployees" runat="server"
 TypeName="DatabaseComponent.EmployeeDB" ... />
```

■ **Note** For this to work, the DatabaseComponent.EmployeeDB class must exist in the App_Code folder or be compiled in an assembly in the Bin folder.

Once you've attached the ObjectDataSource to a class, the next step is to point it to the methods it can use to select and update records.

The ObjectDataSource defines SelectMethod, DeleteMethod, UpdateMethod, and InsertMethod properties that you use to link your data access class to various tasks. Each property takes the name of the method in the data access class. In this example, you simply need to enable querying, so you need to set the SelectMethod property:

```
<asp:ObjectDataSource ID="sourceEmployees" runat="server"
 TypeName="DatabaseComponent.EmployeeDB" SelectMethod="GetEmployees" />
```

Remember, the GetEmployees() method returns a collection of EmployeeDetails objects. These objects fit the criteria of the ObjectDataSource—they provide all the appropriate record data through public properties.

Once you've set up the ObjectDataSource, you can bind your web-page controls in the same way you do with the SqlDataSource. You can even use the same drop-down lists in the Properties window, provided you click the Refresh Schema link in the ObjectDataSource smart tag first. When you click Refresh Schema, Visual Studio retrieves the property names and data types by reflecting on the EmployeeDetails class.

Here's the complete page code, without the formatting details for the GridView:

```
<asp:ObjectDataSource ID="sourceEmployees" runat="server"
 TypeName="DatabaseComponent.EmployeeDB" SelectMethod="GetEmployees"/>
<asp:ListBox ID="ListBox1" runat="server" DataSourceID="sourceEmployees"
 DataTextField="EmployeeID"></asp:ListBox>
<br />
<asp:GridView ID="GridView1" runat="server" DataSourceID="sourceEmployees">
</asp:GridView>
```

Figure 9-10 shows the result.

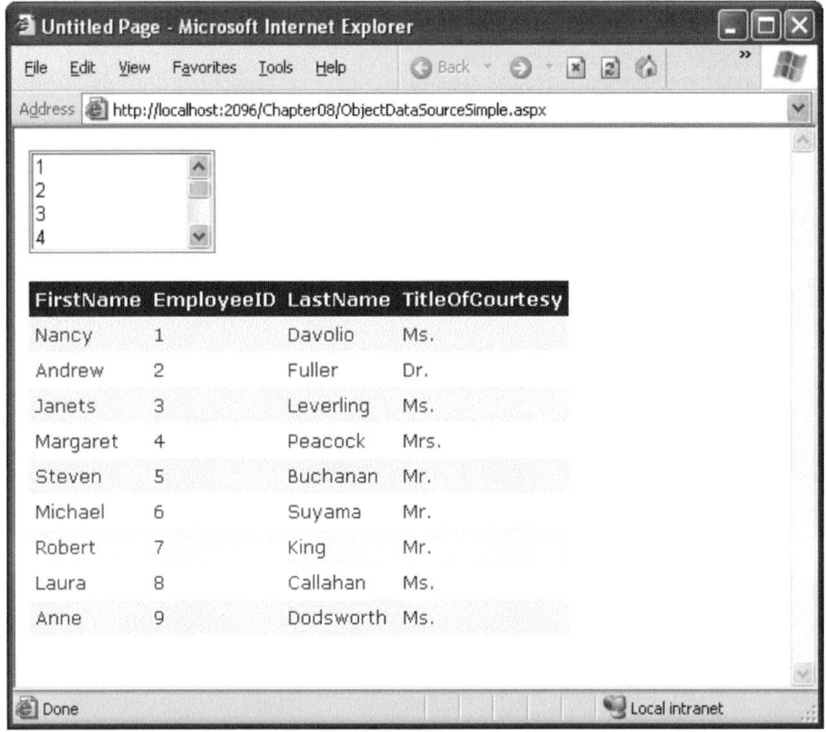

Figure 9-10. *Binding to a data access class*

From the user's perspective, this example is equivalent to the SqlDataSource page shown in Figure 9-6. The only difference is that by default, the columns are shown in the order that the properties are declared in the EmployeeDetails class, whereas the SqlDataSource shows them in the order they're listed in the query. You can easily change the ordering of columns by customizing the GridView.

The apparent similarities conceal some real behind-the-scenes differences. In this example, the web page doesn't require any hard-coded SQL details. Instead, all the work is handed off to the EmployeeDB class. When you run the page, the ListBox and GridView will request data from the ObjectDataSource, which will call the EmployeeDB.GetEmployees() method to retrieve the data (once for each control). This data is then bound and displayed in both controls, with no code required.

■ **Note** Remember, the EmployeeDB class uses error-handling blocks to make sure connections are properly closed, but it doesn't catch exceptions. (Best design practices are to let the exception notify the web page, which can then decide how best to inform the user.) You can handle errors with the ObjectDataSource in the same way you handle them with the SqlDataSource—first, handle the Selected, Inserted, Updated, or Deleted event; second, check for an exception; and third, mark it as handled. For more information, see the "Handling Errors" section earlier in the chapter.

Using a Parameterized Constructor

A key part of extending the data source controls takes place through event handling. For example, by default the ObjectDataSource is able to create your custom data access class only if it provides a zero no-argument constructor. However, you can extend the ObjectDataSource to work with data access classes that don't meet this requirement by writing code that reacts to the ObjectDataSource.ObjectCreating event.

The current EmployeesDB class retrieves the database connection string directly from the web.config file, as shown here:

```
private string connectionString;

public EmployeeDB()
{
    connectionString =
      WebConfigurationManager.ConnectionStrings["Northwind"].ConnectionString;
}
```

However, you might want to add another constructor that lets the web page supply a specific connection string of its choosing:

```
public EmployeeDB(string connectionString)
{
    this.connectionString = connectionString;
}
```

To force the ObjectDataSource to use this constructor, you need to handle the ObjectCreating event, create the EmployeeDB instance yourself, and then assign it to the data source using the ObjectDataSourceEventArgs:

```
protected void sourceEmployees_ObjectCreating(object sender,
 ObjectDataSourceEventArgs e)
{
    e.ObjectInstance = new DatabaseComponent.EmployeeDB("...");
}
```

Clearly, you could perform more complex initialization in the ObjectCreating event. For example, you could call an initialization method, choose to instantiate one of several derived classes, and so on.

■ **Tip** The data source controls expose a rich event model. Events tend to fall into two categories. Events ending in *ing* such as ObjectCreating occur while a task is underway and give you the chance to cancel or customize what's happening. Events ending in *ed* such as ObjectCreated occur when the task is finished and are suitable for logging the action, synchronizing other controls, and handling errors.

You can also react to the ObjectDisposing event to perform cleanup. The ObjectDisposing event is fired just before the data access object is released (before the page is served). Usually, you won't need to use the ObjectDisposing event because a better alternative exists—place your cleanup code in a dedicated Dispose() method inside your data access class. As long as the data access class implements IDisposable, the ObjectDataSource will automatically call your Dispose() method. (To get a painless implementation of IDisposable for free, just derive your data access class from the System.ComponentModel.Component class and override the Dispose() method.)

Using Method Parameters

Earlier, you saw how you could use the SqlDataSource to execute parameterized commands. The same feat is possible with the ObjectDataSource, if you provide a suitable select method that accepts one or more parameters. You can then map each parameter to a control value, query string argument, and so on.

To try this, you can use the EmployeeDB.GetEmployee() method, which retrieves a single employee by ID number. Here's the method declaration:

```
public EmployeeDetails GetEmployee(int employeeID)
{ ... }
```

The test page provides a list with all the employee IDs. This list control uses the GetEmployees() method through an Object data source:

```
<asp:ObjectDataSource ID="sourceEmployeesList" runat="server"
 SelectMethod="GetEmployees" TypeName="DatabaseComponent.EmployeeDB"/>
<asp:ListBox ID="lstEmployees" runat="server" DataSourceID="sourceEmployeesList"
 DataTextField="EmployeeID" AutoPostBack="True"/>
```

When you choose an ID, the page posts back and uses a second data source to call GetEmployee(). The employeeID value is taken from the selected item in the list:

```
<asp:ObjectDataSource ID="sourceEmployee" runat="server"
 SelectMethod="GetEmployee" TypeName="DatabaseComponent.EmployeeDB">
  <SelectParameters>
    <asp:ControlParameter ControlID="lstEmployees" Name="employeeID"
     PropertyName="SelectedValue" />
  </SelectParameters>
</asp:ObjectDataSource>
```

The name you define for the parameter must match the parameter name you use in the method exactly. When the ObjectDataSource calls the method, it uses reflection to examine the method, and it examines the parameter names to determine the order of arguments. This system allows you to use overloaded methods, because the ObjectDataSource is able to correctly identify the overload you want based on the number of parameters you define and their names.

■ **Tip** The data types are not used in the matching process—instead, the ObjectDataSource will attempt to convert the parameter value into the data type of the matching parameter using the appropriate type converter for that data type. If this process fails, an exception is raised.

Now, the single employee record returned from GetEmployee() is displayed in another rich data control—the DetailsView. By default, the DetailsView creates a basic table with one row for each field or property in the data item (assuming the AutoGenerateRows property is true, which is its default value). Here's a basic declaration for the DetailsView:

```
<asp:DetailsView ID="DetailsView1" runat="server"
  DataSourceID="sourceEmployees" />
```

You have one more detail to fill in. The first time the page is requested, there won't be any selected value in the lstEmployees control. However, the DetailsView will still try to bind itself, so the ObjectDataSource will call GetEmployee(). The employeeID parameter is null, but the actual value that's passed is 0, because regular integers aren't nullable. When the GetEmployee() method executes the query, it doesn't find a matching record with an employeeID of 0. This is an error condition, and an exception is thrown.

You could solve this problem by revising the GetEmployee() method to return null in this situation. However, it makes more sense to catch the binding attempt and explicitly cancel it when there's no employeeID parameter. You can do this by handling the ObjectDataSource.Selecting event and looking for the employeeID parameter in the ObjectDataSourceSelectingEventArgs.InputParameters collection, which has every parameter you're using indexed by name.

```
protected void sourceEmployee_Selecting(object sender,
 ObjectDataSourceSelectingEventArgs e)
{
    if (e.InputParameters["employeeID"] == null) e.Cancel = true;
}
```

This is the only code you need to write for the page. Figure 9-11 shows the page in action.

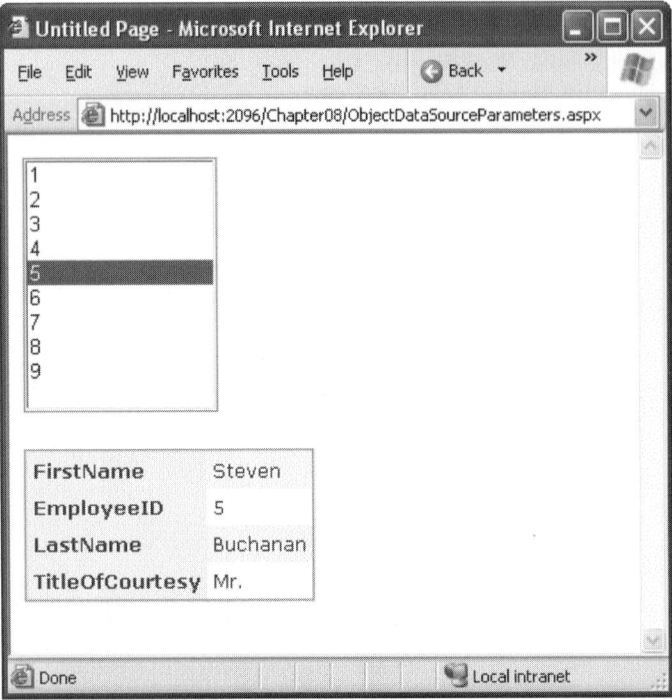

Figure 9-11. Binding to a single employee record

Updating Records

The ObjectDataSource provides the same type of support for updatable data binding as the SqlDataSource. The first step is to specify the UpdateMethod, which needs to be a public instance method in the same class:

```
<asp:ObjectDataSource ID="sourceEmployees" runat="server"
 TypeName="DatabaseComponent.EmployeeDB"
 SelectMethod="GetEmployees" UpdateMethod="UpdateEmployee" />
```

The challenge is in making sure the UpdateMethod has the right signature. As with the SqlDataSource, updates, inserts, and deletes automatically receive a collection of parameters from the linked data control. These parameters have the same names as the corresponding class properties.

To understand how this works, it helps to consider a basic example. Assume you create a grid that shows a list of EmployeeDetails objects. You also add a column with edit links. When the user commits an edit, the GridView fills the ObjectDataSource.UpdateParameters collection with one parameter for each property of the EmployeeDetails class, including EmployeeID, FirstName, LastName, and TitleOfCourtesy. Then, the ObjectDataSource searches for a method named UpdateEmployee() in the EmployeeDB class. This method must have the same parameters, with the same names.

That means this method is a match:

```
public void UpdateEmployee(int employeeID, string firstName, string lastName,
 string titleOfCourtesy)
{ ... }
```

This method is not a match, because the names don't match exactly:

```
public void UpdateEmployee(int id, string first, string last,
 string titleOfCourtesy)
{ ... }
```

This is not a match, because there's an additional parameter:

```
public void UpdateEmployee(int employeeID, string firstName, string lastName,
 string titleOfCourtesy, bool useOptimisticConcurrency)
{ ... }
```

The method matching algorithm is not case-sensitive, and it doesn't consider the order or data type of the parameters. It simply tries to find a method with the right number of parameters and the same names. As long as that method is present, the update can be committed automatically, without any custom code.

Updating with a Data Object

One problem with the UpdateEmployee() method shown in the previous example is that the method signature is a little cumbersome—you need one parameter for each property in the data object. Seeing as you already have a definition for the EmployeeDetails class, it makes sense to create an UpdateEmployee() method that uses it and gets all its information from an EmployeeDetails object. Here's an example:

```
public void UpdateEmployee(EmployeeDetails emp)
{ ... }
```

The ObjectDataSource supports this approach. However, to use it, you must set the DataObjectTypeName to the full name of the class you want to use. Here's how it works:

```
<asp:ObjectDataSource ID="sourceEmployees" runat="server"
 TypeName="DatabaseComponent.EmployeeDB"
 DataObjectTypeName="DatabaseComponent.EmployeeDetails"
 ... />
```

Once this is in place, the ObjectDataSource will match only the UpdateMethod, DeleteMethod, or InsertMethod if it has a single parameter that accepts the type specified in DataObjectTypeName. Additionally, your data object must follow some rules:

- It must provide a default (zero-argument) constructor.
- For every parameter, there must be a property with the same name. (Public variables are ignored.)
- All properties must be public and writable.

You're free to add code to your data object class. For example, you can add methods, constructors, validation, and event-handling logic in your property procedures, and so on.

Dealing with Nonstandard Method Signatures

Sometimes you may run into a problem in which the property names of your data class (for example, EmployeeDetails) don't exactly match the parameter names of your update method (for example, the EmployeeDB.UpdateEmployee() method). If all you need is a simple renaming job, you need to perform the task that was described in the "Updating with Stored Procedures" section earlier, although the syntax is slightly different.

First, you define the additional parameters you need, with the correct names. For example, maybe you need to rename the EmployeeDetails.EmployeeID property to a parameter named id in the update method. Here's the new parameter you need:

```
<asp:ObjectDataSource ID="sourceEmployees" runat="server"
 TypeName="DatabaseComponent.EmployeeDB" SelectMethod="GetEmployees"
 UpdateMethod="UpdateEmployee" OnUpdating="sourceEmployees_Updating" >
  <UpdateParameters>
    <asp:Parameter Name="id" Type="Int32" />
  </UpdateParameters>
</asp:ObjectDataSource>
```

Second, you react to the ObjectDataSource.Updating event, setting the value for these parameters and removing the ones you don't want:

```
protected void sourceEmployees_Updating(object sender,
 ObjectDataSourceMethodEventArgs e)
{
    e.InputParameters["id"] = e.InputParameters["EmployeeID"];
    e.InputParameters.Remove("EmployeeID");
}
```

■ **Tip** The same approach used here for updating applies when you're performing inserts and deletes. The only difference is that you handle the Inserting and Deleting events instead.

You can use a similar approach to add extra parameters. For example, if your method requires a parameter with information that's not contained in the linked data control, just define it as one of the UpdateParameters and then set the value when the ObjectDataSource.Updating event fires.

If you're more ambitious, you can even decide to programmatically point the ObjectDataSource to a different update method in the same class:

```
sourceEmployees.UpdateMethod = "UpdateEmployeeStrict";
```

You'll use this approach to solve a common problem in the section "The Limits of the Data Source Controls" later in this chapter.

In fact, to get really adventurous you could set the ConflictDetection property to ConflictOptions.CompareAllValues so that the old and new values are submitted in the UpdateParameters collection. You can then examine these parameters, determine what fields have changed, and call a different method (with different parameters accordingly). Unfortunately, this isn't a zero-code scenario, and you might end up writing some awkward code for updating and removing parameters. At worst, this code can become messy and difficult to maintain. Still, it gives you an extra layer of flexibility that you may need in some situations.

Handling Identity Values in an Insert

So far, all the examples you've seen have used parameters to supply values to an update operation. However, you can also create a parameter to return a result. With the SqlDataSource, you can use this option to get access to an output parameter. With the ObjectDataSource, you can use this technique to capture the return value.

Figure 9-12 shows an example with a page that includes two data-bound controls. The DetailsView (at the top) allows the user to insert records. The GridView (at the bottom) shows all the records that currently exist and allows the user to delete them. Both records are bound to the same ObjectDataSource.

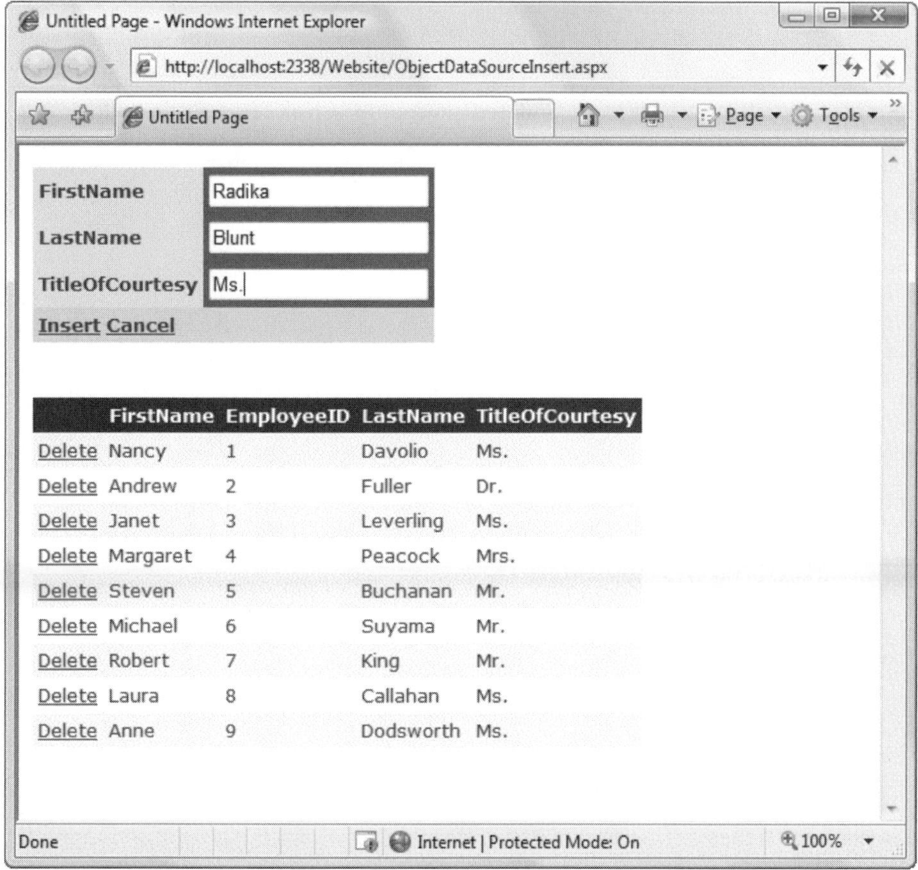

Figure 9-12. *Inserting records (with a DetailsView) and deleting records (with a GridView)*

Here's the stripped-down markup for the data controls, without any formatting details:

```
<asp:DetailsView ID="detailsInsertEmployee" runat="server"
 DataSourceID="sourceEmployees" DefaultMode="Insert"
 AutoGenerateInsertButton="true" />

<asp:Label ID="lblConfirmation" runat="server"
  EnableViewState="false" />
<br /><br />

<asp:GridView ID="gridEmployeeList" runat="server"
 DataSourceID="sourceEmployees" AutoGenerateDeleteButton="true" />
```

When inserting a record, the ObjectDataSource calls the InsertEmployee() method, which adds an employee record and returns the newly generated unique ID value as an integer:

```
public int InsertEmployee(EmployeeDetails emp)
{ ... }
```

You don't need to use the identity value. As you've seen already, linked data controls are bound after any updates are committed, which ensures that the updated information always appears in the linked controls. However, you might want to use the identity for another purpose, such as displaying a confirmation message. To capture this identity value, you need to define a parameter:

```
<asp:ObjectDataSource ID="sourceEmployees" runat="server"
 TypeName="DatabaseComponent.EmployeeDB"
 DataObjectTypeName="DatabaseComponent.EmployeeDetails"
 SelectMethod="GetEmployees"
 DeleteMethod="DeleteEmployee"
 InsertMethod="InsertEmployee" OnInserted="sourceEmployees_Inserted">
  <InsertParameters>
    <asp:Parameter Direction="ReturnValue" Name="EmployeeID" Type="Int32" />
  </InsertParameters>
</asp:ObjectDataSource>
```

Now you can retrieve the parameter by responding to the Inserted event, which fires after the insert operation is finished:

```
protected void sourceEmployees_Inserted(object sender,
 ObjectDataSourceStatusEventArgs e)
{
    if (e.Exception == null)
    {
        lblConfirmation.Text = "Inserted record " + e.ReturnValue.ToString();
    }
    else
    {
        lblConfirmation.Text = e.Exception.Message;
        e.ExceptionHandled = true;
    }
}
```

Identifying Data Classes With Attributes

As you've already learned, Visual Studio can help you configure the markup for the ObjectDataSource using the Configure Data Source Wizard. To start this wizard, select the ObjectDataSource, click the arrow in the top-right corner to show the smart tag, and then click the Configure Data Source link. The wizard will walk you through a series of steps, prompting you to pick a data access class and choose the methods you want to use for selecting, inserting, updating, and deleting data.

When you create a database component, you can take a few simple steps to make sure it works well with tools like the Configure Data Source Wizard. The trick is to add two specialized attributes from the System.ComponentModel namespace that clearly identify that your class is designed for use with the ObjectDataSource.

The first attribute you need is the DataObject attribute. You apply the DataObject attribute directly to the declaration of your data access class, like this:

```
[DataObject]
public class EmployeeDB
{ ... }
```

This indicates that EmployeeDB should be considered a data object—in other words, it's a data source that can supply data to the ObjectDataSource control. When you enable the Show Only Data Components check box option in the Configure Data Source Wizard, you'll only see classes that use the DataObject attribute. This is a great way to cut straight to the data access classes in your solution.

Next, you need to add attributes to the methods you use for your data operations. You do this with the DataObjectMethod attribute, which takes two parameters. The first parameter indicates whether the method is designed for a select, update, insert, delete, or DataSet fill operation. The second parameter is a Boolean. If true, it signals that the method is the default for its type of operation. This is useful if you provide more than one method for a specific type of operation. For example, you might create a data access class that has several select methods. The default method could be the one that returns an unfiltered collection of all the records.

Here's an example that applies the DataObjectMethod attribute:

```
[DataObjectMethod(DataObjectMethodType.Select, true)]
public List<EmployeeDetails> GetEmployees()
{ ... }
```

When you're choosing a method for record selection, the Configure Data Source Wizard will show a list of all the methods that have a DataObjectMethod attribute with a DataObjectMethodType of Select. The Configure Data Source Wizard will preselect the one you've identified as the default method.

The Limits of the Data Source Controls

As a whole, the data source controls are a remarkable innovation for ASP.NET developers. However, you'll still run into situations where you need to step beyond their bounds—or even abandon them completely. In the following sections, you'll see how to use the SqlDataSource and ObjectDataSource to deal with a common design requirement—adding extra items to a data-bound list of information.

The Problem

Earlier, you saw an example that allowed users to browse a list of cities in different regions using two linked controls—a DropDownList and a GridView. Best of all, this example could be created using a SqlDataSource or an ObjectDataSource; either way, it doesn't require any custom code. Figure 9-9 showed this example earlier.

As convenient as this example is, it presents a problem that's difficult to fix. Because it's impossible to create a drop-down list that doesn't have a selected item (unless it's empty), the first city in the list is automatically selected. Many web applications use a different behavior and add an extra item at the top of the list with text such as "(Choose a City)". Selecting this first item has no effect. Additionally, you might want to add an item that allows you to see *every* city in a single list. Figure 9-13 shows the result you want.

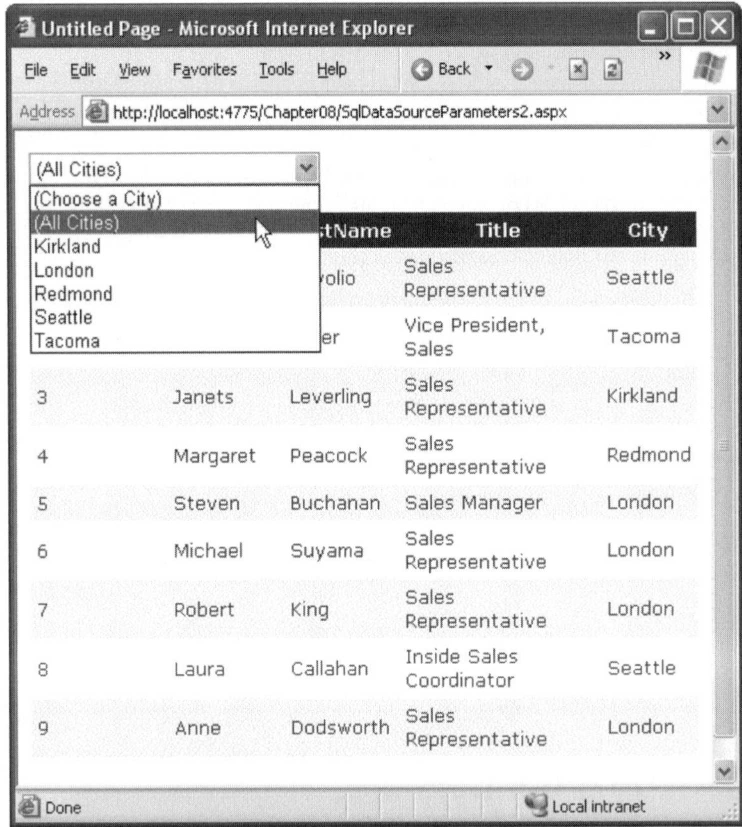

***Figure 9-13.** Data binding with extra options*

So, how can you implement this model with data binding? One of the few weaknesses in the data binding model is that you never explicitly handle or create the data object that's bound to the control. As a result, you don't have the chance to add an extra item. In fact, this example has two challenges—determining how to add the extra options to the list and reacting when they are selected to override the automatic query logic.

Adding the Extra Items

This problem has a few possible workarounds, but none is perfect. You could rewrite the query so that it returns a result set with an extra hard-coded item. Here's an example:

```
SELECT '(Choose a City)' AS City UNION SELECT DISTINCT City FROM Employees
```

The problem with this approach is that it forces you to add presentation details to the data layer. If your query is in a dedicated stored procedure (which is always a good idea), it will be difficult to reuse this query for other purposes, and it will be awkward to maintain the page.

A better choice is to insert this fixed piece of string into the DropDownList programmatically. However, you can't take this step before the data binding takes place, because the data binding process will wipe it from the list. You could override the Page.OnPreRenderComplete() method to perform this task. However, that raises new complications. For one thing, the GridView will have already been filled with data based on the initial DropDownList selection. (Even if you solve this problem, there are other issues related to how changes are detected in the DropDownList selection.)

Ultimately, you'll need to resort to programmatic data binding. In normal operation, data source controls are invoked automatically when a linked control needs data or is ready to commit an update. However, a lesser known fact is that you can also take charge of data source controls programmatically, by calling methods such as Select(), Update(), Insert(), and Delete(). Of course, it's up to you to bind the data you retrieve from Select() and supply the changed data for when committing an update.

To put this into practice, start by removing the DropDownList.DataSourceID property. Instead of using this property, you'll bind the control when the page first loads. This gives you the chance to insert the items immediately, before any other data binding actions take place:

```
protected void Page_Load(object sender, EventArgs e)
{
    if (!Page.IsPostBack)
    {
        // Trigger the sourceEmployeeCities query and bind the results.
        lstCities.DataSource =
          sourceEmployeeCities.Select(DataSourceSelectArguments.Empty);
        lstCities.DataBind();

        // Add the two new items and select the first.
        lstCities.Items.Insert(0, "(Choose a City)");
        lstCities.Items.Insert(1, "(All Cities)");
        lstCities.SelectedIndex = 0;
    }
}
```

In this example, the data binding for the list control is performed only once, when the page is requested for the first time. After that, the values in view state are used instead. This code is identical for the SqlDataSource and the ObjectDataSource. That's not true for the remainder of the example.

Handling the Extra Options with the SqlDataSource

The next challenge is to intercept clicks on either of the first two items. You can accomplish this by handling the data source Selecting event, which occurs just before the query is executed. You can then check the parameters that are about to be supplied and cancel the operation if needed.

Here's the complete code:

```
protected void sourceEmployees_Selecting(object sender,
 SqlDataSourceSelectingEventArgs e)
{
    if ((string)e.Command.Parameters["@City"].Value == "(Choose a City)")
    {
        // Do nothing.
        e.Cancel = true;
    }
    else if ((string)e.Command.Parameters["@City"].Value == "(All Cities)")
    {
        // Manually change the command.
        e.Command.CommandText = "SELECT * FROM Employees";
    }
}
```

This brute-force approach—changing the command using a hard-coded query—is ugly. Another approach is to cancel the operation, call another method that returns the appropriate data, and bind that. However, that forces you to do a fair bit of work manually, and mixing manual and automatic data binding can quickly get confusing. Unfortunately, no perfect solution exists.

Handling the Extra Options with the ObjectDataSource

The object data source handles the problem better, because it gives you the option to reroute the command to another method. If you find that a full list of employees is required, you can remove the City parameter altogether and use a no-parameter method for retrieving all the employees.

Here's how it works:

```
protected void sourceEmployees_Selecting(object sender,
 ObjectDataSourceSelectingEventArgs e)
{
    if (e.InputParameters["employeeID"] == null) e.Cancel = true;
    if ((string)e.InputParameters["City"].Value == "(Choose a City)")
    {
        // Do nothing.
        e.Cancel = true;
    }
    else if ((string)e.InputParameters["City"].Value == "(All Cities)")
    {
        // Manually change the method.
        sourceEmployees.SelectMethod = "GetAllEmployees";
        e.InputParameters.Remove("City");
    }
}
```

This solution isn't possible with the SqlDataSource, because the command logic is embedded into the data source control. Still, this approach can easily be abused and lead to code that is difficult to maintain. For example, you won't receive any warning if you rename, remove, or modify the parameters for the GetAllEmployees() method. In this case, you'll receive an error only when you run the page and click the (All Cities) option.

Summary

In this chapter, you looked at data binding expressions and the ASP.NET data source controls in detail. Along the way, you started using the GridView, ASP.NET's premier rich data control. In the next chapter, you'll explore the three most powerful data-bound controls in detail: the GridView, DetailsView, and FormView. You'll also learn how they work with a few data source features that this chapter didn't cover, such as sorting and filtering.

CHAPTER 10

■■■

Rich Data Controls

In the previous chapter, you saw how to use the data source controls to perform queries, both with and without the assistance of a custom data access class. Along the way, you used some of ASP.NET's rich data controls, such as the GridView. However, you haven't delved into all the features these controls provide.

In this chapter, you'll take a closer look at the three most powerful data controls that ASP.NET offers: the GridView, the DetailsView, the FormView, and the ListView. Using these controls, you'll learn how to fine-tune formatting and use features such as selection, sorting, filtering, and templates. You'll also learn about advanced scenarios such as showing images, calculating summaries, and creating a master-details list in a single control.

Data Control Changes in ASP.NET 4

ASP.NET 4 adds a few minor refinements to its rich data controls. Here they are, in the order you'll encounter them in this chapter:

- **Better selection behavior when sorting or paging:** The GridView and ListView controls gain a new property named EnablePersistedSelection. When set to true, this tells the control to keep the same item selected after a sort or paging operation. When set to false, these controls revert to their traditional (and somewhat annoying) behavior, which keeps the same row *number* selected, even though it probably isn't the same item.
- **Predictable IDs in data templates:** In Chapter 3, you learned how ASP.NET 4 adds a ClientIDMode property that every web control can use to influence how its client-side ID is generated. This allows you to generate simpler, more predictable client-side IDs, which makes it easier to write JavaScript and CSS rules that use these IDs. ASP.NET extends this feature to data controls like the GridView and ListView with the ClientIDRowSuffix property. You'll learn more in the section "Client IDs in Templates."
- **Layout-free ListView controls:** The ListView now renders a default LayoutTemplate if you don't supply one. This is a minor improvement, as most of the time you're using the ListView to get more control of your data layout, and so you need a custom LayoutTemplate anyway.

The GridView

The GridView is an extremely flexible grid control for showing data in a basic grid consisting of rows and columns. It includes a wide range of hard-wired features, including selection, paging, sorting, and editing, and it is extensible through templates. The great advantage of the GridView over the DataGrid is its support for code-free scenarios. Using the GridView, you can accomplish many common tasks, such as paging and selection, without writing any code. With the DataGrid, you were forced to handle events to implement the same features.

You've already seen the GridView at work in the previous chapter. However, you haven't yet considered how to customize it to provide the exact data display you want.

Defining Columns

The GridView examples you've seen so far have set the GridView.AutoGenerateColumns property to true. When this property is set, the GridView uses reflection to examine the data object and finds all the fields (of a record) or properties (of a custom object). It then creates a column for each one, in the order that it finds it.

This automatic column generation is good for creating quick test pages, but it doesn't give you the flexibility you'll usually want. For example, what if you want to hide columns, change their order, or configure some aspect of their display, such as the formatting or heading text? In all of these cases, you'll need to set AutoGenerateColumns to false and define the columns yourself in the <Columns> section of the GridView control tag.

■ **Tip** It's possible to have AutoGenerateColumns set to true and define columns in the <Columns> section. In this case, the columns you explicitly defined are added before the autogenerated columns. This technique was used in the previous chapter to create a GridView with automatically generated bound columns and a manually defined column with edit controls. However, for the most flexibility you'll usually want to explicitly define every column.

Each column can be any of several different types, as described in Table 10-1. The order of your column tags determines the right-to-left order of columns in the GridView.

Table 10-1. *Column Types*

Column	Description
BoundField	This column displays text from a field in the data source.
ButtonField	This column displays a button for each item in the list.
CheckBoxField	This column displays a check box for each item in the list. It's used automatically for true/false fields (in SQL Server, these are fields that use the bit data type).
CommandField	This column provides selection or editing buttons.

Column	Description
HyperLinkField	This column displays its contents (a field from the data source or static text) as a hyperlink.
ImageField	This column displays image data from a binary field (providing it can be successfully interpreted as a supported image format).
TemplateField	This column allows you to specify multiple fields, custom controls, and arbitrary HTML using a custom template. It gives you the highest degree of control but requires the most work.

The most basic column type is the BoundField, which binds to one field in the data object. For example, here's the definition for a single data-bound column that displays the EmployeeID field:

```
<asp:BoundField DataField="EmployeeID" HeaderText="ID" />
```

This achieves one improvement over the autogenerated column—the header text has been changed from EmployeeID to just ID.

When you first create a GridView, the AutoGenerateColumns property is not set (and so the default value of true is used). When you bind it to a data source control, nothing changes. However, if you click the Refresh Schema link of the data source control, the AutoGenerateColumns property is flipped to false, and Visual Studio adds a <asp:BoundField> tag for each field it finds in the data source. This approach has several advantages:

- You can easily fine-tune your column order, column headings, and other details by tweaking the properties of your column object.
- You can hide columns you don't want to show by removing the column tag. (However, don't overuse this technique, because it's better to cut down on the amount of data you're retrieving if you don't intend to display it.)

■ **Tip** You can also hide columns programmatically. To hide a column, use the Columns collection for the GridView. For example, setting GridView1.Columns[2].Visible to false hides the third column. Hidden columns are left out of the rendered HTML altogether.

- Explicitly defined columns are faster than autogenerated columns. That's because auto- generated columns force the GridView to reflect on the data source at runtime.
- You can add extra columns to the mix for selecting, editing, and more.

■ **Tip** If you modify the data source so that it returns a different set of columns, you can regenerate the GridView columns. Just select the GridView, and click the Refresh Schema link in the smart tag. This step will wipe out any custom columns you've added (such as editing controls).

Here's a complete GridView declaration with explicit columns:

```
<asp:GridView ID="gridEmployees" runat="server" DataSourceID="sourceEmployees"
 AutoGenerateColumns="False">
  <Columns>
    <asp:BoundField DataField="EmployeeID" HeaderText="ID" />
    <asp:BoundField DataField="FirstName" HeaderText="First Name" />
    <asp:BoundField DataField="LastName" HeaderText="Last Name" />
    <asp:BoundField DataField="Title" HeaderText="Title" />
    <asp:BoundField DataField="City" HeaderText="City" />
  </Columns>
</asp:GridView>

<asp:SqlDataSource ID="sourceEmployees" runat="server"
  ConnectionString="<%$ ConnectionStrings:Northwind %>"
  ProviderName="System.Data.SqlClient" SelectCommand=
"SELECT EmployeeID, FirstName, LastName, BirthDate, Title, City FROM Employees">
</asp:SqlDataSource>
```

When you explicitly declare a bound field, you have the opportunity to set other properties. Table 10-2 lists these properties.

Table 10-2. *BoundField Properties*

Property	Description
DataField	This property indicates the name of the field (for a row) or property (for an object) of the data item that you want to display in this column.
DataFormatString	This property formats the field. This is useful for getting the right representation of numbers and dates. In previous versions of .NET, it was necessary to set the HtmlEncode property to false in order to use the DataFormatString property. This is no longer required.
ApplyFormatInEditMode	If true, the format string will be used to format the value even when it appears in a text box in edit mode. The default is false, which means only the underlying normal will be used (1143.02 instead of $1,143.02).
HeaderText, FooterText, and HeaderImageUrl	The first two properties set the text in the header and footer region of the grid, if this grid has a header (GridView.ShowHeader is true) and footer (GridView.ShowFooter is true). The header is most commonly used for a descriptive label such as the field name, while the footer can contain a dynamically calculated value such as a summary (a technique demonstrated in the section "Summaries in the GridView" toward the end of this chapter). To show an image in the header *instead* of text, set the HeaderImageUrl property.
ReadOnly	If true, the value for this column can't be changed in edit mode. No edit control will be provided. Primary key fields are often read-only.
InsertVisible	If false, the value for this column can't be set in insert mode. If you want a column value to be set programmatically or based on a default value defined in the database, you can use this feature.

Property	Description
Visible	If false, the column won't be visible in the page (and no HTML will be rendered for it). This property gives you a convenient way to programmatically hide or show specific columns, changing the overall view of the data.
SortExpression	This property specifies an expression that can be appended to a query to perform a sort based on this column. It's used in conjunction with sorting, as described in the "Sorting the GridView" section.
HtmlEncode	If true (the default), all text will be HTML encoded to prevent special characters from mangling the page. You could disable HTML encoding if you want to embed a working HTML tag (such as a hyperlink), but this approach isn't safe. It's always a better idea to use HTML encoding on all values and provide other functionality by reacting to GridView selection events.
NullDisplayText	This property defines the text that will be displayed for a null value. The default is an empty string, although you could change this to a hard-coded value, such as "(not specified)."
ConvertEmptyStringToNull	If this is true, before an edit is committed, all empty strings will be converted to null values.
ControlStyle, HeaderStyle, FooterStyle, and ItemStyle	These properties configure the appearance for just this column, overriding the styles for the row. You'll learn more about styles throughout this chapter.

If you don't want to configure columns by hand, select the GridView, and click the ellipsis (...) next to the Columns property in the Properties window. You'll see a Fields dialog box that lets you add, remove, and refine your columns (see Figure 10-1).

Now that you understand the underpinnings of the GridView, you've still only started to explore its higher-level features. In the following sections, you'll tackle these topics:

Formatting: How to format rows and data values

Selecting: How to let users select a row in the GridView and respond accordingly

Sorting: How to dynamically reorder the GridView in response to clicks on a column header

Paging: How to divide a large result set into multiple pages of data, using both automatic and custom paging code

Templates: How to take complete control of layout, formatting, and editing by defining templates

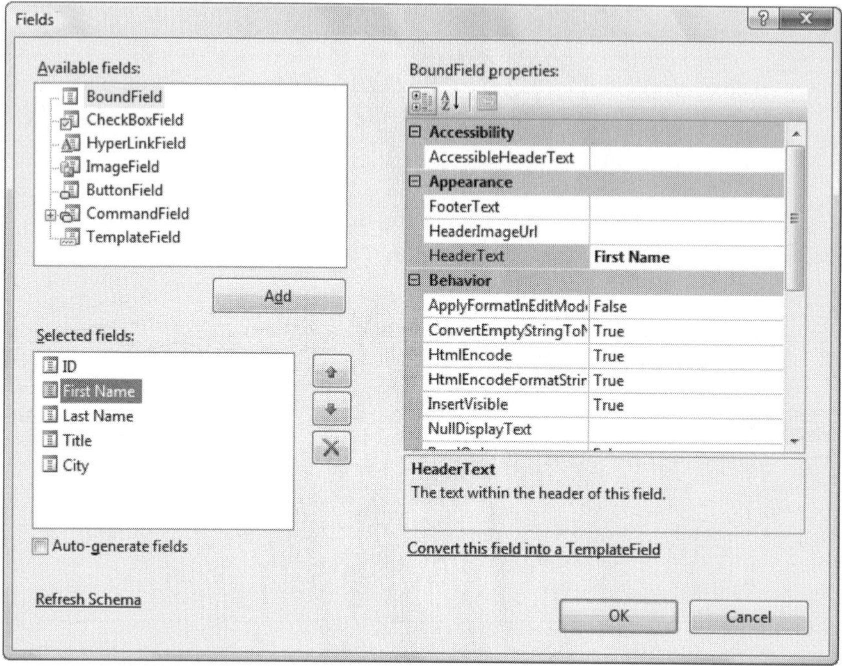

Figure 10-1. *Configuring columns in Visual Studio*

Formatting the GridView

Formatting consists of several related tasks. First, you want to ensure that dates, currencies, and other number values are presented in the appropriate way. You handle this job by setting the DataFormatString property on the column. Next, you'll want to apply the perfect mix of colors, fonts, borders, and alignment options to each aspect of the grid, from headers to data items. The GridView supports these features through styles. Finally, you can intercept events, examine row data, and apply formatting to specific data points programmatically. In the following sections, you'll consider each of these techniques.

The GridView itself also exposes several formatting properties that are self-explanatory and aren't covered here. These include GridLines (for adding or hiding table borders), CellPadding and CellSpacing (for controlling the overall spacing between cells), and Caption and CaptionAlign (for adding a title to the top of the grid).

■ **Tip** Want to create a GridView that scrolls—inside a web page? It's easy. Just place the GridView inside a Panel control, set the appropriate size for the panel, and set the Panel.Scrollbars to Auto, Vertical, or Both.

Formatting Fields

Each BoundField column provides a DataFormatString property that you can use to configure the appearance of numbers and dates using a *format string*.

Format strings are generally made up of a placeholder and format indicator, which are wrapped inside curly brackets. A typical format string looks something like this:

```
{0:C}
```

The 0 represents the value that will be formatted, and the letter indicates a predetermined format style. In this case, C means currency format, which is based on the culture settings that are applied to the current thread. By default, a computer that's configured for the English (United States) region runs with a locale of en-US and displays currencies with the dollar sign (so 3400.34 becomes $3,400.34). A computer that's configured for another locale might display a different currency symbol. Here's a column that uses this format string:

```
<asp:BoundField DataField="UnitPrice" HeaderText="Price"
  DataFormatString="{0:C}" />
```

To use a different currency format, you can change the localization settings of the web server (in the Regional and Language Options section of the Control Panel). Or, you can set a different culture for your web application using code or using the <globalization> element in the web.config file.

■ **Note** If you need to display a variety of different currency strings in your application, the built-in formatting won't work, and it's up to you to solve the problem. One typical strategy is to create a Money structure that wraps the number amount and the culture. You can then override Money.ToString() to return the right string representation.

Table 10-3 shows some of the other formatting options for numeric values.

Table 10-3. *Numeric Format Strings*

Type	Format String	Example
Currency	{0:C}	$1,234.50Brackets indicate negative values: ($1,234.50). The currency sign is locale-specific: €1,234.50.
Scientific (Exponential)	{0:E}	1.234500E+003
Percentage	{0:P}	45.6%
Fixed Decimal	{0:F?}	Depends on the number of decimal places you set. {0:F3} would be 123.400. {0:F0} would be 123.

You can find other examples in the Visual Studio Help. For date or time values, there is also an extensive list. For example, if you want to write the BirthDate value in the format month/day/year (as in 12/30/08), you use the following column:

```
<asp:BoundField DataField="BirthDate" HeaderText="Birth Date"
DataFormatString="{0:MM/dd/yy}" />
```

Table 10-4 shows some more examples.

Table 10-4. *Time and Date Format Strings*

Type	Format String	Example
Short Date	{0:d}	M/d/yyyy (for example: 10/30/2008)
Long Date and Short Time	{0:f}	dddd, MMMM dd, yyyy HH:mm aa (for example: Monday, January 30, 2008 10:00 AM)
Long Date	{0:D}	dddd, MMMM dd, yyyy (for example: Monday, January 30, 2008)
Long Date and Long Time	{0:F}	dddd, MMMM dd, yyyy HH:mm:ss aa (for example: Monday, January 30, 2008 10:00:23 AM)
ISO Sortable Standard	{0:s}	yyyy-MM-ddTHH:mm:ss (for example: 2008-01-30T10:00:23)
Month and Day	{0:M}	MMMM dd (for example: January 30)
General	{0:G}	M/d/yyyy HH:mm:ss aa (depends on locale-specific settings) (for example: 10/30/2008 10:00:23 AM)

The format characters are not specific to the GridView. You can use them with other controls, with data-bound expressions in templates (as you'll see later in this chapter), and as parameters for many methods. For example, the Decimal and DateTime types expose their own ToString() methods that accept a format string, allowing you to format values manually.

Styles

The GridView exposes a rich formatting model that's based on *styles*. Altogether, you can set eight GridView styles, as described in Table 10-5.

Table 10-5. Numeric Format Strings

Style	Description
HeaderStyle	Configures the appearance of the header row that contains column titles, if you've chosen to show it (if ShowHeader is true).
RowStyle	Configures the appearance of every data row.
AlternatingRowStyle	If set, applies additional formatting to every other row. This formatting acts in addition to the RowStyle formatting. For example, if you set a font using RowStyle, it is also applied to alternating rows, unless you explicitly set a different font through the AlternatingRowStyle.
SelectedRowStyle	Configures the appearance of the row that's currently selected. This formatting acts in addition to the RowStyle formatting.
EditRowStyle	Configures the appearance of the row that's in edit mode. This formatting acts in addition to the RowStyle formatting.
EmptyDataRowStyle	Configures the style that's used for the single empty row in the special case where the bound data object contains no rows.
FooterStyle	Configures the appearance of the footer row at the bottom of the GridView, if you've chosen to show it (if ShowFooter is true).
PagerStyle	Configures the appearance of the row with the page links, if you've enabled paging (set AllowPaging to true).

Styles are not simple single-value properties. Instead, each style exposes a Style object that includes properties for choosing colors (ForeColor and BackColor), adding borders (BorderColor, BorderStyle, and BorderWidth), sizing the row (Height and Width), aligning the row (HorizontalAlign and VerticalAlign), and configuring the appearance of text (Font and Wrap). These style properties allow you to refine almost every aspect of an item's appearance. And if you don't want to hard-code all the appearance settings in the web page, you can set the CssClass property of the style object reference to a stylesheet class that's defined in a linked stylesheet (see Chapter 16 for more about styles).

Defining Styles

When setting style properties, you can use two similar syntaxes (and you'll see both of them in this chapter). First, you can use the object-walker syntax to indicate the extended style properties as attributes in the opening tag for the GridView. Here's an example:

```
<asp:GridView runat="server" ID="grid"
  RowStyle-ForeColor="DarkBlue" ... />
  ...
</asp:GridView>
```

Alternatively, you can add nested tags, as shown here:

```
<asp:GridView runat="server" ID="grid" ...>
  <RowStyle ForeColor="DarkBlue" ... />
  ...
</asp:GridView>
```

Both of these approaches are equivalent. However, you make one other decision when setting style properties. You can specify global style properties that affect every column in the grid (as in the previous examples), or you can define column-specific styles. To create a column-specific style, you need to add style attributes or a nested tag inside the appropriate column tag, as shown here:

```
<asp:GridView runat="server" ID="grid" ...>
  <Columns>
    <asp:BoundField DataField="EmployeeID" HeaderText="ID" ItemStyle-Width="30px" />
    ...
  </Columns>
</asp:GridView>
```

Or equivalently, you can use a nested tag:

```
<asp:GridView runat="server" ID="grid" ...>
  <Columns>
    <asp:BoundField DataField="EmployeeID" HeaderText="ID">
      <ItemStyle Width="30px" />
    </asp:BoundField>
    ...
  </Columns>
</asp:GridView>
```

This technique is often used to define specific column widths. If you don't define a specific column width, ASP.NET makes each column just wide enough to fit the data it contains (or, if wrapping is enabled, to fit the text without splitting a word over a line break). If values range in size, the width is determined by the largest value or the width of the column header, whichever is larger. However, if the grid is wide enough, you might want to expand a column so it doesn't appear to be crowded against the adjacent columns. In this case, you need to explicitly define a larger width.

Here's a fully formatted GridView:

```
<asp:GridView ID="GridView1" runat="server" DataSourceID="sourceEmployees"
 Font-Names="Verdana" Font-Size="X-Small" ForeColor="#333333"
 CellPadding="4" GridLines="None" AutoGenerateColumns="False">

  <HeaderStyle BackColor="#990000" Font-Bold="True" ForeColor="White" />
  <RowStyle BackColor="#FFFBD6" ForeColor="#333333" />
  <AlternatingRowStyle BackColor="White" />

  <Columns>
    <asp:BoundField DataField="EmployeeID" HeaderText="ID">
      <ItemStyle Font-Bold="True" BorderWidth="1" />
    </asp:BoundField>
    <asp:BoundField DataField="FirstName" HeaderText="First Name" />
    <asp:BoundField DataField="LastName" HeaderText="Last Name" />
    <asp:BoundField DataField="City" HeaderText="City">
```

```
      <ItemStyle BackColor="LightSteelBlue" />
    </asp:BoundField>
    <asp:BoundField DataField="Country" HeaderText="Country">
      <ItemStyle BackColor="LightSteelBlue" />
    </asp:BoundField>
    <asp:BoundField DataField="BirthDate" HeaderText="Birth Date"
     DataFormatString="{0:MM/dd/yyyy}" />
    <asp:BoundField DataField="Notes" HeaderText="Notes">
      <ItemStyle Wrap="True" Width="400"/>
    </asp:BoundField>
  </Columns>
</asp:GridView>
```

This example uses GridView properties to set the font and adjust the cell spacing and cell gridlines. It uses styles to bold headings and configure the background of rows and alternating rows. Additionally, column-specific style settings highlight the location information with a different background, bold the ID values, and explicitly size the Notes column. A DataFormatString is used to format all date values in the BirthDate field. Figure 10-2 shows the final result.

ID	First Name	Last Name	City	Country	Bith Date	Notes
1	Nancy	Davolio	Seattle	USA	12/08/1948	Education includes a BA in psychology from Colorado State University in 1970. She also completed "The Art of the Cold Call." Nancy is a member of Toastmasters International.
2	Andrew	Fuller	Tacoma	USA	02/19/1952	Andrew received his BTS commercial in 1974 and a Ph.D. in international marketing from the University of Dallas in 1981. He is fluent in French and Italian and reads German. He joined the company as a sales representative, was promoted to sales manager in January 1992 and to vice president of sales in March 1993. Andrew is a member of the Sales Management Roundtable, the Seattle Chamber of Commerce, and the Pacific Rim Importers Association.
3	Janets	Leverling	Kirkland	USA	08/30/1963	Janet has a BS degree in chemistry from Boston College (1984). She has also completed a certificate program in food retailing management. Janet was hired as a sales associate in 1991 and promoted to sales representative in February 1992.
4	Margaret	Peacock	Redmond	USA	09/19/1937	Margaret holds a BA in English literature from Concordia College (1958) and an MA from the American Institute of Culinary Arts (1966). She was assigned to the London office temporarily from July through November 1992.
5	Steven	Buchanan	London	UK	03/04/1955	Steven Buchanan graduated from St. Andrews University, Scotland, with a BSC degree in 1976. Upon joining the company as a sales representative in 1992, he spent 6 months in an orientation program at the Seattle office and then returned to his permanent post in London. He was promoted to sales manager in March 1993. Mr. Buchanan has completed the courses "Successful Telemarketing" and "International Sales Management." He is fluent in French.

Figure 10-2. *A formatted GridView*

Configuring Styles with Visual Studio

There's no reason to code style properties by hand in the GridView control tag, because the GridView provides rich design-time support. To set style properties, you can use the Properties window to modify the style properties. For example, to configure the font of the header, expand the HeaderStyle property to show the nested Font property, and set that. The only limitation of this approach is that it doesn't allow you to set a style for individual columns—if you need that trick, you must first call up the Fields dialog box (shown previously in Figure 10-1) by editing the Columns property. Then, select the appropriate column, and set the style properties accordingly.

You can even set a combination of styles using a preset theme by clicking the Auto Format link in the GridView smart tag. Figure 10-3 shows the Auto Format dialog box with some of the preset styles you can choose. Select Remove Formatting to clear all the style settings.

Once you've chosen a theme, the style settings are inserted into your GridView tag, and you can tweak them by hand or by using the Properties window.

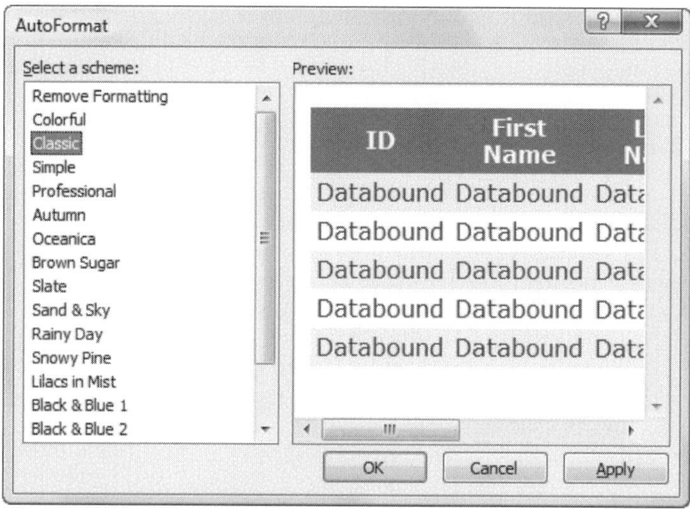

Figure 10-3. *Automatically formatting a GridView*

Formatting-Specific Values

The formatting you've learned so far isn't that fine-grained. At its most specific, this formatting applies to a single column of values. But what if you want to change the formatting for a specific row, or even just a single cell?

The solution is to react to the GridView.RowDataBound event. This event is raised when a part of the grid (the header, footer, or pager or a normal, alternate, or selected item) is being created and bound to the data object. You can access the current row as a GridViewRow control. The GridViewRow.DataItem property provides the data object for the given row, and the GridViewRow.Cells collection allows you to retrieve the row content. You can use the GridViewRow to change colors and alignment, add or remove child controls, and so on.

The following example handles the RowDataBound event and sets the colors according to the following rules:

- The item's background color is set to pink and the foreground color is set to maroon if the title of courtesy is a title for a female—in this case Ms. or Mrs.

- The item's background color is set to dark blue and the foreground color is set to light cyan if the title of courtesy is Mr.
- For other generic titles such as Dr., the item is rendered with the background color specified by the GridView.BackColor property.

Here is the complete code for the RowDataBound event handler that implements these rules:

```
protected void gridEmployees_RowDataBound(object sender, GridViewRowEventArgs e)
{
    if (e.Row.RowType == DataControlRowType.DataRow)
    {
        // Get the title of courtesy for the item that's being created.
        string title = (string)
          DataBinder.Eval(e.Row.DataItem, "TitleOfCourtesy");

        // If the title of courtesy is "Ms.", "Mrs.", or "Mr.",
        // change the item's colors.
        if (title == "Ms." || title == "Mrs.")
        {
            e.Row.BackColor = System.Drawing.Color.LightPink;
            e.Row.ForeColor = System.Drawing.Color.Maroon;
        }
        else if (title == "Mr.")
        {
            e.Row.BackColor = System.Drawing.Color.LightCyan;
            e.Row.ForeColor = System.Drawing.Color.DarkBlue;
        }
    }
}
```

First, the code checks if the item being created is a data row (rather than another part of the grid, such as the pager, footer, or header). If the item is of the right type, the code extracts the TitleOfCourtesy field from the data-bound item and compares it to some hard-coded string values.

Figure 10-4 shows the resulting page.

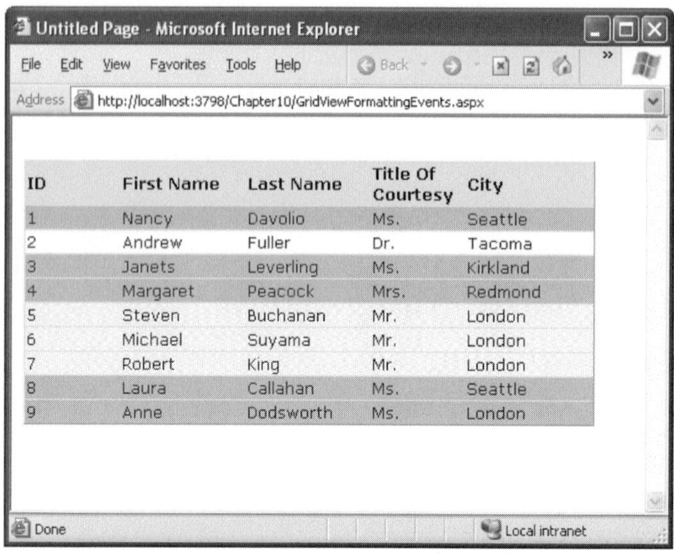

Figure 10-4. *Formatting individual rows based on values*

■ **Tip** This example uses the DataBinder.Eval() method to retrieve a piece of information from the data item using reflection. Alternatively, you could cast the e.Row.DataItem to the correct type (such as EmployeeDetails for the ObjectDataSource), DataRowView (for the SqlDataSource in DataSet mode), or DbDataRecord (for the SqlDataSource in DataReader mode). However, the DataBinder.Eval() approach works in all these scenarios (at the cost of being slightly slower).

This isn't the most useful example of using the RowDataBound event, but it demonstrates how you can handle the event and read all the important information for the item. You could use much more imaginative formatting to change the way the pager's links are represented, add new buttons to the pager or header, render values that you want to highlight with special fonts and colors, create total and subtotal rows, and more.

GridView Row Selection

Selecting a row means that the user can highlight or change the appearance of a row by clicking some sort of button or link. When the user clicks the button, not only will the row change its appearance, but also your code will have the opportunity to handle the event.

The GridView provides built-in support for selection. You simply need to add a CommandField column with the ShowSelectButton property set to true. The CommandField can be rendered as a hyperlink, a button, or a fixed image. You choose the type using the ButtonType property. You can then specify the text through the SelectText property (which defaults to the word Select) or specify the link to the image through the SelectImageUrl property.

Here's an example that displays a select button:

```
<asp:CommandField ShowSelectButton="True" ButtonType="Button"
 SelectText="Select" />
```

And here's an example that shows a small clickable icon:

```
<asp:CommandField ShowSelectButton="True" ButtonType="Image"
 SelectImageUrl="select.gif" />
```

Figure 10-5 shows both types of select buttons. Clicking either one selects the row.

■ **Note** Using a CommandField gives you the most control over where your select column is placed. It also allows you to set the text or image that's used for the select button. However, as you learned in Chapter 9, there's a shortcut that doesn't involve creating a CommandField at all. If you set the GridView.AutoGenerateSelectButton property to true, the GridView will add a select button column automatically. This select column will be placed at the left side of the grid, and it will show a text link with the word *Select*.

When you click a select button, the page is posted back, and a series of steps unfolds. First, the GridView.SelectedIndexChanging event fires, which you can intercept to cancel the operation. Next, the GridView.SelectedIndex property is adjusted to point to the selected row. Finally, the GridView.SelectedIndexChanged event fires, which you can handle if you want to manually update other controls to reflect the new selection. When the page is rendered, the selected row is given the SelectedRowStyle.

■ **Note** For selection to work, you must configure the SelectedRowStyle so that selected rows look different from normal rows. Usually, selected rows will have a different BackColor property.

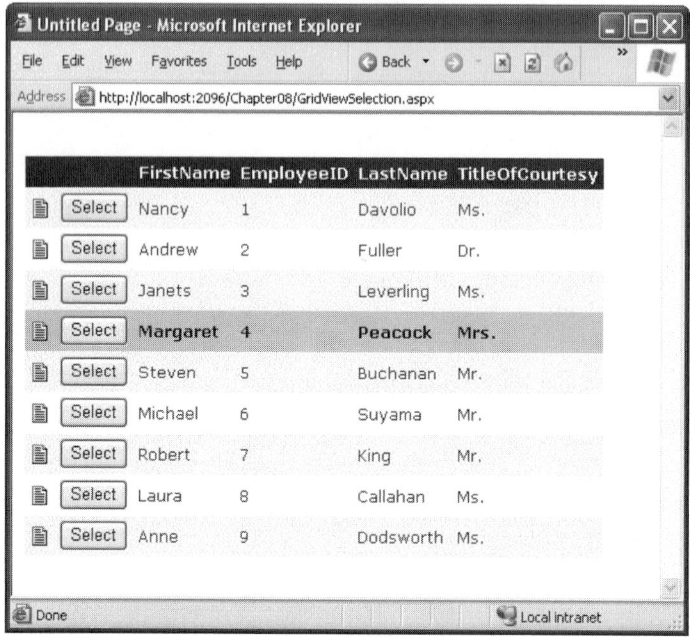

Figure 10-5. *GridView selection*

Using Selection to Create a Master-Details Form

As demonstrated in the previous chapter, you can bind other data sources to a property in a control using parameters. For example, you could add two GridView controls and use information from the first GridView to perform a query in the second.

In the case of the GridView, the property you need to bind is SelectedIndex. However, this has one problem. SelectedIndex returns a zero-based index number representing where the row occurs in the grid. This isn't the information you need to insert into the query that gets the related records. Instead, you need a key field from the corresponding row.

Fortunately, the GridView makes it easy to retrieve this information using the SelectedDataKey property. To use this feature, you must set the GridView.DataKeyNames property, with a comma-separated list of one or more key fields. Each name you supply must match one of the properties of the bound object or one of the fields of the bound record.

Usually, you'll have only one key field, as shown here:

```
<asp:GridView ID="gridEmployees" runat="server" DataSourceID="sourceEmployees"
 DataKeyNames="EmployeeID" ... >
```

Now you can bind the second data source to this field. Here's an example that uses the EmployeeID in a join query to find all the matching records from the Territories table. In other words, this data source retrieves all the regions that the selected employee manages:

```
<asp:SqlDataSource ID="sourceRegions" runat="server"
 ConnectionString="<%$ ConnectionStrings:Northwind %>"
 ProviderName="System.Data.SqlClient" SelectCommand="SELECT Employees.EmployeeID,
```

```
Territories.TerritoryID, Territories.TerritoryDescription FROM Employees INNER JOIN
EmployeeTerritories ON Employees.EmployeeID = EmployeeTerritories.EmployeeID
INNER JOIN Territories ON EmployeeTerritories.TerritoryID = Territories.TerritoryID
WHERE (Employees.EmployeeID = @EmployeeID)" >
  <SelectParameters>
    <asp:ControlParameter ControlID="gridEmployees" Name="EmployeeID"
     PropertyName="SelectedDataKey.Values[&quot;EmployeeID&quot;]" />
    </SelectParameters>
</asp:SqlDataSource>
```

In this example, the SqlDataSource uses a single parameter—the EmployeeID of the selected employee record. The EmployeeID value is retrieved from the SelectedDataKey.Values collection of the first grid. You can look up the EmployeeID field by its index position (which is 0 in this example, because there's only one field in the DataKeyNames list) or by name. The only trick when performing a name lookup is that you need to replace the quotation marks with the corresponding HTML character entity (").

Finally, the second GridView binds to this data source to show the territory records:

```
<asp:GridView ID="gridRegions" runat="server" DataSourceID="sourceRegions" ...>
    ...
    <Columns>
      <asp:BoundField DataField="TerritoryID" HeaderText="ID" />
      <asp:BoundField DataField="TerritoryDescription"
       HeaderText="Description"/>
    </Columns>
</asp:GridView>
```

Figure 10-6 shows this master-details form, which contains the regions assigned to an employee whenever an employee record is selected.

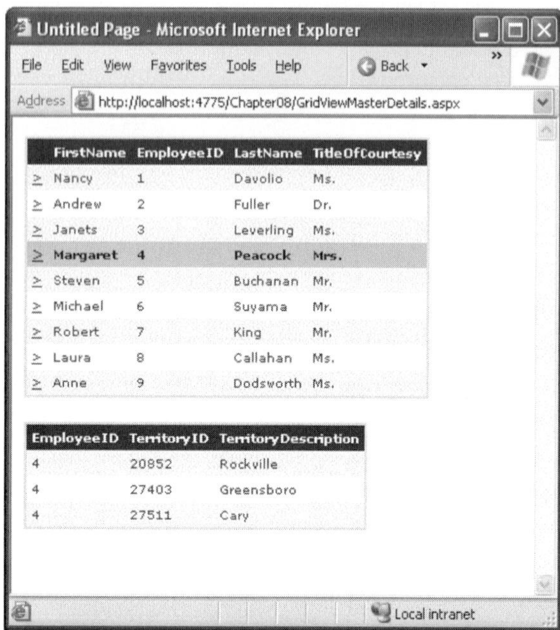

Figure 10-6. *A master-details page*

The SelectedIndexChanged Event

As the previous example demonstrates, you can set up master-details forms declaratively, without needing to write any code. However, there are many cases when you'll need to react to the SelectedIndexChanged event. For example, you might want to redirect the user to a new page (possibly with the selected value in the query string). Or, you might want to adjust other controls on the page.

For example, here's the code you need to add a label describing the child table shown in the previous example:

```
protected void gridEmployees_SelectedIndexChanged(object sender, EventArgs e)
{
    int index = gridEmployees.SelectedIndex;

    // You can retrieve the key field from the SelectedDataKey property.
    int ID = (int)gridEmployees.SelectedDataKey.Values["EmployeeID"];

    // You can retrieve other data directly from the Cells collection,
    // as long as you know the column offset.
    string firstName = gridEmployees.SelectedRow.Cells[2].Text;
    string lastName = gridEmployees.SelectedRow.Cells[3].Text;

    lblRegionCaption.Text = "Regions that " + firstName + " " + lastName +
      " (employee " + ID.ToString() + ") is responsible for:";
}
```

Figure 10-7 shows the result.

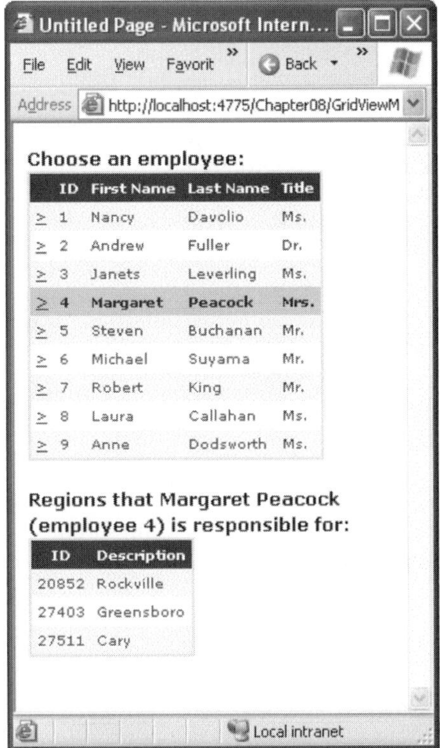

Figure 10-7. Handling the SelectedIndexChanged event

Using a Data Field As a Select Button

You don't need to create a new column to support row selection. Instead, you can turn an existing column into a link. This technique is commonly used to allow users to select rows in a table by the unique ID value.

To use this technique, add a ButtonField column. Set the DataTextField to the name of the field you want to use, as shown here:

```
<asp:ButtonField ButtonType="Button" DataTextField="EmployeeID" />
```

This field will be underlined and turned into a link that, when clicked, will post back the page and trigger the GridView.RowCommand event. You could handle this event, determine which row has been clicked, and programmatically set the SelectedIndex property. However, you can use an easier method. Instead, just configure the link to raise the SelectedIndexChanged event by specifying a CommandName with the text *Select*, as shown here:

```
<asp:ButtonField CommandName="Select" ButtonType="Button"
 DataTextField="EmployeeID" />
```

Now clicking the data field automatically selects the record. You can now remove the CommandField column that was previously used to show the Select link, and you can remove the BoundField column that was previously used to show the EmployeeID, because the ButtonField column effectively fuses these two details in one place.

Sorting the GridView

The GridView sorting features allow the user to reorder the results in the GridView by clicking a column header. It's convenient—and easy to implement.

To enable sorting, you must set the GridView.AllowSorting property to true. Next, you need to define a SortExpression for each column that can be sorted. In theory, a sort expression can use any syntax that's understood by the data source control. In practice, a sort expression almost always takes the form used in the ORDER BY clause of a SQL query. That means the sort expression can include a single field or a list of comma-separated fields, optionally with the word *ASC* or *DESC* added after the column name to sort in ascending or descending order.

Here's how you could define the FirstName column so it sorts by alphabetically ordering rows by first name:

```
<asp:BoundField DataField="FirstName" HeaderText="First Name"
 SortExpression="FirstName"/>
```

If you click the column header for the FirstName column twice in a row, the first click will sort it alphabetically, and the second click will sort it in reverse alphabetical order.

■ **Tip** If you use autogenerated columns, each bound column has its SortExpression property set to match the DataField property. If you don't want a column to be sort-enabled, just don't set its SortExpression property.

Once you've associated a sort expression with the column and set the AllowSorting property to true, the GridView will render the headers with clickable links. However, it's up to the data source control to implement the actual sorting logic. How the sorting is implemented depends on the data source you're using. Not all data sources support sorting, but both the SqlDataSource and the ObjectDataSource do.

Sorting with the SqlDataSource

In the case of the SqlDataSource, sorting is performed using the built-in sorting capabilities of the DataView class. Essentially, when the user clicks a column link, the DataView.Sort property is set to the sorting expression for that column.

■ **Note** As explained in Chapter 8, every DataTable is linked to a default DataView. The DataView is a window onto the DataTable, and it allows you to apply sorting and filtering without altering the structure of the underlying table. You can use a DataView programmatically, but when you use the SqlDataSource it's used implicitly, behind the scenes. However, it's available only when the DataSourceMode property is set to SqlDataSourceMode.DataSet.

With DataView sorting, the data is retrieved unordered from the database, and the results are sorted in memory. This is not the speediest approach (sorting in memory requires more overhead and is slower than having SQL Server do the same work), but it is more scalable when you add caching to the mix. That's because you can cache a single copy of the data and sort it dynamically in several different ways. (Chapter 11 has much more about this essential technique.) Without DataView sorting, a separate query is needed to retrieve the newly sorted data.

Figure 10-8 shows a sortable GridView with column links. Note that no custom code is required for this scenario.

The sort is according to the data type of the column. Numeric and date columns are ordered from smallest to largest. String columns are sorted alphanumerically without regard to case, assuming the underlying DataTable.CaseSensitive property is false (the default setting). Columns that contain binary data (such as images) cannot be sorted.

Sorting with the ObjectDataSource

The ObjectDataSource provides two options:

- If your select method returns a DataSet or DataTable, the ObjectDataSource can use the same automatic sorting used with the SqlDataSource.
- If your select method returns a custom collection, you need to provide a selection method that accepts a sort expression and performs the sorting. Once again, this behavior gives you enough flexibility to build a solution, but it's not necessarily the ideal arrangement. For example, instead of building a GetEmployees() method that can perform sorting, it might make more sense to create a custom EmployeeDetails collection class with a Sort() method. Unfortunately, the ObjectDataSource doesn't support this pattern.

To use the sort parameter, you need to create a select method that accepts a single string parameter. You must then set the ObjectDataSource.SortParameterName property to identify the name of that parameter, as shown here:

```
<asp:ObjectDataSource ID="sourceEmployees" runat="server"
 TypeName="DatabaseComponent.EmployeeDB"
 SelectMethod="GetEmployees" SortParameterName="sortExpression" />
```

■ **Note** When you set SortParameterName, the ObjectDataSource will always call the version of your method that accepts a sort expression. If the data doesn't need to be sorted (for example, the first time the grid is filled), the ObjectDataSource will simply pass an empty string as the sort expression.

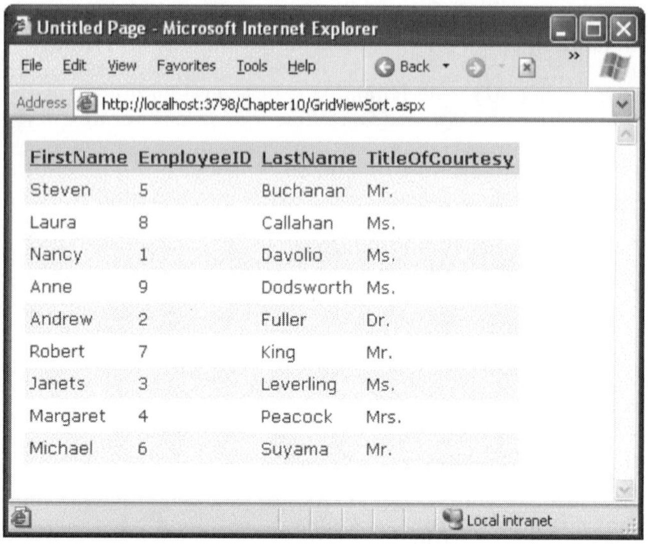
Untitled Page - Microsoft Internet Explorer
File Edit View Favorites Tools Help
Back
Address http://localhost:3798/Chapter10/GridViewSort.aspx
FirstName EmployeeID LastName TitleOfCourtesy
Steven 5 Buchanan Mr.
Laura 8 Callahan Ms.
Nancy 1 Davolio Ms.
Anne 9 Dodsworth Ms.
Andrew 2 Fuller Dr.
Robert 7 King Mr.
Janets 3 Leverling Ms.
Margaret 4 Peacock Mrs.
Michael 6 Suyama Mr.
Local intranet

Figure 10-8. *Automatic sorting by LastName*

Now you have to implement the GetEmployees() method and decide how you want to perform the sorting. The easiest approach is to fill a disconnected DataSet so you can rely on the sorting functionality of the DataView. Here's an example of a GetEmployees() method in a database component that performs the sorting in this way:

```
public EmployeeDetails[] GetEmployees(string sortExpression)
{
    SqlConnection con = new SqlConnection(connectionString);
    SqlCommand cmd = new SqlCommand("GetAllEmployees", con);
    cmd.CommandType = CommandType.StoredProcedure;
    SqlDataAdapter adapter = new SqlDataAdapter(cmd);

    DataSet ds = new DataSet();
    try
    {
        con.Open();
        adapter.Fill(ds, "Employees");
    }
    catch (SqlException err)
    {
        // Replace the error with something less specific.
        // You could also log the error now.
        throw new ApplicationException("Data error.");
    }
    finally
    {
        con.Close();
    }

    // Apply sort.
```

```
    DataView view = ds.Tables[0].DefaultView;
    view.Sort = sortExpression;

    // Create a collection for all the employee records.
    ArrayList employees = new ArrayList();
    foreach (DataRowView row in view)
    {
        EmployeeDetails emp = new EmployeeDetails(
         (int)row["EmployeeID"], (string)row["FirstName"],
         (string)row["LastName"], (string)row["TitleOfCourtesy"]);
        employees.Add(emp);
    }
    return (EmployeeDetails[])employees.ToArray(typeof(EmployeeDetails));
}
```

Another approach is to change the actual query you're executing in response to the sort expression. This way, your database can perform the sorting. This approach is a little more complicated, and no perfect option exists. Here are the two most common possibilities:

- You could dynamically construct a SQL statement with an ORDER BY clause. However, this risks SQL injection attacks, unless you validate your input carefully.
- You could write conditional logic to examine the sort expression and execute different queries accordingly (either in your select method or in the stored procedure). This code is likely to be fragile and involves a fair bit of string parsing.

Sorting and Selection

If you use sorting and selection at the same time, you'll discover another issue. To see this problem in action, select a row, and then sort the data by any column. You'll see that the selection will remain, but it will shift to a new item that has the same index as the previous item. In other words, if you select the second row and perform a sort, the second row will still be selected in the new page, even though this isn't the record you selected.

In the past, the only way to solve this problem was to programmatically change the selection every time the user clicks a header link. But ASP.NET adds a GridView.EnablePersistedSelection property that provides a quick fix. Simply set this property to true, and ASP.NET will ensure that the selected item is identified by its data key. As a result, the selected item will remain selected, even if it moves to a new position in the GridView after a sort.

Advanced Sorting

The GridView's sorting is straightforward—it supports sorting by any sortable column in ascending and descending order. In some applications, the user has more sorting options or can order lengthy result sets with more complex sorting expressions.

Your first avenue for improving sorting with the GridView is to handle the GridView.Sorting event, which occurs just before the sort is applied. At this point, you can change the sorting expression. For example, you could use this approach to turn clicks on different columns into a compound sort. For example, you might want to check if the user clicks LastName and then FirstName. In this case, you could apply a LastName+FirstName sort.

```
protected void gridEmployees_Sorting(object sender, GridViewSortEventArgs e)
{
    if (e.SortExpression == "FirstName" && gridEmployees.SortExpression ==
```

```
"LastName")
    {
        // Based on the current sort and the requested sort, a compound
        // sort makes sense.
        e.SortExpression = "LastName, FirstName";
    }
}
```

You could take this sorting approach one step further and cascade searches over any arbitrary collection of columns by storing the user's past sort selections in view state and using them to build a larger sort expression. Of course, it's important not to go too overboard and create a custom sorting mechanism that's completely unintuitive to your users, which will cause more problems than it solves.

One more technique is available to you. You can sort the GridView programmatically by calling the GridView.Sort() method and supplying a sort expression. This could come in handy if you want to presort a lengthy data report before presenting it to the user. It also makes sense if you want to allow the user to choose from a list of predefined sorting options (listed in another control) rather than use column-header clicks.

Figure 10-9 shows an example. When an item is selected from the list, the sort is applied with this code:

```
protected void lstSorts_SelectedIndexChanged(object sender, EventArgs e)
{
    gridEmployees.Sort(lstSorts.SelectedValue, SortDirection.Ascending);
}
```

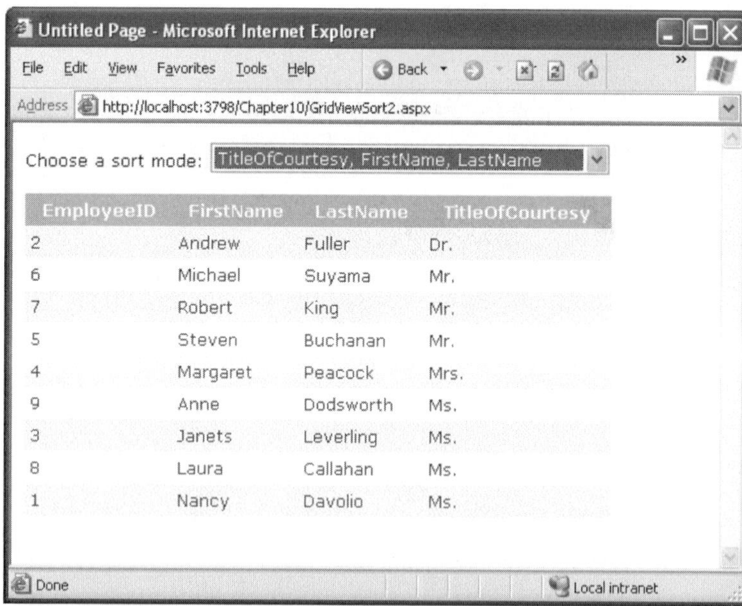

Figure 10-9. Giving sorting options through another control

Paging the GridView

All the examples of repeated-value binding that you've seen so far show all the records of the data source on a single web page. However, this isn't always ideal in real-world situations. Connecting to a data source that contains hundreds or even thousands of records would produce an extremely large page that would take a prohibitively long amount of time to render and transmit to the client browser.

Most websites that display data in tables or lists support record *pagination*, which means showing a fixed number of records per page and providing links to navigate to the previous or next pages to display other records. For example, you have no doubt seen this functionality in search engines that can return thousands of matches.

The GridView control has built-in support for pagination. You can use simple pagination with both the SqlDataSource and ObjectDataSource. If you're using the ObjectDataSource, you also have the ability to customize the way the paging works for a more efficient and scalable solution.

Automatic Paging

By setting a few properties and handling an event, you can make the GridView control manage the paging for you. The GridView will create the links to jump to the previous or next pages and will display the records for the current page without requiring you to manually extract the records by yourself. Before discussing the advantages and disadvantages of this approach, let's see what you need to get this working.

The GridView provides several properties designed specifically to support paging, as shown in Table 10-6.

Table 10-6. *Paging Members of the GridView*

Property	Description
AllowPaging	Enables or disables the paging of the bound records. It is false by default.
PageSize	Gets or sets the number of items to display on a single page of the grid. The default value is 10.
PageIndex	Gets or sets the zero-based index of the currently displayed page, if paging is enabled.
PagerSettings	Provides a PagerSettings object that wraps a variety of formatting options for the pager controls. These options determine where the paging controls are shown and what text or images they contain. You can set these properties to fine-tune the appearance of the pager controls, or you can use the defaults.
PagerStyle	Provides a style object you can use to configure fonts, colors, and text alignment for the paging controls.
PageIndexChanging and PageIndexChanged event	Occurs when one of the page selection elements is clicked, before the navigation (PageIndexChanging) and after (PageIndexChanged).

To use automatic paging, you need to set AllowPaging to true (which shows the page controls), and you need to set PageSize to determine how many rows are allowed on each page. If you don't set the PageSize property, the default value of 10 is used.

Here's an example of a GridView control that sets these properties:

```
<asp:GridView ID="GridView1" runat="server" DataSourceID="sourceEmployees"
 PageSize="5" AllowPaging="True" ...>
  ...
</asp:GridView>
```

This is enough to start using paging. Figure 10-10 shows an example with five records per page (for a total of 16 pages).

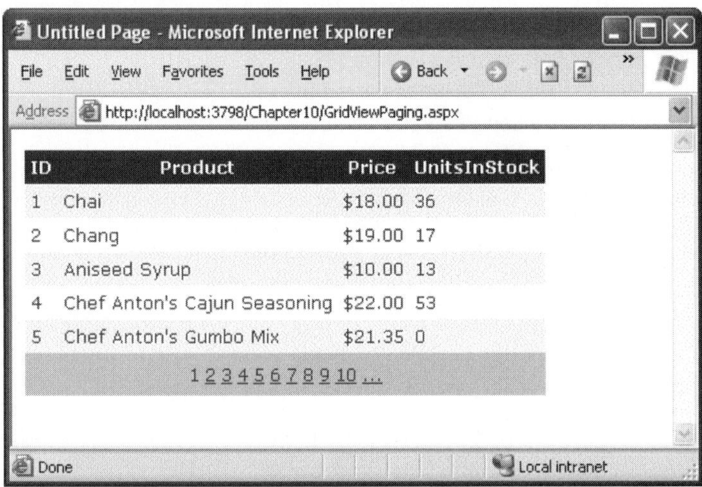

Figure 10-10. *Paging five records at a time*

Automatic paging works with any data source that implements ICollection. This means that the SqlDataSource supports automatic paging, as long as you use DataSet mode. (The DataReader mode won't work and causes an exception.) Additionally, the ObjectDataSource also supports paging, assuming your custom data access class returns an object that implements ICollection—arrays, strongly typed collections, and the disconnected DataSet are all valid options.

Automatic paging doesn't reduce the amount of data you need to query from the database. Instead, all the data is retrieved and bound every time the user navigates to another page. In other words, if you split a table into ten pages and the user steps through each one, you will end up performing the same work ten times (and multiplying the overall database workload for the page by a factor of ten).

Fortunately, you can make automatic paging much more efficient just by switching on automatic caching for the data source control (see Chapter 11). This allows you to reuse the same data object for multiple requests. Of course, storing the data in the cache may not be the ideal solution if you're using paging to deal with an extremely large query. In this case, a prohibitively large amount of server memory is required to keep your data in the cache. That's when custom pagination makes sense.

Paging and Selection

By default, paging and selection don't play nicely together. If you enable both for the GridView, you'll notice that the same row position remains selected as you move from one page to another. For example, if you select the first row on the first page and then move to the second page, the first row on the second page will become selected. To fix this quirk, you can use the GridView's new EnablePersistedSelection property. Set this to true and you'll get very different results. As you move from one page to another, the selection will automatically be removed from the GridView (and the SelectedIndex property will be set to –1). But if you move back to the page that held the originally selected row, that row will be re-selected. This behavior is intuitive, and it neatly ensures that your code won't be confused by a selected row that isn't currently visible.

Custom Pagination with the ObjectDataSource

Custom pagination requires you to take care of extracting and binding only the current page of records for the GridView. The GridView no longer selects the rows that should be displayed automatically. However, the GridView still provides the pager bar with the autogenerated links that allow the user to navigate through the pages.

Although custom pagination is more complex than automatic pagination, it also allows you to minimize the bandwidth usage and avoid storing a large data object in server-side memory. On the other hand, almost all custom pagination strategies requery the database with each postback, which means you may be creating more work for the database.

The ObjectDataSource is the only data source to support custom pagination. The first step to take control of custom paging is to set ObjectDataSource.EnablePaging to true. You can then implement paging through three more properties: StartRowIndexParameterName, MaximumRowsParameterName, and SelectCountMethod.

■ **Tip** To determine whether custom pagination is better than automatic paging with caching, you need to evaluate the way you use data. The larger the amount of data the GridView is using, the more likely you'll need to use custom pagination. On the other hand, the slower the database server and the heavier its load, the more likely you'll want to reduce repeated calls by caching the full data object. Ultimately, you may need to profile your application to determine the optimum paging strategy.

Counting the Records

To have the GridView create the correct number of page links for you, it must know the total number of records and the number of records per page. The records-per-page value is set with the PageSize property, as in the previous example. The total number of pages is a little trickier.

When using automatic pagination, the total number of records is automatically determined by the GridView based on the number of records in the data source. In custom paging, you must explicitly calculate the total number using a dedicated method. The EmployeeDB class already includes a CountEmployees() method that returns this information, which you saw first in Chapter 8. You simply need to bind this method to the ObjectDataSource using the SelectCountMethod property:

```
<asp:ObjectDataSource ID="sourceEmployees" runat="server" EnablePaging="True"
 SelectCountMethod="CountEmployees" ... />
```

When you use custom paging, the SelectCountMethod is executed for every postback. If you want to reduce database work at the risk of providing an incorrect count, you could cache this information and reuse it.

A Stored Procedure to Get Paged Records

The next part of the solution is a little trickier. Instead of retrieving a collection with all the employee records, the GetEmployees() method must retrieve records for the current page only. To accomplish this feat, this example uses a stored procedure named GetEmployeePage. This stored procedure copies all the employee records into a temporary table that has one additional column—a unique autoincrementing ID that will number each row. Next, the stored procedure retrieves a selection from that table that corresponds to the requested page of data, using the supplied @Start and @Count parameters.

Here's the complete stored procedure code:

```
CREATE PROCEDURE GetEmployeePage
@Start int, @Count int
AS
– create a temporary table with the columns we are interested in
CREATE TABLE #TempEmployees
(
  ID                int IDENTITY PRIMARY KEY,
  EmployeeID        int,
  LastName          nvarchar(20),
  FirstName         nvarchar(10),
  TitleOfCourtesy  nvarchar(25),
)

– fill the temp table with all the employees
INSERT INTO #TempEmployees
(
  EmployeeID, LastName, FirstName, TitleOfCourtesy
)
SELECT
  EmployeeID, LastName, FirstName, TitleOfCourtesy
FROM
  Employees ORDER BY EmployeeID ASC

– declare two variables to calculate the range of records
– to extract for the specified page
DECLARE @FromID int
DECLARE @ToID int
– calculate the first and last ID of the range of records we need
SET @FromID = @Start
SET @ToID =  @Start + @Count - 1

– select the page of records
SELECT * FROM #TempEmployees WHERE ID >= @FromID AND ID <= @ToID
```

This stored procedure uses a SQL Server-specific approach. Other databases might have other possible optimizations. For example, Oracle databases allow you to use the ROWNUM operator in the WHERE clause of a query to return a range of rows. For example, the Oracle query SELECT * FROM Employees WHERE ROWNUM > 100 AND ROWNUM < 200 retrieves the page of rows from 101 to 199.

■ **Tip** SQL Server 2005 and later includes a ROWNUMBER() function that lets you return a subset of rows from a large query. For an example that shows how to implement efficient paging using the ROWNUMBER() function, refer to `http://aspnet.4guysfromrolla.com/articles/031506-1.aspx`.

The Paged Selection Method

The final step is to create an overload of the GetEmployees() method that performs paging. This method receives two arguments—the index of the row that starts the page (starting at 0) and the page size (maximum number of rows). You specify the parameter names you want to use for these two details through the StartRowIndexParameterName and MaximumRowsParameterName properties on the ObjectDataSource control. If not set, the default parameter names are startRowIndex and maximumRows.

Here's the GetEmployees() method you need to use the stored procedure shown in the previous example:

```
public EmployeeDetails[] GetEmployees(int startRowIndex, int maximumRows)
{
    SqlConnection con = new SqlConnection(connectionString);
    SqlCommand cmd = new SqlCommand("GetEmployeePage", con);
    cmd.CommandType = CommandType.StoredProcedure;
    cmd.Parameters.Add(new SqlParameter("@Start", SqlDbType.Int, 4));
    cmd.Parameters["@Start"].Value = startRowIndex + 1;
    cmd.Parameters.Add(new SqlParameter("@Count", SqlDbType.Int, 4));
    cmd.Parameters["@Count"].Value = maximumRows;

    // Create a collection for all the employee records.
    ArrayList employees = new ArrayList();

    try
    {
        con.Open();
        SqlDataReader reader = cmd.ExecuteReader();

        while (reader.Read())
        {
            EmployeeDetails emp = new EmployeeDetails(
             (int)reader["EmployeeID"], (string)reader["FirstName"],
             (string)reader["LastName"], (string)reader["TitleOfCourtesy"]);
            employees.Add(emp);
        }
        reader.Close();

        return (EmployeeDetails[])employees.ToArray(typeof(EmployeeDetails));
    }
    catch (SqlException err)
    {
        throw new ApplicationException("Data error.");
    }
    finally
```

```
    {
        con.Close();
    }
}
```

When you run this page, you'll see that the output is the same as the output generated by the previous page using automatic pagination, and the pager controls work the same way.

Customizing the Pager Bar

The GridView paging controls are remarkably flexible. In their default representation, you'll see a series of numbered links (see Figure 10-10). However, you customize them thoroughly using the PagerStyle property (for foreground and background colors, the font, color, size, and so on) and the PagerSettings property.

```
<asp:GridView ID="GridView1" runat="server" DataSourceID="sourceProducts"
 AllowPaging="True" ...>
  <PagerSettings Mode="NextPrevious" PreviousPageText="< Back"
   NextPageText="Forward >" />
  <PagerStyle BackColor="#FFCC66" ForeColor="#333333"
   HorizontalAlign="Center" />
  ...
</asp:GridView>
```

The most important detail is the PagerSettings.Mode property, which specifies how to render the paging links according to one of several styles, as described in Table 10-7.

Table 10-7. *Pager Modes*

Mode	Description
Numeric	The grid will render as many links to other pages as specified by the PagerSettings.PageButtonCount property. If that number of links is not enough to link to every page of the grid, the pager will display ellipsis links (...) that, when clicked, display the previous or next set of page links.
NextPrevious	The grid will render only two links for jumping to the previous and next pages. If you choose this option, you can also define the text for the two links through the NextPageText and PreviousPageText properties on the PagerSettings object (or use image links through NextPageImageUrl and PreviousPageImageUrl).
NumericFirstLast	The same as Numeric, except there are additional links for the first page and the last page.
NextPreviousFirstLast	The same as NextPrevious, except there are additional links for the first page and the last page. You can set the text for these links through FirstPageText and LastPageText properties on the PagerSettings object (or images through FirstPageImageUrl and LastPageImageUrl).

Sorting and Paging Callbacks

One disadvantage with a grid you can sort or page through is that each time you re-sort the grid or move to another page, the browser needs to trigger a postback and render a completely new page of HTML. This means the page flickers and scrolls back to the beginning, which makes the overall user experience a bit jarring.

The GridView has a feature that improves on this situation: the EnableSortingAndPagingCallbacks property. If you set this property to true, the GridView uses a different technique to refresh the page. Rather than forcing a postback when you click a column header or a page link, the browser sends an asynchronous request to the server to get new information. When the browser receives this information, it modifies the current page using the HTML DOM. This technique creates a more seamless, flicker-free browsing experience. Best of all, if a browser doesn't support this feature, the GridView gracefully degrades to the standard postback model. The only limitation is that you can't use sorting and paging callbacks on a grid that uses templates.

The EnableSortingAndPagingCallbacks property uses ASP.NET's callback infrastructure. Under the hood, callbacks are performed using JavaScript and the XMLHttpRequest object. You'll learn more about callbacks and how they work in Chapter 29.

If you don't like the default pager bar, you can implement your own using the template feature described in the next section by creating a PagerTemplate. You can then use any control you want, such as a text box where the user can type the index of the page and a button to submit the request and load the new page. The code for extracting and binding the records for the current page would remain the same.

GridView Templates

So far, the examples have used the GridView control to show data in using separate bound columns for each field. If you want to place multiple values in the same cell, or have the unlimited ability to customize the content in a cell by adding HTML tags and server controls, you need to use a TemplateField.

The TemplateField allows you to define a completely customized *template* for a column. Inside the template you can add control tags, arbitrary HTML elements, and data binding expressions. You have complete freedom to arrange everything the way you want.

For example, imagine you want to create a column that combines the first name, last name, and courtesy fields. To accomplish this trick, you can construct an ItemTemplate like this:

```
<asp:TemplateField HeaderText="Name">
  <ItemTemplate>
    <%# Eval("TitleOfCourtesy") %> <%# Eval("FirstName") %>
    <%# Eval("LastName") %>
  </ItemTemplate>
</asp:TemplateField>
```

Now when you bind the GridView, the GridView fetches the data from the data source and walks through the collection of items. It processes the ItemTemplate for each item, evaluates the data binding expressions, and adds the rendered HTML to the table. This template is quite simple—it simply defines three data-binding expressions. When evaluated, these expressions are converted to ordinary text.

You'll notice that these expressions use Eval(), which is a static method of the System.Web.UI.DataBinder class. Eval()is an indispensable convenience—it automatically retrieves the data item that's bound to the current row, uses reflection to find the matching field (for a DataRow object) or property (for a custom data object), and retrieves the value. This process of reflection adds a little bit of extra work. However, this overhead is unlikely to add much time to the processing of a request. Without the Eval() method, you'd need to access the data object through the Container.DataItem property and use typecasting code like this:

```
<%# ((EmployeeDetails)Container.DataItem)["FirstName"] %>
```

The problem with this approach is that you need to know the exact type of data object. For example, the data-binding expression shown previously assumes you're binding to an array of EmployeeDetails objects through the ObjectDataSource. If you switch to the SqlDataSource, or if you rename the EmployeeDetails class, your page will break. On the other hand, if you use the Eval() method, your data binding expressions will keep working as long as the data object has a property with the given name. In other words, using the Eval() method allows you to create pages that are loosely bound to your data access layer.

■ **Note** If you attempt to bind a field that isn't present in your result set, you'll receive a runtime error. If you retrieve additional fields that are never bound to any template, no problem will occur.

■ **Tip** When binding to a SqlDataSource in DataSet mode, the data item is a DataRowView. When binding to a SqlDataSource in DataReader mode, the data item is a DbDataRecord.

The Eval() method also adds the extremely useful ability to format data fields on the fly. To use this feature, you must use the overloaded version of the Eval() method that accepts an additional format string parameter. Here's an example:

```
<%# Eval("BirthDate", "{0:MM/dd/yy}") %>
```

You can use any of the format strings defined in Table 10-3 and Table 10-4 with the Eval() method.

You're free to mix template columns with other column types. Or, you could get rid of every other column and put all the information from the Employees table into one formatted template:

```
<asp:GridView ID="gridEmployees" runat="server" DataSourceID="sourceEmployees"
 AutoGenerateColumns="False" ...>
  <!-- Styles omitted. -->

  <Columns>
    <asp:TemplateField HeaderText="Employees">
      <ItemTemplate>
        <b>
          <%# Eval("EmployeeID") %> -
          <%# Eval("TitleOfCourtesy") %> <%# Eval("FirstName") %>
          <%# Eval("LastName") %>
        </b>
        <hr />
        <small><i>
```

```
        <%# Eval("Address") %><br />
        <%# Eval("City") %>, <%# Eval("Country") %>,
        <%# Eval("PostalCode") %><br />
        <%# Eval("HomePhone") %></i>
        <br /><br />
        <%# Eval("Notes") %>
      </small>
    </ItemTemplate>
  </asp:TemplateField>
 </Columns>
</asp:GridView>
```

Figure 10-11 shows the result.

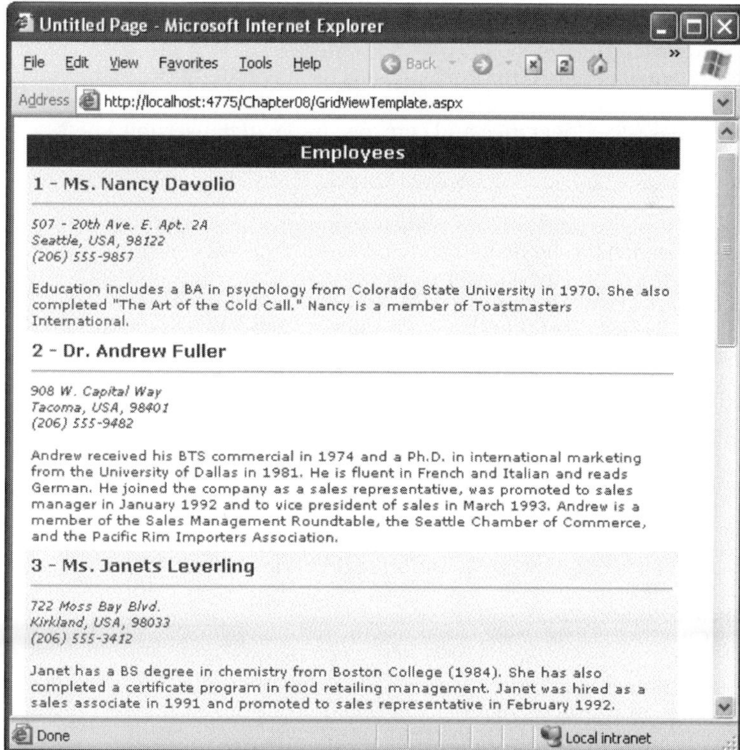

Figure 10-11. Creating a templated column

Using Multiple Templates

The previous example used a single template to configure the appearance of data items. However, the ItemTemplate isn't the only template that the GridView provides. In fact, the GridView allows you to configure various aspects of its appearance with a number of templates. Inside every template column, you can use the templates listed in Table 10-8.

Table 10-8. GridView Templates

Mode	Description
HeaderTemplate	Determines the appearance and content of the header cell
FooterTemplate	Determines the appearance and content of the footer cell
ItemTemplate	Determines the appearance and content of each data cell (if you aren't using the AlternatingItemTemplate) or every odd-numbered data cell (if you are)
AlternatingItemTemplate	Used in conjunction with the ItemTemplate to format even-numbered and odd-numbered rows differently
EditItemTemplate	Determines the appearance and controls used in edit mode
InsertItemTemplate	Determines the appearance and controls used when inserting a new record

Out of the templates listed in Table 10-8, the EditItemTemplate is one of the most useful, as it gives you the ability to control the editing experience for the field. If you don't use template columns, you're limited to ordinary text boxes, and you won't have any validation. The GridView also defines two templates that you can use outside of any column. These are the PagerTemplate, which lets you customize the appearance of pager controls, and the EmptyDataTemplate, which lets you set the content that should appear if the GridView is bound to an empty data object.

Editing Templates in Visual Studio

Visual Studio allows you to edit templates in the web-page designer. To try this, follow these steps:

1. Create a GridView with at least one templated column.
2. Select the GridView and click Edit Templates in the smart tag. This switches the GridView into template editing mode.
3. In the smart tag, use the drop-down Display list to choose the template you want to edit (see Figure 10-12). You can choose either of the two templates that apply to the whole GridView (EmptyDataTemplate or PagerTemplate), or you can choose a specific template for one of the template columns.

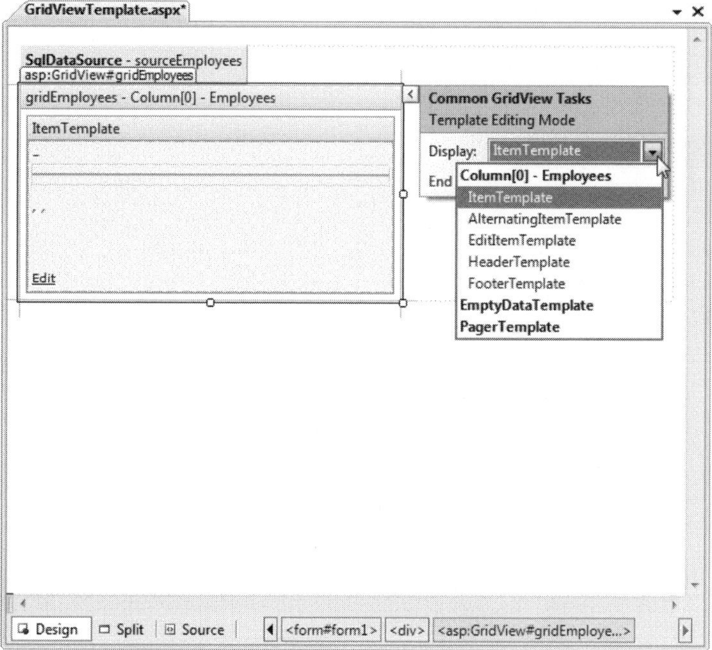

Figure 10-12. *Editing a template in Visual Studio*

4. Enter your content in the control. You can type in static content, drag-and-drop controls, and so on.

5. When you're finished, choose End Template Editing from the smart tag.

Binding to a Method

One of the benefits of templates is that they allow you to use data binding expressions that extend the ways you can format and present bound data. One key technique that recurs in many scenarios is using a method in your page class to process a field value. This removes the limitations of simple data binding and lets you incorporate dynamic information and conditional logic.

For example, you might create a column where you want to display an icon next to each row. However, you don't want to use a static icon—instead, you want to choose the best image based on the data in the row. Figure 10-13 shows an example where check marks indicate when there is a large quantity of a given item in stock (more than 50 units) and an *X* indicates when stock is fully depleted.

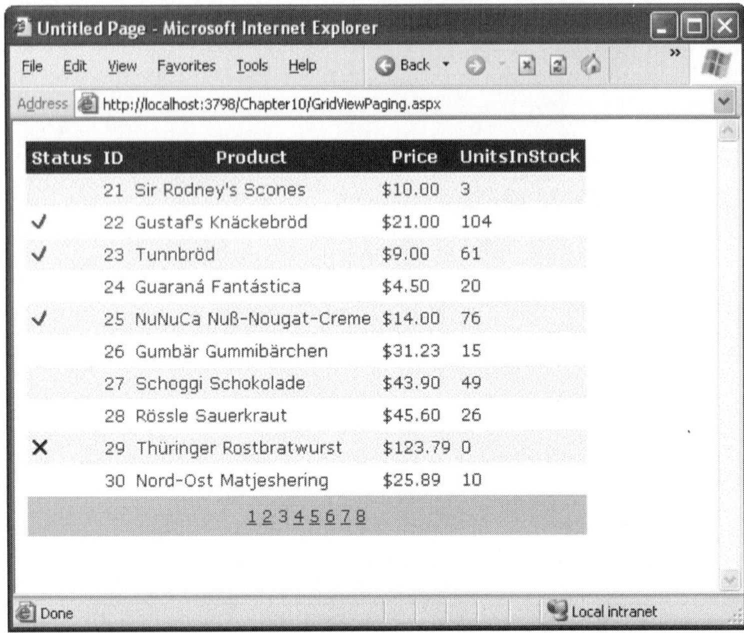

Status	ID	Product	Price	UnitsInStock
	21	Sir Rodney's Scones	$10.00	3
✓	22	Gustaf's Knäckebröd	$21.00	104
✓	23	Tunnbröd	$9.00	61
	24	Guaraná Fantástica	$4.50	20
✓	25	NuNuCa Nuß-Nougat-Creme	$14.00	76
	26	Gumbär Gummibärchen	$31.23	15
	27	Schoggi Schokolade	$43.90	49
	28	Rössle Sauerkraut	$45.60	26
✗	29	Thüringer Rostbratwurst	$123.79	0
	30	Nord-Ost Matjeshering	$25.89	10
		1 2 3 4 5 6 7 8		

Figure 10-13. Flagging rows conditionally

Here's how you would define the status column:

```
<asp:TemplateField HeaderText="Status">
  <ItemTemplate>
    <img src='<%# GetStatusPicture(Container.DataItem) %>' alt="Status" />
  </ItemTemplate>
</asp:TemplateField>
```

And here's the GetStatusPicture() method that examines the data item and chooses the right picture URL:

```
protected string GetStatusPicture(object dataItem)
{
    int units = Int32.Parse(DataBinder.Eval(dataItem, "UnitsInStock").ToString());
    if (units == 0)
        return "Cancel.gif";
    else if (units > 50)
        return "OK.gif";
    else
        return "blank.gif";
}
```

This technique turns up in many scenarios. For example, you could use it to adjust prices to take into consideration the current exchange rates. Or, you could use it to translate a numeric code into a more meaningful piece of text. You might even want to create completely calculated columns—for example, use the EmployeeDateOfBirth field to calculate a value for an EmployeeAge column.

In this example, you might also want to set the alt attribute of the <img> tag using a similar approach. That way the alternate text could provide a more meaningful description (such as OK or Cancel) that would reflect the status of the corresponding product.

■ **Note** If you use data binding expressions to bind to methods, you can no longer use callbacks to optimize the GridView refresh process. To prevent an error, make sure you do not set GridView.EnableSortingAndPagingCallbacks to true. If you don't want to sacrifice the callback features, you can decide not to use templates and get similar functionality by modifying rows when they are first added to the grid, using the GridView.RowDataBound event. This technique is described earlier in the "Formatting-Specific Values" section of this chapter.

Handling Events in a Template

In some cases, you might need to handle events that are raised by the controls you add to a templated column. For example, imagine you changed the previous example so that instead of showing a static status icon, it created a clickable image link through the ImageButton control. This is easy enough to accomplish:

```
<asp:TemplateField HeaderText="Status">
  <ItemTemplate>
    <asp:ImageButton ID="ImageButton1" runat="server"
     ImageUrl='<%# GetStatusPicture(Container.DataItem) %>' />
  </ItemTemplate>
</asp:TemplateField>
```

The problem is that if you add a control to a template, the GridView creates multiple copies of that control, one for each data item. When the ImageButton is clicked, you need a way to determine which image was clicked and which row it belongs to.

The way to resolve this problem is to use an event from the GridView, *not* the contained button. The GridView.RowCommand event serves this purpose, because it fires whenever any button is clicked in any template. This process, where a control event in a template is turned into an event in the containing control, is called *event bubbling*.

Of course, you still need a way to pass information to the RowCommand event to identify the row where the action took place. The secret lies in two string properties of all button controls: CommandName and CommandArgument. CommandName sets a descriptive name you can use to distinguish clicks on your ImageButton from clicks on other button controls in the GridView. The CommandArgument supplies a piece of row-specific data you can use to identify the row that was clicked. You can supply this information using a data binding expression.

Here's the template field containing the revised ImageButton tag:

```
<asp:TemplateField HeaderText="Status">
  <ItemTemplate>
    <asp:ImageButton ID="ImageButton1" runat="server"
     ImageUrl='<%# GetStatusPicture(Container.DataItem) %>'
     CommandName="StatusClick" CommandArgument='<%# Eval("ProductID") %>' />
  </ItemTemplate>
</asp:TemplateField>
```

And here's the code you need to respond when an ImageButton is clicked:

```
protected void GridView1_RowCommand(object sender, GridViewCommandEventArgs e)
{
    if (e.CommandName == "StatusClick")
      lblInfo.Text = "You clicked product #" + e.CommandArgument;
}
```

This example simply displays the ProductID in a label.

■ **Tip** Remembe, you can simplify your life using the GridView's built-in selection support. Just set the CommandName to Select and handle the SelectIndexChanged event, as described in the section "Using a Data Field As a Select Button" earlier in this chapter. Although this approach gives you easy access to the clicked row, it won't help you if you want to provide multiple buttons that perform different tasks.

Editing with a Template

One of the best reasons to use a template is to provide a better editing experience. In the previous chapter, you saw how the GridView provides automatic editing capabilities—all you need to do is switch a row into edit mode by setting the GridView.EditIndex property.

The easiest way to make this possible is to add a CommandField column with the ShowEditButton property set to true (or set the GridView.AutoGenerateEditButton property to true). Either way, you'll end up with a dedicated column that's used to show editing commands. Initially this column will display a link named Edit next to each record. When the user clicks an Edit link, every label in every column of that row will be replaced by a text box, unless the field is read-only.

The standard editing support has several limitations:

It's not always appropriate to edit values using a text box: Certain types of data are best handled with other controls (such as drop-down lists), large fields need multiline text boxes, and so on.

You get no validation: It would be nice to restrict the editing possibilities so that currency figures can't be entered as negative numbers, and so on. You can do that by adding validator controls to an EditItemTemplate.

It's often ugly: A row of text boxes across a grid takes up too much space and rarely seems professional.

In a templated column, you don't have these issues. Instead, you explicitly define the edit controls and their layout using the EditItemTemplate. This can be a somewhat laborious process.

Here's an edit template that allows editing of a single field—the Notes field:

```
<EditItemTemplate>
  <b>
    <%# Eval("EmployeeID") %> -
    <%# Eval("TitleOfCourtesy") %> <%# Eval("FirstName") %>
    <%# Eval("LastName") %>
  </b>
  <hr />
  <small><i>
    <%# Eval("Address") %><br />
    <%# Eval("City") %>, <%# Eval("Country") %>,
    <%# Eval("PostalCode") %><br />
    <%# Eval("HomePhone") %></i>
    <br /><br />
    <asp:TextBox Text='<%# Bind("Notes") %>' runat="server" id="textBox"
     TextMode="MultiLine" Width="413px" />
  </small>
</EditItemTemplate>
```

When binding an editable value to a control, you must use the Bind() method in your data binding expression instead of the ordinary Eval() method. Only the Bind() method creates the two-way link, ensuring that updated values will be sent back to the server.

Another important fact to keep in mind is that when the GridView commits an update, it will submit only the bound, editable parameters. In the previous example, this means the GridView will pass back a single @Notes parameter for the Notes field. This is important, because when you write your parameterized update command (if you're using the SqlDataSource), you must use only one parameter, as shown here:

```
<asp:SqlDataSource ID="sourceEmployees" runat="server"
 ConnectionString="<%$ ConnectionStrings:Northwind %>"
 ProviderName="System.Data.SqlClient"
 SelectCommand="SELECT EmployeeID, FirstName, LastName, Title, City, Country,
Notes, Address, Region, PostalCode, HomePhone, TitleOfCourtesy FROM Employees"
 UpdateCommand="UPDATE Employees SET Notes=@Notes WHERE EmployeeID=@EmployeeID">
</asp:SqlDataSource>
```

Similarly, if you're using the ObjectDataSource, you must make sure your update method takes only one parameter, named Notes.

Figure 10-14 shows the row in edit mode.

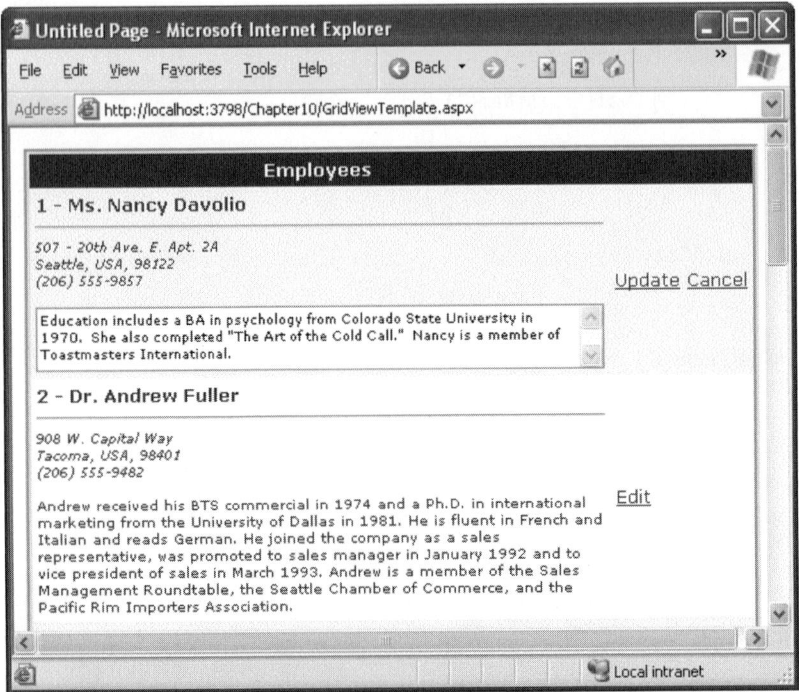

Figure 10-14. *Editing with a template*

Editing with Advanced Controls

Template based-editing really shines if you need to bind to more interesting controls, such as lists. For example, you could change the previous example to make the TitleOfCourtesy field editable through a drop-down list. Here's the template you need, with the new details in bold:

```
<EditItemTemplate>
  <b>
    <%# Eval("EmployeeID") %> -
    <asp:DropDownList runat="server" ID="EditTitle"
     SelectedIndex='<%# GetSelectedTitle(Eval("TitleOfCourtesy")) %>'
     DataSource='<%# TitlesOfCourtesy %>' />
    <%# Eval("FirstName") %>
    <%# Eval("LastName") %>
  </b>
  <hr />
  <small><i>
    <%# Eval("Address") %><br />
    <%# Eval("City") %>, <%# Eval("Country") %>,
    <%# Eval("PostalCode") %><br />
    <%# Eval("HomePhone") %></i>
    <br /><br />
    <asp:TextBox Text='<%# Bind("Notes") %>' runat="server" id="textBox"
```

```
      TextMode="MultiLine" Width="413px" />
  </small>
</EditItemTemplate>
```

This template allows the user to pick a title of courtesy from a limited selection of possible titles. To create this list, you need to resort to a little trick—setting the DropDownList.DataSource with a data binding expression that points to a custom property. This custom property can then return a suitable data source with the available titles of courtesy.

Here's the definition for the TitlesOfCourtesy property in the web-page class:

```
protected string[] TitlesOfCourtesy
{
    get { return new string[]{"Mr.", "Dr.", "Ms.", "Mrs."}; }
}
```

■ **Note** This list of titles of courtesy is by no means complete. There are also Miss, Lord, Lady, Sir, None, and so on. For a real-world application the titles could come from a database table or configuration file.

This step ensures that the drop-down list is populated, but it doesn't solve the related problem of making sure the right title is selected in the list for the current value. The best approach here is to bind the SelectedIndex to a custom method that takes the current title and returns the index of that value. In this example, the GetSelectedTitle() method performs this task. It takes a title as input and returns the index of the respective value in the array returned by TitlesOfCourtesy.

```
protected int GetSelectedTitle(object title)
{
    return Array.IndexOf(TitlesOfCourtesy, title.ToString());
}
```

This code searches the array using the static Array.IndexOf() method. Note that you must explicitly cast the title to a string. That's because the DataBinder.Eval() method returns an object, not a string, and that value is passed to the GetSelectedTitle() method.

Figure 10-15 shows the drop-down list in action.

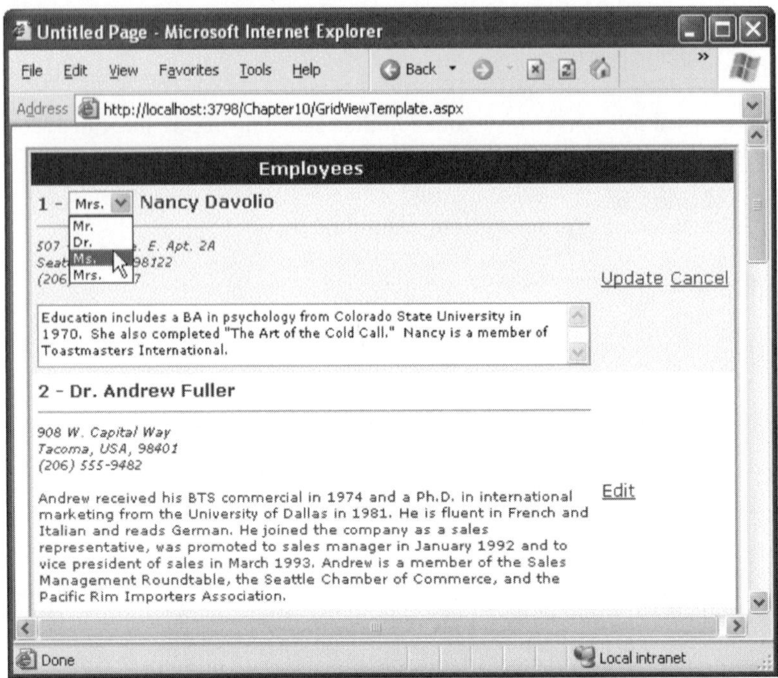

***Figure 10-15.** Editing with a drop-down list of values*

Unfortunately, this still doesn't complete the example. Now you have a list box that is populated in edit mode, with the correct item automatically selected. However, if you change the selection, the value isn't sent back to the data source. In this example, you could tackle the problem by using the Bind() method with the SelectedValue property, because the text in the control exactly corresponds to the text you want to commit to the record. However, sometimes life isn't as easy, because you need to translate the value into a different database representation. In this situation, the only option is to handle the RowUpdating event, find the list control in the current row, and extract the text. You can then dynamically add the extra parameter, as shown here:

```
protected void gridEmployees_RowUpdating(object sender, GridViewUpdateEventArgs e)
{
    // Get the reference to the list control.
    DropDownList title = (DropDownList)
      (gridEmployees.Rows[e.RowIndex].FindControl("EditTitle"));

    // Add it to the parameters.
    e.NewValues.Add("TitleOfCourtesy", title.Text);
}
```

The UpdateCommand in the SqlDataSource must also be updated to use the @TitleOfCourtesy parameter:

```
UpdateCommand="UPDATE Employees SET Notes=@Notes, TitleOfCourtesy=@TitleOfCourtesy
WHERE EmployeeID=@EmployeeID"
```

This will now successfully update both the Notes field and the TitleOfCourtesy. As you can see, editable templates give you a great deal of power, but they often aren't quick to code.

■ **Tip** To make an even more interesting EditItemTemplate, you could add validator controls to verify input values, as discussed in Chapter 4.

Editing Without a Command Column

So far, all the examples you've seen have used a CommandField that automatically generates edit controls. However, now that you've made the transition over to a template-based approach, it's worth considering how you can add your own edit controls.

It's actually quite easy. All you need to do is add a button control to the ItemTemplate and set the CommandName to Edit. This automatically triggers the editing process, which fires the appropriate events and switches the row into edit mode:

```
<ItemTemplate>
  <b>
    <%# Eval("EmployeeID") %> - <%# Eval("TitleOfCourtesy") %>
    <%# Eval("TitleOfCourtesy") %> <%# Eval("FirstName") %>
    <%# Eval("LastName") %>
  </b>
  <hr />
  <small><i>
    <%# Eval("Address") %><br />
    <%# Eval("City") %>, <%# Eval("Country") %>,
    <%# Eval("PostalCode") %><br />
    <%# Eval("HomePhone") %></i>
    <br /><br />
    <%# Eval("Notes") %>
    <br /><br />
    <asp:LinkButton runat="server" Text="Edit"
     CommandName="Edit" ID="cmdEdit" />
  </small>
</ItemTemplate>
```

In the EditItemTemplate, you need two more buttons with a CommandName of Update and Cancel, respectively:

```
<EditItemTemplate>
  <b>
    <%# Eval("EmployeeID") %> -
    <asp:DropDownList runat="server" ID="EditTitle"
     SelectedIndex='<%# GetSelectedTitle(Eval("TitleOfCourtesy")) %>'
     DataSource='<%# TitlesOfCourtesy %>' />
    <%# Eval("FirstName") %>
    <%# Eval("LastName") %>
  </b>
  <hr />
```

```
  <small><i>
    <%# Eval("Address") %><br />
    <%# Eval("City") %>, <%# Eval("Country") %>,
    <%# Eval("PostalCode") %><br />
    <%# Eval("HomePhone") %></i>
    <br /><br />
    <asp:TextBox Text='<%# Bind("Notes") %>' runat="server" id="textBox"
     TextMode="MultiLine" Width="413px" />
    <br /><br />
    <asp:LinkButton runat="server" Text="Update"
     CommandName="Update" ID="cmdUpdate" />
    <asp:LinkButton runat="server" Text="Cancel"
     CommandName="Cancel" ID="cmdCancel" />
  </small>
</EditItemTemplate>
```

As long as you use the right names when setting the CommandName property on your buttons, the GridView editing events will fire and the data source controls will react in the same way as if you were using the automatically generated editing controls. Figure 10-16 shows the custom edit links.

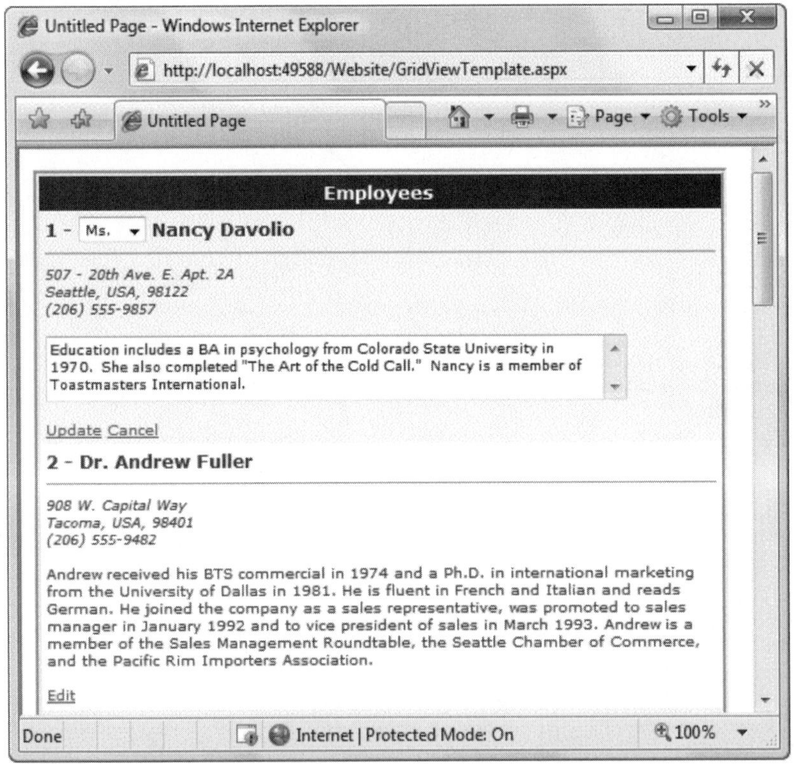

Figure 10-16. Custom edit controls

Client IDs in Templates

As you've seen, the TemplateField in the GridView works by repeating the same block of markup in your web page once for each data item. However, ASP.NET needs the ability to uniquely identify separate instances of the same element. For example, if you place a button in your ItemTemplate, ASP.NET creates one instance of that button for each data item. If the user clicks that button, ASP.NET needs to be able to determine which button triggered the postback. Similarly, if you place a text box in a template, ASP.NET needs to keep its values separate from text box values in other instances of the same template.

Fortunately, this task isn't difficult for ASP.NET, provided each element has a distinct client-side ID in the rendered markup. ASP.NET takes care of this detail for you, by automatically generating unique IDs for each repeated element. In most situations, you can relax and let ASP.NET use its standard ID-generation algorithm, without paying the client IDs any real attention. However, there are situations when you might need more client-side control. For example, you might choose to modify an HTML object using client-side JavaScript. In cases like these, it's important that you know the exact client-side IDs that ASP.NET will generate.

With data bound controls, this isn't always easy. ASP.NET generates unique names by inserting a numeric suffix. This numeric suffix doesn't actually mean anything—it simply separates one item from another. Thus, it's difficult to know what numeric suffix ASP.NET will hand out to a specific data item, and what client-side ID it will generate.

To solve this problem, you can use the ClientIDMode property described in Chapter 3 in conjunction with the GridView's ClientIDRowSuffix property. Essentially, the ClientIDRowSuffix property tells the GridView to use a unique field from the data object as the control suffix. Because you know the value of this field for each data item, you can predict the client IDs that ASP.NET will generate.

To understand this example, consider the grid of employees shown in earlier examples. In the ItemTemplate, the control that creates the Edit link looks like this:

```
<asp:LinkButton runat="server" Text="Edit" CommandName="Edit" ID="cmdEdit" />
```

When rendered to HTML, the LinkButton writes an anchor element, and converts the server-side ID cmdEdit to a unique client-side ID like gridEmployeed_cmdEdit_0:

```
<a id="gridEmployees_cmdEdit_0" href="javascript:__doPostBack(...)">Edit</a>
```

The problem is that the *0* iscompletely arbitrary. It depends on the position of the data item in the GridView, and the number of other records. However, if you use the ClientIDMode to Predictable for the GridView, you can use the ClientIDRowSuffix to choose a data field for the suffic. Here's an example:

```
<asp:GridView ID="gridEmployees" runat="server" ...
 ClientIDMode="Predictable" ClientIDRowSuffix="EmployeeID">
```

Now, the EmployeeID value of each data item is used as a suffix to make its client ID unique. If you have an employee record with an ID of 45HJ77, ASP.NET generates an anchor like this:

```
<a id="gridEmployees_cmdEdit_45HJ77" href="javascript:__doPostBack(...)">Edit</a>
```

This name is used no matter how the employee records are arranged.

The ListView

The ListView is an extremely flexible data-bound control that renders its content based on the templates you define. Unlike the Repeater, the ListView adds higher-level features such as selection and editing, which work in the same way as those in the GridView. But unlike the GridView, the ListView doesn't support a field-based model for creating quick-and-easy grids with a minimum of markup.

Depending on your perspective, the ListView is either a more flexible version of the GridView that requires more work or a more feature-filled version of the simple Repeater that was included with ASP.NET 1.x.

The ListView includes a more extensive set of templates than the GridView. Table 10-9 lists them all.

Table 10-9. *ListView Templates*

Mode	Description
ItemTemplate	Sets the content of every data item (if you aren't using the AlternatingItemTemplate) or every odd-numbered data cell (if you are).
AlternatingItemTemplate	Used in conjunction with the ItemTemplate to format even-numbered and odd-numbered rows differently.
ItemSeparatorTemplate	Sets the content of the separator that's drawn between items.
SelectedItemTemplate	Sets the content of the item that's currently selected. You can use the same content as the ItemSeparatorTemplate, but with different formatting to make it stand out, or you can choose to show an expanded display with additional details for the selected item.
EditItemTemplate	Sets the controls used for an item in edit mode.
InsertItemTemplate	Sets the controls used to insert a new item.
LayoutTemplate	Sets the markup that wraps your list of items.
GroupTemplate	Sets the markup that wraps each group of items, if you're using the grouping feature.
GroupSeparatorTemplate	Sets the content of the separator that's drawn between groups of items.
EmptyItemTemplate	Sets the content that's used to fill empty values in the last group, if you're using grouping. For example, if you create groups of 5 and your data source is a collection of 13 objects, there are 2 items missing from the last group.
EmptyDataTemplate	Sets the markup that's used if the bound data object is empty (doesn't contain any records or objects).

■ **Tip** The most common reason for using the ListView is to create an unusual layout—for example, to create a table that places more than one item in the same row, or to break free from table-based rendering altogether. When building a page to display large amounts of data, ASP.NET developers usually turn to the GridView first and use the ListView in more specialized scenarios.

To display some data with the ListView, you follow the same process that you'd follow with a GridView that's made up of TemplateField columns. First, you create the markup for the templates you want to use. At a bare minimum, you need the ItemTemplate, which represents the content for each item. Here's an example:

```
<asp:ListView ID="listEmployees" DataSourceID="sourceEmployees" runat="server">
  <ItemTemplate>
    <span>
    <b>
      <%# Eval("EmployeeID") %> -
      <%# Eval("TitleOfCourtesy") %> <%# Eval("FirstName") %>
      <%# Eval("LastName") %>
    </b>
    <hr />
    <small>
      <i><%# Eval("Address") %><br />
      <%# Eval("City") %>, <%# Eval("Country") %>,
      <%# Eval("PostalCode") %><br />
      <%# Eval("HomePhone") %></i>
      <br /><br />
      <%# Eval("Notes") %>
      <br /><br />
    </small>
    </span>
  </ItemTemplate>
</asp:ListView>
```

When the ListView renders itself, it iterates over the bound data and renders the ItemTemplate for each item. It places all of this content inside an ordinary <span>.

Often, you'll want to supply a LayoutTemplate to get more control over the arrangement of items. If you include a LayoutTemplate, the list of items is placed *inside* the LayoutTemplate. The default behavior of the ListView with no LayoutTemplate is equivalent to using a LayoutTemplate that looks like this:

```
<asp:ListView ID="listEmployees" DataSourceID="sourceEmployees" runat="server">
  <LayoutTemplate>
    <asp:PlaceHolder ID="itemPlaceHolder" runat="server"></asp:PlaceHolder>
  </LayoutTemplate>

  <ItemTemplate>
    ...
  </ItemTemplate>
</asp:ListView>
```

When creating the LayoutTemplate for a ListView, you need to indicate where the ItemTemplate content should be inserted. You do this by adding a *placeholder*—the element that will be duplicated once for each bound data item. To designate an element as the placeholder, you simply set its ID to itemPlaceholder, as shown in this example. Your placeholder must be a server control—in other words, it needs the runat="server" attribute. This example uses the convenient PlaceHolder web control, but you could substitute a server-side <span> or <div> element instead.

■ **Note** The LayoutTemplate is what allows the ListView to be so flexible. Other data controls use templates for content, but not for the overall structure.

Using the LayoutTemplate, you can easily adapt this example so that it uses a table. For example, if you want to place each item in a separate row (as the GridView does), you would use a table row (the <tr> element) for your item placeholder:

```
<LayoutTemplate>
  <table border="1">
    <tr id="itemPlaceholder" runat="server" />

</LayoutTemplate>
```

Now, each item can start a new row (with <tr>) and add the cells where appropriate (with <td>):

```
<ItemTemplate>
  <tr>
    <td>...<td>
    ...
  </tr>
</ItemTemplate>
```

■ **Note** Compared to the GridView, the ListView has one conceptual drawback—it only has a single template for displaying items. To understand how this can limit you, consider what would happen if you wanted to create a multicolumn display using only the ListView. You'd need to add the column headers above the ListView, and then you'd need to define all the column content in the ItemTemplate. This works perfectly well, but it will cause major headaches if you want to make trivial-seeming changes like reordering your columns.

To make life a little more interesting, you can create a table layout that wouldn't be possible with the ordinary GridView—one that places each item in a separate column. Conceptually, this process is simple. You simply need to use a table cell (the <td> element) as your placeholder:

```
<LayoutTemplate>
      <tr valign="top" border="1"><td id="itemPlaceholder" runat="server" />
</LayoutTemplate>
```

Now the LayoutTemplate must begin with the <td> tag. The result will quickly become difficult to read if you have a somewhat large set of data (unless you also use paging). Figure 10-17 shows the result.

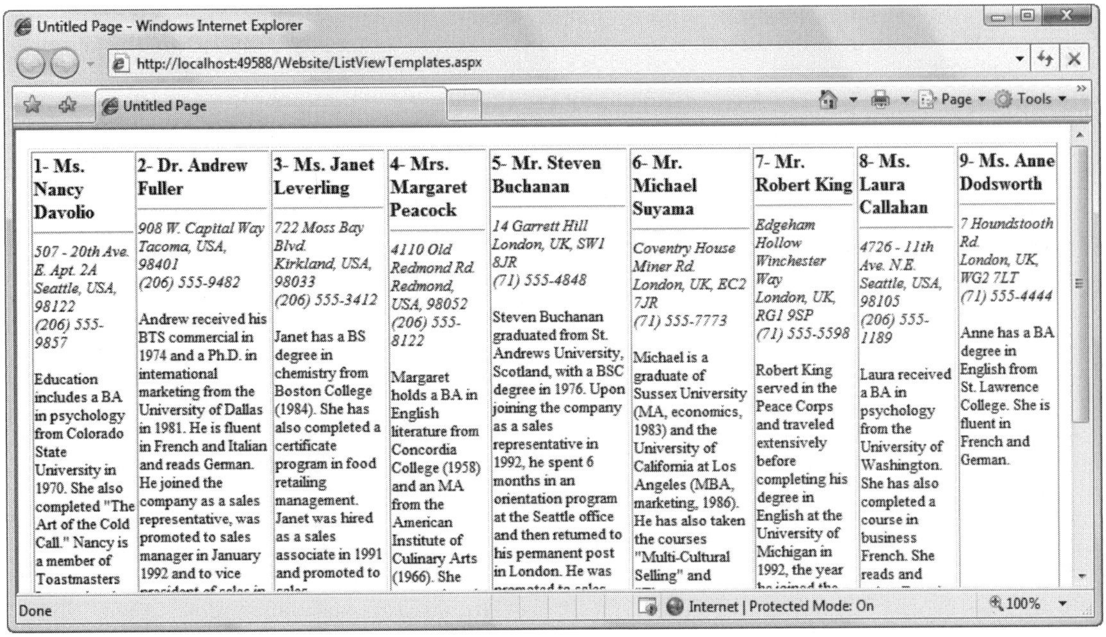

Figure 10-17. *An unusual layout with the ListView*

Grouping

The ListView offers a way to create slightly more structured displays that resolve the problem shown in Figure 10-17. The trick is to use grouping, which allows you to specify an additional level of layout that's used to arrange smaller groups of records inside the overall layout.

To use grouping, you begin by setting the GroupItemCount property, which determines the number of data items in each group:

```
<asp:ListView ID="listEmployees" GroupItemCount="3" ... >
```

Sadly, the ListView's grouping feature doesn't work in conjunction with the information in your bound data. For example, if you bind a collection of Product objects, there's no way to place them into groups based on price ranges or product categories (although you'll see one possible way to solve this problem later in this chapter, in the section "A Parent/Child View in a Single Table"). Instead, the ListView's groups are always fixed in size. The most you can do is make the group size user-configurable (say, by supplying another control like a drop-down list box from which the user can choose the number to use for GroupItemCount).

Once you've set the group size, you need to change the LayoutTemplate. That's because your overall layout no longer contains the data items—instead, it contains the groups, which in turn hold the items. To reflect this fact, you must change the ID from itemPlaceholder to groupPlaceholder. In this example, each group is a separate row:

```
<LayoutTemplate>
  <table border="1">
    <tr id="groupPlaceholder" runat="server">
</LayoutTemplate>
```

Next, you need to supply a GroupTemplate, which is used to wrap each group. The GroupTemplate must provide the item placeholder that was formerly in the LayoutTemplate. In this example, each item is a separate cell:

```
<GroupTemplate>
  <tr><td runat="server" id="itemPlaceholder" valign="top" /></GroupTemplate>
```

■ **Note** Both the group placeholder and the item placeholder need to be server controls, and they need to be content elements—in other words, they need to be able to hold other elements.

Now the ItemTemplate can begin with the <td> tag, so that each item is a cell inside a row. In turn, each row is a group of three data items in the overall table. Figure 10-18 shows the result.

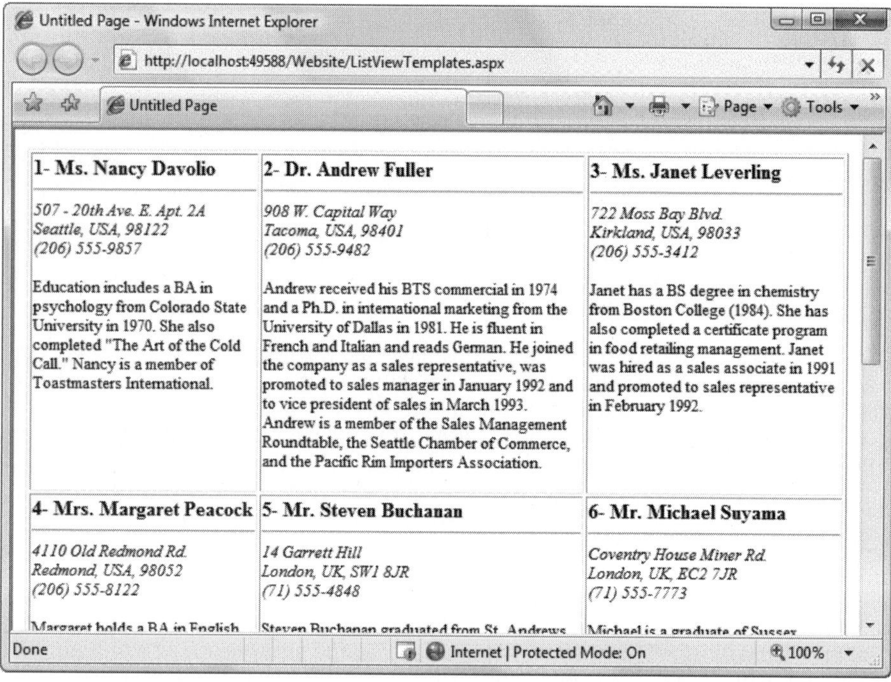

Figure 10-18. A ListView with grouping

When using grouping, the last group may not be completely filled. For example, the previous example creates groups of three. If the number of data items isn't a multiple of three, the last group won't be complete. In many cases, this isn't an issue, but in some situations it might be—for example, if you want to preserve a certain structure or place some alternate content in a table. In this case, you can supply the new content by using the EmptyItemTemplate.

Paging

Unlike the other data controls you'll consider in this chapter, the ListView doesn't have a hard-wired paging feature. Instead, it supports another control whose sole purpose is providing the paging feature: the DataPager.

The idea behind the DataPager is that it gives you a single, consistent way to use paging with a variety of controls. Currently, the ListView is the only control that supports the DataPager. However, it's reasonable to expect the DataPager to work with more ASP.NET controls in future versions.

Another benefit of the DataPager is that you have the flexibility to position it where you want in your overall layout, simply by placing the tag in the right part of the LayoutTemplate. Here's a fairly typical use of the DataPager that puts it at the bottom of the ListView, and gives it buttons for moving forward or backward one page at a time or jumping straight to the first or last page:

```
<LayoutTemplate>
  <table id="groupPlaceholder" runat="server">

  <asp:DataPager runat="server" ID="ContactsDataPager" PageSize="6">
    <Fields>
      <asp:NextPreviousPagerField
       ShowFirstPageButton="true" ShowLastPageButton="true"
       FirstPageText="|&lt;&lt; " LastPageText=" &gt;&gt;|"
       NextPageText=" &gt; " PreviousPageText=" &lt; " />
    </Fields>
  </asp:DataPager>
</LayoutTemplate>
```

The DataPager also pares down the bound data so the ListView only gets the appropriate subset of data. In the current example, pages are limited to six items. Figure 10-19 shows the paging buttons.

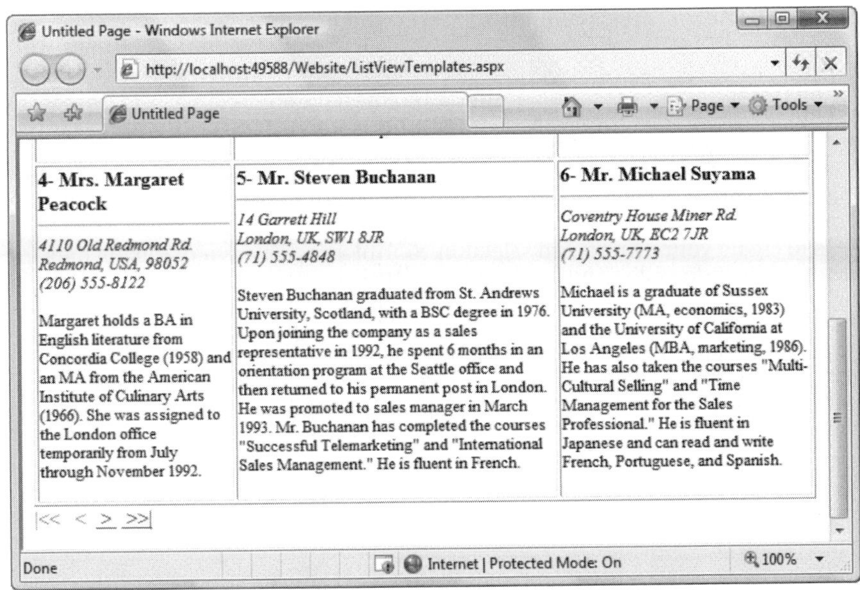

Figure 10-19. A ListView and DataPager working in conjunction

The DetailsView and FormView

The GridView and ListView excel at showing dense tables with multiple rows of information. However, sometimes you want to provide a detailed look at a single record. Although you could work out a solution using a template column in a GridView, ASP.NET also includes two controls that are tailored for this purpose: the DetailsView and FormView. Both show a single record at a time but can include optional pager buttons that let you step through a series of records (showing one per page). Both support templates, but the FormView *requires* them. This is the key distinction between the two controls.

One other difference is the fact that the DetailsView renders its content inside a table, while the FormView gives you the flexibility to display your content without a table. Thus, if you're planning to use templates, the FormView gives you the most flexibility. But if you want to avoid the complexity of templates, the DetailsView gives you a simpler model that lets you build a multirow data display out of field objects, in much the same way that the GridView is built out of column objects.

Now that you understand the features of the GridView and ListView, you can get up to speed with the DetailsView and FormView quite quickly. That's because both the DetailsView and the FormView borrow a portion of the GridView model.

The DetailsView

The DetailsView is designed to display a single record at a time. It places each piece of information (be it a field or a property) in a separate row of a table.

You saw how to create a basic DetailsView to show the currently selected record in Chapter 9. The DetailsView can also bind to a collection of items. In this case, it shows the first item in the group. It also allows you to move from one record to the next using paging controls, if you've set the AllowPaging property to true. You can configure the paging controls using the PagingStyle and PagingSettings properties in the same way as you tweak the pager for the GridView. The only difference is that there's no support for custom paging, which means the full data source object is always retrieved.

Figure 10-20 shows the DetailsView when it's bound to a set of employee records, with full employee information.

It's tempting to use the DetailsView pager controls to make a handy record browser. Unfortunately, this approach can be quite inefficient. First, a separate postback is required each time the user moves from one record to another (whereas a grid control can show multiple records at once). But the real drawback is that each time the page is posted back, the full set of records is retrieved, even though only a single record is shown. If you choose to implement a record browser page with the DetailsView, at a bare minimum you must enable caching to reduce the database work (see Chapter 11). That way, the full set of records is retrieved from the cache when possible and doesn't require a separate database operation.

Often, a better choice is to create your own record selection control using a subset of the full data. For example, you could create a drop-down list and bind this to a data source that queries just the employee names. Then, when a name is selected from the list, you retrieve the full details for just that record using another data source. Of course, several metrics can determine which approach is best, including the size of the full record (how much bigger it is than just the first and last name), the usage patterns (whether the average user browses to just one or two records or needs to see them all), and how many records there are in total. (You can afford to retrieve them all at once if there are dozens of records, but you need to think twice if there are thousands.)

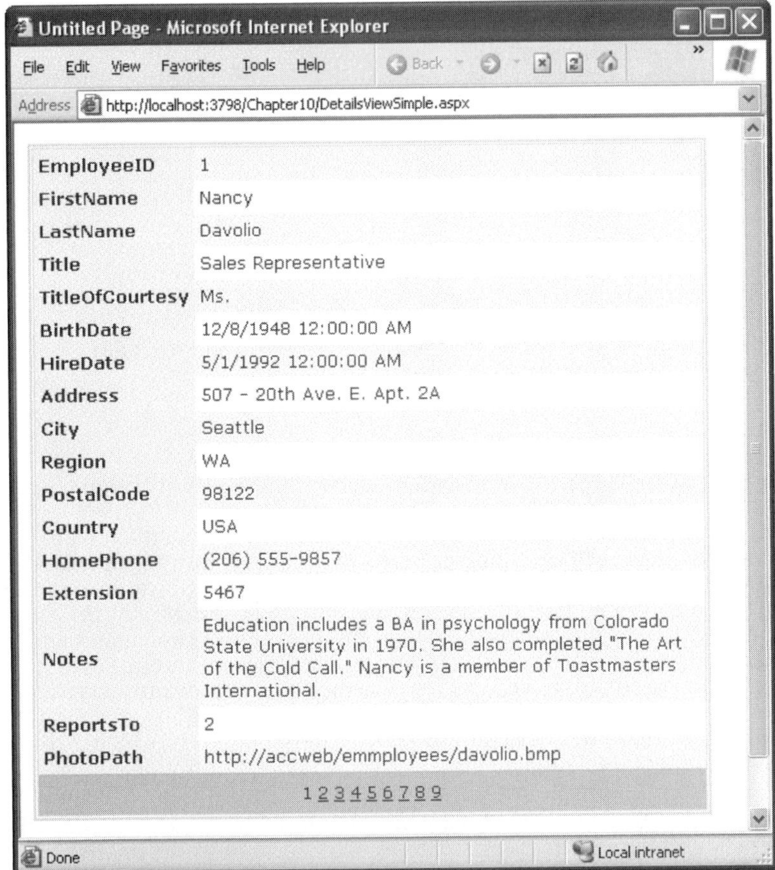

Figure 10-20. The DetailsView with paging

Defining Fields

The DetailsView uses reflection to generate the fields it shows. That means it examines the data object and creates a separate field for each field (in a row) or property (in a custom object), just like the GridView. You can disable this automatic field generation by setting AutoGenerateRows to false. It's then up to you to declare the field objects.

Interestingly, you use the same field object to build a DetailsView as you used to design a GridView. For example, fields from the data item are represented with the BoundField tag, buttons can be created with the ButtonField, and so on. For the full list, refer to Table 10-1.

Following is a portion of the field declarations for a DetailsView:

```
<asp:DetailsView ID="DetailsView1" runat="server" DataSourceID="sourceEmployees"
 AutoGenerateRows="False">
  <Fields>
    <asp:BoundField DataField="EmployeeID" HeaderText="EmployeeID" />
    <asp:BoundField DataField="FirstName" HeaderText="FirstName" />
```

```
        <asp:BoundField DataField="LastName" HeaderText="LastName" />
        <asp:BoundField DataField="Title" HeaderText="Title" />
        <asp:BoundField DataField="TitleOfCourtesy" HeaderText="TitleOfCourtesy" />
        <asp:BoundField DataField="BirthDate" HeaderText="BirthDate" />
        ...
    </Fields>
    ...
</asp:DetailsView>
```

You can use the BoundField tag to set properties such as header text, formatting string, editing behavior, and so on (see Table 10-2 earlier). In addition, you can use the ShowHeader property. When set to false, this instructs the DetailsView to leave the header text out of the row, and the field data takes up both columns.

The field model isn't the only part of the GridView that the DetailsView control adopts. It also uses a similar set of styles, a similar set of events, and a similar editing model.

Record Operations

The DetailsView supports delete, insert, and edit operations. However, unlike the GridView, you don't need to add a CommandField with edit controls. Instead, you simply set the Boolean AutoGenerateDeleteButton, AutoGenerateEditButton, and AutoGenerateInsertButton properties on the DetailsView control. This adds a CommandField at the bottom of the DetailsView with links for these tasks.

When you click the Delete button, the delete operation is performed immediately. However, when you click an Edit or Insert button, the DetailsView changes into edit or insert *mode*. Technically, the DetailsView has three modes (as represented by the DetailsViewMode enumeration). These modes are ReadOnly, Edit, and Insert. You can find the current mode at any time by checking the CurrentMode property, and you can call ChangeMode() to change it. You can also use the DefaultMode property to create a DetailsView that always begins in edit or insert mode.

In edit mode, the DetailsView uses standard text box controls just like the GridView (see Figure 10-21). For more editing flexibility, you'll want to use template fields or the FormView control.

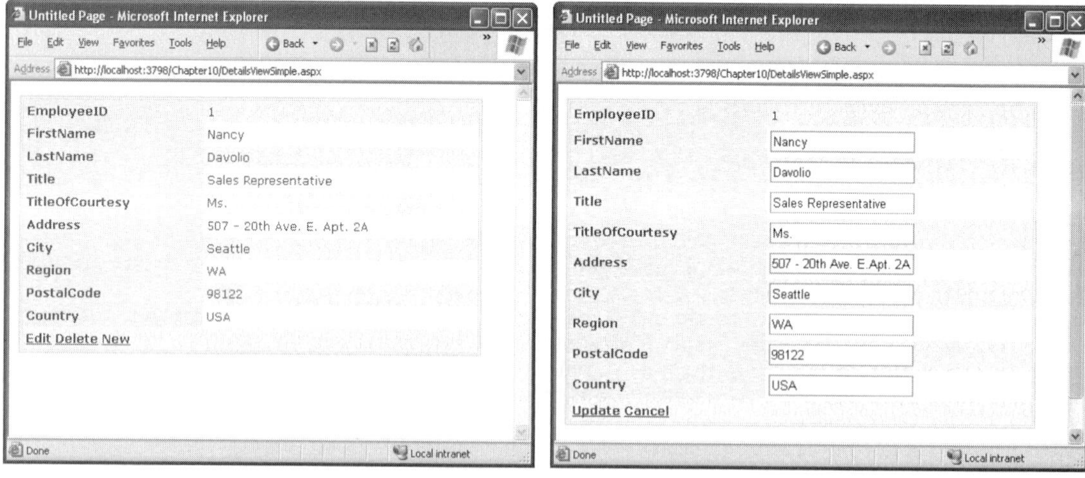

Figure 10-21. Editing in the DetailsView

■ **Note** If you place the DetailsView in edit mode to modify a record, and then navigate to a new record using the pager buttons, the DetailsView remains in edit mode. If this isn't the behavior you want, you can react to the PageIndexChanged event and call the ChangeMode() method to programmatically put it back in read-only mode.

The FormView

If you need the ultimate flexibility of templates, the FormView provides a template-only control for displaying and editing a single record.

The beauty of the FormView template model is that it matches the model of the TemplateField in the GridView quite closely. Therefore, you have the following templates to work with:

- ItemTemplate
- EditItemTemplate
- InsertItemTemplate
- FooterTemplate
- HeaderTemplate
- EmptyDataTemplate
- PagerTemplate

This means you can take the exact template content you put in a TemplateField in a GridView and place it inside the FormView. Here's an example based on the earlier templated GridView:

```
<asp:FormView ID="FormView1" runat="server" DataSourceID="sourceEmployees">
  <ItemTemplate>
    <b>
      <%# Eval("EmployeeID") %> -
      <%# Eval("TitleOfCourtesy") %> <%# Eval("FirstName") %>
      <%# Eval("LastName") %>
    </b>
    <hr />
    <small><i>
      <%# Eval("Address") %><br />
      <%# Eval("City") %>, <%# Eval("Country") %>,
      <%# Eval("PostalCode") %><br />
      <%# Eval("HomePhone") %></i>
      <br /><br />
      <%# Eval("Notes") %>
      <br /><br />
    </small>
  </ItemTemplate>
</asp:FormView>
```

Figure 10-22 shows the result.

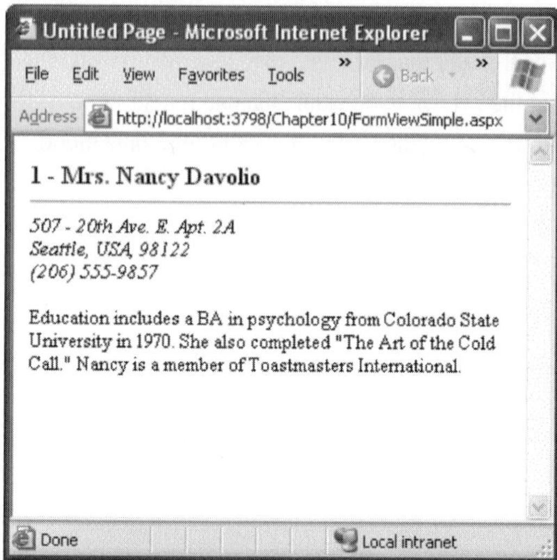

Figure 10-22. *A single record in a FormView*

Much like the DetailsView, the FormView works in three distinct modes: read-only, insert, and edit. However, unlike the DetailsView and the GridView, the FormView control doesn't support the CommandField class that automatically creates editing buttons. Instead, you'll need to create these buttons yourself.

To do so, you simply need to add a Button or LinkButton control and set its CommandName property to the appropriate value. For example, a Button with a CommandName set to Edit switches the FormView into edit mode. This technique is described earlier in this chapter, in the section "Editing Without a Command Column." For a quick refresher, refer to Table 10-10, which lists all the recognized command names you can use.

Table 10-10. *CommandName Values for FormView Editing*

Command Name	Description	Where It Belongs
Edit	Puts the FormView into edit mode. The FormView renders the current record using the EditItemTemplate with the edit controls you've defined.	The ItemTemplate
Cancel	Cancels the edit or insert operation and returns to the mode specified by the DefaultMode property. Usually, this will be normal mode (FormViewMode.ReadOnly), and the FormView will display the current record using the ItemTemplate.	The EditItemTemplate and InsertItemTemplate
Update	Applies the edit and raises the ItemUpdating and ItemUpdated events on the way.	The EditItemTemplate

Command Name	Description	Where It Belongs
New	Puts the FormView in insertion mode. The FormView displays a new, blank record using the InsertItemTemplate with the edit controls you've defined.	The ItemTemplate
Insert	Inserts the newly supplied data and raises the ItemInserting and ItemInserted events on the way.	The InsertItemTemplate
Delete	Removes the current record from the data source, raising the ItemDeleting and ItemDeleted events. Does not change the FormView mode.	The ItemTemplate

Advanced Grids

In the following sections, you'll consider a few ways to extend the GridView. You'll learn how to show summaries, create a complete master-details report on a single page, and display image data that's drawn from a database. You'll also see an example that uses advanced concurrency handling to warn the user about potential conflicts when updating a record.

Summaries in the GridView

Although the prime purpose of a GridView is to show a set of records, you can also add some more interesting information, such as summary data. The first step is to add the footer row by setting the GridView.ShowFooter property to true. This displays a shaded footer row (which you can customize freely), but it doesn't show any data. To take care of that task, you need insert the content into the GridView.FooterRow.

For example, imagine you're dealing with a list of products. A simple summary row could display the total or average product price. In the next example, the summary row displays the total value of all the in-stock products.

The first step is to decide when to calculate this information. If you're using manual binding, you could retrieve the data object and use it to perform your calculations before binding it to the GridView. However, if you're using declarative binding, you need another technique. You have two basic options—you can retrieve the data from the data object before the grid is bound, or you can retrieve it from the grid itself after the grid has been bound. The following example uses the latter approach because it gives you the freedom to use the same calculation code no matter what data source was used to populate the control. It also gives you the ability to total just the records that are displayed on the current page, if you've enabled paging. The disadvantage is that your code is tightly bound to the GridView, because you need to pull out the information you want by position, using hard-coded column index numbers.

In this example, a paged grid of products provides a summary that indicates the total price of all the products that are currently on display (see Figure 10-23 for the results).

```
<asp:GridView ID="gridSummary" runat="server" DataSourceID="sourceProducts"
 AllowPaging="True" OnDataBound="gridSummary_DataBound" ShowFooter="True" ... >
```

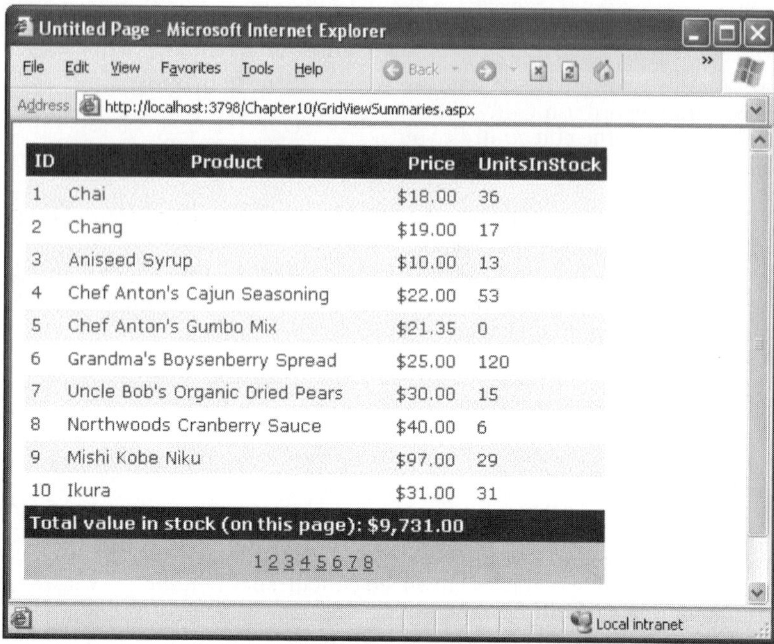

Figure 10-23. *A GridView with a footer summary*

To fill the footer, the code in this example reacts to the GridView.DataBound event. This occurs immediately after the GridView is populated with data. At this point, you can't access the data source any longer, but you can navigate through the GridView as a collection of rows and cells. Once this total is calculated, it's inserted into the footer row.

Here's the complete code:

```
protected void gridSummary_DataBound(object sender, EventArgs e)
{
    decimal valueInStock = 0;

    // The Rows collection includes only the rows that are displayed
    // on the current page (not "virtual" rows).
    foreach (GridViewRow row in gridSummary.Rows)
    {
        decimal price = Decimal.Parse(row.Cells[2].Text);
        int unitsInStock = Int32.Parse(row.Cells[3].Text);
        valueInStock += price * unitsInStock;
    }

    // Update the footer.
    GridViewRow footer = gridSummary.FooterRow;

    // Set the first cell to span over the entire row.
    footer.Cells[0].ColumnSpan = 3;
    footer.Cells[0].HorizontalAlign = HorizontalAlign.Center;
```

```
    // Remove the unneeded cells.
    footer.Cells.RemoveAt(2);
    footer.Cells.RemoveAt(1);

    // Add the text.
    footer.Cells[0].Text = "Total value in stock (on this page): " +
      valueInStock.ToString("C");
}
```

The summary row has the same number of columns as the rest of the grid. As a result, if you want your text to be displayed over multiple cells (as it is in this example), you need to configure cell spanning by setting the ColumnSpan property of the appropriate cell. In this example, the first cell spans over three columns (itself, and the next two on the right).

A Parent/Child View in a Single Table

Earlier in this chapter, you saw a master/detail page that used a GridView and DetailsView. This gives you the flexibility to show the child records for just the currently selected parent record. However, sometimes you want to create a parent/child report that shows all the records from the child table, organized by parent. For example, you could use this to create a complete list of products organized by category. The next example demonstrates how you show a complete, subgrouped product list in a single grid, as shown in Figure 10-24.

The basic technique is to create a GridView for the parent table that contains an embedded GridView for each row. These child GridView controls are inserted into the parent GridView using a TemplateField. The only trick is that you can't bind the child GridView controls at the same time that you bind the parent GridView, because the parent rows haven't been created yet. Instead, you need to wait for the GridView.DataBound event to fire in the parent.

In this example, the parent GridView defines two columns, both of which are the TemplateField type. The first column combines the category name and category description:

```
<asp:TemplateField HeaderText="Category">
  <ItemStyle VerticalAlign="Top" Width="20%"></ItemStyle>
  <ItemTemplate>
    <br />
    <b><%# Eval("CategoryName") %></b>
    <br /><br />
    <%# Eval("Description" ) %>
    <br />
  </ItemTemplate>
</asp:TemplateField>
```

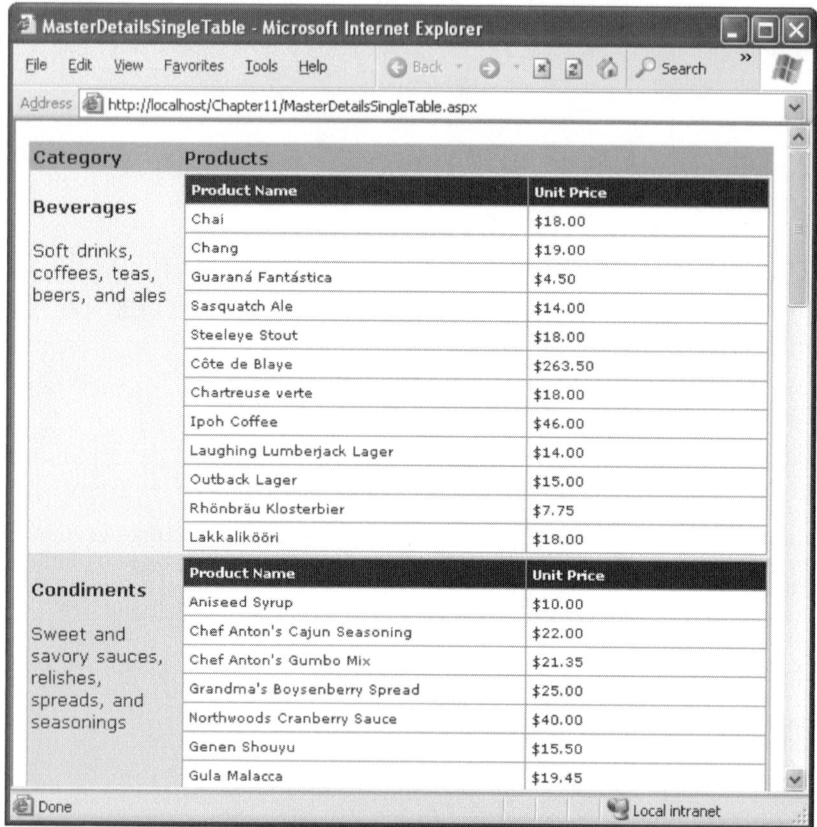

Figure 10-24. *A parent grid with embedded child grids*

The second column contains an embedded GridView of products, with two bound columns. Here's an excerpted listing that omits the style-related attributes:

```
<asp:TemplateField HeaderText="Products">
  <ItemStyle VerticalAlign="Top"></ItemStyle>
  <ItemTemplate>
    <asp:GridView ID="gridChild" runat="server">
      <Columns>
        <asp:BoundField DataField="ProductName"
         HeaderText="Product Name" />
        <asp:BoundField DataField="UnitPrice" HeaderText="Unit Price"
         DataFormatString="{0:C}" />
      </Columns>
    </asp:GridView>
  </ItemTemplate>
</asp:TemplateField>
```

You'll notice that the markup for the second GridView does *not* set the DataSourceID property. That's because the data source for each of these grids is supplied programmatically as the parent grid is being bound to its data source.

Now all you need to do is create two data sources, one for retrieving the list of categories and the other for retrieving all products in a specified category. The first data source provides the query that fills the parent GridView:

```
<asp:SqlDataSource ID="sourceCategories" runat="server"
 ConnectionString="<%$ ConnectionStrings:Northwind %>"
 ProviderName="System.Data.SqlClient"
 SelectCommand="SELECT * FROM Categories">
</asp:SqlDataSource>
```

You can bind the first grid directly to the data source, as shown here:

```
<asp:GridView id="gridMaster" runat="server" DataKeyNames="CategoryID"
 DataSourceID="sourceCategories" OnRowDataBound="gridMaster_RowDataBound" ... >
```

This part of the code is typical. The trick is to bind the child GridView controls. If you leave out this step, the child GridView controls won't appear.

The second data source contains the query that's called multiple times to fill the child GridView. Each time, it retrieves the products that are in a different category. The CategoryID is supplied as a parameter:

```
<asp:SqlDataSource ID="sourceProducts" runat="server"
 ConnectionString="<%$ ConnectionStrings:Northwind %>"
 ProviderName="System.Data.SqlClient"
 SelectCommand="SELECT * FROM Products WHERE CategoryID=@CategoryID">
  <SelectParameters>
    <asp:Parameter Name="CategoryID" Type="Int32" />
  </SelectParameters>
</asp:SqlDataSource>
```

To bind the child GridView controls, you need to react to the GridView.RowDataBound event, which fires every time a row is generated and bound to the parent GridView. At this point, you can retrieve the child GridView control from the second column and bind it to the product information by programmatically calling the Select() method of the data source. To ensure that you show only the products in the current category, you must also retrieve the CategoryID field for the current item and pass it as a parameter. Here's the code you need:

```
protected void gridMaster_RowDataBound(object sender, GridViewRowEventArgs e)
{
    // Look for data items.
    if (e.Row.RowType == DataControlRowType.DataRow)
    {
        // Retrieve the GridView control in the second column.
        GridView gridChild = (GridView)e.Row.Cells[1].Controls[1];

        // Set the CategoryID parameter so you get the products
        // in the current category only.
        string catID =
          gridMaster.DataKeys[e.Row.DataItemIndex].Value.ToString();
```

```
        sourceProducts.SelectParameters[0].DefaultValue = catID;

        // Get the data object from the data source.
        object data = sourceProducts.Select(DataSourceSelectArguments.Empty);

        // Bind the grid.
        gridChild.DataSource = data;
        gridChild.DataBind();
    }
}
```

Editing a Field Using a Lookup Table

In data-driven applications, you'll often encounter fields that are limited to a small list of predetermined values. This is particularly common when you're dealing with related tables. For example, consider the Products and Categories tables in the Northwind database. Clearly, every product must belong to an existing category. As a result, when you edit or create a new product, you must set the Products.CategoryID field to one of the CategoryID values that's in the Categories table.

When dealing with this sort of relationship, it's often helpful to use a *lookup list* for edit and insert operations. That way, you can choose the category from a list by name, rather than remember the numeric CategoryID value. Figure 10-25 shows a DetailsView that uses a lookup list to simplify category picking.

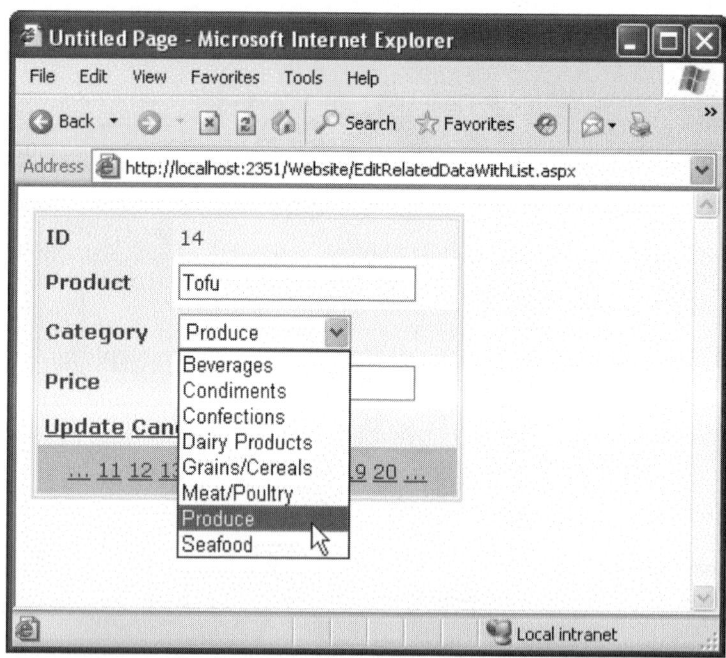

Figure 10-25. A lookup list using another table

You've already seen an example that uses a *fixed* lookup list for the TitleOfCourtesy field in the Employees table. In that example, the data and the currently selected value were retrieved by binding to custom methods in the page. The same approach works with this example, but you have an easier option—you can build the lookup list *declaratively* using a data source control.

Here's how it works. In your page, you need two data source controls. The first one fills the DetailsView, using a join query to get the category name information:

```
<asp:SqlDataSource ID="sourceProducts" runat="server"
 ConnectionString="<%$ ConnectionStrings:Northwind %>"
 ProviderName="System.Data.SqlClient" SelectCommand="SELECT ProductID,
ProductName, Products.CategoryID, CategoryName, UnitPrice FROM Products
INNER JOIN Categories ON Products.CategoryID=Categories.CategoryID"
  UpdateCommand="UPDATE Products SET ProductName=@ProductName,
CategoryID=@CategoryID, UnitPrice=@UnitPrice WHERE ProductID=@ProductID">
</asp:SqlDataSource>
```

This query gets all the rows from the Products table, but it's more likely you'll use a parameter (possibly from the query string or from another control) to select just a single record that interests you. Either way, the lookup list technique is the same.

The second data source control gets the full list of categories to use for the lookup list:

```
<asp:SqlDataSource ID="sourceCategories" runat="server"
 ConnectionString="<%$ ConnectionStrings:Northwind %>"
 ProviderName="System.Data.SqlClient"
 SelectCommand="SELECT CategoryName,CategoryID FROM Categories">
</asp:SqlDataSource>
```

The last step is to define the DetailsView control. This DetailsView is similar to the examples you've seen previously. The difference is that the CategoryID field uses a list box instead of a text box for editing, which requires a template.

```
<asp:DetailsView ID="detailsProducts" runat="server" AllowPaging="True"
 AutoGenerateEditButton="True" AutoGenerateRows="False"
 DataKeyNames="ProductID" DataSourceID="sourceProducts">
  ...
  <Fields>
    <asp:BoundField DataField="ProductID" HeaderText="ID" ReadOnly="True" />
    <asp:BoundField DataField="ProductName" HeaderText="Product" />
    <asp:TemplateField HeaderText="Category" >
      <ItemTemplate> ... </ItemTemplate>
      <EditItemTemplate>... </EditItemTemplate>
    </asp:TemplateField>
    <asp:BoundField DataField="UnitPrice" HeaderText="Price" />
  </Fields>
</asp:DetailsView>
```

In read-only mode, the template field simply shows the category name from the original query (without using the lookup list at all):

```
<ItemTemplate>
  <%# Eval("CategoryName") %>
</ItemTemplate>
```

In edit mode, the template uses a DropDownList control:

```
<EditItemTemplate>
  <asp:DropDownList id="lstCategories" runat="server"
    DataSourceID="sourceCategories"
    DataTextField="CategoryName" DataValueField="CategoryID"
    SelectedValue='<%# Bind("CategoryID")%>' >
  </asp:DropDownList>
</EditItemTemplate>
```

This control is bound in two ways. First, it gets its data from the lookup table of categories using the DataSourceID. The lookup table is bound to the list using the DataTextField and DataValueField properties. This creates a list of category names but keeps track of the matching ID for each item.

The trick is the SelectedValue property, which sets up the binding to the Products table. The SelectedValue property uses a data binding expression that gets (or sets) the current CategoryID value. That way, when you switch in edit mode, the correct category is selected automatically, and when you apply an update, the selected CategoryID is automatically sent to the data source control and applied to the database.

Serving Images from a Database

The data examples in this chapter retrieve text, numeric, and date information. However, databases often have the additional challenge of storing binary data such as pictures. For example, you might have a Products table that contains pictures of each item in a binary field. Retrieving this data in an ASP.NET web page is fairly easy, but displaying it is not as simple.

The basic problem is that in order to show an image in an HTML page, you need to add an image tag that links to a separate image file through the src attribute, as shown here:

```
<img src="myfile.gif" alt="My Image" />
```

Unfortunately, this isn't much help if you need to show image data dynamically. Although you can set the src attribute in code, you have no way to set the image *content* programmatically. You could first save the data to an image file on the web server's hard drive, but that approach would be dramatically slower, waste space, and raise the possibility of concurrency errors if multiple requests are being served at the same time and they are all trying to write the same file.

You can solve this problem in two ways. One approach is to store all your images in separate files. Then your database record simply needs to store the filename, and you can bind the filename to a server-side image. This is a perfectly reasonable solution, but it doesn't help in situations where you want to store images in the database so you can take advantage of the abilities of the RDBMS to cache data, log usage, and back up everything.

In these situations, the solution is to use a separate ASP.NET resource that returns the binary data directly. You can then use this binary data in other web pages in controls. To tackle this task, you also need to step outside the data binding and write custom ADO.NET code. The following sections will develop the solution you need piece by piece.

■ **Tip** As a general rule of thumb, storing images in a database works well as long as the images are not enormous (for example, more than 50 MB) and do not need to be frequently edited by other applications.

Displaying Binary Data

ASP.NET isn't restricted to returning HTML content. In fact, you can use the Response.BinaryWrite() method to return raw bytes and completely bypass the web-page model.

The following page uses this technique with the pub_info table in the pubs database (another standard database that's included with SQL Server). It retrieves the logo field, which contains binary image data. The page then writes this data directly to the page, as shown here:

```
protected void Page_Load(object sender, System.EventArgs e)
{
    string connectionString =
      WebConfigurationManager.ConnectionStrings["Pubs"].ConnectionString;
    SqlConnection con = new SqlConnection(connectionString);
    string SQL = "SELECT logo FROM pub_info WHERE pub_id='1389'";
    SqlCommand cmd = new SqlCommand(SQL, con);

    try
    {
        con.Open();
        SqlDataReader r = cmd.ExecuteReader();
        if (r.Read())
        {
            byte[] bytes = (byte[])r["logo"];
            Response.BinaryWrite(bytes);
        }
        r.Close();
    }
    finally
    {
        con.Close();
    }
}
```

Figure 10-26 shows the result. It doesn't appear terribly impressive (the logo data isn't that remarkable), but you could easily use the same technique with your own database, which can include much richer and larger images.

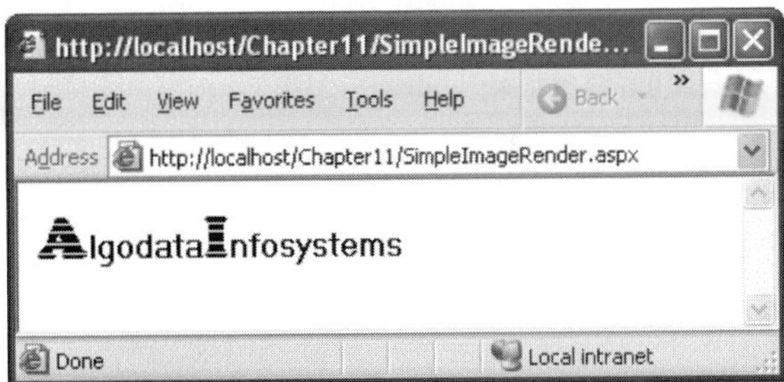

Figure 10-26. Displaying an image from a database

When you use BinaryWrite(), you are stepping away from the web-page model. If you add other controls to your web page, they won't appear. Similarly, Response.Write() won't have any effect, because you are no longer creating an HTML page. Instead, you're returning image data. You'll see how to solve this problem and optimize this approach in the following sections.

Reading Binary Data Efficiently

Binary data can easily grow to large sizes. However, if you're dealing with a large image file, the example shown previously will demonstrate woefully poor performance. The problem is that it uses the DataReader, which loads a single record into memory at a time. This is better than the DataSet (which loads the entire result set into memory at once), but it still isn't ideal if the field size is large.

There's no good reason to load an entire 2 MB picture into memory at once. A much better idea would be to read it piece by piece and then write each chunk to the output stream using Response.BinaryWrite(). Fortunately, the DataReader has a sequential access feature that supports this design. To use sequential access, you simply need to supply the CommandBehavior.SequentialAccess value to the Command.ExecuteReader() method. Then you can move through the row one block at a time, using the DataReader.GetBytes() method.

When using sequential access, you need to keep a couple of limitations in mind. First, you must read the data as a forward-only stream. Once you've read a block of data, you automatically move ahead in the stream, and there's no going back. Second, you must read the fields in the same order they are returned by your query. For example, if your query returns three columns, the third of which is a binary field, you must return the values of the first and second fields before accessing the binary data in the third field. If you access the third field first, you will not be able to access the first two fields.

Here's how you would revise the earlier page to use sequential access:

```
protected void Page_Load(object sender, System.EventArgs e)
{
    string connectionString =
      WebConfigurationManager.ConnectionStrings["Pubs"].ConnectionString;
    SqlConnection con = new SqlConnection(connectionString);
    string SQL = "SELECT logo FROM pub_info WHERE pub_id='1389'";
    SqlCommand cmd = new SqlCommand(SQL, con);

    try
    {
        con.Open();
        SqlDataReader r =
          cmd.ExecuteReader(CommandBehavior.SequentialAccess);

        if (r.Read())
        {
            int bufferSize = 100;                   // Size of the buffer.
            byte[] bytes = new byte[bufferSize];    // The buffer of data.
            long bytesRead;                         // The number of bytes read.
            long readFrom = 0;                      // The starting index.

            // Read the field 100 bytes at a time.
            do
            {
                bytesRead = r.GetBytes(0, readFrom, bytes, 0, bufferSize);
                Response.BinaryWrite(bytes);
                readFrom += bufferSize;
            } while (bytesRead == bufferSize);
        }
        r.Close();
    }
    finally
    {
        con.Close();
    }
}
```

The GetBytes() method returns a value that indicates the number of bytes retrieved. If you need to determine the total number of bytes in the field, you simply need to pass a null reference instead of a buffer when you call the GetBytes() method.

Integrating Images with Other Content

The Response.BinaryWrite() method creates a bit of a challenge if you want to integrate image data with other controls and HTML. That's because when you use BinaryWrite() to return raw image data, you lose the ability to add any extra HTML content.

To attack this problem, you need to create another page that calls your image-generating code. The best way to do this is to replace your image-generating page with a dedicated HTTP handler that generates image output. This way, you save the overhead of the full ASP.NET web form model, which you aren't using anyway. (Chapter 5 introduces HTTP handlers.)

Creating the HTTP handler you need is quite easy. You simply need to implement the IHttpHandler interface and implement the ProcessRequest() method (as you learned in Chapter 5). The HTTP handler will retrieve the ID of the record you want to display from the query string.

Here's the complete HTTP handler code:

```
public class ImageFromDB : IHttpHandler
{
    public void ProcessRequest(HttpContext context)
    {
        string connectionString =
          WebConfigurationManager.ConnectionStrings["Pubs"].ConnectionString;

        // Get the ID for this request.
        string id = context.Request.QueryString["id"];
        if (id == null) throw new ApplicationException("Must specify ID.");

        // Create a parameterized command for this record.
        SqlConnection con = new SqlConnection(connectionString);
        string SQL = "SELECT logo FROM pub_info WHERE pub_id=@ID";
        SqlCommand cmd = new SqlCommand(SQL, con);
        cmd.Parameters.AddWithValue("@ID", id);

        try
        {
            con.Open();
            SqlDataReader r =
              cmd.ExecuteReader(CommandBehavior.SequentialAccess);

            if (r.Read())
            {
                int bufferSize = 100;                   // Size of the buffer.
                byte[] bytes = new byte[bufferSize];    // The buffer.
                long bytesRead;                         // The # of bytes read.
                long readFrom = 0;                      // The starting index.

                // Read the field 100 bytes at a time.
                do
                {
                    bytesRead = r.GetBytes(0, readFrom, bytes, 0, bufferSize);
                    context.Response.BinaryWrite(bytes);
```

```
                readFrom += bufferSize;
            } while (bytesRead == bufferSize);
        }
        r.Close();
    }
    finally
    {
        con.Close();
    }
}

public bool IsReusable
{
    get { return true; }
}
}
```

Once you've created the HTTP handler, you need to register it in the web.config file, as shown here:

```
<httpHandlers>
  <add verb="GET" path="ImageFromDB.ashx"
    type="ImageFromDB" />
</httpHandlers>
```

Now you can retrieve the image data by requesting the HTTP handler URL, with the ID of the row that you want to retrieve. Here's an example:

```
ImageFromDB.ashx?ID=1389
```

To show this image content in another page, you simply need to set the src attribute of an image to this URL, as shown here:

```
<img src="ImageFromDB.ashx?ID=1389" alt="Logo" />
```

Figure 10-27 shows a page with multiple controls and logo images. It uses the following ItemTemplate in a GridView:

```
<ItemTemplate>
  <table border='1'><tr><td>
    <img src='ImageFromDB.ashx?ID=<%# Eval("pub_id")%>'/>
    </tr>
  <b><%# Eval("pub_name") %></b>
  <br />
  <%# Eval("city") %>,
  <%# Eval("state") %>,
  <%# Eval("country") %>
  <br /><br />
</ItemTemplate>
```

And it binds to this data source:

```
<asp:SqlDataSource ID="sourcePublishers"
 ConnectionString="<%$ ConnectionStrings:Pubs %>"
 SelectCommand="SELECT * FROM publishers" runat="server"/>
```

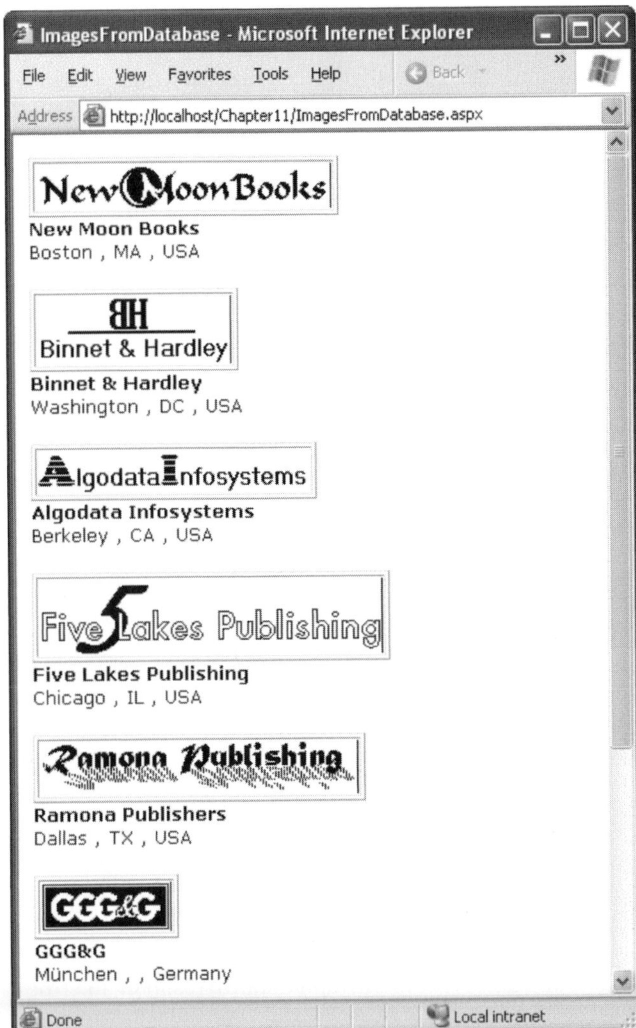

Figure 10-27. *Displaying database images in ASP.NET web page*

This current HTTP handler approach works well if you want to build a detail page with information about a single record. For example, you could show a list of publishers and then display the image for the appropriate publisher when the user makes a selection. However, this solution isn't as efficient if you want to show image data for every publisher at once, such as in a grid control. The approach still works, but it will be inefficient because it uses a separate request to the HTTP handler (and hence a separate database connection) to retrieve each image. You can solve this problem by creating an HTTP handler that checks for image data in the cache before retrieving it from the database. Before you bind the GridView, you would then perform a query that returns all the records with their image data and load each image into the cache.

Detecting Concurrency Conflicts

As discussed in Chapter 8, if a web application allows multiple users to make changes, it's quite possible for two or more edits to overlap. Depending on the way these edits overlap and the concurrency strategy you're using (see the section "Concurrency Strategies" in Chapter 8 for more information), this could inadvertently result in committing stale values back to the database.

To prevent this problem, developers often use match-all or timestamp-based concurrency. The idea here is that the UPDATE statement must match every value from the original record, or the update won't be allowed to continue. Here's an example:

```
UPDATE Shippers SET CompanyName=@CompanyName, Phone=@Phone
 WHERE ShipperID=@original_ShipperID AND CompanyName=@original_CompanyName
 AND Phone=@original_Phone"
```

SQL Server uses the index on the ShipperID primary key to find the record and then compares the other fields to make sure it matches. Now the update can succeed only if the values in the record match what the user saw when making the changes.

■ **Note** As indicated in Chapter 8, timestamps are a better way to handle this problem than explicitly matching every field. However, this example uses the match-all approach because it works with the existing Northwind database. Otherwise, you would need to add a new timestamp column.

The problem with a match-all concurrency strategy is that it can lead to failed edits. Namely, if the record has changed in between the time the user queried the record and applied the update, the update won't succeed. In fact, the data-bound controls won't even warn you of the problem; they'll just execute the UPDATE statement without any effect, because this isn't considered an error condition.

If you decide to use match-all concurrency, you'll need to at least check for lost updates. You can do this by handling the RowUpdated event of the GridView control, or the ItemUpdated event of the DetailsView, FormView, or ListView controls. In your event handler you can check the AffectedRows property of the appropriate EventArgs object (such as GridViewUpdatedEventArgs). If this property is 0, no records were updated, which is almost always because another edit changed the record and the WHERE clause in the UPDATE statement couldn't match anything. (Other errors, such as trying an update that fails because it violates a key constraint or tries to commit invalid data, *do* result in an error being raised by the data source.)

Here's an example that checks for a failed update in the DetailsView control and then informs the user of the problem:

```
protected void DetailsView1_ItemUpdated(object sender,
  DetailsViewUpdatedEventArgs e)
{
    if (e.AffectedRows == 0)
    {
        lblStatus.Text = "A conflicting change has already been made to this " +
          " record by another user. No records were updated.";
    }
}
```

Unfortunately, this doesn't make for the most user-friendly web application. It's particularly a problem if the record has several fields, or if the fields take detailed information, because these edits are simply discarded, forcing the user to start from scratch.

A better solution is to give the user a choice. Ideally, the page would show the current value of the record (taking any recent changes into account) and allow the user to apply the original edited values, cancel the update, or make additional refinements and then apply the update. It's actually quite easy to build a page that provides these niceties. Figure 10-28 shows an example. It warns the user when changing *United Package* to *United Packages* that another user has already modified the record, changing the company name to *United Package Mailer*. The user then has the choice to keep the recently edited name or overwrite it with the new value.

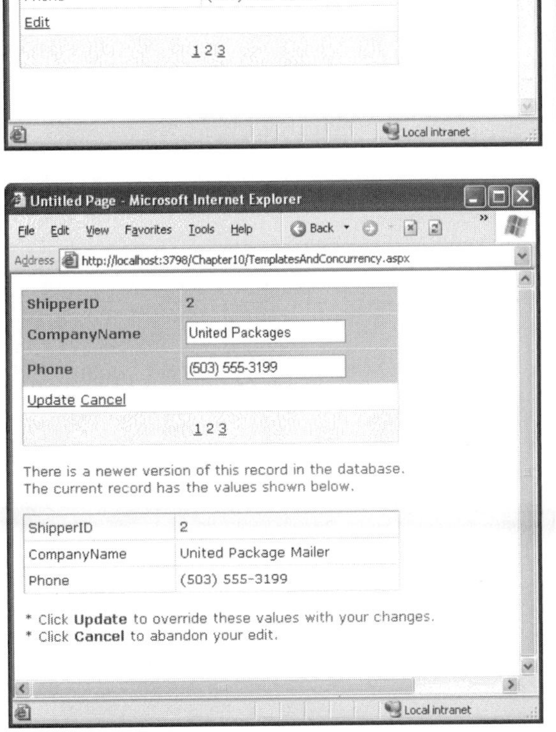

***Figure 10-28.** Detecting a concurrency error during an edit*

First, start with a DetailsView that allows the user to edit individual records from the Shippers table in the Northwind database. (The Shippers table is fairly easy to use with match-all concurrency because it has only three fields. Larger tables work better with the equivalent timestamp-based approach.)

Here's an abbreviated definition of the DetailsView you need:

```
<asp:DetailsView ID="detailsEditing" runat="server"
 DataKeyNames="ShipperID" AllowPaging="True" AutoGenerateRows="False"
 DataSourceID="sourceShippers" OnItemUpdated="detailsEditing_ItemUpdated" ...>
  <Fields>
    <asp:BoundField DataField="ShipperID" ReadOnly="True" />
    <asp:BoundField DataField="CompanyName" />
    <asp:BoundField DataField="Phone" />
    <asp:CommandField ShowEditButton="True" />
  </Fields>
  ...
</asp:DetailsView>
```

The data source control that's bound to the DetailsView uses a match-all UPDATE expression to implement strict concurrency:

```
<asp:SqlDataSource ID="sourceShippers" runat="server"
 ConnectionString="<%$ ConnectionStrings:Northwind %>"
 SelectCommand="SELECT * FROM Shippers" UpdateCommand="UPDATE Shippers SET
CompanyName=@CompanyName, Phone=@Phone WHERE ShipperID=@original_ShipperID AND
CompanyName=@original_CompanyName AND Phone=@original_Phone"
 ConflictDetection="CompareAllValues" OldValuesParameterFormatString="original_{0}">
  <UpdateParameters>
    <asp:Parameter Name="CompanyName" />
    <asp:Parameter Name="Phone" />
    <asp:Parameter Name="original_ShipperID" />
    <asp:Parameter Name="original_CompanyName" />
    <asp:Parameter Name="original_Phone" />
  </UpdateParameters>
</asp:SqlDataSource>
```

You'll notice the SqlDataSource.ConflictDetection property is set to CompareAllValues, which ensures that the values from the original record are submitted as parameters (using the prefix defined by the OldValuesParameterFormatString property).

Most of the work takes place in response to the DetailsView.ItemUpdated event. Here, the code catches all failed updates and explicitly keeps the DetailsView in edit mode.

```
protected void detailsEditing_ItemUpdated(object sender,
 DetailsViewUpdatedEventArgs e)
{
    if (e.AffectedRows == 0)
    {
        e.KeepInEditMode = true;
    ...
```

But the real trick is to rebind the data control. This way, all the original values in the DetailsView are reset to match the values in the database. That means the update can succeed (if the user tries to apply it again).

```
        ...
        detailsEditing.DataBind();
        ...
```

Rebinding the grid is the secret, but there's still more to do. To maintain the values that the user is trying to apply, you need to manually copy them back into the newly bound data control. This is easy but a little tedious.

```
        ...
        // Repopulate the DetailsView with the edit values.
        TextBox txt;
        txt = (TextBox)detailsEditing.Rows[1].Cells[1].Controls[0];
        txt.Text = (string)e.NewValues["CompanyName"];
        txt = (TextBox)detailsEditing.Rows[2].Cells[1].Controls[0];
        txt.Text = (string)e.NewValues["Phone"];
        ...
```

At this point, you have a data control that can detect a failed update, rebind itself, and reinsert the values the user's trying to apply. That means if the user clicks Update a second time, the update will now succeed (assuming the record isn't changed yet again by another user).

However, this still has one shortcoming. The user might not have enough information at this point to decide whether to apply the update. Most likely, he'll want to know what changes were made before he overwrites them. One way to handle this problem is to list the current values in a label or another control. In this example, the code simply unhides a Panel control that contains an explanatory message and another DetailsView:

```
        ...
        ErrorPanel.Visible = true;
    }
}
```

The error panel describes the problem with an informative error message and contains a second DetailsView that binds to the matching row to show the current value of the record in question.

```
<asp:Panel ID="ErrorPanel" runat="server" Visible="False" EnableViewState="False">
  There is a newer version of this record in the database.<br />
  The current record has the values shown below.<br />
  <br />
  <asp:DetailsView ID="detailsConflicting" runat="server"
    AutoGenerateRows="False" DataSourceID="sourceUpdateValues" ...>
    <Fields>
      <asp:BoundField DataField="ShipperID" />
      <asp:BoundField DataField="CompanyName" />
      <asp:BoundField DataField="Phone" />
    </Fields>
    ...
  </asp:DetailsView>

  <br />
  * Click <b>Update</b> to override these values with your changes.<br />
  * Click <b>Cancel</b> to abandon your edit.</span> 
  <asp:SqlDataSource ConnectionString="<%$ ConnectionStrings:Northwind %>"
   ID="sourceUpdateValues" runat="server"
   SelectCommand="SELECT * FROM Shippers WHERE (ShipperID = @ShipperID)"
   OnSelecting="sourceUpdateValues_Selecting">
    <SelectParameters>
      <asp:ControlParameter ControlID="detailsEditing" Name="ShipperID"
```

```
      PropertyName="SelectedValue" Type="Int32" />
    </SelectParameters>
  </asp:SqlDataSource>
</asp:Panel>
```

There's one last detail. To save overhead, there's no point in performing the query for the second DetailsView unless it's absolutely necessary because a concurrency error occurred. To implement this logic, the code reacts to the SqlDataSource.Selecting event for the second SqlDataSource control (sourceUpdateValues) and cancels the query if the error panel isn't currently visible.

```
protected void sourceUpdateValues_Selecting(object sender,
 SqlDataSourceSelectingEventArgs e)
{
    if (!ErrorPanel.Visible) e.Cancel = true;
}
```

To try this example, open two copies of the page in separate browser windows and put both into edit mode for the same row. Apply the first change (by clicking the Update button), and then apply the second one. When you attempt to apply the second one, the error panel will appear, with the explanation (see Figure 10-28). You can then choose to continue with the edit by clicking Update or to abandon it by clicking Cancel.

Summary

In this chapter, you considered everything you need to build rich data-bound pages. You took an exhaustive tour of the GridView and considered its support for formatting, selection, sorting, paging, templates, and editing. You also considered the template-based ListView and the data controls that are designed to work with a single record at a time: the DetailsView and FormView. Finally, the chapter wrapped up by looking at several common advanced scenarios with data-bound pages.

CHAPTER 11

■ ■ ■

Caching and Asynchronous Pages

Caching is the technique of storing an in-memory copy of some information that's expensive to create. For example, you could cache the results of a complex query so that subsequent requests don't need to access the database at all. Instead, they can grab the appropriate object directly from server memory—a much faster proposition. The real beauty of caching is that unlike many other performance-enhancing techniques, caching bolsters both performance and scalability. Performance is better because the time taken to retrieve the information is cut down dramatically. Scalability is improved because you work around bottlenecks such as database connections. As a result, the application can serve more simultaneous page requests with fewer database operations.

Of course, storing information in memory isn't always a good idea. Server memory is a limited resource; if you try to store too much, some of that information will be paged to disk, potentially slowing down the entire system. That's why the best caching strategies (such as those hard-wired into ASP.NET) are self-limiting. When you store information in a cache, you expect to find it there on a future request most of the time. However, the lifetime of that information is at the discretion of the server. If the cache becomes full or other applications consume a large amount of memory, information will be selectively evicted from the cache, ensuring that performance is maintained. It's this self-sufficiency that makes caching so powerful (and so complicated to implement on your own).

With ASP.NET, you get first-rate caching for free, and you have a variety of options. You can cache the completely rendered HTML for a page, a portion of that HTML, or arbitrary objects. You can also customize expiration policies and set up dependencies so that items are automatically removed when other resources—such as files or database tables—are modified.

■ **What's New** ASP.NET 4 adds support for creating custom output cache providers. Ideally, third-party developers will use these features to create components that work with other types of storage—for example, hard drives, databases, the Web, and so on. You'll learn more in the "Output Caching Extensibility" section.

Understanding ASP.NET Caching

Many developers who learn about caching see it as a bit of a frill, but nothing could be further from the truth. Used intelligently, caching can provide a twofold, threefold, or even tenfold performance improvement by retaining important data for just a short period of time.

ASP.NET really has two types of caching. Your applications can and should use both types, because they complement each other:

- **Output caching:** This is the simplest type of caching. It stores a copy of the final rendered HTML page that is sent to the client. The next client that submits a request for this page doesn't actually run the page. Instead, the final HTML output is sent automatically. The time that would have been required to run the page and its code is completely reclaimed.
- **Data caching:** This type of caching is carried out manually in your code. To use data caching, you store important pieces of information that are time-consuming to reconstruct (such as a DataSet retrieved from a database) in the cache. Other pages can check for the existence of this information and use it, thereby bypassing the steps ordinarily required to retrieve it. Data caching is conceptually the same as using application state, but it's much more server-friendly because items will be removed from the cache automatically when it grows too large and performance could be affected. Items can also be set to expire automatically.

Also, two specialized types of caching build on these models:

- **Fragment caching:** This is a specialized type of output caching—instead of caching the HTML for the whole page, it allows you to cache the HTML for a portion of it. Fragment caching works by storing the rendered HTML output of a user control on a page. The next time the page is executed, the same page events fire (and so your page code will still run), but the code for the appropriate user control isn't executed.
- **Data source caching:** This is the caching that's built into the data source controls, including the SqlDataSource, ObjectDataSource, and XmlDataSource. Technically, data source caching uses data caching. The difference is that you don't need to handle the process explicitly. Instead, you simply configure the appropriate properties, and the data source control manages the caching storage and retrieval.

In this chapter, you'll consider every caching option. You'll begin by considering the basics of output caching and data caching. Next, you'll consider the caching in the data source controls. Finally, you'll explore one of ASP.NET's hottest caching features—linking cached items to tables in a database with SQL cache dependencies.

Output Caching

With output caching, the final rendered HTML of the page is cached. When the same page is requested again, the control objects are not created, the page life cycle doesn't start, and none of your code executes. Instead, the cached HTML is served. Clearly, output caching gets the theoretical maximum performance increase, because all the overhead of your code is sidestepped.

■ **Note** An ASP.NET page may use other static resources (such as images) that aren't handled by ASP.NET. Don't worry about caching these items. IIS automatically handles the caching of files in the most efficient way possible.

Declarative Output Caching

To see output caching in action, you can create a simple page that displays the current time of day. Figure 11-1 shows an example.

The code for this page is straightforward. It simply sets the date to appear in a label when the Page.Load event fires:

```
protected void Page_Load(Object sender, EventArgs e)
{
    lblDate.Text = "The time is now:<br />";
    lblDate.Text += DateTime.Now.ToString();
}
```

You have two ways to add this page to the output cache. The most common approach is to insert the OutputCache directive at the top of your .aspx file, just below the Page directive:

```
<%@ OutputCache Duration="20" VaryByParam="None" %>
```

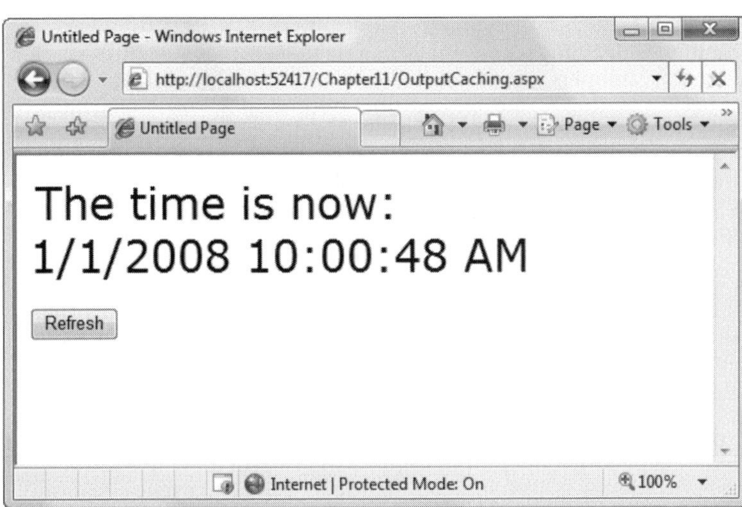

Figure 11-1. *Caching an entire page*

In this example, the Duration attribute instructs ASP.NET to cache the page for 20 seconds. The VaryByParam attribute is also required, but you'll learn about its effect in the next section.

When you run the test page, you'll discover some interesting behavior. The first time you access the page, the current date will be displayed. If you refresh the page a short time later, however, the page will not be updated. Instead, ASP.NET will automatically send the cached HTML output to you (assuming 20 seconds haven't elapsed, and therefore the cached copy of the page hasn't expired). If ASP.NET receives a request after the cached page has expired, ASP.NET will run the page code again, generate a new cached copy of the HTML output, and use that for the next 20 seconds.

Twenty seconds may seem like a trivial amount of time, but in a high-volume site, it can make a dramatic difference. For example, you might cache a page that provides a list of products from a catalog. By caching the page for 20 seconds, you limit database access for this page to three operations per minute. Without caching, the page will try to connect to the database once for each client and could easily make dozens of requests in a minute.

Of course, just because you request that a page should be stored for 20 seconds doesn't mean it actually will be. The page could be evicted from the cache early if the system finds that memory is becoming scarce. This allows you to use caching freely, without worrying too much about hampering your application by using up vital memory.

■ **Tip** When you recompile a cached page, ASP.NET will automatically remove the page from the cache. This prevents problems where a page isn't properly updated because the older, cached version is being used. However, you might still want to disable caching while testing your application. Otherwise, you may have trouble using variable watches, breakpoints, and other debugging techniques, because your code will not be executed if a cached copy of the page is available.

Caching and the Query String

One of the main considerations in caching is deciding when a page can be reused and when information must be accurate up to the latest second. Developers, with their love of instant gratification (and lack of patience), generally tend to overemphasize the importance of real-time information. You can usually use caching to efficiently reuse slightly stale data without a problem, and with a considerable performance improvement.

Of course, sometimes information needs to be dynamic. One example is if the page uses information from the current user's session to tailor the user interface. In this case, full page caching just isn't appropriate (although fragment caching may help). Another example is if the page is receiving information from another page through the query string. In this case, the page is too dynamic to cache—or is it?

The current example sets the VaryByParam attribute to None, which effectively tells ASP.NET that you need to store only one copy of the cached page, which is suitable for all scenarios. If the request for this page adds query string arguments to the URL, it makes no difference—ASP.NET will always reuse the same output until it expires. You can test this by adding a query string parameter manually in the browser window (such as ?a=b).

Based on this experiment, you might assume that output caching isn't suitable for pages that use query string arguments. But ASP.NET actually provides another option. You can set the VaryByParam attribute to * to indicate that the page uses the query string and to instruct ASP.NET to cache separate copies of the page for different query string arguments, as shown here:

```
<%@ OutputCache Duration="20" VaryByParam="*" %>
```

Now when you request the page with additional query string information, ASP.NET will examine the query string. If the string matches a previous request, and a cached copy of that page exists, it will be reused. Otherwise, a new copy of the page will be created and cached separately.

To get a better idea how this process works, consider the following series of requests:

1. You request a page without any query string parameter and receive page copy A.
2. You request the page with the parameter ProductID=1. You receive page copy B.
3. Another user requests the page with the parameter ProductID=2. That user receives copy C.
4. Another user requests the page with ProductID=1. If the cached output B has not expired, it's sent to the user.

5. The user then requests the page with no query string parameters. If copy A has not expired, it's sent from the cache.

You can try this on your own, although you might want to lengthen the amount of time that the cached page is retained to make it easier to test.

Caching with Specific Query String Parameters

Setting VaryByParam="*" allows you to use caching with dynamic pages that vary their output based on the query string. This approach could be extremely useful for a product detail page, which receives a product ID in its query string. With vary-by-parameter caching, you could store a separate page for each product, thereby saving a trip to the database. However, to gain performance benefits you might have to increase the cached output lifetime to several minutes or longer.

Of course, this technique has some potential problems. Pages that accept a wide range of different query string parameters (such as a page that receives numbers for a calculation, client information, or search keywords) just aren't suited to output caching. The possible number of variations is enormous, and the potential reuse is low. Though these pages will be evicted from the cache when the memory is needed, they could inadvertently force other more important information from the cache first or slow down other operations.

In many cases, setting VaryByParam to the wildcard asterisk (*) is unnecessarily vague. It's usually better to specifically identify an important query string variable by name. Here's an example:

```
<%@ OutputCache Duration="20" VaryByParam="ProductID" %>
```

In this case, ASP.NET will examine the query string looking for the ProductID parameter. Requests with different ProductID parameters will be cached separately, but all other parameters will be ignored. This is particularly useful if the page may be passed additional query string information that it doesn't use. ASP.NET has no way to distinguish the "important" query string parameters without your help.

You can specify several parameters, as long as you separate them with semicolons, as follows:

```
<%@ OutputCache Duration="20" VaryByParam="ProductID;CurrencyType" %>
```

In this case, the query string will cache separate versions, provided the query string differs by ProductID or CurrencyType.

■ **Note** Output caching works well with pages that vary only based on server-side data (for example, the data in a database) and the data in query strings. However, output caching doesn't work if the page output depends on user-specific information such as session data or cookies. Output caching also won't work with event-driven pages that use forms. In these cases, events will be ignored, and a static page will be re-sent with each postback, effectively disabling the page. To avoid these problems, use fragment caching instead to cache a portion of the page or use data caching to cache specific information.

Custom Caching Control

Varying by query string parameters isn't the only option when storing multiple cached versions of a page. ASP.NET also allows you to create your own procedure that decides whether to cache a new page version or reuse an existing one. This code examines whatever information is appropriate and then returns a string. ASP.NET uses this string to implement caching. If your code generates the same string for different requests, ASP.NET will reuse the cached page. If your code generates a new string value, ASP.NET will generate a new cached version and store it separately.

One way you could use custom caching is to cache different versions of a page based on the browser type. That way, Firefox browsers will always receive Firefox-optimized pages, and Internet Explorer users will receive Internet Explorer-optimized HTML. To set up this sort of logic, you start by adding the OutputCache directive to the pages that will be cached. Use the VaryByCustom attribute to specify a name that represents the type of custom caching you're creating. (You can pick any name you like.) The following example uses the name browser because pages will be cached based on the client browser:

```
<%@ OutputCache Duration="10" VaryByParam="None" VaryByCustom="browser" %>
```

Next, you need to create the procedure that will generate the custom caching string. This procedure must be coded in the global.asax application file, as shown here:

```
public override string GetVaryByCustomString(
  HttpContext context, string arg)
{
    // Check for the requested type of caching.
    if (arg == "browser")
    {
       // Determine the current browser.
       string browserName;
       browserName = Context.Request.Browser.Browser;
       browserName += Context.Request.Browser.MajorVersion.ToString();

       // Indicate that this string should be used to vary caching.
       return browserName;
    }
    else
    {
        return base.GetVaryByCustomString(context, arg);
    }
}
```

The GetVaryByCustomString() function passes the VaryByCustom name in the arg parameter. This allows you to create an application that implements several types of custom caching in the same function. Each different type would use a different VaryByCustom name (such as Browser, BrowserVersion, or DayOfWeek). Your GetVaryByCustomString() function would examine the VaryByCustom name and then return the appropriate caching string. If the caching strings for different requests match, ASP.NET will reuse the cached copy of the page. Or, to look at it another way, ASP.NET will create and store a separate cached version of the page for each caching string it encounters.

Interestingly, the base implementation of the GetVaryByCustomString() already includes the logic for browser-based caching. That means you don't need to code the method shown previously. The base implementation of GetVaryByCustomString() creates the cached string based on the browser name and major version number. If you want to change how this logic works (for example, to vary based on name, major version, and minor version), you could override the GetVaryByCustomString() method, as in the previous example.

■ **Note** Varying by browser is an important technique for cached pages that use browser-specific features. For example, if your page generates client-side JavaScript that's not supported by all browsers, you should make the caching dependent on the browser version. Of course, it's still up to your code to identify the browser and choose what JavaScript to render. You'll learn more about adaptive pages and JavaScript in Part 5.

The OutputCache directive also has a third attribute that you can use to define caching. This attribute, VaryByHeader, allows you to store separate versions of a page based on the value of an HTTP header received with the request. You can specify a single header or a list of headers separated by semicolons. You could use this technique with multilingual sites to cache different versions of a page based on the client browser language, as follows:

```
<%@ OutputCache Duration="20" VaryByParam="None"
    VaryByHeader="Accept-Language" %>
```

Caching with the HttpCachePolicy Class

Using the OutputCache directive is generally the preferred way to cache a page, because it separates the caching instruction from the rest of your code. The OutputCache directive also makes it easy to configure several advanced properties in one line.

However, you have another choice: You can write code that uses the built-in special Response.Cache property, which provides an instance of the System.Web.HttpCachePolicy class. This object provides properties that allow you to turn on caching for the current page. This allows you to decide programmatically whether you want to enable output caching.

In the following example, the date page has been rewritten so that it automatically enables caching when the page is first loaded. This code enables caching with the SetCacheability() method, which specifies that the page will be cached on the server and that any other client can use the cached copy of the page. The SetExpires() method defines the expiration date for the page, which is set to be the current time plus 60 seconds.

```
protected void Page_Load(Object sender, EventArgs e)
{
    // Cache this page on the server.
    Response.Cache.SetCacheability(HttpCacheability.Public);

    // Use the cached copy of this page for the next 60 seconds.
    Response.Cache.SetExpires(DateTime.Now.AddSeconds(60));

    // This additional line ensures that the browser can't
    // invalidate the page when the user clicks the Refresh button
    // (which some rogue browsers attempt to do).
    Response.Cache.SetValidUntilExpires(true);

    lblDate.Text = "The time is now:<br />" + DateTime.Now.ToString();
}
```

Programmatic caching isn't as clean from a design point of view. Embedding the caching code directly into your page is often awkward, and it's always messy if you need to include other initialization code in your page. Remember, the code in the Page.Load event handler runs only if your page isn't in the cache (either because this is the first request for the page, because the last cached version has expired, or because the request parameters don't match).

■ **Tip** Make sure you use the Response.Cache property of the page, not the Page.Cache property. The Page.Cache property isn't used for output caching—instead, it gives you access to the data cache (discussed in the "Data Caching" section).

Post-Cache Substitution and Fragment Caching

In some cases, you may find that you can't cache an entire page, but you would still like to cache a portion that is expensive to create and doesn't vary. You have two ways to handle this challenge:

Fragment caching: In this case, you identify just the content you want to cache, wrap that in a dedicated user control, and cache just the output from that control.

Post-cache substitution: In this case, you identify just the dynamic content you don't want to cache. You then replace this content with something else using the Substitution control.

Out of the two, fragment caching is the easiest to implement. However, the decision of which you want to use will usually be based on the amount of content you want to cache. If you have a small, distinct portion of content to cache, fragment caching makes the most sense. Conversely, if you have only a small bit of dynamic content, post-cache substitution may be the more straightforward approach. Both approaches offer similar performance.

■ **Tip** The most flexible way to implement a partial caching scenario is to step away from output caching altogether and use data caching to handle the process programmatically in your code. You'll see this technique in the "Data Caching" section.

Fragment Caching

To implement fragment caching, you need to create a user control for the portion of the page you want to cache. You can then add the OutputCache directive to the user control. The result is that the page will not be cached, but the user control will. (Chapter 15 discusses user controls in detail.)

Fragment caching is conceptually the same as page caching. There is only one catch—if your page retrieves a cached version of a user control, it cannot interact with it in code. For example, if your user control provides properties, your web-page code cannot modify or access these properties. When the cached version of the user control is used, a block of HTML is simply inserted into the page. The corresponding user control object is not available.

Post-Cache Substitution

The post-cache substitution feature revolves around a single method that has been added to the HttpResponse class. The method is WriteSubstitution(), and it accepts a single parameter—a delegate that points to a callback method that you implement in your page class. This callback method returns the content for that portion of the page.

Here's the trick: when the ASP.NET page framework retrieves the cached page, it automatically triggers your callback method to get the dynamic content. It then inserts your content into the cached HTML of the page. The nice thing is that even if your page hasn't been cached yet (for example, if it's being rendered for the first time), ASP.NET still calls your callback in the same way to get the dynamic content. In essence, the whole idea is that you create a method that generates some dynamic content, and by doing so you guarantee that your method is always called, and its content is never cached.

The method that generates the dynamic content needs to be static. That's because ASP.NET needs to be able to call this method even when there isn't an instance of your page class available. (Obviously, when your page is served from the cache, the page object isn't created.) The signature for the method is fairly straightforward—it accepts an HttpContext object that represents the current request, and it returns a string with the new HTML. Here's an example that returns a date with bold formatting:

```
private static string GetDate(HttpContext context)
{
    return "<b>" + DateTime.Now.ToString() + "</b>";
}
```

To get this in the page, you need to use the Response.WriteSubstitution() method at some point:

```
protected void Page_Load(object sender, EventArgs e)
{
    Response.Write("This date is cached with the page: ");
    Response.Write(DateTime.Now.ToString() + "<br />");
    Response.Write("This date is not: ");
    Response.WriteSubstitution(new HttpResponseSubstitutionCallback(GetDate));
}
```

Now, even if you apply caching to this page with the OutputCache directive, the second date that's displayed on the page will still be updated for each request. That's because the callback bypasses the caching process. Figure 11-2 shows the result of running the page and refreshing it several times.

The problem with this technique is that post-cache substitution works at a lower level than the rest of your user interface. Usually, when you design an ASP.NET page, you don't use the Response object at all—instead, you use web controls, and those web controls use the Response object to generate their content. One problem is that if you use the Response object as shown in the previous example, you'll lose the ability to position your content with respect to the rest of the page. The only realistic solution is to wrap your dynamic content in some sort of control. That way, the control can use Response.WriteSubstitution() when it renders itself. You'll learn more about control rendering in Chapter 27.

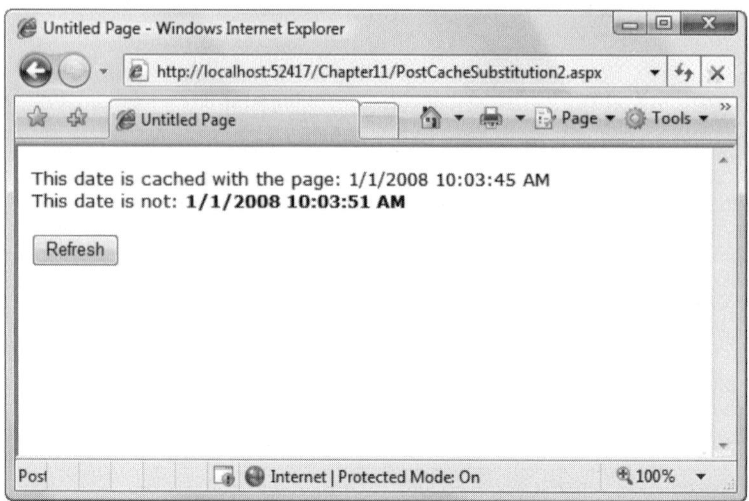

Figure 11-2. Injecting dynamic content into a cached page

However, if you don't want to go to the work of developing a custom control just to get the post-cache substitution feature, ASP.NET has one shortcut—a generic Substitution control that uses this technique to make all its content dynamic. You bind the Substitution control to a static method that returns your dynamic content, exactly as in the previous example. However, you can place the Substitution control alongside other ASP.NET controls, allowing you to control exactly where the dynamic content appears.

Here's an example that duplicates the earlier example using markup in the .aspx portion of the page:

```
This date is cached with the page:
<asp:Label ID="lblDate" runat="server" /><br />
This date is not:
<asp:Substitution ID="Substitution1" runat="server" MethodName="GetDate" />
```

Unfortunately, at design time you won't see the content for the Substitution control.

Remember, post-cache substitution allows you to execute only a static method. ASP.NET still skips the page life cycle, which means it won't create any control objects or raise any control events. If your dynamic content depends on the values of other controls, you'll need to use a different technique (such as data caching), because these control objects won't be available to your callback.

■ **Note** Custom controls are free to use Response.WriteSubstitution() to set their caching behavior. For example, the AdRotator uses this feature to ensure that the advertisement on a page is always rotated, even when the rest of the page is served from the output cache.

Cache Profiles

One problem with output caching is that you need to embed the instruction into the page—either in the .aspx markup portion or in the code of the class. Although the first option (using the OutputCache) is relatively clean, it still produces management problems if you create dozens of cached pages. If you want to change the caching for all these pages (for example, moving the caching duration from 30 to 60 seconds), you need to modify every page. ASP.NET also needs to recompile these pages.

ASP.NET also allows you to apply the same caching settings to a group of pages with a feature called cache profiles. Using cache profiles, you define caching settings in the web.config file, associate a name with these settings, and then apply these settings to multiple pages using the name. That way, you have the freedom to modify all the linked pages at once simply by changing the caching profile in the web.config file.

To define a cache profile, you use the <add> tag in the <outputCacheProfiles> section, as follows. You assign a name and a duration.

```
<configuration>
  <system.web>
    <caching>
      <outputCacheSettings>
        <outputCacheProfiles>
          <add name="ProductItemCacheProfile" duration="60" />
        </outputCacheProfiles>
      </outputCacheSettings>
    </caching>
  ...
  </system.web>
</configuration>
```

You can now use this profile in a page through the CacheProfile attribute:

```
<%@ OutputCache CacheProfile="ProductItemCacheProfile" VaryByParam="None" %>
```

Interestingly, if you want to apply other caching details, such as the VaryByParam behavior, you can set it either as an attribute in the OutputCache directive or as an attribute of the <add> tag for the profile. Just make sure you start with a lowercase letter if you use the <add> tag, because the property names are camel case, as are all configuration settings, and case is important in XML.

Cache Configuration

You can also configure various details about ASP.NET's cache behavior through the web.config file. Many of these options are intended for easier debugging, and may not make sense in a production application.

To configure these settings, you use the <cache> element inside the <caching> element described previously. The <cache> element gives you several options to tweak, as shown here:

```
<configuration>
  <system.web>
    <caching>
      <cache disableMemoryCollection="true|false"
         disableExpiration="true|false"
         percentagePhysicalMemoryUsedLimit="90"
         privateBytesLimit="0"
         privateBytesPollTime="00:02:00"
```

```
        />
        ...
    </caching>
  </system.web>
  ...
</configuration>
```

Use disableMemoryCollection and disableExpiration to stop ASP.NET from collecting items when memory is low (a process called scavenging) and removing expired items. Use caution with these settings, as you could easily cause your application to run out of memory under these settings. Use percentagePhysicalMemoryUsedLimit to set the maximum percentage of a computer's physical memory that ASP.NET will use for the cache. When the cache reaches the memory target, ASP.NET begins to use aggressive scavenging to remove older and less used items. A value of 0 indicates that no memory should be set aside for the cache, and ASP.NET will remove items as fast as they're added. By default, ASP.NET uses up to 90% of physical memory for caching.

The privateBytesLimit setting determines the maximum number of bytes a specific application can use for its cache before ASP.NET begins aggressive scavenging. This limit includes both memory used by the cache as well as normal memory overhead from the running application. A setting of 0 (the default) indicates that ASP.NET will use its own algorithm for determining when to start reclaiming memory. The privateBytesPollTime indicates how often ASP.NET checks the private bytes used. The default value is 2 minutes.

Output Caching Extensibility

The ASP.NET caching model works surprisingly well across a wide variety of web applications. It's simple to use and blisteringly fast, because the cache service runs in the ASP.NET process and stores data in physical memory.

However, ASP.NET's caching system doesn't work as well if you want to cache huge amounts of data for long amounts of time. For example, consider the sprawling product catalog of a giant e-commerce company. Assuming the product catalog changes infrequently, you may want to cache thousands of product pages to avoid the expense of creating them. But with this much data, using web server memory is a risky proposition. Instead, you might prefer to rely on another type of storage that's slower than memory but still faster than recreating the page (and less likely to cause resource bottlenecks). Possibilities include disk-based storage, database-based storage, or a distributed storage system like Windows Server AppFabric.

■ **Note** Any type of external cache storage will be slower than regular in-memory caching. Some storage options even have the potential to introduce new bottlenecks and even reduce scalability. Before you use a non-memory-based type of caching, you need to carefully evaluate the cost of generating pages and the speed and scalability of your cache storage system. Then, you need to profile its performance in a realistic environment, before you roll it out in your web application.

In the past, exotic caching systems have been possible, but their implementation has been completely separate from ASP.NET. As a result, every third-party caching solution has its own programming API. But ASP.NET 4 finally adds the provider model to its caching feature, allowing you to plug in cache providers that use different data stores. However, the following are two caveats:

- ASP.NET doesn't include any pre-built caching providers. However, members of the ASP.NET team have demonstrated prototypes that use file-based caching and Windows Server AppFabric. The intention is to turn these into separate components that you can download for free from `http://www.codeplex.com`. ASP.NET architects have also pledged to release examples that show how to integrate memcached (a popular open-source distributed caching system) with ASP.NET output caching.
- You can only use a custom provider with output caching, not the data caching feature described later in this chapter.

In the following sections, you'll consider a basic example of a file-based caching solution.

Building a Custom Cache Provider

The following example shows a cache provider that stores each cached page (or user control, if you're using fragment caching) in a separate file. Although disk-based caching is an order of magnitude slower than memory-based caching, it does have two important uses:

Durable caching: Because cached output is stored on disk, it remains even when the web application domain is restarted. This makes it a worthwhile consideration if the information you're caching is expensive to generate.

Low memory usage: When a cached page is reused, it's served straight from the hard drive. As a result, it doesn't need to be read back into memory. This is useful for large cached pages. It's particularly useful if you vary the cached output based on a query string parameter and there are many variations. Either way, it can be difficult to implement a successful caching strategy using memory alone.

■ **Note** Although the solution you'll consider works quite well, it lacks the refinements you'll want in a professional application. As with all infrastructure programming, it's always better for you, the application developer, to concentrate on application logic, while letting experienced third-party developers or Microsoft architects build the key bits of plumbing your application needs.

Creating a custom cache provider is easy. You simply derive from the OutputCacheProvider class in the System.Web.Caching namespace. You then need to override the methods listed in Table 11-1.

Table 11-1. Overridable Methods in the OutputCacheProvider

Method	Description
Initialize()	Gives you a place to perform initialization tasks when the provider is first loaded, such as reading other settings from the web.config file. This is the only method in this table that you don't need to override.
Add()	Adds the item to the cache, if it doesn't already exist. If the item does exist, this method should take no action.
Set()	Adds the item to the cache. If the item already exists, this method should overwrite it.
Get()	Retrieves an item from the cache, if it exists. This method must also enforce time-based expiration, by checking the expiration date and removing the item if necessary.
Remove()	Removes the item from the cache.

In this example, the custom cache provider is called FileCacheProvider:

```
public class FileCacheProvider : OutputCacheProvider
{
    // The location where cached files will be placed.
    public string CachePath
    { get; set; }

    ...
}
```

To perform its serialization, it uses a second class named CacheItem, which simply wraps the initial item you want to cache and the expiration date:

```
[Serializable]
public class CacheItem
{
    public DateTime ExpiryDate;
    public object Item;

    public CacheItem(object item, DateTime expiryDate)
    {
        ExpiryDate = expiryDate;
        Item = item;
    }
}
```

Now you simply need to override the Add(), Set(), Get(), and Remove() methods. All of these methods receive a key that uniquely identifies the cached content. The key is based on the file name of the cached page. For example, if you use output caching with a page named OutputCaching.aspx in a web site named CustomCacheProvider, your code might receive a key like this:

```
a2/customcacheprovider/outputcaching.aspx
```

To translate this into a valid file name, the code simply replaces slash characters (\) with dashes (-). It also adds the extension .txt to distinguish this cached content from a real ASP.NET page and to make it easier for you to open it and review its content during debugging. Here's an example of a transformed file name:

```
a2-customcacheprovider-outputcaching.aspx.txt
```

To perform this transformation, the FileOutputCacheProvider uses a private method named ConvertKeyToPath():

```
private string ConvertKeyToPath(string key)
{
    // Flatten it to a single file name, with no path information.
    string file = key.Replace('/', '-');

    // Add .txt extension so it's not confused with a real ASP.NET file.
    file += ".txt";
    return Path.Combine(CachePath, file);
}
```

Other approaches are possible—for example, some caching systems use the types from the System.Security.Cryptography namespace to convert the file name to a unique hash value, which looks like a string of meaningless characters.

Using this method, it's easy to write the Add() and Set() methods. Remember, the difference between the two is that Set() always stores its content, while Add() must check if it already exists. Add() also returns the cached object. The actual serialization code simply uses the BinaryFormatter to convert the rendered page into a stream of bytes, which can then be written to a file.

```
public override object Add(string key, object entry, DateTime utcExpiry)
{
    // Transform the key to a unique filename.
    string path = ConvertKeyToPath(key);

    // Set it only if it is not already cached.
    if (!File.Exists(path))
    {
       Set(key, entry, utcExpiry);
    }
    return entry;
}

public override void Set(string key, object entry, DateTime utcExpiry)
{
    CacheItem item = new CacheItem(entry, utcExpiry);
    string path = ConvertKeyToPath(key);

    // Overwrite it, even if it already exists.
    using (FileStream file = File.OpenWrite(path))
    {
        BinaryFormatter formatter = new BinaryFormatter();
        formatter.Serialize(file, item);
    }
}
```

The Get() method is similarly straightforward. However, it must check the expiration date of the retrieved item, and discard it if it has expired:

```
public override object Get(string key)
{
    string path = ConvertKeyToPath(key);

    if (!File.Exists(path)) return null;

    CacheItem item = null;
    using (FileStream file = File.OpenRead(path))
    {
        BinaryFormatter formatter = new BinaryFormatter();
        item = (CacheItem)formatter.Deserialize(file);
    }

    // Remove expired items.
    if (item.ExpiryDate <= DateTime.Now.ToUniversalTime())
    {
        Remove(key);
        return null;
    }

    return item.Item;
}
```

Finally, the Remove() method simply deletes the file with the cached data:

```
public override void Remove(string key)
{
    string path = ConvertKeyToPath(key);

    if (File.Exists(path)) File.Delete(path);
}
```

Using a Custom Cache Provider

To use a custom cache provider, you first need to add it inside the <caching> section. Here's an example that adds the FileCacheProivder and simultaneously sets it to be the default cache provider for all output caching:

```
<configuration>
  <system.web>
    <caching>
      <outputCache defaultProvider="FileCache">
        <providers>
          <add name="FileCache" type="FileCacheProvider" cachePath="~/Cache" />
        </providers>
      </outputCache>
    </caching>
    ...
  </system.web>
</configuration>
```

This assumes that the FileCacheProvider is a class in the current web application (for example, as a file in the App_Code folder of a projectless web site). If the class were part of a separate assembly, you would need to include the assembly name. For example, a FileCacheProvider in a namespace named CustomCaching and compiled in an assembly named CacheExtensibility would require this configuration:

```
<add name="FileCache" type="CustomCaching.FileCacheProvider, CacheExtensibility"
 cachePath="~/Cache" />
```

There's one other detail here. This example includes a custom attribute, named cachePath. ASP.NET simply ignores this added detail, but your code is free to retrieve it and use it. For example, the FileCacheProvider can use the Initialize() method to read this information and set the path (which, in this case, is a subfolder named Cache in the web application folder).

```
public override void Initialize(string name, NameValueCollection attributes)
{
    base.Initialize(name, attributes);

    // Retrieve the web.config settings.
    CachePath = HttpContext.Current.Server.MapPath(attributes["cachePath"]);
}
```

If you don't use the defaultProvider attribute, it's up to you to tell ASP.NET when to use its standard in-memory caching service, and when to use a custom cache provider. You might expect to handle this with a directive in the page, but you can't, simply because caching acts before the page has been retrieved (and, if it's successful, caching bypasses the page markup altogether).

Instead, you need to override the GetOutputCacheProviderName() method in the global.asax file. This method examines the current request and then returns a string with the name of the cache provider to use while handling this request. Here's an example that tells ASP.NET to use the FileCacheProvider with the page OutputCaching.aspx (but no other):

```
public override string GetOutputCacheProviderName(HttpContext context)
{
    // Get the page.
    string pageAndQuery = System.IO.Path.GetFileName(context.Request.Path);

    if (pageAndQuery.StartsWith("OutputCaching.aspx"))
        return "FileCache";
    else
        return base.GetOutputCacheProviderName(context);
}
```

Data Caching

Data caching is the most flexible type of caching, but it also forces you to take specific additional steps in your code to implement it. The basic principle of data caching is that you add items that are expensive to create to a special built-in collection object (called Cache). This object works much like the Application object. It's globally available to all requests from all clients in the application. However, a few key differences exist:

The Cache object is thread-safe: This means you don't need to explicitly lock or unlock the Cache collection before adding or removing an item. However, the objects in the Cache collection will still need to be thread-safe themselves. For example, if you create a custom business object, more than one client could try to use that object at once, which could lead to invalid data. You can code around this limitation in various ways. One easy approach that you'll see in this chapter is just to make a duplicate copy of the object if you need to work with it in a web page.

Items in the cache are removed automatically: ASP.NET will remove an item if it expires, if one of the objects or files it depends on is changed, or if the server becomes low on memory. This means you can freely use the cache without worrying about wasting valuable server memory, because ASP.NET will remove items as needed. But because items in the cache can be removed, you always need to check if a cached object exists before you attempt to use it. Otherwise, you'll run into a NullReferenceException.

Items in the cache support dependencies: You can link a cached object to a file, a database table, or another type of resource. If this resource changes, your cached object is automatically deemed invalid and released.

As with application state, the cached object is stored in process, which means it doesn't persist if the application domain is restarted, and it can't be shared between computers in a web farm. This behavior is by design, because the cost of allowing multiple computers to communicate with an out-of-process cache would reduce some of its performance benefit. It makes more sense for each web server to have its own cache.

Adding Items to the Cache

As with the Application and Session collections, you can add an item to the Cache collection just by assigning a new key name:

```
Cache["key"] = item;
```

However, this approach is generally discouraged because it does not allow you to have any control over the amount of time the object will be retained in the cache. A better approach is to use the Cache.Insert() method. Table 11-2 lists the four versions of the Insert() method.

Table 11-2. *The Insert() Method Overloads*

Overload	Description
Cache.Insert(key, value)	Inserts an item into the cache under the specified key name, using the default priority and expiration. This is the same as using the indexer-based collection syntax and assigning to a new key name.
Cache.Insert(key, value, dependencies)	Inserts an item into the cache under the specified key name, using the default priority and expiration. The last parameter contains a CacheDependency object that links to other files or cached items and allows the cached item to be invalidated when these change.
Cache.Insert(key, value, dependencies, absoluteExpiration, slidingExpiration)	Inserts an item into the cache under the specified key name, using the default priority and the indicated sliding or absolute expiration policy (you cannot set both at once). This is the most commonly used version of the Insert() method.
Cache.Insert(key, value, dependencies, absoluteExpiration, slidingExpiration, priority, onRemoveCallback)	Allows you to configure every aspect of the cache policy for the item, including expiration, priority, and dependencies. In addition, you can submit a delegate that points to a method you want invoked when the item is removed.

The most important choice you make when inserting an item into the cache is the expiration policy. ASP.NET allows you to set a sliding expiration or an absolute expiration policy, but you cannot use both at the same time. If you want to use an absolute expiration, set the slidingExpiration parameter to TimeSpan.Zero. To set a sliding expiration policy, set the absoluteExpiration parameter to DateTime.Max.

With sliding expiration, ASP.NET waits for a set period of inactivity to dispose of a neglected cache item. For example, if you use a sliding expiration period of 10 minutes, the item will be removed only if it is not used within a 10-minute period. Sliding expiration works well when you have information that is always valid but may not be in high demand, such as historical data or a product catalog. This information doesn't expire because it's no longer valid but shouldn't be kept in the cache if it isn't doing any good.

Here's an example that stores an item with a sliding expiration policy of 10 minutes, with no dependencies:

```
Cache.Insert("MyItem", obj, null,
  DateTime.MaxValue, TimeSpan.FromMinutes(10));
```

■ **Note** The similarity between caching with absolute expiration and session state is no coincidence. When you use the in-process state server for session state, it actually uses the cache behind the scenes! The session state information is stored in a private slot and given an expiration policy to match the timeout value. The session state item is not accessible through the Cache object.

Absolute expirations are best when you know the information in a given item can be considered valid only for a specific amount of time, such as a stock chart or weather report. With absolute expiration, you set a specific date and time when the cached item will be removed.

Here's an example that stores an item for exactly 60 minutes:

```
Cache.Insert("MyItem", obj, null,
  DateTime.Now.AddMinutes(60), TimeSpan.Zero);
```

When you retrieve an item from the cache, you must always check for a null reference. That's because ASP.NET can remove your cached items at any time. One way to handle this is to add special methods that re-create the items as needed. Here's an example:

```
private DataSet GetCustomerData()
{
    // Attempt to retrieve the DataSet from the cache.
    DataSet ds = Cache["CustomerData"] as DataSet;

    // Check if it was retrieved and re-create it if necessary.
    if (ds == null)
    {
        ds = QueryCustomerDataFromDatabase();
        Cache.Insert("CustomerData", ds);
    }

    return ds;
```

```
}

private DataSet QueryCustomerDataFromDatabase()
{
    // (Code to query the database goes here.)
}
```

Now you can retrieve the DataSet elsewhere in your code using the following syntax, without worrying about the caching details:

```
GridView1.DataSource = GetCustomerData();
```

For an even better design, move the QueryDataFromDatabase() method to a separate data component.

There's no method for clearing the entire data cache, but you can enumerate through the collection using the DictionaryEntry class. This gives you a chance to retrieve the key for each item and allows you to empty the class using code like this:

```
foreach (DictionaryEntry item in Cache)
{
    Cache.Remove(item.Key.ToString());
}
```

Or you can retrieve a list of cached items, as follows:

```
string itemList = "";
foreach (DictionaryEntry item in Cache)
{
    itemList += item.Key.ToString() + " ";
}
```

This code is rarely used in a deployed application but is extremely useful while testing your caching strategies.

A Simple Cache Test

The following example presents a simple caching test. An item is cached for 30 seconds and reused for requests in that time. The page code always runs (because the page itself isn't cached), checks the cache, and retrieves or constructs the item as needed. It also reports whether the item was found in the cache.

All the caching logic takes place when the Page.Load event fires.

```
protected void Page_Load(Object sender, EventArgs e)
{
    if (this.IsPostBack)
    {
        lblInfo.Text += "Page posted back.<br />";
    }
    else
    {
        lblInfo.Text += "Page created.<br />";
    }

    DateTime? testItem = (DateTime?)Cache["TestItem"];
```

```
    if (testItem == null)
    {
        lblInfo.Text += "Creating TestItem...<br />";
        testItem = DateTime.Now;

        lblInfo.Text += "Storing TestItem in cache ";
        lblInfo.Text += "for 30 seconds.<br />";
        Cache.Insert("TestItem", testItem, null,
          DateTime.Now.AddSeconds(30), TimeSpan.Zero);
    }
    else
    {
        lblInfo.Text += "Retrieving TestItem...<br />";
        lblInfo.Text += "TestItem is '" + testItem.ToString();
        lblInfo.Text += "'<br />";
    }
    lblInfo.Text += "<br />";
}
```

Figure 11-3 shows the result after the page has been loaded and posted back several times in the 30-second period.

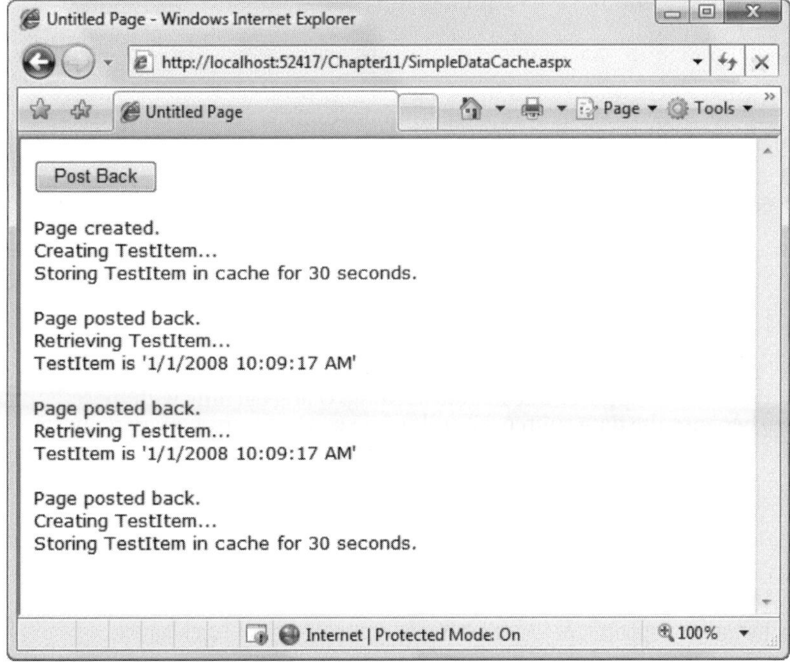

Figure 11-3. *Retrieving data from the cache*

Cache Priorities

You can also set a priority when you add an item to the cache. The priority only has an effect if ASP.NET needs to perform *cache scavenging*, which is the process of removing cached items early because memory is becoming scarce. In this situation, ASP.NET will look for underused items that haven't yet expired. If it finds more than one similarly underused item, it will compare the priorities to determine which one to remove first. Generally, you would set a higher cache priority for items that take more time to reconstruct in order to indicate its heightened importance.

To assign a cache priority, you choose a value from the CacheItemPriority enumeration. Table 11-3 lists all the values.

Table 11-3. *Values of the CachePriority Enumeration*

Value	Description
High	These items are the least likely to be deleted from the cache as the server frees system memory.
AboveNormal	These items are less likely to be deleted than Normal priority items.
Normal	These items have the default priority level. They are deleted only after Low or BelowNormal priority items have been removed.
BelowNormal	These items are more likely to be deleted than Normal priority items.
Low	These items are the most likely to be deleted from the cache as the server frees system memory.
NotRemovable	These items will ordinarily not be deleted from the cache as the server frees system memory.

Caching with the Data Source Controls

In Chapter 9, you spent considerable time working with the data source controls. The SqlDataSource, ObjectDataSource, and XmlDataSource all support built-in data caching. Using caching with these controls is highly recommended, because the data source controls often generate extra query requests. For example, they requery after every postback when parameters change, and they perform a separate query for every bound control, even if those controls use exactly the same command, Even a little caching can reduce this overhead.

■ **Note** Although many data source controls support caching, it's not a required data source control feature, and you'll run into data source controls that don't support it or for which it may not make sense (such as the SiteMapDataSource).

To support caching, the data source controls all use the same properties, which are listed in Table 11-4.

Table 11-4. Cache-Related Properties of the Data Source Controls

Property	Description
EnableCaching	If true, caching is switched on. It's false by default.
CacheExpirationPolicy	Uses a value from the DataSourceCacheExpiry enumeration—Absolute for absolute expiration (which times out after a fixed interval of time) or Sliding for sliding expiration (which resets the time window every time the data object is retrieved from the cache).
CacheDuration	The number of seconds to cache the data object. If you are using sliding expiration, the time limit is reset every time the object is retrieved from the cache. The default value, 0 (or Infinite), keeps cached items perpetually.
CacheKeyDependency and SqlCacheDependency	Allows you to make a cached item dependent on another item in the data cache (CacheKeyDependency) or on a table in your database (SqlCacheDependency). Dependencies are discussed in the "Cache Dependencies" section.

Caching with SqlDataSource

When you enable caching for the SqlDataSource control, you cache the results of the SelectQuery. However, if you create a select query that takes parameters, the SqlDataSource will cache a separate result for every set of parameter values.

For example, imagine you create a page that allows you to view employees by city. The user selects the desired city from a list box, and you use a SqlDataSource control to fill in the matching employee records in a grid (see Figure 11-4). This example was first presented in Chapter 9.

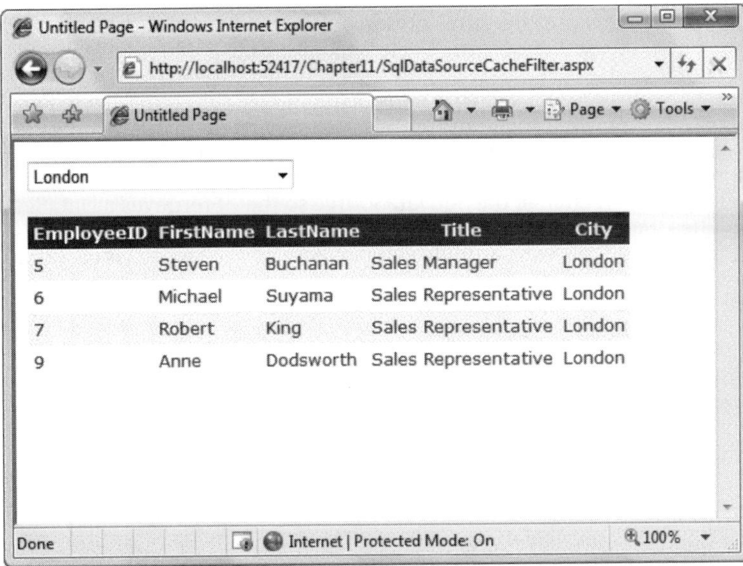

Figure 11-4. Retrieving data from the cache

To fill the grid, you use the following SqlDataSource:

```
<asp:SqlDataSource ID="sourceEmployees" runat="server"
 ProviderName="System.Data.SqlClient"
 ConnectionString="<%$ ConnectionStrings:Northwind %>"
 SelectCommand="SELECT EmployeeID, FirstName, LastName, Title, City FROM Employees
WHERE City=@City">
  <SelectParameters>
    <asp:ControlParameter ControlID="lstCities" Name="City"
     PropertyName="SelectedValue" />
  </SelectParameters>
</asp:SqlDataSource>
```

In this example, each time you select a city, a separate query is performed to get just the matching employees in that city. The query is used to fill a DataSet, which is then cached. If you select a different city, the process repeats, and the new DataSet is cached separately. However, if you pick a city that you or another user has already requested, the appropriate DataSet is fetched from the cache (provided it hasn't yet expired).

■ **Note** SqlDataSource caching works only when the DataSourceMode property is set to DataSet (the default). It doesn't work when the mode is set to DataReader, because the DataReader object maintains a live connection to the database and can't be efficiently cached.

Caching separate results for different parameter values works well if some parameter values are used much more frequently than others. For example, if the results for London are requested much more often than the results for Redmond, this ensures that the London results stick around in the cache even when the Redmond DataSet has been released. Assuming the full set of results is extremely large, this may be the most efficient approach.

On the other hand, if the parameter values are all used with similar frequency, this approach isn't as suitable. One of the problems it imposes is that when the items in the cache expire, you'll need multiple database queries to repopulate the cache (one for each parameter value), which isn't as efficient as getting the combined results with a single query.

If you fall into the second situation, you can change the SqlDataSource so that it retrieves a DataSet with all the employee records and caches that. The SqlDataSource can then extract just the records it needs to satisfy each request from the DataSet. This way, a single DataSet with all the records is cached, which can satisfy any parameter value.

To use this technique, you need to rewrite your SqlDataSource to use *filtering*. First, the select query should return all the rows and not use any SELECT parameters:

```
<asp:SqlDataSource ID="sourceEmployees" runat="server"
 SelectCommand="SELECT EmployeeID, FirstName, LastName, Title, City FROM Employees"
 ...>
</asp:SqlDataSource>
```

Second, you need to define the filter expression. This is the portion that goes in the WHERE clause of a typical SQL query, and you write it in the same way as you used the DataView.RowFilter property in Chapter 9. (In fact, the SqlDataSource uses the DataView's row filtering abilities behind the scenes.) However, this has a catch—if you're supplying the filter value from another source (such as a control), you need to define one or more placeholders, using the syntax {0} for the first placeholder, {1} for the second, and so on. You then supply the filter values using the <FilterParameters> section, in much the same way you supplied the select parameters in the first version.

Here's the completed SqlDataSource tag:

```
<asp:SqlDataSource ID="sourceEmployees" runat="server"
 ProviderName="System.Data.SqlClient"
 ConnectionString="<%$ ConnectionStrings:Northwind %>"
 SelectCommand="SELECT EmployeeID, FirstName, LastName, Title, City FROM Employees"
 FilterExpression="City='{0}'" EnableCaching="True">
  <FilterParameters>
    <asp:ControlParameter ControlID="lstCities" Name="City"
     PropertyName="SelectedValue" />
  </FilterParameters>
</asp:SqlDataSource>
```

■ **Tip** Don't use filtering unless you are using caching. If you use filtering without caching, you are essentially retrieving the full result set each time and then extracting a portion of its records. This combines the worst of both worlds—you have to repeat the query with each postback, and you fetch far more data than you need each time.

Caching with ObjectDataSource

The ObjectDataSource caching works on the data object returned from the SelectMethod. If you are using a parameterized query, the ObjectDataSource distinguishes between requests with different parameter values and caches them separately. Unfortunately, the ObjectDataSource caching has a significant limitation—it works only when the select method returns a DataSet or DataTable. If you return any other type of object, you'll receive a NotSupportedException.

This limitation is unfortunate, because there's no technical reason you can't cache custom objects in the data cache. If you want this feature, you'll need to implement data caching inside your method, by manually inserting your objects into the data cache and retrieving them later. In fact, caching inside your method can be more effective, because you have the ability to share the same cached object in multiple methods. For example, you could cache a DataTable with a list of product categories and use that cached item in both the GetProductCategories() and GetProductsByCategory() methods.

■ **Tip** The only consideration you should keep in mind is to make sure you use unique cache key names that aren't likely to collide with the names of cached items that the page might use. This isn't a problem when using the built-in data source caching, because it always stores its information in a hidden slot in the cache.

If your custom class returns a DataSet or DataTable, and you decide to use the built-in ObjectDataSource caching, you can also use filtering as discussed with the SqlDataSource control. Just instruct your ObjectDataSource to call a method that gets the full set of data, and set the FilterExpression to retrieve just those items that match the current view.

Cache Dependencies

As time passes, the data source may change in response to other actions. However, if your code uses caching, you may remain unaware of the changes and continue using out-of-date information from the cache. To help mitigate this problem, ASP.NET supports cache dependencies. Cache dependencies allow you to make a cached item dependent on another resource so that when that resource changes, the cached item is removed automatically.

ASP.NET includes three types of dependencies:

- Dependencies on other cache items
- Dependencies on files or folders
- Dependencies on a database query

In the following section, you'll consider the first two options. Toward the end of this chapter, you'll learn about SQL dependencies, and you'll learn how to create your own custom dependencies.

File and Cache Item Dependencies

To create a cache dependency, you need to create a CacheDependency object and then use it when adding the dependent cached item. For example, the following code creates a cached item that will automatically be evicted from the cache when an XML file is changed, deleted, or overwritten.

```
// Create a dependency for the ProductList.xml file.
CacheDependency prodDependency = new CacheDependency(
  Server.MapPath("ProductList.xml"));

// Add a cache item that will be dependent on this file.
Cache.Insert("ProductInfo", prodInfo, prodDependency);
```

If you point the CacheDependency to a folder, it watches for the addition, removal, or modification of any files in that folder. Modifying a subfolder (for example, renaming, creating, or removing a subfolder) also violates the cache dependency. However, changes further down the directory tree (such as adding a file into a subfolder or creating a subfolder in a subfolder) don't have any effect.

■ **Tip** CacheDependency monitoring begins as soon as it's created. In this example, that means if the XML file changes before you add the dependent prodItem object to the cache, the item will expire immediately once it's added. If that's not the behavior you want, use the overloaded constructor that accepts a DateTime object. This DateTime indicates when the dependency monitoring will begin.

The CacheDependency provides several constructors. You've already seen how it can make a dependency based on a file by using the filename constructor. You can also specify a directory that needs to be monitored for changes, or you can use a constructor that accepts an array of strings that represent multiple files or directories.

Yet another constructor accepts an array of filenames and an array of cache keys. The following example uses this constructor to create an item that is dependent on another item in the cache:

```
Cache["Key1"] = "Cache Item 1";

// Make Cache["Key2"] dependent on Cache["Key1"].
string[] dependencyKey = new string[1];
dependencyKey[0] = "Key1";
CacheDependency dependency = new CacheDependency(null, dependencyKey);

Cache.Insert("Key2", "Cache Item 2", dependency);
```

Next, when Cache["Key 1"] changes or is removed from the cache, Cache["Key 2"] will automatically be dropped.

Figure 11-5 shows a simple test page that is included with the online samples for this chapter. It sets up a dependency, modifies the file, and allows you to verify that the cache item has been dropped from the cache.

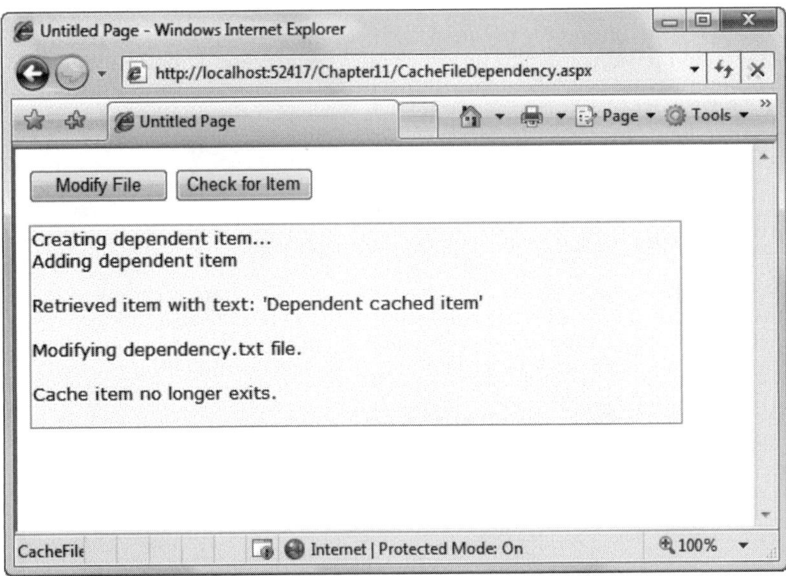

***Figure 11-5.** Testing cache dependencies*

Aggregate Dependencies

Sometimes, you might want to combine dependencies to create an item that's dependent on more than one other resource. For example, you might want to create an item that's invalidated if any one of three files changes. Or, you might want to create an item that's invalidated if a file changes or another cached item is removed. Creating these rules is easy with the AggregateCacheDependency class.

The AggregateCacheDependency can wrap any number of CacheDependency objects. All you need to do is supply your CacheDependency objects in an array using the AggregateCacheDependency.Add() method.

Here's an example that makes a cached item dependent on two files:

```
CacheDependency dep1 = new CacheDependency(
  Server.MapPath("ProductList1.xml"));

CacheDependency dep2 = new CacheDependency(
  Server.MapPath("ProductList2.xml"));

// Create the aggregate.
CacheDependency[] dependencies =  new CacheDependency[]{dep1, dep2};
AggregateCacheDependency aggregateDep = new AggregateCacheDependency();
aggregateDep.Add(dependencies);

// Add the dependent cache item.
Cache.Insert("ProductInfo", prodInfo, aggregateDep);
```

This example isn't particularly practical, because you can already supply an array of files when you create a CacheDependency object to get the same effect. The real value of AggregateCacheDependency appears when you need to wrap different types of objects that derive from CacheDependency. Because the AggregateCacheDependency.Add() method supports any CacheDependency-derived object, you could create a single dependency that incorporates a file dependency, a SQL cache dependency, and even a custom cache dependency.

The Item Removed Callback

ASP.NET also allows you to write a callback method that will be triggered when an item is removed from the cache. You can place the method that handles the callback in your web-page class, or you can use a static method in another accessible class. However, you should keep in mind that this code won't be executed as part of a web request. That means you can't interact with web-page objects or notify the user.

The following example uses a cache callback to make two items dependent on one another—a feat that wouldn't be possible with dependencies alone. Two items are inserted in the cache, and when either one of those items is removed, the item removed callback removes the other.

```
public partial class ItemRemovedCallbackTest : System.Web.UI.Page
{
    protected void Page_Load(object sender, System.EventArgs e)
    {
        if (!this.IsPostBack)
        {
            lblInfo.Text += "Creating items...<br />";
            string itemA = "item A";
            string itemB = "item B";
            Cache.Insert("itemA", itemA, null, DateTime.Now.AddMinutes(60),
              TimeSpan.Zero, CacheItemPriority.Default,
              new CacheItemRemovedCallback(ItemRemovedCallback));
            Cache.Insert("itemB", itemB, null, DateTime.Now.AddMinutes(60),
              TimeSpan.Zero, CacheItemPriority.Default,
              new CacheItemRemovedCallback(ItemRemovedCallback));
        }
    }
```

```
    protected void cmdCheck_Click(object sender, System.EventArgs e)
    {
        string itemList = "";
        foreach(DictionaryEntry item in Cache)
        {
            itemList += item.Key.ToString() + " ";
        }
        lblInfo.Text += "<br />Found: " + itemList + "<br />";
    }

    protected void cmdRemove_Click(object sender, System.EventArgs e)
    {
        lblInfo.Text += "<br />Removing itemA.<br />";
        Cache.Remove("itemA");
    }

    private void ItemRemovedCallback(string key, object value,
      CacheItemRemovedReason reason)
    {
        // This fires after the request has ended, when the
        // item is removed.

        // If either item has been removed, make sure
        // the other item is also removed.
        if (key == "itemA" || key == "itemB")
        {
            Cache.Remove("itemA");
            Cache.Remove("itemB");
        }
    }
}
```

Figure 11-6 shows a test of this page.

When you click Remove in this page, you'll notice that the item removed callback actually fires twice: once for the item you've just removed (itemA) and once for the dependent item (itemB). This doesn't cause a problem, because it's safe to call Cache.Remove() on items that don't exist. However, if you have other cleanup steps (such as deleting a file), you need to make sure that they aren't performed twice.

The callback also provides your code with additional information, including the removed item and the reason it was removed. Table 11-5 shows possible reasons.

There are a few reasons that you might choose to use the item removed callback. As in this example, you might use it to implement complex dependency logic. Or, you might use it to clean up other related resources (such as a temporary file on the hard drive).

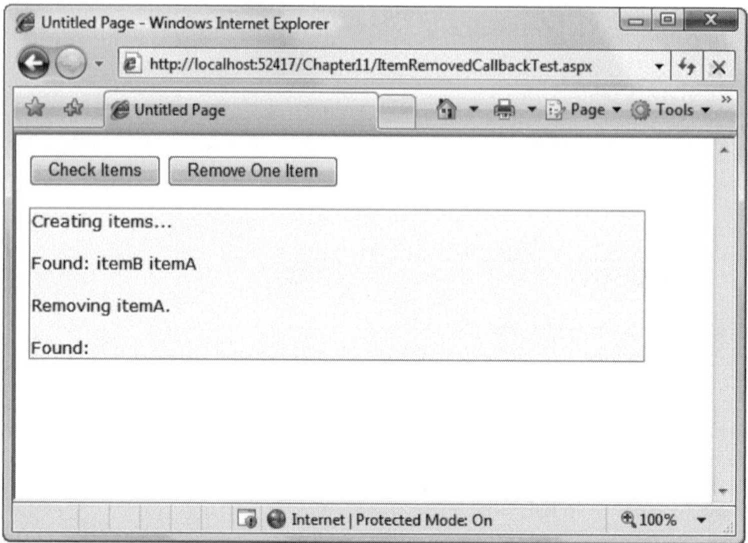

Figure 11-6. *Testing a cache callback*

Table 11-5. *Values for the CacheItemRemovedReason Enumeration*

Value	Description
DependencyChanged	Removed because a file or key dependency changed
Expired	Removed because it expired (according to its sliding or absolute expiration policy)
Removed	Removed programmatically by a Remove method call or by an Insert method call that specified the same key
Underused	Removed because ASP.NET decided it wasn't important enough and wanted to free memory

You can also use the item removed callback to recreate an item when it expires. This is primarily useful if the item is time-consuming to create, and so you want to create it before it's used in a request. (For example, you could use the item removed callback to get data from a remote component or web service.) However, you should be careful when using this technique that you don't waste time generating data that's rarely used. You must also check the reason the item is removed by examining the CacheItemRemovedReason value. If the item has been removed due to normal expiry (Expired) or dependencies (DependencyChanged), you can usually recreate it safely. If the item has been removed manually (Removed) or due to cache scavenging (Underused), you're best not to recreate it, because the item might be quickly discarded again. Above all, you want to ensure that your code doesn't get trapped into a cycle of recreating the same item over and over again in quick succession.

Understanding SQL Cache Notifications

SQL cache dependencies give you the ability to automatically invalidate a cached data object (such as a DataSet) when the related data is modified in the database. This feature works with SQL Server 2005 and later. ASP.NET also provides slightly more limited support for SQL Server 2000, although the underlying plumbing is quite a bit different.

To understand how SQL cache dependencies work, it's important to understand a few flawed solutions that developers have been forced to resort to in the past.

One common technique is to use a marker file. With this technique, you add the data object to the cache and set up a file dependency. However, the file you use is empty—it's just a marker file that's intended to indicate when the database state changes.

Here's how it works. When the user calls a stored procedure that modifies the table you're interested in, your stored procedure removes or modifies the marker file. ASP.NET immediately detects the file change and removes the corresponding data object. This ugly workaround isn't terribly scalable and can introduce concurrency problems if more than one user calls the stored procedure and tries to remove the file at once. It also forces you to clutter your stored procedure code, because every stored procedure that modifies the database needs similar file modification logic. Having a database interact with the file system is a bad idea from the start, because it adds to the complexity and reduces the security of your overall system.

Another common approach is to use a custom HTTP handler that removes cached items at your request. Once again, this only works if you build the appropriate level of support into the stored procedures that modify the corresponding tables. In this case, instead of interacting with a file, these stored procedures call the custom HTTP handler and pass a query string that indicates what change has taken place or what cache key has been affected. The HTTP handler can then use the Cache.Remove() method to get rid of the data.

The problem with this approach is that it requires the considerable complexity of an extended stored procedure. Also, the request to the HTTP handler must be synchronous, which causes a significant delay. Even worse, this delay happens every time the stored procedure executes, because the stored procedure has no way of determining if the call is necessary or if the cached item has already been removed. As a result, the overall time taken to execute the stored procedure increases significantly, and the overall scalability of the database suffers. Like the marker file approach, it works well in small scenarios but can't handle large-scale, complex applications. Both of these approaches introduce a whole other set of complications in web farm scenarios with multiple servers.

What's needed is an approach that can deliver notifications asynchronously, and in a scalable and reliable fashion. In other words, the database server should notify ASP.NET without stalling the current connection. Just as importantly, it should be possible to set up the cache dependency in a loosely coupled way so that stored procedures don't need to be aware of the caching that's in place. The database server should watch for changes that are committed by any means, including from a script, an inline SQL command, or a batch process. Even if the change doesn't go through the expected stored procedures, the change should still be noticed, and the notification should still be delivered to ASP.NET. Finally, the notification method needs to support web farms.

Microsoft put together a team of architects from the ASP.NET, SQL Server, ADO.NET, and IIS groups to concoct a solution. They came up with two different architectures, one for SQL Server 2000 (which is described in earlier editions of this book) and one for all later versions of SQL Server (which is described next). Both of them use the SqlCacheDependency class, which derives from the CacheDependency class you saw earlier.

■ **Tip** Using SQL cache dependencies still entails more complexity than just using a time-based expiration policy. If it's acceptable for certain information to be used without reflecting all the most recent changes (and developers often overestimate the importance of up-to-the-millisecond live information), you may not need it at all.

How Cache Notifications Work

SQL Server 2005 introduced a notification infrastructure and messaging system that's built into the database, called the Service Broker. The Service Broker manages queues, which are database objects that have the same standing as tables, stored procedures, or views.

Using the Service Broker, you can receive notifications for specific database events. The most direct approach is to use the CREATE EVENT NOTIFICATION command to indicate the event you want to monitor. However, .NET offers a higher-level model that's integrated with ADO.NET. Using this model, you simply register a query command, and .NET automatically instructs SQL Server to send notifications for any operations that would affect the results of that query. ASP.NET offers an even higher-level model that builds on this infrastructure, and allows you to invalidate cached items automatically when a query is invalidated.

The SQL Server notification mechanism works in a similar way to indexed views. Every time you perform an operation, SQL Server determines whether your operation affects a registered command. If it does, SQL Server sends a notification message and stops the notification process.

Figure 11-7shows an overview of how cache invalidation works in SQL.

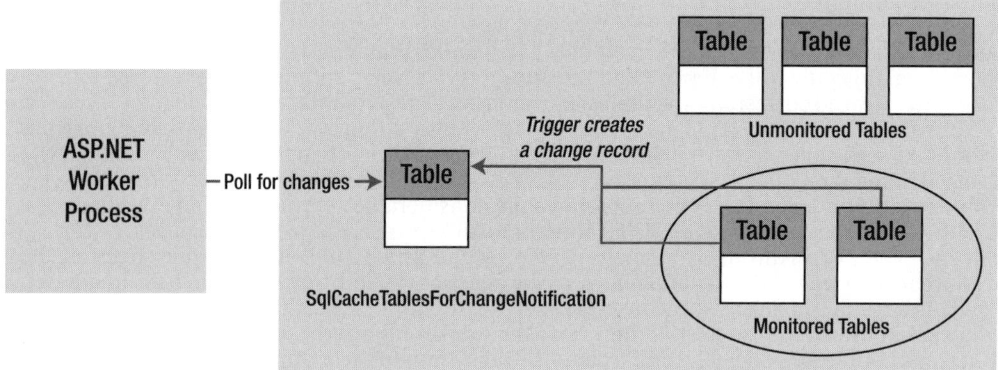

Figure 11-7. *Monitoring a database for changes in SQL Server*

Enabling Notifications

The only configuration step you need to perform is to make sure your database has the ENABLE_BROKER flag set. You can perform this by running the following SQL (assuming you're using the Northwind database):

```
Use Northwind
ALTER DATABASE Northwind SET ENABLE_BROKER
```

Notifications work with SELECT queries and stored procedures. However, some restrictions exist for the SELECT syntax you can use. To properly support notifications, your command must adhere to the following rules:

- You must fully qualify table names in the form [Owner].table, as in dbo.Employees (not just Employees).

- Your query cannot use an aggregate function, such as COUNT(), MAX(), MIN(), or AVERAGE().
- You cannot select all columns with the wildcard * (as in SELECT * FROM Employees). Instead, you must specifically name each column so that SQL Server can properly track changes that do and do not affect the results of your query.

Here's an acceptable command:

```
SELECT EmployeeID, FirstName, LastName, City FROM dbo.Employees
```

These are the most important rules, but SQL Server Books Online has a lengthy list of caveats and exceptions. If you break one of these rules, you won't receive an error. However, the notification message will be sent as soon as you register the command, and the cached item will be invalidated immediately.

Creating the Cache Dependency

When creating a cache dependency, SQL Server needs to know the exact database command you're using to retrieve your data. If you use programmatic caching, you must create the SqlCacheDependency using the constructor that accepts a SqlCommand object. Here's an example:

```
// Create the ADO.NET objects.
string connectionString =  WebConfigurationManager.ConnectionStrings[
 "Northwind"].ConnectionString;
SqlConnection con = new SqlConnection(connectionString);
string query =
 "SELECT EmployeeID, FirstName, LastName, City FROM dbo.Employees";
SqlCommand cmd = new SqlCommand(query, con);
SqlDataAdapter adapter = new SqlDataAdapter(cmd);

// Fill the DataSet.
DataSet ds = new DataSet();
adapter.Fill(ds, "Employees");

// Create the dependency.
SqlCacheDependency empDependency = new SqlCacheDependency(cmd);

// Add a cache item that will be invalidated if one of its records changes
// (or a new record is added in the same range).
Cache.Insert("Employees", ds, empDependency);
```

You also need to call the static SqlDependency.Start() method to initialize the listening service on the web server. This needs to be performed only once for each database connection. One place you can call the Start() method is in the Application_Start() method of the global.asax file.

```
SqlDependency.Start(connectionString);
```

This method opens a new, nonpooled connection to the database. ASP.NET checks the queue for notifications using this connection. The first time you call Start(), a new queue is created with a unique, automatically generated name, and a new notification service is created for that queue. Then, the listening begins. When a notification is received, the web server pulls it from the queue, raises the SqlDependency.OnChange event, and invalidates the cached item.

Even if you have dependencies on several different tables, the same queue is used for all of them. That means you need only a single call to SqlDependency.Start(). If you inadvertently call the Start() method more than once, nothing happens.

Finally, you can use the following code to detach the listener:

```
SqlDependency.Stop(connectionString);
```

Typically, you'll use this when the Application_End() method is called to detach the listener and release all resources.

■ **Tip** Polling works best with data that's used heavily and changes infrequently. That way, you minimize the overhead of the notification process.

Custom Cache Dependencies

ASP.NET gives you the ability to create your own custom cache dependencies by deriving from CacheDependency, in much the same way that SqlCacheDependency does. This feature allows you (or third-party developers) to create dependencies that wrap other databases or to create resources such as message queues, Active Directory queries, and even web service calls.

Designing a custom CacheDependency is remarkably easy. All you need to do is start some asynchronous task that checks when the dependent item has changed. When it has, you call the base CacheDependency.NotifyDependencyChanged() method. In response, the base class updates the values of the HasChanged and UtcLastModified properties, and ASP.NET will remove any linked item from the cache.

You can use one of several techniques to create a custom cache dependency. Here are some typical examples:

Start a timer: When this timer fires, poll your resource to see if it has changed.

Start a separate thread: On this thread, check your resource and, if necessary, pause between checks by sleeping the thread.

Attach an event handler to another component: When the event fires, check your resource. For example, you could use this technique with the FileSystemWatcher to watch for a specific type of file change (such as file deletion).

In every case, you perform the basic initialization (attaching event handlers, creating a separate thread, and so on) in the constructor for your dependency.

A Basic Custom Cache Dependency

The following example shows an exceedingly simple custom cache dependency class. This class uses a timer to periodically check if a cached item is still valid.

The first step is to create the class by deriving from CacheDependency:

```
public class TimerTestCacheDependency : System.Web.Caching.CacheDependency
{ ... }
```

When the dependency is first created, you can set up the timer. In this example, the polling time isn't configurable—it's hard-coded at 5 seconds. That means every 5 seconds the timer fires and the dependency check runs.

```
private System.Threading.Timer timer;
private int pollTime = 5000;

public TimerTestCacheDependency()
{
    // Check immediately and then wait the poll time
    // for each subsequent check (same as CacheDependency behavior).
    timer = new Timer(
      new System.Threading.TimerCallback(CheckDependencyCallback),
      this, 0, pollTime);
}
```

As a test, the dependency check simply counts the number of times it's called. Once it's called for the fifth time (after a total of about 25 seconds), it invalidates the cached item. The important part of this example is how it tells ASP.NET to remove the dependent item. All you need to do is call the base CacheDependency.NotifyDependencyChanged() method, passing in a reference to the event sender (the current object) and any event arguments.

```
private int count = 0;

private void CheckDependencyCallback(object sender)
{
    // Check your resource here. If it has changed, notify ASP.NET:
    count++;
    if (count > 4)
    {
        // Signal that the item is expired.
        base.NotifyDependencyChanged(this, EventArgs.Empty);

        // Don't fire this callback again.
        timer.Dispose();
    }
}
```

The last step is to override DependencyDispose() to perform any cleanup that you need. DependencyDispose() is called soon after you use the NotifyDependencyChanged() method to invalidate the cached item. At this point, the dependency is no longer needed.

```
protected override void DependencyDispose()
{
    // Cleanup code goes here.
    if (timer != null) timer.Dispose();
}
```

Once you've created a custom dependency class, you can use it in the same way as the CacheDependency class, by supplying it as a parameter when you call Cache.Insert():

```
TimerTestCacheDependency dependency = new TimerTestCacheDependency();
Cache.Insert("MyItem", item, dependency);
```

A Custom Cache Dependency Using Message Queues

Now that you've seen how to create a basic custom cache dependency, it's worth considering a more practical example. The following MessageQueueCacheDependency monitors a Microsoft Messaging Queuing (MSMQ) queue. As soon as that queue receives a message, the item is considered expired (although you could easily extend the class so that it waits to receive a specific message). The MessageQueueCacheDependency class could come in handy if you're building the backbone of a distributed system and you need to pass messages between components on different computers to notify them when certain actions are performed or changes are made.

■ **Note** MSMQ is included with Windows but not necessarily installed by default. To install MSMQ, double-click the Programs and Features icon in the Control Panel, and then click Turn Windows Features On or Off. At minimum, you need to place a check mark next to Microsoft Message Queuing (MSMQ) Server and Microsoft Message Queuing (MSMQ) Server Core (which is nested underneath).

Before you can create the MessageQueueCacheDependency, you need to add a reference to the System.Messaging.dll assembly and import the System.Messaging namespace where the MessageQueue and Message classes reside. Then you're ready to build the solution.

In this example, the MessageQueueCacheDependency is able to monitor any queue. When you instantiate the dependency, you supply the queue name (which includes the location information). To perform the monitoring, the MessageQueueCacheDependency fires its private WaitForMessage() method asynchronously. This method waits until a new message is received in the queue, at which point it calls NotifyDependencyChanged() to invalidate the cached item.

Here's the complete code for the MessageQueueCacheDependency:

```
public class MessageQueueCacheDependency : CacheDependency
{
    // The queue to monitor.
    private MessageQueue queue;

    public MessageQueueCacheDependency(string queueName)
    {
        queue = new MessageQueue(queueName);

        // Wait for the queue message on another thread.
        WaitCallback callback = new WaitCallback(WaitForMessage);
        ThreadPool.QueueUserWorkItem(callback);
    }

    private void WaitForMessage(object state)
    {
        // Check your resource here (the polling).
        // This blocks until a message is sent to the queue.
        Message msg = queue.Receive();
```

```
        // (If you're looking for something specific, you could
        //  perform a loop and check the Message object here
        //  before invalidating the cached item.)
        base.NotifyDependencyChanged(this, EventArgs.Empty);
    }
}
```

To test this, you can use a revised version of the file-dependency testing page shown earlier (see Figure 11-8).

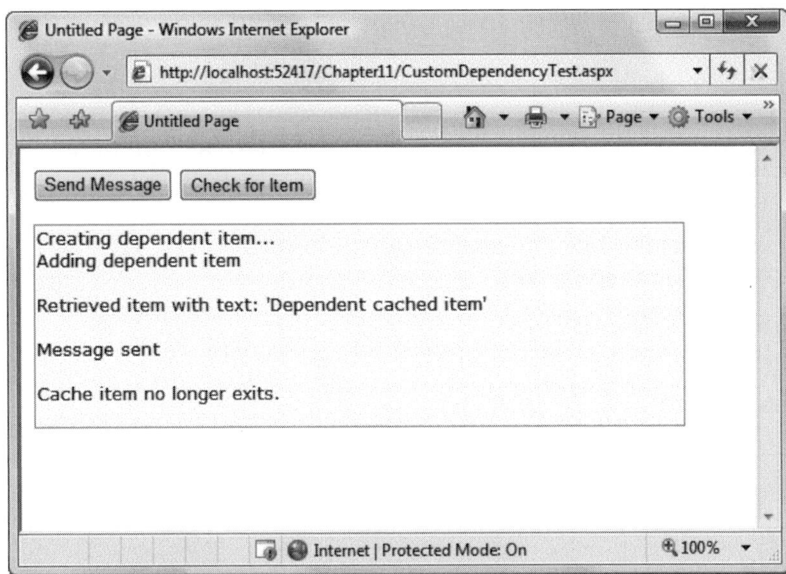

Figure 11-8. *Testing a message queue dependency*

This page creates a new private cache on the current computer and then adds a new item to the cache with a dependency on that queue:

```
private string queueName = @".\Private$\TestQueue";
// The leading . represents the current computer.
// The following Private$ indicates it's a private queue for this computer.
// The TestQueue is the queue name (you can modify this part).

protected void Page_Load(object sender, EventArgs e)
{
    if (!this.IsPostBack)
    {
        // Set up the queue.
        MessageQueue queue;
        if (MessageQueue.Exists(queueName))
        {
            queue = new MessageQueue(queueName);
        }
```

```
        else
        {
            queue = MessageQueue.Create(@".\Private$\TestQueue");
        }

        lblInfo.Text += "Creating dependent item...<br />";
        Cache.Remove("Item");
        MessageQueueCacheDependency dependency = new
          MessageQueueCacheDependency(queueName);
        string item = "Dependent cached item";
        lblInfo.Text += "Adding dependent item<br />";
        Cache.Insert("Item", item, dependency);
    }
}
```

When you click Send Message, a simple text message is sent to the queue, which will be received almost instantaneously by the custom dependency class:

```
protected void cmdModify_Click(object sender, EventArgs e)
{
    MessageQueue queue = new MessageQueue(queueName);

    // (You could send a custom object instead
    //  of a string.)
    queue.Send("Invalidate!");
    lblInfo.Text += "Message sent<br />";
}
```

To learn more about MSMQ, you can refer to the Visual Studio Help.

Asynchronous Pages

Now that you've considered the fundamentals of ASP.NET caching, it's worth taking a detour to consider a different performance-enhancing technique: asynchronous web pages. This specialized feature can help boost the scalability of your website. It's particularly useful in web pages that include time-consuming code that queries a database.

The basic idea behind asynchronous web pages is they allow you to take code that involves significant waiting and move it to a non-ASP.NET thread. To understand the potential benefit of this technique, you need to know a little bit more about how ASP.NET handles requests (a topic that Chapter 18 tackles in more detail).

Essentially, .NET maintains a pool of threads that can handle page requests. When a new request is received, ASP.NET grabs one of the available threads and uses it to process the entire page. That same thread instantiates the page, runs your event handling code, and returns the rendered HTML. If ASP.NET receives requests at a rapid pace—faster than it can serve them—unhandled requests will build up in a queue. If the queue fills up, ASP.NET is forced to reject additional requests with 503 "Server Unavailable" errors.

For most situations, the ASP.NET process model is the best possible compromise. However, there is a possible exception. If your page code involves lengthy waiting—for example, it tries to read a file from a remote location, call an object or web service on a distant computer, or query large amounts of data from a slow database—you'll tie up a request processing thread even though no real work is being performed. In other words, the web server has the processing resources to handle more requests (because your thread isn't using the CPU), but it doesn't have any available threads. Depending on the wait time and the volume of requests on your website, this could adversely affect the overall throughput of your site, preventing it from handling as many requests as it should be able to handle.

■ **Note** The actual number of threads in the pool and the size of the request queue are influenced by several factors, including the version of IIS you're using and the number of CPUs on your computer. It's always best to let ASP.NET handle these details, because it's most successful at balancing all the requirements. If you have too many ASP.NET threads running at once, your threads will tax the CPU (or fight over other limited resources) and ultimately slow down the entire web server. It's always better to stall or reject some requests than have the server attempt to handle too many requests and fail to complete any of them.

If you have a page that involves a fair bit of waiting, you can use the asynchronous page feature to free up the ASP.NET request thread. By doing so, your request is moved to another thread pool. (Technically, you're using the I/O completion port feature, which is built into the Windows operating system.) When your asynchronous work is finished, ASP.NET is notified, and the next available thread in the ASP.NET thread pool finishes the work, rendering the final HTML.

It's important to understand that an asynchronous page is no faster than a normal, synchronous page. In fact, the overhead of switching to the new thread and back again is likely to make it a bit slower. The advantage is that other requests—ones that don't involve long operations—can get served more quickly. This improves the overall scalability of your site. It's also important to realize that the asynchronous processing takes place completely on the web server, and the web page user won't notice any difference—wait times and postbacks will still take just as long.

■ **Note** Asynchronous web pages shouldn't be confused with asynchronous client-side programming techniques (such as Ajax, which is discussed in Chapter 30). The potential advantage of server-side asynchronous web page processing is that it allows you to deal with time-consuming requests more efficiently, so that other users won't need to wait when traffic is heavy. The potential advantage of client-side asynchronous programming is that the page seems more responsive to the end user.

Creating an Asynchronous Page

The first step to building an asynchronous page is setting the Async attribute in the Page directive to true, as shown here:

```
<%@ Page Async="true" ... %>
```

This tells ASP.NET that the page class it generates should implement IHttpAsyncHandler instead of IHttpHandler, which gives it basic support for asynchronous operations.

The next step is to call the AddOnPreRenderCompleteAsync() method of the page, typically when the page first loads. This method takes two delegates, which point to two separate methods. The first method launches your asynchronous task. The second method handles the completion callback for your asynchronous task. Here's the syntax you need:

```
AddOnPreRenderCompleteAsync(new BeginEventHandler(BeginTask),
  new EndEventHandler(EndTask));
```

In fact, C# is intelligent enough to let you use this compressed syntax to supply the two delegates you need:

```
AddOnPreRenderCompleteAsync(BeginTask, EndTask);
```

When ASP.NET encounters this statement, it takes note of it and then completes the normal page-processing life cycle, stopping just after the PreRender event fires. Then, ASP.NET calls the begin method you registered with AddOnPreRenderCompleteAsync(). If coded correctly, the begin method launches an asynchronous task and returns immediately, allowing the ASP.NET thread to be assigned to another request while the asynchronous task continues on another thread. When the task is complete, ASP.NET acquires a thread from its thread pool, runs the end method, and renders the page. Figure 11-9 illustrates this process.

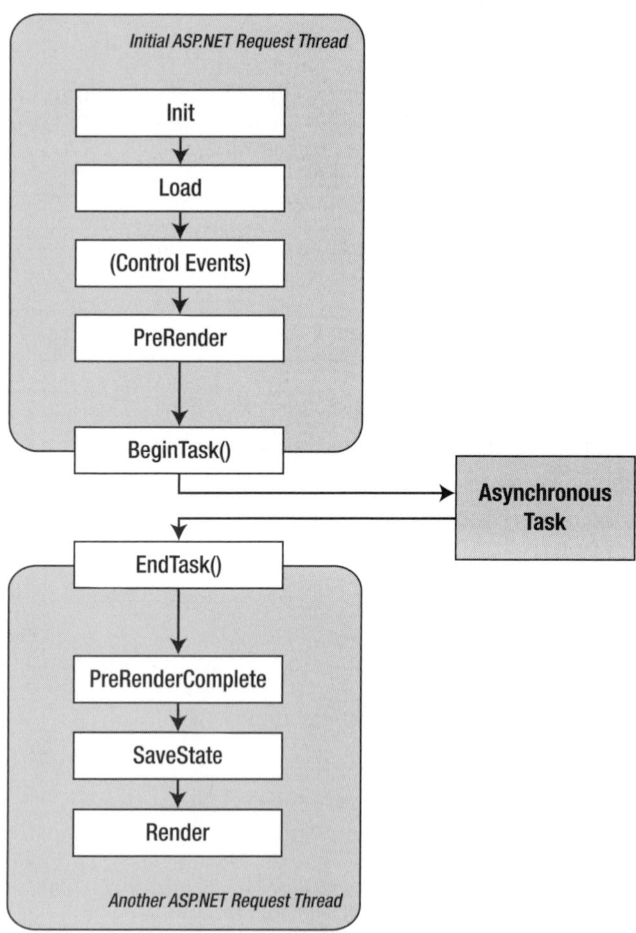

Figure 11-9. *The life cycle of an asynchronous page*

Unfortunately, this has one significant catch. To take advantage of this design, you need to have an asynchronous method that plugs into this infrastructure. This means you need a task that launches itself on a separate thread and returns an IAsyncResult object that allows ASP.NET to determine when it's complete. At first glance, it seems that several possible techniques can accomplish this. However, most of these won't work correctly in an ASP.NET application.

For example, seasoned .NET developers may expect to use the BeginInvoke() method of a delegate or the ThreadPool.QueueUserWorkItem() method. Unfortunately, both of these methods draw from the same thread pool that ASP.NET uses, which makes them ineffective. When you use these techniques in conjunction with an asynchronous page, you relinquish the original page-processing thread, but you acquire a second thread from the same pool. (The online examples include a page named SimpleAsyncPage.aspx that demonstrates how this works.)

Another option is to use the Thread class to explicitly create your own threads. Unfortunately, this is a risky endeavor, because it can easily lead to a page that creates more work than the server can handle. To understand the problem, consider what happens if a page creates a custom thread and that page is requested 100 times in quick succession. The web server winds up managing 100 threads, which taxes performance even if these threads are doing no work at all. In a popular website, you might create so many threads that the server can't complete any requests. Furthermore, the act of thread creation itself has some overhead. A good thread pooling system avoids thread creation and maintains a small set of threads at the ready at all times.

That leaves you with only two options, one of which is writing a custom thread pool. This means you use the low-level Thread class but take care to limit the total number of threads you'll create. This technique is not trivial, and it's beyond the scope of this book. You can find an excellent (although not production-ready) example of a custom thread pool at `http://www.bearcanyon.com/dotnet/#threadpool`.

So, what's the alternative if you wisely decide not to create a custom thread pool? The recommended approach is to use existing support in the .NET class library. For example, .NET includes various classes that provide proper asynchronous support for downloading content from the Web, reading data from a file, contacting a web service, and querying data through a DataReader. In general, this support is provided through matching methods named BeginXxx() and EndXxx(). For example, the System.IO.FileStream class provides a BeginRead() and an EndRead() method for asynchronously retrieving data from a file. These methods use Windows I/O completion ports, so they don't require threads from the shared thread pool that ASP.NET uses. If you use these methods in conjunction with an asynchronous page, you *will* free up another thread to serve ASP.NET web page requests.

In the following section, you'll see a similar example that uses the asynchronous support that's built into the DataReader.

Querying Data in an Asynchronous Page

The data source controls don't have any asynchronous support. However, many of the underlying ADO.NET classes, including SqlCommand and SqlDataReader, have asynchronous support. The following page takes advantage of the BeginReader() and EndReader() methods of the SqlDataReader. To allow the asynchronous query, you need to explicitly enable it in the connection string, as shown in the following snippet from the web.config file:

```
<connectionStrings>
  <add name="NorthwindAsync" connectionString="Data Source=localhost;
Initial Catalog=Northwind;Integrated Security=SSPI;Asynchronous Processing=true"
   providerName="System.Data.SqlClient"/>
</connectionStrings>
```

The first step is to register the methods that perform the asynchronous task. This step is the same in any asynchronous web page:

```
protected void Page_Load(object sender, EventArgs e)
{
    // Register the asynchronous methods for later use.
    // This method returns immediately.
    Page.AddOnPreRenderCompleteAsync(BeginTask, EndTask);
}
```

When the BeginTask() method is called, you can launch the asynchronous operation:

```
// The ADO.NET objects need to be accessible in several different
// event handlers, so they must be declared as member variables.
private SqlConnection con;
private SqlCommand cmd;
private SqlDataReader reader;

private IAsyncResult BeginTask(object sender, EventArgs e,
  AsyncCallback cb, object state)
{
    // Create the command.
    string connectionString = WebConfigurationManager.ConnectionStrings
      ["NorthwindAsync"].ConnectionString;
    con = new SqlConnection(connectionString);
    cmd = new SqlCommand("SELECT * FROM Employees", con);

    // Open the connection.
    // This part is not asynchronous.
    con.Open();

    // Run the query asynchronously.
    // This method returns immediately and provides ASP.NET
    // with the IAsyncResult object it needs to track progress.
    return cmd.BeginExecuteReader(cb, state);
}
```

The EndTask() method fires automatically when the IAsyncResult object indicates the BeginExecuteReader() method has finished its work and retrieved all the data:

```
private void EndTask(IAsyncResult ar)
{
    // You can now retrieve the DataReader.
    reader = cmd.EndExecuteReader(ar);
}
```

If you want to perform more page processing, you can handle the Page.PreRenderComplete event. In this example, this is the point where the grid is filled with the retrieved data:

```
protected void Page_PreRenderComplete(object sender, EventArgs e)
{
    grid.DataSource = reader;
    grid.DataBind();
    con.Close();
}
```

Finally, you need to override the Dispose() method of the page to ensure that the connection is closed in the event of an error:

```
public override void Dispose()
{
    if (con != null) con.Close();
    base.Dispose();
}
```

Overall, the asynchronous data retrieval makes this page more complex. The actual binding needs to be performed by hand (rather than using a data source control), and it spans several methods. However, the end result is a more scalable web application, assuming the query takes a significant amount of time to execute.

Handling Errors

Currently, the asynchronous DataReader page has no error-handling code, which makes it unsuitable for a real-world application. Implementing error handling isn't difficult, but because of the multistage nature of asynchronous pages, it may need to be performed in several places.

The easiest part of error handling is dealing with exceptions that occur during the asynchronous operation. By convention, these exceptions are thrown when you call the EndXxx() method. In the DataReader example, that means any query problems will cause an exception to be thrown when you call EndExecuteReader(). Here's how you catch it:

```
private void EndTask(IAsyncResult ar)
{
    // You can now retrieve the DataReader.
    try
    {
        reader = cmd.EndExecuteReader(ar);
    }
    catch (SqlException err)
    {
        lblError.Text = "The query failed.";
    }
}
```

You can test this code by modifying the query to be intentionally incorrect. (For example, create a query that refers to a nonexistent table.)

The other possible point of failure is when you attempt to open the connection. An exception occurs here if the connection string is invalid or if you're trying to connect a database server that doesn't exist. Although it's easy to catch the resulting exception, it's not as easy to deal with it gracefully. That's because this error occurs in your begin method. Once you've reached the begin method, you're at the point of no return—you've started an asynchronous operation, and ASP.NET expects you to return an IAsyncResult object. If you return a null reference, the page processing will be interrupted with an InvalidOperationException.

The solution is to create a custom IAsyncResult class that signals the operation is complete. This IAsyncResult class can also track the exception details, so you can retrieve them in your end method and use them to report the error. Here's an IAsyncResult-based class that includes these details:

```
public class CompletedSyncResult : IAsyncResult
{
    // Track the offending error.
    private Exception operationException;
    public Exception OperationException
    {
        get { return operationException; }
        set { operationException = value; }
    }

    // Maintain all the details for the asynchronous operation.
    public CompletedSyncResult(Exception operationException,
      AsyncCallback asyncCallback, object asyncState)
    {
        state = asyncState;
        OperationException = operationException;

        // Code that triggers the callback, if it's used.
        if (asyncCallback != null)
        {
            asyncCallback(this);
        }
    }

    // Implement the IAsyncState interface.
    // Use hard-coded values that indicate the task is always considered complete.
    private object state;
    object IAsyncResult.AsyncState
    {
        get { return state; }
    }

    WaitHandle IAsyncResult.AsyncWaitHandle
    {
        get { return null; }
    }

    bool IAsyncResult.CompletedSynchronously
    {
        get { return true; }
    }

    bool IAsyncResult.IsCompleted
    {
        get { return true; }
    }
}
```

Now if a connection error occurs, you can return an instance of this connection object instead of relying on the BeginExecuteReader() method. Here's the changed code:

```
private IAsyncResult BeginTask(object sender, EventArgs e,
  AsyncCallback cb, object state)
{
    ...

    // Open the connection.
    try
    {
        con.Open();
    }
    catch (Exception err)
    {
        return new CompletedSyncResult(err, cb, state);
    }

    // No error, so run the query asynchronously.
    return cmd.BeginExecuteReader(cb, state);
}
```

The only problem with this approach is that you need to explicitly check the type of IAsyncResult object in your end method. That way, you can detect an error condition.

```
private void EndTask(IAsyncResult ar)
{
    if (ar is CompletedSyncResult)
    {
        lblError.Text = "A connection error occurred.<br />";

        // Demonstrate how exception details can be retrieved.
        lblError.Text += ((CompletedSyncResult)ar).OperationException.Message;
        return;
    }

    // Otherwise, you can retrieve the DataReader.
    try
    {
        reader = cmd.EndExecuteReader(ar);
    }
    catch (SqlException err)
    {
        lblError.Text = "The query failed.";
    }
}
```

To try this, modify the connection string to point to an invalid server or database, and run the page. Your begin method will catch the error, and your end method will deal with it appropriately (in this example, by showing a message on the page).

■ **Note** Ideally, this tactic (checking the object type) wouldn't be necessary. Instead, you would simply call the EndExecuteReader() method and pass in the CompletedSyncResult object, and it would rethrow whatever exception object is stored in the CompletedSyncResult.OperationException property. Unfortunately, you can't implement this design because you don't own the EndExecuteReader() code. The only alternative is to wrap the BeginExecuteReader() and EndExecuteReader() methods in another, higher-level class (which is needlessly complex) or inspect the IAsyncResult object as shown here.

Using Caching with Asynchronous Tasks

In the previous example, you saw how you could skip over the asynchronous processing stage when an error occurs by using a custom class that implements IAsyncResult. However, you might want to stop a requested asynchronous operation before it gets started for other reasons. One example is if you've found the data you need in the cache. In this case, you don't need to waste time with a trip to the database.

You can handle this situation in more than one way. One option is to check the cache when the page is first created and register the asynchronous task only if you can't find the data object you need. However, sometimes you won't decide to skip the asynchronous processing stage until later, after your begin method has already been called. In other situations, you might want to make sure that ASP.NET runs the code in your end method, even though you're not performing an asynchronous operation. In both of these situations, you need a way to cancel your asynchronous task and return the data you need immediately.

Once again, the solution is to use a custom IAsyncResult object. In fact, you can use the CompletedSyncResult class developed in the previous section, with just a few minor changes. First, you need a way to store the data that you want to return:

```
private DataTable result;
public DataTable Result
{
    get
    {
        if (OperationException != null)
        {
            throw OperationException;
        }
        return result;
    }
    set { result = value; }
}
```

Notice that this property uses a different error-handling design than the first version of CompletedSyncResult. Now, when you try to read the Result property, CompletedSyncResult checks for the presence of exception information. If an exception has occurred, there won't be any data. This is the perfect time to rethrow the exception to alert the caller.

The second detail you need is another constructor. This constructor should accept the result object but not require any exception information:

```
public CompletedSyncResult(DataTable result, AsyncCallback asyncCallback,
  object asyncState)
{
    state = asyncState;
    Result = result;

    // Code that triggers the callback, if it's used.
    if (asyncCallback != null)
    {
        asyncCallback(this);
    }
}
```

Now you can modify your begin method to implement the caching. In this case, data is stored in a DataTable object. (The DataReader can't be efficiently cached, because it's usable only one time, and it holds an open database connection.)

Here's the code that checks the cache for the DataTable and uses CompletedSyncResult to return it without any asynchronous processing if it's there:

```
private IAsyncResult BeginTask(object sender, EventArgs e,
  AsyncCallback cb, object state)
{
    // Check the cache.
    if (Cache["Employees"] != null)
    {
        return new CompletedSyncResult((DataTable)Cache["Employees"],
          cb, state);
    }

    ...
}
```

The EndTask() method also needs a few changes. First, it checks whether the IAsyncResult object it has received is a CompletedSyncResult instance. If it is, it attempts to read the CompletedSyncResult.Result property. At this point, an error is thrown if needed. If the IAsyncResult isn't a CompletedSyncResult, the code calls EndExecuteReader() to get the DataReader, uses the DataReader to fill a DataTable with the handy DataTable.Load() method, and then stores the DataTable in the cache for 5 minutes so it can be used by subsequent requests.

Here's the complete code for the end method:

```
private DataTable table;

private void EndTask(IAsyncResult ar)
{
    CompletedSyncResult completedSync = ar as CompletedSyncResult;
    if (completedSync != null)
    {
        try
        {
            // Store the DataTable for use in the PreRenderComplete
            // event hander.
            table = completedSync.Result;
            lblError.Text = "Completed with data from the cache.";
```

```
        }
        catch (Exception err)
        {
            lblError.Text = "A connection error occurred.";
        }
    }
    else
    {
        try
        {
            reader = cmd.EndExecuteReader(ar);
            table = new DataTable("Employees");
            table.Load(reader);
            Cache.Insert("Employees", table, null,
              DateTime.Now.AddMinutes(5), TimeSpan.Zero);
        }
        catch (SqlException err)
        {
            lblError.Text = "The query failed.";
        }
    }
}
```

When the Page.PreRenderComplete event fires, the DataTable is bound to the grid:

```
protected void Page_PreRenderComplete(object sender, EventArgs e)
{
    grid.DataSource = table;
    grid.DataBind();
}
```

This example shows the entire process, but the code isn't arranged in the most structured way. You can improve this code by completely wrapping the BeginExecuteReader() and EndExecuteReader() methods in the CompletedSyncResult class. That way, your web page deals with only one type of IAsyncResult object.

■ **Note** To see an example of this more streamlined design, refer to the AsyncDataReaderRefactored.aspx page in the samples for this chapter. This page uses an IAsyncResult-based class named AsyncQueryResult, which supports synchronous use (when an error occurs or the data object is provided in the constructor) and asynchronous use (through the BeginExecuteReader() and EndExecuteReader() methods).

Multiple Asynchronous Tasks and Timeouts

In some situations, you might have a series of asynchronous tasks that can be completed at the same time. For example, maybe you have several web services that you want to call and they all involve a considerable wait. By performing these calls simultaneously, you can collapse your waiting time (in other words, you can wait for a response from all three web services at once).

■ **Tip** Performing simultaneous asynchronous tasks is a good technique when your tasks involve different resources. It's a bad idea if your tasks will compete for the same resource. For example, a page that performs three database queries at once isn't a good candidate for simultaneous execution, because you'll need to open three connections at the same time, which will probably have a negative effect on the overall scalability of your site.

If you use AddOnPreRenderCompleteAsync() to register multiple tasks, they'll be executed sequentially. If you want to execute more than one *simultaneous* task, you need to use the RegisterAsyncTask() method instead. This method takes a PageAsyncTask object that encapsulates all the request details.

Here's an example that has the same end result as the AddOnPreRenderCompleteAsync() statement in the previous example:

```
PageAsyncTask task = new PageAsyncTask(BeginTask, EndTask, null, null);
Page.RegisterAsyncTask(task);
```

To perform simultaneous requests, just create more than one task object and call RegisterAsyncTask for each one:

```
PageAsyncTask taskA = new PageAsyncTask(BeginTaskA, EndTaskA, null, null);
Page.RegisterAsyncTask(taskA);

PageAsyncTask taskB = new PageAsyncTask(BeginTaskB, EndTaskB, null, null);
Page.RegisterAsyncTask(taskB);
```

In this case, the final page rendering stage will be delayed until all the asynchronous tasks have completed their processing.

The RegisterAsyncTask() method has a few other differences as compared to the AddOnPreRenderCompleteAsync() method. You may have noticed that it takes two additional parameters. The first of these allows you to supply a delegate that points to a timeout method:

```
PageAsyncTask task = new PageAsyncTask(BeginTask, EndTask, Timeout, null);
```

This method will be triggered if the asynchronous request times out. You can use this code to display an explanatory error message on the page before it's rendered and returned to the user. Here's an example that's designed for the asynchronous DataReader page:

```
public void Timeout(IAsyncResult result)
{
    if (con != null)
        con.Close();

    lblError.Text = "Task timed out.";
}
```

By default, a timeout occurs after 45 seconds, but you can supply a different timeout value using the AsyncTimeout property of the Page directive, as shown here:

```
<%@ Page Async="true" AsyncTimeout="60" ... %>
```

■ **Note** The timeout affects all tasks. There is no way to set different timeouts to different asynchronous tasks.

The final parameter of the PageAsyncTask() constructor is an optional state object, which you can use to pass any information you need to your begin method.

The other difference with the RegisterAsyncTask() is that the current HttpContext is passed to your end and timeout methods. This means you can use properties such as Page.Request to get information about the current request. This information isn't available to asynchronous tasks that have been registered using AddOnPreRenderCompleteAsync().

Summary

In this chapter, you took a detailed look at caching, which is one of ASP.NET's premier features. As a professional ASP.NET programmer, you should design with caching strategies in mind from the beginning. Caching is particularly important when using the data source controls, because these controls are deceptively simple—they make it easy to build a page that queries a database multiple times for a single request.

CHAPTER 12

■ ■ ■

Files and Streams

Most web applications rely heavily on databases to store information. Databases are unmatched in multiuser scenarios. They handle simultaneous access without a hitch, and they support caching and low-level disk optimizations that guarantee blistering performance. Quite simply, an RDBMS (Relational Database Management System) offers the most robust and best-performing storage for data.

Of course, most web developers inevitably face a scenario where they need to access data in other locations, such as the file system. Common examples include reading information produced by another application, writing a quick-and-dirty log for testing purposes, and creating a management page that allows administrators to upload files and view what's currently on the server. In this chapter, you'll learn how to use the classes in the System.IO namespace to get file system information, work with file paths as strings, write and read files, and serialize objects.

Working with the File System

The simplest level of file access just involves retrieving information about existing files and directories and performing typical file system operations such as copying files and creating directories. These tasks don't involve actually opening or writing a file (both of which are tasks you'll learn about later in this chapter).

The .NET Framework provides a few basic classes for retrieving file system information. They are all located in the System.IO namespace (and, incidentally, can be used in desktop applications in the same way they are used in web applications). They include the following:

- **Directory and File:** These classes provide static methods that allow you to retrieve information about any files and directories that are visible from your server.
- **DriveInfo, DirectoryInfo, and FileInfo:** These classes use similar instance methods and properties to retrieve the same information.

These two sets of classes provide similar methods and properties. The key difference is that you need to create a DirectoryInfo or FileInfo object before you can use any methods, whereas the static methods of the Directory and File classes are always available. Typically, the Directory and File classes are more convenient for one-off tasks. On the other hand, if you need to retrieve several pieces of information, it's better to create DirectoryInfo and FileInfo objects. That way you don't need to keep specifying the name of the directory or file each time you call a method. It's also faster. That's because the FileInfo and DirectoryInfo classes perform their security checks once—when you create the object instance. The Directory and File classes perform a security check every time you invoke a method.

The Directory and File Classes

The Directory and File classes provide a number of useful methods. Tables 12-1 and 12-2 tell the whole story. Note that every method takes the same parameter: a fully qualified path name identifying the directory or file you want the operation to act on.

Table 12-1. *Directory Methods*

Method	Description
CreateDirectory()	Creates a new directory. If you specify a directory inside another nonexistent directory, ASP.NET will thoughtfully create all the required directories.
Delete()	Deletes the corresponding empty directory. To delete a directory along with its contents (subdirectories and files), add the optional second parameter of true.
Exists()	Returns true or false to indicate whether the specified directory exists.
GetCreationTime(), GetLastAccessTime(), and GetLastWriteTime()	Returns a DateTime object that represents the time the directory was created, accessed, or written to. Each "Get" method has a corresponding "Set" method, which isn't shown in this table.
GetDirectories() and GetFiles()	Returns an array of strings, one for each subdirectory or file in the specified directory. These methods can accept a second parameter that specifies a search expression (such as ASP*.*).
GetLogicalDrives()	Returns an array of strings, one for each drive that's defined on the current computer. Drive letters are in this format: c:\.
GetParent()	Parses the supplied directory string and tells you what the parent directory is. You could do this on your own by searching for the \ character (or, more generically, the Path.DirectorySeparatorChar), but this function makes life a little easier.
GetCurrentDirectory() and SetCurrentDirectory()	Allows you to set and retrieve the current directory, which is useful if you need to use relative paths instead of full paths. Generally, you shouldn't rely on these functions—use full paths instead.
Move()	Accepts two parameters: the source path and the destination path. The directory and all its contents can be moved to any path, as long as it's located on the same drive.
GetAccessControl() and SetAccessControl()	Returns or sets a System.Security.AccessControl.Directory- Security object. You can use this object to examine the Windows access control lists (ACLs) that are applied on this directory and even change them programmatically.

Table 12-2. File Methods

Method	Description
Copy()	Accepts two parameters: the fully qualified source filename and the fully qualified destination filename. To allow overwriting, use the version that takes a Boolean third parameter and set it to true.
Delete()	Deletes the specified file but doesn't throw an exception if the file can't be found.
Exists()	Indicates true or false whether a specified file exists.
GetAttributes() and SetAttributes()	Retrieves or sets an enumerated value that can include any combination of the values from the FileAttributes enumeration.
GetCreationTime(), GetLastAccessTime(), and GetLastWriteTime()	Returns a DateTime object that represents the time the file was created, accessed, or last written to. Each "Get" method has a corresponding "Set" method, which isn't shown in this table.
Move()	Accepts two parameters: the fully qualified source filename and the fully qualified destination filename. You can move a file across drives and even rename it while you move it (or rename it without moving it).
Create() and CreateText()	Creates the specified file and returns a FileStream object that you can use to write to it. CreateText() performs the same task but returns a StreamWriter object that wraps the stream.
Open(), OpenText(), OpenRead(), and OpenWrite()	Opens a file (provided it exists). OpenText() and OpenRead() open a file in read-only mode, returning a FileStream or StreamReader. OpenWrite() opens a file in write-only mode, returning a FileStream.
ReadAllText(), ReadAllLines(), and ReadAllBytes()	Reads the entire file and returns its contents as a single string, an array of strings (one for each line), or an array of bytes. Use this method only for very small files. For larger files, use streams to read one chunk at a time and reduce the memory overhead.
WriteAllText(), WriteAllLines(), and WriteAllBytes()	Writes an entire file in one shot using a supplied string, array of strings (one for each line), or array of bytes. If the file already exists, it is overwritten.
GetAccessControl() and SetAccessControl()	Returns or sets a System.Security.AccessControl.FileSecurity object. You can use this object to examine the Windows ACLs that are applied on this directory and even change them programmatically.

■ **Tip** The only feature that the File class lacks (and the FileInfo class provides) is the ability to retrieve the size of a specified file.

The File and Directory methods are completely intuitive. For example, you could use this code to write a dynamic list displaying the name of each file in the current directory:

```
string directoryName = @"c:\Temp";

// Retrieve the list of files, and display it in the page.
string[] fileList = Directory.GetFiles(directoryName);
foreach (string file in fileList)
{
    lstFiles.Items.Add(file);
}
```

In this example, the string with the file path c:\Temp is preceded by an at (@) character. This tells C# to interpret the string exactly as written. Without this character, C# would assume the directory separation character (\) indicates the start of a special character sequence. Another option is to use the escaped character sequence \\, which C# reads as a single literal slash. In this case, you would write the path as c:\\Temp.

Because the list of files is simply an ordinary list of strings, it can easily be bound to a list control, resulting in the following more efficient syntax for displaying the files on a page:

```
string directoryName = @"c:\Temp";
lstFiles.DataSource = Directory.GetFiles(directoryName);
lstFiles.DataBind();
```

For this code to work, the account that is used to run the ASP.NET worker process must have rights to the directory you're using. Otherwise, a SecurityException will be thrown when your web page attempts to access the file system. You can modify the permissions for a directory by right-clicking the directory, selecting Properties, and choosing the Security tab. This typically won't be a problem if you're testing an application with Visual Studio's integrated web server, which runs under your user account. However, it can easily cause issues when you deploy your site. In this case, you need to grant the appropriate permissions to the IIS_USRS group (or modify the account that your web site uses). For more information, refer to Chapter 18.

The DirectoryInfo and FileInfo Classes

The DirectoryInfo and FileInfo classes mirror the functionality in the Directory and File classes. In addition, they make it easy to walk through directory and file relationships. For example, you can easily retrieve the FileInfo objects of files in a directory represented by a DirectoryInfo object.

Note that while the Directory and File classes expose only methods, DirectoryInfo and FileInfo provide a combination of properties and methods. For example, while the File class has separate GetAttributes() and SetAttributes() methods, the FileInfo class exposes a read-write Attributes property.

Another nice thing about the DirectoryInfo and FileInfo classes is that they share a common set of properties and methods because they derive from the common FileSystemInfo base class. Table 12-3 describes the members they have in common.

Table 12-3. DirectoryInfo and FileInfo Members

Member	Description
Attributes	Allows you to retrieve or set attributes using a combination of values from the FileAttributes enumeration.
CreationTime, LastAccessTime, and LastWriteTime	Allows you to set or retrieve the creation time, last access time, and last write time using a DateTime object.
Exists	Returns true or false depending on whether the file or directory exists. In other words, you can create FileInfo and DirectoryInfo objects that don't actually correspond to current physical directories, although you obviously won't be able to use properties such as CreationTime and methods such as MoveTo().
FullName, Name, and Extension	Returns a string that represents the fully qualified name, the directory or filename (with extension), or the extension on its own, depending on which property you use.
Delete()	Removes the file or directory, if it exists. When deleting a directory, it must be empty, or you must specify an optional parameter set to true.
Refresh()	Updates the object so it's synchronized with any file system changes that have happened in the meantime (for example, if an attribute was changed manually using Windows Explorer).
Create()	Creates the specified directory or file.
MoveTo()	Copies the directory and its contents or the file. For a DirectoryInfo object, you need to specify the new path; for a FileInfo object, you specify a path and filename.

In addition, the FileInfo and DirectoryInfo classes have a couple of unique members, as indicated in Tables 12-4 and 12-5.

Table 12-4. Unique DirectoryInfo Members

Member	Description
Parent and Root	Returns a DirectoryInfo object that represents the parent or root directory.
CreateSubdirectory()	Creates a directory with the specified name in the directory represented by the DirectoryInfo object. It also returns a new DirectoryInfo object that represents the subdirectory.
GetDirectories()	Returns an array of DirectoryInfo objects that represent all the subdirectories contained in this directory.
GetFiles()	Returns an array of FileInfo objects that represent all the files contained in this directory.

Table 12-5. Unique FileInfo Members

Member	Description
Directory	Returns a DirectoryInfo object that represents the parent directory.
DirectoryName	Returns a string that identifies the name of the parent directory.
Length	Returns a long (64-bit integer) with the file size in bytes.
CopyTo()	Copies a file to the new path and filename specified as a parameter. It also returns a new FileInfo object that represents the new (copied) file. You can supply an optional additional parameter of true to allow overwriting.
Create() and CreateText()	Creates the specified file and returns a FileStream object that you can use to write to it. CreateText() performs the same task but returns a StreamWriter object that wraps the stream.
Open(), OpenRead(), OpenText(), and OpenWrite()	Opens a file (provided it exists). OpenRead() and OpenText() open a file in read-only mode, returning a FileStream or StreamReader. OpenWrite() opens a file in write-only mode, returning a FileStream.

When you create a DirectoryInfo or FileInfo object, you specify the full path in the constructor, as shown here:

```
DirectoryInfo myDirectory = new DirectoryInfo(@"c:\Temp");
FileInfo myFile = new FileInfo(@"c:\Temp\readme.txt");
```

When you create a new DirectoryInfo or FileInfo object, you'll receive an exception if the path you used isn't properly formed (for example, if it contains illegal characters). However, the path doesn't need to correspond to a real physical file or directory. If you're not sure, you can use Exists to check whether your directory or file really exists.

If the file or directory doesn't exist, you can always use a method such as Create() to create it. Here's an example:

```
// Define the new directory and file.
DirectoryInfo myDirectory = new DirectoryInfo(@"c:\Temp\Test");
FileInfo myFile = new FileInfo(@"c:\Temp\Test\readme.txt");

// Now create them. Order here is important.
// You can't create a file in a directory that doesn't exist yet.
myDirectory.Create();
FileStream stream = myFile.Create();
stream.Close();
```

The FileInfo and DirectoryInfo objects retrieve information from the file system the first time you query a property. They don't check for new information on subsequent use. This could lead to inconsistency if the file changes in the meantime. If you know or suspect that file system information has changed for the given object, you should call the Refresh() method to retrieve the latest information.

The DirectoryInfo class doesn't provide any property for determining the total size information. However, you can calculate the size of all the files in a particular directory quite easily by totaling the FileInfo.Length contribution of each one.

Before you take this step, you need to decide whether to include subdirectories in the total. The following method lets you use either approach:

```
private static long CalculateDirectorySize(DirectoryInfo directory,
 bool includeSubdirectories)
{
    long totalSize = 0;

    // Add up each file.
    FileInfo[] files = directory.GetFiles();
    foreach (FileInfo file in files)
    {
        totalSize += file.Length;
    }

    // Add up each subdirectory, if required.
    if (includeSubdirectories)
    {
        DirectoryInfo[] dirs = directory.GetDirectories();
        foreach (DirectoryInfo dir in dirs)
        {
            totalSize += CalculateDirectorySize(dir, true);
        }
    }
    return totalSize;
}
```

For information about free space, you need to use the DriveInfo class.

The DriveInfo Class

The DriveInfo class allows you to retrieve information about a drive on your computer. Few pieces of information will interest you—typically, the DriveInfo class is just used to retrieve the total amount of used and free space.

Table 12-6 shows the DriveInfo members. Unlike the FileInfo and DriveInfo classes, there is no Drive class to provide instance versions of these methods.

Table 12-6. *DriveInfo Members*

Member	Description
TotalSize	Gets the total size of the drive, in bytes. This includes allocated and free space.
TotalFreeSpace	Gets the total amount of free space, in bytes.
AvailableFreeSpace	Gets the total amount of available free space, in bytes. Available space may be less than the total free space if you've applied disk quotas limiting the space that the ASP.NET process can use.

Member	Description
DriveFormat	Returns the name of the file system used on the drive (such as NTFS or FAT32).
DriveType	Returns a value from the DriveType enumeration, which indicates whether the drive is a fixed, network, CD-ROM, RAM, or removable drive. (It returns Unknown if the drive's type cannot be determined.)
IsReady	Returns whether the drive is ready for reading or writing operations. Removable drives are considered "not ready" if they don't have any media. For example, if there's no CD in a CD drive, IsReady will return false. In this situation, it's not safe to query the other DriveInfo properties. Fixed drives are always readable.
Name	Returns the drive letter name of the drive (such as C: or E:).
VolumeLabel	Gets or sets the descriptive volume label for the drive. In an NTFS-formatted drive, the volume label can be up to 32 characters. If not set, this property returns null.
RootDirectory	Returns a DirectoryInfo object for the root directory in this drive.
GetDrives()	Retrieves an array of DriveInfo objects, representing all the logical drives on the current computer.

■ **Tip** Attempting to read from a drive that's not ready (for example, a CD drive that doesn't currently have a CD in it) will throw an exception. To avoid this problem, check the DriveInfo.IsReady property and attempt to read other properties only if the DriveInfo.IsReady property returns true.

Working with Attributes

The Attributes property of the FileInfo and DirectoryInfo classes represents the file system attributes for the file or directory. Because every file and directory can have a combination of attributes, the Attributes property contains a combination of values from the FileAttributes enumeration. Table 12-7 describes these values.

Table 12-7. *Values for the FileAttributes Enumeration*

Value	Description
Archive	The item is archived. Applications can use this attribute to mark files for backup or removal, although it's really just a holdover from older DOS-based operating systems.
Compressed	The item is compressed.
Device	Not currently used. Reserved for future use.
Directory	The item is a directory.
Encrypted	This item is encrypted. For a file, this means that all data in the file is encrypted. For a directory, this means that encryption is the default for newly created files and directories.
Hidden	This item is hidden and thus is not included in an ordinary directory listing. However, you can still see it in Windows Explorer.
Normal	This item is normal and has no other attributes set. This attribute is valid only if used alone.
NotContentIndexed	This item will not be indexed by the operating system's content indexing service.
Offline	This file is offline and not currently available.
ReadOnly	This item is read-only.
ReparsePoint	This file contains a reparse point, which is a block of user-defined data associated with a file or a directory in an NTFS file system.
SparseFile	The file is a sparse file. Sparse files are typically large files with data consisting of mostly zeros. This item is supported only on NTFS file systems.
System	The item is part of the operating system or is used exclusively by the operating system.
Temporary	This item is temporary and can be deleted when the application is no longer using it.

To find out all the attributes a file has, you can call the ToString() method of the Attributes property. This returns a string with a comma-separated list of attributes:

```
// This displays a string in the format "ReadOnly, Archive, Encrypted"
lblInfo.Text = myFile.Attributes.ToString();
```

When testing for a single specific attribute, you need to use bitwise arithmetic. For example, consider the following faulty code:

```
if (myFile.Attributes == FileAttributes.ReadOnly)
{ ... }
```

This test succeeds only if the read-only attribute is the only attribute for the current file. This is rarely the case. If you want to successfully check whether the file is read-only, you need this code instead:

```
if ((myFile.Attributes & FileAttributes.ReadOnly) != 0)
{ ... }
```

This test succeeds because it filters out just the read-only attribute. Essentially, the Attributes setting consists (in binary) of a series of ones and zeros, such as 00010011. Each 1 represents an attribute that is present, and each 0 represents an attribute that is not. When you use the & operator with an enumerated value, it automatically performs a bitwise and operation, which compares each digit against each digit in the enumerated value. For example, if you combine a value of 00100001 (representing an individual file's archive and read-only attributes) with the enumerated value 00000001 (which represents the read-only flag), the resulting value will be 00000001. It will have a 1 only where it can be matched in both values. You can then test this resulting value against the FileAttributes.ReadOnly enumerated value using the equal sign.

Similar logic allows you to verify that a file does not have a specific attribute:

```
if ((myFile.Attributes & FileAttributes.ReadOnly) != 0)
{ ... }
```

When setting an attribute, you must also use bitwise arithmetic. In this case, you need to ensure that you don't inadvertently wipe out the other attributes that are already set.

```
// This sets the read-only attribute (and keeps all others as is).
myFile.Attributes = myFile.Attributes | FileAttributes.ReadOnly;

// This removes the read-only attribute (and keeps all others as is).
myFile.Attributes = myFile.Attributes & .FileAttributes.ReadOnly;
```

Some attributes can't be set programmatically. For example, the Encrypted attribute is set by the operating system if you're using the EFS (Encrypting File System) feature in Windows. When a file is encrypted using EFS, it's encrypted with a secret key that's linked to the current user account. When the same user reads the file, Windows decrypts it transparently. However, other users won't share the same secret key and won't be able to access the file. (Although EFS rarely makes sense in an ASP.NET application, you can use it programmatically with the Encrypt() and Decrypt() methods of the FileInfo class.)

Filter Files with Wildcards

The DirectoryInfo and Directory objects both provide a way to search the current directories for files or directories that match a specific filter expression. These search expressions can use the standard ? and * wildcards. The ? wildcard represents any single character, and the * wildcard represents any sequence of zero or more characters.

For example, the following code snippet retrieves the names of all the files in the c:\temp directory that have the extension .txt. The code then iterates through the retrieved FileInfo collection of matching files and displays the name and size of each one.

```
DirectoryInfo dir = new DirectoryInfo(@"c:\temp");

// Get all the files with the .txt extension.
FileInfo[] files = dir.GetFiles("*.txt");

// Process each file.
foreach (FileInfo file in files)
{ ... }
```

You can use a similar technique to retrieve directories that match a specified search pattern by using the overloaded DirectoryInfo.GetDirectories() method.

The GetFiles() and GetDirectories() methods search only the current directory. If you want to perform a search through all the contained subdirectories, you'd need to use recursive logic.

Retrieving File Version Information

File version information is the information you see when you look at the properties of an EXE or DLL file in Windows Explorer. Version information commonly includes a version number, the company that produced the component, trademark information, and so on.

The FileInfo and File classes don't provide a way to retrieve file version information. However, you can retrieve it quite easily using the static GetVersionInfo() method of the System.Diagnostics.FileVersionInfo class. The following example uses this technique to get a string with the complete version information and then displays it in a label:

```
string fileName = @"c:\Windows\explorer.exe";
FileVersionInfo info = FileVersionInfo.GetVersionInfo(fileName);
lblInfo.Text = info.FileVersion;
```

Table 12-8 lists the properties you can read.

Table 12-8. *FileVersionInfo Properties*

Property	Description
FileVersion, FileMajorPart, FileMinorPart, FileBuildPart, and FilePrivatePart	Typically, a version number is displayed as [MajorNumber].[MinorNumber].[BuildNumber].[PrivatePartNumber]. These properties allow you to retrieve the complete version as a string (FileVersion) or each individual component as a number.
FileName	Gets the name of the file that this instance of FileVersionInfo describes.
OriginalFilename	Gets the name the file was created with.
InternalName	Gets the internal name of the file, if one exists.
FileDescription	Gets the description of the file.
CompanyName	Gets the name of the company that produced the file.

Property	Description
ProductName	Gets the name of the product this file is distributed with.
ProductVersion, ProductMajorPart, ProductMinorPart, ProductBuildPart, and ProductPrivatePart	These properties allow you to retrieve the complete product version as a string (ProductVersion) or each individual component as a number.
IsDebug	Gets a Boolean value that specifies whether the file contains debugging information or is compiled with debugging features enabled.
IsPatched	Gets a Boolean value that specifies whether the file has been modified and is not identical to the original shipping file of the same version number.
IsPreRelease	Gets a Boolean value that specifies whether the file is a development version, rather than a commercially released product.
IsPrivateBuild	Gets a Boolean value that specifies whether the file was built using standard release procedures.
IsSpecialBuild	Gets a Boolean value that specifies whether the file is a special build.
SpecialBuild	If IsSpecialBuild is true, this property contains a string that specifies how the build differs from an ordinary build.
Comments	Gets the comments associated with the file.
Language	Gets the default language string for the version info block.
LegalCopyright	Gets all copyright notices that apply to the specified file.
LegalTrademarks	Gets the trademarks and registered trademarks that apply to the file.

The Path Class

If you're working with files, you're probably also working with file and directory paths. Path information is stored as an ordinary string. As a result, you'll sometimes need messy string-parsing code to manipulate it.

This is where the System.IO.Path class becomes very useful. The Path class provides static helper methods that perform common path manipulation tasks. For example, the following code snippet uses the Path.Combine() method to fuse together a full directory path with a filename for a file in that directory:

```
DirectoryInfo dirInfo = new DirectoryInfo(@"c:\Upload\Documents");
string file = "test.txt";
string path = Path.Combine(dirInfo.FullName, file);
```

The Path class is also a handy tool when preventing security risks such as a canonicalization error. A canonicalization error is a specific type of application error that can occur when your code assumes that user-supplied values will always be in a standardized form. Canonicalization errors are low-tech but quite serious, and they usually have the result of allowing a user to perform an action that should be restricted.

One infamous type of canonicalization error is SQL injection, whereby a user submits incorrectly formatted values to trick your application into executing a modified SQL command. (Chapter 7 covers SQL injection in detail). Other forms of canonicalization problems can occur with file paths and URLs.

For example, consider the following method that returns file data from a fixed document directory:

```
FileInfo file = new FileInfo(Server.MapPath("Documents\\" + txtBox.Text));
// (Read the file and display it in another control).
```

This code looks simple enough. It concatenates the user-supplied filename with the Documents path, thereby allowing the user to retrieve data from any file in this directory. The problem is that filenames can be represented in multiple formats. Instead of submitting a valid filename, an attacker can submit a qualified filename such as ..\filename. The concatenated path of WebApp\Documents\..\filename will actually retrieve a file from the parent of the Documents directory (WebApp). A similar approach will allow the user to specify any filename on the web application drive. Because the web page is limited only according to the restrictions of the ASP.NET worker process, the user may be allowed to download a sensitive server-side file.

The fix for this code is fairly easy. Once again, you can use the Path class. This time, you use the GetFileName() method to extract just the final filename portion of the string, as shown here:

```
string fileName = Path.GetFileName(txtBox.Text);
FileInfo file = new FileInfo(Server.MapPath(
  Path.Combine("Documents", fileName)));
```

This ensures that the user is constrained to the correct directory. If you are dealing with URLs, you can work similar magic with the System.Uri type. For example, here's how you might remove query string arguments from a URI and make sure it refers to a given server and virtual directory:

```
string uriString = "http://www.wrongsite.com/page.aspx?cmd=run";

Uri uri = new Uri(uriString);
string page = Path.GetFileName(uri.AbsolutePath);
// page is now just "page.aspx"

Uri baseUri = new Uri("http://www.rightsite.com");
uri = new Uri(baseUri, page);
// uri now stores the path http://www.rightsite.com/page.aspx.
```

Table 12-9 lists the most useful methods of the Path class.

Table 12-9. *Path Methods*

Methods	Description
Combine()	Combines a path with a filename or a subdirectory.
ChangeExtension()	Modifies the current extension of the file in a string. If no extension is specified, the current extension will be removed.

Methods	Description
GetDirectoryName()	Returns all the directory information, which is the text between the first and last directory separators (\).
GetFileName()	Returns just the filename portion of a path.
GetFileNameWithoutExtension()	This method is similar to GetFileName(), but it omits the extension from the returned string.
GetFullPath()	This method has no effect on an absolute path, and it changes a relative path into an absolute path using the current directory. For example, if c:\Temp\ is the current directory, calling GetFullPath() on a filename such as test.txt returns c:\Temp\test.txt.
GetPathRoot()	Retrieves a string with the root (for example, C:\), provided that information is in the string. For a relative path, it returns a null reference.
HasExtension()	Returns true if the path ends with an extension.
IsPathRooted()	Returns true if the path is an absolute path and false if it's a relative path.

Although the Path class contains methods for drilling down the directory structure (adding subdirectories to directory paths), it doesn't provide any methods for going back up (removing subdirectories from directory paths). However, you can work around this limitation by using the Combine() method with the relative path .., which means "move one directory up." For good measure, you can also use the GetFullPath() method on the result to return it to a normal form.

Here's an example:

```
string path = @"c:\temp\subdir";

path = Path.Combine(path, "..");
// path now contains the string "c:\temp\subdir\.."

path = Path.GetFullPath(path);
// path now contains the string "c:\temp"
```

■ **Note** In most cases, an exception will be thrown if you supply a path that contains illegal characters to one of these methods. However, path names that contain a wildcard character (* or ?) will not cause the methods to throw an exception.

A File Browser

Using the concepts you've learned so far, it's quite straightforward to put together a simple file-browsing application. Rather than iterating through collections of files and directories manually, this example handles everything using the GridView and some data binding code.

Figure 12-1 shows this program in action.

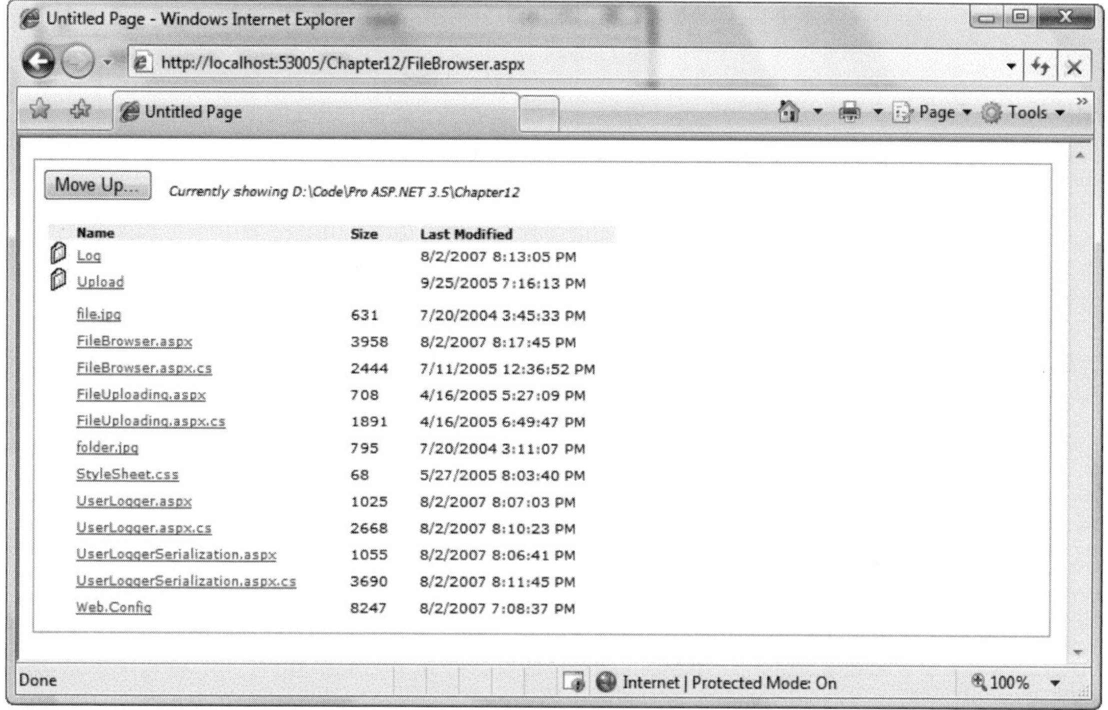

***Figure 12-1.** Browsing the file system*

The directory listing is built using two separate GridView controls, one on top of the other. The topmost GridView shows the directories, and the GridView underneath shows files. The only visible differences to the user are that the directories don't display length information, and they have a folder icon next to their names. The ShowHeader property of the second GridView is set to false so that the two grids blend into each other fairly seamlessly. And because the GridView controls are stacked together, as the list of directories grows, the list of files moves down the page to accommodate it.

Technically, you could handle the directory and file listing using one GridView object. That's because all FileInfo and DirectoryInfo objects have a common parent—the FileSystemInfo object. However, in this grid you want to show the size in bytes of each file, and you want to differentiate the appearance (in this case, through different icons). Because the DirectoryInfo object doesn't provide a Length property, trying to bind to it in a more generic list of FileSystemInfo objects would cause an error.

■ **Note** This problem has another, equally effective solution. You could create a single GridView but not bind directly to the FileInfo.Length property. Instead, you would bind to a method in the page class that examines the current data object and return either the length (for FileInfo objects) or a blank string (for DirectoryInfo objects). You could construct a similar method to hand out the correct icon URL.

Here's the declaration for the GridView control that provides the list of directories, without the formatting-specific style properties:

```
<asp:GridView ID="gridDirList" runat="server" AutoGenerateColumns="False"
 OnSelectedIndexChanged="gridDirList_SelectedIndexChanged"
 GridLines="None" CellPadding="0" CellSpacing="1"
 DataKeyNames="FullName">

  <Columns>
    <asp:TemplateField>
      <ItemTemplate>
        <img src="folder.jpg" alt="Folder" />
      </ItemTemplate>
    </asp:TemplateField>
    <asp:ButtonField DataTextField="Name" CommandName="Select"
     HeaderText="Name" />
    <asp:BoundField HeaderText="Size" />
    <asp:BoundField DataField="LastWriteTime" HeaderText="Last Modified" />
  </Columns>
</asp:GridView>
```

This grid binds to an array of DirectoryInfo objects and displays the Name and LastWriteTime properties. It also creates a Size column, which it doesn't use to display any information—instead, this column simply reserves space so the directory list lines up nicely with the file list that appears immediately underneath. In addition, the DirectoryInfo.FullName property is designated as a key field in the grid so that you can return the full path after the user clicks one of the directories. You'll also notice that one of the columns doesn't actually display any information—that's the BoundColumn for length that displays header text, but it doesn't link to any data field.

The GridView for the files follows immediately. Here's the slightly shortened control tag:

```
<asp:GridView ID="gridFileList" runat="server" AutoGenerateColumns="False"
 OnSelectedIndexChanged="gridFileList_SelectedIndexChanged"
 GridLines="None" CellPadding="0" CellSpacing="1" DataKeyNames="FullName">

  <SelectedRowStyle BackColor="#C0fFF" />
  <Columns>
    <asp:TemplateField>
      <ItemTemplate>
        <img src="file.jpg" alt="File" />
      </ItemTemplate>
    </asp:TemplateField>
    <asp:ButtonField DataTextField="Name" CommandName="Select" />
```

```
    <asp:BoundField DataField="Length" />
    <asp:BoundField DataField="LastWriteTime" />
  </Columns>
</asp:GridView>
```

Note that the GridView for displaying files must define a SelectedRowStyle because it supports file selection. (The GridView for displaying directories handles selection differently. It reacts as soon as a file is clicked by browsing to the new directory and rebinding the controls. Thus, a directory never appears in a selected state.)

The next step is to write the code that fills these controls. The star of the show is a private method named ShowDirectoryContents(), which retrieves the contents of the current folder and binds the two GridView controls. Here's the complete code:

```
private void ShowDirectoryContents(string path)
{
    // Define the current directory.
    DirectoryInfo dir = new DirectoryInfo(path);

    // Get the files and directories in the current directory.
    FileInfo[] files = dir.GetFiles();
    DirectoryInfo[] dirs = dir.GetDirectories();

    // Show the files and directories in the current directory.
    lblCurrentDir.Text = "Currently showing " + path;
    gridFileList.DataSource = files;
    gridDirList.DataSource = dirs;
    Page.DataBind();

    // Clear any selection in the GridView that shows files.
    gridFileList.SelectedIndex = -1;

    // Keep track of the current path.
    ViewState["CurrentPath"] = path;
}
```

When the page first loads, it calls this method to show the current application directory:

```
protected void Page_Load(object sender, System.EventArgs e)
{
    if (!Page.IsPostBack)
    {
        ShowDirectoryContents(Server.MapPath("."));
    }
}
```

You'll notice that the ShowDirectoryContents() method stores the currently displayed directory in view state. That allows the Move Up button to direct the user to a directory that's one level above the current directory:

```
protected void cmdUp_Click(object sender, System.EventArgs e)
{
    string path = (string)ViewState["CurrentPath"];
    path = Path.Combine(path, "..");
```

```
    path = Path.GetFullPath(path);
    ShowDirectoryContents(path);
}
```

To move down through the directory hierarchy, the user simply needs to click a directory link. This is raised as a SelectedIndexChanged event. The event handler then displays the new directory:

```
protected void gridDirList_SelectedIndexChanged(object source, EventArgs e)
{
    // Get the selected directory.
    string dir = (string)gridDirList.DataKeys[gridDirList.SelectedIndex].Value;

    // Now refresh the directory list to
    // show the selected directory.
    ShowDirectoryContents(dir);
}
```

But what happens if a user selects a file from the second GridView? In this case, the code retrieves the full file path, creates a new FileInfo object, and binds it to a FormView control, which uses a template to display several pieces of information about the file. Figure 12-2 shows the result.

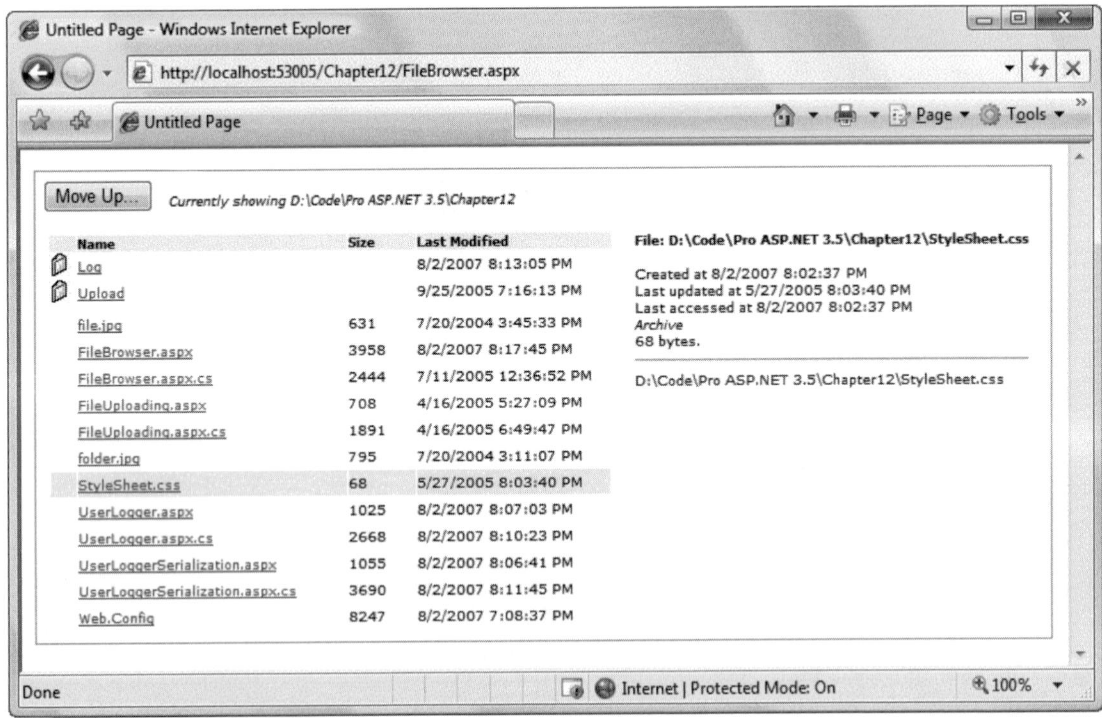

Figure 12-2. Examining a file

Here's the code that binds the file information when a file is selected:

```
protected void gridFileList_SelectedIndexChanged(object sender, System.EventArgs e)
{
    // Get the selected file.
    string file = (string)gridFileList.DataKeys[gridFileList.SelectedIndex].Value;

    // The FormView shows a collection (or list) of items.
    // To accommodate this model, you must add the file object
    // to a collection of some sort.
    ArrayList files = new ArrayList();
    files.Add(new FileInfo(file));

    // Now show the selected file.
    formFileDetails.DataSource = files;
    formFileDetails.DataBind();
}
```

The FormView uses the following template:

```
<asp:FormView id="formFileDetails" runat="server">
  <ItemTemplate>
    <b>File:
    <%# DataBinder.Eval(Container.DataItem, "FullName") %></b><br />
    Created at
    <%# DataBinder.Eval(Container.DataItem, "CreationTime") %><br />
    Last updated at
    <%# DataBinder.Eval(Container.DataItem, "LastWriteTime") %><br />
    Last accessed at
    <%# DataBinder.Eval(Container.DataItem, "LastAccessTime") %><br />
    <i><%# DataBinder.Eval(Container.DataItem, "Attributes") %></i><br />
    <%# DataBinder.Eval(Container.DataItem, "Length") %> bytes.
    <hr />
    <%# GetVersionInfoString(DataBinder.Eval(Container.DataItem, "FullName")) %>
  </ItemTemplate>
</asp:FormView>
```

The data binding expressions are fairly straightforward. The only one that needs any expression is the GetVersionInfoString() method. This method is coded inside the page class. It creates a new FileVersionInfo object for the file and uses that to extract the version information and product name.

```
protected string GetVersionInfoString(object path)
{
    FileVersionInfo info = FileVersionInfo.GetVersionInfo((string)path);
    return info.FileName + " " + info.FileVersion + "<br />" +
    info.ProductName + " " + info.ProductVersion;
}
```

Of course, most developers have FTP tools and other utilities that make it easier to manage files on a web server. However, this page provides an excellent example of how to use the .NET file and directory management classes. With a little more work, you could transform it into a full-featured administrative tool for a web application.

Reading and Writing Files with Streams

The .NET Framework uses a *stream* model in several areas of the framework. Streams are abstractions that allow you to treat different data sources in a similar way—as a stream of ordered bytes. All .NET stream classes derive from the base System.IO.Stream class. Streams represent data in a memory buffer, data that's being retrieved over a network connection, and data that's being retrieved from or written to a file.

Here's how you create a new file and write an array of bytes to it through a FileStream:

```
FileStream fileStream = null;
try
{
    fileStream = new FileStream(fileName, FileMode.Create);
    fileStream.Write(bytes, 0, bytes.Length - 1);
}
finally
{
    if (fileStream != null) fileStream.Close();
}
```

In this example, the FileMode.Create value is specified in the FileStream constructor to indicate that you want to create a new file. You can use any of the FileMode values described in Table 12-10.

Table 12-10. *Values of the FileMode Enumeration*

Value	Description
Append	Opens the file if it exists and seeks to the end of the file, or creates a new file.
Create	Specifies that the operating system should create a new file. If the file already exists, it will be overwritten.
CreateNew	Specifies that the operating system should create a new file. If the file already exists, an IOException is thrown.
Open	Specifies that the operating system should open an existing file.
OpenOrCreate	Specifies that the operating system should open a file if it exists; otherwise, a new file should be created.
Truncate	Specifies that the operating system should open an existing file. Once opened, the file will be truncated so that its size is 0 bytes.

And here's how you can open a FileStream and read its contents into a byte array:

```
FileStream fileStream = null;
try
{
    fileStream = new FileStream(fileName, FileMode.Open);
    byte[] dataArray = new byte[fileStream.Length];
```

```
    for(int i = 0; i < fileStream.Length; i++)
    {
        dataArray[i] = (byte)fileStream.ReadByte();
    }
}
finally
{
    if (fileStream != null) fileStream.Close();
}
```

On their own, streams aren't that useful. That's because they work entirely in terms of single bytes and byte arrays. .NET includes a more useful higher-level model of writer and reader objects that fill the gaps. These objects wrap stream objects and allow you to write more complex data, including common data types such as integers, strings, and dates. You'll see readers and writers at work in the following sections.

■ **Tip** Whenever you open a file through a FileStream, remember to call the FileStream.Close() method when you're finished. This releases the handle on the file and makes it possible for someone else to access the file. In addition, because the FileStream class is disposable, you can use it with the using statement, which ensures that the FileStream is closed as soon as the block ends.

Text Files

You can write to a file and read from a file using the StreamWriter and StreamReader classes in the System.IO namespace. When creating these classes, you simply pass the underlying stream as a constructor argument. For example, here's the code you need to create a StreamWriter using an existing FileStream:

```
FileStream fileStream = new FileStream(@"c:\myfile.txt", FileMode.Create);
StreamWriter w = new StreamWriter(fileStream);
```

You can also use one of the static methods included in the File and FileInfo classes, such as CreateText() or OpenText(). Here's an example that uses this technique to get a StreamWriter:

```
StreamWriter w = File.CreateText(@"c:\myfile.txt");
```

This code is equivalent to the earlier example.

Once you have the StreamWriter, you can use the Write() or WriteLine() method to add information to the file. Both of these methods are overloaded so that they can write many simple data types, including strings, integers, and other numbers. These values are essentially all converted into strings when they're written to a file, and they must be converted back into the appropriate types manually when you read the file. To make this process easier, you should put each piece of information on a separate line by using WriteLine() instead of Write(), as shown here:

```
w.WriteLine("ASP.NET Text File Test");  // Write a string.
w.WriteLine(1000);                      // Write a number.
```

Text Encoding

You can represent a string in binary form using more than one way, depending on the encoding you use. The most common encodings include the following:

- ASCII: Encodes each character in a string using 7 bits. ASCII-encoded data can't contain extended Unicode characters. When using ASCII encoding in .NET, the bits will be padded, and the resulting byte array will have 1 byte for each character.
- Full Unicode (or UTF-16): Represents each character in a string using 16 bits. The resulting byte array will have 2 bytes for each character.
- UTF-7 Unicode: Uses 7 bits for ordinary ASCII characters and multiple 7-bit pairs for extended characters. This encoding is primarily for use with 7-bit protocols such as mail, and it isn't regularly used.
- UTF-8 Unicode: Uses 8 bits for ordinary ASCII characters and multiple 8-bit pairs for extended characters. The resulting byte array will have 1 byte for each character (provided there are no extended characters).

.NET provides a class for each type of encoding in the System.Text namespace. When using the StreamReader and StreamWriter, you can specify the encoding you want to use with a constructor argument, or you can simply use the default UTF-8 encoding.

Here's an example that creates a StreamWriter that uses ASCII encoding:

```
FileStream fileStream = new FileStream(@"c:\myfile.txt", FileMode.Create);
StreamWriter w = new StreamWriter(fileStream, System.Text.Encoding.ASCII);
```

When you finish with the file, you must make sure you close it. Otherwise, the changes may not be properly written to disk, and the file could be locked open. At any time, you can also call the Flush() method to make sure all data is written to disk, as the StreamWriter will perform some in-memory caching of your data to optimize performance (which is usually exactly the behavior you want).

```
// Tidy up.
w.Flush();
w.Close();
```

When reading information, you use the Read() or ReadLine() method of the StreamReader. The Read() method reads a single character, or the number of characters you specify, and returns the data as a char or char array. The ReadLine() method returns a string with the content of an entire line. ReadLine() starts at the first line and advances the position to the end of the file, one line at a time.

Here's a code snippet that opens and reads the file created in the previous example:

```
StreamReader r = File.OpenText(@"c:\myfile.txt");
string inputString;
inputString = r.ReadLine();     // = "ASP.NET Text File Test"
inputString = r.ReadLine();     // = "1000"
```

ReadLine() returns a null reference when there is no more data in the file. This means you can read all the data in a file using code like this:

```
// Read and display the lines from the file until the end
// of the file is reached.
string line;
do
{
    line = r.ReadLine();
    if (line != null)
    {
        // (Process the line here.)
    }
} while (line != null);
```

■ **Tip** You can also use the ReadToEnd() method to read the entire contents of the file and return it as a single string. The File class also includes some shortcuts with static methods such as ReadAllText() and ReadAllBytes(), which are suitable for small files only. Large files should not be read into memory at once—instead, you can reduce the memory overhead by reading them one chunk at a time with the FileStream.

Binary Files

You can also read and write to a binary file. Binary data uses space more efficiently but also creates files that aren't readable. If you open a binary file in Notepad, you'll see a lot of extended characters (politely known as gibberish).

To open a file for binary writing, you need to create a new BinaryWriter class. The class constructor accepts a stream, which you can create by hand or retrieve using the File.OpenWrite() method. Here's the code to open the file c:\binaryfile.bin for binary writing:

```
BinaryWriter w = new BinaryWriter(File.OpenWrite(@"c:\binaryfile.bin"));
```

.NET concentrates on stream objects, rather than the source or destination for the data. This means you can write binary data to any type of stream, whether it represents a file or some other type of storage location, using the same code. In addition, writing to a binary file is almost the same as writing to a text file, as you can see here:

```
string str = "ASP.NET Binary File Test";
int integer = 1000;
w.Write(str);
w.Write(integer);

w.Flush();
w.Close();
```

Unfortunately, when you read data, you need to know the data type you want to retrieve. To retrieve a string, you use the ReadString() method. To retrieve an integer, you must use ReadInt32(), as follows:

```
BinaryReader r = new BinaryReader(File.OpenRead(@"c:\binaryfile.bin"));
string str;
int integer;
str = r.ReadString();
integer = r.ReadInt32();
```

■ **Note** There's no easy way to jump to a location in a text or binary file without reading through all the information in order. While you can use methods such as Seek() on the underlying stream, you need to specify an offset in bytes. This involves some fairly involved calculations to determine variable sizes. If you need to store a large amount of information and move through it quickly, you're best off with a dedicated database, not a binary file.

Uploading Files

ASP.NET includes two controls that allow website users to upload files to the web server. Once the web server receives the posted file data, it's up to your application to examine it, ignore it, or save it to a back-end database or a file on the web server.

The controls that allow file uploading are HtmlInputFile (an HTML server control) and FileUpload (an ASP.NET web control). Both represent the <input type="file"> HTML tag. The only real difference is that the FileUpload control takes care of automatically setting the encoding of the form to multipart/form data. If you use the HtmlInputFile control, it's up to you to make this change using the enctype attribute of the <form> tag—if you don't, the HtmlInputFile control won't work.

Declaring the FileUpload control is easy. It doesn't expose any new properties or events that you can use through the control tag.

```
<asp:FileUpload ID="Uploader" runat="server" />
```

The <input type="file"> tag doesn't give you much choice as far as the user interface is concerned (it's limited to a text box that contains a filename and a Browse button). When the user clicks Browse, the browser presents an Open dialog box and allows the user to choose a file. This behavior is hard-wired into the browser, and you can't change it. Once the user selects a file, the filename is filled into the corresponding text box. However, the file isn't uploaded yet—that happens later, when the page is posted back. At this point, all the data from all the input controls (including the file data) is sent to the server. For that reason, it's common to add a Button control to post back the page.

To get information about the posted file content, you can access the FileUpload.PostedFile object. You can save the content by calling the PostedFile.SaveAs() method, as demonstrated in the following example.

Here's the event-handling code, which reacts to the Button.Click event and copies the uploaded file into a subdirectory named Upload in the web application directory:

```
protected void cmdUpload_Click(object sender, EventArgs e)
{
    // Check if a file was submitted.
    if (Uploader.PostedFile.ContentLength != 0)
    {
        try
        {
            if (Uploader.PostedFile.ContentLength > 1048576)
            {
                // This exceeds the size limit you want to allow (1 MB).
                // You can also use the maxRequestLength attribute
                // of the httpRuntime element (in the web.config file)
                // to refuse large requests altogether.
                lblStatus.Text = "Too large. This file is not allowed";
            }
            else
```

```
            {
                // Retrieve the physical directory path for the Upload
                // subdirectory.
                string destDir = Server.MapPath("./Upload");

                // Extract the filename part from the full path of the
                // original file.
                string fileName = Path.GetFileName(Uploader.PostedFile.FileName);

                // Combine the destination directory with the filename.
                string destPath = Path.Combine(destDir, fileName);

                // Save the file on the server.
                Uploader.PostedFile.SaveAs(destPath);
                lblStatus.Text = "Thanks for submitting your file.";
            }
        }
        catch (Exception err)
        {
            lblStatus.Text = err.Message;
        }
    }
}
```

In the example, if a file has been posted to the server and isn't too large, the file is saved using the HttpPostedFile.SaveAs() method. To determine the physical path you want to use, the code combines the destination directory (Upload) with the name of the posted file using the static utility methods of the Path class.

Figure 12-3 shows the page after the file has been uploaded.

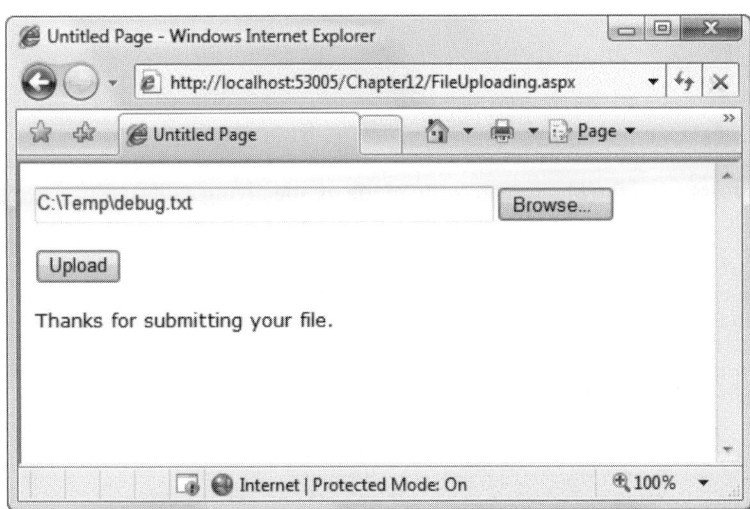

Figure 12-3. Uploading a file

You can also interact with the posted data through the stream model, rather than just saving it to disk. To get access to the data, you use the FileUpload.PostedFile.InputStream property. For example, you could use the following code to display the content of a posted file (assuming it's text-based):

```
// Display the whole file content.
StreamReader r = new StreamReader(Uploader.PostedFile.InputStream);
lblStatus.Text = r.ReadToEnd();
r.Close();
```

■ **Note** By default, the maximum size of the uploaded file is 4 MB. If you try to upload a bigger file, you'll get a runtime error. To change this restriction, modify the maxRequestLength attribute of the <httpRuntime> setting in the application's web.config file. The size is specified in kilobytes, so <httpRuntime maxRequestLength="8192"/> sets the maximum file size to 8 MB. By limiting file size, you can prevent denial-of-service attacks that attempt to fill up your web server's hard drive.

Making Files Safe for Multiple Users

Although it's fairly easy to create a unique filename, what happens in the situation where you really do need to access the same file to serve multiple different requests? Although this situation isn't ideal (and often indicates that a database-based solution would work better), you can use certain techniques to defend yourself.

One approach is to open your files with sharing, which allows multiple processes to access the same file at the same time. To use this technique, you need to use the four-parameter FileStream constructor that allows you to select a FileMode. Here's an example:

```
FileStream fs = new FileStream(fileName, FileMode.Open, FileAccess.Read,
  FileShare.Read);
```

This statement allows multiple users to open the file for reading at the same time. However, no one will be able to update the file.

It is possible to have multiple users open the file in read-write mode by specifying a dif- ferent FileAccess value (such as FileAccess.Write or FileAccess.ReadWrite). In this case, Windows will dynamically lock small portions of the file when you write to them (or you can use the FileStream.Lock() method to lock down a range of bytes in the file). If two users try to write to the same locked portion at once, an exception can occur. Because web applications have high concurrency demands, this technique is not recommended and is extremely difficult to implement properly. It also forces you to use low-level byte-offset calculations, where it is notoriously easy to make small, aggravating errors.

So, what is the solution when multiple users need to update a file at once? One option is to create separate user-specific files for each request. Another option is to tie the file to some other object and use locking. The following sections explain these techniques.

■ **Tip** Another technique that works well if multiple users need to access the same data, especially if this data is frequently used and not excessively large, is to load the data into the cache (as described in Chapter 11). That way, multiple users can simultaneously access the data without a hitch. If another process is responsible for creating or periodically updating the file, you can use a file dependency to invalidate your cached item when the file changes.

Creating Unique Filenames

One solution for dealing with user-concurrency headaches with files is to avoid the conflict altogether by using different files for different users. For example, imagine you want to store a user-specific log. To prevent the chance for an inadvertent conflict if two web pages try to use the same log, you can use the following two techniques:

- Create a user-specific directory for each user.
- Add some information to the filename, such as a timestamp, GUID (global unique identifier), or random number. This reduces the chance of duplicate filenames to a small possibility.

The following sample page demonstrates this technique. It defines a method for creating file- names that are statistically guaranteed to be unique. In this case, the filename incorporates a GUID.

Here's the private method that generates a new unique filename:

```
private string GetFileName()
{
    // Create a unique filename.
    string fileName = "user." +
    Guid.NewGuid().ToString();

    // Put the file in the current web application path.
    return Path.Combine(Request.PhysicalApplicationPath, fileName);
}
```

■ **Note** A GUID is a 128-bit integer. GUID values are tremendously useful in programming because they're statistically unique. In other words, you can create GUID values continuously with little chance of ever creating a duplicate. For that reason, GUIDs are commonly used to uniquely identify queued tasks, user sessions, and other dynamic information. They also have the advantage over sequential numbers in that they can't easily be guessed. The only disadvantage is that GUIDs are long and almost impossible to remember (for an ordinary human being). GUIDs are commonly represented in strings as a series of lowercase hexadecimal digits, like 382c74c3-721d-4f34-80e5-57657b6cbc27.

Using the GetFileName() method, you can create a safer logging application that writes information about the user's actions to a text file. In this example, all the logging is performed by calling a Log() method, which then checks for the filename and assigns a new one if the file hasn't been created yet. The text message is then added to the file, along with the date and time information.

```
private void Log(string message)
{
    // Check for the file.
    FileMode mode;
    if (ViewState["LogFile"] == null)
    {
        // First, create a unique user-specific filename.
        ViewState["LogFile"] = GetFileName();

        // The log file must be created.
        mode = FileMode.Create;
    }
    else
    {
        // Add to the existing file.
        mode = FileMode.Append;
    }

    // Write the message.
    // A using block ensures the file is automatically closed,
    // even in the case of error.
    string fileName = (string)ViewState["LogFile"];
    using (FileStream fs = new FileStream(fileName, mode))
    {
        StreamWriter w = new StreamWriter(fs);
        w.WriteLine(DateTime.Now);
        w.WriteLine(message);
        w.WriteLine();
        w.Close();
    }
}
```

For example, a log message is added every time the page is loaded, as shown here:

```
protected void Page_Load(object sender, EventArgs e)
{
    if (!Page.IsPostBack)
    {
        Log("Page loaded for the first time.");
    }
    else
    {

        Log("Page posted back.");
    }
}
```

The last ingredients are two button event handlers that allow you to delete the log file or show its contents, as follows:

```
protected void cmdRead_Click(object sender, EventArgs e)
{
    if (ViewState["LogFile"] != null)
    {
        StringBuilder log = new StringBuilder();

        string fileName = (string)ViewState["LogFile"];
        using (FileStream fs = new FileStream(fileName, FileMode.Open))
        {
            StreamReader r = new StreamReader(fs);

            // Read line by line (allows you to add
            // line breaks to the web page).
            string line;
            do
            {
                line = r.ReadLine();
                if (line != null)
                {
                    log.Append(line + "<br />");
                }
            } while (line != null);
            r.Close();
        }
        lblInfo.Text = log.ToString();
    }
    else
    {
        lblInfo.Text = "There is no log file."
    }
}

protected void cmdDelete_Click(object sender, EventArgs e)
{
    if (ViewState["LogFile"] != null)
    {
        File.Delete((string)ViewState["LogFile"]);
        ViewState["LogFile"] = null;
    }
}
```

Figure 12-4 shows the web page displaying the log contents.

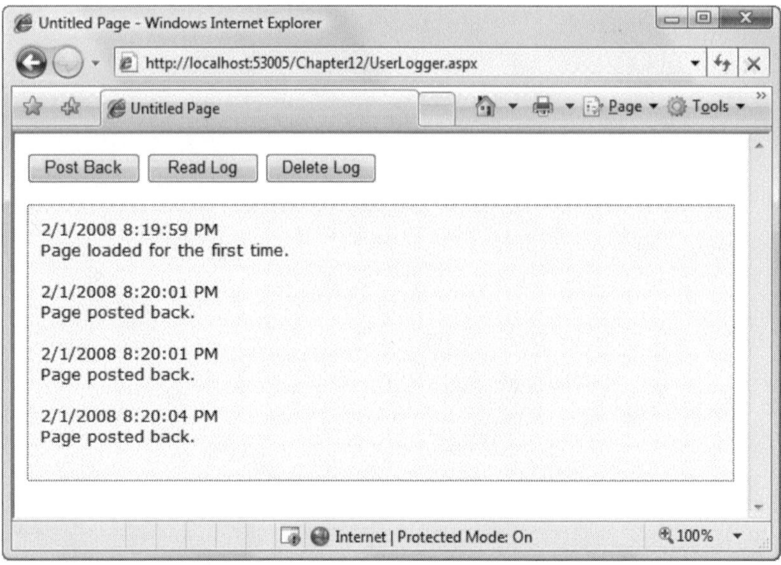

Figure 12-4. *A safer way to write a user-specific log*

Locking File Access Objects

Of course, in some cases you *do* need to update the same file in response to actions taken by multiple users. One approach is to use *locking*. The basic technique is to create a separate class that performs all the work of retrieving the data. Once you've defined this class, you can create a single global instance of it and add it to the Application collection. Now you can use the C# lock statement to ensure that only one thread can access this object at a time (and hence only one thread can attempt to open the file at once).

For example, imagine you create the following Logger class, which updates a file with log information when you call the LogMessage() method, as shown here:

```
public class Logger
{
    public void LogMessage()
    {
        lock (this)
        {
            // (Open the file and update it.)
        }
    }
}
```

The Logger object locks itself before accessing the log file, creating a critical section. This ensures that only one thread can execute the LogMessage() code at a time, removing the danger of file conflicts.

However, for this to work you must make sure every class is using the same instance of the Logger object. You have a number of options here—for example, you could respond to the HttpApplication.Start event in the global.asax file to create a global instance of the Logger class and store it in the Application collection. Alternatively, you could expose a single Logger instance through a static application variable, by adding this code to the global.asax file:

```
private log = new Logger();
public Logger Log
{
    get { return log; }
}
```

Now any page that uses the Logger to call LogMessage() gets exclusive access:

```
// Update the file safely.
Application.Log.LogMessage(myMessage);
```

Keep in mind that this approach is really just a crude way to compensate for the inherent limitations of a file-based system. It won't allow you to manage more complex tasks, such as having individual users read and write pieces of text in the same file at the same time. Additionally, while a file is locked for one client, other requests will have to wait. This is guaranteed to slow down application performance and lead to an exception if the object isn't released before the second client times out. Unless you invest considerable effort refining your threading code (for example, you can use classes in the System.Threading namespace to test if an object is available and take alternative action if it isn't), this technique is suitable only for small-scale web applications. It's for this reason that ASP.NET applications almost never use file-based logs—instead, they write to the Windows event log or a database.

Compression

.NET includes built-in support for compressing data in any stream. This trick allows you to compress data that you write to any file. The support comes from two classes in the new System.IO.Compression namespace: GZipStream and DeflateStream. Both of these classes represent similarly efficient lossless compression algorithms.

To use compression, you need to wrap the real stream with one of the compression streams. For example, you could wrap a FileStream (for compressing data as it's written to disk) or a MemoryStream (for compressing data in memory). Using a MemoryStream, you could compress data before storing it in a binary field in a database or sending it to a web service.

For example, imagine you want to compress data saved to a file. First, you create the FileStream:

```
FileStream fileStream = new FileStream(@"c:\myfile.bin", FileMode.Create);
```

Next, you create a GZipStream or DeflateStream, passing in the FileStream and a CompressionMode value that indicates whether you are compressing or decompressing data:

```
GZipStream compressStream = new GZipStream(fileStream, CompressionMode.Compress);
```

To write your actual data, you use the Write() method of the compression stream, not the FileStream. The compression stream compresses the data and then passes the compressed data to the underlying FileStream. If you want to use a higher-level writer, such as the StreamWriter or BinaryWriter, you supply the compression stream instead of the FileStream:

```
StreamWriter w = new StreamWriter(compressStream);
```

Now you can perform your writing through the writer object. When you're finished, flush the GZipStream so that all the data ends up in the file:

```
w.Flush();
fileStream.Close();
```

Reading a file is just as straightforward. The difference is that you create a compression stream with the CompressionMode.Decompress option, as shown here:

```
FileStream fileStream = new FileStream(@"c:\myfile.bin", FileMode.Open);
GZipStream decompressStream = new GZipStream(fileStream,
  CompressionMode.Decompress);
StreamReader r = new StreamReader(decompressStream);
```

■ **Note** Although GZIP is a industry-standard compression algorithm (see `http://www.gzip.org` for information), that doesn't mean you can use third-party tools to decompress the compressed files you create. The problem is that although the compression algorithm may be the same, the file format is not. Namely, the files you create won't have header information that identifies the original compressed file.

Serialization

You can use one more technique to store data in a file—*serialization*. Serialization is a higher-level model that's built on .NET streams. Essentially, serialization allows you to convert an entire live object into a series of bytes and write those bytes into a stream object such as the FileStream. You can then read those bytes back later to re-create the original object.

For serialization to work, your class must all meet the following criteria:

- The class must have a Serializable attribute preceding the class declaration.
- All the public and private variables of the class must be serializable.
- If the class derives from another class, all parent classes must also be serializable.

If you violate any of these rules, you'll receive a SerializationException when you attempt to serialize the object.

Here's a serializable class that you could use to store log information:

```
[Serializable()]
public class LogEntry
{
    private string message;
    private DateTime date;

    public string Message
    {
        get {return message;}
        set {message = value;}
    }
    public DateTime Date
    {
        get {return date;}
        set {date = value;}
    }

    public LogEntry(string message)
```

```
    {
        Message = message;
        Date = DateTime.Now;
    }
}
```

■ **Tip** In some cases, a class might contain data that shouldn't be serialized. For example, you might have a large field you can recalculate or re-create easily, or you might have some sensitive data that could pose a security request. In these cases, you can add a NonSerialized attribute before the appropriate variable to indicate it shouldn't be persisted. When you deserialize the data to create a copy of the original object, nonserialized variables will return to their default values.

You may remember serializable classes from earlier in this book. Classes need to be serializable in order to be stored in the view state for a page or put into an out-of-process session state store. In those cases, you let .NET serialize the object for you automatically. However, you can also manually serialize a serializable object and store it in a file or another data source of your choosing (such as a binary field in a database).

To convert a serializable object into a stream of bytes, you need to use a class that implements the IFormatter interface. The .NET Framework includes two such classes: BinaryFormatter, which serializes an object to a compact binary representation, and SoapFormatter, which uses the SOAP XML format and results in a longer text-based message. The BinaryFormatter class is found in the System.Runtime.Serialization.Formatters.Binary namespace, and SoapFormatter is found in the System.Runtime.Serialization.Formatters.Soap namespace. (To use SoapFormatter, you also need to add a reference to the assembly System.Runtime.Serialization.Formatters.Soap.dll.) Both methods serialize all the private and public data in a class, along with the assembly and type information needed to ensure that the object can be deserialized exactly.

To create a simple example, let's consider what you need to do to rewrite the logging page shown earlier to use object serialization instead of writing data directly to the file. The first step is to change the Log() method so that it creates a LogEntry object and uses the BinaryFormatter to serialize it into the existing file, as follows:

```
private void Log(string message)
{
    // Check for the file.
    FileMode mode;
    if (ViewState["LogFile"] == null)
    {
        ViewState["LogFile"] = GetFileName();
        mode = FileMode.Create;
    }
    else
    {
        mode = FileMode.Append;
    }

    // Write the message.
    string fileName = (string)ViewState["LogFile"];
```

```
    using (FileStream fs = new FileStream(fileName, mode))
    {
        // Create a LogEntry object.
        LogEntry entry = new LogEntry(message);

        // Create a formatter.
        BinaryFormatter formatter = new BinaryFormatter();

        // Serialize the object to a file.
        formatter.Serialize(fs, entry);
    }
}
```

The last step is to change the code that fills the label with the complete log text. Instead of reading the raw data, it now deserializes each saved instance using the BinaryFormatter, as shown here:

```
protected void cmdRead_Click(object sender, System.EventArgs e)
{
    if (ViewState["LogFile"] != null)
    {
        StringBuilder log = new StringBuilder();

        string fileName = (string)ViewState["LogFile"];
        using (FileStream fs = new FileStream(fileName, FileMode.Open))
        {
            // Create a formatter.
            BinaryFormatter formatter = new BinaryFormatter();

            // Get all the serialized objects.
            while (fs.Position < fs.Length)
            {
                // Deserialize the object from the file.
                LogEntry entry = (LogEntry)formatter.Deserialize(fs);

                // Display its information.
                log.Append(entry.Date.ToString());
                log.Append("<br/>");
                log.Append(entry.Message);
                log.Append("<br /><br />");
            }
        }
        lblInfo.Text = log.ToString();
    }
    else
    {
        lblInfo.Text = "There is no log file."
    }
}
```

So, exactly what information is stored when an object is serialized? Both the BinaryFormatter and the SoapFormatter use a proprietary .NET serialization format that includes information about the class, the assembly that contains the class, and all the data stored in the class member variables. Although the binary format isn't completely interpretable, if you display it as ordinary ASCII text, it looks something like this:

```
?&yuml;&yuml;&yuml;&yuml;? ?GApp_Web_a7ve1ebl, Version=0.0.0.0, Culture=neutral,
PublicKeyToken=null??
?LogEntry??message?date????Page loaded for the first time. ????
```

The SoapFormatter produces more readily interpretable output, although it stores the same information (in a less compact form). The assembly information is compressed into a namespace string, and the data is enclosed in separate elements:

```
<SOAP-ENV:Envelope xmlns:xsi="http://www.w3.org/2001/XMLSchema-instance"
 xmlns:xsd="http://www.w3.org/2001/XMLSchema"
 xmlns:SOAP-ENC="http://schemas.xmlsoap.org/soap/encoding/"
 xmlns:SOAP-ENV="http://schemas.xmlsoap.org/soap/envelope/"
 xmlns:clr="http://schemas.microsoft.com/soap/encoding/clr/1.0"
 SOAP-ENV:encodingStyle="http://schemas.xmlsoap.org/soap/encoding/">
  <SOAP-ENV:Body>
    <a1:LogEntry id="ref-1"
     xmlns:a1=
"http://schemas.microsoft.com/clr/assem/App_Web_m9gesigu%2C%20Version%3D0.0.0.0%2C
%20Culture%3Dneutral%2C%20PublicKeyToken%3Dnull ">
      <message id="ref-3">Page loaded for the first time.</message>
      <date>2008-09-21T22:50:04.8677568-04:00</date>
    </a1:LogEntry>
  </SOAP-ENV:Body>
</SOAP-ENV:Envelope>
```

Clearly, this information (and its structure) is tailored for .NET applications. However, it provides the most convenient, compact way to store the contents of an entire object.

Summary

In this chapter, you learned how to use the .NET classes for retrieving file system information. You also examined how to work with files and how to serialize objects. Along the way you learned how data binding can work with the file classes, how to plug security holes with the Path class, and how to deal with file contention in multiuser scenarios. You also considered data compression using GZIP.

CHAPTER 13

LINQ

One of the most hyped additions to.NET is LINQ (Language Integrated Query), a set of language extensions that allows you to perform *queries* without leaving the comfort of the C# language.

At its simplest, LINQ defines keywords that you use to build query expressions. These query expressions can select, filter, sort, group, and transform data. Different LINQ extensions allow you to use the same query expressions with different data sources. For example, *LINQ to Objects* allows you to query collections of in-memory objects. *LINQ to DataSet* performs the same feat with the in-memory DataSet. Even more interesting are the three LINQ flavors that let you access external data. There's *LINQ to Entities*, which allows you to query a database without writing data access code; *LINQ to XML*, which allows you to read an XML file without using .NET's specialized XML classes; and *Parallel LINQ*, which is a version of LINQ to Objects that processes data using multiple cores or processors simultaneously.

LINQ is a deeply integrated part of .NET and the C# language. However, it isn't an ASP.NET-specific feature, and it can be used equally well in any type of .NET application, from command-line tools to rich Windows clients. Although you can use LINQ anywhere, in an ASP.NET application you're most likely to use LINQ as part of a database component. You can use LINQ in addition to ADO.NET data access code or—with the help of LINQ to Entities—instead of it.

This chapter gives you an overview of LINQ from a web developer's perspective. You'll learn how to use LINQ in your ASP.NET pages, and you'll consider where LINQ improves on other data access approaches (and where it falls short). You'll spend the bulk of the chapter concentrating on LINQ to Entities, which give you a higher-level model for database queries and updates. You'll consider how this system works and how it fits into a typical web application. You'll also learn how to use the EntityDataSource control, which allows you to create surprisingly sophisticated data-bound pages without writing any data access code or SQL queries.

Note You'll learn about one more type of LINQ—LINQ to XML—in Chapter 14.

LINQ Basics

The easiest way to approach LINQ is to consider how it works with in-memory collections. This is LINQ to Objects—the simplest form of LINQ.

Essentially, LINQ to Objects allows you to replace iteration logic (such as a foreach block) with a declarative LINQ expression. For example, imagine you want to get a list of all employees who have a last name that starts with the letter *D*. Using functional C# code, you could loop through the full collection of employees and add each matching employee to a second collection, as shown here:

```
// Get the full collection of employees from a helper method.
List<EmployeeDetails> employees = db.GetEmployees();

// Find the matching employees.
List<EmployeeDetails> matches = new List<EmployeeDetails>();
foreach (EmployeeDetails employee in employees)
{
    if (employee.LastName.StartsWith("D"))
    {
        matches.Add(employee);
    }
}
```

You can then carry on to perform another task with the collection of matches or display it in a web page, as shown here:

```
gridEmployees.DataSource = matches;
gridEmployees.DataBind();
```

You can perform the same task using a LINQ expression. The following example shows how you can rewrite the code, replacing the foreach block with a LINQ query:

```
List<EmployeeDetails> employees = db.GetEmployees();
IEnumerable<EmployeeDetails> matches;

matches = from employee in employees
          where employee.LastName.StartsWith("D")
          select employee;

gridEmployees.DataSource = matches;
gridEmployees.DataBind();
```

The LINQ query uses a set of new keywords, including from, in, where, and select. It gives you a new collection that contains just the matching results.

The end result is identical—you wind up with a collection named matches that's filled with employees who have last names starting with *D*, which is then displayed in a grid (see Figure 13-1). However, there are some differences in the implementation, as you'll learn in the following sections.

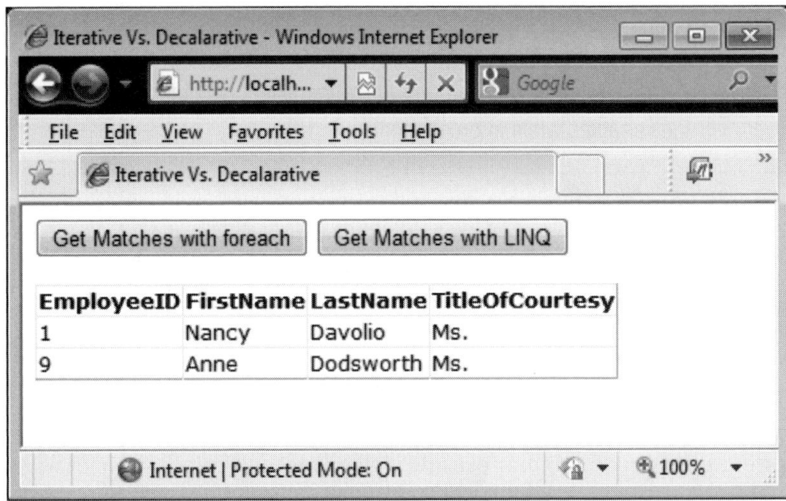

Figure 13-1. Filtering a list of employees with LINQ

■ **Note** The LINQ keywords are a genuine part of the C# language. This fact distinguishes LINQ from technologies like Embedded SQL, which forces you to switch between C# syntax and SQL syntax in a block of code.

Deferred Execution

One obvious difference between the foreach approach and the code that uses the LINQ expression is the way the matches collection is typed. In the foreach code, the matches collection is created as a specific type of collection—in this case, a strongly typed List<T>. In the LINQ example, the matches collection is exposed only through the IEnumerable<T> interface that it implements.

This difference is because of the way that LINQ uses *deferred execution*. Contrary to what you might expect, the matches object isn't a straightforward collection that contains the matching EmployeeDetails objects. Instead, it's a specialized LINQ object that has the ability to fetch the data when you need it.

In the previous example, the matches object is an instance of the WhereIterator<T> class, which is a private class that's nested inside the System.Linq.Enumerable class. Depending on the specific query expression you use, a LINQ expression might return a different object. For example, a union expression that combines data from two different collections would return an instance of the private UnionIterator<T> class. Or, if you simplify the query by removing the where clause, you'll wind up with a simple SelectIterator<T>.

■ **Tip** You don't need to know the specific iterator class that your code uses because you interact with the results through the IEnumerable<T> interface. But if you're curious, you can determine the object type at runtime using the Visual Studio debugger (just hover over the variables while in break mode).

The LINQ iterator objects add an extra layer between defining a LINQ expression and executing it. As soon as you iterate over a LINQ iterator like WhereIterator<T>, it retrieves the data it needs. For example, if you write a foreach block that moves through the matches collection, this action forces the LINQ expression to be evaluated.

The previous example doesn't use a foreach loop at all, because it relies on ASP.NET data binding. However, the background behavior is the same. When you call the GridView.DataBind() method, ASP.NET iterates over the matches collection to get the data that's required and passes it along to the GridView. This step triggers the evaluation of the LINQ expression in the same way as if you were iterating over the results manually.

Depending on the exact type of expression, LINQ may execute it all in one go, or piece by piece as you iterate. In the previous example, the data can be fetched piece by piece, but if you were retrieving the results from a database or applying a sort order to the results, LINQ would use a different strategy and get all the results at the beginning of your loop.

■ **Note** There's no technical reason why LINQ needs to use deferred execution, but there are many reasons why it's a good approach. In many cases, it allows LINQ to use performance optimization techniques that wouldn't otherwise be possible. For example, when using database relationships with LINQ to Entities, you can avoid loading related data that you don't actually use.

How LINQ Works

Here's a quick review of the LINQ basics you've learned so far:

- To use LINQ, you create a LINQ expression. You'll see the rules of expression building later.
- The return value of a LINQ expression is an iterator object that implements IEnumerable<T>.
- When you enumerate over the iterator object, LINQ performs its work.

This raises a good question—namely, how does LINQ execute an expression? What work does it perform to produce your filtered results? The answer depends on the type of data you're querying. For example, LINQ to Entities transforms LINQ expressions into database commands. As a result, the LINQ to Entities plumbing needs to open a connection and execute a database query to get the data you're requesting.

If you're using LINQ to Objects, as in the previous example, the process that LINQ performs is much simpler. In fact, in this case LINQ simply uses a foreach loop to scan through your collections, traveling sequentially from start to finish. Although this doesn't sound terribly impressive, the real advantage of LINQ is that it presents a flexible way to define queries that can be applied to a wide range of different data sources. As you've already learned, the .NET Framework allows you to use LINQ expressions to query in-memory collections, the DataSet, XML documents, and (most usefully) SQL Server databases. However, third-party developers have created their own LINQ providers that support the same expression syntax but work with different data sources—there are data sources available for most commercial and open source databases. LINQ providers simply need to translate LINQ expressions to the appropriate lower-level series of steps. Examples include LINQ providers that query the file system, No-SQL data stores, directory services such as LDAP, and so on.

■ **Note** The code that LINQ to Objects uses to retrieve data is almost always slower than writing a comparable foreach block. Part of this overhead is because there are additional delegates and method calls at work (as you'll see later in this chapter). However, it's extremely unlikely that in-memory object manipulation will be a bottleneck in a server-side application like an ASP.NET website. Instead, tasks such as connecting to a database, contacting a web service, or retrieving information from the file system are all orders of magnitude slower and are much more likely to cause a slowdown. As a result, there's rarely a performance reason to avoid LINQ to Objects. The one exception is if you want to implement a more advanced search routine. For example, a search that drills through a vast collection of ordered information using an index can be more efficient than a LINQ query, which scans through the entire set of data from start to finish.

There's an important symmetry to LINQ. LINQ expressions work on objects that implement IEnumerable<T> (such as the List<EmployeeDetails> collection in the previous example), and LINQ expressions return objects that implement IEnumerable<T> (such as the WhereIterator<T> in the previous example). Thus, you can pass the result from one LINQ expression into another LINQ expression, and so on. This chain of LINQ expressions is evaluated only at the end, when you iterate over the final data. Depending on the type of data source that you're querying, LINQ is often able to fuse your expression chain together into one operation and thus perform it in the most efficient manner possible.

LINQ Expressions

Before you can go much further with LINQ, you need to understand how a LINQ expression is composed. LINQ expressions have a superficial similarity to SQL queries, although the order of the clauses is rearranged.

All LINQ expressions must have a from clause that indicates the data source and a select clause that indicates the data you want to retrieve (or a group clause that defines a series of groups into which the data should be placed). The from clause is placed first:

```
matches = from employee in employees
          ...;
```

The from clause identifies two pieces of information (shown in bold in the preceding code). The word immediately after *in* identifies the data source—in this case, it's the collection object named employees that holds the EmployeeDetails instances. The word immediately after *from* assigns an alias that represents individual items in the data source. For the purpose of the current expression, each EmployeeDetails object is named employee. You can then use this alias later when you build other parts of the expression, like the filtering and selection clauses.

Here's the simplest possible LINQ query. It simply retrieves the full set of data from the employees collection:

```
IEnumerable<EmployeeDetails> matches;
matches = from employee in employees
          select employee;
```

The C# language includes many more LINQ operators that won't be considered in detail in this book. (Instead, this chapter provides an overview of LINQ and a closer examination of the aspects of LINQ programming that are of particular interest to web developers, like LINQ to Entities.) In the following sections, you'll tackle the most important operators, including select, where, orderby, and group. You can review all the LINQ operators in the .NET Framework Help. You can also find a wide range of expression examples on Microsoft's 101 LINQ Samples page at http://msdn2.microsoft.com/en-us/vcsharp/aa336746.aspx.

Projections

You can change the select clause to get a subset of the data. For example, you could pull out a list of first-name strings like this:

```
IEnumerable<string> matches;
matches = from employee in employees
          select employee.FirstName;
```

or a list of strings with both first and last names:

```
matches = from employee in employees
          select employee.FirstName + employee.LastName;
```

As shown here, you can use standard C# operators on numeric data or strings to modify the information as you're selecting it. Even more interestingly, you can dynamically define a new class that wraps just the information you want to return. For example, if you want to get both the first and last names but you want to store them in separate strings, you could create a stripped-down version of the EmployeeDetails class that includes just a FirstName property and a LastName property. To do so, you use the C# *anonymous types* feature. The basic technique is to add the new keyword to the select clause and assign each property you want to create in terms of the object you're selecting. Here's an example:

```
var matches = from employee in employees
          select new {First = employee.FirstName, Last = employee.LastName};
```

This expression, when executed, returns a set of objects that uses an implicitly created class. Each object has two properties: First and Last. You never see the class definition, and you can't pass instances to method calls, because the class is generated by the compiler and given a meaningless, automatically created name. However, you can still use the class locally, access the First and Last properties, and even use it with data binding (in which case ASP.NET extracts the appropriate values by property name, using reflection). The ability to transform the data you're querying into results with a different structure is called *projection*.

There's one trick at work in this example. As you've already learned, LINQ expressions return an iterator object. The iterator class is generic, which means it's locked into a specific type—in this case, an anonymous class that has two properties, named First and Last. However, because you didn't define this class, you can't define the correct IEnumerator<T> reference. The solution is to use the var keyword.

Figure 13-2 shows the result of binding the matches collection to a grid.

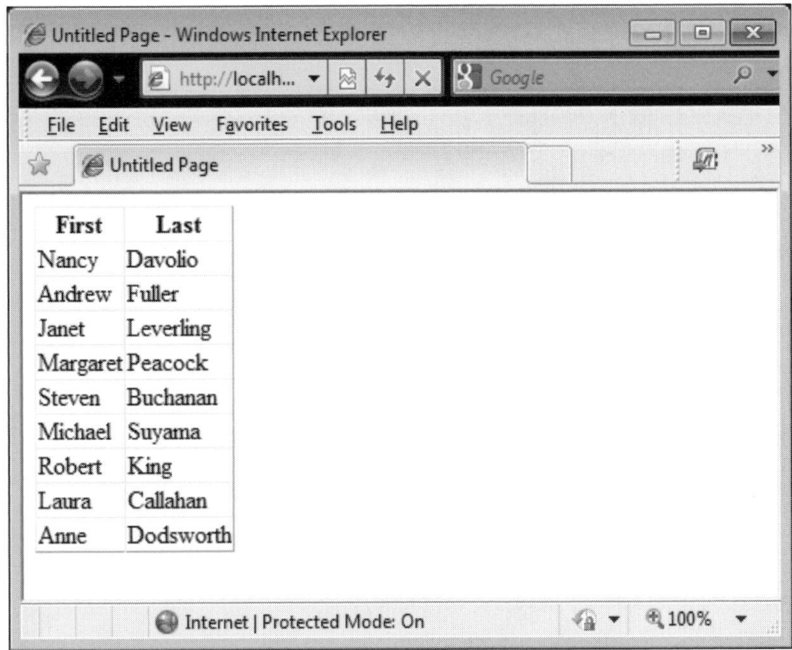

Figure 13-2. *Projecting data to a new representation*

You'll also need to use the var keyword whenever you want to reference an individual object. One example is when performing iteration code through the set of matches returned by the previous LINQ expression:

```
foreach (var employee in matches)
{
    // (Do something here with employee.First and employee.Last.)
}
```

Remember, the var keyword is resolved at compile time and can't be used as a class member variable. As a result, this approach doesn't give you the ability to pass an instance of an anonymous class between methods.

■ **Tip** The var keyword is useful even if you aren't using anonymous types. In this case, it's a shortcut that saves you from writing the full IEnumerable<T> type name.

Of course, you don't need to use anonymous types when perform a projection. You can define the type formally and then use it in your expression. For example, if you created the following EmployeeName class:

```
public class EmployeeName
{
    public string FirstName
    { get; set; }

    public string LastName
    { get; set; }
}
```

you could change EmployeeDetails objects into EmployeeName objects in your query expression like this:

```
IEnumerable<EmployeeName> matches = from employee in employees
  select new EmployeeName {FirstName = employee.FirstName,
  LastName = employee.LastName};
```

This query expression works because the FirstName and LastName properties are publicly accessible and aren't read-only. After creating the EmployeeName object, LINQ sets these properties. Alternatively, you could add a set of parentheses after the EmployeeName class name and supply arguments for a parameterized constructor, like this:

```
IEnumerable<EmployeeName> matches = from employee in employees
  select new EmployeeName(employee.FirstName, employee.LastName);
```

Filtering and Sorting

In the first LINQ example in this chapter, you saw how a where clause can filter the results to include only those that match a specific condition. For example, you can use this code to find employees who have a last name that starts with a specific letter:

```
IEnumerable<EmployeeDetails> matches;
matches = from employee in employees
          where employee.LastName.StartsWith("D")
          select employee;
```

The where clause takes a conditional expression that's evaluated for each item. If it's true, the item is included in the result. However, LINQ keeps the same deferred execution model, which means the where clause isn't evaluated until you actually attempt to iterate over the results.

As you probably already expect, you can combine multiple conditional expressions with the *and* (&&) and *or* (||) operators, and you can use relational operators (such as <, <=, >, and >=). For example, you could create a query like this to filter out products above a certain price threshold:

```
IEnumerable<Product> matches;
matches = from product in products
          where product.UnitsInStock > 0 && product.UnitPrice > 3.00M
          select product;
```

One interesting feature of LINQ expressions is that you can easily call your own methods inline. For example, you could create a function named TestEmployee() that examines an employee and returns true or false based on whether you want to include it in the results:

```
private bool TestEmployee(EmployeeDetails employee)
{
    return employee.LastName.StartsWith("D");
}
```

You could then use the TestEmployee() method like this:

```
IEnumerable<EmployeeDetails> matches;
matches = from employee in employees
          where TestEmployee(employee)
          select employee;
```

The orderby operator is equally straightforward. It's modeled after the syntax of the SELECT statement in SQL. You simply provide a list of one or more values to use for sorting, separated by commas. You can add the word descending after a field name to sort in the reverse order.

Here's a basic sorting example:

```
IEnumerable<EmployeeDetails> matches;
matches = from employee in employees
          orderby employee.LastName, employee.FirstName
          select employee;
```

■ **Note** Sorting is supported on any types that implement IComparable, which includes most core .NET data types (such as numeric data, dates, and strings). It is possible to sort using a piece of data that doesn't implement IComparable, but you need to use the explicit syntax described in the next section. This way, you can pass a custom IComparer object that will be used to sort the data.

Grouping and Aggregation

Grouping allows you to condense a large set of information into a smaller set of summary results.

Grouping is a type of projection, because the objects in the results collections are different from the objects in the source collection. For example, imagine you're dealing with a collection of Product objects, and you decide to place them into price-specific groups. The result is an IEnumerable<T> collection of group objects, each of which represents a separate price range with a subset of products. Each group implements the IGrouping<T, K> interface from the System.Linq namespace.

To use grouping, you need to make two decisions. First, you need to decide what criteria to use to create the group. Second, you need to decide what information to display for each group.

The first task is easy. You use the group, by, and into keywords to choose what objects you're grouping, how groups are determined, and what alias you'll use to refer to individual groups. Here's an example that works with a collection of EmployeeDetails objects and groups them based on the content in the TitleOfCourtesy field (Mr., Ms., and so on):

```
var matches = from employee in employees
  group employee by employee.TitleOfCourtesy into g
  ...
```

■ **Tip** It's a common convention to give the alias g to your groups in a LINQ expression.

Objects are placed into the same group when they share some piece of data. To group data into numeric ranges, you need to write a calculation that produces the same number for each group. For example, if you want to group products by price into ranges like 0–50, 50–100, 100–150, and so on, you'd need to write an expression like this:

```
var matches = from product in products
  group product by (int)(product.UnitPrice / 50) into g
  ...
```

All products less than 50 will have a grouping key of 0, all products from 50 to 100 will have a grouping key of 1, and so on.

Once you've formed your groups, you need to decide what information about them is returned to form your results. Each group is exposed to your code as an object that implements the IGrouping<T, K> interface. For example, the previous LINQ expression created groups of type IGrouping<int, Product>, which means the grouping key type is integer and the element type is Product.

This IGrouping<T, K> interface provides a single property, Key, which returns the value used to create the group. For example, if you want to create a simple list of strings that shows the TitleOfCourtesy of each TitleOfCourtesy group, this is the expression you need:

```
var matches = from employee in employees
  group employee by employee.TitleOfCourtesy into g
  select g.Key;
```

■ **Tip** You could replace the var keyword in this example with IEnumerable<string>, because the final result is a list of strings (showing the different TitleOfCourtesy values). However, it's common to use the var keyword in grouping queries because you'll often use projection and anonymous types to get more useful summary information.

If you bind this to a GridView, you'll see the result shown in Figure 13-3.

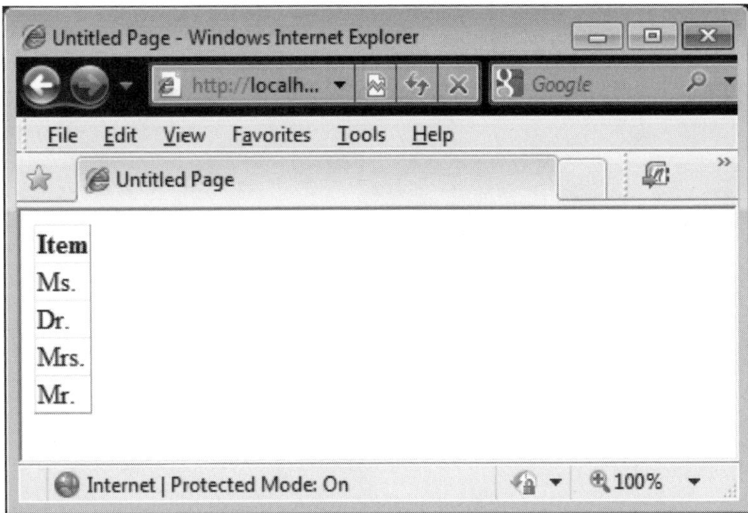

Figure 13-3. A list of employee groups

Alternatively, you can choose to return the entire group, like this:

```
var matches = from employee in employees
  group employee by employee.TitleOfCourtesy into g
  select g;
```

This isn't much help with data binding, because ASP.NET won't be able to display anything useful about each group. However, it gives you the freedom to iterate over each group in code, using code like this:

```
// Look through all the groups.
foreach (IGrouping<string, EmployeeDetails> group in matches)
{
    // Loop through all the EmployeeDetails objects in the current group.
    foreach (EmployeeDetails employee in group)
    {
        // Do something with the employee in the group here.
    }
}
```

This demonstrates that even once you've created groups, you can still give yourself the flexibility to access the individual items in the group.

More practically, you can use an aggregate function to perform a calculation with the data in your group. The LINQ aggregate functions mimic the database aggregate functions you've probably used in the past, allowing you to count and sum data in a group or find the minimum, maximum, and average values. You can also filter out groups based on these calculated values.

The following example returns a new anonymous type that includes the group key value and the number of objects in the group. To work its magic, it uses an inline method call to a method named Count().

```
var matches = from employee in employees
  group employee by employee.TitleOfCourtesy into g
  select new {Title = g.Key, Employees = g.Count()};
```

Figure 13-4 shows the result.

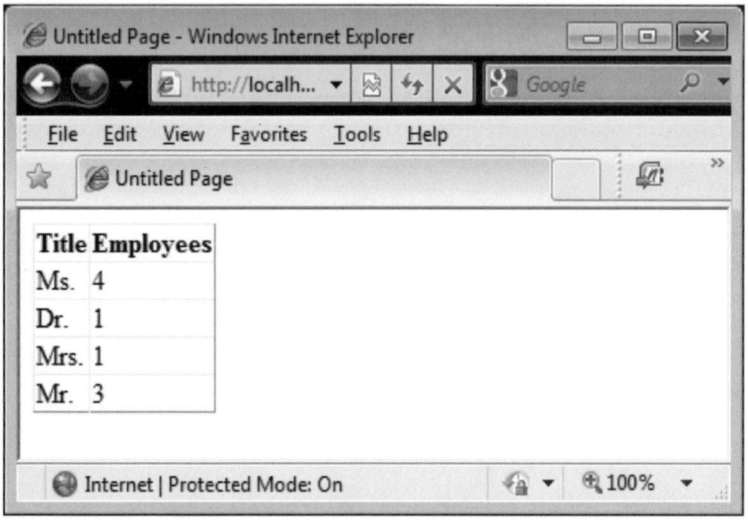

Figure 13-4. *The number of employees in a group*

The preceding LINQ expression is a bit different from the ones you've considered so far because it uses an extension method. Essentially, extension methods are core bits of LINQ functionality that aren't exposed through dedicated C# operators. Instead, you need to invoke the method directly. The Count() method is one example of an extension method.

What differentiates extension methods from ordinary methods is that extension methods aren't defined in the class that uses the method. Instead, LINQ includes a System.Linq.Enumerable class that defines several dozen extension methods that can be called on any object that implements IEnumerable<T>. (These extension methods also work with IGrouping<T, K>, because it extends IEnumerable<T>.)

In other words, this part of the previous LINQ expression tells LINQ to call System.Linq.Enumerable.Count() to calculate the number of items in the group:

```
select new {Title = g.Key, Employees = g.Count()};
```

Along with Count(), LINQ also defines more powerful extension methods that you'll want to use in grouping scenarios, such as the aggregation functions Max(), Min(), and Average(). The LINQ expressions that use these methods are a bit more complicated, because they also use another C# feature known as a *lambda expression*, which allows you to supply additional parameters to the extension method. In the case of the Max(), Min(), and Average() methods, the lambda expression allows you to indicate what property you want to use for the calculation.

Here's an example that uses these extension methods to calculate the maximum, minimum, and average prices of the items in each category:

```
var categories =  from p in products
  group p by p.Category into g
  select new {Category = g.Key,
              MaximumPrice = g.Max(p => p.UnitPrice),
              MinimumPrice = g.Min(p => p.UnitPrice),
              AveragePrice = g.Average(p => p.UnitPrice)};
```

Figure 13-5 shows this grouping.

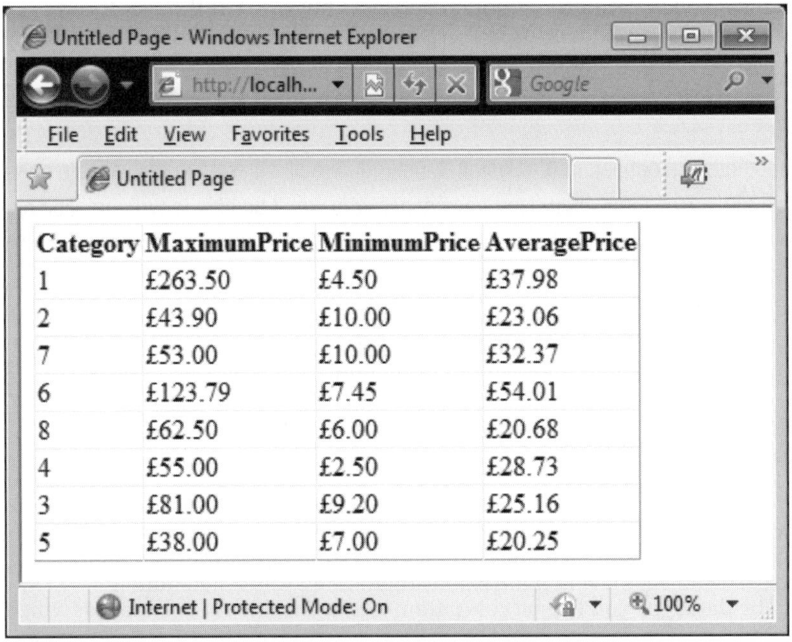

Category	MaximumPrice	MinimumPrice	AveragePrice
1	£263.50	£4.50	£37.98
2	£43.90	£10.00	£23.06
7	£53.00	£10.00	£32.37
6	£123.79	£7.45	£54.01
8	£62.50	£6.00	£20.68
4	£55.00	£2.50	£28.73
3	£81.00	£9.20	£25.16
5	£38.00	£7.00	£20.25

Figure 13-5. *Aggregate information about product groups*

Although this example is fairly intuitive, the lambda syntax looks a little unusual. In the next section, you'll take a deeper look at extension methods and lambda expressions.

LINQ Expressions "Under the Hood"

Although LINQ uses C# keywords (such as from, in, and select), the implementation of these keywords is provided by other classes. In fact, every LINQ query is translated to a series of method calls. Rather than relying on this translation step, you can explicitly call the methods yourself. For example, this simple LINQ expression:

```
matches = from employee in employees
          select employee;
```

can be rewritten using as follows:

```
matches = employees.Select(employee => employee);
```

The syntax here is a bit unusual. It looks as though this code is calling a Select() method on the employees collection. However, the employees collection is an ordinary List<T> collection, and it doesn't include this method. Instead, Select() is an *extension method* that's automatically provided to all IEnumerable<T> classes.

Extension Methods

Essentially, extension methods allow you to define a method in one class but call it as though it were defined in a different class. The LINQ extension methods are defined in the System.Linq.Enumerable class, but they can be called on any IEnumerable<T> object.

■ **Note** Because LINQ extension methods are defined in the System.Linq.Enumerable class, they're available only if this class is in scope. If you haven't imported the System.Linq namespace, you won't be able to write implicit or explicit LINQ expressions—either way, you'll get a compiler error because the necessary methods can't be found.

The easiest way to understand this technique is to take a quick look at an extension method. Here's the definition for the Select() extension method in the System.Linq.Enumerable class:

```
public static IEnumerable<TResult> Select<TSource, TResult>(
  this IEnumerable<TSource> source, Func<TSource, TResult> selector)
{ ... }
```

There is a small set of rules that applies to extension methods. All extension methods must be static. Extension methods can return any data type and take any number of parameters. However, the first parameter is always a reference to the object on which the extension method was called (and it's preceded by the keyword *this*). The data type you use for this parameter determines the classes for which the extension method is available.

For example, with the Select() extension method, the first parameter is IEnumerable<T>:

```
public static IEnumerable<TResult> Select<TSource, TResult>(
 this IEnumerable<TSource> source, Func<TSource, TResult> selector)
```

This indicates that the extension method can be called on an instance of any class that implements IEnumerable<T> (including collections like List<T>). As you can see, the Select<T> method accepts one other parameter—a delegate that's used to pick out the subset of information you're selecting. Finally, the return value of the Select() method is an IEnumerable<T> object—in this case, it's an instance of the private SelectIterator class.

Here's the full code that LINQ uses for the Enumerable.Select() method:

```
public static IEnumerable<TResult> Select<TSource, TResult>(
  this IEnumerable<TSource> source, Func<TSource, TResult> selector)
{
    if (source == null)
    {
        throw new ArgumentNullException("source");
    }
```

```
    if (selector == null)
    {
        throw new ArgumentNullException("selector");
    }
    return SelectIterator<TSource, TResult>(source, selector);
}
```

Lambda Expressions

As mentioned, the lambda expression is another piece of C# syntax in the method-based LINQ expression. The lambda expression is passed to the Select() method, as shown here:

```
matches = employees.Select(employee => employee);
```

As you already know, when the Select() method is called, the employees object is passed as the first parameter. It's the source of the query. The second parameter requires a delegate that points to a method. This method performs the selection work, and it's called once for each item in the collection. The selection method accepts the original value (in this case, an employee object) and returns the selected result. The previous example performs the most straightforward selection logic possible—it takes the original employee object and returns it unchanged.

There's some sleight of hand at work in this example. As described earlier, the Select() method expects a delegate. You could supply an ordinary delegate that points to a named method that you've created elsewhere in your class, but that would make your code much more long-winded.

One simpler approach is to use an anonymous method, which allows you to define the method inline where you use it, as an argument for the Select() method. Anonymous methods start with the word delegate, followed by the declaration of the method signature, followed by a set of braces that contain the code for the method. Here's what the previous expression would look like if you used an anonymous method:

```
var matches = employees
  .Select(
         delegate(EmployeeDetails employee)
           { return employee; }
        );
```

Lambda expressions are simply a way to make code like this even more concise. A lambda expression consists of two portions separated by the => characters. The first portion identifies the parameters that your anonymous method accepts. In the current example, the lambda expression accepts each object from the collection and exposes it through a reference named employee. The second part of the lambda expression defines the value you want to return.

To get a clearer understanding, consider what happens if you create more sophisticated selection logic that performs a projection. You've already seen that LINQ gives you the flexibility to pull out just the properties you want or even declare a new type. For example, this explicit LINQ expression extracts the data from each employee and places it into an instance of a new anonymous type that includes only name information:

```
var matches = employees
  .Select(
         delegate(EmployeeDetails employee)
           { return new { First = employee.FirstName,
                          Last = employee.LastName };
           }
        );
```

Now you can compress the code by replacing the anonymous method with a lambda expression that does the same thing:

```
var matches = employees
  .Select(employee =>
        new { First = employee.FirstName, Last = employee.LastName });
```

Multipart Expressions

Of course, most LINQ expressions are more complex than the examples you've considered in this section. A more realistic LINQ expression might add sorting or filtering, as this one does:

```
IEnumerable<EmployeeDetails> matches = from employee in employees
        where employee.LastName.StartsWith("D")
        select employee;
```

You can rewrite this expression using explicit syntax, as shown here:

```
IEnumerable<EmployeeDetails> matches = employees
          .Where(employee => employee.LastName.StartsWith("D"))
          .Select(employee => employee);
```

One nice thing about the explicit LINQ syntax is that it makes the order of operations clearer. In the previous example, it's easy to see that you begin with the employees collection, then call the Where() method, and finally call the Select() method. If you use more LINQ operators, you'll wind up with a longer series of method calls.

You'll also notice that the Where() method works much like the Select() method. Both Where() and Select() are extension methods, and both use lambda expressions to supply a simple method. The Where() method supplies a lambda expression that tests each item and returns true if it should be included in the results. The Select() method supplies a lambda expression that transforms each data item to the representation you want. You'll find many more extension methods that work the same way in the System.Linq.Enumerable class.

For the most part, you'll use the implicit syntax to create LINQ expressions. However, there may be occasions when you need to use the explicit syntax—for example, if you need to pass a parameter to an extension method that isn't accommodated by the implicit LINQ syntax. In any case, understanding how expressions map to method calls, how extension methods plug into IEnumerable<T> objects, and how lambda expressions encapsulate filtering, sorting, projections, and other details clears up a fair bit about the inner workings of LINQ.

LINQ to DataSet

As you learned in Chapter 8, you can use the DataTable.Select() method to extract a few records that interest you from a DataTable using a SQL-like filter expression. Although the Select() method works perfectly well, it has a few obvious limitations. First, it's string-based, which means it's subject to errors that won't be caught at compile time. It's also limited to filtering and doesn't provide the other features that LINQ operators offer, such as sorting, grouping, and projections. If you need something more, you can use the LINQ querying features with the DataTable.

When using LINQ to DataSet, you use essentially the same expressions that you use to query collections of objects. After all, the DataSet is really just a collection of DataTable instances, each of which is a collection of DataRow objects (along with additional schema information). However, there's one significant limitation to the DataSet—it doesn't expose strongly typed data. Instead, it's up to you to cast field values to the appropriate types. This is a bit of a problem with LINQ expressions, because they return strongly typed data. In other words, the compiler needs to be able to determine at compile time what data type your LINQ expression will return when you run it.

To make this possible, you need the Field<T> extension method, which is provided by the DataRowExtensions class in the System.Data namespace. Essentially, the Field<T> method extends any DataRow object and gives you a strongly typed way to access a field. Here's an example that uses the Field<T> method to avoid typecasting when retrieving the value from the FirstName field:

```
string value = dataRow.Field<string>("FirstName");
```

This isn't the only limitation you need to overcome with the DataSet. As you've already learned, LINQ works on collections that implement IEnumerable<T>. Neither the DataTable nor the DataRowCollection implements this interface—instead, the DataRowCollection implements the weakly typed IEnumerable interface, which isn't sufficient. To bridge this gap, you need another extension method, named AsEnumerable(), which exposes an IEnumerable<T> collection of DataRow objects for a given DataTable. The AsEnumerable() method is defined in the DataTableExtensions class in the System.Data namespace.

```
IEnumerable<DataRow> rows = dataTable.AsEnumerable();
```

To have the Field<T> and AsEnumerable() methods at your fingertips, you must make sure you've imported the System.Data namespace. (You also need a reference to the System.Data.DataSetExtensions.dll assembly, which is automatically added to the web.config file when you create a web application.)

Using DataRowExtensions and DataTableExtensions, you can write a LINQ expression to query a DataTable in a DataSet using the same underlying infrastructure as LINQ to Objects. Here's an example that extracts the employee records that have last names starting with the letter *D* as DataRow objects:

```
DataSet ds = db.GetEmployeesDataSet();

IEnumerable<DataRow> matches = from employee
  in ds.Tables["Employees"].AsEnumerable()
  where employee.Field<string>("LastName").StartsWith("D")
  select employee;
```

This collection isn't suitable for data binding. (If you do bind this collection, the bound control will show only the public properties of the DataRow object, rather than the collection of field values.) The problem is that when data binding ADO.NET data, you need to include the schema. Binding a complete DataTable works because it includes the Columns collection with column titles and other information.

There are two ways to solve this problem. One option is to use the DataTableExtensions.AsDataView() method to get a DataView for the filtered set of rows:

```
DataSet ds = db.GetEmployeesDataSet();

var matches = from employee in ds.Tables["Employees"].AsEnumerable()
  where employee.Field<string>("LastName").StartsWith("D")
  select employee;

gridEmployees.DataSource = matches.AsDataView();
gridEmployees.DataBind();
```

■ **Note** LINQ to DataSet expressions return instances of the EnumerableRowCollection<T> class (which implements the familiar IEnumerable<T> interface). AsDataView() is an extension method that works only on EnumerableRowCollection<T> objects. As a result, you must define the matches variable in the preceding example using the var keyword or as an EnumerableRowCollection<DataRow>. If you declare it as a IEnumerable<DataRow>, you won't have access to the AsDataView() method.

Another equally effective option is to use a projection. For example, this LINQ expression wraps the name details in a new anonymous type that can be bound:

```
DataSet ds = db.GetEmployeesDataSet();

var matches = from employee in ds.Tables["Employees"].AsEnumerable()
  where employee.Field<string>("LastName").StartsWith("D")
  select new { First = employee.Field<string>("FirstName"),
               Last = employee.Field<string>("LastName") };

gridEmployees.DataSource = matches;
gridEmployees.DataBind();
```

Figure 13-6 shows the rather modest result.

Figure 13-6. Filtering a DataSet with LINQ

Both approaches work equally well. The DataView approach is useful in disconnected rich clients, because it gives you the option of manipulating the data without sacrificing DataSet change tracking. The projection approach gives you the ability to reduce the number of fields to include just the ones you want to see.

Of course, there's no need to use LINQ to DataSet to achieve the result that's shown in Figure 13-6. You can accomplish the same thing by using the DataTable.Select() method to filter out the rows that have the right last name and modifying the schema of the GridView so it shows only the two columns you want. However, LINQ to DataSet allows you to take advantage of operators that don't have any direct DataSet equivalent, such as the grouping features discussed earlier.

Typed DataSets

Typed DataSets offer another solution for solving the limitations of the DataSet. Because a typed DataSet uses strongly typed classes, you no longer need to rely on the Field<T> and AsEnumerable() methods, which make for much more readable expressions.

For example, if you use a strongly typed DataSet for the Employees table, you can rewrite the expression in the previous example to this simpler code:

```
var matches = from employee in ds.Employees
  where employee.LastName.StartsWith("D")
  select new { First = employee.FirstName, employee.LastName };
```

Not only is this code simpler to understand, but it also looks a lot more like the expressions you used for querying custom classes in ordinary collections.

Null Values

The Field<T> method plays an important role by giving you strongly typed access to your field values. It also performs another useful trick: it converts null values (represented by DBNull.Value) to a true null reference. (The DataSet doesn't perform this step natively, because when it was created, nullable types weren't part of the framework.) As a result, you can check for a null reference rather than comparing values against DBNull.Value, which streamlines your LINQ expressions.

Here's an example:

```
var matches = from product in ds.Tables["Products"].AsEnumerable()
  where product.Field<DateTime>("DiscontinuedDate") != null
  select product;
```

When using null values, make sure you don't attempt to access a member of a value that could be null. For example, if you want to get discontinued products in a certain date range, you'd need to test for null values before performing the data comparison, as shown here:

```
var matches = from product in ds.Tables["Products"].AsEnumerable()
  where product.Field<DateTime>("DiscontinuedDate") != null &&
        product.Field<DateTime>("DiscontinuedDate").Year > 2006
  select product;
```

Null values aren't handled as nicely with a typed DataSet. Sadly, the property procedures that are hardwired into the custom DataRow classes in a typed DataSet throw exceptions when they encounter null values. To get around this, you'll need to use the more cumbersome Field<T> syntax when accessing a field that might contain a null.

LINQ to Entities

For many developers, the most useful part of LINQ is LINQ to Entities, which allows you to work with the structure and data of a database using standard C# objects. When using LINQ to Entities, your LINQ queries are translated into SQL queries behind the scenes and executed when you need the data, in other words, when you begin enumerating the results. And, if that weren't impressive enough, LINQ to Entities includes change tracking for all the data you retrieve, which means that you can modify the objects you have queries for and commit an entire batch of changes to the database at once.

LINQ to Entities is part of the Entity Framework and has replaced LINQ to SQL as the standard mechanism for using LINQ on databases. The Entity Framework is an industrial-strength Object-Relational Mapping (ORM) system that can be used with a range of databases and can support flexible and complex data models. LINQ to Entities is the part of the Entity Framework that lets you perform LINQ queries using an Entity Framework data model.

What happened to LINQ to SQL?

Microsoft has switched their development focus from LINQ to SQL to the Entity Framework and has announced that no more updates to LINQ to SQL will be made, putting LINQ to SQL in the supported-but-not-recommended category. Using the Entity Framework and LINQ to Entities is similar to using LINQ to SQL, but the additional database support and some of the more advanced modeling features allow you to work with data models that just weren't possible to create with LINQ to SQL. Although you can still use LINQ to SQL in your projects, we recommend you consider the Entity Framework wherever possible to ensure your codebase has long-term support from Microsoft.

LINQ to Entities is an impressive technology, but it's only a small win for most ASP.NET developers. As with the DataSet, ASP.NET developers are far more likely to use the querying features in LINQ to Entities than the batch update features. That's because the updates in a web application usually take place one at a time rather than in a batch. They also tend to take place immediately when the user posts back the page. At this point, you have the original values and the new (updated) values on hand, which makes it easy to use a straightforward ADO.NET command to commit the change.

In short, LINQ to Entities doesn't provide any capability that you can't duplicate with ADO.NET code, your own custom objects, LINQ to Objects (for in-memory filtering), and the DataSet (when change tracking is needed). However, although that is true, there are some compelling reasons to consider using LINQ to Entities:

- **Less code:** You don't need to write ADO.NET code for querying the database. You can also use a tool to generate the data classes you need.
- **Flexible querying capabilities:** Rather than struggle with SQL, you can use the LINQ querying model. Ultimately, you'll be able to use one consistent model (LINQ expressions) to access many different types of data, from databases to XML.
- **Change tracking and batch updates:** You can change multiple details about the data you've queried and commit a batch update, again without writing ADO.NET code.

Generating the Data Model

The Entity Framework relies on a data model to let you query using LINQ to Entities. Rows in tables are converted to instances of C# objects with properties for each of the table columns. The mapping between the schema of your database and the objects in the data model is at the heart of the Entity Framework and essential to how LINQ to Entities works.

Most developers will use Visual Studio to generate the data model automatically—doing so is quicker, and less prone to errors, than creating the mapping objects by hand. (The Entity Framework supports some advanced modeling features that Visual Studio can't generate automatically, but those features are beyond the scope of this book.)

To generate a model, right-click the App_Code folder, click Add New Item, and select ADO.NET Entity Data Model from the list of project templates. Set the name for the file that will be created (like NorthwindModel.edmx), and click Add.

You can generate an empty model and add classes to it manually, but we want to generate a model from an existing database, in this case, the Microsoft Northwind sample database. Select Generate from database in the Entity Data Model Wizard, and configure the connection to the database. You can choose which tables, views, and stored procedures in the database will be included in your data model. You can also pluralize or singularize object names (so that the object that represents a row in the Products table will be called Product, for example) and to include foreign-key relationships. You should select all the tables and then select the Pluralize/Singularize option.

Visual Studio creates a model diagram for the database elements you have selected, which shows the mapping objects that have been created, the fields that each has, and the relationship between each object. Two new files are created in the project:

- **NorthwindModel.edmx:** This XML file defines the schema for your data model.
- **NorthwindModel.Designer.cs:** This is a C# code file containing the mapping objects for your data model.

The Data Model Classes

Of the two files created for the data model, it is NorthwindModel.Designer.cs that we will spend the most time with, because it contains the data types we will query for using LINQ to Entities. You should not made modifications to the NorthwindModel.Designer.cs file, because the contents of the file can be regenerated from the data model and cause your changes to be lost. If you open the file, you will see that there are two code regions, Contexts and Entities.

■ **Tip** You will see a lot of attributes applied to the data model classes; their relationship to the database and to other entity classes is expressed through these attributes. We are not going to cover the meaning and use of the attributes in this book. You will only need to use them if you are creating your own data model by hand, which is something that most ASP.NET developers will never need to do.

The Derived Object Context Class

The first class defined in NorthwindModel.Designer.cs is derived from ObjectContext; ours is called NorthwindEntities. This class has constructors that connect to the database from which the model was generated or let you provide a connection string to connect to a different database (but that has the same schema; otherwise, the data model won't be applicable). The first step in using LINQ to Entities is to create a new instance of the derived ObjectContext class. In our examples, we will use the default constructor, which connects using the connection string we configured when generating the Entity Data Model.

The derived ObjectContext class also contains properties for each of the tables that you included in your data model. Each property is a strongly typed ObjectSet, typed for the entity class it refers to. For example, the Products property is an ObjectSet<Product>, meaning that it can be used to access instances of the Product entity class.

The simplest way to demonstrate using the derived ObjectContext class is to create a new instance and bind one of the ObjectSet properties to a GridView. Here is a sample class:

```
using System;
using NorthwindModel;

public partial class DerivedObjectContext : System.Web.UI.Page {
    protected void Page_Load(object sender, EventArgs e) {

        NorthwindEntities db = new NorthwindEntities();

        GridView1.DataSource = db.Products;
        GridView1.DataBind();
    }
}
```

You import the entity classes and the context using the namespace that was specified when the model was generated, in our case, NorthwindModel. The code in the listing produces the results shown in Figure 13-7.

ProductID	ProductName	SupplierID	CategoryID	QuantityPerUnit	UnitPrice	UnitsInStock	UnitsOnOrder	ReorderLevel	Discontinued
1	Chai Tea	1	1	10 boxes x 20 bags	19.2256	12	0	10	☐
3	Aniseed Syrup	1	2	12 - 550 ml bottles	10.0000	13	70	25	☐
4	Chef Anton's Cajun Seasoning	2	2	48 - 6 oz jars	22.0000	53	0	0	☐
5	Chef Anton's Gumbo Mix	2	2	36 boxes	21.3500	0	0	0	☑
6	Grandma's Boysenberry Spread	3	2	12 - 8 oz jars	25.0000	120	0	25	☐
7	Uncle Bob's Organic Dried Pears	3	7	12 - 1 lb pkgs.	30.0000	15	0	10	☐
8	Northwoods Cranberry Sauce	3	2	12 - 12 oz jars	40.0000	6	0	0	☐
9	Mishi Kobe Niku	4	6	18 - 500 g pkgs.	97.0000	29	0	0	☑
10	Ikura	4	8	12 - 200 ml jars	31.0000	31	0	0	☐
11	Queso Cabrales	5	4	1 kg pkg.	21.0000	22	30	30	☐

Figure 13-7. Binding an ObjectSet to a GridView

The Entity Classes

The entity classes are used to map a record from a database table into a C# object. If you selected the option to pluralize/singularize the entity object names, then a table such as Products will have been used to create an entity object called Product. Each entity object contains the following:

- **A factory method:** You can create new instances of the entity object by calling the default constructor or by using the factory method, which has arguments for the required fields. This can be a useful way to avoid schema errors when you try to store a new data element.
- **Field properties:** Entity objects contain a primitive field property for each column in the database table they are derived from.
- **Navigation properties:** If you included foreign-key relationships in your data model, your entity objects will contain navigation properties that help you access related data. We'll explain more about this in the "Navigation" section.

■ **Tip** Entity classes are declared as partial, meaning that you can create a matching partial class and extend the functionality without losing your changes when the data model is regenerated.

The most common kind of LINQ to Entities query selects objects from an ObjectSet that have specific values for field parameters. For example, to find all the Product instances in the Product ObjectSet with a value of false for the Discontinued field, select the ProductID and ProductName values:

```
using System;
using System.Linq;
using NorthwindModel;

public partial class SimpleLinqToEntitiesQuery : System.Web.UI.Page {

    protected void Page_Load(object sender, EventArgs e) {

        NorthwindEntities db = new NorthwindEntities();

        var results = from p in db.Products
                      where p.Discontinued == false
                      select new {
                          ID = p.ProductID,
                          Name = p.ProductName
                      };

        GridView1.DataSource = results;
        GridView1.DataBind();
    }
}
```

You can see how we have used the derived ObjectContext class. First, by creating a new instance of NorthwindEntities, we have implicitly established a connection to the database. Second, we have used the Products property as the data source for our LINQ query. Since the Products ObjectSet is strongly typed to contain the Product entity type, we are able to use the field parameters to filter the elements in the data source and then to select the fields we want to display in the grid. Figure 13-8 shows the result of binding the result of that query to a GridView.

ID	Name
1	Chai Tea
3	Aniseed Syrup
4	Chef Anton's Cajun Seasoning
6	Grandma's Boysenberry Spread
7	Uncle Bob's Organic Dried Pears
8	Northwoods Cranberry Sauce
10	Ikura
11	Queso Cabrales
12	Queso Manchego La Pastora

Figure 13-8. *The results of a simple LINQ to Entities query*

Entity Relationships

The entity classes contain navigation properties that allow you to move through the data model without having to think about foreign-key relationships. Here is a query that uses the navigation properties:

```
using System;
using System.Linq;
using NorthwindModel;

public partial class OneToManyRelationships : System.Web.UI.Page {

    protected void Page_Load(object sender, EventArgs e) {

        NorthwindEntities db = new NorthwindEntities();

        var result = from c in db.Customers
                     let o = from q in c.Orders
                             where (q.Employee.LastName != "King")
                             select (q)
                     where c.City == "London" && o.Count() > 5
                     select new {
                         Name = c.CompanyName,
                         Contact = c.ContactName,
                         OrderCount = o.Count()
                     };

        GridView1.DataSource = result;
        GridView1.DataBind();
    }
}
```

This query uses the Customers ObjectSet of the derived ObjectContext class and uses the Orders navigation property to query all the Orders associated with each Customer. We use the Employee navigation property of the Order entity type to check the last name of the employee who placed the Order and exclude anywhere the value is King. The where clause of the query filters using fields from the Customer and Order entity types, and the select clause creates a new anonymous type that selects fields from the same types.

Using the navigation properties allowed us to move through the data model without needing to create separate queries for each entity class. We ended up with selected details about customers based in London who have placed more than five orders by employees who are not named King. We obtained data from the Customers, Orders, and Employees tables without worrying about how they are related, which is a great convenience and better than having to split out the query so that we can find all Orders where the CustomerID field has the same value as the primary key of a given Customer instance. The way that one-to-many and one-to-one relationships are implemented differs, as explained in the following sections.

One-to-Many Relationships

The navigation properties for one-to-many relationships are handled using a strongly typed EntityCollection. For example, the Customer entity class has a one-to-many relationship with the Order entity class. To navigate to the Order instances associated with a given Customer, you would use the Customer.Orders navigation property, which is an EntityCollection<Order>. You don't have to worry about selecting appropriate records for a relationship; this is done for you using the foreign keys, so that when you select the Orders for a Customer, for example, you get only the Order instances that have a CustomerID value that matches the CustomerID value of the Customer.

You can use the EntityCollection class as a result directly in a LINQ to Entities query by using the SelectMany extension method; this will include all of the objects contained in the collection in the results collection. Here is an example:

```
NorthwindEntities db = new NorthwindEntities();

IEnumerable<Order> orders = db.Customers
    .Where(c => c.CustomerID == "LAZYK")
    .SelectMany(c => c.Orders);

GridView1.DataSource = orders;
GridView1.DataBind();
```

One-to-One Relationships

There are two navigation properties for one-to-one relationships. The first is always named TReference that returns an EntityReference<T>, where T is the name of the entity type that the relationship refers to; for example, the Order entity type has a navigation property called EmployeeReference, which returns an EntityReference<Employee>. The second navigation property is more useful and is named T, where T is the entity class it refers to; for example, the Order entity type has a convenience property called Employee.

Querying Stored Procedures

You must import a stored procedure into the Entity Framework data model before you can use it with LINQ to Entities. Fortunately, Visual Studio makes doing this pretty straightforward. Double-click the NorthwindModel.edmx file in the Solution Explorer to open the data model diagram. Open the Entity Data Model Browser window (you will find this under the View ~TRA Other Windows menu). Expand the NorthwindModel.Store node, and open the Stored Procedures folder; you will see a list of the stored procedures that have been imported into your model.

■ **Tip** If you did not check the Stored Procedures option when you created the data model, right-click in the drawing surface of the data model diagram, and select Update Model From Database. Select Stored Procedures on the Add tab (or check individual procedures if you don't want them all), and click Finish to regenerate the model.

To import a stored procedure, right-click the one you want, and select Add Function Import from the pop-up menu. The Function Import Name allows you to specify the name of the property that will be added to the derived ObjectContext to represent this stored procedure. We are going to import the Customers_By_City procedure, and we'll use the default name.

You can select which procedure will be imported from the drop-down list, but be careful, because the name used for the ObjectContext property will not be updated automatically. You can end up with the name of one procedure referring to another procedure entirely.

The next step is to click the Get Column Information button; this will read the schema for the stored procedure and infer the columns and data types that will be returned. We want to create a new entity object that represents the result from the stored procedure, so click the Create New Complex Type button. This will select the Complex option in the return type box and create a name for the new entity object (which will be the name of the procedure with _Result appended). You can see the function import dialog box in Figure 13-9. Click OK to import the function.

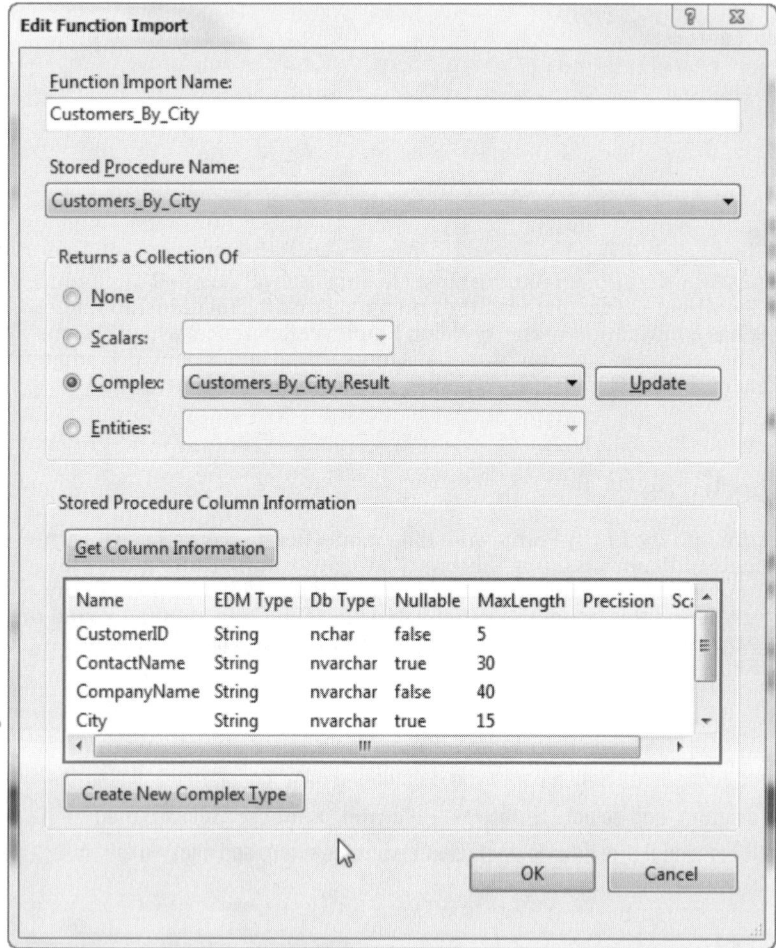

Figure 13-9. The Edit Function Import dialog

Once you have imported a function, you can treat it just the same as any of the EntityCollections in the derived ObjectContext class. Here is an example:

```
using System;
using System.Collections.Generic;
using System.Linq;
```

```
using NorthwindModel;

public partial class StoredProcedure : System.Web.UI.Page {

    protected void Page_Load(object sender, EventArgs e) {

        NorthwindEntities db = new NorthwindEntities();

        IEnumerable<Customers_By_City_Result> results =
            from c in db.Customers_By_City("London")
            select c;

        GridView1.DataSource = results;
        GridView1.DataBind();
    }
}
```

The Customers_By_City stored procedure takes one argument, which is the city to query for. The query returns a collection of the entity class that was created when we imported the function, which we have bound to a data grid.

LINQ to Entities Queries "Under the Hood"

The queries in the previous section showed you that LINQ to Entities is pretty much the same to use as LINQ to Objects. And that is true—at least as a superficial level. One of the nice things about LINQ is that it is largely consistent across data sources, so if you know how to make a basic LINQ query, you can use that knowledge to query objects, databases, XML, and so on.

The drawback is that the similarity comes from hiding away a lot of complexity, and if you are not careful, you can unintentionally generate a significant workload for your database. You should take the time to determine what SQL queries are generated to service your LINQ to Entities queries. The Entity Framework doesn't make it easy to see SQL queries; you have to use some sleight of hand by casting the result of your LINQ to Entities query to an instance of System.Data.Objects.ObjectQuery and calling the ToTraceString method. Here is the technique applied to the query we used to demonstrate navigation properties:

```
using System;
using System.Data.Objects;
using System.Linq;
using NorthwindModel;

public partial class ViewingSQLQuery : System.Web.UI.Page {
    protected void Page_Load(object sender, EventArgs e) {

        NorthwindEntities db = new NorthwindEntities();

        var result = from c in db.Customers
                     let o = from q in c.Orders
                             where (q.Employee.LastName != "King")
                             select (q)
                     where c.City == "London" && o.Count() > 5
                     select new {
                         Name = c.CompanyName,
                         Contact = c.ContactName,
```

```
                        OrderCount = o.Count()
                    };

        Label1.Text = (result as ObjectQuery).ToTraceString();
    }
}
```

View the page associated with this code shows us that the SQL generated to execute the query is as follows:

```
SELECT 1 AS [C1], [Project2].[CompanyName] AS [CompanyName], [Project2].[ContactName] AS
[ContactName], [Project2].[C1] AS [C2] FROM ( SELECT [Project1].[CompanyName] AS
[CompanyName], [Project1].[ContactName] AS [ContactName], (SELECT COUNT(1) AS [A1] FROM
[dbo].[Orders] AS [Extent4] LEFT OUTER JOIN [dbo].[Employees] AS [Extent5] ON
[Extent4].[EmployeeID] = [Extent5].[EmployeeID] WHERE ([Project1].[CustomerID] =
[Extent4].[CustomerID]) AND (N'King' <> [Extent5].[LastName])) AS [C1] FROM ( SELECT
[Extent1].[CustomerID] AS [CustomerID], [Extent1].[CompanyName] AS [CompanyName],
[Extent1].[ContactName] AS [ContactName], [Extent1].[City] AS [City], (SELECT COUNT(1) AS
[A1] FROM [dbo].[Orders] AS [Extent2] LEFT OUTER JOIN [dbo].[Employees] AS [Extent3] ON
[Extent2].[EmployeeID] = [Extent3].[EmployeeID] WHERE ([Extent1].[CustomerID] =
[Extent2].[CustomerID]) AND (N'King' <> [Extent3].[LastName])) AS [C1] FROM
[dbo].[Customers] AS [Extent1] ) AS [Project1] WHERE (N'London' = [Project1].[City]) AND
([Project1].[C1] > 5) ) AS [Project2]
```

Often, it is not practical to print the SQL query like this. If you are using any version of SQL Server other than Express, you can use the SQL Server Profiler tool. If you are using SQL Server Express, then we recommend the excellent, free, and open source SQL Profiler from Anjlab, which you can find at http://sites.google.com/site/sqlprofiler.

Filtering Too Late

One common cause of unnecessary database queries is to filter the data in a query too late. Here is a sample query:

```
NorthwindEntities db = new NorthwindEntities();

IEnumerable<Customer> custs = from c in db.Customers
                              where c.Country == "UK"
                              select c;

IEnumerable<Customer> results = from c in custs
                                where c.City == "London"
                                select c;

GridView1.DataSource = results;
GridView1.DataBind();
```

The problem here is that the first query is performed at the database and retrieves all the records where the Country property equals UK. The second query is applied to the results of the first, but uses LINQ to Objects, which means that we are discarding much of the data that we requested from the database. If you are in doubt, take a look at the SQL queries that are generated. There is only one for this example, and it is as follows:

```
SELECT
[Extent1].[CustomerID] AS [CustomerID],
[Extent1].[CompanyName] AS [CompanyName],
[Extent1].[ContactName] AS [ContactName],
[Extent1].[ContactTitle] AS [ContactTitle],
[Extent1].[Address] AS [Address],
[Extent1].[City] AS [City],
[Extent1].[Region] AS [Region],
[Extent1].[PostalCode] AS [PostalCode],
[Extent1].[Country] AS [Country],
[Extent1].[Phone] AS [Phone],
[Extent1].[Fax] AS [Fax]
FROM [dbo].[Customers] AS [Extent1]
WHERE N'UK' = [Extent1].[Country]
```

The solution, of course, is to combine your filters into a single query. Spotting this problem when the two parts of the query are next to each other is easy, but this problem generally arises when you are consuming data that has been queried by another part of a large project. The wasted overhead can be significant if you are working with large amounts of data.

Using Lazy and Eager Data Loading

To make the navigation properties work seamlessly, LINQ to Entities employs a technique called *lazy loading*, where data is not loaded from the database until it is needed. When you move from one entity type to another via a navigation property, the instances of the second entity type are not loaded until they are needed. Here is an example:

```
using System;
using System.Collections.Generic;
using System.Linq;
using NorthwindModel;

public partial class LazyDataLoading : System.Web.UI.Page {

    protected void Page_Load(object sender, EventArgs e) {

        NorthwindEntities db = new NorthwindEntities();

        IEnumerable<Customer> custs = from c in db.Customers
                                      where c.City == "London" && c.Country == "UK"
                                      select c;

        List<string> names = new List<string>();

        foreach (Customer c in custs) {
            if (c.Orders.Count() > 2) {
                names.Add(c.CompanyName);
            }
        }

        GridView1.DataSource = names;
        GridView1.DataBind();
    }
}
```

In this query, we filter the set of Customers and then iterate through the results, navigating to the related Order instances for the current Customer. We end up with the names of the companies that are based in the city of London in the UK and that have placed more than two orders. Unfortunately, because of lazy loading, the data from the Orders table was only loaded just as it was needed, which means that we generated a SQL query to get the order data for each Customer. That's a lot of queries. Of course, for this simple example, we could have combined everything into a single LINQ query, but we actually want to demonstrate the eager loading feature, which allows you to load related data from other tables in as part of your query. Here is an example:

```
using System;
using System.Collections.Generic;
using System.Linq;
using NorthwindModel;

public partial class EagerDataLoading : System.Web.UI.Page {

    protected void Page_Load(object sender, EventArgs e) {

        NorthwindEntities db = new NorthwindEntities();

        IEnumerable<Customer> custs = from c in db.Customers
                                      .Include("Orders")
                                      where c.City == "London" && c.Country == "UK"
                                      select c;

        List<string> names = new List<string>();

        foreach (Customer c in custs) {
            if (c.Orders.Count() > 2) {
                names.Add(c.CompanyName);
            }
        }

        GridView1.DataSource = names;
        GridView1.DataBind();
    }
}
```

To include related data, we use the Include extension method, marked in bold in the previous listing. This tells the LINQ to Entities engine that the Order instances related to each Customer that we query for should be loaded, even though there is nothing in the query that directly relates to the Orders table. Here is the SQL query that was generated for the LINQ query, edited down for size:

```
SELECT
[Project1].[C1] AS [C1],
[Project1].[CustomerID] AS [CustomerID],
... other projection statements...
[Project1].[ShipCountry] AS [ShipCountry]
FROM ( SELECT
    [Extent1].[CustomerID] AS [CustomerID],
    [Extent1].[CompanyName] AS [CompanyName],
    ...other fields from the customer table...
    [Extent1].[Fax] AS [Fax],
```

```
        1 AS [C1],
        [Extent2].[OrderID] AS [OrderID],
        [Extent2].[CustomerID] AS [CustomerID1],
        ...other fields from the orders table...
        [Extent2].[ShipCountry] AS [ShipCountry],
        CASE WHEN ([Extent2].[OrderID] IS NULL) THEN CAST(NULL AS int) ELSE 1 END AS [C2]
        FROM  [dbo].[Customers] AS [Extent1]
        LEFT OUTER JOIN [dbo].[Orders] AS [Extent2] ON [Extent1].[CustomerID] =
                [Extent2].[CustomerID]
        WHERE (N'London' = [Extent1].[City]) AND
                (N'UK' = [Extent1].[Country])
)  AS [Project1]
ORDER BY [Project1].[CustomerID] ASC, [Project1].[C2] ASC
```

The Entity Framework caches the results, which means that when we come to iterate through the Customer instances and inspect the related Orders, they have already been loaded, and no further queries to the database are generated.

Using Explicit Loading

If you want total control over what data is loaded, then you can use explicit loading. You disable lazy loading using the derived ObjectContext class and then use the EntityCollection.Load method to load data as you require it. You can check to see whether data has already been loaded using the IsLoaded method. Here's an example:

```
using System;
using System.Collections.Generic;
using System.Linq;
using NorthwindModel;

public partial class ExplicitDataLoading : System.Web.UI.Page {

    protected void Page_Load(object sender, EventArgs e) {

        NorthwindEntities db = new NorthwindEntities();
        db.ContextOptions.LazyLoadingEnabled = false;

        IEnumerable<Customer> custs = from c in db.Customers
                                      where c.Country == "UK"
                                      select c;

        foreach (Customer c in custs) {
            if (c.City == "London") {
                c.Orders.Load();
            }
        }

        List<Order> orders = new List<Order>();

        foreach (Customer c in custs) {
            if (c.Orders.IsLoaded) {
                orders.Add(c.Orders.First());
            }
```

```
            }

            GridView1.DataSource = orders;
            GridView1.DataBind();
        }
}
```

We have marked the key statements in bold. The first disabled lazy loading, which means that data referred to by navigation property won't be loaded. We perform a standard LINQ to Entities query to find get the Customer instances that have a Country property with a value of UK. We then use LINQ to Objects to iterate through the results and explicitly load the Orders data for those Customers who have a City property value of London using the Load method; this loads the data from the database into the Entity Framework cache. Finally, we iterate through the LINQ to Entities results again, but this time we check to see which Customers have their Orders data loaded. For those that do, we put the first Order into a collection that we use as the data source for the GridView control. This is a contrived example because we enumerate the results repeatedly, but it should give you the knowledge you need to use explicit data loading in your projects.

Compiling Queries

Another useful "under the hood" aspect of LINQ to Entities queries is the ability to create compiled queries. A compiled query is a strongly typed Func, which takes arguments for a query. Compiling a query performs the translation into a SQL statement, which is then reused each time the compiled query is called. This is not as effective as using a stored procedure because the database still has to create a query plan to execute the SQL, but it does stop the LINQ to Entities engine from having to parse the LINQ query repeatedly. Here is an example of using a compiled query:

```
using System;
using System.Data.Objects;
using System.Linq;
using NorthwindModel;

public partial class CompiledLinqQuery : System.Web.UI.Page {
    Func<NorthwindEntities, string, IQueryable<Customer>> MyCompiledQuery;
    NorthwindEntities db;

    protected void Page_Load(object sender, EventArgs e) {

        MyCompiledQuery = CompiledQuery.Compile<NorthwindEntities, string,
            IQueryable<Customer>>((context, city) =>
                               from c in context.Customers
                               where c.City == city
                               select c);

        db = new NorthwindEntities();

        GridView1.DataSource = MyCompiledQuery(db, "London");
        GridView1.DataBind();
    }

    protected void DropDownList1_SelectedIndexChanged(object sender, EventArgs e) {

        GridView1.DataSource = MyCompiledQuery(db, DropDownList1.SelectedValue);
```

```
        GridView1.DataBind();
    }
}
```

We have compiled a query to load all the customers for a given city; the derived ObjectContext class and the city to look for are passed in as arguments to our Func. We call the CompiledQuery.Compile method, which is strongly typed to match the signature of our Func. Once the Func is generated, it can be used to execute the compiled query again and again. We have reused the query each time a value is selected from a drop-down list. Each time, we pass in an instance of the derived ObjectContext class and the selected value from the list and bind the results to the GridView.

Database Operations

Although there are many projects that will rely only on querying for data, there often comes a point where you need to make a change. In the following sections, we'll show you how to create, modify, and delete database records using the Entity Framework data model.

Inserts

To create a new record in the database, you need to create a new instance of the appropriate entity class, populate the fields, add the entity class to the EntityCollection maintained by the derived ObjectContext, and then write the new record by calling SaveChanges. Here is an example that creates a new Customer:

```
NorthwindEntities db = new NorthwindEntities();

Customer cust = new Customer() {
    CustomerID = "LAWN",
    CompanyName = "Lawn Wranglers",
    ContactName = "Mr. Abe Henry",
    ContactTitle = "Owner",
    Address = "1017 Maple Leaf Way",
    City = "Ft. Worth",
    Region = "TX",
    PostalCode = "76104",
    Country = "USA",
    Phone = "(800) MOW-LAWN",
    Fax = "(800) MOW-LAWO"
};

db.Customers.AddObject(cust);

db.SaveChanges();
```

If you have several inserts (or any other kind of change) to make, then you can do all of the additions and then call SaveChanges just once to write all the new records. The derived ObjectContext keeps track of all the changes you make and applies them all to the database in one go.

Creating Partially Populated Entity Classes

In the previous example, we used the default constructor for the Customer entity class to create an instance that was entirely unpopulated with data. However, we could have used an alternative approach, which minimizes the risk of a database error by forcing you to supply values for the required fields at construction. Each entity class contains a factory method called CreateT, where T is the name of the entity class. For example, the Customer entity class has a factory method called CreateCustomer. Here is the previous example updated to use the factory method:

```
Customer cust = Customer.CreateCustomer("LAWN", "Lawn Wranglers");
cust.ContactName = "Mr. Abe Henry";
cust.ContactTitle = "Owner";
cust.Address = "1017 Maple Leaf Way";
cust.City = "Ft. Worth";
cust.Region = "TX";
cust.PostalCode = "76104";
cust.Country = "USA";
cust.Phone = "(800) MOW-LAWN";
cust.Fax = "(800) MOW-LAWO";

db.Customers.AddObject(cust);

db.SaveChanges();
```

We tend to use the default constructor because it means that we can specify values for properties in a single statement, but the factory method can be useful if you are prone to forgetting to set values for required fields. As you can see from the example, the factory method requires values for the CustomerID and CompanyName fields, both of which will be rejected by the database if null values are supplied.

Inserting Associated Entities

You can use the navigation properties of the entity classes to create a set of related objects and store them in the database in one go – the derived ObjectContext class keeps track of the additions and handles the updates for you. Here is an example of creating a Customer and an Order at the same time:

```
NorthwindEntities db = new NorthwindEntities();

Customer cust = new Customer {
    CustomerID = "LAWN",
    CompanyName = "Lawn Wranglers",
    ContactName = "Mr. Abe Henry",
    ContactTitle = "Owner",
    Address = "1017 Maple Leaf Way",
    City = "Ft. Worth",
    Region = "TX",
    PostalCode = "76104",
    Country = "USA",
    Phone = "(800) MOW-LAWN",
    Fax = "(800) MOW-LAWO",
    Orders = {
        new Order {
            CustomerID = "LAWN",
            EmployeeID = 4,
            OrderDate = DateTime.Now,
            RequiredDate = DateTime.Now.AddDays(7),
            ShipVia = 3,
            Freight = new Decimal(24.66),
```

```
            ShipName = "Lawn Wranglers",
            ShipAddress = "1017 Maple Leaf Way",
            ShipCity = "Ft. Worth",
            ShipRegion = "TX",
            ShipPostalCode = "76104",
            ShipCountry = "USA"
        }
    }
};

// add the new Customer
db.Customers.AddObject(cust);

// save the changes
db.SaveChanges();
```

We created the Order and associated it with the new Customer using the navigation property. We only had to add the Customer to the derived ObjectContext, which detected the relationship with the new Order and ensured that it was written when we called SaveChanges.

However, if we had created the Order and Customer separately, we would have had to add the Order explicitly, like this:

```
NorthwindEntities db = new NorthwindEntities();

Customer cust = new Customer {
    CustomerID = "LAWN",
    CompanyName = "Lawn Wranglers",
    ContactName = "Mr. Abe Henry",
    ContactTitle = "Owner",
    Address = "1017 Maple Leaf Way",
    City = "Ft. Worth",
    Region = "TX",
    PostalCode = "76104",
    Country = "USA",
    Phone = "(800) MOW-LAWN",
    Fax = "(800) MOW-LAWO"
};

Order ord = new Order {
    CustomerID = "LAWN",
    EmployeeID = 4,
    OrderDate = DateTime.Now,
    RequiredDate = DateTime.Now.AddDays(7),
    ShipVia = 3,
    Freight = new Decimal(24.66),
    ShipName = "Lawn Wranglers",
    ShipAddress = "1017 Maple Leaf Way",
    ShipCity = "Ft. Worth",
    ShipRegion = "TX",
    ShipPostalCode = "76104",
    ShipCountry = "USA"
};

cust.Orders.Add(ord);
```

```
db.Customers.AddObject(cust);
db.SaveChanges();
```

If we had not added the Order object explicitly, then it would not have been written to the database. We would not have received an error; it just wouldn't have been written. So, if you are creating sets of associated entities, you must take care to ensure that they are registered with the derived ObjectContext if you want them written to the database correctly.

Updates

Updating entity types is as simple as changing the properties of an entity object, calling the SaveChanges method of the derived ObjectContext. Here is a simple example:

```
NorthwindEntities db = new NorthwindEntities();

Customer cust = (from c in db.Customers
                where c.CustomerID == "LAWN"
                select c).Single();

cust.ContactName = "John Smith";
cust.Fax = "(800) 123 1234";

db.SaveChanges();
```

Deletes

Deleting data via the Entity Framework relies on using the DeleteObject method. You can call this method on the EntityCollection for the entity class you want to delete or on the derived ObjectContext. Here is a simple example:

```
NorthwindEntities db = new NorthwindEntities();

IEnumerable<Order_Detail> ods = from o in db.Order_Details
                                where o.OrderID == 10248
                                select o;

foreach (Order_Detail od in ods) {
    db.Order_Details.DeleteObject(od);
}

db.SaveChanges();
```

As with the other database operations, no changes are made to the database until you call the SaveChanges method. The Entity Framework doesn't delete related entity objects, so you must take care to remove any object that is related by an enforced foreign-key constrain before you call SaveChanges.

Managing Concurrency

The Entity Framework uses an optimistic concurrency model by default, meaning that it doesn't check to see whether anyone has modified the data in the database since you read the data. When you call

SaveChanges, any changes that are pending will be written to the database, even if someone else has updated the same records with conflicting information. If only one instance of your application exists and you are the only user of the database, you might be willing to accept this arrangement, but as soon as you deploy your application to a farm of servers or share the database with a different application, optimistic concurrency will lead to painful data consistency issues.

You can have the Entity Framework check to see whether the database has been modified by another party before it writes changes. This is still optimistic concurrency because nothing is locked in the database while you are working with the entity objects, but it does help by at least alerting you to concurrency issues when they occur.

You have to enable concurrency checking on a per-field basis. If you want all the fields of an entity class to be checked for concurrency conflicts...well, then you need to be sure that you have edited all of the fields—there is no way of telling the Entity Framework that you want every change to an entity type or even every change to the entire Entity Data Model to be checked automatically.

To enable concurrency checking on a field, open the data model view by double-clicking the NorthwindModel.edmx file, and select one of the fields from one of the displayed entity objects. For example, click the CompanyName field in the Customer entity object. In the properties window, set the value for Concurrency Mode to be fixed, as shown in Figure 13-10.

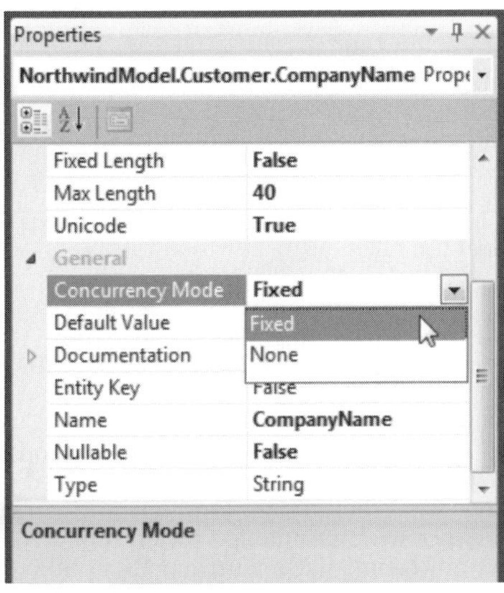

Figure 13-10. *Setting the Concurrency Mode property*

Handling Concurrency Conflicts

Once you have enabled concurrency conflict checking for an entity object field, you will receive an OptimisticConcurrencyException when you try to update data that has been modified since you loaded your entity objects. To simulate a concurrency exception, we have made a change using the Entity Framework and then executed a conflicting change using a direct SQL statement using the ExecuteStatementInDb method:

```
// create the ObjectContext
NorthwindEntities context = new NorthwindEntities();
```

```
Customer cust = context.Customers
    .Where(c => c.CustomerID == "LAZYK")
    .Select(c => c)
    .First();

Console.WriteLine("Initial value {0}", cust.ContactName);

// change the record outside of the entity framework
ExecuteStatementInDb(String.Format(
        @"update Customers
        set ContactName = 'Samuel Arthur Sanders'
        where CustomerID = 'LAZYK'"));

// modify the customer
cust.ContactName = "John Doe";

// save the changes
try {
    context.SaveChanges();
} catch (OptimisticConcurrencyException) {
    Console.WriteLine("Detected concurrency conflict - giving up");
} finally {
    string dbValue = GetStringFromDb(String.Format(
        @"select ContactName from Customers
    where CustomerID = 'LAZYK'"));
    Console.WriteLine("Database value: {0}", dbValue);
    Console.WriteLine("Cached value: {0}", cust.ContactName);
}
```

We obtain the Customer entity object for the record with the CustomerID of LAZYK, change the ContactName field outside of the Entity Framework, make the same change using the Entity Framework, and then call SaveChanges.

We have introduced two convenience methods that use ADO.NET calls to work directly with the database. We don't want to fill a chapter on LINQ with ADO.NET code, so we have included the methods in the sample code for this chapter, which you can download from Apress.com. The methods are called GetStringFromDb and ExecuteStatementInDb, and they do exactly what their names imply.

We wrap the SaveChanges call in a try...catch...finally block. Since we have enabled concurrency checking on the ContactName field, we know that we will receive an OptimisticConcurrencyException when we try to update the database. In the finally block, we print out the ContactName value in the database and the value from the entity object. Running the example code gives us the following output:

```
Initial value John Doe
Executing SQL statement against database with ADO.NET ...
Database updated.
Detected concurrency conflict - giving up
Database value: Samuel Arthur Sanders
Cached value: John Doe
```

We end up with a database that has one value and a cached entity object that has a conflicting value for the same data. That's a step forward—at least we didn't write back an update to the database without checking first. But now we need to resolve the differences in the data values so we are back in sync and can (optionally) try to update again. We do this by using the ObjectContext.Refresh method, as shown here:

```
// create the ObjectContext
NorthwindEntities context = new NorthwindEntities();

Customer cust = context.Customers
    .Where(c => c.CustomerID == "LAZYK")
    .Select(c => c)
    .First();

Console.WriteLine("Initial value {0}", cust.ContactName);

// change the record outside of the entity framework
ExecuteStatementInDb(String.Format(
        @"update Customers
        set ContactName = 'Samuel Arthur Sanders'
        where CustomerID = 'LAZYK'"));

// modify the customer
cust.ContactName = "John Doe";

// save the changes
try {
    context.SaveChanges();
} catch (OptimisticConcurrencyException) {
    Console.WriteLine("Detected concurrency conflict - refreshing data");
    context.Refresh(RefreshMode.StoreWins, cust);
} finally {
    string dbValue = GetStringFromDb(String.Format(
        @"select ContactName from Customers
    where CustomerID = 'LAZYK'"));
    Console.WriteLine("Database value: {0}", dbValue);
    Console.WriteLine("Cached value: {0}", cust.ContactName);
}
```

In this example, we call the Refresh method when we catch the OptimisticConcurrencyException. The Refresh method takes two arguments—the first is a value from the RefreshMode enumeration, and the second is the object that you want to refresh. The RefreshMode enumeration has two values, StoreWins and ClientWins. The StoreWins value refreshes the values for the object you specified using the data in the database. So, in our example, we would expect both the value in the entity object and the value in the database to be Samuel Arthur Adams. Compiling and running the code gives us the expected results:

```
Initial value John Steel
Executing SQL statement against database with ADO.NET ...
Database updated.
Detected concurrency conflict - refreshing data
Database value: Samuel Arthur Sanders
Cached value: Samuel Arthur Sanders
```

Let's just recap what happened there. We tried to write an update on a database row that had been modified by someone else. The Entity Framework detected a concurrency conflict and threw an

OptimisticConcurrencyException to let us know that there was a problem. We refreshed the entity object we modified using the data in the database, which put us back to a consistent state.

But what happened to our update? Well, nothing—we didn't apply it. If you want to apply your changes even when someone else has modified the same data you are using, then you need to use the ClientWins value of the RefreshMode enumeration and call SaveChanges again. Here is an example:

```
// create the ObjectContext
NorthwindEntities context = new NorthwindEntities();

Customer cust = context.Customers
    .Where(c => c.CustomerID == "LAZYK")
    .Select(c => c)
    .First();

Console.WriteLine("Initial value {0}", cust.ContactName);

// change the record outside of the entity framework
ExecuteStatementInDb(String.Format(
        @"update Customers
        set ContactName = 'Samuel Arthur Sanders'
        where CustomerID = 'LAZYK'"));

// modify the customer
cust.ContactName = "John Doe";

// save the changes
try {
    context.SaveChanges();
} catch (OptimisticConcurrencyException) {
    Console.WriteLine("Detected concurrency conflict - refreshing data");
    context.Refresh(RefreshMode.ClientWins, cust);
    context.SaveChanges();
} finally {
    string dbValue = GetStringFromDb(String.Format(
        @"select ContactName from Customers
    where CustomerID = 'LAZYK'"));
    Console.WriteLine("Database value: {0}", dbValue);
    Console.WriteLine("Cached value: {0}", cust.ContactName);
}
```

This time, we have specified the ClientWins value, which is like saying "I know there is a concurrency conflict, but I want to keep my changes." You need to call SaveChanges again; the call to the Refresh method just clears the concurrency conflict for the Entity Framework and doesn't write the changes for you. Running the code gives us the following results:

```
Initial value John Steel
Executing SQL statement against database with ADO.NET ...
Database updated.
Detected concurrency conflict - refreshing data
Database value: John Doe
Cached value: John Doe
```

We can see that the change that we made using the Entity Framework has been written to the database. There is one point we want to make about dealing with a concurrency conflict properly:

someone may have changed the data again while we were refreshing our entity objects. That means that our second call to SaveChanges may result in another OptimisticConcurrencyException. To deal with this, we can use a loop that tries to apply our update repeatedly, as follows:

```
// create the ObjectContext
NorthwindEntities context = new NorthwindEntities();

Customer cust = context.Customers
    .Where(c => c.CustomerID == "LAZYK")
    .Select(c => c)
    .First();

Console.WriteLine("Initial value {0}", cust.ContactName);

// change the record outside of the entity framework
ExecuteStatementInDb(String.Format(
        @"update Customers
        set ContactName = 'Samuel Arthur Sanders'
        where CustomerID = 'LAZYK'"));

// modify the customer
cust.ContactName = "John Doe";

int maxAttempts = 5;
bool recordsUpdated = false;

for (int i = 0; i < maxAttempts && !recordsUpdated; i++) {
    Console.WriteLine("Performing write attempt {0}", i);
    // save the changes
    try {
        context.SaveChanges();
        recordsUpdated = true;
    } catch (OptimisticConcurrencyException) {
        Console.WriteLine("Detected concurrency conflict - refreshing data");
        context.Refresh(RefreshMode.ClientWins, cust);
    }
}
```

We use a loop to try applying our update to the database several times. The bool recordsUpdated will be set to true only if the SaveChanges method doesn't throw an exception. This can be a useful technique, but it should be used carefully.

First, the more attempts we make to write our changes, the more updates from others we are ignoring. We have to be very confident that our update is more important than all the others to keep trying to save our changes.

Second, you will see that we used a loop counter to try writing our update five times and no more. There are very few situations in which you should try to save your changes in an infinite loop. Not only do you have to be super-confident that you have the best data, but there comes a point where you have to question the design of your code or the value of the data you are generating. If the same rows are being updated again and again, the chances are that most of the updates are being discarded as processes keep forcing their changes into the database. So, you should be very careful when automatically trying to save changes when you encounter a concurrency conflict. Just for completeness, here is the code we used in the ExecuteStatementInDb method:

```
static private void ExecuteStatementInDb(string cmd) {
    string connection =
      @"Data Source=.\SQLEXPRESS;Initial Catalog=Northwind;Integrated Security=SSPI;";

    System.Data.SqlClient.SqlConnection sqlConn =
      new System.Data.SqlClient.SqlConnection(connection);

    if (sqlConn.State != ConnectionState.Open) {
        sqlConn.Open();
    }

    System.Data.SqlClient.SqlCommand sqlComm =
      new System.Data.SqlClient.SqlCommand(cmd);

    sqlComm.Connection = sqlConn;
    try {
        Console.WriteLine("Executing SQL statement against database with ADO.NET ...");
        sqlComm.ExecuteNonQuery();
        Console.WriteLine("Database updated.");
    } finally {
        //  Close the connection.
        sqlComm.Connection.Close();
    }
}
```

The EntityDataSource Control

The LINQ to Entities examples in this chapter so far have used pure code to retrieve, manipulate, and bind data. However, ASP.NET also includes a EntityDataSource control that you can use to perform many of these tasks automatically.

Before taking a look at the EntityDataSource control, it's worth asking when it's appropriate. The EntityDataSource occupies a niche in rapid application development when combined with the Entity Data Model generator we saw earlier.

Much like the SqlDataSource control, when you use the EntityDataSource control, you don't need to write any code. But the EntityDataSource control goes one step further—not only can you avoid writing C# code, you can also avoid the messy details of writing SQL queries to select and update data. This makes it a perfect tool for small- or medium-scale applications and applications that don't need to be carefully tuned to get every last ounce of performance. On the other hand, it's also sure to exasperate database purists who prefer to have complete control over every detail. If the EntityDataSource lacks the features, performance, or flexibility you require, you'll need to use custom data access code (possibly with the help of the ObjectDataSource), as described in Chapter 9.

Displaying Data

To get a feel for the capabilities and overall goals of the EntityDataSource, it's worth building a simple example. In the following example, you'll see how to build the web page shown in Figure 13-11, which allows you to insert, delete, and update records in the Employees table of the Northwind sample database.

	LastName	FirstName	EmployeeID	TitleOfCourtesy	City
Select	Davolio	Nancy	1	Ms.	Seattle
Select	Fuller	Andrew	2	Dr.	Tacoma
Select	Leverling	Janet	3	Ms.	Kirkland
Select	Peacock	Margaret	4	Mrs.	Redmond
Select	Buchanan	Steven	5	Mr.	London
Select	Suyama	Michael	6	Mr.	London
Select	**King**	**Robert**	**7**	**Mr.**	**London**
Select	Callahan	Laura	8	Ms.	Seattle
Select	Dodsworth	Anne	9	Ms.	London

EmployeeID	7
LastName	King
FirstName	Robert
Title	Sales Representative
TitleOfCourtesy	Mr.
BirthDate	29/05/1960 00:00:00
HireDate	02/01/1994 00:00:00
Address	Edgeham Hollow Winchester Way
City	London
Region	
PostalCode	RG1 9SP
Country	UK
HomePhone	(71) 555-5598
Extension	465
Notes	Robert King served in the Peace Corps and traveled extensively before completing his degree in English at the University of Michigan in 1992, the year he joined the company. After completing a course entitled "Selling in Europe," he was transferred to the London office in March 1993.
ReportsTo	5
PhotoPath	http://accweb/emmployees/davolio.bmp
Edit Delete New	

***Figure 13-11.** Managing a table with the LinqDataSource*

The first step is to build an Entity Data Model, following the steps in the "Generating the Data Model" section of this chapter. The second step is to create the controls you want to use to display your data. In this example, two controls are used—a GridView that allows you to select an employee and a DetailsView that allows you to change it, remove it, or create a new one. You can add both controls straight from the Toolbox and use the AutoFormat feature to give them a pleasant color scheme to match Figure 13-11.

The third ingredient is the data source that links the derived ObjectContext class to your data controls. In this example, you'll need two data source controls—one that retrieves all the employee records (for the GridView) and one that retrieves a single employee record (for the DetailsView). The latter will also perform the editing, inserting, and deleting operations.

To create your first data source, drop an EntityDataSource control onto your web page. The quickest way to configure it is to use the wizard (select the data source control, click the arrow in the top-right corner, and choose Configure Data Source). The wizard has just two steps. The first step displays all the connection strings known to your application and a list of the derived ObjectContext classes in your project and prompts you to choose one. In this example, the connection and the derived class are both called NorthwindEntities.

The second step asks you what columns you want to include. In most cases, you'll check the Select All option, which includes all the columns (see Figure 13-12). You can then cut down the columns that are actually displayed by modifying the markup for your data-bound controls. If you don't use all the columns, you are essentially asking the EntityDataSource to perform a projection and convert your full-fledged Employee object to an anonymous type. The limitation with this approach is that you won't be able to update the data or display related data from other tables.

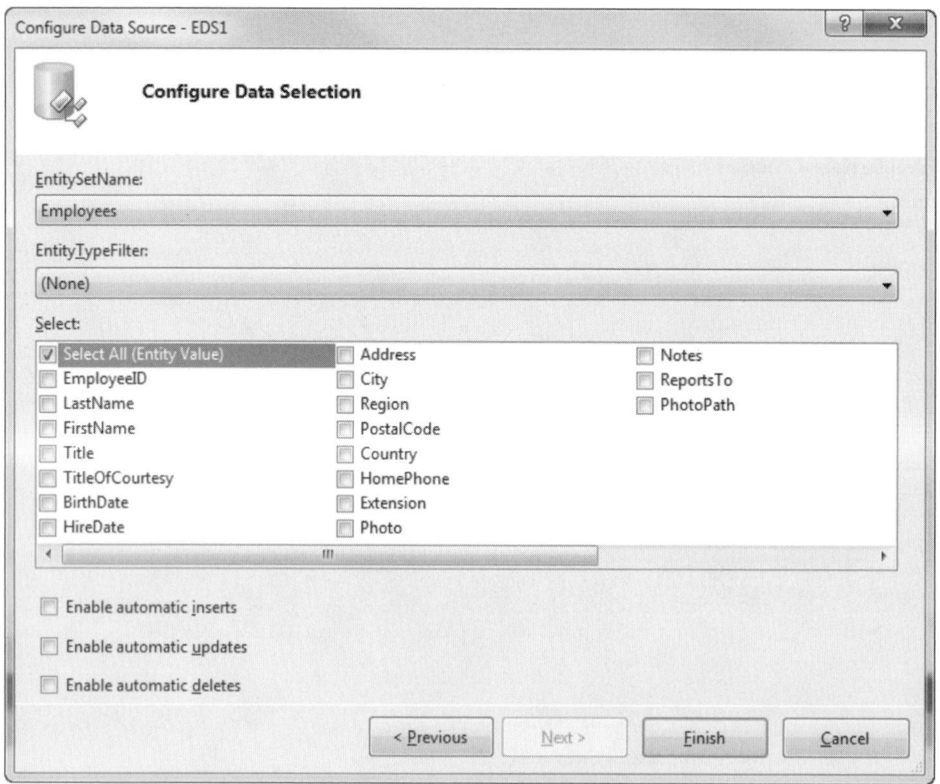

Figure 13-12. Choosing columns

If you have selected the Select All option, you can also select the options to enable inserts, updates, and deletes using this wizard. When you've finished the wizard, you'll end up with a fairly straightforward control tag, like this:

```
<asp:EntityDataSource ID="sourceEmployees" runat="server"
    ConnectionString="name=NorthwindEntities"
    DefaultContainerName="NorthwindEntities" EnableFlattening="False"
    EntitySetName="Employees">
</asp:EntityDataSource>
```

Clearly, the ConnectionString and DefaultContainerName properties relate to the Entity Data Model being used. The EntitySetName specifies the name of the entity class that you are using. If you selected a subset of columns in the second step of the wizard (Figure 13-12), you'll also see a Select property that defines a projection, like this:

```
<asp:EntityDataSource ID="sourceEmployees" runat="server"
    ConnectionString="name=NorthwindEntities"
    DefaultContainerName="NorthwindEntities" EnableFlattening="False"
    EntitySetName="Employees"
    Select="it.[LastName], it.[FirstName], it.[EmployeeID], it.[TitleOfCourtesy],
        it.[City]">
</asp:EntityDataSource>

<asp:LinqDataSource ID="sourceEmployees" runat="server"
  ContextTypeName="DatabaseComponent.NorthwindDataContext"
  TableName="Employees"
  Select="new (EmployeeID, LastName, FirstName, TitleOfCourtesy)">
</asp:LinqDataSource>
```

You can use the sourceEmployees data source to fill the grid shown in Figure 13-11. Simply set the GridView.DataSourceID property to sourceEmployees. Next, remove the columns you don't want to see by deleting the <asp:BoundField> elements from the GridView.Columns collection. Finally, make sure that the GridView supports selection. The DataKeyNames property should be set to EmployeeID, and a Select column should be visible in the grid (to add it, select the Enable Selection option in the GridView smart tag).

The DetailsView shows the currently selected employee in the grid. You learned how to create this design with the SqlDataSource, but the EntityDataSource works a bit differently because it doesn't allow you to define the SELECT command directly. To start, begin by creating a new EntityDataSource that has the same characteristics as the first one. Then, you need to build the where operator for the LINQ expression by setting the EntityDataSource.Where property, which you can edit once you have configured the control with the smart tag. The easiest way to build this part is to click the ellipsis button on the Where item in the Properties window for the EntityDataSource. This opens the Expression Editor, as shown in Figure 13-13. Click the Add Parameter button, and set the name to EmployeeID.

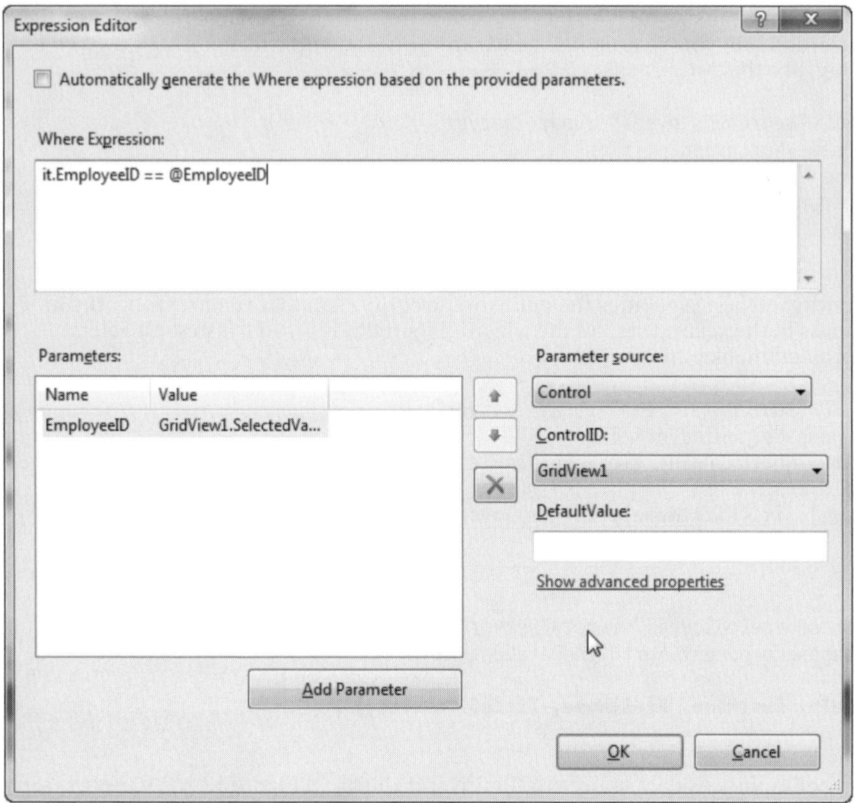

Figure 13-13. *Setting the EntityDataSource Where property*

Set the Parameter Source to be Control, and select the name of your GridView from the drop-down list. Click the Show Advanced Properties link, and set the DbType parameter value to match the type in the database. We are using the EmployeeID field, so we have selected Int32, as shown in Figure 13-14.

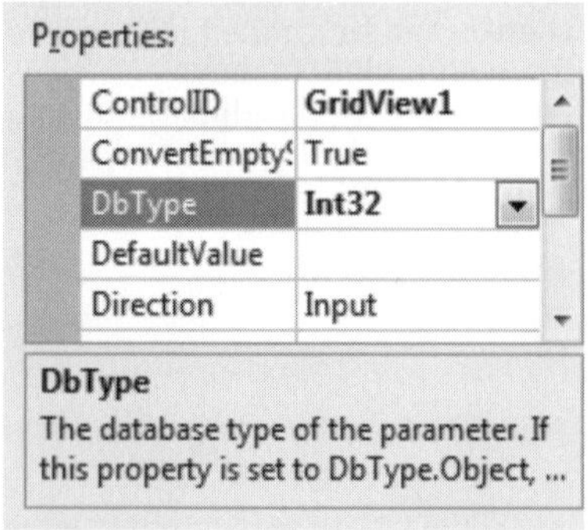

Figure 13-14. *Setting the DbType property for the parameter*

The last step is to enter an expression that uses the parameter we created. The EntityDataSource passes the current entity class to us using the name *it*, and we refer to the parameter we created by prefixing the name with @, so our expression becomes this:

```
it.EmployeeID == @EmployeeID
```

This leaves you with the following easy-to-understand markup:

```
<asp:EntityDataSource ID="sourceSingleEmployee" runat="server"
    ConnectionString="name=NorthwindEntities"
    DefaultContainerName="NorthwindEntities" EnableFlattening="False"
    EntitySetName="Employees" EntityTypeFilter="" Select=""
    Where="it.EmployeeID == @EmployeeID">
    <WhereParameters>
        <asp:ControlParameter ControlID="GridView1" DbType="Int32" Name="EmployeeID"
            PropertyName="SelectedValue" />
    </WhereParameters>
</asp:EntityDataSource>
```

Now, when you select an employee in the GridView, the full details will appear in the DetailsView.

Getting Related Data

When displaying data drawn from the EntityDataSource, you aren't limited to the basic properties in your data class. You can also branch out to consider related data. This is a powerful technique because it allows you to use the LINQ to Entities navigation fields. The only consideration is that you can only use this technique in a TemplateField—the ordinary BoundField doesn't support it.

For example, imagine you want to display the total number of orders that are associated with every employee. You know you can get this information by counting the number of records in the linked Orders table. Here's a TemplateField that uses this detail, which you can add to the end of the <Columns> section of the GridView:

```
<asp:TemplateField HeaderText="Orders">
    <ItemTemplate>
    <%# Eval("Orders.Count") %>
    </ItemTemplate>
</asp:TemplateField>
```

Before you can use the TemplateField, you must tell the EntityDataSource to include records from the Orders table. You do this by setting the Include property to "Orders" in the Properties window or by adding the Include attribute by hand so that the definition for the data source is as follows:

```
<asp:EntityDataSource ID="sourceEmployees" runat="server"
    ConnectionString="name=NorthwindEntities"
    DefaultContainerName="NorthwindEntities" EnableFlattening="False"
    EntitySetName="Employees" Include="Orders">
</asp:EntityDataSource>
```

Figure 13-15 shows the result of adding the TemplateField.

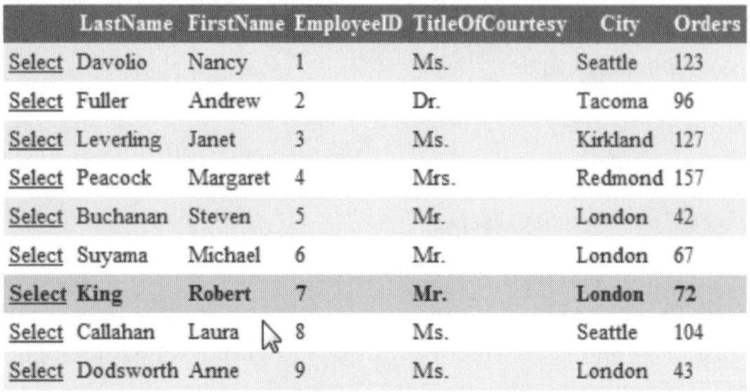

	LastName	FirstName	EmployeeID	TitleOfCourtesy	City	Orders
Select	Davolio	Nancy	1	Ms.	Seattle	123
Select	Fuller	Andrew	2	Dr.	Tacoma	96
Select	Leverling	Janet	3	Ms.	Kirkland	127
Select	Peacock	Margaret	4	Mrs.	Redmond	157
Select	Buchanan	Steven	5	Mr.	London	42
Select	Suyama	Michael	6	Mr.	London	67
Select	**King**	**Robert**	**7**	**Mr.**	**London**	**72**
Select	Callahan	Laura	8	Ms.	Seattle	104
Select	Dodsworth	Anne	9	Ms.	London	43

Figure 13-15. *Adding a TemplateField that uses a navigation property*

If it is not set, you will also need to specify the DataKeyNames property for the GridView, as follows:

```
DataKeyNames="EmployeeID"
```

Editing Data

The final step in this example is to configure the DetailsView and second EntityDataSource to support update, insert, and delete operations.

Select the second EntityDataSource, and use the smart tag to select Configure Data Source. Click the Next button in the wizard, ensure that the Select All item is selected so that all the columns are used, and select the options for Enable automatic inserts, Enable automatic updates, and Enable automatic deletes. This updates the EntityDataSource tag:

```
<asp:EntityDataSource ID="sourceSingleEmployee" runat="server"
    ConnectionString="name=NorthwindEntities"
    DefaultContainerName="NorthwindEntities" EnableFlattening="False"
    EntitySetName="Employees"
    Where="it.EmployeeID == @EmployeeID" EnableDelete="True"
    EnableInsert="True" EnableUpdate="True">
    <WhereParameters>
        <asp:ControlParameter ControlID="GridView1" DbType="Int32" Name="EmployeeID"
            PropertyName="SelectedValue" />
    </WhereParameters>
</asp:EntityDataSource>
```

Select the DetailsView and, using the smart tag, check the options for Enable Inserting, Enable Editing, and Enable Deleting.

Remarkably, this is all you need to complete the example. The EntityDataSource will now automatically use the derived ObjectContext class to perform these record operations against the Northwind database.

■ **Note** There's one quirk in this example. Because there are two data sources at work, the grid isn't properly synchronized when records are inserted or deleted (although changes are handled correctly). To solve this problem, you can set the GridView.EnableViewState property to false so that it always throws out the current data and rebinds itself after every postback.

Validation

To make this example just a bit more realistic, it's worth considering how to add a bit of validation logic to catch invalid data.

As with any validation scenario, there are numerous possible techniques. You could set constraints in the database itself, which will cause exceptions when the web page attempts to commit invalid data. This approach works, but it's fairly low-level, and it forces you to place validation logic where you might not want it (the database) and where it might not perform as well or be as easy to write.

Most powerfully, you can use a TemplateField in conjunction with the ASP.NET validation controls to prevent invalid data from being submitted in the first place. Unfortunately, this requires a lot more work (which takes the EntityDataSource out of its ideal niche as a tool for rapid application development), and it ties your validation code to a single control.

You could also handle the events of the bound DetailsView control or the EntityDataSource. Both of these techniques work, but they constrain your validation unnaturally, limiting it to a single control or a single page. This is less than ideal if you want to deal with the same data in several different places.

A better approach is to extend the Entity Data Model using partial classes. This way, you can plug your own validation logic directly into the entity classes, ensuring that invalid data is impossible no matter how the data objects are manipulated in your application. Each entity class contains two partial methods for each field, one that is called when a new field value has been received (but not applied) and one that is called when the new value has been applied. The partial method names are derived from the names of the field. For example, for the LastName field in the Employee entity object, the partial methods are called OnLastNameChanging and OnLastNameChanged.

If you wanted to prevent a record from being updated or inserted if it has a LastName field with fewer than three characters, you could add the following partial class declaration for the Employee class, which implements the OnLastNameChanging method:

```
using System;

namespace NorthwindModel {

    public partial class Employee {

        partial void OnLastNameChanging(string value) {
            if (value.Length < 3) {
                throw new ArgumentException(String.Format("'{0}' is too short. " +
                 "The last name must be three characters", value));
            }
        }
    }
}
```

Notice that we have used the same namespace that contains the entity classes. The namespace, the name of the class, and the method signature must all match for a partial method to be applied. In our OnLastNameChanging method, we are passed the proposed value as the sole argument; we check the length of the value and throw an instance of ArgumentException if the value length is too short. The Entity Framework wraps up our ArgumentException and rethrows it as a EntityDataSourceValidationException.

Of course, the web page doesn't handle the exception gracefully unless you take extra steps to catch it. As you learned in Chapter 9, you can handle events in the data control, such as ItemUpdated, ItemDeleted, and ItemInserted (or RowUpdated, RowDeleted, and RowInserted in the case of a GridView) to catch and handle the exception. For example, the following code checks for an exception and displays the exception message in a label, provided the exception is an instance of EntityDataSourceValidationException. Either way, the DetailsViewUpdateEventArgs.ExceptionHandled property is set to true to prevent the exception from derailing the current page processing.

```
protected void DetailsView1_ItemUpdated(object sender, DetailsViewUpdatedEventArgs e) {
    if (e.Exception != null) {
        EntityDataSourceValidationException ve = e.Exception
            as EntityDataSourceValidationException;
        if (ve == null) {
            Label1.Text = "Data error";
        } else {
            Label1.Text = ve.Message;
        }
        e.ExceptionHandled = true;
    } else {
        GridView1.DataBind();
    }
}
```

Figure 13-16 shows the error message that appears when the user attempts to supply a last name that is too short.

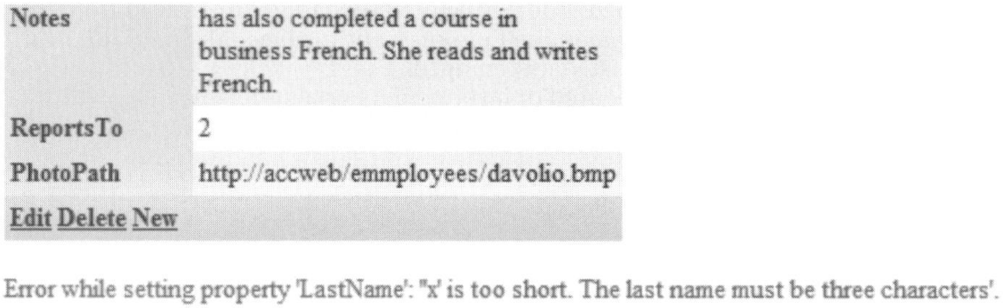

Notes	has also completed a course in business French. She reads and writes French.
ReportsTo	2
PhotoPath	http://accweb/emmployees/davolio.bmp
Edit Delete New	

Error while setting property 'LastName': "x' is too short. The last name must be three characters'.

Figure 13-16. *Validating an attempted change*

Using the QueryExtender Control

An alternative to specifying a where clause for an EntityDataSource control is to use the QueryExtender control. The value in the QueryExtender control is flexibility; the control supports a range of different approaches to how the data is selected, many of which are difficult or impossible to implement using the EntityDataSource where clause directly. The QueryExtender control uses declarative syntax to specify the filter, which can be frustrating until you get used to the format required, but the flexibility that arises as a consequence is worth the effort. In the following sections, we'll look at the most useful of the filtering approaches available with the QueryExtender control.

Using a SearchExpression

The first filter we'll look at is a SearchExpression, which finds all the instances of an entity class where a given property starts with, ends with, or contains an expression. Here is an example, which also demonstrates the declaration of the QueryExtender:

```
<asp:GridView ID="GridView1" runat="server" AutoGenerateColumns="False"
    DataKeyNames="EmployeeID" DataSourceID="EntityDataSource1">
    <Columns>
        <asp:CommandField ShowSelectButton="True" />
        <asp:BoundField DataField="EmployeeID" HeaderText="EmployeeID" ReadOnly="True"
            SortExpression="EmployeeID" />
        <asp:BoundField DataField="LastName" HeaderText="LastName"
            SortExpression="LastName" />
        <asp:BoundField DataField="FirstName" HeaderText="FirstName"
            SortExpression="FirstName" />
        <asp:BoundField DataField="Title" HeaderText="Title" SortExpression="Title" />
        <asp:BoundField DataField="TitleOfCourtesy" HeaderText="TitleOfCourtesy"
            SortExpression="TitleOfCourtesy" />
        <asp:BoundField DataField="City" HeaderText="City" SortExpression="City" />
    </Columns>
</asp:GridView>

<asp:EntityDataSource ID="EntityDataSource1" runat="server"
    ConnectionString="name=NorthwindEntities"
    DefaultContainerName="NorthwindEntities" EnableDelete="True"
    EnableFlattening="False" EnableInsert="True" EnableUpdate="True"
    EntitySetName="Employees">
</asp:EntityDataSource>

<asp:QueryExtender ID="QueryExtender1" runat="server"
    TargetControlID="EntityDataSource1">
        <asp:SearchExpression DataFields="City" SearchType="StartsWith">
            <asp:ControlParameter ControlID="TextBox1" />
        </asp:SearchExpression>
</asp:QueryExtender>

<asp:Label ID="Label1" runat="server" Text="City:"></asp:Label>
<asp:TextBox ID="TextBox1" runat="server"></asp:TextBox>
```

In this example, we have a GridView, which has an EntityDataSource as its data source. The QueryExtender is marked in bold. We use the TargetControlID to specify the data source that we want to filter. We have declared the SearchExpression within the QueryExtender. The DataFields attribute specifies the fields we want to search; the SearchType attribute allows us to choose from StartsWith, EndsWith, and Contains as search options; and the ControlParameter attribute lets us pick up the term to search for from a different control, in this case, a TextBox.

If we view the page, we see that the GridView is populated with the list of Employees. Type in a string, such as the letter *K* in the TextBox and hit Return. The contents of the GridView are filtered so that only those Employees whose City field starts with *K* are displayed.

If you specify more than one field in the DataFields attribute, then your search term will be applied more widely. Here is an example that searches the City and LastName fields:

```
<asp:QueryExtender ID="QueryExtender1" runat="server"
    TargetControlID="EntityDataSource1">
        <asp:SearchExpression DataFields="City, LastName" SearchType="StartsWith">
            <asp:ControlParameter ControlID="TextBox1" />
        </asp:SearchExpression>
</asp:QueryExtender>
```

Now when we enter K into the textbox, we see two results: one resident in the city of Kirkland and one with a last name of King.

Using a RangeExpression

A range expression allows you to select data where the value of a field falls in a specific range. Here is an example that filters for the EmployeeID field between values specified by a pair of TextBoxes:

```
<asp:QueryExtender ID="QueryExtender1" runat="server"
    TargetControlID="EntityDataSource1">
    <asp:RangeExpression DataField="EmployeeID" MinType="Inclusive"
            MaxType="Inclusive">
        <asp:ControlParameter ControlID="TextBox1"/>
        <asp:ControlParameter ControlID="TextBox2"/>
    </asp:RangeExpression>
</asp:QueryExtender>
```

Unlike the SearchExpression, a RangeExpression will work with only a single field, which is specified using the DataField property. The MaxType and MinType properties let you specify whether the search bounds are Inclusive or Exclusive. Figure 13-17 shows the effect of filtering in this way.

EmployeeID	LastName	FirstName	Title	TitleOfCourtesy	City
3	Leverling	Janet	Sales Representative	Ms.	Kirkland
4	Peacock	Margaret	Sales Representative	Mrs.	Redmond
5	Buchanan	Steven	Sales Manager	Mr.	London
6	Suyama	Michael	Sales Representative	Mr.	London
7	King	Robert	Sales Representative	Mr.	London
8	Callahan	Laura	Inside Sales Coordinator	Ms.	Seattle

Min 3

Max 8

Figure 13-17. *Applying a QueryExtender that uses a RangeExpression*

Using a PropertyExpression

A PropertyExpression lets you filter for data where one or more properties exactly match values that you specify. This is not like the SearchExpression that will make partial matches; the comparison is done using the C# == keyword. Here is an example of a QueryExtender that matches values from two TextBoxes to filter for the City and LastName fields:

```
<asp:QueryExtender ID="QueryExtender1" runat="server"
    TargetControlID="EntityDataSource1">
    <asp:PropertyExpression>
        <asp:ControlParameter ControlID="TextBox1" Name="City" />
        <asp:ControlParameter ControlID="TextBox2" Name="LastName" />
    </asp:PropertyExpression>
</asp:QueryExtender>
```

If you specify more than one ControlParameter, as we have done, the filter looks for records that match both conditions. Figure 13-18 shows the effect of filtering for records with a City value of London and a LastName value of King.

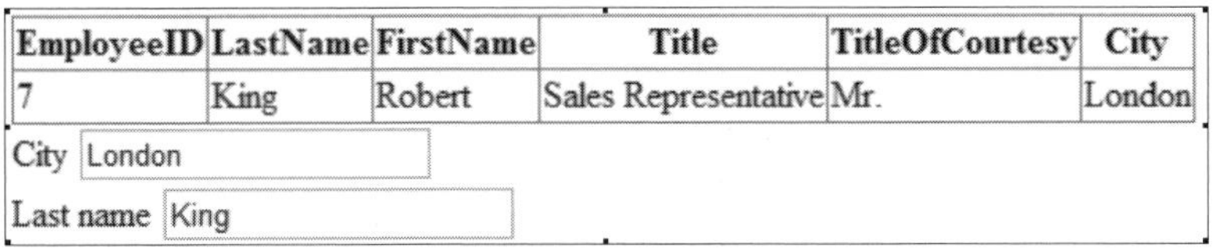

EmployeeID	LastName	FirstName	Title	TitleOfCourtesy	City
7	King	Robert	Sales Representative	Mr.	London

City London

Last name King

***Figure 13-18.** Applying a property expression*

Using a MethodExpression

The last filter option we will consider is the most flexible, in that you specify a method that will be called to execute the filter operation. What you put in that method is entirely open, but it will usually be a LINQ expression. The first step is to define the method. Here is an example:

```
using System.Linq;
using System.Web.UI.WebControls.Expressions;
using NorthwindModel;


public class QueryExtenderMethods {

    public static IQueryable<Employee> FilterEmployees(IQueryable<Employee> data) {

        return from d in data
               where d.City == "London" && d.Country == "UK"
               select d;
    }
}
```

The method you want to use to filter data must accept and return an IQueryable<T>, where T is the entity class you are working with. In our example, we are working with the Employee class again. Our LINQ query filters for instances that have a City value of London and a Country value of UK. Using the method with the QueryExtender is simply a matter of using the TypeName to specify the name of the class that contains your filter method and the MethodName to give the name of the method, as follows:

```
<asp:QueryExtender ID="QueryExtender1" runat="server"
    TargetControlID="EntityDataSource1">
    <asp:MethodExpression TypeName="QueryExtenderMethods" MethodName="FilterEmployees"/>
</asp:QueryExtender>
```

Now when data is loaded into the GridView, it is first filtered through the LINQ expression contained in our method.

Summary

In this chapter, you learned about LINQ, a core feature of the .NET Framework, with deep support in the C# language. LINQ has a wide range of potential applications—simply stated, it provides a declarative model for retrieving and processing data that allows you to use the same (or similar) syntax with a wide range of different types of data. The one unifying principle that underlies all applications of LINQ is that it emphasizes declarative programming over functional programming. In other words, your code states the result it wants rather than the sequence of steps necessary to get that result. Ideally, this shift allows developers to concentrate on business logic and gives the LINQ infrastructure more freedom to automate low-level tasks and optimize how they're performed.

Although LINQ is an exciting and impressive technology, it doesn't suit all applications. LINQ to Collections and LINQ to DataSet are harmless, and LINQ to XML—which you'll examine in Chapter 14—just might be the most practical part of LINQ, because it gives developers a modern, streamlined way to load, search, and construct XML documents. But LINQ to Entities—the real showpiece of LINQ—offers a tricky compromise. On one hand, it gives developers tools to dramatically simplify query logic and data processing. On the other hand, it introduces new potential problems, such as the deferred loading model, which means that database code can be executed at unexpected times (and therefore throw database-related exceptions when you least expect it). At worst, this model breaks down the proper division of layers in a carefully structured component-based application, confuses data retrieval with data processing, and allows database exceptions to migrate to unexpected places where they might not be effectively dealt with. It's no exaggeration to say that LINQ to Entities gives developers the most powerful tool for shooting themselves in the foot that they've had for a long time. If in doubt, and if you don't need the more powerful LINQ to Entities features, it's best to stick to the more modest approach of simple, straightforward ADO.NET commands.

CHAPTER 14

■ ■ ■

XML

Ever since XML (Extensible Markup Language) first arrived on the scene in the late 1990s, it has been the focus of intense activity and overenthusiastic speculation. Based on nothing but ordinary text, XML offers a means of sharing data between just about any two applications, whether they're new or old, written in different languages, built by distinct companies, or even hosted on different operating systems. Now that XML has come of age, it's being steadily integrated into different applications, problem domains, and industries.

The .NET Framework provides a range of options for using XML. But although XML is conceptually simple, processing XML is often tedious (with reams of repetitive code to write) or tricky (with the potential for easily overlooked details to cause future headaches). For this reason, .NET has a constellation of complementary XML APIs, including classes for stream-based XML processing, classes for manipulating XML content in memory, and web controls like Xml and XmlDataSource for quick and convenient XML display and data binding. There's also LINQ to XML, a surprisingly practical XML API that's based on the LINQ extensions described in Chapter 13.

In this chapter, you'll cover a fair bit of ground. You'll learn about the traditional .NET classes for XML processing, LINQ to XML, XML data binding, and the XML support that's built into the ADO.NET DataSet. But first, you'll begin by reviewing the key concepts of XML and its supporting standards.

When Does Using XML Make Sense?

The question that every new ASP.NET developer asks (and many XML proponents don't answer) is when does it make sense to use XML in an ASP.NET web application? It makes sense in a few core scenarios:

- You need to manipulate data that's already stored in XML. This situation might occur if you want to exchange data with an existing application that uses a specific flavor of XML.
- You want to use XML to store your data and open the possibilities of future integration. Because you use XML, you know other third-party applications can be designed to read this data in the future.
- You want to use a technology that depends on XML. For example, web services use various standards that are all based on XML.

Many .NET features use XML behind the scenes. For example, web services use a higher-level model that's built on top of the XML infrastructure. You don't need to directly manipulate XML to use web services—instead, you can work through an abstraction of objects. Similarly, you don't need to manipulate XML to read information from ASP.NET configuration files, save the DataSet to a file, or rely on other .NET Framework features that have XML underpinnings. In all these situations, XML is quietly at work, and you gain the benefits of XML without needing to deal with it by hand.

XML makes the most sense in *application integration* scenarios. However, there's no reason you can't use an XML format to store your own proprietary data. If you do, you'll gain a few minor conveniences, such as the ability to use .NET classes to read XML data from a file. When storing complex, highly structured data, the convenience of using these classes rather than designing your own custom format and writing your own file-parsing logic is significant. It will also make it easier for other developers to understand the system you've created and to reuse or enhance your work.

■ **Note** One of the most important concepts developers must understand is that there are two decisions when storing data—choosing the way data will be structured (the logical format) and choosing the way data will be stored (the physical data store). XML is a choice of format, not a choice of storage. This means if you decide to store data in an XML format, you still need to decide whether that XML will be inserted into a database field, inserted into a file, or just kept in memory in a string or some other type of object.

An Introduction to XML

In its simplest form, the XML specification is a set of guidelines, defined by the W3C (World Wide Web Consortium), for describing structured data in plain text. Like HTML, XML is a markup language based on tags within angled brackets. As with HTML, the textual nature of XML makes the data highly portable and broadly deployable. In addition, you can create and edit XML documents in any standard text editor.

Unlike HTML, XML does not have a fixed set of tags. Instead, XML is a metalanguage that allows for the creation of *other* markup languages. In other words, XML sets out a few simple rules for naming and ordering elements, and you create your own data format with your own custom elements.

For example, the following document shows a custom XML format that stores a product catalog. It starts with some generic product catalog information, followed by a product list with itemized information about two products.

```
<?xml version="1.0" ?>
<productCatalog>
    <catalogName>Acme Fall 2008 Catalog</catalogName>
    <expiryDate>2008-01-01</expiryDate>
    <products>
        <product id="1001">
            <productName>Magic Ring</productName>
            <productPrice>342.10</productPrice>
            <inStock>true</inStock>
        </product>
        <product id="1002">
            <productName>Flying Carpet</productName>
            <productPrice>982.99</productPrice>
            <inStock>true</inStock>
        </product>
    </products>
</productCatalog>
```

This example uses elements such as <productCatalog>, <product>, and <catalogName> to indicate the document structure. However, you're free to use whatever element names describe your data best.

It's because of this flexibility that XML has become extremely successful. Of course, flexibility also has drawbacks. Because XML doesn't define any standard data formats, it's up to you to create data formats that represent product catalogs, invoices, customer lists, and so on. Different companies can easily store similar data using completely different tag names and structures. And even though any application can parse XML data, the writer and the reader of that data still need to agree on a common set of tags and structure in order for the reader to be able to *interpret* that data and extract meaningful information.

Usually, third-party organizations define standards for particular problem domains and industries. For example, if you need to store a mathematical equation in XML, you'll probably choose the MathML format, which is an XML-based format that defines a specific set of tags and a specific structure. Similarly, hundreds more standard XML formats exist for real estate listings, music notation, legal documents, patient records, vector graphics, and much more. Creating a robust, usable XML format takes some experience, so it's always best to use a standardized, agreed-upon, XML-based markup language when possible.

■ **Note** One obvious application XML-based language is XHTML, the modernized version of HTML. In essence, XHTML is an XML-based language that indicates the structure of documents, by dividing text into sections, headings, paragraphs, and lists.

The Advantages of XML

When XML was first introduced, its success was partly due to its simplicity. The rules of XML are much shorter and simpler than the rules of its predecessor, SGML (Standard Generalized Markup Language), and simple XML documents are human-readable. However, in the intervening years many other supporting standards have been added to the XML mix, and as a result, using XML in a professional application isn't simple at all.

■ **Note** Although XML is human-readable in theory, it's often difficult to understand complex documents, and only computer applications, not developers, can read many types of XML.

But if anything, XML is much more useful today than it ever was before. The benefits of using XML in a modern application include the following:

- **Adoption:** XML is ubiquitous. Many companies are using XML to store data or are actively considering it. Whenever data needs to be shared, XML is automatically the first (and often the only) choice that's examined.
- **Extensibility and flexibility:** XML imposes no rules about data semantics and does not tie companies into proprietary networks, unlike EDI (Electronic Data Interchange). As a result, XML can fit any type of data and is cheaper to implement.
- **Related standards and tools:** Another reason for XML's success is the tools (such as parsers) and the surrounding standards (such as XML Schema, XPath, and XSLT) that help in creating and processing XML documents. As a result,

programmers in nearly any language have ready-made components for reading XML, verifying that XML is valid, verifying XML against a set of rules (known as a *schema*), searching XML, and transforming one format of XML into another.

XML acts like the glue that allows different systems to work together. It helps standardize business processes and transactions between organizations. But XML is not just suited for data exchange between companies. Many programming tasks today are all about application integration—web applications integrate multiple web services, e-commerce sites integrate legacy inventory and pricing systems, and intranet applications integrate existing business applications. All these applications are held together by the exchange of XML documents.

Well-Formed XML

XML is a fairly strict standard. This strictness is designed to preserve broad compatibility. If the rules of XML weren't as strict, it would be difficult to distinguish between a harmless variance and a serious error. Even worse, some mistakes might be dealt with differently by different XML parsers, leading to inconsistencies in the way that is processed (or even whether it can be processed at all). These are the sort of quirks that affected one notorious language that isn't based on XML—HTML.

To prevent this sort of problem, all XML parsers perform a few basic quality checks. If an XML document does not meet these standards, it's rejected outright. If the XML document does follow these rules, it's deemed to be *well formed*. Well-formed XML isn't necessarily correct XML—for example, it could still contain incorrect data—but an XML processor can parse it.

To be considered well formed, an XML document must meet these criteria:

- Every start tag must have an end tag.
- An empty element must end with />.
- Elements can nest but not overlap. In other words, <person><firstName></firstName>_</person> is valid, but <person><firstName></person></firstName> is not.
- Elements and attributes must use consistent case. For example, the tags <FirstName></firstName> do not comprise a valid element because they have different case.
- An element cannot have two attributes with the same name because there will be no way to distinguish them from each other. However, an element can contain two nested elements with the same name.
- A document can have only one root element. (The root element is the top-level element that starts the document and contains all its content.)
- All attributes must have quotes around the value.
- Comments can't be placed inside tags. (XML comments have the same format as HTML comments and are bracketed with <!-- and --> markers.)

■ **Tip** To quickly test if an XML document is well formed, try opening it in Internet Explorer. If there is an error, Internet Explorer will report a message and flag the offending line.

XML Namespaces

As the XML standard gained ground, dozens of XML markup languages (often called XML grammars) were created, and many of them are specific to certain industries, processes, and types of information. In many cases, it becomes important to extend one type of markup with additional company-specific elements, or even create XML documents that combine several different XML grammars. This poses a problem. What happens if you need to combine two XML grammars that use elements with the same names? How do you tell them apart? A related, but more typical, problem occurs when an application needs to distinguish between XML grammars in a document. For example, consider an XML document that has order-specific information using a standard called OrderML and client-specific information using a standard called ClientML. This document is sent to an order-fulfillment application that's interested only in the OrderML details. How can it quickly filter out the information that it needs and ignore the unrelated details?

The solution is the XML Namespaces standard. The core idea behind this standard is that every XML markup language has its own namespace that uniquely identifies all related elements. Technically, namespaces *disambiguate* elements by making it clear to which markup language they belong.

All XML namespaces use URIs (universal resource identifiers). Typically, these URIs look like a web-page URL. For example, `http://www.mycompany.com/mystandard` is a typical name for a namespace. Though the namespace looks like it points to a valid location on the Web, this isn't required (and shouldn't be assumed). URIs are used for XML namespaces because they are more likely to be unique. Usually, if you create a new XML language, you'll use a URI that points to a domain or website you control. That way, you can be sure that no one else is likely to use that URI. However, the namespace doesn't need to be a URI—any sequence of text is acceptable.

■ **Note** Sometimes URNs (uniform resource names) are used to prevent confusion with website addresses. URNs start with the prefix urn: and can incorporate a domain name or unique identifier (such as a GUID). One example is urn:schemas-microsoft-com. For more information, see http://en.wikipedia.org/wiki/Uniform_Resource_Name.

To specify that an element belongs to a specific namespace, you simply need to add the xmlns attribute to the start tag and indicate the namespace. For example, the element shown here is part of the `http://mycompany/OrderML` namespace. If you don't take this step, the element will not be part of any namespace.

```
<order xmlns="http://mycompany/OrderML"></order>
```

It would be cumbersome if you needed to type in the full namespace URI every time you wrote an element in an XML document. Fortunately, when you assign a namespace in this fashion, it becomes the default namespace for all child elements. For example, in the XML document shown here, the <order> and <orderItem> elements are both placed in the `http://mycompany/OrderML` namespace:

```
<?xml version="1.0"?>
<order xmlns="http://mycompany/OrderML">
    <orderItem>...</orderItem>
    <orderItem>...</orderItem>
</order>
```

■ **Tip** Namespace names must match exactly. If you change the capitalization in part of a namespace, add a trailing / character, or modify any other detail, the XML parser will interpret it as a different namespace.

You can declare a new namespace for separate portions of the document. The easiest way to deal with this is to use *namespace prefixes*. Namespace prefixes are short character sequences that you can insert in front of a tag name to indicate its namespace. You define the prefix in the xmlns attribute by inserting a colon (:) followed by the characters you want to use for the prefix.

Here's an order document that uses namespace prefixes to map different elements into two different namespaces:

```
<?xml version="1.0"?>
<ord:order xmlns:ord="http://mycompany/OrderML"
           xmlns:cli="http://mycompany/ClientML">
    <cli:client>
        <cli:firstName>...</cli:firstName>
        <cli:lastName>...</cli:lastName>
    </cli:client>

    <ord:orderItem>...</ord:orderItem>
    <ord:orderItem>...</ord:orderItem>
</ord:order>
```

Namespace prefixes are simply used to map an element to a namespace. The actual prefix you use isn't important as long as it remains consistent.

XML Schemas

A good part of the success of the XML standard is due to its remarkable flexibility. Using XML, you can create exactly the markup language you need. This flexibility also raises a few problems. With developers around the world using your XML format, how do you ensure that everyone is following the rules?

The solution is to create a formal document that states the rules of your custom markup language, which is called a schema. These rules won't include syntactical details (such as the requirement to use angle brackets or properly nest tags) because these requirements are already part of the basic XML standard. Instead, the schema document will list the logical rules that pertain to your type of data. They include the following:

- **Document vocabulary:** This determines what element and attribute names are used in your XML documents.
- **Document structure:** This determines where tags can be placed and can include rules specifying that certain tags must be placed before, after, or inside others. You can also specify how many times an element can occur.
- **Supported data types:** This allows you to specify whether data is ordinary text or must be able to be interpreted as numeric data, date information, and so on.
- **Allowed data ranges:** This allows you to set constraints that restrict numbers to certain ranges, limit text to a certain length, force regular expression pattern matching, or allow only a small set of specified values.

The XML Schema standard defines the rules you need to follow when creating a schema document. The following is an XML schema that defines the rules for the product catalog document shown earlier:

```
<?xml version="1.0"?>
<xsd:schema xmlns:xsd="http://www.w3.org/2001/XMLSchema">
   <xsd:element name="productCatalog">
      <xsd:complexType>
         <xsd:sequence>
            <xsd:element name="catalogName" type="xsd:string"/>
            <xsd:element name="expiryDate" type="xsd:date"/>

            <xsd:element name="products">
               <xsd:complexType>
                  <xsd:sequence>
                     <xsd:element name="product"
                      type="productType" maxOccurs="unbounded" />
                  </xsd:sequence>
               </xsd:complexType>
            </xsd:element>
         </xsd:sequence>
      </xsd:complexType>
   </xsd:element>

   <xsd:complexType name="productType">
      <xsd:sequence>
         <xsd:element name="productName" type="xsd:string"/>
         <xsd:element name="productPrice" type="xsd:decimal"/>
         <xsd:element name="inStock" type="xsd:boolean"/>
      </xsd:sequence>
      <xsd:attribute name="id" type="xsd:integer" use="required" />
   </xsd:complexType>
</xsd:schema>
```

Every schema document is an XML document that begins with a root <schema> element. These elements are defined in the XML schema namespace (`http://www.w3.org/2001/XMLSchema`). Your schema documents must use this exact namespace name. However, you're free to map it to whatever namespace prefix you'd like to use in your schema document, although xsd (used here) and xs are the conventional choices.

Inside the <schema> element are two types of definitions—the <element> element, which defines the structure the target document must follow, and one or more <complexType> elements, which define smaller data structures that are used to define the document structure.

The <element> tag is really the heart of the schema, and it's the starting point for all validation. In this example, the <element> tag identifies that the product catalog must begin with a root element named <productCatalog>. Inside the <productCatalog> element is a sequence of three elements. The first, <catalogName>, contains ordinary text. The second, <expiryDate>, includes text that fits the rules for date representation, as set out in the schema standard. The final element, <products>, contains a list of <product> elements.

Each <product> element is a complex type, and the type is defined with the <complexType> element at the end of the document. This complex type (named productType) consists of a sequence of three elements with product information. The elements must store this information as text (<productName>), a decimal value (<productPrice>), and a Boolean value (<inStock>), respectively. The complex type includes one required attribute, named id.

■ **Note** A full discussion of XML Schema is beyond the scope of this book. However, if you want to learn more, you can consider the excellent online tutorials at `http://www.w3schools.com/schema` or the standard itself at `http://www.w3.org/XML/Schema`.

Stream-Based XML Processing

The .NET Framework allows you to manipulate XML data with a set of classes in the System.Xml namespace (and other namespaces that begin with System.Xml). Out of these, the most lightweight way to read and write XML is through two stream-based classes: XmlTextReader and XmlTextWriter. These classes are mandatory if you have huge XML files that make it impractical to hold the whole document in memory at once. They may also be sufficient for simple XML processing.

Writing XML Files

The .NET Framework provides two approaches for writing XML data to a file:

- You can build the document in memory using the XmlDocument or XDocument class and write it to a file when you're finished.
- You can write the document directly to a stream using the XmlTextWriter. This outputs data as you write it, node by node.

Constructing an XML document in memory is a good choice if you need to perform other operations on XML content after you create it, such as searching it, transforming it, or validating it. It's also the only way to write an XML document in a nonlinear way, because it allows you to insert new nodes anywhere. However, the XmlTextWriter provides a much simpler and better performing model for writing directly to a file, because it doesn't store the whole document in memory at once.

■ **Tip** You can use the XmlDocument, XDocument, and XmlTextWriter classes to create XML data that isn't stored in a file. That's because all of these classes allow you to write information to any stream. Using techniques such as these, you could build an XML document and then insert it into another storage location such as a text-based field in a database table.

The next web-page example shows how to use the XmlTextWriter to create a well-formed XML file. The first step is to create a private WriteXML() method that will handle the job. It begins by creating an XmlTextWriter object and passing the physical path of the file you want to create as a constructor argument.

```
private void WriteXML()
{
    string xmlFile = Server.MapPath("DvdList.xml");
    XmlTextWriter writer = new XmlTextWriter(xmlFile, null);
    ...
```

The second parameter to the XML constructor specifies the encoding. You can pass a null reference to use standard UTF-8 encoding.

■ **Note** Keep in mind that when you use the XmlTextWriter to create an XML file, you face all the limitations that you face when writing any other type of file in a web application. In other words, you need to take safeguards (such as generating unique filenames) to ensure that two different clients don't run the same code and try to write the same file at once.

The XmlTextWriter has properties such as Formatting and Indentation, which allow you to specify whether the XML data will be automatically indented with the typical hierarchical structure and to indicate the number of spaces to use as indentation. You can set these two properties as follows:

```
...
writer.Formatting = Formatting.Indented;
writer.Indentation = 3;
...
```

■ **Tip** Remember, in a datacentric XML document, whitespace is almost always ignored. But by adding indentation, you create a file that is easier for a human to read and interpret, so it can't hurt.

Now you're ready to start writing the file. The WriteStartDocument() method writes the XML declaration with version 1.0 (<?xml version="1.0"?>), as follows:

```
writer.WriteStartDocument();
```

The WriteComment() method writes a comment. You can use it to add a message with the date and time of creation:

```
writer.WriteComment("Created @ " + DateTime.Now.ToString());
```

Next, you need to write the real content—the elements, attributes, and so on. This example builds an XML document that represents a DVD list, with information such as the title, the director, the price, and a list of actors for each DVD. These records will be child elements of a parent <DvdList> element, which must be created first:

```
writer.WriteStartElement("DvdList");
```

Now you can create the child nodes. The following code opens a new <DVD> element:

```
writer.WriteStartElement("DVD");
```

Now the code writes two attributes, representing the ID and the related category. This information is added to the start tag of the <DVD> element.

```
...
writer.WriteAttributeString("ID", "1");
writer.WriteAttributeString("Category", "Science Fiction");
...
```

The next step is to add the elements with the information about the DVD inside the <DVD> element. These elements won't have child elements of their own, so you can write them and set their values more efficiently with a single call to the WriteElementString() method. WriteElementString() accepts two arguments: the element name and its value (always as string), as shown here:

```
...
// Write some simple elements.
writer.WriteElementString("Title", "The Matrix");
writer.WriteElementString("Director", "Larry Wachowski");
writer.WriteElementString("Price", "18.74");
...
```

Next is a child <Starring> element that lists one or more actors. Because this element contains other elements, you need to open it and keep it open with the WriteStartElement() method. Then you can add the contained child elements, as shown here:

```
...
writer.WriteStartElement("Starring");
writer.WriteElementString("Star", "Keanu Reeves");
writer.WriteElementString("Star", "Laurence Fishburne");
...
```

At this point the code has written all the data for the current DVD. The next step is to close all the opened tags, in reverse order. To do so, you just call the WriteEndElement() method once for each element you've opened. You don't need to specify the element name when you call WriteEndElement(). Instead, each time you call WriteEndElement() it will automatically write the closing tag for the last opened element.

```
...
// Close the <Starring> element.
writer.WriteEndElement();

// Close the <DVD> element.
writer.WriteEndElement();
...
```

Now let's create another <DVD> element using the same approach:

```
...
writer.WriteStartElement("DVD");

// Write a couple of attributes to the <DVD> element.
writer.WriteAttributeString("ID", "2");
writer.WriteAttributeString("Category", "Drama");

// Write some simple elements.
writer.WriteElementString("Title", "Forrest Gump");
writer.WriteElementString("Director", "Robert Zemeckis");
```

```
    writer.WriteElementString("Price", "23.99");

    // Open the <Starring> element.
    writer.WriteStartElement("Starring");

    // Write two elements.
    writer.WriteElementString("Star", "Tom Hanks");
    writer.WriteElementString("Star", "Robin Wright");

    // Close the <Starring> element.
    writer.WriteEndElement();

    // Close the <DVD> element.
    writer.WriteEndElement();
    ...
```

To complete the document, you simply need to close the <DvdList> item, with yet another call to WriteEndElement(). You can then close the XmlTextWriter, as shown here:

```
    ...
    writer.WriteEndElement();
    writer.Close();
}
```

To try this code, call the WriteXML() procedure from the Page.Load event handler. It will generate an XML file named DvdList.xml in the current folder, as shown in Figure 14-1.

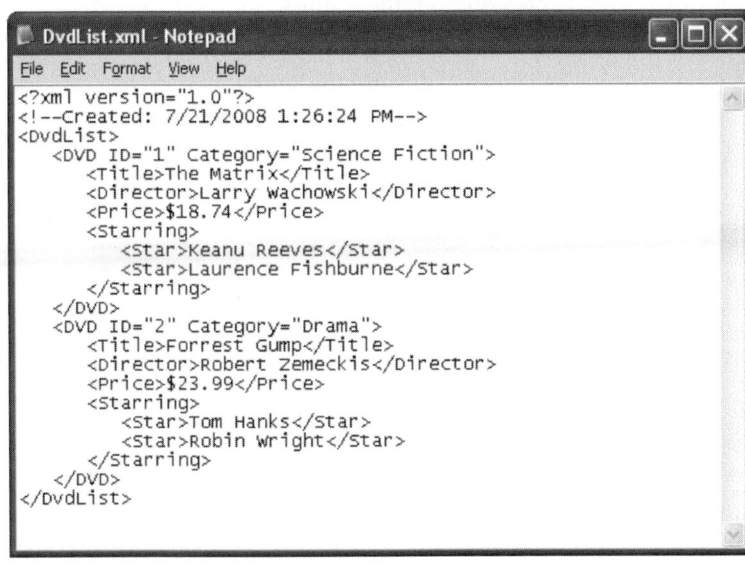

***Figure 14-1.** A dynamically created XML document*

■ **Note** It's always a good idea to identify your XML language by giving it a unique XML namespace, as described earlier in this chapter. Once you do, you'll then want to place your elements into that namespace. To do so, you must first define the namespace prefix as an attribute using the WriteAttributeString() method to write an xmlns attribute. Typically, you'll add this attribute to the root element of your document or to the first element that uses your namespace. Next, you must qualify your element names with the namespace prefix. To do so, you use the overloaded version of the WriteStartElement() method that accepts a namespace URI and a namespace prefix.

Reading XML Files

As when writing XML content, there are two basic strategies when reading it:

- You can read it into memory in one burst using the XmlDocument, XPathNavigator, or XDocument classes. Out of these three, only the XPathNavigator is read-only.
- You can step through the content node by node using the XmlTextReader, which is a stream-based reader.

The stream-based approach reduces the memory overhead and is usually—but not always—more efficient. If you need to perform a time-consuming task with an XML document, you might choose to use the in-memory approach to reduce the amount of time that the file is kept open, if you know other users will also need to access it.

Although reading an XML file with an XmlTextReader object is the simplest approach, it also provides the least flexibility. The file is read in sequential order, and you can't freely move to the parent, child, and sibling nodes as you can with in-memory XML processing. Instead, you read a node at a time from a stream. Usually, you'll write one or more nested loops to dig through the elements in the XML document until you find the content that interests you.

The following code starts by loading the source file in an XmlTextReader object. It then begins a loop that moves through the document one node at time. To move from one node to the next, you call the XmlTextReader.Read() method. This method returns true until it moves past the last node, at which point it returns false. This is similar to the approach used by the DataReader class, which retrieves query results from a database.

Here's the code you need:

```
private void ReadXML()
{
    string xmlFile = Server.MapPath("DvdList.xml");

    // Create the reader.
    XmlTextReader reader = new XmlTextReader(xmlFile);
    StringBuilder str = new StringBuilder();

    // Loop through all the nodes.
    while (reader.Read())
    {
        switch(reader.NodeType)
        {
            case XmlNodeType.XmlDeclaration:
                str.Append("XML Declaration: <b>");
```

```
            str.Append(reader.Name);
            str.Append(" ");
            str.Append(reader.Value);
            str.Append("</b><br />");
            break;
        case XmlNodeType.Element:
            str.Append("Element: <b>");
            str.Append(reader.Name);
            str.Append("</b><br />");
            break;
        case XmlNodeType.Text:
            str.Append(" - Value: <b>");
            str.Append(reader.Value);
            str.Append("</b><br />");
            break;
    }
    ...
```

After handling the types of nodes you're interested in, the next step is to check if the current node has attributes. The XmlTextReader doesn't have an Attributes collection, but an AttributeCount property returns the number of attributes. You can continue moving the cursor forward to the next attribute until MoveToNextAttribute() returns false.

```
        ...
        if (reader.AttributeCount > 0)
        {
            while (reader.MoveToNextAttribute())
            {
                str.Append(" - Attribute: <b>");
                str.Append(reader.Name);
                str.Append("</b> Value: <b>");
                str.Append(reader.Value);
                str.Append("</b><br />");
            }
        }
    }

    // Close the reader and show the text.
    reader.Close();
    lblXml.Text = str.ToString();
}
```

In the last two lines the procedure concludes by flushing the content in the buffer and closing the reader. When using the XmlTextReader, it's imperative you finish your task and close the reader as soon as possible, because it retains a lock on the file.

The XmlTextReader provides additional methods that help make reading XML faster and more convenient if you know what structure to expect. For example, you can use MoveToContent(), which skips over irrelevant nodes (such as comments, whitespace, and the XML declaration) and stops on the declaration of the next element.

You can also use the ReadStartElement() method, which reads a node and performs basic validation at the same time. When you call ReadStartElement(), you specify the name of the element you expect to appear next in the document. The XmlTextReader calls MoveToContent() and then verifies that the current element has the name you've specified. If it doesn't, an exception is thrown. You can also use the ReadEndElement() method to read the closing tag for the element.

Finally, if you want to read an element that contains only text data, you move over the start tag, content, and end tag by using the ReadElementString() method and by specifying the element name. The data you want is returned as a string.

Here's the code that extracts data from the DVD list using this more streamlined approach:

```
// Create the reader.
string xmlFile = Server.MapPath("DvdList.xml");
XmlTextReader reader = new XmlTextReader(xmlFile);

StringBuilder str = new StringBuilder();
reader.ReadStartElement("DvdList");

// Read all the <DVD> elements.
while (reader.Read())
{
    if ((reader.Name == "DVD") && (reader.NodeType == XmlNodeType.Element))
    {
        reader.ReadStartElement("DVD");
        str.Append("<ul><b>");
        str.Append(reader.ReadElementString("Title"));
        str.Append("</b><li>");
        str.Append(reader.ReadElementString("Director"));
        str.Append("</li><li>");
        str.Append(String.Format("{0:C}",
        Decimal.Parse(reader.ReadElementString("Price"))));
        str.Append("</li></ul>");
    }
}
// Close the reader and show the text.
reader.Close();
lblXml.Text = str.ToString();
```

Figure 14-2 shows the result.

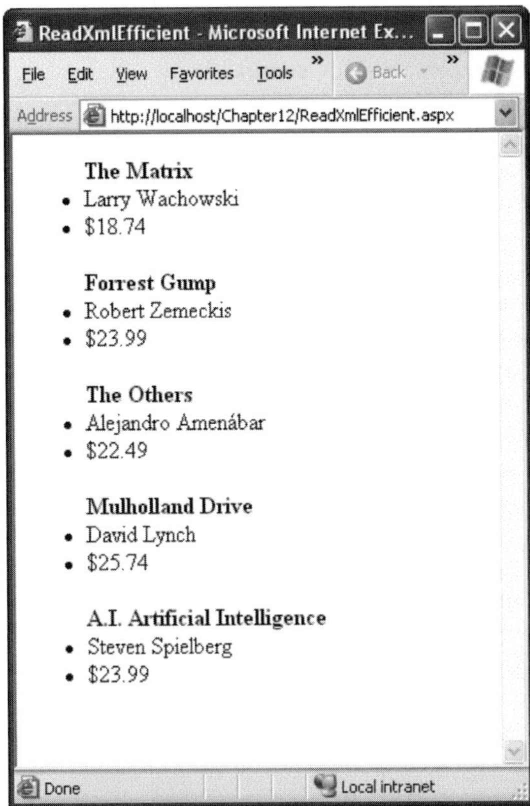

Figure 14-2. Efficient XML reading

In-Memory XML Processing

Stream-based XML processing offers the least overhead but also gives you the least flexibility. In many XML processing scenarios, you don't want to work at such a low level. Instead, you'll want an easy way to pull out the element content you want with a few lines of code (rather than a few dozen). Furthermore, the stream-based processing model makes it easy to make relatively trivial omissions that can cause significant future problems, like failing to anticipate whitespace and comments.

In-memory XML processing is far more convenient. Unfortunately, there's no single, standard approach for in-memory XML processing. All the following classes allow you to read and navigate the content of an XML file:

XmlDocument: The XmlDocument class implements the full XML DOM (Document Object Model) Level 2 Core, as defined by the W3C. It's the most standardized interface to XML data, but it's also a bit clunky at times.

XPathNavigator: Like the XmlDocument, the XPathNavigator holds the entire XML document in memory. However, it offers a slightly faster, more streamlined model than the XML DOM, along with enhanced searching features. Unlike the XmlDocument, it doesn't provide the ability to make changes and save them.

XDocument: The XDocument provides an even more intuitive and efficient API for dealing with XML. Technically, it's part of LINQ to XML, but it's useful even when you aren't constructing LINQ queries. However, because of the newness of the XDocument, it needs to work in conjunction with the older .NET XML classes to perform tasks like validation. You'll also find that some classes that have been around for a long time—like the Xml web control that lets you display XML in a web page more easily—are still based on the XmlDocument, and so won't work with the XDocument.

The following sections demonstrate each of these approaches to loading the DVD list XML document.

The XmlDocument

The XmlDocument stores. information as a tree of nodes. A node is the basic ingredient of an XML file and can be an element, an attribute, a comment, or a value in an element. A separate XmlNode object represents each node. The XmlDocument wraps groups of XmlNode objects that exist at the same level into XmlNodeList collections.

You can retrieve the first level of nodes through the XmlDocument.ChildNodes property. In the DVD list example, that property provides access to the initial comments and the <DvdList> element. The <DvdList> element contains other child nodes, and these nodes contain still more nodes and the actual values. To drill down through all the layers of the tree, you need to use recursive logic, as shown in this example.

Figure 14-3 shows a web page that reads the DvdList.xml document and displays a list of elements. This example uses different levels of indenting to show the overall structure.

When the example page loads, it creates an XmlDocument object and calls the Load() method, which retrieves the XML data from the file. It then calls a recursive function in the page class named GetChildNodesDescr() and displays the result in a Literal control named lblXml:

```
private void Page_Load(object sender, System.EventArgs e)
{
    string xmlFile = Server.MapPath("DvdList.xml");

    // Load the XML file into an XmlDocument.
    XmlDocument doc = new XmlDocument();
    doc.Load(xmlFile);

    // Write the description text to a label.
    lblXml.Text = GetChildNodesDescr(doc.ChildNodes, 0);
}
```

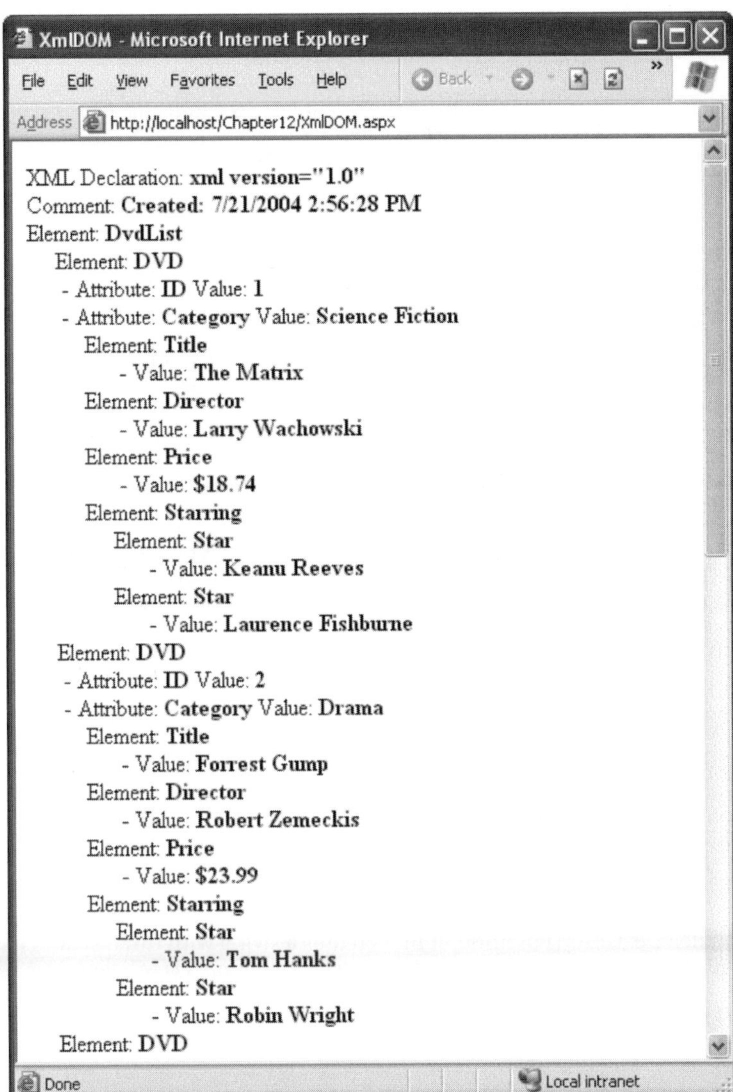

Figure 14-3. *Retrieving information from an XML document*

The XmlDocument and User Concurrency

In a web application, it's extremely important to pay close attention to how your code accesses the file system. If you aren't careful, a web page that reads data from a file can become a disaster under heavy user loads. The problem occurs when two users access a file at the same time. If the first user hasn't taken care to open a shareable stream, the second user will receive an error.

These issues are covered in more detail in Chapter 12. However, all of this raises an excellent question—how does the XmlDocument.Load() method open a file? To find the answer, you need to dig into the IL code of the .NET Framework. What you'll find is that several steps actually unfold to load an XML document into an XmlDocument object. First, the path you supply is examined by an XmlUrlResolver and passed to an XmlDownloadResolver, which determines whether it needs to make a web request (if you've supplied a URL) or can open a FileStream (if you've supplied a path). If it can use the FileStream, it explicitly opens the FileStream with shareable reads enabled. As a result, if more than one user loads the file with the XmlDocument.Load() method at once on different threads, no conflict will occur. Of course, the best approach is to reduce contention by caching the retrieved XML content or the XmlDocument object (see Chapter 11).

The GetChildNodesDescr() method takes two parameters: an XmlNodeList object (a collection of nodes) and an integer that represents the nesting level. When the Page.Load event handler calls GetChildNodesDescr(), it passes an XmlNodeList object that represents the first level of nodes. The code also passes 0 as the second argument of GetChildNodesDescr() to indicate that this is the first level of nesting in the XML document. The processed node content is then returned as a string.

■ **Tip** What if you want to create an XmlDocument and fill it based on XML content you've drawn from another source, such as a field in a database table? In this case, instead of using the Load() method, you would use LoadXml(), which accepts a string that contains the content of the XML document.

The interesting part is the GetChildNodesDescr() method. It first creates a string with three spaces for each indentation level that it will later use as a prefix for each line added to the final HTML text.

```
private string GetChildNodesDescr(XmlNodeList nodeList, int level)
{
    string indent = "";
    for (int i=0; i<level; i++)
       indent += "     ";
    ...
```

Next, the GetChildNodesDescr() method cycles through all the child nodes of the XmlNodeList. For the first call, these nodes include the XML declaration, the comment, and the <DvdList> element. An XmlNode object exposes properties such as NodeType, which identifies the type of item (for example, Comment, Element, Attribute, CDATA, Text, EndElement, Name, and Value). The code checks for node types that are relevant in this example and adds that information to the string, as shown here:

```
    ...
    StringBuilder str = new StringBuilder("");
```

```
foreach (XmlNode node in nodeList)
{
    switch(node.NodeType)
    {
        case XmlNodeType.XmlDeclaration:
        str.Append("XML Declaration: <b>");
        str.Append(node.Name);
        str.Append(" ");
        str.Append(node.Value);
        str.Append("</b><br />");
        break;
    case XmlNodeType.Element:
        str.Append(indent);
        str.Append("Element: <b>");
        str.Append(node.Name);
        str.Append("</b><br />");
        break;
    case XmlNodeType.Text:
        str.Append(indent);
        str.Append(" - Value: <b>");
        str.Append(node.Value);
        str.Append("</b><br />");
        break;
    case XmlNodeType.Comment:
        str.Append(indent);
        str.Append("Comment: <b>");
        str.Append(node.Value);
        str.Append("</b><br />");
        break;
}
...
```

Note that not all types of nodes have a name or a value. For example, for an element such as Title, the name is Title, but the value is empty, because it's stored in the following Text node.

Next, the code checks whether the current node has any attributes (by testing if its Attributes collection is not null). If it does, the attributes are processed with a nested foreach loop:

```
...
if (node.Attributes != null)
{
    foreach (XmlAttribute attrib in node.Attributes)
    {
        str.Append(indent);
        str.Append(" - Attribute: <b>");
        str.Append(attrib.Name);
        str.Append("</b> Value: <b>");
        str.Append(attrib.Value);
        str.Append("</b><br />");
    }
}
...
```

Lastly, if the node has child nodes (according to its HasChildNodes property), the code recursively calls the GetChildNodesDescr function, passing to it the current node's ChildNodes collection and the current indent level plus 1, as shown here:

```
    ...
        if (node.HasChildNodes)
            str.Append(GetChildNodesDescr(node.ChildNodes, level+1));
    }
    return str.ToString();
}
```

When the whole process is finished, the outer foreach block is closed, and the function returns the content of the StringBuilder object.

The XmlDocument also allows you to modify node content (for example, you can change the XmlNode.Name and XmlNode.Value properties) and make more dramatic changes, such as removing a node from a collection by creating a new node. In fact, you can even construct an entire XML document in memory as an XmlDocument and then save it after the fact. To save the current content of an XmlDocument, you call the Save() method and supply the string name of the file or a ready-made stream.

The XPathNavigator

The XPathNavigator class (found in the System.Xml.XPath namespace) works similarly to the XmlDocument class. It loads all the information into memory and then allows you to move through the nodes. The key difference is that it uses a cursor-based approach that allows you to use methods such as MoveToNext() to move through the XML data. An XPathNavigator can be positioned on only one node a time.

You can create an XPathNavigator from an XmlDocument using the XmlDocument.CreateNavigator() method. Here's an example:

```
private void Page_Load(object sender, System.EventArgs e)
{
    string xmlFile = Server.MapPath("DvdList.xml");

    // Load the XML file in an XmlDocument.
    XmlDocument doc = new XmlDocument();
    doc.Load(xmlFile);

    // Create the navigator.
    XPathNavigator xnav = doc.CreateNavigator();
    lblXml.Text = GetXNavDescr(xnav, 0);
}
```

In this case, the returned object is passed to the GetXNavDescr() recursive method, which returns the HTML code that represents the XML structure, as in the previous example.

The code of the GetXNavDescr() method is a bit different from the GetChildNodesDescr() method in the previous example, because it takes an XPathNavigator object that is positioned on a single node, not a collection of nodes. That means you don't need to loop through any collections. Instead, you can simply examine the information for the current node, as follows:

```
private string GetXNavDescr(XPathNavigator xnav, int level)
{
    string indent = "";
    for (int i=0; i<level; i++)
```

```
      indent += "     ";
    StringBuilder str = new StringBuilder("");
    switch(xnav.NodeType)
    {
        case XPathNodeType.Root:
            str.Append("<b>ROOT</b>");
            str.Append("<br />");
            break;
        case XPathNodeType.Element:
            str.Append(indent);
            str.Append("Element: <b>");
            str.Append(xnav.Name);
            str.Append("</b><br />");
            break;
        case XPathNodeType.Text:
            str.Append(indent);
            str.Append(" - Value: <b>");
            str.Append(xnav.Value);
            str.Append("</b><br />");
            break;
        case XPathNodeType.Comment:
            str.Append(indent);
            str.Append("Comment: <b>");
            str.Append(xnav.Value);
            str.Append("</b><br />");
            break;
    }
    ...
```

Note that the values for the NodeType property are almost the same, except for the enumeration name, which is XPathNodeType instead of XmlNodeType. That's because the XPathNavigator uses a smaller, more streamlined set of nodes. One of the nodes it doesn't support is the XmlDeclaration node type.

The function checks if the current node has any attributes. If so, it moves to the first one with a call to MoveToFirstAttribute() and loops through all the attributes until the MoveToNextAttribute() method returns false. At that point it returns to the parent node, which is the node originally referenced by the object. Here's the code that carries this out:

```
    ...
    if (xnav.HasAttributes)
    {
        xnav.MoveToFirstAttribute();
        do {
            str.Append(indent);
            str.Append(" - Attribute: <b>");
            str.Append(xnav.Name);
            str.Append("</b> Value: <b>");
            str.Append(xnav.Value);
            str.Append("</b><br />");
        } while (xnav.MoveToNextAttribute());
        // Return to the parent.
        xnav.MoveToParent();
    }
    ...
```

The function does a similar thing with the child nodes by moving to the first one with MoveToFirstChild() and recursively calling itself until MoveToNext() returns false, at which point it moves back to the original node, as follows:

```
    ...
    if (xnav.HasChildren)
    {
        xnav.MoveToFirstChild();
        do {
            str.Append(GetXNavDescr(xnav, level+1));
        } while (xnav.MoveToNext());

        // Return to the parent.
        xnav.MoveToParent();
    }
    return str.ToString();
}
```

This code produces almost the same output as shown in Figure 14-3.

The XDocument

The XDocument is an all-purpose model for managing in-memory XML. Unlike the XmlDocument and XPathNavigator, it's equally at home constructing XML content. (By comparison, the XmlDocument makes XML construction unnecessarily complex, while the XPathNavigator doesn't support it at all.) If you need to generate XML in a nonlinear fashion—for example, you need to write a collection of elements in the root element, and *then* add more information inside each of these elements, you'll need to use an in-memory class like XDocument.

Much as an XmlDocument object consists of XmlNode objects, an XDocument consists of XNode objects. The XNode is an abstract base class. Other more specific classes, like XElement, XComment, and XText, derive from it. One difference is that attributes are not treated as separate nodes in the LINQ to XML model—instead, they are simply name value pairs that are attached to another element. For that reason, the XAttribute class doesn't derive from XNode.

Technically, the XDocument class is a part of LINQ. It's found in the System.Xml.Linq name- space, and it's a part of the System.Xml.Linq.dll assembly introduced in .NET 3.5. You'll need to add a reference to this assembly to use the XDocument and related classes.

Creating XML with XDocument

You can use XDocument to generate XML content with clean and concise code. Alternatively, you can create XML content that doesn't represent a complete document using the XElement class.

All the LINQ to XML classes provide useful constructors that allow you to create and initialize them in one step. For example, you can create an element and supply text content that should be placed inside using code like this:

```
XElement element = new XElement("Price", "23.99");
```

This is already better than the XmlDocument, which forces you to create nodes and then configure them in a separate statement. But the code savings become even more dramatic when you consider another feature of the LINQ to XML classes—their ability to create a nested tree of nodes in a single code statement.

Here's how it works. Two LINQ to XML classes—XDocument and XElement—include constructors that take a parameter array for the last argument. This parameter array holds a list of nested nodes.

■ **Note** A *parameter array* is a parameter that's preceded with the params keyword. This parameter is always the last parameter, and it's always an array. The advantage is that users don't need to declare the array—instead, they can simply tack on as many arguments as they want, which are grouped into a single array automatically. String.Format() is an example of a method that uses a parameter array. It allows you to supply an unlimited number of values that are inserted into the placeholders of a string.

Here's an example that creates an element with two nested elements and their content:

```
XElement element = new XElement("Starring",
  new XElement("Star", "Tom Hanks"),
  new XElement("Star", "Robin Wright")
);
```

You can extend this technique to create an entire XML document, complete with elements, text content, attributes, and comments. For example, here's the complete code that creates the DvdList.xml sample document:

```
private void WriteXML()
{
    XDocument doc = new XDocument(
      new XDeclaration("1.0", "utf-8", "yes"),
      new XComment("Created: " + DateTime.Now.ToString()),
      new XElement("DvdList",
        new XElement("DVD",
          new XAttribute("ID", "1"),
          new XAttribute("Category", "Science Fiction"),
          new XElement("Title", "The Matrix"),
          new XElement("Director", "Larry Wachowski"),
          new XElement("Price", "18.74"),
          new XElement("Starring",
            new XElement("Star", "Keanu Reeves"),
            new XElement("Star", "Laurence Fishburne")
          )
        ),
        new XElement("DVD",
          new XAttribute("ID", "2"),
          new XAttribute("Category", "Drama"),
          new XElement("Title", "Forrest Gump"),
          new XElement("Director", "Robert Zemeckis"),
          new XElement("Price", "23.99"),
          new XElement("Starring",
            new XElement("Star", "Tom Hanks"),
            new XElement("Star", "Robin Wright")
          )
        ),
        new XElement("DVD",
          new XAttribute("ID", "3"),
          new XAttribute("Category", "Horror"),
```

```
            new XElement("Title", "The Others"),
            new XElement("Director", "Alejandro Amen&aacute;bar"),
            new XElement("Price", "22.49"),
            new XElement("Starring",
            new XElement("Star", "Nicole Kidman"),
              new XElement("Star", "Christopher Eccleston")
            )
          ),
          new XElement("DVD",
            new XAttribute("ID", "4"),
            new XAttribute("Category", "Mystery"),
            new XElement("Title", "Mulholland Drive"),
            new XElement("Director", "David Lynch"),
            new XElement("Price", "25.74"),
            new XElement("Starring",
              new XElement("Star", "Laura Harring")
            )
          ),
          new XElement("DVD",
            new XAttribute("ID", "5"),
            new XAttribute("Category", "Science Fiction"),
            new XElement("Title", "A.I. Artificial Intelligence"),
            new XElement("Director", "Steven Spielberg"),
            new XElement("Price", "23.99"),
            new XElement("Starring",
              new XElement("Star", "Haley Joel Osment"),
              new XElement("Star", "Jude Law")
            )
          )
        )
    );

    doc.Save(Server.MapPath("DvdList.xml"));
}
```

This code exactly replicates the XmlTextWriter code you considered earlier. However, it's shorter and easier to read. It's also far simpler than the equivalent code that you would use to create an in-memory XmlDocument. Unlike the code that uses the XmlTextWriter, there's no need to explicitly close elements—instead, they are delineated by the constructor of the appropriate XElement. Another nice detail is the way the indenting of the code statements mirrors the nesting of the elements in the XML document, allowing you to quickly take in the overall shape of the XML content.

Once the XML content has been created, you can save it using the XDocument.Save() method. Like XmlDocument.Save(), it allows you to supply a string that represents a file name (which is the technique shown previously) or a stream.

Reading XML with XDocument

The XDocument also makes it easy to read and navigate XML content. You can use the XDocument.Load() method to read XML documents from a file, URI, or stream, or you can use the XDocument.Parse() method to load XML content from a string.

Once you have a live XDocument with your content, you can dig into the tree of nodes using a few key properties and methods of the XElement class. Table 14-1 lists the most useful methods.

Table 14-1. Essential Methods of the XElement Class

Method	Description
Attributes()	Gets the collection of XAttribute objects for this element.
Attribute()	Gets the XAttribute with the specific name.
Elements()	Gets the collection of XElement objects that are contained by this element. (This is the top level only—these elements may in turn contain more elements.) Optionally, you can specify an element name, and only those elements will be retrieved.
Element()	Gets the single XElement contained by this element that has a specific name (or null if there's no match).
Nodes()	Gets all the XNode objects contained by this elements. This includes elements and other content, like comments.

Notice that there's an important difference between the XmlDocument and the XDocument model. With the XDocument class, nested elements are exposed through methods rather than properties. This gives you added flexibility to filter out just the elements that interest you. For example, when using the XDocument.Elements() method, you have two overloads to choose from. You can get all the child elements (in which case you would supply no parameters) or get just those child elements that have a specific element name (in which case you would specify the element name as a string).

The XElement class (and other LINQ to XML classes) offer quite a few more members. For example, you'll find members for quickly stepping from one node to the next (FirstNode, LastNode, NextNode, PreviousNode, and Parent), properties for testing for the presence of children (HasElements), attributes (HasAttributes), and content (IsEmpty), and methods for inserting, removing, and otherwise manipulating the XML tree of nodes (Add(), AddAfterSelf(), AddBeforeSelf(), RemoveNodes(), Remove(), ReplaceWith(), and so on).

One further simplification that LINQ to XML uses is that it doesn't force you to distinguish between elements and the text inside, which are represented as two separate nodes in the XML DOM. Instead, you can retrieve the inner value from an XElement by simply casting it to the appropriate data type, as shown here:

```
string title = (string)titleElement;
decimal price = (decimal)priceElement;
```

Setting the text content inside an element is nearly as easy. You simply assign the new content to the Value property, as shown here:

```
priceElement.Value = (decimal)priceElement * 2;
```

You can use the same simplified approach to read and set attributes with the XAttribute class.

Here's a straightforward code routine that mimics the XML processing code you saw earlier with the XPathNavigator. It scans through the elements that are available, and adds title, director, and price information to a bulleted list.

```
private void ReadXML()
{
    // Create the reader.
    string xmlFile = Server.MapPath("DvdList.xml");
```

```
    XDocument doc = XDocument.Load(xmlFile);

    StringBuilder str = new StringBuilder();
    foreach (XElement element in doc.Element("DvdList").Elements())
    {
        str.Append("<ul><b>");
        str.Append((string)element.Element("Title"));
        str.Append("</b><li>");
        str.Append((string)element.Element("Director"));
        str.Append("</li><li>");
        str.Append(String.Format("{0:C}", (decimal)element.Element("Price")));
        str.Append("</li></ul>");
    }
    lblXml.Text = str.ToString();
}
```

This code pulls out individual elements of interest using the XElement.Element() method and iterates over collections of nested XElement objects using the XElement.Elements() method. For example, the opening declaration of the foreach block selects the collection doc.Element("DvdList").Elements(). In other words, it grabs the nested <DvdList> element from the root of the document and examines all the elements inside (which are <DVD> elements). It then retrieves the content from the nested <Title> and <Director> elements inside. From start to finish, the code is noticeably simpler and more intuitive than the XmlTextReader and XmlDocument approaches.

Namespaces

The XDocument class has a particularly elegant way of dealing with namespaces. You simply define an XNamespace object, which you can then use when creating an XElement as part of the name. The XElement class automatically creates the xmlns attribute for you (although you can use the XAttribute object to create it manually, in which case the XElement is intelligent enough to use it).

Here's an example that places some of the elements in the DvdList.xml sample document into a namespace:

```
XNamespace ns = "http://www.somecompany.com/DVDList";
XDocument doc = new XDocument(
  new XDeclaration("1.0", "utf-8", "yes"),
  new XComment("Created: " + DateTime.Now.ToString()),
  new XElement(ns + "DvdList",
    new XElement(ns + "DVD",
      new XAttribute("ID", "1"),
      new XAttribute("Category", "Science Fiction"),
      new XElement(ns + "Title", "The Matrix"),
      new XElement(ns + "Director", "Larry Wachowski"),
      new XElement(ns + "Price", "18.74"),
      new XElement(ns + "Starring",
        new XElement(ns + "Star", "Keanu Reeves"),
        new XElement(ns + "Star", "Laurence Fishburne")
      )
    ),
   ...
)
```

You'll notice that all the elements in this example are placed in the new XML namespace, but the attributes aren't. This isn't a requirement, but it's a common convention of XML languages. Because the elements are already scoped to a specific namespace and the attributes are attached to an element, it's not considered necessary to specifically place the attributes in the same namespace.

Here's the resulting markup with the namespace:

```
<?xml version="1.0" encoding="utf-8" standalone="yes"?>
<!-- Created: 6/19/2008 3:07:15 PM -->
<DvdList xmlns="http://www.somecompany.com/DVDList">
  <DVD ID="1" Category="Science Fiction">
    <Title>The Matrix</Title>
    <Director>Larry Wachowski</Director>
    <Price>18.74</Price>
    <Starring>
      <Star>Keanu Reeves</Star>
      <Star>Laurence Fishburne</Star>
    </Starring>
  </DVD>
  ...
</DvdList>
```

If your elements are in an XML namespace, you must also take that namespace into account when navigating through the XML document. For example, when using the XmlElement.Element() method, you must supply the fully qualified element name by adding an XNamespace object to the string with the element name:

```
XNamespace ns = "http://www.somecompany.com/DVDList";
...
string title = (string)element.Element(ns + "Title");
```

■ **Note** Technically, you don't need to use the XNamespace class, although it makes your code clearer. When you add the XNamespace to an element name string, the namespace is simply wrapped in curly braces. In other words, when you combine the namespace `http://www.somecompany.com/DVDList` with the element name `Title`, it's equivalent to the string `{http://www.somecompany.com/DVDList}Title`. This syntax works because the curly brace characters aren't allowed in ordinary element names, so there's no possibility for confusion.

Searching XML Content

In many situations, you don't need to process the entire XML document. Instead, you need to extract a single piece of information. The exact approach you use depends on the class you're using. With the XmlDocument, you'll use the GetElementsByTagName() for simple scenarios, and the XPath language for more sophisticated cases. With the XDocument, you'll use one of the built-in searching methods (like the Elements() method) for simple scenarios and LINQ expressions when you need more power. In the following sections, you'll see all these approaches.

■ **Note** If you've already learned the LINQ querying syntax, you'll find that it gives you a powerful, strongly typed way to search XML. However, that won't save you from learning more traditional approaches like XPath, because these standards still crop up in other places, including XSL transforms and ASP.NET's XML data binding feature.

Searching with XmlDocument

The simplest way to perform a search with the XmlDocument is to use the XmlDocument.GetElementsByTagName() method, which searches an entire document tree for elements that have a specific name and returns an XmlNodeList that contains all the matches as XmlNode objects.

For example, the following code retrieves the title of each DVD in the document:

```
// Load the XML file.
string xmlFile = Server.MapPath("DvdList.xml");
XmlDocument doc = new XmlDocument();
doc.Load(xmlFile);

// Find all the <Title> elements anywhere in the document.
StringBuilder str = new StringBuilder();
XmlNodeList nodes = doc.GetElementsByTagName("Title");
foreach (XmlNode node in nodes)
{
    str.Append("Found: <b>");

    // Show the text contained in this <Title> element.
    str.Append(node.ChildNodes[0].Value);
    str.Append("</b><br />");
}
lblXml.Text = str.ToString();
```

Figure 14-4 shows the result of running this code in a web page.

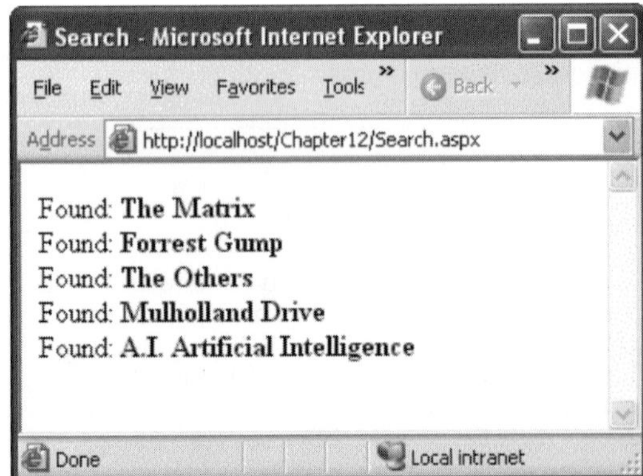

Figure 14-4. Searching for information in an XML document

You can also search portions of an XML document by using the method XmlElement.GetElementsByTagName() on a specific element. In this case, the XmlDocument searches all the descendant nodes looking for a match. To use this method, first retrieve an XmlNode that corresponds to an element and then cast this object to an XmlElement. The following example demonstrates how to use this technique to find the stars of a specific movie:

```
// Load the XML file.
string xmlFile = Server.MapPath("DvdList.xml");
XmlDocument doc = new XmlDocument();
doc.Load(xmlFile);

// Find all the <Title> elements anywhere in the document.
StringBuilder str = new StringBuilder();
XmlNodeList nodes = doc.GetElementsByTagName("Title");
foreach (XmlNode node in nodes)
{
    str.Append("Found: <b>");

    // Show the text contained in this <Title> element.
    string name = node.ChildNodes[0].Value;
    str.Append(name);
    str.Append("</b><br />");

    if (name == "Forrest Gump")
    {
        // Find the stars for just this movie.
        // First you need to get the parent node
        // (which is the <DVD> element for the movie).
        XmlNode parent = node.ParentNode;

        // Then you need to search down the tree.
        XmlNodeList childNodes =
          ((XmlElement)parent).GetElementsByTagName("Star");
        foreach (XmlNode childNode in childNodes)
        {
            str.Append("    Found Star: ");
            str.Append(childNode.ChildNodes[0].Value);
            str.Append("<br />");
        }
    }
}
lblXml.Text = str.ToString();
```

Figure 14-5 shows the result of this test.

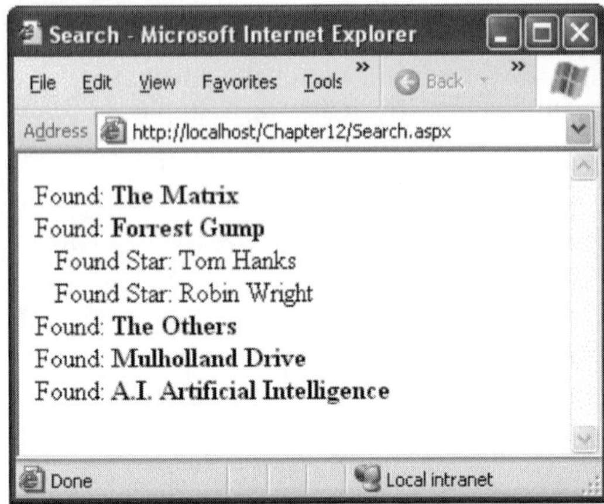

Figure 14-5. Searching portions of an XML document

The code you've seen so far assumes that none of the elements has a namespace. More sophisticated XML documents will always include a namespace and may even have several of them. In this situation, you can use the overload of the method XmlDocument.GetElementsByTagName(), which requires a namespace name as a string argument, as shown here:

```
// Retrieve all <order> elements in the OrderML namespace.
XmlNodeList nodes = doc.GetElementsByTagName("order",
  "http://mycompany/OrderML");
```

Additionally, you can supply an asterisk (*) for the element name if you want to match all tags in the specified namespace:

```
// Retrieve all elements in the OrderML namespace.
XmlNodeList nodes = doc.GetElementsByTagName("*",
  "http://mycompany/OrderML");
```

Searching XmlDocument with XPath

The GetElementsByTagName() method is fairly limited. It allows you to search based on the name of an element only. You can't filter based on other criteria, such as the value of the element or attribute content. XPath is a much more powerful standard that allows you to retrieve the portions of a document that interest you.

XPath uses a pathlike notation. For example, the path / identifies the root of an XML document, and /DvdList identifies the root <DvdList> element. The path /DvdList/DVD selects every <DVD> element inside the <DvdList>. Finally, the period (.) always selects the current node. In addition, the path // is a *recursive path operator* that searches all the descendants of a node. If you start a path with the // characters, the XPath expression will search the entire document for nodes.

These ingredients are enough to build many basic templates, although the XPath standard also defines special selection criteria that can filter out only the nodes in which you are interested. Table 14-2 provides a method overview of XPath characters.

■ **Note** XML distinguishes between two related terms: child node and descendant node. Understanding the difference is a key to understanding how XPath expressions work. A *child node* is a contained node that's just one level below the parent. A *descendant node* is a contained node that's nested at any level. In other words, the term descendant node includes child nodes, and the children of the child nodes, and their children, and so on. In the DVD list example, <Title> is a child of <DVD> and a descendant of <DVD> and <DvdList>, but it's not a child of <DvdList>.

Table 14-2. *Basic XPath Syntax*

Expression	Meaning
/	Searches for child nodes. If you place / at the beginning of an XPath expression, it creates an absolute path that starts from the root node. /DvdList/DVD selects all <DVD> elements that are children of the root <DvdList> element.
//	Searches for child nodes recursively, digging through all the nested layers of nodes. If you place // at the beginning of an XPath expression, it creates a relative path that selects nodes anywhere. //DVD/Title selects all the <Title> elements that are descendants of a <DVD> element.
@	Selects an attribute of a node. /DvdList/DVD/@ID selects the method attribute named ID from all <DVD> elements.
*	Selects any element in the path. /DvdList/DVD/* selects all the child nodes in the <DVD> element (which include <Title>, <Director>, <Price>, and <Starring> in this example).
|	Combines multiple paths. /DvdList/DVD/Title/ DvdList/DVD/Director selects both the <Title> and <Director> elements in the <DVD> element.
.	Indicates the current (default) node.
..	Indicates the parent node. If the current node is <Title>, then .. refers to the <DVD> node.
[]	Defines selection criteria that can test a contained node or attribute value. /DvdList/DVD[Title='Forrest Gump'] selects the <DVD> elements that contain a <Title> element with the indicated value. /DvdList/DVD[@ID='1'] selects the <DVD> elements with the indicated attribute value. You can use the and keyword and the or keyword to combine criteria.
starts-with	This method function retrieves elements based on what text a contained element starts with. /DvdList/DVD[starts-with(Title, 'P')] finds all <DVD> elements that have a <Title> element that contains text that starts with the letter P.

Expression	Meaning
position	This function retrieves elements based on position, using 1-based counting. /DvdList/DVD[position()=2] selects the second <DVD> element. You can also use the shorthand /DvdList/DVD[2].
count	This function counts the number of elements with the matching name. count(DVD) returns the number of <DVD> elements.

To execute an XPath expression in .NET, you can use the Select() method of the XPathNavigator or the SelectNodes() or SelectSingleNode() method of the XmlDocument class. The following code uses this technique method to retrieve specific information:

```
// Load the XML file.
string xmlFile = Server.MapPath("DvdList.xml");
XmlDocument doc = new XmlDocument();
doc.Load(xmlFile);

// Retrieve the title of every science-fiction movie.
XmlNodeList nodes =
  doc.SelectNodes("/DvdList/DVD/Title[../@Category='Science Fiction']");

// Display the titles.
StringBuilder str = new StringBuilder();
foreach (XmlNode node in nodes)
{
    str.Append("Found: <b>");

    // Show the text contained in this <Title> element.
    str.Append(node.ChildNodes[0].Value);
    str.Append("</b><br />");
}
lblXml.Text = str.ToString();
```

Figure 14-6 shows the results.

Figure 14-6. *Extracting information with XPath*

■ **Tip** You can use XPath searches with the XDocument class as well, through extension methods. You simply need to import the System.Xml.XPath namespace. This namespace includes an Extensions class which defines a few methods that extend XNode—most notably, XPathSelectElement() and XPathSelectElements().

Searching XDocument with LINQ

You've already seen how to use the method the XElement.Element() and XElement.Elements() methods to filter out elements that have a specific name. However, both these methods only go one level deep. For example, you can use them on the XElement class that represents the <DVDList> element to find the <DVD> elements, but you won't be able to find the <Title> elements, because these are two levels deep.

There are several ways to resolve this problem. The easiest approach is to use a few more built-in XElement methods that you haven't considered yet, such as ElementsAfterSelf(), ElementsBeforeSelf(), Ancestors(), and Descendants(). All of these return IEnumerable<T> collections of XElement objects.

ElementsAfterSelf() and ElementsBeforeSelf() find the sibling elements. The Ancestors() and Descendants() methods are more noteworthy, because they traverse the XML hierarchy. For example, using Descendants() on the root <DvdList> element returns all the elements in the document, including the directly contained <DVD> elements and more deeply nested elements like <Title> and <Price>.

Using this knowledge, you can find all the movie titles in the document, at any level, using this code:

```
string xmlFile = Server.MapPath("DvdList.xml");
XDocument doc = XDocument.Load(xmlFile);

foreach (XElement element in doc.Descendants("Title"))
{ ... }
```

This gives you functionality that's similar to the XmlDocument.GetElementsByTagName() method. However, it doesn't match the features of XPath. To do that, you need LINQ expressions.

As you learned in Chapter 13, LINQ expressions work with objects that implement IEnumerable<T>. The various LINQ extensions provide ways of bridging the gap between IEnumerable<T> and other data sources. For example, LINQ to DataSet adds extension methods that allow you to get IEnumerable<T> collections of DataRow objects. LINQ to SQL adds the Table<T> class, which provides an IEnumerable<T> implementation over a database query. And LINQ to XML provides the XDocument and XElement classes, which include several ways for getting IEnumerable<T> collections of elements, including the Elements() and Descendants() methods you've just considered.

Once you place your collection of elements in a LINQ expression, you can use all the familiar operators. That means you can use sorting, filtering, grouping, and projections to get the data you want. Here's an example that gets the XElement objects for the <Title> elements that have an ID value less than 3:

```
IEnumerable<XElement> matches = from DVD in doc.Descendants("DVD")
  where (int)DVD.Attribute("ID") < 3
  select DVD.Element("Title");
```

It's often more useful to translate the data to some other form. For example, the following query creates an anonymous type that combines title and price information. The results are sorted in descending order by price and then bound to a GridView for display. Figure 14-7 shows the result.

```
var matches = from DVD in doc.Descendants("DVD")
  orderby (decimal)DVD.Element("Price") descending
```

```
  select new { Movie = (string)DVD.Element("Title"),
               Price = (decimal)DVD.Element("Price")
             };
gridTitles.DataSource = matches;
gridTitles.DataBind();
```

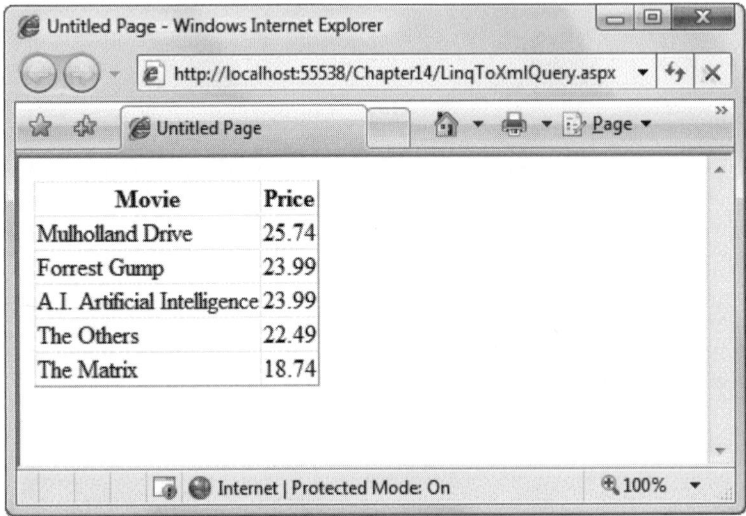

***Figure 14-7.** Extracting information with a LINQ to XML expression*

Notice the casting code that converts the XElement to the expected type (string for the title or decimal for the price). This casting step is required to extract the value from the full XElement object.

The LINQ to XML infrastructure also includes a set of extension methods that work on collections of elements. Here's a query that uses one of them to get a list of titles:

```
IEnumerable<string> matches = from title in
  doc.Root.Elements("DVD").Elements("Title")
  select (string)title;
```

At first glance, this looks like a fairly ordinary usage of the XElement.Elements() method. But closer inspection reveals that something else is happening.

The first call to Elements() gets all the <DVD> elements in the root <DvdList> element. The second call is a bit different, because it's not acting on an XElement object. Instead, it's acting on the collection of XElement objects that's returned by the first Elements() call. In other words, the second call is actually calling the Elements() method on an IEnumerable<T> collection. The IEnumerable<T> interface obviously doesn't include the Elements() method. Instead, the Extensions class in the System.Xml.Linq namespace defines this extension method for any IEnumerable<XElement> type. The end result is that this version of the Elements() method searches the collection and picks out the elements with the matching name.

Of course, you've already seen that you don't need to use this approach to create this query. You can just as easily rely on the XElement.Descendants() method to dig through any branch of your XML document. However, the Elements() extension method might be more useful in other scenarios where you have IEnumerable<XElement> collections that have been constructed in a different way, from different parts of an XML document.

The Extensions class defines several additional extension methods that apply to XElement collections, including Ancestors(), AncestorsAndSelf(), Attributes(), Descendants(), and DescendantsAndSelf().

Validating XML Content

So far you've seen a number of strategies for reading and parsing XML data. If you try to read invalid XML content using any of these approaches, you'll receive an error. In other words, all these classes require well-formed XML. However, none of the examples you've seen so far has validated the XML to check that it follows any application-specific rules.

A Basic Schema

As described at the beginning of this chapter, XML formats are commonly codified with an XML schema that lays out the required structure and data types. For the DVD list document, you can create an XML schema that looks like this:

```
<?xml version="1.0" ?>
<xs:schema id="DvdList" xmlns:xs="http://www.w3.org/2001/XMLSchema">
    <xs:element name="DvdList">
        <xs:complexType>
            <xs:sequence maxOccurs="unbounded">
                <xs:element name="DVD" type="DVDType" />
            </xs:sequence>
        </xs:complexType>
    </xs:element>

    <xs:complexType name="DVDType">
        <xs:sequence>
            <xs:element name="Title" type="xs:string" />
            <xs:element name="Director" type="xs:string"  />
            <xs:element name="Price" type="xs:decimal"  />
            <xs:element name="Starring" type="StarringType" />
        </xs:sequence>
        <xs:attribute name="ID" type="xs:integer" />
        <xs:attribute name="Category" type="xs:string" />
    </xs:complexType>

    <xs:complexType name="StarringType">
        <xs:sequence maxOccurs="unbounded">
            <xs:element name="Star" type="xs:string"/>
        </xs:sequence>
    </xs:complexType>
</xs:schema>
```

This schema defines two complex types, representing the list of stars (named StarringType) and the list of DVDs (each of which is an instance of a complex type named DVDType). The structure of the document is defined using an <element> tag.

Validating with XmlDocument

One approach for validating an XML document against a schema is to use an XmlValidatingReader. To create one, you use the XmlReader.Create() method and pass in an XmlReaderSettings object that specifies the XSD schema you want to use. The validating reader works like the XmlTextReader but includes the ability to verify that the document follows schema rules. The validating reader throws an exception (or raises an event) to indicate errors as you move through the XML file.

The first step when performing validation is to import the System.Xml.Schema namespace, which contains types such as XmlSchema and XmlSchemaCollection:

```
using System.Xml.Schema;
```

The following example shows how you can create a validating reader that uses the DvdList.xsd file and shows how you can use it to verify that the XML in DvdList.xml is valid. The first step is to create the XmlReaderSettings object that specifies the schema you want to use:

```
XmlReaderSettings settings = new XmlReaderSettings();
settings.ValidationType = ValidationType.Schema;
string xsdFile = Server.MapPath("DvdList.xsd");
settings.Schemas.Add("", xsdFile);
...
```

Each schema is used to validate the elements in a specific namespace. If your document contains elements from more than one namespace, you can use separate schemas to validate them. If you don't include a schema that validates the namespace your document uses, no validation will be performed. You specify the namespace name and the schema file path when you call the XmlReaderSettings.Schemas.Add() method.

The simple version of the DVD list that's used in this example doesn't use a namespace. As a result, you need to pass an empty string as the first parameter.

Once you've configured your validation settings, you can create the validating reader and validate the document:

```
...
// Create the validating reader.
string xmlFile = Server.MapPath("DvdList.xml");
FileStream fs = new FileStream(xmlFile, FileMode.Open);
XmlReader vr = XmlReader.Create(fs, settings);

// Read through the document.
while (vr.Read())
{
    // Process document here.
    // If an error is found, an exception will be thrown.
}
vr.Close();
```

Using the current file, this code will succeed, and you'll be able to access the current node through the validating reader in the same way that you can with an ordinary reader. However, consider what happens if you make the minor modification shown here:

```
<DVD ID="A" Category="Science Fiction">
```

Now when you try to validate the document, an XmlSchemaValidationException (from the System.Xml.Schema namespace) will be thrown, alerting you to the invalid data type—the letter A in an attribute that is designated for integer values.

Instead of catching errors, you can react to the ValidationEventHandler event. If you react to this event, you'll be provided with information about the error, but no exception will be thrown. To connect an event handler to this event, assign the method to the XmlSettings.ValidationEventHandler property before you create the validating reader:

```
// Connect to the method named MyValidateHandler.
settings.ValidationEventHandler += ValidateHandler;
```

The event handler receives a ValidationEventArgs class, which contains the exception, a message, and a number representing the severity:

```
private void ValidateHandler(Object sender, ValidationEventArgs e)
{
    lblInfo.Text += "Error: " + e.Message + "<br />";
}
```

To try the validation, you can use the XmlValidation.aspx page in the online samples. This page allows you to validate a valid DVD list as well as another version with incorrect data and an incorrect tag. Figure 14-8 shows the result of a failed validation attempt.

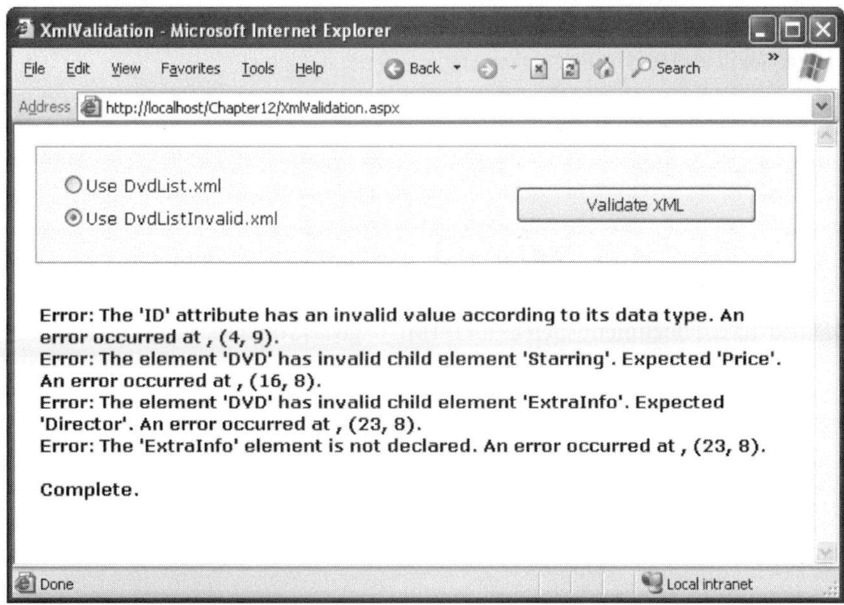

Figure 14-8. *The validation test page*

Validating with XDocument

Although XDocument doesn't have baked-in validation functionality, .NET includes extension methods that allow you to use it with the validation classes you saw in the previous section. To make these available, you need to import the System.Xml.Schema namespace. This namespace contains an Extensions class that includes a Validate() method you can use on an XElement or XDocument.

Here's an example that uses the Validate() extension method to validate the DvdList.xml document:

```
string xmlFile = Server.MapPath("DvdList.xml");
string xsdFile = Server.MapPath("DvdList.xsd");

// Open the XML file.
XDocument doc = XDocument.Load(xmlFile);

// Load the schema.
XmlSchemaSet schemas = new XmlSchemaSet();
schemas.Add("", xsdFile);

// Validate the document (with event handling for errors).
doc.Validate(schemas, ValidateHandler);
```

■ **Note** The validation process is essentially the same with the XmlDocument class. The only difference is that XmlDocument includes a Validate() method, and so it doesn't require an extension method.

Transforming XML Content

XSL (Extensible Stylesheet Language) is an XML-based language for creating stylesheets. Stylesheets (also known as transforms) are special documents that can be used (with the help of an XSLT processor) to convert your XML documents into other documents. For example, you can use an XSLT stylesheet to transform one type of XML to a different XML structure. Or you could use a stylesheet to convert your data-only XML into another text-based document such as an HTML page, as you'll see with the next example.

■ **Note** Of course, XSL stylesheets shouldn't be confused with CSS (Cascading Style Sheets), a standard used to format HTML. Chapter 16 discusses CSS.

Before you can perform a transformation, you need to create an XSL stylesheet that defines how the conversion should be applied. XSL is a complex standard—in fact, it can be considered a genuine language of its own with conditional logic, looping structures, and more.

■ **Note** A full discussion of XSLT is beyond the scope of this book. However, if you want to learn more, you can consider a book such as Jeni Tennison's *Beginning XSLT 2.0: From Novice to Professional* (Apress, 2005), the excellent online tutorials at `http://www.w3schools.com/xsl`, or the standard itself at `http://www.w3.org/Style/XSL`.

A Basic Stylesheet

To transform the DVD list into HTML, you'll use the simple stylesheet shown here:

```
<xsl:stylesheet xmlns:xsl="http://www.w3.org/1999/XSL/Transform" version="1.0">
  <xsl:template match="/">
    <html>
    <body>
      <xsl:apply-templates select="DvdList/DVD" />

  </xsl:template>

  <xsl:template match="DVD">
    <hr/>
    <h3><u><xsl:value-of select="Title" /></u></h3>
    <b>Price: </b> <xsl:value-of select="Price" /><br/>
    <b>Director: </b> <xsl:value-of select="Director" /><br/>
    <xsl:apply-templates select="Starring" />
  </xsl:template>

  <xsl:template match="Starring">
    <b>Starring:</b><br />
    <xsl:apply-templates select="Star" />
  </xsl:template>

  <xsl:template match="Star">
    <li><xsl:value-of select="." /></li>
  </xsl:template>
</xsl:stylesheet>
```

Every XSL file has a root <stylesheet> element. The <stylesheet> element can contain one or more templates (the sample file has four). In this example, the first <template> element matches the root element. When it finds it, it outputs the tags necessary to start an HTML page and then uses the <apply-templates> command to branch off and perform processing for any <DVD> elements that are children of <DvdList>, as follows:

```
<xsl:template match="/">
  <html>
  <body>
    <xsl:apply-templates select="DvdList/DVD" />
  </body>
  </html>
</xsl:template>
```

Each time the <DVD> tag is matched, a horizontal line is added, and a heading is created. Information about the <Title>, <Price>, and <Director> tag is extracted and written to the page using the <value-of> command. Here's the full template for transforming <DVD> elements:

```
<xsl:template match="DVD">
  <hr/>
  <h3><u><xsl:value-of select="Title" /></u></h3>
  <b>Price: </b> <xsl:value-of select="Price" /><br/>
  <b>Director: </b> <xsl:value-of select="Director" /><br/>
  <xsl:apply-templates select="Starring" />
</xsl:template>
```

Using XslCompiledTransform

Using this stylesheet and the XslCompiledTransform class (contained in the System.Xml.Xsl namespace), you can transform the DVD list into formatted HTML. Here's the code that performs this transformation and saves the result to a new file:

```
string xslFile = Server.MapPath("DvdList.xsl");
string xmlFile = Server.MapPath("DvdList.xml");
string htmlFile = Server.MapPath("DvdList.htm");
XslCompiledTransform transform = new XslCompiledTransform();
transform.Load(xslFile);
transform.Transform(xmlFile, htmlFile);
```

Of course, in a dynamic web application you'll want to transform the XML file and return the resulting code directly, without generating an HTML file. To do this you have to create an XPathNavigator for the source XML file. You can then pass the XPathNavigator to the XslCompiledTranform.Transform() method and retrieve the results in any stream object.

The following code demonstrates this technique:

```
// Create an XPathDocument.
string xmlFile = Server.MapPath("DvdList.xml");
XPathDocument xdoc = new XPathDocument(new XmlTextReader(xmlFile));

// Create an XPathNavigator.
XPathNavigator xnav = xdoc.CreateNavigator();

// Transform the XML.
MemoryStream ms = new MemoryStream();
XsltArgumentList args = new XsltArgumentList();
XslCompiledTransform transform = new XslCompiledTransform();
string xslFile = Server.MapPath("DvdList.xsl");
transform.Load(xslFile);
transform.Transform(xnav, args, ms);
```

Once you have the results in a MemoryStream, you can create a StreamReader to retrieve them as a string:

```
StreamReader r = new StreamReader(ms);
ms.Position = 0;
Response.Write(r.ReadToEnd());
r.Close();
```

Figure 14-9 shows the resulting page.

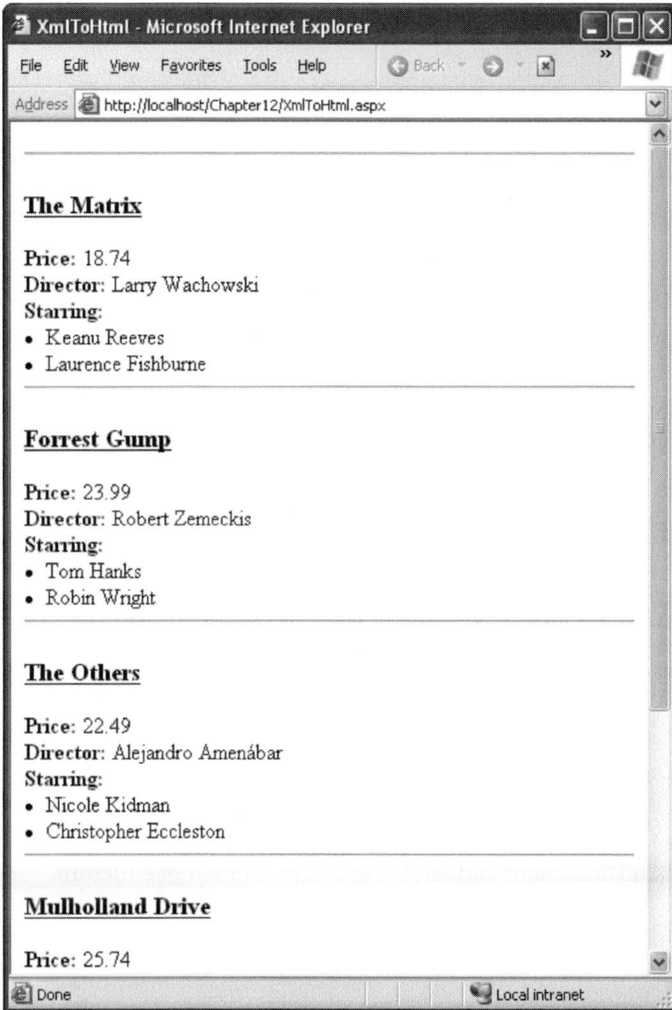

Figure 14-9. *Transforming XML to HTML*

Using the Xml Control

In some cases you might want to combine transformed HTML output with other content and web controls. In this case, you can use the Xml control. The Xml control displays the result of an XSL transformation in a discrete portion of a page.

For example, consider the previous XSLT example, which transformed DvdList.xml using DvdList.xsl. Using the Xml control, all you need is a single tag that sets the DocumentSource and TransformSource properties, as shown here:

```
<asp:Xml runat="server"
  DocumentSource="DvdList.xml" TransformSource="DvdList.xsl" />
```

The best part of this example is that all you need to do is set the XML input and the XSL transform file. You don't need to manually initiate the conversion.

■ **Note** You don't need separate files to use the Xml control. Instead of using the DocumentSource property, you can assign an XmlDocument object to the Document property or assign a string containing the XML content to the DocumentContent property. Similarly, you can supply the XSLT information by assigning an XslTransform object to the Transform property. These techniques are useful if you need to supply XML and XSLT data programmatically (for example, if you extract it from a database record).

Transforming XML with LINQ to XML

XSL is a well-entrenched standard for transforming XML into different representations. However, it's obviously not the only approach. There's nothing that stops you from opening an XDocument, rearranging its nodes manually, and then saving the result—aside from the intrinsic complexity of such an approach, which makes your code difficult to maintain and subject to all kinds of easily missed errors.

So although XSL isn't the only way to change the representation of XML, in the recent past it has been the only reasonably practical way to do so. With LINQ, this reality changes a bit. Although XSL will still continue to be used in a wide range of scenarios, LINQ to XML offers a compelling alternative.

To perform a transformation with LINQ to XML, you need to use a LINQ expression that uses a projection. (As discussed in Chapter 13, a projection takes the data you're searching and rearranges it into a different representation.) The trick is that the projection must return an XElement rather than an anonymous type.

As you've already seen, the XElement constructor allows you to create an entire tree of nodes in a single statement. By using these constructors, your LINQ expression can build an XML tree complete with elements, subelements, attributes, text content, and so on.

The easiest way to understand this technique is to consider an example. The following code extracts some of the information from the DvdList.xml document and rearranges it into a different structure.

```
string xmlFile = Server.MapPath("DvdList.xml");
XDocument doc = XDocument.Load(xmlFile);

XDocument newDoc = new XDocument(
  new XDeclaration("1.0", "utf-8", "yes"),
  new XElement("Movies",
    from DVD in doc.Descendants("DVD")
    where (int)DVD.Attribute("ID") < 3
    select new XElement[] {
      new XElement("Movie",
        new XAttribute("Name", (string)DVD.Element("Title")),
        DVD.Descendants("Star")
      )
    }
  )
);
```

This code does quite a bit in only a few lines. The first two statements open the original XML file and load it into an XDocument object. The third and final code statement does the rest—it creates a new XDocument and fills it with the transformed content.

The document starts with an XML declaration and is followed by the root element, which is named <Movies>. The content for the node is an array of XElement objects, which are used to fill the <Movies> element. The trick is that this array is constructed using a LINQ expression. This expression pulls out all the <DVD> elements in the original documents (wherever they occur, using the Descendants() method) and filters for those that have ID attribute values less than 3. Finally, the select clause applies a projection that creates each nested XElement inside the <Movies> element. Each nested XElement represents a <Movie> element, contains a Name attribute (which has the movie title), and holds a nested collection of <Star> elements.

The final result is as follows:

```
<Movies>
  <Movie Name="The Matrix">
    <Star>Keanu Reeves</Star>
    <Star>Laurence Fishburne</Star>
  </Movie>
  <Movie Name="Forrest Gump">
    <Star>Tom Hanks</Star>
    <Star>Robin Wright</Star>
  </Movie>
</Movies>
```

The syntax for LINQ-based transforms is often easier to understand than an XSL stylesheet, and it's always more concise.

Even better is the fact that the source content doesn't need to be drawn from an XML document. For example, there's no reason that you can't use a LINQ expression that constructs the XElement nodes for an XDocument, but pulls its information from a different type of data. In this example, the expression gets its information from the XDocument by calling the Descendants() method, but you could just as easily substitute another IEnumerable<T> collection, including an in-memory collection or a LINQ to SQL database table. In fact, this feature could easily replace more proprietary technologies, like the awkward FOR XML query syntax in SQL Server.

Here's an example that queries the Employees table you've used in earlier chapters and packages the result into an XML document:

```
public XDocument GetEmployeeXml()
{
    XDocument doc = new XDocument(
      new XDeclaration("1.0", "utf-8", "yes"),
      new XElement("Employees",
          from employee in dataContext.GetTable<EmployeeDetails>()
          select new XElement[] {
            new XElement("Employee",
            new XAttribute("ID", employee.EmployeeID),
            new XElement("Name", employee.FirstName + " " + employee.LastName)
          )}
      )
    );
    return doc;
}
```

And here's the resulting XML that's generated:

```
<Employees>
  <Employee ID="1">
    <Name>Nancy Davolio</Name>
  </Employee>
  <Employee ID="2">
    <Name>Andrew Fuller</Name>
  </Employee>
  <Employee ID="3">
    <Name>Janet Leverling</Name>
  </Employee>
  ...
</Employees>
```

The disadvantage of using LINQ to XML for transformation is that it's not a standard technology, whereas XSLT definitely is. Furthermore, the logic is programmatic, which means you'll need to recompile your code to change your transformation. Although the syntax of XSLT is more complex, its declarative model adds valuable flexibility if you need to share, reuse, or modify the transform.

XML Data Binding

Now that you've learned how to read, write, and display XML by hand, it's worth considering a shortcut that can save a good deal of code—the XmlDataSource control.

The XmlDataSource control works in a declarative way that's analogous to the SqlDataSource and ObjectDataSource controls you learned about in Chapter 9. However, it has two key differences:

- The XmlDataSource extracts information from an XML file, rather than a database or data access class. It provides other controls with an XmlDocument object for data binding.
- XML content is hierarchical and can have an unlimited number of levels. By contrast, the SqlDataSource and ObjectDataSource return flat tables of data.

The XmlDataSource also provides a few features in common with the other data source controls, including caching and rich design support that shows the schema of your data in bound controls.

In the following sections, you'll see how to use the XmlDataSource in simple and complex scenarios.

Nonhierarchical Binding

The simplest way to deal with the hierarchical nature of XML data is to ignore it. In other words, you can bind the XML data source directly to an ordinary grid control such as the GridView.

The first step is to define the XML data source and point it to the file that has the content you want to use:

```
<asp:XmlDataSource ID="sourceDVD" runat="server"
 DataFile="DvdList.xml" />
```

Now you can bind the GridView with automatically generated columns, in the same way you bind it to any other data source:

```
<asp:GridView ID="GridView1" runat="server" AutoGenerateColumns="True"
 DataSourceID="sourceDVD" />
```

■ **Note** Remember, you don't need to use automatically generated columns. If you refresh the schema at design time, Visual Studio will read the DvdList.xml file, determine its structure, and define the corresponding GridView columns explicitly.

Now, when you run the page, the XmlDataSource will extract the data from the DvdList.xml file, provide it to the GridView as an XmlDocument object, and call DataBind(). Because the XmlDocument implements the IEnumerable interface, the GridView can walk through its structure in much the same way as it walks through a DataView. It traverses the XmlDocument.Nodes collection and gets all the attributes for each XmlNode.

■ **Tip** You can use the XmlDataSource programmatically. Call XmlDataSource.GetXmlDocument() to cause it to return the file's content as an XmlDocument object.

However, this has a catch. As explained earlier, the XmlDocument.Nodes collection contains only the first level of nodes. Each of these nodes can contain nested nodes through its own XmlNode.Nodes collection. However, the IEnumerable implementation that the XmlDocument uses doesn't take this into account. It walks over only the upper level of XmlNode objects, and as a result you'll see only the top level of nodes, as shown in Figure 14-10.

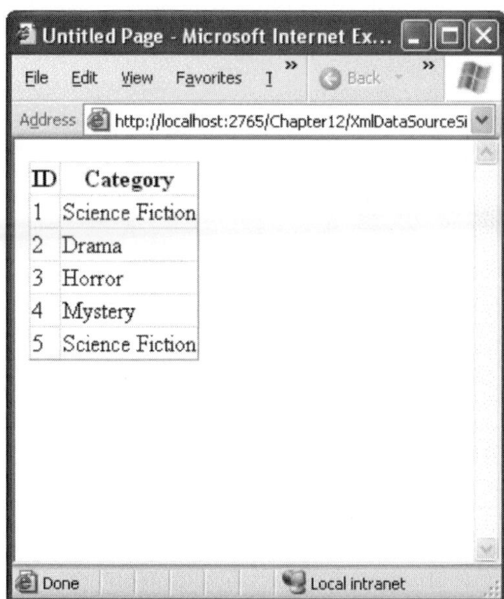

Figure 14-10. *Flattening XML with data binding*

You can make this binding explicit by defining columns for each attribute:

```
<asp:GridView ID="GridView1" runat="server" AutoGenerateColumns="False"
 DataSourceID="sourceDVD">
  <Columns>
    <asp:BoundField DataField="ID" HeaderText="ID" SortExpression="ID" />
    <asp:BoundField DataField="Category" HeaderText="Category"
     SortExpression="Category" />
  </Columns>
</asp:GridView>
```

In other words, if you don't customize the XML data binding process, you can bind only to the top-level of nodes, and you can display text only from the attributes of that node. Furthermore, if there is more than one type of top-level node, the bound control uses the schema of the first node. In other words, if you have a document like this:

```
<DvdList>
  <Retailer ID="..." Name="...">...</Retailer>
  <Retailer ID="..." Name="...">...</Retailer>

  <DVD ID="..." Category="...">...</DVD>
  <DVD ID="..." Category="...">...</DVD>
  <DVD ID="..." Category="...">...</DVD>
</DvdList>
```

the GridView will inspect the first node and create an ID and Name column. It will then attempt to display ID and name information for each node. If no matching attribute is found (for example, the <DVD> specifies a name), then that value will be left blank. Similarly, the Category attribute won't be used, unless you explicitly define it as a column.

All of this raises an obvious question—how do you display other information from deeper down in the XML document? You have a few options:

- You can use XPath to filter out the important elements.
- You can use an XSL transformation to flatten the XML into the structure you want.
- You can nest one data control inside another (similar to the way that the master-child details grid was created in Chapter 10).
- You can use a control that supports hierarchical data. The only ready-made .NET control that fits is the TreeView.

You'll see all of these techniques in the following sections.

Using XPath

Ordinarily, when you bind an XmlNode, you display only attribute values. However, you can get the text from nested elements using XPath data binding expressions.

The most flexible way to do this is to use a template that defines XPath data binding expressions. XPath data binding expressions are similar to Eval() expressions, except instead of supplying the name of the field you want to display, you supply an XPath expression based on the current node.

For example, here's an XPath expression that starts at the current node, looks for a nested node named Title, and gets associated element text:

```
<%# XPath("Title")%>
```

Here's an XPath expression that filters out the text of an ID attribute for the current node:

```
<%# XPath("@ID")%>
```

■ **Tip** You can use the XPath data binding syntax with your own custom data objects, but it isn't easy. The only requirement is that the data item must implement the IXPathNavigable interface.

Finally, here's a GridView with a simple set of XPath expressions:

```
<asp:GridView ID="GridView1" runat="server" AutoGenerateColumns="False"
 DataSourceID="sourceDVD">
  <Columns>
    <asp:TemplateField HeaderText="DVD">
      <ItemTemplate>
        <b><%# XPath("Title") %></b><br />
        <%# XPath("Director") %><br />
      </ItemTemplate>
    </asp:TemplateField>
  </Columns>
</asp:GridView>
```

Figure 14-11 shows the result.

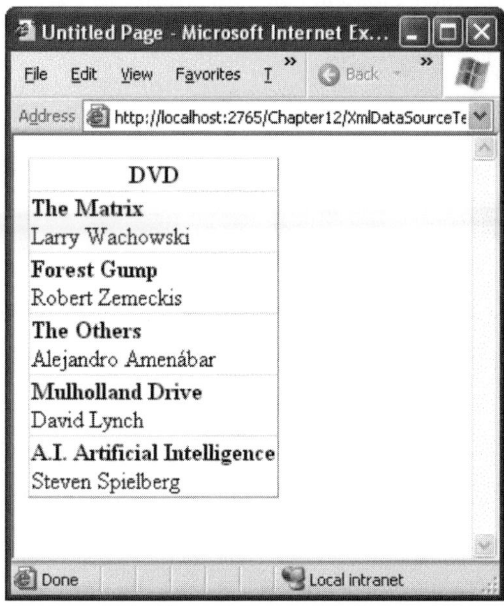

***Figure 14-11.** XML data binding with templates*

As with the Eval() method, you can use an optional second parameter with a format string when calling XPath():

```
<%# XPath("Price", "{0:c}") %>
```

■ **Note** Unfortunately, you need to use a template to gain the ability to write XPath data binding expressions. That limits the usefulness of other controls (such as drop-down lists) in XML data binding scenarios. Although you can bind them to attributes without any problem, you can't bind them to show element content.

You can also use XPath to filter out the initial set of matches. For example, imagine you want to create a grid that shows a list of stars rather than a list of movies. To accomplish this, you need to use the XPath support that's built into the XmlDataSource to prefilter the results.

To use XPath, you need to supply the XPath expression that selects the data you're interested in by using the XmlDataSource.XPath property. This XPath expression extracts an XmlNodeList, which is then made available to the bound controls.

```
<asp:XmlDataSource ID="sourceDVD" runat="server" DataFile="DvdList.xml"
 XPath="/DvdList/DVD/Starring/Star" />
```

If that expression returns a list of nodes, and all the information you need to display is found in attributes, you don't need to perform any extra steps. However, if the information is in element text, you need to create a template.

In this example, the template simply displays the text for each <Star> node:

```
<asp:GridView ID="GridView1" runat="server" DataSourceID="sourceDVD"
 AutoGenerateColumns="False">
  <Columns>
    <asp:TemplateField HeaderText="DVD">
      <ItemTemplate>
        <%# XPath(".") %><br />
      </ItemTemplate>
    </asp:TemplateField>
  </Columns>
</asp:GridView>
```

Figure 14-12 shows the result.

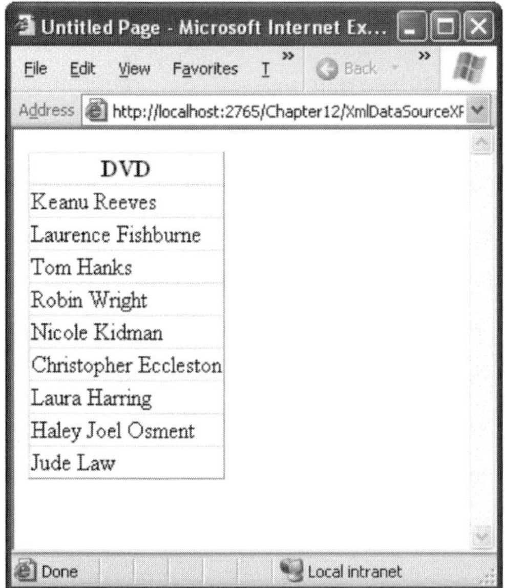

Figure 14-12. *Using XPath to filter results*

You can create a simple record browser using the XmlDataSource.XPath property. Just let the user choose an ID from another control (such as a drop-down list), and then set the XPath property accordingly:

```
sourceDVD.XPath = "/DvdList/DVD[@ID=" + dropDownList1.SelectedValue + "]";
```

This works because data binding isn't performed until the end of the page life cycle.

Nested Grids

Another option is to show nested elements by nesting one grid control inside another. This allows you to deal with much more complex XML structures.

The remarkable part is that ASP.NET provides support for this approach without requiring you to write any code. This is notable, especially because it does require code to create the nested master-details grid display demonstrated in Chapter 10.

The next example uses nested grids to create a list of movies, with a separate list of starring actors in each movie. To accomplish this, you begin by defining the outer grid. Using a template, you can display the title and director information:

```
<asp:GridView ID="GridView1" runat="server" AutoGenerateColumns="False"
 DataSourceID="sourceDVD">
  <Columns>
    <asp:TemplateField HeaderText="DVD">
      <ItemTemplate>
        <b><% #XPath("Title") %></b><br />
        <%# XPath("Director") %><br />
        <br /><i>Starring...</i><br />
        ...
```

Now, you need to define another GridView control inside the template of the first GridView. The trick is in the DataSource property, which you can set using a new XPathSelect() data binding statement, as shown here:

```
...
<asp:GridView id="GridView2" AutoGenerateColumns="False"
 DataSource='<%# XPathSelect("Starring/Star") %>' runat="server">
...
```

When you call XPathSelect(), you supply the XPath expression that retrieves the XmlNodeList based on a search starting at the current node. In this case, you need to drill down to the nested group of <Star> elements.

Once you've set the right data source, all you need to do is define a template in the second GridView that displays the appropriate information. In this case, you need only a single data binding expression to get the element text:

```
        ...
          <Columns>
            <asp:TemplateField>
              <ItemTemplate>
                <%# XPath(".") %><br />
              </ItemTemplate>
            </asp:TemplateField>
          </Columns>
        </asp:GridView>

      </ItemTemplate>
    </asp:TemplateField>
  </Columns>
</asp:GridView>
```

Figure 14-13 shows the grid, with a little extra formatting added for good measure.

Figure 14-13. Showing XML with nested grids

Hierarchical Binding with the TreeView

Some controls have the built-in smarts to show hierarchical data. In .NET, the principal example is the TreeView. When you bind the TreeView to an XmlDataSource, it uses the XmlDataSource.GetHierarchicalView() method and displays the full structure of the XML document (see Figure 14-14).

The TreeView's default XML representation still leaves a lot to be desired. It shows only the document structure (the element names), not the document content (the element text). It also ignores attributes. To improve this situation, you need to set the TreeView.AutoGenerateDataBindings property to false, and you then need to explicitly map different parts of the XML document to TreeView nodes.

```
<asp:TreeView ID="TreeView1" runat="server" DataSourceID="sourceDVD"
 AutoGenerateDataBindings="False">
  ...
</asp:TreeView>
```

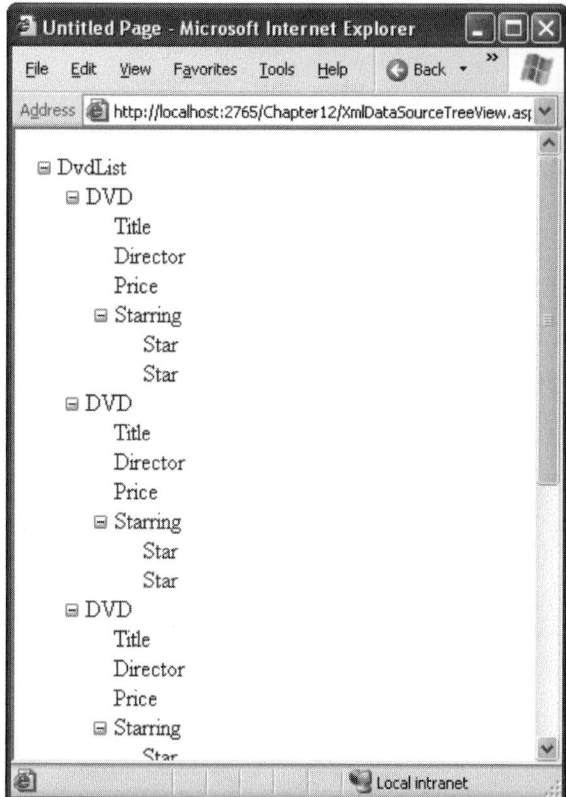

Figure 14-14. *Automatically generated TreeView bindings*

To create a TreeView mapping, you need to add <TreeNodeBinding> elements to the <DataBinding> section. You must start with the root element and then add a binding for each level you want to show. You cannot skip any levels.

Each <TreeNodeBinding> must name the node it binds to (through the DataMember property), the text it should display (TextField), and the hidden value for the node (ValueField). Unfortunately, both TextField and ValueField are designed to bind to attributes. If you want to bind to element content, you can use an ugly hack and specify the #InnerText code. However, this shows all the inner text, including text inside other more deeply nested nodes.

The next example defines a basic set of nodes to show the movie title information:

```
<asp:TreeView ID="TreeView1" runat="server" DataSourceID="sourceDVD"
 AutoGenerateDataBindings="False">
  <DataBindings>
    <asp:TreeNodeBinding DataMember="DvdList" Text="Root" Value="Root" />
    <asp:TreeNodeBinding DataMember="DVD" TextField="ID" />
    <asp:TreeNodeBinding DataMember="Title" TextField="#InnerText" />
  </DataBindings>
</asp:TreeView>
```

Figure 14-15 shows the result.

To get a more practical result with TreeView data binding, you need to use an XSL transform to create a more suitable structure, as described in the next section.

■ **Tip** To learn how to format the TreeView, including how to tweak gridlines and node pictures, refer to Chapter 17.

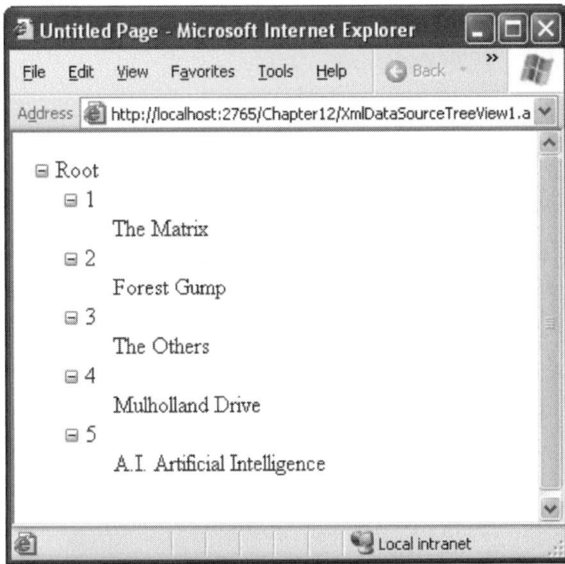

***Figure 14-15.** Binding to specific content*

Using XSLT

The XmlDataSource has similar built-in support for XSL transformations. The difference is that you don't use the stylesheet to convert the XML to HTML. Instead, you use it to convert the source XML document into an XML structure that's easier to data bind. For example, you might generate an XML document with just the results you want and generate a flattened structure (with elements converted into attributes) for easier data binding.

To specify a stylesheet, you can set the XmlDataSource.TransformFile to point to a file with the XSL transform, or you can supply the stylesheet as a single long string using the XmlDataSource.Transform property. You can use both stylesheets and XPath expressions, but the stylesheet is always applied first.

```
<asp:XmlDataSource ID="sourceDVD" runat="server" DataFile="DvdList.xml"
  TransformFile="DVDTreeList.xsl" />
```

One good reason to use the XSLT features of the XmlDataSource is to get your XML data ready for display in a hierarchical control such as the TreeView. For example, imagine you want to create a list of stars grouped by movie. You also want to put all the content into attributes so it's easy to bind.

Here's the final XML you'd like:

```
<Movies>
  <DVD ID="1" Title="The Matrix">
    <Star Name="Keanu Reeves" />
    <Star Name="Laurence Fishburne" />
  </DVD>
  <DVD ID="2" Title="Forest Gump">
    <Star Name="Tom Hanks" />
    <Star Name="Robin Wright" />
  </DVD>
  ...
</Movies>
```

You can transform the original XML into this markup using the following, more advanced XSL stylesheet. It extracts every <DVD> element from the source document and creates a slightly rearranged <DVD> element for it in the result document. The new <DVD> element uses attributes to expose the ID and title information (rather than using nested elements). The transformed <DVD> element also includes nested <Star> elements, but they're also modified. Now, each <Star> element exposes the star name as an attribute (rather than using text content).

```
<xsl:stylesheet xmlns:xsl="http://www.w3.org/1999/XSL/Transform" version="1.0">
  <xsl:output method="xml"/>

  <xsl:template match="/">
    <!-- Rename the root element. -->
    <xsl:element name="Movies">
      <xsl:apply-templates select="DvdList/DVD" />
    </xsl:element>
  </xsl:template>

  <xsl:template match="DVD">
    <!-- Transform the <DVD> element into a new <DVD> element
         with a different structure. -->
    <xsl:element name="DVD">
      <!-- Keep the ID attribute. -->
      <xsl:attribute name="ID">
        <xsl:value-of select="@ID"/>
      </xsl:attribute>
      <!-- Put the nested <Title> text into an attribute. -->
      <xsl:attribute name="Title">
        <xsl:value-of select="Title/text()"/>
      </xsl:attribute>
      <xsl:apply-templates select="Starring/Star" />
    </xsl:element>
  </xsl:template>

  <xsl:template match="Star">
    <xsl:element name="Star">
      <!-- Put the nested <Star> text into an attribute. -->
```

```
      <xsl:attribute name="Name">
        <xsl:value-of select="text()"/>
      </xsl:attribute>
    </xsl:element>
  </xsl:template>

</xsl:stylesheet>
```

Now you can bind this to the TreeView and display it with this set of bindings:

```
<asp:TreeView ID="TreeView1" runat="server" DataSourceID="sourceDVD"
 AutoGenerateDataBindings="False">
  <DataBindings>
    <asp:TreeNodeBinding DataMember="Movies" Text="Movies" />
    <asp:TreeNodeBinding DataMember="DVD" TextField="Title" />
    <asp:TreeNodeBinding DataMember="Stars" TextField="Name" />
  </DataBindings>
</asp:TreeView>
```

Binding to XML Content from Other Sources

So far, all the examples you've seen have bound to XML content in a file. This is the standard scenario for the XmlDataSource control, but it's not your only possibility. The other option is to supply the XML as text through the XmlDataSource.Data property.

You can set the Data property at any point before the binding takes place. One convenient time is during the Page.Load event:

```
protected void Page_Load(object sender, EventArgs e)
{
    string xmlContent;
    // (Retrieve XML content from another location.)
    sourceDVD.Data = xmlContent;
}
```

■ **Tip** If you use this approach, you may find it's still a good idea to set the XmlDataSource.DataFile property at design time in order for Visual Studio to load the schema information about your XML document and make it available to other controls. Just remember to remove this setting when you're finished developing, as the DataFile property overrides the Data property if they are both set.

This allows you to read XML content from another source (such as a database) and still work with the bound data controls. However, it requires adding some custom code.

Even if you do use the XmlDataSource.Data property, XML data binding still isn't nearly as flexible as the .NET XML classes you learned about earlier in this chapter. One of the key limitations is that the XML content needs to be loaded into memory all at once as a string object. If you're dealing with large XML documents, or you just need to ensure the best possible scalability for your web application, you might be able to reduce the overhead considerably by using the XmlReader instead, even though it will require much more code. Handling the XML parsing process yourself also gives you unlimited flexibility to rearrange and aggregate your data into a meaningful summary, which isn't always easy using XSLT alone.

■ **Note** If you do use the XmlDataSource to display XML data from a file, make sure you use caching to reduce the number of times that the file needs to be opened. You can use the CacheDuration, CacheKeyDependency, and CacheExpirationPolicy properties of the XmlDataSource. If your file changes infrequently, you'll be able to keep it in the cache indefinitely, which guarantees good performance. On the other hand, if you need to update the underlying XML document frequently, you're likely to run into multiuser concurrency headaches, as discussed in Chapter 12.

Updating XML Through the XmlDataSource

Unlike the SqlDataSource and the ObjectDataSource, the XmlDataSource doesn't support editable binding. You can confirm this fact with a simple test—just bind the XmlDataSource to a GridView, and add a CommandField with edit buttons. When you try to commit the update, you'll get an error informing you that the data source doesn't support this feature.

However, the XmlDataSource does provide a Save() method. This method replaces the file specified in the DataFile property with the current XML content. Although you need to add code to call the Save() method, some developers have used this technique to provide editable XML data binding.

The basic technique is as follows: when the user commits a change in a control, your code retrieves the current XML content as an XmlDocument object by calling the XmlDataSource.GetXmlDocument() method. Then, your code finds the corresponding node and makes the change using the features of XmlDocument (as described earlier in this chapter). You can find and edit specific nodes, remove nodes, or add nodes. Finally, your code must call the XmlDataSource.Save() method to commit the change.

Although this approach works perfectly well, it's not necessarily a great way to design a website. The XML manipulation code can become quite long, and you're likely to run into concurrency headaches if two users make different changes to the same XmlDocument at once. If you need to change XML content, it's almost always a better idea to implement the logic you need in a separate component, using the XML classes described earlier.

XML and the ADO.NET DataSet

Now that you've taken an exhaustive look at general-purpose XML and .NET, it's worth taking a look at a related topic—the XML support that's built into ADO.NET.

ADO.NET supports XML through the disconnected DataSet and DataTable objects. Both have the built-in intelligence to convert their collection rows into an XML document. You might use this functionality for several reasons. For example, you might want to share data with another application on another platform. Or you might simply use the XML format to serialize to disk so you can retrieve it later. In this case, you still use the same methods, although the actual data format isn't important.

Table 14-3 lists all the XML methods of the DataSet.

Table 14-3. DataSet Methods for Using XML

Method	Description
GetXml()	Retrieves the XML representation of the data in the DataSet as a single string.
WriteXml()	Writes the contents of the DataSet to a file or a TextWriter, XmlWriter, or Stream object. You can choose a write mode that determines if change tracking information and schema information is also written to the file.
ReadXml()	Reads XML data from a file or a TextReader, XmlReader, or Stream object and uses it to populate the DataSet.
GetXmlSchema()	Retrieves the XML schema for the DataSet XML as a single string. No data is returned.
WriteXmlSchema()	Writes just the XML schema describing the structure of the DataSet to a file or a TextWriter, XmlWriter, or Stream object.
ReadXmlSchema()	Reads an XML schema from a file or a TextReader, XmlReader, or Stream object and uses it to configure the structure of the DataSet.
InferXmlSchema()	Reads an XML document with DataSet contents from a file or a TextReader, XmlReader, or Stream object and uses it to infer what structure the DataSet should have. This is an alternative approach to using the ReadXmlSchema() method, but it doesn't guarantee that all the data type information is preserved.

■ **Tip** You can also use the ReadXml(), WriteXml(), ReadXmlSchema(), and WriteXmlSchema() methods of the DataTable to read or write XML for a single table in a DataSet.

Converting the DataSet to XML

Using the XML methods of the DataSet is quite straightforward, as you'll see in the next example. This example uses two GridView controls on a page. The first DataSet is filled directly from the Employees table of the Northwind database. (The code isn't shown here because it's similar to what you've seen in the previous chapters.) The second DataSet is filled using XML.

Here's how it works: once the DataSet has been created, you can generate an XML schema file describing the structure of the DataSet and an XML file containing the contents of every row. The easiest approach is to use the WriteXmlSchema() and WriteXml() methods of the DataSet. These methods provide several overloads, including a version that lets you write data directly to a physical file. When you write the XML data, you can choose between several slightly different formats by specifying an XmlWriteMode. You can indicate that you want to save both the data and the schema in a single file (XmlWriteMode.WriteSchema), only the data (XmlWriteMode.IgnoreSchema), or the data with both the current and the original values (XmlWriteMode.DiffGram).

Here's the code that you need to save a DataSet to an XML file:

```
string xmlFile = Server.MapPath("Employees.xml");
ds.WriteXml(xmlFile, XmlWriteMode.WriteSchema);
```

This code creates an Employees.xml file in the current folder.

Now you can perform the reverse step by creating a new DataSet object and filling it with the data contained in the XML file using the DataSet.ReadXml() method as follows:

```
DataSet dsXml = new DataSet("Northwind");
dsXml.ReadXml(xmlFile);
```

This completely rehydrates the DataSet, returning it to its original state.

If you want to see the structure of the generated Employees.xml file, you can open it in Internet Explorer, as shown in Figure 14-16. Notice how the first part contains the schema that describes the structure of the table (name, type, and size of the fields), followed by the data itself.

The DataSet XML follows a predefined format with a few simple rules:

- The root document element is the DataSet.DataSetName (for example, Northwind).
- Each row in every table is contained in a separate element, using the name of the table. The example with one table means that there are multiple <Employees> elements.
- Every field in the row is contained as a separate tag in the table row tag. The value of the field is stored as text inside the tag.

Unfortunately, the DataSet doesn't make it possible for you to alter the overall structure. If you need to convert the DataSet to another form of XML, you need to manipulate it by using XSLT or by loading it into an XmlDocument object.

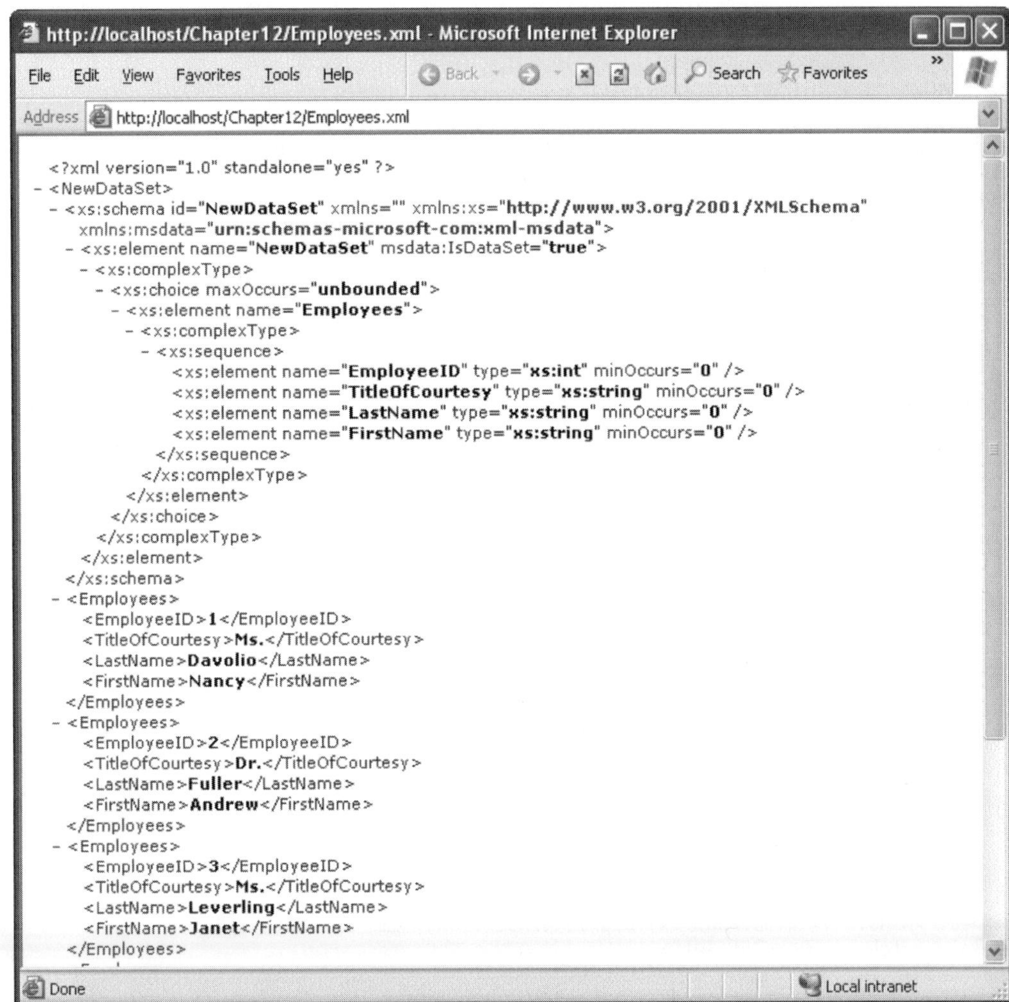

Figure 14-16. *Examining the DataSet XML*

Accessing a DataSet As XML

Another option provided by the DataSet is the ability to access it through an XML interface. This allows you to perform XML-specific tasks (such as hunting for a tag or applying an XSL transformation) with the data you've extracted from a database. To do so, you create an XmlDataDocument that wraps the DataSet. When you create the XmlDataDocument, you supply the DataSet you want as a parameter, as follows:

```
XmlDataDocument dataDocument = new XmlDataDocument(myDataSet);
```

Now you can look at the DataSet in two ways. Because the XmlDataDocument inherits from the XmlDocument class, it provides all the same properties and methods for examining nodes and modifying content. You can use this XML-based approach to deal with your data, or you can manipulate the DataSet through the XmlDataDocument.DataSet property. In either case, the two views are kept automatically synchronized—when you change the DataSet, the XML is updated immediately, and vice versa. This automatic synchronization introduces extra overhead, and as a result the XmlDataDocument is not the most efficient in-memory approach to managing an XML document. (Both the XmlDocument and XDocument classes are far faster.)

For example, consider the pubs database, which includes a table of authors. Using the XmlDataDocument, you could examine a list of authors as an XML document and then apply an XSL transformation with the help of the Xml web control. Here's the complete code you'd need:

```
// Create the ADO.NET objects.
SqlConnection con = new SqlConnection(connectionString);
string SQL = "SELECT * FROM authors WHERE city='Oakland'";
SqlCommand cmd = new SqlCommand(SQL, con);
SqlDataAdapter adapter = new SqlDataAdapter(cmd);
DataSet ds = new DataSet("AuthorsDataSet");

// Retrieve the data.
con.Open();
adapter.Fill(ds, "AuthorsTable");
con.Close();

// Create the XmlDataDocument that wraps this DataSet.
XmlDataDocument dataDoc = new XmlDataDocument(ds);

// Display the XML data (with the help of an XSLT) in the XML web control.
XmlControl.XPathNavigator = dataDoc.CreateNavigator();
XmlControl.TransformSource = "authors.xsl" ;
```

Here's the XSL stylesheet that does the work of converting the XML data into ready-to-display HTML:

```
<?xml version="1.0" encoding="UTF-8" ?>
<xsl:stylesheet xmlns:xsl="http://www.w3.org/1999/XSL/Transform" version="1.0">
  <xsl:template match="AuthorsDataSet">
    <h1>The Author List
      <xsl:apply-templates select="AuthorsTable"/>
    <i>Created through XML and XSLT</i>
  </xsl:template>

  <xsl:template match="AuthorsTable">
    <p><b>Name: </b><xsl:value-of select="au_lname"/>,
    <xsl:value-of select="au_fname"/><br/>
    <b>Phone: </b> <xsl:value-of select="phone"/></p>
  </xsl:template>
</xsl:stylesheet>
```

Figure 14-17 shows the processed data in HTML form.

Remember that when you interact with your data as XML, all the customary database-oriented concepts such as relationships and unique constraints go out the window. The only reason you should interact with your DataSet as XML is if you need to perform an XML-specific task. You shouldn't use

XML manipulation to replace the approaches used in earlier chapters to update data. In most cases, you'll find it easier to use advanced controls such as the GridView, rather than creating a dedicated XSL stylesheet to transform data into the HTML you want to display.

Figure 14-17. *Displaying the results of a query through XML and XSLT*

■ **Tip** If you're using a SQL Server database, you also have the option of performing a FOR XML query to retrieve the results of your query as an XML document. (You'll still be forced to use an XSL stylesheet or some other mechanism to convert it to the HTML you want to show.) To learn more about FOR XML queries, refer to the SQL Server Books Online.

Summary

In this chapter, you got a taste of ASP.NET's XML features. The class libraries for interacting with XML are available to any .NET application, whether it's a Windows application, a web application, or a simple command-line tool. They provide one of the most fully featured toolkits for working with XML and other standards such as XPath, XML Schema, and XSLT. The story gets even better with the XDocument model, which adds streamlined XML processing and full support for LINQ expressions.

XML is a vast topic, and there is much more to cover, such as advanced navigation, search and selection techniques, validation, and serialization. If you want to learn more about XML in .NET, consider a dedicated book on the subject or scour the Visual Studio Help. But remember that you should use XML only where it's warranted. XML is a great tool for persisting file-based data in a readable format and for sharing information with other application components and services. However, it doesn't replace the core data management techniques you've seen in previous chapters.

PART 3

Building ASP.NET Websites

Once you've learned to create solid web pages, you'll begin to consider the big picture—in other words, how to group together a large number of web pages to form a cohesive, integrated website. The previous chapters in this book have already considered some of the fundamentals, like managing state when the user moves from one page to another, and using separate components to factor data access code out of your web pages so they're available wherever you need them. However, web programmers face a few more considerations, such as ensuring consistency on every page and streamlining website navigation. In this part, you'll consider the topics that become important when you stop thinking about individual pages and starting planning an entire web application.

First, you'll look at user controls (Chapter 15), which let you reuse a block of user interface in multiple pages. In Chapter 16, you'll get more sophisticated with two more tools: themes, which let you set control properties automatically, and master pages, which let you reuse a single template to standardize the layout and content in multiple pages. Taken together, these three tools ensure that your web application appears as a single, coherent whole.

In Chapter 17, you'll consider a related topic: how to use site maps and navigation controls to let users move around your website. Finally, in Chapter 18 you'll learn how to bring your web application into a production environment by moving it off a development computer (or test server) to a full-fledged web server running IIS.

CHAPTER 15

■ ■ ■

User Controls

The core set of ASP.NET controls is broad and impressive. It includes controls that encapsulate basic HTML tags and controls that provide a rich higher-level model, such as the Calendar, TreeView, and data controls. Of course, even the best set of controls can't meet the needs of every developer. Sooner or later, you'll want to get under the hood, start tinkering, and build your own user interface components.

In .NET, you can plug into the web forms framework with your own controls in two ways. You can develop either of the following:

User controls: A user control is a small section of a page that can include static HTML code and web server controls. The advantage of user controls is that once you create one, you can reuse it in multiple pages in the same web application. You can even add your own properties, events, and methods.

Custom server controls: Custom server controls are compiled classes that programmatically generate their own HTML. Unlike user controls (which are declared like web-form pages in a plain-text file), server controls are always precompiled into DLL assemblies. Depending on how you code the server control, you can render the content from scratch, inherit the appearance and behavior from an existing web control and extend its features, or build the interface by instantiating and configuring a group of constituent controls.

In this chapter, you'll explore the first option—user controls. User controls are a great way to standardize repeated content across all the pages in a website. For example, imagine you want to provide a consistent way for users to enter address information on several different pages. To solve this problem, you could create an address user control that combines a group of text boxes and a few related validators. You could then add this address control to any web form and program against it as a single object.

User controls are also a good choice when you need to build and reuse site headers, footers, and navigational aids. (Master pages, which are discussed in Chapter 16, complement user controls by giving you a way to standardize web-page layout.) In all of these examples, you could avoid user controls entirely and just copy and paste the code wherever you need to. However, if you do, you'll run into serious problems once you need to modify, debug, or enhance the controls in the future. Because multiple copies of the user interface code will be scattered throughout your website, you'll have the unenviable task of tracking down each copy and repeating your changes. Clearly, user controls provide a more elegant, object-oriented approach.

User Control Basics

User control (.ascx) files are similar to ASP.NET web-form (.aspx) files. Like web forms, user controls are composed of a user interface portion with control tags (the .ascx file) and can use inline script or a .cs code-behind file. User controls can contain just about anything a web page can, including static HTML content and ASP.NET controls, and they also receive the same events as the Page object (like Load and PreRender) and expose the same set of intrinsic ASP.NET objects through properties (such as Application, Session, Request, and Response).

The key differences between user controls and web pages are as follows:

- User controls begin with a Control directive instead of a Page directive.
- User controls use the file extension .ascx instead of .aspx, and their code-behind files inherit from the System.Web.UI.UserControl class. In fact, the UserControl class and the Page class both inherit from the same TemplateControl class, which is why they share so many of the same methods and events.
- User controls can't be requested directly by a client browser. (ASP.NET will give a generic "that file type is not served" error message to anyone who tries.) Instead, user controls are embedded inside other web pages.

Creating a Simple User Control

To create a user control in Visual Studio, select Website ➤ Add New Item, and choose the Web User Control template.

The following is the simplest possible user control—one that merely contains static HTML. This user control represents a header bar.

```
<%@ Control Language="C#" AutoEventWireup="true"
    CodeFile="Header.ascx.cs" Inherits="Header" %>
<table width="100%" border="0" style="background-color: Blue">
    <tr>
        <td style="...">
            <b>User Control Test Page</b>
        </td>
    </tr>
    <tr>
        <td align="right" style="...">
            <b>An Apress Creation © 2008</b>
        </td>
    </tr>
</table>
```

You'll notice that the Control directive identifies the code-behind class. However, the simple header control doesn't require any custom code to work, so you can leave the class empty:

```
public partial class Header : System.Web.UI.UserControl
{}
```

As with ASP.NET web forms, the user control is a partial class, because it's merged with a separate portion generated by ASP.NET. That automatically generated portion has the member variables for all the controls you add at design time.

Now to test the control, you need to place it on a web form. First, you need to tell the ASP.NET page that you plan to use that user control with the Register directive, which you can place immediately after the Page directive, as shown here:

```
<%@ Register TagPrefix="apress" TagName="Header" Src="Header.ascx" %>
```

This line identifies the source file that contains the user control using the Src attribute. It also defines a tag prefix and tag name that will be used to declare a new control on the page. In the same way that ASP.NET server controls have the <asp: ... > prefix to declare the controls (for example, <asp:TextBox>), you can use your own tag prefixes to help distinguish the controls you've created. This example uses a tag prefix of apress and a tag named Header.

The full tag is shown in this page:

```
<%@ Page Language="C#" AutoEventWireup="true" CodeFile="HeaderTest.aspx.cs"
    Inherits="HeaderTest" %>
<%@ Register TagPrefix="apress" TagName="Header" Src="Header.ascx" %>
<html mlns="http://www.w3.org/1999/xhtml">
    <head>
        <title>HeaderHost</title>
    </head>
    <body>
        <form id="Form1" method="post" runat="server">
            <apress:Header id="Header1" runat="server"></apress:Header>
        </form>
    </body>
</html>
```

At a bare minimum, when you add a user control to your page, you should give it a unique ID and indicate that it runs on the server, like all ASP.NET controls. Figure 15-1 shows the sample page with the custom header.

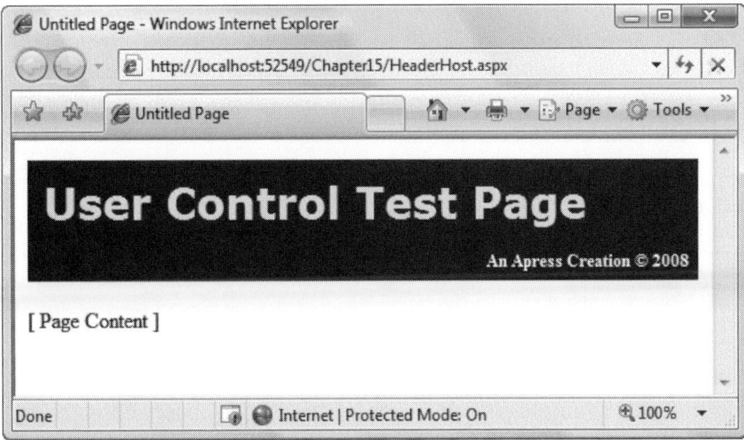

Figure 15-1. *Testing the header user control*

In Visual Studio, you don't need to code the Register directive by hand. Instead, once you've created your user control, simply select the .ascx file in the Solution Explorer and drag it onto the design area of a web form (not the source view). Visual Studio will automatically add the Register directive for you as well as an instance of the user control tag.

The header control is the simplest possible user control example, but it can already provide some realistic benefits. Think about what might happen if you had to manually copy the header's HTML code into all your ASP.NET pages, and then you had to change the title, add a contact link, or something else. You would need to change and upload all the pages again. With a separate user control, you just update that one file. Best of all, you can use any combination of HTML, user controls, and server controls on an ASP.NET web form.

Converting a Page to a User Control

Sometimes the easiest way to develop a user control is to put it in a web page first, test it on its own, and then translate the page to a user control. Even if you don't follow this approach, you might still end up with a portion of a user interface that you want to extract from a page and reuse in multiple places.

Overall, this process is a straightforward cut-and-paste operation. However, you need to watch for a few points:

- Remove all <html>, <head>, <body>, and <form> tags. These tags appear once in a page, so they can't be added to user controls (which might appear multiple times in a single page). Also, remove the doctype.
- If there is a Page directive, change it to a Control directive and remove the attributes that the Control directive does not support, such as AspCompat, Buffer, ClientTarget, CodePage, Culture, EnableSessionState, EnableViewStateMac, ErrorPage, LCID, ResponseEncoding, Trace, TraceMode, and Transaction.
- If you aren't using the code-behind model, make sure you still include a class name in the Control directive by supplying the ClassName attribute. This way, the web page that consumes the control can be strongly typed, which allows it to access properties and methods you've added to the control. If you are using the code-behind model, you need to change your code-behind class so that it inherits from UserControl rather than Page.
- Change the file extension from .aspx to .ascx.

Adding Code to a User Control

The previous user control didn't include any code. Instead, it simply provided a useful way to reuse a static block of a web-page user interface. In many cases, you'll want to add some code to your user control creation, either to handle events or to add functionality that the client can access. Just like a web form, you can add this code to the user control class in a <script> block directly in the .ascx file, or you can use a separate .cs code-behind file.

Handling Events

To get a better idea of how this works, the next example creates a simple TimeDisplay user control with some event-handling logic. This user control encapsulates a single LinkButton control. Whenever the link is clicked, the time displayed in the link is updated. The time is also refreshed when the control first loads.

Here's the user control markup:

```
<%@ Control Language="c#" AutoEventWireup="true"
    CodeFile="TimeDisplay.ascx.cs" Inherits="TimeDisplay" %>
<asp:LinkButton id="lnkTime" runat="server" OnClick="lnkTime_Click" />
```

And here's the corresponding code-behind class:

```
public partial class TimeDisplay : System.Web.UI.UserControl
{
    protected void Page_Load(object sender, EventArgs e)
    {
        if (!Page.IsPostBack)
            RefreshTime();
    }
    protected void lnkTime_Click(object sender, EventArgs e)
    {
        RefreshTime();
    }
    public void RefreshTime()
    {
        lnkTime.Text = DateTime.Now.ToLongTimeString();
    }
}
```

Note that the lnkTime_Click event handler calls a method named RefreshTime(). Because this method is public, the code on the hosting web form can trigger a label refresh programmatically by calling RefreshTime().

Figure 15-2 shows the resulting control.

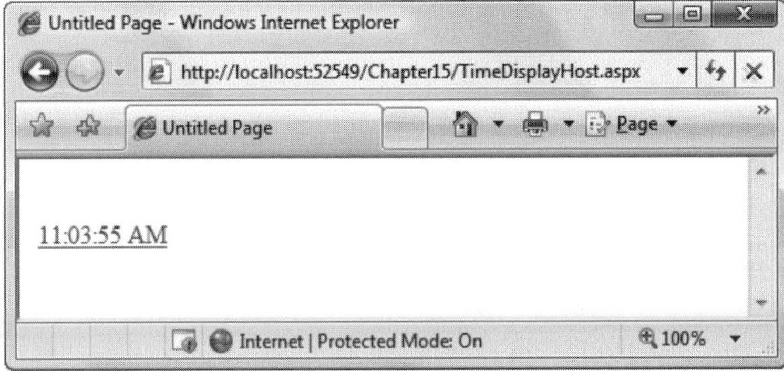

Figure 15-2. *A user control that handles its own events*

Note that in this example, the user control receives and handles a Page.Load event. This event and event handler are completely separate from the Page.Load event that the web form can respond to (although they are both raised as a consequence of the same thing—a page being created). This makes it easy for you to add initialization code to a user control.

Adding Properties

Currently, the TimeDisplay user control allows only limited interaction with the page that hosts it. All you can really do in your web-form code is call RefreshTime() to update the display. To make a user control more flexible and much more reusable, developers often add properties.

The next example shows a revised TimeDisplay control that adds a public Format property. This property accepts a standard .NET format string, which configures the format of the displayed date. The RefreshTime() method has been updated to take this information into account.

```
public class TimeDisplay : System.Web.UI.UserControl
{
    protected void Page_Load(object sender, EventArgs e)
    {
        if (!Page.IsPostBack)
            RefreshTime();
    }

    private string format;
    public string Format
    {
        get { return format; }
        set { format = value; }
    }

    protected void lnkTime_Click(object sender, EventArgs e)
    {
        RefreshTime();
    }

    public void RefreshTime()
    {
        if (format == null)
        {
            lnkTime.Text = DateTime.Now.ToLongTimeString();
        }
        else
        {
            // This will throw an exception for invalid format strings,
            // which is acceptable.
            lnkTime.Text = DateTime.Now.ToString(format);
        }
    }
}
```

In the hosting page, you have two choices. For one, you can set the Format property at some point in your code by manipulating the control object, as shown here:

```
TimeDisplay1.Format = "dddd, dd MMMM yyyy HH:mm:ss tt (GMT z)";
```

Your second option is to configure the user control when it's first initialized by setting the value in the control tag, as shown here:

```
<apress:TimeDisplay id="TimeDisplay1"
  Format="dddd, dd MMMM yyyy HH:mm:ss tt (GMT z)" runat="server" />
<hr />
<apress:TimeDisplay id="TimeDisplay2" runat="server" />
```

In this example, two versions of the TimeDisplay control are created, one with a control that displays the date in the default format and another one with a custom format applied. Figure 15-3 shows the resulting page in the browser.

■ **Tip** If you use simple property types such as int, DateTime, float, and so on, you can still set them with string values when declaring the control on the host page. ASP.NET will automatically convert the string to the property type defined in the class. Technically, ASP.NET employs a *type converter*—a special type of object often used to convert data types to and from string representations.

When you begin adding properties to a user control, it becomes more important to understand the sequence of events. Essentially, page initialization follows this order:

1. The page is requested.
2. The user control is created. If you have any default values for your variables, or if you perform any initialization in a class constructor, it's applied now.
3. If any properties are set in the user control tag, these are applied now.
4. The Page.Load event in the page executes, potentially initializing the user control.
5. The Page.Load event in the user control executes, potentially initializing the user control.

Once you understand this sequence, you'll realize that you shouldn't perform user control initialization in the Page.Load event of the user control that might overwrite the settings specified by the client.

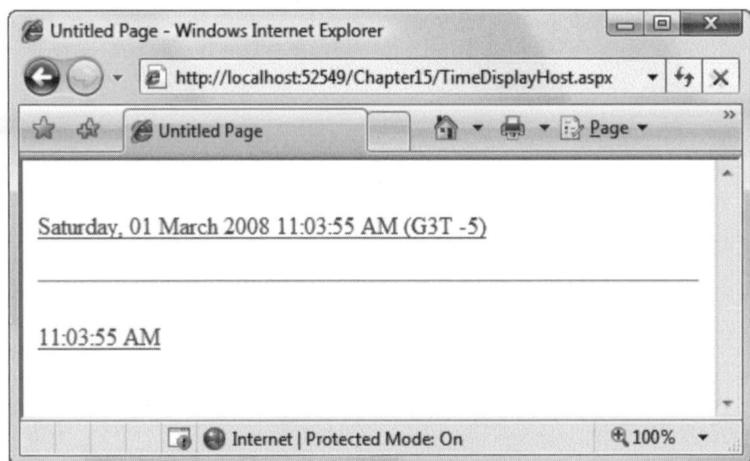

Figure 15-3. *Two instances of a dynamic user control*

Using Custom Objects

Many user controls are designed to abstract away the details of common scenarios with a higher-level control model. For example, if you need to enter address information, you might group several text box controls into one higher-level AddressInput control. When you're modeling this sort of control, you'll need to use more complex data than individual strings and numbers. Often, you'll want to create custom classes designed expressly for communication between your web page and your user control.

To demonstrate this idea, the next example develops a LinkTable control that renders a set of hyperlinks in a formatted table. Figure 15-4 shows the LinkTable control.

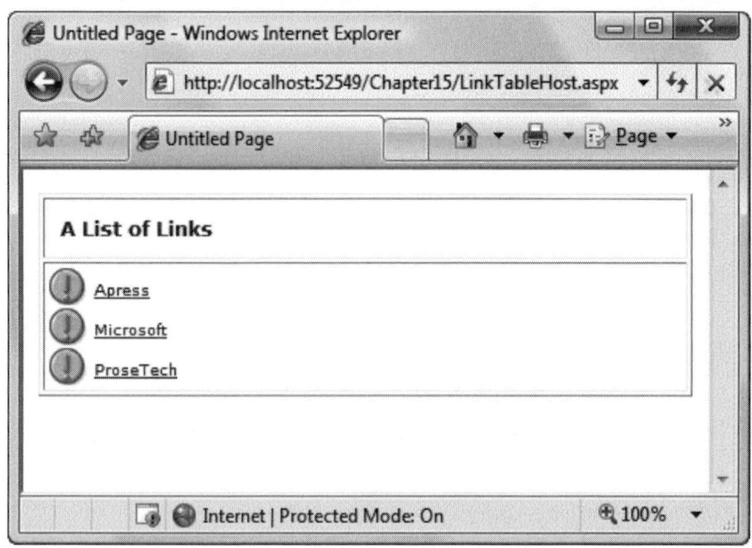

Figure 15-4. *A user control that displays a table of links*

To support this control, you need a custom class that defines the information needed for each link:

```
public class LinkTableItem
{
    private string text;
    public string Text
    {
        get { return text; }
        set { text = value; }
    }

    private string url;
    public string Url
    {
        get { return url; }
        set { url = value; }
    }

    // Default constructor.
```

```
    public LinkTableItem()
    {}

    public LinkTableItem(string text, string url)
    {
        this.text = text;
        this.url = url;
    }
}
```

This class could be expanded to include other details, such as an icon that should appear next to the control. The LinkTable simply uses the same icon for every item.

Next, consider the code-behind class for the LinkTable user control. It defines a Title property that allows you to set a caption and an Items collection that accepts an array of LinkTableItem objects, one for each link that you want to display in the table.

```
public partial class LinkTable : System.Web.UI.UserControl
{
    public string Title
    {
        get { return lblTitle.Text; }
        set { lblTitle.Text = value; }
    }

    private LinkTableItem[] items;
    public LinkTableItem[] Items
    {
        get { return items; }
        set
        {
            items = value;

            // Refresh the grid.
            gridContent.DataSource = items;
            gridContent.DataBind();
        }
    }
}
```

The control itself uses data binding to render most of its user interface. Whenever the Items property is set or changed, a GridView in the LinkTable control is rebound to the item collection. The GridView contains a single template that, for each link, displays each HyperLink control, which appears with an exclamation mark icon next to it.

```
<%@ Control Language="c#" AutoEventWireup="true" CodeFile="LinkTable.ascx.cs"
    Inherits="LinkTable" %>
<table border="1" cellpadding="2">
    <tr>
        <td>
          <asp:Label id="lblTitle" runat="server" ForeColor="#C00000"
            Font-Bold="True" Font-Names="Verdana" Font-Size="Small">
            [Title Goes Here]</asp:Label>
        </td>
```

```
    </tr>
    <tr>
        <td>
          <asp:GridView id="gridLinkList" runat="server"
           AutoGenerateColumns="false" ShowHeader="false" GridLines="None">
            <Columns>
              <asp:TemplateField>
                <ItemTemplate>
                  <img height="23" src="exclaim.gif"
                    alt="Menu Item" style="vertical-align: middle" />
                  <asp:HyperLink id="lnk" NavigateUrl=
                   '<%# DataBinder.Eval(Container.DataItem, "Url") %>'
                   Font-Names="Verdana" Font-Size="XX-Small" ForeColor="#0000cd"
                   Text='<%# DataBinder.Eval(Container.DataItem, "Text") %>'
                   runat="server" />
                </ItemTemplate>
              </asp:TemplateField>
            </Columns>
          </asp:GridView>
        </td>
    </tr>
</table>
```

Finally, here's the typical web-page code you would use to define a list of links and display it by binding it to the LinkTable user control:

```
protected void Page_Load(object sender, EventArgs e)
{
    // Set the title.
    LinkTable1.Title = "A List of Links";

    // Set the hyperlinked item list.
    LinkTableItem[] items = new LinkTableItem[3];
    items[0] = new LinkTableItem("Apress", "http://www.apress.com");
    items[1] = new LinkTableItem("Microsoft", "http://www.microsoft.com");
    items[2] = new LinkTableItem("ProseTech", "http://www.prosetech.com");
    LinkTable1.Items = items;
}
```

Once it's configured, the web-page code never needs to interact with this control again. When the user clicks one of the links, the user is just forwarded to the new destination without needing any additional code. Another approach would be to design the LinkTable so that it raises a server-side click event. You'll see that approach in the next section.

Adding Events

Another way that communication can occur between a user control and a web page is through events. With methods and properties, the user control reacts to a change made by the web-page code. With events, the story is reversed—the user control notifies the web page about an action, and the web-page code responds.

Usually, you'll delve into events when you create a user control that the user can interact with. After the user takes a certain action—such as clicking a button or choosing an option from a list—your user control intercepts a web control event and then raises a new, higher-level event to notify your web page.

The first version of the LinkTable control is fairly functional, but it doesn't use events. Instead, it simply creates the requested links. To demonstrate how events can be used, the next example revises the LinkTable so that it notifies the user when an item is clicked. Your web page can then determine what action to take based on which item was clicked.

The first step to implement this design is to define the events. Remember that to define an event you must use the event keyword with a delegate that represents the signature of the event. The .NET standard for events specifies that every event should use two parameters. The first one provides a reference to the control that sent the event, and the second one incorporates any additional information. This additional information is wrapped into a custom EventArgs object, which inherits from the System.EventArgs class. (If your event doesn't require any additional information, you can just use the generic System.EventArgs class, which doesn't contain any additional data. Many events in ASP.NET, such as Page.Load or Button.Click, follow this pattern.)

In the LinkTable example, it makes sense to transmit basic information about what link was clicked. To support this design, you can create the following custom EventArgs object, which adds a read-only property that has the corresponding LinkTableItem object:

```
public class LinkTableEventArgs : EventArgs
{
    private LinkTableItem selectedItem;
    public LinkTableItem SelectedItem
    {
        get { return selectedItem; }
    }

    private bool cancel = false;
    public bool Cancel
    {
        get { return cancel; }
        set { cancel = value; }
    }

    public LinkTableEventArgs(LinkTableItem item)
    {
        selectedItem = item;
    }
}
```

Notice that the LinkTableEventArgs class defines two new details—a SelectedItem property that allows the user to get information about the item that was clicked and a Cancel property that the user can set to prevent the LinkTable from navigating to the new page. One reason you might set Cancel is if you want to respond to the event in your web-page code and handle the redirect yourself. For example, you might want to show the target link in a server-side <iframe> or use it to set the content for an <img> tag rather than navigating to a new page.

Next, you need to create a new delegate that represents the LinkClicked event signature. Here's what it should look like:

```
public delegate void LinkClickedEventHandler(object sender,
  LinkTableEventArgs e);
```

You can add the delegate definition anywhere you'd like, but it's customary to place it at the namespace level, just before or after the declaration of the class that uses it (in this case, LinkTableEventArgs).

Using the LinkClickedEventHandler, the LinkTable class defines a single event:

```
public event LinkClickedEventHandler LinkClicked;
```

To intercept the server click, you need to replace the HyperLink control with a LinkButton, because only the LinkButton raises a server-side event. (The HyperLink simply renders as an anchor that directs the user straight to the target when clicked.) Here's the new template you need:

```
<ItemTemplate>
  <img height="23" src="exclaim.gif"
   alt="Menu Item" style="vertical-align: middle" />
  <asp:LinkButton ID="lnk" Font-Names="Verdana"
   Font-Size="XX-Small" ForeColor="#0000cd" runat="server"
   Text='<%# DataBinder.Eval(Container.DataItem, "Text") %>'
   CommandName="LinkClick"
   CommandArgument='<%# DataBinder.Eval(Container.DataItem, "Url") %>'>
  </asp:LinkButton>
</ItemTemplate>
```

You can then intercept the server-side click event by handling the GridView.RowCommand event, which fires when a command is triggered by any control in the grid:

```
<asp:GridView id="gridLinkList" runat="server"
 OnRowCommand="gridLinkList_RowCommand" ... />
```

Then you can write the event-handling code that passes the event along to the web page as a LinkClicked event:

```
protected void gridLinkList_RowCommand(object source,
  GridViewCommandEventArgs e)
{
    // Make sure there is at least one registered event handler before
    // raising the event.
    if (LinkClicked != null)
    {
        // Get the LinkButton object that was clicked.
        LinkButton link = (LinkButton)e.CommandSource;

        // Construct the event arguments.
        LinkTableItem item = new LinkTableItem(link.Text, link.CommandArgument);
        LinkTableEventArgs args = new LinkTableEventArgs(item);

        // Fire the event.
        LinkClicked(this, args);

        // Navigate to the link if the event recipient didn't
        // cancel the operation.
        if (!args.Cancel)
        {
            Response.Redirect(item.Url);
        }
    }
}
```

Note that when you raise an event, you must first check to see if the event variable contains a null reference. If it does, it signifies that no event handlers are registered yet (perhaps the control hasn't been created). Trying to fire the event at this point will generate a null reference exception. If the event variable isn't null, you can fire the event by using the name and passing along the appropriate event parameters.

Consuming this event isn't quite as easy as it is for the standard set of ASP.NET controls. The problem is that user controls don't provide much in the way of design-time support. (Custom controls, which you'll look at in Chapter 27, do provide design-time support.) As a result, you can't use the Properties window to wire up the event handler at design time. Instead, you need to write the event handler and the code that attaches it yourself.

Here's an example of an event handler that has the required signature (as defined by the LinkClickedEventHandler delegate):

```
protected void LinkClicked(object sender, LinkTableEventArgs e)
{
    lblInfo.Text = "You clicked '" + e.SelectedItem.Text +

      "' but this page chose not to direct you to '" +
    e.SelectedItem.Url + "'.";
    e.Cancel = true;
}
```

You have two options to wire up the event handler. You can do it manually in the Page.Load event handler using this code:

```
LinkTable1.LinkClicked += new LinkClicked;
```

Alternatively, you can do it in the control tag. Just add the prefix On in front of the event name, as shown here:

```
<apress:LinkTable ID="LinkTable1" runat="server" OnLinkClicked="LinkClicked" />
```

Figure 15-5 shows the result when a link is clicked.

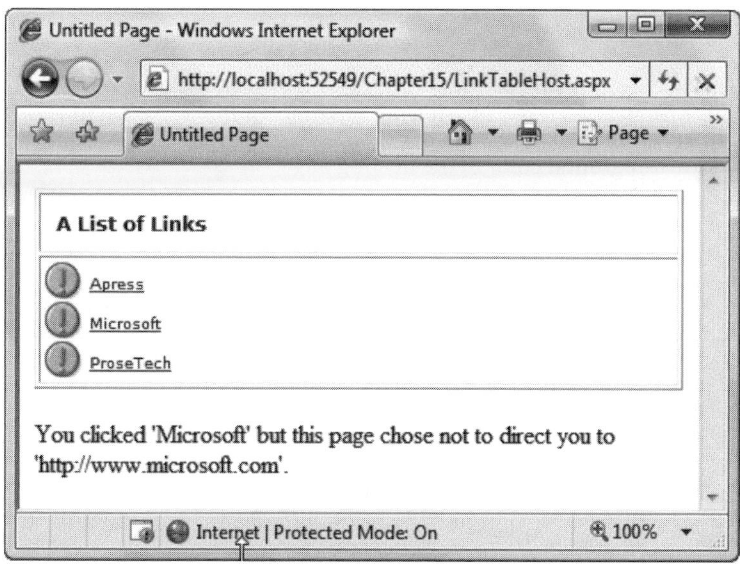

Figure 15-5. A user control that fires an event

Exposing the Inner Web Control

One important detail to remember is that the user control's constituent controls can be accessed only by the user control. That means the web page that hosts the user control cannot receive the events, set the properties, or call the methods of these contained controls. For example, in the TimeDisplay user control, the web page has no ability to access the LinkButton control that it uses.

Usually, this behavior is exactly what you want. It means your user control can add public properties to expose specific details without giving the web page free reign to tamper with everything and potentially introduce invalid or inconsistent changes. For example, if you want to give the web page the ability to tweak the foreground color of the LinkButton control, you might add a ForeColor property to your user control. Here's an example:

```
public Color ForeColor
{
    get { return lnkTime.ForeColor; }
    set { lnkTime.ForeColor = value; }
}
```

To change the foreground color in your web-page code, you would now use code like this:

```
TimeDisplay1.ForeColor = System.Drawing.Color.Green;
```

This example maps the lnkTime.ForeColor property to the ForeColor property of the user control. This trick is usually the best approach, but it can become tedious if you need to expose a large number of properties. For example, your user control might render a table, and you might want to let the user configure the formatting of each table cell.

In this case, it might make sense to expose the complete control object. Here's an example that exposes the lnkTime control for the TimeDisplay user control:

```
public LinkButton InnerLink
{
    get { return lnkTime; }
}
```

Notice that you need to use a read-only property, because it's not possible for the web page to replace the control with something different.

Now you can use this code to set the foreground color in the hosting page:

```
TimeDisplay1.InnerLink.ForeColor = System.Drawing.Color.Green;
```

Keep in mind that when you use this practice, you expose all the details of the inner control. This means the web page can call methods and receive events from that control. This approach gives unlimited flexibility, but it reduces the reusability of the code. It also increases the chance that your web page will become tightly coupled to the internal details of the current implementation of your control, thereby making it less likely that you can revise or enhance the user control without disrupting the web pages that use it. As a general rule, it's always better to create dedicated methods, events, and properties to expose just the functionality you need, rather than opening a back door that could be used to create messy workarounds.

Dynamically Loading User Controls

So far you've seen how you can add user controls to a page by registering the type of user control and adding the corresponding tag. You can also create user controls dynamically—in other words, create them on the fly using nothing but a little web-page code.

This technique is similar to the technique you used to add ordinary web controls dynamically (as described in Chapter 3). As with ordinary controls, you should do the following:

- Add user controls when the Page.Load event fires (so that your user control can properly restore its state and receive postback events).
- Use container controls and the PlaceHolder control to make sure the user controls end up exactly where you want.
- Give the user control a unique name by setting its ID property. You can use this information to retrieve a reference to the control when you need it with the Page.FindControl() method.

This has one additional wrinkle. You can't create a user control object directly, like you can with an ordinary control. That's because user controls aren't entirely based on code—they also require the control tags that are defined in the .ascx file. To use a user control, ASP.NET needs to process this file and initialize the corresponding child control objects.

To perform this step, you need to call the Page.LoadControl() method. When you call LoadControl(), you pass the filename of the .ascx user control markup file. LoadControl() returns a UserControl object, which you can then add to the page and cast to the specific class type to access control-specific functionality.

Here's an example that loads the TimeDisplay user control dynamically and adds it to the page using a PlaceHolder control:

```
protected void Page_Load(object sender, EventArgs e)
{
    TimeDisplay ctrl = (TimeDisplay)Page.LoadControl("TimeDisplay.ascx");
    PlaceHolder1.Controls.Add(ctrl);
}
```

Despite this slightly awkward detail, dynamically loading is a powerful technique when used in conjunction with user controls. It's commonly used to create highly configurable portal frameworks.

Portal Frameworks

Although it takes a fair bit of boilerplate code to create a complete portal framework, you can see the most important principles with a simple example. Consider the page shown in Figure 15-6. It includes a panel that contains three controls—a DropDownList (with its AutoPostBack property set to true), a Label, and a PlaceHolder control.

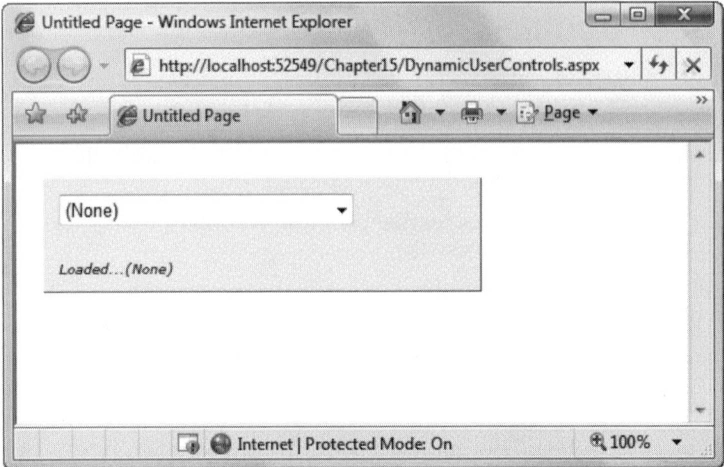

Figure 15-6. A panel for holding user controls

When the user selects an item from the drop-down list, the page posts back, and the appropriate user control is loaded dynamically and inserted into the placeholder. Figure 15-7 shows the result.

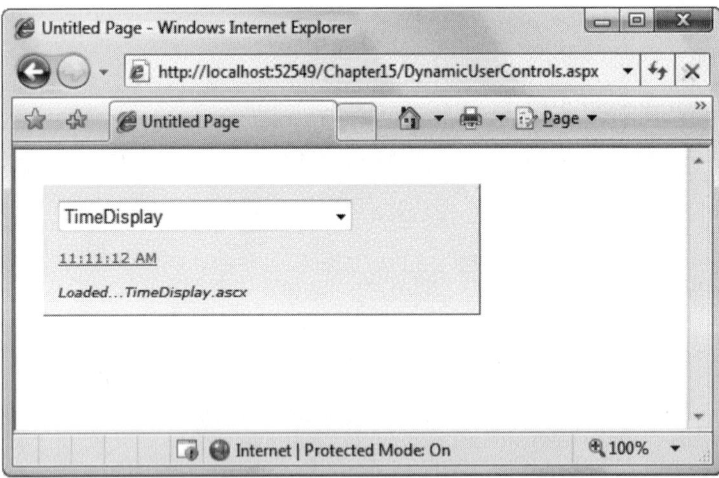

Figure 15-7. A dynamically loaded user control

Here's the code that loads the selected control:

```
protected void Page_Load(object sender, EventArgs e)
{
    // Remember that the control must be loaded in the Page.Load event handler.
    // The DropDownList.SelectedIndexChanged event fires too late.
    string ctrlName = listControls.SelectedItem.Value;
```

```
        if (ctrlName.EndsWith(".ascx"))
        {
            placeHolder.Controls.Add(Page.LoadControl(ctrlName));
        }
        lbl.Text = "Loaded..." + ctrlName;
}
```

This example demonstrates a number of interesting features. First, because the PlaceHolder is stored in a formatted container, the user controls you load automatically acquire the container's font, background color, and so on (unless they explicitly define their own fonts and colors).

Best of all, because you're loading these controls when the Page.Load event fires, the control objects are able to handle their own events. You can try this by loading the TimeDisplay user control and then clicking the link to refresh the time.

■ **Note** Because the TimeDisplay control isn't loaded until the page is posted back at least once, it won't show the time until you click the link at least once. Instead, it will start with the generic control name text. You can solve this problem in a number of ways, including calling the RefreshTime() method from your web page when the control is loaded. An even better approach is to create an interface for all your user controls that defines certain basic methods, such as InitializeControl(). That way, you can initialize any control generically. Most portal frameworks use interfaces to provide this type of standardization.

It's not too difficult to extend this example to provide an entire configurable web page. All you need to do is create more panels and organize them on your web page, possibly using tables and other panels to group them. (The following example loads user controls into <div> elements that have the runat="server" attribute set to make them server controls.)

This might seem like a tedious task, but you can actually use it quite effectively by writing some generic code that deals with all the panels on your page. One option is to create a user control that loads other user controls. Another approach is to use a custom method in the web-page class (as shown in the following code) to handle user control loading for three panels.

```
protected void Page_Load(object sender, EventArgs e)
{
    LoadControls(div1);
    LoadControls(div2);
    LoadControls(div3);
}

private void LoadControls(Control container)
{
    DropDownList list = null;
    PlaceHolder ph = null;
    Label lbl = null;

    // Find the controls for this panel.
    foreach (Control ctrl in container.Controls)
    {
        if (ctrl is DropDownList)
        {
            list = (DropDownList)ctrl;
```

```
        }
        else if (ctrl is PlaceHolder)
        {
            ph = (PlaceHolder)ctrl;
        }
        else if (ctrl is Label)
        {
            lbl = (Label)ctrl;
        }
    }

    // Load the dynamic content into this panel.
    string ctrlName = list.SelectedItem.Value;
    if (ctrlName.EndsWith(".ascx"))
    {
        ph.Controls.Add(Page.LoadControl(ctrlName));
    }
    lbl.Text = "Loaded..." + ctrlName;
}
```

Figure 15-8 shows this example in action.

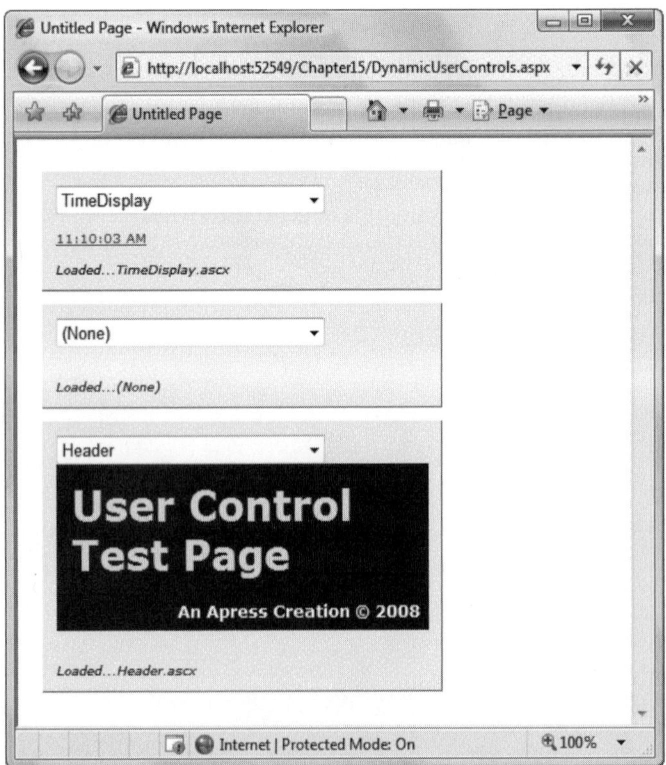

Figure 15-8. *A dynamic web page with multiple user controls*

Using this technique to build an entire web portal framework is possible, but it requires significant work before it would be practical. Creating this framework is a tedious, time-consuming task. In Chapter 31 you'll learn about web parts, a native ASP.NET solution for building web portals that doesn't force you to reinvent the wheel. Web parts are based, at least in part, on user controls.

Partial Page Caching

In Chapter 11, you learned how you can cache a web page by adding the OutputCache directive to the .aspx page. This type of caching, called output caching, caches a rendered HTML version of the page, which ASP.NET can reuse automatically for future requests without executing any of your page code.

One of the drawbacks with output caching is that it works on an all-or-nothing basis. It doesn't work if you need to render a portion of your page dynamically. For example, you might want to cache a table that's filled with records read from a data source so that you can limit the round-trips to the database server, but you might still need to get fresh output for the rest of the page. If that's your situation, user controls can provide exactly what you're looking for because they can cache their own output. This feature is called partial caching, or fragment caching, and it works in almost the same way as output caching. The only difference is that you add the OutputCache directive to the user control, instead of the page.

To test this feature, add the following line to the .ascx portion of a user control such as the TimeDisplay:

```
<%@ OutputCache Duration="10" VaryByParam="None" %>
```

Now in the hosting page you'll see that the displayed time won't change for 10 seconds. Refreshing the page has no effect. The VaryByParam parameter has the same meaning as it did with web pages—it allows to you to generate and cache fresh HTML output when the parameters in the query string portion of the URL change.

Alternatively, you can enable caching by adding the following attribute to the declaration of your user control class:

```
[PartialCaching(10)]
public class MyUserControl : System.Web.UI.UserControl
{ ... }
```

There's one caveat when using fragment caching. When a user control is cached, the user control essentially becomes a block of static HTML. As a result, the user control object won't be available to your web-page code. Instead, ASP.NET instantiates one of two more generic object types, depending on how the user control was created. If the user control was created declaratively (by adding a user tag to the web page), a StaticPartialCachingControl object is added. If the user control was created programmatically (using the LoadControl() method), a PartialCachingControl object is added. ASP.NET places the object into the logical position that a user control would occupy in the page's control hierarchy if it were not cached. However, these objects are just placeholders—they won't allow you to interact with the user control through its properties or methods. If you aren't sure if caching is in effect, you should test for a null reference before you attempt to use the user control object.

VaryByControl

If your user control contains input controls, it's difficult to use caching. The problem occurs if the content in the input controls affects the cached content that the user control displays. With ordinary caching, you're stuck reusing the same copy of the user control, regardless what the user types into an input control. (A similar problem exists with web pages, which is why it seldom makes sense to cache a web page that includes input controls.)

The VaryByControl property solves this problem. VaryByControl takes a semicolon-delimited string of control names that are used to vary the cached content in much the same way that VaryByParameter varies the cached content for query string values.

For example, consider the following user control, named VaryingDate:

```
<%@ Control Language="C#" AutoEventWireup="true"
    CodeFile="VaryByControl.ascx.cs" Inherits="VaryingDate" %>

<asp:DropDownList id="lstMode" runat="server" Width="187px">
  <asp:ListItem>Large</asp:ListItem>
  <asp:ListItem>Small</asp:ListItem>
  <asp:ListItem>Medium</asp:ListItem>
</asp:DropDownList> <br />
<asp:Button ID="cmdSubmit" text="Submit" runat="server" />
<br /><br />
Control generated at:<br />
<asp:Label id="TimeMsg" runat="server" />
```

When the button is clicked, it displays the current date in one of three formats.

```
protected void Page_Load(object sender, EventArgs e)
{
    switch (lstMode.SelectedIndex)
    {
        case 0:
            TimeMsg.Font.Size = FontUnit.Large;
            break;
        case 1:
            TimeMsg.Font.Size = FontUnit.Small;
            break;
        case 2:
            TimeMsg.Font.Size = FontUnit.Medium;
            break;
    }
    TimeMsg.Text = DateTime.Now.ToString("F");
}
```

It's not sufficient to keep one cached copy of this page, because the display format changes depending on the selection in the lstMode control (see Figure 15-9).

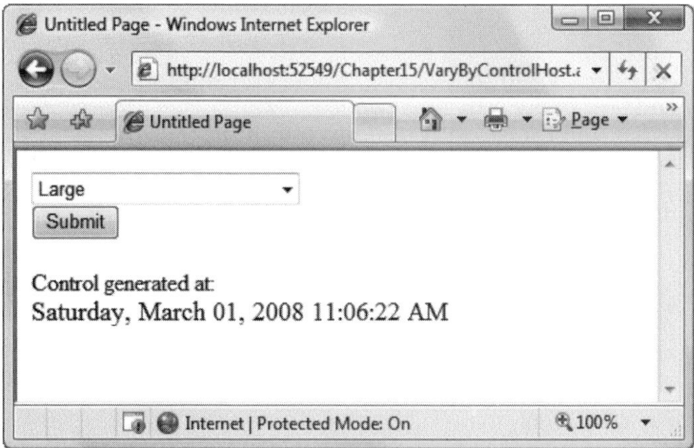

Figure 15-9. *Content that varies by control selection*

You can handle this using the VaryByControl attribute in the .ascx file for the user control and referring specifically to the property of the control that varies:

```
<%@ OutputCache Duration="30" VaryByControl="lstMode.SelectedItem" %>
```

When you try this example, you'll see a different date for each option, which emphasizes that ASP.NET maintains a separate cached copy for each list selection.

Sharing Cached Controls

If you use the same user control in ten different pages, ASP.NET will cache ten separate versions of that control. This gives each page the chance to customize the user control the first time it's executed, before the user control is cached. However, in many cases you might find that you reuse the same user control on multiple pages and you don't need to introduce page-specific customizations. In this case, you can save memory by telling ASP.NET to share the cached copy of the control.

ASP.NET enables this scenario through the Shared property of the OutputCache directive. The Shared property works only when you are applying the directive to a user control, not a web form. Here's an example:

```
<%@ OutputCache Duration="10" VaryByParam="None" Shared="True" %>
```

You can also make the same request by adding the PartialCaching attribute to the class declaration for the user control:

```
[PartialCaching(10, null, null, null, true)]
public class MyUserControl : System.Web.UI.UserControl
{ ... }
```

The null parameters here represent VaryByParam, VaryByControl, and VaryByCustom.

Summary

In this chapter, you learned how to create some simple and some sophisticated user controls. You also saw how to load user controls dynamically and how to use fragment caching.

Though user controls are easy to create, they don't solve every custom control challenge. In fact, user controls are quite limited in scope (they can't be easily shared across applications), and they have limited design-time support (for example, you can't attach event handlers in the Properties window). User controls also lack advanced features and aren't well suited to rendering HTML and JavaScript on the fly. To improve on this situation, you can step up to custom controls, which are much more sophisticated and quite a bit more complicated to create. Chapter 27 describes custom controls.

■ **Note** Although server controls are more powerful than user controls, most of the concepts you've learned in this chapter apply to server controls in the same way that they apply to user controls. For example, you can create server controls that include properties and methods, use custom objects, fire events, and expose child controls.

CHAPTER 16

■ ■ ■

Themes and Master Pages

Building a professional web application involves much more than designing individual web pages. You also need the tools to integrate your web pages into a complete, unified website. In this chapter, you'll consider two ASP.NET features that let you do that.

First up is a feature called *themes*, which let you define the formatting details for various types of controls and seamlessly reuse these formats in multiple pages. Themes make it much easier to standardize your website's look and feel and tweak it later. Once a theme is in place, you can give your entire website a face-lift just by changing the theme definition.

A more impressive innovation is *master pages*, which let you create reusable page templates. Using a master page, you can define the layout for your website pages, complete with all the usual details such as headers, menu bars, and ad banners. Once you've formalized this structure, you can use the master page throughout your website, ensuring that all pages have the same design. Visitors can then surf from one section to another without noticing any change.

In this chapter, you'll learn how to use themes and master pages to standardize your websites.

Cascading Style Sheets

The first step you can follow to create a seamless, unified website is to adopt a consistent visual style. In other words, standardize ruthlessly. If you want to tweak the font or border of a button, make sure you change it for *every* button you include. Being consistent isn't always easy. To help manage the details, you can use CSS or themes.

CSS provides a cross-platform solution for formatting web pages that works in conjunction with HTML or XHTML and is supported by virtually all modern browsers. In fact, early versions of Visual Studio automatically generated a Styles.css file for you to use in your website. (Later versions of Visual Studio abandoned this practice in favor of less clutter.)

■ **Tip** You can get the technical lowdown on CSS at `http://www.w3.org/Style/CSS`, or you can visit `http://www.w3schools.com/css` for a thorough tutorial.

Creating a Stylesheet

With CSS, you use a stylesheet to define a set of formatting presets. You then link this stylesheet to the appropriate control using the CssClass property. To try it and add an (almost) empty stylesheet to your web project, choose Website ➤ Add New Item in Visual Studio (or Project ➤ Add New Item if you're using the web project model). Then select Style Sheet, edit the filename, and click OK.

Stylesheets consist of *rules*. Each rule defines how a single ingredient in your web page should be formatted. For example, if you want to define a rule for formatting headings, you start by defining a rule with a descriptive name, like this:

```
.heading1
{
}
```

Each rule name has two parts. The portion before the period indicates the HTML element to which the rule applies. In this example, nothing appears before the period, which means the rule can apply to any tag. The portion after the period is a unique name (called the CSS *class name*) that you choose to identify your rule. CSS class names are case-sensitive.

Once you've defined a rule, you can add the appropriate formatting information. Here's an example the sets the heading1 style to use large, bold text with a green foreground color. The font is set to Verdana (if it's available), Arial (if it's not), or the browser's default sans-serif typeface (if neither Verdana nor Arial is installed).

```
.heading1
{
    font-weight: bold;
    font-size: large;
    color: lime;
    font-family: Verdana, Arial, Sans-Serif;
}
```

You can also create rules that are applied to HTML tags automatically. To do this, specify the tag name for the rule name. Here's a rule that affects all <h2> tags on the page that uses the stylesheet:

```
h2
{ ... }
```

Although this automatic stylesheet application sounds useful, it's less convenient in ASP.NET because you're usually dealing with controls, not individual HTML tags. You can't always be certain what tags will be used to render a given control, so it's best to explicitly specify the rule you want to use through the class name.

■ **Tip** If hand-writing CSS rules seems like too much work, don't worry—Visual Studio allows you to build a style rule using the same designer you use to format HTML tags. To use this feature, start by adding your rule declaration. Then, right-click between the two curly braces, and select Build Style. You'll see the Modify Style dialog box where you can point and click your way to custom fonts, borders, backgrounds, and alignment.

A typical stylesheet defines a slew of rules. In fact, stylesheets are often used to formally define the formatting for every significant piece of a website's user interface. The following stylesheet serves this purpose by defining five rules. The first rule sets the font for the <body> element, which ensures that the entire page shares a consistent default font. The rest of the rules are class-based, and need to be applied explicitly to the elements that use them. Two rules define size and color formatting for headings, and the final rule configures the formatting that's needed to create a bordered, shaded box of text.

```
body
{
    font-family: Verdana, Arial, Sans-Serif;
    font-size: small;
}

.heading1
{
    font-weight: bold;
    font-size: large;
    color: lime;
}

.heading2
{
    font-weight: bold;
    font-size: medium;
    font-style: italic;
    color: #C0BA72;
}

.blockText
{
    padding: 10px;
    background-color: #FFFFD9;
    border-style: solid;
    border-width: thin;
}
```

Visual Studio includes a CSS Outline window, which shows you an overview of the rules in your stylesheet. To show the CSS Outline window when you're editing a stylesheet, choose View ➤ Other Windows ➤ Document Outline.

While you're editing the stylesheet just shown, you'll see the outline shown in Figure 16-1. It clearly indicates that your stylesheet includes one element rule (the one that formats the body) and three class rules. You can jump immediately to a specific rule by clicking it in the CSS Outline window.

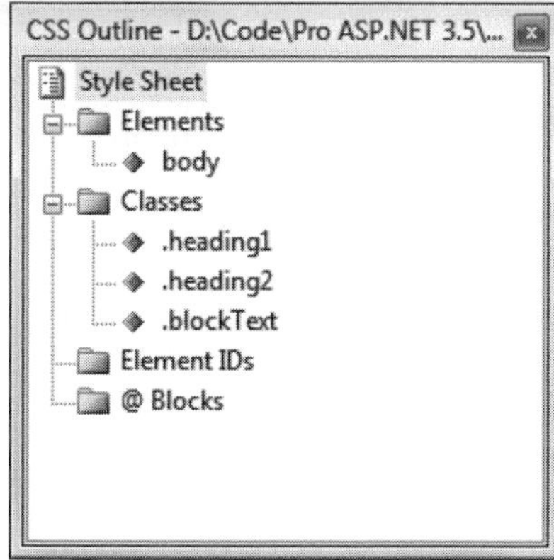

Figure 16-1. Navigating a stylesheet with the CSS Outline window

Rule names are technically known as *selectors*, because they identify the parts of an HTML document that should be selected for formatting. You've seen how to write selectors that use element types and selectors that use class names. CSS also supports a few more options for building advanced selectors that aren't described in this chapter. For example, you can create selectors that only apply to a specific element type *inside* another element (for example, a link inside a specific <div> container). Or, you can create selectors that apply formatting to individual elements that have a specific id values. (These appear in the CSS Outline window under the Element IDs group.) To learn more about CSS, consult a dedicated book such as *CSS: The Definitive Guide*, by Eric Meyer.

Applying Stylesheet Rules

To use a rule in a web page, you first need to link the page to the appropriate stylesheet. You do this by adding a <link> element in the <head> section of your page. The <link> element references the file with the styles you want to use. Here's an example that allows the page to use styles defined in the file StyleSheet.css, assuming it's in the same folder as the web page:

```
<link href="StyleSheet.css" rel="stylesheet" type="text/css" />
```

Now you can bind any static HTML element or control to your style rules. For example, if you want an ordinary label to use the heading1 format, set the Label.CssStyle property to heading1, as shown here:

```
<asp:Label ID="Label1" runat="server" Text="This Label uses the heading1 style."
 CssClass="heading1"></asp:Label>
```

To apply a style to an ordinary piece of HTML, you set the class attribute. Here's an example that applies a style to a <div> element, which groups together a paragraph of text for easy formatting:

```
<div class="blockText" id="paragraph" runat="server" >
  <p>This paragraph uses the blockText style.</p>
</div>
```

There's no reason that you need to attach style sheets and apply styles by hand. You can also use the support that's built into Visual Studio. To add the <link> element to a web page, drag your stylesheet from the Solution Explorer and drop it onto the design surface of the page (or the <head> section in source view). To apply a style, you can use Visual Studio's Apply Styles window.

To show the Apply Styles window, open a web page and choose View ➤ Apply Styles. The Apply Styles window appears on the left with the Toolbox and Server Explorer, just like the other CSS windows you've seen so far.

The Apply Styles window shows a list of all the styles that are available in the attached stylesheets, along with a preview of each one (see Figure 16-2). To apply a style, simply select an element on your web page and then click the appropriate style in the Apply Styles window.Visual Studio is intelligent enough to figure out the appropriate way to apply a style based on what you've selected in your web page:

- If you select a web control, it adds or changes the CssClass property.
- If you select an ordinary HTML element, it adds or changes the class attribute.
- If you select a section of HTML content, it adds a <span> or <div> element (depending on the type of content you've selected) and then sets its class attribute.

■ **Tip** Click the Options button to tweak the way the Apply Styles window works. For example, you can choose to preview styles in a different order, or include just those styles that are being used in the current page.

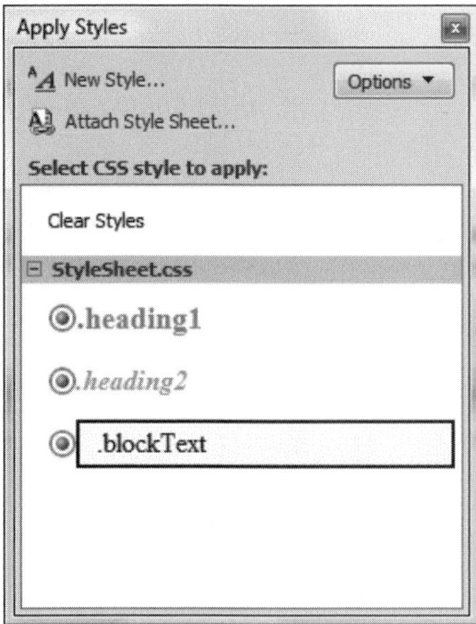

***Figure 16-2.** Applying a style with the Apply Styles window*

Visual Studio has even more stylesheet assistance for you to explore. Here are a few more features that can help with the daily drudgery of managing styles:

- **The Manage Styles window:** This window gives you an at-a-glance overview of all the styles that are in scope in the current web page, in a single list. To show it, open a web page and choose View ➤ Manage Styles. Using this window, you can view the style definition (hover over a style), edit it (right-click the style and choose Go To Code), or design it with the style builder (right-click the style and choose Modify).
- **The Style Sheet toolbar:** This toolbar is useful when designing a stylesheet, and provides buttons for modifying an existing style or adding a new style. To show this toolbar, right-click the toolbar strip and add a check mark next to Style Sheet.
- **The CSS Properties window:** This window allows you to examine a style in detail and modify its formatting properties. To use it, choose View ➤ CSS Properties. Then, select find an element that has a style, and select it on the design surface of your web page. The CSS Properties window will show a detailed, sub-grouped list of all the CSS style properties (see Figure 16-3), which looks similar to the list of web control properties in the Properties window.

■ **Note** If more than one style rule applies to the currently selected element, the CSS Properties window shows a list of all the style rules in order of precedence. You can then select one to view or edit it. Properties that are set in a parent but don't apply to the currently selected element (either because they aren't inherited or because they're overridden by another style) are crossed out with a red line.

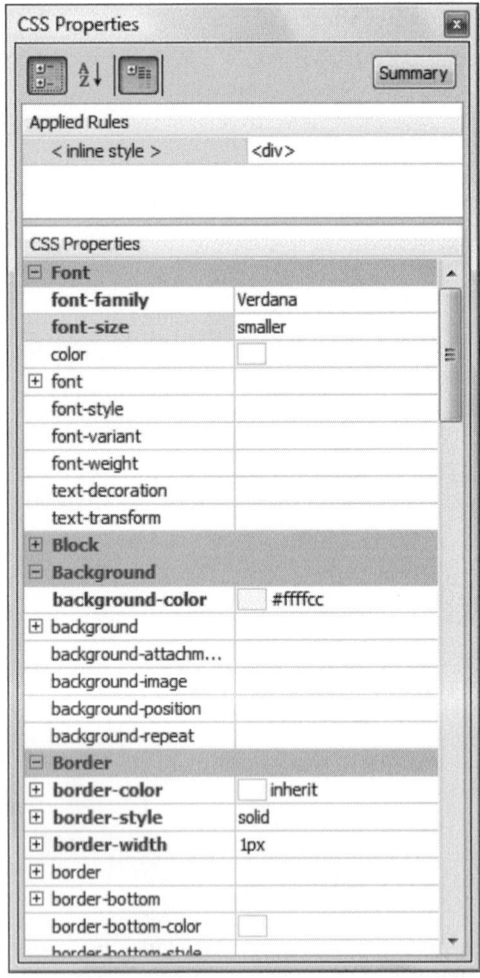

Figure 16-3. Modifying a style with the CSS Properties window

Using stylesheets accomplishes two things. First, it standardizes your layout so that you can quickly format pages without introducing minor mistakes or idiosyncrasies. Second, it separates the formatting information so that it doesn't appear in your web pages at all, allowing you to modify the format without tracking down each page or recompiling your code. And although CSS isn't a .NET-centric standard, Visual Studio still provides rich support for it.

Themes

With the convenience of CSS styles, you might wonder why developers need anything more. The problem is that CSS rules are limited to a fixed set of style attributes. They allow you to reuse specific formatting details (fonts, borders, foreground and background colors, and so on), but they obviously can't control other aspects of ASP.NET controls. For example, the CheckBoxList control includes properties that control how it organizes items into rows and columns. Although these properties affect the visual appearance of the control, they're outside the scope of CSS, so you need to set them by hand. Additionally, you might want to define part of the behavior of the control along with the formatting. For example, you might want to standardize the selection mode of a Calendar control or the wrapping in a TextBox. This obviously isn't possible through CSS.

Themes fill this gap. Like CSS, themes allow you to define a set of style attributes that you can apply to controls in multiple pages. However, unlike CSS, themes aren't implemented by the browser. Instead, they're a native ASP.NET solution that's implemented on the server. Although themes don't replace styles, they have some features that CSS can't provide. Here are the key differences:

Themes are control-based, not HTML-based: As a result, themes allow you to define and reuse almost any control property. For example, themes allow you to specify a set of common node pictures and use them in numerous TreeView controls or to define a set of templates for multiple GridView controls. CSS is limited to style attributes that apply directly to HTML.

Themes are applied on the server: When a theme is applied to a page, the final styled page is sent to the user. When a stylesheet is used, the browser receives both the page and the style information and then combines them on the client side.

Themes can be applied through configuration files: This lets you apply a theme to an entire folder or your whole website without modifying a single web page.

Themes don't cascade in the same way as CSS: Essentially, if you specify a property in a theme *and* in the individual control, the value in the theme overwrites the property in the control. However, you have the choice of changing this behavior and giving precedence to the properties in the page, which makes themes behave more like stylesheets.

It would be overstating it to say that themes replace CSS. Instead, themes represent a higher-level model. To implement your formatting properties, ASP.NET will frequently render inline style rules. In addition, if you've crafted the perfect stylesheet, you can still use it. It's up to you whether you want to use one or both solutions. As you'll see later in this chapter (in the section "Using CSS in a Theme"), it's possible to use a stylesheet as part of a theme.

Theme Folders and Skins

All themes are application-specific. To use a theme in a web application, you need to create a folder that defines it. You need to place this folder in a folder named App_Themes, which must be inside the top-level directory for your web application. In other words, a web application named SuperCommerce might have a FunkyTheme theme in the SuperCommerce\App_Themes\FunkyTheme folder.

An application can contain definitions for multiple themes, as long as each theme is in a separate folder. Only one theme can be active on a given page at a time. In the "Applying Themes Dynamically" section, you'll discover how you can dynamically change the active theme when your page is processing.

To actually make your theme accomplish something, you need to create at least one *skin* file in the theme folder. A skin file is a text file with the .skin extension. ASP.NET never serves skin files directly—instead, they're used behind the scenes to define a theme.

A skin file is essentially a list of control tags—with a twist. The control tags in a skin file don't need to completely define the control. Instead, they need to set only the properties you want to standardize. For example, if you're trying to apply a consistent color scheme, you might be interested in setting properties such as ForeColor and BackColor only. When you add a control tag for the ListBox control in the skin file, it might look like this:

```
<asp:ListBox runat="server" ForeColor="White" BackColor="Orange"/>
```

The runat="server" portion is always required. Everything else is optional. The id attribute is not allowed in a theme, because it's required to uniquely identify each control in the actual web page.

It's up to you whether you create multiple skin files or place all your control tags in a single skin file. Both approaches are equivalent, because ASP.NET treats all the skin files in a theme directory as part of the same theme definition. Often, it makes sense to separate the control tags for complex controls (such as the data controls) into separate skin files. Figure 16-4 shows the relationship between themes and skins in more detail.

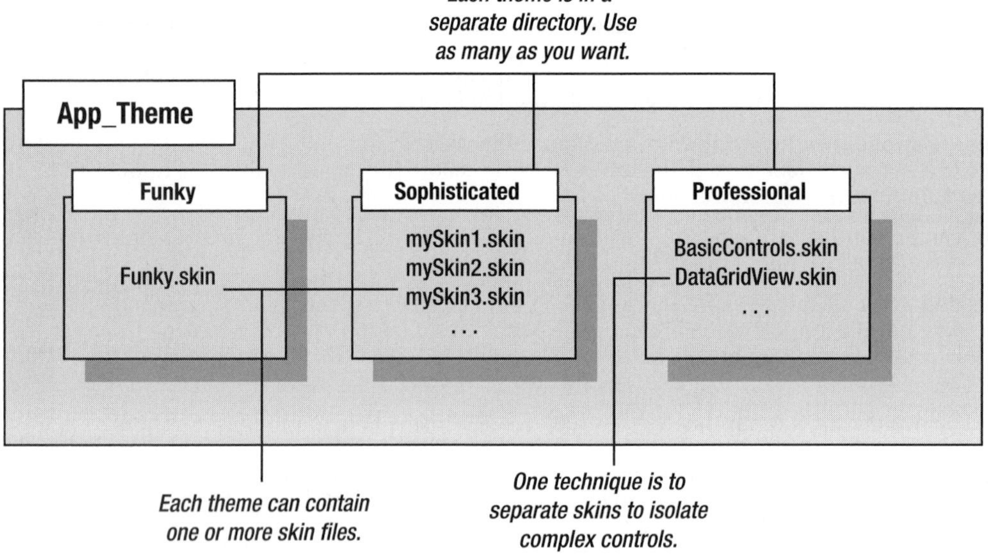

***Figure 16-4.** Themes and skins*

ASP.NET also supports global themes. These are themes you place in the c:\Inetpub\wwwroot\aspnet_client\system_web\[Version]\Themes directory (assuming c:\Inetpub\wwwroot is the web root for the IIS web server, which is the default configuration). However, it's recommended that you use local themes, even if you want to create more than one website that has the same theme. Using local themes makes it easier to deploy your web application, and it gives you the flexibility of introducing site-specific differences in the future.

If you have a local theme with the same name as a global theme, the local theme takes precedence, and the global theme is ignored. The themes are *not* merged together.

■ **Tip** ASP.NET doesn't ship with any predefined themes. That means you'll need to create your own from scratch or download sample themes from other websites such as `http://www.asp.net`.

Applying a Simple Theme

To add a theme to your project, select Website ➤ Add New Item (or Project ➤ Add New Item) and choose Skin File. Visual Studio will warn you that skin files need to be placed in a subfolder of the App_Themes folder and will ask you if that's what you intended. If you choose Yes, Visual Studio will create a folder with the same name as your theme file. You can then rename the folder and the file to whatever you'd like to use. Figure 16-5 shows an example with a theme that contains a single skin file.

Visual Studio doesn't include any design-time support for creating themes, so it's up to you to copy and paste control tags from other web pages. Here's a sample skin that sets background and foreground colors for several common controls:

```
<asp:ListBox runat="server" ForeColor="White" BackColor="Orange"/>
<asp:TextBox runat="server" ForeColor="White" BackColor="Orange"/>
<asp:Button runat="server" ForeColor="White" BackColor="Orange"/>
```

To apply the theme in a web page, you need to set the Theme attribute of the Page directive to the folder name for your theme. (ASP.NET will automatically scan all the skin files in that theme.)

```
<%@ Page Language="C#" AutoEventWireup="true" ... Theme="FunkyTheme" %>
```

Figure 16-5. *A theme in the Solution Explorer*

You can make this change by hand, or you can select the DOCUMENT object in the Properties window at design time and then set the Theme property (which provides a handy drop-down list of all your web application's themes). Visual Studio will modify the Page directive accordingly.

When you apply a theme to a page, ASP.NET considers each control on your web page and checks your skin files to see if they define any properties for that control. If ASP.NET finds a matching tag in the skin file, the information from the skin file overrides the current properties of the control.

Figure 16-6 shows the result of applying the FunkyTheme to a simple page. The first picture shows the Themes.aspx page in its natural state, with no theme. The second picture shows the same page with the FunkyTheme applied. All the settings in FunkyTheme are applied to the controls in Themes.aspx, even if they overwrite values you've explicitly set in the page (such as the background for the list box). However, details that were in the original page but that don't conflict with the theme (such as the custom font for the buttons) are left in place.

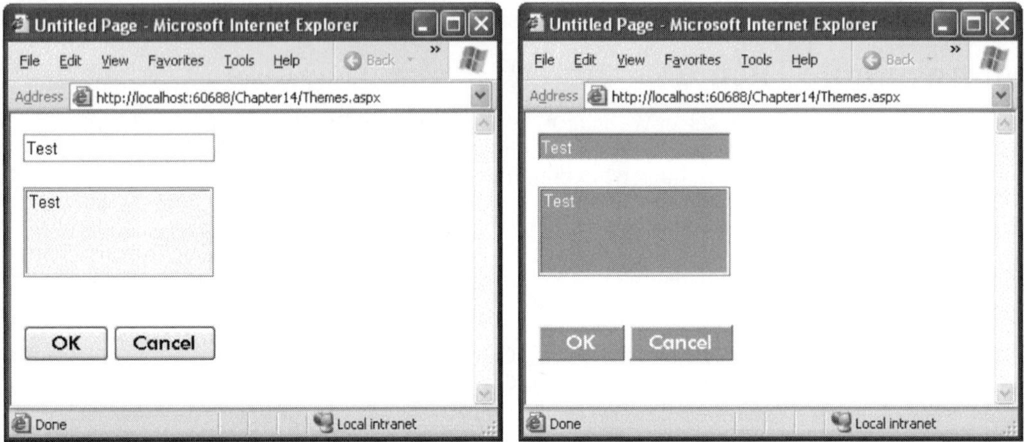

Figure 16-6. *A simple page before and after applying a theme*

Handling Theme Conflicts

As you've seen, when properties conflict between your controls and your theme, the theme wins. However, in some cases you might want to change this behavior so that your controls can fine-tune a theme by specifically overriding certain details. ASP.NET gives you this option, but it's an all-or-nothing setting that applies to all the controls on the entire page.

To make this change, just use the StyleSheetTheme attribute instead of the Theme attribute in the Page directive. (The StyleSheetTheme setting works more like CSS.) Here's an example:

```
<%@ Page Language="C#" AutoEventWireup="true" ... StyleSheetTheme="FunkyTheme" %>
```

Now the custom yellow background of the ListBox takes precedence over the background color specified by the theme. Figure 16-7 shows the result—and a potential problem. Because the foreground color has been changed to white, the lettering is now difficult to read. Overlapping formatting specifications can cause glitches such as this, which is why it's often better to let your themes take complete control by using the Theme attribute.

■ **Note** It's possible to use both the Theme attribute and the StyleSheetTheme attribute at the same time so that some settings are always applied (those in the Theme) and others are applied only if they aren't already specified in the control (those in the StyleSheetTheme). Depending on your point of view (and level of comfort with themes and styles), this is either a terribly confusing design or a useful way to make a distinction between settings you want to enforce (Theme) and settings you want to use as defaults (StyleSheetTheme).

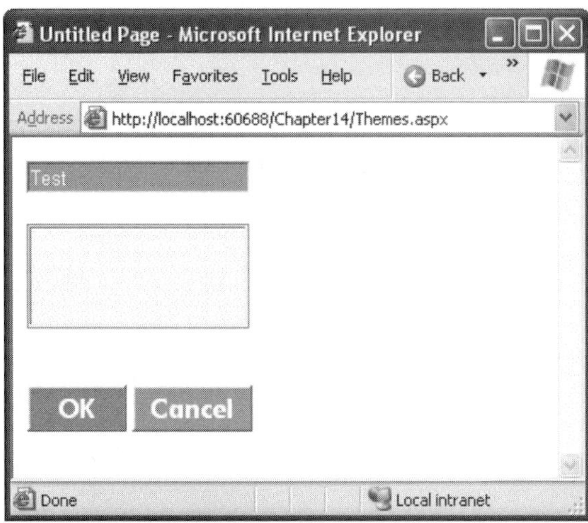

Figure 16-7. Giving the control tag precedence over the theme

Another option is to configure specific controls so they opt out of the theming process entirely. To do this, simply set the EnableTheming property of the control on the web page to false. ASP.NET will still apply the theme to other controls on the page, but it will skip over the control you've configured.

```
<asp:Button ID="Button1" runat="server" ... EnableTheming="false" />
```

Creating Multiple Skins for the Same Control

Having each control locked into a single format is great for standardization, but it's probably not flexible enough for a real-world application. For example, you might have several types of text boxes that are distinguished based on where they're used or what type of data they contain. Labels are even more likely to differ, depending on whether they're being used for headings or for body text. Fortunately, ASP.NET allows you to create multiple declarations for the same control.

Ordinarily, if you create more than one theme for the same control, ASP.NET will give you a build error stating that you can have only a single default skin for each control. To get around this problem, you need to create a named skin by supplying a SkinID attribute. Here's an example:

```
<asp:ListBox runat="server" ForeColor="White" BackColor="Orange" />
<asp:TextBox runat="server" ForeColor="White" BackColor="Orange" />
<asp:Button runat="server" ForeColor="White" BackColor="Orange" />
<asp:TextBox runat="server" ForeColor="White" BackColor="DarkOrange"
 Font-Bold="True" SkinID="Dramatic" />
<asp:Button runat="server" ForeColor="White" BackColor="DarkOrange"
 Font-Bold="True" SkinID="Dramatic" />
```

The catch is that named skins aren't applied automatically like default skins. To use a named skin, you need to set the SkinID of the control on your web page to match. You can choose this value from a drop-down list that Visual Studio creates based on all your defined skin names, or you can type it in by hand:

```
<asp:Button ID="Button1" runat="server" ... SkinID="Dramatic" />
```

If you don't like the opt-in model for themes, you can make all your skins named. That way, they'll never be applied unless you set the control's SkinID.

■ **Note** Using named themes is similar to using CSS rules that are based on class name (as shown at the beginning of this chapter). CSS class rules are applied only if you set the class attribute of the corresponding HTML tag.

ASP.NET is intelligent enough to catch if you try to use a skin name that doesn't exist, in which case you'll get a build warning. The control will then behave as though you set EnableTheming to false, which means it will ignore the corresponding default skin.

■ **Tip** The SkinID doesn't need to be unique. It just has to be unique for each control. For example, imagine you want to create an alternate set of skinned controls that use a slightly smaller font. These controls match your overall theme, but they're useful on pages that display a large amount of information. In this case, you can create new Button, TextBox, and Label controls, and give each one the same skin name (such as Smaller).

Skins with Templates and Images

So far, the theme examples have applied relatively simple properties. However, you can create much more detailed control tags in your skin file. Most control properties support themes. If a property can't be declared in a theme, you'll receive a build error when you attempt to launch your application.

■ **Note** Control developers can choose which properties you can set in a skin file by applying the Themeable attribute to the property declaration. If this attribute isn't present, the property can't be set in a theme.

For example, many controls support styles that specify a range of formatting information. The data controls are one example, and the Calendar control provides another. Here's how you might define Calendar styles in a skin file to match your theme:

```
<asp:Calendar runat="server" BackColor="White" ForeColor="Black"
 BorderColor="Black" BorderStyle="Solid" CellSpacing="1"
 Font-Names="Verdana" Font-Size="9pt" Height="250px" Width="500px"
 NextPrevFormat="ShortMonth" SelectionMode="Day">
  <SelectedDayStyle BackColor="DarkOrange" ForeColor="White" />
  <DayStyle BackColor="Orange" Font-Bold="True" ForeColor="White" />
  <NextPrevStyle Font-Bold="True" Font-Size="8pt" ForeColor="White" />
  <DayHeaderStyle Font-Bold="True" Font-Size="8pt" ForeColor="#333333"
   Height="8pt" />
```

```
  <TitleStyle BackColor="Firebrick" BorderStyle="None" Font-Bold="True"
   Font-Size="12pt" ForeColor="White" Height="12pt" />
  <OtherMonthDayStyle BackColor="NavajoWhite" Font-Bold="False"
   ForeColor="DarkGray" />
</asp:Calendar>
```

This skin defines the font, colors, and styles of the Calendar. It also sets the selection mode, the formatting of the month navigation links, and the overall size of the calendar. As a result, all you need to use this formatted calendar is the following streamlined tag:

```
<asp:Calendar ID="Calendar1" runat="server" />
```

Figure 16-8 shows how this Calendar control would ordinarily look and how it looks when the page uses the corresponding theme.

■ **Caution** When you create skins that specify details such as sizing, be careful. When these settings are applied to a page, they could cause the layout to change with unintended consequences. If you're in doubt, set a SkinID so that the skin is applied only if the control specifically opts in.

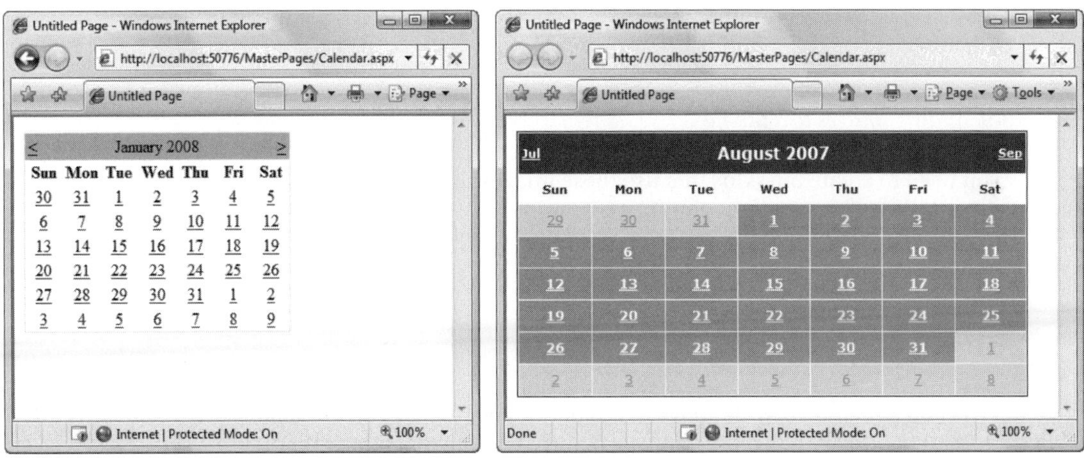

Figure 16-8. An unformatted Calendar on an unthemed and themed page

Another powerful technique is to reuse images by making them part of your theme. For example, imagine you perfect an image that you want to use for OK buttons throughout your website and you have another image for all the Cancel buttons. The first step in implementing this design is to add the images to your theme folder. For the best organization, it makes sense to create one or more subfolders just for holding images. In Figure 16-9, the images are stored in a folder named ButtonImages.

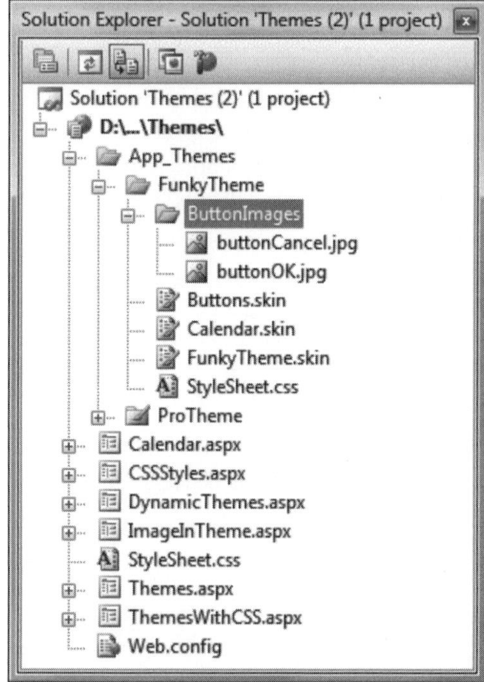

Figure 16-9. *Adding images to a theme*

Now you need to create the skins that use these images. In this case, both of these tags should be named skins. That's because you're defining a specific type of standardized button that should be available to the page when needed. You aren't defining a default style that should apply to all buttons.

```
<asp:ImageButton runat="server" SkinID="OKButton"
 ImageUrl="ButtonImages/buttonOK.jpg" />
<asp:ImageButton runat="server" SkinID="CancelButton"
 ImageUrl="ButtonImages/buttonCancel.jpg" />
```

When you add a reference to an image in a skin file, always make sure the image URL is relative to the theme folder, not the folder where the page is stored. When this theme is applied to a control, ASP.NET automatically inserts the Themes\ThemeName portion at the beginning of the URL.

Now to apply these images, simply create an ImageButton in your web page that references the corresponding skin name:

```
<asp:ImageButton ID="ImageButton1" runat="server" SkinID="OKButton" />
<asp:ImageButton ID="ImageButton2" runat="server" SkinID="CancelButton" />
```

You can use the same technique to create skins for other controls that use images. For example, you can standardize the node pictures used in a TreeView, the bullet image used for the BulletList control, or the icons used in a GridView.

Using CSS in a Theme

ASP.NET also gives you the ability to use a stylesheet as part of a theme. You might use this feature for a few reasons:

- You want to style HTML elements that might not correspond to server controls.
- You prefer to use a stylesheet because it is more standardized or because it can also be used to format static HTML pages.
- You have already invested effort in creating a stylesheet, and you don't want to create themes to implement the same formatting.

To use a stylesheet in a theme, you first need to add the stylesheet to your theme folder. ASP.NET searches this folder for all .css files and dynamically binds them to any page that uses the theme.

This has one catch, however. To bind the page to the stylesheet, ASP.NET needs to be able to insert a <link> tag in the <head> section of the web page. This is possible only if the <head> tag has the runat="server" attribute (which is the default in the web pages generated by Visual Studio).

```
<head runat="server">
    <title>...</title>
</head>
```

This turns the <head> element into a server-side control that ASP.NET can modify to insert the stylesheet links. Once this detail is in place, you simply need to set the Theme attribute of the page to gain access to the stylesheet rules. You can then set the CssClass property of the controls you want to format, as you saw earlier in the chapter. Any style rules that are linked directly to HTML tags are applied automatically.

You can use as many stylesheets as you want in a theme. ASP.NET will add multiple <link> tags, one for each stylesheet in the theme.

Applying Themes Through a Configuration File

Using the Page directive, you can bind a theme to a single page. However, you might decide that your theme is ready to be rolled out for the entire web application. The cleanest way to apply this theme is to configure the <pages> element in the web.config file for your application, as shown here:

```
<configuration>
  <system.web>
   <pages theme="FunkyTheme" />
  </system.web>
</configuration>
```

If you want to use the stylesheet behavior so that the theme doesn't overwrite conflicting control properties, use the styleSheetTheme attribute instead of the theme attribute:

```
<configuration>
  <system.web>
   <pages styleSheetTheme="FunkyTheme" />
  </system.web>
</configuration>
```

Either way, when you specify a theme in the web.config file, the theme you specify will be applied throughout all the pages in your website, provided these pages don't have their own theme settings. If a page specifies the Theme or StyleSheetTheme attribute, the page setting will take precedence over the web.config setting.

Using this technique, it's just as easy to apply a theme to part of a web application. For example, you can create a separate web.config file for each subfolder and use the <pages> setting to configure different themes.

■ **Tip** If you apply themes through a configuration file, you can still disable them for specific pages. Just include the EnableTheming attribute in the Page directive, and set it to false. No themes will be applied to the page.

Applying Themes Dynamically

In some cases, themes aren't used to standardize website appearance but to make that appearance configurable for each user. In this scenario, your web application gives the user the chance to specify the theme that your pages will use.

This technique is remarkably easy. All you need to do is set the Page.Theme or Page.StyleSheet property dynamically in your code. The trick is that this step needs to be completed in the Page.PreInit event stage. After this point, attempting to set the property causes an exception.

Here's an example that applies a dynamic theme by reading the theme name from the current Session collection:

```
protected void Page_PreInit(object sender, EventArgs e)
{
    if (Session["Theme"] == null)
    {
        // No theme has been chosen. Choose a default
        // (or set a blank string to make sure no theme
        // is used).
        Page.Theme = "";
    }
    else
    {
        Page.Theme = (string)Session["Theme"];
    }
}
```

Of course, you could also store the selected theme in a cookie, a session state, a profile (see Chapter 24), or any other user-specific location.

If you want to create a page that allows the user to choose a theme, you need a little more sleight of hand. The problem is that the user's selection can't be read until after the page has been loaded and has passed the PreInit stage. However, at this point, it is too late to set the theme. One way around this problem is to trigger a refresh by redirecting the page back to itself. The most efficient way to accomplish this is to use Server.Transfer() so that all the processing takes place on the server. (Response.Redirect() sends a redirect header to the client and so requires an extra round-trip.) You'll see this technique in the next example.

■ **Note** Other approaches are possible, but the best real-world solution is probably to make users perform theme selection on a separate web page. You can store the theme selection in a cookie, session state, or some other type of storage. The chosen theme will then always be available to the Page.PreInit event handler on other pages.

Here's the code that presents the list of selections when the page loads and then records the selection and transfers the page when a button is clicked:

```
protected void Page_Load(object sender, EventArgs e)
{
    if (!Page.IsPostBack)
    {
        // Fill the list box with available themes
        // by reading the folders in the App_Themes folder.
        DirectoryInfo themeDir = new DirectoryInfo(Server.MapPath("App_Themes"));
        lstThemes.DataTextField = "Name";
        lstThemes.DataSource = themeDir.GetDirectories();
        lstThemes.DataBind();
    }
}

protected void cmdApply_Click(object sender, EventArgs e)
{
    // Set the chosen theme.
    Session["Theme"] = lstThemes.SelectedValue;

    // Refresh the page (so the Page.PreInit event handler can apply the theme).
    Server.Transfer(Request.FilePath);
}
```

Remember, you still need the event handler for the Page.PreInit event to actually apply the selected theme to the page. Figure 16-10 shows the result.

***Figure 16-10.** Allowing the user to choose a theme*

If you use named skins, you can set the SkinID of a control declaratively when you design the page, or you can specify it dynamically in your code.

■ **Caution** If you use named skins, you'll need to be careful that every theme uses the same names and provides tags for the same controls. If a control specifies the SkinID attribute and ASP.NET can't find a matching skin for that control in the theme, the control won't be themed, and it will keep its current formatting.

Standardizing Website Layout

Standardizing the formatting of your website is only half the battle. You also need to make sure that common elements, such as your website header and site navigation controls, appear in the same position on every page.

The challenge is to create a simple, flexible layout that can be replicated throughout your entire website. You can use three basic approaches:

User controls: User controls allow you to define a "pagelet"—a portion of a web page, complete with markup and server-side code, that can be reused on as many web forms as you want. User controls are a great way to standardize a common page element. However, they can't solve the layout problem on their own, because there's no way to ensure that user controls are placed in the same position on every page. Chapter 15 describes user controls.

HTML frames: Frames are a basic tool of HTML that allow you to show more than one page in a browser window at once. The key disadvantage of frames is that each page is retrieved through a separate request to the server, and as a result the code on each page must be completely independent. That means a page in one frame can't communicate with or influence a page in another frame (at least not through server-side code).

Master pages: Master pages are an ASP.NET feature that's designed specifically for standardizing web-page layout. Master pages are web-page templates that can define fixed content and declare the portion of the web page where you can insert custom content. If you use the same master page throughout your website, you're guaranteed to keep the same layout. Best of all, if you change the master page definition after applying it, all the web pages that use it acquire the change automatically.

In ASP.NET, master pages are the preferred option for standardizing website layout, and you'll see them at work throughout the rest of this chapter. Frames offer a clumsier programming model but are required if you want to fix a portion of your page in place while allowing scrolling in another section. If you want to learn more about frames, refer to Chapter 29 for the basics and for several ASP.NET workarounds.

Master Page Basics

To provide a practical, flexible solution for page templating, a number of requirements must be met:

- The ability to define a portion of a page separately and reuse it on multiple pages.
- The ability to create a locked-in layout that defines editable regions. Pages that reuse this template are then constrained to adding or modifying content in the allowed regions.

- The ability to allow some customization of the elements you reuse on each page.
- The ability to bind a page to a page template declaratively (with no code) or to bind to a page dynamically at runtime.
- The ability to design a page that uses a page template with a tool such as Visual Studio.

Master pages meet all of these requirements. They provide a system for reusing templates, a way to limit how templates can be modified, and rich design-time support.

For this to work, ASP.NET defines two specialized types of pages: master pages and content pages. A master page is a page template. Like an ordinary ASP.NET web page, it can contain any combination of HTML, web controls, and even code. In addition, master pages can include *content placeholders*—defined regions that can be modified. Each *content page* references a single master page and acquires its layout and content. In addition, the content page can add page-specific content in any of the placeholders. In other words, the content page fills in the missing pieces that the master page doesn't define.

For example, in a typical website, a master page might include a fixed element such as a header and a content placeholder for the rest of the page. The content page then acquires the header for free and supplies additional content.

To take a closer look at how this works, it helps to consider the example presented in the following sections.

A Simple Master Page

To create a master page in Visual Studio, select Website ➤ Add New Item from the menu. Select Master Page, give it a filename (such as SiteTemplate.master), and click Add.

A master page is similar to an ordinary ASP.NET web form. Like a web form, the master page can include HTML, web controls, and code (either in an inline script block or in a separate file). One difference is that while web forms start with the Page directive, a master page starts with a Master directive that specifies the same information, as shown here:

```
<%@ Master Language="C#" AutoEventWireup="true" CodeFile="SiteTemplate.master.cs"
    Inherits="SiteTemplate" %>
```

Another difference between master pages and ordinary web forms is that master pages can use the ContentPlaceHolder control, which isn't allowed in ordinary pages. The ContentPlaceHolder is a portion of the page where the content page can insert content.

When you create a new master page in Visual Studio, you start with a blank page that includes two ContentPlaceHolder controls. One is defined in the <head> section, which gives content pages the ability to add page metadata, such as search keywords and stylesheet links. The second, more important ContentPlaceHolder is defined in the <body> section, and represents the displayed content of the page. It appears on the page as a faintly outlined box. If you click inside it or hover over it, the name of the ContentPlaceHolder appears in a tooltip (see Figure 16-11). To create more sophisticated page layouts, you can add additional markup and ContentPlaceHolder controls.

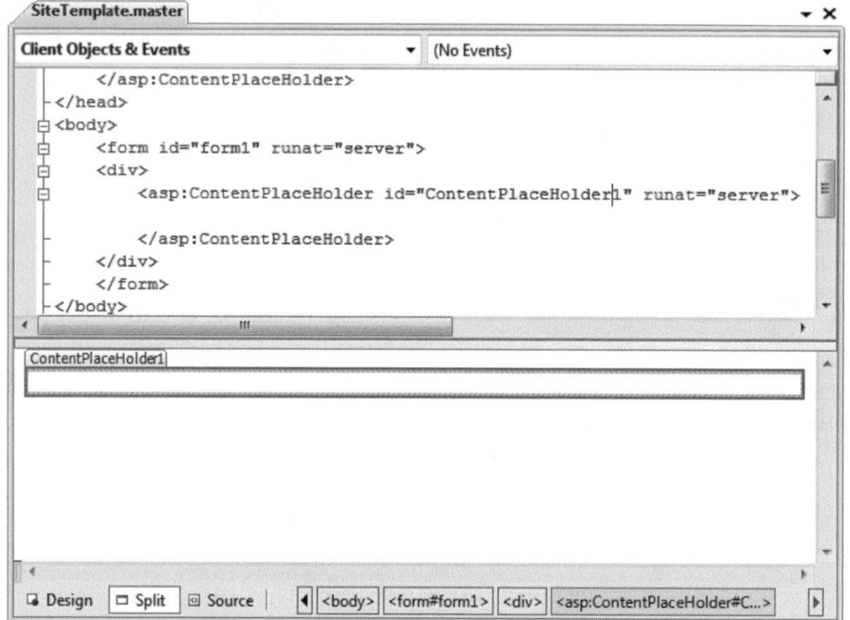

Figure 16-11. *A new master page*

The ContentPlaceHolder doesn't have any remarkable properties. Here's an example that creates a master page with a static banner followed by a ContentPlaceHolder and then a footer (shown in Figure 16-12):

```
<%@ Master Language="C#" AutoEventWireup="true" CodeFile="SiteTemplate.master.cs"
    Inherits="SiteTemplate" %>

<html xmlns="http://www.w3.org/1999/xhtml" >
<head runat="server">
    <title>Untitled Page</title>
</head>
<body>
    <form id="form1" runat="server">
    <div style="...">
         <img align="left" src="headerleft.jpg" alt="" />
          <img align="right" src="headerright.jpg" alt="" />
          <br />My Site<br />
    </div>
    <br />
    <asp:ContentPlaceHolder id="ContentPlaceHolder1" runat="server">
    </asp:ContentPlaceHolder>
    <br />
    <em>Copyright © 2008.</em>
    </form>
</body>
</html>
```

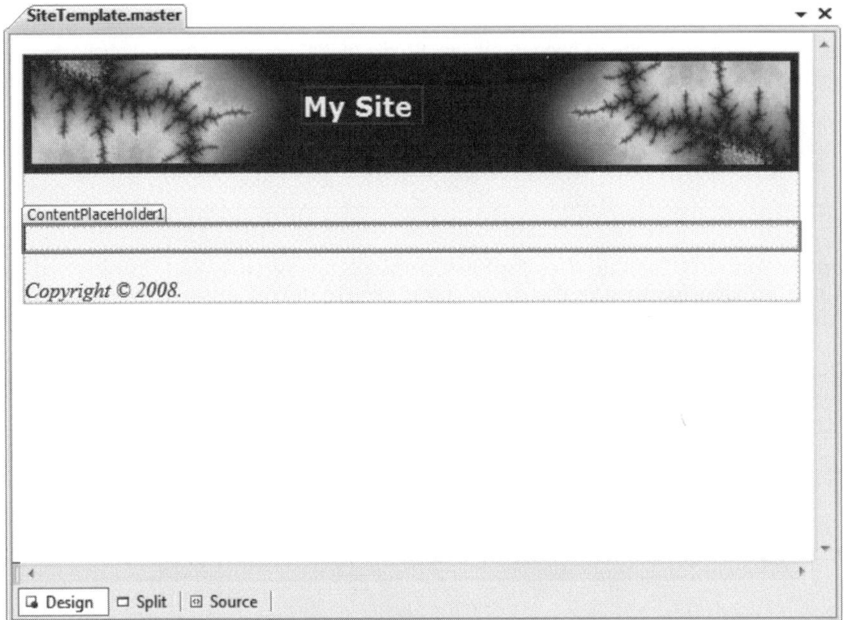

Figure 16-12. *A master page at design time*

Master pages can't be requested directly. To use a master page, you need to build a linked content page.

A Simple Content Page

To use your master page in another web page, you need to add the MasterPageFile attribute to the Page directive. This attribute indicates the filename of the master page you want to use:

```
<%@ Page Language="C#" MasterPageFile="./SiteTemplate.master" ... %>
```

Notice that the MasterPageFile attribute begins with the path ./ to specify the root website folder.

Setting the MasterPageFile attribute isn't enough to transform an ordinary page into a content page. The problem is that content pages have a single responsibility—to define the content that will be inserted in one or more ContentPlaceHolder controls (and to write any code you need for these controls). A content page doesn't define the page, because the outer shell is already provided by the master page. As a result, attempting to include elements such as <html>, <head>, and <body> will fail, because they're already defined in the master page.

To provide content for a ContentPlaceHolder, you use another specialized control, called Content. The ContentPlaceHolder control and the Content control have a one-to-one relationship. For each ContentPlaceHolder in the master page, the content page supplies a matching Content control (unless you don't want to supply any content at all for that region). ASP.NET links the Content control to the appropriate ContentPlaceHolder by matching the ID of the ContentPlaceHolder with the Content.ContentPlaceHolderID property of the corresponding Content control. If you create a Content control that references a nonexistent ContentPlaceHolder, you'll receive an error at runtime.

■ **Tip** To make it even easier to create a new content page, let Visual Studio guide you. Just select Website ➤ Add New Item from the menu. Select Web Form, click the Select Master Page check box, and click OK. Visual Studio will prompt you to choose a master page file from your current web project. When you take this step, Visual Studio automatically creates a Content control for every ContentPlaceHolder in the master page.

Thus, to create a complete content page that uses the SiteTemplate master page, you simply need to fill in the content for the ContentPlaceHolder with the ID ContentPlaceHolder1. Here's an example that shows the complete page code:

```
<%@ Page Language="C#" MasterPageFile="./SiteTemplate.master"
    AutoEventWireup="true" CodeFile="SimpleContentPage.aspx.cs"
    Inherits="SimpleContentPage" Title="Content Page" %>

<asp:Content ID="Content1" ContentPlaceHolderID="ContentPlaceHolder1"
  runat="Server">
    <span style="...">Far out in the uncharted backwaters of the unfashionable end
of the western spiral arm of the Galaxy lies a small unregarded yellow sun.</span>
</asp:Content>
```

In this example, the Page directive sets the MasterPageFile attribute and the Title attribute. The Title attribute allows you to specify the title for your content page, thereby overriding the title that's set in the master page. This works as long as the master page has the runat="server" attribute in the <head> tag, which is the default.

As you can see, content pages are refreshingly clean, because they don't include any of the details defined in the master page. Even better, this makes it easy to update your website. All you need to is modify a single master page. As long as you keep the same ContentPlaceHolder controls, the existing content pages will keep working and will fit themselves into the new layout wherever you specify.

Figure 16-13 shows this sample content page.

Master Pages and Formatting

Master pages provide a few interesting possibilities for standardizing formatting. For example, you can link to a stylesheet without using themes by adding a <link> element in the <head> section of the master page. That way, the stylesheet is automatically applied to all the content pages that use this master page.

You can also use a more fine-grained model and have your master page help you apply different formatting to different sections of a content page. All you need to do is set the appropriate foreground and background colors, fonts, and alignment options using container tags in the master page. For example, you might set these on a table, a table cell, a <div> tag, or a Panel control. The information from the content page can then flow seamlessly into these containers, acquiring the appropriate style attributes automatically.

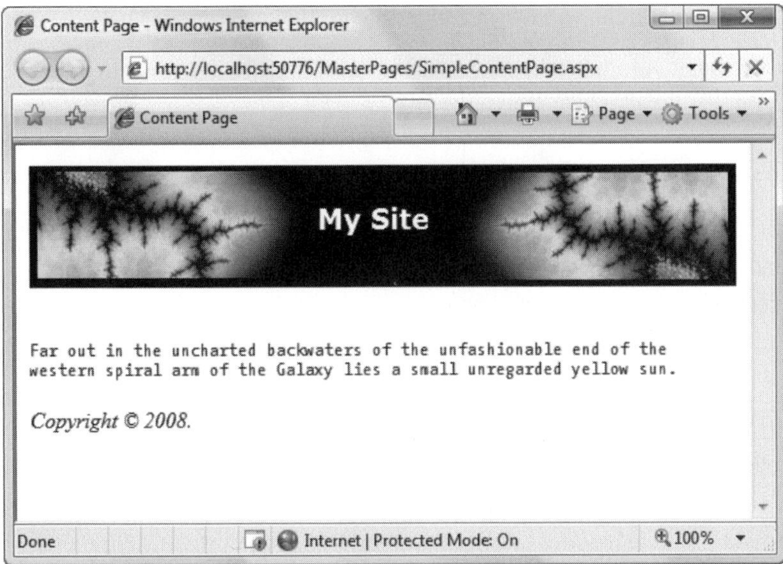

Figure 16-13. A content page at runtime

To get a better understanding of how master pages work under the hood, it's worth taking a look at a content page with tracing (add the Trace="true" attribute in the Page directive). That way you can study the control hierarchy. What you'll discover is that ASP.NET creates the control objects for the master page first, including the ContentPlaceHolder, which acts as a container. It then adds the controls from the content page into the ContentPlaceHolder.

If you need to dynamically configure your master page or content page, you can react to the Page.Load event in either class. Sometimes you might use initialization code in both the master page and the content page. In this situation, it's important to understand the order in which the respective events fire. ASP.NET begins by creating the master page controls and then the child controls for the content page. It then fires the Page.Init event for the master page and follows it up by firing the Page.Init event for the content page. The same step occurs with the Page.Load event. Thus, customizations that you perform in the content page (such as changing the page title) will take precedence over changes you make at the same stage in the master page, if they conflict.

Default Content

When the master page defines a ContentPlaceHolder, it can also include default content—content that will be used only if the content page doesn't supply a corresponding Content control.

To get this effect, all you need to do is place the appropriate HTML or web controls in the ContentPlaceHolder tag. (You can do this by hand using the .aspx markup or just by dragging and dropping controls into the ContentPlaceHolder.)

Here's an example that adds default content to the banner text from the previous example:

```
<asp:ContentPlaceHolder id="TitleContent" runat="server">
Master Pages Website
</asp:ContentPlaceHolder>
```

If you create a content page in Visual Studio, you won't notice any immediate change. That's because Visual Studio automatically creates a <Content> tag for each ContentPlaceHolder. When a content page includes a <Content> tag, it automatically overrides the default content. However, if you delete the <Content> tag, you'll see the default content in its place—the new "Master Pages Website" banner text.

■ **Note** Content pages can't use just a portion of the default content or just edit it slightly. This isn't possible because the default content is stored only in the master page, not in the content page. As a result, you need to decide between using the default content as is or replacing it completely.

Master Pages with Tables and CSS Layout

For the most part, HTML uses a flow-based layout. That means as more content is added, the page is reorganized and other content is bumped out of the way. This layout can make it difficult to get the result you want with master pages. For example, if you aren't careful, you could craft the perfect layout, only to have the structure distorted by a huge block of information that's inserted into a <Content> tag.

To control these problems, most master pages will use either HTML tables or CSS positioning to control the layout.

With tables, the basic principle is to divide all or a portion of the page into columns and rows. You can then add a ContentPlaceHolder in a single cell, ensuring that the other content is aligned more or less the way you want. With CSS positioning, the idea is to separate your content into <div> tags and position these <div> tags by using absolute coordinates or by floating them on one side of the page. You'll then place the ContentPlaceHolder in the <div> tag.

■ **Tip** For some great examples of CSS-based layout, see the sites `http://www.csszengarden.com` and `http://www.bluerobot.com/web/layouts`.

The following example shows how you can use master pages to create a traditional web application with a header, footer, and navigation bar, all of which are defined with tables. Figure 16-14 shows how this structure is broken up into a table.

Here's the markup for the table that contains the ContentPlaceHolder:

```
<table style="width: 100%">
    <tr><td colspan="2">My Header</td></tr>
    <tr>
        <td width="150px">Navigation Controls</td>
        <td>
            <asp:ContentPlaceHolder id="ContentPlaceHolder1" runat="server">
            </asp:ContentPlaceHolder>
        </td>
     </tr>
     <tr><td colspan="2">My Footer</td></tr>
</table>
```

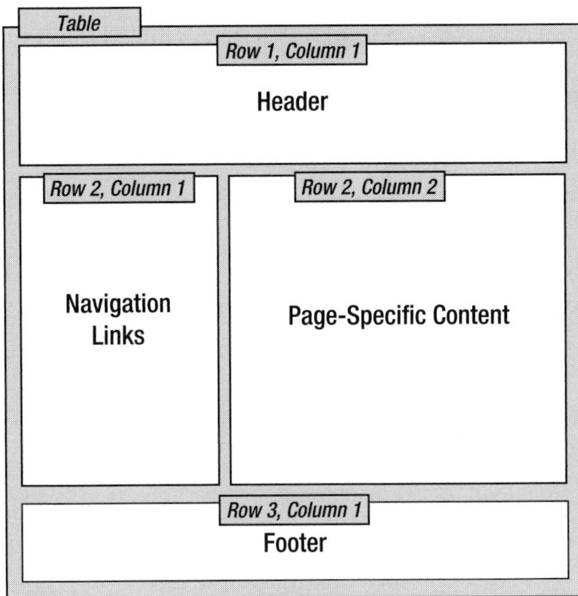

Figure 16-14. A table-based layout

■ **Tip** To get a quick refresher on HTML tables, complete with information about how to specify borders, cell sizes, alignment, and more, refer to the examples at `http://www.w3schools.com/html/html_tables.asp`.

Figure 16-15 shows the resulting master page and a content page that uses the master page. Using style rules, dotted lines have been added around all the cells that are fixed (in other words, cells that don't have a ContentPlaceHolder control that the content page can use to insert additional content.)

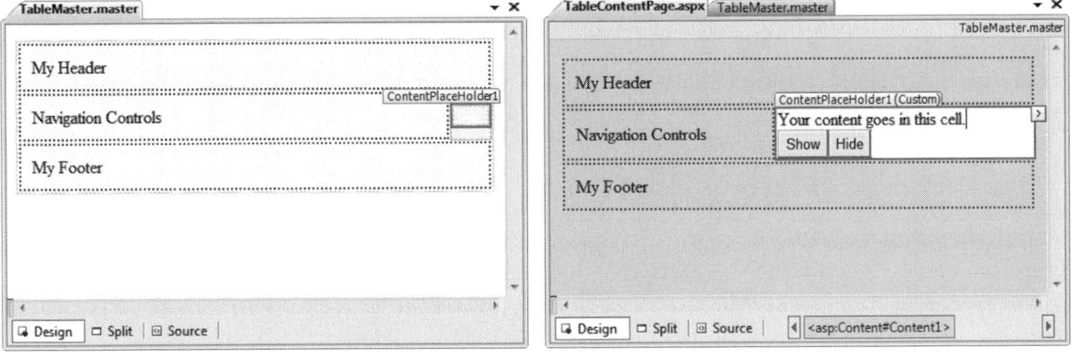

Figure 16-15. A master page and content page that use a table

To convert this example into something more practical, just replace the static text in the master page with the actual header, footer, and navigation controls (using the ASP.NET navigation features discussed in Chapter 17). All the child pages will acquire these features automatically. This is the first step for defining a practical structure for your entire website.

Many professional web developers prefer to use more modern CSS-based layout techniques. CSS-based layout allows you to write markup that's easier to read and easier to revise later on, which makes for fewer long-term headaches.

Fortunately, it's just as easy to use the ContentPlaceHolder with CSS-based layout as it is to use it with tables. Instead of placing the ContentPlaceHolder objects in the cells of a table, you simply place the ContentPlaceHolder objects in different <div> elements. Your stylesheet then applies the positioning to each <div> using the position, left, right, top, and bottom attributes.

For example, one common page design is to divide the page into three columns. The columns on either edge of the page are set to a fixed size, while the column in the middle takes the remaining space. Here's a simple stylesheet that puts this design into action by creating a 150-pixel-wide panel on either side of the page:

```
.leftPanel
{
    position: absolute;
    top: 70px;
    left: 10px;
    width: 150px;
}

.rightPanel
{
    position: absolute;
    top: 70px;
    right: 10px;
    width: 150px;
}

.centerPanel
{
    margin-left: 151px;
    margin-right: 151px;
    padding-left: 12px;
    padding-right: 12px;
}
```

You can now divide your page into columns using the styles, and place a ContentPlaceHolder in the appropriate region. For example, you might use the left panel for navigation controls, the right panel for an advertisement, and the middle panel for the content that's supplied by the content page:

```
<div class="leftPanel">...</div>
<div class="centerPanel">
  <asp:ContentPlaceHolder id="ContentPlaceHolder1" runat="server">
  </asp:ContentPlaceHolder>
</div>
<div class="rightPanel">...</div>
```

Remember, in order for this technique to work, the master page must use the stylesheet you've created—in other words, it needs to include the <link> element that attaches the stylesheet and makes the styles available to your web page markup, as described at the beginning of this chapter in the "Applying Stylesheet Rules" section.

There are a variety of tutorials online about CSS-based layout. You can find a concise set of examples for common layouts at http://www.glish.com/css, and some thought-provoking examples that demonstrate how the same content can be given an entirely different layout and appearance with an advanced stylesheet at http://www.csszengarden.com.

Master Pages and Relative Paths

One quirk that can catch unsuspecting developers is the way that master pages handle relative paths. If all you're using is static text, this issue won't affect you. However, if you've added <img> tags or any other HTML tag that points to another resource, problems can occur.

The problem shows up if you place the master page in a different directory from the content page that uses it. This is a recommended best practice for large websites. In fact, Microsoft encourages you to use a dedicated folder for storing all your master pages. However, if you're not suitably careful, this can cause problems when you use relative paths.

For example, imagine you put a master page in a subfolder named MasterPages and add the following <img> tag to the master page:

```
<img src="banner.jpg" />
```

Assuming the file \MasterPages\banner.jpg exists, this appears to work fine. The image will even appear in the Visual Studio design environment. However, if you create a content page in another subfolder, the path is interpreted relative to that folder. If the file doesn't exist there, you'll get a broken link instead of your graphic. Even worse, you could conceivably get the wrong graphic if another image has the same filename.

This problem occurs because the <img> tag is ordinary HTML. As a result, ASP.NET won't touch it. Unfortunately, when ASP.NET builds your content page, this tag is no longer appropriate. The same problem occurs with <a> tags that provide relative links to other pages, and with the <link> element, which you can use to connect the master page to a stylesheet.

To solve your problem, you could try to think ahead and write your URL relative to the content page where you want to use it. But this creates confusion, limits where your master page can be used, and has the unwelcome side effect of displaying your master page incorrectly in the design environment.

Another quick fix is to make your image tag into a server-side control, in which case ASP.NET will fix the mistake:

```
<img src="banner.jpg" runat="server"/>
```

This works because ASP.NET uses this information to create an HtmlImage server control. This object is created after the Page object for the master page is instantiated. At this point, ASP.NET interprets all the paths relative to the location of the master page. You could use the same technique to fix <a> tags that provide relative links to other pages.

You can also use the root path syntax and start your URL with the . character. For example, this <img> tag points unambiguously to the banner.jpg file in the MasterPages subfolder of the website:

```
<img src="./MasterPages/banner.jpg" runat="server" />
```

Unfortunately, this syntax works only with server-side controls. If you want a similar effect with ordinary HTML, you need to change the link to a full relative path incorporating your domain name. This makes for ugly, unportable HTML, and it's not recommended.

Applying Master Pages Through a Configuration File

It's worth noting that you can also apply a master page to all the pages in your website at once using the web.config file. All you need to do is add the <pages> attribute and set its masterPageFile attribute, as shown here:

```
<configuration>
  <system.web>
    <pages masterPageFile ="SiteTemplate.master"/>
  </system.web>
</configuration>
```

The problem is that this approach tends to be quite inflexible. Any web page you have that doesn't play by the rules (for example, that includes a root <html> tag or defines a content region that doesn't correspond to a ContentPlaceHolder) will be automatically broken. If you must use this feature, don't apply it site-wide. Instead, create a subfolder for your content pages, and create a web.config file in just that subfolder to apply the master page.

■ **Note** Even if a master page is applied through the web.config, you have no guarantee that an individual page won't override your setting by supplying a MasterPageFile attribute in the Page directive. And if the MasterPageFile attribute is specified with a blank string, the page won't have any master page at all, regardless of what the web.config file specifies.

Advanced Master Pages

Using what you've learned, you can create and reuse master pages across your website. However, you can use other tricks and techniques to refine the way master pages work. In the following sections, you'll see how to interact with a master page from your content, how to set master pages dynamically, and how to nest one master page inside another.

Interacting with the Master Page Class

One issue with master pages is how their model assumes you either want to copy something exactly across every page (in which case you include it in the master page) or vary it on each and every page (in which case you add a ContentPlaceHolder for it and include the information in each content page). This distinction works well for many pages, but it runs into trouble if you want to allow a more nuanced interaction between the master page and content pages.

For example, you might want the master page to give a choice of three display modes. The content page would then choose the correct display mode, which would change the appearance of the master page. However, the content page shouldn't have complete freedom to change the master page indiscriminately. Instead, anything other than these three presets should be disallowed.

To enable scenarios such as these, you need some level of programmatic interaction between the content page and the master page. This isn't too difficult, because you can access the current instance of your master page using the Page.Master property, as described in the previous section.

The first step in allowing interaction between your content page and master page is to add public properties or methods to your master page class. The content page can then set these properties or call these methods accordingly. For example, maybe you want to make the banner text customizable (as shown in a previous example) but you don't want to let the content page insert any type of content there. Instead, you want to restrict it to a single descriptive string. To accomplish this, you can add a server-side label control to the header and provide access to that control through a BannerText property in the master page class:

```
public string BannerText
{
    get { return lblTitleContent.Text; }
    set { lblTitleContent.Text = value; }
}
```

The content page can now change the text. The only caveat is that the Master property returns an object that's typed as the generic MasterPage class. You need to cast it to your specific master page class to get access to any custom members you've added.

```
protected void Page_Load(object sender, EventArgs e)
{
    SiteTemplate master =
      (SiteTemplate)Master;
    master.BannerText = "Content Page #1";
}
```

Another way to get strongly typed access to the master page is to add the MasterType directive to the content page. All you need to do is indicate the virtual path of the corresponding .master file:

```
<%@ MasterType VirtualPath="./SiteTemplate.master" %>
```

Now you can use simpler strongly typed code when you access the master page:

```
protected void Page_Load(object sender, EventArgs e)
{
    Master.BannerText = "Content Page #1";
}
```

You should note one point about these examples: when you navigate from one page to another, all the web-page objects are re-created. This means that even if you move to another content page that uses the same master page, ASP.NET creates a different instance of the master page object. As a result, the Text property of the Label control in the header is reset to its default value (a blank string) every time the user navigates to a new page. To change this behavior, you need to store the information in another location (such as a cookie) and write initialization code in the master page to check for it.

You can also get access to an individual control on a master page through brute force. The trick is to use the MasterPage.FindControl() method to search for the object you want based on its unique name. When you have the control, you can then modify it directly. Here's an example that uses this technique to look for a label:

```
Label lbl = Master.FindControl("lblTitleContent") as Label;
if (lbl != null)
{
    lbl.Text = "Content Page #1";
}
```

Of course, this type of interaction breaks all the rules of proper class-based design and encapsulation. If you really need to access a control in a master page, you are far better off wrapping it (or, ideally, just the properties you're interested in) by adding properties to your master page class. That way, the interaction between the content page and the master page is clear, documented, and loosely coupled. If your content page tinkers directly with the internals of another page, it's likely to lead to fragile code models with dependencies that break when you edit the master page.vb

Dynamically Setting a Master Page

Sometimes you might want to change your master page on the fly. This might occur in a couple of cases:

- Several types of users exist, and you want to adjust the complexity of the layout or the visible features according to the user. You may perform this customization based on accessibility considerations, available bandwidth, or user preferences.
- You are in partnership with another company, and you need your website to adjust itself to have a different look and layout accordingly. For example, you might cobrand your website, providing the same features with two or more different layouts.

Changing the master page programmatically is easy. All you need to do is set the Page.MasterPageFile property. The trick is that this step needs to be completed in the Page.Init event stage. After this point, attempting to set this property causes an exception.

You can implement this technique in much the same way that you implemented dynamic themes earlier in this chapter. However, this technique has a potential danger—a content page isn't necessarily compatible with an arbitrary master page. If your content page includes a Content tag that doesn't correspond to a ContentPlaceHolder in the master, an error will occur. To prevent this problem, you need to ensure that all the master pages you set dynamically include the same placeholders.

Nesting Master Pages

You can nest master pages so that one master page uses another master page. This is not used too often, but it could allow you to standardize your website to different degrees. For example, you might have two sections of your website. Each section might warrant its separate navigation controls. However, both sections may need the same header. In this case, you could create a top-level master page that adds the header. Here's an example:

```
<%@ Master Language="C#" AutoEventWireup="true"
    CodeFile="NestedMasterRoot.master.cs" Inherits="NestedMasterRoot" %>

<html xmlns="http://www.w3.org/1999/xhtml" >
<head runat="server">
    <title>Untitled Page</title>
</head>
<body style="background: #ccffff">
    <form id="form1" runat="server">
    <div>
        <h1>The Root</h1>
        <asp:ContentPlaceHolder  id="RootContent" runat="server">
        </asp:ContentPlaceHolder >
    </div>
    </form>
</body>
</html>
```

Next, you would create a second master page that uses the first master page (through the MasterPageFile attribute). This second master page gets the header from the first master page and adds the navigation controls in a panel on the left. Here's an example:

```
<%@ Master Language="C#" AutoEventWireup="true"
    CodeFile="NestedMasterSecondLevel.master.cs"
    Inherits="NestedMasterSecondLevel"
    MasterPageFile="~/NestedMasterRoot.master"%>

<asp:Content ID="Content1" ContentPlaceHolderID="RootContent" Runat="Server">
    <table style="background: #ccff00; width: 100%">
      <tr>
        <td colspan="2">
          <h2>The Second Level</h2>
        </td>
      <tr>
        <td style="width: 200px"></td>
        <td style="background: white">
          <asp:ContentPlaceHolder id="NestedContent" runat="server">
          </asp:ContentPlaceHolder>
        </td>
      </tr>
    </table>
</asp:Content>
```

■ **Tip** You don't need to add the MasterPageFile attribute to your master page by hand. Instead, you can use the Select Master Page check box when creating the second master page, just as you can when creating a new web page.

Presumably, your goal would be to create more than one version of the second master page—one for each section of your website. These would acquire the same standard header.

Finally, each content page could use one of the second-level master pages to standardize its layout:

```
<%@ Page Language="C#" MasterPageFile="./NestedMasterSecondLevel.master"
    AutoEventWireup="true" CodeFile="NestedContentPage.aspx.cs"
    Inherits="NestedContentPage" Title="Nested Content Page" %>

<asp:Content ID="Content1" ContentPlaceHolderID="NestedContent" Runat="Server">
<br />This is the nested content!<br />
</asp:Content>
```

Figure 16-16 shows the result.

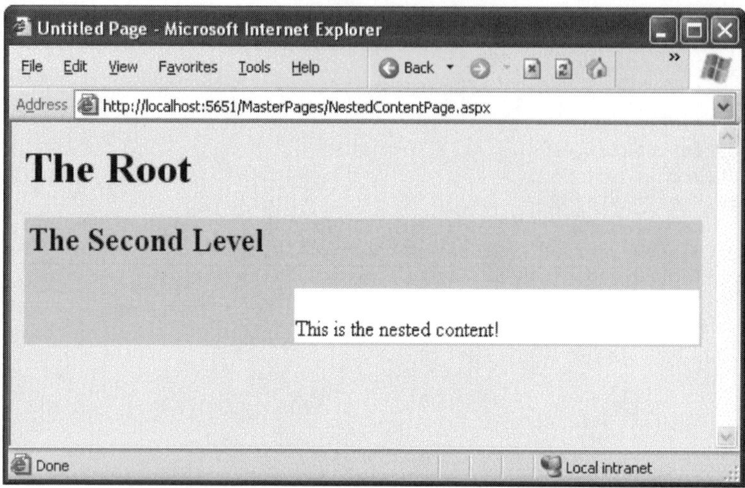

Figure 16-16. *A content page that uses a nested master page*

You can use as many layers of nested master pages as you want. However, be careful when implementing this approach—although it sounds like a nifty way to make a modular design, it can tie you down more than you realize. For example, you'll need to reword your master page hierarchy if you decide later that the two website sections need similar but slightly different headers. For that reason, it might be better to use only one level of master pages and copy the few common elements. In most cases, you won't be creating many master pages, so this won't add a significant amount of duplication.

Summary

In this chapter, you tackled two key enhancements that were first introduced in ASP.NET 2.0—themes and master pages. Both of these features remain unchanged in ASP.NET 4. Armed with these tools, you can create a complete web application that has a unified look and feel and a consistent layout.

In the next chapter, you'll learn how to add navigation controls to the mix.

CHAPTER 17

■ ■ ■

Website Navigation

Navigation is a fundamental component of any website. Although it's easy enough to transfer the user from one page to another, creating a unified system of navigation that works across an entire website takes more effort. While you could build your own navigation system with a few links (and a lot of work), ASP.NET has a built-in navigation system that makes it easy.

In this chapter, you'll tackle three core topics:

- **The MultiView and Wizard controls:** These let you boil down a series of steps into a single page. With the help of these controls, you can combine several pages of work into one place, simplifying your navigation needs.
- **The site map model:** This lets you define the navigation structure of your website and bind it directly to rich controls. You'll also learn how to extend this framework to support different types of controls and different site map storage locations.
- **The rich navigational controls:** These include the TreeView and Menu. Although these controls aren't limited to navigation, they're an ideal match. In this chapter, you'll learn about their wide range of features.

Using these controls, the site map model, and master pages, you can build a complete navigation system with minimal effort. Best of all, ASP.NET cleanly separates the data (the information about the structure of your website) from its implementation (the navigational controls). That means you can reorganize, replace, and rename web pages without disturbing your website or editing any code. All you need to do is make the corresponding changes to your application's site map file.

Navigation Changes in ASP.NET 4

In this chapter, you'll find one significant new feature and two minor refinements. They are:

- **Routing:** First introduced as a part of ASP.NET MVC, it's now possible to use routing to process URLs and redirect requests to a suitable web form. The chief advantage is supporting a clearer, more logical URL system, which allows search engines to discover and index the content of your web site more easily. You'll learn more in the "URL Mapping and Routing" section.
- **A more flexible Wizard:** The Wizard control sports a new LayoutTemplate that gives you even more control if you want to replace its built-in layout with your own design. You'll get the details in the "Wizard Styles, Templates, and Layout" section.
- **A more standardized Menu:** The Menu control now creates its output using a list with a proper set of CSS styles, rather than an HTML table. You'll learn more in the "Menu Templates" section.

Pages with Multiple Views

Most websites split tasks across several pages. For example, if you want to add an item to your shopping cart and take it to the checkout in an e-commerce site, you'll need to jump from one page to another. This is the cleanest approach, and it's easy to program—provided you use some sort of state management technique (from query strings to session state) to transfer information from one page to another.

In other situations, you might want to embed the code for several different pages inside a single page. For example, you might want to provide several views of the same data (such as a grid-based view and a chart-based view) and allow the user to switch from one view to the other without leaving the page. Or, you might want to handle a small multistep task (such as supplying user information for an account sign-up process), without worrying about how to transfer the relevant information between web pages.

■ **Tip** From the user's point of view, it probably doesn't make much difference whether you use multiple pages or a page with multiple views. In a well-designed site, the only difference the user will see is that the multiple view approach keeps the same URL. The prime difference is the coding model. With multiple pages, you get improved separation but extra work in determining how the pages should interact (the way they share or transmit information). With multiple views, you lose your separation but get easier coding for small, nondivisible tasks.

In ASP.NET 1.*x*, the only way to model a page with multiple views was to add several Panel controls to a page so that each panel represents a single view or a single step. You could then set the Visible property of each Panel so that you see only one at a time. The problem with this approach is that it clutters your page with extra code for managing the panels. Additionally, it's not very robust—with a minor mistake, you can end up with two panels showing at the same time.

With ASP.NET 4, there's no need to design your own multiple view system from scratch. Instead, you can use one of two higher-level controls that make these designs much easier—the MultiView and the Wizard.

The MultiView Control

The MultiView is the simpler of the two multiple view controls. Essentially, the MultiView gives you a way to declare multiple views and show only one at a time. It has no default user interface—you get only whatever HTML and controls you add. The MultiView is equivalent to the custom panel approach explained earlier.

Creating a MultiView is suitably straightforward. You add the <asp:MultiView> tag to your .aspx page file and then add one <asp:View> tag inside it for each separate view.

```
<asp:MultiView ID="MultiView1" runat="server">
  <asp:View ID="View1" runat="server">...</asp:View>
  <asp:View ID="View2" runat="server">...</asp:View>
  <asp:View ID="View3" runat="server">...</asp:View>
</asp:MultiView>
```

Inside the <asp:View> tag, you add the HTML and web controls for that view.

```
<asp:MultiView ID="MultiView1" runat="server" ActiveViewIndex="0">
  <asp:View ID="View1" runat="server">
    <b>Showing View #1<br />
    <br />
    <asp:Image ID="Image1" runat="server"
     ImageUrl="./cookies.jpg" /></b>
  </asp:View>
  <asp:View ID="View2" runat="server">
    <b>Showing View #2</b><br />
    <br />
    Text content.
  </asp:View>
  <asp:View ID="View3" runat="server">
    <b>Showing View #3</b><br />
    <br />
    <asp:Calendar ID="Calendar1" runat="server"></asp:Calendar>
  </asp:View>
</asp:MultiView>
```

■ **Tip** You can also add views programmatically (like any other control) by instantiating a new view object and adding it to the MultiView with the Add() or AddAt() methods of the Views collection.

Visual Studio shows all your views at design time, one after the other (see Figure 17-1). You can edit these regions in the same way you design any other part of the page.

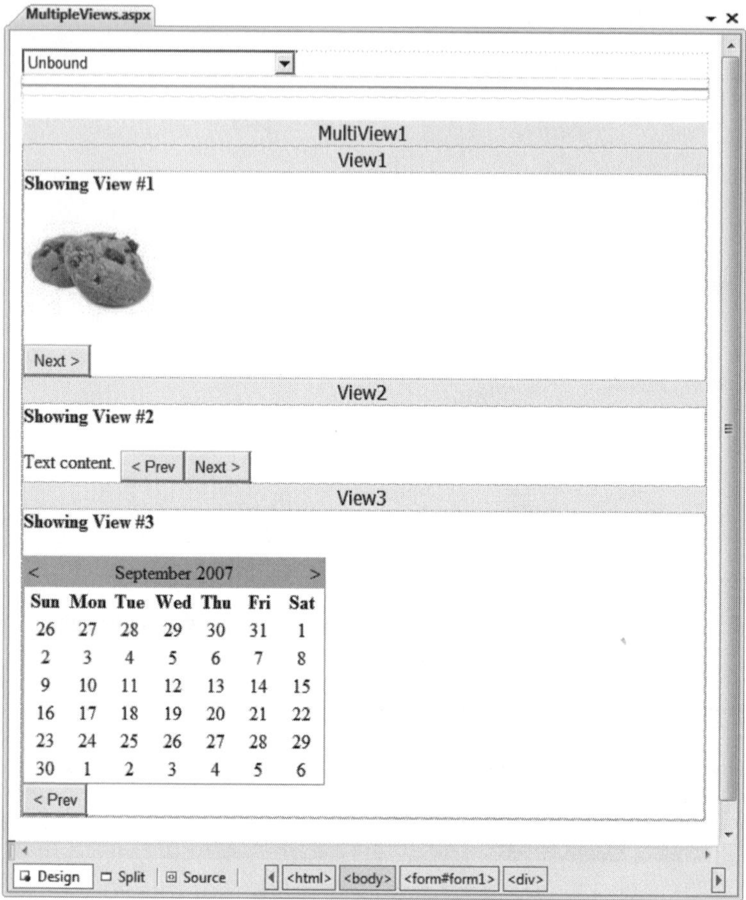

Figure 17-1. Designing multiple views

■ **Note** You can get a similar effect to the MultiView using the Accordion control, which is a part of the ASP.NET AJAX Control Toolkit. The Accordion control allows you to create a group of collapsible panels. The user clicks a header to expand one of the panels and close all the others. The Accordion has dramatically different underpinnings than the MultiView, and does most of its work on the client. You'll learn more about the Accordion in Chapter 30.

The MultiView.ActiveViewIndex determines what view will be shown. This is the only view that's rendered in the page. The default ActiveViewIndex value is -1, which means no view is shown. One option is to use a list control that lets users choose from the full list of views. Here's some sample code that binds the list of views to a list box:

```
protected void Page_Load(object sender, EventArgs e)
{
    if (!Page.IsPostBack)
    {
        DropDownList1.DataSource = MultiView1.Views;
        DropDownList1.DataTextField = "ID";
        DropDownList1.DataBind();
     }
}
```

And here's the code that sets the current view based on the list index:

```
protected void DropDownList1_SelectedIndexChanged(object sender, EventArgs e)
{
    MultiView1.ActiveViewIndex = DropDownList1.SelectedIndex;
}
```

Figure 17-2 shows the result.

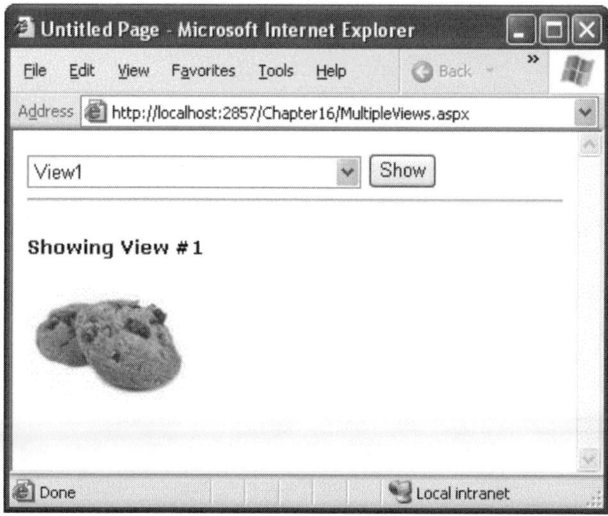

Figure 17-2. Switching views with a list control

If you want to give the views more descriptive names, you simply fill the list box by hand. Just make sure the order matches the order of views.

There's actually no need to write this code, because the MultiView includes some built-in smarts. Like some of the rich data controls, the MultiView recognizes specific command names in button controls. (A button control is any control that implements IButtonControl, including the Button, ImageButton, and LinkButton.) If you add a button control to the view that uses one of these recognized command names, the button will have some automatic functionality. Table 17-1 lists all the recognized command names. Each command name also has a corresponding static field in the MultiView class, so you can easily get the right command name if you choose to set it programmatically.

Table 17-1. Recognized Command Names for the MultiView

Command Name	MultiView Field	Description
PrevView	PreviousViewCommandName	Moves to the previous view.
NextView	NextViewCommandName	Moves to the next view.
SwitchViewByID	SwitchViewByIDCommandName	Moves to the view with a specific ID (string name). The ID is taken from the CommandArgument property of the button control.
SwitchViewByIndex	SwitchViewByIndexCommandName	Moves to the view with a specific numeric index. The index is taken from the CommandArgument property of the button control.

To try this, add this button to your first two views (remembering to change the ID for each one):

```
<asp:Button ID="cmdNext" runat="server" Text="Next >" CommandName="NextView" />
```

And add this button to your second and third views:

```
<asp:Button ID="cmdPrev" runat="server" Text="< Prev" CommandName="PrevView" />
```

Finally, make sure the drop-down list shows the correct view when you use the buttons by adding this code to handle the MultiView.ActiveViewIndexChanged event:

```
protected void MultiView1_ActiveViewChanged(object sender, EventArgs e)
{
    DropDownList1.SelectedIndex = MultiView1.ActiveViewIndex;
}
```

The Performance of MultiView Pages

The most important detail you need to know about the MultiView is that unlike the rich data controls (the GridView, FormsView, and so on), the MultiView is *not* a naming container. This means that if you add a control named textBox1 to a view, you can't add another control named textBox1 to another view. In fact, in terms of the page model, there's no real difference between controls you add to a view and controls in the rest of the page. Either way, the controls you create will be accessible through member variables in your page class. This means it's easy to configure a control in the second view when an event is raised by a control in the first view.

As a result, the pages you create using the MultiView tend to be heavier than normal pages. That's because the entire control model—including the controls from every view—is created on every postback and persisted to view state. For the most part, this won't be a significant factor, unless you are manipulating a large number of controls programmatically (in which case you might want to turn EnableViewState off for these controls) or you are using several data sources. For example, if you have three views and each view has a different data source control, each time the page is posted back all three data source controls will perform their queries, and every view will be bound, including those that aren't currently visible. To avoid this overhead, you can use the techniques described in Chapter 9, such as leaving your controls unbound and binding them programmatically, or canceling the binding process for views that aren't currently visible.

Of course, not all uses of the MultiView need to involve data binding. The perfect scenario for the MultiView is an extended set of input controls—for example, an online survey form that's split into separate views just to spare the user a lot of scrolling. This example works well with the MultiView because at the end when the survey is complete, you can read all the data from the controls of every view.

Now you can move from view to view using the buttons (see Figure 17-3).

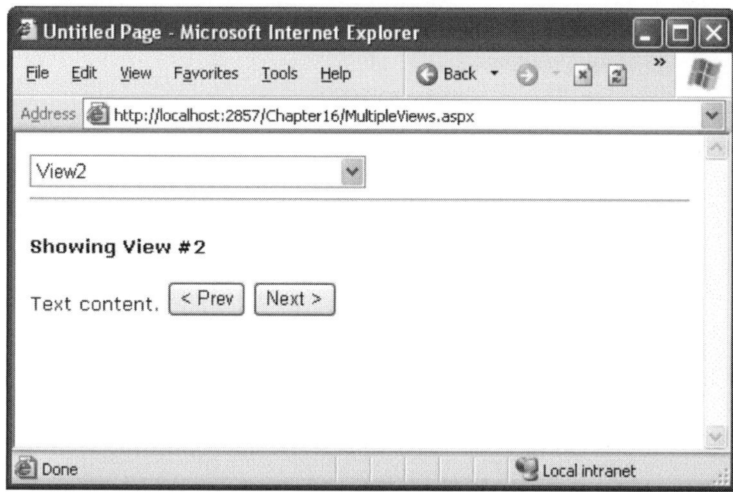

Figure 17-3. Switching views with recognized command names

The Wizard Control

The Wizard control is a more glamorous version of the MultiView control. It also supports showing one of several views at a time, but it includes a fair bit of built-in yet customizable behavior, including navigation buttons, a sidebar with step links, styles, and templates.

Usually, wizards represent a single task, and the user moves linearly through them, moving from the current step to the one immediately following it (or the one immediately preceding it in the case of a correction). The ASP.NET Wizard control also supports nonlinear navigation, which means it allows you to decide to ignore a step based on the information the user supplies.

By default, the Wizard control supplies navigation buttons and a sidebar with links for each step on the left. You can hide the sidebar by setting the Wizard.DisplaySideBar property to false. Usually, you'll take this step if you want to enforce strict step-by-step navigation and prevent the user from jumping out of sequence. You supply the content for each step using any HTML or ASP.NET controls. Figure 17-4 shows the region where you can add content to an out-of-the-box Wizard instance.

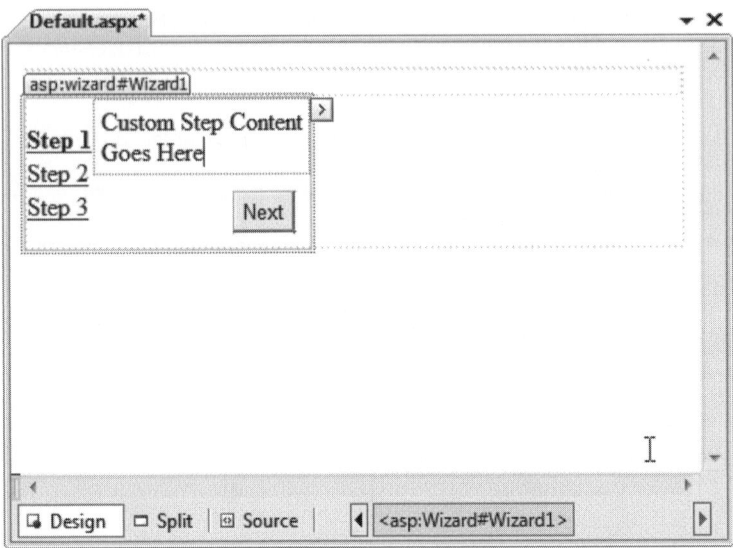

Figure 17-4. The region for step content

Wizard Steps

To create a wizard in ASP.NET, you simply define the steps and their content using <asp:WizardStep> tags. Each step takes a few basic pieces of information. The most important ones are listed in Table 17-2.

Table 17-2. WizardStep Properties

Property	Description
Title	The descriptive name of the step. This name is used for the text of the links in the sidebar.
StepType	The type of step, as a value from the WizardStepType enumeration. This value determines the type of navigation buttons that will be shown for this step. Choices include Start (shows a Next button), Step (shows Next and Previous buttons), Finish (shows a Finish and Previous button), Complete (show no buttons and hides the sidebar, if it's enabled), and Auto (the step type is inferred from the position in the collection). The default is Auto, which means that the first step is Start, the last step is Finish, and all other steps are Step.
AllowReturn	Indicates whether the user can return to this step. If false, once the user has passed this step, the user will not be able to return. The sidebar link for this step will have no effect, and the Previous button of the following step will either skip this step or be hidden completely (depending on the AllowReturn value of the preceding steps).

The following wizard contains four steps that, taken together, represent a simple survey. The StepType adds a Complete step at the end, with a summary. The navigation buttons and sidebar links are added automatically.

```
<asp:Wizard ID="Wizard1" runat="server" Width="467px"
 BackColor="#EFF3FB" BorderColor="#B5C7DE" BorderWidth="1px">
  <WizardSteps>
    <asp:WizardStep ID="WizardStep1" runat="server" Title="Personal">
      <h3>Personal Profile</h3>
      Preferred Programming Language:
      <asp:DropDownList ID="lstLanguage" runat="server">
        <asp:ListItem>C#</asp:ListItem>
        <asp:ListItem>VB</asp:ListItem>
        <asp:ListItem>J#</asp:ListItem>
        <asp:ListItem>Java</asp:ListItem>
        <asp:ListItem>C++</asp:ListItem>
        <asp:ListItem>C</asp:ListItem>
      </asp:DropDownList>
      <br />
    </asp:WizardStep>
    <asp:WizardStep ID="WizardStep2" runat="server" Title="Company">
      <h3>Company Profile</h3>
      Number of Employees: <asp:TextBox ID="txtEmpCount" runat="server"/>
      Number of Locations: <asp:TextBox ID="txtLocCount" runat="server"/>
    </asp:WizardStep>
    <asp:WizardStep ID="WizardStep3" runat="server" Title="Software">
      <h3>Software Profile</h3>
      Licenses Required:
      <asp:CheckBoxList ID="lstTools" runat="server">
        <asp:ListItem>Visual Studio 2008</asp:ListItem>
        <asp:ListItem>Office 2007</asp:ListItem>
        <asp:ListItem>Windows Server 2008</asp:ListItem>
        <asp:ListItem>SQL Server 2008</asp:ListItem>
      </asp:CheckBoxList>
    </asp:WizardStep>
    <asp:WizardStep ID="Complete" runat="server" Title="Complete"
     StepType="Complete">
      <br />
      Thank you for completing this survey.<br />
      Your products will be delivered shortly.<br />
    </asp:WizardStep>
  </WizardSteps>
</asp:Wizard>
```

Figure 17-5 shows the wizard steps.

***Figure 17-5.** A wizard with four steps*

Unlike the MultiView control, you can see only one step at a time on the design surface of your web page in Visual Studio. To choose which step you're currently designing, select it from the smart tag, as shown in Figure 17-6. But be warned—every time you do, Visual Studio changes the Wizard.ActiveStepIndex property to the step you choose. Make sure you set this back to 0 before you run your application so it starts at the first step.

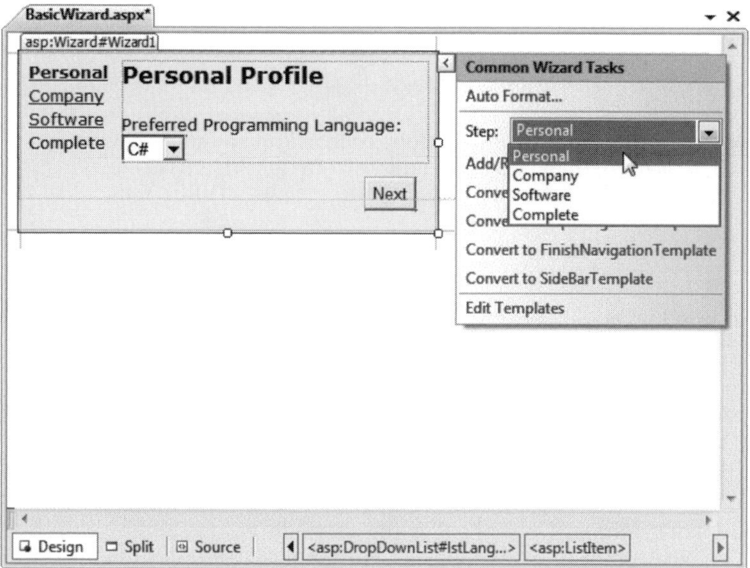

Figure 17-6. Designing a step

■ **Note** Remember, when you add controls to separate steps on a wizard, they are all instantiated and persisted in view state, regardless of the current step. If you need to slim down a complex wizard, you'll need to split it into separate pages, use the Server.Transfer() method to move from one page to the next, and tolerate a less elegant programming model.

Wizard Events

You can write the code that underpins your wizard by responding to several events (as listed in Table 17-3).

Table 17-3. Wizard Events

Event	Description
ActiveStepChanged	Occurs when the control switches to a new step (either because the user has clicked a navigation button or your code has changed the ActiveStepIndex property).
CancelButtonClick	Occurs when the Cancel button is clicked. The cancel button is not shown by default, but you can add it to every step by setting the Wizard.DisplayCancelButton property. Usually, a cancel button exits the wizard. If you don't have any cleanup code to perform, just set the CancelDestinationPageUrl property, and the wizard will take care of the redirection automatically.

Event	Description
FinishButtonClick	Occurs when the Finish button is clicked.
NextButtonClick and PreviousButtonClick	Occurs when the Next or Previous button is clicked on any step. However, because there is more than one way to move from one step to the next, it's better to handle the ActiveStepChanged event.
SideBarButtonClick	Occurs when a button in the sidebar area is clicked.

On the whole, two wizard programming models exist:

Commit-as-you-go: This makes sense if each wizard step wraps an atomic operation that can't be reversed. For example, if you're processing an order that involves a credit card authorization followed by a final purchase, you can't allow the user to step back and edit the credit card number. To support this model, you set the AllowReturn property to false on some or all steps, and you respond to the ActiveStepChanged event to commit changes for each step.

Commit-at-the-end: This makes sense if each wizard step is collecting information for an operation that's performed only at the end. For example, if you're collecting user information and plan to generate a new account once you have all the information, you'll probably allow a user to make changes midway through the process. You execute your code for generating the new account when the wizard is finished by reacting to the FinishButtonClick event.

To implement commit-at-the-end with the current example, just respond to the FinishButtonClick event. Here's an example that simply displays every selection in the summary:

```
protected void Wizard1_FinishButtonClick(object sender, WizardNavigationEventArgs e)
{
    StringBuilder sb = new StringBuilder();
    sb.Append("<b>You chose: <br />");
    sb.Append("Programming Language: ");
    sb.Append(lstLanguage.Text);
    sb.Append("<br />Total Employees: ");
    sb.Append(txtEmpCount.Text);
    sb.Append("<br />Total Locations: ");
    sb.Append(txtLocCount.Text);
    sb.Append("<br />Licenses Required: ");
    foreach (ListItem item in lstTools.Items)
    {
        if (item.Selected)
        {
            sb.Append(item.Text);
            sb.Append(" ");
        }
    }
    sb.Append("</b>");
    lblSummary.Text = sb.ToString();
}
```

For this to work, you must add a Label control named lblSummary. In this example, lblSummary is placed in the final summary step.

■ **Tip** If you want to find out the path the user has taken through your wizard, you can use the Wizard.GetHistory() method. It returns a collection of WizardStepBase objects that have been accessed so far, arranged in reverse chronological order. That means the first item in the collection represents the previous step, the second item represents the step before that, and so on.

Wizard Styles, Templates, and Layout

Without a doubt, the Wizard control's greatest strength is the way it lets you customize its appearance. This means that if you want the basic model (a multistep process with navigation buttons and various events), you aren't locked into the default user interface.

Depending on how radically you want to change the wizard, you have different options. For less dramatic modifications, you can set various top-level properties. For example, you can control the colors, fonts, spacing, and border style, as you can with any ASP.NET control. You can also tweak the appearance of every button. For example, to change the Next button, you can use the following properties: StepNextButtonType (use a button, link, or clickable image), StepNextButtonText (customize the text for a button or link), StepNextButtonImageUrl (set the image for an image button), and StepNextButtonStyle (use a style from a stylesheet). You can also add a header using the HeaderText property.

More control is available through styles. You can use styles to apply formatting options to various portions of the Wizard control just as you can use styles to format different parts of rich data controls such as the GridView. Table 17-4 lists all the styles you can use. As with other style-based controls, more specific style settings (such as SideBarStyle) override more general style settings (such as ControlStyle) when they conflict. Similarly, StartNextButtonStyle overrides NavigationButtonStyle on the first step.

Table 17-4. *Wizard Styles*

Style	Description
ControlStyle	Applies to all sections of the Wizard control
HeaderStyle	Applies to the header section of the Wizard control, which is visible only if you set some text in the HeaderText property
SideBarStyle	Applies to the sidebar area of the Wizard control
SideBarButtonStyle	Applies to just the buttons in the sidebar
StepStyle	Applies to the section of the control where you define the step content
NavigationStyle	Applies to the bottom area of the control where the navigation buttons are displayed
NavigationButtonStyle	Applies to just the navigation buttons in the navigation area
StartNextButtonStyle	Applies to the next navigation button on the first step (when StepType is Start)

Style	Description
StepNextButtonStyle	Applies to the next navigation button on intermediate steps (when StepType is Step)
StepPreviousButtonStyle	Applies to the previous navigation button on intermediate steps (when StepType is Step)
FinishPreviousButtonStyle	Applies to the previous navigation button on the last step (when StepType is Finish)
CancelButtonStyle	Applies to the cancel button, if you have Wizard.DisplayCancel-Button set to true

Finally, if you can't get the level of customization you want through properties and styles, you can use templates to completely define the appearance of the Wizard control. Ordinarily, you can supply the markup only for the step content (as shown in Figure 17-1). With templates, you supply the markup for one of the other regions, such as the header, sidebar, or buttons. All templates are declared separately from the step content. Figure 17-7 shows where templates fit in.

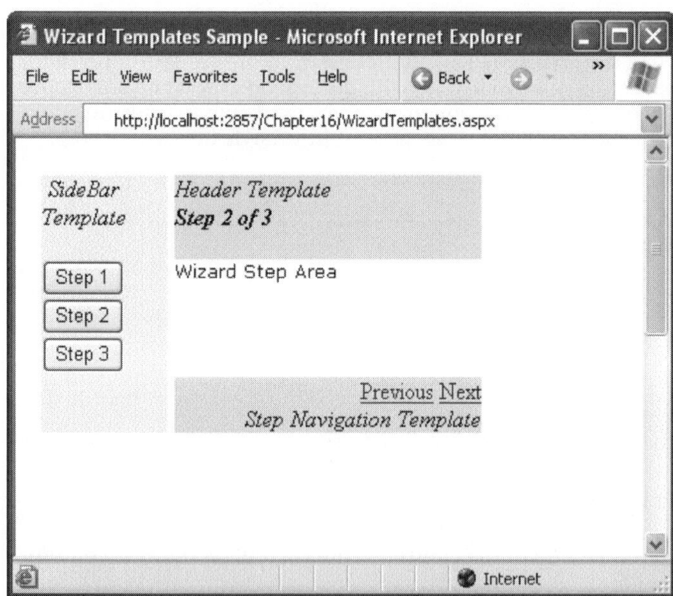

Figure 17-7. Template regions in the Wizard control

Table 17-5 shows the full list of templates.

Table 17-5. Wizard Templates

Style	Description
HeaderTemplate	Defines the content of the header region
SideBarTemplate	Defines the sidebar, which typically includes navigation links for each step
StartNavigationTemplate	Defines the navigation buttons for the first step (when StepType is Start)
StepNavigationTemplate	Defines the navigation buttons for intermediate steps (when StepType is Step)
FinishNavigationTemplate	Defines the navigation buttons for the final step (when StepType is Finish)
LayoutTemplate	Defines the overall arrangement of the header, sidebar, step area, and navigation buttons.

For example, here's a header template that uses a data binding expression to show the title of the current step:

```
<asp:Wizard ID="Wizard1" runat="server" ...>
  <WizardSteps>
    ...
  </WizardSteps>

  <HeaderTemplate>
    <i>Header Template</i> -
    <b><%= Wizard1.ActiveStep.Title %></b>
    <br /><br />
  </HeaderTemplate>
</asp:Wizard>
```

You can also add the following templates to customize the navigation buttons. This example keeps the standard buttons (by declaring them explicitly) and adds a piece of italicized text so you can see when each template is being used.

```
<StartNavigationTemplate>
  <i>StartNavigationTemplate</i><br />
  <asp:Button ID="StartNextButton" runat="server" Text="Next"
   CommandName="MoveNext" />
</StartNavigationTemplate>

<StepNavigationTemplate>
  <i>StepNavigationTemplate</i><br />
  <asp:Button ID="StepPreviousButton" runat="server" CausesValidation="False"
   CommandName="MovePrevious"
  Text="Previous" />
```

```
    <asp:Button ID="StepNextButton" runat="server" Text="Next"
     CommandName="MoveNext" />
  </StepNavigationTemplate>

  <FinishNavigationTemplate>
    <i>FinishNavigationTemplate</i><br />
    <asp:Button ID="FinishPreviousButton" runat="server" CausesValidation="False"
      Text="Previous" CommandName="MovePrevious" />
    <asp:Button ID="FinishButton" runat="server" Text="Finish"
     CommandName="MoveComplete" />
  </FinishNavigationTemplate>
```

The secret to using templates is making sure you use the right command names so that the Wizard control will hook up the standard logic. Otherwise, you'll need to implement the navigation and sequencing code, which is tedious and error-prone. For example, clicking on a button with a command name of MoveNext automatically moves to the next step. If you are unsure about the correct command name to use, you can use a convenient shortcut. Select the Wizard control in Visual Studio, and choose one of the template generation links in the smart tag, such as Convert to StartNavigationTemplate. When you do, Visual Studio inserts a template that duplicates the default button appearance and behavior.

■ **Note** You can use the validation controls in a Wizard without any problem. If the validation controls detect invalid data, they will prevent the user from clicking any of the sidebar links (to jump to another step) and they will prevent the user from continuing by clicking the Next button. However, by default the Previous button has its CausesValidation property set to false, which means the user *will* be allowed to step back to the previous step. If this isn't the behavior you want, you can create your own custom template and set the CausesValidation property of your controls accordingly.

Finally, you can use the LayoutTemplate to break out of the tabular structure shown in Figure 17-7. Essentially, the LayoutTemplate allows you to tell ASP.NET how to position the other templates relative to each other. You insert each template using a PlaceHolder control with the right name (headerPlaceholder, sideBarPlaceholder, wizardStepPlaceholder, and navigationPlaceholder). For example, if you simply want to stack the header at the top, put the sidebar underneath, put the step section under that, and add the navigation buttons at the bottom, all with no additional markup, you would configure the LayoutTemplate like this:

```
<LayoutTemplate>
  <asp:PlaceHolder ID="headerPlaceholder" runat="server" />
  <asp:PlaceHolder ID="sideBarPlaceholder" runat="server" />
  <asp:PlaceHolder id="wizardStepPlaceholder" runat="server" />
  <asp:PlaceHolder id="navigationPlaceholder" runat="server" />
</LayoutTemplate>
```

To get a more sophisticated layout, you would arrange the individual Placeholder objects in the cells of a table or in <div> elements that you position with CSS style attributes.

Site Maps

If your website has more than a handful of pages, you'll probably need some sort of navigation system to let the user move from one page to the next. As you saw in Chapter 16, you can use master pages to define a template for your site that includes a navigation bar. However, it's still up to you to fill this navigation bar with content.

Obviously, you can use the ASP.NET toolkit of controls to implement almost any navigation system, but it still requires you to perform all the hard work. Fortunately, ASP.NET includes a set of navigation features that you can use to dramatically simplify the task.

As with all the best ASP.NET features, ASP.NET navigation is flexible, configurable, and pluggable. It consists of three components:

- A way to define the navigational structure of your website. This part is the XML site map, which is (by default) stored in a file.
- A convenient way to parse the site map file and convert its information into a suitable object model. This part is performed by the SiteMapDataSource control and the XmlSiteMapProvider.
- A way to use the site map information to display the user's current position and give the user the ability to easily move from one place to another. This part is provided through the controls you bind to the SiteMapDataSource control, which can include breadcrumb links, lists, menus, and trees.

You can customize or extend each of these ingredients separately. For example, if you want to change the appearance of your navigation controls, you simply need to bind different controls to the SiteMapDataSource. On the other hand, if you want to read a different format of site map information or read it from a different location, you need to change your site map provider.

Figure 17-8 shows how these pieces fit together.

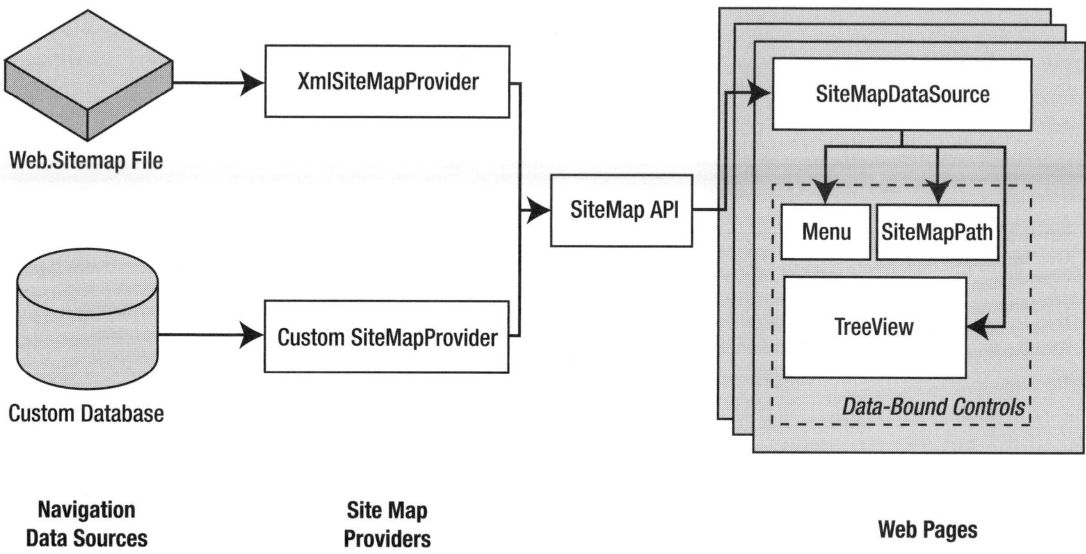

Figure 17-8. ASP.NET navigation with site maps

Defining a Site Map

The starting point in site map-based navigation is the site map provider. ASP.NET ships with a single site map provider, named XmlSiteMapProvider, which is able to retrieve site map information from an XML file. If you want to retrieve a site map from another location or in a custom format, you'll need to create your own site map provider—a topic covered in the section "Creating a Custom SiteMapProvider."

The XmlSiteMapProvider looks for a file named Web.sitemap in the root of the virtual directory. Like all site map providers, its task is to extract the site map data and create the corresponding SiteMap object. This SiteMap object is then made available to other controls through the SiteMapDataSource.

To try this, you need to begin by creating a Web.sitemap file and defining the website structure using the <siteMap> and <siteMapNode> elements. To add a site map using Visual Studio, choose Website ➤ Add New Item (or Project ➤ Add New Item in a web project), choose the Site Map template, and then click Add.

Here's the bare-bones structure that the site map file uses:

```
<siteMap xmlns="http://schemas.microsoft.com/AspNet/SiteMap-File-1.0">
  <siteMapNode>
    <siteMapNode>...</siteMapNode>
    <siteMapNode>...</siteMapNode>
    ...
  </siteMapNode>
</siteMap>
```

To be valid, your site map must begin with the root <siteMap> node, followed by a single <siteMapNode> element, representing the default home page. You can nest other <siteMapNode> elements in the root <siteMapNode> as many layers deep as you want. Each site map node should have a title, description, and URL, as shown here:

```
<siteMapNode title="Home" description="Home" url="./default.aspx">
```

In this example, the URL uses the ./ relative path syntax, which indicates the root of the web application. This style isn't necessary, but it is strongly recommended, as it ensures that your site map links are interpreted correctly regardless of the current folder.

You can now use the <siteMapNode> to create a site map. The only other restriction is that you can't create two site map nodes with the same URL.

■ **Note** The restriction to avoid duplicate URLs is not baked into the navigation system. It's simply required by the XmlSiteMapProvider, because the XmlSiteMapProvider uses the URL as a unique key. If you create your own site map provider or use a third-party provider, you may allow duplicate URLs and require separate key information. However, you can't get around the rule that every site must begin with one root node, because that's implemented in the base SiteMapProvider class. (As you'll see shortly, you still have options for tailoring the display of the site map tree, but you must start with a single home node.)

Here's a sample site map:

```
<siteMap xmlns="http://schemas.microsoft.com/AspNet/SiteMap-File-1.0">
  <siteMapNode title="Home" description="Home" url="./default.aspx">
    <siteMapNode title="Products" description="Our products"
```

```
      url="./Products.aspx">
      <siteMapNode title="Hardware" description="Hardware choices"
        url="./Hardware.aspx" />
      <siteMapNode title="Software" description="Software choices"
        url="./Software.aspx" />
    </siteMapNode>
    <siteMapNode title="Services" description="Services we offer"
        url="./Services.aspx">
        <siteMapNode title="Training" description="Training classes"
          url="./Training.aspx" />
        <siteMapNode title="Consulting" description="Consulting services"
          url="./Consulting.aspx" />
        <siteMapNode title="Support" description="Support plans"
          url="./Support.aspx" />
    </siteMapNode>
  </siteMapNode>
</siteMap>
```

■ **Tip** In this example, all the nodes have URLs, which means they are clickable (and take the user to specific pages). However, if you simply want to use these nodes as categories to arrange other links, just omit the url attribute. You'll still see the node in your bound controls; it just won't be rendered as a link.

Binding to a Site Map

Once you've defined the Web.sitemap file, you're ready to use it in a page. This is a great place to use master pages so that you can define the navigation controls as part of a template and reuse them with every page. Here's how you might define a basic structure in your master page that puts navigation controls on the left and creates the SiteMapDataSource that provides navigational information to other controls:

```
<form id="form1" runat="server">
  <table>
    <tr>
      <td style="width: 226px;vertical-align: top;">
        <!-- Navigation controls go here. -->
      </td>
      <td style="vertical-align: top;">
        <asp:ContentPlaceHolder id="ContentPlaceHolder1" runat="server" />
      </td>
    </tr>
  </table>
  <asp:SiteMapDataSource ID="SiteMapDataSource1" runat="server" />
</form>
```

Then you can create a child page with some simple static content:

```
<asp:Content ID="Content1" ContentPlaceHolderID="ContentPlaceHolder1"
  runat="Server">
    <br />
```

```
    <br />
    Default.aspx page (home).
</asp:Content>
```

The only remaining task is to choose the controls you want to use to display the site map data. One all-purpose solution is the TreeView control. You can add the TreeView and bind it to the SiteMapDataSource in the master page using the DataSourceID, as shown here:

```
<asp:TreeView ID="treeNav" runat="server" DataSourceID="SiteMapDataSource1" />
```

Alternatively, you could use the fly-out Menu control just as easily:

```
<asp:Menu ID="Menu1" runat="server" DataSourceID="SiteMapDataSource1" />
```

Figure 17-9 shows both options.

You can do a lot more to customize the appearance of your navigation controls and the processing of your site map. You'll consider these more advanced topics in the following sections.

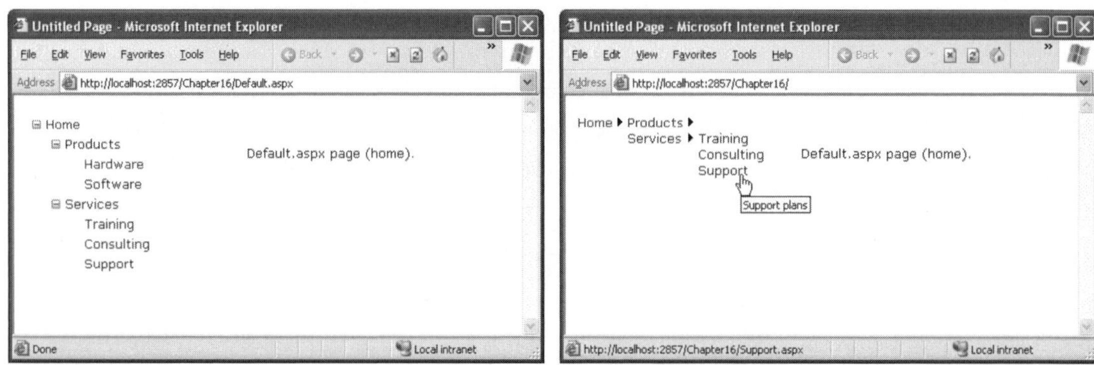

Figure 17-9. *TreeView and Menu navigation*

Breadcrumbs

ASP.NET actually defines three navigation controls: the TreeView, Menu, and SiteMapPath. The SiteMapPath provides *breadcrumb navigation*, which means it shows the user's current location and allows the user to navigate back up the hierarchy to a higher level using links. Figure 17-10 shows an example with a SiteMapPath control when the user is on the Software.aspx page. Using the SiteMapPath control, the user can return to the Products.aspx page or the Home.aspx page.

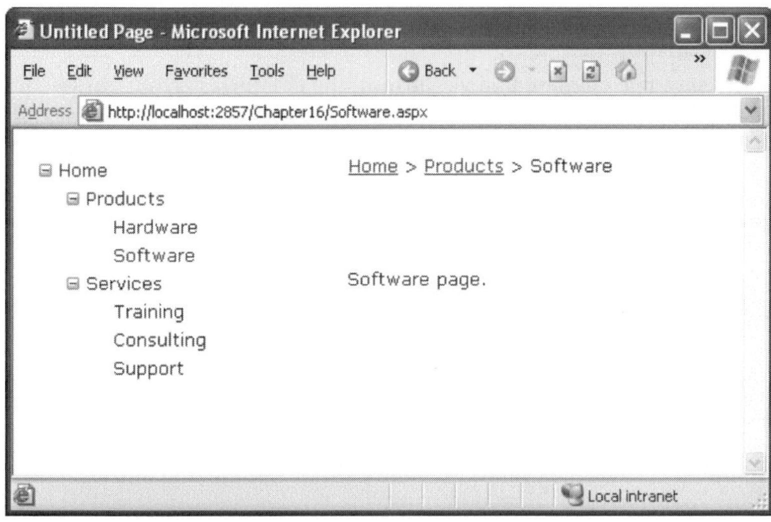

Figure 17-10. Breadcrumb navigation with SiteMapPath

The SiteMapPath has a subtle but important difference from other navigational controls such as the TreeView and Menu. Unlike these controls, the SiteMapPath works directly with the ASP.NET navigation model—in other words, it doesn't need to get its data through the SiteMapDataSource. As a result, you can use the SiteMapPath on pages that don't have a SiteMapDataSource, and changing the properties of the SiteMapDataSource won't affect the SiteMapPath.

Here's how you define the SiteMapPath control:

```
<asp:SiteMapPath ID="SiteMapPath1" runat="server" />
```

Typically, you'll place the SiteMapPath on your master page so it can be displayed on all your content pages.

The SiteMapPath control is useful both for an at-a-glance view that provides the current position and for a way to move up the hierarchy. However, you always need to combine it with other navigation controls that let the user move down the site map hierarchy.

The SiteMapPath control is also thoroughly customizable. Table 17-6 lists some of its most commonly configured properties.

***Table 17-6.** SiteMapPath Appearance-Related Properties*

Property	Description
ShowToolTips	Set this to false if you don't want the description text to appear when the user hovers over a part of the site map path.
ParentLevelsDisplayed	Sets the maximum number of parent levels that will be shown at once. By default, this setting is -1, which means all levels will be shown.
RenderCurrentNodeAsLink	If true, the portion of the page that indicates the current page is turned into a clickable link. By default, this is false because the user is already at the current page.

Property	Description
PathDirection	You have two choices: RootToCurrent (the default) and CurrentToRoot (which reverses the order of levels in the path).
PathSeparator	Indicates the characters that will be placed between each level in the path. The default is the greater-than (>) symbol. Another common path separator is the colon (:).

For even more control, you can configure the SiteMapPath control with styles or even redefine the controls and HTML with templates (see Table 17-7).

Table 17-7. *SiteMapPath Styles and Templates*

Style	Template	Applies To
NodeStyle	NodeTemplate	All parts of the path except the root and current node.
CurrentNodeStyle	CurrentNodeTemplate	The node representing the current page.
RootNodeStyle	RootNodeTemplate	The node representing the root. If the root node is the same as the current node, the current node template or styles are used.
PathSeparatorStyle	PathSeparatorTemplate	The separator between each node.

For example, the following SiteMapPath uses an arrow image as a separator and a fixed string of bold text for the root node. The final part of the path, which represents the current page, is italicized.

```
<asp:SiteMapPath ID="SiteMapPath1" runat="server">
  <PathSeparatorTemplate>
    <asp:Image ID="Image1" ImageUrl="./images/arrow.jpg"
     runat="server" GenerateEmptyAlternateText="True" />
  </PathSeparatorTemplate>
  <RootNodeTemplate>
    <b>Root</b>
  </RootNodeTemplate>
  <CurrentNodeTemplate>
    <i><asp:Label ID="Label1" runat="server" Text='<%# Eval("title") %>'>
     </asp:Label></i>
  </CurrentNodeTemplate>
</asp:SiteMapPath>
```

Notice how the CurrentNodeTemplate uses a data binding expression to bind to the title property of the current node. You can also get the url and description attributes that you declared in the site map file in the same way.

Showing a Portion of the Site Map

In the examples so far, the page controls replicate the structure of the site map file exactly. However, this isn't always what you want. For example, showing a large site map might distract the user from the portion of the website they're currently exploring. Or, the site map might have so many levels that the entire tree doesn't fit neatly into your web page.

In this situation, you can choose to cut down on the total amount of information and show just a portion of your site map. The following sections explain the different techniques you can use.

Skipping the Root Node

Ordinarily, the site map tree begins with the single root node from the site map. Often, this isn't what you want. It adds an extra layer of nesting to your site map structure, making it take more room), and introduces a top-level link that might not be very useful.

In the previous example (Figure 17-10), you may not like the way the Home node sticks out. To clean this up, you can set the SiteMapDataSource.ShowStartingNode property to false. If you still want to show the Home entry, modify the site map file so it defines the Home node in the first group of pages (just before Products). The real root node won't be shown, so it doesn't need any URL.

Here's the revised site map:

```
<siteMap xmlns="http://schemas.microsoft.com/AspNet/SiteMap-File-1.0">
  <siteMapNode title="Root" description="Root">
    <siteMapNode title="Home" description="Home" url="./default.aspx"/>
    <siteMapNode title="Products" description="Our products"
      url="./Products.aspx">
    ...
  </siteMapNode>
</siteMap>
```

Figure 17-11 shows the nicer result.

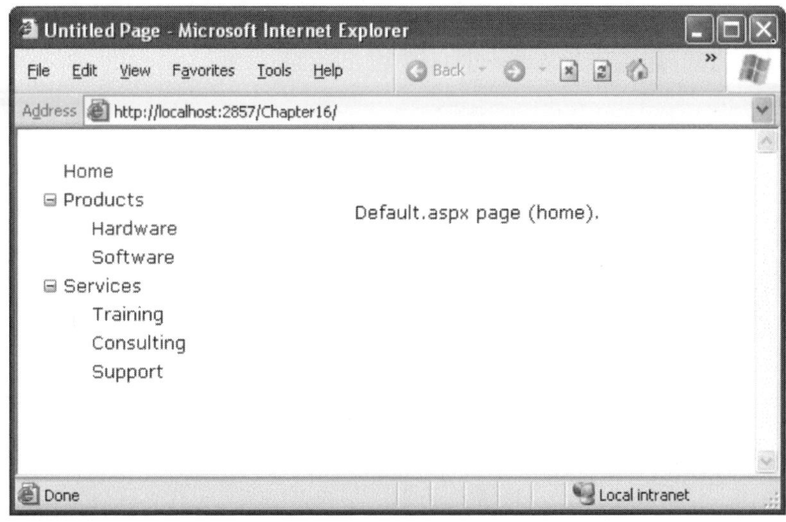

Figure 17-11. *A site map without the root node*

Starting from the Current Node

The previous example shows how you can skip the root node. Another option you have is to show just a portion of the complete site map, starting from the current node. For example, you might use a control such as the TreeView to show everything in the hierarchy starting from the current node. If the user wants to move up a level, they could use another control (such as a SiteMapPath).

To implement this design, simply set the SiteMapDataSource.StartFromCurrentNode property to true. The SiteMapPath will still show the complete hierarchy, because it doesn't use the SiteMapDataSource. (Thus, the user can click a link in the SiteMapPath to move up to a higher-level page.) However, bound navigational controls such as the TreeView will show only the pages beneath the current page, allowing the user to move down the hierarchy.

You still have the choice of whether to use ShowStartingNode, but now it determines whether you show the current node, because that's the starting point for the navigation tree. Figure 17-12 shows an example where both StartFromCurrentNode and ShowStartingNode are true. The current page is Products.aspx. The SiteMapPath shows higher-level pages, and the TreeView shows the nodes underneath the Products.aspx node (Hardware.aspx and Software.aspx).

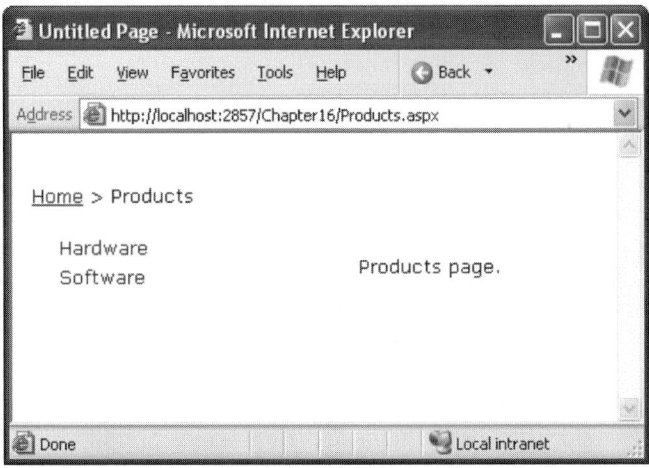

Figure 17-12. Binding to child nodes only

For this technique to work, ASP.NET must be able to find a page in the Web.sitemap file that matches the current URL. Otherwise, it won't know where the current position is, and it won't provide any navigation information to the bound controls.

Starting from a Specific Node

The SiteMapDataSource has two more properties that can help you configure the navigation tree: StartingNodeOffset and StartingNodeUrl.

StartingNodeUrl is the easiest to understand—it takes the URL of the node that should be the first node in the tree. This value must match the url attribute of the node in the Web.sitemap file exactly. For example, if you specify a StartingNodeUrl of "./home.aspx", then the first node in the tree is the Home node, and you will see only nodes underneath that node.

The StartingNodeUrl property is particularly useful if you want to vary between a small number of different site maps (say, fewer than ten). The ideal solution is to define multiple site map files and bind to the one you want to use. Unfortunately, the default XmlSiteMapProvider supports only a single site map file, so you need to find a different mechanism. In this case, the solution is to separate the different site maps into distinct branches of the Web.sitemap file.

For example, imagine you want to have a dealer section and an employee section on your website. You might split this into two different structures and define them both under different branches in the same file, like this:

```
<siteMap xmlns="http://schemas.microsoft.com/AspNet/SiteMap-File-1.0" >
  <siteMapNode title="Root" description="Root" url="./">
    <siteMapNode title="Dealer Home" description="Home" url="./default.aspx">
      ...
    </siteMapNode>
    <siteMapNode title="Employee Home" description="Home" url="./default_emp.aspx">
      ...
    </siteMapNode>
  </siteMapNode>
</siteMap>
```

Now, to bind the menu to the dealer view, you set the StartingNodeUrl property to "./default.aspx". You can do this programmatically or, more likely, by creating an entirely different master page and implementing it in all your dealer pages. In your employee pages, you set the StartingNodeUrl property to "./default_emp.aspx". This way, you'll show only the pages under the Employee Home branch of the site map.

You can even make your life easier by breaking a single site map into separate files using the siteMapFile attribute, like this:

```
<siteMap xmlns="http://schemas.microsoft.com/AspNet/SiteMap-File-1.0" >
  <siteMapNode title="Root" description="Root" url="./">
    <siteMapNode siteMapFile="Dealers.sitemap" />
    <siteMapNode siteMapFile="Employees.sitemap" />
  </siteMapNode>
</siteMap>
```

Even with this technique, you're still limited to a single site map tree, and it always starts with the Web.sitemap file. However, you can manage your site map more easily because you can factor some of its content into separate files. (You can also use security trimming, which is discussed later in the "Security Trimming" section, to create user-specific, personalized site maps.)

■ **Note** This technique is greatly limited because the XmlSiteMapProvider doesn't allow duplicate URLs. That means there's no way to reuse the same page in more than one branch of a site map. Although you can try to work around this problem by creating different URLs that are equivalent (for example, by adding extra query string parameters on the end), this raises more headaches. If these limitations won't work in your scenario, the best approach is to design your own site map provider.

The SiteMapDataSource.StartingNodeOffset property takes the most getting used to. It takes an integer that instructs the SiteMapDataSource to move that many levels down the tree (if the number is positive) or up the tree (if the number is negative). The important detail that's often misunderstood is that when the SiteMapDataSource moves down the tree, it moves *toward* the current node. If it's already at the current node, or your offset takes it beyond the current node, the SiteMapDataSource won't know where to go, and you'll end up with a blank navigation control.

To understand how this works, it helps to consider an example. Imagine you're at this location in a website:

```
Home > Products > Software > Custom > Contact Us
```

If the SiteMapDataSource is starting at the Home node (the default), and you apply a StartingNodeOffset of 2, it will move down the tree two levels and bind the tree from that node down. In this example, that node is Software:

```
Software > Custom > Contact Us
```

That means you'll be able to jump to any links in the Software or Custom groups, but you won't be able to go anywhere else (at least not without stepping up a level first or clicking another control).

If you attempt to move down too many levels—for example, if the user is on a second-level page and you supply a StartingNodeOffset of 3—the SiteMapDataSource will run out of levels and your bound controls will be left blank.

Another useful technique is to move *up* from the current node. For example, if you set StartFromCurrentNode to true and use a StartingNodeOffset of -3, the SiteMapDataSource will move up three levels from the current page (Contact Us) and bind to this tree:

```
Products > Software > Custom > Contact Us
```

This technique is a bit more useful, because it ensures that your navigational controls will always show the same number of levels. If you attempt to step up past the root node, you'll simply see as many levels as possible. For example, if you specify a StartingNodeOffset of -3 and the user is currently at a second-level page (such as Software), you'll bind to this tree:

```
Products > Software
```

It may take a bit of experimenting to decide the right combination of SiteMapDataSource settings that you want to use.

■ **Note** StartingNodeOffset and StartFromCurrentNode are specialized properties that many websites never use. However, they can be useful if you have a deeply nested, complex site map tree. In this case, you can use these properties to cut down the number of levels that are shown at once. This makes the navigation links easier to read and understand (or at least more compact, so they don't waste valuable web page space). To get a similar effect with the SiteMapPath (which doesn't use the SiteMapDataSource), you can set the SiteMapPath.ParentLevelsDisplayed property.

The Site Map Objects

You aren't limited to no-code data binding in order to display navigation hierarchies. You can interact with the navigation information programmatically. Two reasons exist for using programmatic navigation:

To change the display of the page: For example, you can retrieve the current node information and use that to configure details such as the page heading and title.

To implement different navigation logic: For example, you might want to display just a portion of the full list of child nodes for the current page in a newsreader, or you might want to create previous/next navigation buttons.

The site map API is remarkably straightforward. To use it, you need to work with two classes from the System.Web namespace. The starting point is the SiteMap class, which provides the static properties CurrentNode (the site map node representing the current page) and RootNode (the root site map node). Both of these properties return a SiteMapNode object. Using the SiteMapNode, you can retrieve information from the site map, including the title, description, and URL values. You can branch out to consider related nodes using the navigational properties in Table 17-8.

■ **Note** You can also search for nodes using the methods of the current SiteMapProvider object, which is available through the SiteMap.Provider static property. For example, the SiteMap.Provider.FindSiteMapNode() method allows you to search for a node by its URL.

***Table 17-8.** SiteMapNode Navigational Properties*

Property	Description
ParentNode	Returns the node one level up in the navigation hierarchy, which contains the current node. On the root node, this returns a null reference.
ChildNodes	Provides a collection of all the child nodes. Check the HasChildNodes property to determine if there are child nodes.
PreviousSibling	Returns the previous node that's at the same level (or a null reference if no such node exists).
NextSibling	Returns the next node that's at the same level (or a null reference if no such node exists).

To see this in action, consider the following code, which configures two labels on a page to show the heading and description information retrieved from the current node:

```
protected void Page_Load(object sender, EventArgs e)
{
    lblHead.Text = SiteMap.CurrentNode.Title;
    lblDescription.Text = SiteMap.CurrentNode.Description;
}
```

The next example is a little more ambitious. It provides a Next button, which allows the user to traverse an entire set of subnodes. The code checks for the existence of sibling nodes, and if there aren't any in the required position, it simply hides the link.

```
protected void Page_Load(object sender, EventArgs e)
{
    if (SiteMap.CurrentNode.NextSibling != null)
```

```
    {
        lnkNext.NavigateUrl = SiteMap.CurrentNode.NextSibling.Url;
        lnkNext.Visible = true;
    }
    else
    {
        lnkNext.Visible = false;
    }
}
```

Adding Custom Site Map Information

In the site maps you've seen so far, the only information that's provided for a node is the title, description, and URL. This is the bare minimum of information that you'll want to use. However, the schema for the XML site map is open, which means you're free to insert custom attributes with your own data.

You might want to insert additional node data for a number of reasons. This additional information might be descriptive information that you intend to display or contextual information that describes how the link should work. For example, you could add attributes that specify a target frame or indicate that a link should be opened in a pop-up window. The only catch is that it's up to you to act on the information later. In other words, you need to configure your user interface so it uses this extra information.

For example, the following code shows a site map that uses a target attribute to indicate the frame where the link should be opened. This technique is useful if you're using frames-based navigation (rather than a master page), as described in Chapter 29. In this example, one link is set with a target of _blank so it will open in a new (pop-up) browser window.

```
<siteMap xmlns="http://schemas.microsoft.com/AspNet/SiteMap-File-1.0" >
  <siteMapNode title="Home" description="Root" url="./Default.aspx">
    <siteMapNode title="Products" description="Our products"
     url="./Products.aspx" target="_blank" />
    ...
  </siteMapNode>
</siteMap>
```

Now in your code, you have several options. If you're using a template in your navigation control, you can bind directly to the new attribute you've added. If your navigation control doesn't support templates (or you don't want to create one), you'll need to find another approach. Both the TreeView and Menu classes expose an event that fires when an individual item is bound (TreeNodeDataBound and MenuItemDataBound). You can then customize the current item. To apply the new target, you use this code:

```
protected void TreeView1_TreeNodeDataBound(object sender, TreeNodeEventArgs e)
{
    e.Node.Target = ((SiteMapNode)e.Node.DataItem)["target"];
}
```

Notice that you can't retrieve the custom attribute from a strongly typed property. Instead, you retrieve it by name using the SiteMapNode indexer.

Creating a Custom SiteMapProvider

To really change how the ASP.NET navigation model works, you need to create your own site map provider. You might choose to create a custom site map provider for several reasons:

- You need to store site map information in a different data source (such as a relational database).
- You need to store site map information with a different schema from the XML format expected by ASP.NET. This is most likely if you have an existing system in place for storing site maps.
- You need a highly dynamic site map that's generated on the fly. For example, you might want to generate a different site map based on the current user, the query string parameters, and so on.
- You need to change one of the limitations in the XmlSiteMapProvider implementation. For example, maybe you want the ability to have nodes with duplicate URLs.

You have two choices when implementing a custom site map provider. All site map providers derive from the abstract base class SiteMapProvider in the System.Web namespace. You can derive from this class to implement a new provider from scratch. However, if you want to keep the same logic but use a different data store, just derive from the StaticSiteMapProvider class instead. It gives you a basic implementation of many methods, including the logic for node storing and searching.

In the following sections, you'll see a custom provider that lets you store site map information in a database.

Storing Site Map Information in a Database

In this example, all navigation links are stored in a single database table. Because databases don't lend themselves easily to hierarchical data, you need to be a little crafty. In this example, each navigation link is linked to a parent link in the same table, except for the root node. This means that although the navigational links are flattened into one table, you can re-create the right structure by starting with the home page and then searching for the subset of rows at each level.

Figure 17-13 shows the SiteMap table with some sample data that roughly duplicates the site map you saw earlier in this chapter.

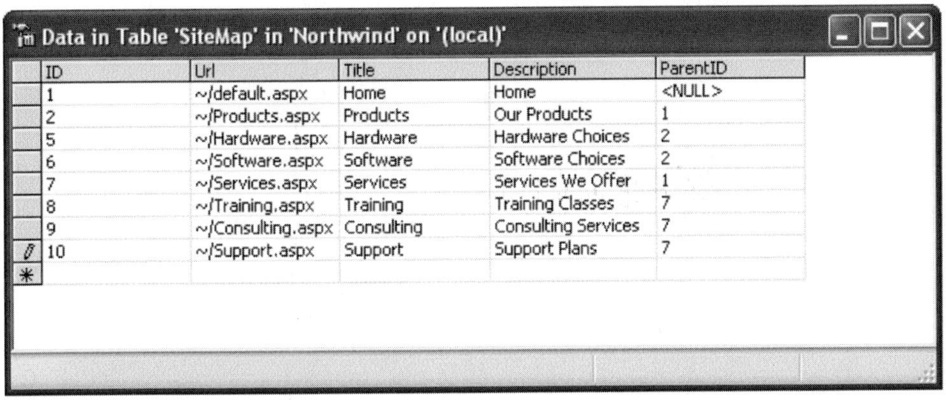

Data in Table 'SiteMap' in 'Northwind' on '(local)'

ID	Url	Title	Description	ParentID
1	~/default.aspx	Home	Home	<NULL>
2	~/Products.aspx	Products	Our Products	1
5	~/Hardware.aspx	Hardware	Hardware Choices	2
6	~/Software.aspx	Software	Software Choices	2
7	~/Services.aspx	Services	Services We Offer	1
8	~/Training.aspx	Training	Training Classes	7
9	~/Consulting.aspx	Consulting	Consulting Services	7
10	~/Support.aspx	Support	Support Plans	7

Figure 17-13. *The SiteMap table*

In this solution, the site map provider won't access the table directly. Instead, it will use a stored procedure. This gives some added flexibility and potentially allows you to store your navigation information with a different schema, as long as you return a table with the expected column names from your stored procedure.

Here's the stored procedure used in this example:

```
CREATE PROCEDURE GetSiteMap AS
SELECT * FROM SiteMap ORDER BY ParentID, Title
```

Creating the Site Map Provider

Because this site map provider doesn't change the underlying logic of site map navigation, you can derive from StaticSiteMapProvider instead of deriving from SiteMapProvider and reimplementing all the tracking and navigation behavior (which is a much more tedious task).

Here's the class declaration for the provider:

```
public class SqlSiteMapProvider : StaticSiteMapProvider
{ ... }
```

The first step is to override the Initialize() method to get all the sitemap-related information you need from the web.config file. The Initialize() method gives you access to the configuration element in the web.config that defines the site map provider.

In this example, your provider needs three pieces of information:

- The connection string for the database where the site map data is stored.
- The name of the stored procedure that returns the site map.
- The provider name for the database. This allows you to use provider-agnostic coding (as described in Chapter 7). In other words, you can support SQL Server, Oracle, or another database equally easily, as long as there's a .NET provider factory installed.

You can configure your web application to use the custom provider (SqlSiteMapProvider) and supply the required three pieces of information using the <siteMap> section of the web.config file:

```
<configuration>
  <system.web>
    <siteMap defaultProvider="SqlSiteMapProvider">
      <providers>
        <add name="SqlSiteMapProvider" type="SqlSiteMapProvider"
         providerName="System.Data.SqlClient"
         connectionString=
"Data Source=localhost;Initial Catalog=SiteMap;Integrated Security=SSPI"
         storedProcedure="GetSiteMap" />
      </providers>
    </siteMap>
    ...
  </system.web>
  ...
</configuration>
```

Now in your provider you simply need to retrieve these three pieces of information and store them for later. Here's the code you need to add to the SqlSiteMapProvider class:

```
private string connectionString;
private string providerName;
private string storedProcedure;
private bool initialized = false;

public override void Initialize(string name,
  System.Collections.Specialized.NameValueCollection attributes)
{
    if (!IsInitialized)
    {
        base.Initialize(name, attributes);

        // Retrieve the web.config settings.
        providerName = attributes["providerName"];
        connectionString = attributes["connectionString"];
        storedProcedure = attributes["storedProcedure"];

        if (String.IsNullOrEmpty(providerName))
          throw new ArgumentException("The provider name was not found.");
        else if (String.IsNullOrEmpty(connectionString))
          throw new ArgumentException("The connection string was not found.");
        else if (String.IsNullOrEmpty(storedProcedure))
          throw new ArgumentException("The stored procedure name was not found.");

        initialized = true;
    }
}

public virtual bool IsInitialized
{
    get { return initialized; }
}
```

The real work that the provider does is in the BuildSiteMap() method, which constructs the SiteMapNode objects that make up the navigation tree. In the lifetime of an application, you'll typically construct the SiteMapNode once and reuse it multiple times. To make that possible, the provider needs to store the site map in memory, so add the following field to the SqlSiteMapProvider class:

```
private SiteMapNode rootNode;
```

The root SiteMapNode contains the first level of nodes, which then contain the next level of nodes, and so on. Thus, the root node is the starting point for the whole navigation tree.

You override the BuildSiteMap() method to actually create the site map. The first step is to check if the site map has already been generated and then create it. Because multiple pages could share the same instance of the site map provider, it's a good idea to lock the object before you update any shared information (such as the in-memory navigation tree).

```
public override SiteMapNode BuildSiteMap()
{
    lock (this)
    {
        // Don't rebuild the map unless needed.
        // If your site map changes often, consider using caching.
        if (rootNode == null)
```

```
{
    // Start with a clean slate.
    Clear();
    ...
```

Next, you need to create the database provider and use it to call the stored procedure that gets the navigation history. The navigation history is stored in a DataSet (a DataReader won't work because you need back-and-forth navigation to traverse the structure of the site map).

Here's the code you need (which assumes you've imported the System.Data.Common namespace):

```
...
// Get all the data (using provider-agnostic code).
DbProviderFactory provider =
  DbProviderFactories.GetFactory(providerName);

// Use this factory to create a connection.
DbConnection con = provider.CreateConnection();
con.ConnectionString = connectionString;

// Create the command.
DbCommand cmd = provider.CreateCommand();
cmd.CommandText = storedProcedure;
cmd.CommandType = CommandType.StoredProcedure;
cmd.Connection = con;

// Create the DataAdapter.
DbDataAdapter adapter = provider.CreateDataAdapter();
adapter.SelectCommand = cmd;

// Get the results in a DataSet.
DataSet ds = new DataSet();
adapter.Fill(ds, "SiteMap");
DataTable dtSiteMap = ds.Tables["SiteMap"];
...
```

The next step is to navigate the DataTable to create the SiteMapNode objects, beginning with the root node. You can find the root node by searching for the node with no parent (where ParentID is null). In this example, no attempt is made to check for all the possible error conditions (such as duplicate root nodes).

```
...
// Get the root node.
DataRow rowRoot = dtSiteMap.Select("ParentID IS NULL")[0];
...
```

Now to create a SiteMapNode, you need to supply the key, URL, title, and description. In the default implementation of a site map provider, the key and URL are the same, which makes searching by URL easier. The custom SqlSiteMapProvider also uses this convention.

```
...
rootNode = new SiteMapNode(this,
  rowRoot["Url"].ToString(),
  rowRoot["Url"].ToString(),
```

```
            rowRoot["Title"].ToString(),
            rowRoot["Description"].ToString());
          ...
```

Now it's time to fill in the rest of the hierarchy. This is a step that needs to be performed recursively so that you can drill down through a hierarchy that's an unlimited number of levels deep. To make this work, the SqlSiteMapProvider uses a private AddChildren method, which fills in one level at a time. Once this process is complete, the root node that provides access to the full site map is returned.

```
          ...
          string rootID = rowRoot["ID"].ToString();
          AddNode(rootNode);

          // Fill down the hierarchy.
          AddChildren(rootNode, rootID, dtSiteMap);
        }
    }
    return rootNode;
}
```

The AddChildren() method simply searches the DataTable for records where the ParentID is the same as the current ID—in other words, it finds all the parents for the current node. Each time it finds a child, it adds the child to the SiteMapNode.ChildNodes collection using the AddNode method that's inherited from StaticSiteMapProvider.

Here's the complete code:

```
private void AddChildren(SiteMapNode rootNode, string rootID, DataTable dtSiteMap)
{
    DataRow[] childRows = dtSiteMap.Select("ParentID = " + rootID);
    foreach (DataRow row in childRows)
    {
        SiteMapNode childNode = new SiteMapNode(this,
          row["Url"].ToString(),
          row["Url"].ToString(),
          row["Title"].ToString(),
          row["Description"].ToString());
        string rowID = row["ID"].ToString();

        // Use the SiteMapNode AddNode method to add
        // the SiteMapNode to the ChildNodes collection.
        AddNode(childNode, rootNode);

        // Check for children in this node.
        AddChildren(childNode, rowID, dtSiteMap);
    }
}
```

The only remaining details are to fill a few other required overloads that retrieve the site map information:

```
protected override SiteMapNode GetRootNodeCore()
{
    return BuildSiteMap();
```

```
}

public override SiteMapNode RootNode
{
    get { return BuildSiteMap(); }
}

protected override void Clear()
{
    lock (this)
    {
        rootNode = null;
        base.Clear();
    }
}
```

This completes the example. You can now request the same pages you created earlier, using the new site map provider (as configured in the web.config file). In fact, you use exactly the same markup. The custom provider plugs in easily and neatly. The new information will flow through the custom provider and arrive in your pages without any indication that the underlying plumbing has changed.

Adding Sorting

Currently, the SqlSiteMapProvider returns the results ordered alphabetically by title. This means the About page always appears before the Contact Us page. This make sense for a quick test, but it isn't practical in a real site, where you probably want the ability to control the order in which pages appear.

Fortunately, an easy solution exists. In fact, you don't even need to touch the SqlSiteMapProvider code. All you need to do is introduce a new field in the SiteMap table (say, OrdinalPosition) and modify the GetSiteMap procedure to use it:

```
ALTER PROCEDURE GetSiteMap AS
SELECT * FROM SiteMap ORDER BY ParentID, OrdinalPosition, Title
```

First, records are sorted into groups based on the parent (which node they fall under). Next, they're ordered according to the OrdinalPosition values, if you've supplied them. Finally, they're sorted by title.

Sorting is only applied with a group of pages that are at the same level. For example, you can use the same ordinal numbers (say, 1, 2, 3) to order pages in the Products branch as you do in the Services branch. If two pages in the same group have the same ordinal number, they're ordered alphabetically by title with respect to one another. (As a side effect, if you don't set any ordinal numbers, the nodes will all be sorted alphabetically by title, just like they were in the previous example.)

■ **Note** Strictly speaking, you don't need to sort by ParentID. The SqlSiteMapDataProvider code processes nodes one batch at a time, and each batch is made up of nodes that have the same ParentID. However, sorting by ParentID makes it easier to test your sorting. This way, you can run the GetSiteMap stored procedure, look over the results, and get a good overview of how your nodes are organized.

Adding Caching

One issue you might notice with the SqlSiteMapProvider is that it stores the root node for the current site map in memory indefinitely. This means the SqlSiteMapProvider uses the same site map until the application domain is restarted (for example, when you rebuild your website or change its configuration settings). If you plan to change your site map regularly, you have several choices to make sure your application notices the change and refreshes the site map. The best option is to use the data cache to keep the root note around for a limited amount of time.

You can use time-based expiry (for example, so the site map is refreshed once an hour). The cache time is added to the web.config file (as a value in seconds):

```
<add name="SqlSiteMapProvider" ... cacheTime="600" />
```

And it's retrieved in the SqlSiteMapProvider constructor using this statement:

```
cacheTime = Int32.Parse(attributes["cacheTime"]);
```

Here's a revised version of the BuildSiteMap() method that keeps the site map in the cache for the desired period of time:

```
public override SiteMapNode BuildSiteMap()
{
    SiteMapNode rootNode;

    lock (this)
    {
        rootNode = HttpContext.Current.Cache["rootNode"] as SiteMapNode;
        if (rootNode == null)
        {
            ...
            // Store the root node in the cache.
            HttpContext.Current.Cache.Insert("rootNode", rootNode,
              null, DateTime.Now.AddSeconds(cacheTime), TimeSpan.Zero);
        }
    }
    return rootNode;
}
```

Lastly, the SqlSiteMapProvider.Clear() method requires minor changes so that it removes the site map from the cache:

```
protected override void Clear()
{
    lock (this)
    {
        HttpContext.Current.Cache.Remove("rootNode");
        base.Clear();
    }
}
```

If you want to get even more sophisticated, you can use SQL Server cache invalidation to automatically remove your cached site map when a change takes place in the SiteMap table. The only disadvantage is that this is a SQL Server-specific feature, so it breaks the broad database compatibility enjoyed by the SqlSiteMapProvider (which currently supports any data source that has an ADO.NET data provider and data factory).

If you decide to implement database cache invalidation, you need to take care to ensure that it's an optional feature. For example, you might decide to use the time-based caching approach shown here unless you find a specific attribute in the custom provider tag that indicates database cache invalidation is supported.

■ **Note** Some developers have created custom site map providers that expose the directory structure of a website using the site map model. These providers simply create nodes for every file and subdirectory they find in your website directory. This approach allows you to provide basic navigation without actually creating a site map file (or table). Of course, you sacrifice considerable flexibility, because you can't control what pages are shown or how they're ordered. For an example of a custom provider that implements this file-and-folder approach, see `http://msdn2.microsoft.com/en-us/library/aa479338.aspx`.

Security Trimming

In Chapter 23, you'll learn how to protect specific pages and folders using *authorization rules.* These authorization rules can prevent anonymous users from accessing sensitive content, regardless of what type of authentication system you're using. You can also use authorization rules to lock out specific users, roles, or Windows groups.

This creates a bit of a challenge if you're using a single site map for all users. The problem is that the site map may include some pages that are accessible only to certain classes of users. For example, all users will see a link to an Admin.aspx page, even though you may have used authorization rules that explicitly prevent most people from accessing this page. To prevent the confusion, you can use an often-overlooked site map feature called *security trimming.*

When security trimming is switched on, all the pages that a user wouldn't be allowed to access (based on authorization rules) are left out of the site map altogether. This means non-admin users won't see the link to the Admin.aspx page. And if you've used authorization rules to create separate groups of pages for separate roles, every user will see just the appropriate pages.

To turn on security trimming, you need to use the securityTrimmingEnabled attribute when you register the site map provider in the web.config file. Although you could edit the root web.config file on the web server, the easiest option is to simply add the standard site map provider with the new configuration settings, as shown here:

```
<configuration>
  <system.web>
    <providers>
      <siteMap defaultProvider="SecureSiteMapProvider" >
        <add name="SecureSiteMapProvider"
          type="System.Web.XmlSiteMapProvider "
          siteMapFile="Web.sitemap"
          securityTrimmingEnabled="true"  />
    </providers>
    </siteMap>
    ...
  </system.web>
</configuration>
```

When you switch on security trimming, it automatically applies to all the nodes in your site map file. However, you can opt out. If you know specific sections of your site map should be shown to all people or if you don't want to use security trimming to hide certain pages, you can explicitly turn security trimming off for a portion of the site map. To do so, you need to set the roles attribute for that node to an asterisk (*), as shown here:

```
<siteMapNode title="Admin" description="Administration"
  url="./Admin.aspx" roles="*" >
```

Now the Services node is visible to everyone, regardless of their role, even if security trimming is switched on. You might take this step for several reasons:

To ensure good performance: The fewer nodes ASP.NET needs to check, the less overhead it applies to each request.

To make it easier for people to use a secure page as a starting point: For example, an administrator might want to surf to your website and click the Admin.aspx link before logging in. At this point, the administrator will be sent to a login page (assuming you're using forms authentication), authenticated, and then redirected back to the Admin.aspx page. But if the Admin.aspx page isn't visible, the site isn't quite as easy to use. The administrator would need to surf to the login page first and then surf to the Admin.aspx page.

To prevent child nodes from being hidden: For example, if the Administration node contains other nodes that aren't secured (such as Meet Our Administrators), these nodes will be hidden when the Administration node is hidden. This problem usually indicates a poor site map design.

The value of the roles attribute is not passed down to nested nodes. This means if there are other nodes contained inside the Administration node and these nodes point to protected pages that you want to show in the site map, you'll need to add the roles="*" attribute to each one.

■ **Tip** Security trimming imposes extra work on each request. If your site map contains a large number of nodes, this additional overhead can reduce performance. Microsoft recommends using security trimming with site maps that have fewer than 150 nodes. Or, to ensure good performance, turn off security trimming for sections of the site map where it's not needed using the roles attribute.

The roles node hints at another, less commonly used possibility. You can use it to explicitly set a comma-separated list of roles (or, in the case of Windows authentication, Windows groups) that are allowed to see the page. However, this usage is confusing. You can't use it to limit access to a node; instead, it only *expands* access. In other words, when you enable security trimming, ASP.NET determines who should see a site map node based on the authorization settings for that page in the web.config file. Then, it *also* shows the node for explicitly named roles.

■ **Note** Remember, the roles attribute controls whether a node appears in the site map. It has no effect on whether a user can actually access the page, which is determined by the web.config authorization rules. To learn more about authorization rules, refer to Chapter 23.

URL Mapping and Routing

The site map model is designed around a simple principle: each entry has a separate URL. Although you can distinguish URLs by adding query string arguments, in many web sites, there is one-to-one correspondence between web forms and site map entries.

When this doesn't suit, ASP.NET has two tools that may be able to help you out. The first is URL mapping, which is a clean, no-nonsense way to map one URL to another. The second is URL routing, which is a slightly more elaborate but much more flexible system that performs a similar task. URL mapping is an ideal way to deal with "one-off" redirection. For example, mapping is a quick way to deal with old or recently moved pages, or to allow extra entry points for a few popular pages. On the other hand, URL routing can serve as the basis for a more sophisticated redirection system that deals with many more pages. For example, you could use it to replace long, complex product page URLs with a simpler syntax, and implement that across your entire web site. Routing is particularly useful if you want to offer cleaner URLs so that search engines can index your web site more easily and comprehensively.

URL Mapping

In some situations, you might want to have several URLs lead to the same page. This might be the case for a number of reasons—maybe you want to implement your logic in one page and use query string arguments but still provide shorter and easier-to-remember URLs to your website users (often called *friendly* URLs). Or maybe you have renamed a page, but you want to keep the old URL functional so it doesn't break user bookmarks. Although web servers sometimes provide this type of functionality, ASP.NET includes its own URL mapping feature.

The basic idea behind ASP.NET URL mapping is that you map a request URL to a different URL. The mapping rules are stored in the web.config file, and they're applied before any other processing takes place. Of course, for ASP.NET to apply the remapping, it must be processing the request, which means the request URL must use a file type extension that's mapped to ASP.NET. (See Chapter 18 for more information about how to configure ASP.NET to handle file extensions that it wouldn't ordinarily handle.)

You define URL mapping in the <urlMappings> section of the web.config file. You supply two pieces of information—the request URL (as the attribute url) and the new destination URL (mappedUrl). Here's an example:

```
<configuration>
  <system.web>
    <urlMappings enabled="true">
      <add url="./Category.aspx"
       mappedUrl="./Default.aspx?category=default" />
      <add url="./Software.aspx"
       mappedUrl="./Default.aspx?category=software" />
    </urlMappings>
    ...
  </system.web>
</configuration>
```

To make a match, the incoming URL must be requesting the same page. However, the case of the request URL is ignored, as are query string arguments. Unfortunately, there's no support for advanced matching rules, such as wildcards or regular expressions.

When you use URL mapping, the redirection is performed in the same way as the Server.Transfer() method, which means there is no round-trip and the URL in the browser will still show the original request URL, not the remapped URL. In your code, the Request.Path and Request.QueryString properties reflect the new (mapped) URL. The Request.RawUrl property returns the original friendly request URL.

This can introduce some complexities if you use it in conjunction with site maps—namely, does the site map provider try to use the original request URL or the destination URL when looking for the current node in the site map? The answer is both. It begins by trying to match the request URL (provided by the Request.RawUrl property), and if no value is found, it then uses the Request.Path property instead. This is the behavior of the XmlSiteMapProvider, so you could change it in a custom provider if desired.

URL Routing

Routing is a core feature for ASP.NET MVC, and you'll consider it in detail in Chapter 32. However, ASP.NET also allows you to use the same routing techniques in a traditional web application that consists of web forms.

Unlike URL mapping, URL routing doesn't take place in the web.config file. Instead, it's implemented using code. Typically, you'll use the Application_Start() method in the global.asax file to register all the routes for your application.

To register a route, you use the RouteTable class from the System.Web.Routing namespace. It provies a static property named Routes, which holds a collection of Route objects that are defined for your application. Initially, this collection is empty, but you can create your own custom routes by calling the MapPageRoute() method, which takes three arguments:

routeName: This is a name that uniquely identifies the route. It can be whatever you want.

routeUrl: This specifies the URL format that browsers will use. Typically, a route URL consists of one or more pieces of variable information, separated by slashes, which are extracted and provided to your code. For example, you might request a product page using a URL such as */products/4312*.

physicalFile: This is the target web form—the place where users will be redirected when they use the route. The information from the original routeUrl will be parsed and made available to this page as a collection through the Page.RouteData property.

Here's an example that adds two routes to a web application when it first starts:

```
void Application_Start(object sender, EventArgs e)
{
    RouteTable.Routes.MapPageRoute("product-details",
      "product/{productID}", "~/productInfo.aspx");

    RouteTable.Routes.MapPageRoute("products-in-category",
      "products/category/{categoryID}", "~/products.aspx");
}
```

The route URL can include one or more parameters, which is represented by a placeholder in curly brackets. For example, the first route shown here includes a parameter named productID. This piece of information will be pulled out of the URL and passed along to the target page.

Here's a URL that uses this route to request a product with the ID FI_00345:

```
http://localhost:[PortNumber]/Routing/product/FI_00345
```

The ASP.NET routing infrastructure then redirects the user to the productInfo.aspx page. All the parameters are provided through the Page.RouteData property. Technically, Page.RouteData provides a RouteData object. It's most useful property is the Values collection, which provides all the parameters from the original request, indexed by name.

Here's an example that shows how the productInfo.aspx page can retrieve the requested product ID from the original URL:

```
protected void Page_Load(object sender, EventArgs e)
{
    string productID = (string)Page.RouteData.Values["productID"];
    lblInfo.Text = "You requested " + productID;
}
```

Similarly, the second route in this example acceptsURLs in this form:

```
http://localhost:[PortNumber]/Routing/products/category/342
```

Although you can hard-code this sort of URL, there's a Page.GetRouteUrl() helper method that does it for you automatically, avoiding potential mistakes. Here's an example that looks up a route (using its registered name), supplies the parameter information, and then retrieves the corresponding URL:

```
hyperLink.NavigateUrl = Page.GetRouteUrl("product-details", new { productID = "FI_00345" });
```

The result is a routed URL that points to the FI_00345 product, as shown in the first example.

You'll learn quite a bit more about the routing system when you consider ASP.NET MVC in Chapter 32.

The TreeView Control

The TreeView is one of the most impressive navigation controls. Not only does it allow you to render rich tree views, it also supports filling portions of the tree on demand (and without refreshing the entire page). But most important, it supports a wide range of styles that can transform its appearance. By setting just a few basic properties, you can change the TreeView from a help topic index to a file-and-folder directory listing. In fact, the TreeView doesn't have to be rendered as a tree at all—it can also tackle nonindented hierarchical data such as a table of contents with the application of just a few style settings.

You've already seen two basic TreeView scenarios. In Chapter 14, you used a TreeView to display bound XML data. In this chapter, you used a TreeView to display site map data. Both of these examples used the ability of the TreeView to bind to hierarchical data sources. But you can also fill a TreeView by binding to an ordinary data source (in which case you'll get only a single level of nodes) or by creating the nodes yourself, either programmatically or through the .aspx declaration.

The latter option is the simplest. For example, by adding <asp:TreeNode> tags to the <Nodes> section of a TreeView control, you can create several nodes:

```
<asp:TreeView ID="TreeView1" runat="server">
  <Nodes>
    <asp:TreeNode Text="Products">
      <asp:TreeNode Text="Hardware"/>
    </asp:TreeNode>
    <asp:TreeNode Text="Services"/>
  </Nodes>
</asp:TreeView>
```

And here's how you can add a TreeNode programmatically when the page loads:

```
TreeNode newNode = new TreeNode("Software");

// Add as a child of the first root node
// (the Products node in the previous example).
TreeView1.Nodes[0].ChildNodes.Add(newNode);
```

When the TreeView is first displayed, all the nodes are shown. You can control this behavior by setting the TreeView.ExpandDepth property. For example, if ExpandDepth is 2, only the first three levels are shown (level 0, level 1, and level 2). To control how many levels the TreeView includes altogether (collapsed or uncollapsed), you use the MaxDataBindDepth property. By default, MaxDataBindDepth is -1, and you'll see the entire tree. However, if you use a value such as 2, you'll see only two levels under the starting node. You can also programmatically collapse and expand individual nodes by setting the TreeNode.Expanded property to true or false.

This just scratches the surface of how a TreeView works. To get the most out of the TreeView, you need to understand how to customize several other details for a TreeNode.

The TreeNode

Each node in the tree is represented by a TreeNode object. As you already know, every TreeNode has an associated piece of text, which is displayed in the tree. The TreeNode object also provides navigation properties such as ChildNodes (the collection of nodes it contains) and Parent (the containing node, one level up the tree). Along with this bare minimum, the TreeNode provides all the useful properties detailed in Table 17-9.

Table 17-9. *TreeNode Properties*

Property	Description
Text	The text displayed in the tree for this node.
ToolTip	The tooltip text that appears when you hover over the node text.
Value	Stores a nondisplayed value with additional data about the node (such as a unique ID you'll use when handling click events to identify the node or look up more information).
NavigateUrl	If set, the user will be automatically forwarded to the corresponding URL when this node is clicked. Otherwise, you'll need to react to the TreeView.SelectedNodeChanged event to decide what action you want to perform.
Target	If the NavigateUrl property is set, this sets the target window or frame for the link. If Target isn't set, the new page is opened in the current browser window. The TreeView also exposes a Target property, which you can set to apply a default target for all TreeNode instances.
ImageUrl	The image that's displayed next to this node.
ImageToolTip	The tooltip text for the image displayed next to the node.

One unusual detail about the TreeNode is that it can be in one of two modes. In *selection mode,* clicking the node posts back the page and raises the TreeView.SelectedNodeChanged event. This is the default mode for all nodes. In *navigation mode,* clicking a node navigates to a new page, and the SelectedNodeChanged event is not raised. The TreeNode is placed in navigation mode as soon as you set the NavigateUrl property to anything other than an empty string. A TreeNode that's bound to site map data is in navigational mode, because each site map node supplies URL information.

The next example fills a TreeView with the results of a database query. You want to use the TreeView's ability to show hierarchical data to create a master-details list. Because ASP.NET doesn't include any data source control that can query a database and expose the results as a hierarchical data source, you can't use data binding. Instead, you need to programmatically query the table and create the TreeNode structure by hand.

Here's the code that implements this approach:

```
protected void Page_Load(object sender, EventArgs e)
{
    if (!Page.IsPostBack)
    {
        // Fill a DataSet with two DataTable objects, representing
        // the Products and Categories tables.
        DataSet ds = GetProductsAndCategories();

        // Loop through the category records.
        foreach (DataRow row in ds.Tables["Categories"].Rows)
        {
            // Use the constructor that requires just text
            // and a nondisplayed value.
            TreeNode nodeCategory = new TreeNode(
              row["CategoryName"].ToString(),
              row["CategoryID"].ToString());

            TreeView1.Nodes.Add(nodeCategory);

            // Get the children (products) for this parent (category).
            DataRow[] childRows = row.GetChildRows(ds.Relations[0]);

            // Loop through all the products in this category.
            foreach (DataRow childRow in childRows)
            {
                TreeNode nodeProduct = new TreeNode(
                  childRow["ProductName"].ToString(),
                  childRow["ProductID"].ToString());
                nodeCategory.ChildNodes.Add(nodeProduct);
            }

            // Keep all categories collapsed (initially).
            nodeCategory.Collapse();
        }
    }
}
```

Now when a node is clicked, you can handle the SelectedNodeChanged event to show the node information:

```
protected void TreeView1_SelectedNodeChanged(object sender, EventArgs e)
{
    if (TreeView1.SelectedNode == null) return;
    if (TreeView1.SelectedNode.Depth == 0)
    {
        lblInfo.Text = "You selected Category ID: ";
    }
    else if (TreeView1.SelectedNode.Depth == 1)
    {
        lblInfo.Text = "You selected Product ID: ";
    }
    lblInfo.Text += TreeView1.SelectedNode.Value;
}
```

Figure 17-14 shows the result.

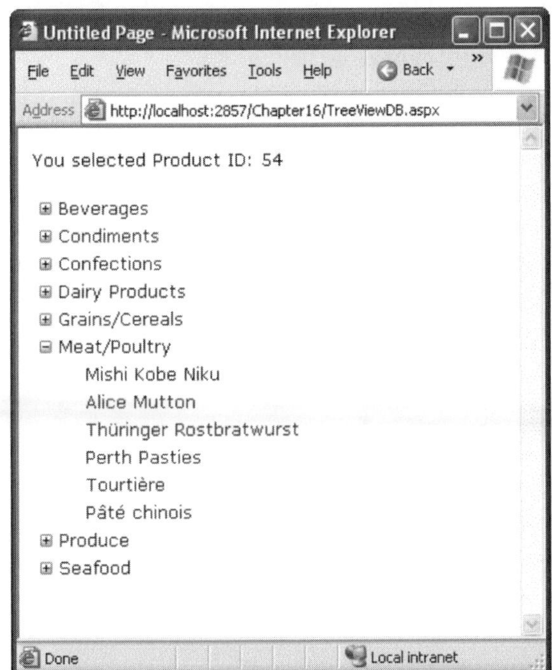

***Figure 17-14.** Filling a TreeView with database data*

A few options exist to simplify the page code in this example. One option is to bind to XML data instead of relational data. Seeing as SQL Server 2000 and later have the ability to perform XML queries with FOR XML, you could retrieve the data shaped in a specific XML markup and then bind it through the XmlDataSource control. The only trick is that because the XmlDataSource assumes you'll be binding to a file, you need to set the Data property by hand with the XML extracted from the database.

Populating Nodes on Demand

If you have an extremely large amount of data to display in a TreeView, you probably don't want to fill it in all at once. Not only will that increase the time taken to process the initial request for the page, it will also dramatically increase the size of the page and the view state. Fortunately, the TreeView includes a populate-on-demand feature that makes it easy to fill in branches of the tree as they are expanded. Even better, you can use populate-on-demand on selected portions of the tree, as you see fit.

To use populate-on-demand, you set the PopulateOnDemand property to true for any TreeNode that has content you want to fill in at the last minute. When the user expands this branch, the TreeView will fire a TreeNodePopulate event, which you can use to add the next level of nodes. If you want, this level of nodes can contain another level of nodes that are populated on demand.

Although the programming model remains fixed, the TreeView actually supports two techniques for filling in the on-demand nodes. When the TreeView.PopulateNodesFromClient property is true (the default), the TreeView performs a client-side callback to retrieve the nodes it needs from your event, without posting back the entire page. If PopulateNodesFromClient is false, or if it's true but the TreeView detects that the current browser doesn't appear to support client callbacks, the TreeView triggers a normal postback to get the same result. The only difference is that the entire page will be refreshed in the browser, generating a less seamless interface. (It also allows other page events to fire, such as control change events.)

You can use the populate-on-demand feature with the previous example. Instead of filling the whole tree when the page loads, you would begin by adding just the category nodes and setting them to populate on demand:

```
protected void Page_Load(object sender, EventArgs e)
{
    if (!Page.IsPostBack)
    {
        DataTable dtCategories = GetCategories();

        // Loop through the category records.
        foreach (DataRow row in dtCategories.Rows)
        {
            TreeNode nodeCategory = new TreeNode(
              row["CategoryName"].ToString(),
              row["CategoryID"].ToString());

            // Use the populate-on-demand feature for this
            // node's children.
            nodeCategory.PopulateOnDemand = true;

            // Make sure the node is collapsed at first,
            // so it's not populated immediately.
            nodeCategory.Collapse();
            TreeView1.Nodes.Add(nodeCategory);
        }
    }
}
```

■ **Note** Chapter 29 has more information about how client callbacks work and how you can use them directly. However, the TreeView support is particularly nice because it hides the underlying model, allowing you to write an ordinary .NET event handler.

Now you need to react to the TreeNodePopulate event to fill a category when it's expanded. In this example, the only nodes that populate themselves on demand are the categories. However, if there were several levels of nodes that use populate-on-demand, you could check the TreeNode.Depth to determine what type of node is being expanded.

```
protected void TreeView1_TreeNodePopulate(object sender, TreeNodeEventArgs e)
{
    int categoryID = Int32.Parse(e.Node.Value);
    DataTable dtProducts = GetProducts(categoryID);

    // Loop through the product records.
    foreach (DataRow row in dtProducts.Rows)
    {
        // Use the constructor that requires just text
        // and a nondisplayed value.
        TreeNode nodeProduct = new TreeNode(
          row["ProductName"].ToString(),
          row["ProductID"].ToString());

        e.Node.ChildNodes.Add(nodeProduct);
    }
}
```

A given node is populated on demand only once. After that, the values remain available on the client, and no callback is performed if the same node is collapsed and expanded.

TreeView Styles

The TreeView has a fine-grained style model that lets you completely control its appearance. Each style applies to a type of node. Styles are represented by the TreeNodeStyle class, which derives from the more conventional Style class.

As with other rich controls, the styles give you options to set background and foreground colors, fonts, and borders. Additionally, the TreeNodeStyle class adds the node-specific style properties shown in Table 17-10. These properties deal with the node image and the spacing around a node.

Table 17-10. *TreeNodeStyle Added Properties*

Property	Description
ImageUrl	The URL for the image shown next to the node
NodeSpacing	The space (in pixels) between the current node and the node above and below
VerticalPadding	The space (in pixels) between the top and bottom of the node text and border around the text
HorizontalPadding	The space (in pixels) between the left and right of the node text and border around the text
ChildNodesPadding	The space (in pixels) between the last child node of an expanded parent node and the following sibling node

Because a TreeView is rendered using an HTML table, you can set the padding of various elements to control the spacing around text, between nodes, and so on. One other property that comes into play is TreeView.NodeIndent, which sets the number of pixels of indentation (from the left) in each subsequent level of the tree hierarchy. Figure 17-15 shows how these settings apply to a single node.

The TreeView also allows you to configure some of its internal rendering through higher-level properties. You can turn off the node lines in a tree using the TreeView.ShowExpandCollapse property. You can also use the CollapseImageUrl and ExpandImageUrl properties to set the collapsed and expanded indicators of the TreeView (usually represented by plus and minus icons) and the NoExpandImageUrl property to set what's displayed next to nodes that have no children. Finally, you can show check boxes next to every node (set TreeView.ShowCheckBoxes to true) or individual nodes (set TreeNode.ShowCheckBox to true). You can determine if a given node is checked by examining the TreeNode.Checked property.

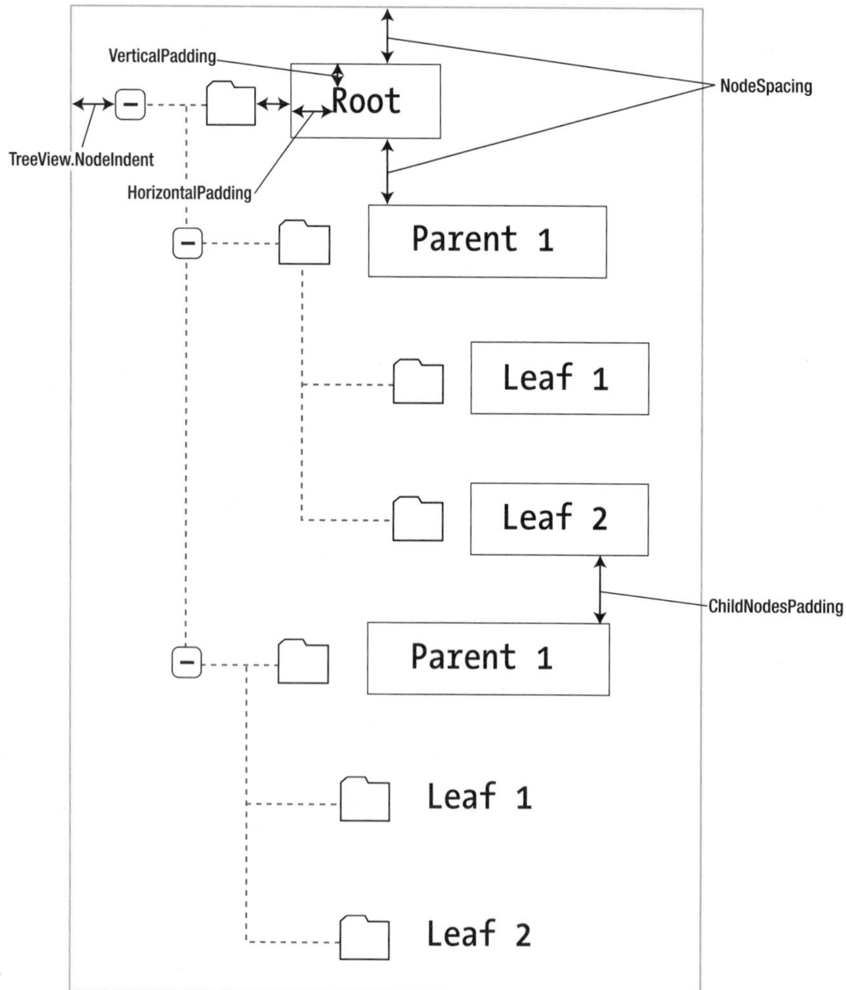

Figure 17-15. Node spacing

Applying Styles to Node Types

The TreeView allows you to individually control the styles for different types of nodes—for example, root nodes, nodes that contain other nodes, selected nodes, and so on.

To apply node style settings to all the nodes of a tree, you can use the TreeView.NodeStyle property. You can isolate individual regions of the TreeView using a more specific style, as listed in Table 17-11.

Styles are listed in this table in order of most general to most specific. That means the SelectedNodeStyle style settings override any conflicting settings in a RootNodeStyle, for exam- ple. (If you don't want a node to be selectable, set TreeNode.SelectAction to None.) However, the RootNodeStyle, ParentNodeStyle, and LeafNodeStyle settings never conflict, because the definitions for root, parent, and leaf nodes are mutually exclusive. You can't have a node that is simultaneously a parent and a root node, for example—the TreeView simply designates this as a root node.

Table 17-11. *TreeView Style Properties*

Property	Description
NodeStyle	Applies to all nodes.
RootNodeStyle	Applies only to the first-level (root) node.
ParentNodeStyle	Applies to any node that contains other nodes, except root nodes.
LeafNodeStyle	Applies to any node that doesn't contain child nodes and isn't a root node.
SelectedNodeStyle	Applies to the currently selected node.
HoverNodeStyle	Applies to the node the user is hovering over with the mouse. These settings are applied only in up-level clients that support the necessary dynamic script.

Applying Styles to Node Levels

Being able to apply styles to different types of nodes is interesting, but a more useful feature is being able to apply styles based on the node *level*. That's because most trees use a rigid hierarchy (for example, the first level of nodes represents categories, the second level represents products, the third represents orders, and so on). In this case, it's not so important to determine whether a node has children. Instead, it's important to determine the node's depth.

The only problem is that a TreeView can have a theoretically unlimited number of node levels. Thus, it doesn't make sense to expose properties such as FirstLevelStyle, SecondLevelStyle, and so on. Instead, the TreeView has a LevelStyles collection that can have as many entries as you want. The level is inferred from the position of the style in the collection, so the first entry is considered the root level, the second entry is the second node level, and so on. For this system to work, you must follow the same order, and you must include an empty style placeholder if you want to skip a level without changing the formatting.

For example, here's a TreeView that doesn't use any indenting but instead differentiates levels by applying different amounts of spacing and different fonts:

```
<asp:TreeView runat="server" HoverNodeStyle-Font-Underline="true"
 ShowExpandCollapse="false" NodeIndent="0">
  <LevelStyles>
    <asp:TreeNodeStyle ChildNodesPadding="10" Font-Bold="true" Font-Size="12pt"
     ForeColor="DarkGreen"/>
```

```
    <asp:TreeNodeStyle ChildNodesPadding="5" Font-Bold="true" Font-Size="10pt" />
    <asp:TreeNodeStyle ChildNodesPadding="5" Font-UnderLine="true"
     Font-Size="10pt" />
  </LevelStyles>
  ...
</asp:TreeView>
```

If you apply this to the category and product list shown in earlier examples, you'll see a page like the one shown in Figure 17-16.

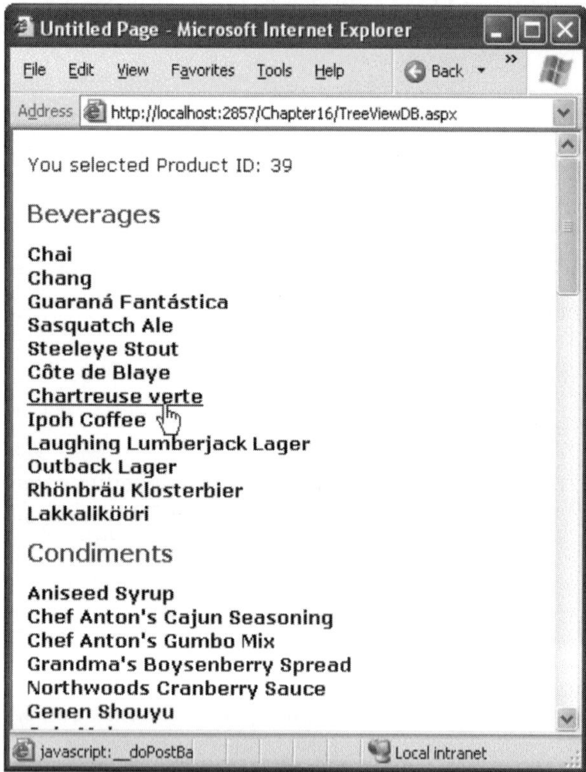

Figure 17-16. A nonindented TreeView

TreeView Images

As you've already learned, you can set the image for a single node using the TreeViewNode.ImageUrl property. Fortunately, you don't need to use this fine-grained approach if you want to assign a consistent set of images to your entire tree. Instead, you can use three TreeView properties to set images for all your nodes. You can choose the picture that is shown next to all collapsed nodes (CollapseImageUrl), all expanded nodes (ExpandImageUrl), and all nodes that don't have any children and thus aren't expandable (NoExpandImageUrl). If you set these properties and you specify an image for a specific node using the TreeViewNode.ImageUrl property, the node-specific image takes precedence.

The TreeView also has some stock images that you can use if you don’t want to go to the trouble of creating your own custom node images. To access these images, you use the TreeView.ImageSet property, which takes one of 16 values from the TreeViewImageSet enumeration. Each set includes an image for collapsed, expanded, and no-children nodes. When using the ImageSet property, you don't need to use any of the other image-related properties.

Figure 17-17 shows several of the available ImageSet options. For example, an ImageSet value of TreeViewImageSet.Faq creates a tree with help-style icons that show a question mark (for nodes that have no children) or a question mark superimposed over a folder (for nodes that do contain children).

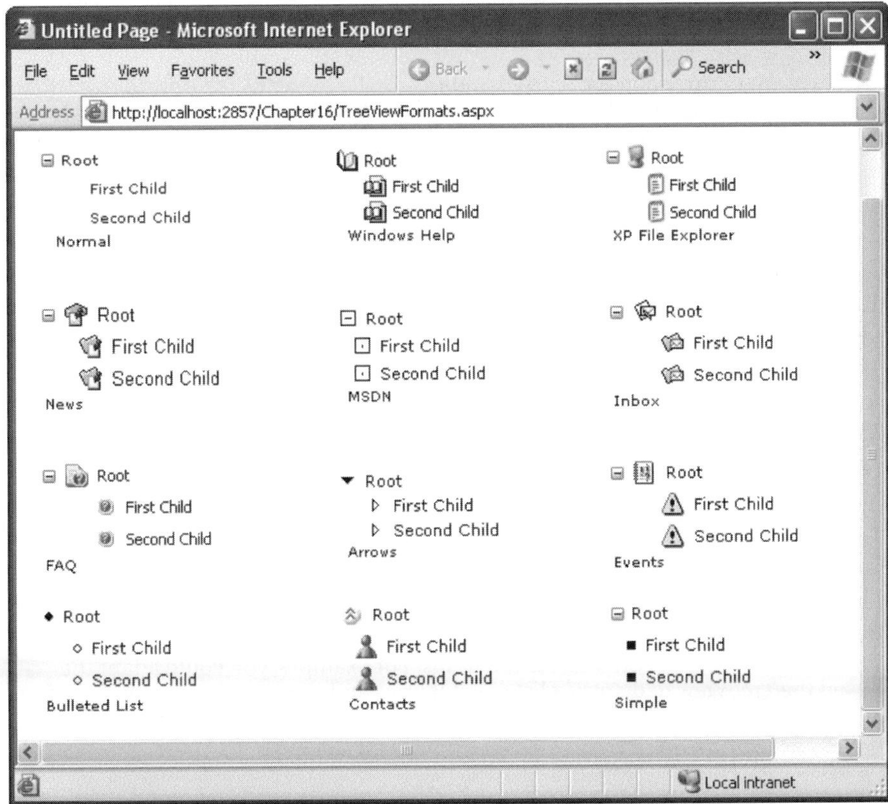

Figure 17-17. Different looks for a TreeView

The Menu Control

The Menu control is another rich control that supports hierarchical data. Like the TreeView, you can bind the Menu to a data source, or you can fill it by hand (declaratively or programmatically) using MenuItem objects.

The MenuItem class isn’t quite as rich as the TreeNode class—for example, MenuItem objects don’t support check boxes or the ability to programmatically set their expanded/collapsed state. However, they still have many similar properties, including those for setting images, determining whether the item is selectable, and specifying a target link. Table 17-12 has the defaults.

Table 17-12. MenuItem Properties

Property	Description
Text	The text displayed in the menu for this item (when displayed).
ToolTip	The tooltip text that appears when you hover over the menu item.
Value	Stores a nondisplayed value with additional data about the menu item (such as a unique ID you'll use when handling click events to identify the node or look up more information).
NavigateUrl	If set, when this node is clicked, it automatically forwards the user to this URL. Otherwise, you'll need to react to the Menu.MenuItemClick event to decide what action you want to perform.
Target	If the NavigateUrl property is set, this sets the target window or frame for the link. If Target isn't set, the new page is opened in the current browser witndow. The Menu also exposes a Target property, which you can set to apply a default target for all MenuItem instances.
Selectable	If false, this item can't be selected. Usually you'll set this to false only if the item is a subheading that contains selectable child items.
ImageUrl	If set, it's the image that's displayed next to the menu item (on the right of the text). By default, no image is used.
PopOutImageUrl	The image that's displayed next to the menu item (on the right) if it contains subitems. By default, this is a small solid arrow.
SeparatorImageUrl	The image that's displayed immediately underneath this menu item, to separate it from the following item.

You can walk over the structure of a Menu control in much the same way as the structure of a TreeView. The Menu contains a collection of MenuItem objects in the Items property, and each MenuItem has a ChildItems collection that contains nested items. For example, you could adapt the previous example that used the TreeView to display a list of categories and products by simply changing a few class names. Here's the code you need, with the surprisingly few changes highlighted:

```
protected void Page_Load(object sender, EventArgs e)
{
    if (!Page.IsPostBack)
    {
        DataSet ds = GetProductsAndCategories();

        // Loop through the category records.
        foreach (DataRow row in ds.Tables["Categories"].Rows)
        {
            // Create the menu item for this category.
            MenuItem itemCategory = new MenuItem(
              row["CategoryName"].ToString(),
              row["CategoryID"].ToString());
            Menu1.Items.Add(itemCategory);
```

```
            // Create the menu items for the products in this category.
            DataRow[] childRows = row.GetChildRows(ds.Relations[0]);
            foreach (DataRow childRow in childRows)
            {
                MenuItem itemProduct = new MenuItem(
                  childRow["ProductName"].ToString(),
                  childRow["ProductID"].ToString());
                itemCategory.ChildItems.Add(itemProduct);
            }
        }
    }
}

protected void Menu1_MenuItemClick(object sender,
  System.Web.UI.WebControls.MenuEventArgs e)
{
    if (Menu1.SelectedItem.Depth == 0)
    {
        lblInfo.Text = "You selected Category ID: ";
    }
    else if (Menu1.SelectedItem.Depth == 1)
    {
        lblInfo.Text = "You selected Product ID: ";
    }
    lblInfo.Text += Menu1.SelectedItem.Value;
}
```

Figure 17-18 shows the result.

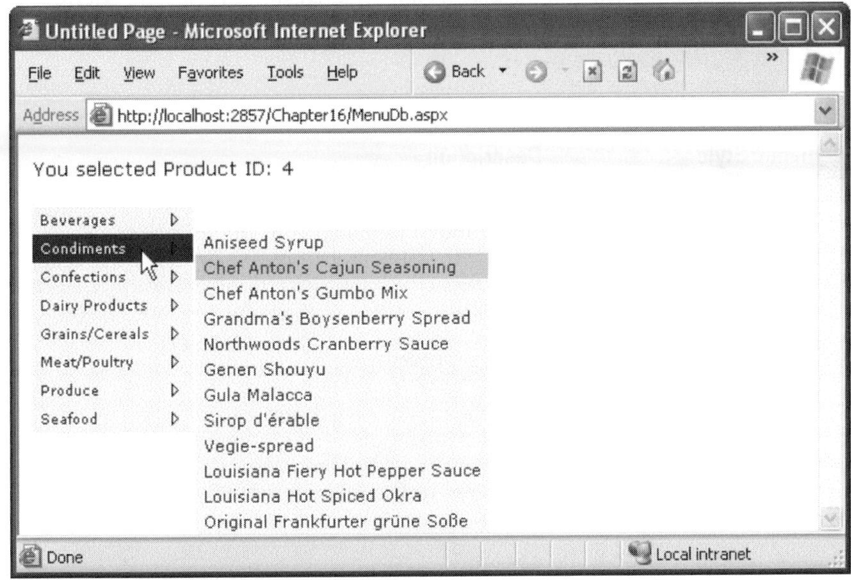

Figure 17-18. Displaying a menu with information from a database

Overall, the Menu and TreeView controls expose strikingly similar programming models, even though they render themselves quite differently. They also have a similar style-based formatting model. But a few noteworthy differences exist:

- The Menu displays a single submenu. The TreeView can expand an arbitrary number of node branches at a time.
- The Menu displays a root level of links in the page. All other items are displayed using fly-out menus that appear over any other content on the page. The TreeView shows all its items inline in the page.
- The TreeView supports on-demand filling and client callbacks. The Menu does not.
- The Menu supports templates. The TreeView does not.
- The TreeView supports check boxes for any node. The Menu does not.
- The Menu supports horizontal and vertical layouts, depending on the Orientation property. The TreeView supports only vertical layouts.

Menu Styles

The Menu control provides an overwhelming number of styles. Like the TreeView, the Menu derives a custom class from the Style base class—in fact, it derives two (MenuStyle and MenuItemStyle). These styles add spacing properties (ItemSpacing, HorizontalPadding, and VerticalPadding). However, you can't set menu item images through the style, because there is no ImageUrl property.

Much like the TreeView, the Menu supports defining different menu styles for different menu levels. However, the key distinction that the Menu control encourages you to adopt is between *static* items (the root level items that are displayed in the page when it's first generated) and *dynamic* items (the items in fly-out menus that are added when the user moves the mouse over a portion of the menu). In most websites, there is a definite difference in the styling of these two elements. To support this, the Menu class defines two parallel sets of styles, one that applies to static items and one that applies to dynamic items, as shown in Table 17-13.

***Table 17-13.** Menu Styles*

Static Style	Dynamic Style	Description
StaticMenuStyle	DynamicMenuStyle	Sets the appearance of the overall "box" in which all the menu items appear. In the case of StaticMenuStyle, this box is shown on the page, whereas with DynamicMenuStyle it's shown as a pop-up.
StaticMenuItemStyle	DynamicMenuItemStyle	Sets the appearance of individual menu items.
StaticSelectedStyle	DynamicSelectedStyle	Sets the appearance of the selected item. Note that the selected item isn't the item that's currently being hovered over. It's the item that was previously clicked (and triggered the last postback).
StaticHoverStyle	DynamicHoverStyle	Sets the appearance of the item that the user is hovering over with the mouse.

Along with these styles, you can set level-specific styles so that each level of menu and submenu is different. You do this using three collections: LevelMenuItemStyles, LevelSubMenuStyles, and LevelSelectedStyles. These collections apply to ordinary menus, menus that contain other items, and selected menu items, respectively.

It might seem like there's a fair bit of unnecessary work here in separating dynamic and static styles. The reason for this model becomes obvious when you consider another remarkable feature of the Menu control—it allows you to choose the number of static levels. By default, there is only one static level, and everything else is displayed as a fly-out menu when the user hovers over the corresponding parent. But you can set the Menu.StaticDisplayLevels property to change all that. If you set it to 2, for example, the first two levels of the menu will be rendered in the page, using the static styles. (You can control the indentation of each level using the StaticSubMenuIndent property.)

Figure 17-19 shows the previous example with this change. Note that the items still change as you hover over them, and selection works in the same way. If you want, you can make your entire menu static.

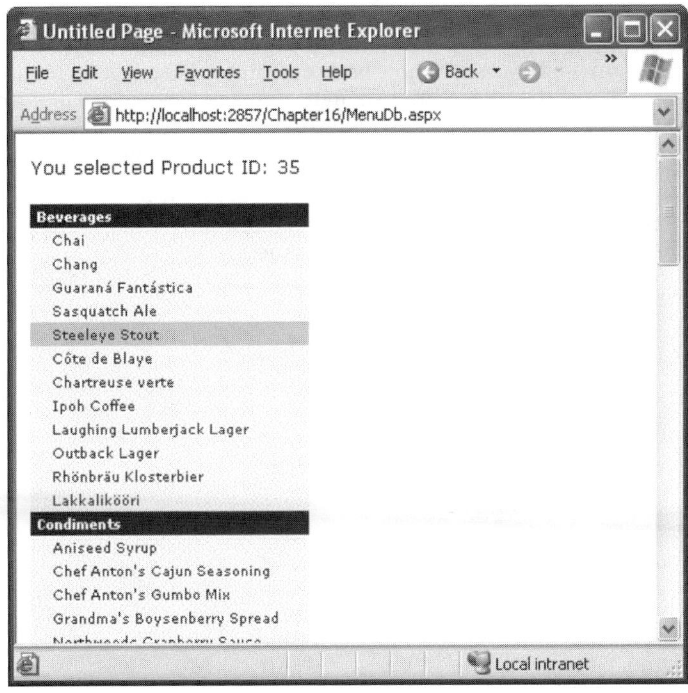

Figure 17-19. *A menu with two static levels*

■ **Tip** The Menu control exposes many more top-level properties for tweaking specific rendering aspects. For example, you can set the delay before a pop-up menu disappears (DisappearAfter), the default images used for expansion icons and separators, the scrolling behavior (which kicks into gear when the browser window is too small to fit a pop-up menu), and much more. Consult the Visual Studio help for a full list of properties.

Menu Templates

The Menu control also supports templates through the StaticMenuItemTemplate and DynamicMenuItemTemplate properties. These templates determine the HTML that's rendered for each menu item, giving you complete control.

Interestingly, whether you fill the Menu class declaratively or programmatically, you can still use a template. From the template's point of view, you're always binding to a MenuItem object. That means your template always needs to extract the value for the item from the MenuItem.Text property, as shown here:

```
<asp:Menu ID="Menu1" runat="server">
  <StaticItemTemplate>
    <%# Eval("Text") %>
  </StaticItemTemplate>
</asp:Menu>
```

One reason you might want to use the template features of the Menu is to show multiple pieces of information from a data object. For example, you might want to show both the title and the description from the SiteMapNode for this item (rather than just the title). Unfortunately, that's not possible. The problem is that the Menu binds directly to the MenuItem object. The MenuItem object does expose a DataItem property, but by the time it's being added into the menu, that DataItem no longer has the reference to the SiteMapNode that was used to populate it. So, you're mostly out of luck.

If you're really desperate, you can write a custom method in your class that looks up the SiteMapNode based on its URL. This is extra work that should be unnecessary, but it solves the problem. The GetDescriptionFromTitle() method shown here demonstrates this technique:

```
private string matchingDescription = "";

protected string GetDescriptionFromTitle(string title)
{
    // This assumes there's only one node with this title.
    SiteMapNode node = SiteMap.RootNode;
    SearchNodes(node, title);
    return matchingDescription;
}

private void SearchNodes(SiteMapNode node, string title)
{
    if (node.Title == title)
    {
        matchingDescription = node.Description;
        return;
    }
    else
    {
        foreach (SiteMapNode child in node.ChildNodes)
        {
            // Perform recursive search.
            SearchNodes(child, title);
        }
    }
}
```

Now you can use the GetDescriptionFromTitle() method in a template:

```
<asp:Menu ID="Menu1" runat="server" DataSourceID="SiteMapDataSource1">
  <StaticItemTemplate>
    <%# Eval("Text") %><br />
    <small>
    <%# GetDescriptionFromTitle(((MenuItem)Container.DataItem).Text) %>
    </small>
  </StaticItemTemplate>
  <DynamicItemTemplate>
    <%# Eval("Text") %><br />
    <small>
    <%# GetDescriptionFromTitle(((MenuItem)Container.DataItem).Text) %>
    </small>
  </DynamicItemTemplate>
</asp:Menu>
```

Finally, you can declare data bindings for the Menu control that specifically map out what property in the bound object should be used for the MenuItem text. This isn't much help if you want to display both the title and description, because it accepts only one field. However, it's fairly easy to show the title as the text and the description as the tooltip text:

```
<asp:Menu ID="Menu1" runat="server" DataSourceID="SiteMapDataSource1">
  <DataBindings>
    <asp:MenuItemBinding DataMember="SiteMapNode" TextField="Title"
     ToolTipField="Description" />
  </DataBindings>
</asp:Menu>
```

■ **Note** In ASP.NET 4, the Menu no longer renders itself using HTML tables. Instead, it renders itself as an unordered list of items (using the <ul> and <li> elements), and it applies style rules to create the correct formatting.

The Menu renders all its styles in a style block at the top of the page, rather than inline with the rendered HTML. However, you can set the new Menu.IncludeStyleBlock property to false to tell the Menu not to render its styles at all. This allows you to take full control over the Menu styling, and even apply styles from an external style sheet. (If you need a starting point, run your web page with IncludeStyleBlock set to true, copy the styles from the rendered HTML, and then adapt them to fit your needs.)

Summary

In this chapter, you explored a variety of navigation features. You started with the multipane MultiView and Wizard controls. You then delved into ASP.NET's navigation model and learned how to define site maps, bind the navigation data, and extend the site map provider infrastructure. Finally, you considered two rich controls that are especially suited for navigation data: the TreeView and Menu.

CHAPTER 18

■ ■ ■

Website Deployment

In production projects, you will almost certainly have one of more servers that you will use to service client requests for your website. These servers may be owned and operated by you or your infrastructure team or by a third-party hosting company. Either way, there comes a time when the coding and testing is complete and it is time to publish your work to the world, and you do that by *deploying* your website. In this chapter, we'll walk you through the different deployment options. The basic premise for all the options is the same, though. You have a completed website on your development workstation that you want to deploy to a server in order that it is available to clients. For ASP.NET, the server in this scenario is Internet Information Services (IIS), and the current version is IIS 7. IIS started out as a basic web server when it was first released. Over the years, IIS has evolved into a sophisticated application server with a wide range of features, key among them being support for hosting ASP.NET applications.

We don't have the space to cover all the features of IIS (and as an ASP.NET developer, we suspect that you won't be interested in the gory details). But we will show you how to get the basic IIS features up and running and how to configure and use each of the approaches available for deployment.

The approach you use for deployment will be driven by your hosting arrangements. If you are using a hosting company, they will send you details of their preferred technique. Similarly, if you have an IT team that runs your server for you, they will have already set up an approach and expect you to use it. If you have a free choice in which approach to use, then we suggest picking the simplest.

Installing and Configuring IIS

In this chapter, we focus on IIS 7. Although we refer to the machine running IIS 7 as the *server* in this chapter, you can run IIS on both the workstation and server versions of Windows. Some features are not available on workstations, but most of them are, and you can host complex websites this way. We recommend using Windows Server if you can, but using Windows 7 or Windows Vista can be a low-cost alternative.

Microsoft ties the release of IIS to the release of Windows. Windows Server 2008 and Windows Vista run IIS version 7.0, while Windows Server 2008 R2 and Windows 7 run IIS version 7.5. Confusingly, Microsoft refers collectively to versions 7.0 and 7.5 as *IIS 7*. You can't change the version of IIS that your operating system supports—Windows Server 2008 will only ever run IIS 7.0. You can't upgrade to the version 7.5 that Windows Server 2008 R2 uses, for example.

Installing IIS 7

IIS is included as part of the installation of Windows (both the server and workstation varieties) and needs to be activated and configured. The simplest way of activating and configuring IIS 7 on any version of Windows is using the Web Platform Installer (known as *WebPI*). WebPI provides a standard interface and has a catalog of add-on components to expand the IIS feature set. In this section, we'll show you how to use WebPI to get IIS running. As we look at different deployment options, we'll return to WebPI to install additional features.

■ **Note** In this chapter, we assume that you have the Administrator password and are logged in to the server using the Administrator account in order to install and manage IIS 7.

To get started with WebPI, open your server's browser, and go to http://www.microsoft.com/web/downloads/platform.aspx. You will see a link to download the installer. Depending on your operating system and browser settings, you will see a number of security warnings. Download and run the installer. This installs WebPI, not IIS. When the installation has completed, WebPI will start, and you'll see a window similar to Figure 18-1.

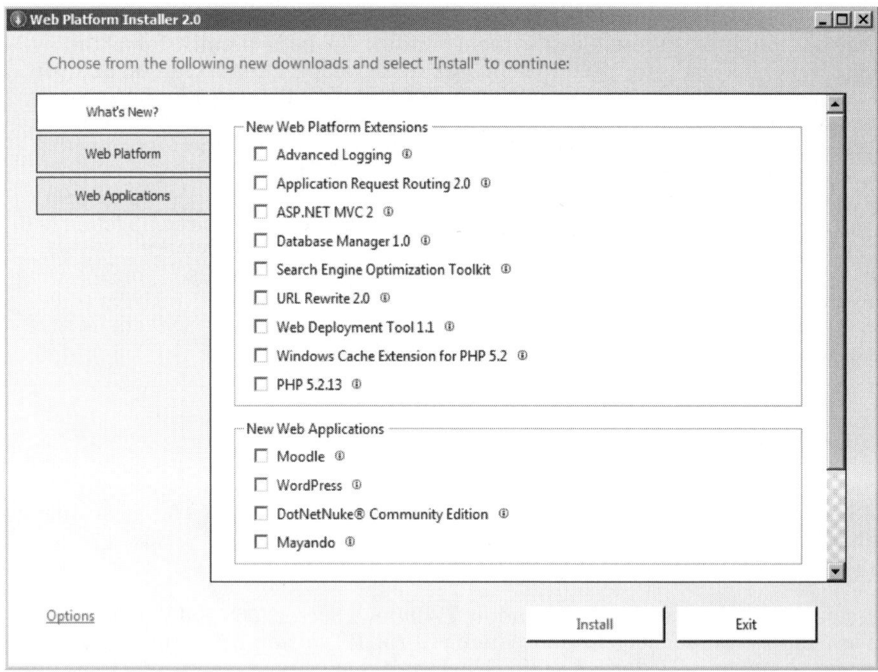

Figure 18-1. The WebPI What's New? screen

Click the Web Platform tab. You will see that WebPI is able to install more than just IIS 7. It can also install SQL Server Express, various web application frameworks, and some support tools. We are going to keep things simple and install only the items we need for this chapter.

First select the IIS 7 components you want. Click the "Click to include the recommended products" link in the Web Server section. A green check mark will appear. Now click the Customize link in the Web Server section. This will show a list of the individual IIS 7 features available—select the ASP.NET option.

Return to the Web Platform tab, and select .NET Framework 4.0 from the Frameworks and Runtimes section. We don't need anything else for the moment, so now you can click the Install button. You will see a list of the components that will be installed and the license terms that they require. Accept the terms to begin the download and installation.

Much of the software you need is already included in the Windows installation. The WebPI downloads any missing pieces and configures IIS for you. When the installation and configuration have been completed, you will see a summary screen. Exit WebPI.

To test that everything has worked properly, open a web browser on the server, and go to localhost. You should see the default IIS 7 welcome page.

Managing IIS 7

Now that you have IIS 7 installed and running, you can manage it. You do that through the IIS Manager tool, which was installed on the server by WebPI. You can find IIS Manager in the Start menu. The location can vary based on which version of Windows you use; it will be in the Programs section or the Administrative Tools section. Figure 18-2 shows the IIS Manager's Start Page.

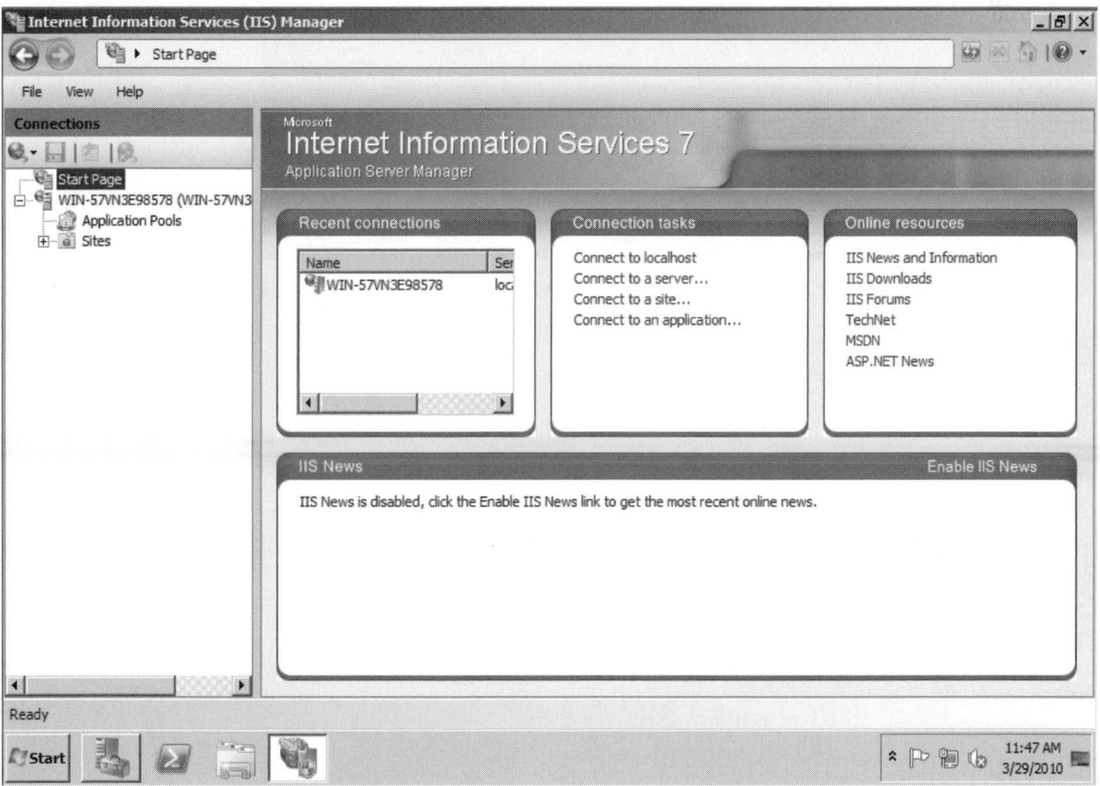

Figure 18-2. *IIS Manager's Start Page*

We now need to introduce some IIS terminology. If you look at the left side of IIS Manager, you will see the Start Page and then an entry with the name of your server. Our server has the catchy name of

WIN-57VN3E98578—this is the default name generated for us by Windows Server 2008 R2, which we'll be using for most of the examples in this chapter. If you click the name, you'll get the Server View, as shown by Figure 18-3.

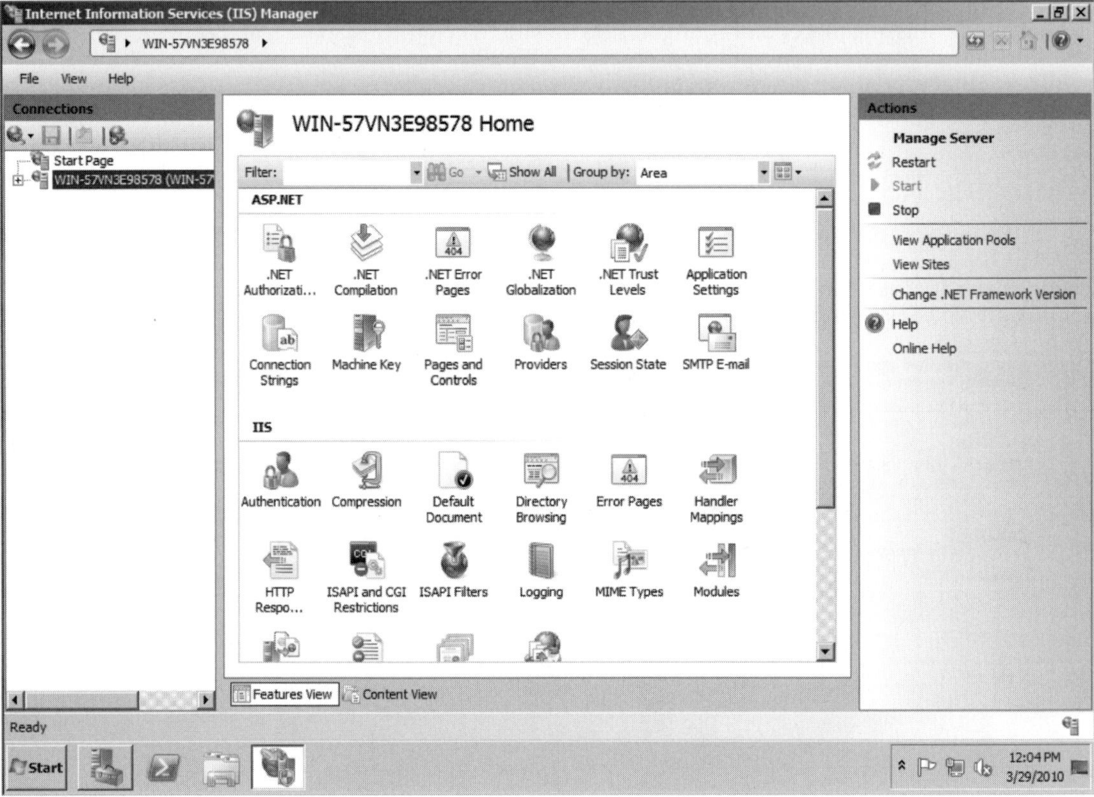

Figure 18-3. *IIS Manager's Server View*

The Server View presents a series of icons that allow you to configure the settings for your server. On the right side of the screen, you will see a series of actions. In this view, you can start, stop, and restart your server, for example. If you expand the server item in the tree control on the left of the screen, you will see an item named Sites, which contains a single entry called Default Web Site. A *site* is a collection of files and directories that make up a website. IIS can support multiple sites on a single server, typically on different TCP/IP ports (the default being port 80). The combination of the server name and the site port give you the first part of the URL. For example, if you have a server called mywebserver with a site on port 80, your URL would be as follows:

```
http://mywebserver:80
```

Each site can contain multiple files and directories. Each of these makes up part of the URL. If you have a directory called myfiles that contains a static page called mypage.html, then you get the following URL:

```
http://mywebserver:80/myfiles/mypage.html
```

■ **Note** In some situations, the name that you know a server by and the name that clients use to retrieve content will be different. We are going to gloss over this, but your server administrator or hosting company will give you the details you need if this applies to your server.

So, to summarize, each *server* can support multiple *sites*, each running on a different port or IP address. Each site can have multiple files and directories, and the combination of these items gives you the information for the URL. We'll return to the URL and using IIS Manager as we cover each deployment approach.

Deploying a Website

Now that you have IIS 7 running and know how to manage it, you can begin to deploy websites. At its simplest, you can deploy an ASP.NET web application by doing nothing more than copying the directory structure of your application to the target machine and configuring the environment. For simple applications, that's almost always true. But if your application uses databases or accesses other resources, you have to perform some additional steps. Here are some common factors that will require additional configuration steps:

- Copy all required application files to the target machine. You don't need to do anything else. But if you are using global assemblies accessed through the GAC, you have to verify whether these assemblies are in place. If not, you have to install them using the gacutil.exe command-line utility of the .NET Framework.
- Create and configure the database for the application. It's important not only to create the database and its tables but to configure the database server logins and database users. Don't forget that if you are using integrated authentication for connecting to a SQL Server database, you must configure the account under which ASP.NET is executed (the application pool account or aspnet_wp.exe account) as a user for the application's database. The web deployment approach can simplify your database deployment—see the "Using Web Deployment" section later in the chapter. If you do not use web deployment, you will have to configure and populate your databases manually.
- Configure IIS as required for the application. Therefore, create necessary application pools, share the application directory as a virtual directory, and configure the virtual directory appropriately. See the "Using Application Pools" section later in this chapter for more details.
- Set up Windows account permissions for the worker process user. The user who is used for running the worker process (w3wp.exe) needs read access to the application directories. If your application accesses other resources such as the registry or event log, you have to configure the permission for the worker process account to access these resources.
- Add IIS file mappings if you want to process any URLs with filename extensions that are different from the extensions registered on a default ASP.NET installation.
- Configure ASP.NET (and IIS 7.0 application-specific configuration settings) through the web.config file for production environments. That means add (or modify) any connection strings and application settings as well as security and authorization settings, session state settings, and globalization settings appropriately.

- In some cases, it is also required to modify machine.config. For example, if you are in a web hosting environment and your application runs on multiple web servers for load balancing, you have to synchronize any encryption keys used for encrypting forms authentication tickets or view state on all those machines. These keys are stored in machine.config and need to be equal on every machine in the web farm so that one machine is able to decrypt information encrypted by another machine that previously processed the request.

The core activity is deploying the contents of your application to IIS7. In the following sections, we'll show you how to use the three most common deployment approaches.

■ **Note** In this chapter, we assume that you have the Administrator credentials and are logged in to the server using the Administrator account. If you are using a shared server or a hosting provider, the provider will send you account details to use when deploying websites. We have assumed Administrator for simplicity, but if you are managing your own server, then you should consider using a less privileged account.

Deploying by Copying Files

The simplest way to deploy a website is to copy the files from your development workstation to the server. Although simple, this approach does require you to have direct access to the server, which is why some IT departments and hosting companies won't support this option. But this could be your easiest option if you control your own server or you have an especially understanding hosting arrangement.

■ **Note** This deployment technique works for all versions of IIS 7 running on all versions of Windows.

Preparing IIS

You must prepare IIS before you deploy your website. The main decision is where you want to place the content and how this affects the URL you then end up with. Let's start with an obvious approach—we would like the URL for our example content to be as follows:

```
http://<servername>:80/WebsiteDeployment/FileCopy
```

We need to prepare IIS so we have somewhere to copy our file to. Using IIS Manager, select the Default Web Site item. This is, as the name suggests, the default site on the server. Right-click and select Explore to open a Windows Explorer window for the default IIS directory, which is the inetpub\wwwroot directory of the system volume (typically C:\). Create a directory called WebsiteDeployment, and create another, called FileCopy, nested inside of it (so the path inetpub\wwwroot\WebsiteDeployment\FileCopy exists). Close the File Explorer window to return to IIS Manager. Right-click the Default Web Site item, and select Refresh to see the new directories.

The Website

We have created a very simple website to demonstrate this deployment technique. We have included all the websites used in this chapter in the source code download, available from Apress.com. This project contains a single ASP.NET form with a single label, as shown in Figure 18-4.

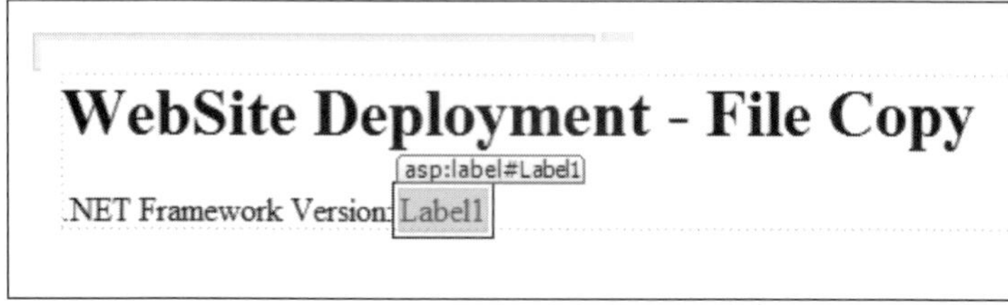

Figure 18-4. *The ASP.NET form for the sample website*

In the code behind the form, we set the label text to show us which version of the .NET Framework is being used to host our site, as follows:

```
using System;

public partial class Default : System.Web.UI.Page
{
    protected void Page_Load(object sender, EventArgs e)
    {
        Label1.Text = System.Environment.Version.Major.ToString();
    }
}
```

Deploying the Website

In this deployment technique, we just copy the files into the directory we created. Transfer the website files to the server by whatever means suits you—shared network drive, USB key, DVD, and so on—and copy the Default.aspx and Default.aspx.cs files into the FileCopy directory you created on the server. When you have copied the files into place, return to IIS Manager on the server, right-click the FileCopy item in the tree control, and select Refresh. At the bottom of the screen, click the Content View button. You should see the two website files in the center part of the display, as shown in Figure 18-5.

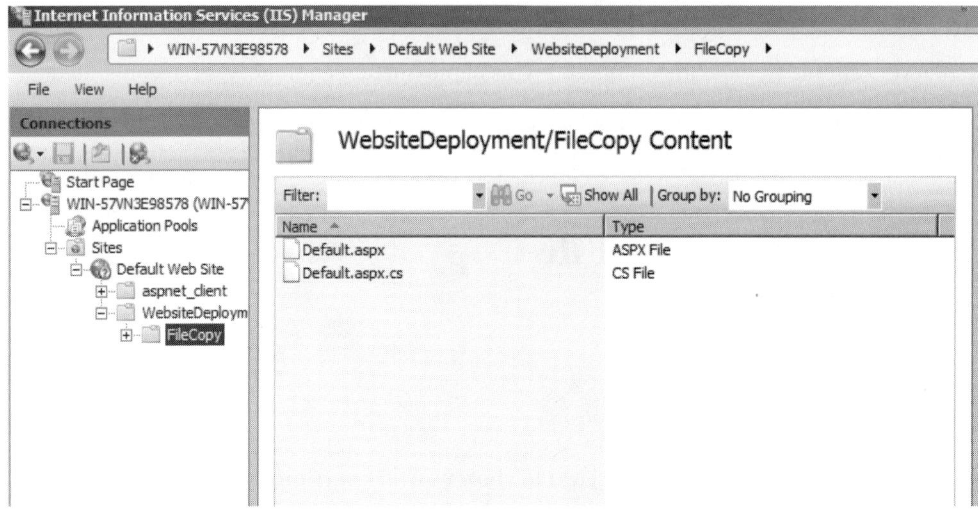

Figure 18-5. The deployed website items

That's the most important part of this deployment technique—you create the directory structure that represents the URL you require and then copy your website files into place. Let's see how it looks. To do that, select the FileCopy item in IIS Manager, and click the Browse link on the right side of the window. This will open a web browser and point it at the URL for the folder you created. You should see something similar to Figure 18-6.

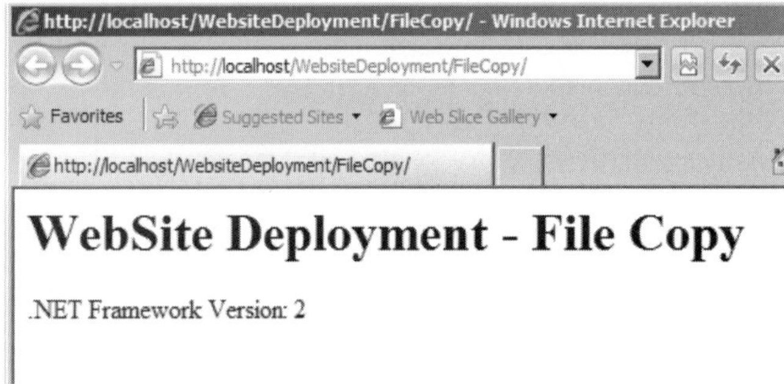

Figure 18-6. Browsing the deployed website

If we look at the URL, we can see that we got the result we were looking for. The browser has loaded the website from here:

```
http://localhost/WebsiteDeployment/FileCopy/
```

You might already know that localhost is a special name that refers to the current machine and that a URL that doesn't specify a port will use port 80. Just to prove the point, we get the same result if we point the browser at the following URL:

```
http://win-57vn3e9857:80/WebsiteDeployment/FileCopy/
```

Configuring the Deployment

You may have noticed that the .NET Framework version is being reported as 2 in Figure 18-6. This would be a problem for any website that depends on ASP.NET 4 features. We are not quite done yet—we need to configure the website we deployed to use .NET version 4. We do this by changing the settings for the default application pool. Don't worry about application pools for the moment; we explain more about them in the "Managing a Website" section later in this chapter. For the moment, it is enough to know that we need to make a change so that our website uses version 4 of the .NET Framework.

Using IIS Manager, expand the server item, and click Application Pools.
Click the Set Application Pool Defaults link, which is on the right side of the display. In the dialog box that appears, change the .NET Framework Version setting to be 4.0, as shown in Figure 18-7.

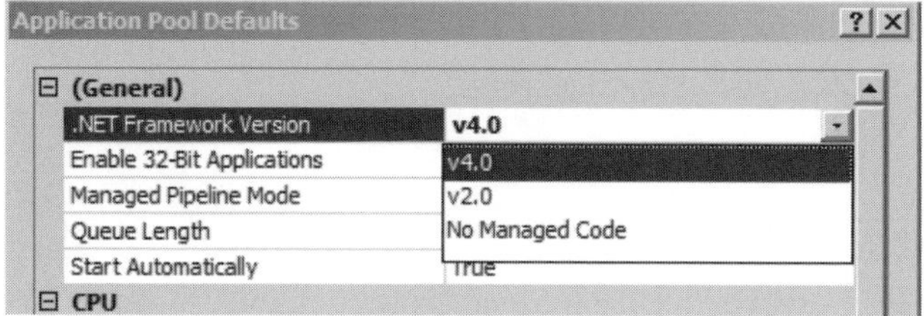

Figure 18-7. Setting the .NET Framework version in the Application Pool Defaults dialog box

Return to your web browser, and reload the page. You should not see that the .NET Framework version reported by the website page is 4, as shown in Figure 18-8.

Figure 18-8. The website running under version 4 of the .NET Framework

---

■ **Tip** If you see error 500.21 with the message “Handler "WebServiceHandlerFactory-Integrated" has a bad module "ManagedPipelineHandler" in its module list,” then your ASP.NET installation has not completed properly. We have noticed this happens most with Windows Vista. You can fix this by running the following command (for 32-bit systems):

C:\Windows\Microsoft.NET\Framework\v4.0.<build_number>\aspnet_regiis –i

You will need to correctly enter the build number where we have included <build_number> in the command string. For 64-bit systems, the command is as follows:

C:\Windows\Microsoft.NET\Framework64\v4.0.<build_number>\aspnet_regiis –i

---

We also want to tell IIS that our deployed site is an application. This is optional, but you’ll almost certainly want to do this when deploying ASP.NET applications—it enables session state and other ASP.NET features. Right-click the FileCopy folder item in the IIS Manager Connections area, and select Convert to Application, as shown in Figure 18-9.

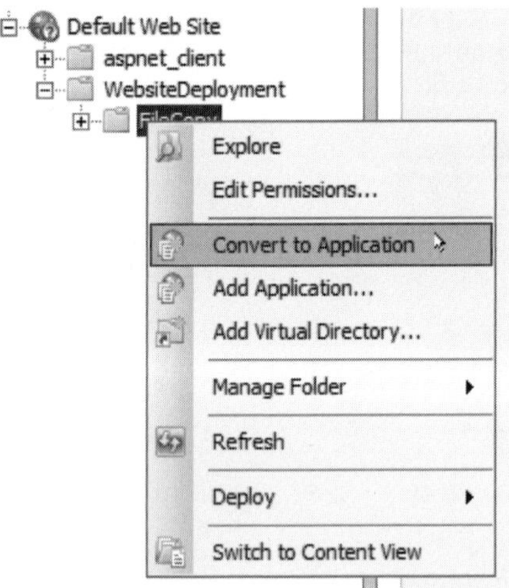

Figure 18-9. *Converting to an application*

This will open the Add Application dialog box. You can change the application pool used for your application by clicking the Select button. We will have more to say on applications pools later in the chapter. You can configure the user account that IIS will use to access the content in your site using the Connect as... and Test Settings... buttons. For now, though, simply click the OK button. You may have to select Refresh from the View menu (or, as we often find, close and reopen IIS Manager), but the FileCopy entry in the tree control should now have a different icon.

Using Web Deployment

Web deployment allows you to deploy your website directly from Visual Studio 2010 using HTTP—but only if you have created a project, rather than used the project-less website feature. Don't confuse web deployment with Front Page Server Extensions (FPSE). FPSE has been phased out, although you can download and install them for IIS 7.0 on Windows Server 2008 and Windows Vista.

■ **Note** This deployment technique works only on the server versions of Windows.

Preparing IIS

You need to add two components to IIS to use the web deploy feature. You do this by using WebPI again. When you installed and configured IIS 7 at the start of the chapter, WebPI was installed on your machine. Start WebPI from your Start menu, and select Customize from the Web Server section of the Web Platform tab.

In the Deployment and Publishing section, select the Web Deployment Tool option. At the time we wrote this book, the current version was 1.1. In the Management section, check the Management Service option. It is important that you install both of them to make this deployment approach works properly.

When installation has completed, start IIS Manager, and select the server item in the Connections tree control. Scroll to the bottom of the screen, and if everything has been installed correctly, you should see two new icons—one called Management Service and one called Management Service Delegation.

You need to configure and start a Windows Service that will listen for remote IIS management requests. Double-click the Management Service icon to see the Management Service feature page. Select the Enable remote connections option, click Apply, and then click Start.

By enabling remote connections, you are allowing other machines to perform management operations on IIS. You will use this feature to publish directly from Visual Studio in this section and to publish a package from IIS Manager in the next section. We'll be demonstrating these features using the Administrator account, but you can use other accounts and configure exactly what each can do using the Management Service Delegation icon.

■ **Tip** By default, the Management Service does not start automatically when the server is booted. If you want it to start automatically, you should change the setting of the Web Management Service in the Services tool.

The Website

You can use web deployment from Visual Studio 2010 for ASP.NET application projects—but not project-less websites. To demonstrate this kind of deployment, we have created a project that contains a single page that reports on the .NET Framework version, just like we used in the previous example. The only difference between the website we created for this example and the previous one is the use of the Visual Studio project.

To create this project yourself, create a new Visual Studio project using the ASP.NET Empty Web Application template, and add a new web form to the project with the name Default.aspx. You can put any components you like on this form—we have followed the same format as before, as shown in Figure 18-10.

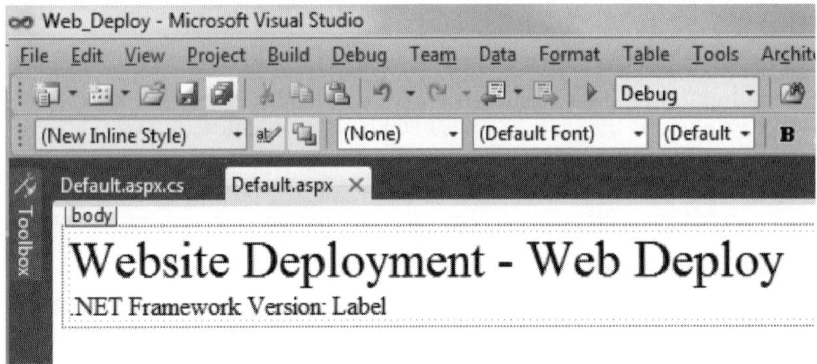

Figure 18-10. *The sample website*

And, because we want to be sure that our site is run under the correct version of the .NET so we can rely on ASP.NET 4, we have added code to display the major version of the framework, as follows:

```
using System;

namespace Web_Deploy {
    public partial class Default : System.Web.UI.Page {
        protected void Page_Load(object sender, EventArgs e) {
            Label1.Text = System.Environment.Version.Major.ToString();
        }
    }
}
```

You can download the project from Apress.com as part of the source code for this book—this is the simplest way of following along with this example.

Transforming web.config

Many projects go through a series of deployment phases as they move from development through testing and into production, where each step involves deploying to staging servers that have different configurations. The Web Deployment model includes a useful feature for simplifying this process by transforming the web.config file to work at each stage as part of the deployment process.

If you expand web.config in the Solution Explorer, you'll see that there are items listed for each build configuration in your project; these are the web.config transformation files. By default, Visual Studio 2010 creates Debug and Release configurations, but you can add custom configurations using the Configuration Manager.

During web deployment, XML statements in the transformation file for the active build configuration are applied to the source web.config in your project to add, modify, and delete configuration settings. When the project is deployed, the transformed settings are included, which means that, for example, you don't have to change connection strings by hand to work with the databases in a different staging area. Not only is this convenient, but it reduces the chances of a configuration error breaking your environment when you deploy. In the following sections, we'll show you the most useful transformations you can apply to a configuration file. We'll use the same source web.config file for each example, the contents of which are as follows:

```
<?xml version="1.0"?>
<configuration>

  <connectionStrings>
    <add name="NorthwindConnectionString" connectionString="Data
Source=.\SQLEXPRESS;AttachDbFilename=|DataDirectory|\Northwind.mdf;Integrated
Security=True;User Instance=True"
      providerName="System.Data.SqlClient" />
  </connectionStrings>

  <system.web>
    <compilation debug="true" targetFramework="4.0" />
  </system.web>
</configuration>
```

This contains the connection string for the Northwind database on our development workstation and targets .NET 4 with debugging symbols.

Setting an Attribute

The most common transformation is to change an attribute for a setting in the source web.config—for example, changing the connection string for a database. Here is a web.release.config transformation file that changes the connection string so that it points at our Windows Server 2008 R2 machine:

```
<?xml version="1.0"?>
<configuration xmlns:xdt="http://schemas.microsoft.com/XML-Document-Transform">

    <connectionStrings>
      <add name="NorthwindConnectionString"
        connectionString="Data Source=WIN-57VN3E98578;Initial Catalog=Northwind;Integrated
            Security=True"
        xdt:Transform="SetAttributes" xdt:Locator="Match(name)"/>
    </connectionStrings>

</configuration>
```

To set an existing attribute, you use the same definition as the source file (in this case, adding a named item to connectionStrings) and add the Transform and Locator elements. Setting the value of Transform to SetAttributes replaces the matching elements with the transformed data—our revised connection string in this example. The Locator element says that we want to match the element source element using the name attribute, in this case NorthwindConnectionString. Being able to specify which element to match is useful when there are multiple attributes of the same type.

We have included an example project in the source code download for this book that contains this transformation and the ones that follow—you can download the source code from Apress.com. When we deploy the project using the Release configuration, the transformation will be applied, and the web.config that is installed on IIS will contain the new connection string value, as shown here:

```
<?xml version="1.0"?>
<configuration>

  <connectionStrings>
    <add name="NorthwindConnectionString" connectionString="Data Source=WIN-
57VN3E98578;Initial Catalog=Northwind;Integrated Security=True"
providerName="System.Data.SqlClient" />
```

```
  </connectionStrings>

  <system.web>
    <compilation debug="true" targetFramework="4.0" />
  </system.web>
</configuration>
```

You can see that the transformation engine has replaced our development connection string (which uses an attached file to SQL Server Express) with our deployment connection string (which connects to a server). The transformation is not applied until deployment, so even if you switch the build configuration and rebuild the project, the values in your project web.config will still be used on your workstation.

Inserting Elements

You specify the Insert value for the Transform attribute to insert an element into the configuration file. We've added a transformation that adds a second connection string, marked in bold:

```
<?xml version="1.0"?>
<configuration xmlns:xdt="http://schemas.microsoft.com/XML-Document-Transform">

  <connectionStrings>
    <add name="NorthwindConnectionString"
      connectionString="Data Source=WIN-57VN3E98578;Initial Catalog=Northwind;Integrated
Security=True"
      xdt:Transform="SetAttributes" xdt:Locator="Match(name)"/>
  </connectionStrings>

  <connectionStrings>
    <add name="Connection2"
      connectionString="Data Source=MyServer;Initial Catalog=MyDB;Integrated Security=True"
      xdt:Transform="Insert"/>
  </connectionStrings>

</configuration>
```

We have left the first example to show you the format for specifying multiple transformations. When we deploy our project, we get the following transformed web.config, with the addition highlighted:

```
<?xml version="1.0"?>
<configuration>

  <connectionStrings>
    <add name="NorthwindConnectionString" connectionString="Data
Source=.\SQLEXPRESS;AttachDbFilename=|DataDirectory|\Northwind.mdf;Integrated
Security=True;User Instance=True" providerName="System.Data.SqlClient" />
    <add name="Connection2" connectionString="Data Source=MyServer;Initial
Catalog=MyDB;Integrated Security=True" />
  </connectionStrings>

  <system.web>
    <compilation debug="true" targetFramework="4.0" />
```

```
  </system.web>
</configuration>
```

Replacing Sections

To replace an entire section of web.config, use the Replace value for the Transform attribute, as follows:

```
<?xml version="1.0"?>
<configuration xmlns:xdt="http://schemas.microsoft.com/XML-Document-Transform">

  <system.web xdt:Transform="Replace">
    <customErrors defaultRedirect="GenericError.htm"
      mode="RemoteOnly">
      <error statusCode="500" redirect="InternalError.htm"/>
    </customErrors>
  </system.web>

</configuration>
```

This transformation specifies that the entire system.web block of web.config should be replaced with the content in the transformation file. When we deploy the project, we get the following result:

```
<?xml version="1.0"?>
<configuration>

  <connectionStrings>
    <add name="NorthwindConnectionString" connectionString="Data
Source=.\SQLEXPRESS;AttachDbFilename=|DataDirectory|\Northwind.mdf;Integrated
Security=True;User Instance=True" providerName="System.Data.SqlClient" />
  </connectionStrings>

  <system.web>
    <customErrors defaultRedirect="GenericError.htm" mode="RemoteOnly">
      <error statusCode="500" redirect="InternalError.htm" />
    </customErrors>
  </system.web>
</configuration>
```

Our development connection string has been left untouched, but our target for the framework version has been replaced.

Removing Elements

To remove a configuration section, you declare the section using the Remove value for the Transform attribute, as follows:

```
<?xml version="1.0"?>
<configuration xmlns:xdt="http://schemas.microsoft.com/XML-Document-Transform">
  <connectionStrings xdt:Transform="Remove"/>
</configuration>
```

This transformation removes the connectionStrings section, giving us the following when we deploy:

```
<?xml version="1.0"?>
<configuration>

  <system.web>
    <compilation debug="true" targetFramework="4.0" />
  </system.web>
</configuration>
```

You can remove individual attributes with RemoveAttributes, specifying the attributes you want to remove in a comma-separated list:

```
<?xml version="1.0"?>
<configuration xmlns:xdt="http://schemas.microsoft.com/XML-Document-Transform">
  <system.web>
    <compilation xdt:Transform="RemoveAttributes(debug,targetFramework)"/>
  </system.web>
</configuration>
```

This transformation removes the debug and targetFramework attributes from the compilation element, giving us the following deployed result:

```
<?xml version="1.0"?>
<configuration>

  <connectionStrings>
    <add name="NorthwindConnectionString" connectionString="Data
Source=.\SQLEXPRESS;AttachDbFilename=|DataDirectory|\Northwind.mdf;Integrated
Security=True;User Instance=True" providerName="System.Data.SqlClient" />
  </connectionStrings>

  <system.web>
    <compilation />
  </system.web>
</configuration>
```

Publishing Databases

Another useful feature for web deployment is to publish your database when you publish your project. A SQL script containing either the database scheme or the scheme and the data is generated as part of the deployment process and used to populate your deployment environment. Some caution is required to use this feature—it would be very easy to overwrite your production database with test data.

Configuring database publishing is a two-step process. On the Package/Publish Web properties tab for your project, select "Include all databases configured in the Package/Publish SQL tab" to enable the feature.

To specify the details, move to the Package/Publish SQL tab. The Database Entries table contains one entry for each database that will be published. You can use the connection strings already defined in your project by clicking the Import from web.config button. If you do import your connection strings, many of the details in the form will be populated for you, leaving you to add only the connection string for the target database. If you leave the target connection string blank, the value from web.config will be used, and if you have specified a transformation for that connection string, the transformed result will be used. See the preceding section for details of web.config transformations. If you have multiple databases, you can change the order in which they will be published using the up and down arrows for the Database Entries table. You can specify what the SQL script will contain—just the schema for your database or the schema and the data.

A useful option is to include statements in the SQL script that will drop the existing table and data during deployment. To enable this, you have to enable the project file directly—there is no UI option within Visual Studio. Open the file with the .csproj suffix, and look for the PublishDatabaseSettings section. Find the PreSource tag and add ScriptData="False" to that line, as marked in bold here:

```
<PublishDatabaseSettings>
      <Objects>
        <ObjectGroup Name="NorthwindConnectionString-Deployment" Order="1">
          <Destination Path="Data Source=WIN-57VN3E98578\SQLEXPRESS%3bInitial
Catalog=Northwind%3bPersist Security Info=True%3bUser ID=sa_deploy%3bPassword=sa" />
          <Object Type="dbFullSql">
            <PreSource Path="Data Source=.\sqlexpress%3bInitial Catalog=Northwind%3bPersist
Security Info=True%3bUser ID=sa_deploy%3bPassword=sa" ScriptDropsFirst="true"
ScriptSchema="True" ScriptData="False" CopyAllFullTextCatalogs="False" />
            <Source Path="obj\Debug\AutoScripts\NorthwindConnectionString-
Deployment_SchemaOnly.sql" Transacted="True" />
          </Object>
        </ObjectGroup>
   </Objects>
</PublishDatabaseSettings>
```

Visual Studio will prompt you to reload the project file, at which point the new setting will take effect. Once you have configured your publishing settings, you deploy your project as shown in the following sections.

Be very, very careful with these features and options—an inadvertent selection will have you looking for the backup tapes. There is nothing quite like the sick feeling in your stomach when you realize you have wiped the deployment database.

Deploying the Website

To deploy the website from within Visual Studio, open the website project, and select the Publish item from the Build menu. The exact name of the menu item will depend on the name you gave your project. If you are using our sample project, the item will be called Publish Web_Deploy.

You will see the Publish dialog box, as shown in Figure 18-11. This is the heart of the Web Deploy feature. For Publish method, select Web Deploy. In the Service URL box, enter the name of the server you will publish to—our Windows Server 2008 R2 server has the catchy name of WIN-57VN3E98578.

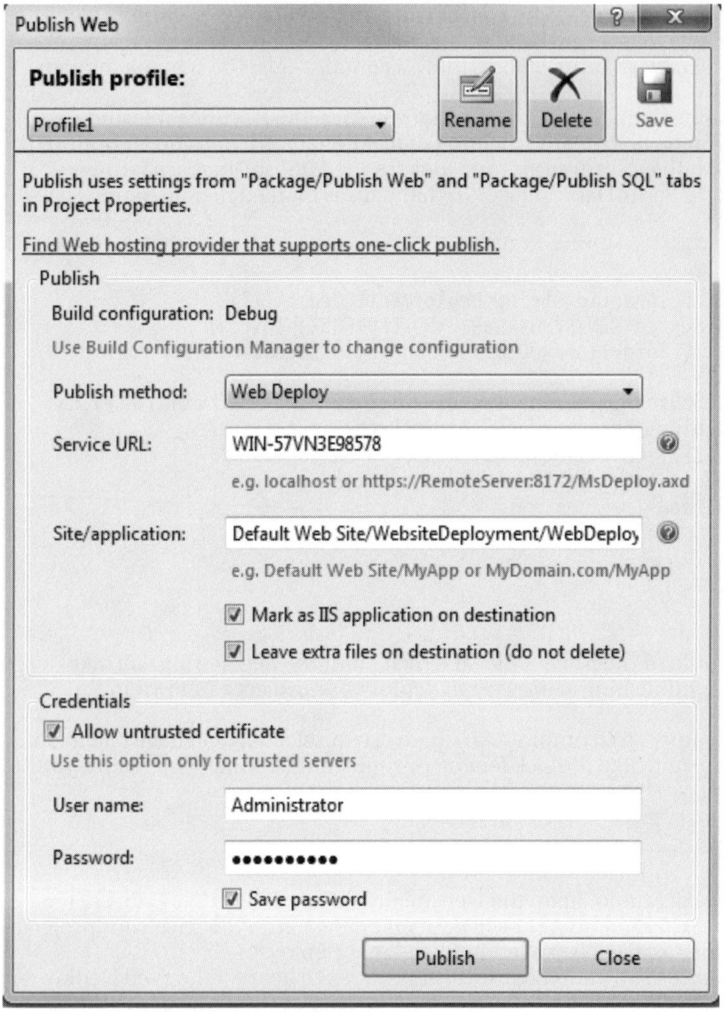

Figure 18-11. The Visual Studio Publish dialog box

The Site/application field lets you specify where the site will be deployed, and, as we have explained, this forms the URL that clients will use. For this example, we want our URL to be as follows:

```
http://<servername>/WebsiteDeployment/WebDeploy/
```

This URL will place our example alongside the one we deployed by copying files in the previous section. To achieve this, we have put Default Web Site/WebsiteDeployment/WebDeploy in the Site/application field.

Select the “Mark as IIS application on destination” option; this is equivalent to the manual process we followed with the previous technique.

In the Credentials section, enable “Allow untrusted certificate” if you have not installed a certificate on IIS 7 from a certificate authority—we haven’t on our server, so we need to enable this option to be able to publish using web deploy. Finally, enter the username and password for the account you want to use to publish—we have used the Administrator account. Your hosting company or server administrator will give you details of the account you should use.

That's it—you can now deploy your site by clicking the Publish button. If you refresh (or restart) IIS Manager, you can see the new application you have deployed, as shown in Figure 18-12. Any web.config transformations will have been performed, and any databases you configured will have been published.

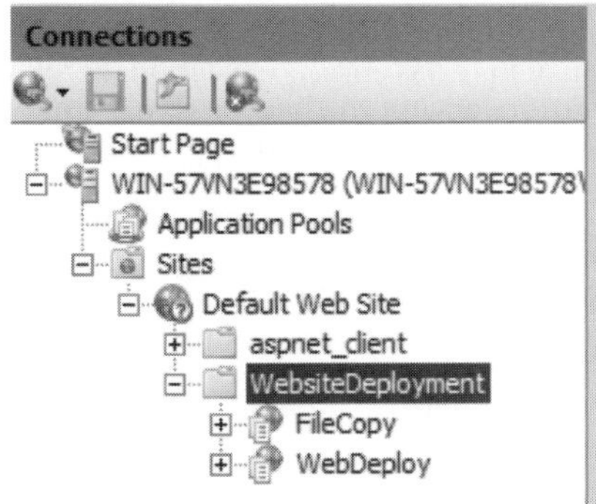

Figure 18-12. *The web-deployed site*

Finally, you can test the deployment to see whether your example application works. You use a web browser to open the URL:

```
http://WIN-57VN3E98578/WebsiteDeployment/WebDeploy
```

If you have followed along with this example, you should see the result shown in Figure 18-13.

Figure 18-13. *Testing the deployment*

Using FTP Deployment

FTP deployment deploys your project to the server using the File Transfer Protocol (FTP). The main advantage of FTP deploy is the wider range of platform support. The main disadvantage is that there can be more firewall issues with FTP deployment than with web deployment.

■ **Note** This deployment approach is supported on all versions of IIS 7 on all operating system versions.

Preparing IIS

The simplest way to install and configure FTP deployment is using our old friend, the Web Platform Installer. Start WebPI, click the Web Platform tab, and select Customize in the Web Server section. Scroll down, and select the FTP Publishing Service item. Click the Install button, accept the license terms, and begin the installation. IIS won't have detected the new changes if it was running during the installation, so exit and restart it now if need be.

First, we need to enable FTP deployment to our IIS site; expand the Connections tree control in IIS Manager, right-click Default Web Site, and select Add FTP Publishing. You will see the first page of the Add FTP Site Publishing Wizard, as shown in Figure 18-14. If your server has more than one network interface, you can use the settings in the Binding section of the screen to select the one that will be listened to for deployment requests. If your server has only one interface or you want to listen for requests on every interface installed, leave the IP Address value as All Unassigned. The Port field defaults to 21, which is the standard TCP port for FTP.

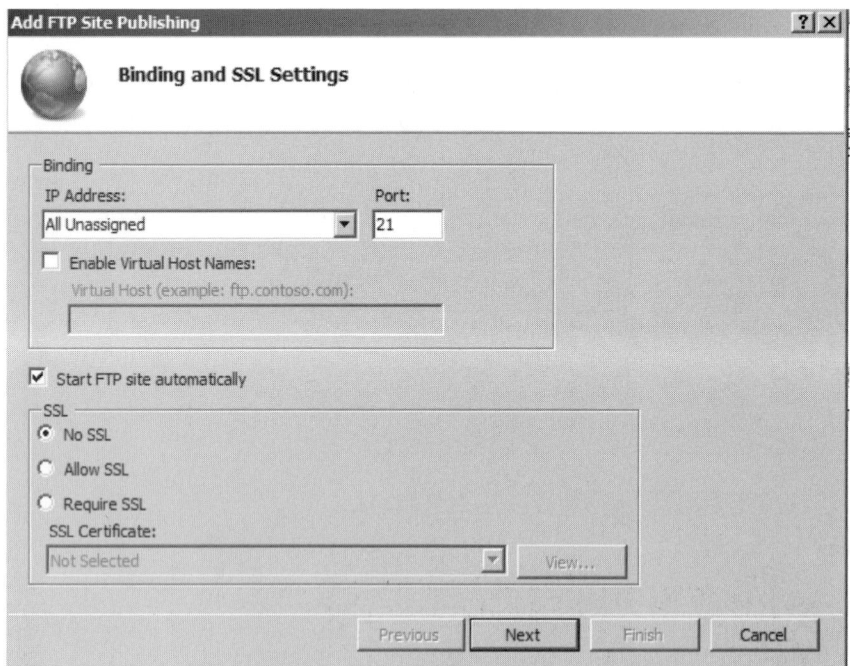

Figure 18-14. *The first page of the Add FTP Site Publishing Wizard*

You can require that encryption is used to secure your FTP deployment network traffic in the SSL section of the screen. We have not installed an SSL certificate on our test server, so we have selected the No SSL option. Click Next to move to the next screen, which lets you specify who can use the FTP deployment feature. We want to restrict access to the Administrator account, so we have enabled authentication by selecting the Basic option, selecting Specified users, and entering Administrator in the account name field. We want to be able to read and write content when we deploy, so we have selected both of those options. Your configuration may differ depending on your server administration policy. Click the Finish button to complete the configuration.

We have to create the target directory for our application before deploying it for the first time. This is because we won't be able to specify that the directory should be treated as an application as we can with web deployment.

The Website

The website we will use for this deployment technique is identical to the one covered when discussing web deployment, except we have changed the text of the (only) page, as shown in Figure 18-15.

Figure 18-15. *The FTP Deploy website*

This is a project-based website, and you can download everything in the project from the Apress website. See the variation in the following section for details of how to use FTP to deploy a project-less website.

Deploying the Website

Before we deploy our site for the first time, we need to create the destination directory on the server and tell IIS that it contains a web application. We would like our URL for this example to be as follows:

```
http://<servername>/WebsiteDeployment/FTPDeploy
```

To achieve this, we use IIS Manager to right-click the Default Website item in the tree control and select Explore. We then use the Explorer window to create a directory called WebsiteDeployment and then one called FTPDeploy inside it.

Refresh IIS Manager, and open the tree control until you can see the FTPDeploy folder, right-click it, and select the Convert to Application menu item. Accept the default values. We have now created a destination for our deployment and told IIS that it will contain an application.

To perform the deployment, open the sample project in Visual Studio 2010, and select the Publish FTP_Deploy from the Build menu. You will now see the same dialog box we used for Web Deployment. Select FTP from the Publish Method list; the dialog box layout will change, as shown in Figure 18-16.

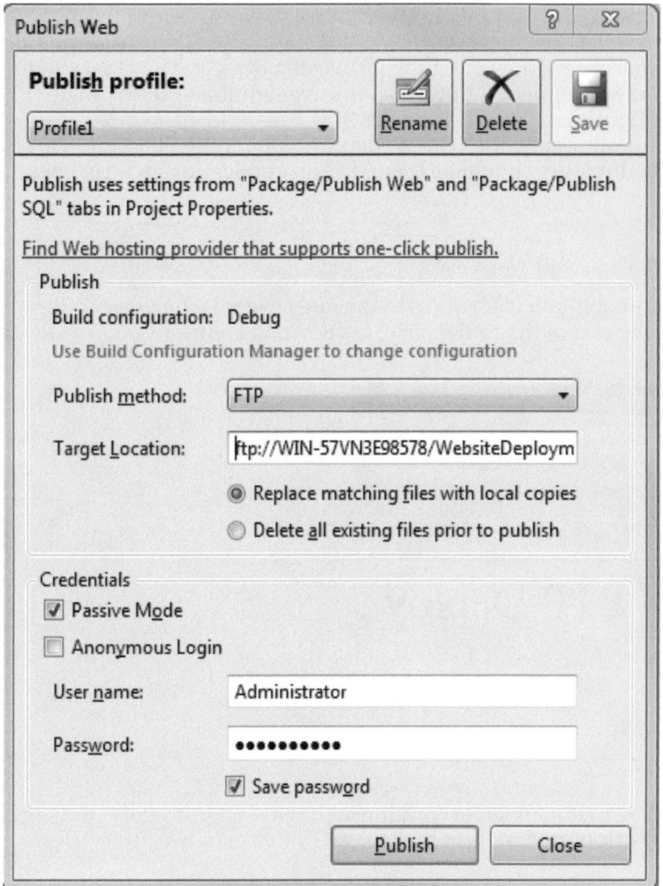

Figure 18-16. *The Publish Web dialog box*

The Target Location format for FTP is slightly different from the previous example. It is of the following form:

```
ftp://<servername>/targetlocation
```

The ftp and the servername parts are obvious enough, but the important thing is that we don't specify the site name in this URL. IIS knows which site we enabled FTP deployment for and so the targetlocation part of the URL is relative to the root of that site. You can't see it all on the figure, but the URL we specified was as follows:

```
ftp://WIN-57VN3E98578/WebsiteDeployment/FTPDeploy
```

This URL is relative to the root of Default Web Site and corresponds to both the HTTP URL we want for our content and the directories we created at the start of this section. Be careful with the options under the Target Location field. You are likely to want the Replace option; the Delete option will remove any files that are on the server but that are not part of your project.

You will see that we have selected the Passive Mode option; you will probably want to do the same thing for your deployments to increase the chances of your deployment working through firewalls without having to reconfigure them. Finally, we have specified the Administrator account and password for our server. If you are using a different account to deploy your site, then you would enter the details here. When you are ready to deploy, click the Publish button.

■ **Tip** One of the most common causes of problems when using FTP deployment is firewall configuration. If you do encounter problems, check the configuration of the Windows firewall on both the server and the client as well as the configuration of any physical firewalls in your infrastructure.

When the deployment is complete, we can check the deployed site by loading our desired URL. You can see the result in Figure 18-17.

Figure 18-17. Testing the FTP deployment

Variation: Deploying a Project-less Website

You can use FTP to deploy your project-less website, although the process is not quite as effortless. To demonstrate this deployment approach, we have created a very simple project-less site, following the pattern of our other examples. You can find the website in the source code download for this book, available from Apress.com. It is in the FTP_Projectless_Deploy folder. The Default.aspx.cs file contains the code that sets the label text to the .NET Framework version used to run the application.

Prior to deploying for the first time, you must create the target directory on the server and convert it to an application—just as we did for project-based FTP deployment previously. We won't repeat the instructions; you can see them in the previous section. To keep our examples separate, we created a directory called FTPProjectlessDeploy inside the WebsiteDeployment directory.

Once that is done, you select Copy Web Site... from the Visual Studio Website menu, which opens the Copy Web tab, as shown in Figure 18-18. On the left side of the display, you can see the files that make up the site—it looks a little silly with just two files, but you can imagine how it would look for a more complex site.

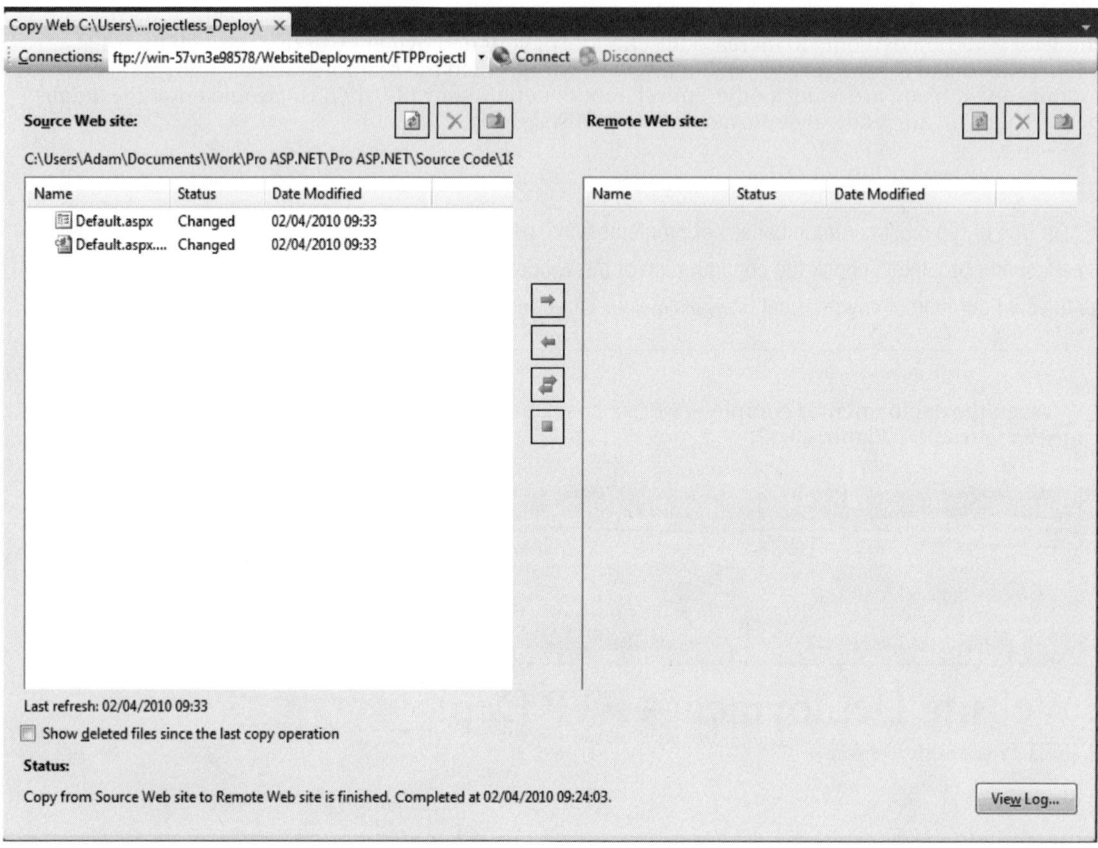

Figure 18-18. *The Visual Studio Copy Web tab*

The next step is to connect to IIS. Click the Connect button at the top of the Copy Web tab. This will display the Open Web Site dialog box, as shown by Figure 18-19. Select FTP Site by clicking the button on the left side of the display.

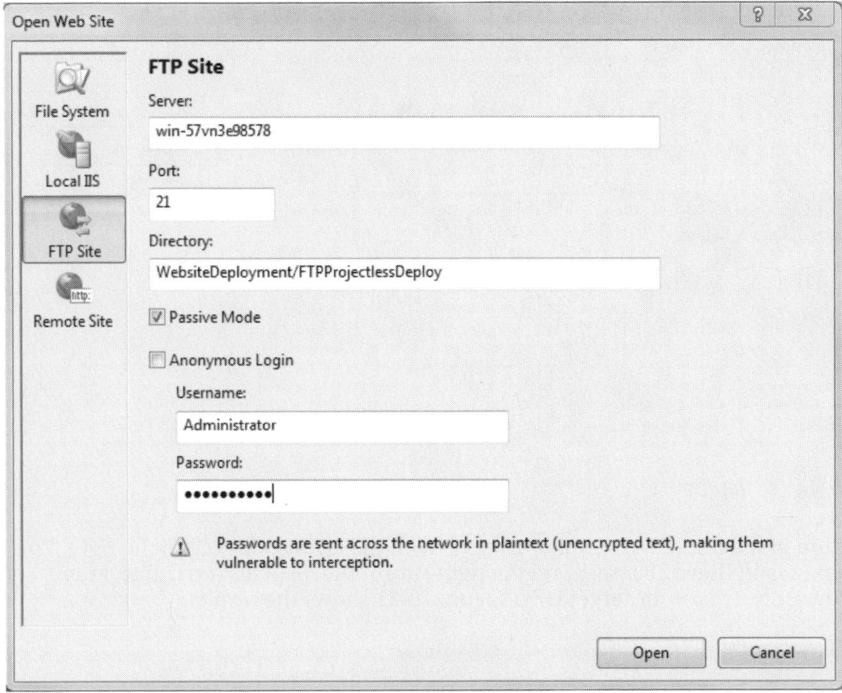

Figure 18-19. *The Open Web Site dialog box*

Filling out the fields uses the same information as for project-based site deployment. The server field requires the name of the server you want to deploy to. The port defaults to 21, which is what is generally used for FTP. The directory is the location you want to deploy your content to, relative to the root of your site. In our case, we want to deploy to WebsiteDeployment/FTPProjectlessDeploy. Passive Mode is selected by default; we recommend that you leave this selected, because it reduces the chances of problems if there are firewalls between your workstation and the server.

Deselect the Anonymous Login option, and enter the account and password you are using for deployment. We are using the Administrator account, as with our previous examples. When you have filled out all of the details, click the Open button. The right side of the Copy Web tab will now show the contents of the directory you created on the server. Since this is your initial deployment, there is nothing on the server, so the right side of the display is empty.

Select both of the files on the left side of the display. Doing so will cause some of the buttons in the middle of the tab to light up, as shown in Figure 18-20. This is where you need to pay particular attention—only the files you select will be deployed. If you miss a file, it won't be pushed to the server, and you'll get odd behavior from your site.

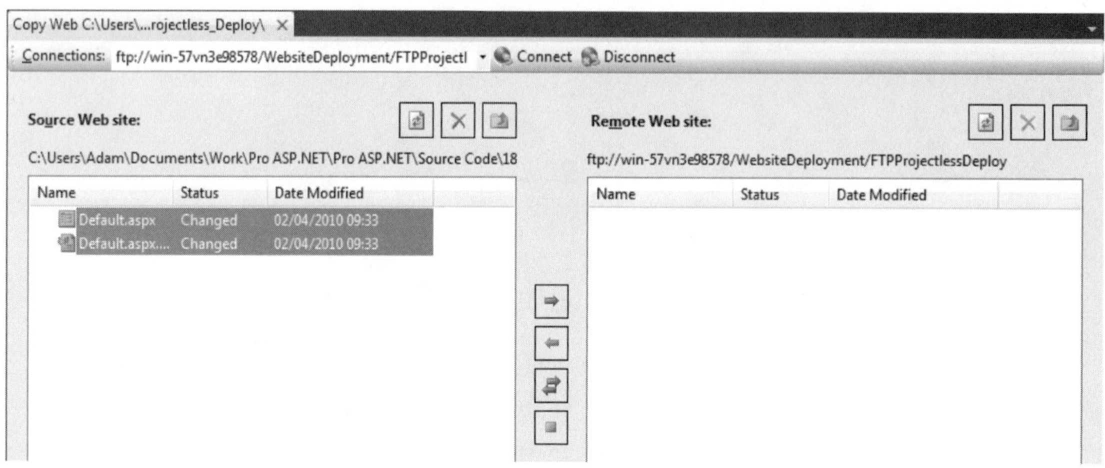

Figure 18-20. *Selecting the files to deploy*

Click the topmost button in the middle of the tab—the one with the arrow pointing to the right. This will copy the files to the server, and they will appear on the right side of the display. You can test the deployment by using a browser to open your target URL. Figure 18-21 shows the results.

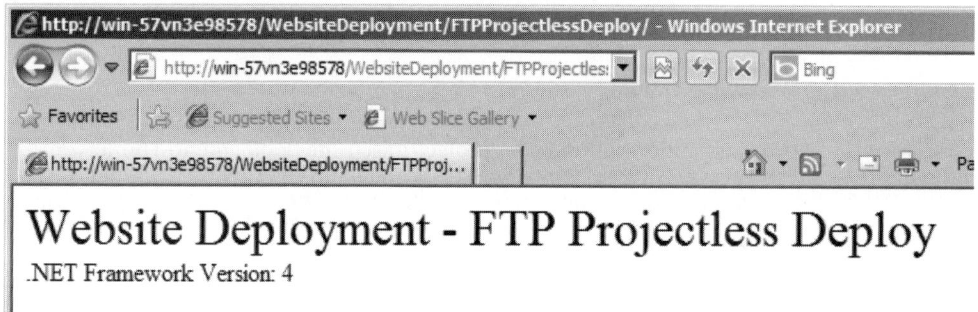

Figure 18-21. *Testing the deployment*

Although you need to be careful when selecting the files to deploy, Visual Studio does provide some helpful hits. If we modify one of our site files and then select Copy Web Site..., again, the changes are marked with an arrow, as shown in Figure 18-22. This is very useful in ensuring that you keep things in sync.

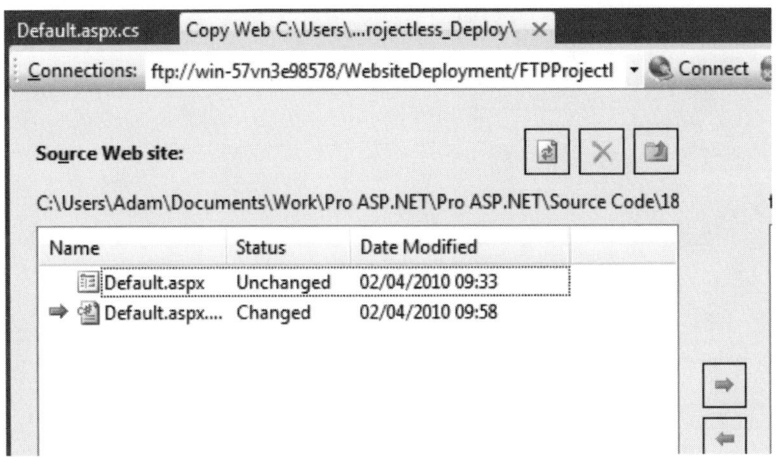

Figure 18-22. *Highlighted changes in the Copy Web tab*

Managing a Website

Once you have deployed a site, you can use the features of IIS to manage the way that it is hosted and executed. In this part of the chapter, we'll show you the most useful configuration options and how to use them.

Creating a New Site

IIS 7 is able to support multiple sites on a single server. In our example deployments, we have added content to the default server, but in this section, we'll show you how to create a new one. To create a new site, expand the tree control in IIS Manager, right-click Sites, and select the Add Web Site... menu item. This will show the Add Web Site dialog box, as shown in Figure 18-23.

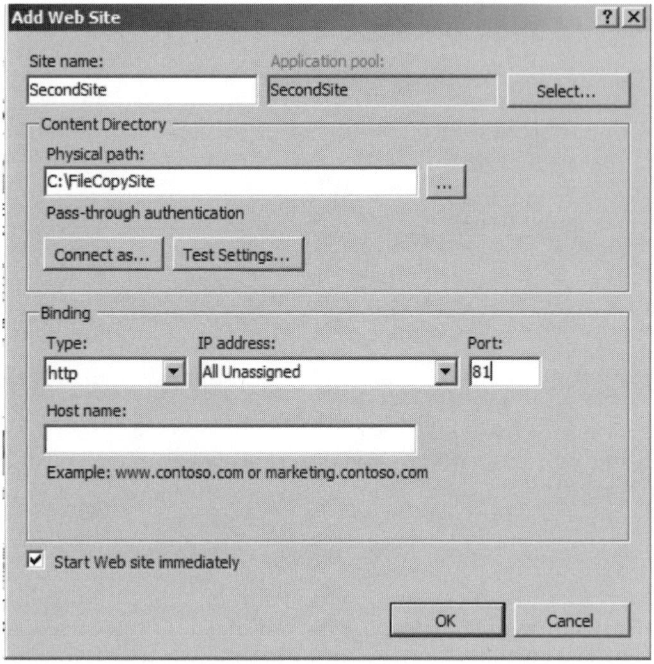

Figure 18-23. The Add Web Site dialog box

The Site name field should be something meaningful to you. It is used to identify the site in IIS Manager but does not affect the site content. We have left the application pool as it is (we'll talk about application pools later in this chapter). The Physical path setting specifies where IIS 7 will look for content to service requests for your new site. We have created a new directory on the server, C:\FileCopySite. The Connect as and Test Settings buttons allow you to specify different user credentials to access the site content.

In the Bindings section of the dialog box, you can specify how IIS 7 will listen for requests from clients. IIS 7 supports a wide range of network protocols, but we will focus on HTTP, since it is the most widely used. To do that, we select the http option for Type. The IP address menu allows you to select which network interface your server will listen to for requests. We have left this as All Unassigned, meaning that IIS will listen on all interfaces except those where another site is being serviced using the same TCP port. The Port value allows you to specify the TCP port on which IIS 7 will listen for client requests; in general each site must be served on a unique port, so we have selected port 81 so as not to conflict with the default website on port 80.

We have selected the Start Web site immediately option, which means that as soon as we click OK, IIS will create the website and start listing for requests. There is nothing further you need to configure here, so click OK to create and start the website. Each of the deployment options we have shown you in this chapter allows you to specify the site to deploy to—remember that the sites are differentiated by name for the purposes of deployment and you use the port numbers when deploying.

Creating Virtual Directories

When we set up the destinations for our example websites, we placed our content in the directory in which IIS 7 looks for content by default. We could have done things differently by placing the content elsewhere and then using a virtual directory to reference it. To demonstrate this, we'll create a new directory on our server and copy our site content there. The path for our new directory is as follows:

```
C:\WebsiteDeployment\VirtualDirectory
```

To associate our new directory with IIS, go to IIS Manager, expand the tree view, right-click the Default Web Site item, and select the Add Virtual Directory... menu item. This will show the Add Virtual Directory dialog box, which is shown in Figure 18-24.

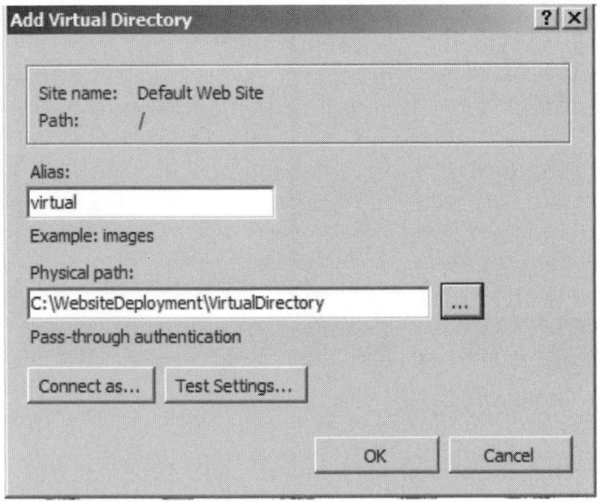

Figure 18-24. *The Add Virtual Directory dialog box*

We would like the URL of this website to be as follows:

```
http://<servername>/virtual
```

In the Alias box, enter virtual. We selected the root of the default website, which means that whatever we put in the Alias box will be appended directly to the URL after the server name. In the Physical path box, enter the path to one of the deployment directories you created previously. Click the OK button to create the virtual directory. To test the virtual directory, open a browser on the server, and point it at the URL http://localhost/virtual. Once again, you see your simple website, but this time the content was sourced from your new directory and accessed using the custom URL you specified.

Using the VirtualPathProvider

The VirtualPathProvider class provides an alternative approach to virtual directories, such that the content can be generated programmatically or from a database, rather than sourced from the file system.

The best way to understand the capabilities of the VirtualPathProvider class is with an example. We will show how to create a simple VirtualPathProvider class that can read ASPX files from a SQL Server table.

To do this, you need a database table like the one shown in Figure 18-25, which contains three pages stored in a table. We have included the database in the source code download for this book, which you can get from Apress.com.

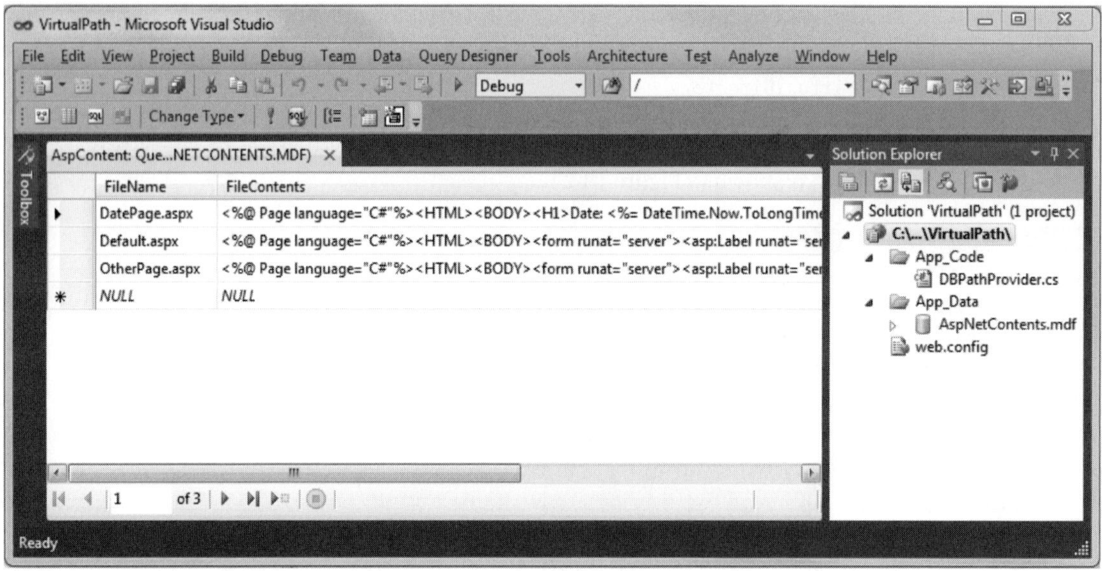

Figure 18-25. The SQL Server database used for the VirtualPathProvider

As you can see, the table includes a filename (which is the primary key) and the actual content. The content could be any type of code that ASP.NET understands—in this example, because we are going to serve simple pages, the content could be anything that the page parser is capable of compiling.

The VirtualPathProvider class is defined in the System.Web.Hosting namespace. Just add a new class to the App_Code directory and inherit from VirtualPathProvider. The class needs to implement at least the following methods:

```
Using System;
using System.Data.SqlClient;
using System.IO;
using System.Text;
using System.Web.Hosting;


public class DBPathProvider : VirtualPathProvider {

    public static void AppInitialize() {
        HostingEnvironment.RegisterVirtualPathProvider(
            new DBPathProvider());
    }

    public override bool FileExists(string virtualPath) {
       throw new Exception("The method or operation is not implemented.");
    }

    public override VirtualFile GetFile(string virtualPath) {
       throw new Exception("The method or operation is not implemented.");
    }
}
```

A provider must implement the static AppInitialize method, in which you should create an instance of your class and register it as a provider with the framework. The FileExists method is used to test whether a path can be served by the provider, and the GetFile method is called to retrieve the content for a path, returning an instance of the abstract VirtualFile class—there are no concrete implementations of VirtualFile, meaning that you must extend the abstract class to support your provider.

The following is our implementation of the VirtualFile class to accompany our provider, which we have placed in the same code file:

```
public class DBVirtualFile : VirtualFile {

    private string _FileContent;

    public DBVirtualFile(string virtualPath, string fileContent)
        : base(virtualPath) {
        _FileContent = fileContent;
    }

    public override Stream Open() {
        Stream stream = new MemoryStream();
        StreamWriter writer = new StreamWriter(stream, Encoding.Unicode);

        writer.Write(_FileContent);
        writer.Flush();
        stream.Seek(0, SeekOrigin.Begin);
        return stream;
    }
}
```

The constructor gets the virtual path as well as the content of the file. In the Open method, the content string is stored in a MemoryStream, which is returned as the method result. ASP.NET uses the stream for reading the contents as if they were read from the file system—thanks to the abstraction of bytes through Stream classes.

Returning to complete our provider class, we need to add support to get the content from the database. If a file doesn't exist in the database, the provider just forwards the request to its previous provider (which has been selected by the infrastructure while registering in the static AppInitialize method). Add a method for retrieving the contents from the database to the DBPathProvider class:

```
private string GetFileFromDB(string virtualPath) {
    string contents;
    string fileName = virtualPath.Substring(
                        virtualPath.IndexOf('/', 1) + 1);

    // Read the file from the database
    SqlConnection conn = new SqlConnection();
    conn.ConnectionString = "Data Source=.\\SQLEXPRESS;Initial
Catalog=\"ASPNETCONTENTS\";Integrated Security=True";
    conn.Open();

    try {
        SqlCommand cmd = new SqlCommand(
            "SELECT FileContents FROM AspContent " +
            "WHERE FileName=@fn", conn);
        cmd.Parameters.AddWithValue("@fn", fileName);
```

```
            contents = cmd.ExecuteScalar() as string;
            if (contents == null)
                contents = string.Empty;
        } catch {
            contents = string.Empty;
        } finally {
            conn.Close();
        }

        return contents;
    }
```

The GetFileFromDB function gets the filename from the virtual path and reads the corresponding content from the database. This method is then used by both the FileExists and GetFile methods, as shown in the following code snippet:

```
public override bool FileExists(string virtualPath) {
    string contents = this.GetFileFromDB(virtualPath);
    if (contents.Equals(string.Empty)) {
        return false;
    } else {
        return true;
    }
}

public override VirtualFile GetFile(string virtualPath) {
    string contents = this.GetFileFromDB(virtualPath);
    if (contents.Equals(string.Empty)) {
        return Previous.GetFile(virtualPath);
    } else {
        return new DBVirtualFile(virtualPath, contents);
    }
}
```

You can implement a few additional methods in your provider that can be useful for more complex models, such as verifying a directory exists (DirectoryExists), computing file hashes (GetFileHash), and performing cache verification (GetCacheDependency). With the basic functions in place, we are ready to test our provider. You can see three browsers in Figure 18-26—each displaying one of the pages from the database.

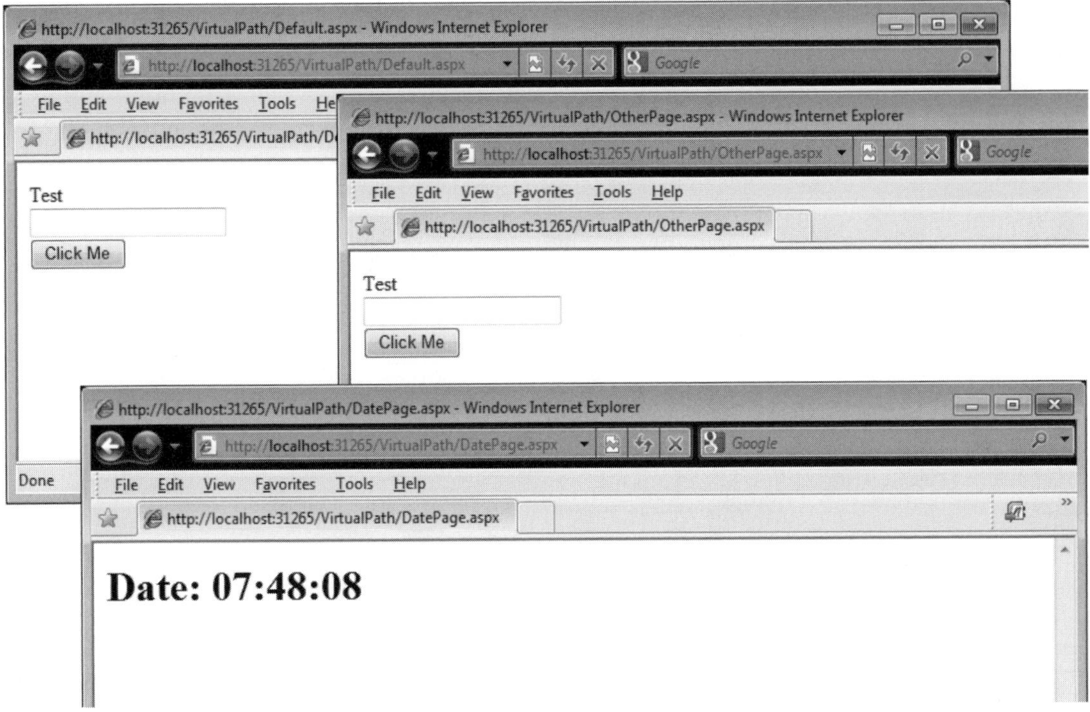

Figure 18-26. *The VirtualPathProvider in action*

Using Application Pools

Application pools let you group together similar or related applications to make configuration and management easier. Equally, applications that are assigned to application pools are isolated so that problems in one pool don't affect applications in different pools. There are no hard and fast rules for how you assign applications to pools. You can group applications together because they have similar performance profiles or belong to the same department or, well, for any reason that makes sense in your environment. One of the most useful features, as we'll see, is the ability to have different application pools use different versions of the .NET Framework. In this section, we'll show you how to create, configure, and assign your applications to application pools.

IIS 7 creates a number of application pools automatically, including one that is used by default when you create a new application. You can see and manage application pools using IIS Manager—expand the server item in the tree control, and click Application Pools. This will show you the pools on your server. You can see the ones on our Windows Server 2008 R2 machine in Figure 18-27.

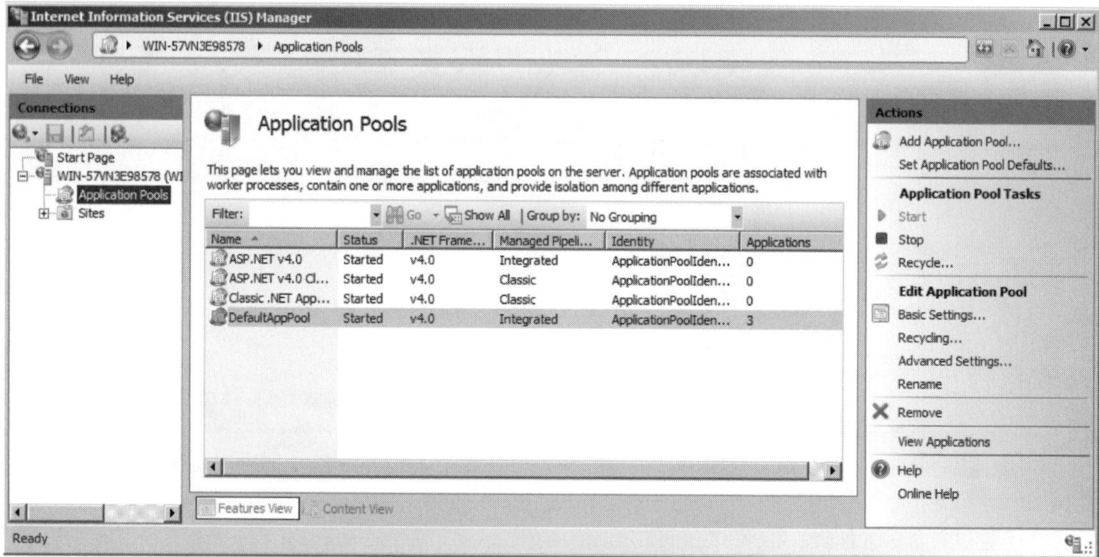

Figure 18-27. *The standard application pools*

The application pools are listed in the table in the middle of the screen. The table columns show us the most important characteristics of the pools, as we have described in Table 18-1. When you deploy an application, it is assigned to the default application pool. When you deployed an application previously, we had you change the settings for the default application pool so that it would use .NET 4.

Table 18-1. *Application Pool Characteristics Shown in the Main IIS Manager Window*

Column	Description
Name	This is the name of the application pool. You can't change the name of a pool once it has been created.
Status	This shows whether the application pool is running—meaning that requests for applications assigned to the pool will be responded to. See the "Starting and Stopping an Application Pool" section for more information.
.NET Framework Version	The version of the .NET Framework that will be used to execute managed code—we had you change the setting for the default pool during the deployment examples. See the "Using Side-by-Side Execution" section for more information about specifying framework versions.
Managed Pipeline Mode	IIS 7 supports two pipeline modes for handling requests—Integrated and Classic. See the "Extending the Integrated Pipeline" section for details of how to extend the pipeline.
Identity	This is the Windows account used to run the applications in the pool.
Applications	This is the number of applications assigned to the pool—you can see that we have three applications in the DefaultAppPool.

Creating a New Application Pool

You can create a custom application pool by clicking the Add Application Pool action on the right of the IIS Manager screen. This shows the Add Application Pool dialog box, which is shown in Figure 18-28. Enter the name for your new pool (we have used CustomAppPool), select the version of the .NET Framework that will be used to run applications assigned to the pool, and choose whether you want to use the Integrated or Classic pipeline mode (the Classic mode is for legacy applications—if you are unsure, select Integrated here).

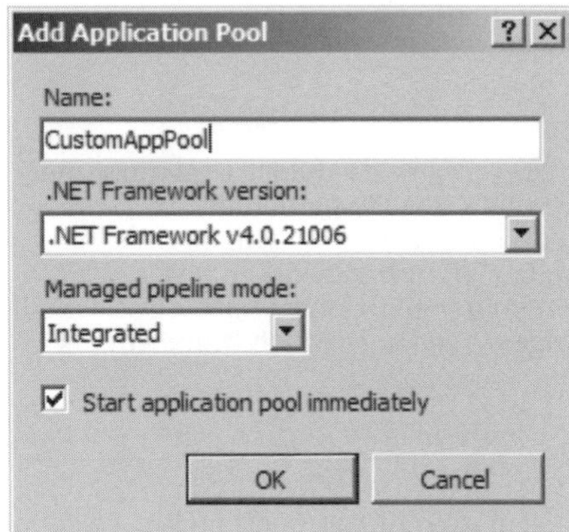

Figure 18-28. The Add Application Pool dialog box

Click OK, and the new pool will be created and added to the IIS Manager list. If you click the Advanced Settings... action, you will be able to configure the fine detail of the pool (these settings are beyond the scope of this book).

Assigning an Application to an Application Pool

To assign an application to an application pool, select the application using IIS Manager, and then click the Basic Settings action on the right of the screen. This will open the Edit Application dialog box. Click the Select button, and choose an application pool from the drop-down list, as shown in Figure 18-29. We selected the custom application pool we created in the previous section.

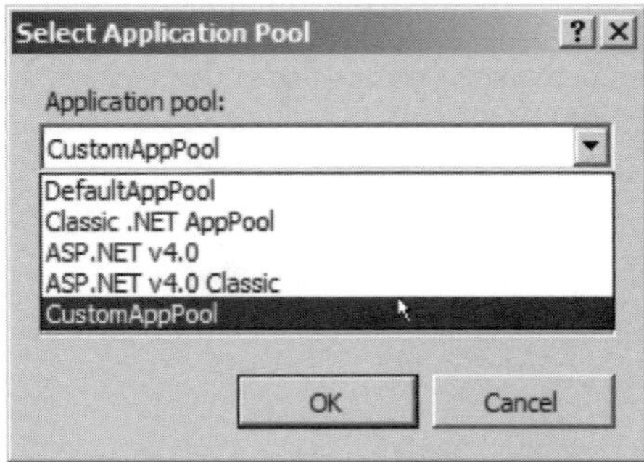

Figure 18-29. The Select Application Pool dialog box

Click OK. Click the Application Pools item in IIS Manager, and you will see that one application is listed in the Applications column for CustomAppPool and one fewer for DefaultAppPool.

Starting and Stopping an Application Pool

If you click an application pool, you will see three actions listed under Application Pool Tasks on the right side of the IIS Manager window. The Start and Stop actions determine whether requests to the applications assigned to the pool are serviced. If the pool is stopped, clients will receive an error. The Recycle action resets the application pool; this is useful if you are encountering problems that build gradually and that are difficult to diagnose.

Using Side-by-Side Execution

Application pools allow you to run applications that require different versions of ASP.NET on the same server. If you have legacy applications or are upgrading applications to ASP.NET 4 gradually, you can mix and match applications pools to ensure that each application operates with the right features.

In the example sites we deployed, we displayed the version of the .NET Framework that was used to process requests—this is why. If you change the framework version for a pool to what you have assigned one of the example deployments, you will see that the output changes to indicate which framework is used by the pool.

■ **Tip** If you want to change the .NET version used for a site that you created with a Visual Studio project, you'll need to change the project settings to use that version and deploy again. If you don't, you'll see a configuration error when making requests to the site.

Using Application Warm-Up

You may have noticed that when you tested the deployment techniques earlier in the chapter, the first request you made took a while to return in the browser, but subsequent requests were faster. This is because IIS 7 doesn't do anything with the files you deployed until the first request for your content arrives. At that point, IIS prepares your application; the code portions of your site are compiled, database connections are created, data is loaded, and so on. This can take some time, which is why that first request is so slow. If you restart IIS, the process is repeated.

For large and complex applications, the amount of time taken to respond to the initial request can be significant. The application warm-up feature is new to IIS 7.5. For each application you configure to use the warm-up feature, IIS 7 will perform a set of requests (which you specify) at startup. This means that by the time the first request comes in from a real user, everything is ready to go.

■ **Tip** If you don't want to use application warm-up, you can still improve the initial performance of your application through precompilation using the aspnet_compiler.exe command-line tool. You can get more details at http://msdn.microsoft.com/en-us/library/ms229863(VS.100).aspx.

Preparing IIS 7

The simplest way of preparing IIS 7 to use application warm-up is to use the Web Platform Installer again. At the time we wrote this chapter, the component to configure warm-up was in beta and available on the What's New? tab of WebPI.

■ **Note** Application warm-up works with IIS 7.5 only, meaning that Windows Server 2008 and Windows Vista are not supported by this feature.

Select Application Warm-Up for IIS 7.5, and click Install to begin the usual download and installation process. When the installation has completed, refresh or restart IIS Manager so that you can use the newly installed features.

Configuring Application Warm-Up

Select the application you want to configure in IIS Manager, and double-click the newly installed Application Warm-Up icon, as shown in Figure 18-30.

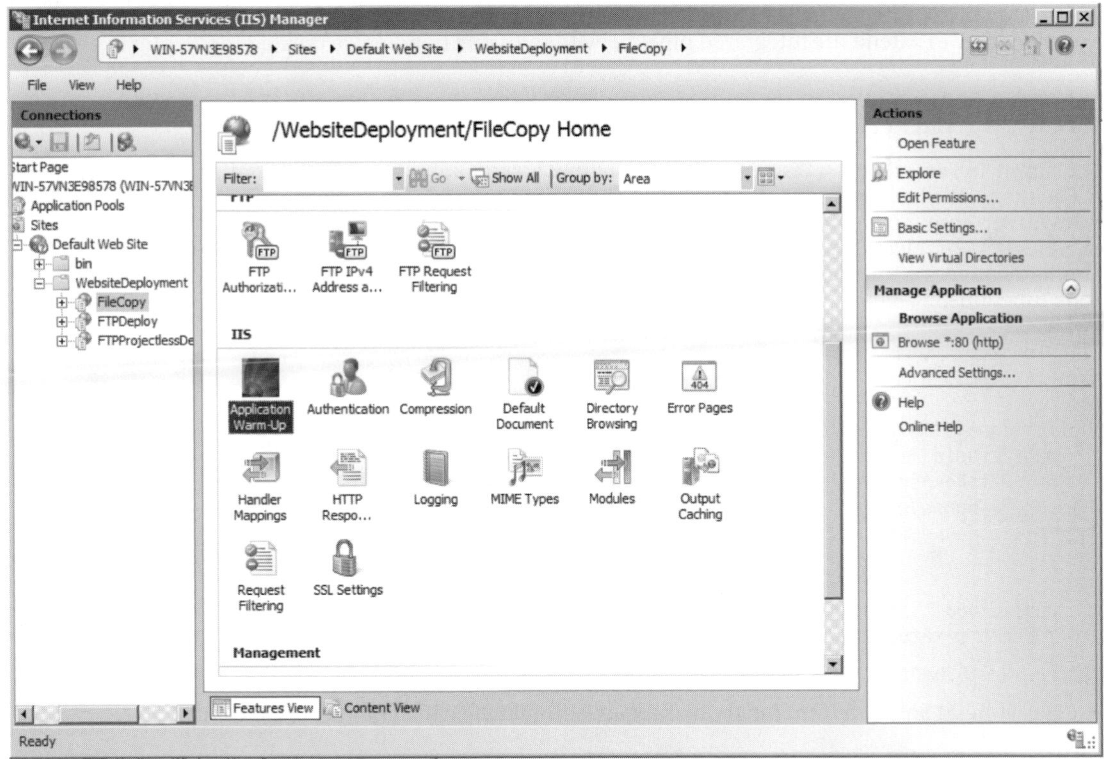

Figure 18-30. Selecting the Application Warm-Up icon

This will display the empty Application Warm-Up summary screen. Click the Add Request action on the right side of the screen, and fill out the form to add a request to be performed during warm-up.

Enter the URL for the application. Our samples in this chapter are all very simple, so we just want to request the root, which is /. The Status Codes field allows you to specify the range of HTTP codes that you expect in the response from your application—if the code is outside the expected range, an error will be logged (but subsequent requests will still be made). You can use the Request Context Parameter field to attach a string to the request URL so that you can differentiate between requests made by real clients and warm-up requests.

The Request Send Mode allows you to choose between asynchronous and synchronous requests. Application warm-up sends all the asynchronous requests, followed by synchronous requests, waiting for the result from each synchronous response before making the next request. This feature can be useful if you want to warm up your application via a series of related requests.

Returning to the main display, click the Settings action on the right side of the window and select both the Enable Application Warm-Up and Start Application Pool options. This will ensure that your application is warmed up when IIS is started or restarted and when the application pool is recycled.

Extending the Integrated Pipeline

IIS 7 supports two modes for processing requests. The first, known as Classic, is the model that earlier versions used and is supported today for legacy applications. The second mode, known as Integrated, offers better performance and a different model for extending IIS 7 using the IHttpHandler interface that we covered in Chapter 5. You should use the integrated pipeline mode by default. In this section, we'll show you how to extend the integrated pipeline with the same handler we created in Chapter 5.

Creating the Handler

For simplicity, we created a Visual Studio project that just contains the SimpleHandler class we created in Chapter 5. We have included this project in the source code for the book, which you can download from Apress.com. To create the handler from scratch, select New and then Project in the Visual Studio File menu; then select Class Library. Name the project SimpleHandler. Rename the C# code file to SimplerHandler.cs, and paste the code in the listing into the file. See Chapter 5 for details of how this code functions.

```
using System;
using System.Web;

public class SimpleHandler : IHttpHandler {
    public void ProcessRequest(System.Web.HttpContext context) {
        HttpResponse response = context.Response;
        response.Write("<html><body><h1>Rendered by the SimpleHandler");
        response.Write("</h1></body></html>");
    }

    public bool IsReusable {
        get { return true; }
    }
}
```

Select Build Solution from the Build menu to compile the code and create a DLL file.

Deploying the Handler

Find the DLL that Visual Studio created; it will be in the bin/Debug or bin/Release directory of your project and will be called SimpleHandler.dll. Copy this file to the server, placing it in the bin directory at the root of your application. If the bin directory does not exist, create it. For example, if you want to apply your handler to the FileCopy application you deployed earlier in the chapter, you would place the DLL in the C:\inetpub\wwwroot\WebsiteDeployment\FileCopy\bin directory.

Configuring the Handler

Using IIS Manager, select the application you want to modify. For us that will be the FileCopy application we deployed previously. Double-click the Handler Mappings icon to open the Handler Mappings summary screen, as shown in Figure 18-31.

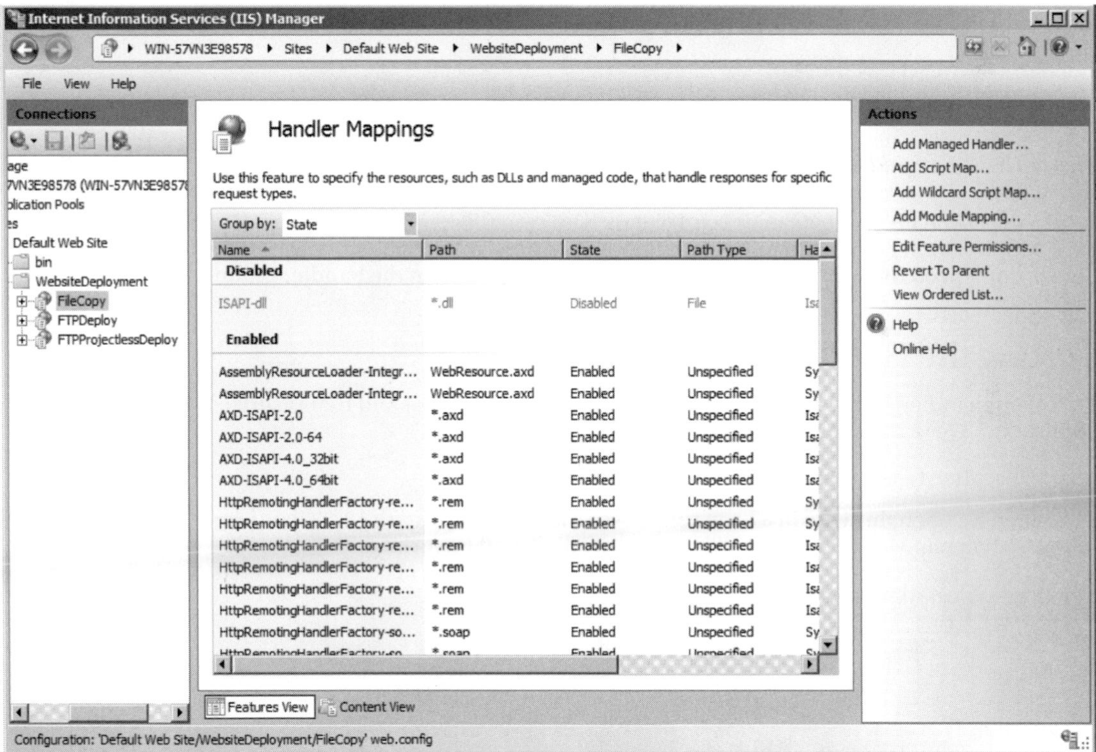

***Figure 18-31.** The Handler Mappings summary screen*

Click the Add Managed Handler action on the right side of the window to open the Add Managed Handler dialog box, shown in Figure 18-32. In the Request Path field, specify what requests the handler will service. We want our simple handler to be used only for requests that end in .htest. In the Type field, enter the name of the handler class. If you have used a namespace for your class, you must include it in this field.

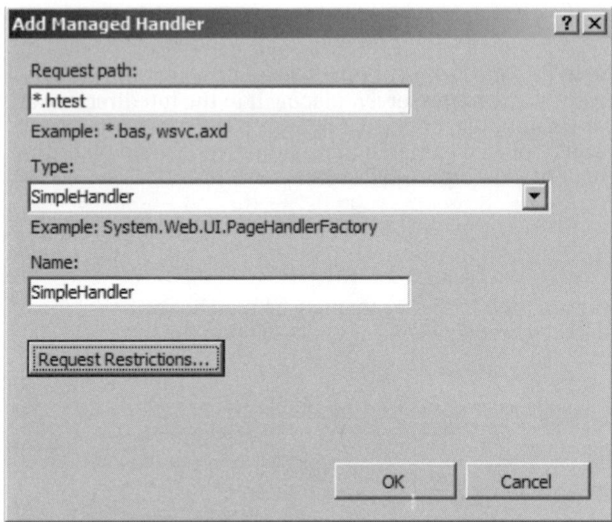

Figure 18-32. *The Add Managed Handler dialog box*

In the Name field, enter a name you will recognize in the handler summary page. We have called ours SimpleHandler. You can configure additional options by clicking the Request Restrictions button, but we don't need these for our simple handler. Click OK to create the handler mapping.

Testing the Handler

To test our handler, we need to request a URL that ends with .htest and that is serviced by the FileCopy application. We will use the following:

```
http://localhost/WebsiteDeployment/FileCopy/help.htest
```

When we open this URL in a browser, we see the results in Figure 18-33, confirming that our integrated pipeline handler has been installed properly and is working.

Figure 18-33. *Testing the integrated pipeline handler*

Summary

In this chapter, you learned how to install and configure IIS 7 and use the three most common deployment techniques—copy files, web deployment, and FTP deployment. We also showed you how to manage application pools, warm up an application so that the initial client request doesn't take a long time to execute, and extend the integrated pipeline with a simple request handler.

As we have mentioned a few times in this chapter, the deployment technique you use is driven by your service environment. Unless you manage your own servers, you will have to fit in to whatever approach has been adopted for other projects and users—increasingly this will be web deployment, but a wide variety will remain.

IIS 7 is a complex and capable server that goes beyond ASP.NET and the scope of this book. We have given you enough information to deploy and configure the basics for your application, but time spent learning more about the advanced options can pay dividends.

PART 4

■■■

Security

Devising a proper security strategy is a key part of any distributed application, particularly a large-scale web application that's exposed over the public Internet. In this book, you'll find no less than eight chapters that cover ASP.NET security features.

In Chapter 19, you'll begin with a high-level overview of three security fundamentals: authentication, authorization, and confidentiality. Once you have this perspective in mind, you're ready to consider ASP.NET's two key systems for authenticating users: forms authentication (Chapter 20), which provides a simple yet flexible framework for securing a public website, and Windows authentication (Chapter 22), which uses existing Windows accounts to authenticate users and is most commonly used in local intranet sites. You'll also explore ASP.NET's higher-level security services, such as membership, roles, and profiles. Membership (Chapter 21) provides prebuilt security controls and allows ASP.NET to manage the back-end database that stores user credentials. Roles (Chapter 24) allows you to place users into logical groups, which can then have different privileges. Profiles (Chapter 25) allows you to store user-specific information in a server-side database without writing your own ADO.NET code. Although these features are powerful, they drive many details behind the scenes. To truly customize the way these features work, you need to build a custom provider, a topic you'll tackle in Chapter 26.

Finally, you'll find that Chapter 25 takes a detour into .NET's cryptography features, which are essentially for securing sensitive information before you store it in a file or database. Unlike the other security features that are described in this part, the .NET cryptography classes aren't limited to ASP.NET, although they're frequently useful in web applications, allowing you to perform feats like building a tamper-proof query string.

CHAPTER 19

■ ■ ■

The ASP.NET Security Model

Security is an essential part of web applications and should be taken into consideration from the first stage of the development process. Essentially, security is all about protecting your assets from unauthorized actions. You use several mechanisms to this end, including identifying users, granting or denying access to sensitive resources, and protecting the data that's stored on the server and transmitted over the wire. In all of these cases, you need an underlying framework that provides basic security functionality. ASP.NET fills this need with built-in functionality that you can use for implementing security in your web applications.

The ASP.NET security framework includes classes for authenticating and authorizing users as well as for dealing with authenticated users in your applications. It also includes a higher-level model for managing users and roles, both programmatically and with built-in administrative tools. Furthermore, the .NET Framework on its own provides you with a set of base classes for implementing confidentiality and integrity through encryption and digital signatures.

This chapter provides a road map to the security features in ASP.NET. In subsequent chapters, you'll dig deeper into each of the topics covered in this chapter. Here, you'll get a quick introduction to the key features of .NET security. Most importantly, you'll get a basic understanding of how you can incorporate security into your application architecture and design, and you'll see what the most important factors are for creating secure software.

What It Means to Create Secure Software

Although the security framework provided by .NET and ASP.NET is powerful, it's essential to keep some basic principles in mind and use the features correctly and at the right time. In all too many projects, security is treated as an afterthought, and architects and developers fail to consider it in the early stages. But when you don't keep security in mind from the beginning—which means in your application architecture and design—how can you use all the security features offered by the .NET Framework correctly and at the right time?

Therefore, it's essential to include security from the first moment of your development process. That's the only way to make the right security-related decisions when creating your architecture and designs.

Understanding Potential Threats

Creating a secure architecture and design requires that you have an in-depth understanding of your application's environment. You can't create secure software if you don't know who has access to your application and where possible points of attack might be. Therefore, the most important factor for creating a secure application architecture and design lies in a good understanding of environmental factors such as users, entry points, and potential possible threats with points of attack.

That's why *threat modeling* has become more important in today's software development processes. Threat modeling is a structured way of analyzing your application's environment for possible threats, ranking those threats, and then deciding about mitigation techniques based on those threats. With this approach, a decision for using a security technology (such as authentication or SSL encryption) is always based on an actual reason: the threat itself.

But threat modeling is important for another reason. As you probably know, not all potential threats can be mitigated with security technologies such as authentication or authorization. In other words, some of them can't be solved technically. For example, a bank's online solution can use SSL for securing traffic on its website. But how do users know they are actually using the bank's page and not a hacker's fake website? Well, the only way to know this is to look at the certificate used for establishing the SSL channel. But users have to be aware of that, and therefore you have to inform them of this somehow. So, the "mitigation technique" is not a security technology. It just involves making sure all your registered users know how to look at the certificate. (Of course, you can't force them to do so, but if your information is designed appropriately, you might get most of them to do it.) Threat modeling as an analysis method helps you determine issues such as these, not merely the technical issues.

■ **Tip** Threat modeling is a big topic that is beyond the scope of this book. For more information, you can refer to a number of books, including Michael Howard and David LeBlanc's *Writing Secure Code, Second Edition* (Microsoft Press, 2002) and Frank Swiderski and Window Snyder's *Threat Modeling* (Microsoft Press, 2004). Additionally, the book *Security Development Lifecycle* by Michael Howard and Steve Lipner (Microsoft Press, 2006) is extremely useful for project managers and architects. This book focuses on how to make sure that security gets an integral part in your software development life cycle, from the first planning steps through architecture, development, testing, and maintenance. It summarizes how Microsoft's project management makes sure security is an integral part of the project in a smooth and pragmatic way.

Secure Coding Guidelines

Of course, a secure architecture and design alone doesn't make your application completely secure. It's only one of the most important factors. After you have created a secure architecture and design, you have to write secure code as well. Again, *Writing Secure Code, Second Edition* by Michael Howard and David C. LeBlanc (Microsoft Press, 2002) and *Threat Modeling* by Frank Swiderski and Window Snyder (Microsoft Press, 2004), as well as *The Security Development Lifecycle* by Michael Howard and Steve Lipner (Microsoft Press, 2006) are excellent sources for detailed information for every developer. In terms of web applications, you should always keep the following guidelines in mind when writing code:

Never trust user input: Assume that every user is evil until you have proven the opposite. Therefore, always strongly validate user input. Write your validation code in a way that it verifies input against only allowed values and not invalid values. (There are always more invalid values than you might be aware of at the time of writing the application.)

Never use string concatenation for creating SQL statements: Always use parameterized statements so that your application is not SQL injectable, as discussed in Chapter 7.

Never output data entered by a user directly on your web page before validating and encoding it: The user might enter some HTML code fragments (for example, scripts) that lead to cross-site scripting vulnerabilities. Therefore, always use HttpUtility.HtmlEncode() for escaping special characters such as < or > before outputting them on the page, or use a web control that performs this encoding automatically.

Never store sensitive data, business-critical data, or data that affects internal business rule decisions made by your application in hidden fields on your web page: Hidden fields can be changed easily by just viewing the source of the web page, modifying it, and saving it to a file. Then an attacker simply needs to submit the locally saved, modified web page to the server. Browser plug-ins are available to make this approach as easy as writing an e-mail with Microsoft Outlook.

Never store sensitive data or business-critical data in view state: View state is just another hidden field on the page, and it can be decoded and viewed easily. View state encryption (as described in Chapter 6) helps to protect information that's only valuable for a limited interval of time, but keep in mind that even encrypted data can eventually be cracked if an attacker has enough time, resources, and motivation.

Enable SSL when using Basic authentication or ASP.NET forms authentication: Chapter 20 discusses forms authentication. SSL is discussed later in this chapter in the section "Understanding SSL."

Protect your cookies: Always protect your authentication cookies when using forms authentication, and set timeouts as short as possible and only as long as necessary.

Use SSL: In general, if your web application processes sensitive data, secure your whole website using SSL. Don't forget to protect even image directories or directories with other files not managed by the application directly through SSL.

Of course, these are just a few general, important issues. To get a complete picture of the situation in terms of your concrete application, you have to create threat models in order to compile a complete list of potential dangers. In addition, invest in ongoing education, because hackers' techniques and technologies evolve just as other techniques and technologies do.

If you forget about just one of these guidelines, all the other security features are more or less useless. Never forget the following principle: Security is only as good as your weakest link.

Understanding Gatekeepers

A good way to increase the security of your application is to have many components in place that enforce security. *Gatekeepers* are a conceptual pattern that apply a pipelining model to a security infrastructure. This model helps you tighten your security.

The gatekeeper model assumes that a secure application always has more security mechanisms in place than necessary. Each of these mechanisms is implemented as a gatekeeper that is responsible for enforcing some security-related conditions. If one of these gatekeepers fails, the attacker will have to face the next gatekeeper in the pipeline. The more gatekeepers you have in your application, the harder the attacker's life will be. Actually, this model supports a core principle for creating secure applications: be as secure as possible, and make attackers' lives as hard as possible.

In Figure 19-1, you can see a pipeline of gatekeepers. At the end of the pipeline, you can see the protected resource (which can be anything, even your custom page code). The protected resource will be accessed or executed only if every gatekeeper grants access. If just one gatekeeper denies access, the request processing is returned to the caller with a security exception.

Implementing a central security component in such a way is generally a good idea. You can also secure your business layer in this way. The ASP.NET application infrastructure leverages this mechanism as well. ASP.NET includes several gatekeepers, each one enforcing a couple of security conditions and therefore protecting your application. In the next sections of this chapter, you will learn which gatekeepers the ASP.NET framework includes and what those gatekeepers' responsibilities are.

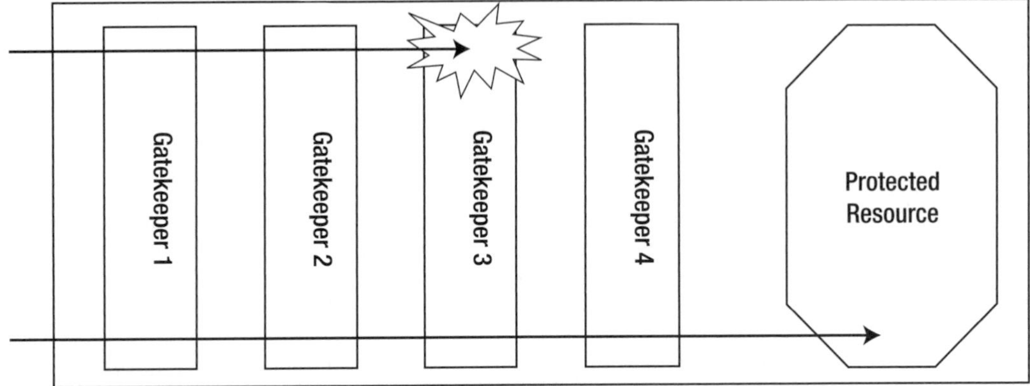

Figure 19-1. A pipeline of gatekeepers

Understanding the Levels of Security

Basically, for mainstream web applications, the fundamental tasks for implementing security (besides the issues you identify during your threat modeling session) are always the same:

Authentication: First, you have to authenticate users. Authentication asks the question, who goes here? It determines who is working with your application on the other end.

Authorization: Second, as soon as you know who is working with your application, your application has to decide which operations the user may execute and which resources the user may access. In other words, authorization asks the question, what is your clearance level?

Confidentiality: While the user is working with the application, you have to ensure that nobody else is able to view sensitive data processed by the user. Therefore, you have to encrypt the channel between the client's browser and the web server. Furthermore, you possibly have to encrypt data stored on the backend (or in the form of cookies on the client) even if you have to prevent database administrators or other staff of the company where the web application is hosted from viewing the data of your application.

Integrity: Finally, you have to make sure data transmitted between the client and the server is not changed by unauthorized actors. Digital signatures provide you with a way to mitigate this type of threat.

ASP.NET includes a basic infrastructure for performing authentication and authorization. The .NET Framework base class library includes some classes in the System.Security namespace for encrypting and signing data. Furthermore, SSL is a standardized way for ensuring confidentiality and integrity of data transmitted between the client browser and the web server. Now you will take a closer look at each of these concepts.

Authentication

Authentication is the process of discovering a user's identity and ensuring the authenticity of this identity. The process of authentication is analogous to checking in at a conference registration table. First, you provide some credentials to prove your identity (such as a driver's license or a passport). Second, once your identity is verified with this information, you are issued a conference badge, or *token*, that you carry with you when you are at the conference. Anyone you meet at the conference can immediately determine your identity by looking at your badge, which typically contains basic identity information, such as your first and last name. This whole process is an example of authentication. Once your identity is established, your token identifies you so that everywhere you go within a particular area, your identity is known.

In an ASP.NET application, authentication is implemented through one of several possible authentication systems:

- Windows authentication
- Forms authentication
- A custom authentication process

In each of these, the user provides credentials when logging in. The user's identity is tracked in different ways depending on the type of authentication. For example, the Windows operating system uses a 96-bit number called an SID (security identifier) to identify each logged-on user. In ASP.NET forms authentication (which is covered in detail in Chapter 20), the user is given a forms authentication ticket, which is a combination of values that are encrypted and placed in a cookie.

All authentication does is allow the application to identify who a user is on each request. This works well for personalization and customization, because you can use the identity information to render user-specific messages on the web pages, alter the appearance of the website, add custom content based on user preferences, and so on. However, on its own, authentication isn't enough to restrict the tasks that a user is allowed to perform based on that user's identity. For that, you need authorization, described in a moment. However, before you learn about authorization, you will take a look at impersonation, which is related to authentication.

Impersonation

Impersonation is the process of executing code in the context (or on behalf) of another user identity. By default, all ASP.NET code is executed using a fixed machine-specific account (typically the Network Service on IIS 7.x). To execute code using another identity, you can use the built-in impersonation capabilities of ASP.NET. You can use a predefined user account, or you can assume the user's identity, if the user has already been authenticated using a Windows account.

One reason you might want to use impersonation is to make use of existing Windows user accounts and their permissions. For example, consider an application that retrieves information from various files that already have user-specific or group-specific permissions set. Rather than code the authorization logic in your ASP.NET application, you can use impersonation to assume the identity of the end user. That way, Windows will perform the authorization for you, checking permissions as soon as you attempt to access a file. You might event choose to switch on impersonation for a short period of time, rather than the entire request. You'll learn more about these options in Chapter 22.

Authorization

Authorization is the process of determining the rights and restrictions assigned to an authenticated user. In the conference analogy, authorization is the process of being granted permission to a particular type of session, such as the keynote speech. At most conferences it is possible to purchase different types of access, such as full access, preconference only, or exhibition hall only. This means if you want to attend the keynote address at Microsoft's Professional Developer Conference to hear what Bill Gates has to say, you must have the proper permissions (the correct conference pass). As you enter the keynote presentation hall, a staff member will look at your conference badge. Based on the information on the badge, the staff member will let you pass or will tell you that you cannot enter. This is an example of authorization. Depending on information related to your identity, you are either granted or denied access to the resources you request.

The conference example is a case of *role-based authorization*—authorization being based on the role or group the user belongs to, not on who the user is. In other words, you are authorized to enter the room for the keynote address based on the role (type of pass), not your specific identity information (first and last name). In many cases, role-based authorization is preferable because it's much easier to implement. If the staff member needed to consult a list with the name of each allowed guest, the process of authorization would be much more awkward. The same is true in a web application, although the roles are more likely to be managers, administrators, guests, salespeople, clients, and so on.

In a web application, different types of authorization happen at different levels. For example, at the topmost level, your code can examine the user identity and decide whether to continue with a given operation. On a lower level, you can configure ASP.NET to deny access to specific web pages or directories for certain users or roles. At an even lower level, when your code performs various tasks such as connecting to a database, opening a file, writing to an event log, and so on, the Windows operating system checks the permissions of the Windows account that's executing the code. In most situations, you won't rely on this bottommost level, because your code will always run under a fixed account. In IIS 7.x, this is by default the fixed Network Service account.

Sound reasons exist for using a fixed account to run ASP.NET code. In almost all applications, the rights allocated to the user don't match the rights needed by your application, which works on behalf of the user. Generally, your code needs a broader set of permissions to perform incidental tasks, and you won't want to give these permissions to every user who might access your web application. For example, your code may need to create a log record when a failure occurs, even though the current user isn't allowed to directly write to the Windows event log, file, or database. Similarly, ASP.NET applications always require rights to the c:\[WinDir]\Microsoft.NET\Framework\[Version]\Temporary ASP.NET Files directory to create and cache a compiled machine-language version of your web pages. Finally, you might want to use an authentication system that has nothing to do with Windows. For example, an e-commerce application might verify user e-mail addresses against a server-side database. In this case, the user's identity doesn't correspond to a Windows account.

In a few rare cases, you'll want to give your code the ability to temporarily assume the identity of the user. This type of approach is much more common when creating ASP.NET applications for local networks where users already have a carefully defined set of Windows privileges. In this case, you need to supplement your security arsenal with impersonation, as mentioned in the previous section and described in Chapter 22.

Confidentiality and Integrity

Confidentiality means ensuring that data cannot be viewed by unauthorized users while being transmitted over a network or stored in a data store such as a database. *Integrity* is all about ensuring that nobody can change the data while it is transmitted over a network or stored in a data store. Both are based on encryption.

Encryption is the process of scrambling data so that it's unreadable by other users. Encryption in ASP.NET is a completely separate feature from authentication, authorization, and impersonation. You can use it in combination with these features or on its own.

As mentioned previously, you might want to use encryption in a web application for two reasons:

To protect communication (data over the wire): For example, you might want to make sure an eavesdropper on the public Internet can't read a credit card number that's used to purchase an item on your e-commerce site. The industry-standard approach to this problem is to use SSL. SSL also implements digital signatures for ensuring integrity. SSL isn't implemented by ASP.NET. Instead, it's a feature provided by IIS. Your web-page (or web service) code is identical whether or not SSL is used.

To protect permanent information (data in a database or in a file): For example, you might want to store a user's credit card in a database record for future use. Although you could store this data in plain text and assume the web server won't be compromised, this is never a good idea. Instead, you should use the encryption classes that are provided with .NET to manually encrypt data before you store it.

It's worth noting that the .NET encryption classes aren't directly tied to ASP.NET. In fact, you can use them in any type of .NET application. You'll learn about encryption and digital signatures as well as how to take control of custom encryption in Chapter 25.

Pulling It All Together

So, how do authentication, authorization, and impersonation all work together in a web application?

When users first come to your website, they are anonymous. In other words, your application doesn't know (and doesn't care) who they are. Unless you authenticate them, this is the way it stays.

By default, anonymous users can access any ASP.NET web page. But when a user requests a web page that doesn't permit anonymous access, several steps take place (as shown in Figure 19-2):

1. The request is sent to the web server. Since the user identity is not known at this time, the user is asked to log in (using a custom web page or a browser-based login dialog box). The specific details of the login process depend on the type of authentication you're using.
2. The user provides his or her credentials, which are then verified, either by your application (in the case of forms authentication) or automatically by IIS (in the case of Windows authentication).
3. If the user credentials are legitimate, the user is granted access to the web page. If his or her credentials are not legitimate, then the user is prompted to log in again, or the user is redirected to a web page with an "access denied" message.

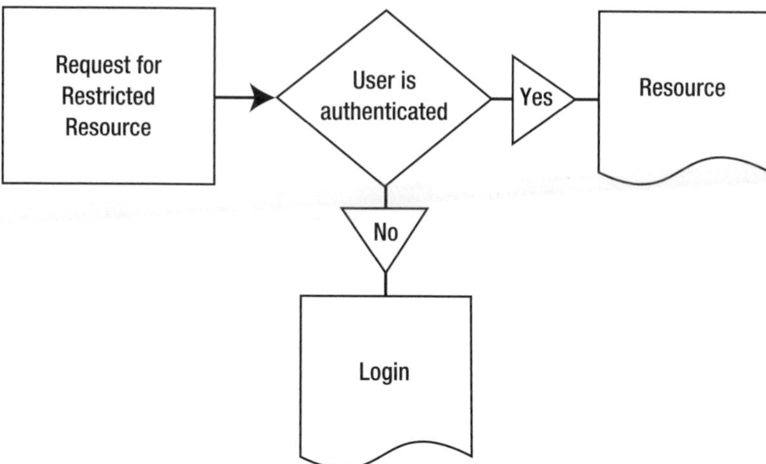

Figure 19-2. *Requesting a web page that requires authentication*

When a user requests a secure web page that allows only specific users or users in specific roles, the process is similar, but an extra step takes place (see Figure 19-3):

1. The request is sent to the web server. Since the user identity is not known at this time, the user is asked to log in (using a custom web page or a browser-based login dialog box). The specific details of the login process depend on the type of authentication you're using.
2. The user provides his or her credentials, which are verified with the application. This is the authentication stage.
3. The authenticated user's credentials or roles are compared to the list of allowed users or roles. If the user is in the list, then the user is granted access to the resource; otherwise, access is denied.
4. Users who have access denied are either prompted to log in again, or they are redirected to a web page with an "access denied" message.

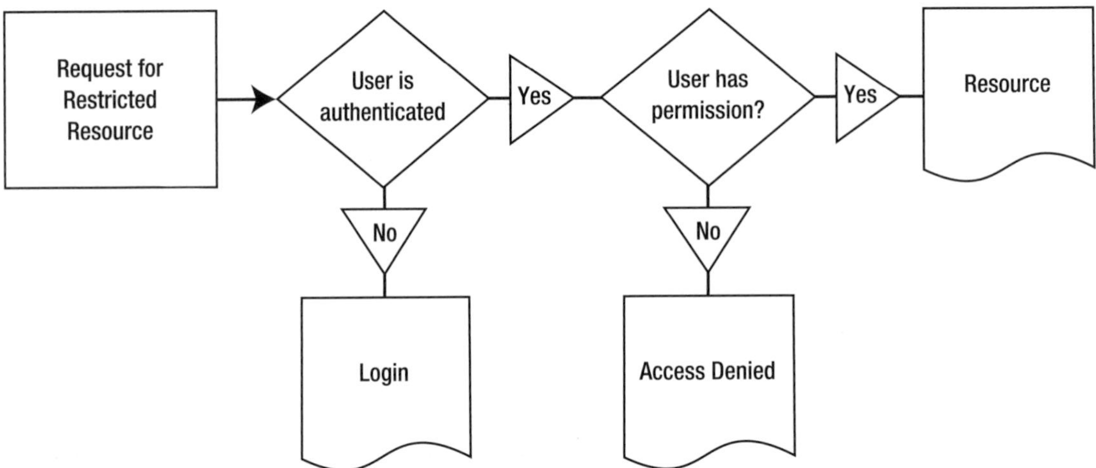

Figure 19-3. *Requesting a web page that requires authentication and authorization*

Understanding Secure Sockets Layer

The SSL technology encrypts communication over HTTP. SSL is supported by a wide range of browsers and ensures that an eavesdropper can't easily decipher information exchanged between a client and a web server. SSL is important for hiding sensitive information such as credit card numbers and confidential company details, but it's also keenly important for user authentication. For example, if you create a login page where the user submits a user name and password, you must use SSL to encrypt this information. Otherwise, a malicious user could intercept the user credentials and use them to log on to the system.

IIS provides SSL out of the box. Because SSL operates underneath HTTP, using SSL does not change the way you deal with HTTP requests. All the encryption and decryption work is taken care of by the SSL capabilities of the web server software (in this case, IIS). The only difference is that the URL for addresses protected by SSL begins with https:// rather than http://. SSL traffic also flows over a different port (typically web servers use port 443 for SSL requests and port 80 for normal requests).

For a server to support SSL connections, it must have an installed X.509 certificate (the name X.509 was chosen to correspond with the X.500 directory standard). To implement SSL, you need to purchase a certificate, install it, and configure IIS appropriately. We'll cover these steps in the following sections.

Understanding Certificates

Before sending sensitive data, a client must decide whether to trust a website. *Certificates* were designed to serve this purpose, by making it possible to partially verify a user's identity. Certificates can be installed on any type of computer, but they are most often found on web servers.

With certificates, an organization purchases a certificate from a known certificate authority (CA) and installs it on its web server. The client implicitly trusts the CA and is therefore willing to trust certificate information signed by the CA. This model works well because it is unlikely that a malicious user will go to the expense of purchasing and installing a falsified certificate. The CA also retains information about each registered user. However, a certificate does not in any way ensure the trustworthiness of the server, the safety of the application, or the legitimacy of the business. In these ways, certificates are fundamentally limited in scope.

The certificate itself contains certain identifying information. It is signed with the CA's private key to guarantee that it is authentic and has not been modified. The industry-standard certificate type, known as x.509v3, contains the following basic information:

- The holder's name, organization, and address
- The holder's public key, which will be used to negotiate an SSL session key for encrypting communication
- The certificate's validation dates
- The certificate's serial number

In addition, a certificate might also include business-specific information, such as the certificate holder's industry, the length of time they have been in business, and so on.

The two biggest CAs are as follows:

- Thawte: `http://www.thawte.com`
- VeriSign: `http://www.verisign.com`

If you don't need the identity validation function of CAs (for example, if your certificates will be used only on a local intranet), you can create and use your own certificates and configure all clients to trust them. This requires Active Directory and Certificate Server (which is a built-in part of Windows 2003 Server and Windows 2000 Server). For more information, consult a dedicated book about Windows network administration.

Understanding SSL

As described in the previous section, every certificate includes a public key. A public key is part of an *asymmetric key pair*. The basic idea is that the public key is freely provided to anyone who is interested. The corresponding private key is kept carefully locked away and is available only to the server. The interesting twist is that anything that's encrypted with one of the keys is decipherable with the other. That means a client can retrieve the public key and use it to encode a secret message that can be decrypted only with the corresponding private key. In other words, the client can create a message that only the server can read.

This process is called *asymmetric encryption*, and it's a basic building block of SSL. An important principle of asymmetric encryption is that you can't determine a private key by analyzing the corresponding public key. To do so would be computationally expensive (even more difficult than cracking one of the encrypted messages). However, asymmetric encryption also has its limitations—namely, it's much slower and generates much larger messages than symmetric encryption.

Symmetric encryption is the type of encryption that most people are intuitively familiar with. It uses the same secret key to encrypt a message as to decrypt it. The drawback with symmetric encryption is that both parties need to know the secret value in order to have a conversation. However, you can't transmit this information over the Internet, because a malicious user might intercept it and then be able to decipher the following encrypted conversation. The great trick of SSL is to combine asymmetric and symmetric encryption. Asymmetric encryption manages the initial key exchange—in other words, agrees on a secret value. Then, this secret value symmetrically encrypts all subsequent messages, which ensures the best possible performance.

The whole process works like this, where the *client* refers to the web browser running on the end user's machine and the *server* refers to the web server hosting the websites the user wants to get access to:

1. The client sends a request to connect to the server.
2. The server signs its certificate and sends it to the client. This concludes the handshake portion of the exchange.
3. The client checks whether the certificate was issued by a CA it trusts. If so, it proceeds to the next step. In a web browser scenario, the client may warn the user with an ominous-sounding message if it does not recognize the CA, and allows the user to decide whether to proceed. The client recognizes CAs when their certificate is stored in the Trusted Root Certification Authorities store of the operating system. You can find certificates stored in this store through the Internet Explorer options by clicking the Certificates button on the Content tab.
4. The client compares the information in the certificate with the information received from the site (including its domain name and its public key). The client also verifies that the server-side certificate is valid, has not been revoked, and is issued by a trusted CA. Then the client accepts the connection.
5. The client tells the server what encryption keys it supports for communication.
6. The server chooses the strongest shared key length and informs the client.
7. Using the indicated key length, the client randomly generates a symmetric encryption key. This will be used for the duration of the transaction between the server and the client. It ensures optimum performance, because symmetric encryption is much faster than asymmetric encryption.
8. The client encrypts the session key using the server's public key (from the certificate), and then it sends the encrypted session key to the server.
9. The server receives the encrypted session key and decrypts it using its private key. Both the client and server now have the shared secret key, and they can use it to encrypt all communication for the duration of the session.

You'll notice that the symmetric key is generated randomly and used only for the duration of a session. This limits the security risk. First, it's harder to break encrypted messages using cryptanalysis, because messages from other sessions can't be used. Second, even if the key is determined by a malicious user, it will remain valid only for the course of the session.

Another interesting point is that the client must generate the symmetric key. This is because the client has the server's public key, which can be used to encrypt a message that only the server can read. The server does not have corresponding information about the client and thus cannot yet encrypt a message. This also means that if the client supplies a weak key, the entire interaction could be compromised. For example, older versions of the Netscape browser used a weak random number generator to create the symmetric key. This would make it much easier for a malicious user to guess the key.

When deploying an application, you will probably want to purchase certificates from a genuine CA such as VeriSign. This is particularly the case with websites and Internet browsers, which recognize a limited number of CAs automatically. If you use a test certificate to encrypt communication with a secured portion of a website, for example, the client browser will display a warning that the certificate is not from a known CA.

Configuring SSL in IIS 7.x

First of all, you need to issue a certificate for your web server. For this purpose you have to select the web server root node in the navigation tree of the management console, and select the Server Certificates feature, as shown in Figure 19-4.

***Figure 19-4.** The Server Certificates option in IIS 7.x*

When opening the details, the management console will list all the server certificates installed on your web server. The first interesting part in IIS 7.x is the fact that you can install multiple server certificates on one web server, which can be used for different websites configured on your web server (see Figure 19-5). This is a nice improvement compared to older IIS versions, which allowed you to install just one server certificate per web server.

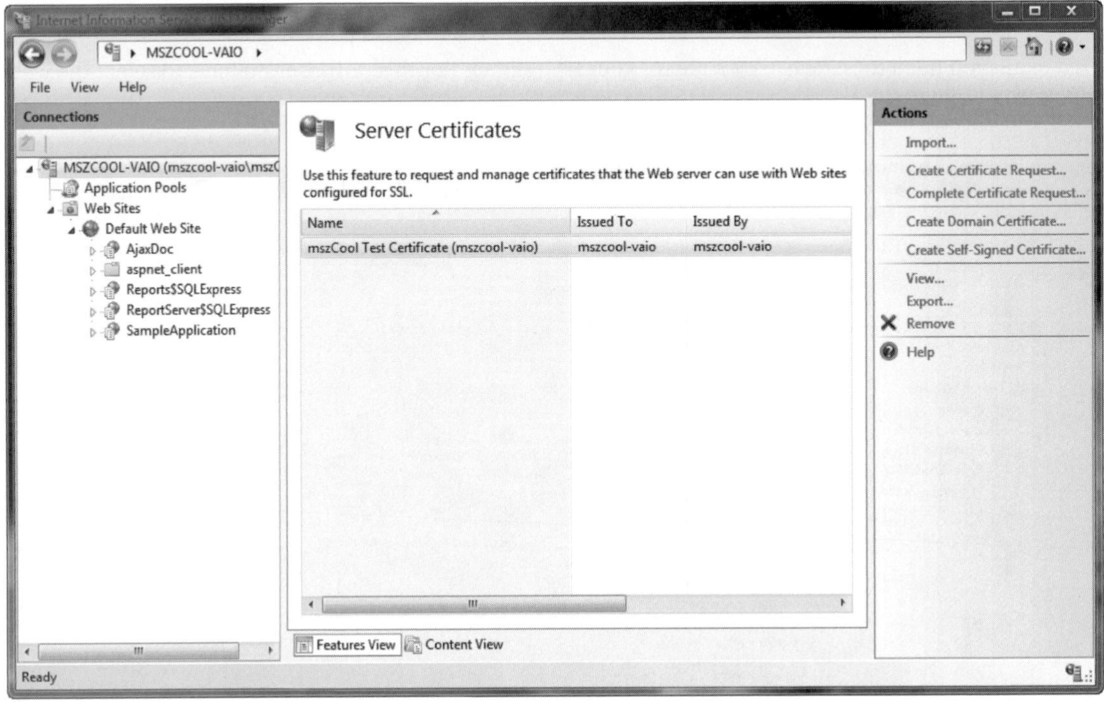

***Figure 19-5.** List of server certificates installed in IIS 7.x*

In the Server Certificates feature details view, the task pane on the right side of the management console shows the necessary task for installing server certificates. It allows you to create a certificate request automatically that you can use for requesting a new certificate at a CA. To create a new request, you just use the Create Certificate Request task link on the task pane, which creates the same Base64-encoded request as the previous IIS versions did. You use this Base64-encoded request file to submit your request at the CA. After you have retrieved the certificate from your CA, you can complete the running request by clicking the Complete Certificate Request task link in the task pane within the server certificates feature of the management console. This way you can request and configure an SSL certificate for a standalone web server. If you want to request a certificate for your own CA, you can use the Online Certification Authority wizard by clicking the Create Domain Certificate wizard. This certificate is then configured in your own CA and is used for signing certificates issued by this CA.

Honestly, this process is really cumbersome if you are just a developer who wants to test SSL with your own web applications. Therefore, IIS 7.x includes an additional option that was not available in previous IIS versions out of the box: creating a self-signed certificate for your own machine. All you need to specify for a self-signed certificate is a friendly name to be displayed in the list. Afterward, the wizard creates a certificate by using cryptographic functions of your machine and installs that certificate in your web server! It is important to understand that these certificates should be used for testing purposes only, because no other browser than yours running on your developer machine will know the certificate, and therefore will include warnings that the certificate is invalid.

After you have configured and installed your server certificates, you can leverage them for SSL-based communication within the websites configured on your IIS. For this purpose you need to configure protocol bindings for SSL, as well as the SSL options for your web applications within the websites.

Configuring Bindings for SSL

As outlined in detail in Chapter 18, bindings are used for making contents of websites available through specific protocols, IP addresses, and ports. Host headers for accessing several web applications through the same IP address and port are configured in bindings, as well. If you want to leverage SSL for applications configured within a website, you need to configure a protocol binding for SSL for the website. For that purpose, just select your website (such as the Default Web Site) in the navigation tree of the IIS management console and select the Bindings link from the task pane on the right-hand side of the console. A dialog that allows you to configure your bindings appears. Now you can add new bindings to make contents available through different IP addresses, ports, and protocols. Figure 19-6 shows this dialog.

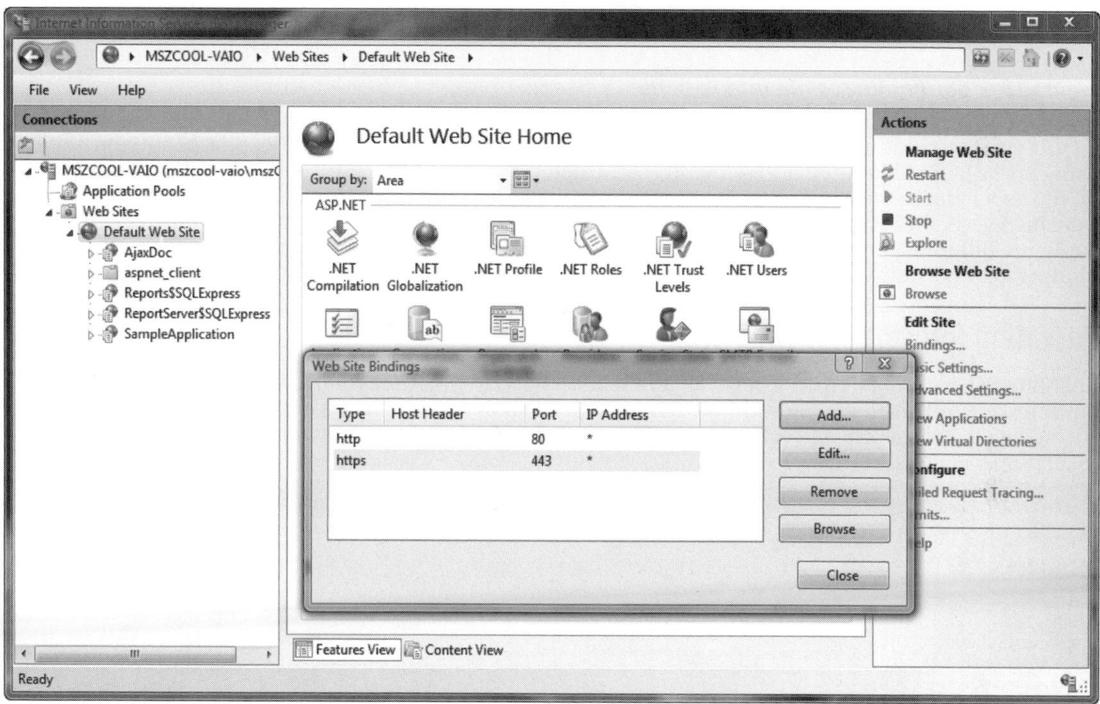

Figure 19-6. Configuring bindings for a website

By clicking the Add button you can add new bindings to your website, and by clicking the Edit button you can modify existing bindings in the list. Figure 19-7 shows the binding configuration for enabling SSL on your website.

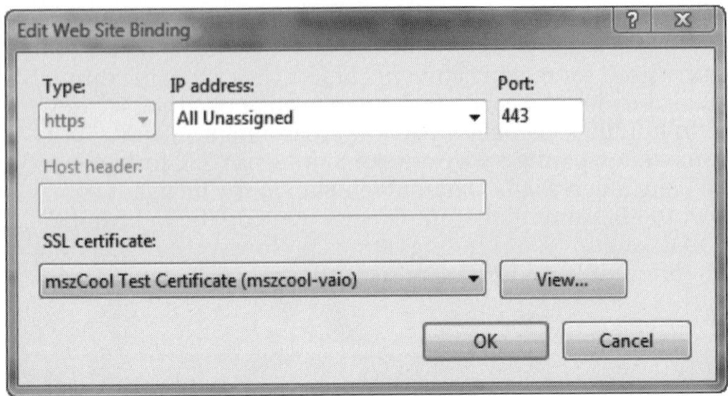

***Figure 19-7.** SSL binding configuration in IIS 7.x*

As you can see, the protocol is configured to https running on the default IP address for your server, using port 443 for SSL-based access (which is the default port for SSL). Furthermore, in the combo box on the lower end of the window you can select the certificate that's used for SSL traffic on the selected website. Every certificate you installed previously is available for selection in this list, and you can configure different certificates for each website on your web server. After you have configured the SSL binding for your website, you can enable SSL for web applications within the website.

Encoding Information with SSL

Enabling SSL is configured on a per-web application basis in IIS. After you have configured your bindings at a website level, you can select a web application of your choice in the navigation tree of the IIS management console and activate the SSL feature configuration as shown in Figure 19-8.

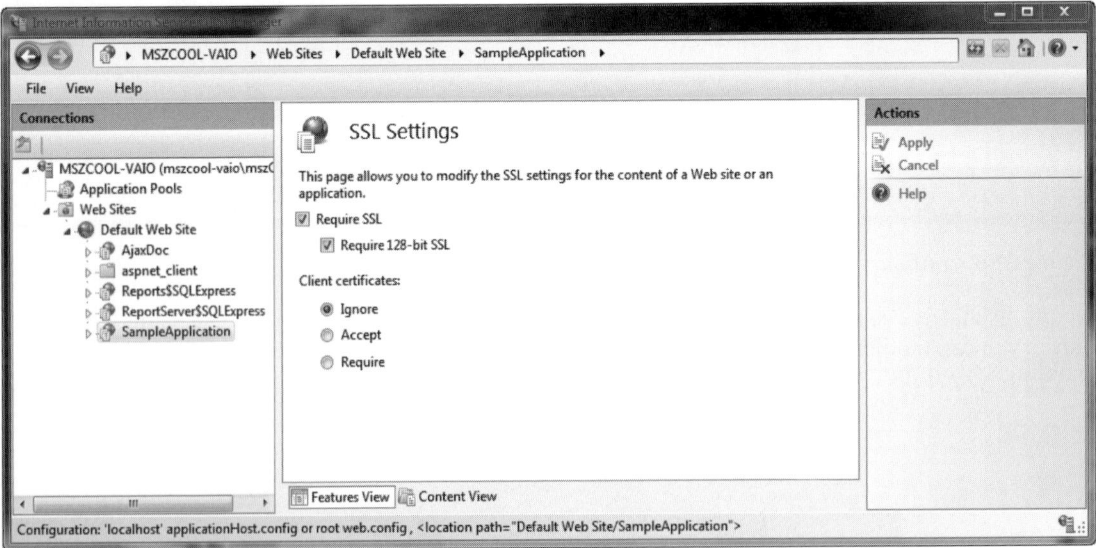

***Figure 19-8.** Enabling SSL traffic on your website*

You can specify if you want to require SSL encoding for the selected web application and whether you require client certificates for authenticating users. When using client certificate authentication you need to configure certificate mappings from certificates to users that are finally authenticated by IIS when retrieving a certain certificate. Again, you need to configure these mappings in your web.config configuration file through the <iisClientCertificateMapping> configuration section within the <system.webServer> section. For more information on configuring client certificate mappings, refer to the Microsoft documentation available at MSDN or TechNet: `http://msdn2.microsoft.com/en-us/library/Aa347495.aspx`.

Summary

With ASP.NET, programmers finally have a comprehensive, full-featured set of security tools. As with many other features in the world of ASP.NET, the presence of a security framework simply means that there is less work for you to do to implement a variety of authentication and authorization scenarios. ASP.NET provides two types of authentication providers: Windows authentication and forms authentication. Additionally, ASP.NET also includes all the necessary interfaces and classes you need to build your own authentication and authorization system. In the following chapters, you'll learn about all of these features.

CHAPTER 20

■ ■ ■

Forms Authentication

In the previous chapter, you learned about the basic structure of ASP.NET security. In this chapter, you will learn how you can authenticate your users using *forms authentication*. You should use this type of authentication whenever there is a reason for not using Windows-based accounts in your applications. We will discuss such reasons in this chapter, as well as in Chapter 22 when discussing Windows authentication itself.

Forms authentication is an all-purpose authentication system that's based around two concepts. First is a login page that can validate users (usually, by comparing a user name and password combination against a database or some other data store). Second, is a mechanism for preserving and reestablishing the security context on each request (usually, using a cookie). This way, the user needs log in only once.

As you'll see in this chapter, ASP.NET includes all the infrastructure that you need. With forms authentication, ASP.NET creates the security cookie for logged-in users, maintains it, and automatically establishes the security context on subsequent requests. Best of all, it manages the process in a way that's efficient and highly resistant to tampering.

Introducing Forms Authentication

Forms authentication is a *ticket-based* (also called *token-based*) system. This means when users log in, they receive a ticket with basic user information. This information is stored in an encrypted cookie that's attached to the response so it's automatically submitted on each subsequent request.

When a user requests an ASP.NET page that is not available for anonymous users, the ASP.NET runtime verifies whether the forms authentication ticket is available. If it's not available, ASP.NET automatically redirects the user to a login page. At that moment, it's your turn. You have to create this login page and validate the credentials within this login page. If the user is successfully validated, you just tell the ASP.NET infrastructure about the success (by calling a method of the FormsAuthentication class), and the runtime automatically sets the authentication cookie (which actually contains the ticket) and redirects the user to the originally requested page. With this request, the runtime detects that the authentication cookie with the ticket is available and grants access to the page. You can see this process in Figure 20-1.

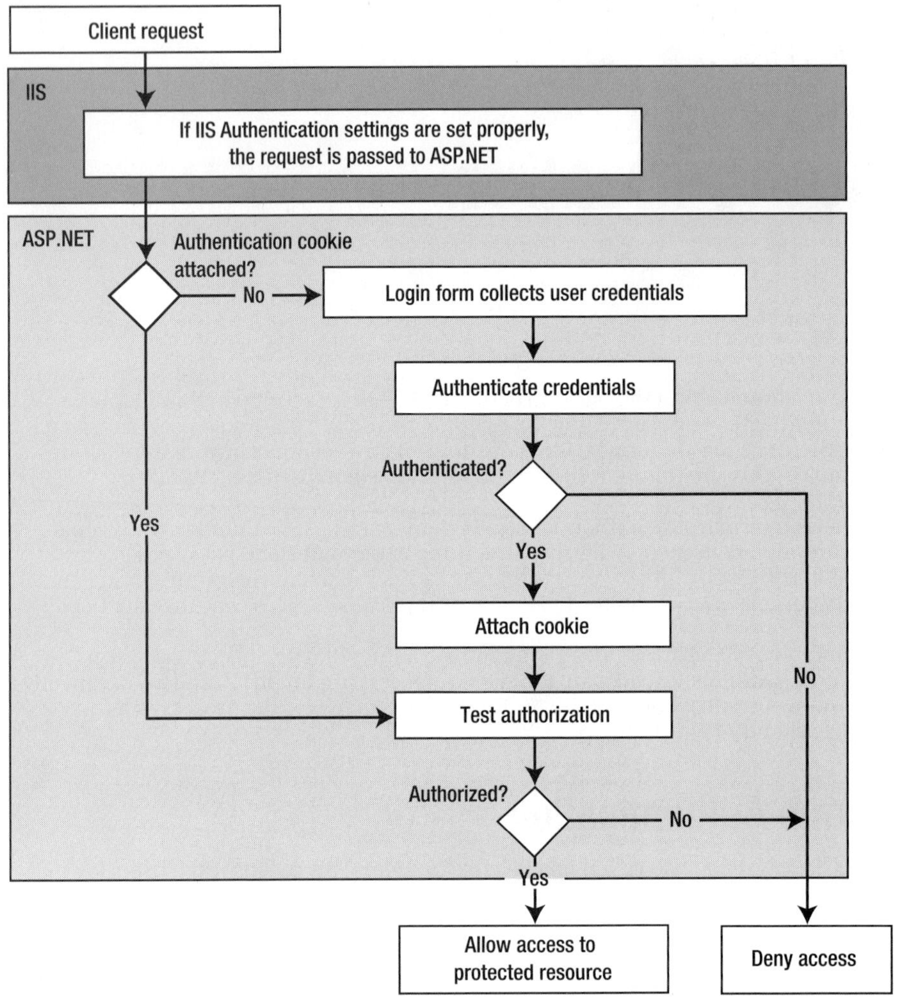

Figure 20-1. *The forms authentication process*

All you need to do is configure forms authentication in the web.config file, create the login page, and validate the credentials in the login page.

Why Use Forms Authentication?

Forms authentication is an attractive option for developers for a number of reasons:

- You have full control over the authentication code.
- You have full control over the appearance of the login form.
- It works with any browser.

- It allows you to decide how to store user information.

Let's look at each of these in turn.

Controlling the Authentication Code

Because forms authentication is implemented entirely within ASP.NET, you have complete control over how authentication is performed. You don't need to rely on any external systems, as you do with Windows or Passport authentication. You can customize the behavior of forms authentication to suit your needs, as you will see in the section "Persistent Cookies in Forms Authentication."

Controlling the Appearance of the Login Form

You have the same degree of control over the appearance of forms authentication as you do over its functionality. In other words, you can format the login form in any way you like. Or, if you don't want to do any of this work, you can use the higher-level membership API and the ASP.NET security controls. These security controls contain a ready-to-use and highly customizable Login control. We will discuss the membership API and the security controls in the next chapter in detail.

This flexibility in appearance is not available in the other authentication methods. Windows authentication needs the browser to collect credentials, and Passport authentication requires that users leave your website and visit the Passport site to enter their credentials.

Working with a Range of Browsers

Forms authentication uses standard HTML as its user interface, so all browsers can handle it. Because you can format the login form in any way you like, you can even use forms authentication with browsers that do not use HTML, such as those on mobile devices. To do this, you need to detect the browser being used and provide a form in the correct format for the device (such as WML for most mobile phones).

■ **Caution** Forms authentication uses standard HTML forms for collecting and submitting the user's credentials. Therefore, you have to use SSL to encrypt and transmit the user's credentials securely. If you don't use SSL, the information is transmitted as clear text in the postback data in the request to the server.

Storing User Information

Forms authentication stores users in the web.config file by default, but as you will see in the section "Custom Credentials Store," you can store the information anywhere you like. You just need to create the code that accesses the data store and retrieves the required information. (And if you use the membership API introduced in Chapter 21, you don't even need to do that.) A common example is to store the user information in a custom database.

This flexibility in the storage of user information also means you can control how user accounts are created and administered, and you can attach additional information to user accounts, such as personal preferences for customizing the appearance of your website. You can also attach business-specific information such as, for example, encrypted credit card information if you have an online shop. In addition to the membership API mentioned earlier and covered in Chapter 21, ASP.NET includes the profiles API, which allows you to store additional user information independent from your user accounts themselves. The profiles API is covered in Chapter 24. By comparison, Windows authentication (discussed in Chapter 22) is much less flexible. It requires that you set up a Windows user account for each user you want to authenticate. This is obviously a problem if you want to serve a large number of users or if you want to register users programmatically. It also doesn't allow you to store additional information about users. (In the case of Active Directory, you have the possibility of extending the Active Directory schema, which defines contents and types for data structures stored in an Active Directory. However, this is something that needs to be planned well and is often not seen gladly by IT administrators.) Instead, you have to store this information separately. Passport authentication has similar limitations. Although Passport stores more user information, it doesn't allow you to add custom information, and it doesn't allow you to take part in user registration or account management.

Why Would You Not Use Forms Authentication?

So far, you've considered the reasons that make forms authentication an attractive choice for user authentication. However, forms authentication also has downsides:

- You have to create the user interface for users to log in. You can either create the login page completely on your own or use the ASP.NET security controls (which are covered in the next chapter).
- You have to maintain a catalog with user credentials.
- You have to take additional precautions against the interception of network traffic.

The following sections explore these issues. You can solve the first two of these downsides by using the membership API framework, which offers prebuilt controls and a prebuilt schema for credential storage and runs on SQL Server databases out of the box. You will learn about the membership API framework in Chapter 21.

Creating Your Own Login Interface

As mentioned earlier, forms authentication gives you control over the interface that users use to log into your web application. Along with its benefits, this approach also creates extra work, because you have to build the login page. Other forms of authentication supply some prebuilt portions. For instance, if you're using Windows authentication, the browser provides a standard dialog box. In Passport authentication, the user interface of the Passport site is always used for logging in.

Creating the login page for forms authentication doesn't require a lot of work, though. It's just worth noting that forms authentication is merely a framework for building an authentication system, rather than an all-in-one system that's complete and ready to use.

The new membership API, on the other hand, includes a prebuilt Login control that can be used either on a separate login page or within any page of your application that provides a prebuilt login user interface. This user interface is customizable and communicates with the membership API to log the user in automatically. The control does most of the work of creating custom login pages. In most cases, creating a custom login page requires nothing more than adding an .aspx page to your solution with a Login control on it. You don't need to catch any events or write any code if you are fine with the default behavior of the control (which will usually be the case). You will learn more details about this control in Chapter 21.

Maintaining User Details

When you use forms authentication, you are responsible for maintaining the details of the users who access your system. The most important details are the credentials that the user needs in order to log into the system. Not only do you need to devise a way to store them, but you also need to ensure that they are stored securely. Also, you need to provide some sort of administration tools for managing the users stored in your custom store.

The membership API framework ships with a prebuilt schema for storing credentials in a SQL Server database. So, you can save lots of time using this existing schema; furthermore, the schema is extensible. Still, you are responsible for backing up the credentials store securely so that you can restore it in case of a system failure.

All these considerations don't apply to most other types of authentication. In Windows authentication, user credentials are stored by the underlying operating system. Windows uses a variety of techniques to keep them secure automatically so that you don't need to perform any work of your own. In Passport authentication, the credentials are stored securely on Passport servers.

Intercepting Network Traffic

When a user enters credentials for forms authentication, the credentials are sent from the browser to the server in plain-text format. This means anyone intercepting them will be able to read them. This is obviously an insecure situation.

The usual solution to this problem is to use SSL (as described in the previous chapter). Now, a valid argument might be that you just need to use SSL for securing the login page, not the entire application. You can configure forms authentication to encrypt and sign the cookie, and therefore it's extremely difficult for an attacker to get any information from it. In addition, the cookie should not contain any sensitive information and therefore won't include the password that was used for authentication.

But what if the attacker intercepts the unencrypted traffic and just picks the (already encrypted) cookie and uses it for replay? The attacker doesn't need to decrypt it; she just needs to send the cookie with her own request across the wire. You can mitigate such a *replay attack* only if you run the entire website with SSL.

Other authentication mechanisms don't require this extra work. With Windows authentication, you can use a protocol that automatically enforces a secure login process (with the caveat that this is not supported by all browsers and all network environments). With Passport authentication, the login process is handled transparently by the Passport servers, which always use SSL.

Why Not Implement Cookie Authentication Yourself?

Depending on the configuration you will learn about in the next sections of this chapter, forms authentication uses cookies for assigning authentication tickets to clients and users. A more generic term for this approach is cookie authentication. *Cookie authentication* is, on the surface, a fairly straightforward system. You might wonder why you shouldn't just implement it yourself using cookies or session variables.

The answer is the same reason developers don't implement features in ASP.NET ranging from session state to the web control framework. Not only does ASP.NET save you the trouble, but it also provides an implementation that's secure, well tested, and extensible. Some of the advantages provided by ASP.NET's implementation of forms authentication include the following:

- The authentication cookie is secure.
- Forms authentication is a well-tested system.
- Forms authentication integrates with the .NET security classes.

Keeping the Authentication Cookie Secure

Cookie authentication seems simple, but if it's not implemented correctly, you can be left with an insecure system. On their own, cookies are not a safe place to store sensitive information, because a malicious user can easily view and edit cookie data. If your authentication is based on unprotected cookies, attackers can easily compromise your system.

By default, the forms authentication module encrypts its authentication information before placing it in a cookie. It also attaches a hash code and validates the cookies when they return to the server to verify that no changes have been made. The combination of these two processes makes these cookies very secure and saves you from needing to write your own security code. Most examples of homemade cookie authentication are far less secure.

Forms Authentication Is Well Tested

Forms authentication is an integral part of ASP.NET, so it has already been used in a number of web applications and websites. Because so many people use the same system, flaws are quickly discovered, publicized, and solved. As long as you keep up-to-date with patches, you have a high level of protection. On the other hand, if you create your own cookie authentication system, you do not have the advantage of this widespread testing. The first time you'll notice a vulnerability will probably be when your system is compromised.

Integrating with the ASP.NET Security Framework

All types of ASP.NET authentication use a consistent framework. Forms authentication is fully integrated with this security framework. For example, it populates the security context (IPrincipal) object and user identity (IIdentity) object, as it should. This makes it easy to customize the behavior of forms authentication.

The Forms Authentication Classes

The most important part of the forms authentication framework is the FormsAuthenticationModule, which is an HttpModule class that detects existing forms authentication tickets in the request. If the ticket is not available and the user requests a protected resource, it automatically redirects the request to the login page configured in your web.config file before this protected resource is even touched by the runtime.

If the ticket is present, the module automatically creates the security context by initializing the HttpContext.Current.User property with a default instance of GenericPrincipal, which contains a FormsIdentity instance with the name of the currently logged-in user. Basically, you don't work with the module directly. Your interface to the module consists of the classes in Table 20-1, which are part of the System.Web.Security namespace.

Table 20-1. *The Forms Authentication Framework Classes*

Class Name	Description
FormsAuthentication	This is the primary class for interacting with the forms authentication infrastructure. It provides basic information about the configuration and allows you to create the ticket, set the cookie, and redirect from the login page to the originally requested page if the validation of credentials was successful.
FormsAuthenticationEventArgs	The FormsAuthenticationModule raises an Authenticate event that you can catch. The event arguments passed are encapsulated in an instance of this class. It contains basic information about the authenticated user.
FormsAuthenticationTicket	This class represents the user information that will be encrypted and stored in the authentication cookie.

Class Name	Description
FormsIdentity	This class is an implementation of IIdentity that is specific to forms authentication. The key addition to the FormsIdentity class, in addition to the members required when implementing the IIdentity interface, is the Ticket property, which exposes the forms authentication ticket. This allows you to store and retrieve additional information in the ticket, such as caching role information for simple scenarios.
FormsAuthenticationModule	This is the core of the forms authentication infrastructure that establishes the security context and performs the automatic page redirects to the login page if necessary.

Mostly you will use the FormsAuthentication class and the FormsIdentity class, which represents a successfully authenticated user in your application. Next you will learn how to use forms authentication in your application.

Implementing Forms Authentication

You need to complete the following steps to use forms authentication in your application:

1. Configure forms authentication in the web.config file.
2. Configure IIS to *allow* anonymous access to the virtual directory, and configure ASP.NET to *restrict* anonymous access to the web application.
3. Create a custom login page that collects and validates a user name and password and then interacts with the forms authentication infrastructure for creating the ticket.

The following sections describe these steps.

■ **Note** The cookie is encrypted with a machine-specific key that's defined in the machine.config file. Usually, this detail isn't important. However, in a web farm you need to make sure all servers use the same key so that one server can decrypt the cookie created by another.

Configuring Forms Authentication

You have to configure forms authentication appropriately in your web.config file. Remember from the previous chapter that every web.config file includes the <authentication /> configuration section. Forms authentication works if you configure this section with the value Forms for the mode attribute:

```
<authentication mode="Forms">
    <!-- Detailed configuration options -->
</authentication>
```

The <authentication /> configuration is limited to the top-level web.config file of your application. If the mode attribute is set to Forms, ASP.NET loads and activates the FormsAuthenticationModule, which does most of the work for you. The previous configuration uses default settings for forms authentication that are hard-coded into the ASP.NET runtime. You can override any default settings by adding settings to the <system.web> section of the machine.config file. You can override these default settings in your application by specifying additional settings in the <forms /> child tag of this section. The following code snippet shows the complete set of options for the forms tag:

```
<authentication mode="Forms">
    <!-- Detailed configuration options -->
    <forms name="MyCookieName"
           loginUrl="DbLogin.aspx"
           timeout="20"
           slidingExpiration="true"
           cookieless="AutoDetect"
           protection="All"
           requireSSL="false"
           enableCrossAppRedirects="false"
           defaultUrl="MyDefault.aspx"
           domain="www.mydomain.com"
           path="/" />
</authentication>
```

■ **Note** In the preceding example, the domain property is set to a value representing your domain. However, usually when developing and debugging an application, you run your web application either on your local server or a test server within your intranet (for example, by using the URL `http://localhost:<port>` when using the integrated web development server). In that case the URL you use to access the application is different from your actual domain. Therefore, forms authentication would not work, as it matches the name of the cookie domain with the URL used for accessing the web server. If you need to test cross-application domain authentication, we recommend setting the domain property to the name of your local machine or your test machine and accessing the application by using your machine's name instead of localhost (for example, `http://your-machine-name:<port>` instead of `http://localhost:<port>`).

The properties are listed in the order you will use them in most cases. Table 20-2 describes the details of these properties and their default configuration.

Table 20-2. *The Forms Authentication Options*

Option	Default	Description
name	.ASPXAUTH	The name of the HTTP cookie to use for authentication. If multiple applications are running on the same web server, you should give each application's security cookie a unique name.
loginUrl	login.aspx	Defines which page the user should be redirected to in order to log into the application. This could be a page in the root folder of the application, or it could be in a subdirectory.
timeout	30	The number of minutes before the authentication cookie expires. ASP.NET will refresh the cookie when it receives a request, as long as half of the cookie's lifetime has expired. The expiry of cookies is a significant concern. If cookies expire too often, users will have to log in often, and the usability of your application may suffer. If they expire too seldom, you run a greater risk of cookies being stolen and misused.
slidingExpiration	true	This attribute enables or disables sliding expiration of the authentication cookie. If enabled, the expiration of an authentication cookie will be reset by the runtime with every request a user submits to the page. This means with every request the expiration of the cookie will be extended.
cookieless	UseDeviceProfile	Allows you to specify whether the runtime uses cookies for sending the forms authentication ticket to the client. Possible options are AutoDetect, UseCookies, UseUri, and UseDeviceProfile. These settings are covered in detail in Table 20-3 later in this chapter.
protection	All	Allows you to specify the level of protection for the authentication cookie. The option All encrypts and signs the authentication cookie. Other possible options are None, Encryption (encrypts only), and Validation (signs only).
requireSSL	false	If set to true, this property has the effect that the browser simply doesn't transmit the cookie if SSL is not enabled on the web server. Therefore, forms authentication will not work in this case if SSL is not activated on the web server.

Option	Default	Description
enableCrossAppRedirects	false	Enables cross-application redirects when using forms authentication for different applications on your server. Of course, this makes sense only if both applications rely on the same credential store and use the same set of users and roles.
defaultUrl	default.aspx	If the FormsAuthenticationModule redirects a request from the user to the login page, it includes the originally requested page when calling the login page. Therefore, when returning from the login page, the module can use this URL for a redirect after the credentials have been validated successfully. But what if the user browses to the login page directly? This option specifies the page to redirect to if the user accesses the login page directly by typing its URL into the address bar of the browser.
domain	<empty string>	Specifies the domain for which this cookie is valid. Overriding this property is useful if you want to enable the cookie to be used for more applications on your web server.
path	/	The path for cookies issued by the application. The default value (/) is recommended, because case mismatches can prevent the cookie from being sent with a request.

As explained in Table 20-2, you can disable cookie validation and encryption. However, it's reasonable to wonder why you would want to remove this protection. The only case in which you might make this choice is if you are not authenticating users for security reasons but simply identifying users for personalization purposes. In these cases, it does not really matter if a user impersonates another user, so you might decide that the overhead of encrypting, decrypting, and validating the authentication cookies will adversely affect performance without offering any benefits. Think carefully before taking this approach, however—you should use this approach only in situations where it really does not matter if the authentication system is subverted.

Credentials Store in web.config

When using forms authentication, you have the choice of where to store credentials for the users. You can store them in a custom file or in a database; basically, you can store them anywhere you want if you provide the code for validating the user name and password entered by the user with the values stored in your credential store.

The easiest place to store credentials is directly in the web.config file through the <credentials /> subelement of the <forms /> configuration tag introduced previously.

```
<authentication mode="Forms">
    <!-- Detailed configuration options -->
    <forms name="MyCookieName"
```

```
        loginUrl="DbLogin.aspx"
        timeout="20">
      <credentials passwordFormat="Clear">
         <user name="Admin" password="(Admin1)"/>
         <user name="Mario" password="Szpuszta"/>
         <user name="Matthew" password="MacDonald"/>
      </credentials>
   </forms>
</authentication>
```

■ **Note** First, using web.config as a credential store is possible for simple solutions with just a few users only. In larger scenarios, you should use the membership API, which is described in Chapter 21. Second, you can hash password values for credentials stored in the web.config file. Hashing is nothing more than applying one-way encryption to the password. This means the password will be encrypted in a way that it can't be decrypted anymore. You will learn how you can hash passwords correctly when creating a custom membership provider in Chapter 26.

Denying Access to Anonymous Users

As mentioned earlier, you do not need to restrict access to pages in order to use authentication. It is possible to use authentication purely for personalization so that anonymous users view the same pages as authenticated users (but see slightly different, personalized content). However, to demonstrate the redirection functionality of forms authentication, it's useful to create an example that denies access to anonymous users. This will force ASP.NET to redirect anonymous users to the login page.

Chapter 23 describes authorization in detail. For now, you'll use the simple technique of denying access to all unauthenticated users. To do this, you must use the <authorization> element of the web.config file to add a new authorization rule, as shown here:

```
<configuration>
   <system.web>
      <!-- Other settings omitted. -->
      <authorization>
         <deny users="?" />
      </authorization>
   </system.web>
</configuration>
```

The question mark (?) is a wildcard character that matches all anonymous users. By including this rule in your web.config file, you specify that anonymous users are not allowed. Every user must be authenticated, and every user request will require the forms authentication ticket (which is a cookie). If you request a page in the application directory now, ASP.NET will detect that the request isn't authenticated and attempt to redirect the request to the login page (which will probably cause an error, unless you've already created this page).

■ **Tip** Unlike the <authentication> element, the <authorization> element is not limited to the web.config file in the root of the web application. Instead, you can use it in any subdirectory, thereby allowing you to set different authorization settings for different groups of pages. You'll learn much more about authorization in Chapter 23.

Creating a Custom Login Page

Next, you have to create a custom login page. This page collects a user name and password from the user and validates it against the credentials stored in the credential store. If credentials are stored in web.config, this is extremely easy. However, at the same time, it is not much harder to store credentials in any other store, such as an external database.

The login page you have to create must contain the parts shown in Figure 20-2. Furthermore, you must include the code for validating the credentials. The ASP.NET page shown in Figure 20-2 contains the text boxes for entering the values. Note that the URL in the address bar of the browser shown in Figure 20-2 includes the originally requested page as a query parameter. This parameter is used by the FormsAuthentication class later for redirecting to the originally requested page. If not present, it uses the page configured in the defaultUrl attribute of the <forms /> configuration tag.

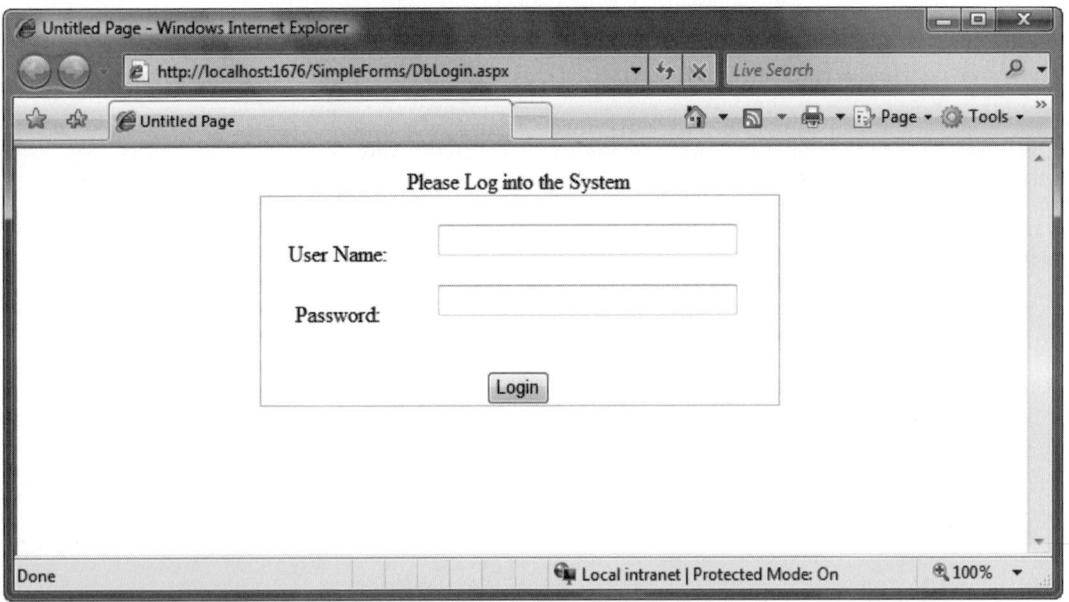

***Figure 20-2.** A typical login page for a web application*

What you cannot see in Figure 20-2 are validation controls. Validation controls are especially important to let the user enter only valid values for a user name and a password. Remember what we mentioned in the previous chapter: never trust user input. Validation adheres to this principle by ensuring that only valid values are entered. Here you can see all the controls contained on the login page:

```
<form id="form1" runat="server">
    <div style="text-align: center">
    Please Log into the System<br />
    <asp:Panel ID="MainPanel" runat="server" Height="90px" Width="380px"
        BorderColor="Silver" BorderStyle="Solid" BorderWidth="1px">
        <br />
        <table width="100%" border="0" cellpadding="0" cellspacing="0">
                            <td width="30%" style="height: 43px">
                    User Name:
                <td width="70%" style="height: 43px">
                    <asp:TextBox ID="UsernameText"
                                    runat="server" Width="80%" />
                    <asp:RequiredFieldValidator
                        ID="UsernameRequiredValidator" runat="server"
                        ErrorMessage="*" ControlToValidate="UsernameText" />
                    <br />
                    <asp:RegularExpressionValidator
                        ID="UsernameValidator" runat="server"
                        ControlToValidate="UsernameText"
                        ErrorMessage="Invalid username"
                        ValidationExpression="[\w| ]*" />

                                        <td width="30%" style="height: 26px">
                    Password:
                <td width="70%" style="height: 26px">
                    <asp:TextBox ID="PasswordText" runat="server"
                                    Width="80%" TextMode="Password" />
                    <asp:RequiredFieldValidator ID="PwdRequiredValidator"
                        runat="server" ErrorMessage="*"
                        ControlToValidate="PasswordText" />
                    <br />
                    <asp:RegularExpressionValidator ID="PwdValidator"
                        runat="server" ControlToValidate="PasswordText"
                        ErrorMessage="Invalid password"
                        ValidationExpression='[\w| !"§$%&amp;/()=\-?\*]*' />


        <br />
        <asp:Button ID="LoginAction" runat="server"
                    OnClick="LoginAction_Click" Text="Login" /><br />
        <asp:Label ID="LegendStatus" runat="server"
                    EnableViewState="false" Text="" />
    </asp:Panel>
    </div>
</form>
```

As mentioned previously, the validation controls serve two purposes. First, the RequiredFieldValidator controls ensure that both a user name and password are entered in a valid format containing only the characters allowed for user names and passwords. Second, the RegularExpressionValidator controls ensure that only valid values are entered in the User Name text field and in the Password text field. For example, the user name may contain letters, digits, and spaces only. Therefore, the validation expression looks like this:

```
ValidationExpression="[\w| ]*"
```

The \w character class is equivalent to [a-zA-Z_0-9], and the space afterward allows spaces in the user name. The password, for example, may also contain special characters. Therefore, the validation expression looks different from the previous one, as shown here:

```
ValidationExpression='[\w| !"§$%&amp;/()=\-?\*]*'
```

Note that the single quote is used for enclosing the attribute value, because this uses the double quote as the allowed special character. Furthermore, because the attribute is contained in the tag code (and therefore the HTML entity), & indicates that the ampersand (&) character is allowed in the password. You can see the validation controls in action in Figure 20-3.

As you can see in Figure 20-3, with validation controls in place you can stop users from entering values for the user name or password that would lead to a SQL injection attack. In addition to using parameterized SQL queries (introduced in Chapter 7 and Chapter 8), you should always use validation controls to mitigate this type of attack in your applications.

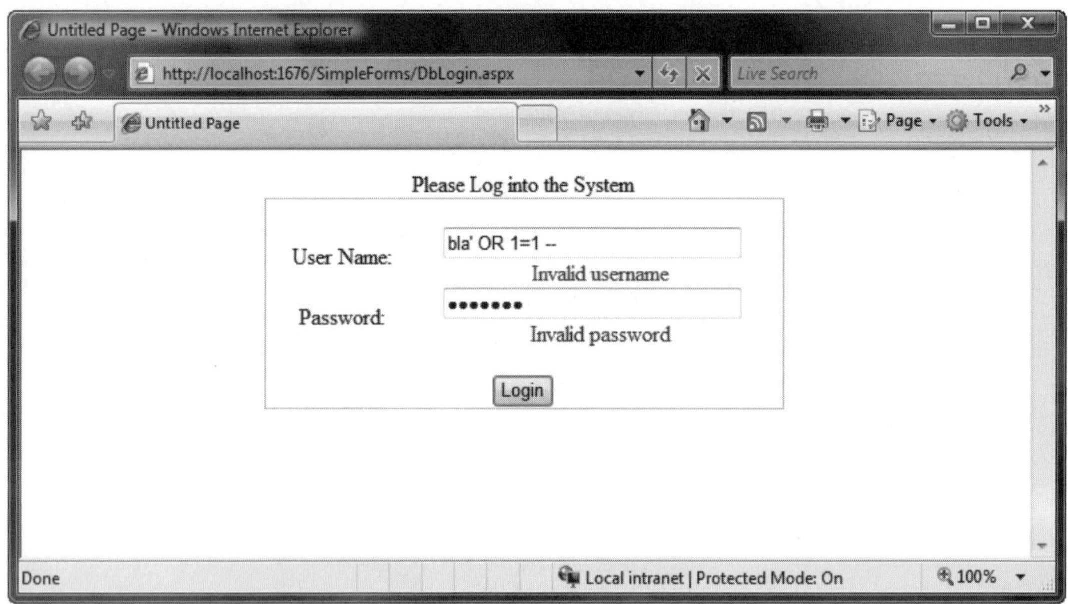

Figure 20-3. Validation controls in action

The last step for creating the login page is to write the code for validating the credentials against the values entered by the user. You have to add the necessary code to the Click event of the login button. Because the following Click event is using the credentials store of the web.config file, validation is fairly easy:

```
protected void LoginAction_Click(object sender, EventArgs e)
{
    Page.Validate();
    if (!Page.IsValid) return;

    if (FormsAuthentication.Authenticate(UsernameText.Text, PasswordText.Text))
```

```
    {
        // Create the ticket, add the cookie to the response,
        // and redirect to the originally requested page
        FormsAuthentication.RedirectFromLoginPage(UsernameText.Text, false);
    }
    else
    {
        // User name and password are not correct
        LegendStatus.Text = "Invalid username or password!";
    }
}
```

■ **Note** Because forms authentication uses standard HTML forms for entering credentials, the user name and password are sent over the network as plain text. This is an obvious security risk—anyone who intercepts the network traffic will be able to read the user names and passwords that are entered into the login form. For this reason, it is strongly recommended that you encrypt the traffic between the browser and the server using SSL (as described in Chapter 19), at least while the user is accessing the login page.

Furthermore, it's important to include the Page.IsValid condition at the beginning of this procedure. The reason for this is that validation controls by default use JavaScript for client-side validation. When calling Page.Validate(), the validation takes place on the server. This is important for browsers that either have JavaScript turned off or don't support it. Therefore, if you don't include this part, validation will not happen if the browser doesn't support JavaScript or doesn't have JavaScript enabled. So, you should always include server-side validation in your code.

The FormsAuthentication class provides two methods that are used in this example. The Authenticate() method checks the specified user name and password against those stored in the web.config file and returns a Boolean value indicating whether a match was found. Remember that the methods of FormsAuthentication are static, so you do not need to create an instance of FormsAuthentication to use them—you simply access them through the name of the class.

```
if (FormsAuthentication.Authenticate(UsernameText.Text, PasswordText.Text))
```

If a match is found for the supplied credentials, you can use the RedirectFromLoginPage() method, as shown here:

```
FormsAuthentication.RedirectFromLoginPage(UsernameText.Text, false);
```

This method performs several tasks at once:

1. It creates an authentication ticket for the user.
2. It encrypts the information from the authentication ticket.
3. It creates a cookie to persist the encrypted ticket information.
4. It adds the cookie to the HTTP response, sending it to the client.
5. It redirects the user to the originally requested page (which is contained in the query string parameter of the login page request's URL).

The second parameter of RedirectFromLoginPage() indicates whether a persistent cookie should be created. Persistent cookies are stored on the user's hard drive and can be reused for later visits. Persistent cookies are described in the section "Persistent Cookies in Forms Authentication" later in this chapter.

Finally, if Authenticate() returns false, an error message is displayed on the page. Feedback such as this is always useful. However, make sure it doesn't compromise your security. For example, it's all too common for developers to create login pages that provide separate error messages depending on whether the user has entered a user name that isn't recognized or a correct user name with the wrong password. This is usually not a good idea. If a malicious user is trying to guess a user name and password, the user's chances increase considerably if your application gives this sort of specific feedback.

Logging Out

Logging a user out of forms authentication is as simple as calling the FormsAuthen- tication.SignOut() method. You can create a logout button and add this code, as shown here:

```
protected void SignOutAction_Click(object sender, EventArgs e)
{
    FormsAuthentication.SignOut();
    FormsAuthentication.RedirectToLoginPage();
}
```

When you call the SignOut() method, you remove the authentication cookie. Depending on the application, you may want to redirect the user to another page when the user logs out. If the user requests another restricted page, the request will be redirected to the login page. You can also redirect to the login page immediately after calling the SignOut method. Or you can use the Response.Redirect method.

■ **Tip** In a sophisticated application, your login page might not actually be a page at all. Instead, it might be a separate portion of the page—either a distinct HTML frame or a separately coded user control. Using these techniques, you can keep a login and logout control visible on every page. The membership API framework includes ready-to-use controls for providing this type of functionality.

Hashing Passwords in web.config

Forms authentication includes the possibility of storing the password in different formats. In the <credentials /> configuration section of the <forms /> element, the format of the password is specified through the passwordFormat attribute, which has three valid values:

- **Clear:** The passwords are stored as clear text in the <user /> elements of the <credentials /> section.
- **MD5:** The hashed version of the password is stored in the <user /> elements, and the algorithm used for hashing the password is the MD5 hashing algorithm.
- **SHA1:** The <user /> elements in the <credentials /> section of the web.config file contain the hashed password, and the algorithm used for hashing the password is the SHA1 algorithm. This value is the default for the passwordFormat option.

When using the hashed version of the passwords, you have to write a tool or some code that hashes the passwords for you and stores them in the web.config file. This could be either code such as the following, included in some administrative applications for your web application, or a separate Windows application for managing the users of your web application (which then needs to run on the web server). For storing the password, you should then use the FormsAuthentica-tion.HashPasswordForStoringInConfigFile method instead of passing in the clear-text password as follows:

```
string hashedPwd =
   FormsAuthentication.HashPasswordForStoringInConfigFile(
                                  clearTextPassword, "SHA1");
```

The first parameter specifies the clear-text password, and the second one specifies the hash algorithm you should use. The result of the method call is the hashed version of the password. This result needs to be stored in the web.config (when using web.config as a storage for your user accounts) or can be stored in your own users database (when using a custom database for storing user information).

If you want to modify users stored in web.config as shown previously, you have to use the configuration API of the .NET Framework. You cannot edit this section with the web-based configuration tool. The following code snippet shows how you can modify the section through the configuration API. This code typically is implemented as part of an administrative application for managing your web application, which should be available for administrators only.

```
Configuration MyConfig = WebConfigurationManager.OpenWebConfiguration("./");

ConfigurationSectionGroup SystemWeb = MyConfig.SectionGroups["system.web"];
AuthenticationSection AuthSec =
     (AuthenticationSection)SystemWeb.Sections["authentication"];
AuthSec.Forms.Credentials.Users.Add(
    new FormsAuthenticationUser(UsernameText.Text, PasswordText.Text));

MyConfig.Save();
```

To use this configuration API, you need to import the System.Web.Configuration namespace into your application. Furthermore, you need to make sure to have a reference to the System.Configuration.dll assembly (which is the case, by default).

Of course, only privileged users such as website administrators should be allowed to execute the previous code, and the process executing the code must have write access to your web.config file. Also, this sort of code should not be included in the actual web application. You should include it in an administration application only. You will learn more about hashing passwords in Chapters 25 and 26.

Cookieless Forms Authentication

ASP.NET supports cookieless forms authentication out of the box. If you don't want the runtime to use cookies, you configure this through the cookieless attribute of the <forms /> tag in the <authentication /> section:

```
<authentication mode="Forms">
    <!-- Detailed configuration options -->
    <forms name="MyCookieName"
           loginUrl="DbLogin.aspx"
           cookieless="AutoDetect" />
</authentication>
```

The cookieless option includes the possible settings in Table 20-3.

Table 20-3. *Cookieless Options in the <forms /> Configuration*

Option	Description
UseCookies	Forces the runtime to use cookies when working with forms authentication. This requires the client browser to support cookies. If the browser does not support cookies, forms authentication will simply not work with that setting activated. As it will never receive a valid authentication cookie from the browser, ASP.NET redirects back to the login page over and over again, and you end up in an endless loop of presented login pages.
UseUri	If this configuration option is selected, cookies will not be used for authentication. Instead, the runtime encodes the forms authentication ticket into the request URL, and the infrastructure processes this specific portion of the URL for establishing the security context.
AutoDetect	Results in the use of cookies if the client browser supports cookies. Otherwise, URL encoding of the ticket will be used. This is established through a probing mechanism.
UseDeviceProfile	Results in the use of cookies or URL encoding based on a device profile configuration stored on the web server. These profiles are stored in .browser files in the c:\[WinDir]\Microsoft.NET\Framework\[Version]\CONFIG\Browsers directory.

Custom Credentials Store

As mentioned previously, the credential store in web.config is useful for simple scenarios only. You won't want to use web.config as the credential store for a number of reasons:

- **Potential lack of security:** Even though users aren't able to directly request the web.config file, you may still prefer to use a storage medium where you can secure access more effectively. As long as this information is stored on the web server, passwords are accessible to any administrator, developer, or tester who has access.
- **No support for adding user-specific information:** For example, you might want to store information such as addresses, credit cards, personal preferences, and so on.
- **Poor performance with a large number of users:** The web.config file is just a file, and it can't provide the efficient caching and multiuser access of a database. Furthermore, whenever you change the web.config file, the HttpApplication is restarted, which results in losing all AppDomains, Session state, and so on. Reestablishing all these things affects performance.

Therefore, in most applications you will use your own custom credential store for user name and password combinations, and mostly it will be a database such as SQL Server. In ASP.NET 1.*x*, you had to implement this scenario on your own. In your login form you then had to connect to the database, verify whether the user existed, compare the password stored in the database to the one entered by the user, and then call FormsAuthentication.RedirectFromLoginPage if the user name and password entered by the user were valid. The following example demonstrates this, and it assumes that you have written a function MyAuthenticate that connects to a SQL Server database and reads the corresponding user entry. It returns true if the entered user name and password match the ones stored in the database.

```
protected void LoginAction_Click(object sender, EventArgs e)
{
    Page.Validate();
    if (!Page.IsValid) return;

    if (this.MyAuthenticate(UsernameText.Text, PasswordText.Text))
    {
        FormsAuthentication.RedirectFromLoginPage(UsernameText.Text, false);
    }
    else
    {
        LegendStatus.Text = "Invalid username or password!";
    }
}
```

Fortunately, ASP.NET provides a ready-to-use infrastructure as well as a complete set of security-related controls that do this for you. The membership API includes a SQL Server-based data store for storing users and roles, and has functions for validating user names and passwords against users of this store without knowing any details about the underlying database, as you will learn in Chapter 21. It also includes powerful security controls, such as a ready-to-use Login control, which sits on top of the membership API. Furthermore, this infrastructure is completely extensible through custom providers, as you will learn in Chapter 26.

Persistent Cookies in Forms Authentication

The examples you've seen so far have used a nonpersistent authentication cookie to maintain the authentication ticket between requests. This means that if the user closes the browser, the cookie is immediately removed. This is a sensible step that ensures security. It's particularly important with shared computers to prevent another user from using a previous user's ticket. Nonpersistent cookies also make *session hijacking* attacks (where a malicious user gains access to the network and steals another user's cookie) more difficult and more limited.

Despite the increased security risks of using persistent authentication cookies, it is appropriate to use them in certain situations. If you are performing authentication for personalization rather than for controlling access to restricted resources, you may decide that the usability advantages of not requiring users to log in on every visit outweigh the increased danger of unauthorized use.

Once you have decided to use persistent cookies, implementing them is easy. You simply need to supply a value of true rather than false for the second parameter of the RedirectFromLoginPage() or SetAuthCookie() method of the FormsAuthentication class. Here's an example:

```
FormsAuthentication.RedirectFromLoginPage(UsernameText.Text,true);
```

Persistent cookies do not expire when the browser is closed. Like nonpersistent cookies, they do expire when you call the FormsAuthentication.SignOut() method or when they reach the time limit set in the timeout attribute of the <forms> element (by default, 30 minutes). This raises a potential problem. In some applications, you might want to give users the choice of using a short-term nonpersistent cookie or storing a long-lived persistent cookie. However, you can only set the timeout attribute to one value. The solution is to use the GetAuthCookie() method of the FormsAuthentication class to create your persistent cookie, set the expiry date and time by hand, and then write the persistent cookie to the HTTP response yourself.

The following example rewrites the code that authenticates the user when the login button is clicked. It creates a persistent cookie but performs additional steps to give the cookie a 10-day life span:

```
protected void LoginAction_Click(object sender, EventArgs e)
{
    Page.Validate();
    if (!Page.IsValid) return;

    if (FormsAuthentication.Authenticate(UsernameText.Text, PasswordText.Text))
    {
        // Create the authentication cookie
        HttpCookie AuthCookie;
        AuthCookie = FormsAuthentication.GetAuthCookie(
                                   UsernameText.Text, true);
        AuthCookie.Expires = DateTime.Now.AddDays(10);

        // Add the cookie to the response
        Response.Cookies.Add(AuthCookie);

        // Redirect to the originally requested page
        Response.Redirect(FormsAuthentication.GetRedirectUrl(
                             UsernameText.Text, true));
    }
    else
    {
        // User name and password are not correct
        LegendStatus.Text = "Invalid username or password!";
    }
}
```

The code for checking the credentials is the same in this scenario. The only difference is that the authentication cookie isn't added automatically. Instead, it's created with a call to GetAuthCookie(), which returns a new instance of HttpCookie, as shown here:

```
HttpCookie AuthCookie;
AuthCookie = FormsAuthentication.GetAuthCookie(
                                   UsernameText.Text, true);
```

Once you've created the authentication cookie, you can retrieve the current date and time (using the DateTime.Now static property), add ten days to it (using the DateTime.AddDays() method), and use this value as the expiry date and time of the cookie:

```
AuthCookie.Expires = DateTime.Now.AddDays(10);
```

Next, you have to add the cookie to the HTTP response:

```
Response.Cookies.Add(AuthCookie);
```

Finally, you can redirect the user to the originally requested URL, which you can obtain by using the GetRedirectUrl() method:

```
Response.Redirect(FormsAuthentication.GetRedirectUrl(
                                   UsernameText.Text, true));
```

The end result is a cookie that will persist beyond the closing of the browser but that will expire after ten days, at which point the user will need to reenter credentials to log into the website.

IIS 7.x and Forms Authentication

IIS 7.x ships with an ASP.NET integrated mode that—among many other things—integrates the ASP.NET HTTP processing pipeline with the IIS HTTP processing pipeline. This gives you a tremendous set of new capabilities you can leverage with your existing ASP.NET knowledge. For example, one capability is the possibility of using ASP.NET forms authentication for other web applications configured in IIS 7.x, which do not necessarily need to be built with ASP.NET.

Furthermore, IIS 7.x leverages web.config files for storing many parts of its configuration for web applications configured within the web server. That means you can configure many options of your web application either by using the IIS 7.x management console or by directly modifying the web.config file. Due to the tight integration of configuration features for ASP.NET and IIS 7.x, any changes made to the web.config file directly are reflected to the management console immediately, and vice versa.

Let's first take a look at the possibilities of configuring forms authentication from within the IIS 7.x management console. You can configure forms authentication by using the authentication configuration feature of the IIS 7.x management console, as you can see in Figure 20-4.

After enabling forms authentication in this way, you also need to configure the required authorization rules. The most important one is to add a "deny" rule for all anonymous users using the authorization configuration feature of the IIS 7.x management console, as shown in Figure 20-5.

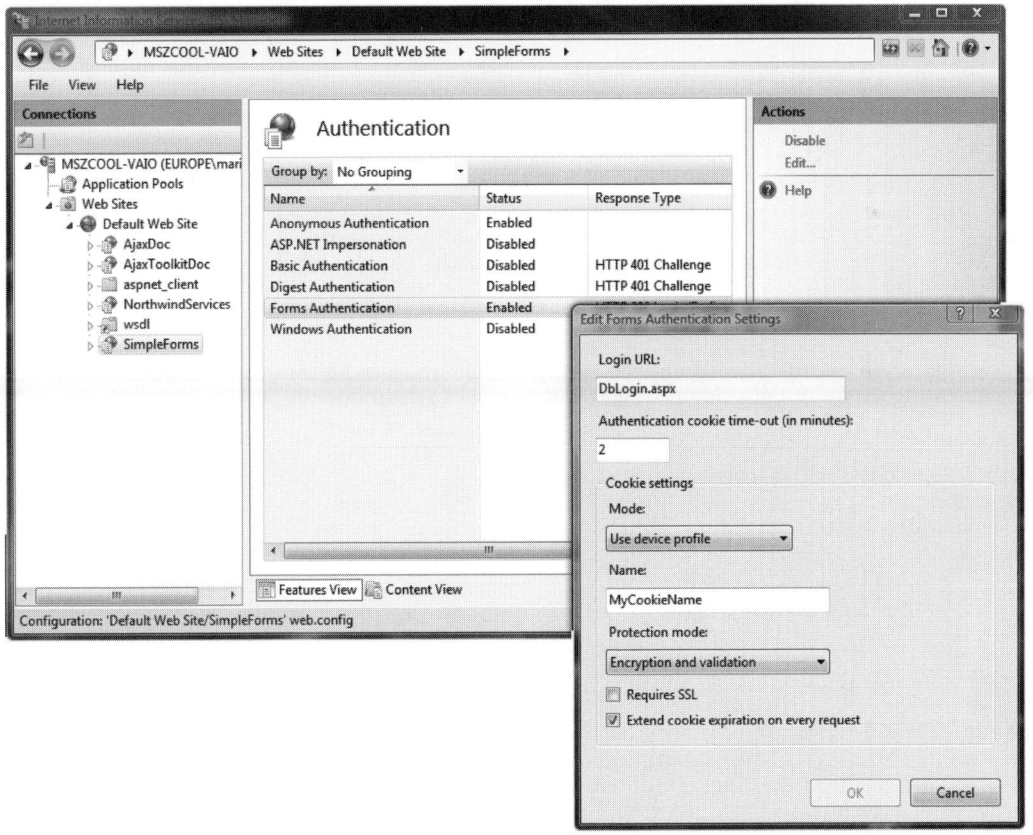

Figure 20-4. Configuring forms authentication from the IIS 7.x management console

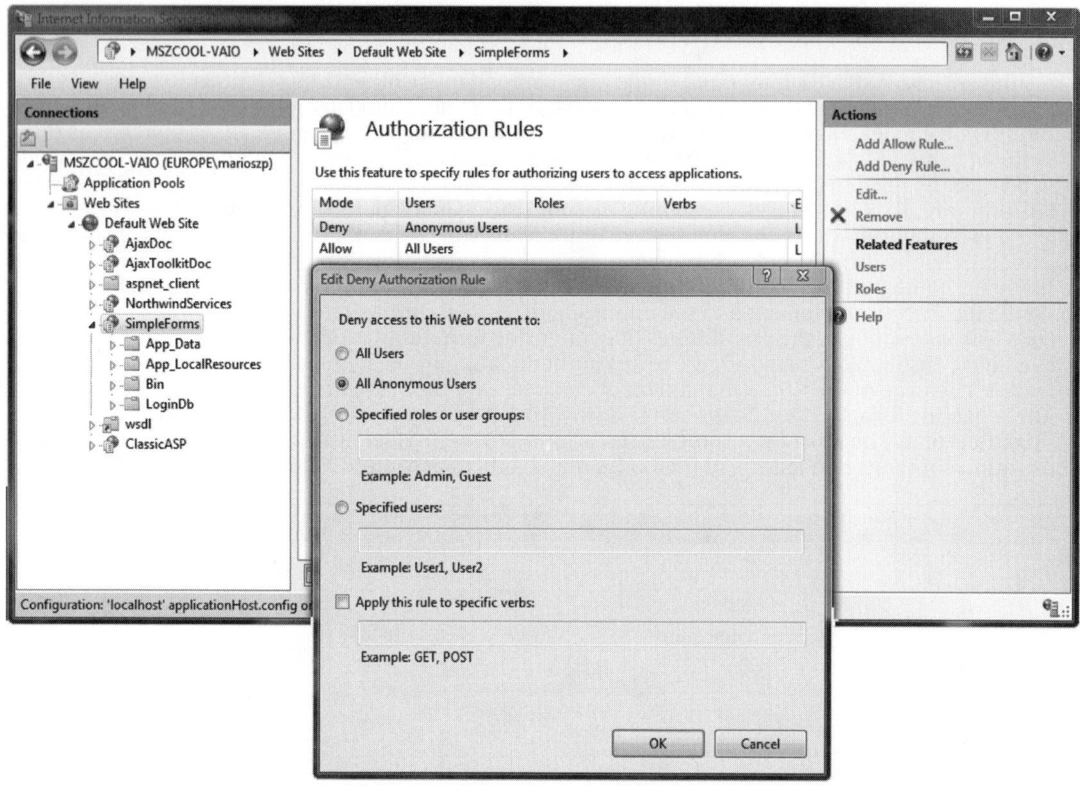

Figure 20-5. Denying access to all anonymous users using the IIS 7.x authorization feature

Both configuration settings affect your web.config file, and the web server takes this information from the web.config file for its behavior as well, as you can see in the following code snippet:

```
<configuration>
  <!-- Other sections such as connectionStrings, etc. -->
  <system.web>
    <authentication mode="Forms">
      <forms name="MyCookieName"
             loginUrl="DbLogin.aspx"
             timeout="2" />
    </authentication>
  </system.web>
  <!-- Other configuration sections -->
  <system.webServer>
     <!-- Other modules, handlers configuration,
          but no security-related configuration according
          to configuration settings selected in Figures
          20-4 and 20-5.
  </system.webServer>
</configuration>
```

You will notice that IIS configured forms authentication for you as expected, in the <system.web> section. But by default (and if you haven't added it manually before), you won't find any authorization rule. As mentioned in Chapter 18, not all configuration options are directly placed in the web.config configuration file by default. URL authorization is one of these configuration options. You will learn the details about URL authorization in general and any IIS 7.x specifics in Chapter 23.

In any case, the unified management console is very neat, as you don't need to configure IIS security and ASP.NET security through different tools, and many options are stored directly in your web.config by default. As you learned in Chapters 18 and 19, and as you will find in Chapter 23, you even can configure IIS so that nearly all configuration options are stored directly in web.config. However, as mentioned earlier, the ASP.NET integration gives us many more possibilities when running IIS 7.x in ASP.NET integrated mode.

When running IIS 7.x in integrated mode (which is the default), IIS uses one HTTP processing pipeline for processing both ASP.NET-based HTTP modules and IIS 7.x native HTTP modules. As forms authentication is implemented as an ASP.NET HTTP module, you can use it for any web application and virtual directory configured on IIS 7.x when running in integrated mode. That means you can even use forms authentication together with other types of applications, such as static HTML sites, classic ASP applications, or even PHP applications. All you need to do is configure the web application as a virtual directory and then configure forms authentication through the IIS 7.x management console. That adds a web.config configuration to your application automatically. You need to take care of one additional detail, so let's walk through configuring forms authentication for a non-ASP.NET application in this section. Suppose you have the following classic ASP application running on your web server:

```
<%@ Language=VBScript %>
<html>
    <head>
        <title>Example 2</title>
    </head>
    <body>
        <%
            FirstVar = "Hello world!<br>"
        %>
        <%FOR i=1 TO 10%>
        <%=FirstVar%>
        <%NEXT%>
    </body>
</html>
```

Now just share the folder where you have stored this classic ASP page file (for example, TestClassic.asp) as a virtual directory or web application from within IIS. Afterwards, you can configure forms authentication and authorization settings as described earlier. As IIS 7.x natively supports forms authentication by leveraging the HTTP forms authentication module delivered with ASP.NET, it works the same way as it would work with an ASP.NET application itself. All you need is to make sure you have the required login page, which on its own is an ASP.NET page. You also need the parts required by this ASP.NET page, available within the web application (or within another virtual directory if you use cross-application forms authentication cookies). Figure 20-6 .shows the classic ASP page together with an ASP.NET login page in a virtual directory. Forms authentication is simply configured via the IIS 7.x management console as outlined earlier.

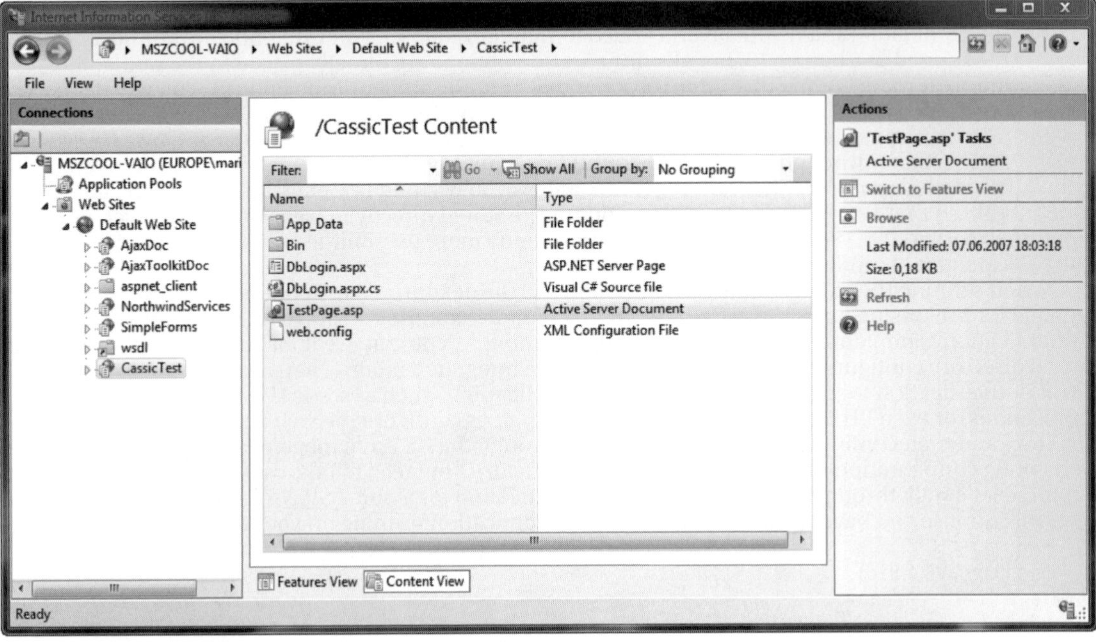

Figure 20-6. ASP.NET content mixed together with classic ASP

However, just putting ASP content together with your ASP.NET-based login pages and configuring forms authentication is not enough yet. When you try navigating to the classic ASP page, forms authentication will not work yet. Depending on your authentication and authorization rules, you will either get an "unauthorized" response or you will just be able to navigate to the classic ASP page without being prompted for login (you will learn more about authorization rules and their behavior in Chapter 23).

The reason for that is that by default, managed HTTP modules such as the forms authentication module are configured so that they are only executed for requests to ASP.NET-based code. Therefore, to make forms authentication work you need to change this behavior by selecting the HTTP Modules configuration feature of the IIS 7.x management console while having your web application selected. Then, open the details for the FormsAuthentication module configured in the list of modules, as shown in Figure 20-7 and Figure 20-8.

After you have opened the HTTP Modules configuration feature, you need to find the FormsAuthentication entry and double-click it, or select the Edit link from the task pane on the right border of the management console. In the settings dialog that opens, you just need to disable the option Invoke Only for Requests to ASP.NET Applications or Managed Handlers, as shown in Figure 20-8.

After having completed this configuration when accessing the classic ASP page in your web application directory, the request is authenticated by using ASP.NET forms authentication. The web.config of your web application then looks as follows:

```
<?xml version="1.0" encoding="UTF-8"?>
<configuration>
    <system.web>
        <authentication mode="Forms">
            <forms cookieless="UseCookies" loginUrl="dblogin.aspx" />
        </authentication>
        <authorization>
```

```
            <deny users="?" />
        </authorization>
    </system.web>
    <system.webServer>
        <modules>
            <remove name="FormsAuthentication" />
            <add name="FormsAuthentication"
                type="System.Web.Security.FormsAuthenticationModule"
                preCondition="" />
        </modules>
    </system.webServer>
    <connectionStrings>
        <add connectionString="..." name="..." />
    </connectionStrings>
</configuration>
```

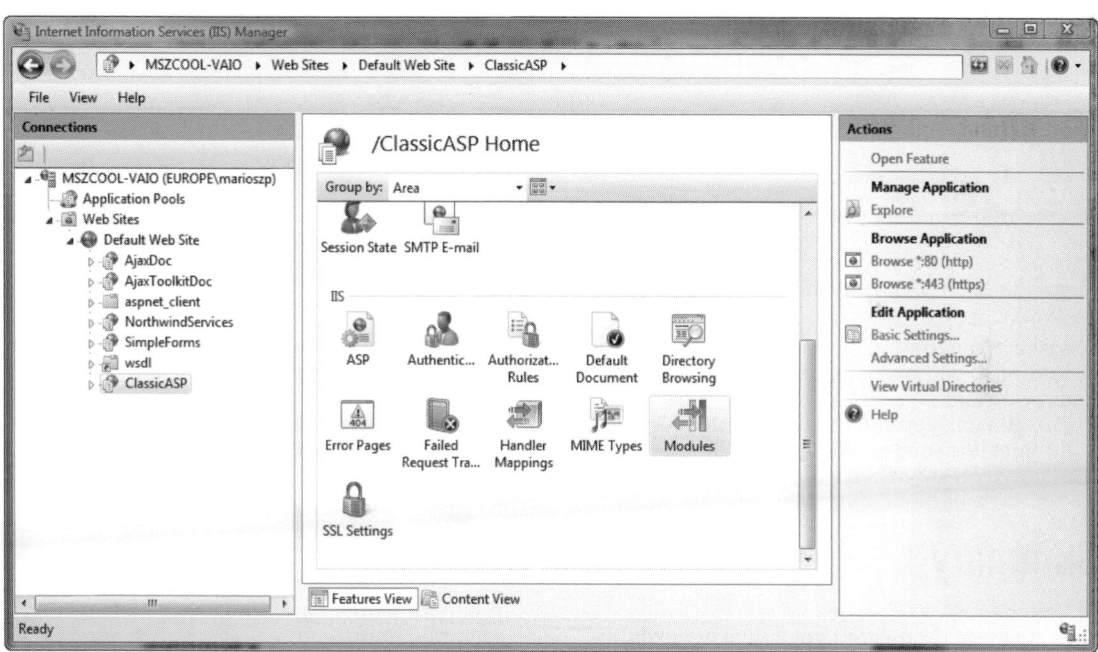

Figure 20-7. Selecting the HTTP Modules configuration feature in your web application

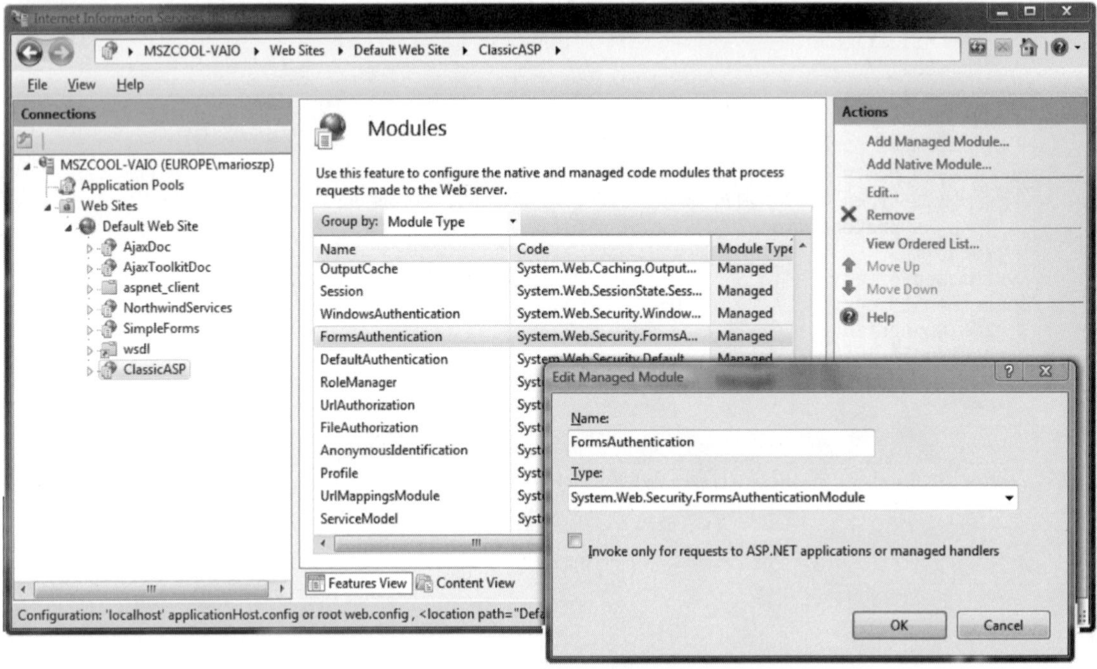

Figure 20-8. Configuration details of the FormsAuthenticationModule

The configuration of the FormsAuthenticationModule is important. The check mark you configured according to Figure 20-8 manifests itself in the setting preCondition="", which by default is set to managedHandler.

In general, you can use this way to leverage powerful ASP.NET features, such as forms authentication or even the membership API introduced in Chapter 21, with all your web applications configured on your IIS 7.x-based web server.

Summary

In this chapter, you learned how to use forms authentication to implement authentication systems that simplify life and provide a great deal of flexibility. You also learned how to protect passwords, and how you can use any data source for credential storage. In the next chapter, you'll learn about the new features that are built on top of forms authentication and that make it even easier to create login pages and deal with user authentication without writing all the code yourself.

Finally, you learned about how IIS 7.x allows you to configure forms authentication and the necessary simple authorization rules directly from within the management console of IIS 7.x. The most interesting part is that you can leverage ASP.NET-based forms authentication across all of your web applications on the web server—independent from the platform they are developed with. You learned how you can leverage the IIS 7.x integrated mode to use forms authentication with other web applications based on static HTML pages, classic ASP, or even PHP. This is a powerful technology and a huge improvement compared to older versions of IIS.

CHAPTER 21

■ ■ ■

Membership

On one hand, forms authentication solves the critical fundamentals for implementing secure, custom login forms for your ASP.NET applications. On the other hand, the tasks you have to accomplish for implementing the login forms and communicating with the underlying credential store are almost always the same for every web application, and they're tedious. You should keep in mind one more point: forms authentication provides the infrastructure for authenticating users only. If you are using a custom credentials store, you have to write administration applications for managing users, which need to implement functionality for adding users, removing users, resetting passwords, and much more. Implementing such functionality is fairly similar for every web application and gets boring quickly.

To address this issue, ASP.NET 2.0 added a feature called the membership API, which remains essentially unchanged in ASP.NET 4. The membership API is a framework based on top of the existing forms authentication infrastructure. When using the membership API, you even don't need to implement login pages or credential storage. In this chapter, you will learn about the details of the membership API.

Introducing the ASP.NET Membership API

The membership API framework provides you with a complete set of user management functions out of the box:

- The ability to create and delete users either programmatically or through the ASP.NET web configuration utility.
- The ability to reset passwords, with the possibility of automatically sending password reset e-mails to the users if an e-mail address is stored for the affected user.
- The ability to automatically generate passwords for users if these users are created programmatically in the background. Of course, these passwords can be sent to these users automatically if e-mail addresses are available for them.
- The ability to find users in the underlying data store as well as retrieve lists of users and details for every user. This is necessary for typical management tasks, such as assigning users to roles through a management user interface, or for simple things such as creating statistics about how many users are leveraging your website's offerings.
- A set of prebuilt controls for creating login pages and registration pages and for displaying login states and different views for authenticated and unauthenticated users.

- A layer of abstraction for your application so that the application has no dependency on the underlying data store through membership provider classes. Any functionality listed until now therefore works completely independently from the underlying data store, and the data store can be replaced with other types of data stores without needing to modify the application at all. By default, the membership API leverages a SQL Server Express database for storing user and role information.

Figure 21-1 shows the fundamental architecture of the membership API, which consists of providers, an API, and controls for creating appropriate user interfaces.

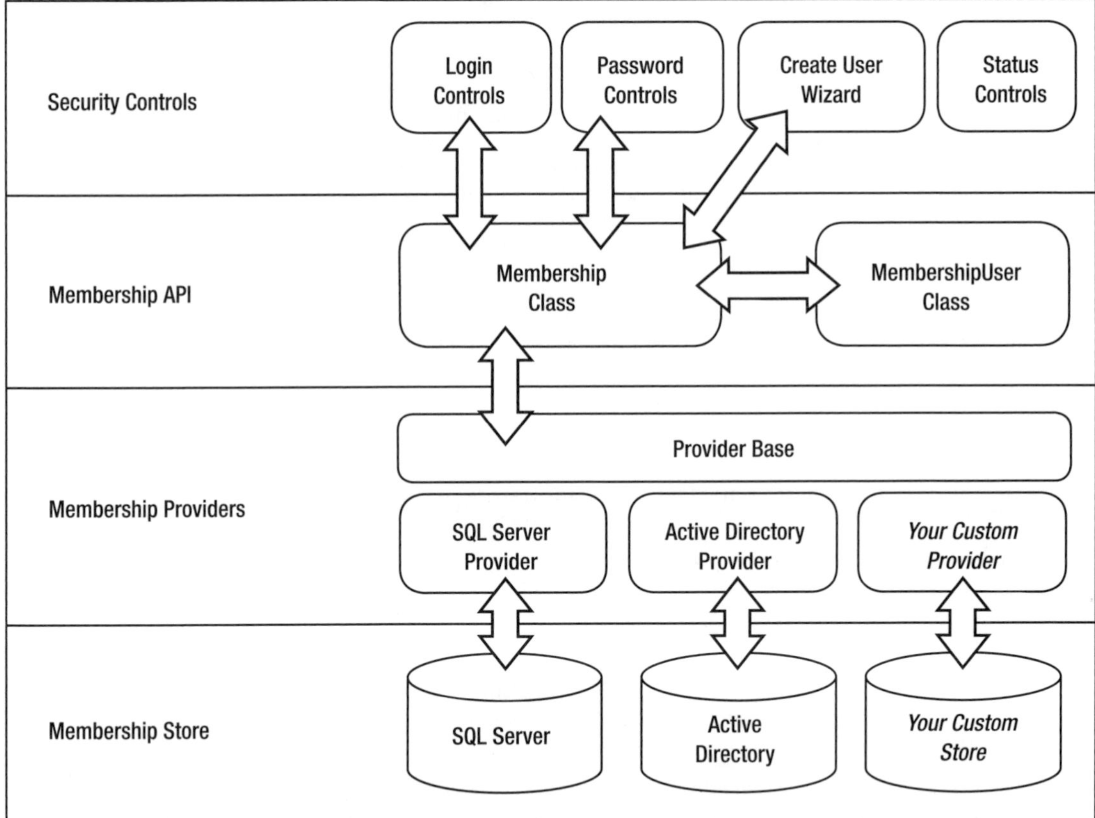

Figure 21-1. *Architecture of the membership API*

The membership API is designed to work completely independently from its underlying data store. You, as the application developer, primarily work with the controls provided by ASP.NET as well as the Membership class. The Membership class provides you with a set of static methods and static properties for programmatically accessing users and roles of the store. These methods work with a membership provider. This provider implements the access to the underlying data store. All membership API-related classes are placed in the System.Web.Security namespace. Table 21-1 lists and describes these classes.

Table 21-1. The Membership API-Related Classes of the System.Web.Security Namespace

Component	Description
Membership	The Membership class is the primary point of interaction with the membership API. It provides methods for managing users, validating users, and resetting user passwords.
MembershipCreateUserException	An exception is thrown if an error occurs when you try to create a user through the Membership class.
MembershipUser	Represents a single user stored in a membership API credential store. This object contains all information about this user and is returned through several methods of the Membership class, such as GetUser.
MembershipUserCollection	A collection of membership users. For example, the GetAllUsers method of the Membership class returns an instance of this collection.
MembershipProvider	This is the base class that you derive from if you want to create a custom membership provider that authenticates users against your custom credential store.
MembershipProviderCollection	A collection of available membership providers on the machine and for this web application.
SqlMembershipProvider	An implementation of the MembershipProvider class that works with SQL Server databases.
ActiveDirectoryMembershipProvider	An implementation of the MembershipProvider class that works with Active Directory.
ActiveDirectoryMembershipUser	This class inherits all the functionality from MembershipUser and adds some Active Directory-specific properties.

ASP.NET ships with a membership provider for SQL Server and Active Directory (which enables you to create custom login pages for users stored in Active Directory). But the idea of providers is that they give you the ability to completely extend the infrastructure. Therefore, you can write your own membership provider, which is a class that inherits from System.Web.Security.MembershipProvider. You configure membership providers primarily through your web.config configuration file, which includes a <membership /> section. You will learn more about custom membership providers in Chapter 26.

■ **Note** Although the membership API supports Active Directory as a provider, there is still a big difference between using Windows authentication and using the membership API for authenticating users in your web application. When you configure your application to use membership APIs, which are based on forms authentication, credentials are sent as clear text across the line (except you should use SSL), and a forms authentication ticket is used for authentication, as you learned in the previous chapter. On the other hand, when configuring Windows authentication, the user is authenticated either through NTLM or through Kerberos (in the case of Windows Server domains). Both methods are much more secure, because credentials are never sent across the line.

■ **Note** In Table 21-1, you will find a dedicated class called ActiveDirectoryMembershipUser that is used in conjunction with the ActiveDirectoryMembershipProvider. However, you won't find a class called SqlMembershipProviderUser, which means that the SqlMembershipProvider uses the base class MembershipUser for representing users. This is simply because the Active Directory provider version extends the MembershipUser class with a number of Active Directory-specific attributes that are available for AD-based users. There are no such specific properties available for the SqlMembershipProvider; therefore, creating a separate SqlMembershipUser class is simply unnecessary.

The membership API is just used for managing and authenticating users. It does not implement any authorization functionality and doesn't provide you with functionality for managing user roles. For this purpose, you have to use the roles API. You will learn more about authorization and the role management functionality in Chapter 23.

Using the Membership API

Before you can use the ASP.NET membership API and the security controls of ASP.NET, you have to complete a couple of steps:

1. Configure forms authentication in your web.config file as usual, and deny access to anonymous users.
2. Set up the membership data store. For example, if you are using SQL Server, you have to create a couple of tables and stored procedures in a SQL Server database of your choice.
3. Configure the database connection string and the membership provider you want to use in the application's web.config file.
4. Create users in your membership store using the ASP.NET web configuration utility or using a custom administration page that you can implement in your web application using the membership API functions.

5. Create a login page that uses the prebuilt Login control, or create a login page that uses the Membership class for validating the entered credentials and authenticating the user.

You can perform every configuration step except the provider configuration through the ASP.NET WAT, which includes a security wizard. Just select the Web Site ➤ ASP.NET Configuration menu from within Visual Studio. Figure 21-2 shows the WAT.

If you are using ASP.NET on a machine with SQL Server Express Edition, you don't even need to set up a data store and configure a membership provider. Just launch the security wizard in the WAT, as shown in Figure 21-2, and start by adding users to your membership storage. The required underlying data store will be created automatically for you when you create the first user. It will be created automatically even if you programmatically access the membership store, because this functionality is provided through the SqlMembershipProvider. However, be aware that this only works with the SQL Server Express Edition! If you are using one of the other SQL Server editions, then you need to configure your data store manually, as described later in the section "Creating the Data Store."

When using SQL Server Express Edition, the SqlMembershipProvider automatically creates a new database in the website's App_Data special directory called ASPNETDB.MDB. This database implements the complete schema, which is necessary for storing and managing user information, role information, user-role assignments, or even more, such as personalization and user profiles. You'll learn about this database in Chapters 24 and 30.

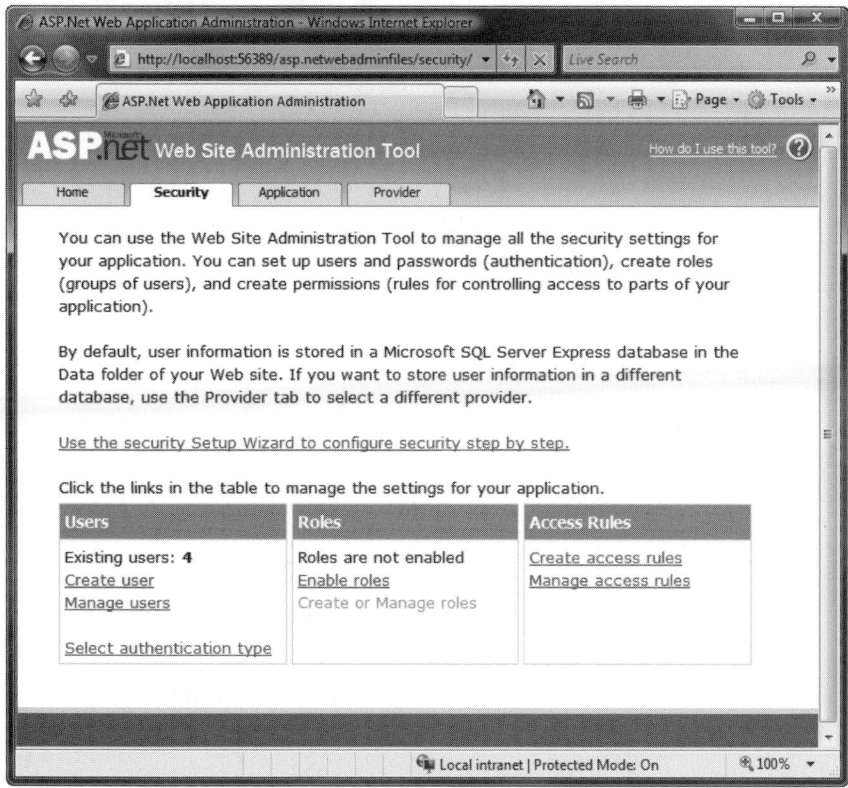

Figure 21-2. *Setting up security in the WAT*

If you want to use your own database for storing user information and role information instead of this automatically created one, you have to configure the membership provider and connection information for the provider before you launch the security wizard in the WAT. You will learn more about the configuration steps and how the membership API works behind the scenes in the next sections of this chapter.

Configuring Forms Authentication

The membership API is based on top of forms authentication and provides you with an out-of-the-box infrastructure for managing and authenticating users. Therefore, as the first step, you have to configure your application for forms authentication as usual. But you will structure the solution a little bit differently this time. Often, the root directory of the web application grants access to anonymous users, while restricted resources are stored in subdirectories with restricted access. These subdirectories have their own web.config file that denies access to anonymous users. As soon as someone tries to access resources stored in this secured directory, the ASP.NET runtime automatically redirects the user to the login page. Typically, the root directory, which is accessible to anonymous users, includes features such as a login page and a registration page. You can see the structure of the web application in Figure 21-3, which displays the Solution Explorer of an already structured Visual Studio project.

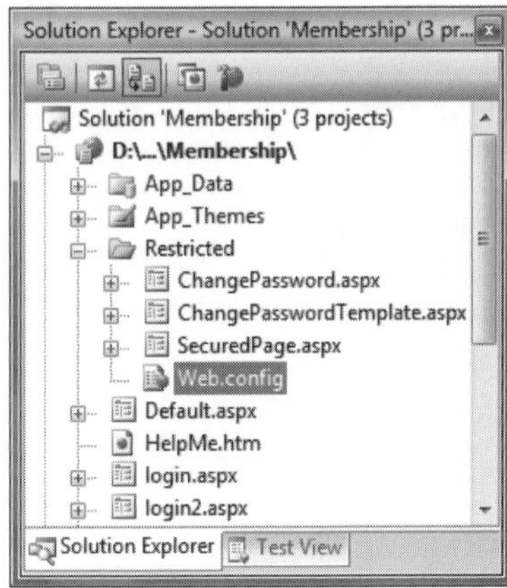

Figure 21-3. *The folder and file structure of a web application with a secured area*

Therefore, in the root directory of the web application, you just configure forms authentication by including the following:

```
<system.web>
    <authentication mode="Forms" />
</system.web>
```

As you can see, this configuration specifies forms authentication and allows anonymous access to the pages. In the secured subdirectory, you add an extra web.config file with the following contents:

```
<configuration>
    <system.web>
        <authorization>
            <deny users="?" />
```

```
        </authorization>
    </system.web>
</configuration>
```

This configuration denies any anonymous user access to the website's secured subfolder. If someone who is not authenticated tries to access resources placed in this directory, the ASP.NET runtime automatically redirects the user to the (publicly available) login page. Of course, you have to create the login page on your own, but it's much easier and much less work with the membership API, as you will see when you learn about the Login control in the section "Using the Security Controls."

Creating the Data Store

When using the membership API, you have to set up a data store that will be used by your membership provider. As mentioned earlier, when using SQL Server Express Edition in conjunction with ASP.NET, the SqlMembershipProvider is able to create this storage automatically for you. However, when using any other edition of SQL Server, you have to create this data storage manually. There are some other reasons for not using these auto-attached, file-based databases: performance and concurrency. Let's give you some background. SQL Server Express Edition can leverage databases in two ways. The first way is the classic way, which means you create or attach a database to the SQL Server Service as you are used to from previous versions. SQL Server then has full control over the database and is able to provide this database to multiple applications and multiple users concurrently. The second mode in which SQL Server Express Edition can be used is a file-based mode. This means your application can access a SQL Server database file directly without attaching it to your SQL Server instance. SQL Server dynamically attaches and detaches the database to the locally running SQL Server Express Edition whenever data from the database is needed. Therefore, the database file is just locked for a short amount of time (compared to attached databases, which are locked by SQL Server all the time when the SQL Server service is running). That makes copying the database file easy, as it is not locked (for example, if you want to copy changes you've made to a deployment location, and so on). However, at the same time, it requires some additional performance overhead when accessing the file-based database, as it needs to be attached automatically. Furthermore, for the time the database is attached for a dedicated application, no other application has access to it, as it is locked for the currently active application. The file-based mode is neat for Windows-based client applications that are using SQL Server Express Edition on the client as some kind of client-based storage, where one user and one application are accessing the database at the same time. It is nice for development purposes as well, as you do not need to manage databases for all projects in your SQL Server installation through Management Studio. However, this option is not well suited for production environments where multiple users of your (and maybe other) web application(s) access contents of the database.

Therefore, for production environments we recommend manual creation of the membership database as described in this section. In the case of the SqlMembershipProvider, creating such a data storage means creating a SQL Server database and a number of tables and stored procedures in this database. ASP.NET ships with a number of SQL scripts that allow you to manually create the necessary database and database tables required for storing user and role information used by the membership API. However, ASP.NET also ships with a tool that creates these database tables and stored procedures in a database of your choice for you. This tool is called aspnet_regsql.exe, and you can easily call it from within a Visual Studio Command Prompt window. In the case of a custom provider, you have to prepare and configure the data store used by the custom provider according to the custom provider's documentation and requirements.

You can use the aspnet_regsql.exe tool in two ways: either through a wizard interface or through the command line using dedicated command-line switches. In any case, you should launch the tool from a Visual Studio Command Prompt window, as it includes the necessary path information to the .NET Framework directory containing the necessary tools. If you just launch the tool without any parameters, the tool fires up the wizard interface that guides you through the process of creating a database, as shown in Figure 21-4. In Figure 21-4 you are creating the database in a SQL Server Express Edition.

Therefore, you manually add the \SQLEXPRESS post-fix to the (local) machine identifier for identifying the named instance SQLEXPRESS. That means your new database gets created in the SQL Server instance named SQLEXPRESS. Also note that it gets created as a full-blown, attached database (rather than the file-based version that gets created automatically). So, this would be the way you would create the database manually for the full edition of SQL Server: you just would either skip the instance name (in this case, SQLEXPRESS) or use your own instance name. You have the option of choosing an instance name for your SQL Server when installing SQL Server on your target machine.

The wizard provides you with the option of either creating the necessary database or removing the tables from an existing database. If you select the <default> option for the database, it looks for a database called aspnetdb on the server you have specified. If it doesn't exist already, aspnet_regsql.exe creates this database and creates the tables in this database. If the tables already exist in the target database, the wizard leaves them as they are.

As already mentioned, you can use the aspnet_regsql.exe tool from the command line as well. Actually, that's a good way to automate your application's setup—just call this tool from the command line and automatically set up the ASP.NET database tables required by your application. For example, to set up the membership API database tables, you can execute the following command:

```
aspnet_regsql -S (local)\SQLEXPRESS -E -A all -d MyDatabase
```

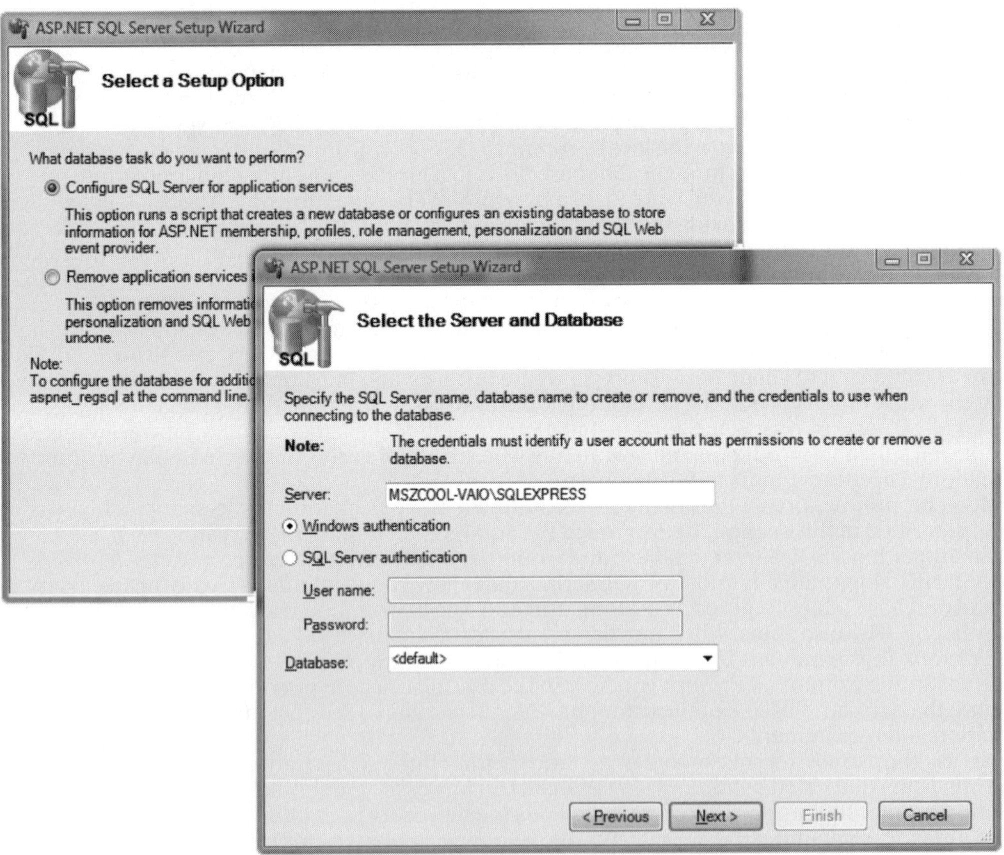

Figure 21-4. The apsnet_regsql.exe wizard user interface

Figure 21-5 shows the result of executing this command. Again, note that you are working against a local SQL Server instance called SQLEXPRESS (which is the SQL Server Express Edition installed on your machine). However, as you are creating a full-blown, attached database here, this would work with any version and edition of SQL Server. On a default installation of the full-blown SQL Server edition (Standard or Enterprise Edition), you would just skip the instance name (\SQLEXPRESS), or use the instance name you specified during the installation of your SQL Server, instead.

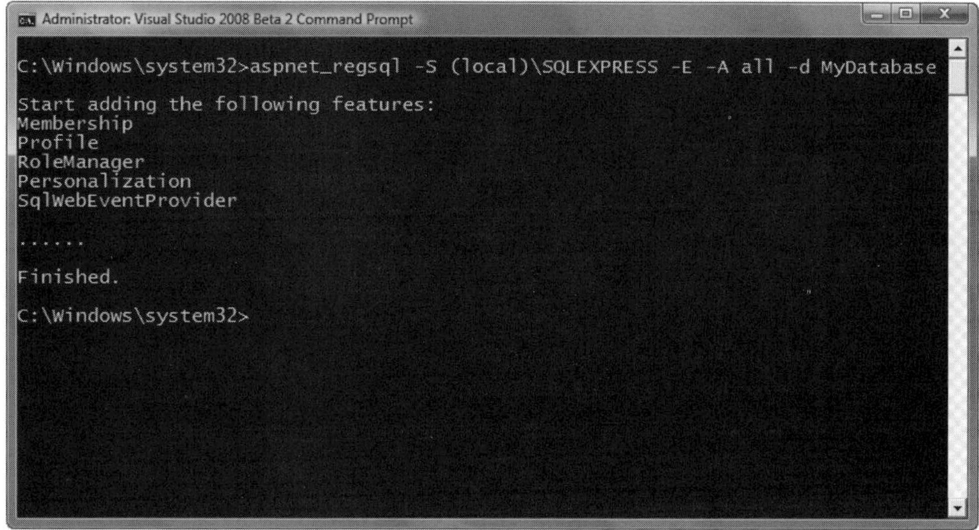

Figure 21-5. *Executing aspnet_regsql.exe for installing the database*

Table 21-2 describes the most important command-line switches of the aspnet_regsql.exe tool needed for the membership API and related ASP.NET application services.

Table 21-2. *Command-Line Switches of aspnet_regsql.exe*

Switch	Description
-S servername	Specifies the SQL Server and instance for which you want to install the ASP.NET database tables. You can use SQL Server 7.0 or newer as an under- lying storage for the membership API.
-U username	The SQL Server database user with which you want to connect to SQL Server. This is required if you do not want to use Windows authentication to connect only to SQL Server.
-P password	If the -U switch is specified, you need to specify the password switch as well. This is required if you do not want to use Windows authentication to connect only to SQL Server.

Switch	Description
-E	If you don't specify -U and -P, you automatically connect through Windows authentication to the SQL Server instance specified in -S. With -E, you can explicitly specify to connect through Windows authentication to the SQL Server.
-C	Allows you to specify a full-fledged ODBC or OLEDB connection string for connecting to the database.
-sqlexportonly	Creates the SQL scripts for adding or removing the specified features to the database without installing them on a dedicated SQL Server instance.
-A	Installs application services. The valid options for this switch are all, m, r, p, c, and w. The command in the previous example used the option all for installing all application services; m is dedicated to membership. r means role services, p means ASP.NET profiles for supporting user profiles, c stands for personalization of web part pages, and finally, w means SQL web event provider.
-R	Uninstalls application services. This switch supports the same option as -A and uninstalls the corresponding database tables for the application services.
-d	Lets you optionally specify the name of the database into which you want to install the application services. If you don't specify this parameter, a database named aspnetdb is created automatically (as is the case with the <default> option for the database in the wizard interface).

The aspnet_regsql.exe tool contains a couple of additional switches for installing SQL Server-based session state as well as for configuring the SQL cache dependency. For session state, please refer to Chapter 6. You will learn more about caching and cache dependencies in Chapter 11.

Database Scripts for ASP.NET Services

The aspnet_regsql.exe tool executes a couple of scripts for creating (or dropping) the membership-related database and database tables. These scripts ship with the .NET Framework; you can find them in the .NET Framework directory, as shown in Figure 21-6.

Two types of scripts exist: InstallXXX and the corresponding UninstallXXX scripts. When an InstallXXX script installs a set of database tables such as the set needed for the membership API, the corresponding UninstallXXX script drops the same tables and databases. Table 21-3 describes some of the SQL scripts included with the .NET Framework.

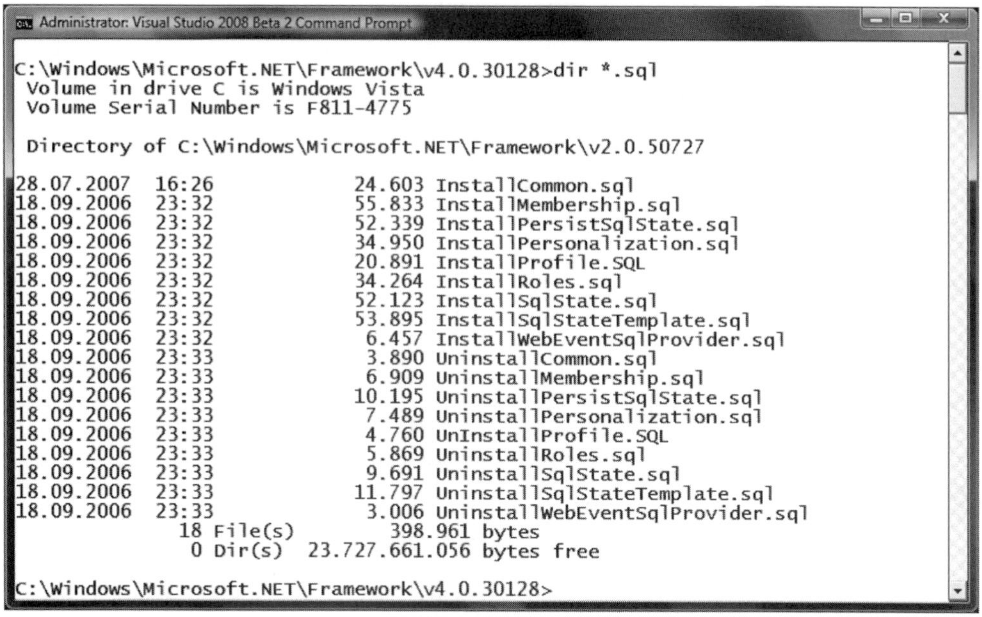

```
Administrator: Visual Studio 2008 Beta 2 Command Prompt

C:\Windows\Microsoft.NET\Framework\v4.0.30128>dir *.sql
 Volume in drive C is Windows Vista
 Volume Serial Number is F811-4775

 Directory of C:\Windows\Microsoft.NET\Framework\v2.0.50727

28.07.2007  16:26            24.603 InstallCommon.sql
18.09.2006  23:32            55.833 InstallMembership.sql
18.09.2006  23:32            52.339 InstallPersistSqlState.sql
18.09.2006  23:32            34.950 InstallPersonalization.sql
18.09.2006  23:32            20.891 InstallProfile.SQL
18.09.2006  23:32            34.264 InstallRoles.sql
18.09.2006  23:32            52.123 InstallSqlState.sql
18.09.2006  23:32            53.895 InstallSqlStateTemplate.sql
18.09.2006  23:32             6.457 InstallWebEventSqlProvider.sql
18.09.2006  23:33             3.890 UninstallCommon.sql
18.09.2006  23:33             6.909 UninstallMembership.sql
18.09.2006  23:33            10.195 UninstallPersistSqlState.sql
18.09.2006  23:33             7.489 UninstallPersonalization.sql
18.09.2006  23:33             4.760 UnInstallProfile.SQL
18.09.2006  23:33             5.869 UninstallRoles.sql
18.09.2006  23:33             9.691 UninstallSqlState.sql
18.09.2006  23:33            11.797 UninstallSqlStateTemplate.sql
18.09.2006  23:33             3.006 UninstallWebEventSqlProvider.sql
              18 File(s)        398.961 bytes
               0 Dir(s)  23.727.661.056 bytes free

C:\Windows\Microsoft.NET\Framework\v4.0.30128>
```

Figure 21-6. *The SQL scripts for installing and uninstalling SQL databases*

Table 21-3. *Membership API Installation Scripts*

Script	Description
InstallCommon.sql	Installs some common tables and stored procedures necessary for both the membership and roles APIs. This includes tables for identifying ASP.NET applications that use other ASP.NET features, such as the membership API, role service, or personalization.
InstallMembership.sql	Installs the database tables, stored procedures, and triggers used by the membership API. This includes tables for users, additional user properties, and stored procedures for accessing this information.
InstallRoles.sql	Installs all database tables and stored procedures required for associating users with application roles. These roles will be used for authorization, as you will learn in Chapter 23.
InstallPersonalization.sql	Contains DDL for creating any table and stored procedure required for creating personalized portal applications with web parts. You will learn more about web part pages in Chapter 31.

Script	Description
InstallProfile.sql	Creates all the necessary tables and stored procedures for supporting ASP.NET user profiles.
InstallSqlState.sql	Installs tables for persistent session state in the TEMP database of SQL Server. That means every time the SQL Server service is shut down, the session state gets lost.
InstallPersistSqlState.sql	Installs tables for persistent session state in a separate ASPState database. That means the state stays alive even if the SQL Server service gets restarted.

If you do not want to use aspnet_regsql.exe or you cannot use aspnet_regsql.exe, you can execute these scripts by either using the sqlcmd.exe command-line tool. For example, to install the common database tables on a SQL Server Express Edition, you can execute the following command:

```
sqlcmd -S (local)\SQLExpress -E -i InstallCommon.sql
```

Remember that you do not need to execute these scripts if you are using aspnet_regsql.exe, as it executes these SQL scripts for you. We recommend using aspnet_regsql.exe whenever possible, and explain this way only for situations where you cannot use aspnet_regsql.exe for some reason (whatever that reason might be—IT policy, SQL script customization, or inclusion of the standard SQL scripts in your own SQL scripts you use for deploying your application. But instead of including these SQL scripts in your own SQL deployment scripts, we recommend including either custom code or batch files in your deployment packages for calling aspnet_regsql.exe manually, as well).

The -S switch specifies the server and instance name for the target SQL Server. Usually you will not use an instance name (which is specified after the \), but SQL Server Express Edition will be installed as a named instance so that you can install more versions and instances of SQL Server on the same machine. Remember that for SQL Server Express Edition, you have to specify the instance name, which is SQLExpress by default. With the -E switch, you specify to access SQL Server through Windows authentication, and finally through the -i switch you can specify the input SQL script that should be executed. Figure 21-7 shows the result of executing the previous command.

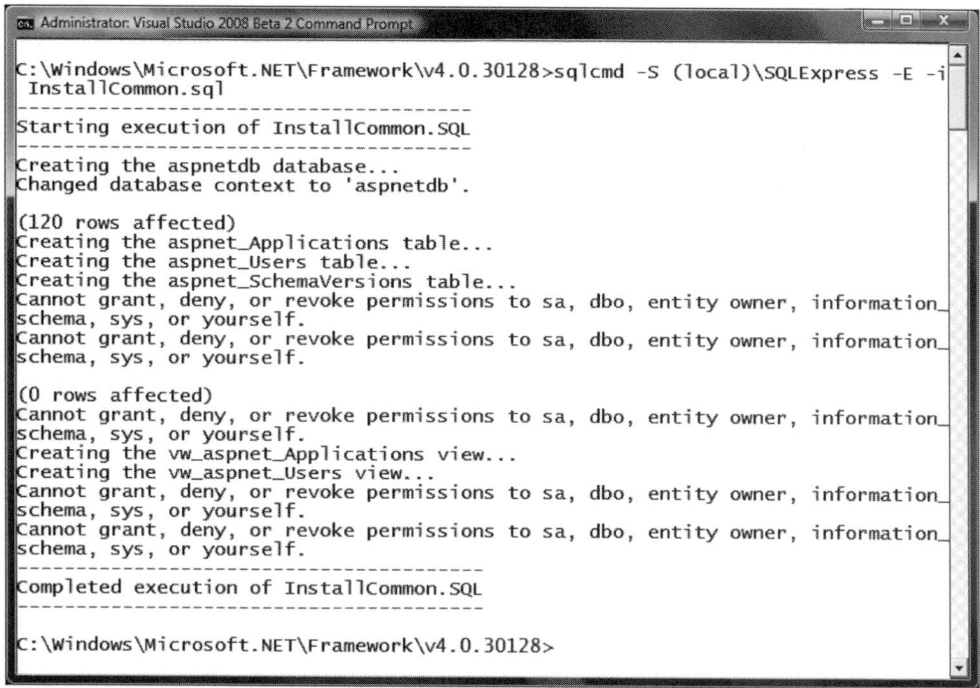

Figure 21-7. ***Installing ASP.NET database tables on SQL Server Express***

Don't be confused by the error messages. Because the command was executed by the administrator, the error messages appear because you cannot grant, revoke, or deny permissions to the system administrator (sa, db owner, or system—the administrator owns all these permissions).

File-Based SQL Server Store

SQL Server Express Edition supports a file-only database mode that allows you to access SQL Server databases directly through their MDF files without creating or attaching them in a SQL Server instance—as explained briefly earlier in this chapter. With this feature it is possible to just copy the application's database file with the application files onto the target server and run the application. The SQL Server provider then uses a connection string that accesses the database file directly. SQL Server automatically attaches the database (temporarily) and allows you to access it directly through the file without any additional configuration steps. The only prerequisite is that SQL Server Express Edition is installed on the target machine. Also remember that file-based mode works only with the Express Edition. The large editions do not support this mode (as it typically is not practicable for highly scalable production environments).

These database files are located in the special App_Data subdirectory of the application. When running ASP.NET with the default configuration, this file will be created automatically for you. But what causes the file to be created for you? Well, the answer is simple: when a feature that requires a specific type of functionality is used for the first time, the provider automatically creates the database file with the necessary contents. Therefore, when you first run the security wizard of the web-based administration tool WAT you saw previously, the database will be created automatically when you create the first user. This functionality is provided by the SqlMembershipProvider class. (The actual implementation is also included in a utility class used by all SQL provider classes, such as the

SqlRoleProvider.) Remember that we do not recommend this mode for production environments, as it has some performance and concurrency drawbacks explained in the section "Creating the Data Store" earlier in this chapter.

Configuring Connection String and Membership Provider

With the default configuration and SQL Server Express Edition installed, you don't have to prepare the data store and configure a membership provider, because the ASP.NET runtime uses the file-based SQL Server provider and automatically creates the database file for you. When having no SQL Server Express Edition installed, you need to create the storage manually, as outlined in the preceding section, and configure the provider of the membership API as outlined in this section. Remember that a membership provider should be configured at the root web.config file of your web application (meaning the web.config that is placed in the root directory within your web application). That means the following configuration happens in the root web.config, and not in a web.config in a subdirectory of your website, as it affects the whole web application!

But if you want to use your own SQL Server database, or even your custom membership provider and store, you have to configure the provider as well as the connection string to the membership store database appropriately. For this purpose, you have to touch the web.config file directly or edit the configuration through the IIS MMC snap-in if you are running your application on IIS.

In the case of using SQL Server storage (or other database-based storage), you have to configure the connection string as your first step. You can do this through the <connectionStrings /> section of the web.config file. For example, if you want to use a local database called MyDatabase where you have installed the database tables through the aspnet_regsql.exe tool as shown previously, you have to configure the connection string as follows (remember, the <connectionStrings /> section is located directly below the <configuration /> element):

```
<connectionStrings>
  <add name="MyMembershipConnString"
       connectionString="data source=(local)\SQLEXPRESS;
                         Integrated Security=SSPI;
                         initial catalog=MyDatabase" />
</connectionStrings>
```

After you have configured the connection string for your custom membership storage, you must configure the membership provider for the application. For this purpose, you have to add the <membership> section to your web.config file (if it's not already there) below the <system.web> section, as follows (again in your root web.config as outlined at the beginning of this section—a rule of thumb is that provider configurations are always placed in the root web.config, as they affect the whole web application):

```
<system.web>

    <authentication mode="Forms" />

    <membership defaultProvider="MyMembershipProvider">
        <providers>
            <add name="MyMembershipProvider"
                    connectionStringName="MyMembershipConnString"
                    applicationName="MyMembership"
                    enablePasswordRetrieval="false"
                    enablePasswordReset="true"
                    requiresQuestionAndAnswer="true"
```

```
                requiresUniqueEmail="true"
                passwordFormat="Hashed"
                type="System.Web.Security.SqlMembershipProvider" />
        </providers>
    </membership>

</system.web>
```

Within the <membership> section, you can add multiple providers as child elements of the <providers> section. In the previous code, you can see a valid configuration for the included SqlMembershipProvider. It's important not to forget about the defaultProvider attribute on the <membership> element. This attribute indicates the membership provider that your application will use. Configured providers are shown in the ASP.NET web configuration when selecting the option Select a Different Provider for Each Feature in the provider configuration. This enables you selecting a separate provider for each feature as shown in Figure 21-8.

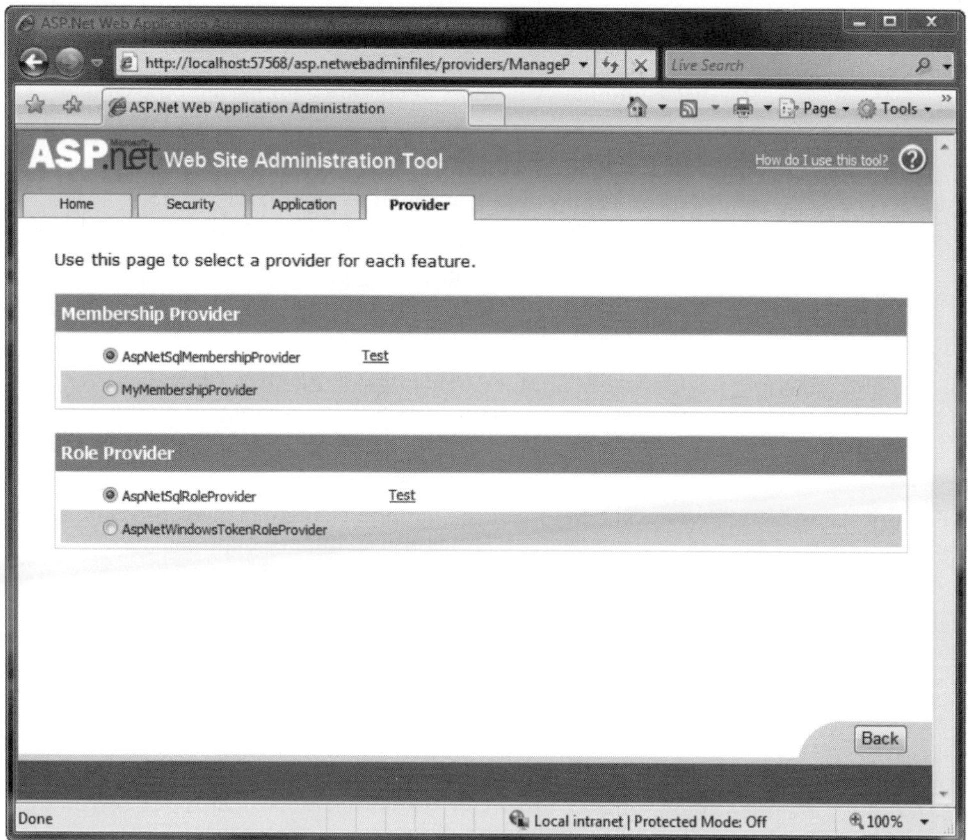

***Figure 21-8.** The configured provider selected in the WAT*

Table 21-4 describes the most important properties you can configure for the SqlMembershipProvider.

Table 21-4. *The SqlMembershipProvider's Properties*

Property	Description
name	Specifies a name for the membership provider. You can choose any name you want. You can use this name later for referencing the provider when programmatically accessing the list of configured membership providers. Furthermore, the WAT will use this name to display the provider.
applicationName	String value of your choice that specifies the name of the application for which the membership provider manages users and their settings. This setting allows you to use one membership database for multiple applications. Users and roles are always associated with an application. If you do not specify an application name, a root application name called "/" will be used automatically. More details are outlined after the table.
description	An optional description for the membership provider.
passwordFormat	Gets or sets the format in which passwords will be stored in the underlying credential store. Valid options are Clear for clear-text password storage, Encrypted for encrypting passwords in the data store (uses the locally configured machine key for encryption), and Hashed for hashing passwords stored in the underlying membership store.
minRequiredNonalphanumeric Characters	Specifies the number of nonalphanumeric characters the password needs to have. This is an important part for the validation of the password and enables you to specify strength requirements for the passwords used by your users.
minRequiredPasswordLength	Allows you to specify the minimum length of passwords for users of your application. This is also an important property for specifying password strength properties.
passwordStrengthRegular Expression	If the previously mentioned properties are not sufficient for specifying password strength conditions, then you can use a regular expression for specifying the format of valid passwords. With this option you are completely flexible in terms of specifying password format criteria.
enablePasswordReset	The membership API contains functionality for resetting a user's password and optionally sending an e-mail if an SMTP server is configured for the application.
enablePasswordRetrieval	When set to true, you can retrieve the password of a MembershipUser object by calling its GetPassword method. Of course, this works only if the password is not hashed.

Property	Description
maxInvalidPasswordAttempts	Specifies the number of invalid validation attempts before the user gets locked. The default value of this setting is 5. In many cases, you'll likely want to set this to a lower level depending on your security policy.
passwordAttemptWindow	Here you can set the number of minutes in which a maximum number of invalid password or password question-answer attempts are allowed before the user is completely locked out from the application. In that case, the user gets locked out, so the administrator must activate the account again. Again, the default value is ten minutes. Depending on your security policies, you might want to lower or raise the value.
requiresQuestionAndAnswer	Specifies whether the password question with an answer is required for this application. This question can be used if the user has forgotten his password. With the answer he gets the possibility of retrieving an automatically generated, new password via e-mail.
requiresUniqueEmail	Specifies whether e-mail addresses must be unique for every user in the underlying membership store.

Now, after you have set up the data store and configured the membership provider, you can use your configuration in your application, or for example, by creating users through the WAT. There is just one last important thing you have to bear in mind: the effects of the applicationName property of the membership configuration. You can use one membership provider database for more than one application by leveraging this property. Every user, role, profile—actually, any object in the membership database—is connected to an application entry. If you don't specify an applicationName property in the membership configuration, the API (and therefore any administration tool such as WAT) associates objects to the root application with the "/" name. If you specify the applicationName property in the membership provider configuration, any object created by the membership API will be associated with an application specified with the name. Validation of credentials through the Login control (as outlined in the section "Using the Security Controls") or through the membership API (as you will learn in the section "Using the Membership Class") works only against objects associated with the application configured in the applicationName property. That means if you configure your membership provider with the application name TestApp and you try to log in, the membership API (and therefore any controls sitting on top of it) will validate user names and passwords only against users associated with the application entry TestApp—even if users with the same name and password exist in the database, associated with other applications. This can be a little pitfall when switching from test configuration to production system and changing the applicationName property but using the same membership database.

Creating and Authenticating Users

To create new users in your previously created membership provider store, launch the WAT by selecting the Website ➤ ASP.NET Web Configuration menu from within Visual Studio. Now switch to the Security tab, and select Create User, as shown in Figure 21-9.

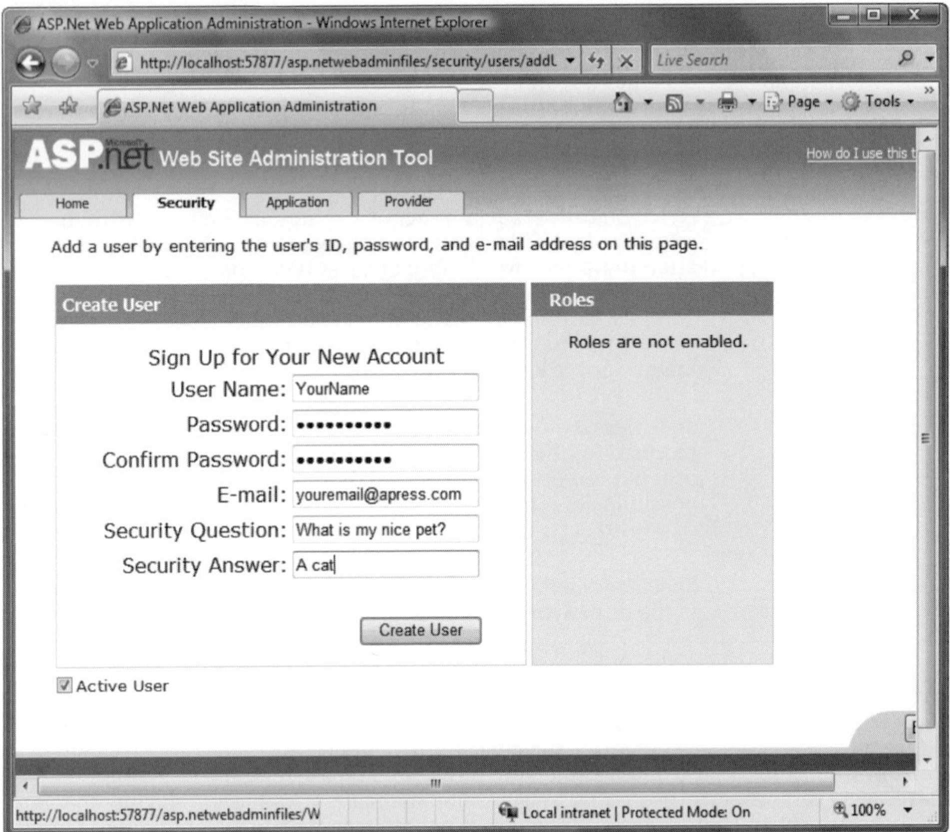

Figure 21-9. Creating users with the WAT

After you have created a couple of users, you can connect to the database through Visual Studio's Server Explorer (which requires you to add a database connection in Server Explorer to your membership database) or with the SQL Server Management Studio, and look at the aspnet_Users and aspnet_Membership tables in the database, as shown in Figure 21-10.

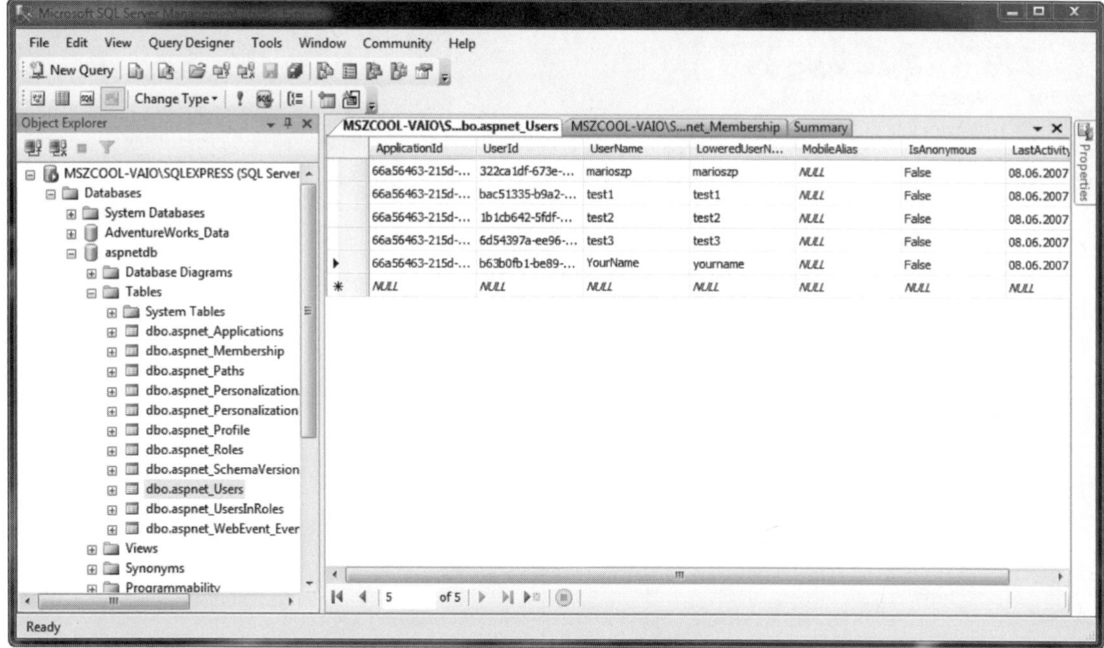

Figure 21-10. The aspnet_Users table in the membership database

Both the password and the answer for the password question are stored as a salted hash in the database because you have selected the passwordFormat="Hashed" option for the provider in the <membership> configuration section. You can see this when opening the aspnet_Membership table where these values are stored as you can see in Figure 21-11.

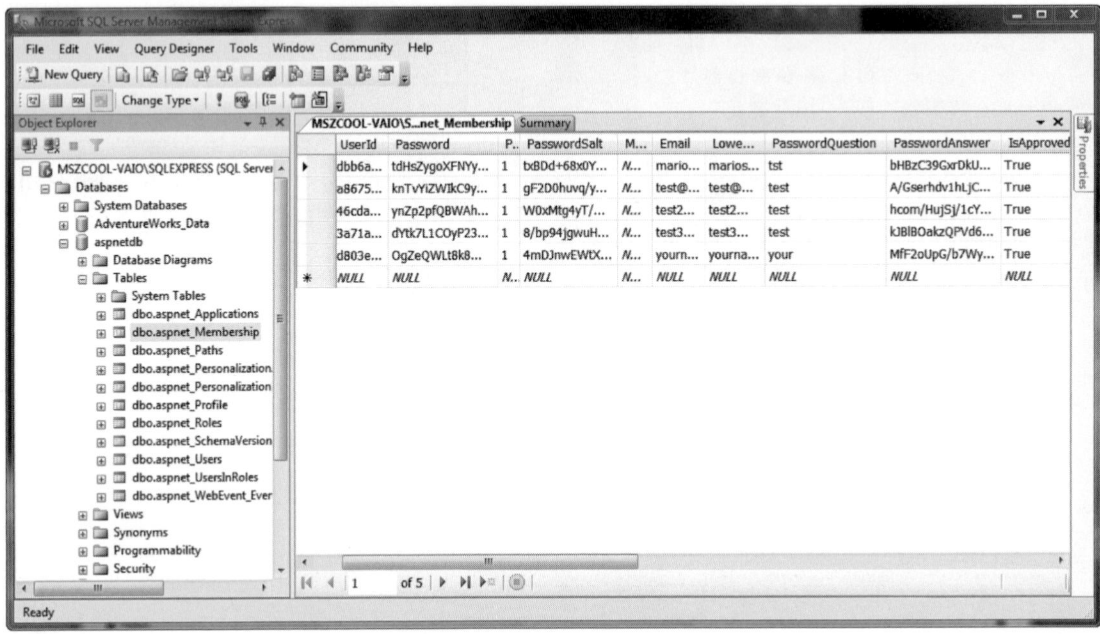

Figure 21-11. The aspnet_Membership table with the password-hash and salt values

After you have added users to the membership store, you can authenticate those users with the membership API. For that purpose, you have to create a login page that queries the user name and password from the user and then validates those credentials against the credential store, as follows:

```
protected void LoginAction_Click(object sender, EventArgs e)
{
    if (Membership.ValidateUser(UsernameText.Text, PasswordText.Text))
    {
        FormsAuthentication.RedirectFromLoginPage(UsernameText.Text, false);
    }
    else
    {
        LegendStatus.Text = "Invalid user name or password!";
    }
}
```

You don't need to know which provider is actually used by the application. If you want to use a different membership provider, you just need to change the configuration so that the membership API uses this different provider. Your application doesn't know about any details of the underlying provider. Furthermore, in the next section you will learn about the new security controls. You will see that you don't need to create the controls for the login page manually anymore.

Using the Security Controls

Now, after you have prepared your provider and storage for user information, you can start building the user interfaces for authenticating users, registering users, or giving users the chance of resetting their passwords. All these purposes require building some ASP.NET pages (such as login.aspx, as was necessary with forms authentication, introduced in the previous chapter).

ASP.NET ships with several controls you can use in your ASP.NET pages that simplify the process of creating login pages, for example, as well as other related pages (for example, registering users, resetting passwords using password question and answer combinations, and so on). In this section, you will learn more about these security controls included with ASP.NET. These security controls rely on the underlying forms authentication and the membership API infrastructure. Table 21-5 describes the security controls that ship with ASP.NET and summarizes their typical usage scenarios. We've also included some hints where these controls are typically used. However, these are just recommendations. You can use these controls on any ASP.NET page in your web application.

Table 21-5. *The New ASP.NET Security Controls*

Control	Primary Purpose
Login	The Login control is a composite control that solves the most common task for forms authentication-based applications—displaying a user name and password text box with a login button. Furthermore, if events are caught through custom event procedures, it automatically validates the user against the default membership provider. This control is typically placed on a login.aspx page used for forms authentication. However, you can place it on any page where you want to allow users to sign in to your website.
LoginStatus	The login status is a simple control that validates the authentication state of the current session. If the user is not authenticated, it offers a login button that redirects to the configured login page. Otherwise, it displays a sign-out button for the possibility of logging off. This control encapsulates behavior that should typically be available on all your pages. Therefore, placing it on a master page is very useful. However, you can use it on any page where you think displaying the login status with direct links to a login page or for signing out is useful for your users.
LoginView	This is really a powerful control that allows you to display different sets of controls for authenticated and unauthenticated users. Furthermore, it allows you to display different controls for users who are in different roles, as you will see in Chapter 23. This control is typically placed on content pages, as it displays contents of your website depending on the user currently working with a web page.
PasswordRecovery	This allows the user to retrieve the password if the user has provided an e-mail address during registration. It requests the user name from the user and then automatically displays a user interface that displays the password question and requests the appropriate answer from the user. If the answer is correct, it uses the membership API to send the password to the user. Typically, you put this control on a separate page in your website, which allows the user to reset the password. This page can be referred from the login page, for example, as you will see later in this chapter.

Control	Primary Purpose
ChangePassword	This control is a composite control that requests the old password from the user and lets the user enter a new password, including the password confirmation. Again, you usually put this on a separate ASP.NET page, which allows the user to change his password.
CreateUserWizard	Includes a complete wizard that guides the user (or an administrator) through the process of creating a user. This control is typically placed on a separate ASP.NET page in your website, which allows users to register themselves on your website.

You can use these controls with any other control. For example, you can use the Login control either on your main page or on a separate login page. Every control works in the same way: if you don't handle any custom events, all these controls work with the membership API by default. As soon as you handle events provided by the controls, you are responsible for completing the task. For example, the Login control supports an Authenticate event. If you don't handle this event, it uses the membership API automatically. But if you do handle this event, you are responsible for validating user credentials on your own.

The Login Control

The Login control simplifies the creation of a login page for forms authentication in conjunction with the membership API. It provides you with a ready-to-use user interface that queries the user name and password from the user and offers a Log In button for logging the user in. Behind the scenes, it encapsulates functionality you learned about in the previous chapter: validating user credentials against the membership API and encapsulating the basic forms authentication functionality, such as redirecting back to the originally requested page in a restricted area of your application after a successful login.

That means it encapsulates things such as Membership.ValidateUser() or FormsAuthentication.RedirectFromLoginPage() for you, and you do not have to write this code on your own. Figure 21-12 shows an example of the Login control in action.

Figure 21-12. The Login control in action

Whenever the user hits the Log In button, the control automatically validates the user name and password using the membership API function Membership.ValidateUser(), and then calls FormsAuthenication.RedirectFromLoginPage() if the validation was successful. All options on the UI of the Login control affect the input delivered by the control to these methods. For example, if you click the "Remember me next time" option, it passes the value true to the createPersistentCookie parameter of the RedirectFromLoginPage() method. Therefore, the FormsAuthenticationModule creates a persistent cookie, as you learned about in the previous chapter.

Behind the scenes, the UI of the Login control is nothing more than an ASP.NET composite control. It's completely extensible in that it allows you to override any layout styles and properties, as well as handle events thrown by the control for overriding its default behavior. If you leave the Login control as it is and you don't handle any of its events, it automatically uses the membership provider configured for your application. The simplest form of a Login control on your page is as follows:

```
<form id="form1" runat="server">
    <div style="text-align: center">
        <asp:Login ID="Login1" runat="server">
        </asp:Login>
    </div>
</form>
```

You can use several properties for changing the appearance of the control. You can use the different style settings supported by the Login control as follows:

```
<form id="form1" runat="server">
<div style="text-align: center">
 <asp:Login ID="Login1" runat="server"
           BackColor="aliceblue" BorderColor="Black" BorderStyle="double">
```

```
        <LoginButtonStyle BackColor="darkblue" ForeColor="White" />
        <TextBoxStyle BackColor="LightCyan" ForeColor="Black" Font-Bold="true" />
        <TitleTextStyle Font-Italic="true" Font-Bold="true" Font-Names="Verdana" />
    </asp:Login>
</div>
</form>
```

You can also use CSS classes for customizing the Login control's appearance. Every style property supported by the Login control includes a CssClass property. As is the case for every other ASP.NET control, this property allows you to set a CSS class name for your Login control that was added to the website previously. Imagine you added the following CSS stylesheet with the filename MyStyles.css to your project:

```
.MyLoginTextBoxStyle
{
    cursor: crosshair;
    background-color: yellow;
    text-align: center;
    border-left-color: black;
    border-bottom-color: black;
    border-top-style: dotted;
    border-top-color: black;
    border-right-style: dotted;
    border-left-style: dotted;
    border-right-color: black;
    border-bottom-style: dotted;
    font-family: Verdana;
    vertical-align: middle;
}
```

The content of the CSS file defines the style .MyLoginTextBoxStyle that you will use for the text boxes displayed on your Login control. You can include this style file in your login page so that you can use the style for the Login control as follows:

```
<html xmlns="http://www.w3.org/1999/xhtml" >
<head runat="server">
    <title>Your Login Page</title>
    <link href="MyStyles.css" rel="stylesheet" type="text/css" />
</head>
<body>
    <form id="form1" runat="server">
    <div style="text-align: center">
        <asp:Login ID="Login1" runat="server"
                   BackColor="aliceblue"
                   BorderColor="Black" BorderStyle="double">
            <LoginButtonStyle BackColor="darkblue" ForeColor="White" />
            <TextBoxStyle CssClass="MyLoginTextBoxStyle" />
            <TitleTextStyle Font-Italic="true" Font-Bold="true"
                            Font-Names="Verdana" />
        </asp:Login>
    </div>
    </form>
```

Anonymous Access to StyleSheets Used by Your Login Page

If you try running the page and if the CSS file is placed in a directory where anonymous access is denied, the styles will not be applied to the Login control because the CSS file is protected by the ASP.NET runtime (because its file extension is mapped to ASP.NET). This is also the case if you deny access to anonymous users in the root directory and put your CSS file there. Therefore, if you want to use CSS files with the Login control (where the user is definitely the anonymous user), either you have to put the CSS file into a directory that allows anonymous users access or you have to add the following configuration for the CSS file to your web.config file:

```
<location path="MyStyles.css">
    <system.web>
        <authorization>
            <allow users="*" />
        </authorization>
    </system.web>
</location>
```

In the preceding example, assume you're restricting access to the overall application, which means you have an <authorization> element in the root web.config that restricts access to the whole application. That means you have to add this configuration to the root web.config file to make the CSS file accessible to the login page, which gets accessed anonymously. If you just have a restricted area in your web application in a subfolder, and the root part of your web application is accessible to anonymous users as well (as shown earlier in Figure 21-3), you do not need to add this configuration if you just put the CSS file in the root folder of your application. If you put the CSS file in the restricted area of your web application and make it accessible to the publicly accessible login page, you need to use the following configuration:

```
<location path="Restricted/MyStyles.css">
    <system.web>
        <authorization>
            <allow users="*" />
        </authorization>
    </system.web>
</location>
```

We prefer having publicly available resources in a separate folder and restricting access to any other location of the web application, or the other way round. You will learn more about authorization and the configuration steps for it in Chapter 23.

Table 21-6 lists the styles supported by the Login control. Every style works in the same way. You can set color and font properties directly, or you use the CssClass property for assigning a CSS class.

Table 21-6. *The Styles Supported by the Login Control*

Style	Description
CheckBoxStyle	Defines the style properties for the Remember Me check box.
FailureTextStyle	Defines the style for the text displayed if the login was not successful.
HyperLinkStyle	The Login control allows you to define several types of hyperlinks, for example, to a registration page. This style defines the appearance of these hyperlinks.

Style	Description
InstructionTextStyle	The Login control allows you to specify help text that is displayed directly in the Login control. This style defines the appearance of this text.
LabelStyle	Defines the style for the UserName and Password labels.
LoginButtonStyle	Defines the style for the login button.
TextBoxStyle	Defines the style for the User Name and Password text boxes.
TitleTextStyle	Defines a style for the title text of the Login control.
ValidatorTextStyle	Defines styles for validation controls that are used for validating the user name and password.

The UI of the Login control is not just customizable through these styles—other, additional properties are dedicated to specific content parts of the control, such as the Log In button, which allows you to customize the UI as well. For example, you can select the text displayed for the login button, and you have the choice of displaying a login link instead of a login button (which is the default). Furthermore, you can add several hyperlinks to your Login control, such as a hyperlink to a help text page or a hyperlink to a registration page. Both pages must be available for anonymous users, because the help should be provided to anonymous users (remember, if someone sees the Login control, she potentially is an anonymous user). If you want to include some additional links in your Login control, modify the previously displayed control as follows:

```
<asp:Login ID="Login1" runat="server"
           BackColor="aliceblue"
           BorderColor="Black" BorderStyle="double"
           CreateUserText="Register"
           CreateUserUrl="Register.aspx"
           HelpPageText="Additional Help"
           HelpPageUrl="HelpMe.htm"
           InstructionText="Please enter your user name and password for <br>
                            logging into the system.">
    <LoginButtonStyle BackColor="DarkBlue" ForeColor="White" />
    <TextBoxStyle CssClass="MyLoginTextBoxStyle" />
    <TitleTextStyle Font-Italic="True" Font-Bold="True" Font-Names="Verdana" />
</asp:Login>
```

This code displays two additional links—one for a help page and one for a registration page—and adds some short, instructional text below the heading of the Login control. The styles discussed previously are applied to these properties. Table 21-7 describes the most important properties for customizing the Login control.

Table 21-7. The Relevant Customization Properties for the Login Control

Property	Description
TitleText	The text displayed as the heading of the control.
InstructionText	You have already used this property in the previous code snippet, which contains text that is displayed below the heading of the control.
FailureText	The text displayed by the Login control if the login attempt was not successful.
UserNameLabelText	The text displayed as a label in front of the user name text box.
PasswordLabelText	The text displayed as a label in front of the password text box.
UserName	Initial value filled into the user name text box.
UsernameRequiredErrorMessage	Error message displayed if the user has not entered a user name.
PasswordRequiredErrorMessage	Error message displayed if the user has not entered a password.
LoginButtonText	The text displayed for the login button.
LoginButtonType	The login button can be displayed as a link, button, or image. For this purpose, you have to set this property appropriately. Supported values are Link, Button, and Image.
LoginButtonImageUrl	If you display the login button as an image, you have to provide a URL to an image that is displayed for the button.
DestinationPageUrl	If the login attempt was successful, the Login control redirects the user to this page. This property is empty by default. If empty, it uses the forms authentication infrastructure for redirecting either to the originally requested page or to the defautlUrl configured in web.config for forms authentication.
DisplayRememberMe	Enables you to show and hide the Remember Me check box. By default this property is set to true.
FailureAction	Defines the action the control performs after a login attempt failed. The two valid options are Refresh and RedirectToLoginPage. The first one refreshes just the current page, and the second one redirects to the configured login page. The second one is useful if you use the control anywhere else instead of the login page.
RememberMeSet	Defines the default value for the Remember Me check box. By default this option is set to false, which means the check box is not checked by default.

Property	Description
VisibleWhenLoggedIn	If set to false, the control automatically hides itself if the user is already logged in. If set to true (default), the Login control is displayed even if the user is already logged in.
CreateUserUrl	Defines a hyperlink to a page in the website that allows you to create (register!) a user. Therefore, this is typically used for enabling the user to access a registration page. Typically this page displays the CreateUserWizard control.
CreateUserText	Defines the text displayed for the CreateUserUrl hyperlink.
CreateUserIconUrl	Defines a URL to an image displayed together with the text for the CreateUserUrl hyperlink.
HelpPageUrl	URL for redirecting the user to a help page.
HelpPageText	Text displayed for the hyperlink configured in the HelpPageUrl property.
HelpPageIconUrl	URL to an icon displayed together with the text for the HelpPageUrl hyperlink.
PasswordRecoveryUrl	URL for redirecting the user to a password recovery page. This page is used if the user has forgotten the password. Typically this page displays the PasswordRecovery control.
PasswordRecoveryText	The text displayed for the hyperlink configured in PasswordRecoveryUrl.
PasswordRecoveryIconUrl	Icon displayed together with the text for the PasswordRecoveryUrl.

Templates and the Login Control

As you can see, the control is nearly completely customizable through these properties. But as you probably have seen, you cannot define any validation expressions for validating the input. Of course, you can do validation on the server side within the event procedures offered by the Login control. However, generally, if you want to add any controls to the Login control, you can't do that through the properties introduced previously. For example, what if you have an additional text box for strong authentication with a second password or user access key as on some governmental pages?

Fortunately, the Login control supports templates just as other controls such as the GridView control do. With templates, you can customize the contents of the Login control without any limitations. You can add any controls you want to your Login control. You can use a custom template for the Login control through the LayoutTemplate tag as follows:

```
<asp:Login ID="LoginCtrl" runat="server"
           BackColor="aliceblue"
           BorderColor="Black"
```

```
        BorderStyle="double">
    <LayoutTemplate>
        <h4>Log-In to the System</h4>
                            <td>
            User Name:

            <td>
            <asp:TextBox ID="UserName" runat="server" />
            <asp:RequiredFieldValidator ID="UserNameRequired"
                            runat="server"
                            ControlToValidate="UserName"
                            ErrorMessage="*" />
            <asp:RegularExpressionValidator ID="UsernameValidator"
                            runat="server"
                            ControlToValidate="UserName"
                            ValidationExpression="[\w| ]*"
                            ErrorMessage="Invalid User Name" />

                                <td>
            Password:

            <td>
            <asp:TextBox ID="Password" runat="server" TextMode="Password" />
            <asp:RequiredFieldValidator ID="PasswordRequired"
                            runat="server"
                            ControlToValidate="Password"
                            ErrorMessage="*" />
            <asp:RegularExpressionValidator ID="RegularExpressionValidator1"
                            runat="server"
                            ControlToValidate="Password"
                            ValidationExpression='[\w| !"§$%&amp;/()=\-?\*]*'
                            ErrorMessage="Invalid Password" />


        <asp:CheckBox ID="RememberMe" runat="server" Text="Remember Me" />
        <asp:Literal ID="FailureText" runat="server" /><br />
        <asp:Button ID="Login" CommandName="Login"
                    runat="server" Text="Login"  />
    </LayoutTemplate>
</asp:Login>
```

Now, one question arises when taking a look at the preceding code: when customizing the template, you have to write so much UI code (or design it in a visual designer)—so why not write a custom login page without using the Login control? This is a valid question. However, as explained at the beginning of this section, the UI part is just one part of the Login control. Under the hood, meaning whenever the user clicks the login button, for example, the Login control contains all the code for automatically validating the user against the membership API storage and redirecting the user back to the originally requested page through the forms authentication infrastructure. So, you still save yourself from writing this code.

With the right controls and the correct ID values for these controls in place, you don't need to write any code for handling events. The code just works as usual, except that you define the set of controls and the layout of these controls. Actually, the Login control requires at least two text boxes with the IDs UserName and Password. If those two text boxes are missing (or don't have these ID values), the control throws an exception. All the other controls are optional, but if you specify corresponding ID values (such as Login for the login button), the Login control automatically handles their events and behaves as when you used the predefined layouts for the control. Table 21-8 lists the special ID values, their required control types, and whether they are required or optional.

Table 21-8. *Special Controls for the Login Template*

Control ID	Control Type	Required?
UserName	System.Web.UI.WebControls.Textbox	Yes
Password	System.Web.UI.WebControls.Textbox	Yes
RememberMe	System.Web.UI.WebControls.CheckBox	No
FailureText	System.Web.UI.WebControls.Literal	No
Login	Any control that supports event bubbling and a CommandName	No

The control with the ID Login can be any control that supports event bubbling (as you will learn in Chapter 27 in detail) and a CommandName property. It is important that you set the CommandName property to Login, because otherwise the Login control won't recognize it in the event-handling process. If you don't add a control with the CommandName set to Login, you have to handle the event of the control yourself and write the appropriate code for validating the user name and password and for redirecting to the originally requested page. You can also add controls with other IDs that are not related to the Login control at all. The previous code includes RequiredFieldValidator and RegularExpressionValidator controls for validating the UserName and Password fields appropriately.

When using the LayoutTemplate, many of the properties originally offered by the Login control are not available anymore. Only the following properties are available when using the template:

- DestinationPageUrl
- VisibleWhenLoggedIn
- FailureAction
- MembershipProvider
- Password
- Username
- RememberMeSet

All the style properties and several properties for configuring text contents of default controls are not available in Visual Studio's property editor anymore, because you can add them manually as separate controls or static text to the template for the Login control. If you still add them to the Login control when using the template mode, they simply get ignored because the template overrides the default UI of the Login control, which leverages these properties.

Programming the Login Control

The Login control supports several events and properties that you can use to customize the behavior of the control. This gives you complete control over customizing the Login control (used along with the other customization possibilities such as templates or custom style properties). The Login control supports the events listed in Table 21-9.

Table 21-9. The Events of the Login Control

Event	Description
LoggingIn	Raised before the user gets authenticated by the control.
LoggedIn	Raised after the user has been authenticated by the control.
LoginError	Raised when the login of the user failed for some reason (such as a wrong password or user name).
Authenticate	Raised to authenticate the user. If you handle this event, you have to authenticate the user on your own, and the Login control completely relies on your authentication code.

You can handle the first three events (in the previous table) to perform some actions before the user gets authenticated, after the user has been authenticated, and if an error has happened during the authentication process. For example, you can use the LoginError event to automatically redirect the user to the password recovery page after a specific number of attempts, as follows:

```
protected void Page_Load(object sender, EventArgs e)
{
    if (!this.IsPostBack)
        ViewState["LoginErrors"] = 0;
}

protected void LoginCtrl_LoginError(object sender, EventArgs e)
{
    // If the "LoginErrors" state does not exist, create it
    If(ViewState["LoginErrors"] == null)
        ViewState["LoginErrors"] = 0;

    // Increase the number of invalid logins
    int ErrorCount = (int)ViewState["LoginErrors"] + 1;
    ViewState["LoginErrors"] = ErrorCount;

    // Now validate the number of errors
    if ((ErrorCount > 3) && (LoginCtrl.PasswordRecoveryUrl != string.Empty))
        Response.Redirect(LoginCtrl.PasswordRecoveryUrl);
}
```

The Login control fires the events in the order shown in Figure 21-13.

As mentioned previously, if you handle the event, you have to add your own code for validating the user name and password. The Authenticate event receives an instance of AuthenticateEventArgs as a parameter. This event argument class has a property called Authenticated. If you set this property to true, the Login control assumes that authentication was successful and raises the LoggedIn event. If set to false, it displays the FailureText and raises the LoginError event.

```
protected void LoginCtrl_Authenticate(object sender, AuthenticateEventArgs e)
{
    if (YourValidationFunction(LoginCtrl.UserName, LoginCtrl.Password))
```

```
    {
        e.Authenticated = true;
    }
    else
    {
        e.Authenticated = false;
    }
}
```

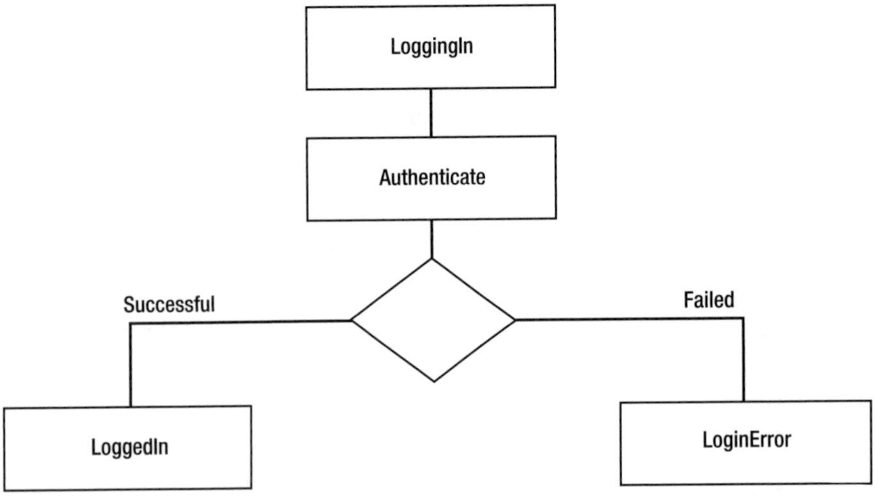

Figure 21-13. The order of the Login control events

As you can see, you have direct access to the entered values through the UserName and Password properties that contain the text entered in the corresponding text boxes. If you are using template controls and require the value of another control in addition to the controls with the IDs UserName and Password, you can use the control's FindControl method to get the control. This method requires the ID of the control and returns an instance of System.Web.UI.Control. You then just cast the control to the appropriate type and read the values you require for your custom credential validation method. The following Login control uses a template with an additional control that you will use later in the Authenticate event in your code:

```
<asp:Login ID="OtherLoginCtrl" runat="server"
            BackColor="aliceblue"
            BorderColor="Black"
            BorderStyle="double"
            PasswordRecoveryUrl="./pwdrecover.aspx"
            OnAuthenticate="OtherLoginCtrl_Authenticate">

    <LayoutTemplate>
        <div style="font-family: Courier New">
        Userskey: <asp:Textbox ID="AccessKey" runat="server" /><br />
        User Name: <asp:TextBox ID="UserName" runat="server" /><br />
        Password: <asp:TextBox ID="Password" runat="server"
                              TextMode="password" Width="149px" /><br />
```

```
        <asp:Button runat="server" ID="Login"
                    CommandName="Login" Text="Login" />
        </div>
    </LayoutTemplate>

</asp:Login>
```

In the previous code example, the user's key is an additional value that must be provided by the user for successfully logging in. To include this value into your credential validation process, you have to modify the contents of the Authenticate event as follows:

```
protected void OtherLoginCtrl_Authenticate(
                                   object sender, AuthenticateEventArgs e)
{
    TextBox AccessKeyText = (TextBox)OtherLoginCtrl.FindControl("AccessKey");

    if (YourValidation(AccessKeyText.Text,
                  OtherLoginCtrl.UserName, OtherLoginCtrl.Password))
    {
        e.Authenticated = true;
    }
    else
    {
        e.Authenticated = false;
    }
}
```

Of course, in this case you cannot use any default membership provider. You have to implement your own validation function that accepts these additional parameters. But the Login control forces you not to use membership at all. The validation function can be any type of function you want. You just need to set the e.Authenticated property appropriately. Then you can use the Login control for whatever login mechanism you want.

The LoginStatus Control

The LoginStatus control is a simple control that displays either a login link if the user is not authenticated or a logout link if the user is authenticated. The login link automatically redirects to the configured login page, and the logout link automatically calls the method FormsAuthentication.SignOut for logging off the user. The control is fairly simple, and therefore customization is simple as well.

```
<asp:LoginStatus ID="LoginStatus1" runat="server"
        LoginText="Sign In"
        LogoutText="Sign Out"
        LogoutPageUrl="./Default.aspx"
        LogoutAction="Redirect" />
```

The LoginStatus control offers a couple of properties for customizing the text shown for the links and the URLs to redirect to when the user clicks the link. You can find the most important properties in Table 21-10.

Table 21-10. Properties for Customizing the LoginStatus Control

Property	Description
LoginText	The text displayed if the user is not signed in.
LoginImageUrl	A URL for an image displayed as an icon for the login link.
LogoutText	The text displayed if the user is authenticated.
LogoutImageUrl	A URL for an image displayed as an icon for the logout link.
LogoutAction	Configures the action the control performs if the user clicks the logout link that is displayed when the user is authenticated. Valid options are Refresh, Redirect, and RedirectToLoginPage. The first option just refreshes the current page, the second option redirects to the page configured in the LogoutPageUrl, and the last option redirects to the login page.
LogoutPageUrl	A page to redirect to if the user clicks the logout link and the LogoutAction is set to Redirect.

The LoginView Control

This control is fairly simple but extremely powerful. It allows you to display a different set of controls for anonymous and authenticated users. Further, it even allows you to display different content based on which roles the currently logged-in user is assigned to. You will learn more about roles and their connection to the LoginView control in Chapter 23. For now you will learn how to display different content for anonymous users and for authenticated users.

The LoginView control is a template control with different types of templates—one for anonymous users, one for authenticated users, and one for supporting role-based templates. Within those templates, you just add the controls to display for the corresponding situation as follows (role-based templates are encapsulated into RoleGroup controls, but you will learn more about them in Chapter 23):

```
<asp:LoginView ID="LoginViewCtrl" runat="server">
    <AnonymousTemplate>
        <h2>You are anonymous</h2>
    </AnonymousTemplate>
    <LoggedInTemplate>
        <h2>You are logged in</h2>
        Submit your comment: <asp:TextBox runat="server" ID="CommentText" />
        <br />
        <asp:Button runat="server" ID="SubmitCommentAction" Text="Submit" />
    </LoggedInTemplate>
</asp:LoginView>
```

The previous control displays some simple text for anonymous users and some text in a text box together with a button for logged-in users. Furthermore, the control supports two events you can handle for initializing content controls of different templates appropriately before they are displayed:

- ViewChanging, which is raised before the control displays content defined in another template
- ViewChanged, which is raised after the control has changed the content display from one template to another

The PasswordRecovery Control

The PasswordRecovery control is useful if a user has forgotten his password. This queries the user name from the user and afterward automatically displays the password question stored for the user in the credential store. If the user enters the correct answer for the password question, the password is mailed automatically to the e-mail address configured for the user. Figure 21-14 shows the PasswordRecovery control in action.

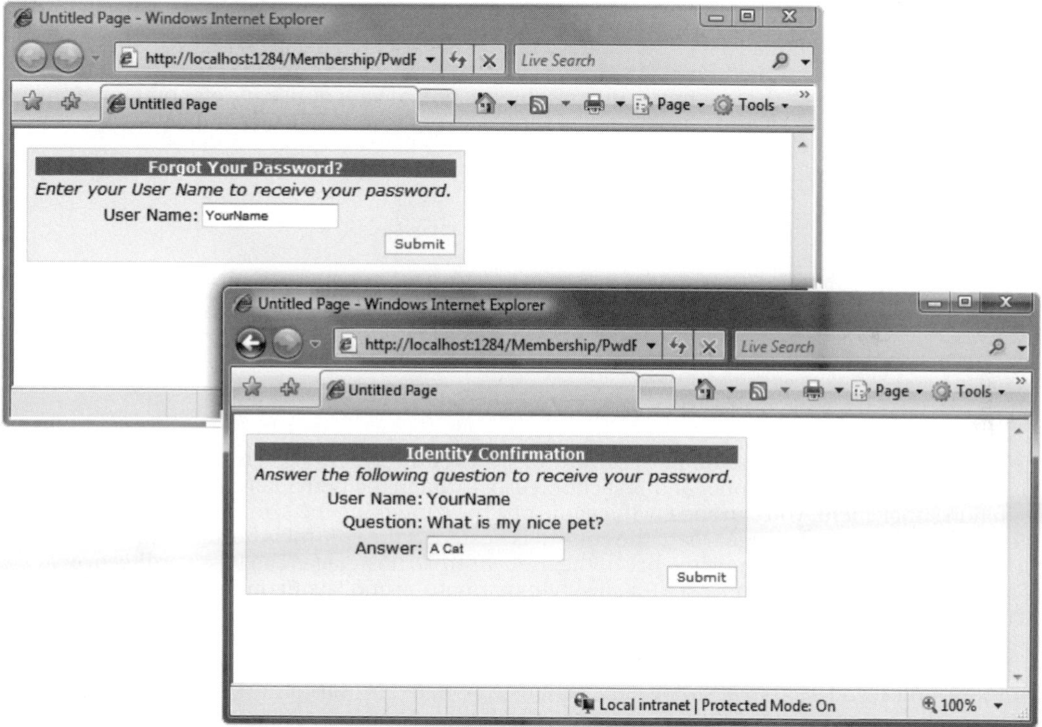

Figure 21-14. *The PasswordRecovery control in action*

The control includes three customizable view modes. First, the user has to enter his user name. When the user clicks the submit button, the control queries the password question through the membership API from the underlying credential store. Second, this question is then displayed, and the user is requested to enter the correct answer. When the user enters the correct answer, an automatically generated password or the stored password is sent to the user's e-mail address. This e-mail address was specified during the registration process (or when the user was created through the WAT). If sent successfully, the control displays a confirmation view. Any mail configuration takes place through the control's properties, as follows. Of course, the password can be sent to the user only if it is not hashed. Therefore, the membership provider must be configured in a way that it stores the passwords either encrypted or in clear-text format. If the membership provider stores the password in a hashed form, it automatically generates a new, random password and sends the new password in the e-mail.

```
<asp:PasswordRecovery ID="PasswordRecoveryCtrl" runat="server"
                        BackColor="Azure"
                        BorderColor="Black" BorderStyle="solid">
    <MailDefinition From="proaspnet2@apress.com"
                    Subject="Forgotten Password"
                    Priority="high" />
    <TitleTextStyle Font-Bold="true" Font-Italic="true" BorderStyle="dotted" />
    <TextBoxStyle BackColor="Yellow" BorderStyle="double" />
    <FailureTextStyle Font-Bold="true" ForeColor="Red" />
</asp:PasswordRecovery>
```

The control requires an e-mail SMTP server for sending the e-mail message. It relies on the SmtpClient class in the System.Net.Mail namespace, which you can use in any type of application. You can configure this class in the <system.net> configuration section of your application's configuration file. Therefore, you have to configure the SMTP mail server in your web.config file, as follows:

```
<system.net>
    <mailSettings>
        <smtp deliveryMethod="Network" from="proaspnet@apress.com">
            <network
            host="localhost"
            port="25"
            defaultCredentials="true" />
        </smtp>
    </mailSettings>
</system.net>
```

The MailDefinition subelement of the PasswordRecovery control allows you to set basic properties, as you can see in the first code snippet of this section. Also, through the BodyFileName of the MailDefinition subelement, you can specify the name of a file containing the e-mail text. This file has to be in the same directory as the page where the control is hosted. If the control is hosted within another user control, the file has to be in the directory of the user control's host page. The PasswordRecovery control supports different style properties for specifying formatting and layout options for the different parts of the control (just as the Login control does). For a complete list of the supported properties, refer to the MSDN documentation; these properties are similar to the properties introduced with the Login control. The control raises several different events during the password recovery process. You can handle these events if you want to customize the actions completed by the control. Table 21-11 lists these events.

Table 21-11. Events of the PasswordRecovery Control

Event	Description
VerifyingUser	Raised before the control starts validating the user name entered. Validating the user name means looking for the user in the membership store and retrieving the password question information.
UserLookupError	If the user name entered in the user name text box doesn't exist in the membership store, this event is raised before the failure text is displayed.
VerifyingAnswer	When the user clicks the submit button in the second step, the answer for the question is compared to the one stored in the membership store. This event is raised before this action takes place.
AnswerLookupError	If the answer provided by the user is not correct, this event is raised by the control.
SendingMail	This event is raised by the control after the answer submitted by the user has been identified as the correct answer and before the e-mail is sent through the mail server.
SendMailError	If the e-mail cannot be sent for some reason (for example, the mail server is not available), this event is raised by the control.

You can use these events for preparing information before that information gets processed by the control. For example, if you want to convert all letters in the user name to lowercase letters before the control compares contents with the data stored in the membership store, you can do this in the VerifyingUser event. Similarly, you can use the VerifyingAnswer for preprocessing information before it gets processed by the control. Both events get event arguments of type LoginCancelEventArgs, which contains a Cancel property. If you set this property to true, you can cancel the whole processing step.

When handling the SendingMail event, you have the chance to modify the contents of the e-mail message before the control actually sends the e-mail to the user. The passed MailMessageEventArgs contains a Message property that represents the actual e-mail message. By modifying the Message's properties, such as the Attachments collection, you can add attachments, configure a CC address, or do anything else related to the e-mail message.

PasswordRecovery Templates

Like the Login control, the PasswordRecovery control can be customized completely if customization through the previously mentioned properties and styles is not sufficient for some reason. The control supports templates for every view:

- The UserNameTemplate contains all the controls displayed for the first step of the password recovery process when the user is required to enter the user name.
- Controls for the second step, the password question step, are placed in the QuestionTemplate.
- Finally, the control supports a SuccessTemplate that consists of the controls displayed for the confirmation, which are shown after the password has been sent successfully to the user.

Every template has certain required controls. For example, the UserNameTemplate requires a text box for entering the user name. The QuestionTemplate requires a text box for entering the question, and the SuccessTemplate requires a Literal control for displaying the final confirmation message. A template PasswordRecovery control might look like this:

```
<asp:PasswordRecovery ID="PasswordTemplateCtrl" runat="server">
    <MailDefinition From="pwd@apress.com"
                    Priority="high"
                    Subject="Important information" />
    <UserNameTemplate>
        <span style="text-align: center">
        <font face="Courier New">
            <h2>Forgotten your Password?</h2>
            Please enter your user name:<br />
            <asp:TextBox ID="UserName" runat="server" />
            <br />
            <asp:Button ID="SubmitButton" CommandName="Submit"
                        runat="server" Text="Next" />
            <br />
            <span style="color: Red">
            <asp:Literal ID="FailureText" runat="server" />
            </span>
        </font>
        </span>
    </UserNameTemplate>
    <QuestionTemplate>
        <span style="text-align: center">
        <font face="Courier New">
            <h2>Forgotten your Password?</h2>
            Hello <asp:Literal ID="UserName" runat="server" />! <br />
            Please answer your password-question:<br />
            <asp:Literal ID="Question" runat="server" /><br />
            <asp:TextBox ID="Answer" runat="server" /><br />
            <asp:Button ID="SubmitButton" CommandName="Submit"
                        runat="Server" Text="Send Answer" /><br />
            <asp:Literal ID="FailureText" runat="server" />
            </span>
        </font>
        </span>
    </QuestionTemplate>
    <SuccessTemplate>
        Your password has been sent to your email address
        <asp:Label ID="EmailLabel" runat="server" />!
    </SuccessTemplate>
</asp:PasswordRecovery>
```

Again, if you use controls with the appropriate ID values and use the appropriate CommandName values for buttons, you don't have to write any code for the control to work, as in the previous examples where you didn't use templates. In the previous code, these special controls are in bold. Some of these controls are required for the templates, and others are optional. Table 21-12 lists the controls for PasswordRecovery templates.

Table 21-12. Special Controls for PasswordRecovery Templates

Additional Template	ID	Control Type	Required?	Comments
UserNameTemplate	UserName	System.Web.UI.Web Controls.	Yes	TextBox
UserNameTemplate	SubmitButton	All controls that support Command-event bubbling.	No	Name must be set to Submit.
UserNameTemplate	FailureText	System.Web.UI.Web Controls.	No	Literal
QuestionTemplate	UserName	System.Web.UI.Web Controls.	No	Literal
QuestionTemplate	Question	System.Web.UI.Web Controls.	No	Literal
QuestionTemplate	Answer	System.Web.UI.Web Controls.	Yes	TextBox
QuestionTemplate	SubmitButton	All controls that support Command-event bubbling.	No	Name must be set to Submit.
QuestionTemplate	FailureText	System.Web.UI.Web Controls.	No	Literal

Again, the submit button can be any control that supports event bubbling and a CommandName property. Typically you can use the controls Button, ImageButton, or LinkButton for this purpose. The CommandName must be set to Submit; otherwise, the command is not recognized by the control (the ID is not evaluated and can therefore be set to any value). The SuccessTemplate doesn't require any type of control with any special IDs. Therefore, you can add any control you want there; it's just for displaying the confirmation. In the previous example, it includes a Literal control that should display the e-mail address to which the password has been sent. You can set this Literal control through the SendingMail event procedure. Again, you can use the FindControl method for finding the control (which is actually a child control of the PasswordRecovery template control) in the appropriate template, as follows:

```
protected void PasswordTemplateCtrl_SendingMail(object sender,
                                                MailMessageEventArgs e)
{
    Label lbl =
      (Label)PasswordTemplateCtrl.SuccessTemplateContainer.FindControl(
                                                         "EmailLabel");
    lbl.Text = e.Message.To[0].Address;
}
```

Because the PasswordRecovery control includes more than one template, you cannot call the FindControl method directly on the PasswordRecovery control instance. You have to select the appropriate template container (UserNameTemplateContainer, QuestionTemplateContainer, or SuccessTemplateContainer). Afterward, you can work with the control as usual. In the previous example, you just set the text of the label to the first e-mail recipient. Usually for a password recovery, the list has only one mail recipient.

The ChangePassword Control

You can use this control as a standard control for allowing the user to change her password. The control simply queries the user name as well as the old password from the user. Then it requires the user to enter the new password and confirm the new password. You can use the control on a secured page as follows:

```
<asp:ChangePassword ID="ChangePwdCtrl" runat="server"
                    BorderStyle="groove" BackColor="aliceblue">
    <MailDefinition From="pwd@apress.com"
                    Subject="Changes in your profile"
                    Priority="high" />
    <TitleTextStyle Font-Bold="true" Font-Underline="true"
                    Font-Names="Verdana" ForeColor="blue" />
</asp:ChangePassword>
```

Again, the control includes a MailDefinition child element with the same settings as the PasswordRecovery control. This is because after the password has been changed successfully, the control automatically can send an e-mail to the user's e-mail address if a mail server is configured for the web application. As for all the other controls, this control is customizable through both properties and styles and a template-based approach. But this time two templates are required when customizing the control:

- The ChangePasswordTemplate displays the fields for entering the old user name and password as well as the new password, including the password confirmation field.
- The SuccessTemplate displays the success message, telling the user if the reset completed successfully or not.

The ChangePasswordTemplate requires you to add some special controls with special IDs and CommandName property values. You can find these control ID values and CommandName values in bold in the following code snippet:

```
<asp:ChangePassword ID="ChangePwdCtrl" runat="server">
    <ChangePasswordTemplate>
        Old Password: 
        <asp:TextBox ID="CurrentPassword" runat="server"
                     TextMode="Password" /><br />
        New Password: 
        <asp:TextBox ID="NewPassword" runat="server"
                     TextMode="Password" /><br />
        Confirmation: 
        <asp:TextBox ID="ConfirmNewPassword" runat="server"
                     TextMode="Password" /><br />
        <asp:Button ID="ChangePasswordPushButton" CommandName="ChangePassword"
                    runat="server" Text="Change Password" />
        <asp:Button ID="CancelPushButton" CommandName="Cancel"
                    runat="server" Text="Cancel" /><br />
        <asp:Literal ID="FailureText" runat="server"
                     EnableViewState="False" />
```

```
    </ChangePasswordTemplate>
    <SuccessTemplate>
        Your password has been changed!
        <asp:Button ID="ContinuePushButton" CommandName="Continue"
                    runat="server" Text="Continue" />
    </SuccessTemplate>
</asp:ChangePassword>
```

The text box controls of the ChangePasswordTemplate are all required. The other controls are optional. If you select the ID properties and the CommandName properties for the buttons appropriately, you don't have to write any additional code.

The CreateUserWizard Control

The CreateUserWizard control is the most powerful control of the login controls. It enables you to create registration pages within a couple of minutes. This control is a wizard control with two default steps: one for querying general user information and one for displaying a confirmation message. As the CreateUserWizard inherits from the base Wizard control, you can add as many wizard steps as you want. But when you just add a CreateUserWizard control to your page as follows, the result is really amazing, as shown in Figure 21-15.

```
<asp:CreateUserWizard ID="RegisterUser" runat="server"
                      BorderStyle="ridge" BackColor="aquamarine">
    <TitleTextStyle Font-Bold="true" Font-Names="Verdana" />
    <WizardSteps>
        <asp:CreateUserWizardStep runat="server">
        </asp:CreateUserWizardStep>
        <asp:CompleteWizardStep runat="server">
        </asp:CompleteWizardStep>
    </WizardSteps>
</asp:CreateUserWizard>
```

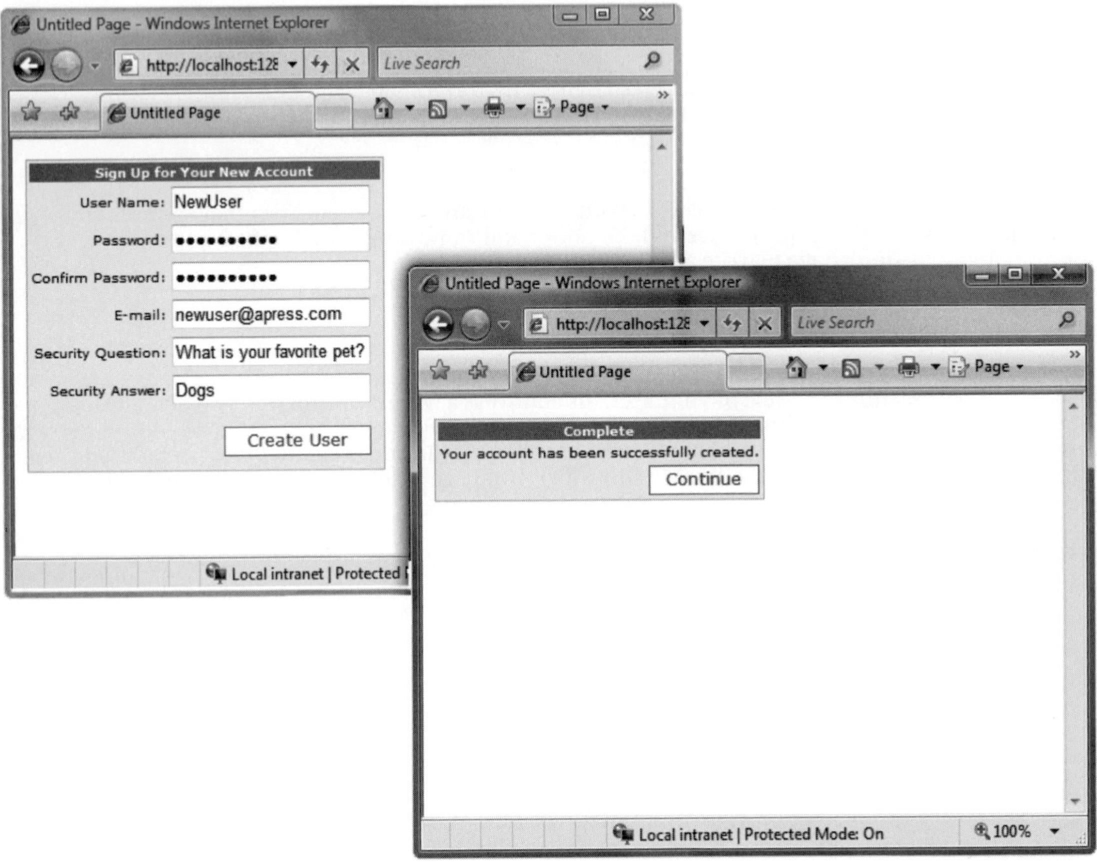

***Figure 21-15.** A simple CreateUserWizard control*

The default appearance of the control is, again, customizable through properties and styles. The control offers lots of styles, but the meaning of the styles is similar to the styles covered for the previous controls. In fact, this control includes the most complete list of styles, as it includes most of the fields presented in the previous controls as well. When you use the CreateUserWizard control as shown previously, you don't need to perform any special configuration. It automatically uses the configured membership provider for creating the user, and it includes two steps: the default CreateUserWizardStep that creates controls for gathering the necessary information and the CompleteWizardStep for displaying a confirmation message. Both steps are customizable through styles and properties or through templates. Although you can customize these two steps, you cannot remove them. If you use templates, you are responsible for creating the necessary controls, as follows:

```
<asp:CreateUserWizard ID="RegisterUser" runat="server"
                      BorderStyle="ridge" BackColor="aquamarine">
    <TitleTextStyle Font-Bold="True" Font-Names="Verdana" />
    <WizardSteps>
        <asp:CreateUserWizardStep runat="server">
            <ContentTemplate>
```

```
                <div align="right">
                <font face="Courier New">
                User Name:
                <asp:TextBox ID="UserName" runat="server" /><br />
                Password:
                <asp:TextBox ID="Password" runat="server"
                             TextMode="Password" /><br />
                Conform Password:
                <asp:TextBox ID="ConfirmPassword" runat="server"
                             TextMode="Password" /><br />
                Email:
                <asp:TextBox ID="Email" runat="server" /><br />
                Security Question:
                <asp:TextBox ID="Question" runat="server" /><br />
                Security Answer:
                <asp:TextBox ID="Answer" runat="server" /><br />
                <asp:Literal ID="ErrorMessage" runat="server"
                             EnableViewState="False" />
                </font>
                </div>
            </ContentTemplate>
        </asp:CreateUserWizardStep>
        <asp:CompleteWizardStep runat="server">
            <ContentTemplate>
                Your account has been successfully created.
                <asp:Button ID="ContinueButton" CommandName="Continue"
                            runat="server" Text="Continue" />
            </ContentTemplate>
        </asp:CompleteWizardStep>
    </WizardSteps>
</asp:CreateUserWizard>
```

Because the control is a wizard control, the first step doesn't require any buttons because a Next button is automatically displayed by the hosting wizard control. Depending on the configuration of the membership provider, some of the controls in the first step are required, and others are not, as listed in Table 21-13.

Table 21-13. *Required Controls and Optional Controls*

ID	Type	Required?	Comments
UserName	System.Web.UI.WebControls.TextBox	Yes	Always required
Password	System.Web.UI.WebControls.TextBox	Yes	Always required
ConfirmPassword	System.Web.UI.WebControls.TextBox	Yes	Always required
Email	System.Web.UI.WebControls.TextBox	No	Required only if the RequireEmail property of the CreateUserWizard control is set to true

ID	Type	Required?	Comments
Question	System.Web.UI.WebControls.TextBox	No	Required only if the underlying membership provider requires a password question
Answer	System.Web.UI.WebControls.TextBox	No	Required only if the underlying membership provider requires a password question
ContinueButton	Any control that supports bubbling	No	Not required at all, but if present, you need to set the CommandName to Continue

As soon as you start creating additional wizard steps, you will need to handle events and perform some actions within the event procedures. For example, if you collect additional information from the user with the wizard, you will have to store this information somewhere and therefore will need to execute some SQL statements against your database (assuming you are storing the information in a SQL Server database, for example). Table 21-14 lists the events specific to the CreateUserWizard control. The control also inherits all the events you already know from the Wizard control.

Table 21-14. *The CreateUserWizard Events*

Event	Description
ContinueButtonClick	Raised when the user clicks the Continue button in the last wizard step.
CreatingUser	Raised by the wizard before it creates the new user through the membership API.
CreatedUser	After the user has been created successfully, the control raises this event.
CreateUserError	If the creation of the user was not successful, this event is raised.
SendingMail	The control can send an e-mail to the created user if a mail server is configured. This event is raised by the control before the e-mail is sent so that you can modify the contents of the mail message.
SendMailError	If the control was unable to send the message—for example, because the mail server was unavailable—it raises this event.

Now you can just add a wizard step for querying additional user information, such as the first name and the last name, and automatically save this information to a custom database table. A valid point might be storing the information in the profile. But when running through the wizard, the user is not authenticated yet, so you cannot store the information into the profile, as this is available for authenticated users only. Therefore, you either have to store it in a custom database table or include a way for the user to edit the profile after the registration process.

Furthermore, the CreatedUser event is raised immediately after the CreateUserWizardStep has been completed successfully. Therefore, if you want to save additional data within this event, you have to collect this information in previous steps. For this purpose, it's sufficient to place other wizard steps prior to the <asp:CreateUserWizardStep> tag. In any other case you have to save the information in one of the other events (for example, the FinishButtonClick event). But because you cannot make sure that the user really runs through the whole wizard and clicks the Finish button, it makes sense to collect all the required information prior to the CreateUserWizardStep and then save any additional information through the CreatedUser event.

```
<asp:CreateUserWizard ID="RegisterUser" runat="server"
                        BorderStyle="ridge" BackColor="aquamarine"
                        OnCreatedUser="RegisterUser_CreatedUser"
    <TitleTextStyle Font-Bold="True" Font-Names="Verdana" />
    <WizardSteps>
        <asp:WizardStep ID="NameStep" AllowReturn="true">
            Firstname:
            <asp:TextBox ID="FirstnameText" runat="server" /><br />
            Lastname:
            <asp:TextBox ID="LastnameText" runat="server" /><br />
            Age:
            <asp:TextBox ID="AgeText" runat="server" />
        </asp:WizardStep>
        <asp:CreateUserWizardStep runat="server">
            ...
        </asp:CreateUserWizardStep>
        <asp:CompleteWizardStep runat="server">
            ...
        </asp:CompleteWizardStep>
    </WizardSteps>
</asp:CreateUserWizard>
```

With the previous wizard step alignment, you now can store additional information in your data store when the CreatedUser event is raised by the control, as follows:

```
protected void RegisterUser_CreatedUser(object sender, EventArgs e)
{
    short _Age;
    string _Firstname, _Lastname;

    // Find the correct wizard step
    WizardStepBase step = null;
    for (int i = 0; i < RegisterUser.WizardSteps.Count; i++)
    {
        if (RegisterUser.WizardSteps[i].ID == "NameStep")
        {
            step = RegisterUser.WizardSteps[i];
            break;
        }
    }

    if (step != null)
    {
        _Firstname = ((TextBox)step.FindControl("FirstnameText")).Text;
        _Lastname = ((TextBox)step.FindControl("LastnameText")).Text;
        _Age = short.Parse(((TextBox)step.FindControl("AgeText")).Text);
```

```
        // Store the information
        // This is just simple code you need to replace with code
        // for really storing the information
        System.Diagnostics.Debug.WriteLine(
           string.Format("{0} {1} {2}", _Firstname, _Lastname, _Age));
    }
}
```

In the CreatedUser event, the code just looks for the wizard step with the ID set to NameStep. Then it uses the FindControl method several times for getting the controls with the actual content. As soon as you have retrieved the controls where the user entered his first name, last name, and age, you can access their properties and perform any action you want with them.

In summary, the CreateUserWizard control is a powerful control based on top of the membership API and is customizable, just as the other login controls that ship with ASP.NET. With template controls, you have complete flexibility and control over the appearance of the login controls, and the controls still perform lots of work—especially interaction with membership—for you. And if you still want to perform actions yourself, you can handle several events of the controls.

Configuring Membership in IIS 7.x

The management console of IIS 7.x includes a full set of administration tools for configuring the ASP.NET membership API and providers. Furthermore, as the membership API is used in conjunction with ASP.NET forms authentication, you also can use the membership API with web applications not developed with ASP.NET, such as classic ASP or PHP applications.

Configuring Providers and Users

The first step for using the membership API after configuring forms authentication is the configuration of a membership provider. For that purpose, the IIS 7.x management console offers the new "Providers" feature configuration in the .NET category section, as outlined in Figure 21-16.

As you can see, this applet allows you to select different features through the combo box at the top of the screen. The features you can select in this combo box map to appropriate providers in ASP.NET. You can configure users, roles, and profiles this way directly from within the IIS management console (roles and authorization are covered in Chapter 23 in detail, and profiles are covered in Chapter 24 in detail). For example, the .NET Users feature shown in Figure 21-16 that's selected in the combo box maps to the membership API provider that is responsible for managing users of a web application. Just click the Add link in the task pane on the right border of the management console to add a new provider. This opens a dialog that lets you select the type of the provider supported by both the runtime and your application if you have custom provider classes deployed with it (you will read more on custom membership provider development in Chapter 26). Figure 21-17 shows the dialog for configuring a new provider for your application.

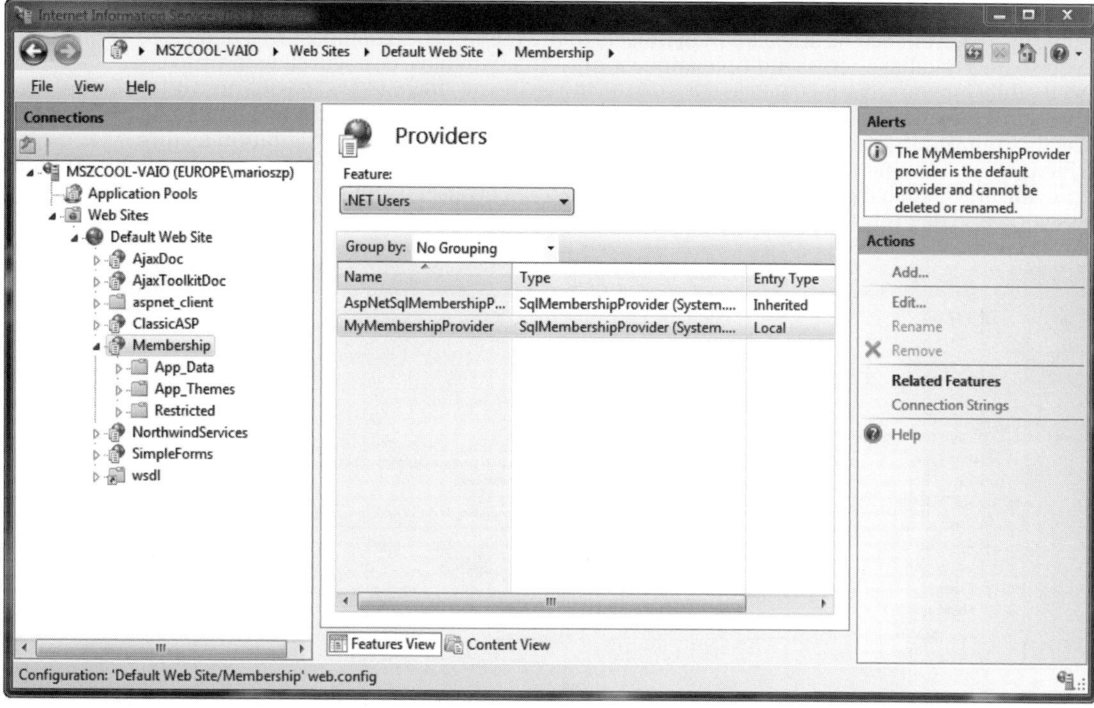

Figure 21-16. *The IIS 7.x .NET providers feature configuration*

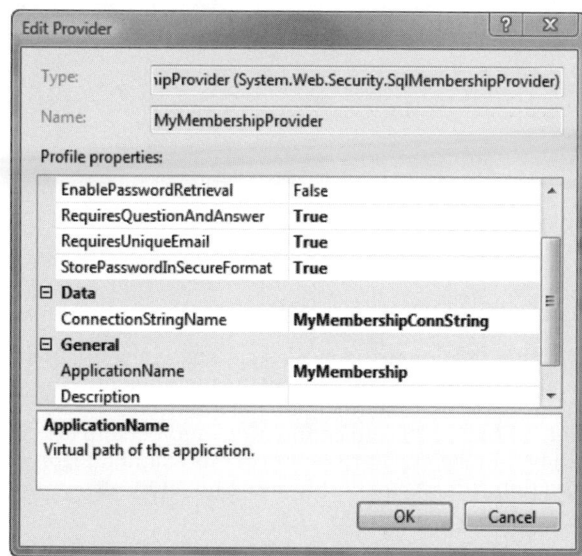

Figure 21-17. *Adding a new provider to your application*

This dialog allows you to configure the most common properties, including the applicationName property, which affects the association of objects in the membership database to a dedicated application if you share a database across multiple applications. After you have configured your provider successfully for your feature (such as .NET Users in Figures 21-16 and 21-17), you can work with the other administration features of the management console. For example, you can add and delete users directly from within the IIS management console using the .NET Users configuration feature, as shown in Figure 21-18. Within this configuration, the IIS 7.x management console uses the membership API for retrieving and displaying all the users available, creating new users, modifying users, resetting a user's password, and deleting users.

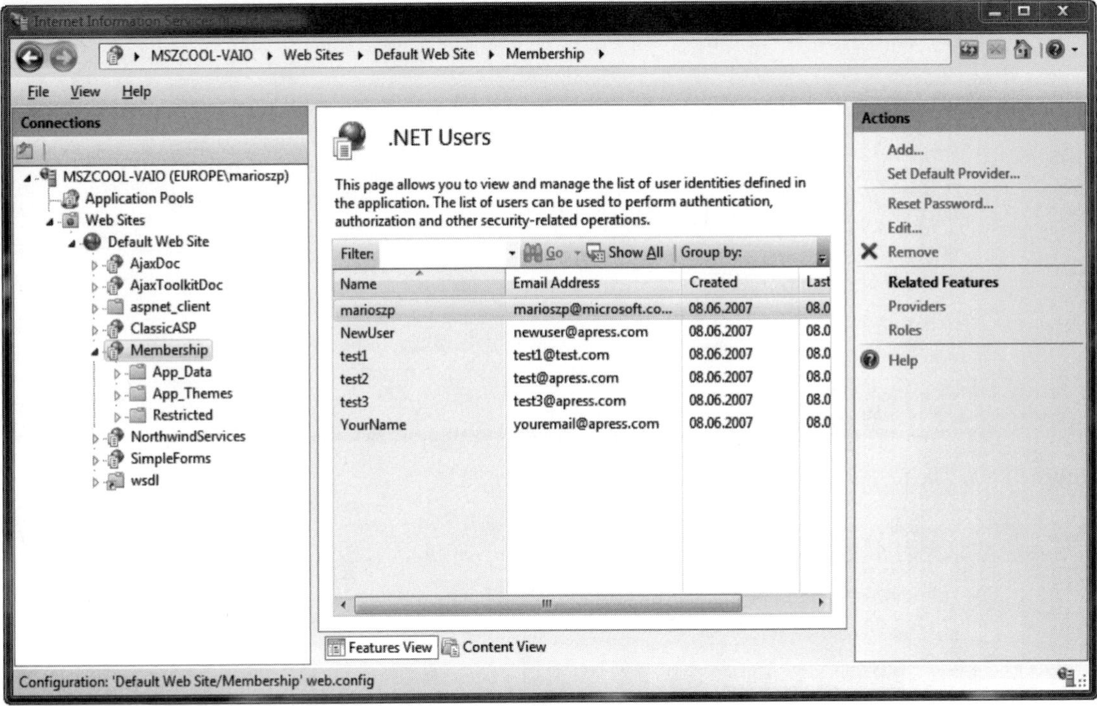

Figure 21-18. *Managing users directly from within IIS 7.x*

Using the Membership API with Other Applications

As outlined in Chapter 20, it is possible to use forms authentication with any web application configured in IIS 7.x when running IIS in ASP.NET integrated mode. That means you can use the membership API with any web application as well. You do so by configuring forms authentication for your web application (such as classic ASP or PHP), as explained in Chapter 20, and configuring membership providers for .NET users as well as .NET users, as outlined in the previous section of this chapter. Figure 21-19 shows the classic ASP page introduced in the section "IIS 7.x and Forms Authentication" in Chapter 20, together with an ASP.NET login page hosting the Login control.

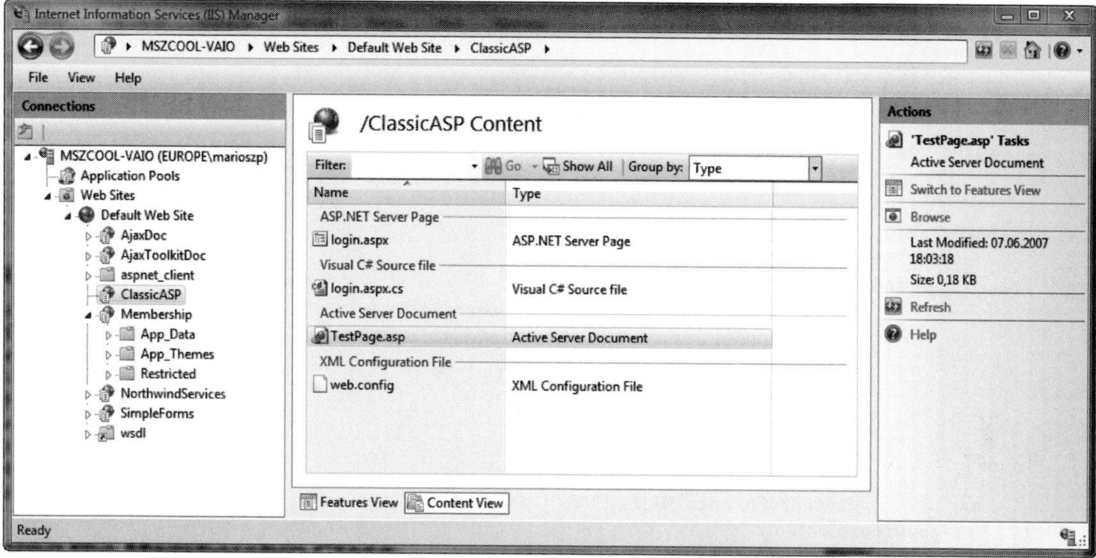

Figure 21-19. An ASP.NET login page hosting the Login control with a classic ASP page

Using Basic Authentication with Membership API

The extensibility model of IIS 7.x goes one step further and allows you to use the ASP.NET membership API and providers even for other types of authentication methods, such as HTTP Basic authentication. This is only possible when running IIS 7.x in ASP.NET integrated mode. That's because when running IIS in ASP.NET integrated mode, native HTTP modules and managed HTTP modules are executed in the same request-processing pipeline. This allows you to easily replace standard functionality implemented as an HTTP module with your own implementations.

For example, this allows you to create a custom module that implements the HTTP Basic authentication scheme and validates user accounts against your custom database using the membership API. You can use this module to replace the existing Basic authentication module. You need to know how Basic authentication works in detail to implement such a module. Unfortunately, you cannot extend the existing modules by using a .NET-based language directly, as most of these modules are native implementations (not even COM-based).

In the IIS online community at `http://www.iis.net`, you can find an article demonstrating how to implement a Basic authentication module using C# and how to plug it into IIS 7.x to replace the default Basic authentication module. This implementation allows you to use other accounts than Windows accounts (which are the default) in conjunction with Basic authentication. You can find this article at `http://learn.iis.net/page.aspx/170/developing-a-module-using-net`.

Now, you just configure the membership provider through the IIS management console as outlined in the previous section and that's it—membership is used together with forms authentication and a classic ASP page. The web.config looks as follows after completing the configuration:

```
<configuration>
    <system.web>
        <authentication mode="Forms">
            <forms cookieless="UseCookies" loginUrl="login.aspx" />
        </authentication>
        <authorization>
            <deny users="?" />
        </authorization>
        <membership defaultProvider="TestMembership">
            <providers>
                <add name="TestMembership"
                     type="System.Web.Security.SqlMembershipProvider"
                     connectionStringName="MembershipConn"
                     enablePasswordRetrieval="false"
                     enablePasswordReset="false"
                     requiresQuestionAndAnswer="false"
                     applicationName="MyMembership"
                     requiresUniqueEmail="false"
                     passwordFormat="Hashed" />
            </providers>
        </membership>
    </system.web>
    <system.webServer>
        <modules>
            <remove name="FormsAuthentication" />
            <add name="FormsAuthentication"
                 type="System.Web.Security.FormsAuthenticationModule"
                 preCondition="" />
        </modules>
    </system.webServer>
    <connectionStrings>
        <add connectionString="..." name="MembershipConn" />
    </connectionStrings>
</configuration>
```

You can integrate the membership API this way into any other web application configured on IIS 7.x as well. That allows a unification of your authentication infrastructure across all web applications if you want.

Using the Membership Class

In the following sections of this chapter, you will learn how you can use the underlying membership programming interface that is used by all the controls and the whole membership API infrastructure you just used. You will see that the programming interface is simple. It consists of a class called Membership with various properties and methods, and a class called MembershipUser that encapsulates the properties for a single user. The methods of the Membership class perform fundamental operations:

- Creating new users
- Deleting existing users
- Updating existing users

- Retrieving lists of users
- Retrieving details for one user
- Validating user credentials against the store

Many methods of the Membership class accept an instance of MembershipUser as a parameter or return one or even a collection of MembershipUser instances. For example, by retrieving a user through the Membership.GetUser method, setting properties on this instance, and then passing it to the UpdateUser method of the Membership class, you can simply update user properties. The Membership class and the MembershipUser class both provide the necessary abstraction layer between the actual provider and your application. Everything you do with the Membership class depends on your provider. This means if you exchange the underlying membership provider, this will not affect your application if the implementation of the membership provider is complete and supports all features propagated by the MembershipProvider base class.

All classes used for the membership API are defined in the System.Web.Security namespace. The Membership class just contains lots of static methods and properties. We will now walk you through the different types of tasks you can perform with the Membership class and related classes such as the MembershipUser.

Retrieving Users from the Store

The first task you will do is retrieve a single user and a list of users through the Membership class from the membership store. For this purpose, you just create a simple page with a GridView control for binding the users to the grid, as follows:

```
<html xmlns="http://www.w3.org/1999/xhtml" >
<head runat="server">
    <title>Display Users Page</title>
</head>
<body>
    <form id="form1" runat="server">
    <div>
        <asp:GridView ID="UsersGridView" runat="server"
                      DataKeyNames="UserName"
                      AutoGenerateColumns="False">
            <Columns>
                <asp:BoundField DataField="UserName" HeaderText="Username" />
                <asp:BoundField DataField="Email" HeaderText="Email" />
                <asp:BoundField DataField="CreationDate"
                                HeaderText="Creation Date" />
                <asp:CommandField ShowSelectButton="True" />
            </Columns>
        </asp:GridView>
        </div>
    </form>
```

As you can see, the GridView defines the UserName field as DataKeyName. This enables you to access the UserName value of the currently selected user directly through the grid's SelectedValue property. As most of the methods require the user name for retrieving more details, this is definitely useful. With this page in place, you can now add the following code to the Page_Load event procedure for loading the users from the membership store and binding them to the grid:

```
public partial class _Default : System.Web.UI.Page
{
    MembershipUserCollection _MyUsers;

    protected void Page_Load(object sender, EventArgs e)
    {
        _MyUsers = Membership.GetAllUsers();
        UsersGridView.DataSource = _MyUsers;

        if (!this.IsPostBack)
        {
            UsersGridView.DataBind();
        }
    }
}
```

Figure 21-20 shows the application in action.

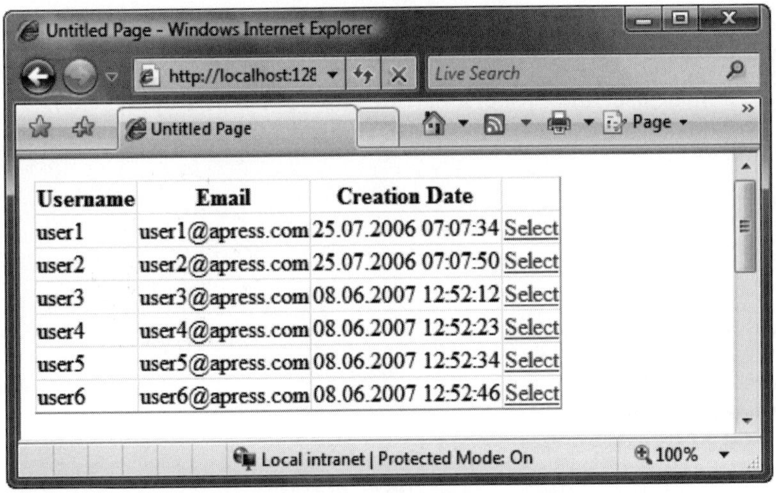
Untitled Page - Windows Internet Explorer
http://localhost:128
Live Search
Untitled Page
Page
Username
Email
Creation Date
user1
user1@apress.com
25.07.2006 07:07:34
Select
user2
user2@apress.com
25.07.2006 07:07:50
Select
user3
user3@apress.com
08.06.2007 12:52:12
Select
user4
user4@apress.com
08.06.2007 12:52:23
Select
user5
user5@apress.com
08.06.2007 12:52:34
Select
user6
user6@apress.com
08.06.2007 12:52:46
Select
Local intranet | Protected Mode: On
100%

Figure 21-20. *The custom user management application in action*

As you can see, the Membership class includes a GetAllUsers method, which returns an instance of type MembershipUserCollection. You can use this collection just like any other collection. Every entry contains all the properties of a single user. Therefore, if you want to display the details of a selected user, you just need to add a couple of controls for displaying the contents of the selected user in the previously created page, as follows:

```
Selected User:<br />
<table border="1" bordercolor="blue">
            <td>User Name:
        <td><asp:Label ID="UsernameLabel" runat="server" />
                <td>Email:
        <td><asp:TextBox ID="EmailText" runat="server" />
                <td>Password Question:
```

```
<td><asp:Label ID="PwdQuestionLabel" runat="server" />
        <td>Last Login Date:
<td><asp:Label ID="LastLoginLabel" runat="server" />
        <td>Comment:
<td><asp:TextBox ID="CommentTextBox" runat="server"
                TextMode="multiline" />
        <td>
<asp:CheckBox ID="IsApprovedCheck" runat="server" Text="Approved" />

<td>
<asp:CheckBox ID="IsLockedOutCheck" runat="Server" Text="Locked Out" />
```

You can then handle the SelectedIndexChanged event of the previously added GridView control for filling these fields with the appropriate values, as follows:

```
protected void UsersGridView_SelectedIndexChanged(object sender, EventArgs e)
{
    if (UsersGridView.SelectedIndex >= 0)
    {
        MembershipUser Current = _MyUsers[(string)UsersGridView.SelectedValue];

        UsernameLabel.Text = Current.UserName;
        PwdQuestionLabel.Text = Current.PasswordQuestion;
        LastLoginLabel.Text = Current.LastLoginDate.ToShortDateString();
        EmailText.Text = Current.Email;
        CommentTextBox.Text = Current.Comment;
        IsApprovedCheck.Checked = Current.IsApproved;
        IsLockedOutCheck.Checked = Current.IsLockedOut;
    }
}
```

As you can see, the MembershipCollection object requires the user name for accessing users directly. Methods from the Membership class such as GetUser require the user name as well. Therefore, you used the UserName field as content for the DataKeyNames property in the GridView previously. With an instance of the MembershipUser in your hands, you can access the properties of the user as usual.

Updating Users in the Store

Updating a user in the membership store is nearly as easy as retrieving the user from the store. As soon as you have an instance of MembershipUser in your hands, you can update properties such as the e-mail and comments as usual. Then you just call the UpdateUser method of the Membership class. You can do that by extending the previous code by adding a button to your page and inserting the following code in the button's Click event-handling routine:

```
protected void ActionUpdateUser_Click(object sender, EventArgs e)
{
    if (UsersGridView.SelectedIndex >= 0)
    {
        MembershipUser Current = _MyUsers[(string)UsersGridView.SelectedValue];

        Current.Email = EmailText.Text;
        Current.Comment = CommentTextBox.Text;
```

```
        Current.IsApproved = IsApprovedCheck.Checked;

        Membership.UpdateUser(Current);

        // Refresh the GridView
        UsersGridView.DataBind();
    }
}
```

The UpdateUser method just accepts the modified MembershipUser you want to update. Before the method is called, you have to update the properties on your instance. This has just one exception: the IsLockedOut property cannot be set. This property gets automatically set if the user has too many failed login attempts. If you want to unlock a user, you have to call the MembershipUser's UnlockUser method separately. Similar rules apply to the password. You cannot change the password directly by setting some properties on the MembershipUser. Furthermore, the MembershipUser class has no property for directly accessing the password at all. For this purpose, the Membership class itself supports a GetPassword method and a ChangePassword method that requires you to pass in the old and the new password. Retrieving the password through the GetPassword method is possible, but only if the password is not hashed in the underlying store. Therefore, GetPassword works only if the membership provider is configured to store the password either in clear text or encrypted in the underlying membership store.

Creating and Deleting Users

Creating users is as simple as using the rest of the membership API. You can create users by just calling the CreateUser method of the Membership class. Therefore, if you want to add the feature of creating users to your website, you can add a new page containing the necessary text boxes for entering the required information, then add a button, and finally handle the Click event of this button with the following code:

```
protected void ActionAddUser_Click(object sender, EventArgs e)
{
    try
    {
        MembershipCreateStatus Status;

        Membership.CreateUser(UserNameText.Text,
                              PasswordText.Text,
                              UserEmailText.Text,
                              PwdQuestionText.Text,
                              PwdAnswerText.Text, true,
                              out Status);

        StatusLabel.Text = "User created successfully!";
    }
    catch(Exception ex)
    {
        Debug.WriteLine("Exception: " + ex.Message);
        StatusLabel.Text = "Unable to create user!";
    }
}
```

The CreateUser method exists with several overloads. The easiest overload just accepts a user name and a password, while the more complex versions require a password question and answer as well. The CreateUser() method returns a new instance of MembershipUser representing the created user, while the MembershipCreateStatus object returns additional information about the creation status of the user. As the CreateUser() method already has a MembershipUser as a return value, the method returns the status as an output parameter. Depending on the provider's configuration, your call to simpler versions of CreateUser will succeed or fail. For example, the default membership provider requires you to include a password question and answer; therefore, if you don't provide them, a call to CreateUser will result in an exception.

Deleting users is as simple as creating users. The Membership class offers a DeleteUser() method that requires you to pass the user name as a parameter. It deletes the user as well as all related information, if you want, from the underlying membership store.

Validating Users

Last but not least, the Membership class provides a method for validating a membership user. If a user has entered his user name and password in a login mask, you can use the ValidateUser() method for programmatically validating the information entered by the user, as follows:

```
if (Membership.ValidateUser(UserNameText.Text, PasswordText.Text))
{
    FormsAuthentication.RedirectFromLoginPage(UserNameText.Text, false);
}
else
{
    // Invalid user name or password
}
```

Summary

In this chapter, you learned about the membership API, which provides you with a full-fledged infrastructure for managing users of your application. You can either use the WAT, the new security controls, or the membership API for accessing these base services. The membership API is provider-based. In other words, you can exchange the underlying store by changing the underlying provider without touching your application. In this chapter you used only SQL Server as a provider. Furthermore, you learned how you can configure membership providers and users directly from within the IIS 7.x management console, due to its tight integration with ASP.NET. You learned how to use the membership API even with non-ASP.NET applications, such as classic ASP applications or PHP applications. It is also possible to replace existing authentication modules of IIS 7.x to integrate the membership API with them. In Chapter 26 you will learn the necessary details for creating and configuring a custom membership provider. In the next chapter, you'll look at a different approach to validating user identity—Windows authentication.

CHAPTER 22

■ ■ ■

Windows Authentication

Forms authentication is a great approach if you want to roll your own authentication system using a back-end database and a custom login page. But what if you are creating a web application for a smaller set of known users who already have Windows user accounts? In these situations, it makes sense to use an authentication system that can leverage the existing user and group membership information.

The solution is *Windows authentication*, which matches web users to Windows user accounts that are defined on the local computer or another domain on the network. In this chapter, you'll learn how to use Windows authentication in your web applications. You'll also learn how to apply impersonation to temporarily assume another identity.

Introducing Windows Authentication

Unlike forms authentication, Windows authentication isn't built into ASP.NET. Instead, Windows authentication hands over responsibility of authentication to IIS. IIS asks the browser to authenticate itself by providing credentials that map to a Windows user account. If the user is successfully authenticated, IIS allows the web-page request and passes the user and role information onto ASP.NET so that your code can act on it in much the same way that it works with identity information in a forms authentication scenario.

Figure 22-1 shows the end-to-end flow.

Why Use Windows Authentication?

You would want to use Windows authentication for four main reasons:

- It involves little programming work on the developer's part.
- It allows you to use existing user logins.
- It provides a single authentication model for multiple types of applications.
- It allows you to use impersonation and Windows security.

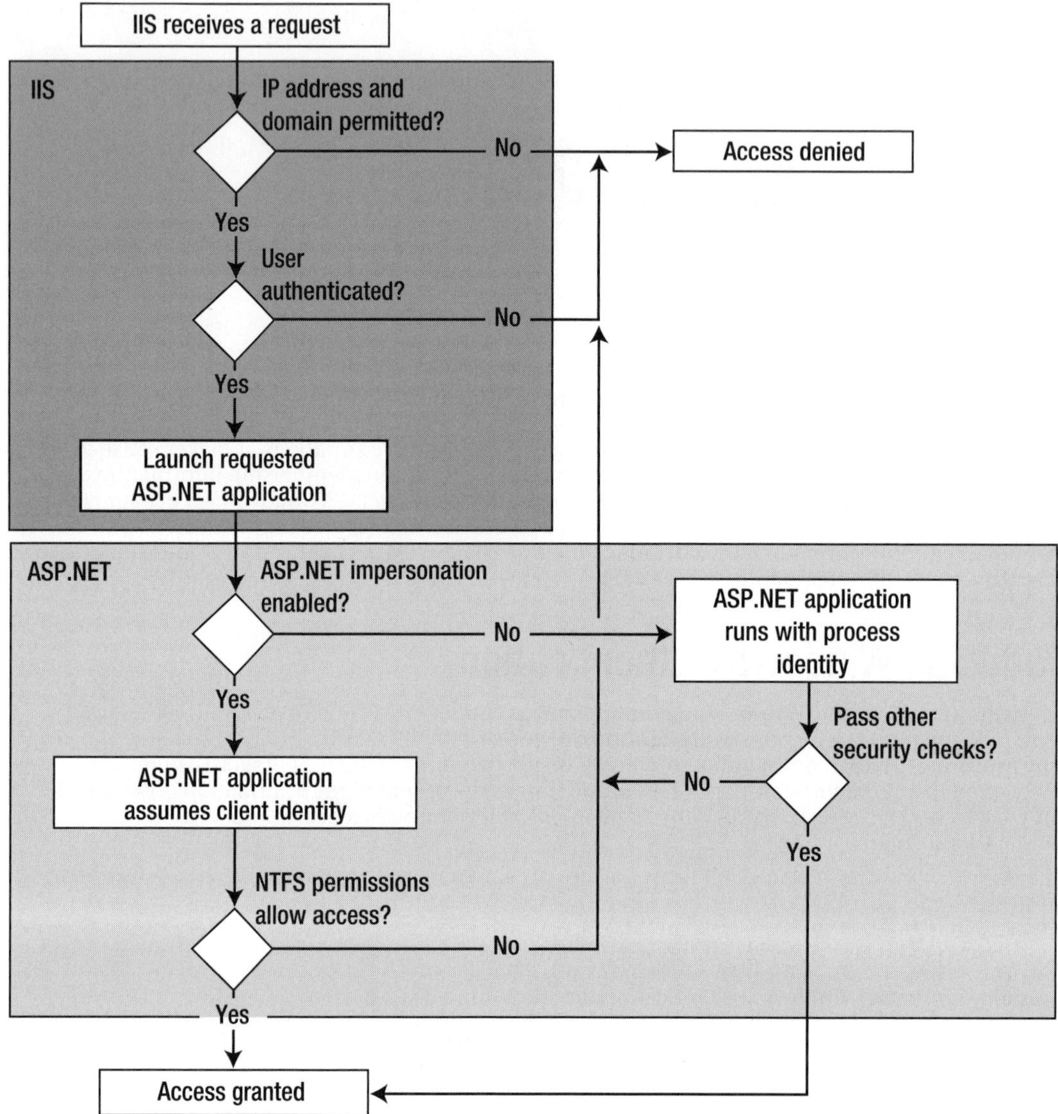

Figure 22-1. *The Windows authentication process*

The first reason is quite simple—using Windows authentication allows IIS and the client browser to take care of the authentication process so you don't need to create a login page, check a database, or write any custom code. Similarly, Windows already supports basic user account features such as password expiry, account lockout, and group membership.

The second, most important reason for using Windows authentication is that it allows you to leverage existing Windows accounts. Typically, you use Windows authentication for applications where the users are part of the same local network or intranet as your web server. This means you can authenticate users with the same credentials they use to log into their computers. Best of all, depending on the settings you use and the network architecture, you may be able to provide "invisible" authentication that works without forcing a separate login step. Instead, the browser simply uses the logged-in identity of the current user.

The third reason is really an appealing one. When working with Windows authentication, you have a single authentication model across different types of applications. For example, you can use the same authentication model for web services, ASP.NET applications, and Windows Communication Foundation-based services (wherever they are hosted). Therefore, Windows authentication can save you from the challenge of flowing identities between machine boundaries. With Kerberos in place, Windows offers a well-established mechanism for such scenarios. Actually, this goes along with the fourth reason for using Windows authentication.

Windows authentication allows you to take advantage of existing Windows security settings. For example, you can control access to files by setting Windows file-access permissions. However, it's important to remember that these permissions don't take effect automatically. That's because by default your web application runs using a fixed account (typically Network Service on IIS 7.x). You can change this behavior by carefully using Windows authentication and impersonation, as described in the "Impersonation" section of this chapter.

Why Would You Not Use Windows Authentication?

So, why would you not want to use Windows authentication?

- It's tied to Windows users.
- It's tied to Windows client machines.
- It doesn't provide much flexibility or control and can't be customized easily.

The first problem is that Windows authentication won't work unless the users you are authenticating already have valid Windows accounts. In a public website, this probably isn't the case. Even if you could create a Windows account for each visitor, it wouldn't be as efficient as a database approach for large numbers of users. It also has a potential security risk, because Windows user accounts can have permissions to the web server computer or other network computers. You might not want to risk granting these abilities to your website users.

The second problem is that some of the authentication methods that IIS uses require users to have compatible software on their computers. This limits your ability to use Windows authentication for users who are using non-Microsoft operating systems or for users who aren't using Internet Explorer.

The final main problem is that Windows authentication doesn't give you any control over the authentication process. Also, you have no easy way to add, remove, and manage Windows account information programmatically or to store other user-specific information with the user credentials. As you learned in the previous chapter, all these features are easy to add to forms authentication, but they don't play any part in Windows authentication.

Mechanisms for Windows Authentication

When you implement Windows authentication, IIS uses one of three possible authentication strategies to authenticate each request it receives:

Basic authentication: The user name and password are passed as clear text. This is the only form of authentication supported by all browsers as part of the HTML standard.

Digest authentication: The user name and password are not transmitted. Instead, a cryptographically secure hash with this information is sent.

Integrated Windows authentication: The user name and password are not transmitted. Instead, the identity of a user already logged into Windows is passed automatically as a token. This is the only form of authentication that takes place transparently (without user intervention).

The following sections discuss these options.

■ **Note** There are other less commonly used protocols for Windows authentication. One example is certificate-based authentication. If you use this approach, you must distribute a digital certificate to each client and map each certificate to the appropriate Windows account. Unfortunately, this technique is rife with administrative and deployment headaches. Another option is Advanced Digest authentication, which works essentially the same way as Digest authentication but stores the passwords more securely.

Basic Authentication

The most widely supported authentication protocol is Basic authentication. Almost all web browsers support it. When a website requests client authentication using Basic authentication, the web browser displays a login dialog box for user name and password, like the one shown in Figure 22-2.

Figure 22-2. *A login dialog box for Basic authentication*

After a user provides this information, the data is transmitted to the web server (in this case localhost). Once IIS receives the authentication data, it attempts to authenticate the user with the corresponding Windows account.

The key limitation of Basic authentication is that it isn't secure—at least not on its own. User name and password credentials obtained via Basic authentication are transmitted between the client and server as clear text. The data is encoded (not encrypted) into a Base64 string that eavesdroppers can easily read. In Windows Vista Microsoft has even modified the login dialog to display a warning if the connection is not secure (meaning SSL/TLS is not used for communicating with the web server), and

Basic authentication is used, as you can see in Figure 22-2. For this reason, you should use Basic authentication only in situations where there's no need to protect user credentials, or only in conjunction with an HTTP wire encryption protocol such as SSL. This way, the data that would otherwise be clearly visible to any network sniffing utility will be encrypted using complex algorithms. (You can find more information on SSL in Chapter 19.)

Digest Authentication

Digest authentication, like Basic authentication, requires the user to provide account information using a login dialog box that is displayed by the browser. Unlike Basic authentication, however, Digest authentication passes a hash of the password, rather than the password. (*Digest* is another name for *hash*, which explains the name of this authentication scheme.) Because a hash is used, the password is never sent across the network, thereby preventing it from being stolen even if you aren't using SSL.

The process of authenticating a user with Digest authentication works like this:

1. The unauthenticated client requests a restricted web page.
2. The server responds with an HTTP 401 response. This response includes a *nonce* value—a randomly generated series of bytes. The web server ensures that each nonce value is unique before it issues it.
3. The client uses the nonce, the password, the user name, and some other values to create a hash. This hash value, known as the `digest`, is sent back to the server along with the plain-text user name.
4. The server uses the nonce value, its stored password for the user name, and the other values to create a hash. It then compares this hash to the one provided by the client. If they match, then the authentication succeeds.

Since the nonce value changes with each authentication request, the digest is not very useful to an attacker. The original password cannot be extracted from it. Similarly, because it incorporates a random nonce, the digest cannot be used for *replay attacks*, in which an attacker attempts to gain access at a later time by resending a previously intercepted digest.

In theory, Digest authentication is a standard, and web servers and web browsers should all be able to use Digest authentication to exchange authentication information. Unfortunately, Microsoft interpreted a part of the Digest authentication specification in a slightly different way than other organizations, such as the Apache Foundation (which provides the Apache web server) and the Mozilla project (which provides the Mozilla web browser). Currently, IIS Digest authentication works only with Internet Explorer 5.0 and later.

Another limitation of Digest authentication in IIS is that it functions only when the virtual directory being authenticated is running on or controlled by a Windows Active Directory domain controller.

Integrated Windows Authentication

Integrated Windows authentication is the most convenient authentication standard for WAN-based and LAN-based intranet applications, because it performs authentication without requiring any client interaction. When IIS asks the client to authenticate itself, the browser sends a token that represents the Windows user account of the current user. If the web server fails to authenticate the user with this information, a login dialog box is shown where the user can enter a different user name and password.

For Integrated Windows authentication to work, both the client and the web server must be on the same local network or intranet. That's because Integrated Windows authentication doesn't actually transmit the user name and password information. Instead, it coordinates with the domain server or Active Directory instance where it is logged in and gets that computer to send the authentication information to the web server.

The protocol used for transmitting authentication information is either NTLM (NT LAN Manager) authentication or Kerberos 5—depending on the operating system version of the client and the server. If both are running Windows 2000 or higher and both machines are running in an Active Directory domain, Kerberos is used as the authentication protocol; otherwise, NTLM authentication will be used. Both protocols are extremely secure (Kerberos is the most secure protocol currently available), but they are limited. Therefore, in general, integrated authentication works only on Internet Explorer and is not supported in non-Internet Explorer clients. Kerberos works only for machines running Windows 2000 or higher, and neither protocol can work across a proxy server. In addition, Kerberos requires some additional ports to be open on firewalls. In the following section, you will learn the basics of the authentication protocols used for Integrated Windows authentication. These concepts will help you understand the configuration steps, especially for impersonation and delegation.

NT LAN Manager Authentication

NTLM authentication is integrated into the Windows operating system since it has built-in network support. NTLM authenticates clients through a challenge/response mechanism that is based on a three-way handshake between the client and the server. Everything you will learn about in this section takes place on the operating system automatically. Of course, this works only if the client and the server are running Windows.

The client starts the communication by sending a message to the server, which indicates that the client wants to talk to the server. The server generates a 64-bit random value called the *nonce*. The server responds to the client's request by returning this nonce. This response is called the *challenge*. Now the client operating system asks the user for a user name and password. Immediately after the user has entered this information, the system hashes the password. This password hash—called the *master key*—will then be used for encrypting the nonce. Together with the user name, the client transmits the encrypted nonce in his *response* to the server (completing the challenge/response mechanism).

The server now needs to validate the returned nonce. Depending on whether the user is a local user or a domain user, this validation takes place locally or remotely on the domain controller. In both cases, the user's master key, which is the hashed version of the password, is retrieved from the security account database. This master key then encrypts the clear-text nonce again on the server (of course, the server has cached the clear-text nonce before it transmits the data to the client). If the re-created encrypted version of the nonce matches the encrypted version returned from the client, the user is authenticated successfully, and a logon session is created on the server for the user. Figure 22-3 shows the process flow.

As you can see, the password is never transmitted across the wire. Even the hashed version of the password is never transmitted. This makes NTLM really secure. But there is an even more secure protocol with additional possibilities, as you will see in the next section.

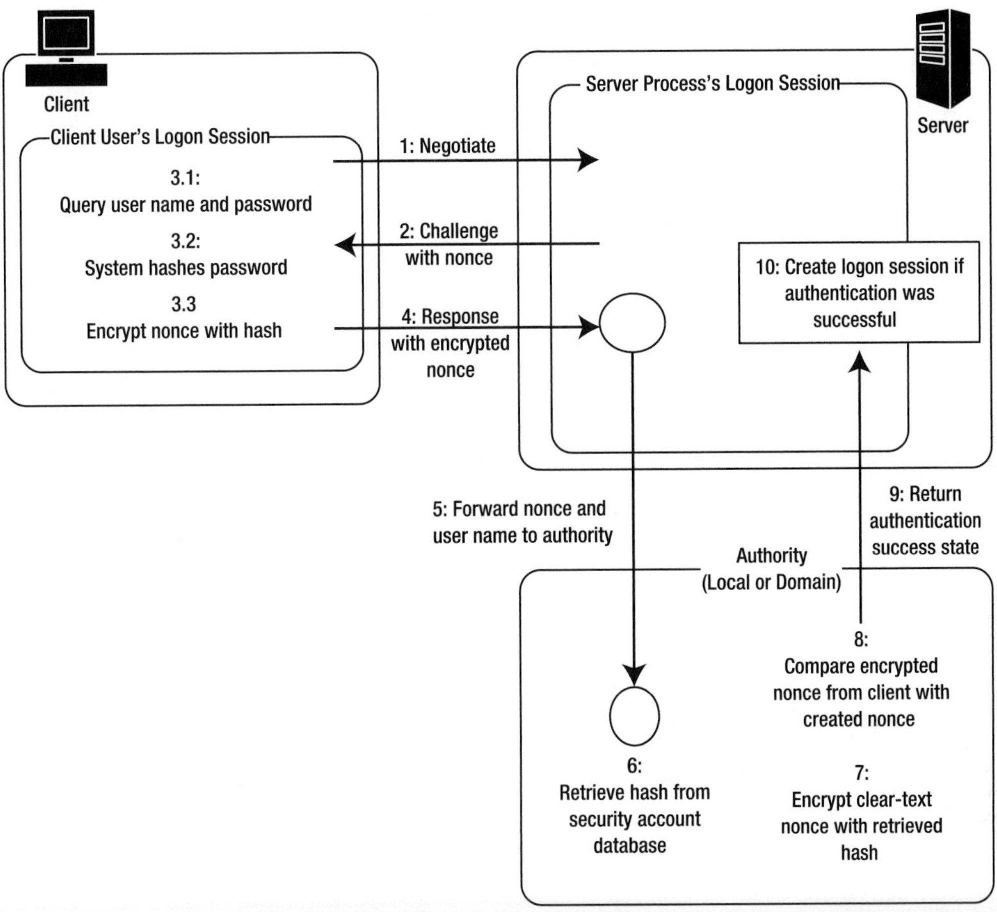

Figure 22-3. The NTLM protocol at a glance

Kerberos Authentication: A Short Introduction

Currently, Kerberos 5 is the most secure authentication protocol available. It is a well-known public standard created by the IETF (Internet Engineering Task Force), and it implements a ticket-based authentication protocol. When activating Integrated Windows authentication, Windows will use Kerberos automatically under the following circumstances:

- The client and the server are running Windows 2000 or higher.
- An Active Directory Domain with a primary domain controller (which automatically plays the role of the key distribution center) is available in the network.

In any other case, Windows will select NTLM as the authentication protocol. Although covering Kerberos in detail requires a book of its own, you will learn about the basic concepts in this chapter. These concepts will help you understand the necessary configuration tasks and when each feature will work. For example, one of the big differences between NTLM and Kerberos is that Kerberos supports both impersonation and delegation, while NTLM supports impersonation only.

Delegation is based on the same concept as impersonation. It involves merely performing actions on behalf of the client's identity. But while impersonation just works within the scope of one machine, delegation works across the network as well. This means the authentication ticket of the original client's identity can be passed to another server in the network if the originally accessed server machine has the permission to do so. You will learn more about impersonation and delegation later, in the "Impersonation" section. For now, it's important to understand that Kerberos supports both impersonation and delegation, while NTLM and other Windows authentication techniques such as Basic or Digest authentication support impersonation only.

The core component of a Kerberos system is the KDC (key distribution center), which is responsible for issuing tickets and managing credentials. In the Windows world, an Active Directory primary domain controller plays the role of the KDC. Every actor (meaning all the clients and all the servers) involved in the authentication process has to trust the KDC. It manages all the user and computer accounts and issues so-called *authentication tickets* and *session tickets*. Authentication tickets are issued after a successful authentication of a user or a machine, and are used for requesting any further tickets, such as session tickets. Session tickets are then used for establishing secure communication sessions between machines in the domain. This is another big difference when comparing Kerberos to NTLM: while NTLM works for workgroup scenarios without a central authority, Kerberos requires a central authority for issuing any type of ticket. Therefore, for Kerberos to work, you require a connection to an Active Directory domain controller. Figure 22-4 shows the flow for authenticating a user and then establishing a session between the client and the simple member server of a domain.

The following section explains the basics about Kerberos authentication and tickets, which are demonstrated in Figure 22-4 (the steps in the numbered list map to the numbers in the figure):

1. Every user authentication process starts with submitting a request to the authentication service, which runs on the KDC (Active Directory Domain Controller in Figure 22-4). This request contains the user name of the user to be authenticated. The KDC reads the user's master key from the security account database. Again, this is the hashed version of the user's password.
2. Afterward, it creates a TGT (ticket-granting ticket). This ticket contains a session key for the user's session as well as an expiration date and time. Before the ticket is returned to the client, the server encrypts it using the user's master key.
3. With only the correct password entered on the client, the client operating system can create the correct master key (the hash) for successfully decrypting the TGT received from the server. If decryption of the TGT succeeds on the client, the user is authenticated successfully.
4. Finally, the client caches the TGT locally.
5. When the client wants to communicate with another member server in the network, it first has to ask the KDC for a session ticket. For this purpose, it sends the locally cached TGT to a ticket-granting service that runs on the KDC. This service validates the TGT, and if it's still valid (not expired, not tampered with, and so on), it generates a session key for the communication session between the client and the member server. This session key is then encrypted with the client's master key. In addition, the session key is packaged into an ST (session ticket), which contains additional expiration information for the server. This session ticket is encrypted with the member server's master key. Of course, both the server and the client are well known to the KDC, as somewhere in the past both have been *joined* to the domain (joining a machine to a domain means establishing a trust relationship between this machine and the KDC). Therefore, the KDC knows the client's and the member server's master keys and can use them for encrypting the information accordingly.

6. Both the encrypted session key and the encrypted session ticket are forwarded to the client.
7. The client decrypts the session key and keeps a local copy of this session key in a local cache.
8. Afterwards the client forwards the encrypted session ticket to the server. The KDC has encrypted the session ticket for the server using the server's master key, as outlined in step 5.
9. If the server can successfully decrypt and validate the session ticket received from the client, the communication session will be established.
10. Both the client and the server use the previously generated session key for encrypting the communication traffic. As soon as the session ticket has expired, the whole operation takes place again.

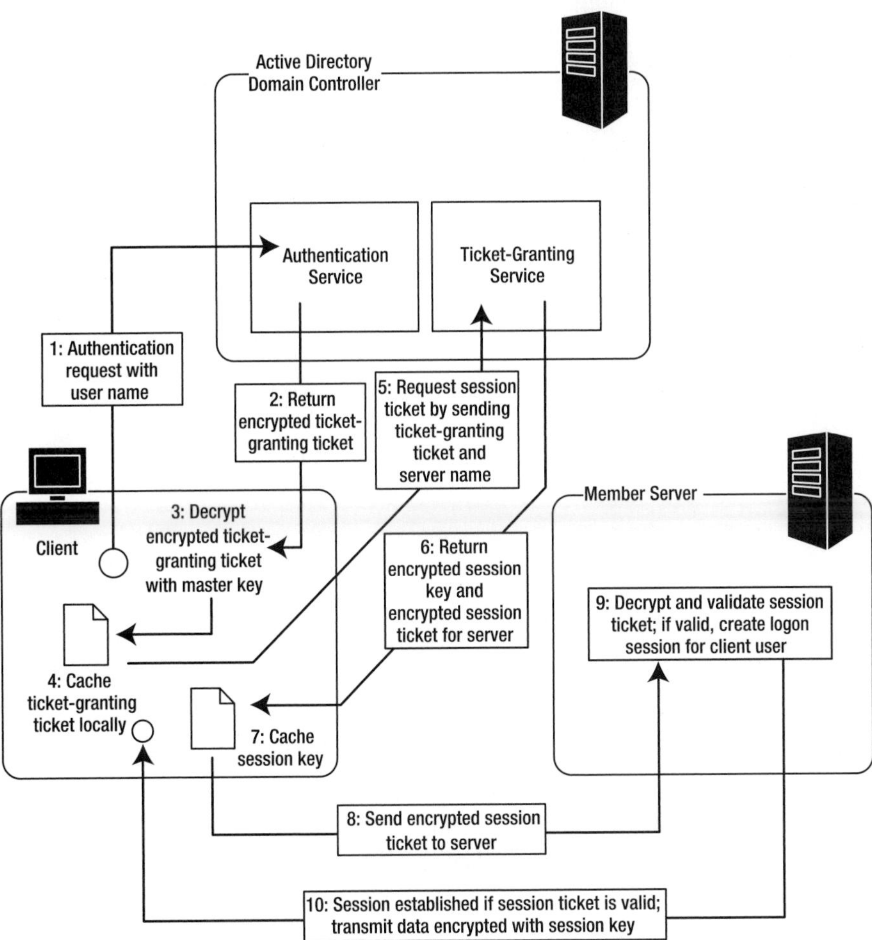

Figure 22-4. Kerberos authentication and tickets

Every ticket—session tickets and ticket-granting tickets—is equipped with capabilities. Capabilities of a ticket are a set of defined properties that are required for certain features, such as impersonation or delegation. For example, equipped with the right set of properties (capabilities), tickets can be used for impersonating the client user on the server or delegating the client's identity to another server. If the client and the KDC do not include these capabilities (set of properties) into the ticket, features related to these capabilities would not work. For example, if the ticket does not include the necessary information for impersonating a user, impersonation will not work. From the security perspective, this is a good design, as the client and the server can decide whether certain features are allowed or not just by including or not including certain properties in the ticket. Exactly for this purpose, the user account and the server account need additional permissions, as you will see in the "Impersonation" section of this chapter.

Covering these concepts in detail would require a book on its own. The idea of this discussion of the basic concepts of NTLM and Kerberos is to give you enough understanding to complete the necessary configuration steps to make impersonation and delegation work in your environment. In most cases, if something doesn't work with impersonation (or delegation), it's because the domain controller or the KDC is incorrectly configured (if you are not using Active Directory) or because the expiration date of the ticket is not set appropriately (it should not be set too long, but not too short either).

Although covering these topics in great detail requires an entire book, this overview will allow you to understand how the protocol works and what the requirements for different usage scenarios are.

Implementing Windows Authentication

To use Windows authentication in an ASP.NET application and have access to the user identity in ASP.NET, you need to take three steps:

1. Configure the type of Windows authentication in IIS.
2. Configure ASP.NET to use the IIS authentication information using the web.config file.
3. Restrict anonymous access for a web page, a subdirectory, or the entire application.

The first two steps are just one step in IIS 7.x when running in ASP.NET integrated mode, as its new management console directly configures your application's web.config file as required, in addition to the IIS configuration.

Configuring IIS 7.x

When running IIS 7.x, Windows authentication is implemented through a module in the HTTP modules pipeline. This pipeline is a mixture of native modules shipping with IIS and managed modules shipping with ASP.NET. The big advantage of this model is that you can use standard ASP.NET HTTP modules for all applications configured in IIS 7.x—even applications not based on ASP.NET.

Another big advantage of IIS 7.x is a unification of the configuration system as introduced in Chapter 18, which means you do not need to configure certain configuration options in IIS 7.x and ASP.NET separately. You can do all the configuration directly through the IIS management console. IIS performs the configuration in its central configuration store (applicationHost.config, as you learned in Chapter 18) and in the application's web.config as necessary. In IIS 7.x you can configure the authentication methods via the authentication configuration feature of the management console, as you can see in Figure 22-5.

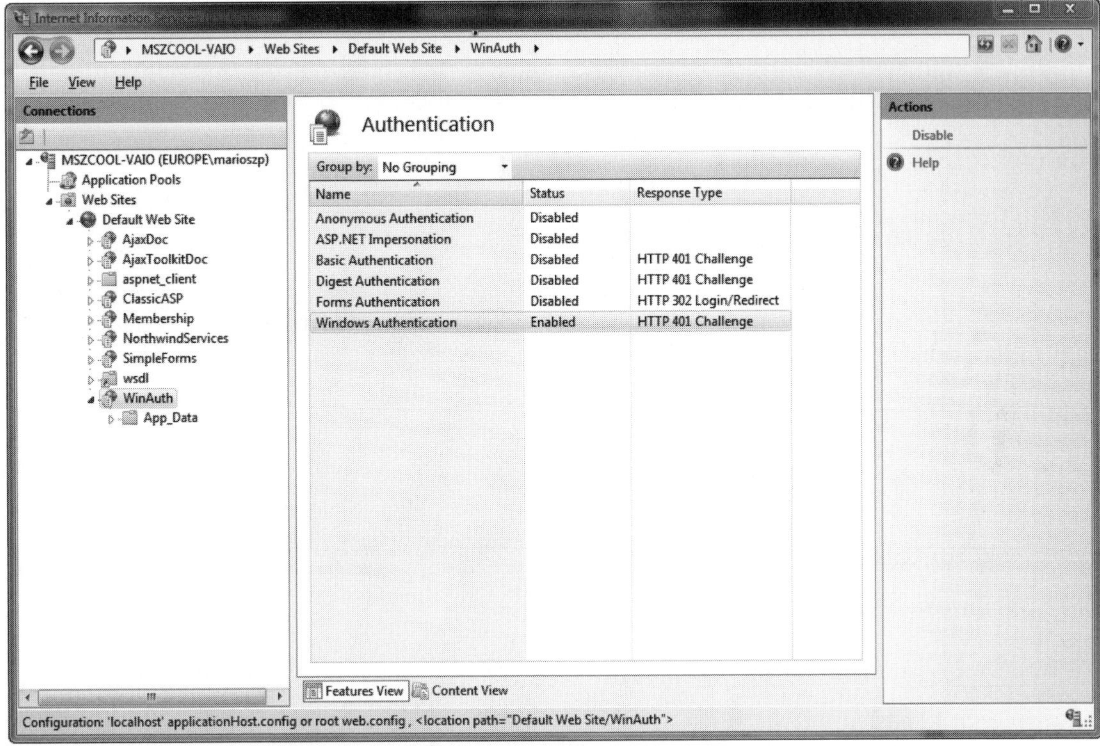

Figure 22-5. *Authentication configuration feature of IIS 7.x*

You can just enable or disable some authentication modules, such as the Windows authentication module, by clicking the appropriate link in the Actions task pane on the right border of the console (for example, Enable or Disable). Other authentication modules, such as the Basic authentication module, offer more detailed settings by clicking the Edit link on the Actions task pane, as you can see in Figure 22-6.

As shown in Figure 22-6, these are the default domain settings used for Basic authentication. This domain is used as a default domain if the user logs into the website without specifying a domain in the format DOMAIN\Username when logging in through the authentication dialog.

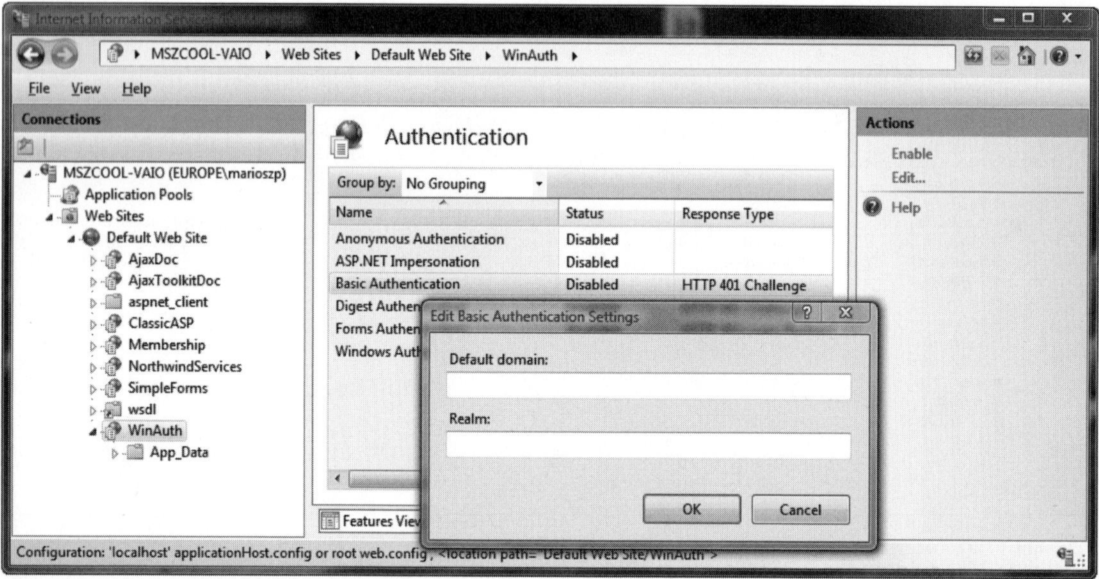

Figure 22-6. Configuring Basic authentication details

Whenever performing this configuration, IIS 7.x updates your application's web.config file, and if necessary its central applicationHost.config configuration file, which you learned about in Chapter 18. How the files get updated and which settings reside in which of these two files depends on the feature delegation configuration you learned about in Chapter 18. By default, web server-specific modules are configured centrally in the applicationHost.config configuration file, and ASP.NET-based configurations are automatically updated in your application's web.config file. In any case, that means after performing this configuration through the IIS 7.x management console you do not need to perform any additional, manual configuration steps in your application's web.config.

Configuring ASP.NET

Once you've configured IIS, the authentication process happens automatically. However, if you are using the Visual Studio test web server and you want to be able to access the identity information for the authenticated user in your ASP.NET application, you need to manually configure the web.config file of your ASP.NET application to use Windows. This configuration looks as follows:

```
<configuration>
    <system.web>
        <!-- Other settings omitted. -->
        <authentication mode="Windows"/>
    </system.web>
</configuration>
```

The preceding configuration tells ASP.NET that you want to use the Windows authentication module. The WindowsAuthenticationModule HTTP module will then handle the AuthenticateRequest event of the application to extract the identity previously authenticated by the web server and provide it to the web application. This is true independent from the underlying version of IIS!

Deeper Into the IIS 7.x Pipeline

So far, you've considered the configuration essentials. However, when you configure IIS 7.x to use Basic or Windows authentication, it actually perform a bit more configuration work that you probably realize.

To understand why, you first need to know that IIS uses two HTTP modules for performing dedicated parts of the authentication process, as you can see in Figure 22-7. One of these modules is the native one shipping with IIS 7.x, and the other one is the module shipping with ASP.NET itself.

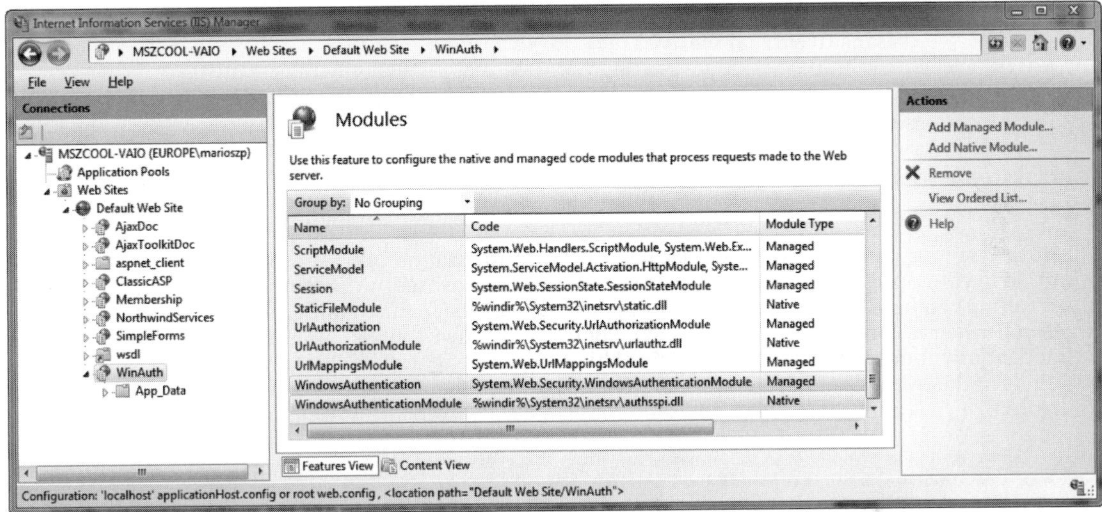

***Figure 22-7.** Modules implementing Windows authentication*

The WindowsAuthenticationModule module is a native HTTP module provided by IIS 7.x, while the module named only WindowsAuthentication is the managed module provided by ASP.NET. The native module is the web server's implementation of the authentication protocol itself. For Basic authentication, this is the BasicAuthenticationModule, and for Windows authentication, it is the WindowsAuthenticationModule. These modules are responsible for handling the native authentication protocol. For example, in the case of Windows authentication, the module is responsible for handling the NTLM challenge/response or the Kerberos handshake, as outlined in the section "Integrated Windows Authentication" earlier in this chapter. The managed module ships with ASP.NET. The managed module is responsible for extracting Windows user information for the user authenticated by the native module. After extracted, the Windows user information is available in your application—as is the case on any version of IIS.

That means that when configuring Windows, Basic, or Digest authentication through the IIS 7.x management console, two configurations need to be performed: first it needs to configure ASP.NET for Windows authentication as outlined earlier, and second it needs to configure the native authentication module. The native module is configured either in the central applicationHost.config configuration of the web server, or in the web.config file of your application, depending on the feature delegation configuration of the web server. The central configuration applicationHost.config is located in the inetsrv\config subdirectory of your system directory. For example, on a 32-bit Windows version this would be \Windows\system32\inetsrv\config.

By default, IIS 7.x feature delegation is configured so that your web.config inherits the settings from the central applicationHost.config configuration for the native authentication modules, such as the native BasicAuthenticationModule. That means your web.config file contains only the ASP.NET-specific configuration. You configure the native module in the central applicationHost.config configuration, as follows:

```
<location path="Default Web Site/WinAuth">
    <system.webServer>
        <security>
            <authentication>
                <anonymousAuthentication enabled="true" />
                <windowsAuthentication enabled="false" />
                <basicAuthentication enabled="false"
                                     realm=""
                                     defaultLogonDomain="MSZCOOL-VAIO" />
            </authentication>
        </security>
    </system.webServer>
</location>
```

However, you can change your feature delegation configuration of IIS 7.x so that even these settings are stored in your application's web.config file. This would allow xcopy deployment of your application, as any setting can be stored directly in the web.config file (if the feature configuration delegation of the target web server is configured appropriately). Figure 22-8 shows the IIS 7.x feature configuration with authentication modules selected. You can find the feature configuration option when clicking the top-level node of the tree view on the left side of the management console. Feature delegation is always configured for the whole web server, and therefore affects any web application or virtual directory!

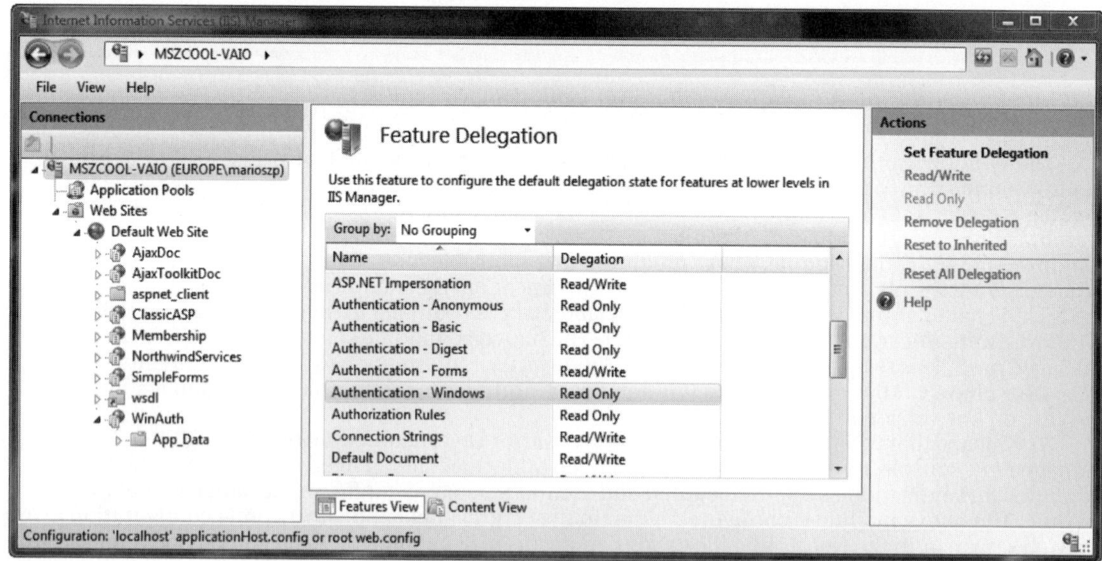

Figure 22-8. *The IIS 7.x feature configuration for authentication modules*

As you can see, the feature delegation for authentication modules provided by IIS 7.x natively, such as Basic, Digest, and Windows authentication, is set to Read Only. That means these settings are configured by the management console in the central applicationHost.config configuration file, and inherited by your local web.config file. It even means that configuration settings for these modules are not allowed to appear in an application's web.config configuration. Therefore, you will not find any configuration settings for these modules in your local web.config file, by default.

If you change the feature delegation configuration for these modules (or one of these modules) to Read/Write, the configuration will be included in your web.config file as well. That means if you configure the feature delegation for Basic authentication and Windows authentication to the setting Read/Write, the following section will be added to your web.config file. It will be added when configuring one (or both) of these authentication methods for your web application using the authentication configuration feature of the IIS 7.x management console:

```
<configuration>
    <appSettings />
    <connectionStrings />
    <system.web>
            <compilation debug="true" />
                <authentication mode="Windows" />
    </system.web>
    <system.webServer>
              <security>
                    <authentication>
                           <windowsAuthentication enabled="true" />
                           <basicAuthentication enabled="true"
                             realm=""
                             defaultLogonDomain="TestDomain" />
                    </authentication>
              </security>
    </system.webServer>
</configuration>
```

As you can see in the preceding web.config file, the configuration of the Windows authentication HTTP module shipping with ASP.NET resides in the <system.web> section. Any configuration specific to native HTTP modules typically shipping with IIS 7.x is added to the <system.webServer> configuration section. However, you need to bear one additional thing in mind. If you configure settings for native modules in the <system.webServer> section of your web.config, even though the central feature delegation configuration is set to Read Only, you will retrieve an HTTP 500 internal server error when trying to request the page. Even the IIS 7.x management console will respond with an error message when trying to configure the affected features, as shown in Figure 22-9.

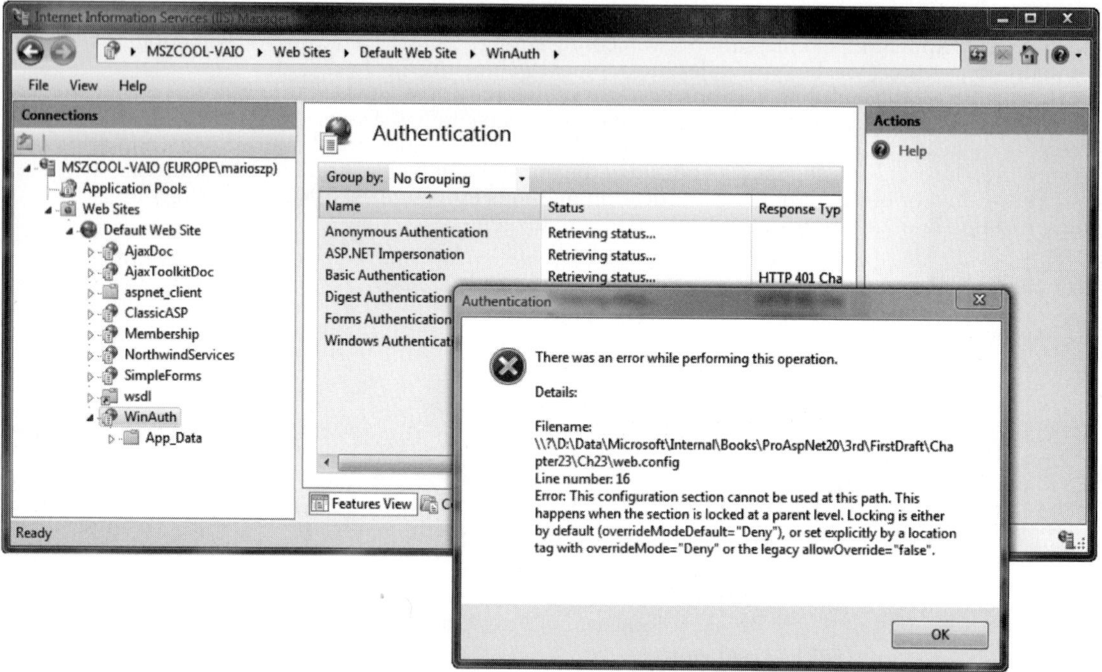

Figure 22-9. *Configuration error with invalid web.config according to feature delegation*

In that case, you need to manually remove invalid web.config configuration entries from your web.config file.

In general, unifying the configuration model and feature delegation is a powerful utility for administrators and developers. Having feature delegation enabled as outlined earlier would allow xcopy deployment of your web applications to IIS. All you need to do is add a virtual directory or web application, and all the remaining configuration settings reside directly in your web.config file of your application. At the same time, administrators can determine exactly which settings can be overridden in web.config files to strengthen security. Remember that by default, feature delegation configuration is disabled for many modules. These modules are configured in the central applicationHost.config configuration of IIS 7.x and not through the application's web.config. You can find a complete list just by opening the feature configuration of your local web server, as outlined earlier and in Chapter 18.

Denying Access to Anonymous Users

As described earlier, you can force users to log on by modifying IIS virtual directory settings or by using authorization rules in the web.config file. The second approach is generally preferred. Not only does it give you more flexibility, but it also makes it easier to verify and modify authorization rules after the application is deployed to a production web server.

Chapter 23 describes authorization in detail. For now, you'll consider only the simple technique of denying access to all unauthenticated users. To do this, you must use the <authorization> element of the web.config file to add a new authorization rule, as follows:

```
<configuration>
    <system.web>
        <!-- Other settings omitted. -->
        <authorization>
            <deny users="?" />
        </authorization>
    </system.web>
</configuration>
```

The question mark (?) is a wildcard character that matches all anonymous users. By including this rule in your web.config file, you specify that anonymous users are not allowed. Every user must be authenticated using one of the configured Windows authentication protocols.

When using IIS 7.x, you can configure authorization rules directly from within the IIS management console, as shown in Figure 22-10.

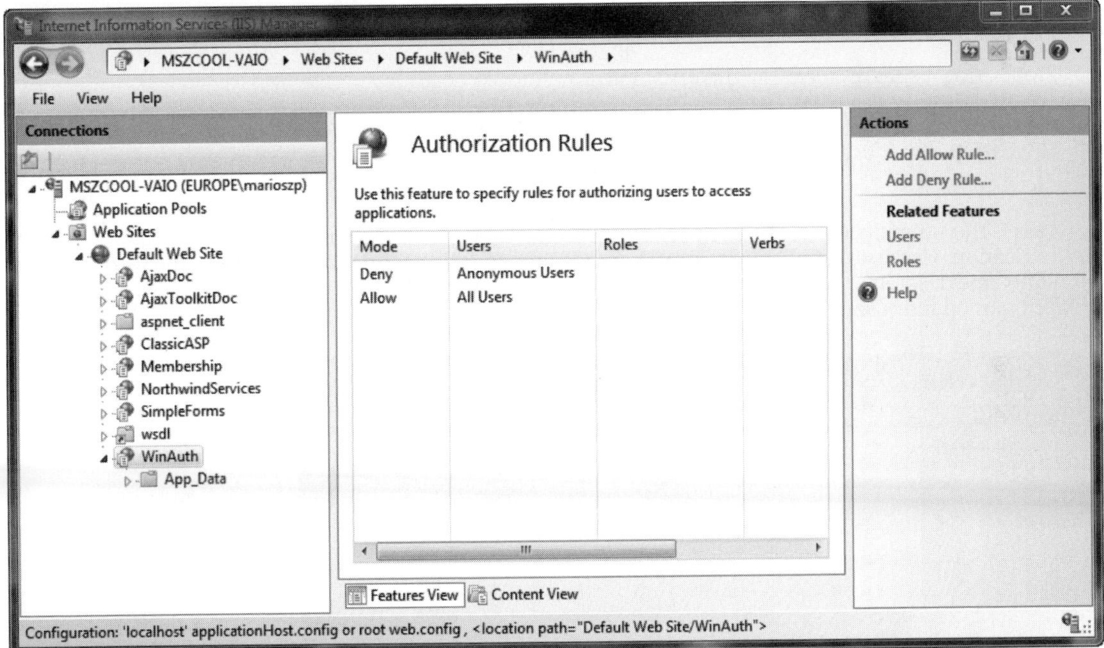

Figure 22-10. IIS authorization configuration for Windows authentication

By default, the feature delegation configuration of IIS 7.x is configured so that authorization rules are added to the central applicationHost.config configuration of the web server. That means if you configure these rules with the IIS management console, they will not be reflected in your web.config file. However, you can configure them manually in the <authorization> element of the <system.web> section of your web.config as outlined earlier, and the resulting behavior will be exactly the same as when configuring them through the IIS management console—at least from the user's perspective. What does that mean? Well, when configuring authorization rules through the IIS 7.x management console, they will be configured in the <system.webServer> section, which is evaluated by the web server's native authorization module. That means the web server itself rejects the request. On the other hand, when configuring the settings in the <system.web> section, ASP.NET will reject the request (which is at a later point in time in the processing pipeline).

Furthermore, when you disable the Anonymous Authentication module in IIS 7.x, you don't even need to configure any authorization rules, as the web server itself rejects the request before it even comes to evaluating authorization rules. However, according to "defense in-depth" and "secure-by-default," we would recommend you configure authorization rules either through the management console or your web.config file anyway.

Accessing Windows User Information

One of the nice things about Windows authentication is that no login page is required. When the user requests a page that requires authentication, the browser transmits the credentials to IIS. Your web application can then retrieve information directly from the User property of the web page.

Here's an example that displays the currently authenticated user:

```
if (Request.IsAuthenticated)
{
    // Display generic identity information.
    lblInfo.Text = "<b>Name: </b>" + User.Identity.Name;
    lblInfo.Text += "<br><b>Authenticated With: </b>";
    lblInfo.Text += User.Identity.AuthenticationType;
}
```

This is the same code you can use to get information about the current identity when using forms authentication. However, you'll notice one slight difference. The user name is always in the form DomainName\UserName or ComputerName\UserName. Figure 22-11 shows an example with a user account named marioszp of the domain EUROPE.

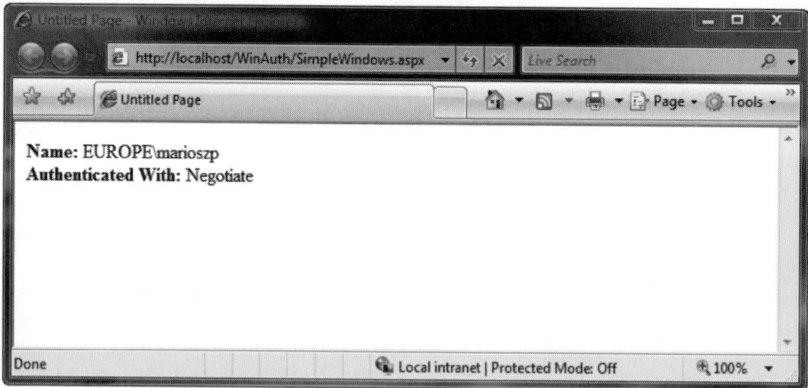

Figure 22-11. Displaying user information

The WindowsPrincipal Class

As you've learned in the past two chapters, the User property returns an IPrincipal object. When you use Windows authentication, this is an instance of the WindowsPrincipal class. The WindowsPrincipal class provides access to a WindowsIdentity object through the Identity property.

The WindowsPrincipal class implements four overloads of IsInRole() that all check whether the user is in a specified Windows user group. The IsInRole(string) overload (which is the only one required to be implemented when implementing IPrincipal) is implemented so that it accepts the name of the user group to be checked. IsInRole(int) expects an integer RID (Role Identifier) that refers to a user group. Furthermore, an overload is provided that expects a member of the WindowsBuiltInRole enumeration, which provides a list of predefined Windows account types (such as Guest, Administrator, and so on). Finally, there is an overload accepting a SecurityIdentifier instance. You will learn more about the SecurityIdentifier classes in the section "IdentityReference and Role Information" later in this chapter. You can find the WindowsPrincipal, WindowsIdentity, and WindowsBuiltInRole types in the System.Security.Principal namespace.

Here's a simple example that tests whether the user is in a predefined Windows role:

```
if (Request.IsAuthenticated)
{
    lblInfo.Text = "<b>Name: </b>" + User.Identity.Name;
    if(User is WindowsPrincipal)
    {
        WindowsPrincipal principal = (WindowsPrincipal)User;
        lblInfo.Text += "<br><b>Power user? </b>";
        lblInfo.Text += principal.IsInRole(
          WindowsBuiltInRole.PowerUser).ToString();
    }
}
```

Note that you must cast the User object to a WindowsPrincipal to access this Windows-specific functionality. Also notice that this cast will not work with forms authentication enabled and with the roles API enabled. (Chapter 23 covers the roles API in detail.) When having the roles API enabled, ASP.NET will create a RolePrincipal even when Windows authentication is configured for the application. Figure 22-12 shows the result of the previous code sample.

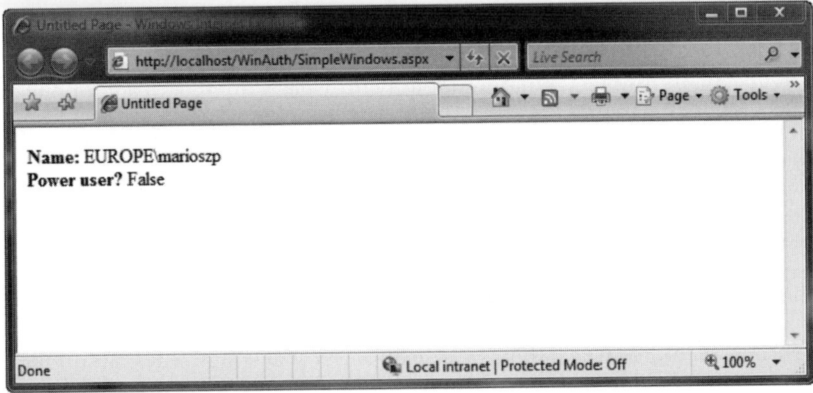

Figure 22-12. Testing group membership

Table 22-1 lists all the possible roles provided through the WindowsBuiltInRole enumeration. You can also test for membership with any arbitrary group you've created. Chapter 23 discusses this technique.

Table 22-1. *Values for the WindowsBuiltInRole Enumeration*

Role	Description
AccountOperator	Users with the special responsibility of managing the user accounts on a computer or domain.
Administrator	Users with complete and unrestricted access to the computer or domain.
BackupOperator	Users who can override certain security restrictions only as part of backing up or restoring operations.
Guest	Like the User role but even more restrictive.
PowerUser	Similar to Administrator but with some restrictions.
PrintOperator	Like a User but with additional privileges for taking control of a printer.
Replicator	Like a User but with additional privileges to support file replication in a domain.
SystemOperator	Similar to Administrator but with some restrictions. Generally, system operators manage a particular computer.
User	Users are restricted accounts that are prevented from making system-wide changes.

The WindowsIdentity Class

You can access some additional information about the currently authenticated user by casting the general identity object to a WindowsIdentity object. WindowsIdentity provides a number of additional members, as described in Table 22-2.

Table 22-2. *Additional Members of the WindowsIdentity*

Member	Description
IsAnonymous	This property returns true if the user is anonymous (has not been authenticated).
IsGuest	This property returns true if the user is using a Guest account. Guest accounts are designed for public access and do not confer many privileges.
IsSystem	Returns true if the user account has the Act As Part of the Operating System permission, which means it is a highly privileged system account.

Member	Description
Groups	Retrieves a collection that contains instances of IdentityReference classes, which returns the SID values for the groups the user is in.
Token	Returns the Windows account token for the identity.
Owner	Gets the SID for the token owner.
User	Gets the user's SID. For example, you can use this SID if you want to modify permissions for this user on ACLs through the classes provided in the System.Security.AccessControl namespace.
Impersonate()	This method instructs ASP.NET to run the following code under the corresponding Windows account. You'll learn much more about impersonation in the next section.
GetAnonymous()	This static method creates a WindowsIdentity that represents an anonymous user.
GetCurrent()	This static method creates a WindowsIdentity that represents the identity tied to the current security context (the user whose identity the current code is running under). If you use this method in an ASP.NET application, you'll retrieve the user account under which the code is running, not the user account that was authenticated by IIS and is provided in the User object.

The following code displays extra Windows-specific information about the user:

```
if (Request.IsAuthenticated)
{
    lblInfo.Text = "<b>Name: </b>" + User.Identity.Name;

    WindowsIdentity identity = (WindowsIdentity)User.Identity;
    lblInfo.Text += "<br><b>Token: </b>";
    lblInfo.Text += identity.Token.ToString();
    lblInfo.Text += "<br><b>Guest? </b>";
    lblInfo.Text += identity.IsGuest.ToString();
    lblInfo.Text += "<br><b>System? </b>";
    lblInfo.Text += identity.IsSystem.ToString();
}
```

Figure 22-13 shows the result.

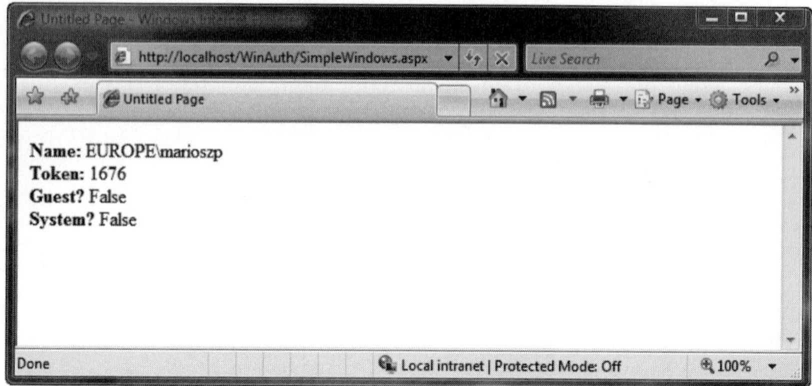

Figure 22-13. Showing Windows-specific user information

IdentityReference and Role Information

The .NET Framework ships with a set of IdentityReference classes. An IdentityReference is a reference to a valid Windows identity that is expressed through a SID. Valid Windows identities are computer and user accounts as well as Windows groups. When you create a user, when you create a group, or when you set up a new machine with Windows, it gets a worldwide unique SID assigned by the system. Actually, this SID is used for uniquely identifying system objects such as users. You can find an IdentityReference wherever a system object such as a user is referenced. For example, if you grant a user on your machine access to a file through the Security tab of the file properties, an IdentityReference gets added to the access control list of the file and contains the SID of the user to whom you are granting access. When adding a user to a group, a reference to the user in the form of a SID gets added to the group's user list as well (and to the user's group list).

The .NET Framework includes three classes for SID references in the System.Security.Principal namespace: IdentityReference, SecurityIdentifier, and NTAccount. These classes are key for enumerating groups of a Windows user through a WindowsIdentity instance. The IdentityReference is an abstract base class for any class representing a SID. Therefore, it is the base class for two classes: SecurityIdentifier and NTAccount. The first one represents the real, unique code of a SID—which looks similar to a Universally Unique ID (UUID)—whereas the second one represents the human-readable string for a SID (such as the readable name of the user or the group). The IdentityReference base class defines a method called Translate that allows you to convert an existing IdentityReference instance from one type to another, such as the conversion from NTAccount to SecurityIdentifier.

With that knowledge, enumerating the groups of the currently logged on Windows user account is simple, as shown in the following code sample:

```
protected void Page_Load(object sender, EventArgs e)
{
  if (User is WindowsPrincipal)
  {
    // First of all, get general user information
    WindowsPrincipal principal = (WindowsPrincipal)User;
    // ...
    WindowsIdentity identity = (WindowsIdentity)principal.Identity;
    // ...

    // Now get the roles for the user
```

```
        lblInfo.Text += "<hr/>";
        lblInfo.Text += "<h2>Roles:</h2>";

        foreach (IdentityReference SIDRef in identity.Groups)
        {
          lblInfo.Text += "<br/>--";

          // Get the system code for the SID
          SecurityIdentifier sid =
            (SecurityIdentifier)SIDRef.Translate(
                typeof(SecurityIdentifier));
          lblInfo.Text += "<br><b>SID (code): </b></br>";
          lblInfo.Text += sid.Value;

          // Get the human-readable SID
          NTAccount account = (NTAccount)SIDRef.Translate(typeof(NTAccount));
          lblInfo.Text += "<br><b>SID (human-readable): </b></br>";
          lblInfo.Text += account.Value;
        }
    }
}
```

The WindowsIdentity class includes a property called Groups, which is nothing other than a collection of IdentityReference objects. All you need to do is enumerate this collection and translate the IdentityReference to the type of reference you need for your purpose. As already mentioned, the .NET Framework comes with two types of representations of IdentityReferences: a SecurityIdentifier representing the SID because it's system-internal code, and the NTAccount representing the human-readable version of the SID. Through the Value property of the IdentityReference classes, you can access the actual value of the reference, which is the SID code for the SecurityIdentifier instance and the readable name of the user or group for the NTAccount instancehe NTAccount instance.

■ **Note** The IdentityReference classes are used by the System.Security.AccessControl classes as well. These classes provide a fully managed API that allows you to access file system access control lists programmatically from .NET-based applications. Access control list entries always bind to IdentityReference instances in this API, representing the user for which you have created the access control list entry. Finally, this is a great possibility for setting file system or registry access rights correctly when installing your applications on target machines (or modifying file system or registry access rights programmatically). Actually, you can use the System.Security.AccessControl classes to secure even more than just file system objects or registry objects. Indeed, you can secure any system object that can be secured through access control lists, such as named pipes, that are used for interprocess communication.

Impersonation

Everything that ASP.NET does is executed under a Windows account. When using IIS 7.x, this identity is the identity of the worker processes created for an application pool configured in IIS. Each application pool can have its own identity configured as you learned in Chapter 18. In any case, as each page request is processed, the configured identity determines what ASP.NET can and cannot do.

Impersonation provides you with a way to make this system more flexible. Instead of using a fixed account for all users, web pages, and applications, you can temporarily change the identity that ASP.NET uses for certain tasks. This process of temporarily assuming the identity of another Windows account is *impersonation*.

One potential reason to use impersonation is to use the permissions that are defined for the currently authenticated user. This means the actions ASP.NET performs will be limited according to the person who is using the application. For example, your web server might be set up with a number of personalized directories, one for each user. By impersonating the user in your web application, you ensure that your application cannot inadvertently give the user access to any files except the ones in that user's directory. If you attempt to access a restricted file, the Windows operating system will intervene, and an exception will be raised in your code.

■ **Note** Impersonation does not give you the ability to circumvent Windows security. You must still have the credentials for the user you want to impersonate, whether you write them into your code or a user provides them at runtime.

ASP.NET has two types of impersonation. *Configured* (web.config) impersonation allows you to specify that page requests should be run under the identity of the user who is making the request. *Programmatic* impersonation gives you the ability to switch to another identity within the code and switch back to the original identity when a specific task is finished. You'll learn about both of these techniques in the following sections.

Impersonation and Delegation in Windows

In order to use impersonation, the account that's running your website requires a specific operating system privilege, which is called "Impersonate a client after authentication." You can configure this privilege through the Local Security Policy management console (search for it in the Start menu), but you usually won't need to. That's because the built-in accounts Local Service and Network Service both have this privilege by default (see Figure 22-14). That means as long as you run your application pools under Network Service or Local Service, you don't need to configure anything for enabling impersonation. If you run your applications under a custom user account, you need to configure this privilege for the user you are going to use for the application pool.

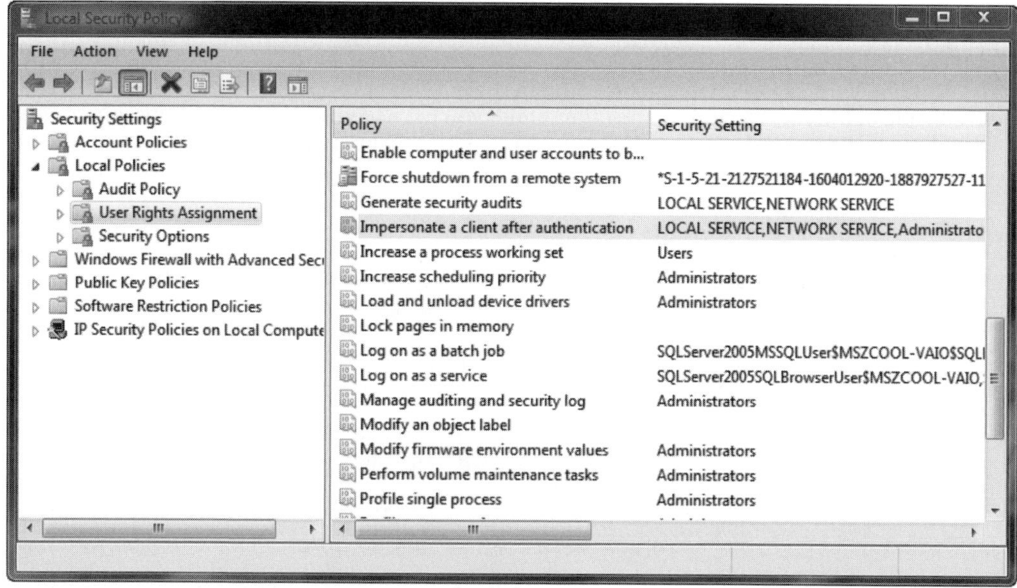

Figure 22-14. Impersonation privilege in Windows Vista

But delegation is different. As mentioned previously, delegation means that a server that has authenticated the client can pass the client's authentication ticket to another server in this network. This means that this server (and therefore your application) acts on behalf of the client across the network. Figure 22-15 shows this in detail.

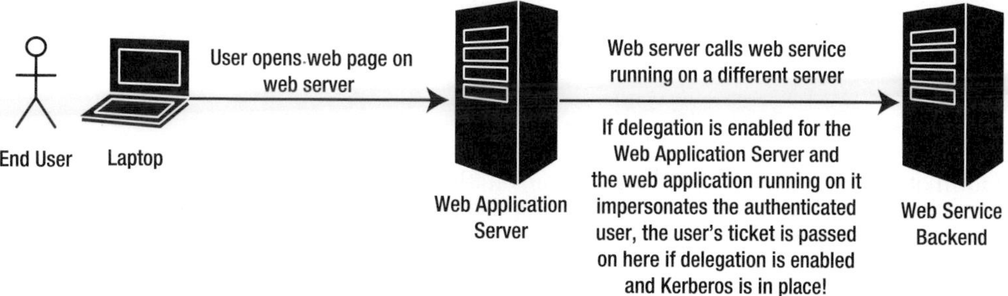

Figure 22-15. Identity flows across network hops

In Figure 22-15, you can see the big difference of impersonation. While impersonation takes place on the local machine only, delegation brings the concept of impersonation to calls across the network. Of course, if every server could do that in an uncontrolled fashion, this feature would definitely lead to a security risk. Therefore, Windows provides you with a way to specify which computer is trusted for delegation. By default no computer in the network except the domain controller is trusted for delegation. In Figure 22-15, the server you would configure for delegation would be the Web Application Server, as this is the one that needs to pass the credentials on to the next server.

You need to configure delegation explicitly using the Windows Server 2008 Active Directory Computers and Users configuration through the server management console. On the one hand, you need to permit machines to pass Kerberos tickets to other machines that allow impersonation (this is the "Trusted for delegation" privilege, which can be found in the local or global security policies management console of the server), and on the other hand, you have to give the same permission to the domain user under which your web application process is running. You need to do this configuration on the domain controller on Windows Server 2008.

■ **Caution** We suggest not using impersonation or delegation if it's not really necessary. If you use impersonation or delegation, this includes flowing the original client user's identity from the front-end to the backend. On the backend, all the ACLs and operating system security-related authorization settings must be configured properly for every single user. This configuration gets harder and harder with an increasing number of users. A simple configuration mistake can lead to either an application that doesn't work or a (probably huge) security leak. And think about the additional security configurations necessary! Instead, you should group users to roles and perform any security configuration based on roles or groups. You will learn more about roles and groups in Chapter 23.

■ **Caution** Enabling delegation for a server is something you should do carefully. Thoroughly review applications running on such a server, because malicious applications can lead to repudiation attacks. Imagine a malicious application (or a malicious part of an application that has not been reviewed) running on this server and performing some "illegal" actions under an impersonated or delegated user's identity. Applications (and therefore servers) should be allowed only for performing delegation if it's really necessary so that applications running on such servers cannot do any "illegal" things based on other, impersonated or delegated user identities.

Configured Impersonation

The simplest form of impersonation is configured impersonation, where you use the web.config file to define the impersonation behavior you want. You accomplish this by adding the <identity> element shown here:

```
<configuration>
    <system.web>
        <!-- Other settings omitted. -->
        <identity impersonate="true" />
    </system.web>
</configuration>
```

You can configure the <identity> element in more than one way, depending on the result you want. If you want to impersonate the Windows account authenticated by IIS, then you should use the setting as shown in the previous code snippet—just set the impersonate attribute to true.

Keep in mind that if you allow anonymous access, you can use the IUSR_[ComputerName] account. When using this approach, the impersonated account must have all the permissions required to run ASP.NET code, including read-write access to the c:\[WinDir]\Microsoft.NET\Framework\[Version]\Temporary ASP.NET Files directory where the compiled ASP.NET files are stored. Otherwise, an error will occur and the page will not be served.

Programmatic Impersonation

Configured impersonation allows you to impersonate a user for the entire duration of a request. If you want more control, such as the ability to impersonate a user for only part of the page request, you have to do the impersonation yourself in your code.

The key to impersonating a user programmatically is the WindowsIdentity.Impersonate() method. This method sets up impersonation for a specific account. You identify the account you want to impersonate by using its *account token*. Account tokens are what Windows uses to track users once their credentials are approved. If you have the token for a user, you can impersonate that user.

The general process is as follows:

1. Obtain an account token for the account you want to impersonate.
2. Use WindowsIdentity.Impersonate() to start impersonation. This method returns a WindowsImpersonationContext object.
3. Call the Undo() method of the WindowsImpersonationContext object to revert to the original identity.

Getting a Token

You can get an account token in two main ways. The most common approach is to retrieve the token for the currently authenticated user. You can access this token through the current security context, using the WindowsIdentity.Token property. Tokens are represented in .NET as IntPtr objects, which are representations of pointers to unmanaged memory locations. However, you never need to interact with this directly. Instead, you simply need to pass the token to the WindowsIdentity.Impersonate() method.

Here's an example that extracts the token for the current user:

```
IntPtr token = ((WindowsIdentity)User.Identity).Token;
```

The only other way to get a user token is to programmatically log in with a specific user name and password. Unfortunately, .NET does not provide managed classes for logging a user in. Instead, you must use the LogonUser() function from the unmanaged Win32 security API.

To use the LogonUser() function, you must first declare it as shown in the following code snippet. This code uses the DllImport attribute, which tells the runtime that you are going to access a native Windows API located in the native DLL advapi32.dll in the Windows system directory. The types of the parameters in the function prototype where this attribute is applied to need to map to the types of the functions encapsulated into the native DLL. Although every call to this method in your code looks like a call to any other static method of a .NET class, in reality the call gets routed to the native method encapsulated in the DLL specified in the DllImport attribute, and the information transmitted gets marshaled accordingly. For more information on consuming functionality implemented in a native Windows DLL, take a look at the MSDN article at `http://msdn2.microsoft.com/en-us/library/26thfadc.aspx`.

```
[DllImport(@"c:\Windows\System32\advapi32.dll")]
public static extern bool LogonUser(string lpszUserName,
  string lpszDomain, string lpszPassword, int dwLogonType,
  int dwLogonProvider, out int phToken);
```

As you can see, the LogonUser() function exists in advapi32.dll. It takes a user name, domain, password, logon type, and logon provider input parameters, along with an output parameter that allows you to access the token following a successful logon. The parameter names aren't important. In this example, the somewhat cryptic names from the Windows API reference are used. A Boolean result is returned to indicate whether the logon was successful.

■ **Note** Windows XP or later operating systems impose restrictions on the use of blank passwords to prevent network-based attacks. As a result of these restrictions, you won't be able to use the LogonUser() function to impersonate an account with a blank password.

Once you have imported the LogonUser() function, you can use it in your code to log the user in, as shown here:

```
// Define required variables.
string user = "matthew";
string password = "secret";
string machine = "FARIAMAT";
int returnedToken;

// Try to log on.
if (LogonUser(user, machine, password, 3, 0, out returnedToken))
{
    // The attempt was successful. Get the token.
    IntPtr token = new IntPtr(returnedToken);
}
```

Note that you must convert the integer value returned by LogonUser() into an IntPtr in order to use it with the WindowsIdentity.Impersonate() method.

Performing the Impersonation

Once you have an account token, you can use the WindowsIdentity.Impersonate() method to start impersonating the corresponding identity. You can use the Impersonate() method in two ways. You can use the static version, which requires an account token. Alternatively, you can use the instance version, which impersonates the identity represented by the corresponding WindowsIdentity object. In either case, the Impersonate() method returns a WindowsImpersonationContext object that has a single function—it allows you to revert to the original identity by calling its Undo() method.

Here's an example of programmatic impersonation at its simplest, using the static version of the Impersonate() method:

```
WindowsImpersonationContext impersonateContext;
impersonateContext = WindowsIdentity.Impersonate(token);

// (Now perform tasks under the impersonated ID.
// This code will not be able to perform any task
// that the user would not be allowed to do.)

impersonateContext.Undo();
```

At any time, you can determine the identity that your code is currently executing under by calling the WindowsIdentity.GetCurrent() method. Here's a function that uses this technique to determine the current identity and display the corresponding user name in a label on a web page:

```
private void DisplayIdentity()
{
    // Get the identity under which the code is currently executing.
    WindowsIdentity identity = WindowsIdentity.GetCurrent();
    lblInfo.Text += "Executing as: " + identity.Name + "<br>";
}
```

Using the method, you can create a simple test that impersonates the authenticated IIS identity and then reverts to the standard identity:

```
private void Page_Load(object sender, System.EventArgs e)
{
    if (User is WindowsPrincipal)
    {
        DisplayIdentity();

        // Impersonate the IIS identity.
        WindowsIdentity id;
        id = (WindowsIdentity)User.Identity;
        WindowsImpersonationContext impersonateContext;
        impersonateContext = id.Impersonate();
        DisplayIdentity();

        // Revert to the original ID as shown here.
        impersonateContext.Undo();
        DisplayIdentity();
    }
    else
    {
        // User isn't Windows authenticated.
        // Throw an error or take other steps.
    }
}
```

Figure 22-16 shows the result.

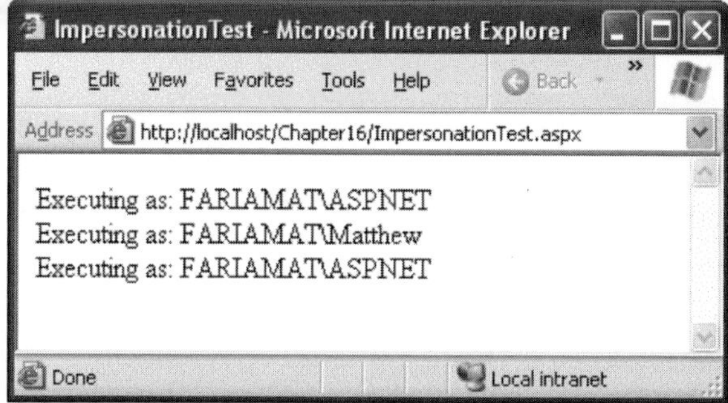

Figure 22-16. *Impersonating a user programmatically*

Summary

In this chapter, you learned how to use Windows authentication with ASP.NET to let IIS validate user identities. You also learned about the different types of authentication, how to retrieve user information, and how to impersonate users so your code runs under a different Windows account. Furthermore, you learned how IIS 7.x and ASP.NET work together when it comes to Windows authentication. The IIS 7.x management console is able to configure both ASP.NET-specific and web server-specific settings for you. This configuration is done in your web.config as well as in the web server's central configuration (applicationHost.config), depending on the feature delegation configuration. By default, features shipping with the web server are configured centrally, and ASP.NET-specific features are configured in web.config. However, you can change this behavior by modifying the feature delegation configuration.

In the next chapter, you'll learn about using advanced authorization rules that apply to Windows authentication and forms authentication.

CHAPTER 23

■ ■ ■

Authorization and Roles

So far, you've seen how to confirm that users are who they say they are and how to retrieve information about those authenticated identities. This gives your application the basic ability to distinguish between different users, but it's only a starting point. To create a truly secure web application, you need to act upon that identity at various points using *authorization*.

Authorization is the process of determining whether an authenticated user has sufficient permissions to perform a given action. This action could be requesting a web page, accessing a resource controlled by the operating system (such as a file or database), or performing an application-specific task (such as placing an order in an order management system or assigning a project in a project management application such as Microsoft Project Server). Windows performs some of these checks automatically, and you can code others declaratively using the web.config file. You'll need to perform still others directly in your code using the IPrincipal object.

In this chapter, you'll learn how ASP.NET authorization works, how to protect different resources, and how to implement your own role-based security.

URL Authorization

The most straightforward way to set security permissions is on individual web pages, web services, and subdirectories. Ideally, a web application framework should support resource-specific authorization without requiring you to change code and recompile the application. ASP.NET supports this requirement with declarative *authorization rules*, which you can define in the web.config file.

The rules you define are acted upon by the UrlAuthorizationModule, a specific HTTP module. This module examines these rules and checks each request to make sure users can't access resources you've specifically restricted. This type of authorization is called *URL authorization* because it considers only two details—the security context of the user and the URL of the resource that the user is attempting to access. If the page is forbidden and you're using forms authentication, the user will be redirected to the login page. If the page is forbidden and you're using Windows authentication, the user will receive an "access denied" (HTTP 401) error page, as shown in Figure 23-1, or a more generic error message or custom error page, depending on the <customErrors> element.

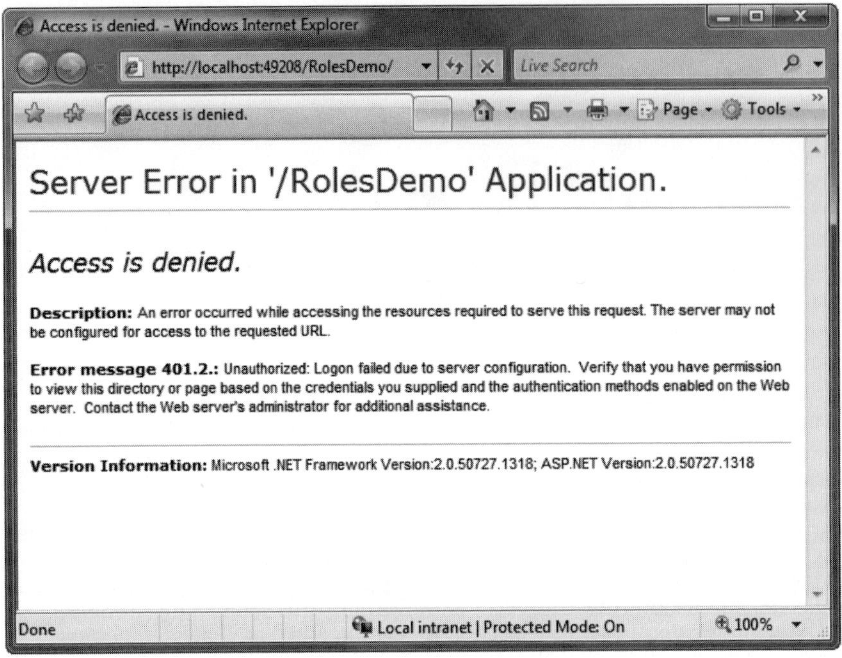

***Figure 23-1.** Trying to request a forbidden web page*

Authorization Rules

You define the authorization rules in the <authorization> element within the <system.web> section of the web.config file. The basic structure is as follows:

```
<authorization>
  <allow users="comma-separated list of users"
         roles="comma-separated list of roles"
         verbs="comma-separated list of verbs" />
  <deny  users="comma-separated list of users"
         roles="comma-separated list of roles"
         verbs="comma-separated list of verbs" />
</authorization>
```

In other words, two types of rules exist: allow and deny. You can add as many allow and deny rules as you want. Each rule identifies one or more users or roles (groups of users). In addition, you can use the verbs attribute to create a rule that applies only to specific types of HTTP requests (GET, POST, HEAD, or DEBUG).

You've already seen the simplest example in the previous chapters. To deny access to all anonymous users, you can use a <deny> rule like this:

```
<authorization>
  <deny users="?" />
</authorization>
```

In this case, the question mark (?) is a wildcard that represents all users with unknown identities. This rule is almost always used in authentication scenarios. That's because you can't specifically deny other, known users unless you first force all users to authenticate themselves.

You can use an additional wildcard—the asterisk (*), which represents all users. For example, the following <authorization> section allows access by authenticated and anonymous users:

```
<authorization>
  <allow users="*" />
</authorization>
```

This rule is rarely required, because it's already present in the machine.config file. After ASP.NET applies all the rules in the web.config file, it applies rules from the machine.config file. As a result, any user who is not explicitly denied access automatically gains access.

Now consider what happens if you add more than one rule in the authorization section:

```
<authorization>
    <allow users="*" />
    <deny users="?" />
</authorization>
```

When evaluating rules, ASP.NET scans through the list from top to bottom. As soon as it finds an applicable rule, it stops its search. Thus, in the previous case, it will determine that the rule <allow users="*"> applies to the current request and will not evaluate the second line. That means these rules will allow all users, including anonymous users. Reversing the order of these two lines, however, will deny anonymous users (by matching the first rule) and allow all other users (by matching the second rule).

```
<authorization>
    <deny users="?" />
    <allow users="*" />
</authorization>
```

When you add authorization rules to the web.config file in the root directory of the web application, the rules automatically apply to all the web resources that are part of the application. If you've denied anonymous users, ASP.NET will examine the authentication mode. If you've selected forms authentication, ASP.NET will direct the user to the login page. If you're using Windows authentication, IIS will request user credentials from the client browser, and a login dialog box may appear (depending on the protocols you've enabled).

In the following sections, you'll learn how to fine-tune authorization rules to give them a more carefully defined scope.

Controlling Access for Specific Users

The <allow> and <deny> rules don't need to use the asterisk or question mark wildcards. Instead, they can specifically identify a user name or a list of comma-separated user names. For example, the following authorization rule specifically restricts access from three users. These users will not be able to access the pages in the directory having a web.config containing these entries in place. All other authenticated users will be allowed.

```
<authorization>
  <deny users="?" />
  <deny users="dan" />
  <deny users="jenny" />
```

```
  <deny users="matthew" />
  <allow users="*" />
</authorization>
```

You can also use a comma-separated list to deny multiple users at once. Here's an equivalent version of the previous example that uses only two authorization rules:

```
<authorization>
  <deny users="?" />
  <deny users="dan,jenny,matthew" />
  <allow users="*" />
</authorization>
```

Note that in both these cases the order in which the three users are listed is unimportant. However, it is important that these users are denied before you include the <allow> rule. For example, the following authorization rules won't affect the user jenny, because ASP.NET matches the rule that allows all users and doesn't read any further:

```
<authorization>
  <deny users="?" />
  <deny users="dan,matthew" />
  <allow users="*" />
  <deny users="jenny" />
</authorization>
```

When creating secure applications, it's often a better approach to explicitly allow specific users or groups and then deny all others (rather than denying specific users, as in the examples so far). Here's an example of authorization rules that explicitly allow two users. All other user requests will be denied access, even if they are authenticated.

```
<authorization>
  <deny users="?" />
  <allow users="dan,matthew" />
  <deny users="*" />
</authorization>
```

You should consider one other detail. The format of user names in these examples assumes forms authentication. In forms authentication, you assign a user name when you call the Redirect-FromLoginPage() method. At this point, the UrlAuthorizationModule will use that name and check it against the list of authorization rules. Windows authentication is a little different, because names are entered in the format DomainName\UserName or ComputerName\UserName. You need to use the same format when listing users in the authorization rules. For example, if you have the user accounts dan and matthew on a computer named FARIAMAT, you can use these authorization rules:

```
<authorization>
  <deny users="?" />
  <allow users="FARIAMAT\dan,FARIAMAT\matthew" />
  <deny users="*" />
</authorization>
```

■ **Note** Make sure you specify the computer or domain name in the users attribute when you use Windows authentication. You can't use an alias such as localhost, because this will not be successfully matched.

Controlling Access to Specific Directories

A common application design is to place files that require authentication into a separate directory. With ASP.NET configuration files, this approach is easy. Just leave the <authorization> element in the normal parent directory empty, and add a web.config file that specifies stricter settings in the secured directory.

Remember that when you add the web.config file in the subdirectory, it shouldn't contain any of the application-specific settings. In fact, it should contain only the authorization information, as shown here:

```
<configuration>
  <system.web>
    <authorization>
      <deny users="?" />
    </authorization>
  </system.web>
</configuration>
```

■ **Note** You cannot change the <authentication> tag settings in the web.config file of a subdirectory in your application. Instead, all the directories in the application must use the same authentication system. However, each directory can have its own authorization rules.

When using authorization rules in a subdirectory, ASP.NET still reads the authorization rules from the parent directory. The difference is that it applies the rules in the subdirectory *first*. This is important, because ASP.NET stops as soon as it matches an authorization rule. For example, consider an example in which the root virtual directory contains this rule:

```
<allow users="dan" />
```

and a subdirectory contains this rule:

```
<deny users="dan" />
```

In this case, the user dan will be able to access any resource in the root directory but no resources in the subdirectory. If you reverse these two rules, dan will be able to access resources in the subdirectory but not the root directory.

To make life more interesting, ASP.NET allows an unlimited hierarchy of subdirectories and authorization rules. For example, it's quite possible to have a virtual directory with authorization rules, a subdirectory that defines additional rules, and then a subdirectory inside that subdirectory that applies even more rules. The easiest way to understand the authorization process in this case is to imagine all the rules as a single list, starting with the directory where the requested page is located. If all those rules are processed without a match, ASP.NET then begins reading the authorization rules in the parent directory, and then its parent directory, and so on, until it finds a match. If no authorization rules match, ASP.NET will ultimately match the <allow users="*"> rule in the machine.config file.

Controlling Access to Specific Files

Generally, setting file access permissions by directory is the cleanest and easiest approach. However, you also have the option of restricting specific files by adding <location> tags to your web.config file.

The <location> tags sit outside the main <system.web> tag and are nested directly in the base <configuration> tag, as shown here:

```
<configuration>
    <system.web>
        <!-- Other settings omitted. -->
        <authorization>
            <allow users="*" />
        </authorization>
    </system.web>

    <location path="SecuredPage.aspx">
        <system.web>
            <authorization>
                <deny users="?" />
            </authorization>
        </system.web>
    </location>

    <location path="AnotherSecuredPage.aspx">
        <system.web>
            <authorization>
                <deny users="?" />
            </authorization>
        </system.web>
    </location>

</configuration>
```

In this example, all files in the application are allowed, except SecuredPage.aspx and AnotherSecuredPage.aspx, which have an access rule that denies anonymous users.

Controlling Access for Specific Roles

To make website security easier to understand and maintain, users are often grouped into categories, called *roles*. If you need to manage an enterprise application that supports thousands of users, you can understand the value of roles. If you needed to define permissions for each individual user, it would be tiring, difficult to change, and nearly impossible to complete without error.

In Windows authentication, roles are automatically available and naturally integrated. In this case, roles are actually Windows groups. You might use built-in groups (such as Administrator, Guest, PowerUser, and so on), or you can create your own to represent application-specific categories (such as Manager, Contractor, Supervisor, and so on). Roles aren't provided intrinsically in forms authentication alone, but together with membership, ASP.NET employs the roles API, which is an out-of-the-box implementation for supporting and managing roles in your application. Furthermore, if you don't want to use this infrastructure, it's fairly easy to create your own system that slots users into appropriate groups based on their credentials. You'll learn details about the two ways of supporting roles in the section "Using the Roles API for Role-Based Authorization" in this chapter.

Once you have defined roles, you can create authorization rules that act on these roles. In fact, these rules look essentially the same as the user-specific rules you've seen already.

For example, the following authorization rules deny all anonymous users, allow two specific users (dan and matthew), and allow two specific groups (Manager and Supervisor). All other users are denied.

```
<authorization>
  <deny users="?" />
  <allow users="FARIAMAT\dan,FARIAMAT\matthew" />
  <allow roles="FARIAMAT\Manager,FARIAMAT\Supervisor" />
  <deny users="*" />
</authorization>
```

Using role-based authorization rules is simple conceptually, but it can become tricky in practice. The issue is that when you use roles, your authorization rules can overlap. For example, consider what happens if you allow a group that contains a specific user and then explicitly deny that user. Or consider the reverse—allowing a user by name but denying the group to which the user belongs. In these scenarios, you might expect the more fine-grained rule (the rule affecting the user) to take precedence over the more general rule (the rule affecting the group). Or, you might expect the more restrictive rules to always take precedence, as in the Windows operating system. However, neither of these approaches is used in ASP.NET. Instead, ASP.NET simply uses the first matching rule. As a result, rule ordering can become important.

Consider this example:

```
<authorization>
  <deny users="?" />
  <allow users="FARIAMAT\matthew" />
  <deny roles="FARIAMAT\Guest" />
  <allow roles="FARIAMAT\Manager" />
  <deny users="FARIAMAT\dan" />
  <allow roles="FARIAMAT\Supervisor" />
  <deny users="*" />
</authorization>
```

Here's how ASP.NET parses these rules:

- In this example, the user matthew is allowed, regardless of the group to which he belongs.
- All users in the Guest role are then denied. If matthew is in the Guest role, matthew is still allowed because the user-specific rule is matched first.
- Next, all users in the Manager group are allowed. The only exception is users who are in both the Manager and Guest groups. The Guest rule occurs earlier in the list, so those users would have already been denied.
- Next, the user dan is denied access. But if dan belongs to the allowed Manager group, dan will already have been allowed, because this rule won't be executed.
- Any users who are in the Supervisor group, and who haven't been explicitly allowed or denied by one of the preceding rules, are allowed.
- Finally, all other users are denied.

Keep in mind that these overlapping rules can also span multiple directories. For example, a subdirectory might deny a user, while a parent directory allows a user in that group. In this example, when accessing files in the subdirectory, the user-specific rule is matched first.

File Authorization

URL authorization is one of the cornerstones of ASP.NET authorization. However, ASP.NET also uses another type of authorization that's often overlooked or ignored by many developers. This is file-based authorization, and it's implemented by the FileAuthorizationModule. File-based authorization takes effect only if you're using Windows authentication. If you're using custom authentication or forms authentication, it's not used.

To understand file authorization, you need to understand how the Windows operating system enforces file system security. If your file system uses the NTFS format, you can set ACLs that specifically identify users and roles that are allowed or denied access to individual files. The FileAuthorizationModule simply checks the Windows permissions for the file you're requesting. For example, if you request a web page, the FileAuthorizationModule checks that the currently authenticated IIS user has the permissions required to access the underlying .aspx file. If the user doesn't, the page code is not executed, and the user receives an "access denied" message.

New ASP.NET users often wonder why file authorization needs to be implemented by a separate module—shouldn't it take place automatically at the hands of the operating system? To understand why the FileAuthorizationModule is required, you need to remember how ASP.NET executes code. Unless you've enabled impersonation, ASP.NET executes under a fixed user account, such as ASPNET. The Windows operating system will check that the ASPNET account has the permissions it needs to access the .aspx file, but it wouldn't perform the same check for a user authenticated by IIS. The FileAuthorizationModule fills the gap. It performs authorization checks using the security context of the current user. As a result, the system administrator can set permissions to files or folders and control access to portions of an ASP.NET application. Generally, it's clearer and more straightforward to use authorization rules in the web.config file. However, if you want to take advantage of existing Windows permissions in a local network or an intranet scenario, you can.

Authorization Checks in Code

With URL authorization and file authorization, you can control access only to individual web pages. The next step in ensuring a secure application is to build checks into your application before attempting specific tasks or allowing certain operations. To use these techniques, you'll need to write some code.

Using the IsInRole() Method

As you saw in earlier chapters, all IPrincipal objects provide an IsInRole() method, which lets you evaluate whether a user is a member of a group. This method accepts the role name as a string name and returns true if the user is a member of that role.

For example, here's how you can check if the current user is a member of the Supervisors role:

```
if (User.IsInRole("Supervisors"))
{
    // Do nothing, the page should be accessed as normal because the
    // user has administrator privileges.
}
else
{
```

```
    // Don't allow this page. Instead, redirect to the home page.
    Response.Redirect("default.aspx");
}
```

Remember that when using Windows authentication, you need to use the format DomainName\GroupName or ComputerName\GroupName. Here's an example:

```
if (User.IsInRole(@"FARIAMAT\Supervisors"))
{ ... }
```

This approach works for custom groups you've created but not for built-in groups that are defined by the operating system. If you want to check whether a user is a member of one of the built-in groups, you use this syntax:

```
if (User.IsInRole(@"BUILTIN\Administrators"))
{ ... }
```

Of course, you can also cast the User object to a WindowsPrincipal and use the overloaded version of IsInRole() that accepts the WindowsBuiltInRole enumeration, as described in Chapter 22.

■ **Note** The @ prefix when using strings in C# just enables you to use the backslash without escaping it with an additional backslash. This is especially useful if you have strings with lots of backslashes. But this also means you cannot use any escape sequence (such as \n or \r) in the string. If you want to use these escape sequences, you may not use the @ prefix. However, in this case, you have to escape any backslash; otherwise, the backslash would be used as the start of an escape sequence. This means with the @ prefix you would have to write FARIAMAT\\Supervisors, for example.

Using the PrincipalPermission Class

.NET includes another way to enforce role and user rules. Instead of checking with the IsInRole() method, you can use the PrincipalPermission class from the System.Security.Permissions namespace.

The basic strategy is to create a PrincipalPermission object that represents the user or role information you require. Then, invoke the PrincipalPermission.Demand() method. If the current user doesn't meet the requirements, a SecurityException will be thrown, which you can catch (or deal with using a custom error page).

There are four overloads of the constructor of the PrincipalPermission, from one up to three parameters, which are in turn evaluated by the Demand() method of the class. One parameter is for the user name, another one is for the role name, and the third one specifies a flag that asks the PrincipalPermission's Demand() method to verify if the user is authenticated or not (isAuthenticated). The last and fourth overload accepts a PermissionState parameter as the only parameter. This parameter is inherited by the base class of the PrincipalPermission class. It is out of scope for this book and not relevant for the further sections in this chapter. You can omit either one of these parameters by supplying a null reference in its place. For example, the following code tests whether the user is a Windows administrator:

```
try
{
    PrincipalPermission pp = new PrincipalPermission(null,
      @"BUILTIN\Administrators");
    pp.Demand();

    // If the code reaches this point, the demand succeeded.
    // The current user is an administrator.
}
catch (SecurityException err)
{
    // The demand failed. The current user isn't an administrator.
}
```

The advantage of this approach is that you don't need to write any conditional logic. Instead, you can simply demand all the permissions you need. This works particularly well if you need to verify that a user is a member of multiple groups. The disadvantage is that using exception handling to control the flow of your application is slower. Often, PrincipalPermission checks are used in addition to web.config rules as a failsafe. In other words, you can call Demand() to ensure that even if a web.config file has been inadvertently modified, users in the wrong groups won't be allowed.

Merging PrincipalPermission Objects

The PrincipalPermission approach also gives you the ability to evaluate more complex authentication rules. For example, consider a situation where UserA and UserB, who belong to different groups, are both allowed to access certain functionality. If you use the IPrincipal object, you need to call IsInRole() twice. An alternate approach is to create multiple PrincipalPermission objects and merge them to get one PrincipalPermission object. Then you can call Demand() on just this object.

Here's an example that combines two roles:

```
try
{
    PrincipalPermission pp1 = new PrincipalPermission(null,
      @"BUILTIN\Administrators");
    PrincipalPermission pp2 = new PrincipalPermission(null,
      @"BUILTIN\Guests");

    // Combine these two permissions.
    PrincipalPermission pp3 = (PrincipalPermission)pp1.Union(pp2);
    pp3.Demand();

    // If the code reaches this point, the demand succeeded.
    // The current user is in one of these roles.
}
catch (SecurityException err)
{
    // The demand failed. The current user is in none of these roles.
}
```

This example checks that a user is a member of either one of the two Windows groups, Administrators or Guests. You can also ensure that a user is a member of *both* groups. In this case, use the PrincipalPermission.Intersect() method instead of PrincipalPermission.Union().

Using the PrincipalPermission Attribute

The PrincipalPermission attribute provides another way of validating the current user's credentials. It serves the same purpose as the PrincipalPermission class, but it's used declaratively. In other words, you attach it to a given class or method, and the CLR checks it automatically when the corresponding code runs. The exception handling now works a little bit differently: this time you cannot catch the exception within the function on which the attribute has been applied. You have to catch the exception in the function that actually calls this function. If you apply the PrincipalPermission attribute on an event procedure (such as Button_Click), you have to catch the exception in the global Application_Error event, which you can find in the Global.asax file.

When you use a PrincipalPermission attribute, you can restrict access to a specific user or a specific role. Here's an example that requires the user accessing the page to be in the server's Administrators group. If the user is not member of the web server's Administrators group, the ASP.NET runtime throws a security exception.

```
[PrincipalPermission(SecurityAction.Demand,
 Role=@"BUILTIN\Administrators")]
public partial class MyWebPage : System.Web.UI.Page
{ ... }
```

Again, with the previous example you have to catch the exception in the global error handler (Application_Error) because your code is not the caller of this web page. Otherwise, ASP.NET would raise the exception and display the ASP.NET error page according to the web.config configuration. The following example restricts a particular method to a specific role:

```
[PrincipalPermission(SecurityAction.Demand, Role=@"FARIAMAT\finance")]
private void DoSomething()
{ ... }
```

The caller of this method can catch the SecurityException with a try/catch block.

PrincipalPermission attributes give you another way to safeguard your code. You won't use them to make decisions at runtime, but you might use them to ensure that even if web.config rules are modified or circumvented, a basic level of security remains.

■ **Note** Changing declarative permissions means that you need to recompile the application. But why use them if every change requires recompilation? Don't you want to have the possibility of managing roles in terms of adding, deleting, and changing them? Yes, and that requires more generic code, but it can't be done with declarative permissions. So, when is it helpful to use declarative permissions? Well, declarative permissions are especially suited for fixed roles in your application that cannot be deleted anyway. For example, an Administrators role is required in most applications and therefore cannot be deleted. So, you can secure functionality that should be accessible to only administrators with declarative permissions. Typical examples in Windows are all the built-in groups such as Administrators, Power Users, Backup Operators, and Users.

Using the Roles API for Role-Based Authorization

ASP.NET ships with a ready-to-use infrastructure for managing and using roles (as well as the membership API introduced in Chapter 21). This infrastructure—which is completely extensible through providers such as the membership API—includes prebuilt functionality for managing roles, assigning roles to users, and accessing all the role information from code. In more detail, the roles infrastructure includes the following:

- A provider-based extensible mechanism for including different types of role data stores.
- A ready-to-use implementation of a provider for SQL Server and the necessary database tables based on the Membership database introduced in Chapter 21. These tables associate membership user entries with roles in a many-to-many relationship and are automatically created when calling the aspnet_regsql.exe tool (also introduced in Chapter 21).
- The prebuilt RolePrincipal class that is automatically initialized for authenticated users through the RoleManagerModule (also included with the roles infrastructure).
- Complete programmatic access to the roles through the Roles class.

To use this infrastructure, you have to first enable it. You can do this either by checking the Enable Roles for This Web Site box when running through the Security Setup Wizard or by clicking the Enable Roles link in the Security tab of the WAT. Figure 23-2 shows both of these possibilities.

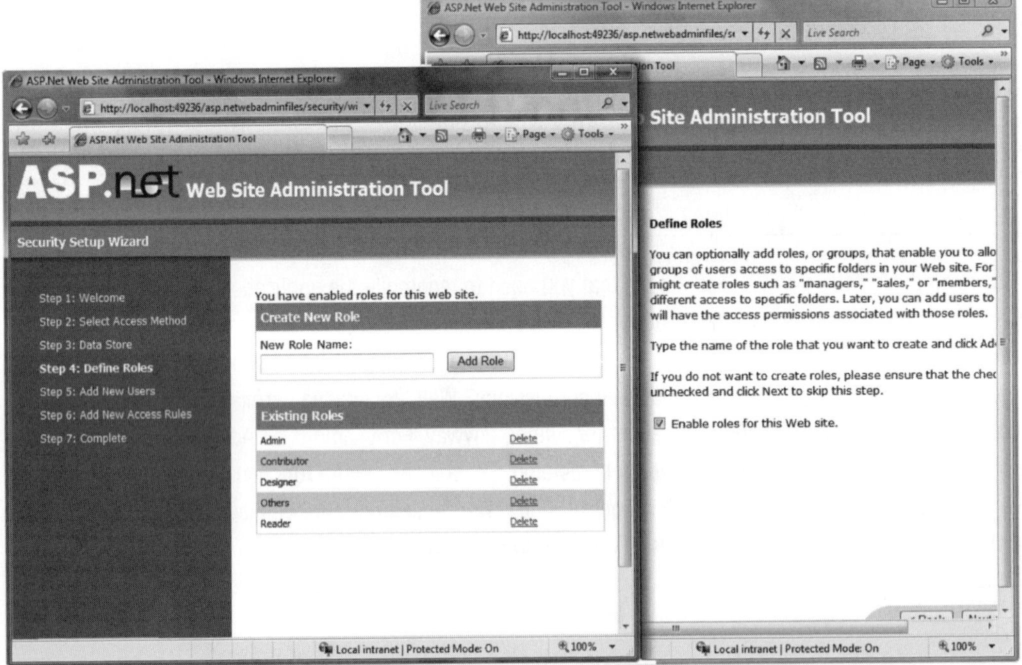

Figure 23-2. Configuring the roles API

In both cases, the tool adds a little configuration entry to the application's web.config file. You can do this manually, just as you can enable the roles API.

```
<configuration>
    <system.web>
        <roleManager enabled="true" />
        <!-- Note that you can use roles with Windows authentication
             as well; you do not need to use forms authentication. Often
             it is very useful to map Windows accounts to custom roles
             as well. But now we use forms auth. for our examples. -->
        <authentication mode="Forms" />
    </system.web>
</configuration>
```

With this configuration in place, ASP.NET automatically creates a file-based database, ASPNETDB.MDF, in the application's App_Data directory, as already described in Chapter 21. If you want to use a custom store, you have to complete the following steps:

1. Create the data store either by using aspnet_regsql.exe or by executing the TSQL command scripts included in the .NET Framework directory. Both were introduced in Chapter 21.
2. Configure the roles provider to use the previously created custom store.

You can configure the roles provider through the <roleManager> tag. You can either use a different database or use a completely different store if you want. In addition, you can configure certain properties through the <roleManager> tag that can't be configured in the WAT.

```
<configuration>
    <connectionStrings>
        <add name="MySqlStore"
             connectionString="data source=(local);
                    Integrated Security=SSPI;initial catalog=MySqlDB"/>
    </connectionStrings>
    <system.web>
        <roleManager enabled="true"
                     defaultProvider="CustomSqlProvider"
                     cacheRolesInCookie="true"
                     cookieName=".MyRolesCookie"
                     cookieTimeout="30"
                     cookieSlidingExpiration="true"
                     cookieProtection="All">
            <providers>
                <add name="CustomSqlProvider"
                     type="System.Web.Security.SqlRoleProvider"
                     connectionStringName="MySqlStore"
                     applicationName="RolesDemo"/>
            </providers>
        </roleManager>
        <authentication mode="Forms"/>
        <compilation debug="true"/>
    </system.web>
</configuration>
```

As soon as you have added this configuration entry to your web.config file, you can select the provider through the WAT. Just switch to the Provider tab, and then click the link Select a Different Provider for Each Feature. Figure 23-3 shows the provider selection in the WAT.

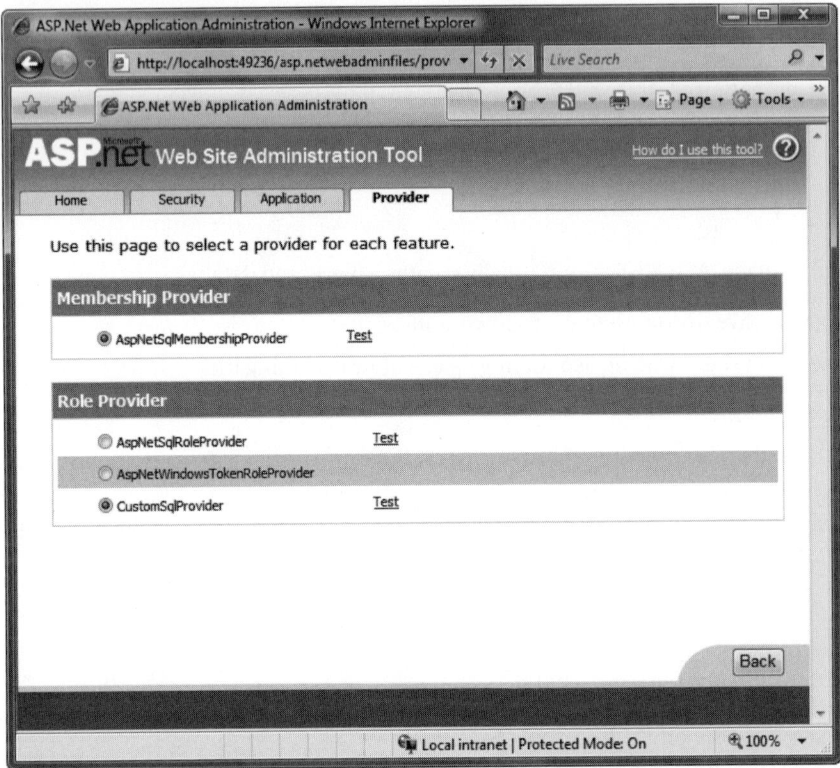

Figure 23-3. *The roles provider in the web-based configuration tool*

Table 23-1 lists the properties you can configure through the <roleManager> configuration tag.

Table 23-1. *Options for the <roleManager> Configuration*

Option	Description
enabled	Indicates whether the roles API is enabled (true) or not (false).
defaultProvider	Optional attribute for specifying the currently active provider for storing role information. If you want to use a different provider, you have to configure it and set the defaultProvider attribute to the name of the provider you want to use.
cacheRolesInCookie	Instead of reading the roles every time from the back-end store, you can store roles in a cookie. This attribute indicates whether a cookie is used.

Option	Description
cookieName	If roles are cached in a cookie, you can specify a name for this cookie through this attribute.
cookiePath	Specifies the path of the cookie where roles are cached for your application. This allows you to specify the part of your application for which the cookie is valid. The default value is /.
cookieProtection	The roles cookie can be encrypted and signed. You specify the level of protection through this attribute. Valid values are All (encrypt and sign), Encryption, Validation, and None.
cookieRequireSSL	Specifies whether the cookie will be returned by ASP.NET only if SSL is enabled (true) or in any other case (false). If this attribute is set to true and SSL is not activated, the runtime simply doesn't return the cookie, and therefore role checks always happen against the underlying roles provider.
cookieTimeout	Gets or sets a timeout for the roles cookie in minutes with a default of 30 minutes.
cookieSlidingExpiration	Specifies whether the cookie's timeout will be extended with each request the user is performing against the ASP.NET application (true) or not (false). The default is true.
createPersistentCookie	If set to true, the cookie will be stored persistently on the client machine. Otherwise, the cookie is just a session cookie that will be deleted when the user is closing the browser.
domain	Specifies the valid domain for the role cookie.
maxCachedResults	Specifies the maximum number of role names persisted in the cookie.

In the previous example, you configured the SqlRoleProvider. The provider includes a couple of additional settings you can configure through web.config, as shown in Table 23-2.

Table 23-2. *Additional Properties of the SqlRoleProvider*

Property	Description
name	Name of the provider. This name can be used in the defaultProvider attribute described in Table 23-1 for specifying the provider by the application.
applicationName	Name of the application for which the roles are managed.
description	Short, friendly description of the provider.
connectionStringName	Name of the connection string specified in the web.config file's <connectionStrings> section that will be used for connecting to the back-end roles store.

In addition to the SqlRoleProvider, ASP.NET ships with a provider that can be used on Windows Server 2003 with Authorization Manager. You can also create and use your own custom providers, as you will learn in Chapter 26. Table 23-3 shows the classes included in the roles API framework.

Table 23-3. *The Fundamental Roles API Classes*

Class	Description
RoleManagerModule	This module ensures that roles will be assigned to the currently logged-on user for every request. It attaches to the Application_AuthenticateRequest event and creates an instance of RolePrincipal containing the roles the user is assigned to automatically if the roles API is enabled in web.config.
RoleProvider	Base class for every roles provider that defines the interface you must implement for a custom RoleProvider. Every custom provider must be inherited from this class.
RoleProviderCollection	A collection of roles providers. This collection allows you to iterate through the configured roles providers on your system and for your application, which is handy when writing an administration application or pages for your application.
SqlRoleProvider	Implementation of a roles provider for SQL Server-based databases.
WindowsTokenRoleProvider	Gets role information for an authenticated Windows user based on Windows group associations.
AuthorizationStoreRoleProvider	Implementation of a roles provider for storing roles in an Authorization Manager-based store. Authorization Manager ships with Windows Server 2003 and allows you to declaratively define application roles and permissions for this role. Your application can use Authorization Manager for programmatically authorizing users.
Roles	You use the Roles class as your primary interface to the roles store. This class includes methods for programmatically managing roles.
RolePrincipal	This is a IPrincipal implementation that connects the configured roles with the authenticated user. It is created automatically by the RoleManagerModule if the roles API is enabled.

As soon as you have configured the roles API, you can create users and roles and then assign users to these roles using either the WAT or the Roles class in your code. On the Security tab, just click the Create or Manage Roles link. Then you can create roles and add users to roles, as shown in Figure 23-4.

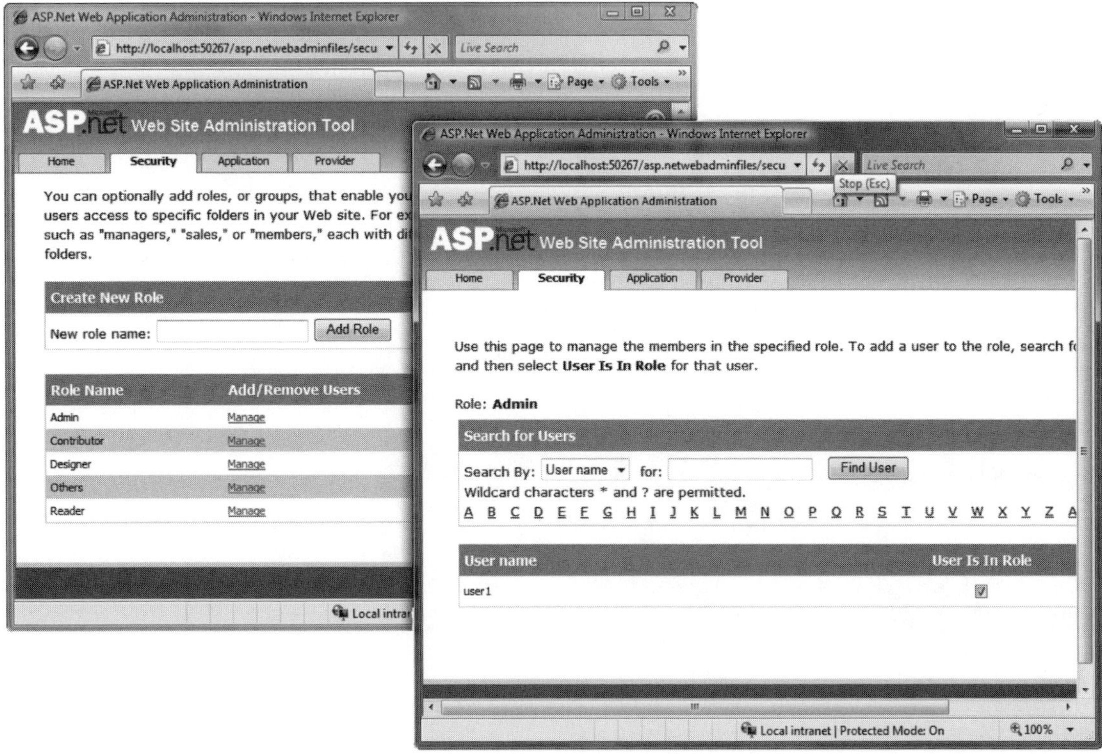

Figure 23-4. Adding users to roles

After you have configured users and roles, you need to configure the authorization rules for your application. You have already learned all the necessary details. Just configure the appropriate <authorization> sections in the different directories of your application. Fortunately, you even don't have to do this manually. When selecting the Security tab, you just need to click one of the links in the Add New Access Rule section, as shown in Figure 23-5.

When the roles API is enabled, the RoleManagerModule automatically creates a RolePrincipal instance containing both the authenticated user's identity and the roles of the user. The RolePrincipal is just a custom implementation of IPrincipal, which is the base interface for all principal classes. It therefore supports the default functionality, such as access to the authenticated identity and a method for verifying a role membership condition through the IsInRole() method. Furthermore, it employs a couple of additional properties for accessing more detailed information about the principal. You can use the properties in the following code for extracting information from the instance as well as for performing authorization checks by calling the IsInRole() method:

```
protected void Page_Load(object sender, EventArgs e)
{
    if (User.Identity.IsAuthenticated)
    {
        RolePrincipal rp = (RolePrincipal)User;

        StringBuilder RoleInfo = new StringBuilder();
```

```
        RoleInfo.AppendFormat("<h2>Welcome {0}</h2>", rp.Identity.Name);
        RoleInfo.AppendFormat("<b>Provider:</b> {0}<BR>", rp.ProviderName);
        RoleInfo.AppendFormat("<b>Version:</b> {0}<BR>", rp.Version);
        RoleInfo.AppendFormat("<b>Expires at:</b> {0}<BR>", rp.ExpireDate);
        RoleInfo.Append("<b>Roles:</b> ");

        string[] roles = rp.GetRoles();
        for (int i = 0; i < roles.Length; i++)
        {
            if (i > 0) RoleInfo.Append(", ");
            RoleInfo.Append(roles[i]);
        }

        LabelRoleInformation.Text = RoleInfo.ToString();
    }
}
```

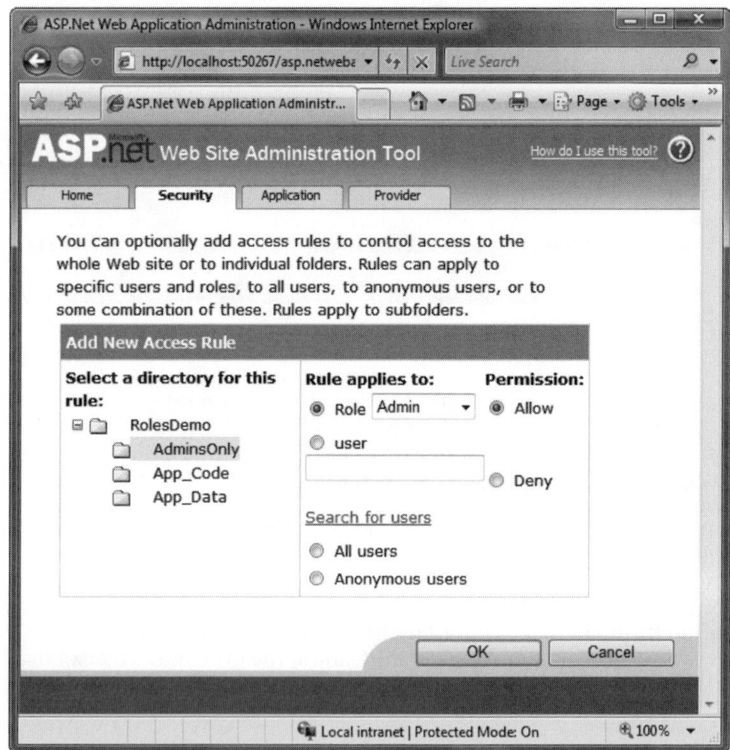

Figure 23-5. Configuring access rules with the WAT

Using the LoginView Control with Roles

In the previous chapter, you learned details about the security controls that ship with ASP.NET. One of these controls is the LoginView control. You used this control in Chapter 21 for displaying different controls for anonymous and logged-in users. The control uses templates for implementing this functionality. In Chapter 21 you used the <LoggedInTemplate> and <AnonymousTemplate> templates.

The control supports one additional template that enables you to create different views based on the roles to which a user belongs. For this purpose you need to add a RoleGroups template with <asp:RoleGroup> controls. Within every <asp:RoleGroup> control, you specify a comma-separated list of roles in the Roles attribute for which its <ContentTemplate> will be displayed, as follows:

```
<asp:LoginView runat="server" ID="MainView">
    <LoggedInTemplate>
        <h2>This is the logged in template</h2>
    </LoggedInTemplate>
    <RoleGroups>
        <asp:RoleGroup Roles="Admin">
            <ContentTemplate>
                <h2>Only Admins will see this</h2>
            </ContentTemplate>
        </asp:RoleGroup>
        <asp:RoleGroup Roles="Contributor">
            <ContentTemplate>
                <h2>This is for contributors!</h2>
            </ContentTemplate>
        </asp:RoleGroup>
        <asp:RoleGroup Roles="Reader, Designer">
            <ContentTemplate>
                <h2>This is for web designers and readers</h2>
            </ContentTemplate>
        </asp:RoleGroup>
    </RoleGroups>
</asp:LoginView>
```

The LoginView control in the previous code displays different content for logged-in users and for users assigned to specific roles. For example, for users in the Admin role the control displays the text "Only Admins will see this," while for users in the Contributor role it displays the text "This is for contributors!" Also, for users who are associated with the Reader or Designer role, it displays different content.

It's important to understand that just one of these templates will be displayed. The control simply displays the first template that fits the logged-in user. For example, if you have a user associated with the Contributor, Reader, and Designer roles, the first matching template is the <asp:RoleGroup> for contributors. The other role group will simply not be displayed. The LoggedInTemplate, for example, will be displayed only for authenticated users with no matching <asp:RoleGroup> element. As soon as a matching role group is found, the contents of the LoggedInTemplate will not be displayed.

Accessing Roles Programmatically

As is the case for the membership API introduced in Chapter 21, the roles API includes an API that allows you to perform all tasks from code. You can programmatically add new roles, read role information, and delete roles from your application. Furthermore, you can associate users with roles as well as get users associated with a specific role. You can do all this by calling methods of the Roles class.

Most of the properties included in the Roles class just map to the settings for the <roleManager> tag described in Table 23-1. Therefore, Table 23-4 includes the additional properties and the Roles class's methods that you can use for managing and accessing the roles API programmatically.

Table 23-4. *Members of the Roles Class*

Member	Description
Provider	Returns the provider currently used by your application.
Providers	Returns a collection of all the available providers on the system and for your application. It therefore returns the providers configured in machine.config and in web.config of your application.
AddUserToRole	Accepts a user name and a role name as a string parameter and adds the specified user to the specified role.
AddUserToRoles	Accepts a user name as a string parameter and role names as an array of strings and adds the specified user to all the roles specified in the role names parameter.
AddUsersToRole	Accepts a string array with user names and a string parameter that specifies a role name and adds all the specified users to the role specified in the second parameter.
AddUsersToRoles	Accepts a string array with user names and a second one with role names and adds all the users in the user names parameter to all the roles in the role names parameter.
CreateRole	Creates a new role.
DeleteRole	Deletes an existing role.
FindUsersInRole	Accepts a string representing the role name and a second string specifying a pattern for user names to match. The method returns a list of users that are associated with the role, and matches the pattern of the second parameter of the method (usernameToMatch).
GetAllRoles	Returns a string array containing all the role names of the roles available in the role store of the configured provider.
GetRolesForUser	Returns a string array containing all the roles the specified user is associated with. There is also a version that doesn't take any parameters, which gets the roles of the currently logged on user.
GetUsersInRole	Returns a list of users who are associated with the role passed in as a parameter.
IsUserInRole	Returns true if the specified user is a member of the specified role.
RemoveUserFromRole	Removes a single user from the specified role.

Member	Description
RemoveUserFromRoles	Removes the specified user from all roles specified.
RemoveUsersFromRole	Removes all the specified users from a single role.
RemoveUsersFromRoles	Removes all the specified users from all the specified roles.
RoleExists	Returns true if a role exists and otherwise false.

A good use for accessing roles programmatically is to associate users to roles automatically when they register themselves. Of course, this is useful only for specific roles. Imagine that your application supports a role called Everyone, and every single user should be a member of this role. If you register users on your own, you can enter this relationship manually. But if your application supports self-registration for Internet users, you can't do this. Therefore, you somehow have to make sure users will be associated with the Everyone role automatically.

With your first attempt, you might want to catch the CreatedUser event of the CreateUserWizard control, but that's not sufficient. Remember the existence of the ASP.NET WAT, where you can create users. In this case, catching the CreatedUser event of the control placed in your application won't help. Therefore, you have to find a different solution. You need an application-wide event for this purpose, although this will not be raised by the configuration application because it is a different application. One possibility is to catch the Application_AuthenticateRequest event; within the event you verify whether the user is a member of the Everyone class. If not, you can add the user automatically. This shifts the task of adding a user automatically to the role to the point of authentication, which affects every user. To do so, you just have to add a global application class to your project and add the following code.

■ **Caution** You should do something like this only for the lowest privileged roles, such as Everyone. It's never a good idea to perform such an action for any other type of role.

```
protected void Application_AuthenticateRequest(Object sender, EventArgs e)
{
    if (User != null)
    {
        if (User.Identity.IsAuthenticated && Roles.Enabled)
        {
            string EveryoneRoleName =
                     ConfigurationManager.AppSettings["EveryoneRoleName"];

            if (!Roles.IsUserInRole(EveryoneRoleName) &&
                 Roles.RoleExists(EveryoneRoleName))
            {
                Roles.AddUserToRole(User.Identity.Name, EveryoneRoleName);
            }
        }
    }
}
```

The previous code reads the name of the Everyone role from the configuration file so that it is not hard-coded into the application. It then uses the Roles class to check whether the user is already associated with the role, and if not, it checks whether the role exists. If the user is not associated with the role, and the user exists in the system, it uses the Roles.AddUsersToRole method for programmatically adding the user to the Everyone role.

■ **Caution** You might want to use User.IsInRole() in the previous code; however, this is not valid. When the application-wide Application_AuthenticateRequest is called, the RoleManagerModule itself has not been called yet. Therefore, the RolePrincipal with the association of the user and its roles has not been created yet, so a call such as User.IsInRole("Everyone") would return false. Later in your page code—for example, in a Page_Load routine—the RolePrincipal is already initialized, and the call to User.IsInRole("Everyone") will work appropriately.

Using the Roles API with Windows Authentication

The roles API comes with a provider that integrates with Windows roles for Windows authentication: the WindowsTokenRoleProvider. This provider retrieves the Windows group membership information for the currently logged-on user and provides it in the same way for your application as you saw previously with the SqlRoleProvider. When using the WindowsTokenRoleProvider, you have to configure your application using Windows authentication and then configure the WindowsTokenRoleProvider as follows:

```
<configuration>
    <system.web>
        <authentication mode="Windows"/>
        <authorization>
            <deny users="?" />
        </authorization>
        <roleManager enabled="true"
                     cacheRolesInCookie="false"
                     defaultProvider="WindowsRoles">
            <providers>
                <add name="WindowsRoles"
                     type="System.Web.Security.WindowsTokenRoleProvider" />
            </providers>
        </roleManager>
    </system.web>
</configuration>
```

With this configuration in place, the user is authenticated through Windows authentication. The RoleManagerModule automatically creates an instance of RolePrincipal and associates it with the HttpContext.Current.User property. Therefore, you can use the RolePrincipal as follows—there is no difference compared to other roles providers in terms of usage:

```
protected void Page_Load(object sender, EventArgs e)
{
    if ((User != null) && (User.Identity.IsAuthenticated))
    {
        RolePrincipal rp = (RolePrincipal)User;

        StringBuilder Info = new StringBuilder();
        Info.AppendFormat("<h2>Welcome {0}!</h2>", User.Identity.Name);
        Info.AppendFormat("<b>Provider: </b>{0}<br>", rp.ProviderName);
```

```
        Info.AppendFormat("<b>Version: </b>{0}<br>", rp.Version);
        Info.AppendFormat("<b>Expiration: </b>{0}<br>", rp.ExpireDate);
        Info.AppendFormat("<b>Roles: </b><br>");

        string[] Roles = rp.GetRoles();
        foreach (string role in Roles)
        {
            if (!role.Equals(string.Empty))
                Info.AppendFormat("-) {0}<br>", role);
        }

        LabelPrincipalInfo.Text = Info.ToString();
    }
}
```

You can see the result of the previous code in Figure 23-6.

The provider-based architecture enables you to use Windows authentication with Windows groups without changing the inner logic of your application. Everything works the same as with the SqlRoleProvider. The same is true for the membership API introduced in Chapter 21. When configuring another provider, you don't have to change your code; however, you should have some programmatic authorization checks with hard-coded role names in your code, because the Windows groups include the domain qualifier and the custom roles do not. To avoid this, you can add functionality to your application that allows you to associate roles with permissions in either a database or a configuration file. The way you do this depends on the requirements of your application.

Figure 23-6. Results of querying the RolePrincipal with Windows authentication

We suggest not using Windows groups for authorization in your application directly except for a few of the built-in groups such as the Administrators group. In most cases, it's useful to define roles that are specific to your application. This is why:

- Windows groups other than the built-in groups depend on the name of the domain or machine on which they exist.
- In most cases, Windows groups in a domain are structured according to the organizational and network management requirements of the enterprise. Often these requirements do not map to the application requirements.
- Structuring application roles independently from the network groups makes your application more flexible and usable across multiple types of network structures.

A good example that introduces such a design is Windows SharePoint Services. SharePoint (currently available in version 2007) is a ready-to-use portal solution built on ASP.NET that can be used for free with Windows Server. SharePoint includes prebuilt functionality for document libraries, meeting workspaces, and lists. You can use SharePoint for collaboratively working in teams—sharing documents, planning meetings, and more.

For example, SharePoint defines application-specific roles that are typical for a collaborative portal solution. You can assign both Windows users and Windows groups to these roles. SharePoint by default includes the roles Administrator, Web Author, Designer, and Reader. All of these roles are optimized for performing authorization within the portal. For example, while a Web Author automatically gets permission to create new workspaces for meetings and to structure contents displayed on the portal, a Reader is just able to view information on the portal. Every Windows user assigned to one of these roles, or every Windows user who is a member of a Windows group assigned to one of these roles, automatically gets the appropriate permissions. Therefore, SharePoint is independent of the network structure deployed in the Windows network where it is used. You will learn more details about implementing such concepts in your own application in Chapter 26, where you will learn details about custom membership and roles providers.

Authorization and Roles in IIS 7.x

IIS 7.x natively supports the same URL-based authorization mechanisms as ASP.NET does. On the one hand, IIS 7.x ships with its own UrlAuthorizationModule. This allows configuration of URL-based authorization in the <authorization> configuration option as a part of the <system.webServer> section of the web.config configuration file. On the other hand, when running IIS in ASP.NET integrated mode you can also configure web applications hosted in IIS 7.x to leverage the ASP.NET-based URL authorization module directly. You can therefore leverage existing <authorization> configurations within the <system.web> section.

IIS 7.x allows you to manage access rules for your own, native authorization module for websites directly from within the management console. Even more, you can manage roles stored in your configured roles API provider's data store directly from the management console, as well. You already saw how to configure access rules using the IIS management console on IIS 7.x in Chapter 20, where you configured some Basic authentication rules for enabling forms authentication for ASP.NET and non-ASP.NET applications. Figure 23-7 shows the authorization configuration feature of the IIS 7.x management console, again. In this section we will drill into some details about IIS 7.x authorization mechanisms.

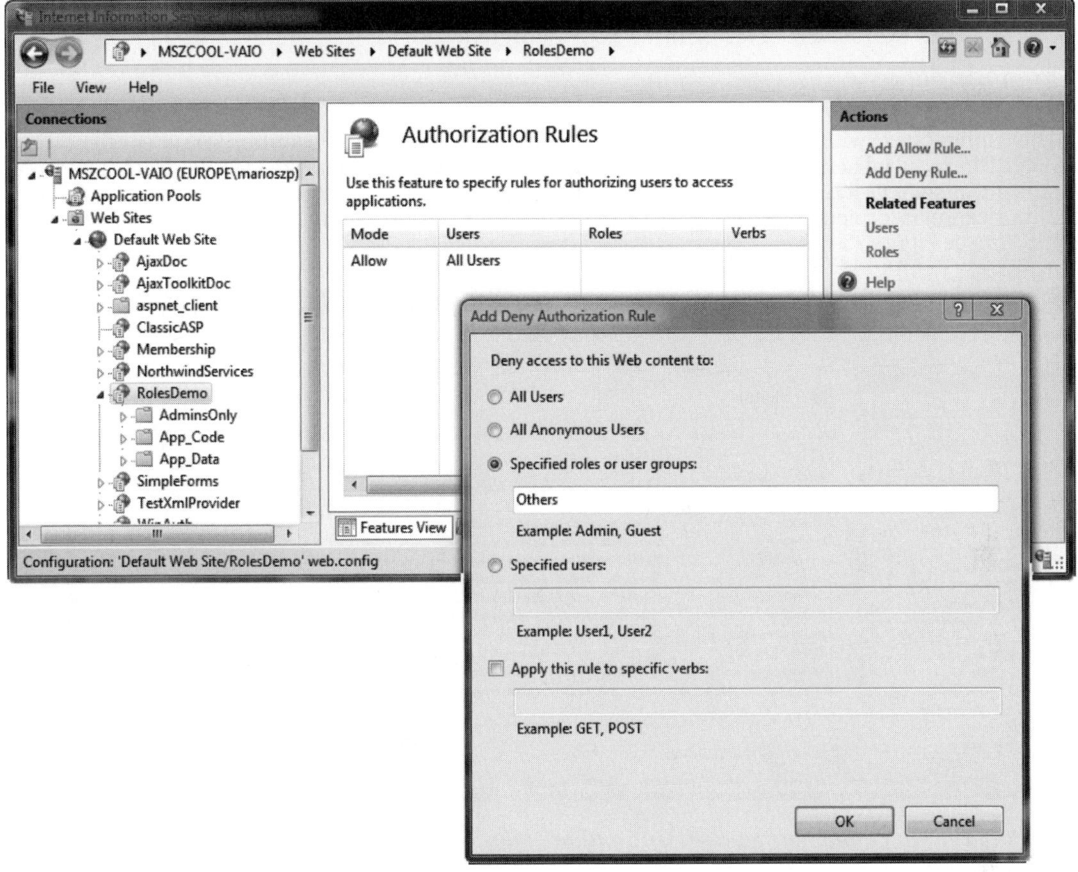

Figure 23-7. Configuring authorization rules in IIS 7.x

The IIS 7.x URL authorization feature works completely independently of ASP.NET; it is implemented in its own, native HTTP module shipping with IIS 7.x. As mentioned earlier, it is configured in a separate configuration section within your web.config configuration file. Any authorization rule you configure through the IIS 7.x management console gets added to an <authorization> configuration section within the <system.webServer> section of the web.config file. You learned about the details of the IIS 7.x configuration architecture in Chapter 18. A typical IIS 7.x authorization configuration in a web.config file looks similar to the following one and conceptually works the same way as ASP.NET authorization rules do.

```
<system.webServer>
      <security>
          <authorization>
              <remove users="*" roles="" verbs="" />
              <add accessType="Deny" users="?" />
              <add accessType="Allow" users="*" />
          </authorization>
      </security>
```

```
        ...
        <!-- Other system.webServer related configuration -->
        ...
</system.webServer>
```

The configuration within that section adheres to the same rules that the authorization configuration of ASP.NET introduced at the beginning of this chapter does. IIS 7.x evaluates these rules from top to bottom, and as soon as it finds an applicable rule it stops searching immediately. Again, don't forget that the authorization is implemented in its own, native UrlAuthorizationModule.dll module, which ships with IIS 7.x (see Figure 23-8).

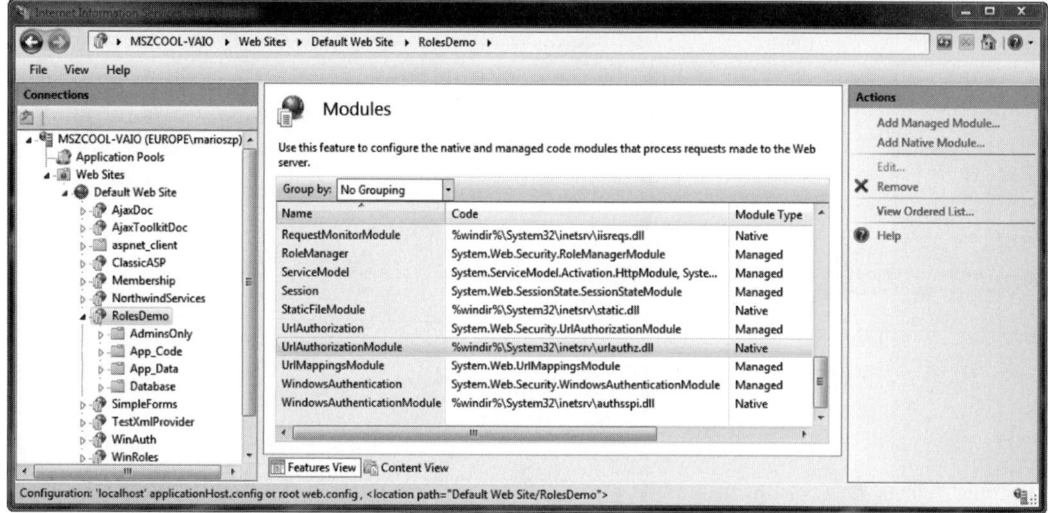

Figure 23-8. *The native and the managed URL authorization modules*

Why is it important to understand this difference? First of all, you can use the IIS 7.x UrlAuthorizationModule.dll independently from ASP.NET. When you install IIS 7.x on a machine without installing ASP.NET in the web server, you still could use URL-based authorization through the native module. However, a second reason is much more important for an ASP.NET developer. The native URL authorization module shipping with IIS 7.x is able to correctly identify logged in users authenticated by all possible authentication modules, including Basic authentication, Windows authentication, and even forms authentication. This is because the module has been developed so that it understands the forms authentication ticket (either encoded in a cookie or the query string) correctly. But unfortunately it has not been implemented with ASP.NET roles in mind.

What is the reason for that? Well, roles are extracted by the ASP.NET infrastructure at a certain stage within the application's life cycle from a storage (for example, a database configured for the roles provider). Role information is then encapsulated in managed objects implementing the IPrincipal interface, and therefore stored in pure, managed .NET objects that are not accessible to native modules of IIS 7.x. Therefore, native modules of IIS 7.x such as the UrlAuthorizationModule cannot make use of this information. So, you cannot configure any ASP.NET-based roles in conjunction with the native IIS 7.x URL authorization module within the <authorization> configuration of the <system.webServer> section. In reality, that means you can use only Windows Roles principal names when using the native UrlAuthorizationModule shipping with IIS 7.x.

As mentioned before, in the case of user names you can fully leverage the authorization management of IIS 7.x. This is because the native module is implemented in a way that recognizes users authenticated by native modules and users authenticated by managed modules such as the FormsAuthenticationModule. To make use of the FormsAuthentication module in conjunction with the native UrlAuthorizationModule, the FormsAuthentication module needs to be enabled for the native processing queue, as you learned in Chapter 20.

Finally, that means role-based authorization is one of the few exceptions where you still have to keep IIS-based and ASP.NET-based configuration in mind separately.

Authorization with ASP.NET Roles in IIS 7.x

Now we know that the native URL authorization module shipping with IIS 7.x does not understand ASP.NET-specific role information, as this information is only encapsulated into managed objects implementing managed interfaces. On the other hand, running IIS 7.x in ASP.NET integrated mode provides a unified HTTP processing pipeline where native and managed modules are processed within the same HTTP module pipeline. Therefore, you can use any managed HTTP module written with the .NET language of your choice to extend the default behavior of IIS 7.x.

That means you can write your own HTTP modules with .NET and integrate them into the IIS 7.x processing pipeline. But it also means that you can integrate existing ASP.NET modules such as the FormsAuthentication or even the UrlAuthorization modules directly into the processing pipeline. That enables you to achieve the following two things much more easily compared to previous versions of IIS:

- Protect non-ASP.NET resources as outlined in the previous section
- Use ASP.NET security for any other web application, even if it's not written with ASP.NET

Both targets can be achieved the same way—you just need to enable the managed UrlAuthorization module shipping with ASP.NET to be processed in the native pipeline together with other IIS 7.x modules (and ASP.NET modules) as well. You can enable this configuration option in the IIS 7.x modules configuration feature, as outlined in Figure 23-9.

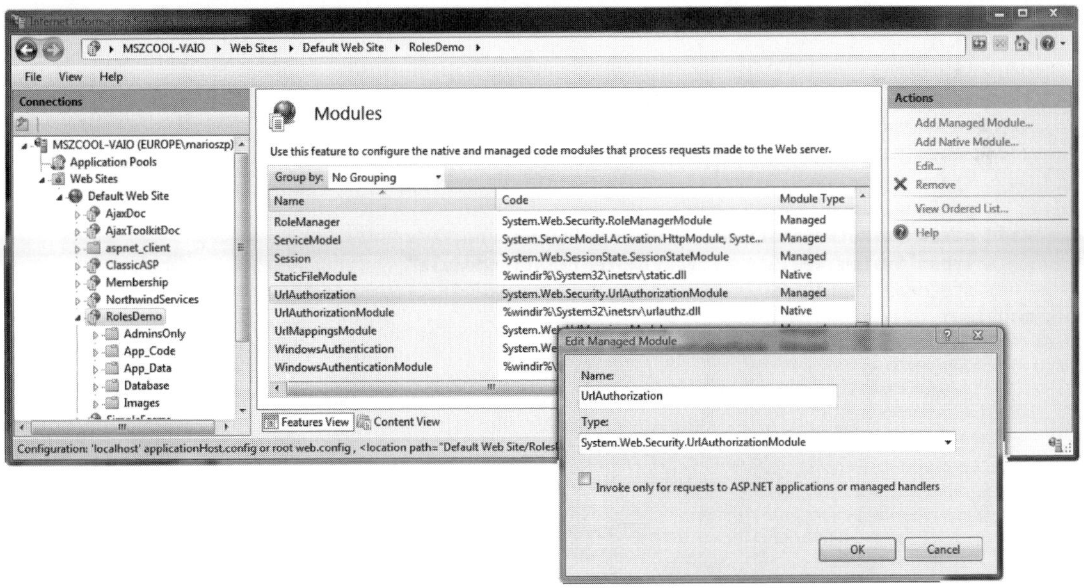

Figure 23-9. Enabling the UrlAuthorization managed module for native processing

As soon as you have enabled the managed UrlAuthorization module, any resource of the website gets protected by ASP.NET security, as well. That's true for images, text files, or any other type of file such as classic ASP pages or even PHP pages. Now you can configure authorization roles for accessing all of these resources through the <authorization> configuration section within the <system.web> section of your web.config file. Figure 23-10 illustrates the power of this IIS 7.x and ASP.NET integrated way of security. Even though IIS 7.x authorization is configured to allow anyone access to the site, whenever the browser is accessing an image, it gets redirected to the forms authentication login page because of ASP.NET authorization configuration.

The configuration within the web.config file looks similar to the following one for the case demonstrated in Figure 23-10.

```
<configuration>
  <!-- More configuration settings here ... -->
  <system.web>
    <authentication mode="Forms">
      <forms cookieless="UseUri" />
    </authentication>
    <authorization>
      <deny users="?" />
    </authorization>
    <!-- More configuration settings here ... -->
  </system.web>

  <system.webServer>
    <validation validateIntegratedModeConfiguration="false" />
    <security>
      <authorization>
        <remove users="*" roles="" verbs="" />
        <add accessType="Allow" users="*" roles="" />
      </authorization>
    </security>
    <modules>
      <remove name="UrlAuthorization" />
      <remove name="FormsAuthentication" />
      <add name="FormsAuthentication"
           type="System.Web.Security.FormsAuthenticationModule"
           preCondition="" />
      <add name="UrlAuthorization"
           type="System.Web.Security.UrlAuthorizationModule"
           preCondition="" />
    </modules>
    <!-- More configuration settings here ... -->
  </system.webServer>
</configuration>
```

Figure 23-10. *The ASP.NET UrlAuthorization module in action for other file types*

As you can see in the preceding configuration, the IIS 7.x authorization allows access to the website to any user, whereas the ASP.NET authorization clearly denies access to anonymous users. Furthermore, the IIS 7.x configuration includes both the ASP.NET FormsAuthenticationModule and the ASP.NET UrlAuthorizationModule in its processing pipeline, which means they will affect access to any resource—whether ASP.NET-based or not ASP.NET-based—within the web application directory. This also means that you can leverage roles managed by ASP.NET through the roles API and roles API framework for any resource hosted in an IIS 7.x web application.

Using the UrlAuthorization module of ASP.NET for the native processing pipeline only makes sense when not using Windows authentication. That's because with Windows authentication you can configure any declarative authorization rules directly through the IIS 7.x management console to leverage the out-of-the-box functionality provided by the native UrlAuthorizationModule shipping with IIS 7.x.

Managing ASP.NET Roles with IIS 7.x

Although the native UrlAuthorization module shipping with IIS 7.x does not understand application roles managed by ASP.NET through the roles API or through any other managed-only mechanism, it allows you to manage roles for the roles API with any provider configured in your web.config directly through its management console. You can do this through the .NET Roles configuration feature, as shown in Figure 23-11.

You can add, delete, or modify roles directly through the IIS management console using this feature, whereas IIS leverages the roles API provider configured in your web.config. You can use any provider, even custom providers, as you will learn in Chapter 26. You can configure providers through the Providers configuration feature of the IIS 7.x management console, as shown in Figure 23-12.

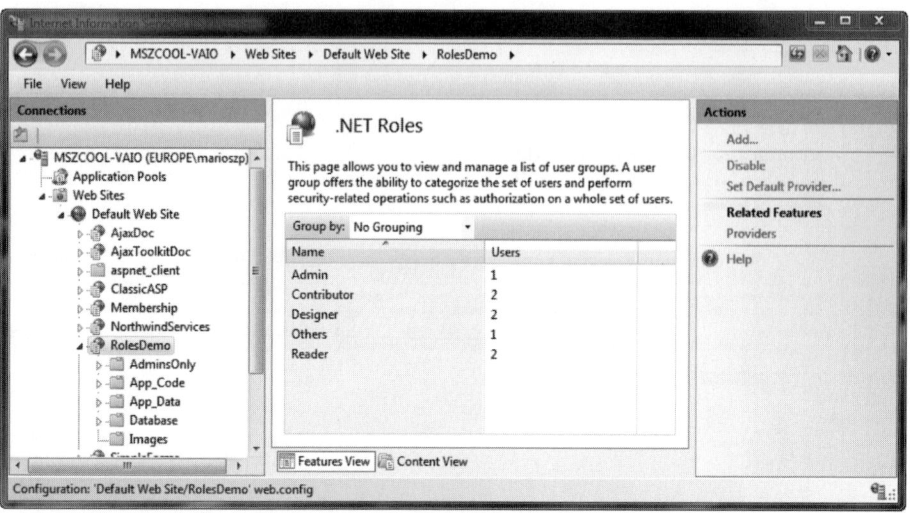

Figure 23-11. The .NET Roles configuration feature in action

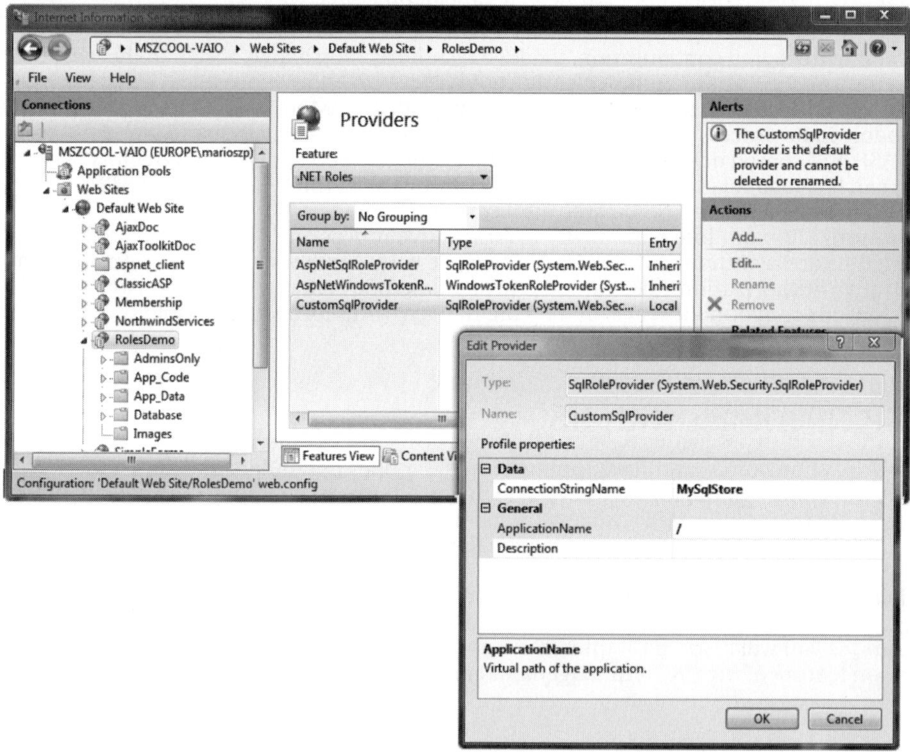

Figure 23-12. Configuring roles providers with IIS 7.x

The provider feature allows you to configure providers for .NET users (membership API, Chapter 21), .NET Roles as shown in Figure 23-12, and .NET Profiles (see Chapter 24 for more details). The configuration feature shown in Figure 23-11 leverages the provider configured for .NET Roles for any management operation.

Together with the possibilities introduced in the previous section of this chapter (authorization with ASP.NET Roles in IIS 7.x) and the possibilities introduced in Chapters 20 and 21, this allows you to leverage the full power of the ASP.NET framework, including forms authentication, the membership API, and the roles API for any web application hosted in IIS 7.x—even if it is not ASP.NET-based. This is an extremely useful and powerful possibility provided by IIS 7.x, thanks to its new architecture.

Summary

Authorization provides an effective way to control access to resources. In this chapter, you learned how to safeguard different pages, directories, and code routines in your web application using authorization. You also saw how to use the roles API for managing and associating users with roles for simpler authorization. Finally, you learned about the new authorization possibilities introduced with IIS 7.x. IIS 7.x ships with its own, native UrlAuthorization module that allows declarative authorization even without ASP.NET being involved. Although the native authorization module shipping with IIS 7.x is able to understand all types of authenticated users (Basic, Windows, and forms), it is unable to extract ASP.NET roles from managed applications, as they are encapsulated behind pure managed objects. However, you learned how to solve this problem by leveraging the ASP.NET integrated mode of IIS 7.x and configuring the UrlAuthorization module shipping with ASP.NET. You configured these to be available even for applications that aren't ASP.NET-based as a general authorization mechanism across many IIS 7.x-based web applications.

In the next chapter, you'll take a look at a few advanced security techniques that you can use to extend ASP.NET authentication and authorization.

CHAPTER 24

■ ■ ■

Profiles

In previous chapters, you learned how to use a range of ASP.NET security features. Many of these features are geared to identifying individual users (authentication) and then determining what actions they should be able to perform (authorization). But you need to uniquely identify and authenticate users for another important reason—to keep track of user-specific information.

In ASP.NET 1.x, the only practical option to store user-specific information was to create your own data access component (a topic covered in Chapter 8). Your web page could call the methods of your data access component to retrieve the current user's data and then save any changes. As you'll see in this chapter, this approach still makes a lot of sense in many scenarios. However, ASP.NET 2.0 introduced another option with the *profiles* feature, which remains unchanged in ASP.NET 4. When you use profiles, ASP.NET handles retrieving and updating user-specific data automatically by using a back-end data source (typically a database).

Conceptually, the profiles feature is a lot like creating your own database component. However, it adds some neat conveniences. Most impressively, it integrates with the ASP.NET authentication model in such a way that user information is automatically retrieved for the current user when needed and (if this information is changed) written back to the database at the end of the current request. Best of all, your web-page code can access the current user's profile data using strongly typed properties.

In this chapter, you'll learn how to use profiles, how the profiles system works, and when profiles make the most sense. You'll also learn how to extend the Profiles API with a custom profile provider.

Understanding Profiles

One of the most significant differences between profiles and other types of state management (as discussed in Chapter 6) is that profiles are designed to store information permanently by using a back-end data source such as a database. Most other types of state management are designed to maintain information for a series of requests that occur in a relatively short space of time (such as session state and caching) or in the current browser session (such as non-persistent cookies and view state) or to transfer information from one page to another (such as the query string and cross-page posting). If you need to store information for the longer term in a database, profiles simply provide a convenient model that manages the retrieval and persistence of this information for you.

Before you begin using profiles, you need to assess them carefully. In the following sections, you'll learn how they stack up.

Profile Performance

The goal of ASP.NET's profiles feature is to provide a transparent way to manage user-specific information, without forcing you to write custom data access code using the ADO.NET data classes. Unfortunately, many features that seem convenient suffer from poor performance or scalability. This is particularly a concern with profiles, because they involve database access, and database access can easily become a scalability bottleneck for any distributed application.

So, do profiles suffer from scalability problems? This question has no simple answer. It all depends on how much data you need to store and how often you plan to access it. To make an informed decision, you need to know a little more about how profiles work.

Profiles plug into the page life cycle in two ways:

- The first time you access the Profile object in your code, ASP.NET retrieves the complete profile data for the current user from the database. From this point onward, you can read the profile information in your code without any further database work (until the next postback).
- If you change any profile data, the update is deferred until the page processing is complete. At that point (after the PreRender, PreRenderComplete, and Unload events have fired for the page), the profile is written back to the database. This way, multiple changes are batched into one operation. If you don't change the profile data, no extra database work is incurred.

■ **Note** Profile reading and saving is implemented by a dedicated ProfileModule, which runs during each request. Chapter 5 discusses HTTP modules in more detail.

Overall, the profiles feature could result in two extra database trips for each request (in a read-write scenario) or one extra database trip (if you are simply reading profile data). The profiles feature doesn't integrate with caching, so every request that uses profile data requires a database connection.

From a performance standpoint, profiles work best when the following is true:

- You have a relatively small number of pages that access the profile data.
- You are storing small amounts of data.
- They tend to work less well when the following is true:
- You have a large number of pages that need to use profile information.
- You are storing large amounts of data. This is particularly inefficient if you need to use only some of that data in a given request (because the profile model always retrieves the full block of profile data).

Of course, you can combine profiles with another type of state management. For example, imagine your website includes an order wizard that walks the user through several steps. At the beginning of this process, you could retrieve the profile information and store it in session state. You could then use the Session collection for the remainder of the process. Assuming you're using the in-process or out-of-process state server to maintain session data, this approach is more efficient because it saves you from needing to connect to the database repeatedly.

How Profiles Store Data

The most significant limitation with profiles doesn't have anything to do with performance—instead, it's a limitation of how the profiles are serialized. The default profile provider included with ASP.NET serializes profile information into a block of data that's inserted into a single field in a database record. For example, if you serialize address information, you'll end up with something like this:

```
Marty Soren315 Southpart DriveLompocCalifornia93436U.S.A.
```

Another field indicates where each value starts and stops, using a format like this:

```
Name:S:0:11:Street:S:11:19:City:S:30:6:State:S:36:10:ZipCode:S:46:5:Country:S:51:6
```

Although this approach gives you the flexibility to store just about any type of data, it makes it more difficult to use this data in other applications. You can write custom code to parse the profile data in order to find the information you want, but depending on the amount of data and the data types you're using, this can be an extremely tedious process. And even if you do this, you're still limited in the ways you can reuse this information. For example, imagine you use profiles to store customer address information. Because of the proprietary format, it's no longer possible to generate customer lists in an application such as Microsoft Word or perform queries that filter or sort records using this profile data. (For example, you can't easily perform a query to get all the customers living in a specific city.)

This problem has two solutions:

- Use custom data access components instead of profiles to store and retrieve data in a database.
- Create a custom profile provider that's designed to store information using your database schema.

Out of the two options, creating a custom data access component is easier, and it gives you more flexibility. You can design your data component to have any interface you want, and you can then reuse that component with other .NET applications. Currently, ASP.NET developers are more likely to use this approach because it has been around since .NET 1.0 and is well understood.

The second option is interesting because it allows your page to keep using the profile model. In fact, you could create an application that uses the standard profile serialization with the SqlProfileProvider and then switch it later to use a custom provider. To make this switch, you don't need to change any code. Instead, you simply modify the profile settings in the web.config file. As it becomes more common for websites to use profiles, custom profile providers will become more attractive.

■ **Note** It's also important to consider the type of data that works best in a profile. As with many other types of state management, you can store any serializable types into a profile, including simple types and custom classes.

Profiles and Authentication

One significant difference between profiles and other types of state management is that profiles are stored as individual records, each of which is uniquely identified by user name. This means that profiles require you to use some sort of authentication system. It makes no difference what type of authentication system you use (Windows, forms, or a custom authentication system)—the only requirement is that authenticated users are assigned a unique user name. That user name is used to find the matching profile record in the database.

■ **Note** Later in this chapter (in the section "Anonymous Profiles"), you'll also learn how the anonymous identification feature lets you temporarily store profile information for users who haven't logged in.

Profiles vs. Custom Data Components

Profiles are a natural competitor with custom data components of the kind you saw in Chapter 8. Clearly, data components are far more flexible. They allow you not only to maintain user-specific information but also to store other types of information and perform more complex business tasks.

For example, an e-commerce website could realistically use profiles to maintain customer address information (with the limitations discussed in the previous section). However, you wouldn't use a profile to store information about previous orders. Not only is it far too much information to store efficiently, it's also awkward to manipulate.

The standard profile provider that's included with ASP.NET (named SqlProfileProvider) doesn't provide any features beyond basic database storage and retrieval. The following list includes some features that you can easily add through a custom database component but aren't available if you're using the SqlProfileProvider. If you need any of these features, you'll need to abandon profiles and create your own data access component, or you'll need to design a custom profile provider.

Encryption: Profile data can be serialized into a string, XML, or a binary representation. But no matter what you choose, you'll always end up storing the raw text. If you have sensitive information, your only option is to encrypt it manually before you store it, which has the undesirable result of putting encryption logic in your UI code.

Validation: You can't restrict the type of information that can be placed in a profile. You need to use other tools (such as validator controls and custom data classes) to prevent invalid data.

Caching: If profile information is used in a page, it's always retrieved from the database. You can't keep profile information around in memory. Although you can copy profile information into the cache, it becomes more difficult to track this information.

Auditing: When you design a custom database component, you have the ability to add any logging or tracing code you want. You can use this to diagnose unexpected errors or monitor the performance of your web application. However, if you want these features with profiles, you'll need to build a custom profile provider that has the logging code.

Now that you know the ins and outs of profiles, you're ready to try them.

Using the SqlProfileProvider

The SqlProfileProvider allows you to store profile information in a SQL Server 7.0 or later database. You can choose to create the profile tables in any database. However, you can't change any of the other database schema details, which means you're locked into specific table names, column names, and serialization formats.

From start to finish, you need to perform the following steps to use profiles:

1. Create the profile tables. (If you're using SQL Server Express Edition, this step happens automatically.)
2. Configure the profile provider.
3. Define some profile properties.
4. Enable authentication for a portion of your website.
5. Use the profile properties in your web-page code.

You'll tackle these steps in the following sections.

Creating the Profile Tables

If you're not using SQL Server Express, you must create the profile tables manually. To do so, you use the aspnet_regsql.exe command-line utility, which is the same tool that allows you to generate databases for other ASP.NET features, such as SQL Server-based session state, membership, roles, database cache dependencies, and web parts personalization. You can find the aspnet_regsql.exe tool in the c:\Windows\Microsoft.NET\Framework\[Version] folder.

■ **Note** If you're using SQL Server Express Edition, you don't need to create your database by hand. Instead, the first time you use the profiles feature, ASP.NET will create a new database named aspnetdb.mdf, place it in the App_Data subdirectory of your web application, and add the profiles tables. If you already have an aspnetdb.mdf database (because you're using it for another feature), ASP.NET will simply add the profiles tables to the existing aspnetdb.mdf database.

To create the tables, views, and stored procedures required for profiles, you use aspnet_regsql.exe with the -A p command-line option. The only other detail you need to supply is the server location (-S), database name (-d), and authentication information for connecting to the database (use -U and -P to supply a password and user name, or use -E to use the current Windows account). If you leave the other server location and database name, aspnet_regsql.exe uses the default instance on the current computer and creates a database named aspnetdb.

Here's an example that creates the aspnetdb database with the default name on the current computer by logging into the database using the current Windows account:

```
aspnet_regsql.exe -A p -E
```

Table 24-1 shows the tables that aspnet_regsql.exe creates. (The rather unexciting views aren't included.)

Table 24-1. Database Tables Used for Profiles

Table Name	Description
aspnet_Applications	Lists all the web applications that have records in this database. It's possible for several ASP.NET applications to use the same aspnetdb database. In this case, you have the option of separating the profile information so that it's distinct for each application (by giving each application a different application name when you register the profile provider), or of sharing it (by giving each application the same application name).
aspnet_Profile	Stores the user-specific profile information. Each record contains the complete profile information for a single user. The PropertyNames field lists the property names, and the PropertyValuesString and PropertyValuesBinary fields list all the property data, although you'll need to do some work if you want to parse this information for use in other non-ASP.NET programs. Each record also includes the last update date and time (LastUpdatedDate).
aspnet_SchemaVersions	Lists the supported schemas for storing profile information. In the future, this could allow new versions of ASP.NET to provide new ways of storing profile information without breaking support for old profile databases that are still in use.
aspnet_Users	Lists user names and maps them to one of the applications in aspnet_Applications. Also records the last request date and time (LastActivityDate) and whether the record was generated automatically for an anonymous user (IsAnonymous). Anonymous user support is discussed later in this chapter (in the section "Anonymous Profiles").

■ **Note** Even if you don't use the default database name (aspnetdb), you should use a new, blank database that doesn't include any other custom tables. That's because aspnet_regsql.exe creates several tables for profiles (see Table 24-1), and you shouldn't risk confusing them with business data. The examples in the rest of this chapter assume you're using aspnetdb.

Figure 24-1 shows the relationships between the most important profile tables.

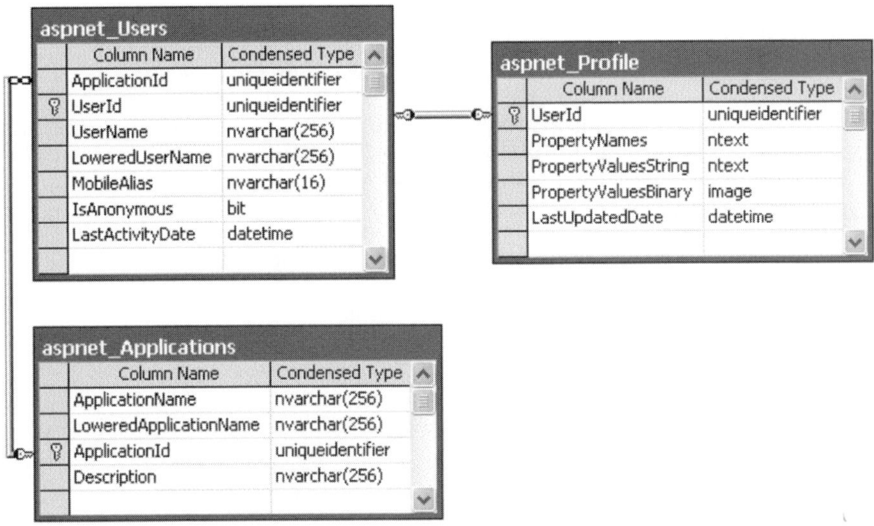

Figure 24-1. *The profile tables*

ASP.NET also creates several stored procedures that allow it to manage the information in these tables more easily. Table 24-2 lists the most noteworthy stored procedures.

Table 24-2. *Database Stored Procedures Used for Profiles*

Stored Procedure	Description
aspnet_Applications_CreateApplications	Checks whether a specific application name exists in the aspnet_Applications table and creates the record if needed.
aspnet_CheckSchemaVersion	Checks for support of a specific schema version for a specific feature (such as profiles) using the aspnet_SchemaVersions table.
aspnet_Profile_GetProfiles	Retrieves the user name and update times for all the profile records in the aspnet_Profile table for a specific web application. Doesn't return the actual profile data.
aspnet_Profile_GetProperties	Retrieves the profile information for a specific user (which you specify by user name). The information is not parsed in any way—instead, this stored procedure simply returns the underlying fields (PropertyNames, PropertyValuesString, PropertyValuesBinary).

Stored Procedure	Description
aspnet_Profile_SetProperties	Sets the profile information for a specific user (which you specify by user name). This stored procedure requires values for the PropertyNames, PropertyValuesStrings, and PropertyValuesBinary fields. There's no way to update just a single property in a profile.
aspnet_Profile_GetNumberOfInactiveProfiles	Returns profile records that haven't been used within a time window you specify.
aspnet_Profile_DeleteInactiveProfiles	Removes profile records that haven't been used within a time window you specify.
aspnet_Users_CreateUser	Creates a new record in the aspnet_Users table for a specific user. Checks whether the user exists (in which case no action is taken) and creates a GUID to use for the UserID field if none is specified.
aspnet_Users_DeleteUser	Removes a specific user record from the aspnet_Users table.

Configuring the Provider

Now that you have the database in place, you can register the SqlProfileProvider using the web.config file. First, define a connection string for the profile database. Then, use the <profile> section to remove any existing providers (with the <clear> element), and add a new instance of the System.Web.Profile.SqlProfileProvider class (with the <add> element). Here are the configuration settings you need:

```
<configuration>
  <connectionStrings>
    <add name="SqlServices" connectionString=
      "Data Source=localhost;Integrated Security=SSPI;Initial Catalog=aspnetdb;" />
  </connectionStrings>

  <system.web>
    <profile defaultProvider="SqlProvider">
      <providers>
        <clear />
        <add name="SqlProvider"
          type="System.Web.Profile.SqlProfileProvider"
          connectionStringName="SqlServices"
          applicationName="TestApplication" />
      </providers>
    </profile>
    ...
  </system.web>
</configuration>
```

When you define a profile provider, you need to supply a name (which the <profile> element can then reference as the default provider), the exact type name, a connection string, and a web application name. Use different application names to separate the profile information between web applications (or use the same application name to share it).

Defining Profile Properties

Before you can store anything in the aspnet_Profile table, you need to define it specifically. You do this by adding the <properties> element inside the <profile> section of the web.config file. Inside the <properties> element, you place one <add> tag for each user-specific piece of information you want to store. At a minimum, the <add> element supplies the name for the property, like this:

```
<profile defaultProvider="SqlProvider">
  <providers>
    ...
  </providers>
  <properties>
    <add name="FirstName"/>
    <add name="LastName"/>
  </properties>
</profile>
```

Usually, you'll also supply the data type. (If you don't, the property is treated as a string.) You can specify any serializable .NET class as the type, as shown here:

```
<add name="FirstName" type="String"/>
<add name="LastName" type="String"/>
<add name="DateOfBirth" type="DateTime"/>
```

You can set a few more property attributes to create the more advanced properties shown in Table 24-3.

Table 24-3. *Profile Property Attributes*

Attribute (for the <add> Element)	Description
name	The name of the property.
type	The fully qualified class name that represents the data type for this property. By default, this is System.String.
serializeAs	Indicates the format to use when serializing this value (String, Binary, Xml, or ProviderSpecific). You'll look more closely at the serialization model in the section "Profile Serialization."
readOnly	Add this attribute with a value of true to create a property that can be read but not changed. (Attempting to change the property will cause a compile-time error.) By default, this is false.

Attribute (for the <add> Element)	Description
defaultValue	A default value that will be used if the profile doesn't exist or doesn't include this particular piece of information. The default value has no effect on serialization—if you set a profile property, the ProfileModule will commit the current values to the database, even if they match the default values.
allowAnonymous	A Boolean value that indicates whether this property can be used with the anonymous profiles feature discussed later in this chapter. By default, this is false.
provider	The profile provider that should be used to manage just this property. By default, all properties are managed using the provider specified in the <profile> element, but you can assign different properties to different providers.

Using Profile Properties

Because profiles are stored in a user-specific record, you need to authenticate the current user before you can read or write profile information. You can use any type of authentication system (Windows, forms, or custom). You simply need to add an authorization rule to prevent anonymous access for the page or folder where you plan to use the profile. Here's an example:

```
<configuration>
  ...
  <system.web>
    <authentication mode="Windows"/>
    <authorization>
      <deny users="?"/>
    </authorization>
    ...
  </system.web>
</configuration>
```

Chapter 23 has much more information about authorization rules.

With these details in place, you're ready to access the profile information using the Profile property of the current page. When you run your application, ASP.NET creates a new class to represent the profile by deriving from System.Web.Profile.ProfileBase, which wraps a collection of profile settings. ASP.NET adds a strongly typed property to this class for each profile property you've defined in the web.config file. These strongly typed properties simply call the GetPropertyValue() and SetPropertyValue() methods of the ProfileBase base class to retrieve and set the corresponding profile values.

For example, if you've defined a string property named FirstName, you can set it in your page like this:

```
Profile.FirstName = "Henry";
```

Figure 24-2 presents a complete test page that allows the user to display the profile information for the current user or set new profile information.

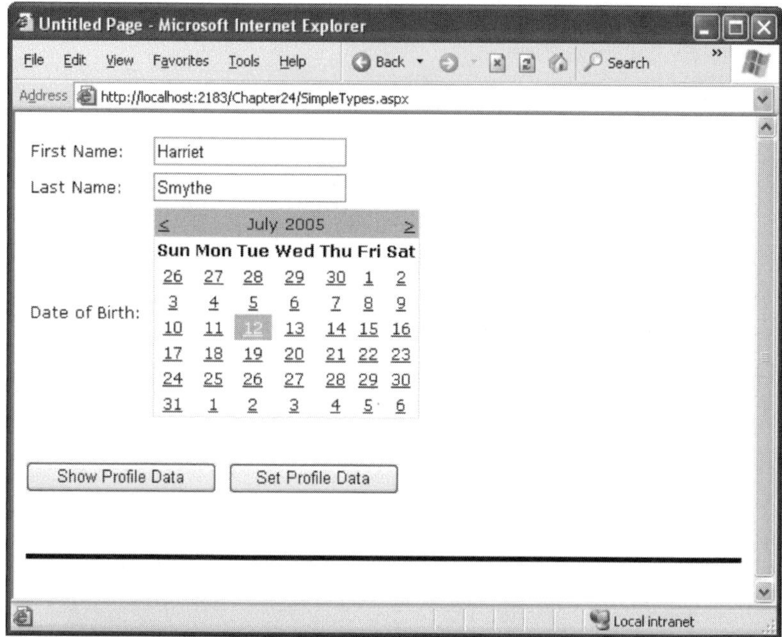

Figure 24-2. Testing profiles

The first time this page runs, no profile information is retrieved, and no database connection is used. However, if you click the Show Profile Data button, the profile information is retrieved and displayed on the page:

```
protected void cmdShow_Click(object sender, EventArgs e)
{
    lbl.Text = "First Name: " + Profile.FirstName + "<br />" +
      "Last Name: " + Profile.LastName + "<br />" +
      "Date of Birth: " + Profile.DateOfBirth.ToShortDateString();
}
```

At this point, an error will occur if the profile database is missing or the connection can't be opened. Otherwise, your page will run without a hitch, and you'll see the newly retrieved profile information. Technically, the complete profile is retrieved when your code accesses the Profile.FirstName property in the first line and is used for the subsequent code statements.

■ **Note** Profile properties behave like any other class member variable. That means if you read a profile value that hasn't been set, you'll get a default initialized value (like an empty string or the number 0).

If you click the Set Profile Data button, the profile information is set based on the current control values:

```
protected void cmdSet_Click(object sender, EventArgs e)
{
    Profile.FirstName = txtFirst.Text;
    Profile.LastName = txtLast.Text;
    Profile.DateOfBirth = Calendar1.SelectedDate;
}
```

Now the profile information is committed to the database when the page request finishes. If you want to commit some or all of the information earlier (and possibly incur multiple database trips), just call the Profile.Save() method. As you can see, the profiles feature is unmatched for simplicity.

■ **Tip** The Profile object doesn't include just the properties you've defined. It also provides LastActivityDate and LastUpdatedDate properties with information drawn from the database.

Profile Serialization

Earlier, you learned how properties are serialized into a single string. For example, if you save a FirstName of Harriet and a LastName of Smythe, both values are crowded together in the PropertyValuesString field, saving space:

```
HarrietSmythe
```

The PropertyNames field gives the information you need to parse each value from the PropertyValuesString field. Here's what you'll see in the PropertyNames field in this example:

```
FirstName:S:0:7:LastName:S:7:6:
```

The colons (:) are used as delimiters. The basic format is as follows:

```
PropertyName:StringOrBinarySerialization:StartingCharacterIndex:Length:
```

Something interesting happens if you create a profile with a DateTime data type. When you look at the PropertyValuesString field, you'll see something like this:

```
<?xml version="1.0" encoding="utf-16"?><dateTime>2007-07-12T00:00:00-04:00
</dateTime>HarrietSmythe
```

Initially, it looks like the profile data is serialized as XML, but the PropertyValuesString clearly doesn't contain a valid XML document (because of the text at the end). What has actually happened is that the first piece of information, the DateTime, is serialized (by default) as XML. The following two profile properties are serialized as ordinary strings.

The PropertyNames field makes it slightly clearer:

```
DateOfBirth:S:0:81:FirstName:S:87:7:LastName:S:94:6:
```

Interestingly, you have the ability to change the serialization format of any profile property by adding the serializeAs attribute to its declaration in the web.config file. Table 24-4 lists your choices.

Table 24-4. Serialization Options

SerializeAs	Description
String	Converts the type to a string representation. Requires a type converter that can handle the job. (See Chapter 28 for more information about type converters.)
Xml	Converts the type to an XML representation, which is stored in a string, using the System.Xml.XmlSerialization.XmlSerializer (the same class that's used with web services).
Binary	Converts the type to a proprietary binary representation that only .NET understands using the System.Runtime.Serialization.Formatters.Binary.BinaryFormatter. This is the most compact option but the least flexible. Binary data is stored in the PropertyValuesBinary field instead of the PropertyValues.
ProviderSpecific	Performs customized serialization that's implemented in a custom provider.

For example, here's how you can change the serialization for the profile settings:

```
<add name="FirstName" type="String" serializeAs="Xml"/>
<add name="LastName" type="String" serializeAs="Xml"/>
<add name="DateOfBirth" type="DateTime" serializeAs="String"/>
```

Now the next time you set the profile, the serialized representation in the PropertyValuesString field will take this form:

```
2007-07-12<?xml version="1.0" encoding="utf-16"?><string>Harriet</string>
<?xml version="1.0" encoding="utf-16"?><string>Smythe</string>
```

If you use the binary serialization mode, the property value will be placed in the PropertyValuesBinary field instead of the PropertyValuesString field. The only indication of this shift is the use of the letter B instead of S in the PropertyNames field. Here's an example where the FirstName property is serialized in the PropertyValuesBinary field:

```
DateOfBirth:S:0:9:FirstName:B:0:31:LastName:S:9:64:
```

All of these serialization details raise an important question—what happens when you change profile properties or the way they are serialized? Profile properties don't have any support for versioning. However, you can add or remove properties with relatively minor consequences. For example, the ProfileModule will ignore properties that are present in the aspnet_Profile table but not defined in the web.config file. The next time you modify part of the profile, these properties will be replaced with the new profile information. Similarly, if you define a profile in the web.config file that doesn't exist in the serialized profile information, the ProfileModule will just use the default value. However, more dramatic changes—such as renaming a property, changing its data type, and so on, are likely to cause an exception when you attempt to read the profile information. Even worse, because the serialized format of the profile information is proprietary, you have no easy way to migrate existing profile data to a new profile structure.

■ **Tip** Not all types are serializable in all ways. For example, classes that don't provide a parameterless constructor can't be serialized in Xml mode. Classes that don't have the Serializable attribute can't be serialized in Binary mode. You'll consider this distinction when you learn how to use custom types with profiles, but for now just keep in mind that you may run across types that can be serialized only if you choose a different serialization mode.

Profile Groups

If you have a large number of profile settings, and some settings are logically related to each other, you may want to use profile groups to achieve better organization.

For example, you may have some properties that deal with user preferences and others that deal with shipping information. Here's how you could organize these profile properties using the <group> element:

```
<profile defaultProvider="SqlProvider">
  <properties>
    <group name="Preferences">
      <add name="LongDisplayMode" defaultValue="true" type="Boolean" />
      <add name="ShowSummary" defaultValue="true" type="Boolean" />
    </group>
    <group name="Address">
      <add name="Name" type="String" />
      <add name="Street" type="String" />
      <add name="City" type="String" />
      <add name="ZipCode" type="String" />
      <add name="State" type="String" />
      <add name="Country" type="String" />
    </group>
  </properties>
</profile>
```

Now you can access the properties through the group name in your code. For example, here's how you retrieve the country information:

```
lblCountry.Text = Profile.Address.Country;
```

Groups are really just a poor man's substitute for a full-fledged custom structure or class. For example, you could achieve the same effect as in the previous example by declaring a custom Address class. You'd also have the ability to add other features (such as validation in the property procedures). The next section shows how.

Profiles and Custom Data Types

Using a custom class with profiles is easy. You need to begin by creating the class that wraps the information you need. In your class, you can use public member variables or full-fledged property procedures. The latter choice, though longer, is the preferred option because it ensures your class will support data binding and gives you the flexibility to add property procedure code later.

Here's a slightly abbreviated Address class that ties together the same information you saw in the previous example. For the sake of conciseness, it uses automatic properties (which store data in automatically generated private fields).

```
[Serializable()]
public class Address
{
    public string Name {get; set;}
    public string Street {get; set;}
    public string City {get; set;}
    public string ZipCode {get; set;}
    public string State {get; set;}
    public string Country {get; set;}

    public Address(string name, string street, string city,
      string zipCode, string state, string country)
    {
        Name = name;
        Street = street;
        City = city;
        ZipCode = zipCode;
        State = state;
        Country = country;
    }
    public Address() { }
}
```

You can place this class in the App_Code directory (or compile it and place the DLL assembly in the Bin directory). The final step is to add a property that uses it:

```
<properties>
  <add name="Address" type="Address" />
  ...
</properties>
```

Now you can manipulate it in your code like this:

```
Profile.Address = new Address("Joe Pasta", "34 Parkside Ave", "New York",
  "10002", "New York", "U.S.A.");
lbl.Text = "You are in " + Profile.Address.Country;
```

Custom Type Serialization

You need to keep in mind a few points, depending on how you decide to serialize your custom class. By default, all custom data types use XML serialization with the XmlSerializer. This class is relatively limited in its serialization ability. It simply copies the value from every public property or member variable into a straightforward XML format like this:

```
<Address ...>
  <Name>...</Name>
  <Street>...</Street>
  <City>...</City>
  <ZipCode>...</ZipCode>
```

```
  <State>...</State>
  <Country>...</Country>
</Address>
```

You can alter this XML representation by adding attributes from the System.Xml.Serialization namespace to the public properties in your class. For example, you can use XmlElement to change the XML element name that's used to store a property, XmlAttribute to make sure a property is stored as an XML attribute instead of an XML element, and XmlIgnore to prevent a property value from being serialized altogether. For more information, refer to the .NET Framework reference for the System.Xml.Serialization namespace.

When deserializing your class, the XmlSerializer needs to be able to find a parameterless public constructor. In addition, none of your properties can be read-only. If you violate either of these rules, the deserialization process will fail.

If you decide to use binary serialization instead of XmlSerialization, .NET uses a completely different approach.

```
<add name="Address" type="Address" serializeAs="Binary"/>
```

In this case, the ProfileModule enlists the help of the BinaryFormatter. The BinaryFormatter can serialize the full public and private contents of any class, provided the class is decorated with the Serializable attributes. (Additionally, any class it derives from or references must also be serializable.) You can learn much more about the binary formatter in Chapter 12.

Finally, you can decide to use string serialization:

```
<add name="Address" type="Address" serializeAs="String"/>
```

In this case, you need a type converter that can translate between an instance of your class and its string representation.

Automatic Saves

The ProfileModule that saves profile information isn't able to detect changes in complex data types (anything other than strings, simple numeric types, Boolean values, and so on). This means if your profile includes complex data types, the ProfileModule saves the profile information at the end of every request that accesses the Profile object.

This behavior obviously adds unnecessary overhead. To optimize performance when working with complex types, you have several choices. One option is to set the corresponding profile property to be read-only (if you know it never changes). Another approach is to disable the autosave behavior completely by adding the automaticSaveEnabled attribute on the <profile> element and setting it to false, as shown here:

```
<profile defaultProvider="SqlProvider" automaticSaveEnabled="false">...</profile>
```

If you choose this approach, it's up to you to call Profile.Save() to explicitly commit changes. Generally, this approach is the most convenient, because it's easy to spot the places in your code where you modify the profile. Just add the Profile.Save() call at the end:

```
Profile.Address = new Address(txtName.Text, txtStreet.Text, txtCity.Text,
  txtZip.Text, txtState.Text, txtCountry.Text);
Profile.Save();
```

One final option is to handle the ProfileModule.ProfileAutoSaving event in the global.asax file. At this point, you can check to see if a save is really necessary and cancel the save if it isn't.

With this technique, the obvious problem is determining whether the automatic save should be cancelled. You could store the original profile data in memory and then compare these objects with the current objects when the ProfileAutoSaving event fires. However, this approach would be awkward and slow. A better option is to make the page keep track of whether a change has been made. If a change has been made, your code can then set a flag to indicate that the update should go ahead.

For example, consider the test page shown in Figure 24-3 that allows you to retrieve and modify address information.

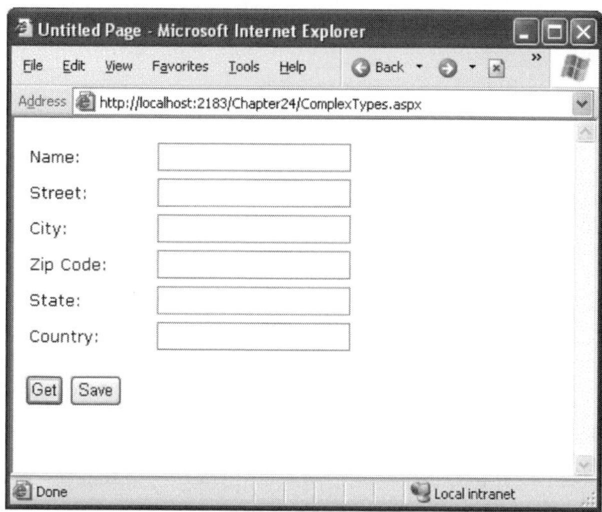

Figure 24-3. Modifying a complex type in a profile

All the text boxes on this page use the same event handler for their TextChanged event. This event handler indicates that a change has been made by storing a Boolean value in the context for the current request:

```
protected void txt_TextChanged(object sender, EventArgs e)
{
    Context.Items["AddressDirtyFlag"] = true;
}
```

■ **Tip** The Page.Context property provides an HttpContext object. The HttpContext.Items collection provides a handy place where you can temporarily store data that needs to be used later during the same postback. View state and session state can be used to similar effect, but they assume longer-term storage.

Keep in mind that a value stored in this way lasts only for the duration of the current request. In this example, that's not a problem because the user has only two options after making a change—rejecting the change (by clicking Get) or applying the change (by clicking Save). However, if you create a page where the user can make changes over several steps and then apply them later, you would need to do more work to maintain the flag. Storing the flag in other locations such as session state or view state won't work, because they aren't available when the ProfileAutoSaving event fires in the global.asax file.

Finally, here's the event handler you need that allows the autosave to carry on only if a change has been made:

```
void Profile_ProfileAutoSaving(Object sender, ProfileAutoSaveEventArgs e)
{
    if ((e.Context.Items["AddressDirtyFlag"] == null) ||
      ((bool)e.Context.Items["AddressDirtyFlag"] == false))
    {
        e.ContinueWithProfileAutoSave = false;
    }
}
```

Remember, the ProfileAutoSaving event fires for any change. If you have more than one page that modifies different profile details, you might need to write conditional code that checks which page was requested and restricts or permits the save accordingly. In this situation, it's usually easier to turn off automatic saving altogether and force the page to use the Profile.Save() method.

The Profiles API

Although your page automatically gets the profile information for the current user, that doesn't prevent you from retrieving and modifying the profiles of other users. In fact, you have two tools to help you—the ProfileBase class and the ProfileManager class.

The ProfileBase object (provided by the Page.Profile property) includes a useful GetProfile() function that retrieves, by user name, the profile information for a specific user. Figure 24-4 shows an example with a Windows authenticated user.

Here's the code that gets the profile:

```
protected void cmdGet_Click(object sender, EventArgs e)
{
    ProfileCommon profile = Profile.GetProfile(txtUserName.Text);
    lbl.Text = "This user lives in " + profile.Address.Country;
}
```

Figure 24-4. Retrieving a profile manually

GetProfile() returns a ProfileCommon object. However, you won't find ProfileCommon in the .NET class library. That's because ProfileCommon is a dynamically generated class that ASP.NET creates to hold the profile information for your web application. In this example, the profile defines a property named Address so that you can retrieve this information using the ProfileCommon.Address property.

Notice that once you have a ProfileCommon object, you can interact with it in the same way as you interact with the profile for the current user. You can even make changes. The only difference is that changes aren't saved automatically. If you want to save a change, you need to call the Save() method of the ProfileCommon object. The ProfileCommon also adds the LastActivityDate and LastUpdatedDate properties, which you can use to determine the last time a specific profile was accessed and modified.

■ **Note** If you try to retrieve a profile that doesn't exist, you won't get an error. Instead, you'll simply end up with blank data. If you change and save the profile, a new profile record will be created. You can test for this condition by examining the ProfileCommon.LastUpdatedDate property. If the profile hasn't been created yet, this value will be a zero-date value (in other words, day 0 on month 0 in year 0000).

If you need to perform other tasks with profiles, you can use the ProfileManager class in the System.Web.Profile namespace, which exposes the useful static methods described in Table 24-5. Many of these methods work with a ProfileInfo class, which provides information about a profile. The ProfileInfo includes the user name (UserName), last update and last activity dates (LastActivityDate and LastUpdateDate), the size of the profile in bytes (Size), and whether the profile is for an anonymous user (IsAnonymous). It doesn't provide the actual profile values.

Table 24-5. *ProfileManager Methods*

Method	Description
DeleteProfile()	Deletes the profile for the user you specify.
DeleteProfiles()	Deletes multiple profiles at once. You supply a collection of user names.
DeleteInactiveProfiles()	Deletes profiles that haven't been used since a time you specify. You also must supply a value from the Profile-AuthenticationOption enumeration to indicate what type of profiles you want to remove (All, Anonymous, or Authenticated).
GetNumberOfProfiles()	Returns the number of profile records in the data source.
GetNumberOfInactiveProfiles()	Returns the number of profiles that haven't been used since the time you specify.
GetAllInactiveProfiles()	Retrieves profile information for profiles that haven't been used since the time you specify. The profiles are returned as ProfileInfo objects.

Method	Description
GetAllProfiles()	Retrieves all the profile data from the data source as a collection of ProfileInfo objects. You can choose what type of profiles you want to retrieve (All, Anonymous, or Authenticated). You can also use an overloaded version of this method that uses paging and retrieves only a portion of the full set of records based on the starting index and page size you request.
FindProfilesByUserName()	Retrieves a collection of ProfileInfo objects that match a specific user name. The SqlProfileProvider uses a LIKE clause when it attempts to match user names. That means you can use wildcards such as the % symbol. For example, if you search for the user name user%, you'll return values like user1, user2, user_guest, and so on. You can use an overloaded version of this method that uses paging.
FindInactiveProfilesByUserName()	Retrieves profile information for profiles that haven't been used since the time you specify. You can also filter out certain types of profiles (All, Anonymous, or Authenticated) or look for a specific user name (with wildcard matching). The return value is a collection of ProfileInfo objects.

For example, if you want to remove the profile for the current user, you need only a single line of code:

```
ProfileManager.DeleteProfile(User.Identity.Name);
```

And if you want to display the full list of users in a web page (not including anonymous users), just add a GridView with AutoGenerateColumns set to true and use this code:

```
protected void Page_Load(object sender, EventArgs e)
{
    GridView1.DataSource = ProfileManager.GetAllProfiles(
      ProfileAuthenticationOption.Authenticated);
    GridView1.DataBind();
}
```

Figure 24-5 shows the result.

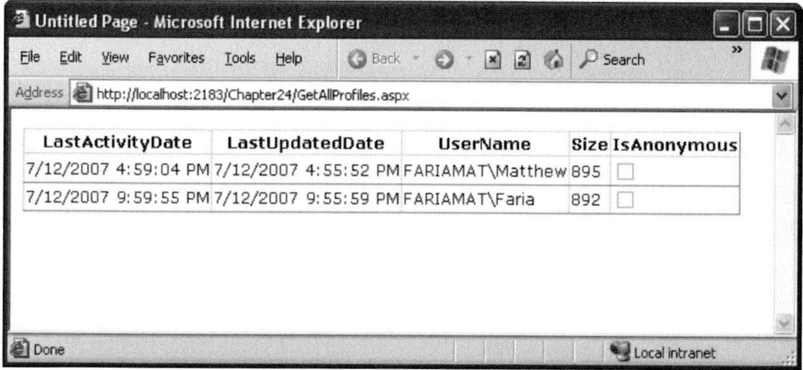

***Figure 24-5.** Retrieving information about all the profiles in the data source*

Anonymous Profiles

So far, all the examples have assumed that the user is authenticated before any profile information is accessed or stored. Usually, this is the case. However, sometimes it's useful to create a temporary profile for a new, unknown user. For example, most e-commerce websites allow new users to begin adding items to a shopping cart before registering. If you want to provide this type of behavior and you choose to store shopping cart items in a profile, you'll need some way to uniquely identify anonymous users.

ASP.NET provides an anonymous identification feature that fills this gap. The basic idea is that the anonymous identification feature automatically generates a random identifier for any anonymous user. This random identifier stores the profile information in the database, even though no user ID is available. The user ID is tracked on the client side using a cookie (or in the URL, if you've enable cookieless mode). Once this cookie disappears (for example, if the anonymous user closes and reopens the browser), the anonymous session is lost and a new anonymous session is created.

Anonymous identification has the potential to leave a lot of abandoned profiles, which wastes space in the database. For that reason, anonymous identification is disabled by default. However, you can enable it using the <anonymousIdentification> element in the web.config file, as shown here:

```
<configuration>
  ...
  <system.web>
    <anonymousIdentification enabled="true" />
    ...
  </system.web>
</configuration>
```

You also need to flag each profile property that will be retained for anonymous users by adding the allowAnonymous attribute and setting it to true. This allows you to store just some basic information and restrict larger objects to authenticated users.

```
<properties>
  <add name="Address" type="Address" allowAnonymous="true" />
  ...
</properties>
```

If you're using a complex type, the allowAnonymous attribute is an all-or-nothing setting. You configure the entire object to support anonymous storage or not.

The <anonymousIdentification> element also supports numerous optional attributes that let you set the cookie name and timeout, specify whether the cookie will be issued only over an SSL connection, control whether cookie protection (validation and encryption) is used to prevent tampering and eavesdropping, and configure support for cookieless ID tracking. Here's an example:

```
<anonymousIdentification enabled="true" cookieName=".ASPXANONYMOUS"
  cookieTimeout="43200" cookiePath="/" cookieRequireSSL="false"
  cookieSlidingExpiration="true" cookieProtection="All"
  cookieless="UseCookies"/>
```

For more information, refer to the configuration settings for forms authentication (Chapter 20) and role management (Chapter 23), which use the same settings.

■ **Tip** If you use anonymous identification, it's a good idea to delete old anonymous sessions regularly using the aspnet_Profile_DeleteInactiveProfiles stored procedure, which you can run at scheduled intervals using the SQL Server Agent. You can also delete old profiles using the ProfileManager class, as described in the previous section.

Migrating Anonymous Profiles

A challenge that occurs with anonymous profiles is what to do with the profile information when a previously anonymous user logs in. For example, in an e-commerce website a user might select several items and then register or log in to complete the transaction. At this point, you need to make sure the shopping cart information is copied from the anonymous user's profile to the appropriate authenticated (user) profile.

Fortunately, ASP.NET provides a solution through the ProfileModule.MigrateAnonymous event. This event (which can be handled in the global.asax file) fires whenever an anonymous identifier is available (either as a cookie or in the URL if you're using cookieless mode) and the current user is authenticated.

The basic technique when handling the MigrateAnonymous event is to load the profile for the anonymous user by calling Profile.GetProfile() and passing in the anonymous ID, which is provided to your event handler through the ProfileMigrateEventArgs.

Once you've loaded this data, you can then transfer the settings to the new profile manually. You can choose to transfer as few or as many settings as you want, and you can perform any other processing that's required. Finally, your code should remove the anonymous profile data from the database and clear the anonymous identifier so the MigrateAnonymous event won't fire again.

```
void Profile_MigrateAnonymous(Object sender, ProfileMigrateEventArgs pe)
{
    // Get the anonymous profile.
    ProfileCommon anonProfile = Profile.GetProfile(pe.AnonymousID);

    // Copy information to the authenticated profile
    // (but only if there's information there).
    if (anonProfile.Address.Name != null && anonProfile.Address.Name != "")
    {
        Profile.Address = anonProfile.Address;
```

```
    }

    // Delete the anonymous profile from the database.
    // (You could decide to skip this step to increase performance
    //  if you have a dedicated job scheduled on the database server
    //  to remove old anonymous profiles.)
    System.Web.Profile.ProfileManager.DeleteProfile(pe.AnonymousID);

    // Remove the anonymous identifier.
    AnonymousIdentificationModule.ClearAnonymousIdentifier();
}
```

You need to handle this task with some caution. If you've enabled anonymous identification, every time a user logs in, the MigrateAnonymous event fires, even if the user hasn't entered any information into the anonymous profile. That's a problem, because if you're not careful, you could easily overwrite the real (saved) profile for the user with the blank anonymous profile. The problem is further complicated because complex types (such as the Address object) are created automatically by the ProfileModule, so you can't just check for a null reference to determine whether the user has anonymous address information.

In the previous example, the code tests for a missing Name property in the Address object. If this information isn't a part of the anonymous profile, no information is migrated. A more sophisticated example might test for individual properties separately or might migrate an anonymous profile only if the information in the user profile is missing or out of date.

A Shopping Cart Example

To see a more comprehensive end-to-end example of profiles, you can refer to the online samples. They include a page named ShoppingCartTest.aspx (in the SqlProfileProviderWindowsAuthentication website), which uses profiles to store a complete shopping cart stocked full of items.

The ShoppingCartTest.aspx example provides a good demonstration of how you can store complex objects in a profile. However, most professional websites won't use profiles in this way, because it forces you to give up too much control over data storage. You're more likely to use session state instead (and possibly use SQL Server-backed session storage if you want partially complete shopping carts to persist between user visits). In fact, the ShoppingCart and ShoppingCartItem classes that the ShoppingCartTest.aspx page uses work equally well if you want to store shopping cart data in session state.

Custom Profile Providers

The profile model plugs neatly into ASP.NET web pages. However, it isn't very configurable. You might decide you need to create a custom profile provider for a number of reasons:

- You need to store profile information in a data source other than a SQL Server database, such as an Oracle database.
- You need your profile data to be available to other applications. Parsing the information in the PropertyValuesString and PropertyValuesBinary fields is tedious, error-prone, and inflexible. If you need to use this information in other queries or applications, you need to store your profile information in a database table that's split into distinct fields.

- You need to implement additional logic when storing or retrieving profile data. For example, you could apply validation, caching, logging, encryption, or compression. (In some cases, you can get these features by simply extending the ProfileBase class that wraps profile settings, rather than creating an entirely new ProfileProvider.)

In the following sections, you'll focus on the second scenario. You'll see how to build a custom provider that keeps its property values in separate fields and can be adapted to fit any existing database.

The Custom Profile Provider Classes

To implement a profile provider, you need to create a class that derives from the ProfileProvider abstract class from the System.Web.Profile namespace. The ProfileProvider abstract class itself inherits the SettingsProvider abstract class from the System.Configuration namespace, which inherits from the ProviderBase abstract class from the System.Configuration.Provider namespace. As a result, you also need to implement members from the SettingsProvider and ProviderBase classes. Altogether, more than a dozen members must be implemented before you can compile your custom profile provider.

However, these methods aren't all of equal importance. For example, you can create a basic provider that saves and retrieves profile information by implementing two or three of these methods. Many of the other methods support functionality that's exposed by the ProfileManager class, such as the ability to delete profiles or find inactive profiles.

In the following example, you'll consider a simple profile provider that includes the core logic that's needed to plug into a page but doesn't support most other parts of the Profiles API. Methods that aren't supported should simply throw a NotImplementedException, like this:

```
public override int DeleteProfiles(string[] usernames)
{
    throw new NotImplementedException("The method or operation is not implemented.");
}
```

All of these methods are conceptually easy to implement (all you need is some basic ADO.NET code). However, properly coding each method requires a fairly substantial amount of code.

Table 24-6 lists the overridable properties and methods and indicates which class defines them. Those that are implemented in the following example are marked with an asterisk. To be considered truly complete, a provider must implement all of these members.

Table 24-6. *Abstract Members for Profile Providers*

Class	Member	Description
*ProviderBase	Name	A read-only property that returns the name (set in the web.config file) for the current provider.
*ProviderBase	Initialize()	Gets the configuration element from the web.config file that initializes this provider. Gives you the chance to read custom settings and store the information in member variables.
SettingsProvider	ApplicationName	A name (set in the web.config file) that allows you to separate the users of different applications that are stored in the same database.

Class	Member	Description
*SettingsProvider	GetPropertyValues()	Retrieves the profile information for a single user. This method is called automatically when a web page accesses the Page.Profile property. This method is provided with a list of all the profile properties that are defined in the application. You must return a value for each of these properties.
*SettingsProvider	SetPropertyValues()	Updates the profile information for a single user. This method is called automatically at the end of a request when profile information is changed. This method is provided with a list of all the profile properties that are defined in the application and their current values.
ProfileProvider	DeleteProfiles()	Deletes one or more user profile records from the database.
ProfileProvider	DeleteInactiveProfiles()	Similar to DeleteProfiles() but looks for profiles that haven't been accessed since a specific time. To support this method, you must keep track of when profiles are accessed or updated in your database.
ProfileProvider	GetAllProfiles()	Returns information about a group of profile records. This method must support paging so that it returns only a subset of the total records. Refer to the aspnet_Profile_GetProfiles stored procedure that aspnet_regsql creates for a sample paging implementation.
ProfileProvider	GetAllInactiveProfiles()	Similar to GetAllProfiles() but looks for profiles that haven't been accessed since a specific time. To support this method, you must keep track of when profiles are accessed or updated in your database.
ProfileProvider	FindProfilesByUserName()	Retrieves profile information based on the user name of one or more (if you support wildcard matching) users. The actual profile information isn't returned—only some standard information such as the last activity date is returned.

Class	Member	Description
ProfileProvider	FindInactiveProfilesByUserName()	Similar to FindProfilesByUserName() but looks for profiles that haven't been accessed since a specific time.
ProfileProvider	GetNumberOfInactive Profiles()	Counts the number of profiles that haven't been accessed since a specific time.

** Implemented in the following example*

Designing the FactoredProfileProvider

The FactoredProfileProvider stores property values in a series of fields in a database table, rather than in a single block. This makes the values easier to use in different applications and with different queries. Essentially, the FactoredProfileProvider unlocks the profiles table so that it's no longer using a proprietary schema. The only disadvantage to this approach is that it's no longer possible to change the profile or add information to it without modifying the schema of your database.

When implementing a custom profile provider, you need to determine how generic you want your solution to be. For example, if you decide to implement compression using the classes in the System.IO.Compression namespace (see Chapter 12) or encryption with the classes in the System.Security.Cryptography namespace (see Chapter 25), you'll also need to decide whether you want to create an all-purpose solution or a more limited provider that's fine-tuned for your specific scenario.

Similarly, the FactoredProfileProvider has two possible designs:

- You can create a provider that's designed specifically for your database schema.
- You can create a generic provider that can work with any database table by making certain assumptions. For example, you can simply assume that profile properties match field names.

The first approach is the most straightforward and in some cases will be the easiest to secure and optimize. However, it also limits your ability to reuse your provider or change your database schema later. The second approach is the one you'll see in the following example.

The basic idea behind the FactoredProfileProvider is that it will perform its two key tasks (retrieving and updating profile information) through two stored procedures. That gives you a powerful layer of flexibility, because you can modify the stored procedures at any time to use different tables, field names, data types, and even serialization choices.

The critical detail in this example is that the web application chooses which stored procedures to use by using the provider declaration in the web.config file. Here's an example of how you might use the FactoredProfileProvider in an application:

```
<profile defaultProvider="FactoredProfileProvider">
  <providers >
    <clear />
    <add name="FactoredProfileProvider"
         type="FactoredProfileProvider"
         connectionStringName="SqlServices"
         updateUserProcedure="Users_Update"
         getUserProcedure="Users_GetByUserName"/>
  </providers>
  <properties>...</properties>
</profile>
```

Along with the expected attributes (name, type, and connectionStringName), the <add> tag includes two new attributes: updateUserProcedure and getUserProcedure. The updateUserProcedure indicates the name of the stored procedure that's used to insert and update profile information. The getUserProcedure indicates the name of the stored procedure that's used to retrieve profile information.

This design allows you to use the FactoredProfileProvider with any database table. But what about mapping the properties to the appropriate columns? You could take a variety of approaches to make this possible, but the FactoredProfileProvider takes a convenient shortcut. When updating, it simply assumes that every profile property you define corresponds to the name of a stored procedure parameter. So, if you define the following properties:

```
<properties>
  <add name="FirstName"/>
  <add name="LastName"/>
</properties>
```

the FactoredProfileProvider will call the update stored procedure you've specified and pass the value in for parameters named @FirstName and @LastName. When querying profile information, the FactoredProfileProvider will look for the field names FirstName and LastName.

This is similar to the design used by the SqlDataSource and ObjectDataSource controls. Although it forces you to follow certain conventions in your two stored procedures, it imposes no other restrictions on the rest of your database. For example, the update stored procedure can insert the information into any series of fields in any table, and the stored procedure used to query profile information can use aliases or joins to construct the expected table.

Coding the FactoredProfileProvider

The first step of creating the FactoredProfileProvider is to derive the class from ProfileProvider:

```
public class FactoredProfileProvider : ProfileProvider
{ ... }
```

All the methods that aren't implemented in this example (see Table 24-6) are simply filled with a single line of code that throws an exception.

■ **Tip** One quick way to fill all the methods with exception-throwing logic is to right-click ProfileProvider in the class declaration and choose Refactor ➤ Implement Abstract Class.

Initialization

The FactoredProfileProvider needs to keep track of a few basic details, such as the provider name, the connection string, and the two stored procedures. These details are all exposed through read-only properties, as shown here:

```
private string name;
public override string Name
{
    get { return name; }
}
```

```
private string connectionString;
public string ConnectionString
{
    get { return connectionString; }
}

private string updateProcedure;
public string UpdateUserProcedure
{
    get { return updateProcedure; }
}

private string getProcedure;
public string GetUserProcedure
{
    get { return getProcedure; }
}
```

To set these details, you need to override the Initialize() method. At this point, you receive a collection that contains all the attributes of the <add> element that registered the provider. If any of the necessary details are absent, you should raise an exception. The following code demonstrates this (and assumes you've imported the System.Collections.Specialized namespace).

```
public override void Initialize(string name, NameValueCollection config)
{
    this.name = name;

    // Initialize values from web.config.
    ConnectionStringSettings connectionStringSettings =
      ConfigurationManager.ConnectionStrings[config["connectionStringName"]];
    if (connectionStringSettings == null ||
        connectionStringSettings.ConnectionString.Trim() == "")
    {
        throw new HttpException("You must supply a connection string.");
    }
    else
    {
        connectionString = connectionStringSettings.ConnectionString;
    }

    updateProcedure = config["updateUserProcedure"];
    if (updateProcedure.Trim() == "")
    {
        throw new HttpException(
          "You must specify a stored procedure to use for updates.");
    }

    getProcedure = config["getUserProcedure"];
    if (getProcedure.Trim() == "")
    {
        throw new HttpException(
         "You must specify a stored procedure to use for retrieving user records.");
    }
}
```

Reading Profile Information

When the web page accesses any profile information, ASP.NET calls the GetPropertyValues() method. It passes in two parameters—a SettingsContext object that includes the current user name and a SettingsPropertyCollection object that contains a collection of all the profile properties that the application has defined (and expects to be able to access). You need to return a SettingsPropertyValueCollection with the corresponding values.

Before doing anything, you should create a new SettingsPropertyValueCollection:

```
public override SettingsPropertyValueCollection GetPropertyValues(
  SettingsContext context, SettingsPropertyCollection properties)
{
    // This collection will store the retrieved values.
    SettingsPropertyValueCollection values = new SettingsPropertyValueCollection();
    ...
```

Now create the ADO.NET objects that you need in order to execute the stored procedure that retrieves the profile information. The connection string and stored procedure name are specified through the configuration attributes that were retrieved in the Initialize() method.

```
    ...
    SqlConnection con = new SqlConnection(connectionString);
    SqlCommand cmd = new SqlCommand(getProcedure, con);
    cmd.CommandType = CommandType.StoredProcedure;
    ...
```

The only nonconfigurable assumption in this code is that the stored procedure accepts a parameter named @UserName. You could add other configuration attributes to make this parameter name configurable.

```
    ...
    cmd.Parameters.Add(new SqlParameter("@UserName", (string)context["UserName"]));
    ...
```

This code retrieves the current user name from the SettingsContext dictionary that's passed as an argument to the GetPropertyValues() method. The SettingsContext object includes two pieces of information—a Boolean flag that indicates if the user was authenticated (indexed under the name IsAuthenticated) and the user name of the currently authenticated user (indexed under the name UserName).

Now you're ready to execute the command and retrieve the matching record. Depending on the design of the database, this record may actually represent the joining of two tables (one with a list of users and one with profile information), or all the information may come from a single table.

```
    ...
    try
    {
        con.Open();
        SqlDataReader reader = cmd.ExecuteReader(CommandBehavior.SingleRow);

        // Get the first row.
        reader.Read();
        ...
```

Once you have the row, the next task is to loop through the SettingsPropertyCollection. For each defined property, you should retrieve the value from the corresponding field. However, it's perfectly valid for a user to exist without any profile information. In this case (when reader.HasRows is false), you should still create the SettingsPropertyValue objects for each requested property, but don't bother setting the property values. They'll simply keep their defaults.

```
        ...
        foreach (SettingsProperty property in properties)
        {
            SettingsPropertyValue value = new SettingsPropertyValue(property);

            if (reader.HasRows)
            {
                value.PropertyValue = reader[property.Name];
            }
            values.Add(value);
        }
        ...
```

The final step is to close the reader and connection and to return the collection of values.

```
        ...
        reader.Close();
    }
    finally
    {
        con.Close();
    }
    return values;
}
```

■ **Note** If you want to mimic the behavior of the SqlProfileProvider, you should also update the database with the last activity time whenever the GetPropertyValues() method is called.

Updating Profile Information

The job of updating profile properties in SetPropertyValues() is just as straightforward as reading property values. This time, the update stored procedure is used, and every supplied value is translated into a parameter with the same name.

Here's the complete code:

```
public override void SetPropertyValues(SettingsContext context,
  SettingsPropertyValueCollection values)
{
    // Prepare the command.
    SqlConnection con = new SqlConnection(connectionString);
    SqlCommand cmd = new SqlCommand(updateProcedure, con);
    cmd.CommandType = CommandType.StoredProcedure;
```

```
    // Add the parameters.
    // The assumption is that every property maps exactly
    // to a single stored procedure parameter name.
    foreach (SettingsPropertyValue value in values)
    {
        cmd.Parameters.Add(new SqlParameter(value.Name, value.PropertyValue));
    }
    // Again, this provider assumes the stored procedure accepts a parameter named
    // @UserName.
    cmd.Parameters.Add(new SqlParameter("@UserName", (string)context["UserName"]));

    // Execute the command.
    try
    {
        con.Open();
        cmd.ExecuteNonQuery();
    }
    finally
    {
        con.Close();
    }
}
```

This completes the code you need for the simple implementation of the FactoredProfileProvider.

■ **Note** If you want to mimic the behavior of the SqlProfileProvider, you should also update the database with the last update time whenever the SetPropertyValues() method is called.

Testing the FactoredProfileProvider

To try this example, you need to create, at a bare minimum, a database with a Users table and the two stored procedures. The following example demonstrates an example with a Users table that provides address information (see Figure 24-6).

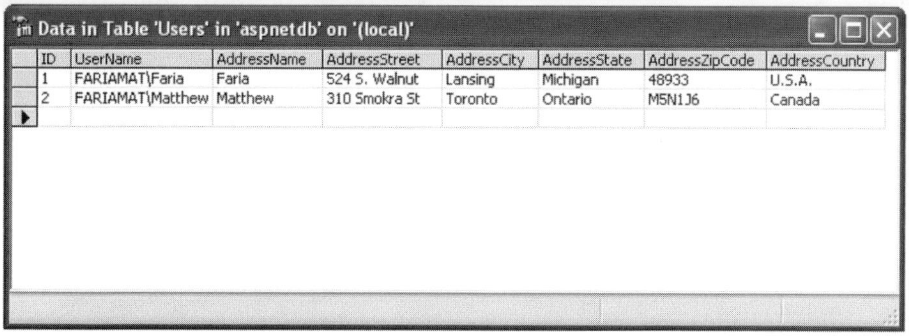

Data in Table 'Users' in 'aspnetdb' on '(local)'

ID	UserName	AddressName	AddressStreet	AddressCity	AddressState	AddressZipCode	AddressCountry
1	FARIAMAT\Faria	Faria	524 S. Walnut	Lansing	Michigan	48933	U.S.A.
2	FARIAMAT\Matthew	Matthew	310 Smokra St	Toronto	Ontario	M5N1J6	Canada

Figure 24-6. *A custom Users table*

A straightforward procedure named Users_GetByUserName queries the profile information from the table:

```
CREATE PROCEDURE Users_GetByUserName
  @UserName varchar(50)
AS
  SELECT * FROM Users WHERE UserName = @UserName
```

The Users_Update stored procedure is a little more interesting. It begins by checking for the existence of the specified user. If the user doesn't exist, a record is created with the profile information. If the user does exist, that record is updated. This design meshes with the behavior of the SqlProfileProvider.

■ **Note** Remember, all profile providers assume the user has already been authenticated. If you're using the same table to store user authentication information and profile information, an unauthenticated user must have a record in this table. However, this isn't the case if you use separate tables or Windows authentication.

Here's the complete code for the Users_Update stored procedure:

```
CREATE PROCEDURE [Users_Update]
  (@UserName       [varchar](50),
   @AddressName    [varchar](50),
   @AddressStreet  [varchar](50),
   @AddressCity    [varchar](50),
   @AddressState   [varchar](50),
   @AddressZipCode [varchar](50),
   @AddressCountry [varchar](50))
AS
  DECLARE @Match int
  SELECT @Match = COUNT(*) FROM Users
    WHERE  UserName = @UserName

  IF (@Match = 0)
    INSERT INTO Users
      (UserName, AddressName, AddressStreet, AddressCity,
       AddressState, AddressZipCode, AddressCountry)
    VALUES
      (@UserName, @AddressName, @AddressStreet, @AddressCity,
       @AddressState, @AddressZipCode, @AddressCountry)

  IF (@Match = 1)
    UPDATE Users SET
      [UserName] = @UserName,
      [AddressName] = @AddressName,
      [AddressStreet] = @AddressStreet,
      [AddressCity] = @AddressCity,
      [AddressState] = @AddressState,
      [AddressZipCode] = @AddressZipCode,
```

```
    [AddressCountry] = @AddressCountry
  WHERE
    (UserName = @UserName)
```

■ **Note** You can download a script to create this table and the corresponding stored procedures with the sample code for this chapter.

To use this table, you simply need to configure the FactoredProfileProvider, identify the stored procedures you're using, and define all the fields of the Users table that you need to access. Here are the complete web.config configuration details:

```
<profile defaultProvider="FactoredProfileProvider">
  <providers >
    <clear />
    <add name="FactoredProfileProvider"
         type="FactoredProfileProvider"
         connectionStringName="ProfileService"
         updateUserProcedure="Users_Update"
         getUserProcedure="Users_GetByUserName"/>
  </providers>
  <properties>
    <add name="AddressName"/>
    <add name="AddressStreet"/>
    <add name="AddressCity"/>
    <add name="AddressState"/>
    <add name="AddressZipCode"/>
    <add name="AddressCountry"/>
  </properties>
</profile>
```

It assumes you've added a connection string named ProfileServer to the <connectionStrings> section of your web.config file:

```
<connectionStrings>
  <add name="ProfileService" connectionString=
"Data Source=localhost;Integrated Security=SSPI;Initial Catalog=CustomProfiles;" />
</connectionStrings>
```

From this point, you can access the profile details exactly as you would with the SqlProfile- Provider. For example, here's the code you need to copy the information in a series of text boxes into the profile record:

```
protected void cmdSave_Click(object sender, EventArgs e)
{
    Profile.AddressName = txtName.Text;
    Profile.AddressStreet = txtStreet.Text;
    Profile.AddressCity = txtCity.Text;
    Profile.AddressZipCode = txtZip.Text;
```

```
    Profile.AddressState = txtState.Text;
    Profile.AddressCountry = txtCountry.Text;
}
```

And here's the code that reads the current values in the text boxes and applies them to the profile, completing the test page:

```
protected void cmdGet_Click(object sender, EventArgs e)
{
    txtName.Text = Profile.AddressName;
    txtStreet.Text = Profile.AddressStreet;
    txtCity.Text = Profile.AddressCity;
    txtZip.Text = Profile.AddressZipCode;
    txtState.Text = Profile.AddressState;
    txtCountry.Text = Profile.AddressCountry;
}
```

Figure 24-7 shows the test page.

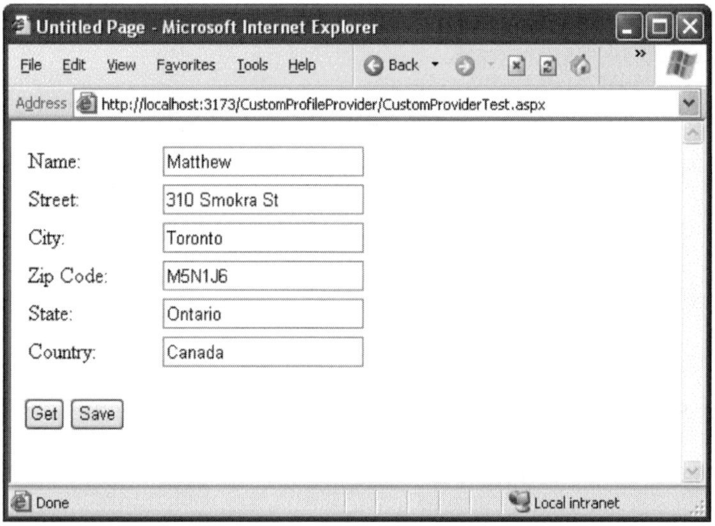

Figure 24-7. *Testing a custom profile provider*

Summary

In this chapter, you took a detailed look at the profiles feature. You considered how it works behind the scenes, when it makes the most sense, and how to configure its behavior.

The final part of this chapter explored how to create a simple profile provider of your own. Using these techniques, you can overcome many of the limitations of the profiles feature (such as the way it serializes all information into a single, opaque field). The ultimate decision of whether to use profiles or a custom database component still depends on several factors, but with this ability profiles become a valid alternative.

CHAPTER 25

■ ■ ■

Cryptography

In Chapters 19–23, you learned how to identify users through several supported authentication mechanisms and how to implement authorization for those users in your applications. ASP.NET supports rich services, such as the membership and roles APIs, that help you implement this functionality. However, although authentication and authorization are two important factors for securing applications, you have to keep much more in mind. Therefore, .NET has a bit more functionality in store. One of the most important examples is .NET's support for *cryptography*—the science of scrambling data to ensure confidentiality and adding hash codes to detect tampering.

.NET includes the rich CryptoAPI for a wide range of cryptographic tasks, such as creating hashes of different types (MD5, SHA1, and so on) and implementing the most important symmetric and asymmetric encryption algorithms. And if that's not enough, the .NET Framework ships with separate functions for protecting secrets on the local machine or on a per-user basis through a completely managed wrapper for the Windows data protection API (DPAPI). In this chapter, you'll learn when to use these APIs and how to use them correctly.

Encrypting Data: Confidentiality Matters

In Chapter 20, you learned how to use hashing to protect passwords using methods of the FormsAuthentication class. With hashing, you store a digital fingerprint of the original data, not the data itself. As a result, you have no way to reverse the hashing process to retrieve the original data. All you can do is hash new data and perform a comparison.

The hashing approach is the most secure practice for validating passwords. However, it's not much help when you want to protect sensitive data that you need to decrypt later. For example, if you're creating an e-commerce application, you probably want to store a user's credit card information so it can be reused in later orders. In this scenario, your application needs to be able to retrieve the credit card details on its own. Hashing doesn't give you what you really need.

Often developers deal with this situation by storing sensitive data in clear text. They assume that because the data is kept in a secure server-side storage location, they don't need to go to the additional work of encrypting it. However, security experts know this is not true. Without encryption, a malicious user needs to gain access to the server for only a matter of minutes or even seconds to retrieve passwords or credit card numbers for every customer. Security breaches can occur because of poor administrative policies, weak administrator passwords, or other exploitable software on the server. Problems can even occur because of hardware maintenance; in fact, dozens of companies have reported selling or discarding old server hard drives without properly erasing the sensitive customer data they contained. Finally, many organizations have a privacy policy that explicitly pledges to keep customer information confidential and encrypted at all times. If a security breach occurs and the company is forced to notify users that their data is at risk because it wasn't properly encrypted, the company can face significant embarrassment and loss of trust. To avoid these problems and ensure that data is safe, you need to encrypt sensitive information stored by your application.

The .NET Cryptography Namespace

In the System.Security.Cryptography namespace, you can find the necessary classes for encrypting and decrypting information in your application. Furthermore, you find all the fundamental classes for creating different types of hashes in this namespace. If you then reference the additional assembly System.Security.dll, you have access to even more advanced security functionality such as an API for modifying Windows ACLs (the System.Security.AccessControl namespace), the DPAPI, and classes for creating key-hashed message authentication codes (HMAC). Table 25-1 shows the categories of classes.

Table 25-1. *Categories of Security Classes in the System.Security.Cryptography Namespace*

Category	Description
Encryption algorithms	The namespace includes the most important hashing and encryption algorithms and classes for creating digital signatures. You will learn more about the details of these classes in the section "Understanding the .NET Cryptography Classes."
Helper classes	If you need to create true cryptographic random numbers, you will find helper classes in the System.Security.Cryptography namespace. The helper classes are for interacting with the underlying Windows cryptography system (the CryptoAPI).
X509 certificates	In the namespace System.Security.Cryptography.X509Certificates, you will find all the necessary classes for working with X509 certificates and classes for accessing the Windows certificate store.
XML signature and encryption	You can find complete support of the XML signature and encryption standards in the System.Security.Cryptography.Xml namespace. The classes in this namespace are used for encrypting and signing XML documents according to the standards published by the W3C.
CMS/PKCS#7	The framework has managed support for creating CMS/PKCS-enveloped messages directly without unmanaged calls. (CMS stands for Cryptographic Message Syntax, and PKCS stands for Public-Key Cryptography Standard.)

In the world of the Web, X509 certificates play an important role. They establish SSL communications and perform certificate authentication to secure traffic between the web server and its clients. An X509 certificate is a binary standard for encapsulating keys for asymmetric encryption algorithms together with a signature of a special organization that has issued the certificate (usually such organizations are called *certificate authorities*).

For simple SSL connections, you don't need access to the certificate store, but if you want to call web services or web applications in your code hosted on a different server that requires you to authenticate with an X509 certificate, your application has to read the certificate from the Windows certificate store and then add the certificate to the web request (or the web service proxy) before actually sending the request. For this purpose, the System.Security.Cryptography.X509Certificates namespace includes several classes you can use, as follows:

- **X509Certificate and X509Certificate2:** These classes encapsulate X509 certificates. They allow you to load certificates from various stores such as the file system and give you access to the properties of a certificate. The X509Certificate class is the one provided originally with the very first versions of the .NET Framework. The X509Certificate2 is an extension to the X509Certificate class and includes a number of additional methods and properties.

- **X509Store:** This class gives you access to the Windows certificate storage, which is a special storage area where Windows stores all certificates. For every user, Windows creates such a store (accessible through StoreLocation.CurrentUser), and for the machine it manages exactly one store (StoreLocation.LocalMachine). User storages are accessible only for the users they are created for, while the machine store stores certificates that are accessible for all users working with a machine.
- **X509CertificateCollection:** This is a simple class representing a collection of X509Certificate and X509Certificate2 instances that represent single certificates. The X509Store allows you to retrieve either a list of certificates or single certificates based on one of their unique identifiers (such as the certificate's subject key, subject name, or hash).

You can read a certificate from the store and assign it to a web request in your application, as follows:

```
X509Certificate2 Certificate = null;

// Read the certificate from the store
X509Store store = new X509Store(StoreName.My, StoreLocation.LocalMachine);
store.Open(OpenFlags.ReadOnly);
try
{
    // Try to find the certificate
    // based on its common name
    X509Certificate2Collection Results =
        store.Certificates.Find(
            X509FindType.FindBySubjectDistinguishedName,
            "CN=Mario, CN=Szpuszta", false);

    if (Results.Count == 0)
        throw new Exception("Unable to find certificate!");
    else
        Certificate = Results[0];
}
finally
{
    store.Close();
}
```

This code opens the personal certificate store of the local machine by using the X509Store class. It then tries to find a certificate with the subject name "CN=Mario, CN=Szpuszta" in this store. The syntax used here is the common name syntax that you probably know from LDAP directory systems as well.

Windows supports several types of certificate stores that are called *store locations*. The local machine store, for example, is accessible to all applications running on the local machine with the appropriate permissions. You can create a separate store for each Windows service of a machine, and every user has a separate certificate store. Certificates are stored securely in those stores. While the local machine store is encrypted with a key managed by the local security authority of the machine, the user store is encrypted with a key stored in the user's profile. Within a store location, Windows differentiates between stores used for different purposes. The most important stores are the Personal ("my") store and the Trusted Root Certification Authorities. Usually, the "my" store contains all the certificates used by applications (and users if it's a user store), while the Trusted Root Certification Authorities store contains certificates of authorities issuing certificates. VeriSign is an example of a well-known authority from which you can buy certificates. If you place a certificate into the Trusted Root Certification Authorities store, you indicate that any certificates issued by this authority are trusted by the system and therefore can be used by any application without any fear. Other certificates by default are not trusted and therefore marked with a special flag. Of course, you should use only valid certificates issued by a trusted authority for critical operations such as authenticating or setting up SSL on the server, because any other certificate could lead to a potential security risk.

In ASP.NET web applications, you have to use either the local machine store or a service account's store (which is nothing more than the user store of the service account under which a Windows service is executed). Therefore, the code introduced previously opens the store with the flag StoreLocation.LocalMachine. The second possible flag for this option is StoreLocation.CurrentUser, which opens a current user's or service account's store. Because the certificate is a "usage" certificate, you will read it from the personal store. You can view the certificates of a store by opening a Microsoft Management Console and then adding the Certificates snap-in, as shown in Figure 25-1.You can open this console by starting the management console (mmc.exe) and then selecting File ➤ Add/Remove Snap In. In the dialog box that appears after selecting this menu entry, you select the Certificates snap-in from the list of available snap-ins and add it to the selected snap-ins list. When doing so, you have to select the store you want to display in the snap-in. Afterward, you can close the dialog, and the certificates snap-in displaying all stores and certificates in these stores for the selected account appears in the management console. You can create test certificates through the makecert.exe command. For example, the following command creates a certificate in the personal store of the local machine:

```
makecert -ss my -sr LocalMachine -n "CN=Mario, CN=Szpuszta"
```

As soon as you have the certificate from the store in place, you can use it when sending requests through SSL to a server that requires certificate authentication, as follows:

```
// Now create the web request
HttpWebRequest Request = (HttpWebRequest)WebRequest.Create(url);
Request.ClientCertificates.Add(Certificate);
HttpWebResponse Response = (HttpWebResponse)Request.GetResponse();
// ...
```

For the preceding code, you need to import the System.Net namespace in your code file. Useful cases where this code makes sense are, for example, use cases where your application needs to retrieve data from another web application or send data to another web application using HTTP GET/POST requests and the other web application requires authentication through certificates.

Another useful example of security is a class for generating cryptographically strong random numbers. This class is important for generating random key values or salt values when you want to store salted password hashes. A *salted password hash* is a hash created from a password and a so-called salt. A salt is a random value. This ensures that even if two users select the same passwords, the results stored in the back-end store will look different, because the random salt value is hashed with the password. It also requires you to store the salt value in a separate field together with the password, because you will need it for password validation. You will learn more about salted hash values when creating a custom membership provider in Chapter 26. For now, this shows how you can create random number values with the System.Security.Cryptography.RandomNumberGenerator class:

```
byte[] RandomValue = new byte[16];
RandomNumberGenerator RndGen = RandomNumberGenerator.Create();
RndGen.GetBytes(RandomValue);
ResultLabel.Text = Convert.ToBase64String(RandomValue);
```

For more information about the random number generator, refer to the Cryptographic Service Provider documentation of Windows, because this class is just a wrapper around the native implementation (http://msdn2.microsoft.com/en-us/library/aa380245.aspx).

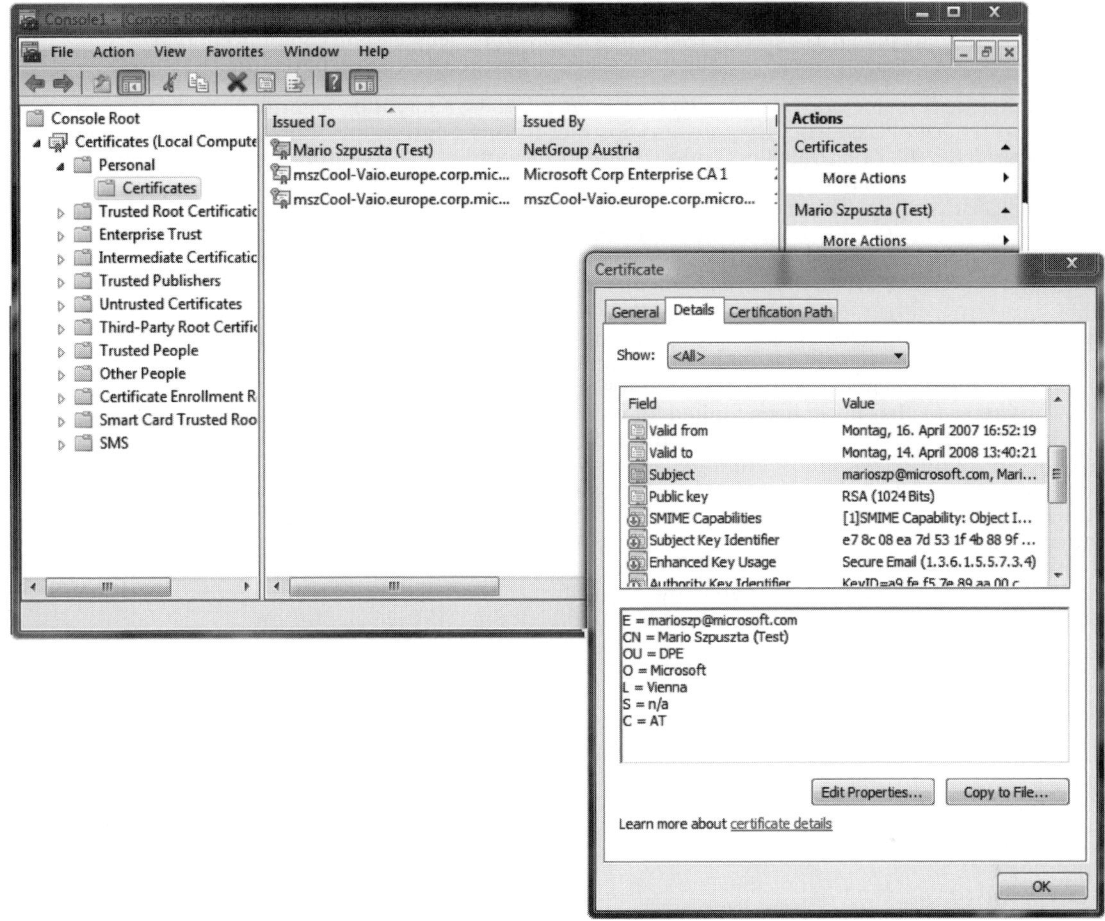

Figure 25-1. The Windows Certificates snap-in

Understanding the .NET Cryptography Classes

Before you can perform cryptography in .NET, you need to understand a little more about the underlying plumbing. The .NET encryption classes are divided into three layers. The first layer is a set of abstract base classes; these classes represent an encryption task. These include the following:

- **AsymmetricAlgorithm:** This class represents asymmetric encryption, which uses a public/private key pair. Data encrypted with one key can be decrypted only with the other key.
- **SymmetricAlgorithm:** This class represents symmetric encryption, which uses a shared secret value. Data encrypted with the key can be decrypted using only the same key.

- **HashAlgorithm:** This class represents hash generation and verification. Hashes are also known as *one-way encryption algorithms*, because you can only encrypt but not decrypt data. You can use hashes to ensure that data is not tampered with.

The second level includes classes that represent a specific encryption algorithm. They derive from the encryption base classes, but they are also abstract classes. For example, the DES algorithm class, which represents the DES (Data Encryption Standard) algorithm, derives from SymmetricAlgorithm.

The third level of classes is a set of encryption implementations. Each implementation class derives from an algorithm class. This means a specific encryption algorithm such as DES could have multiple implementation classes. Although some .NET Framework encryption classes are implemented entirely in managed code, most are actually thin wrappers over the CryptoAPI library. The classes that wrap the CryptoAPI functions have *CryptoServiceProvider* in their name (for example, DESCryptoServiceProvider), while the managed classes typically have *Managed* in their name (for example, RijndaelManaged). Essentially, the managed classes perform all their work in the .NET world under the supervision of the CLR, while the unmanaged classes use calls to the unmanaged CryptoAPI library. This might seem like a limitation, but it's actually an efficient reuse of existing technology.

The CryptoAPI has never been faulted for its technology, just for its awkward programming interface. Figure 25-2 shows the classes in the System.Security.Cryptography namespace. This three-layer organization allows almost unlimited extensibility. You can create a new implementation for an existing cryptography class by deriving from an existing algorithm class. For example, you could create a class that implements the DES algorithm entirely in managed code by creating a new DESManaged class and inheriting from DESCryptoServiceProvider. Similarly, you can add support for a new encryption algorithm by adding an abstract algorithm class (for example, the CAST128 algorithm, which is similar to the DES algorithm but is not provided in the framework) and a concrete implementation class (such as, for example, CAST128Managed if you want to implement the CAST128 algorithm).

■ **Note** The encryption classes are one of the few examples in the .NET class library where the standard naming and case rules are not followed. For example, you'll find classes such as TripleDES and RSA rather than TripleDes and Rsa.

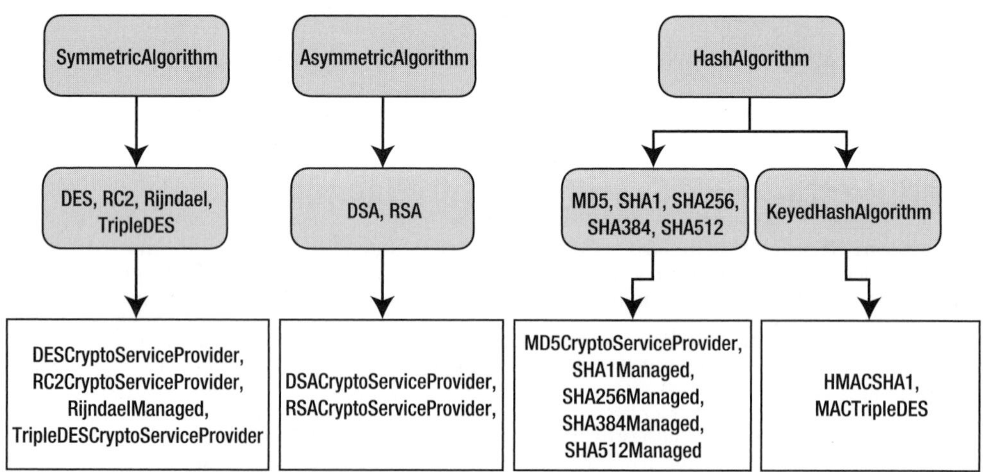

***Figure 25-2.** The cryptographic class hierarchy*

Symmetric Encryption Algorithms

As mentioned in the previous section, the .NET Framework supports three types of encryption: symmetric, asymmetric, and one-way encryption (hashes). Symmetric algorithms always use the same key for encryption and decryption. Symmetric algorithms are fast for encryption and decryption. Table 25-2 lists the most important symmetric algorithms supported by the .NET Framework.

Table 25-2. *Symmetric Algorithms Supported by .NET*

	Abstract Algorithm	Default Implementation	Valid Key Size	Maximum Key Size
DES	DES	DESCryptoServiceProvider	64	64
TripleDES	TripleDES	TripleDESCryptoServiceProvider	128, 192	192
RC2	RC2	RC2CryptoServiceProvider	40-128	128
Rijndael	Rijndael	RijndaelManaged	128, 192, 256	256

The strength of the encryption corresponds to the length of the key. Keep in mind that the greater the key size, the harder it is for a brute-force attack to succeed, because there are far more possible key values to test. Of course, greater symmetric key sizes also lead to larger messages and slower encryption times. For most purposes, a good standard choice is Rijndael. It offers solid performance and support for large key sizes.

■ **Note** DES, TripleDES, and RC2 are all implemented using the CryptoAPI and thus need the high encryption pack on Windows 2000. Note also that the key length for DES and TripleDES includes parity bits that don't contribute to the strength of the encryption. TripleDES with a 192-bit key uses only 168 bits, while a 128-bit key uses 112 bits. In DES, the 64-bit key uses only 56 bits. For that reason, it's considered fairly weak, and you should use other key algorithms instead. For additional information about the relative strengths of these algorithms, consult a dedicated book or Internet resource about encryption theory, such as Bruce Schneier's *Applied Cryptography: Protocols, Algorithms, and Source Code in C, Second Edition* (Wiley, 1995).

As mentioned, the big advantage of symmetric algorithms is performance. Conversely, the major problems with symmetric algorithms are as follows:

Key exchange: If you are using symmetric algorithms to exchange data between two applications hosted by different parties, you have to exchange the key in a secure way.

Brute-force attacks: If you use the symmetric key for a longer period of time, attackers might have enough time to decrypt traffic by just trying any valid combination of bits in a key. Therefore, with an increasing bit size, the strength of the key increases, as explained previously. But generally this means you should use a different key in regular intervals anyway.

Long-term key management: If you have to update keys in regular intervals, you have to exchange them in regular intervals, which might lead to additional security risks. Furthermore, you have to store the key in a secure place.

Symmetric algorithms are not enough for secure systems, and that's why asymmetric algorithms exist.

Asymmetric Encryption

Asymmetric algorithms try to solve some of the problems of symmetric algorithms. They are based on mathematical methods that require different keys for encryption and decryption. Usually the key used for encryption is called a *public key*. You can give this key to anyone who wants to send encrypted information to you. On the other hand, the private key is the only key that can be used for decryption. Therefore, if you are the only one with access to the private key, you are the only person who is able to decrypt the information. This fact makes key exchange between parties definitely easier, because you don't need to transmit the key that can decrypt sensitive data. Table 25-3 lists the asymmetric algorithms supported by the .NET Framework.

Table 25-3. *Asymmetric Algorithms Supported by .NET*

	Abstract Algorithm	Default Implementation	Valid Key Size	Default Key Size
RSA	RSA	RSACryptoServiceProvider	384-16384 (8-bit increments)	1024
DSA	DSA	DSACryptoServiceProvider	512-1024 (64-bit increments)	1024

When you use RSA (its name comes from the inventors of the algorithm—Ron Rivest, Adi Shamir, and Leonard Adleman) and DSA (Digital Signature Algorithm), you will recognize that only RSA supports the direct encryption and decryption of values. The DSA algorithm—as its name Digital Signature Algorithm implies—can be used only for signing information and verifying signatures.

The big problem is that asymmetric algorithms are much slower (depending on the size of the data you want to encrypt) than symmetric algorithms. This will affect the performance of your application if you need to exchange data through lots of requests. Therefore, technologies such as SSL use asymmetric algorithms at the beginning when establishing a connection session. Through the first communication steps, traffic between the client and the server is secured through asymmetric encryption (the client encrypts with a public key, and the server decrypts with a private key). With these steps, the client and the server can exchange a symmetric key securely. This symmetric key then secures traffic for any subsequent communication through symmetric encryption. This combines the advantages of symmetric and asymmetric encryption. You do have to find a way to securely store the private key so that unauthorized people don't have a chance to access it.

■ **Note** If you don't store the private key on an external device such as a smart card, you create a chance of someone gaining unauthorized access (and even the smart card is not completely secure, because you can lose it), especially users who have administrative privileges on machines. However, you should always make your solution as secure as possible and "raise the bar" for attackers. Therefore, any additional security mechanism (gatekeeper) will make life for a potential attacker harder.

The Abstract Encryption Classes

The abstract encryption classes serve two purposes. First, they define the basic members that encryption implementations need to support. Second, they provide some functionality through the static Create() method, which you can use to indirectly create a class instance for you. This method allows you to create one of the concrete implementation classes without needing to know how it is implemented.

For example, consider the following line of code:

```
DES crypt = DES.Create();
```

The static Create() method returns an instance of the default DES implementation class. In this case, the class is DESCryptoServiceProvider. The advantage of this technique is that you can code generically, without creating a dependency on a specific implementation. Best of all, if Microsoft updates the framework and the default DES implementation class changes, your code will pick up the change seamlessly. This is particularly useful if you are using a CryptoAPI class, which could be replaced with a managed class equivalent in the future.

In fact, you can work at an even higher level if you want by using the static Create() method in one of the cryptographic task classes. For example, consider this code:

```
SymmetricAlgorithm crypt = SymmetricAlgorithm.Create();
```

This creates an instance of whatever cryptography class is defined as the default symmetric algorithm. In this case, it isn't DES but is Rijndael. The object returned is an instance of the RijndaelManaged implementation class. For more information on configuring default implementations and configuring friendly names used with the Create() method, take a look at the document about "Mapping Algorithm Names to Cryptography Classes" on MSDN at `http://msdn2.microsoft.com/en-us/library/693aff9y.aspx`.

■ **Tip** It is good practice to code generically using the abstract algorithm classes. This allows you to know which type of algorithm you are using (and any limitations it may have) without worrying about the underlying implementation.

Note that most of the algorithm classes support a GenerateKey() method as well, in addition to methods for encrypting and decrypting data with an algorithm. This method generates a random key that adheres to the key requirements of the corresponding algorithm. The key is generated on strong cryptographic random number generators that are part of the Windows platform so that the value is really unpredictable and random.

The ICryptoTransform Interface

.NET uses a stream-based architecture for encryption and decryption, which makes it easy to encrypt and decrypt different types of data from different types of sources. This architecture also makes it easy to perform multiple cryptographic operations in succession, on the fly, independent of the low-level details of the actual cryptography algorithm you're using (such as the block size).

To understand how all this works, you need to consider the core types—the ICryptoTransform interface and the CryptoStream class. The ICryptoTransform interface represents blockwise cryptographic transformation. This could be an encryption, decryption, hashing, Base64 encoding/decoding, or formatting operation. To create an ICryptoTransform object for a given algorithm, you use the CreateEncryptor() and CreateDecryptor() methods on the cryptography algorithm class instance (such as an instance of DES or any other algorithm you have created earlier).

Use the CreateEncryptor() method if you want to encrypt data, and use the CreateDecryptor() method if you want to decrypt data. Here's a code snippet that creates an ICryptoTransform for encrypting with the DES algorithm:

```
DES crypt = DES.Create();
ICryptoTransform transform = crypt.CreateEncryptor();
```

Various cryptographic tasks execute in the same way, even though the actual cryptographic function performing the transformation may be different. Every cryptographic operation requires that data be subdivided into blocks of a fixed size before it can be processed. You can use an ICryptoTransform instance directly, but in most cases you'll take an easier approach and simply pass it to another class: the CryptoStream.

The CryptoStream Class

The CryptoStream wraps an ordinary stream and uses an ICryptoTransform to perform its work behind the scenes. The key advantage is that the CryptoStream uses buffered access, thereby allowing you to perform automatic encryption without worrying about the block size required by the algorithm. The other advantage of the CryptoStream is that, because it wraps an ordinary .NET stream-derived class, it can easily "piggyback" on another operation, such as file access (through a FileStream), memory access (through a MemoryStream), a low-level network call (through a NetworkStream), and so on.

To create a CryptoStream, you need three pieces of information: the underlying stream, the mode (read or write), and the ICryptoTransform you want to use. For example, the following code snippet creates an ICryptoTransform using the DES algorithm implementation class and then uses it with an existing stream to create a CryptoStream:

```
DES crypt = DES.Create();
ICryptoTransform transform = crypt.CreateEncryptor();
CryptoStream cs = new CryptoStream(fileStream, transform,
  CryptoStreamMode.Write);

// (Now you can use cs to write encrypted information to the file.)
```

Note that the CryptoStream can be in one of two modes: read mode or write mode, as defined by the CryptoStreamMode enumeration. In read mode, the transformation is performed as it is retrieved from the underlying stream (as shown in Figure 25-3).

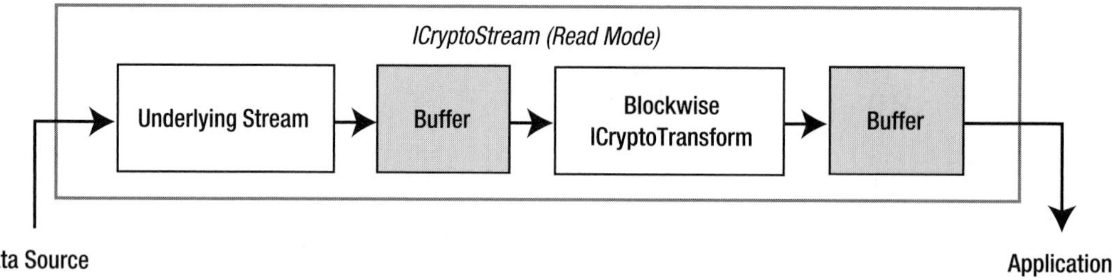

Figure 25-3. Reading and decrypting data

In write mode, the transformation is performed before the data is written to the underlying stream (as shown in Figure 25-4).

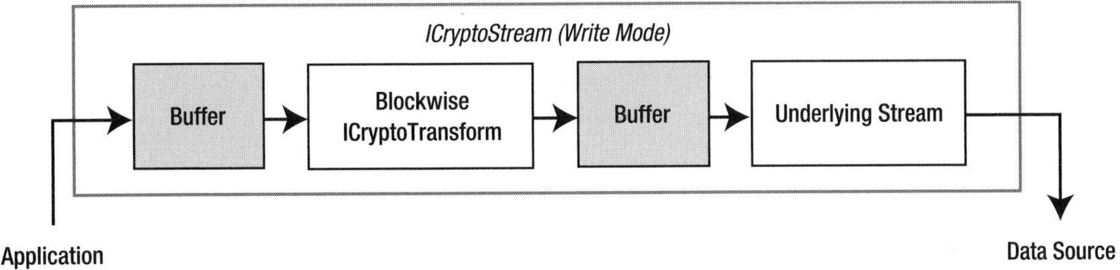

Figure 25-4. *Writing and encrypting data*

You cannot combine both modes to make a readable and writable CryptoStream (which would have no meaning anyway). Similarly, the Seek() method and the Position property of the CryptoStream class, which are used to move to different positions in a stream, are not supported for the CryptoStream and will throw a NotSupportedException if called. However, you can often use these members with the underlying stream.

Encrypting Sensitive Data

Now that you've taken an in-depth look at .NET cryptography, it's time to put it all together. In the following sections, you will create two utility classes that use symmetric and asymmetric algorithms. In the section "Encrypting Sensitive Data in a Database," you will use one of these classes to encrypt sensitive information such as a credit card number stored in a database, and in the section "Encrypting the Query String" you will learn how to encrypt the URL query string of an HTTP GET/POST request. You need to perform the following steps to encrypt and decrypt sensitive information; we will cover these steps in this and the subsequent sections:

1. Choose and create an algorithm.
2. Generate and store the secret key.
3. Encrypt or decrypt information through a CryptoStream.
4. Close the source and target streams appropriately.

After you have created and tested your encryption utility classes, you will prepare a database to store secret information and then write the code for encrypting and decrypting this secret information in the database.

Managing Secrets

Before you learn the details of using the encryption classes, you have to think about one additional thing: where do you store the key? The key used for encryption and decryption is a secret, so it must be stored securely. Often developers think the best way to store such a key is in source code. However, storing secrets in source code is one of the biggest mistakes you can make in your application. Imagine that you have the following code in the code of a class library that will be compiled into a binary DLL:

```
public static class MyEncryptionUtility
{
    // Shhh!!! Don't tell anybody!
    private const string MyKey = "m$%&kljasldk$%/65asjdl";

    public static byte[] Encrypt(string data)
    {
        // Use "MyKey" to encrypt data
        return null;
    }
}
```

Keys such as this can easily be revealed through disassembling tools. You just need to open ILDASM and analyze your class. Of course, you definitely will be able to find this secret, as shown in Figure 25-5.

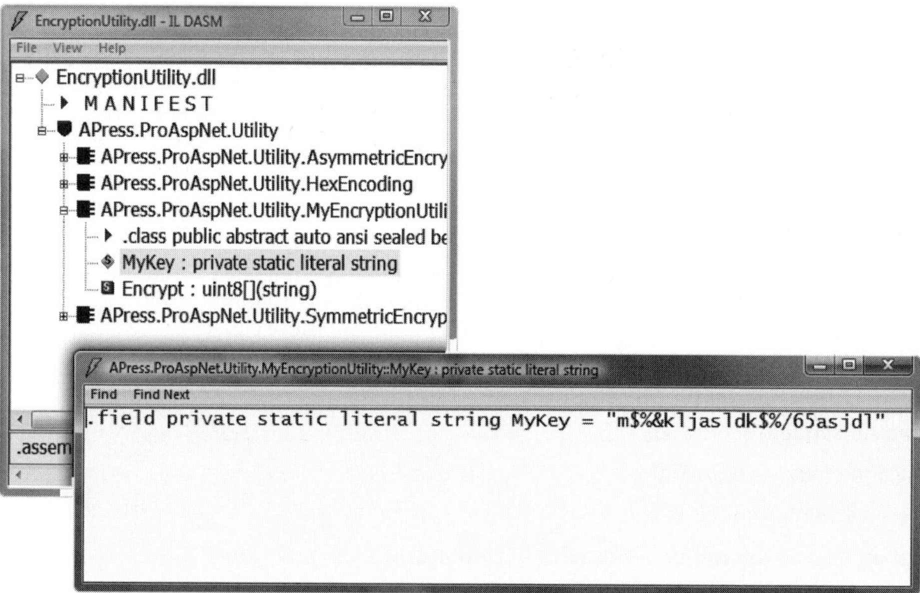

Figure 25-5. ILDASM with the previous class and the secret

If you think this is a problem in the managed world only, try something similar with an unmanaged C++ application. Create a class, and include the secret as a constant value in your application. Because constant values are stored in a special section of native executables, perform the following steps:

1. Install the Microsoft platform SDK.
2. Open a command shell, and execute the following command:

   ```
   dumpbin /all BadProtectCPlus.exe /out:test.txt
   ```

3. Open the generated file test.txt with Notepad, and scroll to the .rdata section. Somewhere in this section you will find your hard-coded secret.

So, you definitely have to protect the key somehow. You might want to encrypt the key on its own, but then you need another encryption key.

Windows supports a built-in mechanism for storing and protecting secrets. This mechanism uses a machine key generated with the system installation for encrypting data. Only the local operating system (the system's local security authority) has access to this machine key. Of course, the machine key is unique for every installation. Windows supports the DPAPI for protecting data with this key. You don't have direct access to the key when using this API; you just tell the system to encrypt or decrypt something with the machine's key. So, this solves the problem of key management: your application could encrypt the key used by your application through the DPAPI. For this purpose, the .NET Framework supports the class System.Security.Cryptography.ProtectedData, which you can use as follows:

```
byte[] ProtData = ProtectedData.Protect(
    ClearBytes, null, DataProtectionScope.LocalMachine);
```

You need to add a reference to the System.Security.dll assembly and import the System.Security.Cryptography namespace when you want to use the ProtectedData class for protecting sensitive information. Possible scopes are LocalMachine and CurrentUser. While the first option uses the machine key, the second one uses a key generated for the currently logged-on user's profile. (In the case of Active Directory roaming profiles that allow reusing a Windows user profile on several Windows machines within an Active Directory domain, this key is machine independent.) If a user is the administrator of the machine and has the necessary know-how, he can decrypt the data by writing a program that calls the previous function. However, this definitely "raises the bar" and makes it harder to access the key. And if the user is not the administrator and has no permission to use the DPAPI, she cannot decrypt data encrypted with the machine key.

■ **Caution** Don't use the DPAPI to encrypt information in your database. Although it is easy to use the DPAPI with the .NET Framework, this method has one problem: encrypted data is bound to the machine if you use the DataProtectionScope.LocalMachine setting. Therefore, if the machine crashes and you have to restore your data on another machine, you will lose all the encrypted information. If you use the DPAPI for encrypting the key as described previously, you should have a backup of the key in another secure place. If you want to use the DPAPI in web farm scenarios, you have to run your application under a domain user account and use the key created for the user's profile (DataProtectionScope.CurrentUser). We recommend creating a separate domain for your web farm so that you don't have to use a domain user of your company's internal domain network.

Using Symmetric Algorithms

As mentioned, symmetric encryption algorithms use one key for encrypting and decrypting data. In the next section, you will learn the details by creating a utility class that performs the encryption and decryption of sensitive data. You can then reuse this class across several web applications. The utility class you will create has the following structure and can be used for encrypting and decrypting string data. (Note that based on the _ProtectKey Boolean, you will write code later that decides whether to protect the key using the DPAPI or not by querying this Boolean value. A true value means it should protect the key using the DPAPI, as you will see when you implement the class.)

```
public static class SymmetricEncryptionUtility
{
    private static bool _ProtectKey;
    private static string _AlgorithmName;

    public static string AlgorithmName
    {
        get { return _AlgorithmName; }
        set { _AlgorithmName = value; }
    }

    public static bool ProtectKey
    {
        get { return _ProtectKey; }
        set { _ProtectKey = value; }
    }

    public static void GenerateKey(string targetFile) { }
    public static void ReadKey(SymmetricAlgorithm algorithm, string file) { }
    public static byte[] EncryptData(string data, string keyFile) { }
    public static string DecryptData(byte[] data, string keyFile) { }
}
```

Because the class is just a utility class with static members only, you can make it a static class so that nobody can create an instance of it. You can specify the name of the algorithm (DES, TripleDES, RijnDael, or RC2) through the AlgorithmName property. It also supports operations for generating a new key, reading this key from the file specified directly into the key property of an algorithm instance, and encrypting and decrypting data. To use this class, you must set the algorithm name appropriately and then generate a key if none exists already. Then you need to call the EncryptData and DecryptData methods, which internally will call the ReadKey method for initializing the algorithm. The ProtectKey property allows the user of the class to specify whether the key should be protected through the DPAPI.

You can generate encryption keys through the algorithm classes. The GenerateKey() method looks like this:

```
public static void GenerateKey(string targetFile)
{
    // Create the algorithm
    SymmetricAlgorithm Algorithm = SymmetricAlgorithm.Create(AlgorithmName);
    Algorithm.GenerateKey();

    // Now get the key
    byte[] Key = Algorithm.Key;

    if (ProtectKey)
    {
        // Use DPAPI to encrypt key
        Key = ProtectedData.Protect(
            Key, null, DataProtectionScope.LocalMachine);
    }

    // Store the key in a file called key.config
    using (FileStream fs = new FileStream(targetFile, FileMode.Create))
    {
```

```
            fs.Write(Key, 0, Key.Length);
        }
    }
```

The GenerateKey() method of the SymmetricAlgorithm class generates a new key through cryptographically strong random number algorithms via the GenerateKey() method supplied by the created algorithm and initializes the Key property with this new key. If the calling code has set the ProtectKey flag of your utility class to true, your implementation encrypts the key using the DPAPI.

The ReadKey method reads the key from the file created by the GenerateKey method, as follows:

```
public static void ReadKey(SymmetricAlgorithm algorithm, string keyFile)
{
    byte[] Key;

    using (FileStream fs = new FileStream(keyFile, FileMode.Open))
    {
        Key = new byte[fs.Length];
        fs.Read(Key, 0, (int)fs.Length);
    }

    if (ProtectKey)
        algorithm.Key = ProtectedData.Unprotect(
                  Key, null, DataProtectionScope.LocalMachine);
    else
        algorithm.Key = Key;
}
```

If the key was protected previously, the ReadKey method uses the DPAPI for unprotecting the encrypted key when reading it from the file. Furthermore, ReadKey() requires you to pass in an existing instance of a symmetric algorithm. It directly initializes the key property of the algorithm so that this key will be used automatically for all subsequent operations. Finally, both the EncryptData() and DecryptData() functions use the ReadKey() function.

```
public static byte[] EncryptData(string data, string keyFile) { }
public static string DecryptData(byte[] data, string keyFile) { }
```

As you can see, both methods require a keyFile parameter with the path to the file that stores the key. They subsequently call the ReadKey method for initializing their algorithm instance with the key. While the EncryptData method accepts a string and returns a byte array with the encrypted representation, the DecryptData method accepts the encrypted byte array and returns the clear-text string.

Let's get started with the EncryptData method:

```
public static byte[] EncryptData(string data, string keyFile)
{
    // Convert string data to byte array
    byte[] ClearData = System.Text.Encoding.UTF8.GetBytes(data);

    // Now create the algorithm
    SymmetricAlgorithm Algorithm = SymmetricAlgorithm.Create(AlgorithmName);
    ReadKey(Algorithm, keyFile);

    // Encrypt information
```

```
    MemoryStream Target = new MemoryStream();

    // Generate a random initialization vector (IV) to use for the algorithm
    Algorithm.GenerateIV();
    Target.Write(Algorithm.IV, 0, Algorithm.IV.Length);

    // Encrypt actual data
    CryptoStream cs = new CryptoStream(Target,
            Algorithm.CreateEncryptor(), CryptoStreamMode.Write);
    cs.Write(ClearData, 0, ClearData.Length);
    cs.FlushFinalBlock();

    // Return the encrypted stream of data as a byte array
    return Target.ToArray();
}
```

First, the method converts the incoming clear-text string value into a byte array because all the encryption functions of the algorithms require byte arrays as input parameters. You can use the Encoding class of the System.Text namespace to do this easily. Next, the method creates the algorithm according to the AlgorithmName property of the class. This value can be one of the names RC2, Rijndael, DES, or TripleDES. The factory method of the SymmetricAlgorithm creates the appropriate instance, while you can register additional cryptography classes through the <cryptographySettings> section in the machine.config file. You can read more about configuring cryptography providers at http://msdn2.microsoft.com/en-us/library/bke5we9a.aspx.

Afterward, the method creates a memory stream that will be the target of your encryption operation in this case. Before the class starts with the encryption operation through the CryptoStream class, it generates an initialization vector (IV) and writes the IV to the target stream on the first position. The IV adds random data to the encrypted stream of data.

Imagine the following situation: if your application exchanges the same information multiple times between a client and a server, simple encryption will always result in the same encrypted representation of the information. This makes brute-force attacks easier. To add some sort of random information, symmetric algorithms support IV. These IVs are not only added to the encrypted stream of bytes themselves but are also used as input for encrypting the first block of data. When using the CryptoStream for encrypting information, don't forget to call the FlushFinalBlock method to make sure the last block of encrypted data is written appropriately to the target.

You have to add the IV itself to the encrypted set of bytes because you need the information later to be able to decrypt the encrypted content completely:

```
public static string DecryptData(byte[] data, string keyFile)
{
    // Create the algorithm
    SymmetricAlgorithm Algorithm = SymmetricAlgorithm.Create(AlgorithmName);
    ReadKey(Algorithm, keyFile);

    // Decrypt information
    MemoryStream Target = new MemoryStream();

    // Read IV and initialize the algorithm with it
    int ReadPos = 0;
    byte[] IV = new byte[Algorithm.IV.Length];
    Array.Copy(data, IV, IV.Length);
    Algorithm.IV = IV;
    ReadPos += Algorithm.IV.Length;
```

```
    CryptoStream cs = new CryptoStream(Target,
           Algorithm.CreateDecryptor(), CryptoStreamMode.Write);
    cs.Write(data, ReadPos, data.Length - ReadPos);
    cs.FlushFinalBlock();

    // Get the bytes from the memory stream and convert them to text
    return Encoding.UTF8.GetString(Target.ToArray());
}
```

The decryption function is structured the other way around. It creates the algorithm and creates a stream for the decrypted target information. Before you can start decrypting the data, you have to read the IV from the encrypted stream, because it is used by the algorithm for the last transformation. You then use the CryptoStream as you did previously, except you create a decryptor transformer this time. Finally, you get the decrypted byte representation of the string you have created through Encoding.UTF8.GetBytes(). To reverse this operation, you need to call the GetString() method of the UTF-8 encoding class for getting the clear-text representation of the string.

Using the SymmetricEncryptionUtility Class

Now you can create a page for testing the class you created previously. Just create a page that allows you to generate a key and enter clear-text data through a text box. You can output the encrypted data through Convert.ToBase64String() easily. For decryption, you need to decode the Base64-encoded portion back to its byte array. You do so by calling the counterpart method called Convert.FromBase64String() to get the encrypted bytes back and pass them into the DecryptData method.

```
private string KeyFileName;
private string AlgorithmName = "DES";

protected void Page_Load(object sender, EventArgs e)
{
    SymmetricEncryptionUtility.AlgorithmName = AlgorithmName;
    KeyFileName = Server.MapPath("./") + "\\symmetric_key.config";
}

protected void GenerateKeyCommand_Click(object sender, EventArgs e)
{
        SymmetricEncryptionUtility.ProtectKey = EncryptKeyCheck.Checked;
        SymmetricEncryptionUtility.GenerateKey(KeyFileName);
        Response.Write("Key generated successfully!");
}

protected void EncryptCommand_Click(object sender, EventArgs e)
{
    // Check for encryption key
    if (!File.Exists(KeyFileName))
    {
        Response.Write("Missing encryption key. Please generate key!");
    }

    byte[] data = SymmetricEncryptionUtility.EncryptData(
                        ClearDataText.Text, KeyFileName);
    EncryptedDataText.Text = Convert.ToBase64String(data);
```

```
}

protected void DecryptCommand_Click(object sender, EventArgs e)
{
    // Check for encryption key
    if (!File.Exists(KeyFileName))
    {
        Response.Write("Missing encryption key. Please generate key!");
    }

    byte[] data = Convert.FromBase64String(EncryptedDataText.Text);
    ClearDataText.Text = SymmetricEncryptionUtility.DecryptData(
                                          data, KeyFileName);
}
```

The previous page uses the DES algorithm because you set the AlgorithmName of your utility class appropriately. Within the Click event of the GenerateKeyCommand button, it calls the GenerateKey() method. Depending on the check box of the page, it encrypts the key itself through the DPAPI or not. After the data has been encrypted through your utility class within the Click event of the EncryptCommand button, it converts the encrypted bytes to a Base64 string and then writes it to the EncryptedDataText text box. Therefore, if you want to decrypt information again, you have to create a byte array based on this Base64 string representation and then call the method for decryption. You can see the result in Figure 25-6.

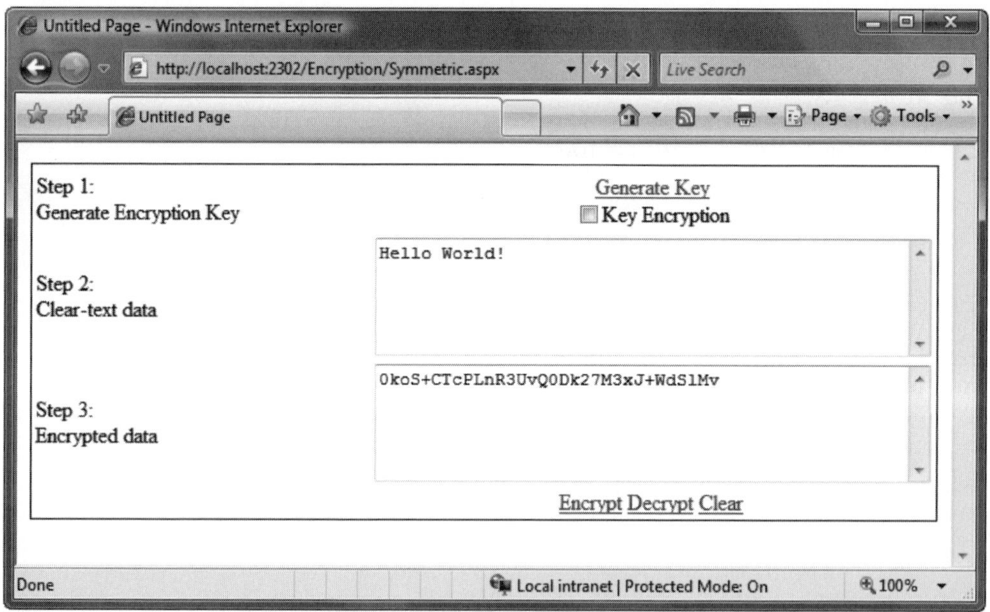

Figure 25-6. *The resulting test page for symmetric algorithms*

Using Asymmetric Algorithms

Using asymmetric algorithms is similar to using symmetric algorithms. You will see just a handful of differences. The major difference has to do with key management. Symmetric algorithms just have one key, and asymmetric algorithms have two keys: one for encrypting data (public key) and one for decrypting data (private key). While the public key can be available to everyone who wants to encrypt data, the private key should be available only to those decrypting information. In this section, you will create a utility class similar to the previous one.

Because the .NET Framework ships with only one asymmetric algorithm for real data encryption (RSA; remember, DSA is used for digital signatures only), you don't need to include a way to select the algorithm (for a while).

```
public static class AsymmetricEncryptionUtility
{
    public static string GenerateKey(string targetFile) { }
    private static void ReadKey(
            RSACryptoServiceProvider algorithm, string keyFile) { }
    public static byte[] EncryptData(string data, string publicKey) { }
    public static string DecryptData(byte[] data, string keyFile) { }

}
```

The GenerateKey method creates an instance of the RSA algorithm for generating the key. It stores only the private key in the file secured through the DPAPI and returns the public key representation as an XML string using the ToXmlString() method of the algorithm. This is a fairly realistic concept—the private key is usually kept as a secret by the application, while the public key is shared with others to be able to encrypt information that then is decrypted by the application using its secret private key.

```
public static string GenerateKey(string targetFile)
{
    RSACryptoServiceProvider Algorithm = new RSACryptoServiceProvider();

    // Save the private key
    string CompleteKey = Algorithm.ToXmlString(true);
    byte[] KeyBytes = Encoding.UTF8.GetBytes(CompleteKey);

    KeyBytes = ProtectedData.Protect(KeyBytes,
                    null, DataProtectionScope.LocalMachine);

    using (FileStream fs = new FileStream(targetFile, FileMode.Create))
    {
        fs.Write(KeyBytes, 0, KeyBytes.Length);
    }

    // Return the public key
    return Algorithm.ToXmlString(false);
}
```

The caller of the function needs to store the public key somewhere; this is necessary for encrypting information. You can retrieve the key as an XML representation through a method called ToXmlString(). The parameter specifies whether private key information is included (true) or not (false). Therefore, the GenerateKey function first calls the ToXmlString() function with the true parameter to store the complete key information in the file and then calls it with the false parameter to include the public key only. Subsequently, the ReadKey() method just reads the key from the file and then initializes the passed algorithm instance through FromXml(), the opposite of the ToXmlString() method:

```
private static void ReadKey(RSACryptoServiceProvider algorithm, string keyFile)
{
    byte[] KeyBytes;

    using(FileStream fs = new FileStream(keyFile, FileMode.Open))
    {
        KeyBytes = new byte[fs.Length];
        fs.Read(KeyBytes, 0, (int)fs.Length);
    }

    KeyBytes = ProtectedData.Unprotect(KeyBytes,
                    null, DataProtectionScope.LocalMachine);

    algorithm.FromXmlString(Encoding.UTF8.GetString(KeyBytes));
}
```

This time the ReadKey() method is used by the decryption function only. The EncryptData() function requires the caller to pass in the XML string representation of the public key returned by the GenerateKey() method, because the private key is not required for encryption. Encryption and decryption with RSA takes place as follows:

```
public static byte[] EncryptData(string data, string publicKey)
{
    // Create the algorithm based on the public key
    RSACryptoServiceProvider Algorithm = new RSACryptoServiceProvider();
    Algorithm.FromXmlString(publicKey);

    // Now encrypt the data
    return Algorithm.Encrypt(
                Encoding.UTF8.GetBytes(data), true);
}

public static string DecryptData(byte[] data, string keyFile)
{
    RSACryptoServiceProvider Algorithm = new RSACryptoServiceProvider();
    ReadKey(Algorithm, keyFile);

    byte[] ClearData = Algorithm.Decrypt(data, true);
    return Convert.ToString(
                Encoding.UTF8.GetString(ClearData));
}
```

Now you can build a test page, as shown in Figure 25-7. (You can find the source code of this page in the book's downloadable code in the Source Code/Download area on the Apress website at `http://www.apress.com`.)

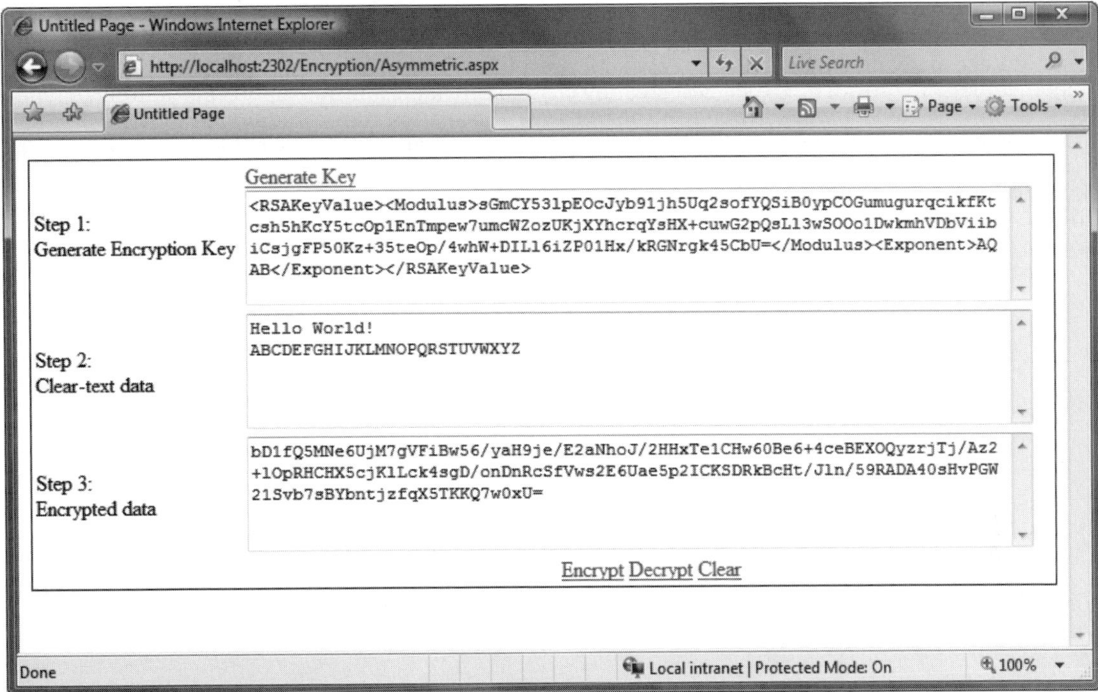

Figure 25-7. A sample test page for asymmetric algorithms

Encrypting Sensitive Data in a Database

In this section, you will learn how to create a simple test page for encrypting information stored in a database table. This table will be connected to a user registered in the Membership Service. We suggest not creating a custom membership provider with custom implementations of MembershipUser that support additional properties. As long as you stay loosely coupled with your own logic, you can use it with multiple membership providers. In this sample, you will create a database table that stores additional information for a MembershipUser without creating a custom provider. It just connects to the MembershipUser through the ProviderUserKey—this means the actual primary key of the underlying data store. Therefore, you have to create a table on your SQL Server as follows:

```
CREATE DATABASE ExtendedUser
GO
USE ExtendedUser
GO
CREATE TABLE ShopInfo
(
  UserId UNIQUEIDENTIFIER PRIMARY KEY,
  CreditCard VARBINARY(80),
  Street VARCHAR(80),
  ZipCode VARCHAR(6),
  City VARCHAR(60)
)
```

The primary key, UserId, will contain the same key as the MembershipUser for which this information is created. That's the only connection to the underlying Membership Service. As mentioned, the advantage of not creating a custom provider for just these additional fields is that you can use it for other membership providers. We suggest creating custom providers only for supporting additional types of data stores for the Membership Service. The sensitive information is the CreditCard field, which now is not stored as VARCHAR but as VARBINARY instead. Now you can create a page that looks like this:

```
<form id="form1" runat="server">
<div>
<asp:LoginView runat="server" ID="MainLoginView">
    <AnonymousTemplate>
        <asp:Login ID="MainLogin" runat="server" />
    </AnonymousTemplate>
    <LoggedInTemplate>
        Credit Card: <asp:TextBox ID="CreditCardText" runat="server" /><br />
        Street: <asp:TextBox ID="StreetText" runat="server" /><br />
        Zip Code: <asp:TextBox ID="ZipCodeText" runat="server" /><br />
        City: <asp:TextBox ID="CityText" runat="server" /><br />
        <asp:Button runat="server" ID="LoadCommand" Text="Load"
                    OnClick="LoadCommand_Click" /> 
        <asp:Button runat="server" ID="SaveCommand" Text="Save"
                    OnClick="SaveCommand_Click" />
    </LoggedInTemplate>
</asp:LoginView>
</div>
</form>
```

The page includes a LoginView control to display the Login control for anonymous users and display some text fields for the information introduced with the CREATE TABLE statement. Within the Load button's Click event handler, you will write code for retrieving and decrypting information from the database, and within the Save button's Click event handler, you will obviously do the opposite. Before doing that, though, don't forget to configure the connection string appropriately.

```
<configuration>
    <connectionStrings>
        <add name="DemoSql"
             connectionString="data source=(local);
                               Integrated Security=SSPI;
                               initial catalog=ExtendedUser"/>
    </connectionStrings>
    <system.web>
        <authentication mode="Forms" />
    </system.web>
</configuration>
```

Now you should use the ASP.NET WAT to create a couple of users in your membership store. After you have done that, you can start writing the actual code for reading and writing data to the database. The code doesn't include anything special. It just uses the previously created encryption utility class for encrypting the data before updating the database and decrypting the data stored on the database.

Let's take a look at the Page_Load method, which initializes the ADO.NET Connection instance, and then at the update method implemented in the SaveCommand's Click event handler first. Remember that you leverage the previously created utility class (SymmetricEncryptionUtility), which requires you to specify a filename for storing the protected private key. Also note that in the previous ASP.NET page code, you used the LoginView control. This means that you have to manually find the TextBox controls using FindControl() on the LoginView control and associate them to your own members, as shown in the following code snippet:

```
// Private member of our current page representing the Connection
// to our custom database configured in the previous web.config
SqlConnection DemoDb;

// We need some TextBox controls that we find in the
// LoginView control template through FindControl() because
// they are only contained in a template of the LoginView
private TextBox CreditCardText;
private TextBox StreetText;
private TextBox ZipCodeText;
private TextBox CityText;

// Used for storing the encryption key based on the code
// introduced previously with our SymmetricEncryptionUtility class
private string EncryptionKeyFile;

protected void Page_Load(object sender, EventArgs e)
{
    // Configure Encryption Utility
    EncryptionKeyFile = Server.MapPath("key.config");
    SymmetricEncryptionUtility.AlgorithmName = "DES";
    if (!System.IO.File.Exists(EncryptionKeyFile))
    {
        SymmetricEncryptionUtility.GenerateKey(EncryptionKeyFile);
    }

    // Create the connection
    DemoDb = new SqlConnection(
        ConfigurationManager.ConnectionStrings["DemoSql"].ConnectionString);

    // Associate with Textfields
    CreditCardText = (TextBox)MainLoginView.FindControl("CreditCardText");
    StreetText = (TextBox)MainLoginView.FindControl("StreetText");
    ZipCodeText = (TextBox)MainLoginView.FindControl("ZipCodeText");
    CityText = (TextBox)MainLoginView.FindControl("CityText");
}

protected void SaveCommand_Click(object sender, EventArgs e)
{
    DemoDb.Open();

    try
    {
        string SqlText = "UPDATE ShopInfo " +
                         "SET Street=@street, ZipCode=@zip, " +
                             "City=@city, CreditCard=@card " +
                         "WHERE UserId=@key";

        SqlCommand Cmd = new SqlCommand(SqlText, DemoDb);

        // Add simple values
```

```
        Cmd.Parameters.AddWithValue("@street", StreetText.Text);
        Cmd.Parameters.AddWithValue("@zip", ZipCodeText.Text);
        Cmd.Parameters.AddWithValue("@city", CityText.Text);
        Cmd.Parameters.AddWithValue("@key",
                    Membership.GetUser().ProviderUserKey);

        // Now add the encrypted value
        byte[] EncryptedData =
            SymmetricEncryptionUtility.EncryptData(
                    CreditCardText.Text, EncryptionKeyFile);
        Cmd.Parameters.AddWithValue("@card", EncryptedData);

        // Execute the command
        int results = Cmd.ExecuteNonQuery();
        if (results == 0)
        {
            Cmd.CommandText = "INSERT INTO ShopInfo VALUES" +
                              "(@key, @card, @street, @zip, @city)";
            Cmd.ExecuteNonQuery();
        }
    }
    finally
    {
        DemoDb.Close();
    }
}
```

The two key parts of the previous code are the part that retrieves the ProviderUserKey from the currently logged-on MembershipUser for connecting the information to a membership user and the position where the credit card information is encrypted through the previously created encryption utility class. Only the encrypted byte array is passed as a parameter to the SQL command. Therefore, the data is stored encrypted in the database.

The opposite of this function, reading data, looks quite similar, as shown here:

```
protected void LoadCommand_Click(object sender, EventArgs e)
{
    DemoDb.Open();

    try
    {
        string SqlText = "SELECT * FROM ShopInfo WHERE UserId=@key";
        SqlCommand Cmd = new SqlCommand(SqlText, DemoDb);
        Cmd.Parameters.AddWithValue("@key",
                    Membership.GetUser().ProviderUserKey);
        using (SqlDataReader Reader = Cmd.ExecuteReader())
        {
            if (Reader.Read())
            {
                // Cleartext Data
                StreetText.Text = Reader["City"].ToString();
                ZipCodeText.Text = Reader["ZipCode"].ToString();
                CityText.Text = Reader["City"].ToString();
```

```
                // Encrypted Data
                byte[] SecretCard = (byte[])Reader["CreditCard"];
                CreditCardText.Text =
                    SymmetricEncryptionUtility.DecryptData(
                                SecretCard, EncryptionKeyFile);
            }
        }
    }
    finally
    {
        DemoDb.Close();
    }
}
```

Again, the function uses the currently logged-on MembershipUser's ProviderUserKey property for retrieving the information. If successfully retrieved, it reads the clear-text data and then retrieves the encrypted bytes from the database table. These bytes are then decrypted and displayed in the credit card text box. You can see the results in Figure 25-8.

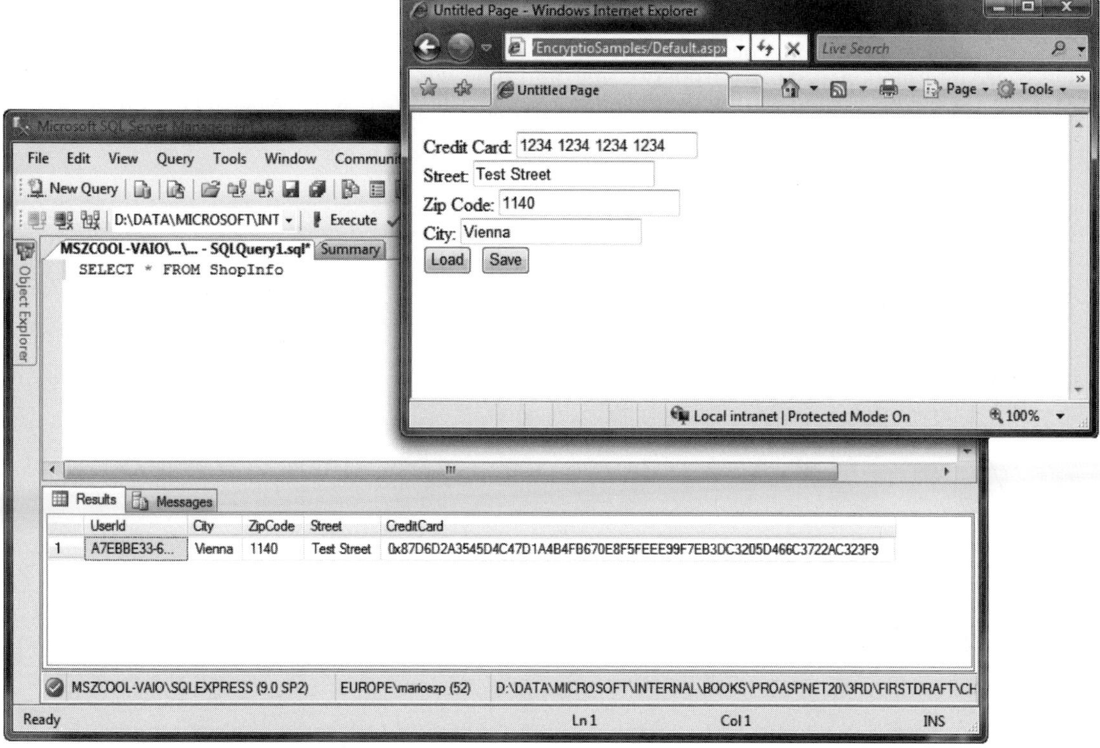

Figure 25-8. Encrypting sensitive information on the database

Encrypting the Query String

In this book, you've seen several examples in which ASP.NET security works behind the scenes to protect your data. For example, in Chapter 20 you learned how ASP.NET uses encryption and hash codes to ensure that the data in the form cookie is always protected. You have also learned how you can use the same tools to protect view state. Unfortunately, ASP.NET doesn't provide a similar way to enable automatic encryption for the query string (which is the extra bit of information you add to URLs to transmit information from one page to another). In many cases, the URL query information corresponds to user-supplied data, and it doesn't matter whether the user can see or modify it. In other cases, however, the query string contains information that should remain hidden from the user. In this case, the only option is to switch to another form of state management (which may have other limitations) or devise a system to encrypt the query string.

In the next example, you'll see a simple way to tighten security by scrambling data before you place it in the query string. Once again, you can rely on the cryptography classes provided with .NET. In fact, you can leverage the DPAPI. (You can do this only if you are not in a server farm environment. In that case, you could use the previously created encryption classes and deploy the same key file to any machine in the server farm.)

Wrapping the Query String

The starting point is to build an EncryptedQueryString class. This class should accept a collection of string-based information (just like the query string) and allow you to retrieve it in another page. Behind the scenes, the EncryptedQueryString class needs to encrypt the data before it's placed in the query string and decrypt it seamlessly on the way out.

Here's the starting point for the EncryptedQueryString class you need:

```
public class EncryptedQueryString :
    System.Collections.Specialized.StringDictionary
{
    public EncryptedQueryString()
    {
        // Nothing to do here
    }

    public EncryptedQueryString(string encryptedData)
    {
        // Decrypt information and add to
        // the dictionary
    }

    public override string ToString()
    {
        // Encrypt information and return as
        // HEX-encoded string
    }
}
```

You should notice one detail immediately about the EncryptedQueryString class: it derives from the StringDictionary class, which represents a collection of strings indexed by strings. By deriving from StringDictionary, you gain the ability to use the EncryptedQueryString like an ordinary string collection. As a result, you can add information to the EncryptedQueryString in the same way you add information to the Request.QueryString collection. Here's an example:

```
encryptedQueryString["value1"] = "Sample Value";
```

Best of all, you get this functionality for free, without needing to write any additional code. So, with just this rudimentary class, you have the ability to store a collection of name/value strings. But how do you actually place this information into the query string? The EncryptedQueryString class provides a ToString() method that examines all the collection data and combines it in a single encrypted string.

First, the EncryptedQueryString class needs to combine the separate collection values into a delimited string so that it's easy to split the string back into a collection on the destination page. In this case, the ToString() method uses the conventions of the query string, separating each value from the name with an equal sign (=) and separating each subsequent name/value pair with the ampersand (&). However, for this to work, you need to make sure the names and values of the actual item in the collection don't include these special characters. To solve this problem, the ToString() method uses the HttpServerUtility.UrlEncode() method to escape the strings before joining them.

Here's the first portion of the ToString() method, which escapes and joins the collection settings into one string:

```
public override string ToString()
{
    StringBuilder Content = new StringBuilder();

    // Go through the contents and build a
    // typical query string
    foreach (string key in base.Keys)
    {
        Content.Append(HttpUtility.UrlEncode(key));
        Content.Append("=");
        Content.Append(HttpUtility.UrlEncode(base[key]));
        Content.Append("&");
    }

    // Remove the last '&'
    Content.Remove(Content.Length-1, 1);
    ...
```

The next step is to use the ProtectedData class to encrypt the data. This class uses the DPAPI to encrypt the information and its Protect method to return a byte array, so you need to take additional steps to convert the byte array to a string form that's suitable for the query string. One approach that seems reasonable is the static Convert.ToBase64String() method, which creates a Base64-encoded string. Unfortunately, Base64 strings can include symbols that aren't allowed in the query string (namely, the equal sign). Although you could create a Base64 string and then URL-encode it, this further complicates the decoding stage. The problem is that the ToBase64String() method may also introduce a series of characters that look like URL-encoded character sequences. These character sequences will then be incorrectly replaced when you decode the string.

A simpler approach is to use a different form of encoding. This example uses hex encoding, which replaces each character with an alphanumeric code. The following example shows the simple implementation of such a helper class implementing hexadecimal-based encodings:

```
public static class HexEncoding
{
    public static string GetString(byte[] data)
    {
        StringBuilder Results = new StringBuilder();
        foreach (byte b in data)
        {
```

```
            Results.Append(b.ToString("X2"));
        }

        return Results.ToString();
    }

    public static byte[] GetBytes(string data)
    {
        // GetString encodes the hex numbers with two digits
        byte[] Results = new byte[data.Length / 2];
        for (int i = 0; i < data.Length; i += 2)
        {
            Results[i / 2] = Convert.ToByte(data.Substring(i, 2), 16);
        }

        return Results;
    }
}
```

The GetString() method just returns a string with hexadecimal digits created from a byte array, while GetBytes() converts a string with hexadecimal digits back to the byte array for further processing. This is fairly simple to implement, because it uses existing conversion methods encapsulated in the .NET Framework's convert class. These methods are then simple to use, as the following code excerpt shows:

```
    ...
    // Now encrypt the contents using DPAPI
    byte[] EncryptedData = ProtectedData.Protect(
                Encoding.UTF8.GetBytes(Content.ToString()),
                null, DataProtectionScope.LocalMachine);

    // Convert encrypted byte array to a URL-legal string
    // This would also be a good place to check that data
    // is not larger than typical 4 KB query string
    return HexEncoding.GetString(EncryptedData);
}
```

You can place the string returned from EncryptedQueryString.ToString() directly into a query string using the Response.Redirect() method.

The destination page that receives the query data needs a way to deserialize and decrypt the string. The first step is to create a new EncryptedQueryString object and supply the encrypted data. To make this step easier, it makes sense to add a new constructor to the EncryptedQueryString class that accepts the encrypted string, as follows:

```
public EncryptedQueryString(string encryptedData)
{
    // Decrypt data passed in using DPAPI
    byte[] RawData = HexEncoding.GetBytes(encryptedData);
    byte[] ClearRawData = ProtectedData.Unprotect(
                RawData, null, DataProtectionScope.LocalMachine);
    string StringData = Encoding.UTF8.GetString(ClearRawData);

    // Split the data and add the contents
    int Index;
```

```
    string[] SplittedData = StringData.Split(new char[] { '&' });
    foreach (string SingleData in SplittedData)
    {
        Index = SingleData.IndexOf('=');
        base.Add(
            HttpUtility.UrlDecode(SingleData.Substring(0, Index)),
            HttpUtility.UrlDecode(SingleData.Substring(Index + 1))
        );
    }
}
```

This constructor first decodes the hexadecimal information from the string passed in and uses the DPAPI to decrypt information stored in the query string. It then splits the information back into its parts and adds the key/value pairs to the base StringCollection.

Now you have the entire infrastructure in place to create a simple test page and transmit information from one page to another in a secure fashion.

Creating a Test Page

To try the EncryptedQueryString class, you need two pages—one that sets the query string and redirects the user and another that retrieves the query string. The first one contains a text box for entering information, as follows:

```
<form id="form1" runat="server">
<div>
Enter some data here: <asp:TextBox runat="server" ID="MyData" />
<br />
<br />
<asp:Button ID="SendCommand" runat="server" Text="Send Info"
            OnClick="SendCommand_Click" />
</div>
</form>
```

When the user clicks the SendCommand button, the page sends the encrypted query string to the receiving page, as follows:

```
protected void SendCommand_Click(object sender, EventArgs e)
{
    EncryptedQueryString QueryString = new EncryptedQueryString();

    QueryString.Add("MyData", MyData.Text);
    QueryString.Add("MyTime", DateTime.Now.ToLongTimeString());
    QueryString.Add("MyDate", DateTime.Now.ToLongDateString());

    Response.Redirect("QueryStringRecipient.aspx?data=" +
                      QueryString.ToString());
}
```

Notice that the page enters the complete encrypted data string as one parameter called *data* into the query string for the destination page. Figure 25-9 shows the page in action.

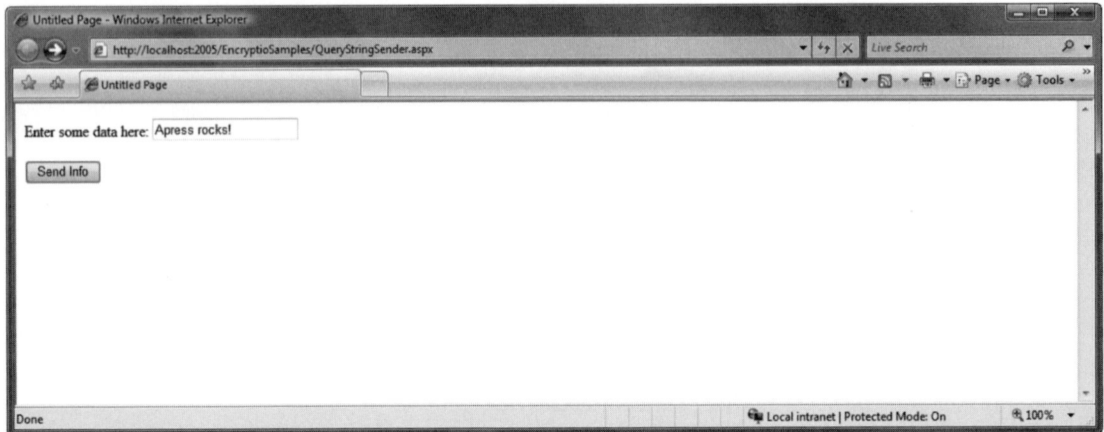

Figure 25-9. The source page in action

The destination page deserializes the query string passed in through the data query string parameter with the previously created class, as follows:

```
protected void Page_Load(object sender, EventArgs e)
{
    // Deserialize the encrypted query string
    EncryptedQueryString QueryString =
        new EncryptedQueryString(Request.QueryString["data"]);

    // Write information to the screen
    StringBuilder Info = new StringBuilder();
    foreach (String key in QueryString.Keys)
    {
        Info.AppendFormat("{0} = {1}<br>", key, QueryString[key]);
    }
    QueryStringLabel.Text = Info.ToString();
}
```

This code adds the information to a label on the page. You can see the result of the previously posted information in Figure 25-10.

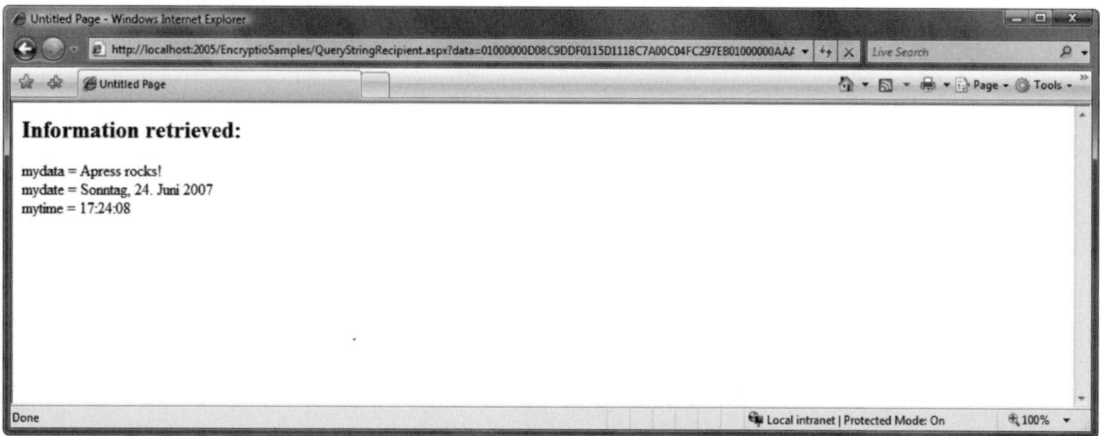

Figure 25-10. The results of the received query string information

Summary

In this chapter, you learned how to take control of .NET security with advanced techniques. You saw how to use stream-based encryption to protect stored data and the query string. In the next chapter, you'll learn how to use powerful techniques to extend the ASP.NET security model.

CHAPTER 26

■■■

Custom Membership Providers

In the previous chapters, you learned all the necessary details for authenticating and authorizing users with ASP.NET through both forms authentication and Windows authentication. You learned that with forms authentication on its own, you are responsible for managing users (and roles if you want to implement role-based authorization in your application) in a custom store.

Fortunately, ASP.NET ships with the membership API and the roles API, which provide you with a framework for user and roles management. You learned the details about the membership API in Chapter 21, and you learned about the roles API in Chapter 23. You can extend the framework through providers that implement the actual access to the underlying data store. In both of those chapters, you used the default provider for SQL Server that ships with ASP.NET.

You can exchange the default implementation that works with SQL Server by implementing custom membership and roles providers. This gives you the possibility of exchanging the underlying storage used for user and role information, without affecting your web application.

In this chapter, you will learn how you can extend the membership API and the roles API by implementing custom membership and roles providers. Furthermore, you will learn how you can configure and debug your custom provider for web applications. With the information in this chapter, you will also be equipped to create other custom providers—for example, providers for the profiles API and the personalization engine of web parts (see Chapter 31)—because the creation process is always the same.

Architecture of Custom Providers

In Chapters 21 and 23 you learned many details about the integrated membership and roles services. These services provide you with an out-of-the-box solution for managing users and roles with forms authentication. As explained earlier, you can extend the model through providers, as shown in Figure 26-1. When implementing custom providers, you should always keep the architecture shown in Figure 26-1 in mind. A custom provider is always based on the lowest level in the layered model introduced by the ASP.NET membership and roles framework. It's important to know that every other provider-based API in ASP.NET is structured in the same way. Therefore, implementing custom providers for the profiles API or the personalization engine of ASP.NET is similar.

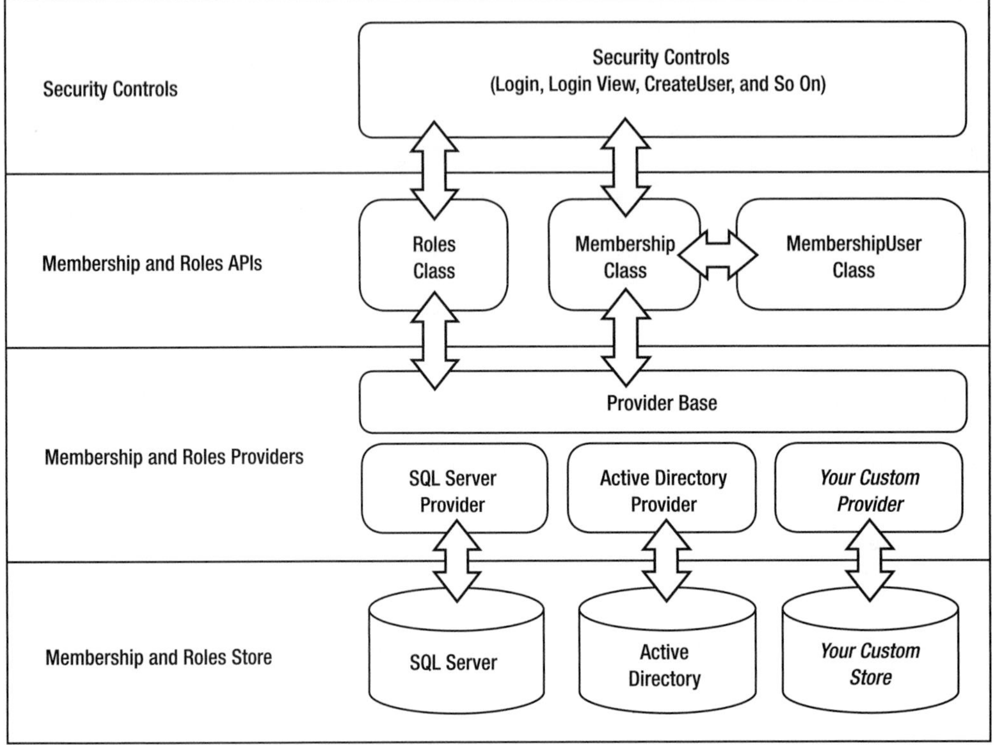

Figure 26-1. *The membership and roles framework*

As you can see from their basic architectures, the membership and roles services are independent from each other. Therefore, membership providers and roles providers have separate base classes; in addition, you can store membership users and roles in different back-end systems. A good example is when using the roles service with Windows authentication. Remember what you learned in Chapter 23 about application-specific roles that are used for authorization within the application instead of within Windows groups: this provides you with a way to decouple your application from an underlying Active Directory infrastructure.

Before you learn about the details of implementing custom providers, it's important to understand why you might want to create a custom membership provider. Some common reasons include the following:

- You want to use an existing user and roles database that has a different schema than the ASP.NET standard.
- You want to use a database other than Microsoft SQL Server.
- You want to use an unusual data store (such as an XML file, web service, or LDAP directories of your choice).
- You want to implement additional authentication logic. A good example of this is often implemented for governmental websites where users have to authenticate by specifying three values: a user name, a subscription ID, and a password.

If you just want to store your own information in addition to the information stored by the default implementation, we recommend not implementing a custom provider. Because the membership API gives you access to a key that uniquely identifies a user in the store, we recommend adding your own tables for storing your additional information and connecting information stored in your tables through the user's unique key with the actual user of the membership provider's storage; alternatively, you could implement user profiles for these additional properties. This is far easier than implementing a custom provider for adding a few extra values.

From within the application, you can access the user's unique key through the ProviderUserKey property of the MembershipUser class. In this chapter, you will learn how the unique key is propagated to the ProviderUserKey of the MembershipUser class.

Basic Steps for Creating Custom Providers

You will now learn how to implement your custom provider for the membership and roles services. Creating a custom provider involves the following steps:

1. Design and create the underlying data store.
2. Create utility classes for accessing the underlying data store.
3. Create a class that inherits from the MembershipProvider.
4. Create a class that inherits from the RoleProvider.
5. Create a provider test application.
6. Configure the custom providers in your test application.
7. Use the custom providers in your custom application.

Implementing custom providers is fairly straightforward but will require some time, because you have to implement lots of methods and properties. In the following sections, you will create a custom membership and roles provider that uses an XML file as the underlying data store. XML files are not a good solution for highly scalable applications but may be a nice alternative if you write a simple application and need to host this application on a provider site and don't have access to a database such as SQL Server.

Overall Design of the Custom Provider

Before creating a custom provider, you have to think about the overall design of the solution. Your goal is to keep the underlying functionality as simple as possible so that you can concentrate on the actual membership and roles provider implementation. In terms of XML, the easiest way to load and save data to XML files is XML serialization. This allows you to store a complete object graph with just one function call in a file and to read it with one function call.

```
Serializer = new XmlSerializer(typeof(List<SimpleUser>));
using (XmlTextReader reader = new XmlTextReader(fileName))
{
    _Users = (List<SimpleUser>)Serializer.Deserialize(reader);
}
```

Remember that you have to tell the XmlSerializer the type you want to serialize and deserialize at the time of instance creation of the serializer. Also don't forget that you need to import the System.Xml and System.Xml.Serialization namespaces in your code before you can use the XmlTextReader, XmlTextWriter, and XmlSerializer classes.

Because classes such as MembershipUser don't allow you to access some information—for example, the password—you cannot use them with XML serialization directly; XML serialization requires all properties and members that need to be stored as public properties or members. Therefore, you will create your own representation of users and roles as utility classes for the back-end store. These classes will never be passed to the application, which simply relies on the existing membership classes. (You will include some mapping logic, which is fairly simple, between this internal user representation and the MembershipUser class.) Figure 26-2 shows the overall design of the custom provider solution.

As mentioned, the SimpleUser and SimpleRole classes make XML serialization possible. Although this requires some mapping logic for supporting MembershipUser, this makes the whole implementation much easier. UserStore and RoleStore are both utility classes for encapsulating the access to the XML file. These classes include functions for loading and saving XML files as well as some basic utility functions for searching information in the store.

Finally, the model includes the XmlMembershipProvider and XmlRoleProvider classes. XmlMembershipProvider inherits basic functionality from MembershipProvider, while XmlRoleProvider is inherited from RoleProvider. Both base classes are defined in the System.Web.Security namespace.

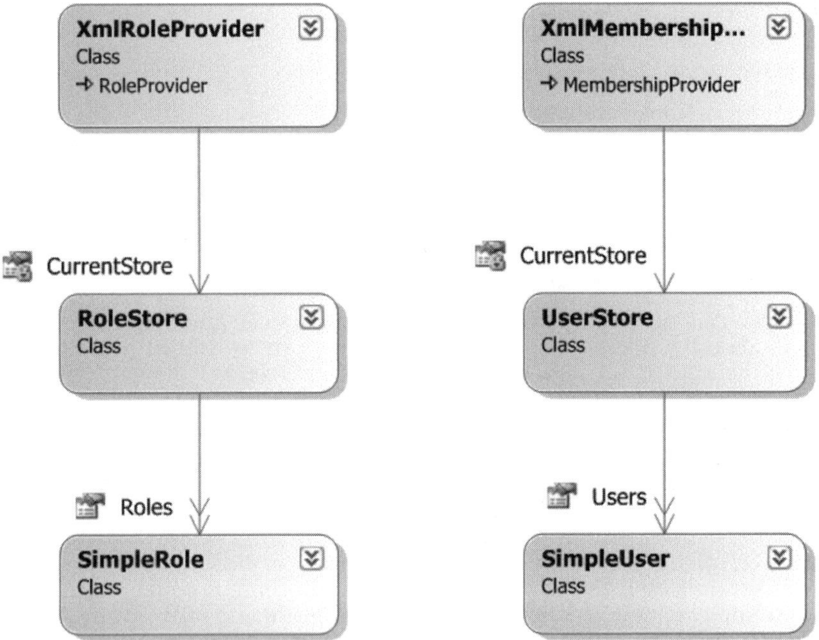

Figure 26-2. *The design of your custom provider solution*

Designing and Implementing the Custom Store

After you have designed your overall architecture, you can start thinking about the underlying data store. In the example, the data store will consist of an XML file for the users and an XML file for the roles. To make access to these files as simple as possible, you will use XML serialization as the primary mechanism for reading from and writing to these files. Therefore, you need some classes to hold the data stored to the XML files either as public fields or as properties, as follows:

```
public class SimpleUser
{
    public Guid UserKey = Guid.Empty;

    public string UserName = "";
    public string Password = "";

    public string Email = "";
    public DateTime CreationDate = DateTime.Now;
    public DateTime LastActivityDate = DateTime.MinValue;
    public DateTime LastLoginDate = DateTime.MinValue;
    public DateTime LastPasswordChangeDate = DateTime.MinValue;
    public string PasswordQuestion = "";
    public string PasswordAnswer = "";
    public string Comment;
}

public class SimpleRole
{
    public string RoleName = "";
    public System.Collections.Specialized.StringCollection AssignedUsers
            = new System.Collections.Specialized.StringCollection();
}
```

In this example, you will use a GUID as ProviderUserKey for uniquely identifying users in your store, similar to a primary key used for uniquely identifying records in a table of a database. For every user you will then store a user name, a password (hashed), an e-mail, some date information, a password question and answer, and some comments. For the roles, you will store a name as well as the association to the users. For simplicity, every role will contain an array of user names (which are strings) that are associated with this role. The serialized version of an array of users will be the user store, while the serialized version of an array of roles will be the roles store, as shown in Figure 26-3.

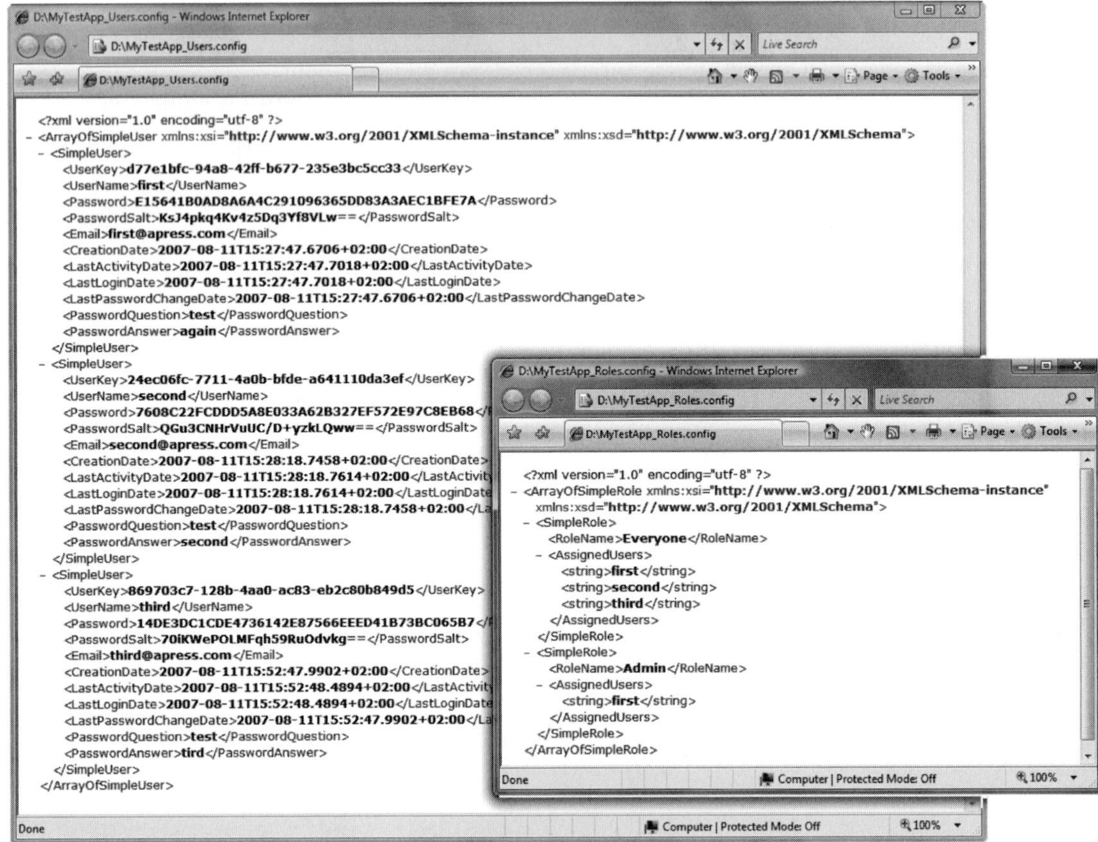

Figure 26-3. *Serialized versions of the SimpleUser and SimpleRole arrays*

Note that Figure 26-3 shows a serialized version of your users and roles from the finished version of the provider you are developing. You are using passwords with a salted hash, as you will see in this chapter. Furthermore, you might ask why no comment has been serialized to the XML file. Well, the XmlSerializer serializes fields only if they have another value than null (except if specified through XmlSerializer attributes applied to properties of your class).

Another design aspect you have to think about is how to access the store. You need only one instance of each store class in memory (UserStore and RoleStore) to save resources and avoid loading the XML files too often. You can implement this through the Singleton pattern, which is a solution for ensuring that only one instance of a class exists within a process. It does this by making the constructor private and providing a static public method for retrieving an instance. This public method verifies whether the instance already exists, and if not, it automatically creates an instance of its own, which is then returned. Now, you might ask why you are not just using a static class with lots of static methods and members. When looking at the following code snippet, you will recognize that you're keeping storage information in memory, and that way you would support opening more, isolated storages at the same time without reloading XML files all the time. This logic is encapsulated through the singleton pattern implementation of your storage classes, as you can see in the following code. Taking a look at the following code snippet, for each XML file storage—for example, of a set of users—you keep one UserStore instance in memory, which encapsulates access to one store in an isolated fashion (the same logic applies to the RoleStore for roles). Although you do not use this feature in your provider, it might be an interesting pattern for other scenarios.

Let's examine all these aspects based on the UserStore class introduced in Figure 26-3:

```
public class UserStore
{
  private string _FileName;
  private List<SimpleUser> _Users;
  private XmlSerializer _Serializer;

  private static Dictionary<string, UserStore> _RegisteredStores;

  private UserStore(string fileName)
  {
      _FileName = fileName;
      _Users = new List<SimpleUser>();
      _Serializer = new XmlSerializer(typeof(List<SimpleUser>));

      LoadStore(_FileName);
  }

  public static UserStore GetStore(string fileName)
  {
      // Create the registered store if it does not exist yet
      if (_RegisteredStores == null)
          _RegisteredStores = new Dictionary<string, UserStore>();

      // Now return the appropriate store for the filename passed in
      if (!_RegisteredStores.ContainsKey(fileName))
      {
          _RegisteredStores.Add(fileName, new UserStore(fileName));
      }

      return _RegisteredStores[fileName];
  }
}
```

The class includes a few private members for the filename of the store, the list of users, and an XmlSerializer instance used for reading and writing data.

Because the constructor is private, instances can't be created outside the class. Outside classes can retrieve instances only by calling the public static GetStore() method. The implementation of the Singleton pattern is special in this case. It creates single instances based on the filenames. For every file processed by the provider, one instance of the UserStore class is created. If more than one web application using this provider is running in the same process, you need to ensure that different instances are created for different filenames. Therefore, the class doesn't manage one static variable for a single instance; instead, it has a dictionary containing all the instances of the class, one for every filename.

Because you are using XML serialization to save and load data to and from the store, the functions for loading the store and saving data back to the store are fairly easy:

```
private void LoadStore(string fileName)
{
    try
```

```
    {
        // Note that if the file does not exist we ignore it at this
        // point in time. On a save operation, the storage file gets
        // created automatically by our store implementation
        if (System.IO.File.Exists(fileName))
        {
            using (XmlTextReader reader = new XmlTextReader(fileName))
            {
                _Users = (List<SimpleUser>)_Serializer.Deserialize(reader);
            }
        }
    }
    catch (Exception ex)
    {
        throw new Exception(
            string.Format("Unable to load file {0}", fileName), ex);
    }
}

private void SaveStore(string fileName)
{
    try
    {
        if (System.IO.File.Exists(fileName))
            System.IO.File.Delete(fileName);

        using (XmlTextWriter writer =
                    new XmlTextWriter(fileName, System.Text.Encoding.UTF8))
        {
            _Serializer.Serialize(writer, _Users);
        }
    }
    catch (Exception ex)
    {
        throw new Exception(
            string.Format("Unable to save file {0}", fileName), ex);
    }
}
```

Both functions are private, because they are called only within the class itself. The LoadStore() method is called within the constructor of the UserStore class. Within the method, the private variable _Users is initialized. Every subsequent query happens based on querying the _Users collection of the store class. The SaveStore() method, on the other hand, just serializes the _Users collection to the file specified in the private _FileName member, which is passed in through the constructor (and indirectly through the static GetStore() method). Finally, the class supports a couple of methods for querying information in the _Users collection.

```
public List<SimpleUser> Users
{
    get { return _Users; }
}

public void Save()
{
```

```
    SaveStore(_FileName);
}

public SimpleUser GetUserByName(string name)
{
    return _Users.Find(delegate(SimpleUser user)
            {
                return string.Equals(name, user.UserName);
            });
}

public SimpleUser GetUserByEmail(string email)
{
    return _Users.Find(delegate(SimpleUser user)
            {
                return string.Equals(email, user.Email);
            });
}

public SimpleUser GetUserByKey(Guid key)
{
    return _Users.Find(delegate(SimpleUser user)
    {
        return (user.UserKey.CompareTo(key) == 0);
    });
}
```

The Users property is a simple property that allows the actual provider (XmlMembership Provider) to access users of the store. After the provider implementation has changed something within the store (has changed properties of a user, for example), it calls the public Save() method, which internally calls the SaveStore() to serialize information back to the file specified in the private _FileName variable of this instance. The remaining methods are for searching users based on different criteria. For this purpose, the generic List<> includes a find method. This find method accepts a reference to another method that is called for every element while iterating through the list for comparison. If the comparison function returns true for an element, the element is included in the results.

```
public SimpleUser GetUserByKey(Guid key)
{
    return _Users.Find(delegate(SimpleUser user)
    {
        return (user.UserKey.CompareTo(key) == 0);
    });
}
```

In this code, you pass in a delegate (which is a reference to a function) that compares the internal SimpleUser's key with the key passed in. If this is true, the current user that is passed in as a parameter from the List<> is returned as a result; otherwise, the List<> continues iterating through its elements. The inline implementation of the method, without explicitly creating a method with a separate prototype, is called an *anonymous method* and is a special feature of C# for saving additional code for short algorithm parameters.

The UserStore includes the implementation for saving user information only. Roles are not included. For this purpose, you have to implement the RoleStore class (which is similar to the UserStore class), as shown here:

```
public class RoleStore
{
    XmlSerializer _Serializer;
    private string _FileName;
    List<SimpleRole> _Roles;

    #region "Singleton Implementation"

    private static Dictionary<string, RoleStore> _RegisteredStores;

    private RoleStore(string fileName)
    {
        _FileName = fileName;
        _Roles = new List<SimpleRole>();
        _Serializer = new XmlSerializer(typeof(List<SimpleRole>));

        LoadStore(_FileName);
    }

    public static RoleStore GetStore(string fileName)
    {
        // Create the registered stores
        if (_RegisteredStores == null)
            _RegisteredStores = new Dictionary<string, RoleStore>();

        // Now return the appropriate store
        if (!_RegisteredStores.ContainsKey(fileName))
        {
            _RegisteredStores.Add(fileName, new RoleStore(fileName));
        }

        return _RegisteredStores[fileName];
    }

    #endregion

    #region "Private Helper Methods"

    private void LoadStore(string fileName)
    {
        try
        {
            // Again we create the storage automatically when
            // saving it - see SaveStorage method.
            if (System.IO.File.Exists(fileName))
            {
                using (XmlTextReader reader = new XmlTextReader(fileName))
                {
                    _Roles = (List<SimpleRole>)_Serializer.Deserialize(reader);
                }
            }
        }
        catch (Exception ex)
```

```
    {
        throw new Exception(string.Format(
            "Unable to load file {0}", fileName), ex);
    }
}

private void SaveStore(string fileName)
{
    try
    {
        if (System.IO.File.Exists(fileName))
            System.IO.File.Delete(fileName);

        using (XmlTextWriter writer =
                new XmlTextWriter(fileName, Encoding.UTF8))
        {
            _Serializer.Serialize(writer, _Roles);
        }
    }
    catch (Exception ex)
    {
        throw new Exception(string.Format(
            "Unable to save file {0}", fileName), ex);
    }
}

#endregion

public List<SimpleRole> Roles
{
    get { return _Roles; }
}

public void Save()
{
    SaveStore(_FileName);
}

public List<SimpleRole> GetRolesForUser(string userName)
{
    List<SimpleRole> Results = new List<SimpleRole>();
    foreach (SimpleRole r in Roles)
    {
        if (r.AssignedUsers.Contains(userName))
            Results.Add(r);
    }
    return Results;
}

public string[] GetUsersInRole(string roleName)
{
    SimpleRole Role = GetRole(roleName);
    if (Role != null)
    {
```

```
                string[] Results = new string[Role.AssignedUsers.Count];
                Role.AssignedUsers.CopyTo(Results, 0);
                return Results;
            }
            else
            {
                throw new Exception(string.Format(
                      "Role with name {0} does not exist!", roleName));
            }
        }

        public SimpleRole GetRole(string roleName)
        {
            return Roles.Find(delegate(SimpleRole role)
                {
                    return role.RoleName.Equals(
                        roleName, StringComparison.OrdinalIgnoreCase);
                });
        }
}
```

This implementation looks fairly similar to the UserStore. The major differences are that it uses the SimpleRole class instead of the SimpleUser class, and it initializes the XmlSerializer class with a different type. Also, the functions for querying the store are different. While the UserStore implements functions for finding users by e-mail, by unique IDs, or by names, this store class finds roles by name, enables returning users of a role, and queries all roles for one dedicated user. Note that in the preceding GetRole() method, you compare the role names using the Equals method of the string instance by passing in the parameter StringComparison.OrdinalIgnoreCase. This means you compare the role names without case sensitivity. So, if a role name gets passed in with different case letters, you still find it in your method.

Now the classes for accessing the underlying stores are complete, which means you can start implementing the custom provider classes.

Implementing the Provider Classes

In this section, you will create the XmlMembershipProvider class, which fulfills the role of an adapter between your custom store and the requirements of the membership API. (The code for the complete provider implementation is included in this book's downloads on the Apress website at `http://www.apress.com`.) In this section you will go through the most important parts of creating a membership provider.

Every custom membership provider must be inherited from System.Web.Security.MembershipProvider, as follows:

```
public class XmlMembershipProvider : MembershipProvider
{
    // ...
}
```

When inheriting from MembershipProvider, you have to implement lots of properties and methods to fulfill the requirements of the membership API. These properties and methods are used for querying, creating, updating, and deleting users as well as retrieving specific information about the provider such as password requirements. These types of properties are queried by the security controls introduced in

Chapter 21. (For example, the RequiresQuestionAndAnswer property is queried by the CreateUserWizard to decide whether to display the text boxes for entering password questions and answers.) You should start by implementing the properties of the provider, because this is the easiest part of the whole task. For every property, you should provide one private variable that contains the state of the appropriate property.

```
public override string ApplicationName { }
public override bool EnablePasswordReset { }
public override bool EnablePasswordRetrieval { }
public override int MaxInvalidPasswordAttempts { }
public override int MinRequiredNonAlphanumericCharacters { }
public override int MinRequiredPasswordLength { }
public override int PasswordAttemptWindow { }
public override MembershipPasswordFormat PasswordFormat { }
public override string PasswordStrengthRegularExpression { }
public override bool RequiresQuestionAndAnswer { }
public override bool RequiresUniqueEmail { }
```

For a detailed description of these properties, you can refer to Chapter 21. The properties of providers are described there, and they have the same meaning as in the underlying provider implementation. Many of these properties just have get accessors and no setters. So, how can the ASP.NET infrastructure initialize these properties with values configured in web.config? You can find the answer in the original base class for all providers, which is in the System.Configuration.Provider.ProviderBase class. The ProviderBase class in turn is the base class for the MembershipProvider class, and therefore all classes that inherit from MembershipProvider are indirectly inherited from ProviderBase and have the basic properties of ProviderBase. All you have to do is override the Initialize method. This method accepts two parameters: a name (which is configured through the name attribute in web.config) and a NameValueCollection (which contains keys and their appropriate values for all settings configured through web.config). Within this method you can initialize the private members of the properties shown previously.

Let's examine the contents of this function for the XmlMembershipProvider step-by-step:

```
public override void Initialize(string name,
            System.Collections.Specialized.NameValueCollection config)
{
    if (config == null)
    {
        throw new ArgumentNullException("config");
    }
    if (string.IsNullOrEmpty(name))
    {
        name = "XmlMembershipProvider";
    }
    if (string.IsNullOrEmpty(config["description"]))
    {
        config.Remove("description");
        config.Add("description", "XML Membership Provider");
    }

    // Initialize the base class
    base.Initialize(name, config);
    ...
```

First, you have to verify whether any configuration is passed in. If nothing is configured for the provider, it won't work. Second, if no name is specified, you have to initialize a default name, which is required by the configuration tool for displaying the provider in the list of providers. Finally, you have to add a default description if no description is configured for the provider. This final step is optional but useful for configuration tools that query provider information.

Don't forget to call the base class's Initialize implementation for initializing basic properties properly. You do this in the last line of code in the previous code.

Next, you can start initializing your properties:

```
...

// Initialize default values
_ApplicationName = "DefaultApp";
_EnablePasswordReset = false;
_PasswordStrengthRegEx = @"[\w| !§$%&/()=\-?\*]*";
_MaxInvalidPasswordAttempts = 3;
_MinRequiredNonAlphanumericChars = 1;
_MinRequiredPasswordLength = 5;
_RequiresQuestionAndAnswer = false;
_PasswordFormat = MembershipPasswordFormat.Hashed;

// Now go through the properties and initialize custom values
foreach (string key in config.Keys)
{
    switch(key.ToLower())
    {
        case "name":
            _Name = config[key];
            break;
        case "applicationname":
            _ApplicationName = config[key];
            break;
        case "filename":
            _FileName = config[key];
            break;
        case "enablepasswordreset":
            _EnablePasswordReset = bool.Parse(config[key]);
            break;
        case "passwordstrengthregex":
            _PasswordStrengthRegEx = config[key];
            break;
        case "maxinvalidpasswordattempts":
            _MaxInvalidPasswordAttempts = int.Parse(config[key]);
            break;
        case "minrequirednonalphanumericchars":
            _MinRequiredNonAlphanumericChars = int.Parse(config[key]);
            break;
        case "minrequiredpasswordlength":
            _MinRequiredPasswordLength = int.Parse(config[key]);
            break;
        case "passwordformat":
            _PasswordFormat = (MembershipPasswordFormat)Enum.Parse(
                        typeof(MembershipPasswordFormat), config[key]);
            break;
```

```
        case "requiresquestionandanswer":
            _RequiresQuestionAndAnswer = bool.Parse(config[key]);
            break;
    }
```

■ **Caution** In our first implementation, we tried to derive the default application name from the current HTTP context automatically based on the virtual root directory. The effect was that our provider worked properly as long as we used the management functions from within the application. As soon as we tried to use it from the ASP.NET WAT, though, it failed with an exception. When debugging, we discovered that in this case the provider doesn't have access to members of the application's HTTP context. Therefore, you should avoid using the HttpContext.Current in your membership provider and instead keep it as simple as possible.

The previous code starts by initializing some default values for your options, just in case they are not included in the web.config configuration file. After initializing these default values, you can go through the entries of the config parameter passed into the method (which is a simple NameValueCollection). As you can see, you even can include custom settings such as the filename setting, which is not included in the default set of properties of the membership provider. This filename property is a custom property for your specific provider that points to the XML file that contains the user information. You will pass this filename to the UserStore class in a separate property that you will use in the remaining functions of the implementation.

```
private UserStore CurrentStore
{
    get
    {
        if (_CurrentStore == null)
            _CurrentStore = UserStore.GetStore(_FileName);
        return _CurrentStore;
    }
}
```

Next, you have a large number of methods in your provider. These methods are for creating, updating, and deleting users as well as for accessing and retrieving user details. The methods access the information through the previously created store classes. The following code snippet lists these methods to give you an overview of what you have to implement while reading through the subsequent sections.

```
public override MembershipUser CreateUser(string username, string password,
                        string email, string passwordQuestion,
                        string passwordAnswer, bool isApproved,
                        object providerUserKey,
                        out MembershipCreateStatus status)
public override bool DeleteUser(string username, bool deleteAllRelatedData)
public override MembershipUser GetUser(string username, bool userIsOnline)
public override MembershipUser GetUser(object providerUserKey,
                                       bool userIsOnline)
public override string GetUserNameByEmail(string email)
public override void UpdateUser(MembershipUser user)
```

```
public override bool ValidateUser(string username, string password)
public override bool ChangePassword(string username,
              string oldPassword, string newPassword)
public override bool ChangePasswordQuestionAndAnswer(string username,
        string password, string newPasswordQuestion, string newPasswordAnswer)
public override MembershipUserCollection FindUsersByEmail(string emailToMatch,
                            int pageIndex, int pageSize, out int totalRecords)
public override MembershipUserCollection FindUsersByName(
                       string usernameToMatch,
                       int pageIndex, int pageSize, out int totalRecords)
public override MembershipUserCollection GetAllUsers(int pageIndex,
                                 int pageSize, out int totalRecords)
public override int GetNumberOfUsersOnline()
public override string GetPassword(string username, string answer)
public override string ResetPassword(string username, string answer)
public override bool UnlockUser(string userName)
```

Within those methods, you just have to call the appropriate methods of the UserStore class through the previously introduced CurrentStore property. These are the only methods defined by the provider. Any additional method introduced in this chapter is a helper method that you have to include on your own. (In this book, you will see the most important implementations of these methods but not all of them. The complete code is available with the book's downloadable code.)

Let's get started with the CreateUser method.

Creating Users and Adding Them to the Store

The CreateUser method is interesting because it needs to make sure that the user name and e-mail are unique and that the password is valid and adheres to the password strength requirements.

```
public override MembershipUser CreateUser(string username, string password,
    string email, string passwordQuestion,
    string passwordAnswer, bool isApproved,
    object providerUserKey, out MembershipCreateStatus status)
{
    try
    {
        // Validate the user name and e-mail
        if (!ValidateUsername(username, email, Guid.Empty))
        {
            // If the user name is invalid because it already
            // exists or the e-mail is duplicated and the provider
            // is configured to not allow duplicated e-mails, then
            // we return the InvalidUserName status through the
            // output parameter "status"
            status = MembershipCreateStatus.InvalidUserName;
            return null;
        }

        // Raise the event before validating the password
        // This event is handled by the membership API class, which
        // in turn forwards the event to any subscribers in custom code
        // to allow writing custom code for validating password formats
        // without the need to understand the internals of
```

```
        // the membership provider implementation
        base.OnValidatingPassword(
            new ValidatePasswordEventArgs(
                    username, password, true));

        // Validate the password
        if (!ValidatePassword(password))
        {
            status = MembershipCreateStatus.InvalidPassword;
            return null;
        }
        ...
```

In the first section, the function calls the private methods ValidateUserName and ValidatePassword. These methods make sure the user name and e-mail are unique in the store and the password adheres to the password strength requirements. After these checks succeed, you can create the user for the underlying store (SimpleUser), add the user to the store, and then save the store.

```
        ...
        // Everything is valid, create the user
        SimpleUser user = new SimpleUser();
        user.UserKey = Guid.NewGuid();
        user.UserName = username;
        // Note - the TransformPassword() method creates
        // the salted hash value for storing the password
        user.Password = this.TransformPassword(password);
        user.Email = email;
        user.PasswordQuestion = passwordQuestion;
        user.PasswordAnswer = passwordAnswer;
        user.CreationDate = DateTime.Now;
        user.LastActivityDate = DateTime.Now;
        user.LastPasswordChangeDate = DateTime.Now;

        // Add the user to the store
        CurrentStore.Users.Add(user);
        CurrentStore.Save();

        status = MembershipCreateStatus.Success;
        return CreateMembershipFromInternalUser(user);
    }
    catch
    {
        // If an exception is raised while saving the storage
        // or while serializing contents we just forward it to the
        // caller. It would be cleaner to work with custom exception
        // classes here and pass more detailed information to the caller
        // but we leave as is for simplicity.
        throw;
    }
}
```

Finally, the method needs to return an instance of MembershipUser to the calling Membership class with the details of the created user. For this purpose, you just need to match the properties of your SimpleUser instance to the properties of the MembershipUser, as shown in the following function:

```
private MembershipUser CreateMembershipFromInternalUser(SimpleUser user)
{
    MembershipUser muser = new MembershipUser(base.Name,
        user.UserName, user.UserKey, user.Email, user.PasswordQuestion,
        string.Empty, true, false, user.CreationDate, user.LastLoginDate,
        user.LastActivityDate, user.LastPasswordChangeDate, DateTime.MaxValue);

    return muser;
}
```

As you can see, this mapping creates an instance of MembershipUser and passes the appropriate properties from your own SimpleUser as constructor parameters.

Next, take a look at the validation functions for validating the user name, e-mail, and password:

```
private bool ValidatePassword(string password)
{
    bool IsValid = true;
    System.Text.RegularExpressions.Regex HelpExpression;

    // Validate simple properties
    IsValid = (password.Length >= this.MinRequiredPasswordLength);

    // Validate non-alphanumeric characters
    HelpExpression = new Regex(@"\W");
    IsValid = IsValid && (
             HelpExpression.Matches(password).Count >=
                this.MinRequiredNonAlphanumericCharacters);

    // Validate regular expression
    HelpExpression = new Regex(this.PasswordStrengthRegularExpression);
    IsValid = IsValid && (HelpExpression.Matches(password).Count > 0);

    return IsValid;
}
```

The password validation first verifies the length of the password. If the password is too short, it returns false. Through the .NET Framework, it then verifies regular expression classes to see whether the number of nonalphanumeric characters in the password is high enough according to the MinRequireNonAlphanumericCharacters. Afterward, the password validation function performs a check on the password through regular expression functions of the .NET Framework of the System.Text.RegularExpressions namespace against the PasswordStrengthRegularExpression. If all these checks pass, the function returns true. If these checks don't pass, it returns false.

Now let's take a closer look at the method for validating the user name and the e-mail. Both need to be unique in the underlying store.

```
private bool ValidateUsername(string userName, string email, Guid excludeKey)
{
    bool IsValid = true;
```

```
    UserStore store = UserStore.GetStore(_FileName);
    foreach (SimpleUser user in store.Users)
    {
        if (user.UserKey.CompareTo(excludeKey) != 0)
        {
            if (string.Equals(user.UserName, userName,
                    StringComparison.OrdinalIgnoreCase))
            {
                IsValid = false;
                break;
            }

            if (string.Equals(user.Email, email,
                    StringComparison.OrdinalIgnoreCase))
            {
                IsValid = false;
                break;
            }
        }
    }

    return IsValid;
}
```

As you can see in the previous snippet, user validation is fairly simple. The code goes through the users in the CurrentStore and verifies whether there is any user with the same user name or e-mail. If that's the case, the function returns false or otherwise true.

The last interesting part in the CreateUser method is how the password is set for the user. Through the PasswordFormat property, every provider has three types for storing the password: clear, hashed, and encrypted. The CreateUser method uses a private helper method of the XmlMembershipProvider class called TransformPassword, as follows:

```
user.Password = this.TransformPassword(password);
```

This method queries the current setting for the PasswordFormat property, and according to the setting it leaves the password as clear text, creates a hash for the password, or encrypts the password, as follows:

```
private string TransformPassword(string password)
{
    string ret = string.Empty;

    switch (PasswordFormat)
    {
        case MembershipPasswordFormat.Clear:
            ret = password;
            break;
        case MembershipPasswordFormat.Hashed:
            ret = FormsAuthentication.HashPasswordForStoringInConfigFile(
                                                password, "SHA1");
            break;
        case MembershipPasswordFormat.Encrypted:
            byte[] ClearText = Encoding.UTF8.GetBytes(password);
            byte[] EncryptedText = base.EncryptPassword(ClearText);
```

```
                ret = Convert.ToBase64String(EncryptedText);
                break;
        }

        return ret;
    }
```

If the password format is set to Clear, the method just returns the clear-text password. In the case of the Hashed setting, it creates the simple hash through the forms authentication utility method and then returns the hash for the password. The last possible option encrypts the password with a two-way encryption algorithm, which has the advantage that the password can be retrieved from the underlying storage through decryption. In that case, the method uses the EncryptPassword method from the base class implementation for encrypting the password. This method uses a key stored in machine.config for encrypting the password. If you are using this in a web farm environment, you have to sync the key stored in machine.config on every machine so that a password encrypted on one machine of the farm can be decrypted on another machine on the web farm properly.

Validating Users on Login

The Membership class supports a method for programmatically validating a password entered by a user. This method is used by the Login control as well. This means every time the user tries to log in, the ValidateUser method of the Membership class is involved. This method on its own calls the ValidateUser method of the underlying membership provider. According to the settings of the PasswordFormat property, the method has to retrieve the user from the store based on the user name and then somehow validate the password. If the password is clear text, validating the password involves a simple string comparison. Encrypted passwords have to be decrypted and compared afterward, while last but not least validating hashed passwords means re-creating the hash and then comparing the hash values.

```
public override bool ValidateUser(string username, string password)
{
    try
    {
        SimpleUser user = CurrentStore.GetUserByName(username);
        if(user == null)
            return false;

        if (ValidateUserInternal(user, password))
        {
            user.LastLoginDate = DateTime.Now;
            user.LastActivityDate = DateTime.Now;
            CurrentStore.Save();
            return true;
        }
        else
        {
            return false;
        }
    }
    catch
    {
        // If an exception is raised while saving the storage
        // or while serializing contents we just forward it to the
        // caller. It would be cleaner to work with custom exception
```

```
            // classes here and pass more detailed information to the caller
            // but we leave as is for simplicity.
            throw;
        }
    }
```

This method retrieves the user from the store. It then validates the password against the password passed in (which is the one entered by the user for login) through a private helper method called ValidateUserInternal. Finally, if the user name and password are fine, it updates the LastLoginDate and the LastActivityDate for the user and then returns true. It's always useful to encapsulate password validation functionality into a separate function, because it may be used more than once in your provider. A typical example for reusing this functionality is the ChangePassword method, where the user has to enter the old password and the new password. If validation of the old password fails, the provider should not change the password, as shown here:

```
public override bool ChangePassword(string username,
                                    string oldPassword, string newPassword)
{
    try
    {
        // Get the user from the store
        SimpleUser user = CurrentStore.GetUserByName(username);
        if (user == null)
           throw new Exception("User does not exist!")

        if (ValidateUserInternal(user, oldPassword))
        {
            // Raise the event before validating the password
            base.OnValidatingPassword(
                new ValidatePasswordEventArgs(
                        username, newPassword, false));

            if (!ValidatePassword(newPassword))
                throw new ArgumentException(
                      "Password doesn't meet password strength requirements!");

            user.Password = TransformPassword(newPassword);
            user.LastPasswordChangeDate = DateTime.Now;
            CurrentStore.Save();

            return true;
        }

        return false;
    }
    catch
    {
        throw;
    }
}
```

Only if the old password is entered correctly by the user does the change take place. The ChangePassword method again uses the TransformPassword method to generate the protected version (hashed, encrypted) of the password if necessary. You can reuse the function introduced previously with the CreateUser method. But now let's take a look at the password validation functionality:

```
private bool ValidateUserInternal(SimpleUser user, string password)
{
    if (user != null)
    {
        string passwordValidate = TransformPassword(password);
        if (string.Compare(passwordValidate, user.Password) == 0)
        {
            return true;
        }
    }

    return false;
}
```

This method uses the TransformPassword method for creating the protected version of the password (hashed, encrypted) if necessary. The results are then compared through simple string comparison. (Even the encrypted version returns a Base64-encoded string that will be stored in the XML file; therefore, string comparison is fine.) This is why validating hashed passwords works at all, for example. Just re-create the hash, and then compare the hashed version of the password.

Using Salted Password Hashes

If you want to change this to include a salt value as mentioned, you have to complete the following steps:

1. Add a new field to your SimpleUser class called PasswordSalt.
2. Extend your TransformPassword method to accept a salt value. This salt is necessary for re-creating the hash, which actually will be based on both the password and the salt.
3. When creating a new password, you simply have to create the random salt value and then store it with your user. For any validation, pass the previously generated salt value to the TransformPassword function for validation.

The best way to do this is to extend the TransformPassword so that it generates the salt value automatically if necessary. Therefore, it accepts the salt as a second parameter. This parameter is not just a simple parameter—it's a reference parameter, as shown here:

```
private string TransformPassword(string password, ref string salt)
{
    ...
}
```

Whenever you pass in string.Empty or null for the salt value, the function automatically generates a new salt. The method therefore is called as follows from other methods that create the new password hash. These methods are CreateUser, ChangePassword, and ResetPassword, as they all update the password value of your SimpleUser class.

```
SimpleUser user = ...
...
user.PasswordSalt = string.Empty;
user.Password = this.TransformPassword(password, ref user.PasswordSalt);
...
```

This means every method that updates the password field of your user store sets the PasswordSalt value to string.Empty before it calls TransformPassword and passes in a reference to the user.PasswordSalt field. When validating the password, you don't want the method to regenerate a new salt value. Therefore, you have to pass in the salt value stored with the hashed version of the password in the data store. Having said that, the previously introduced ValidateUserInternal() method now looks like this:

```
private bool ValidateUserInternal(SimpleUser user, string password)
{
    if (user != null)
    {
        string passwordValidate = TransformPassword(
                         password, ref user.PasswordSalt);
        if (string.Compare(passwordValidate, user.Password) == 0)
        {
            return true;
        }
    }

    return false;
}
```

The only thing that changes compared to the original version is that the method now passes in an initialized version of the salt value that will be used by the TransformPassword method to regenerate the password hash based on the existing salt and the password entered by the user. Therefore, internally the TransformPassword method now looks as follows for validating and optionally generating a salt value:

```
private string TransformPassword(string password, ref string salt)
{
    string ret = string.Empty;

    switch (PasswordFormat)
    {
        case MembershipPasswordFormat.Clear:
            ret = password;
            break;

        case MembershipPasswordFormat.Hashed:

            // Generate the salt if not passed in
            if (string.IsNullOrEmpty(salt))
            {
                byte[] saltBytes = new byte[16];
                System.Security.Cryptography.RandomNumberGenerator rng =
                  System.Security.Cryptography.RandomNumberGenerator.Create();
                rng.GetBytes(saltBytes);
                salt = Convert.ToBase64String(saltBytes);
            }
            ret = FormsAuthentication.HashPasswordForStoringInConfigFile(
                                          (salt + password), "SHA1");
            break;

        case MembershipPasswordFormat.Encrypted:
```

```
            byte[] ClearText = Encoding.UTF8.GetBytes(password);
            byte[] EncryptedText = base.EncryptPassword(ClearText);
            ret = Convert.ToBase64String(EncryptedText);
            break;
    }

    return ret;
}
```

When the provider is configured for storing the passwords as salted hashes, it verifies whether the passed-in salt value is empty or null. If the provider is configured for using salted hashes, it generates a new salt value using the cryptographic random number generator of the System.Security.Cryptography namespace to generate a real random number. The functions CreateUser, ChangePassword, and ResetPassword will pass in null or string.Empty to generate a new salt value, while the ValidateUserInternal method passes in the already initialized salt value from the underlying data store of the provider. Afterward, the method again uses the HashPasswordForStoringInConfigFile, but this time it passes a combination of the random salt value and the actual password. The result is returned to the caller.

The Remaining Functions of the Provider

Initializing the provider and creating and validating users are the most important and hardest functions to implement in the provider. The rest of the functions are just for reading information from the store and for updating the users in the store. These functions call the underlying methods of the UserStore class or try to find users in the UserStore.Users collection. A typical example is the GetUser() method, which retrieves a single user from the data store based on its user name or key:

```
public override MembershipUser GetUser(string username, bool userIsOnline)
{
    try
    {
        SimpleUser user = CurrentStore.GetUserByName(username);
        if (user != null)
        {
            if (userIsOnline)
            {
                user.LastActivityDate = DateTime.Now;
                CurrentStore.Save();
            }
            return CreateMembershipFromInternalUser(user);
        }
        else
        {
            return null;
        }
    }
    catch
    {
        // If an exception is raised while saving the storage
        // or while serializing contents we just forward it to the
        // caller. It would be cleaner to work with custom exception
        // classes here and pass more detailed information to the caller
```

```
        // but we leave as is for simplicity.
        throw;
    }
}
```

This example accepts the name of the user as a parameter and another parameter that indicates whether the user is online. The Membership class automatically initializes this parameter when it calls your provider's method. In your method, you can query this parameter; if it is set to true, you must update the LastActivityDate of your user in the store. The function does nothing other than find the user in the underlying store by calling the UserStore's GetUserByName method. It then creates an instance of MembershipUser based on the information of the store by calling the private CreateMembershipFromInternalUser utility method. The provider implementation requires you to implement a couple of methods that work this way. You just need to call the methods of the UserStore appropriately. Some of the methods require you to return not just a MembershipUser but a whole MembershipUserCollection, as follows:

```
public override MembershipUserCollection FindUsersByEmail(string emailToMatch,
                            int pageIndex, int pageSize, out int totalRecords)
{
    try
    {
        List<SimpleUser> matchingUsers =
            CurrentStore.Users.FindAll(delegate(SimpleUser user)
                {
                    return user.Email.Equals(emailToMatch,
                       StringComparison.OrdinalIgnoreCase);
                });

        totalRecords = matchingUsers.Count;
        return CreateMembershipCollectionFromInternalList(matchingUsers);
    }
    catch
    {
        // If an exception is raised while saving the storage
        // or while serializing contents we just forward it to the
        // caller. It would be cleaner to work with custom exception
        // classes here and pass more detailed information to the caller
        // but we leave as is for simplicity.
        throw;
    }
}
```

For example, the FindUsersByEmail method finds all users with a specific e-mail (which is possible only if you have configured the provider to not require the e-mail to be unique or if you use pattern matching for e-mails through regular expressions). It returns a collection of Membership users. But as you can see, the method again leverages the FindAll method of the List<> class and an anonymous method for specifying the filter criteria. Therefore, the collection returned from this method is a collection of SimpleUser instances that you use in the back-end store. You can create another helper method for mapping this type of collection to a MembershipUserCollection, as follows:

```
private MembershipUserCollection CreateMembershipCollectionFromInternalList(
                                                List<SimpleUser> users)
{
```

```
    MembershipUserCollection ReturnCollection = new MembershipUserCollection();

    foreach (SimpleUser user in users)
    {
        ReturnCollection.Add(CreateMembershipFromInternalUser(user));
    }

    return ReturnCollection;
}
```

Finally, the LastActivityDate property stored for every user is used by the Membership class to determine the number of current users online in the application. You have to implement this method in your custom provider through the GetNumberOfUsersOnline method, as follows:

```
public override int GetNumberOfUsersOnline()
{
    int ret = 0;

    foreach (SimpleUser user in CurrentStore.Users)
    {
        if (user.LastActivityDate.AddMinutes(
                Membership.UserIsOnlineTimeWindow) >= DateTime.Now)
        {
            ret++;
        }
    }

    return ret;
}
```

This method just goes through all users in the store and uses the UserIsOnlineTimeWindow, which is a property managed through the Membership class and specifies the number of minutes a user is online without any activity. As long as the LastActivityDate with this number of minutes is larger than the current date and time, the user is considered to be online. The LastActivityDate is updated automatically by the different overloads of the GetUser method and the ValidateUser method.

Implementing the remaining functions of the provider does not involve any new concepts, and therefore we will skip them. They merely update some values on users and then call the CurrentStore.Save method to save it to the XML file on the file system. You can download the complete implementation of this provider with the source code for the book.

Implementing the XmlRoleProvider

Implementing the roles provider is much easier than implementing the membership provider, because the structures are much simpler for managing roles. Implementing the roles provider does not introduce any new concepts. It merely requires calling the appropriate methods of the previously introduced RoleStore class for creating roles, deleting roles, assigning users to roles, and deleting users from roles. The complete interface of the roles provider looks like this:

```
public class XmlRoleProvider : RoleProvider
{
    public override void Initialize(string name, NameValueCollection config)
```

```
    public override string ApplicationName { get; set; }

    public override void CreateRole(string roleName)
    public override bool DeleteRole(string roleName, bool throwOnPopulatedRole)
    public override bool RoleExists(string roleName)
    public override void AddUsersToRoles(
                            string[] usernames, string[] roleNames)
    public override void RemoveUsersFromRoles(
                            string[] usernames, string[] roleNames)
    public override string[] GetAllRoles()
    public override string[] GetRolesForUser(string username)
    public override string[] GetUsersInRole(string roleName)
    public override bool IsUserInRole(string username, string roleName)
    public override string[] FindUsersInRole(
                              string roleName, string usernameToMatch)
}
```

As you can see, the class derives from the base class RoleProvider. Again, it overrides the Initialize method for initializing custom properties. But this time initialization of the provider is much simpler because the roles provider supports only a handful of properties. The only property provided by the base class is the ApplicationName property. Everything else is up to you. Therefore, initialization is fairly simple here:

```
public override void Initialize(string name, NameValueCollection config)
{
    if (config == null)
    {
        throw new ArgumentNullException("config");
    }
    if (string.IsNullOrEmpty(name))
    {
        name = "XmlRoleProvider";
    }
    if (string.IsNullOrEmpty(config["description"]))
    {
        config.Remove("description");
        config.Add("description", "XML Role Provider");
    }

    // Base initialization
    base.Initialize(name, config);

    // Initialize properties
    _ApplicationName = "DefaultApp";
    foreach (string key in config.Keys)
    {
        if (key.ToLower().Equals("applicationname"))
            ApplicationName = config[key];
        else if (key.ToLower().Equals("filename"))
            _FileName = config[key];
    }
}
```

Again, the initialization routine checks the name and description configuration parameters and initializes them with default values if they are not configured. It then calls the base class's Initialize implementation. Do not forget to call the base class's Initialize method; otherwise, the default configuration values managed by the base class will not be initialized. Next it initializes the properties while your implementation of the XmlRoleProvider just knows about the ApplicationName and FileName settings. Again, the FileName specifies the name of the XML file where role information is stored.

Next, the class supports a few methods for managing the roles: CreateRole, DeleteRole, and RoleExists. Within these methods, you have to access the underlying RoleStore's methods, as you can see in this example of CreateRole:

```
public override void CreateRole(string roleName)
{
    try
    {
        SimpleRole NewRole = new SimpleRole();
        NewRole.RoleName = roleName;
        NewRole.AssignedUsers = new StringCollection();

        CurrentStore.Roles.Add(NewRole);
        CurrentStore.Save();
    }
    catch
    {
        // If an exception is raised while saving the storage
        // or while serializing contents we just forward it to the
        // caller. It would be cleaner to work with custom exception
        // classes here and pass more detailed information to the caller
        // but we leave as is for simplicity.
        throw;
    }
}
```

Compared to the CreateUser method introduced previously, this method is fairly simple. It creates a new instance of SimpleRole and then adds this new role to the underlying RoleStore. Again, it is useful to add a CurrentStore property to your membership provider's implementation. This gives you easy access to the underlying store, as shown in the following code snippet (this property was already used in the previous snippet).

```
private RoleStore CurrentStore
{
    get
    {
        if (_CurrentStore == null)
            _CurrentStore = RoleStore.GetStore(_FileName);
        return _CurrentStore;
    }
}
```

The RoleExists method goes through the CurrentStore.Roles list and verifies whether the role with the name passed in through its parameter exists in the list. The DeleteRole tries to find the role in the roles list of the underlying role store, and if it exists, it deletes the role from the store and then saves the store back to the file system by calling CurrentStore.Save. Most of the methods for your custom roles provider are that simple. The most complex operations are adding a user to a role and removing the user from the role. The following is the first method—adding users to roles:

```
public override void AddUsersToRoles(string[] usernames, string[] roleNames)
{
    try
    {
        // Get the roles to be modified
        foreach (string roleName in roleNames)
        {
            SimpleRole Role = CurrentStore.GetRole(roleName);
            if (Role != null)
            {
                foreach (string userName in usernames)
                {
                    if (!Role.AssignedUsers.Contains(userName))
                    {
                        Role.AssignedUsers.Add(userName);
                    }
                }
            }
        }

        CurrentStore.Save();
    }
    catch
    {
        // If an exception is raised while saving the storage
        // or while serializing contents we just forward it to the
        // caller. It would be cleaner to work with custom exception
        // classes here and pass more detailed information to the caller
        // but we leave as is for simplicity.
        throw;
    }
}
```

Although the Roles class you used in Chapter 23 provides more overloads for this type of method, your provider has to implement the most flexible one: adding all users specified in the first parameter array to all roles specified in the second parameter array. Therefore, you have go through the list of supported roles stored in your XML file, and for every role specified in the roleNames parameter you have to add all users specified in the usernames parameter to the corresponding role. That's what this method is doing. Within the first foreach, it iterates through the array of role names passed in. It retrieves the role from the store by calling the RoleStore's GetRole method and then adds all the users specified in the usernames parameter to this role. Finally, it calls CurrentStore.Save() for serializing the roles back to the XML file. The RemoveUsersFromRoles method is doing the opposite, as follows:

```
public override void RemoveUsersFromRoles(string[] usernames, string[] roleNames)
{
    try
    {
        // Get the roles to be modified
        List<SimpleRole> TargetRoles = new List<SimpleRole>();
        foreach (string roleName in roleNames)
        {
            SimpleRole Role = CurrentStore.GetRole(roleName);
            if (Role != null)
```

```
            {
                foreach (string userName in usernames)
                {
                    if (Role.AssignedUsers.Contains(userName))
                    {
                        Role.AssignedUsers.Remove(userName);
                    }
                }
            }
        }

        CurrentStore.Save();
    }
    catch
    {
        // If an exception is raised while saving the storage
        // or while serializing contents we just forward it to the
        // caller. It would be cleaner to work with custom exception
        // classes here and pass more detailed information to the caller
        // but we leave as is for simplicity.
        throw;
    }
}
```

The only difference in this method from the one introduced previously is that it removes the users specified in the usernames parameter from all the roles specified in the roleNames parameter. The remaining logic of the method is the same. The remaining methods of the custom roles provider are easy to implement; in most cases, they just iterate through the roles that exist in the store and return some information, mostly arrays of strings with user names or role names, as shown here:

```
public override string[] GetRolesForUser(string username)
{
    try
    {
        List<SimpleRole> RolesForUser = CurrentStore.GetRolesForUser(username);
        string[] Results = new string[RolesForUser.Count];
        for (int i = 0; i < Results.Length; i++)
            Results[i] = RolesForUser[i].RoleName;
        return Results;
    }
    catch
    {
        // If an exception is raised while saving the storage
        // or while serializing contents we just forward it to the
        // caller. It would be cleaner to work with custom exception
        // classes here and pass more detailed information to the caller
        // but we leave as is for simplicity.
        throw;
    }
}

public override string[] GetUsersInRole(string roleName)
{
    try
```

```
    {
        return CurrentStore.GetUsersInRole(roleName);
    }
    catch
    {
        // If an exception is raised while saving the storage
        // or while serializing contents we just forward it to the
        // caller. It would be cleaner to work with custom exception
        // classes here and pass more detailed information to the caller
        // but we leave as is for simplicity.
        throw;
    }
}

public override bool IsUserInRole(string username, string roleName)
{
    try
    {
        SimpleRole Role = CurrentStore.GetRole(roleName);
        if (Role != null)
        {
            return Role.AssignedUsers.Contains(username);
        }
        else
        {
            // Requires import of System.Configuration.Provider
            throw new ProviderException("Role does not exist!");
        }
    }
    catch
    {
        // If an exception is raised while saving the storage
        // or while serializing contents we just forward it to the
        // caller. It would be cleaner to work with custom exception
        // classes here and pass more detailed information to the caller
        // but we leave as is for simplicity.
        throw;
    }
}
```

The first method returns all roles for a single user. It therefore calls the RoleStore's GetRolesForUsers method, which returns a list of SimpleRole objects. The result is then mapped to an array of strings and returned to the caller. Retrieving users for one role is even simpler, because the functionality is provided by the RoleStore class. Finally, the IsUserInRole method verifies whether a user is assigned to a role by retrieving the role and then calling the StringCollection's Contains method to verify whether the user exists in the SimpleRole's AssignedUsers collection.

You should take a look at one last method—FindUsersInRoles:

```
public override string[] FindUsersInRole(string roleName, string usernameToMatch)
{
    try
    {
        List<string> Results = new List<string>();
        Regex Expression = new Regex(usernameToMatch.Replace("%", @"\w*"));
```

```
            SimpleRole Role = CurrentStore.GetRole(roleName);
            if (Role != null)
            {
                foreach (string userName in Role.AssignedUsers)
                {
                    if (Expression.IsMatch(userName))
                        Results.Add(userName);
                }
            }
            else
            {
                throw new ProviderException("Role does not exist!");
            }

            return Results.ToArray();
        }
        catch
        {
            // If an exception is raised while saving the storage
            // or while serializing contents we just forward it to the
            // caller. It would be cleaner to work with custom exception
            // classes here and pass more detailed information to the caller
            // but we leave as is for simplicity.
            throw;
        }
    }
```

This method tries to find users based on pattern matching in the role specified through the roleName parameter. For this purpose, it retrieves the role from the store and then creates a regular expression. The SQL membership provider uses the % character for pattern matching, and because it is a good idea to have a provider that is compatible to existing implementations, you will use it for pattern matching again in your provider. But regular expressions don't understand the % as a placeholder for any characters in the string; therefore, you need to replace it with a representation that regular expressions understand: \w*. When the Membership class now passes in this character as a placeholder, your pattern matching function will still work, and therefore this function is compatible with the SqlMembershipProvider's implementation (which also uses the % as a placeholder). The remaining part of the function goes through the users assigned to the role; if the user name matches the pattern, it is added to the resulting list of strings that will be returned as a simple string array.

As you can see, implementing the custom roles provider is easy if you have previously implemented the custom membership provider. The process does not require you to understand any new concepts. In general, when you know how to implement one provider, you know how to implement another provider. Therefore, it should be easy for you to implement custom profile and personalization providers. Again, you can download the complete source code for the roles provider from the Apress website (http://www.apress.com). Now it's time to discuss how you can use these providers.

Using the Custom Provider Classes

Using providers in a custom web application is fairly easy. The steps for using custom providers are as follows (besides the typical ones such as configuring forms authentication):

1. If you have encapsulated the custom provider in a separate class library (which is definitely useful, because you want to use it in several web applications), you need to add a reference to this class library through the Visual Studio Add References dialog box.
2. Afterward, you must configure the custom provider appropriately in your web.config file.
3. Next you have to select your custom provider as the default provider either through the ASP.NET WAT or through web.config manually.
4. After you have completed these configuration steps, you are ready to use the provider. If you have not added any special functionality and have just implemented the inherited classes straightforwardly as shown in this chapter, you don't even need to change any code in your application.

The configuration of the previously created XmlMembershipProvider and XmlRoleProvider in the web.config configuration file within the <system.web> section looks like this:

```
<membership defaultProvider="XmlMembership">
    <providers>
        <add name="XmlMembership"
                applicationName="MyTestApp"
                fileName="C:\Work\MyTestApp_Users.config"
                type="Apress.ProAspNet.Providers.XmlMembershipProvider,
                      Apress.ProAspNet.Providers"
                requiresQuestionAndAnswer="true"/>
    </providers>
</membership>

<roleManager enabled="true"
                defaultProvider="XmlRoles">
    <providers>
        <add name="XmlRoles"
                applicationName="MyTestApp"
                fileName="C:\Work\MyTestApp_Roles.config"
                type="Apress.ProAspNet.Providers.XmlRoleProvider,
                      Apress.ProAspNet.Providers" />
    </providers>
</roleManager>
```

In the previous example, the providers will be configured to use files stored on c:\Work for saving user and role information appropriately. With this configuration, you will find the providers in the ASP.NET WAT (under Providers/Advanced Configuration), as shown in Figure 26-4.

Don't try to test the provider in the WAT; it will fail in this case. Testing providers in the WAT is just supported for providers that are using database connection strings to connect to the underlying back-end store. Because you are using XML files, testing will not work for the custom provider in this case.

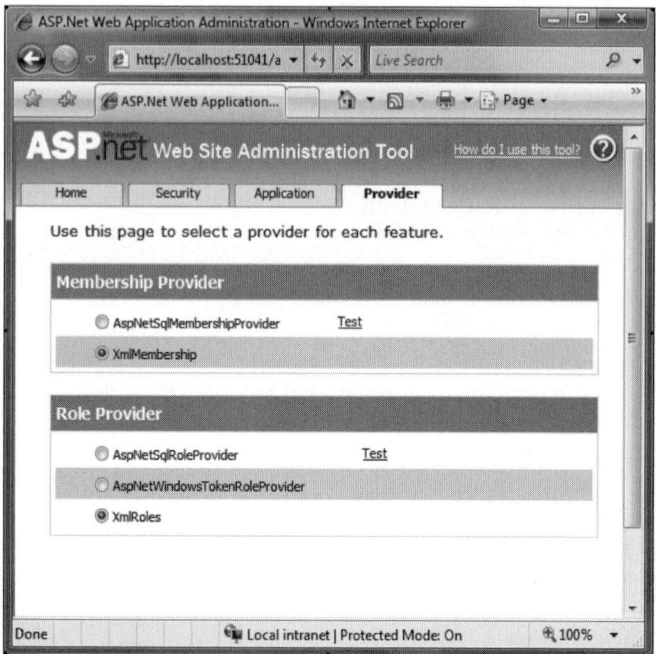

Figure 26-4. Custom providers in the ASP.NET WAT

■ **Caution** You should use absolute filenames and path values when storing the provider configuration settings. If you use a relative path, the provider will attempt to create the configuration files in the working directory of the web server. This will cause an exception if the account running your web application doesn't have permission to access this folder.

Debugging Using the WAT

The ASP.NET WAT uses the Membership and Roles classes for retrieving and updating data stored through the membership provider. Although we suggest building your own test driver classes by calling all the methods of the Membership and Roles classes, it is definitely useful to have the possibility of debugging from within the ASP.NET WAT, especially if you experience any problems you did not encounter while testing with your own applications.

For debugging through the WAT, you just need to launch the configuration utility through the Website ➤ ASP.NET Configuration menu and then attach to the web server process hosting the configuration tool. If you are using the file-based web server for development purposes, launch Visual Studio's Attach to Process dialog box by selecting Debug ➤ Attach to Process. Next, find the appropriate web server process. As in most cases, two of these processes will run when using the file-based web server, so you have to attach to the one with the right port number. Match the port number displayed in the address bar of the browser using the ASP.NET WAT with the one displayed in the Attach to Process dialog box. Then your breakpoints in the provider classes will be hit appropriately. Figure 26-5 shows how to attach to the web service process that hosts the ASP.NET WAT.

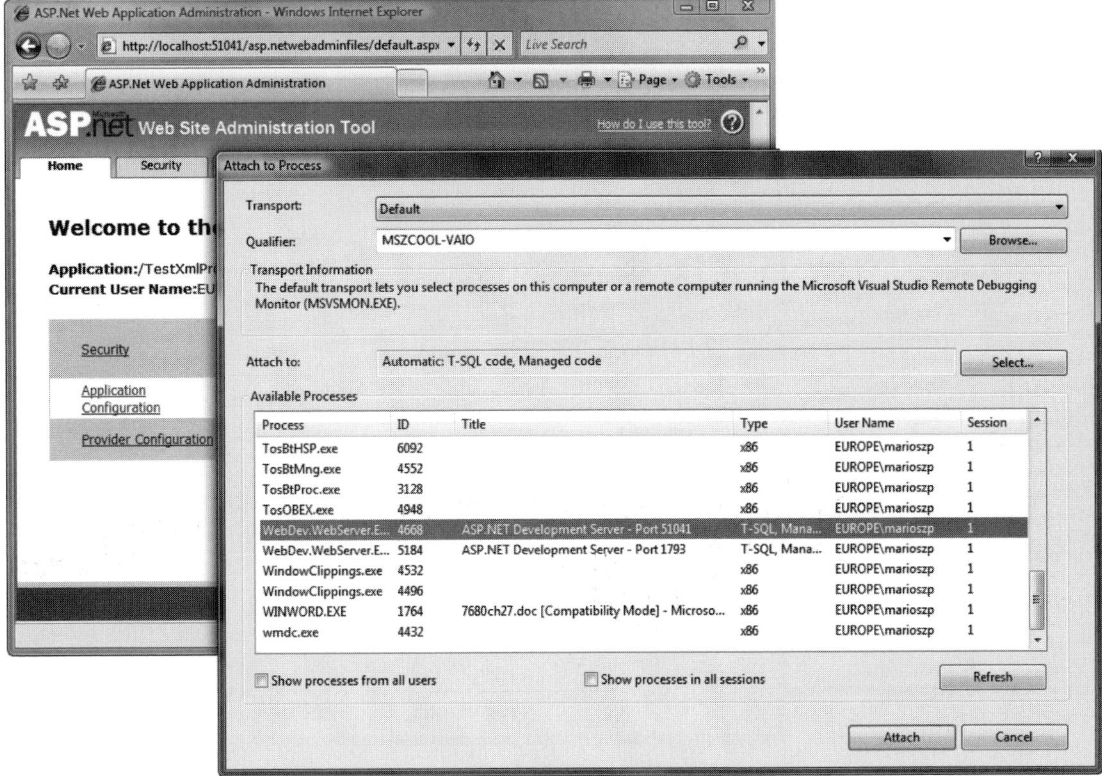

Figure 26-5. Attaching to the Configuration utility web server process

Using Custom Providers with IIS 7.x

Using custom membership providers through IIS is fairly straightforward and is exactly the same as configuring membership providers the way you learned in Chapter 21.

As soon as you have a custom membership provider or roles API provider implementation in your application's bin directory (or installed globally in the global assembly cache), IIS allows you to configure this provider through its management console, as you can see in Figure 26-6.

After you have configured your custom provider for .NET Users (as in Figure 26-6) and for .NET roles, you can add, edit, and remove users directly from within the management console of IIS 7.x. You don't need to fulfill any special requirements in your provider implementations. The only exception is that you may not include any dependencies to a running instance of a web application, such as accessing the HttpContext, which is not available from within the management console. However, you should always adhere to this rule when implementing custom providers.

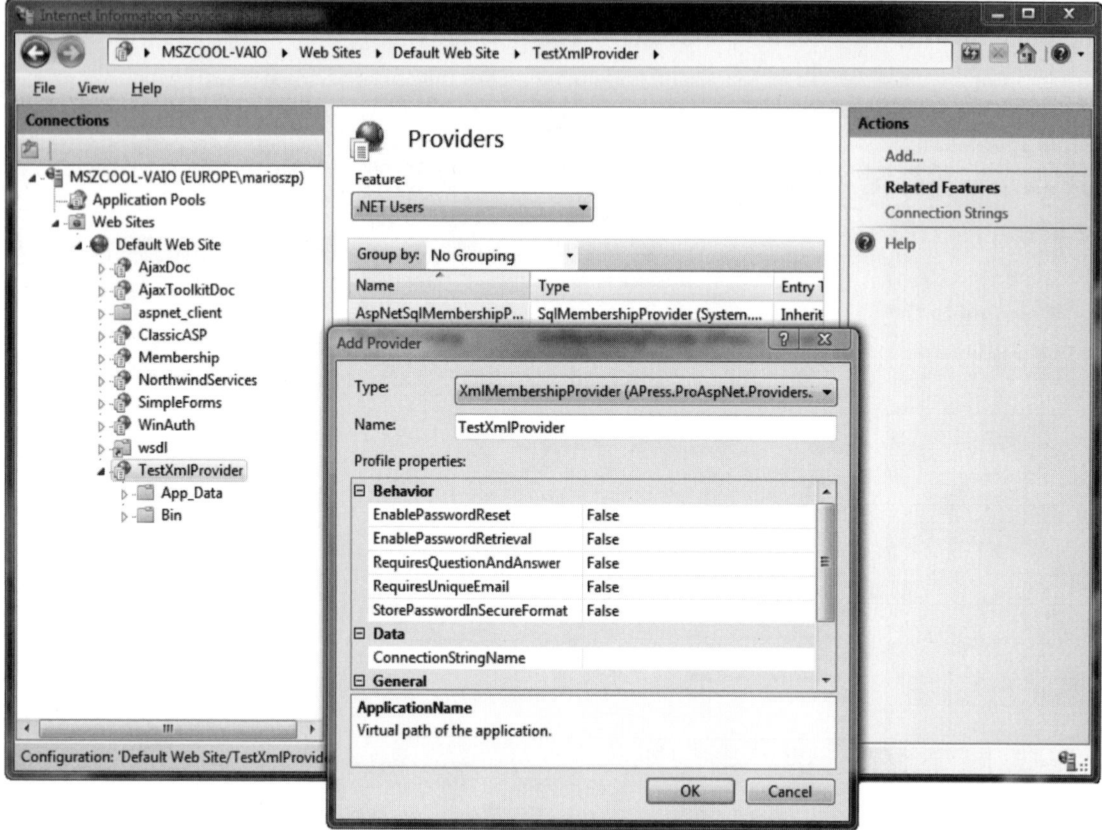

Figure 26-6. *Adding your custom provider through the IIS 7.x management console*

The final question we need to answer right now is, "How can you debug custom membership providers when they are used from within the IIS management console?" Why? Well, it can happen that your program logic works fine from within WAT but does not work properly from within the IIS management console (for example, you accidentally use a dependency to a running web application such as the HttpContext). Finding these errors is easier when you can debug the application. Again, this is fairly straightforward. Instead of attaching to the web server process hosting WAT, you attach to the IIS management process (called InetMgr.exe), as you can see in Figure 26-7.

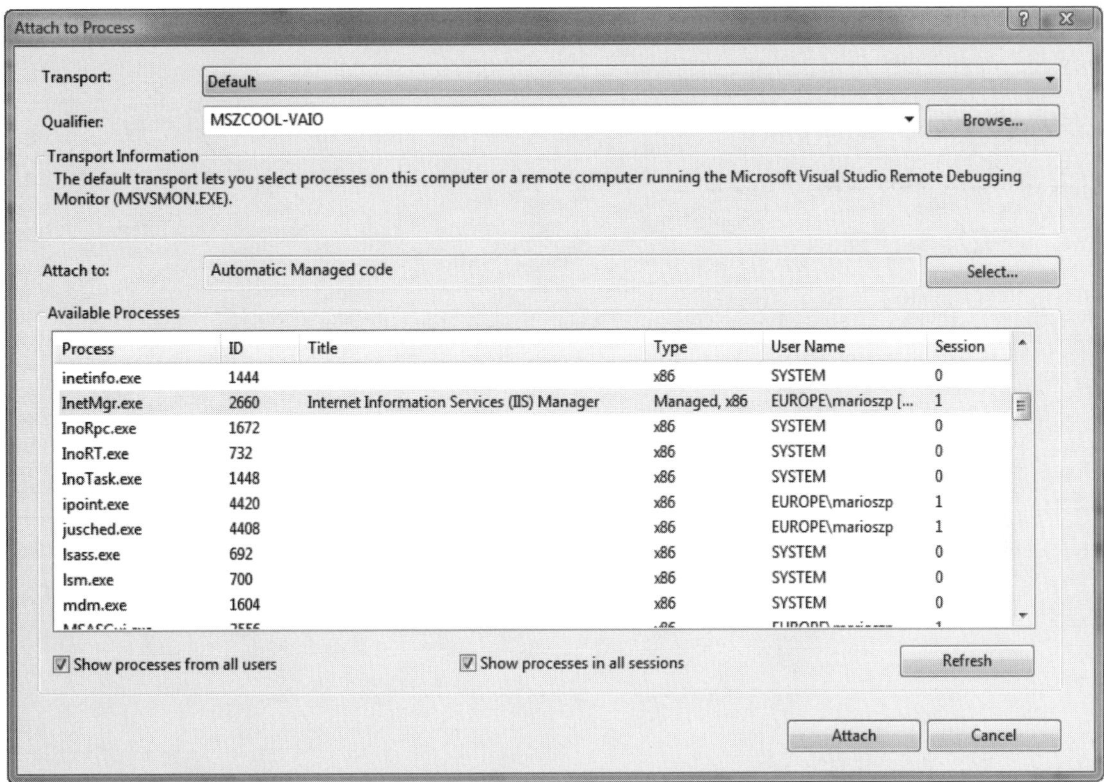

Figure 26-7. Debugging a provider from within the IIS management console

You need to be aware of a few things. Usually you run the IIS management console with administrative privileges. Debugging an application running with administrative privileges requires running Visual Studio with administrative privileges as well. To do so, right-click the Visual Studio shortcut and choose Run As Administrator. Next—as shown in Figure 26-7—you need to make sure to check the check marks on the bottom of the Attach to Process dialog from Visual Studio.

Summary

In this chapter, you saw how to extend the ASP.NET membership API and roles API through custom membership providers and roles providers. As an example, you developed a custom, XML-based provider for the membership and roles services. An XML-based provider is appropriate only for simple applications, but you learned the most important concepts for developing a custom membership and roles provider. These providers should conform as much as possible to the suggested interfaces so that you don't have to change your application when using a different provider. Furthermore, when using IIS 7.x in ASP.NET integrated mode, you can use your custom provider to manage users and roles directly from within the IIS 7.x management console. You don't need to fulfill any special requirements, because this is new functionality included with IIS out of the box. You should always test your custom providers against both the IIS 7.x management console and WAT to ensure the broadest availability of your custom providers.

PART 5

■■■

Advanced User Interface

As you already know, one of ASP.NET's greatest strengths is its extensible architecture. Throughout this book, you've learned how to customize the way ASP.NET processes requests, reads configuration files, and uses countless provider-based features from membership to profiles. Custom controls are one more avenue of advancement—they allow you to build your own well-encapsulated graphical widgets that you can drop into any page in any web application. Sometimes, the goal of a first-rate custom control is to provide a nice wrapper around a fancy piece of HTML markup. More often, custom controls are used to standardize a piece of page functionality and formalize the way it interacts with the page code so that you can reuse it effortlessly.

In Chapter 27, you'll learn how to build basic ASP.NET controls. You'll begin with simple controls that render their HTML from scratch. You'll learn a host of important techniques, including mechanisms to retain state information, support style attributes, preserve compatibility with different browsers, and trigger postback events. Later, you'll consider other types of custom controls, such as composite controls that are built out of smaller pieces and derived controls that extend ASP.NET staples.

In Chapter 28, you'll tackle a different technique for web-page design and learn how you can render custom image content that you can then place in a web page (with the help of the familiar <img> tag). You'll also learn how to streamline the process by wrapping your drawing logic in a custom control.

In Chapter 29 and Chapter 30, you'll dive into client-side programming and see how you can outfit your pages with JavaScript and use Ajax techniques to create more dynamic, responsive user interfaces.

Finally, in Chapter 31 you'll consider a whole new family of web controls—the web parts that allow you to build flexible portal-style web pages. You'll learn how to use the existing set of ASP.NET web parts and how to create your own reusable web parts.

CHAPTER 27

■ ■ ■

Custom Server Controls

Each type of custom control has its own advantages and disadvantages. In Chapter 15, you learned about user controls. User controls are easier to create than custom server controls, but server controls are far more powerful. Server controls beat user controls in two key areas:

Server controls give you complete control over the HTML you generate: In other words, you can create a control such as the ASP.NET Calendar, which provides a single object interface but renders itself as a complex combination of elements.

Server controls provide better design-time support: You can add them to the Toolbox in Visual Studio and set properties and add event handlers at design time. You can even configure the description that Visual Studio will show for each property, along with other design-time niceties.

All of ASP.NET's web controls are server controls. In this chapter, you'll learn how you can build your own.

Custom Server Control Basics

Server controls are .NET classes that derive directly or indirectly from System.Web.UI.Control. The Control class provides properties and methods that are common across all server controls (such as ID, ViewState, and the Controls collection). Most controls don't derive directly from Control; instead, they derive from System.Web.UI.WebControls.WebControl, which adds a few features that help you implement standard styles. These include properties such as Font, ForeColor, and BackColor.

Ideally, you'll create your server controls in a separate class library project and compile the project into a separate DLL assembly. Although you can create a custom control and place the source code directly in the App_Code directory of a web application, this limits your ability to reuse the control in pages written in different languages. If you place controls in a separate assembly, you'll also have better design-time support, which makes it easier to add them to web pages using Visual Studio.

To get a better idea of how custom controls work, the following sections demonstrate a few simple custom control examples.

■ **Tip** To create a new assembly for your custom server controls, start by creating a new project in Visual Studio by choosing File ➤ New ➤ Project. In the New Project dialog box, browse to the Visual C# ➤ Web section. Then, choose the ASP.NET Server Control project type. The ASP.NET Server Control project template is essentially the same as an ordinary class library assembly project, except it already has the references you need to the ASP.NET assemblies.

Creating a Bare-Bones Custom Control

To create a basic custom control, you derive from the Control class and override the Render() method. The Render() method receives an HtmlTextWriter object that you use to generate the HTML for the control.

The simplest way to generate your HTML is to use the HtmlTextWriter.Write() method, which writes a string of raw HTML into the page. Obviously, you can't use Write() to output ASP.NET tags and other server-side content, because you're rendering the content for the final page just before it's sent to the client.

Here's an example control that generates a simple hyperlink using the HtmlTextWriter in the Render() method:

```
public class LinkControl : Control
{
    protected override void Render(HtmlTextWriter output)
    {
        output.Write(
          "<a href='http://www.apress.com'>Click to visit Apress</a>");
    }
}
```

The HtmlTextWriter class not only lets you write raw HTML but also provides some helpful methods to help you manage style attributes and tags. The next example presents the same control, with a couple of minor differences. First, it renders the start tag and the end tag for the anchor separately, using the RenderBeginTag() and RenderEndTag() methods. Second, it adds style attributes that configure how the control will appear. Here's the complete code:

```
public class LinkControl : Control
{
    protected override void Render(HtmlTextWriter output)
    {
        // Specify the URL for the upcoming anchor tag.
        output.AddAttribute(HtmlTextWriterAttribute.Href,
          "http://www.apress.com");

        // Add the style attributes.
        output.AddStyleAttribute(HtmlTextWriterStyle.FontSize, "20");
        output.AddStyleAttribute(HtmlTextWriterStyle.Color, "Blue");

        // Create the anchor tag.
        output.RenderBeginTag(HtmlTextWriterTag.A);

        // Write the text inside the tag.
        output.Write("Click to visit Apress");

        // Close the tag.
        output.RenderEndTag();

    }
}
```

You should note a few important points in this example. First, to make life easier, the example uses several enumerations. These enumerations help avoid minor typographic mistakes that would cause unexpected problems. The enumerations include the following:

HtmlTextWriterTag: This enumeration defines dozens of HTML tags, such as <a>, <p>, <font>, and many more.

HtmlTextWriterAttribute: This enumeration defines a large set of common HTML tag attributes such as onClick, href, align, alt, and more.

HtmlTextWriterStyle: This enumeration defines 14 style attributes, including BackgroundColor, BackgroundImage, BorderColor, BorderStyle, BorderWidth, Color, FontFamily, FontSize, FontStyle, FontWeight, Height, and Width. All these pieces of information are joined in a semicolon-delimited list of CSS style information, which is used to set the style attribute of the rendered tag.

When the Render() method executes, it begins by defining all the attributes that will be added to the upcoming tag. Then when the start tag is created (using the RenderBeginTag() method), all of these attributes are placed into the tag. The final rendered tag looks like this:

```
<a href="http://www.apress.com" style="font-size:20;color:Blue;">
Click to visit Apress</a>
```

Table 27-1 provides an overview of the key methods of the HtmlTextWriter.

***Table 27-1.** HtmlTextWriter Methods*

Method	Description
AddAttribute()	Adds any HTML attribute and its value to an HtmlTextWriter output stream. This attribute is automatically used for the next tag you create by calling RenderBeginTag(). Instead of using the exact attribute name, you can choose a value from the HtmlTextWriterAttribute enumeration.
AddStyleAttribute()	Adds an HTML style attribute and its value to an HtmlTextWriter output stream. This attribute is automatically used for the next tag you create by calling RenderBeginTag(). Instead of using the exact style name, you can choose a value from the HtmlTextWriterStyle enumeration, and it will be rendered appropriately depending on whether the browser is an up-level or down-level client.
RenderBeginTag()	Writes the start tag for the HTML element. For example, if you are writing an anchor tag, this writes <a>. Instead of using the exact tag name, you can choose a value from the HtmlTextWriterTag enumeration.
RenderEndTag()	Writes the end tag for the current HTML element. For example, if you are in the process of writing an anchor tag, this writes the closing </a>. You don't need to specify the tag name.
WriteBeginTag()	This method is similar to the RenderBeginTag() method, except it doesn't write the closing > character for the start tag. That means you can call WriteAttribute() to add more attributes to the tag. To close the start tag, you can call Write(HtmlTextWriter.TagRightChar), which writes the closing >.

Method	Description
WriteAttribute()	Writes an HTML attribute to the output stream. This must follow the WriteBeginTag() method.
WriteEndTag()	Writes the end tag for the current HTML element (the one that was last opened using the WriteBeginTag() method).

Using a Custom Control

To use a custom control, you need to make it available to your web application. You have two choices—you can copy the source code to the App_Code directory, or you can compile in a separate assembly, which you will then place in the Bin directory (using Visual Studio's Add Reference command).

For the page to have access to a custom control, you must use the Register directive, just as you did with user controls in Chapter 15. However, this time you need to indicate slightly different information. Not only must you include a TagPrefix, but you also need to specify the assembly file (without the DLL extension) and the namespace where the control class is located. You don't need to specify the TagName, because the server control's class name is used automatically.

Here's an example of the Register directive:

```
<%@ Register TagPrefix="apress" Namespace="CustomServerControlsLibrary"
  Assembly="CustomServerControlsLibrary" %>
```

If the control is in the App_Code directory of the current web application, you don't need to include the Assembly attribute:

```
<%@ Register TagPrefix="apress" Namespace="CustomServerControlsLibrary" %>
```

You can reuse tag prefixes. In other words, it's completely valid to map two different namespaces or two completely different assemblies to the same tag prefix.

If you want to use a control in several pages of the same web application, ASP.NET has a helpful shortcut—you can register the tag prefix in the web.config file like this:

```
<configuration>
  <system.web>
    <pages>
      <controls>
        <add tagPrefix="apress" namespace="CustomServerControlsLibrary"
             assembly="CustomServerControlsLibrary" />
      </controls>
    </pages>
    ...
  </system.web>
</configuration>
```

This is particularly handy if you want to standardize on a specific tag prefix. Otherwise, Visual Studio chooses a default prefix (such as cc1 for custom control 1) when you drop a control from the Toolbox.

Once you've registered the control, you can declare it with a standard control tag, as shown here:

```
<apress:LinkControl id="LinkControl1" runat="server"/>
```

Figure 27-1 shows the custom LinkControl in action.

Figure 27-1. *A bare-bones server control*

Custom Controls in the Toolbox

To make it easier to use your custom control, you probably want to allow it to appear in the Toolbox. Impressively, Visual Studio has built-in Toolbox support for custom controls, provided you create them in a separate assembly.

■ **Note** Remember, Visual Studio supports projectless development, which means it hides solution files away in a user-specific directory. This means that it's fairly easy to lose the solution file (for example, by moving the website to another computer or renaming the website directory outside of Visual Studio). If you lose your solution file, the next time you open your website, the custom control project won't appear in the design environment—instead, you'll need to choose File ➤ Add ➤ Existing Project to get it back. To avoid this problem in a solution that has multiple projects, you can explicitly save a solution file to a well-known location and use the solution file to open your web application later. To do so, select the first line in the Solution Explorer (which has text such as *Solution "MyWebApp" (2 projects)*), and then choose File ➤ Save [SolutionName].sln As.

Once you've created your project, you can define your controls. You develop your control library project in the same way you work with any other DLL component. You can build the project at any time, but you can't start it directly because it isn't an actual application.

To test your controls, you need to use them in another application. You can use two approaches. First, you can add a reference in the same way that you add a reference to any other .NET assembly. Just right-click your website in the Solution Explorer, and choose Add Reference. Choose the Projects tab, pick the custom control project you've created, and click OK. This copies the compiled control assembly to your Bin directory in your website, making it available to your pages.

An easier approach is to use the automatic Toolbox support in Visual Studio. When you compile a project that contains custom server controls, Visual Studio examines each control and adds each one dynamically to a temporary, project-specific section of the Toolbox at the top (see Figure 27-2). That means you can easily add controls to any page. When you drop the control on the page, Visual Studio automatically copies the assembly to the Bin directory if you haven't already created a reference, adds the Register directive if it's not already present in the page, and then adds the control tag.

Figure 27-2. A custom control in the Toolbox

■ **Tip** As with any other type of reference in Visual Studio, every time you compile your project, the most recent version of the referenced assembly is copied into your web application's Bin directory. This means that if you change and recompile a custom control after adding it to the Toolbox, you have no reason to remove and re-add it.

The only limitation of the automatic Toolbox support is that your custom controls will appear in the Toolbox only when the custom control project is loaded in the design environment. If you want to make a control available to any web application but you don't want the web application developers to be able to change your custom control code, you need another approach. In this case, it makes sense to deploy just the compiled assembly. You can then add the controls to the Toolbox permanently so the application developers don't need to worry about finding the control.

To do this, right-click the Toolbox, and select Choose Items. On the .NET Framework Components tab, click the Browse button. Then choose the custom control assembly from the file browser. The controls will be added to the list of available .NET controls, as shown in Figure 27-3.

All checked controls will appear in the Toolbox. Note that controls aren't added on a per-project basis. Instead, they will remain in the Toolbox until you delete them. To remove a control, right-click it, and select Delete. This action removes the icon only, not the referenced assembly.

Visual Studio gives you quite a bit of basic design-time support. For example, after you add a custom control to a web page, you can modify its properties in the Properties window (they will appear under the Misc group) and attach event handlers.

■ **Tip** You can extend the design-time support of your control using special .NET attributes, control designer classes, and other techniques. However, design-time programming is complex, it's out of the scope of this chapter, and it's often best left to developers who want to create and sell custom controls packages. If you want to learn more, you can get started with the "Design-Time Support" chapter from the previous edition of this book, which is provided as downloadable bonus content on the web page for this book. See the introduction for more details.

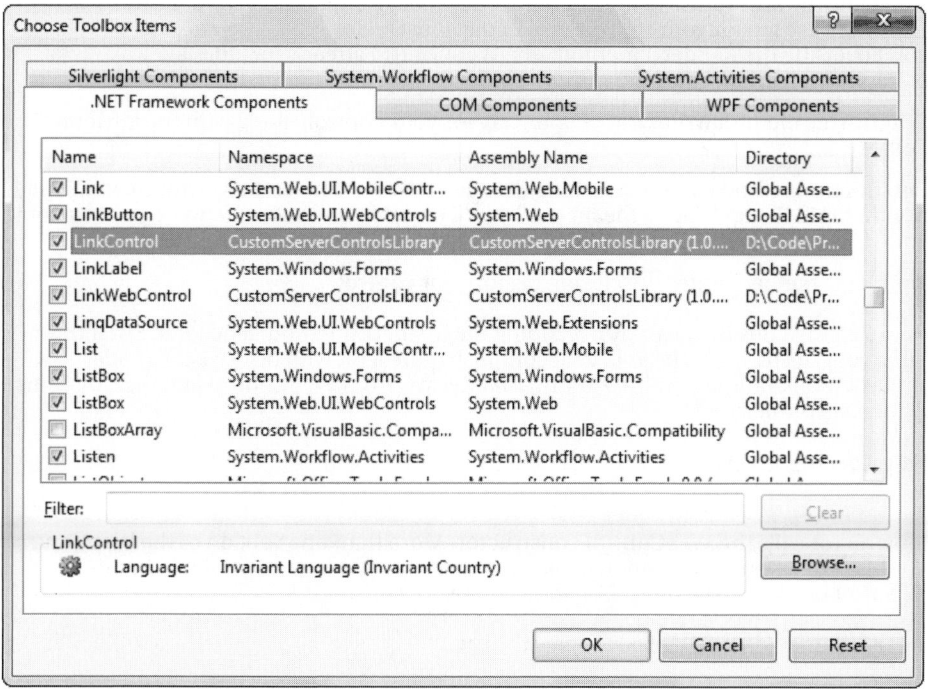

Figure 27-3. Adding a custom control to the Toolbox

Creating a Web Control That Supports Style Properties

The previous custom control example doesn't allow the web page to customize the control's appearance. The LinkControl doesn't provide any properties for setting foreground or background colors, the font, or other attributes of the HTML tag that you generate. In other words, the LinkControl is in complete control of its rendering and doesn't allow outside code (the web page) to alter the HTML it generates. To make the LinkControl more flexible, you need to explicitly add public properties for various formatting-related details. You then need to read these properties in the Render() method and generate the appropriate HTML code.

Of course, style properties are a basic part of infrastructure that many HTML controls need to use. Ideally, all controls should follow a single, streamlined model for style information and not force custom control developers to write this generic functionality themselves. ASP.NET does this with the WebControl base class (in the System.Web.UI.WebControls namespace). Every web control that's included with ASP.NET derives from WebControl, and you can derive your custom controls from it as well.

Not only does the WebControl class include basic style-related properties such as Font, ForeColor, BackColor, and so on, but it also renders them automatically in the control tag. Here's how it works: the WebControl assumes that it should add the attributes to a single HTML tag, called the *base tag*. If you're writing multiple elements, the attributes are added to the outermost element that contains the other elements. You specify the base tag for your web control in the constructor.

Finally, you don't override the Render() method. The WebControl already includes an implementation of Render() that farms out the work to the following three methods:

RenderBeginTag(): This method writes the opening tag for your control, along with the attributes you've specified.

RenderContents(): This method writes everything between the start and end tag, which can include text content or other HTML tags. This is the method you'll override most often to write your custom control content.

RenderEndTag(): This method writes the closing tag for your control.

Of course, you can change this behavior by overriding the Render() method, if needed. But if this basic framework suits your needs, you'll be able to accomplish quite a bit with little custom code.

The next example demonstrates a new link control that derives from WebControl and thereby gains automatic support for style properties.

```
public class LinkWebControl : WebControl
{ ... }
```

The default constructor calls the WebControl constructor. More than one version of the WebControl constructor exists—this code uses the version that allows you to specify a base control tag. In this example, the base control tag is the <a> anchor, as shown here:

```
public LinkWebControl() : base(HtmlTextWriterTag.A)
{}
```

The LinkWebControl constructor doesn't require any actual code. It's just important that you use this opportunity to call the WebControl constructor to set the base control tag. If you use the default (zero-parameter) WebControl constructor, a <span> tag is used automatically. You can then render additional HTML inside this <span> tag, which ensures that all elements will have the same style attributes.

The LinkWebControl also defines two properties that allow the web page to set the text and the target URL:

```
private string text;
public string Text
{
    get {return text;}
    set {text = value;}
}

private string hyperLink;
public string HyperLink
{
    get {return hyperLink;}
    set
    {
        if (value.IndexOf("http://") == -1)
        {
            throw new ApplicationException("Specify HTTP as the protocol.");
        }
        else
        {
            hyperLink = value;
        }
    }
}
```

You could set the text and hyperLink variables to empty strings when you define them. However, this example overrides the OnInit() method to demonstrate how you can initialize a control programmatically:

```
protected override void OnInit(EventArgs e)
{
    base.OnInit(e);

    // If no values were set in the control tag, apply the defaults now.
    if (hyperLink == null)
        hyperLink = "http://www.google.com";
    if (text == null)
        text = "Click to search";
}
```

The LinkWebControl presents a minor challenge. To successfully create an <a> tag, you need to specify a target URL and some text. The text is placed between the start and end tags. However, the URL is added as an attribute (named href) to the start tag. As you've already learned, the WebControl manages the attributes for the start tag automatically. Fortunately, the WebControl class gives you the ability to add extra tags by overriding the method AddAttributesToRender(), as shown here:

```
protected override void AddAttributesToRender(HtmlTextWriter output)
{
    output.AddAttribute(HtmlTextWriterAttribute.Href, HyperLink);
    base.AddAttributesToRender(output);
}
```

Note that whenever a custom control overrides a method, it should call the base class implementation using the base keyword. This ensures that you don't inadvertently suppress any code that needs to run. Often, all the base method does is fire a related event, but that's not always the case. For example, if you override RenderBeginTag() and don't call the base implementation, the rendering code will fail with an unhandled exception because the tag isn't opened.

Finally, the RenderContents() method adds the text inside the anchor:

```
protected override void RenderContents(HtmlTextWriter output)
{
    output.Write(Text);
    base.RenderContents(output);
}
```

Custom Server Controls in Visual Studio

When you create an ASP.NET server control project, it begins with one server control (named, rather unhelpfully, WebCustomControl1). You can create additional controls by adding new code files and writing the code by hand, as in the previous example. Or, you can create a new control with a bit more help from Visual Studio by choosing Project ➤ Add New Item, browsing to the Visual C# Items ➤ Web section, and choosing the ASP.NET Server Control template.

There's one important difference between the controls you create by hand and the ones Visual Studio generates. Controls created by Visual Studio include some automatically generated boilerplate code:

- The file begins with a number of using statements that import useful ASP.NET namespaces.
- The control class adds a Text property, which is stored in view state (a technique you'll start using later in this chapter).
- The control class overrides the RenderContents() method to write out the contents of the Text property.
- The control class declaration and the Text property are decorated with attributes that configure design-time support. (For example, the control class declaration begins with a DefaultProperty attribute that indicates what property Visual Studio should highlight in the Properties window when you select the control at design time.)

It's quite easy to add these details without Visual Studio's help, so don't be afraid to begin with a blank code file and write your custom control class by hand (as many control developers do).

Note that the code doesn't use the style properties. Instead, ASP.NET applies these automatically when it renders the base tag.

Now that you have created the control, you can use it in any ASP.NET web page. You can set the style properties in code or in the control tag. You can even use the Properties window. Here's an example:

```
<apress:LinkWebControl id="LinkWebControl1" runat="server"
  BackColor="#FFFF80" Font-Names="Verdana" Font-Size="Large"
  ForeColor="#C00000" Text="Click to visit Apress"
  HyperLink="http://www.apress.com"></apress:LinkWebControl>
```

The HyperLink and Text attributes are automatically mapped to the corresponding public properties of the custom control. The same is true of the style-related properties, which are defined in the base WebControl class.

Figure 27-4 shows this control in a web browser.

***Figure 27-4.** A custom control that supports style properties*

■ **Tip** As a general guideline, you should derive from the WebControl class if your control needs to add any visible content to the page. Of course, exceptions exist. For example, if you know you want only a subset of the UI features or you want to combine multiple controls, which will each have their own specific style properties, you might want to derive from Control instead of WebControl. However, the basic rule of thumb that the .NET class library follows is always to derive from WebControl, even if some of the properties aren't relevant.

The Rendering Process

The previous example introduced several new rendering methods. Before going any further, it's a good idea to look at how they all work together.

The starting point for the rendering process is the RenderControl() method. The RenderControl() method is the public rendering method that ASP.NET uses to render each control on a web page to HTML. You should not override RenderControl(). Instead, RenderControl() calls the protected Render() method that starts the rendering process. You *can* override Render(), as demonstrated in the first example in this chapter. However, if you override Render() and don't call the base implementation of the Render() method, none of the other rendering methods will fire.

The base implementation of the Render() method calls RenderBeginTag(), RenderContents(), and then RenderEndTag(), as you saw in the previous example. However, this has one more twist. The base implementation of the RenderContents() method calls another rendering method—RenderChildren(). This method loops through the collection of child controls in the Controls collection and calls the RenderControl() method for each individual control. By taking advantage of this behavior, you can easily build a control from other controls. This approach is demonstrated later in this chapter with composite controls (see the section "Composite Controls").

So, which rendering method should you override? If you want to replace the entire rendering process with something new or if you want to add HTML content *before* your base control tag (such as a block of JavaScript code), you can override Render(). If you want to take advantage of the automatic style attributes, you should define a base tag (by specifying a tag name parameter such as HtmlTextWriterTag.A when you call the base constructor) and then override RenderContents(). If you want to prevent child controls from being displayed or customize how they are rendered (for example, by rendering them in the reverse order), you can override RenderChildren().

Figure 27-5 summarizes the rendering process.

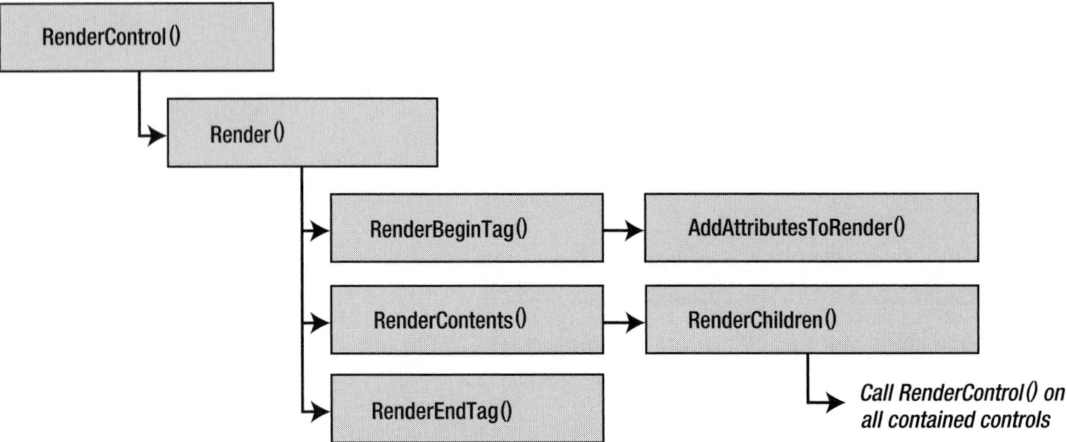

***Figure 27-5.** The control rendering methods*

It's worth noting that you can call RenderControl() yourself to examine the HTML output for a control. In fact, this technique can be a convenient shortcut when debugging. Here's an example that gets the rendered HTML for a control and displays it in a label on a web page:

```
// Create the in-memory objects that will catch the rendered output.
StringWriter writer = new StringWriter();
HtmlTextWriter output = new HtmlTextWriter(writer);

// Render the control to an in-memory string.
LinkWebControl1.RenderControl(output);

// Display the HTML (and encode it properly so that
// it appears as text in the browser).
lblHtml.Text = "The HTML for LinkWebControl1 is<br /><blockquote>" +
  Server.HtmlEncode(writer.ToString()) + "</blockquote>";
```

Figure 27-6 shows the page with the control and its HTML.

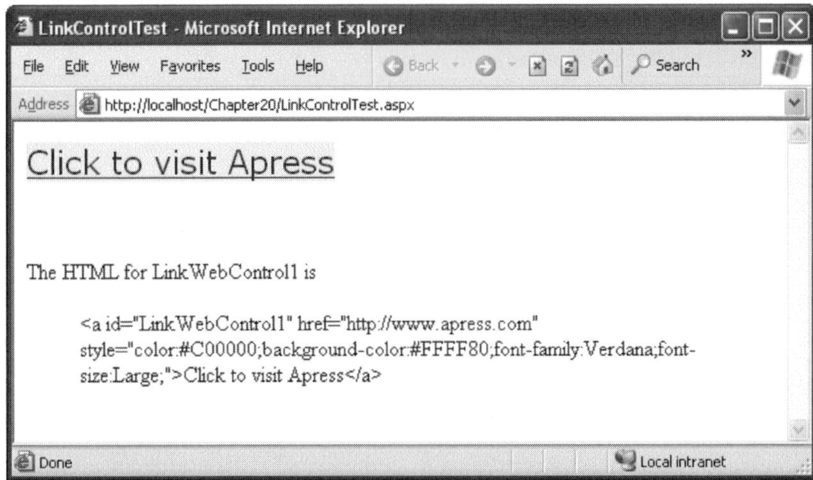

Figure 27-6. *Getting the HTML representation of a control*

■ **Tip** This technique isn't just for debugging. You could also use it to simplify your rendering code. For example, you might find it easier to create and configure an HtmlTable control and then call its RenderControl() method, rather than write tags such as <table>, <td>, and <tr> directly to the output stream.

Dealing with Different Browsers

Because of the wide variation in the features supported by different browsers, it's a challenge to create applications that work across all the browsers and still provide the best possible user experience. ASP.NET provides a few features that can help you write the correct type of markup for different devices.

The HtmlTextWriter

First, ASP.NET makes a broad distinction in the type of markup that a client sees so that some clients get HTML 3.2, others get HTML 4.0, and others get XHTML 1.1. You might not even realize that this differentiation is taking place.

It all works through the HtmlTextWriter class, which has several derived classes. HtmlTextWriter itself is designed to write HTML 4.0 markup. But its derived classes are different—so, the Html32TextWriter writes HTML 3.2 markup for down-level clients, and the XhtmlTextWriter writes XHTML 1.1. Because all these classes derive from HtmlTextWriter, you're free to use the same basic set of HtmlTextWriter methods in your rendering code. However, the implementations of many of these methods differ, so depending on which object you get, the output might not be the same.

For example, if you use this rendering code:

```
output.RenderBeginTag(HtmlTextWriterTag.Div);
```

you expect the following:

```
<div>
```

But here's the result you'll see with the Html32TextWriter (assuming Html32TextWriter.ShouldPerformDivTableSubstitution is true):

```
<table cellpadding="0" cellspacing="0" border="0" width="100%"><tr><td>
```

On the other hand, if you use the following code, your rendered output is completely inflexible and never changes, regardless of the capabilities of the target device:

```
output.Write("<div>");
```

Similarly, if you derive from WebControl to get automatic support for style properties, this support is implemented differently depending on the renderer.

The lesson here is that you should avoid writing raw HTML (using the Write() method) and instead use higher-level methods (such as RenderBeginTag(), RenderEndTag(), and so on) wherever possible. That way, your controls are more flexible. ASP.NET will create and pass in the correct HtmlTextWriter, based on the capabilities of the browser that's requesting the page, and your HTML markup can adapt itself. This issue isn't quite as critical as it was in the past, because the most commonly used browsers all support XHTML. However, it's still good design, and it ensures your code will continue to work flawlessly if ASP.NET is updated to support newer types of rendering that don't have the same broad range of support.

Browser Detection

So, how does ASP.NET decide which type of text writer suits a particular client? It's all based on the user-agent string that the client supplies when it makes a request. ASP.NET tries to match this string against a large catalog of known browsers. You can find this catalog in c:\[WinDir]\Microsoft.NET\Framework\[Version]\Config\Browsers. There you'll see a number of .browser files. Each one is an XML file that maps a user-agent string to a set of capabilities and a text writer.

Every .browser file has this basic structure:

```
<browsers>
  <browser id="..." parentID="...">
    <identification>
      <!-- Here is one regular expression that attempts to match the
           user-agent string.
           There may also be multiple nonmatches, which disqualify
           user-agent strings that otherwise match the desired pattern. -->
      <userAgent match="..." />
      <userAgent nonMatch="..." />
    </identification>

    <capabilities>
      <!-- Assuming the user-agent string matches, here are the
           capabilities ASP.NET should assume that the client has. -->
    </capabilities>

    <controlAdapters>
      <!-- For this client, some controls may need nondefault rendering
           of specific controls. This is made possible through adapters.
```

```
        Here is a list of all the control-specific adapters ASP.NET
        should use. -->
    </controlAdapters>
  </browser>

  <!-- More browsers can be defined here. -->
</browsers>
```

Further complicating the model is that you can create subcategories of browsers. To do this, the <browser> element includes the parentID attribute, which refers to another <browser> definition from which it should inherit settings.

You probably think this is a somewhat brittle system—and unfortunately, it is. You have no guarantee that a browser won't appear with a browser string that doesn't match any of the known patterns or that a browser won't submit the wrong string. However, this is a necessary compromise in the loosely coupled world of the Web, and the ASP.NET team has worked hard to make sure the browser information that ships with ASP.NET 4 is much more reliable and up-to-date than the information from any earlier versions of ASP.NET. You're also free to customize the browser presets completely or even add new definitions for different user-agent strings.

Browser Properties

You can detect the current browser configuration using the Browser property of the HttpRequest object, which returns a reference to an HttpBrowserCapabilities object. (You can also get the user-agent string from the UserAgent property.) When a client makes an HTTP request, an HttpBrowserCapabilities object is created and filled with information about the capabilities of the browser based on the corresponding .browser file. The information provided in the HttpBrowserCapabilities class includes the kind of browser and its version, whether scripting support is available on the client side, and so on. By detecting the capabilities of the browser, you can choose to customize your output to provide different behaviors on different browsers. This way, you can fully exploit the potential capabilities of up-level clients without breaking down-level clients.

Table 27-2 summarizes the properties of HttpBrowserCapabilities class.

Table 27-2. *HttpBrowserCapabilities Properties*

Property	Description
Browser	Gets the browser string that was sent with the request in the user-agent header.
MajorVersion	Gets the major version number of the client browser. (For example, this returns 4 for version 4.5.)
MinorVersion	Gets the minor version number of the client browser. (For example, this returns 5 for version 4.5.)
Type	Gets the name and the major version number of the client browser.
Version	Gets the full version number of the client browser.
Beta	Returns true if the client browser is a beta release.

Property	Description
AOL	Returns true if the client is an AOL (America Online) browser.
Platform	Provides the name of the operating system platform that the client uses.
Win16	Returns true if the client is a Win16-based computer.
Win32	Returns true if the client is a Win32-based computer.
ClrVersion	Provides the highest version number of the .NET CLR installed on the client computer. You can also use the GetClrVersions() method to retrieve information about all the installed CLR versions. This setting is significant only if you have embedded .NET Windows Forms controls in your web page. Client browsers don't need the CLR to run ordinary ASP.NET web pages.
ActiveXControls	Returns true if the client browser supports ActiveX controls.
BackgroundSounds	Returns true if the client browser supports background sounds.
Cookies	Returns true if the client browser supports cookies.
Frames	Returns true if the client browser supports frames.
Tables	Returns true if the client browser supports HTML tables.
JavaScript	Indicates whether the client browser supports JavaScript. This is considered obsolete, and it's recommended that you test the EcmaScriptVersion property instead.
VBScript	Returns true if the client browser supports VBScript.
JavaApplets	Returns true if the client browser supports embedded Java applets.
EcmaScriptVersion	Gets the version number of ECMA script that the client browser supports.
MSDomVersion	Gets the version of Microsoft HTML DOM that the client browser supports.
Crawler	Returns true if the client browser is a web crawler search engine.

The HttpBrowserCapabilities class has one glaring limitation—it's limited to evaluating the *expected* built-in functionality of the browser. It does *not* evaluate the current state of a browser's functionality. For example, imagine you are evaluating the client-side JavaScript support provided by the browser. If the requesting browser is Internet Explorer 7, this will return true since the browser supports client-side JavaScript support. However, if the user has the scripting capabilities turned off, the JavaScript property still returns true. In other words, you don't learn what the browser is capable of doing, just what it *should* be capable of doing. In fact, all ASP.NET really does is read the user-agent information that's passed from the browser to the server during the request and compare this string against the predefined user-agent information in the .browser files. It's the .browser files that list the corresponding browser capabilities, such as whether the browser supports scripting, styles, frames, and so on. Unfortunately, the client just doesn't send any information about how the browser is configured.

This situation leaves you with two options. You can rely on the HttpBrowserCapabilities class to tell you whether certain browser features should be available and base your programming logic on that information. In this case, you may need to tolerate the occasional error. If you need a more robust approach, you need to write your own code to actually test the support for the features you need. For example, with cookies you could (over two web pages) attempt to set a cookie and then attempt to read it. If the second test doesn't succeed, cookie support isn't enabled. You could use similar workarounds to check for other features such as JavaScript support. For example, you could add a piece of JavaScript code to the page that writes to a hidden form variable and then check it on the server. These steps are awkward and messy, but they're the only way to be absolutely certain of specific browser features. Unfortunately, when creating custom controls, you usually don't have the luxury of performing these tests.

Overriding Browser Type Detection

ASP.NET gives you the ability to explicitly set how a page is rendered instead of relying on automatic browser detection. The trick is to set the Page.ClientTarget property either programmatically (in the Page.PreInit stage) or declaratively (using the Page directive). When you set the ClientTarget property, automatic browser detection is disabled, and ASP.NET uses the browser setting you specified for the remainder of the request.

The only trick to using the ClientTarget property is that you can use only defined *aliases*. Each alias is mapped to a specific user-agent string (and the browser settings for that user agent are declared in the corresponding .browser file).

For example, imagine you want to test how your page will render with a legacy browser such as Internet Explorer 5. First, you need to create an alias in the <clientTarget> section that maps the right user agent string to any name you pick. In this case, the alias is ie5:

```
<configuration>
  <system.web>
    <clientTarget>
      <add alias="ie5" userAgent="Mozilla/4.0 (compatible; MSIE 5.5; Windows NT 4.0)" />
    </clientTarget>
    ...
  </system.web>
</configuration>
```

Now you can force a page to use this alias and render itself as though Internet Explorer 5 were making the request by setting the ClientTarget attribute in the Page directive. Here's how:

```
<%@ Page ClientTarget="ie5" ... />
```

Adaptive Rendering

Ideally, you'll be able to render markup that works on all major browsers. But in some cases, you may find yourself writing browser-specific rendering logic. At its worst, that looks like this:

```
protected override void RenderContents(HtmlTextWriter output)
{
    base.RenderContents(output);

    if (Page.Request.Browser.EcmaScriptVersion.Major >= 1)
```

```
    {
        output.Write("<i>You support JavaScript.</i><br />");
    }
    if (Page.Request.Browser.Browser == "IE")
    {
        output.Write("<i>Output configured for IE.</i><br />");
    }
    else if (Page.Request.Browser.Browser == "Netscape")
    {
        output.Write("<i>Output configured for Netscape.</i><br />");
    }
}
```

A better approach is to use the control to output standard rendering and create a *control adapter* that uses specialized rendering for a specific browser. The control adapter model makes it possible to create a single control that can be adapted for multiple types of devices. Best of all, because of the separation between controls and control adapters, third-party developers can write adapters for existing controls, allowing them to work with other platforms.

You can link any control to an adapter through the .browser file. For example, you could create a FirefoxSlideMenuAdapter that changes the rendered code for your SlideMenu control so that it works better with Firefox. You would then edit the mozilla.browser file to specifically indicate that this adapter should be used for your control with all Firefox browsers.

The control adapter works by plugging into the rendering process. ASP.NET calls the adapter at each state of the web control's life cycle, which allows the adapter to adjust the rendering process and handle other details, such as device-specific view state logic.

To create an adapter, derive a new class from System.Web.UI.Adapters.ControlAdapter (if your custom control derives from Control) or System.Web.UI.WebControls.Adapters.WebControlAdapter (if your custom control derives from WebControl). You can then implement the functionality you want by overriding methods. Each method corresponds to a method in the custom control class, and when you override the method in a control adapter, the control adapter method is used *instead* of the control method.

■ **Note** As with server controls, you should place your control adapters in a separate DLL assembly. If your adapters are relatively simple, you may choose to place them in the same assembly that contains your controls. However, if your adapters are complex and they're designed to support a specialized usage scenario, you might choose to place them in a dedicated assembly of their own.

For example, in the ControlAdapter you can override methods such as OnInit(), Render(), and RenderChildren(). In the WebControlAdapter you can also override RenderBeginTag(), RenderEndTag(), and RenderContents(). Here's an example:

```
public class LinkControlAdapter : ControlAdapter
{
    // Replace the ordinary rendering logic so it uses different color
    // and doesn't change the font.
    protected override void Render(HtmlTextWriter output)
    {
        // Specify the URL for the upcoming anchor tag.
```

```
        output.AddAttribute(HtmlTextWriterAttribute.Href,
          "http://www.apress.com");

        // Add the style attributes.
        output.AddStyleAttribute(HtmlTextWriterStyle.Color, "Red");

        // Create the anchor tag.
        output.RenderBeginTag(HtmlTextWriterTag.A);
        output.Write("Click to visit Apress");
        output.RenderEndTag();
    }
}
```

Control State and Events

ASP.NET uses web controls to create an object-oriented layer of abstraction over the lower-level details of HTML and HTTP. Two cornerstones of this abstraction are view state (the mechanism that lets you store information between requests) and postback (the technique wherein a web page posts back to the same URL with a collection of form data). To create realistic server controls, you need to know how to create classes that plug into both of these parts of the web-page infrastructure.

View State

Controls need to store information in state just like your web pages. Fortunately, all controls provide a ViewState property that you can use to store and retrieve information just as you do with a web page. You'll need to use the ViewState collection to restore private information after a postback.

A common design pattern with web controls is to access the ViewState collection in your property procedures. For example, consider the LinkWebControl presented earlier. Currently, this control doesn't use view state, which means that if you change its Text and HyperLink properties programmatically, the changes will be lost in subsequent postbacks. (This isn't true of the style properties such as Font, ForeColor, and BackColor, which are stored in view state automatically.) To change the LinkWebControl to ensure that state information is retained for the Text and HyperLink properties, you need to remove the text and hyperLink fields from the LinkButton class and rewrite the Text and HyperLink properties as shown here:

```
public string Text
{
    get {return (string)ViewState["Text"];}
    set {ViewState["Text"] = value;}
}

public string HyperLink
{
    get {return (string)ViewState["HyperLink"];}
    set
    {
        if (value.IndexOf("http://") == -1)
        {
            throw new ApplicationException("Specify HTTP as the protocol.");
        }
        else
```

```
            {
                ViewState["HyperLink"] = value;
            }
        }
    }

    protected override void OnInit(EventArgs e)
    {
        base.OnInit(e);
        if (ViewState["HyperLink"] == null)
            ViewState["HyperLink"] = "http://www.apress.com";

        if (ViewState["Text"] == null)
            ViewState["Text"] = "Click here to visit Apress";
    }
```

You can also request that the page encrypts the view state information by calling Page.RegisterRequiresViewStateEncryption() when your control initializes. This is useful if you need to store potentially sensitive data.

```
protected override void OnInit(EventArgs e)
{
    base.OnInit(e);
    Page.RegisterRequiresViewStateEncryption();
}
```

It's important to realize that the ViewState property of a control is separate from the ViewState property of the page. In other words, if you add an item in your control code, you can't access it in your web page, and vice versa. When the page is rendered to HTML, ASP.NET takes the view state of the page and all the combined controls and then merges it into a special tree structure.

Although view state is easy to use in a control, you have to consider a couple of issues. First, you shouldn't store large objects because they will reduce page transmission times. For example, the ASP.NET controls that support data binding don't store the DataSource property in view state. They simply hold it in memory until you call the DataBind() method. This makes programming a little more awkward—for example, it forces you to rebind data controls after every postback—but it ensures that pages don't become ridiculously bloated.

Another consideration with view state is that it's at the mercy of the containing page. If the page sets the EnableViewState property of your control to false, all your view state information will be lost after each postback. If you have critical information that you require in order for your control to work, you should store it in control state instead (see the next section).

■ **Note** Even if the EnableViewState property is set to false, the ViewState collection will still be accessible to your code. The only difference is that the information you place in that collection will be discarded once the control is finished processing and the page is rendered.

Finally, keep in mind that you can't assume data is in the ViewState collection. If you try to retrieve an item that doesn't exist, you'll run into a NullReferenceException. To prevent this problem, you should check for null values or set default view state information in the OnInit() method or the custom control constructor. For example, the LinkWebControl won't run into null references because it uses OnInit() to set initial view state values.

■ **Note** Although the WebControl provides a ViewState property, it doesn't provide properties such as Cache, Session, and Application. However, if you need to use these objects to store or retrieve data, you can access them through the static HttpContext.Current property.

Occasionally, you might want more flexibility to customize how view state information is stored. You can take control by overriding the LoadViewState() and SaveViewState() methods. The SaveViewState() method is always called before a control is rendered to HTML. You can return a single serializable object from this method, which will be stored in view state. Similarly, the LoadViewState() method is called when your control is re-created on subsequent postbacks. You receive the object you stored as a parameter, and you can now use it to configure control properties. In most simple controls, you'll have no reason to override these methods. However, sometimes it does become useful, such as when you've developed a more compact way of storing multiple pieces of information in view state using a single object or when you're deriving from an existing control and you want to prevent it from saving its state. You also need this method when you're managing how a complex control saves the state of nested child controls. You'll see an example of this last technique at the end of this chapter

Control State

ASP.NET includes a feature called *control state* for storing the data a control is currently using. Technically, control state works in the same way as view state—it stores serializable information that's stuffed into a hidden field when the page is rendered. In fact, ASP.NET puts the view state information and the control state information into the same hidden field. The difference is that control state is not affected by the EnableViewState property. Even if this is set to false, your control can still store and retrieve information from control state.

■ **Note** The LinkWebControl doesn't require control state. If the developer sets EnableViewState to true, it's probably because the developer expects to set the HyperLink and Text properties in every postback.

Because control state cannot be disabled, you should carefully restrict the amount of information you store. Usually, it should be limited to something critical such as a current page index or a data key value. To use control state, you must begin by overriding the OnInit() method and call Page.RegisterRequiresControlState() to signal that your control needs to access control state.

```
protected override void OnInit(EventArgs e)
{
    base.OnInit(e);
    Page.RegisterRequiresControlState(this);
}
```

Unlike view state, you can't access control state directly through a collection. (This limitation is likely in place to prevent developers from overusing control state when view state is better suited.) Instead, you must override two methods: SaveControlState() and LoadControlState().

These methods use a slightly unusual pattern. The basic idea is that you want to take any control state that has been serialized by the base class and combine that with an object that contains your new serializable object. You can accomplish this with the System.Web.Pair class, as shown here:

```
string someData;

protected override object SaveControlState()
{
    // Get the state from the base class.
    object baseState = base.SaveControlState();

    // Combine it with the state object you want to store,
    // and return final object.
    return new Pair(baseState, someData);
}
```

This technique allows you to store only a single object. If you need to store several pieces of information, consider making a custom class that encapsulates all these details (and make sure it includes the Serializable attribute, as discussed in Chapter 6). Alternatively, you can create a chain of Pair objects:

```
private string stringData;
private int intData;

protected override object SaveControlState()
{
    // Get the state from the base class.
    object baseState = base.SaveControlState();

    // Combine it with the state objects you want to store,
    // and return final object.
    Pair pair1 = new Pair(stringData, intData);
    Pair pair2 = new Pair(baseState, pair1);
    return pair2;
}
```

Unfortunately, this approach quickly becomes confusing.

In the LoadControlState(), you pass on the base class control state and then cast your part of the Pair object to the appropriate type:

```
protected override void LoadControlState(object state)
{
    Pair p = state As Pair;
    if (p != null)
    {
        // Give the base class its state (from p.First).
        base.LoadControlState(p.First);

        // Now you can process the state you saved (from p.Second).
        Pair pair1 = p.Second;
```

```
        stringData = (string)pair1.First
        intData = (int)pair2.Second;
    }
}
```

Postback Data and Change Events

View state and control state help you keep track of your control's contents, but they're not enough for input controls. That's because input controls have an additional ability—they allow users to change their data. For example, consider a text box that's represented as an <input> tag in a form. When the page posts back, the data from the <input> tag is part of the information in the control collection. The TextBox control needs to retrieve this information and update its state accordingly.

To process the data that's posted to the page in your custom control, you need to implement the IPostBackDataHandler interface. By implementing this interface, you indicate to ASP.NET that when a postback occurs, your control needs a chance to examine the postback data. Your control will get this opportunity regardless of which control actually triggers the postback.

The IPostBackDataHandler interface defines two methods:

LoadPostData(): ASP.NET calls this method when the page is posted back, before any control events are raised. It allows you to examine the data that's been posted back and update the state of the control accordingly. However, you shouldn't fire change events at this point, because other controls won't be updated yet.

RaisePostDataChangedEvent(): After all the input controls on a page have been initialized, ASP.NET gives you the chance to fire a change event, if necessary, by calling the RaisePostDataChangedEvent() method.

The best way to understand how these methods work is to examine a basic example. The next control emulates the basic TextBox control. Here's the basic control definition:

```
public class CustomTextBox : WebControl, IPostBackDataHandler
{ ... }
```

As you can see, the control inherits from WebControl and implements IPostBackDataHandler.

The control requires only a single property, Text. The Text is stored in view state and initialized to an empty string in the control constructor. The constructor also sets the base tag to <input>.

```
public CustomTextBox() : base(HtmlTextWriterTag.Input)
{
    Text = "";
}

public string Text
{
    get {return (string)ViewState["Text"];}
    set {ViewState["Text"] = value;}
}
```

Because the base tag is already set to <input>, there's little extra rendering work required. You can handle everything by overriding the AddAttributesToRender() method and adding a type attribute that indicates the <input> control represents a text box and a value attribute that contains the text you want to display in the text box, as follows:

```
protected override void AddAttributesToRender(HtmlTextWriter output)
{
    output.AddAttribute(HtmlTextWriterAttribute.Type, "text");
    output.AddAttribute(HtmlTextWriterAttribute.Value, Text);
    output.AddAttribute("name", this.UniqueID);
    base.AddAttributesToRender(output);
}
```

You must also add the UniqueID for the control using the name attribute. That's because ASP.NET matches this string against the posted data. If you don't add the UniqueID, the LoadPostData() method will never be called, and you won't be able to retrieve posted data.

■ **Tip** Alternatively, you can call the Page.RegisterRequiresPostback() method in the OnInit() method of your custom control. In this case, ASP.NET will add the unique ID if you don't explicitly render it, ensuring that you can still receive the postback.

All that's left is to implement the IPostBackDataHandler methods to give the control the ability to respond to user changes.

The first step is to implement the LoadPostData() method. This method uses two parameters. The second parameter is a collection of values posted to the page. The first parameter is the key value that identifies the data for the current control. Thus, you can access the data for your control using syntax like this:

```
string postedValue = postData[postDataKey];
```

The LoadPostData() also needs to tell ASP.NET whether a change event is required. You can't fire an event at this point, because the other controls may not be properly updated with the posted data. However, you can tell ASP.NET that a change has occurred by returning true. If you return true, ASP.NET will call the RaisePostDataChangedEvent() method after all the controls are initialized. If you return false, ASP.NET will not call this method.

Here's the complete code for the LoadPostData() method in the CustomTextBox:

```
public bool LoadPostData(string postDataKey, NameValueCollection postData)
{
    // Get the posted value and the most recent view state value.
    string postedValue = postData[postDataKey];
    string viewstateValue = Text;

    // If the value changed, then reset the value of the text property
    // and return true so the RaisePostDataChangedEvent will be fired.
    if (viewstateValue != postedValue)
    {
        Text = postedValue;
        return true;
    }
    else
    {
        return false;
    }
}
```

The RaisePostDataChangedEvent() has the relatively simple task of firing the event. However, most ASP.NET controls use an extra layer, whereby the RaisePostDataChangedEvent() calls an On*Xxx*() method and the On*Xxx*() method actually raises the event. This extra layer gives other developers the ability to derive a new control from your control and alter its behavior by overriding the On*Xxx*() method.

Here's the remaining code:

```
public event EventHandler TextChanged;

public void RaisePostDataChangedEvent()
{
    // Call the method to raise the change event.
    OnTextChanged(new EventArgs());
}

protected virtual void OnTextChanged(EventArgs e)
{
    // Check for at least one listener, and then raise the event.
    if (TextChanged != null)
        TextChanged(this, e);
}
```

Figure 27-7 shows a sample page that tests the CustomTextBox control and responds to its event.

***Figure 27-7.** Retrieving posted data in a custom control*

Triggering a Postback

By implementing IPostBackDataHandler, you're able to participate in every postback and retrieve the posted data that belongs to your control. But what if you want to *trigger* a postback? The simplest example of such a control is the Button control. Here, the support is automatic, because according to the HTML Forms standard, a submit button always posts back the page. However, many other rich web controls—including the Calendar and GridView—allow you to trigger a postback by clicking an element or a link somewhere in the rendered HTML. The support for this behavior is provided through another ASP.NET mechanism: a JavaScript function named __doPostBack(). The __doPostBack() function accepts two parameters: the name of the control that's triggering the postback and a string representing additional postback data.

ASP.NET makes it easy to access the __doPostBack() function with the Page.ClientScript.GetPostBackEventReference() method. This method creates a reference to the client-side __doPostBack() function, which you can then render into your control. Usually, you'll place this reference in the onClick attribute of one of the HTML elements in your control. That way, when that HTML element is clicked, the __doPostBack() function is triggered. Of course, JavaScript provides other attributes that you can use, some of which you'll see in Chapter 29.

The best way to see postbacks in action is to create a simple control. The following example demonstrates a clickable image. When clicked, the page is posted back without any additional data.

This control is based on the <img> tag and requires just a single property:

```
public CustomImageButton() : base(HtmlTextWriterTag.Img)
{
    ImageUrl = "";
}

public string ImageUrl
{
    get {return (string)ViewState["ImageUrl"];}
    set {ViewState["ImageUrl"] = value;}
}
```

The only customization you need to do is add a few additional attributes to render. These include the unique control name, the image URL, and the onClick attribute that wires the image up to the __doPostBack() function, as follows:

```
protected override void AddAttributesToRender(HtmlTextWriter output)
{
    output.AddAttribute("name", UniqueID);
    output.AddAttribute("src", ImageUrl);
    output.AddAttribute("onClick",
      Page.ClientScript.GetPostBackEventReference(this, String.Empty));
}
```

This is enough to trigger the postback, but you need to take additional steps to participate in the postback and raise an event. This time, you need to implement the IPostBackEventHandler interface. This interface defines a single method named RaisePostBackEvent():

```
public class CustomImageButton : WebControl, IPostBackEventHandler
{ ... }
```

When the page is posted back, ASP.NET determines which control triggered the postback (by looking at each control's UniqueID property), and if that control implements IPostBackEventHandler, ASP.NET then calls the RaisePostBackEvent() method with the event data. At this point, all the controls on the page have been initialized, and it's safe to fire an event, as shown here:

```
public event EventHandler ImageClicked;

public void RaisePostBackEvent(string eventArgument)
{
    OnImageClicked(new EventArgs());
}

protected virtual void OnImageClicked(EventArgs e)
{
```

```
    // Check for at least one listener, and then raise the event.
    if (ImageClicked != null)
        ImageClicked(this, e);
}
```

Figure 27-8 shows a sample page that tests the CustomImageButton control and responds to its event.

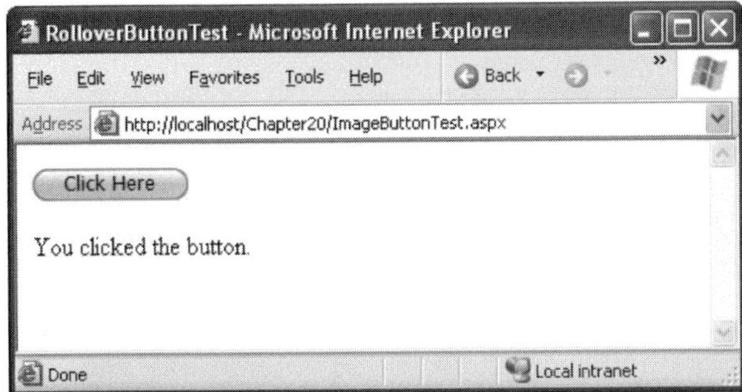

Figure 27-8. Triggering a postback in a custom control

This control doesn't offer any functionality you can't already get with existing ASP.NET web controls, such as the ImageButton. However, it's a great starting point for building something that's much more useful. In Chapter 29, you'll see how to extend this control with JavaScript code to create a rollover button—something with no equivalent in the .NET class library.

■ **Note** Rather than posting back the entire page, you can use a callback to fetch some specific information from the server. Callbacks are described in Chapter 29.

Extending Existing Web Controls

In many situations, you don't need to create a new control from scratch. Some of the functionality might already exist in the basic set of ASP.NET web controls. Because all ASP.NET controls are ordinary classes, you can use their functionality with basic object-oriented practices such as composition (creating a class that uses instances of other classes) and inheritance (creating a class that extends an existing class to change its functionality). In the following sections, you'll see how both tasks apply to custom control design.

Composite Controls

So far you've seen a few custom controls that programmatically generate all the HTML code they need (except for the style properties, which can be inherited from the WebControl class). If you want to write a series of controls, you need to output all the HTML tags, one after the other. Fortunately, ASP.NET includes a feature that can save you this work by allowing you to build your control class out of other, existing web controls.

The basic technique is to create a control class that derives from System.Web.UI.WebControls.CompositeControl (which itself derives from WebControl). Then, you must override the CreateChildControls() method to add the child controls. At this point, you can create one or more control objects, set their properties and event handlers, and finally add them to the Controls collection of the current control. The best part about this approach is that you don't need to customize the rendering code at all. Instead, the rendering work is delegated to the constituent server controls. You also don't need to worry about details such as triggering postbacks and getting postback data, because the child controls will handle these details themselves.

The following example creates a TitledTextBox control that pairs a label (on the left) with a text box (on the right). Here's the class definition for the control:

```
public class TitledTextBox : CompositeControl
{ ... }
```

The CompositeControl implements the INamingContainer interface. This interface doesn't have any methods. It simply instructs ASP.NET to make sure all the child controls have unique ID values. ASP.NET does this by prepending the ID of the server control before the ID of the control. This ensures that there won't be any naming conflict, even if you add several instances of the TitleTextBox control to a web form.

To make life easier, you should track the constituent controls with member variables. This allows you to access them in any method in your control. However, you shouldn't create these controls yet, because that's the function of the CreateChildControls() method.

```
protected Label label;
protected TextBox textBox;
```

The web page won't be able to directly access either of these controls. If you want to allow access to certain properties, you need to add property procedures to your custom control class, as follows:

```
public string Title
{
    get {return (string)ViewState["Title"];}
    set {ViewState["Title"] = value;}
}


public string Text
{
    get {return (string)ViewState["Text"];}
    set {ViewState["Text"] = value;}
}
```

Note that these properties simply store information in view state—they don't directly access the child controls. That's because the child controls might not yet exist. These properties will be applied to the child controls in the CreateChildControls() method. All the controls are rendered in a <span>, which works well. It ensures that if the web page applies font, color, or position attributes to the TitledTextBox control, it will have the desired effect on all the child controls.

Now you can override the CreateChildControls() method to create the Label and TextBox control objects. These objects are separated with one additional control object—a LiteralControl, which simply represents a scrap of HTML. In this example, the LiteralControl wraps two nonbreaking spaces. Here's the complete code for the CreateChildControls() method:

```
protected override void CreateChildControls()
{
    // Add the label.
    label = new Label();
    label.EnableViewState = false;
```

```
        label.Text = Title;
        Controls.Add(label);

        // Add a space.
        Controls.Add(new LiteralControl("  "));

        // Add the text box.
        textBox = new TextBox();
        textBox.EnableViewState = false;
        textBox.Text = Text;
        textBox.TextChanged += new EventHandler(OnTextChanged);
        Controls.Add(textBox);
}
```

The CreateChildControls() code attaches an event handler to the TextBox.TextChanged event. When this event fires, your TitledTextBox should pass it along to the web page as the TitledTextBox.TextChanged event. Here's the code you need to implement the rest of this design:

```
public event EventHandler TextChanged;

protected virtual void OnTextChanged(object sender, EventArgs e)
{
    if (TextChanged != null)
        TextChanged(this, e);
}
```

Figure 27-9 shows a sample page that tests the TitledTextBox control and responds to its event.

You may prefer to follow the earlier approach and use an HtmlTextWriter to get full control over the HTML markup you render. But if you want to handle postbacks and events and create complex controls (such as an extended GridView or a navigational aid), using composite controls can simplify your life dramatically.

Better Design Support for the TitledTextBox

There's one more detail worth adding to this example. If you change the Title or Text properties after the CreateChildControls() method has been called to render the control, you need to make sure that the child controls are regenerated. Although this won't happen in most scenarios (because the controls won't be rendered until the page is rendered), it can happen in the design environment when you tweak the control in the Properties window.

Here's the code that deals with this scenario when the Title property is set. It calls the RecreateChildControls() method, which ensures that the HTML is updated after each change.

```
public string Title
{
    get {return (string)ViewState["Title"];}
    set
    {
        ViewState["Title"] = value;
        if (this.ChildControlsCreated) this.RecreateChildControls();
    }
}
```

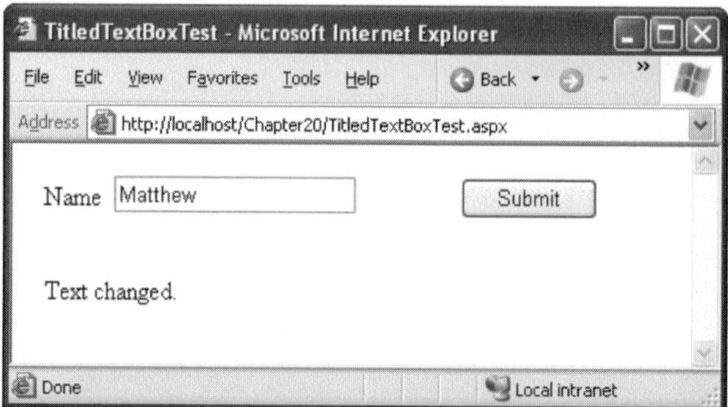

Figure 27-9. Creating a composite control with a label and text box

Derived Controls

Another approach to creating controls is to derive a more specialized control from one of the existing control classes. You can then override or add just the functionality you need, rather than re-creating the whole control. This approach isn't always possible, because some controls keep key pieces of their infrastructure out of site in private methods you can't override. However, when it does work, it can save a lot of work.

Sometimes, you might create a derived control so that you can preinitialize an existing control with certain styles or formatting properties. For example, you could create a custom Calendar or GridView that sets styles in the OnInit() method. That way, when you add this Calendar control, it's already formatted with the look you need. In other cases, you might add entirely new functionality in the form of new methods or properties, as demonstrated in the following example.

Creating a Label for Specific Data

One common reason for creating customized controls is to fine-tune a control for specific types of data. For example, consider the Label control. In its standard form, it's a flexible all-purpose tool that you can use to render text content and insert arbitrary HTML. However, in many situations it would be nice to have a higher-level way to output text—a way that automatically takes care of some of the presentation by applying some built-in rules to translate your content to an HTML-worthy representation. The following example is designed for one of these scenarios. It shows how you can customize the rendering of a derived Label control for a specific type of content.

In Chapter 14, you learned about the Xml control, which allows you to display XML content in a page using an XSLT stylesheet. However, the Xml control doesn't give you any way to show XML content without using an XSLT stylesheet to transform it first. So, what should you do if you want to duplicate the Internet Explorer behavior, which shows a color-coded tree of XML tags? You could implement this approach using an XSLT stylesheet. However, another interesting choice is to create a custom Label control that's designed for XML content. This Label control can apply the formatting you want automatically.

First, consider what happens if you try to display XML content *without* taking any extra steps. In this case, all the XML tags will be interpreted as meaningless HTML tags, and they won't be shown. The display will simply show a jumbled block of text that represents all the content of all elements from start to finish. You can improve upon this situation slightly by using the HttpServerUtility.HtmlEncode() method, which replaces all special HTML characters with the equivalent character entities. However, the XML display you'll create with this approach is still far from ideal. For one thing, all the whitespace will be collapsed, and all the line breaks will be ignored, leading to a long string of text that's not easy to interpret. Figure 27-10 shows this approach with the DvdList.xml document used in Chapter 14.

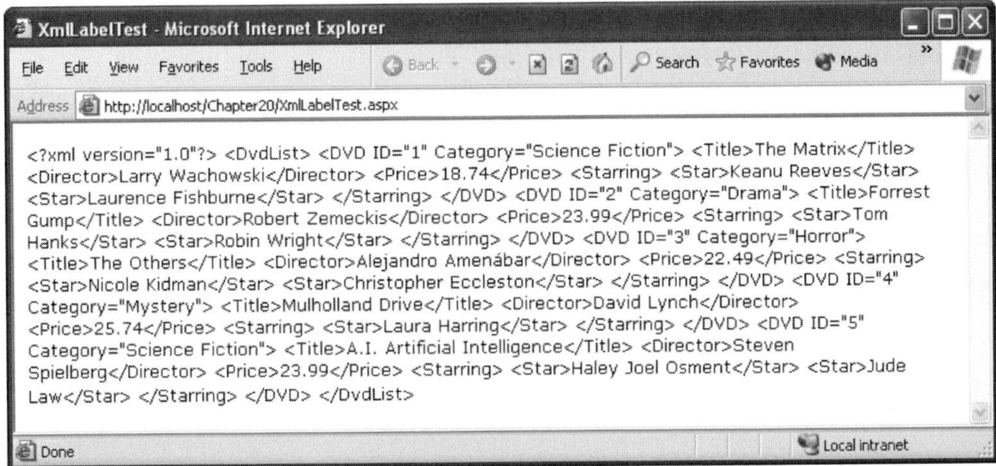

***Figure 27-10.** Displaying XML data with HTML escaping*

The custom XmlLabel control solves this problem by applying formatting to XML start and end tags. This functionality is wrapped into a static method called ConvertXmlTextToHtmlText(), which accepts a string with XML content and returns a string with formatted HTML content. This functionality is implemented as a static method rather than an instance method so that you can call it to format text for display in other controls.

The ConvertXmlTextToHtmlText() method uses a regular expression to find all the XML tags in the string. Here's the expression you need:

```
<([^>]+)>
```

This expression matches the less-than sign (<) that starts the tag, followed by a sequence of one or more characters that aren't greater-than signs (>). The match ends as soon as a greater-than sign is found. This expression matches both start tags (such as <DvdList>) and end tags (such as </DvdList>).

■ **Tip** You might think you could use a simpler regular expression such as <.+> to match a tag. The problem is that regular expressions use *greedy matching*, which means they often match as much as possible. As a result, an expression such as <.+> will match everything between the less-than sign of the first tag and the greater-than sign in the last tag at the end of document. In other words, you'll end up with a single match that obscures other embedded matches. To prevent this behavior, you need to create a regular expression that explicitly specifies what characters you *don't* want to match.

Once you have a match, the next step is to replace this text with the text you really want. The replacement expression is as follows:

```
&lt;<b>$1&gt;</b>
```

This replacement uses the HTML entities for the less-than and greater-than signs (< and >), and it adds an HTML <b> tag to format the text in bold. The $1 is a *back reference* that refers to the bracketed text in the search expression. In this example, the bracketed text includes the full opening tag of the XML element—everything between the opening < and the closing >.

Once the tags are in bold, the last step is to replace the spaces in the string with the   character entity so that whitespace will be preserved. At the same time, it makes sense to replace all the line feeds with an HTML <br />.

Here's the complete code for formatting the XML text. To use this code as written, you must import the System.Text.RegularExpressions namespace.

```
public static string ConvertXmlTextToHtmlText(string inputText)
{
    // Replace all start and end tags.
    string startPattern = @"<([^>]+)>";
    Regex regEx = new Regex(startPattern);
    string outputText = regEx.Replace(inputText, "&lt;<b>$1&gt;</b>");

    outputText = outputText.Replace(" ", " ");
    outputText = outputText.Replace("\r\n", "<br />");
    return outputText;
}
```

The rest of the XmlLabel code is remarkably simple. It doesn't add any new properties. Instead, it simply overrides RenderContents() to ensure that the formatted text is rendered instead of the ordinary text:

```
protected override void RenderContents(HtmlTextWriter output)
{
    string xmlText = XmlLabel.ConvertXmlTextToHtmlText(Text);
    output.Write(xmlText);
}
```

Note that this code doesn't call the base implementation of RenderContents(). That's because the goal of the XmlLabel control is to *replace* the rendering logic for the label text, not to supplement it.

Figure 27-11 shows what ordinary XML data looks like when displayed in the XmlLabel control. Of course, now that you have the basic framework in place, you could do a lot more to perfect this output, including color-coding and automatic indenting.

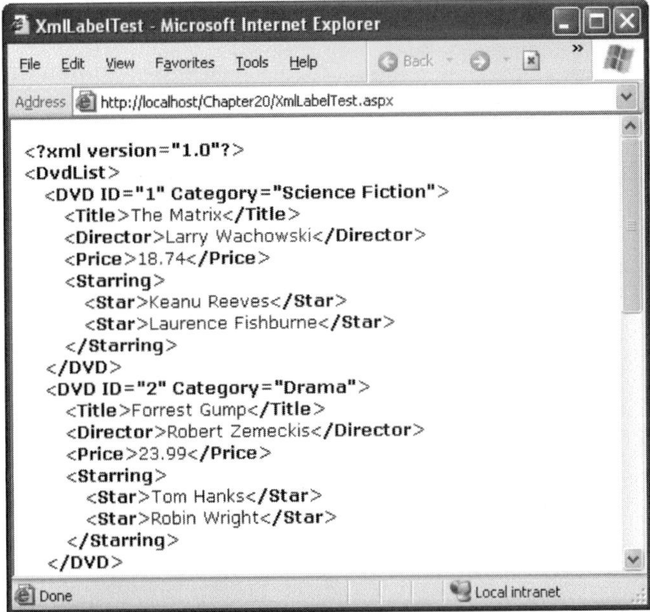

Figure 27-11. Displaying formatted XML data

■ **Tip** You can use a similar technique to create a label that automatically converts mail addresses and URLs to links (wrapped by the <a> tag), formats multiple lines of text into a bulleted list, and so on.

Summary

In this chapter, you learned how to use a variety of techniques to create custom controls. In Chapter 28 and Chapter 29, you'll see examples of custom controls that use GDI+ and JavaScript for advanced solutions.

Even after you've read all these chapters, you still will not have learned everything there is to know about ASP.NET custom control creation. If you want to continue your exploration into the tricks, techniques, and idiosyncrasies of custom control programming, you might be interested in a dedicated book about the topic. You may also be interested in examining third-party control offers at the ASP.NET control gallery (`http://www.asp.net/community/control-gallery`). If you want to learn more about designing proper design-time support for your controls, refer to the bonus "Design-Time Support" chapter that's available for download from the book web page.

CHAPTER 28

■ ■ ■

Graphics, GDI+, and Charting

In Chapter 4, you learned about basic web controls for displaying graphics, such as the Image and ImageButton controls. Both allow you to display an image, and the ImageButton control also fires a Click event that gives you the exact mouse coordinates. But in a modern web application, you'll often want much more.

In this chapter, you'll learn about three features that give you greater control over the look and feel of your website. First, you'll learn about the ImageMap control, which allows you to define invisible shaped regions over an image and react when they're clicked. Next you'll tackle GDI+, a .NET model for rendering dynamic graphics. You'll learn how to render custom graphics with GDI+, how to embed these graphics in a web page, and how to create custom controls that use GDI+. Finally, we'll show you the Chart control, which allows you to create complex and sophisticated charts.

The ImageMap Control

Web pages commonly include complex graphics, where different actions are taken depending on what part of the graphic is clicked. ASP.NET developers can use several tricks to implement this design:

Stacked image controls: Multiple borderless pictures will look like one graphic when carefully positioned next to each other. You can then handle the clicks of each control separately. This approach works well for buttons and navigational controls that have defined, rectangular edges.

ImageButton: When an ImageButton control is clicked, it provides the coordinates where the click was made. You can examine these coordinates in your server-side code and determine what region was clicked programmatically. This technique is flexible but tedious and error-prone to code.

ImageMap: With the ImageMap control, you can define separate regions and give each one a unique name. One advantage of this approach is that as the user moves the mouse pointer over the image, it changes to a hand only when the user is positioned over a defined region. Thus, this approach works particularly well for detailed images that have small hotspots.

The ImageMap control provides a server-side abstraction over the HTML <map> and <area> tags, which define an image map. The ImageMap control renders itself as a <map> tag. You define regions by adding HotSpot objects to the ImageMap.HotSpots collection, and each region is rendered as an <area> tag inside the <map> tag. Just before the <map> tag, ASP.NET renders the linked <img> tag that shows the picture and uses the image map.

For example, if you create a map named ImageMap1 with three circular hotspots, the ImageMap control will render markup like this:

```
<img id="ImageMap1" src="cds.jpg" usemap="#ImageMapImageMap1"
 style="border-width:0px;" />
```

```
<map name="ImageMapImageMap1">
  <area shape="circle" coords="272,83,83"
   href="javascript:__doPostBack('ImageMap1','0')" title="DVDs" alt="DVDs" />
  <area shape="circle" coords="217,221,83"
   href="javascript:__doPostBack('ImageMap1','1')" title="Media" alt="Media" />
  <area shape="circle" coords="92,173,83"
   href="javascript:__doPostBack('ImageMap1','2')" title="CDs" alt="CDs" />
</map>
```

Creating Hotspots

You can add an ImageMap control to a form in much the same way as an Image control. Just drop it onto the page, and set the ImageUrl property to the name of the image file you want to use. You can also use the usual ImageAlign, BorderStyle, BorderWidth, and BorderColor properties.

To define the clickable regions, you need to add HotSpot objects to the ImageMap.HotSpots property. You can use three derived classes: CircleHotSpot, RectangleHotSpot, and PolygonHotSpot, matching the three shape types defined by HTML.

You need to know the exact coordinates of the hotspot you want to create. The Visual Studio ImageMap designer doesn't let you define regions visually. We tend to use Expression Web, as shown in Figure 28-1, but any HTML authoring program will do.

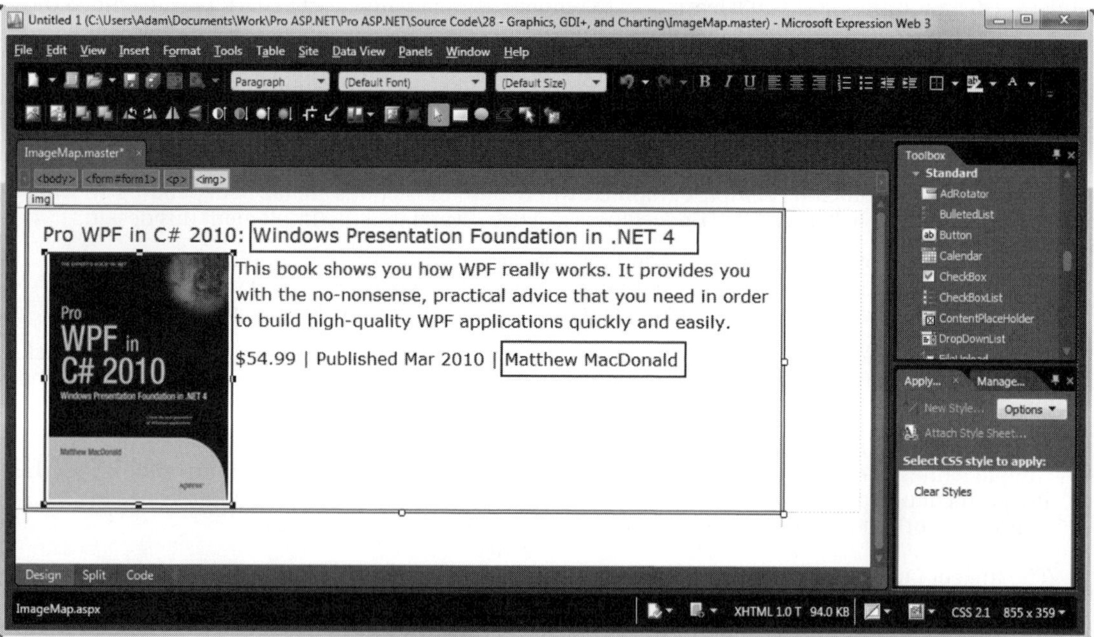

Figure 28-1. Configuring hotspots in Microsoft Expression Web

Once you've tweaked the hotspots to perfection, you can look at the source code to find the coordinates. When defining a rectangle, you define the top-left and bottom-right corners. The order of coordinates is left X, top Y, right X, and bottom Y. When defining a polygon, you can have as many points as you like. The browser draws a line from one point to another to create the shape. You list the X and Y coordinates for your points in pairs like this: X1, Y1, X2, Y2, X3, Y3, and so on. The HTML standard recommends that you end at the same point with which you started.

In the case of a circle, three details are important: the X coordinate, the Y coordinate, and the radius. They appear in that order in the <area> tag:

```
<area shape="circle" coords="272, 83, 83" ...>
```

The circles center is at (272, 83), and the radius is 83 pixels.

■ **Tip** You can define overlapping hotspots, but the hotspot that is defined first will handle the click.

Once you've determined your hotspots, you can add the corresponding HotSpot objects. Here's the ImageMap for Figure 28-1, with three hotspots:

```
<asp:ImageMap ID="ImageMap1" runat="server" ImageUrl="CoverShot.png" HotSpotMode="PostBack"
    OnClick="ImageMap1_Click">
    <asp:RectangleHotSpot Top="41" Left="16" Bottom="285" Right="206"/>
    <asp:RectangleHotSpot Top="125" Left="475" Bottom="160" Right="659"/>
    <asp:RectangleHotSpot Top="10" Left="222" Bottom="41" Right="671"/>
</asp:ImageMap>
```

Rather than coding this by hand, you can select your ImageMap and click the ellipsis next to the HotSpots property in the Properties window. This opens a collection editor where you can add and modify each hotspot.

Once you've defined the hotspots, you can test them in a browser. When you move the mouse pointer over a hotspot, it changes into a hand.

Handling Hotspot Clicks

The next step is to make the hotspots clickable. A hotspot can trigger one of two actions—it can navigate to a new page, or it can post back your page (and fire the ImageMap.Click event). To choose which option you prefer, simply set the ImageMap.HotSpotMode property.

■ **Tip** When you set the ImageMap.HotSpotMode property, it applies to all hotspots. You can also override this setting for individual hotspots by setting the HotSpot.HotSpotMode property. This allows you to have some hotspots that post back the page and others that trigger page navigation.

To disable hotspots completely, use HotSpotMode.Inactive. If you use HotSpotMode.Navigate, you need to set the URL for each hotspot using the HotSpot.NavigateUrl property. If you use HotSpotMode.PostBack, you should give each hotspot a unique HotSpot.PostBackValue. This allows you to identify which hotspot triggered the postback in the Click event.

Here's the revised ImageMap control declaration that adds these details:

```
<asp:ImageMap ID="ImageMap1" runat="server" ImageUrl="CoverShot.png"
    HotSpotMode="PostBack" OnClick="ImageMap1_Click">
    <asp:RectangleHotSpot Top="41" Left="16" Bottom="285" Right="206"
        PostBackValue="Cover" />
    <asp:RectangleHotSpot Top="125" Left="475" Bottom="160" Right="659"
        PostBackValue="Name" />
    <asp:RectangleHotSpot Top="10" Left="222" Bottom="41" Right="671"
        PostBackValue="Subtitle" />
</asp:ImageMap>
```

Here's the Click event handler, which simply displays the name of the clicked hotspot:

```
protected void ImageMap1_Click(object sender, ImageMapEventArgs e)
{
    Label1.Text = "You clicked: " + e.PostBackValue;
}
```

Figure 28-2 shows the resulting page.

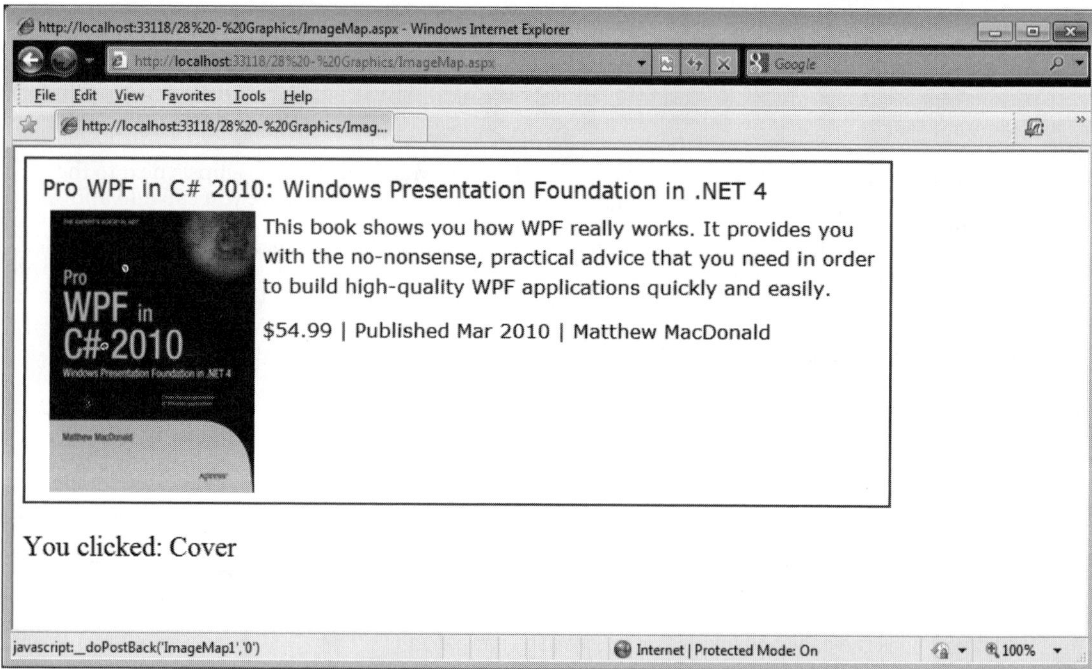

Figure 28-2. *Handling a hotspot click*

A Custom Hotspot

The ImageMap control supports any HotSpot-derived class. ASP.NET includes the three that correspond to the basic types of <area> shapes defined by HTML. However, you can create your own hotspots by deriving your own custom class from HotSpot.

Obviously, a custom hotspot class can't do anything that falls outside the HTML standard. For example, it would be nice to have an ellipse and other curved shapes, but that just isn't available. However, you can create a variety of complex multisided shapes, such as triangles, octagons, diamonds, and so on, using the polygon type. By deriving a custom HotSpot, you can create a higher-level model that generates the appropriate polygon based on a few basic pieces of information (such as the center coordinate and the radius).

For example, the following class presents a simple custom triangle. This triangle is created based on a center point, width, and height.

```
namespace CustomHotSpots
{
    public class TriangleHotSpot : HotSpot
    {
        public TriangleHotSpot()
        {
            Width = 0;
            Height = 0;
            X = 0;
            Y = 0;
        }

        public int Width
        {
            get { return (int)ViewState["Width"]; }
            set { ViewState["Width"] = value; }
        }

        public int Height
        {
            get { return (int)ViewState["Height"]; }
            set { ViewState["Height"] = value; }
        }
        // X and Y are the coordinates of the center point.
        public int X
        {
            get { return (int)ViewState["X"]; }
            set { ViewState["X"] = value; }
        }

        public int Y
        {
            get { return (int)ViewState["Y"]; }
            set { ViewState["Y"] = value; }
        }
        ...
```

When creating a custom HotSpot, you must override the MarkupName property to return the type of shape you are creating. The valid choices are circle, rectangle, and polygon. This information is placed into the shape attribute of the <area> tag.

```
        ...
        protected override string MarkupName
        {
            get { return "polygon"; }
        }
        ...
```

Finally, you need to override the GetCoordinates() method to return the string for the cords attribute. For a polygon, this must be a comma-separated series of points in X, Y pairs. Here's the code that creates a simple triangle, with a bottom edge and a single point in the top center:

```
        ...
        public override string GetCoordinates()
        {
            // Top coordinate.
            int topX = X;
            int topY = Y - Height / 2;

            // Bottom-left coordinate.
            int btmLeftX = X - Width / 2;
            int btmLeftY = Y + Height / 2;

            // Bottom-right coordinate.
            int btmRightX = X + Width / 2;
            int btmRightY = Y + Height / 2;

            return topX.ToString() + "," + topY.ToString() + "," +
              btmLeftX.ToString() + "," + btmLeftY.ToString() + "," +
              btmRightX.ToString() + "," + btmRightY.ToString();
        }
    }
}
```

Now you can use your custom hotspot much as you use a custom control. The first step is to register a tag prefix for your namespace, as shown here:

```
<%@ Register TagPrefix="chs" Namespace="CustomHotSpots" %>
```

And here's an ImageMap that uses the TriangleHotSpot and redirects users to a new URL when the triangle is clicked:

```
<asp:ImageMap ID="ImageMap1" runat="server" ImageUrl="./triangle.gif">
  <chs:TriangleHotSpot AlternateText="Triangle"
   NavigateUrl="http://en.wikipedia.org/wiki/Triangle"
   X="140" Y="50" Height="75" Width="85" />
</asp:ImageMap>
```

Drawing with GDI+

GDI+ is an general-purpose drawing model for .NET applications. GDI+ has a number of uses in .NET, including writing documents to the printer, displaying graphics in a Windows application, and rendering graphics in a web page.

Using GDI+ code to draw a graphic is slower than using a static image file. However, it gives you much more freedom and enables several possibilities that weren't possible (or were prohibitively difficult) in earlier web development platforms, such as classic ASP. For example, you can create graphics that incorporate user-specific information, and you can render charts and graphs on the fly based on the records in a database.

The heart of GDI+ programming is the System.Drawing.Graphics class. The Graphics class encapsulates a GDI+ drawing surface, whether it is a window, a print document, or an in-memory bitmap. ASP.NET developers rarely have the need to paint windows or print documents, so it is the last option that is the most commonly used in web applications.

To use GDI+ in ASP.NET, you need to follow a sequence of four steps:

1. Create an in-memory bitmap image where you'll perform all your drawing.
2. Create a GDI+ graphics context for the image. This gives you an instance of System.Drawing.Graphics.
3. Perform the drawing using the methods of the Graphics instance. You can draw and fill lines and shapes, and you can copy bitmap content from existing files.
4. Write the image to the browser, using the Response.OutputStream property.

In the following sections, you'll see several examples of web pages that use GDI+. Before continuing, you may want to ensure that the following namespaces are imported:

```
using System.Drawing;
using System.Drawing.Drawing2D;
using System.Drawing.Imaging;
```

The System.Drawing namespace defines many of the fundamental ingredients for drawing, including pens, brushes, and bitmaps. The System.Drawing.Drawing2D namespace adds other useful details such as the flexible GraphicsPath class, while System.Drawing.Imaging includes the ImageFormat namespace that lets you choose the graphics format in which your bitmap will be rendered when it is sent to the client.

Simple Drawing

The following example demonstrates the simplest possible GDI+ page. All the work is performed in the event handler for the Page.Load event.

The first step is to create the in-memory bitmap by creating an instance of the System.Drawing.Bitmap class. When you create this object, you need to specify the height and width of the image in pixels as constructor arguments. You should make the size as small as possible. Not only will a larger bitmap consume additional server memory while your code is executing, but the size of the rendered content you send to the client will also increase, slowing down the transmission.

```
// Create the in-memory bitmap where you will draw the image.
// This bitmap is 300 pixels wide and 50 pixels high.
Bitmap image = new Bitmap(300, 50);
```

The next step is to create a GDI+ graphics context for the image, which is represented by the System.Drawing.Graphics object. This object provides the methods that allow you to draw on the in-memory bitmap. To create a Graphics object from an Bitmap object, you use the static Graphics.FromImage method, as shown here:

```
Graphics g = Graphics.FromImage(image);
```

Now comes the interesting part. Using the methods of the Graphics class, you can draw text, shapes, and images on the bitmap. In this example, the drawing code is exceedingly simple. It fills the graphic with a solid white background using the FillRectangle method of the Graphics object. (Every pixel is initially set to black in a new bitmap.)

```
// Draw a solid white rectangle.
// Start from point (1, 1).
// Make it 298 pixels wide and 48 pixels high.
g.FillRectangle(Brushes.White, 1, 1, 298, 48);
```

The FillRectangle method requires several arguments. The first argument sets the color, the next two parameters set the starting point, and the final two parameters set the width and height. When measuring pixels, the point (0, 0) is the top-left corner of your image in (X, Y) coordinates. The X coordinate increases as you go farther to the right, and the Y coordinate increases as you go farther down. In the example, the image is 300 pixels wide and 50 pixels high, which means the point (299, 49) is the bottom-right corner.

In the example, we have left a 1-pixel border unfilled. This has the effect of leaving a narrow border of the original black color. The next portion of the drawing code renders a static label message. To do this, we create a System.Drawing.Font object representing the font we want to use. This shouldn't be confused with the FontInfo object you use with ASP.NET controls to specify the requested font for a web page. Unlike FontInfo, Font represents a single, specific font (including typeface, size, and style) that's installed on the current computer. When you create a Font object, you specify the font name, point size, and style, as shown here:

```
Font font = new Font("Impact", 20, FontStyle.Regular);
```

■ **Tip** Because this image is generated on the server, you can use any font that the server has installed when creating the graphic. The client won't need to have the same font, because the client receives the text as a rendered image.

To render the text, you use the DrawString method of the Graphics object. As with the FillRectangle object, you need to specify the coordinates where the drawing should begin. This point represents the top-left corner of the text block. In this case, the point (10, 5) is used, which gives a distance of 10 pixels from the left and 5 pixels from the top.

```
g.DrawString("This is a test.", font, Brushes.Blue, 10, 5);
```

Once the image is complete, you can send it to the browser using the Image.Save method. You are saving the image to the browser's response stream. It gets sent to the client and displayed in the browser. When you write directly to the response stream like this, your image replaces any other web-page data and bypasses the web control model.

```
// Render the image to the output stream.
image.Save(Response.OutputStream,
  System.Drawing.Imaging.ImageFormat.Gif);
```

■ **Tip** You can save an image to any valid stream, including a FileStream. This technique allows you to save dynamically generated images to disk so you can use them later in other web pages.

Finally, call the Dispose method for the image and graphics context as shown next. Both hold onto some unmanaged resources that won't be released right away, and if you are generating a high volume of images, the resource demands can impact your server.

```
g.Dispose();
image.Dispose();
```

Figure 28-3 shows the completed web page created by this code.

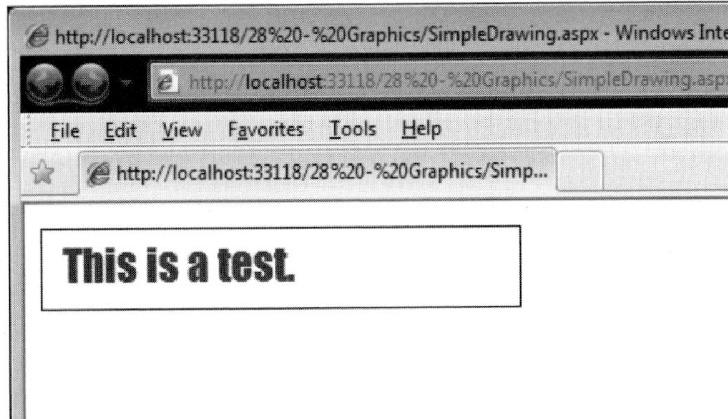

Figure 28-3. *A graphical label*

Image Format and Quality

When you save the image, you can choose the format you want to use. JPEG offers the best color support and graphics, although it uses compression that can lose detail and make text look fuzzy. GIF is often a better choice for graphics containing text, but it doesn't offer good support for color. In .NET, every GIF uses a fixed palette with 256 generic colors. If you use a color that doesn't map to one of these presets, the color will be dithered, leading to a less-than-optimal graphic.

■ **Tip** Another choice is the PNG format, which gives you the best of both the JPEG and GIF formats. However, the PNG format doesn't work directly in a web page—instead, you need to wrap it in an <img> tag. Later, in the section "Embedding Dynamic Graphics in a Web Page," you'll see how to take this step.

Quality isn't just determined by the image format. It also depends on the way you render the original bitmap. GDI+ allows you to choose between optimizing your drawing code for appearance or speed. When you choose to optimize for the best appearance, .NET uses rendering techniques such as *antialiasing* to improve the drawing.

Antialiasing smoothes jagged edges in shapes and text. It works by adding shading at the border of an edge. For example, gray shading might be added to the edge of a black curve to make a corner look smoother. Figure 28-4 shows a close-up of an antialiased ellipse.

Figure 28-4. *Antialiasing with an ellipse*

To use smoothing in your applications, you set the SmoothingMode property of the Graphics object. You can choose between None (the default), HighSpeed, AntiAlias, and HighQuality (which is similar to AntiAlias but uses other, slower optimizations that improve the display on LCD screens). The Graphics.SmoothingMode property is one of the few stateful Graphics members. This means you set it before you begin drawing, and it applies to any text or shapes you draw until the Graphics object is disposed of.

```
g.SmoothingMode = SmoothingMode.AntiAlias;
```

■ **Tip** Antialiasing makes the most difference when you're displaying curves. That means it will dramatically improve the appearance of ellipses, circles, and arcs, but it won't make any difference with straight lines, squares, and rectangles.

You can also use antialiasing with fonts to soften jagged edges on text. You can set the Graphics.Text-RenderingHint property to ensure optimized text. You can choose between SingleBitPerPixelGridFit (fastest performance and lowest quality), AntiAlias (good quality due to smoothing), AntiAliasGridFit (better quality due to smoothing and hinting but slower performance), and ClearTypeGridFit (the best quality on an LCD display). Or you can use the SystemDefault value to apply whatever font-smoothing settings the user has configured. SystemDefault is the default setting, and the default system settings for most computers enable text antialiasing. Even if you don't set this, your dynamically rendered text will usually be drawn in high quality. However, because you can't necessarily control the system settings of the web server, it's a good practice to specify this setting explicitly if you need to draw text in an image.

The Graphics Class

The Graphics class also provides methods for drawing specific kinds of shapes, images, and text. Table 28-1 describes these methods, some of which are used in the examples in this chapter.

Table 28-1. *Graphics Class Methods for Drawing*

Method	Description
DrawArc()	Draws an arc representing a portion of an ellipse specified by a pair of coordinates, a width, and a height.
DrawBezier() and DrawBeziers()	Draws the infamous and attractive Bezier curve, which is defined by four control points.
DrawClosedCurve()	Draws a curve and then closes it off by connecting the endpoints.
DrawCurve()	Draws a curve (technically, a cardinal spline).
DrawEllipse()	Draws an ellipse defined by a bounding rectangle specified by a pair of coordinates, a height, and a width.
DrawIcon() and DrawIconUnstreched()	Draws the icon represented by an Icon object and (optionally) stretches it to fit a given rectangle.
DrawImage	Draws the image represented by an Image-derived object (for example, a Bitmap object that's been loaded from a file) and stretches it to fit a rectangular region.
DrawImageUnscaled() and DrawImageUnscaledAndClipped()	Draws the image represented by an Image-derived object with no scaling and (optionally) clips it to fit the rectangular region you specify.
DrawLine() and DrawLines()	Draws one or more lines. Each line connects the two points specified by coordinate pairs.
DrawPath()	Draws a GraphicsPath object, which can represent a combination of curves and shapes.
DrawPie()	Draws a "piece-of-pie" shape defined by an ellipse specified by a coordinate pair, a width, a height, and two radial lines.
DrawPolygon()	Draws a multisided polygon defined by an array of points.
DrawRectangle() and DrawRectangles()	Draws one or more rectangles. Each rectangle is defined by a starting coordinate pair and width and height.
DrawString()	Draws a string of text in a given font.

Method	Description
FillClosedCurve()	Draws a curve, closes it off by connecting the endpoints, and fills it.
FillEllipse()	Fills the interior of an ellipse.
FillPath()	Fills the shape represented by a GraphicsPath object.
FillPie()	Fills the interior of a "piece-of-pie" shape.
FillPolygon()	Fills the interior of a polygon.
FillRectangle() and FillRectangles()	Fills the interior of one or more rectangles.

The DrawXxx() methods draw outlines (for example, the edge around a rectangle). The FillXxx() methods paint solid regions (for example, the actual surface inside the borders of a rectangle). The only exception is the DrawString() method, which draws filled-in text using a font you specify, and DrawIcon() and DrawImage(), which copy bitmap images onto the drawing surface.

If you want to create a shape that has both an outline in one color and a fill in another color, you need to combine both a draw and a fill method. Here's an example that first paints a white rectangle and then adds a green border around it:

```
g.FillRectangle(Brushes.White, 0, 0, 300, 50);
g.DrawRectangle(Pens.Green, 0, 0, 299, 49);
```

■ **Note** You won't receive an exception if you specify coordinates that are not in the drawing area, but the content you draw that's off the edge won't appear in the final image. In some cases, this means a partial shape may appear (which might be exactly the effect you want).

You'll notice that when you use a fill method, you need to specify a Brush object. When you use a draw method, you need to specify a Pen object. In the example, the code uses a prebuilt Pen and Brush object, which can be retrieved from the Pens and Brushes classes, respectively. Brushes retrieved in this way always correspond to solid colors. Pens retrieved in this way are always 1 pixel wide. Later in this chapter (in the Pens and Brushes sections), you'll learn how to create your own custom pens and brushes.

Using the techniques you've learned, it's easy to create a simple web page that draws a more complex GDI+ image. The next example uses the Graphics class to draw an ellipse, a text message, and an image from a file.

Here's the code you'll need:

```
protected void Page_Load(Object sender, EventArgs e)
{
    // Create the in-memory bitmap where you will draw the image.
    // This bitmap is 450 pixels wide and 100 pixels high.
    Bitmap image = new Bitmap(450, 100);
```

```
    Graphics g = Graphics.FromImage(image);

    // Ensure high-quality curves.
    g.SmoothingMode = SmoothingMode.AntiAlias;

    // Paint the background.
    g.FillRectangle(Brushes.White, 0, 0, 450, 100);

    // Add an ellipse.
    g.FillEllipse(Brushes.PaleGoldenrod, 120, 13, 300, 50);
    g.DrawEllipse(Pens.Green, 120, 13, 299, 49);

    // Draw some text using a fancy font.
    Font font = new Font("Harrington", 20, FontStyle.Bold);
    g.DrawString("Oranges are tasty!", font, Brushes.DarkOrange, 150, 20);

    // Add a graphic from a file.
    System.Drawing.Image orangeImage =
      System.Drawing.Image.FromFile(Server.MapPath("oranges.gif"));
    g.DrawImageUnscaled(orangeImage, 0, 0);

    // Render the image to the output stream.
    image.Save(Response.OutputStream,
     System.Drawing.Imaging.ImageFormat.Jpeg);

    // Clean up.
    g.Dispose();
    image.Dispose();
}
```

Figure 28-5 shows the resulting web page.

***Figure 28-5.** Using multiple elements in a drawing*

Using a GraphicsPath

Two interesting methods that we haven't covered yet are DrawPath and FillPath, which work with the GraphicsPath class in the System.Drawing.Drawing2D namespace.

The GraphicsPath class encapsulates a series of connected lines, curves, and text. To build a GraphicsPath object, you simply create a new instance and use the methods in Table 28-2 to add all the required elements.

```
GraphicsPath path = new GraphicsPath();
path.AddEllipse(0, 0, 100, 50);
path.AddRectangle(new Rectangle(100, 50, 100, 50));
```

Once you've created a GraphicsPath object, you can use the Graphics.DrawPath method to draw its outline and the Graphics.FillPath method to paint its fill region:

```
g.DrawPath(Pens.Black, path);
g.FillPath(Brushes.Yellow, path);
```

Table 28-2. *GraphicsPath Methods*

Method	Description
AddArc()	Draws an arc representing a portion of an ellipse specified by a pair of coordinates, a width, and a height.
AddBezier() and AddBeziers()	Draws the infamous and attractive Bezier curve, which is defined by four control points.
AddClosedCurve()	Draws a curve and then closes it off by connecting the endpoints.
AddCurve()	Draws a curve (technically, a cardinal spline).
AddEllipse()	Draws an ellipse defined by a bounding rectangle specified by a pair of coordinates, a height, and a width.
AddLine() and AddLines()	Draws a line connecting the two points specified by coordinate pairs.
AddPath()	Adds another GraphicsPath object to this GraphicsPath object.
AddPie()	Draws a "piece-of-pie" shape defined by an ellipse specified by a coordinate pair, a width, a height, and two radial lines.
AddPolygon()	Draws a multisided polygon defined by an array of points.
AddRectangle() and AddRectangles()	Draws an ordinary rectangle specified by a starting coordinate pair and width and height.
AddString()	Draws a string of text in a given font.

Method	Description
StartFigure() and CloseFigure()	StartFigure() defines the start of a new closed figure. When you use CloseFigure(), the starting point will be joined to the endpoint by an additional line.
Transform(), Warp(), and Widen()	Applies a matrix transform, a warp transform (defined by a rectangle and parallelogram), and an expansion, respectively.

Optionally, you can also create a solid, filled figure from separate line segments. To do this, you first call the StartFigure method. Then you add the required curves and lines using the appropriate methods. When finished, you call the CloseFigure method to close off the shape by drawing a line from the endpoint to the starting point. You can use these methods multiple times to add several closed figures to a single GraphicsPath object. Here's an example that draws a single figure based on an arc and a line:

```
GraphicsPath path = new GraphicsPath();
path.StartFigure();
path.AddArc(10, 10, 100, 100, 20, 50);
path.AddLine(20, 100, 70, 230);
path.CloseFigure();
```

Pens

When you use the DrawXxx methods from the Graphics class, the border of the shape or curve is drawn with the Pen object you supply. You can retrieve a standard pen using one of the static properties from the System.Drawing.Pens class. These pens all have a width of 1 pixel and differ only in their color.

```
Pen myPen = Pens.Black;
```

You can create a custom Pen object to configure all the properties described in Table 28-3. Here's an example:

```
Pen myPen = new Pen(Color.Red);
myPen.DashCap = DashCap.Triangle;
myPen.DashStyle = DashStyle.DashDotDot;
g.DrawLine(myPen, 0, 0, 10, 0);
```

Table 28-3. *Pen Members*

Member	Description
DashPattern	Defines a dash style for broken lines using an array of dashes and spaces.
DashStyle	Defines a dash style for broken lines using the DashStyle enumeration.
LineJoin	Defines how connecting lines in a shape will be joined.
PenType	Defines the type of fill that will be used for the line. Typically this will be SolidColor, but you can also use a gradient, bitmap texture, or hatch pattern by supplying a brush object when you create the pen. You cannot set the PenType through this property, however, because it is read-only.

Member	Description
StartCap and EndCap	Determines how the beginning and ends of lines will be rendered. You can also define a custom line cap by creating a CustomLineCap object (typically by using a GraphicsPath) and then assigning it to the CustomStartCap or CustomEndCap property.
Width	Defines the pixel width of lines drawn by this pen.

The easiest way to understand the different LineCap and DashStyle properties is to create a test page that enumerates the options. The following web-page code creates a drawing that does exactly that:

```
protected void Page_Load(object sender, System.EventArgs e)
{
    // Create the in-memory bitmap where you will draw the image.
    // This bitmap is 500 pixels wide and 400 pixels high.
    Bitmap image = new Bitmap(500, 400);
    Graphics g = Graphics.FromImage(image);

    // Paint the background.
    g.FillRectangle(Brushes.White, 0, 0, 500, 400);

    // Create a pen to use for all the examples.
    Pen myPen = new Pen(Color.Blue, 10);

    // The y variable tracks the current y (up/down) position
    // in the image.
    int y  = 60;

    // Draw an example of each LineCap style in the first column (left).
    g.DrawString("LineCap Choices", new Font("Tahoma", 15, FontStyle.Bold),
      Brushes.Blue, 0, 10);
    foreach (LineCap cap in System.Enum.GetValues(typeof(LineCap)))
    {
        myPen.StartCap = cap;
        myPen.EndCap = cap;
        g.DrawLine(myPen, 20, y, 100, y);
        g.DrawString(cap.ToString(), new Font("Tahoma", 8),
          Brushes.Black, 120, y - 10);
        y += 30;
    }

    // Draw an example of each DashStyle in the second column (right).
    y = 60;
    g.DrawString("DashStyle Choices", new Font("Tahoma", 15,
      FontStyle.Bold), Brushes.Blue, 200, 10);
    foreach (DashStyle dash in System.Enum.GetValues(typeof(DashStyle)))
    {
        // Configure the pen.
        myPen.DashStyle = dash;

        // Draw a short line segment.
```

```
        g.DrawLine(myPen, 220, y, 300, y);

        // Add a text label.
        g.DrawString(dash.ToString(), new Font("Tahoma", 8), Brushes.Black,
          320, y - 10);

        // Move down one line.
        y += 30;
    }

    // Render the image to the output stream.
    image.Save(Response.OutputStream,
      System.Drawing.Imaging.ImageFormat.Gif);

    g.Dispose();
    image.Dispose();
}
```

Figure 28-6 shows the resulting web page.

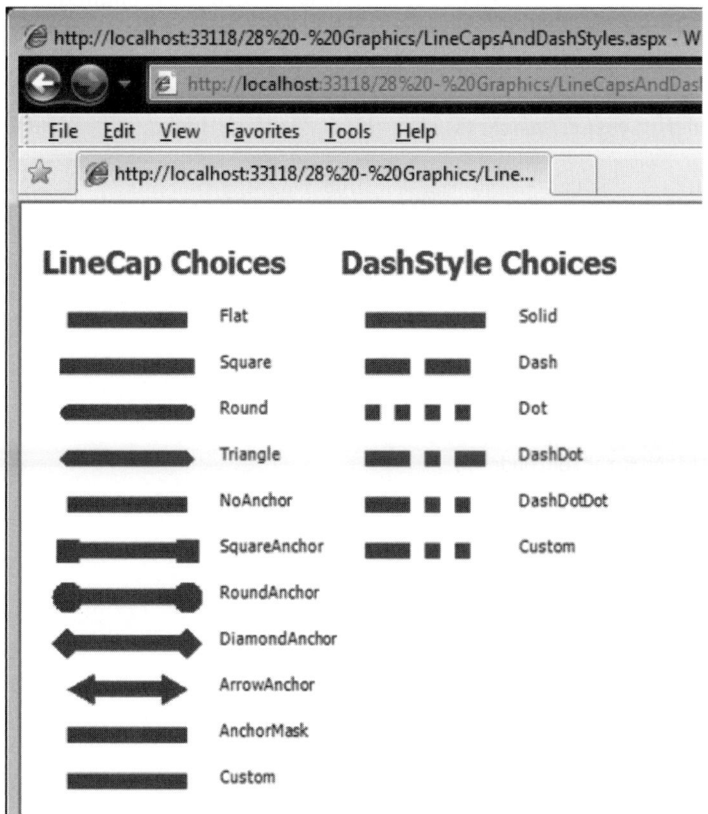

Figure 28-6. Different pen options

Brushes

Brushes are used to fill the space between lines. Brushes are used when drawing text or when using any of the FillXxx methods of the Graphics class for painting the inside a shape. You can quickly retrieve a predefined solid brush using a static property from the Brushes class, as shown here:

```
Brush myBrush = Brushes.White;
```

You can also create a custom brush. Simple solid brushes are created from the SolidBrush class, and more complex brushes are available through other classes:

HatchBrush: A HatchBrush has a foreground color, a background color, and a hatch style that determines how these colors are combined. Typically, colors are interspersed using stripes, grids, or dots, but you can even select unusual pattern styles such as bricks, confetti, weave, and shingles.

LinearGradientBrush: The LinearGradientBrush allows you to blend two colors in a gradient pattern. You can choose any two colors (as with the hatch brush) and then choose to blend horizontally (from left to right), vertically (from top to bottom), diagonally (from the top-left corner to the bottom-right corner), or diagonally backward (from the top-right corner to the bottom-left corner). You can also specify the origin point for either side of the gradient.

TextureBrush: The TextureBrush attaches a bitmap to a brush. The image is tiled in the painted portion of the brush, whether it is text or a simple rectangle.

Here's an example of the drawing logic you need to test all the styles of LinearGradientBrush:

```
protected void Page_Load(object sender, System.EventArgs e)
{
    // Create the in-memory bitmap.
    Bitmap image = new Bitmap(300, 300);
    Graphics g = Graphics.FromImage(image);

    // Paint the background.
    g.FillRectangle(Brushes.White, 0, 0, 300, 300);

    // Show a rectangle with each type of gradient.
    LinearGradientBrush myBrush;
    int y = 20;
    foreach (LinearGradientMode gradientStyle in
      System.Enum.GetValues(typeof(LinearGradientMode)))
    {
        // Configure the brush.
        myBrush = new LinearGradientBrush(new Rectangle(20, y, 100, 60),
          Color.Violet, Color.White, gradientStyle);

        // Draw a small rectangle and add a text label.
        g.FillRectangle(myBrush, 20, y, 100, 60);
        g.DrawString(gradientStyle.ToString(), new Font("Tahoma", 8),
          Brushes.Black, 130, y + 20);

        // Move to the next line.
        y += 70;
    }

    // Render the image to the output stream.
```

```
    image.Save(Response.OutputStream,
     System.Drawing.Imaging.ImageFormat.Jpeg);

    g.Dispose();
    image.Dispose();
}
```

Figure 28-7 shows the result.

■ **Tip** You can also create a pen that draws using the fill style of a brush. This allows you to draw lines that are filled with gradients and textures. To do so, begin by creating the appropriate brush and then create a new pen. One of the overloaded pen constructor methods accepts a reference to a brush—that's the one you need to use for a brush-based pen.

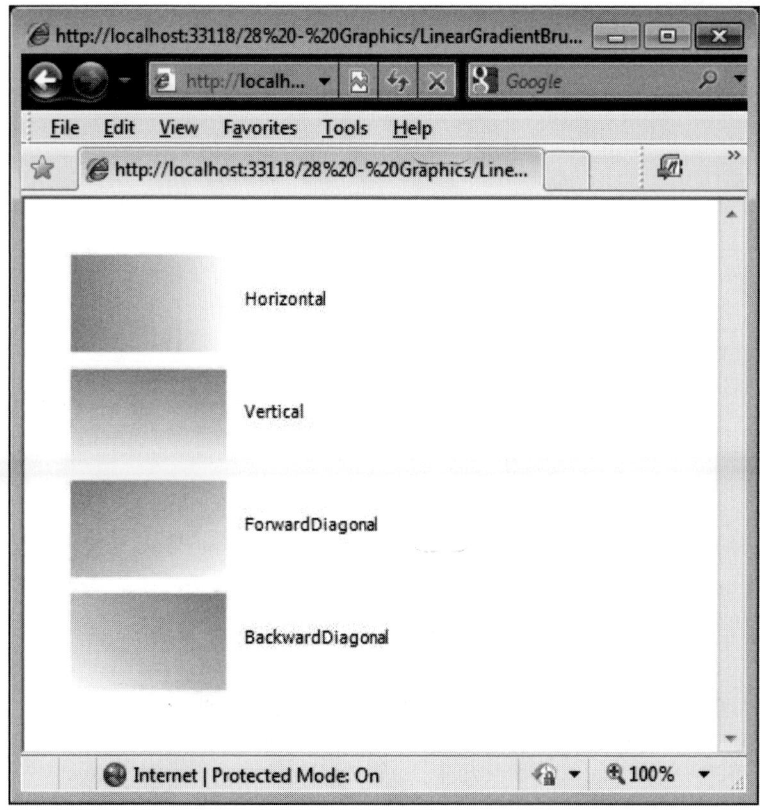

Figure 28-7. Testing gradient styles

Embedding Dynamic Graphics in a Web Page

Using the Image.Save method to write the image to the response stream overwrites whatever information ASP.NET would otherwise use. Fortunately, a simple solution exists. You can use the HTML <img> tag or the Image web control, but instead of specifying a static image as the source, you link to the .aspx file that generates a dynamic image.

For example, consider the graphic shown earlier in Figure 28-1. It's stored in a file named SimpleDrawing.aspx, and it writes a dynamically generated image to the response stream. In another page, you could show the dynamic image by adding an Image web control and setting the ImageUrl property to SimpleDrawing.aspx. You could then add other controls or even multiple Image controls that link to the same content.

Figure 28-8 shows an example that uses two <img> tags that point to SimpleDrawing.aspx, along with additional ASP.NET web controls in between.

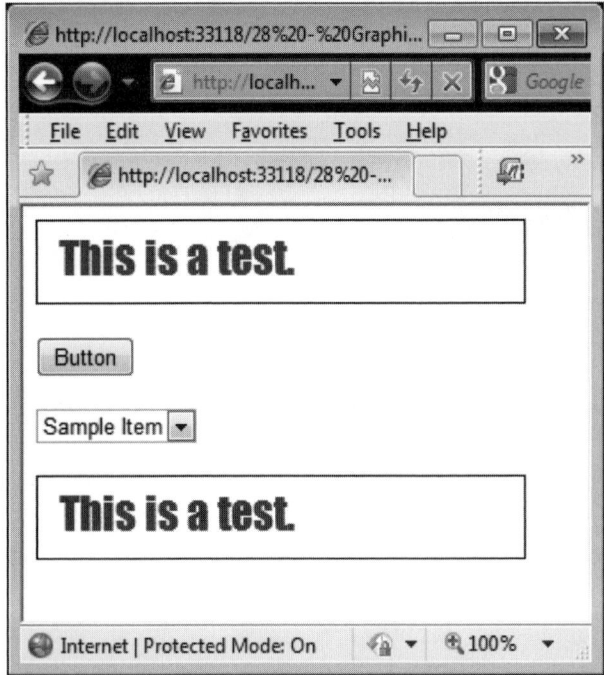

Figure 28-8. Mixing dynamically drawn content and ordinary web controls

---

■ **Tip** Remember that creating a GDI+ drawing is usually an order of magnitude slower than serving a static image. As a result, it's probably not a good idea to implement graphical buttons and other elements that you'll repeat multiple times on a page using GDI+. (If you do, consider caching or saving the image file once you've generated it to increase performance.)

Using the PNG Format

PNG is an all-purpose format that always provides high quality by combining the lossless compression of GIFs with the rich color support of JPEGs. Some browsers (especially older version of Internet Explorer) don't display PNG images correctly when they are returned dynamically from a page. Instead of seeing the picture content, the user receives a message prompting them to download the picture content and open it in another program. You can use the <img> tag approach discussed previously to address this problem.

The other issue with dynamically generating PNG images is that you can't use the Bitmap.Save method shown in earlier examples. Response.OutputStream is a linear stream, meaning data must be written sequentially from beginning to end. To create a PNG file, .NET needs to be able to move back and forth in a file, which requires a stream that can seek specific locations. The solution is fairly simple. Instead of saving directly to Response.OutputStream, you create a System.IO.MemoryStream, which is an in-memory buffer of data. Use Bitmap.Save your image to the MemoryStream and then write the MemoryStream to the Response.OutputStream.

Here's the code you need to implement this solution, assuming you've imported the System.IO namespace:

```
Response.ContentType = "image/png";

// Create the PNG in memory.
MemoryStream mem = new MemoryStream();
image.Save(mem, System.Drawing.Imaging.ImageFormat.Png);

// Write the MemoryStream data to the output stream.
mem.WriteTo(Response.OutputStream);

// Clean up.
g.Dispose();
image.Dispose();
```

Passing Information to Dynamic Images

When you generate graphics in web pages, you can send information from the page to the code that generates the graphic to create truly dynamic images. The following example creates a data-bound list that shows a thumbnail of every bitmap in a given directory. Figure 28-9 shows the final result.

Figure 28-9. *A data-bound thumbnail list*

This page needs to be designed in two parts: the page that contains the GridView and the page that dynamically renders a single thumbnail. The GridView page will call the thumbnail page multiple times (using <img> tags) to fill the list.

It makes sense to design the page that creates the thumbnail first. In this example, the page is named ThumbnailViewer.aspx. To make this component as generic as possible, you shouldn't hard-code any information about the directory to use or the size of a thumbnail. Instead, this information will be retrieved through three query string arguments. The first step that you need to perform is to check that all this information is supplied when the page first loads, as shown here:

```
protected void Page_Load(object sender, System.EventArgs e)
{
    if ((String.IsNullOrEmpty(Request.QueryString["X"])) ||
        (String.IsNullOrEmpty(Request.QueryString["Y"])) ||
        (String.IsNullOrEmpty(Request.QueryString["FilePath"])))
    {
        // There is missing data, so don't display anything.
        // Other options include choosing reasonable defaults
        // or returning an image with some static error text.
    }
    else
```

```
    {
        int x = Int32.Parse(Request.QueryString["X"]);
        int y = Int32.Parse(Request.QueryString["Y"]);
        string file = Server.UrlDecode(Request.QueryString["FilePath"]);
        ...
```

Once you have the basic set of data, you can create your Bitmap and Graphics objects as always. In this case, the Bitmap dimensions should correspond to the size of the thumbnail, because you don't want to add any additional content:

```
        ...
        // Create the in-memory bitmap where you will draw the image.
        Bitmap image = new Bitmap(x, y);
        Graphics g = Graphics.FromImage(image);
        ...
```

Creating the thumbnail is easy. All you need to do is load the image (using the static Image.FromFile method) and then draw it on the drawing surface. When you draw the image, you specify the starting point, (0, 0), and the height and width. The height and width correspond to the size of the Bitmap object. The Graphics class will automatically scale your image to fit these dimensions, using antialiasing to create a high-quality thumbnail:

```
        ...
        // Load the file data.
        System.Drawing.Image thumbnail =
        System.Drawing.Image.FromFile(file);

        // Draw the thumbnail.
        g.DrawImage(thumbnail, 0, 0, x, y);
        ...
```

Lastly, you can render the image and clean up, as follows:

```
        ...
        // Render the image.
        image.Save(Response.OutputStream, ImageFormat.Jpeg);
        g.Dispose();
        image.Dispose();
    }
}
```

The next step is to use this page in the page that contains the GridView. In this example, the page that uses ThumbnailViewer.aspx is named ThumbnailsInDirectory.aspx.

The basic idea behind ThumbnailsInDirectory.aspx is that the user will enter a directory path and click the submit button. At this point, your code can perform a little work with the System.IO classes. First, you need to create a DirectoryInfo object that represents the user's choice of directory. Second, you need to retrieve a collection of FileInfo objects that represent files in that directory using the DirectoryInfo.GetFiles method. Finally, the code binds the array of FileInfo objects to a GridView, as shown here:

```
protected void cmdShow_Click(object sender, EventArgs e)
{
    // Get a string array with all the image files.
```

```
    DirectoryInfo dir = new DirectoryInfo(txtDir.Text);
    gridThumbs.DataSource = dir.GetFiles();

    // Bind the string array.
    gridThumbs.DataBind();
}
```

It's up to the GridView template to determine how the bound FileInfo objects are displayed. In this example, you need to show two pieces of information—the short name of the file and the corresponding thumbnail. Showing the short name is straightforward. You simply need to bind to the FileInfo.Name property. Showing the thumbnail requires using an <img> tag to invoke the ThumbnailViewer.aspx page. However, constructing the right URL can be a little tricky, so the best solution is to hand the work off to a method in the web-page class called GetImageUrl.

Here's the complete GridView declaration with the template:

```
<asp:GridView ID="gridThumbs" runat="server"
 AutoGenerateColumns="False" Font-Names="Verdana"
 Font-Size="X-Small" GridLines="None">
  <Columns>
    <asp:TemplateField>
      <ItemTemplate>
        <img src='<%# GetImageUrl(Eval("FullName")) %>' />
        <%# Eval("Name") %>
        <hr/>
      </ItemTemplate>
    </asp:TemplateField>
  </Columns>
</asp:GridView>
```

The GetImageUrl method examines the full file path, encodes it, and adds it to the query string so ThumbnailViewer.aspx can find the required file. At the same time, the GetImageUrl method also chooses a thumbnail size of 50 by 50 pixels. Note that the file path is URL-encoded. That's because filenames commonly include characters that aren't allowed in URLs, like the space:

```
protected string GetImageUrl(object path)
{
    return "ThumbnailViewer.aspx?x=50&y=50&FilePath=" +
      Server.UrlEncode((string)path);
}
```

Custom Controls That Use GDI+

Based on everything you learned in Chapter 27, you're probably eager to use GDI+ to create your own well-encapsulated custom controls. Unfortunately, ASP.NET doesn't make it easy, because of the way you need to embed GDI+ images in a page.

As you've seen, if you want to use GDI+, you need to create a separate web page. You can then embed the content of this page in another page by using an <img> tag. As a result, you can't just drop a custom control that uses GDI+ onto a web page. What you *can* do is create a custom control that wraps an <img> tag. This control can then provide a convenient programming interface, complete with properties, methods, and events. But the custom control won't actually generate the image. It will collect the data from its properties, use it to build the query string portion of a URL, and then render itself as an <img> tag pointing to a page that generates the dynamic image. The custom control provides a higher-level wrapper that abstracts the process of transferring information to your GDI+ page.

Figure 28-10 shows how this process works for the example we'll use to demonstrate this technique. We use custom control approach to create a simple label that renders with a gradient background. The custom control is named GradientLabel and the GDI+ code in a separate page named GradientLabel.aspx. To see this example at work, you can request the GradientTest.aspx web page, which hosts a single instance of the GradientLabel control.

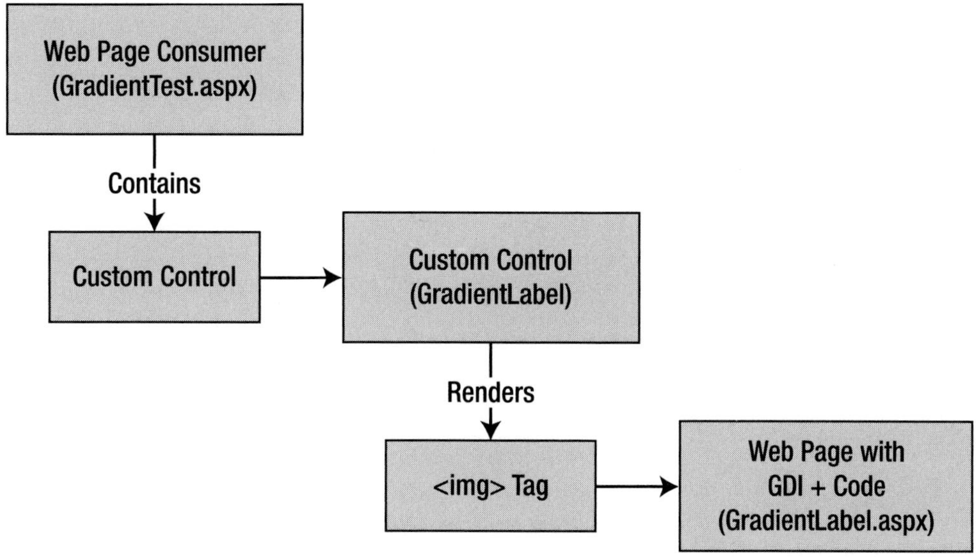

Figure 28-10. *Using custom controls with GDI+*

■ **Tip** If you're worried about confusing your real web pages with the web pages you use to supply GDI+ drawing, consider using a custom HTTP handler to generate the image. With an HTTP handler, your image generators can have a custom extension and use essentially the same code in the ProcessRequest() method. HTTP handlers were first demonstrated in Chapter 5.

The Custom Control Class

The first step is to create the control class. As with any custom control, you can place it in the App_Code folder of a website or, ideally, in a separate class library project, as described in Chapter 27.

The custom control class (named GradientLabel) derives from Control rather than WebControl. That's because it won't be able to support the rich set of style properties because it renders a dynamic graphic, not an HTML tag.

```
public class GradientLabel : Control
{ ... }
```

The GradientLabel class provides five properties, which allow the user to specify the text, the font size, and the colors that are used for the gradient and text, as follows:

```
public string Text
{
    get { return (string)ViewState["Text"]; }
    set { ViewState["Text"] = value; }
}

public int TextSize
{
    get { return (int)ViewState["TextSize"]; }
    set { ViewState["TextSize"] = value; }
}

public Color GradientColorStart
{
    get { return (Color)ViewState["ColorStart"]; }
    set { ViewState["ColorStart"] = value; }
}

public Color GradientColorEnd
{
    get { return (Color)ViewState["ColorEnd"]; }
    set { ViewState["ColorEnd"] = value; }
}

public Color TextColor
{
    get { return (Color)ViewState["TextColor"]; }
    set { ViewState["TextColor"] = value; }
}
```

The properties are set to some sensible defaults in the GradientLabel constructor, as shown here:

```
public GradientLabel()
{
    Text = "";
    TextColor = Color.White;
    GradientColorStart = Color.Blue;
    GradientColorEnd = Color.DarkBlue;
    TextSize = 14;
}
```

The GradientLabel renders itself as an <img> tag that points to the GradientLabel.aspx page. It's the GradientLabel.aspx page that contains the GDI+ drawing code. When the GradientLabel is rendered, it reads the information from all the properties and supplies the information in the query string.

```
protected override void Render(HtmlTextWriter writer)
{
    HttpContext context = HttpContext.Current;
    writer.Write("<img src='" + "GradientLabel.aspx?" +
      "Text=" + context.Server.UrlEncode(Text) +
```

```
        "&TextSize=" + TextSize.ToString() +
        "&TextColor=" + TextColor.ToArgb() +
        "&GradientColorStart=" + GradientColorStart.ToArgb() +
        "&GradientColorEnd=" + GradientColorEnd.ToArgb() +
        "'>");
}
```

The Rendering Page

The first step for the GradientLabel.aspx page is to retrieve the properties from the query string, as follows:

```
protected void Page_Load(object sender, System.EventArgs e)
{
    string text = Server.UrlDecode(Request.QueryString["Text"]);
    int textSize = Int32.Parse(Request.QueryString["TextSize"]);
    Color textColor = Color.FromArgb(
      Int32.Parse(Request.QueryString["TextColor"]));
    Color gradientColorStart = Color.FromArgb(
      Int32.Parse(Request.QueryString["GradientColorStart"]));
    Color gradientColorEnd = Color.FromArgb(
      Int32.Parse(Request.QueryString["GradientColorEnd"]));
    ...
```

The GradientLabel.aspx page has an interesting challenge. The text and font size are supplied dynamically, so it's impossible to use a fixed bitmap size without running the risk of making it too small (so that some text content is cut off) or too large (so that extra server memory is wasted and the image takes longer to send to the client). One way to try to resolve this problem is to create the Font object you want to use and then invoke the Graphics.MeasureString argument to determine how many pixels are required to display the desired text. The only caveat is that you need to be careful not to allow the bitmap to become too large. For example, if the user submits a string with hundreds of characters, you don't want to create a bitmap that's dozens of megabytes in size! To avoid this risk, the rendering code imposes a maximum height and width of 800 pixels.

■ **Tip** You can also use an alternative version of the DrawString method that accepts a rectangle in which you want to place the text. This version of DrawString automatically wraps the text if there's room for more than one line. You could use this approach to allow the display of large amounts of text over several lines.

Here's the portion of the drawing code that retrieves the query string information and measures the text:

```
    ...
    // Define the font.
    Font font = new Font("Tahoma", textSize, FontStyle.Bold);

    // Use a test image to measure the text.
    Bitmap image = new Bitmap(1, 1);
    Graphics g = Graphics.FromImage(image);
```

```
    SizeF size = g.MeasureString(text, font);
    g.Dispose();
    image.Dispose();

    // Using these measurements, try to choose a reasonable bitmap size.
    // If the text is large, cap the size at some maximum to
    // prevent causing a serious server slowdown.
    int width = (int)Math.Min(size.Width + 20, 800);
    int height = (int)Math.Min(size.Height + 20, 800);
    image = new Bitmap(width, height);
    g = Graphics.FromImage(image);
    ...
```

You'll see that in addition to the size needed for the text, an extra 20 pixels are added to each dimension. This allows for a padding of 10 pixels on each side.

Finally, you can create the LinearGradientBrush, paint the drawing surface, and then add the text, as follows:

```
    ...
    LinearGradientBrush brush = new LinearGradientBrush(
      new Rectangle(new Point(0,0), image.Size),
    gradientColorStart, gradientColorEnd, LinearGradientMode.ForwardDiagonal);

    // Draw the gradient background.
    g.FillRectangle(brush, 0, 0, width, height);

    // Draw the label text.
    g.DrawString(text, font, new SolidBrush(textColor), 10, 10);

    // Render the image to the output stream.
    image.Save(Response.OutputStream,
     System.Drawing.Imaging.ImageFormat.Jpeg);

    g.Dispose();
    image.Dispose();
}
```

To test the label, you can create a control tag like this:

```
<cc1:gradientlabel id="GradientLabel1" runat="server"
  Text="Test String" GradientColorStart="MediumSpringGreen"
  GradientColorEnd="RoyalBlue"></cc1:gradientlabel>
```

Figure 28-11 shows the rendered result.

Figure 28-11. *A GDI+ label custom control*

■ **Tip** Passing information from one page to another is a useful way of using GDI+, but the limits on the size of the query string means that it works only for relatively small amounts of data. For larger amounts of data, we can use the Session collection. This has more overhead because everything you put in the Session collection uses server memory, but it allows you to transmit any serializable data.

Using the Chart Control

One of the most common graphics tasks is to create a chart. The ASP.NET Chart control provides a very wide range of chart types and configuration options. The Chart control was available as a download for .NET version 3.5 SP1 but is included in.NET version 4.0.

The Chart Control has so many different features and options that we can't cover them all in this section. We'll show you how to create some of the different types of types available, bind the chart to different data sources, and perform some useful charting functions, but if you want a more comprehensive set of examples, take a look at the samples library at `http://code.msdn.microsoft.com/mschart`, which contains more than 200 different Chart control examples.

Creating a Basic Chart

As with much of ASP.NET, the best place to start with the Chart control is with an example. Figure 28-12 shows a simple chart. We'll show you how we created this chart and then show some of different ways to customize and adapt the chart. To help explain how the Chart control works, we have annotated the figure to indicate the major elements.

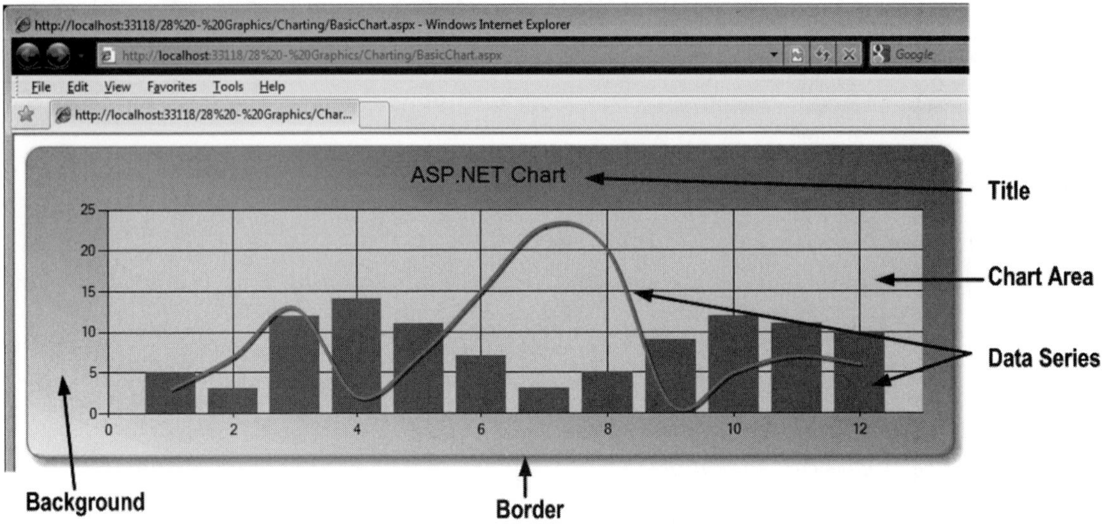

Figure 28-12. *A simple ASP.NET Chart control*

You can add a chart by dragging the Chart control from the design palette (it is in the Data group) or by adding the <asp:Chart> tag to your markup. Here is the basic declaration for our sample chart:

```
<asp:Chart ID="Chart1" runat="server" Width="900px">
   <ChartAreas>
      <asp:ChartArea Name="ChartArea1" />
   </ChartAreas>
</asp:Chart>
```

Each chart has one or more chart areas where data can be plotted. Our basic declaration has one chart, which we will use to plot two sets of data. As with most ASP.NET controls, you can use a code-behind file to drive the control or continue to use the markup. We'll show you the code-behind approach first. We start by configuring the chart appearance, as follows:

■ **Note** When using a code file with the Chart control, you'll need to import the System.Web.UI.DataVisualization.Charting namespace.

```
using System;
using System.Drawing;
using System.Web.UI.DataVisualization.Charting;

public partial class Charting_BasicChart : System.Web.UI.Page {

    protected void Page_Load(object sender, EventArgs e) {
```

```
// format the chart
Chart1.BackColor = Color.Gray;
Chart1.BackSecondaryColor = Color.WhiteSmoke;
Chart1.BackGradientStyle = GradientStyle.DiagonalRight;
...
```

The chart background is the area that surrounds the chart area. We decided that our chart background should be a graduated fill from Gray to WhiteSmoke in a diagonal pattern, which we specified using the BackColor, BackSecondaryColor, and BackGradientStyle properties. When the chart is rendered, the background is created using our chosen color scheme. We then move on to the border. The BorderlineDashStyle controls the very edge of the border. The Solid value from the ChartDashStyle enumeration gives us a single pixel line drawn around edge of the chart, drawn in the color specified by the BorderlineColor property, which we have set to Gray. The BorderSkin property has many options, but we have set the SkinStyle to be Emboss, which gives us the raised 3D effect with a shadow.

```
...
Chart1.BorderlineDashStyle = ChartDashStyle.Solid;
Chart1.BorderlineColor = Color.Gray;
Chart1.BorderSkin.SkinStyle = BorderSkinStyle.Emboss;
...
```

Our next step is to set the color we want for the background of the chart area and set our title. You'll notice that we refer to the chart area by an index value. This is because charts can have more than one area in which data can be plotted. We'll show you how to do this later in the section. Our chart has only one area, and we have chosen to use the Wheat color.

```
// format the chart area
Chart1.ChartAreas[0].BackColor = Color.Wheat;

// add and format the title
Chart1.Titles.Add("ASP.NET Chart");
Chart1.Titles[0].Font = new Font("Utopia", 16);
```

A chart can have more than one title, so we must add a new title to the Titles collection using the Add method and then refer to the title by index in order to format it. The formatting is simply to set a font and size. Figure 28-13 shows our chart so far.

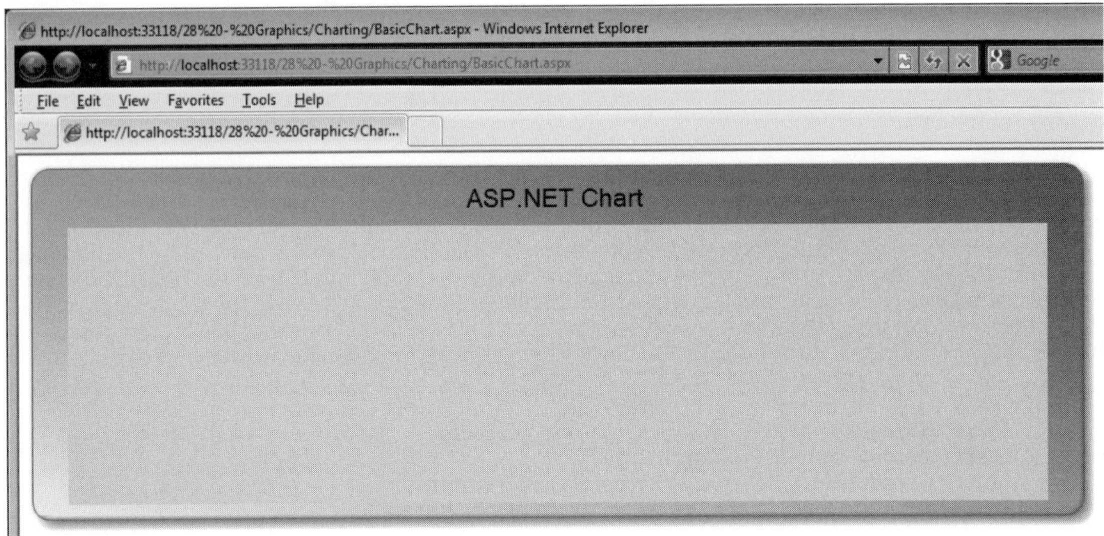

Figure 28-13. *The formatted, but empty, chart*

There are many different ways of formatting a chart, and it can take a while to find the permutation of options that you are looking for. We have started with the appearance of our example chart because, ironically, the process of adding in the data is easier than finding a satisfactory color scheme. The Chart control is so flexible and has so many options that the tyranny of choice makes itself felt.

Once we have the basic presentation settings out of the way, we can start to work on the data. We represent sets of data using the Series class, and each Series class we create must be added to the Chart.Series collection using the Add method. We usually combine creating and adding the Series class in a single step, as follows:

```
...
Chart1.Series.Add(new Series("ColumnSeries") {
     ChartType = SeriesChartType.Column,
 });
...
```

We created a new series with the name ColumnSeries and specified that the data in the series should be plotted using a column chart by setting the Series.ChartType property to SeriesChartType.Column. The SeriesChartType has 35 different values, each representing a different kind of chart. We'll stick to the basic types in this book, but they are worth exploring. The ChartType property defaults to Column if you don't specify a value.

You can configure a range of properties on the series. Here is the code we used to create the second Series for our chart, which contains some customizations:

```
Chart1.Series.Add(new Series("SplineSeries") {
    ChartType = SeriesChartType.Spline,
    BorderWidth = 3,
    ShadowOffset = 2,
    Color = Color.PaleVioletRed
});
```

We have set the chart type to be Spline (a smoothed line plot). The BorderWidth value control the width of the line plot and setting a value for the ShadowOffset property creates a 3D shadow effect under the line when it is drawn. The Color property sets the color used to draw the plot. We have picked the fetching PaleVioletRed shade.

The last step is to add the data to the series. There are lots of different ways of associating data with your chart. We use the simplest in this example, which is to specify static values, as follows:

```
Chart1.Series[0].Points.DataBindY(
    new int[] { 5, 3, 12, 14, 11, 7, 3, 5, 9, 12, 11, 10 });
Chart1.Series[1].Points.DataBindY(
    new int[] { 3, 7, 13, 2, 7, 15, 23, 20, 1, 5, 7, 6 });
```

Each Series has a Points collection. We have used the DataBindY method, which consumes an IEnumerable, allowing us to use an array of integers to specify the data. The index into the data is used as the x-axis value for each Y value in the data arrays. When we load the page containing our chart control, we see the result shown in Figure 28-12.

The Chart control is fully configurable using markup as well. Here is the same chart defined in that form:

```
<asp:Chart ID="Chart2" runat="server" Width="900px" BackColor="Gray"
    BackSecondaryColor="WhiteSmoke" BackGradientStyle="DiagonalRight"
    BorderlineDashStyle="Solid" BorderlineColor="Gray">
    <BorderSkin SkinStyle="Emboss" />
    <Titles>
        <asp:Title Text="ASP.NET Chart" Font="Utopia,16" />
    </Titles>
    <Series>
        <asp:Series Name="ColumnSeries" ChartType="Column">
            <Points>
                <asp:DataPoint YValues="5" />
                <asp:DataPoint YValues="3" />
                <asp:DataPoint YValues="12" />
                <asp:DataPoint YValues="14" />
                <asp:DataPoint YValues="11" />
                <asp:DataPoint YValues="7" />
                <asp:DataPoint YValues="3" />
                <asp:DataPoint YValues="5" />
                <asp:DataPoint YValues="9" />
                <asp:DataPoint YValues="12" />
                <asp:DataPoint YValues="11" />
                <asp:DataPoint YValues="10" />
            </Points>
        </asp:Series>
        <asp:Series Name="SplineSeries" ChartType="Spline" BorderWidth="3" ShadowOffset="2"
            Color="PaleVioletRed">
            <Points>
                <asp:DataPoint YValues="3" />
                <asp:DataPoint YValues="7" />
                <asp:DataPoint YValues="13" />
                <asp:DataPoint YValues="2" />
                <asp:DataPoint YValues="7" />
                <asp:DataPoint YValues="15" />
                <asp:DataPoint YValues="23" />
```

```
                <asp:DataPoint YValues="20" />
                <asp:DataPoint YValues="1" />
                <asp:DataPoint YValues="5" />
                <asp:DataPoint YValues="7" />
                <asp:DataPoint YValues="6" />
            </Points>
        </asp:Series>
    </Series>
    <ChartAreas>
        <asp:ChartArea Name="ChartArea1" BackColor="Wheat" />
    </ChartAreas>
</asp:Chart>
```

Part of the flexibility of the Chart control is that the various elements are isolated from one another. To demonstrate this, we'll show you how to create a second chart area in the same chart and have one data series drawn on each. Here's the additional code we need to add to the Page_Load method:

```
Chart1.ChartAreas.Add("SecondArea");
Chart1.Series[1].ChartArea = "SecondArea";
```

To get the same effect using markup, we make the following additions:

```
        <asp:Series Name="SplineSeries" ChartType="Spline" BorderWidth="3" ShadowOffset="2"
            Color="PaleVioletRed" ChartArea="ChartArea2">
            <Points>
                <asp:DataPoint YValues="3" />
                <asp:DataPoint YValues="7" />
                <asp:DataPoint YValues="13" />
                <asp:DataPoint YValues="2" />
                <asp:DataPoint YValues="7" />
                <asp:DataPoint YValues="15" />
                <asp:DataPoint YValues="23" />
                <asp:DataPoint YValues="20" />
                <asp:DataPoint YValues="1" />
                <asp:DataPoint YValues="5" />
                <asp:DataPoint YValues="7" />
                <asp:DataPoint YValues="6" />
            </Points>
        </asp:Series>
    </Series>
    <ChartAreas>
        <asp:ChartArea Name="ChartArea1" BackColor="Wheat" />
        <asp:ChartArea Name="ChartArea2"/>
    </ChartAreas>
```

That's it. And if we look at the web page, we get the result shown in Figure 28-14.

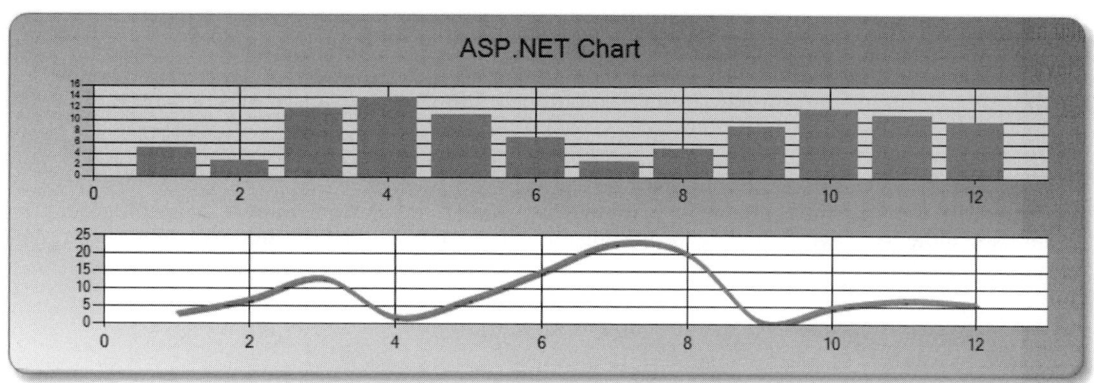

Figure 28-14. A chart with two chart areas

We are not going to dig into all the presentation options available, but one common task is to generate 3D charts. To transform our simple chart into a 3D chart, we add the following to the Page_Load method:

```
Chart1.ChartAreas[0].Area3DStyle.Enable3D = true;
```

You enable 3D at the ChartArea level. If you have a chart with multiple ChartAreas, then you can elect to mix and match 2D and 3D plots as you need. Figure 28-15 shows our basic chart in 3D. The equivalent change in markup is as follows:

```
<ChartAreas>
   <asp:ChartArea Name="ChartArea1" BackColor="Wheat" Area3DStyle-Enable3D="true"/>
</ChartAreas>
```

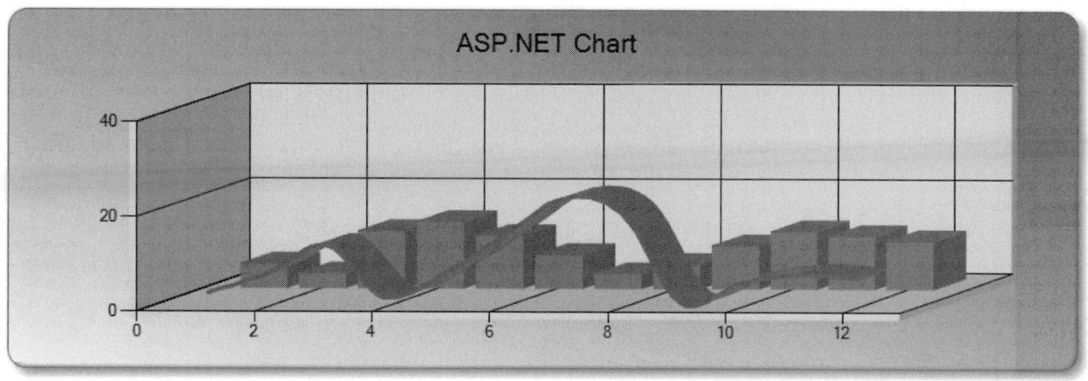

Figure 28-15. The example chart in 3D

Populating a Chart with Data

In addition to the static data we used in the previous example, the Chart control can be populated with data from a range of different sources. In this section, we'll show you the most commonly used.

Binding to a Database Table

In this example, we'll use the Products table in the Northwind database to demonstrate binding a chart to a database table. We have started by formatting our Chart control, largely as in the previous example:

```
using System;
using System.Configuration;
using System.Data.SqlClient;
using System.Drawing;
using System.Web.UI.DataVisualization.Charting;

public partial class Charting_TableBinding : System.Web.UI.Page {

    protected void Page_Load(object sender, EventArgs e) {
        // format the chart
        Chart1.BackColor = Color.Gray;
        Chart1.BackSecondaryColor = Color.WhiteSmoke;
        Chart1.BackGradientStyle = GradientStyle.DiagonalRight;

        Chart1.BorderlineDashStyle = ChartDashStyle.Solid;
        Chart1.BorderSkin.SkinStyle = BorderSkinStyle.Emboss;
        Chart1.BorderlineColor = Color.Gray;

        // format the chart area
        Chart1.ChartAreas[0].BackColor = Color.Wheat;
        // add and format the title
        Chart1.Titles.Add("Table Bound Chart");
        Chart1.Titles[0].Font = new Font("Utopia", 16);
        ...
```

We use the standard ADO.NET classes from the System.Data.SqlClient namespace to define a connection to the Northwind database using a connection string property. We then define the query that will be used to generate the data in the chart. We have chosen to query for the ProductName and UnitsInStock columns of the Products table, selecting products that have not been discontinued and limiting our results to five rows. We open the connection and create an SqlDataReader—all standard ADO.NET code.

```
        ...
        // create the connection to the database
        SqlConnection conn = new SqlConnection(
           ConfigurationManager.ConnectionStrings["Northwind"].ConnectionString);

        // define the command
        SqlCommand command = new SqlCommand("SELECT TOP (5) ProductName, UnitsInStock "
            + "FROM Products WHERE (Discontinued = 'FALSE')", conn);

        // open the command and create the reader
        command.Connection.Open();
        SqlDataReader reader = command.ExecuteReader();
        ...
```

We have formatted our chart and created a connection to our data. Now it is time to bind the data to the chart. We start by clearing the Chart.Series collection. This is because when we bind a table, the Chart control automatically creates a new Series instance for each numeric column that it finds in the data. We will end up with a Series called UnitsInStock. But the default Series isn't removed (it is called Series1), and this can cause problems if you change the Series.ChartType property to a value that cannot be plotted on the same ChartArea as a Column chart, which is the default chart type of the default series. It is good practice to remove the default Series class before binding to the data so that you end up only with the Series class associated with your data.

```
        // clear the chart series and bind to the table
        Chart1.Series.Clear();
        Chart1.DataBindTable(reader);
        Chart1.Series["UnitsInStock"].ChartType = SeriesChartType.StackedBar;

        // close the reader and the connection
        reader.Close();
        conn.Close();
    }
}
```

We then perform the binding, using the DataBindTable method, which takes our previously created SqlDataReader as its argument. As we mentioned previously, binding to a table automatically creates one data series per numeric column in the data. In our case, we query for the ProductName and UnitsInStock columns. The Chart control will ignore the text ProductName column and create a new Series for the UnitsInStock column. We can't format the Series until after it has been created, so we set the ChartType property after we have bound the table to the control. Finally, we close the SqlDataReader and the SqlCommand. The chart we get from this code is shown in Figure 28-16.

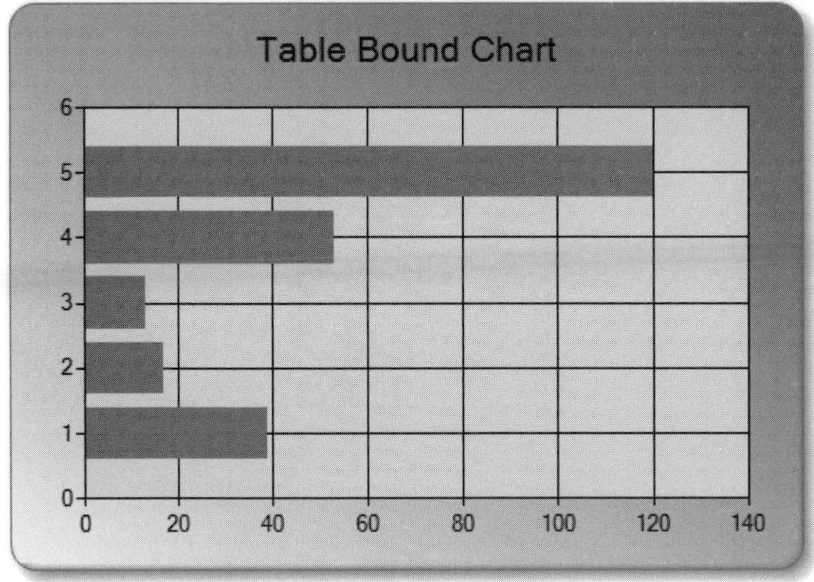

***Figure 28-16.** A chart bound to a database table*

The problem with this chart is that the ProductName column was ignored. During the binding process, the Chart control worked on the basis that all the SQL data was intended to be interpreted as values on the y-axis and discarded anything that couldn't be used that way.

If we want to use one of the columns as x-axis values, then we must explicitly instruct the Chart control by binding the data using the Points.DataBindXY method of the Series class. To adapt the previous example, comment out the first three lines, and add two new lines to the code-behind file as follows:

```
// clear the chart series and bind to the table
//Chart1.Series.Clear();
//Chart1.DataBindTable(reader);
//Chart1.Series["UnitsInStock"].ChartType = SeriesChartType.StackedBar;

// bind the X and Y values to the default series and format the chart
Chart1.Series[0].Points.DataBindXY(reader, "ProductName", reader, "UnitsInStock");
Chart1.Series[0].ChartType = SeriesChartType.StackedBar;
```

The DataBindXY method allows you to supply the source of the data and the column name that should be used for the x- and y-axes. For our example, the source of the data for both axes is our SqlDataReader, and the column names are ProductName and UnitsInStock. Notice that we didn't clear the Series collection this time. The DataBindXY method is applied to an already-existing Series (and doesn't create a new one), and in our example, we used the one that is created by default. When we view our revised page, we get the chart shown in Figure 28-17.

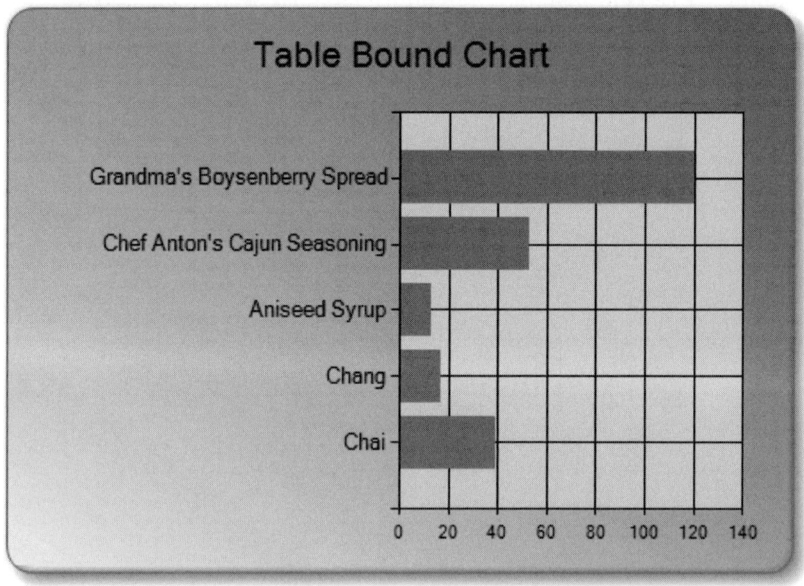

Figure 28-17. *Explicitly binding X and Y values to a chart*

Binding to a Object DataSource

One of the most flexible mechanisms for populating a chart is to use an object data source, such that you define an object that can retrieve your data and use an ObjectDataSource to bridge between the retrieval logic in your code and the Chart control. You should create your retrieval class in the App_Code folder. Here is our example, which returns some simple static data:

```
public class MyObjectDataSource {

    public class DataItem {
        public string Name {get; set;}
        public double Popularity {get; set;}
    }

    public DataItem[] GetData() {
        return new DataItem[] {
            new DataItem() {Name = "Cheesecake", Popularity = 30},
            new DataItem() {Name = "Ice Cream", Popularity = 30},
            new DataItem() {Name = "Fudge", Popularity = 20},
            new DataItem() {Name = "Milkshake", Popularity = 20}
        };
    }
}
```

We have defined a DataItem class that has a Name and Popularity properties. The GetData method generates and returns an array of DataItems. This binding technique will also work with methods that return DataSets and DataTables. The flexibility of using an ObjectDataSource is that the means by which you source your data are abstracted from the chart, so you can change your business logic freely. To use our data, we create a new instance of ObjectDataSource, passing the name of the retrieval class we have created and the name of the method that should be called to get the data. In our case that is MyObjectDataSource and GetData, respectively. We have marked the important statements, which appear after the usual chart formatting preamble:

```
using System;
using System.Drawing;
using System.Web.UI.DataVisualization.Charting;
using System.Web.UI.WebControls;

public partial class Charting_ObjectAdaptorBinding : System.Web.UI.Page {

    protected void Page_Load(object sender, EventArgs e) {

        // format the chart
        Chart1.BackColor = Color.Gray;
        Chart1.BackSecondaryColor = Color.WhiteSmoke;
        Chart1.BackGradientStyle = GradientStyle.DiagonalRight;

        Chart1.BorderlineDashStyle = ChartDashStyle.Solid;
        Chart1.BorderSkin.SkinStyle = BorderSkinStyle.Emboss;
        Chart1.BorderlineColor = Color.Gray;

        // format the chart area
        Chart1.ChartAreas[0].BackColor = Color.Wheat;
```

```
        Chart1.ChartAreas[0].Area3DStyle.Enable3D = true;

        // add and format the title
        Chart1.Titles.Add("Table Object Adaptor Chart");
        Chart1.Titles[0].Font = new Font("Utopia", 16);

        // create the object data source
        ObjectDataSource ds = new ObjectDataSource("MyObjectDataSource", "GetData");
        // bind the source to the chart
        Chart1.DataSource = ds;
        Chart1.Series[0].XValueMember = "Name";
        Chart1.Series[0].YValueMembers = "Popularity";

        // format the series
        Chart1.Series[0].ChartType = SeriesChartType.Pie;
    }
}
```

Once we have created the ObjectDataSource, we bind it to the control using the Chart.DataSource property. At this point, the data source is acting as a bridge between our retrieval class and the chart, but the chart doesn't know what to do with the data that is available. We provide that information using the Series.XValueMember and Series.YValueMember properties, which allows us to specify which of the members in the type provided by the ObjectDataSource should be used for the x- and y-axes. Figure 28-18 shows the chart that we produced using this technique.

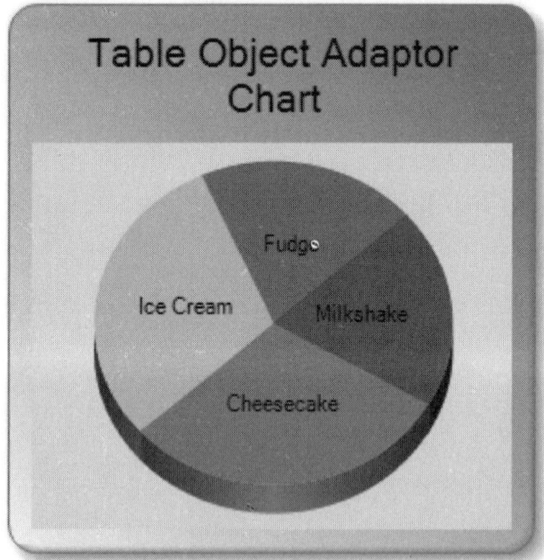

Figure 28-18. *A chart creating with an object data source*

Binding to an XML File

You can populate your chart with data from an XML file by using the System.Data.DataSet class. Here is a simple XML file that we will use as an example:

```
<?xml version="1.0" encoding="utf-8" ?>
<Data>
  <Product>
    <Name>Apple</Name>
    <Quantity>40</Quantity>
  </Product>
  <Product>
    <Name>Orange</Name>
    <Quantity>20</Quantity>
  </Product>
  <Product>
    <Name>Banana</Name>
    <Quantity>30</Quantity>
  </Product>
  <Product>
    <Name>Mango</Name>
    <Quantity>22</Quantity>
  </Product>
  <Product>
    <Name>Cherry</Name>
    <Quantity>38</Quantity>
  </Product>
</Data>
```

To demonstrate using XML data to populate a chart, we have created an example in the XMLBinding.aspx file. In the associated code-behind file, we have added the following to the Page_Load method:

```
using System;
using System.Data;
using System.Drawing;
using System.Web.UI.DataVisualization.Charting;

public partial class Charting_XMLBinding : System.Web.UI.Page {

    protected void Page_Load(object sender, EventArgs e) {

        // format the chart
        Chart1.BackColor = Color.Gray;
        Chart1.BackSecondaryColor = Color.WhiteSmoke;
        Chart1.BackGradientStyle = GradientStyle.DiagonalRight;

        Chart1.BorderlineDashStyle = ChartDashStyle.Solid;
        Chart1.BorderSkin.SkinStyle = BorderSkinStyle.Emboss;
        Chart1.BorderlineColor = Color.Gray;

        // format the chart area
        Chart1.ChartAreas[0].BackColor = Color.Wheat;
        Chart1.ChartAreas[0].Area3DStyle.Enable3D = true;

        // add and format the title
        Chart1.Titles.Add("XML Chart");
        Chart1.Titles[0].Font = new Font("Utopia", 16);
```

```
            // format the data series
            Chart1.Series[0].ChartType = SeriesChartType.Radar;

            // define the path to the xml file
            string dataPath = MapPath(".") + "\\sampledata.xml";

            // create a DataSet and read the XML data
            DataSet dataSet = new DataSet();
            dataSet.ReadXml(dataPath);
            // create a DataView from the DataSet
            DataView dataView = new DataView(dataSet.Tables[0]);
            // bind the XML ata to the chart
            Chart1.Series[0].Points.DataBindXY(dataView, "Name", dataView, "Quantity");
        }
    }
```

Once the chart has been formatted, we create a new DataSet and use the ReadXml method to load our file, which we have placed alongside our web page. We then create a DataView, using the first item in the DataSet.Tables collection as the constructor argument. To bind the data, we use DataBindXY method of the Points collection of the default Series, specifying that the Name property should be used for the x-axis and the Quantity property should be used for the y-axis. The chart that this creates is shown in Figure 28-19.

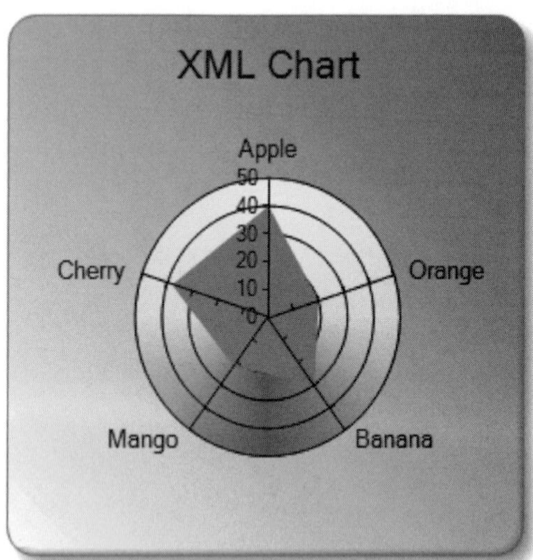

Figure 28-19. A chart populated with XML data

Binding to LINQ

Another flexible way to bind data to a chart is to use LINQ, and you can do this consistently whether you are using LINQ to Objects, LINQ to XML, or LINQ to Entities. In this section, we'll show you how to use LINQ to Entities. We started by creating a data model for the Northwind database; see Chapter 13 for details of how to do this.

We then created a new web page that contains a Chart control and added the following to the Page_Load method. As ever with the Chart control, it takes more effort to format the chart than it does to bind the data; we have highlighted the binding statements:

```
using System;
using System.Drawing;
using System.Linq;
using System.Web.UI.DataVisualization.Charting;
using NorthwindModel;

public partial class Charting_LINQBinding : System.Web.UI.Page {

    protected void Page_Load(object sender, EventArgs e) {

        // format the chart
        Chart1.BackColor = Color.Gray;
        Chart1.BackSecondaryColor = Color.WhiteSmoke;
        Chart1.BackGradientStyle = GradientStyle.DiagonalRight;

        Chart1.BorderlineDashStyle = ChartDashStyle.Solid;
        Chart1.BorderSkin.SkinStyle = BorderSkinStyle.Emboss;
        Chart1.BorderlineColor = Color.Gray;

        // format the chart area
        Chart1.ChartAreas[0].BackColor = Color.Wheat;

        // add and format the title
        Chart1.Titles.Add("LINQ Chart");
        Chart1.Titles[0].Font = new Font("Utopia", 16);

        // add and format a new data series
        Chart1.Series.Add("StockLevel");
        Chart1.Series["StockLevel"].ChartType = SeriesChartType.Spline;
        Chart1.Series["StockLevel"].BorderWidth = 3;
        Chart1.Series["StockLevel"].Color = Color.PaleVioletRed;

        // create a new EF context
        NorthwindEntities context = new NorthwindEntities();

        // perform a query
        var data = context.Products
            .Where(item => !item.Discontinued)
            .Select(item => item)
            .Take(5);

        // bind the default data series to the data
        Chart1.Series[0].Points.DataBind(data, "ProductName", "UnitPrice", "");
        Chart1.Series[1].Points.DataBind(data, "ProductName", "UnitsInStock", "");
    }
}
```

We create a new instance of the NorthwindEntities class, which was generated when we created the Entity Framework data model. Then, using LINQ, we query for all products that have not been discontinued, limiting the results to five items.

We then bind the results of the query to two Series in the Chart using the DataBind method. This lets us specify the source of the data (the result of the LINQ query) and the members of the result type that should be used for the x-axis and y-axis. We bind the UnitPrice values to one Series and the UnitsInStock values to another, both of them using the ProductName values as x-axis values. The chart that we produced is shown in Figure 28-20.

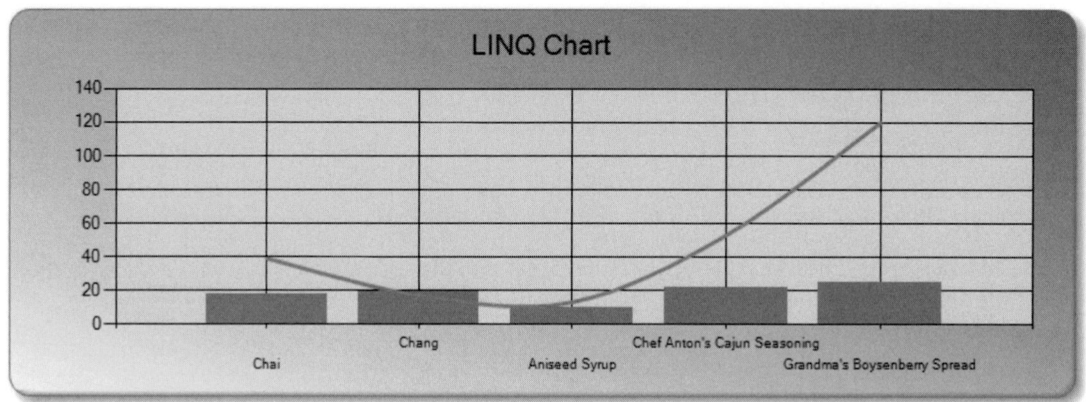

Figure 28-20. *A LINQ populated chart*

Summary

In this chapter, you learned how to master GDI+. Although GDI+ isn't right for every web page, it does give you a set of features that can't be matched by many other web application programming frameworks. You also explored how to create server-side image maps with the ImageMap control. For more graphical power, you might be interested in using the client-side drawing features of Silverlight, a next-generation browser plug-in discussed in Chapter 33. Finally, we showed you how to use the Chart control, a powerful and flexible charting tool that offers many different chart formats and can consume data from a wide range of sources. We showed you that with very little effort, it is possible to use the Chart control to create high-quality results.

CHAPTER 29

■ ■ ■

JavaScript and Ajax Techniques

ASP.NET provides a rich server-based programming model. The postback architecture allows you to perform all your work with object-oriented programming languages on the server, which ensures that your code is secure and compatible with all browsers. However, the postback architecture has its weaknesses. Because posting back the page always involves some small but noticeable overhead, it's impossible to react efficiently to mouse movements and key presses. Additionally, certain tasks—such as showing pop-up windows, providing a real-time status messages, and communicating between frames—need browser interaction and just aren't possible with server-side programming.

To compensate for these problems, experienced ASP.NET developers often use client-side programming to supplement their server-side web-page code. This client-side script allows you to make more responsive pages and accomplish some feats that wouldn't otherwise be possible. Often, these considerations occur when creating custom controls that render rich user interfaces (such as rollover buttons). For the greatest browser compatibility, the client-side script language of choice is JavaScript.

In this chapter, you'll learn some tried-and-true techniques for integrating JavaScript with ASP.NET. You'll even build a few JavaScript-fortified controls and learn how to strengthen your pages with Ajax, a particularly savvy style of JavaScript coding. These examples will also provide you with valuable insight into the workings of ASP.NET AJAX works, which you'll consider in the next chapter.

■ **What's New** ASP.NET's request validation feature—which catches suspicious values in query strings, cookies, headers, and posted-back form values—is now extensible. That means you can write a class that adds your own validation logic or overrides the built-in behavior. You'll learn more in the "Script Injection Attacks" section.

JavaScript Essentials

JavaScript is an embedded language. This means that JavaScript code is inserted directly into another document—typically, an HTML web page. The code is downloaded to the client computer and executed by the browser.

You have two ways to embed JavaScript code in a web page:

- You can embed the code directly in an event attribute for an HTML element. This is the most straightforward approach for small amounts of code.
- You can add a <script> tag that contains the JavaScript code. You can choose to run this code automatically when the page loads, or you can create a JavaScript function that will be called in response to a client-side event.

■ **Note** By convention, named JavaScript code routines are called *functions*, even when they don't explicitly return a value. JavaScript code routines are not called *methods*, because the JavaScript language doesn't support true object-oriented programming.

In many cases, you'll use both of these techniques at the same time. For example, you might define a function in a <script> block and then wire this function up to a client-side event using an event attribute. ASP.NET follows this pattern when it performs automatic postbacks. The __doPostBack() function includes the code needed to trigger a postback and send the event information for every control. It's rendered inside a <script> block. The __doPostBack() function is then connected to different controls using JavaScript event attributes, such as onchange, so that a client-side change causes a postback to the server.

It's important to realize that whether you use <script> blocks, event attributes, or both, you still have two choices about how you create your JavaScript code. Your first option is to embed fixed JavaScript code in the .aspx portion of your page. This is the simplest approach. Your second option is to add JavaScript code dynamically by using the methods of the Page class. This gives you the greatest flexibility, including the ability to tweak the JavaScript code on the fly and decide what you want to render at runtime. For example, you could tailor the JavaScript code to suit different browsers or different property settings. When you create custom controls, the controls render the JavaScript code they need in this way.

The followings sections explore the basic techniques for using JavaScript. You'll learn how to interact with the objects in your web page, handle client-side events, set properties, and move your script into a separate .js file.

■ **Note** You can also use VBScript if your web application exists on a company intranet where Internet Explorer is the standard. However, JavaScript is the only standard supported by a wide range of browsers.

The HTML Document Object Model

As a server-side programmer, you're used to interacting with your web pages as a collection of control objects. As a client-side programmer, you'll work with a similar abstraction. The difference is that each object you work with maps directly to an individual HTML tag. This means there aren't any higher-level controls, such as ASP.NET's Calendar and GridView. Instead, almost everything boils down to paragraphs, headings, images, form controls, and tables. For example, if you create a page with an <h1> tag for a heading, two <p> tags for paragraphs, and an <input> tag for a text box, you'll wind up with four controls that you can manipulate individually on the client side. It makes no difference whether you created these tags by writing raw HTML in the .aspx file or whether they were rendered by ASP.NET server controls.

The ability to interact with your web page as a tree of objects is provided by the HTML DOM (Document Object Model). The combination of JavaScript and the HTML DOM is called DHTML (Dynamic HTML). In other words, DHTML isn't a separate technology. Instead, it's a name that encompasses a specific way to use JavaScript. You'll see a similar distinction when you learn about Ajax later in this chapter. Ajax isn't a new technology—it's a small set of client-side programming techniques.

As is common in the world of the Web, not all browsers support the same level of JavaScript and HTML DOM functionality. However, in this chapter, you'll focus on techniques that are known to work on the majority of modern browsers (including Firefox). As usual, if you are creating a web application for a large number of users, you should perform extensive testing.

■ **Tip** You can find event compatibility tables on the Internet (see, for example, `www.quirksmode.org/js/events_compinfo.html`). For a comprehensive introduction to DHTML, you can refer to the MSDN website, at `http://msdn2.microsoft.com/en-us/library/ms533044.aspx`.

Client-Side Events

JavaScript supports a rich set of client-side events, which are listed in Table 29-1.

Table 29-1. *Common Events of HTML Objects*

Event	Description	Applies To
onchange	Occurs when the user changes the value in an input control. In text controls, this event fires after the user changes focus to another control.	select, text, text area
onclick	Occurs when the user clicks a control.	button, check box, radio, link, area
onmouseover	Occurs when the user moves the mouse pointer over a control.	link, area
onmouseout	Occurs when the user moves the mouse pointer away from a control.	link, area
onkeydown	Occurs when the user presses a key.	text, text area
onkeyup	Occurs when the user releases a pressed key.	text, text area
onselect	Occurs when the user selects a portion of text in an input control.	text, text area
onfocus	Occurs when a control receives focus.	select, text, text area
onblur	Occurs when focus leaves a control.	select, text, text area
onabort	Occurs when the user cancels an image download.	image

Event	Description	Applies To
onerror	Occurs when an image can't be downloaded (probably because of an incorrect URL).	image
onload	Occurs when a new page finishes downloading.	window, location
onunload	Occurs when a page is unloaded. (This typically occurs after a new URL has been entered or a link has been clicked. It fires just before the new page is downloaded.)	window

■ **Note** If you're coding your pages in XHTML, you must write the JavaScript names in all lowercase, as in onmouseover. If you aren't using XHTML, you can use mixed-case, as in onMouseOver, which is easier to read.

Using the event attributes listed in Table 29-1, you can insert JavaScript code that will be triggered when a specific action occurs. For example, the following web-page code adds the onmouseover attribute to two TextBox controls:

```
protected void Page_Load(object sender, EventArgs e)
{
    TextBox1.Attributes.Add("onmouseover",
      "alert('Your mouse is hovering on TextBox1.');");
    TextBox2.Attributes.Add("onmouseover",
      "alert('Your mouse is hovering on TextBox2.');");
}
```

When the user moves the mouse over the appropriate text box, the client-side onmouseover event occurs and the JavaScript alert() function is called, which shows a message box (as shown in Figure 29-1).

Figure 29-1. Responding to a JavaScript event

■ **Note** Keep in mind that ASP.NET already uses the onchange event to support the automatic postback feature. If you add the onchange attribute and set the AutoPostBack property to true, ASP.NET is intelligent enough to add both your JavaScript and the __doPostBack() function call to the attribute. Your client-side JavaScript code will be executed first, followed by the __doPostBack() function.

Adding JavaScript Attributes Declaratively

The example you just looked at adds the JavaScript code programmatically, by manipulating the Attributes collection that's provided by every server control. Another option is to add your event attributes declaratively to the control tag, like so:

```
<asp:TextBox id="TextBox1" runat="server"
  onmouseover="alert('Your mouse is hovering on TextBox1.');" />
```

In this example, ASP.NET is unable to match the onmouseover attribute to a control property or server-side event, so it simply passes it along to the rendered tag (although Visual Studio IntelliSense will flag this as an error). This technique obviously won't work if the JavaScript event name matches a C# event, like the onclick attribute on a button.

The OnClientClick Property

Usually, you attach client-side JavaScript events to the appropriate event-handling functions by adding attributes. If you're using ordinary HTML elements, you can set the attributes directly. If you're using web controls, you can manipulate them through the Attributes collection.

However, ASP.NET provides an alternative way to handle button clicks with JavaScript code. Instead of using the Attributes collection in code, you can set the OnClientClick property, which is defined in the Button, ImageButton, and LinkButton web controls. The OnClientClick property accepts a string with JavaScript code. It's up to you whether this code does its work directly or calls another JavaScript function.

Here's an example that uses OnClientClick to display a confirmation message before a page is posted back:

```
<asp:Button id="btnClick" runat="server"
 OnClientClick="return confirm('Post back to the server?');"
 Text="Click Me"/>
```

The button click still posts back the page and raises server-side events. The difference is that the OnClientClick client-side logic fires first and *then* triggers the server-side postback.

■ **Tip** You can use the OnClientClick attribute to cancel a postback. The basic pattern is to call a JavaScript method. If this method returns false, the postback is canceled.

Script Blocks

It's impractical to place a large amount of JavaScript code in an attribute, particularly if you need to use the same code for several controls. A more common approach is to place a JavaScript function in a <script> block and then call that function using an event attribute. The <script> tag can appear anywhere in the header or the body of an HTML document, and a single document can have any number of <script> tags in it.

The <script> tag takes a type attribute that specifies the script language. Browsers will ignore <script> blocks for languages they don't support.

A typical inline script looks like this:

```
<script type="text/javascript">
  <!--
  window.alert('This window displayed through JavaScript.');
  // -->
</script>
```

In this case, the HTML comment markers (<!-- and -->) hide the content from browsers that don't understand script. Additionally, the closing HTML comment marker (-->) is preceded by a JavaScript comment (//). This is because extremely old versions of Netscape will throw a JavaScript parsing exception when encountering the closing HTML comment marker. Modern browsers don't suffer from these problems, and most browsers now recognize the <script> tag (even if they don't support JavaScript).

In this example, the script code is processed as soon as the browser encounters it while rendering the page. If you want your code to occur later, when a specific event occurs, it makes more sense to wrap it inside a function in the script block, like so:

```
<script type="text/javascript">
  function ShowAlert()
  {
      window.alert('This window displayed through JavaScript.');
  }
</script>
```

Now you can hook it up to one or more HTML elements using an event attribute:

```
<asp:TextBox id="TextBox1" runat="server" onmouseover="ShowAlert();" />
```

A script block can contain any number of functions. You can also declare page-level variables that you can access in any function:

```
<script type="text/javascript">
  var counter = 0;
  ...
</script>
```

■ **Note** Although JavaScript code has a superficial similarity to C#, it's a much looser language. When declaring variables and function parameters, you don't need to specify their data types. Similarly, when defining a function, you don't indicate its return type.

If you have too much JavaScript to fit neatly in a page or if you need to reuse the same set of functions in more than one page, it makes sense to move your code to another file. Once you make the transition, you can create a <script> block that points to your external file. The trick is to set the src attribute to point to the file, as shown here:

```
<script type="text/javascript" src="ExternalJavaScript.js">
</script>
```

The .js file will contain the contents of the <script> block. In other words, it will include the functions and variable declarations, but it won't include the opening <script> tag and closing </script> tag.

Moving JavaScript code to an external file is a common technique when dealing with complex JavaScript routines. You can also embed a JavaScript resource in a DLL assembly when you build a custom control using the WebResource attribute.

Placing the Script Block

The content in an HTML document is processed in the order in which it appears, from top to bottom. If you have a script block that uses immediate JavaScript code (loose JavaScript statements that are not wrapped in a function), this code is executed as soon as it is processed. In order to avoid problems, you must place this script block *after* any elements that it manipulates.

However, if your script block uses functions that are called later in the page life cycle (for example, event-handling functions that are triggered in response to a client-side event), you don't need to worry. In this situation, the browser will process the entire page before your functions are triggered. As a result, you can place your script block anywhere in the HTML document, with the <head> section being a popular choice.

■ **Note** Placing JavaScript in a separate file or even embedding it in an assembly doesn't prevent users from retrieving it and examining it (and even modifying their local copy of the web page to use a tampered version of the script file). Therefore, you should never include any secret algorithms or sensitive information in your JavaScript code. You should also make sure you repeat any JavaScript validation steps on the server, because the user can circumvent client-side code.

Manipulating HTML Elements

Reacting to events is only half the story. Most JavaScript-enabled pages also need the ability to change the content in the page. For example, you might want to refresh a label with up-to-date text or inject entirely new content somewhere on a page. The HTML DOM makes this easy—all you need to do is find the element you want and manipulate its innerHTML property.

■ **Note** The innerHTML property represents the content between the start and end tag of an HTML element. Some web pages use the innerText property instead, which automatically escapes HTML tags (for example, it converts <b> to <b>). However, innerText is discouraged because it isn't supported on Mozilla-based browsers such as Firefox.

Unlike in your server-side code, JavaScript doesn't provide member variables that give you access to the HTML elements on your page. Instead, you need to look up the element you need using the document.getElementById() method. Here's an example:

```
var paragraph = document.getElementById("textParagraph1");
```

This task is exceedingly common in JavaScript code. The only consideration is that you need to make sure the elements you want to manipulate have unique identifiers (as set in the ID attribute).

Once you've retrieved the object that represents the HTML tag you want to change, you read and set its properties. All HTML objects have a wide range of basic properties, as well as a number of tag-specific properties. Table 29-2 lists just a few that you may want to manipulate.

Table 29-2. *Common Properties of HTML Objects*

Event	Description
innerHTML	The HTML content between the start and end tag. May include other elements.
style	Returns a style object that exposes all the CSS style properties for your element. For example, you could use myObject.style.fontSize to change the font size of an element. You can use the style object to set colors, borders, fonts, and even positioning.
value	In HTML form controls, the value attribute indicates the current state of the control. For example, in a check box it indicates whether the check box is checked, in a text box it indicates the text inside the box, and so on.
tagName	Provides the name of the HTML tag for this object (without the angle brackets).
parentElement	The HTML object for the tag that contains this tag. For example, if the current element is a <b> tag in a paragraph, this gets the object for the <p> tag. You can use this property (and other related properties) to move from one element to another.

Debugging JavaScript

Visual Studio includes integrated JavaScript debugging. If you're using Internet Explorer 8, you don't need to take any steps to switch on client-side debugging. Visual Studio sets it up automatically, regardless of your Internet Explorer settings.

Debugging JavaScript with Older Versions of IE

With versions of Internet Explorer before IE 8, you need to explicitly enable script debugging. To do so, follow these steps:

1. Choose Tools ➤ Internet Options from the menu in Internet Explorer.
2. In the Internet Options dialog box, choose the Advanced tab.
3. In the list of settings, under the Browsing group, remove the check mark next to Disable Script Debugging (Internet Explorer). You can also remove the check mark

next to Disable Script Debugging (Other) to allow debugging for Internet Explorer windows hosted in other applications.

4. Click OK to apply your change.

When script debugging is switched on, you'll be prompted to debug web pages with script errors, even on websites that you don't control. This can be more than a little annoying because script errors are common, and one script error usually leads to more. In other words, it won't be long before your web browsing is interrupted with a series of dialog boxes, each one prompting you to begin debugging the current page.

You might think you can solve this problem by turning off the Display a Notification About Every Script Error setting, which appears just under the Disable Script Debugging settings. Unfortunately, this setting only applies when debugging is off. For this reason, most developers who test and surf in Internet Explorer switch the script debugging option on while testing and off while surfing.

You can try script debugging out by placing a breakpoint in a JavaScript block, as shown in Figure 29-2. Now, when the browser reaches this point in the code, it enters debug mode in Visual Studio. You can now single-step through your code, hover over variables to see their contents, use the Watch window, and so on, just as you would with server-side C# code.

There's a bit of magic that makes this work. When you place a breakpoint in your JavaScript, you add it to the server-side ASP.NET page (the .aspx source file). However, when the browser reaches your breakpoint, it's using the rendered client-side HTML, which is a bit different. If you look closely at a page while you're debugging it in Visual Studio, you'll notice that you're dealing with the client-side version. For that reason, you won't see ASP.NET control tags—instead, you'll see the HTML that they've rendered. (This is the reason the breakpoint in Figure 29-2 looks a bit different than normal, and has a white dot in the center. The white dot indicates that this isn't the actual breakpoint, just a marker that tells the browser where to place its breakpoint in the rendered HTML.) If your web page markup uses the JavaScript code in a separate .js file, you'll also see that file appear in the Solution Explorer. You can use all the same debugging tools with .js files, including breakpoints and single-step debugging.

The Solution Explorer makes this distinction a bit clearer. It shows both versions of your page, with the runtime version added under a special section named Windows Internet Explorer (as shown in Figure 29-3). You can't modify the rendered version of your page (because doing so wouldn't make any lasting change), but you can edit the original server-side version and then run your page to see the changes.

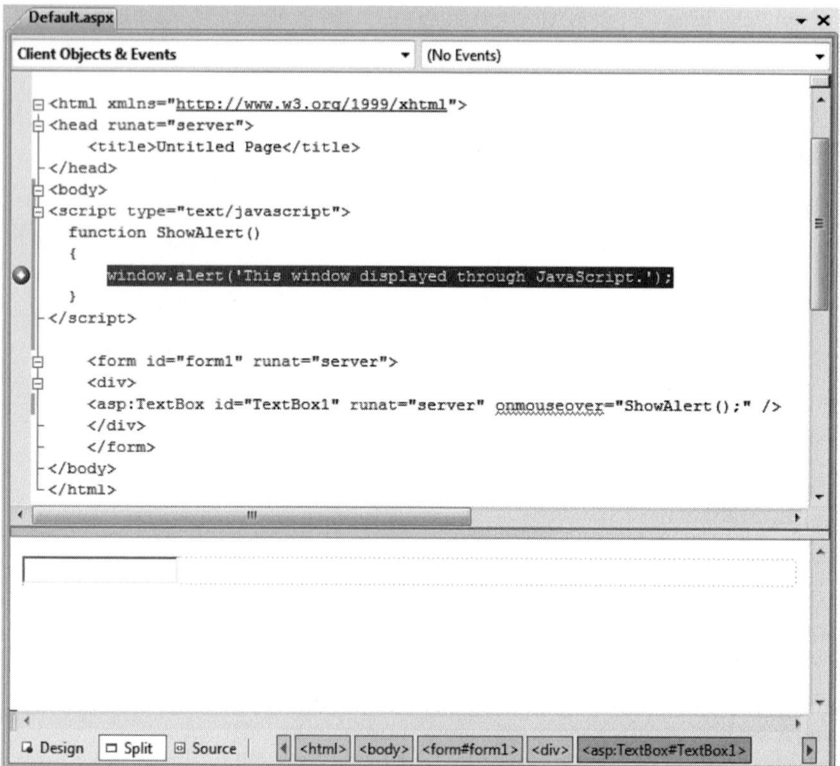

Figure 29-2. *A client-side breakpoint*

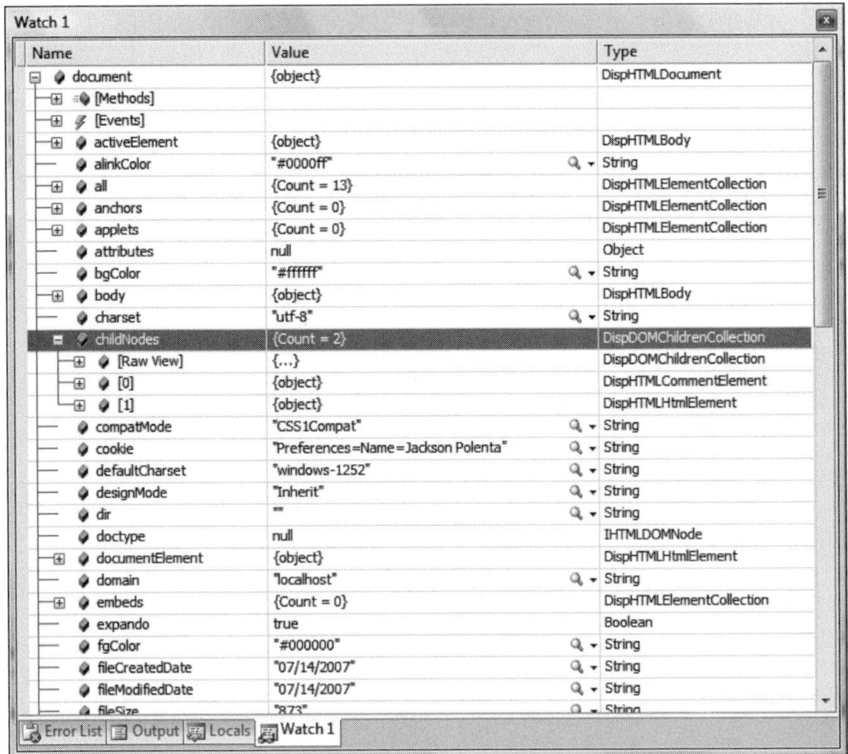

Figure 29-3. Debugging the rendered page

There's one more neat trick you can pull off using Visual Studio's JavaScript debugging. You can add a reference to the JavaScript document object in the Watch window to take a look at the DOM for the current web page. You can then browse through its properties (and even take a look at its methods and events). For example, Figure 29-3 shows an expanded view of the document.childNodes collection, which contains the nested elements of the page. This first node contains the doctype, while the second node is the top-level <html> element. Expand it and look at its childNodes collection, and you'll find the next level of elements (the <head> and <body> elements). You can continue this process to dig deeper into your page until you arrive at the form and its controls.

Basic JavaScript Examples

Now that you've learned the key points of JavaScript, it's easy to enhance your pages with a dash of client-side code. In the following sections, you'll use JavaScript to put a pretty face on pages and pictures that take a long time to download.

Creating a JavaScript Page Processor

How many times have you clicked a web page just to watch the Internet Explorer globe spin for what seems like an eternity? Did your Internet connection go down? Was there any error connecting to a back-end system? Or is the system just that slow? These issues often complicate new web-based solutions, particularly if you're replacing a more responsive rich client application (such as a Windows application). In this situation, the easiest way to reassure your application users is to provide them with progress messages that let them know the system is currently working on their request.

One common way to give a status message is to use JavaScript to create a standard page processor. When the user navigates to a page that takes a long time to process, the page processor appears immediately and shows a standard message (perhaps with scrolling text). At the same time, the requested page is downloaded in the background. Once the results are available, the page processor message is replaced by the requested page.

You can't solve the processing delay problem by adding JavaScript code to the target page, because this code won't be processed until the page has finished processing and the rendered HTML is returned to the user. However, you *can* create a generic page processor that handles requests for any time-consuming page in your site.

To create a page processor, you need to react to the onload and onunload events. Here's a page (named PageProcessor.aspx) that demonstrates this pattern. It shows a table with the message text "Loading Page - Please Wait." The <body> element is wired up to two functions, which you'll consider shortly.

```
<html>
  <head>
    <title>LoadPage</title>
    <script type="text/javascript" >
      <!-- JavaScript functions go here. -->
    </script>
  </head>

  <body onload="BeginPageLoad();"
        onunload="EndPageLoad();">
    <form id="frmPageLoader" method="post" runat="server">
      <table border="0" width="99%">
        <tr><td align="center" valign="center">
            <span id="MessageText">Loading Page - Please Wait</span>
            <span id="ProgressMeter"></span>
        </td></tr>
      </table>
    </form>
  </body>
</html>
```

To use the page processor, you request this page and pass the desired page as a query string argument. For example, if you want to load TimeConsumingPage.aspx in the background, you would use this URL:

```
PageProcessor.aspx?Page=TimeConsumingPage.aspx
```

The page processor needs very little server-side code. In fact, all it does is retrieve the originally requested page from the query string and store it in a protected page class variable. (This is useful because you can then expose this variable to your JavaScript code using an ASP.NET data binding expression, as you'll see in a moment.) Here's the complete server-side code for the PageProcessor.aspx page:

```
public partial class PageProcessor : System.Web.UI.Page
{
    protected string PageToLoad;

    protected void Page_Load(object sender, EventArgs e)
    {
        PageToLoad = Request.QueryString["Page"];
    }
}
```

The rest of the work is performed with client-side JavaScript. When the page processor first loads, the onload event fires, which calls the client-side BeginPageLoad() function. The BeginPageLoad() function keeps the current window open and begins retrieving the page that the user requested. To accomplish this, it uses the window.setInterval() method, which sets a timer that calls the custom UpdateProgressMeter() function periodically.

Here's the code for the BeginPageLoad() JavaScript function:

```
var iLoopCounter = 1;
var iMaxLoop = 6;
var iIntervalId;

function BeginPageLoad()
{
    // Redirect the browser to another page while keeping focus.
    location.href = "<%=PageToLoad %>";

    // Update progress meter every 1/2 second.
    iIntervalId = window.setInterval
      ("iLoopCounter=UpdateProgressMeter(iLoopCounter,iMaxLoop);", 500);
}
```

The first code statement points the page to its new URL. Notice that the page you want to download isn't hard-coded in the JavaScript code. Instead, it's set with the data binding expression <%=PageToLoad %>. When the page is rendered on the server, ASP.NET automatically inserts the value of the PageToLoad variable in its place.

The last code statement starts a timer using the window.setInterval() function. Every 500 milliseconds, this timer fires and executes the line of code that's specified. This line of code calls another JavaScript function, which is named UpdateProgressMeter(), and keeps track of the current loop counter.

The UpdateProgressMeter() function simply changes the status message periodically to make it look more like an animated progress meter. The status message cycles repeatedly from 0 to 5 periods. Here's the JavaScript code that makes it work:

```
function UpdateProgressMeter(iCurrentLoopCounter, iMaximumLoops)
{
    // Find the object for the <span> element with the progress text.
    var progressMeter = document.getElementById("ProgressMeter")

    iCurrentLoopCounter += 1;
    if(iCurrentLoopCounter <= iMaximumLoops)
    {
        progressMeter.innerText += ".";
        return iCurrentLoopCounter;
    }
```

```
    else
    {
        // Reset the progress meter.
        ProgressMeter.innerText = "";
        return 1;
    }
}
```

Finally, when the page is fully loaded, the client-side onunload event fires. In this example, the onunload event is hooked up to a function named EndPageLoad(). This function stops the timer, clears the progress message, and sets a temporary transfer message that disappears as soon as the new page is rendered in the browser. Here's the code:

```
function EndPageLoad()
{
    window.clearInterval(iIntervalId);

    var progressMeter = document.getElementById("ProgressMeter")
    progressMeter.innerText = "Page Loaded - Now Transferring";
}
```

No postbacks are made through the whole process. The end result is a progress message (see Figure 29-4) that remains until the target page is fully processed and loaded.

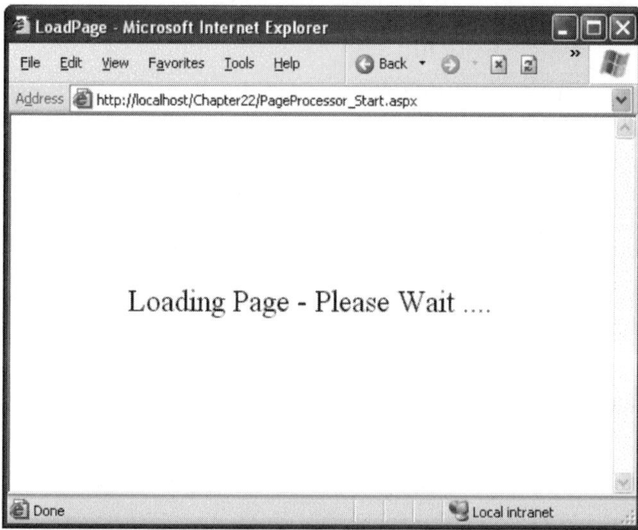

Figure 29-4. *An automated progress meter*

To test the page processor, you simply need to use a target page that takes a long time to execute on the server (because of the work performed by the code) or to be downloaded in the client (because of the size of the page). You can simulate a slow page by placing the following time delay code in the target page, like this:

```
protected void Page_Load(object sender, EventArgs e)
{
    // Simulate a slow page loading (wait five seconds).
    System.Threading.Thread.Sleep(5000);
}
```

Now when you request this page through the page processor, you'll have five seconds to study the progress message.

■ **Note** To try this with the sample code included for this chapter, request the PageProcessor_Start.aspx page, which includes a button that takes you to the time-consuming PageProcessor_Target.aspx using the page processor.

As you can see, with just a small amount of client-side JavaScript code, you can keep the user informed that a page is processing. By keeping users informed, the level of perceived performance increases.

Using JavaScript to Download Images Asynchronously

The previous example demonstrated how JavaScript can help you create a more responsive interface. This advantage isn't limited to page processors. You can also use JavaScript to download time-consuming portions of a page in the background. Often, this requires a little more work, but it can provide a much better user experience.

For example, consider a case where you're displaying a list of records in a GridView. One of the fields displays a small image. This technique, which was demonstrated in Chapter 10, requires a dedicated page to retrieve the image, and, depending on your design, it may require a separate trip to the file system or database for each record. In many cases, you can optimize this design (for example, by preloading images in the cache before you bind the grid), but this isn't possible if the images are retrieved from a third-party source. This is the case in the next example, which displays a list of books and retrieves the associated images from the Amazon website.

Rendering the full table can take a significant amount of time, especially if it has a large number of records. You can deal with this situation more effectively by using placeholder images that appear immediately. The actual images can be retrieved in the background and displayed once they're available. The time required to display the complete grid with all its pictures won't change, but the user will be able to start reading and scrolling through the data before the images have been downloaded, which makes the slowdown easier to bear.

The first step in this example is to create the page (named IncrementalDownloadGrid.aspx) that displays the GridView. For the purposes of this example, the code fills a DataSet with a static list of books from an XML file.

```
protected void Page_Load(object sender, EventArgs e)
{
    if (!Page.IsPostBack)
    {
        // Get data.
        DataSet ds = new DataSet();
        ds.ReadXml(Server.MapPath("Books.xml"));
```

```
        GridView1.DataSource = ds.Tables["Book"];
        GridView1.DataBind();
    }
}
```

Here's the content of the XML file:

```
<?xml version="1.0" encoding="utf-8" ?>
<Books>
    <Book Title="Expert C# Business Objects" isbn="1590593448"
     Publisher="Apress"></Book>
    <Book Title="C# and the .NET Platform" isbn="1590590554"
     Publisher="Apress"></Book>
    <Book Title="Beginning XSLT" isbn="1590592603"
     Publisher="Apress"></Book>
    <Book Title="SQL Server Security Distilled" isbn="1590592190"
     Publisher="Apress"></Book>
</Books>
```

As you can see, the XML data doesn't include any picture information. Instead, these details need to be retrieved from the Amazon website. The GridView binds directly to the columns that are available (Title, isbn, and Publisher) and then uses another page (named GetBookImage.aspx) to find the corresponding image for this ISBN.

Here's the GridView control tag without the style information:

```
<asp:GridView id="GridView1" runat="server" AutoGenerateColumns="False">
  <Columns>
    <asp:BoundField DataField="Title" HeaderText="Title"/>
    <asp:BoundField DataField="isbn" HeaderText="ISBN"/>
    <asp:BoundField DataField="Publisher" HeaderText="Publisher"/>
    <asp:TemplateField>
      <HeaderTemplate>
        Book Cover
      </HeaderTemplate>
      <ItemTemplate>
        <img src="UnknownBook.gif"
         onerror="this.src='Unknownbook.gif';"
         onload=
"GetBookImage(this, '<%# DataBinder.Eval(Container.DataItem, "isbn") %>');"
      </ItemTemplate>
    </asp:TemplateField>
  </Columns>
</asp:GridView>
```

The innovative part is the last column, which contains an <img> tag. Rather than pointing this tag directly to GetBookImage.aspx, the src attribute is set to a local image file (UnknownBook.gif), which can be quickly downloaded and displayed. Then the onload event (which occurs as soon as the UnknownBook.gif image is first displayed) begins downloading the real image in the background. When the real image is retrieved, it's displayed, unless an error occurs during the download process. The onerror event is handled in order to ensure that if an error occurs, the UnknownBook.gif image remains (rather than the red X error icon).

The onload event completes its work with the help of a custom JavaScript function named GetBookImage(). When the page calls GetBookImage(), it passes a reference to the current image control (the one that needs the new picture) and the ISBN for the book, which is extracted through a data binding expression. The GetBookImage() function calls another page, named GetBookImage.aspx, to get the picture for the book. It indicates the picture it wants by passing the ISBN as a query string argument.

```
<script language="javascript" type="text/javascript">
  function GetBookImage(img, url)
  {
      // Detach the event handler (the code makes just one attempt
      // to get the picture).
      img.onload = null;

      // Try to get the picture from the GetBookImage.aspx page.
      img.src = 'GetBookImage.aspx?isbn=' + url;
  }
</script>
```

The GetBookImage.aspx page performs the time-consuming task of retrieving the image you want, which might involve contacting a web service or connecting to a database. In this case, the GetBookImage.aspx page simply hands the work off to a dedicated class named FindBook that does the work. Once the URL is retrieved, it redirects the page:

```
protected void Page_Load(object sender, System.EventArgs e)
{
    FindBook findBook = new FindBook();
    string imageUrl = findBook.GetImageUrl(Request.QueryString["isbn"]);
    Response.Redirect(imageUrl);
}
```

The FindBook class is more complex. It uses screen scraping to find the <img> tag for the picture on the Amazon website. Unfortunately, Amazon's image thumbnails don't have a clear naming convention that would allow you to retrieve the URL directly. However, based on the ISBN you can find the book detail page, and you can look through the HTML of the book detail page to find the image URL. That's the task the FindBook class performs.

Two methods are at work in the FindBook class. The GetWebPageAsString() method requests a URL, retrieves the HTML content, and converts it to a string, as shown here:

```
public string GetWebPageAsString(string url)
{
    // Create the request.
    WebRequest requestHtml = WebRequest.Create(url);

    // Get the response.
    WebResponse responseHtml = requestHtml.GetResponse();

    // Read the response stream.
    StreamReader r = new StreamReader(responseHtml.GetResponseStream());
    string htmlContent = r.ReadToEnd();
    r.Close();
    return htmlContent;
}
```

The GetImageUrl() method uses GetWebPageAsString() and a little regular expression wizardry.

Amazon image URLs are notoriously cryptic. However, most currently take the following form:

`http://ec1.images-amazon.com/images/I/[ImageName].jpg.`

For example, a typical URL is

`http://ec1.images-amazon.com/images/I/51M6SPXWT5L._BO2,204,203,200_PIsitb-dp-500-arrow,TopRight,45,-64_OU01_AA240_SH20_.jpg.`

Using the regular expression, the code matches the full URL for the book image (with the ending character sequence) and returns it. Here's the complete code for the GetImageUrl() method:

```
public string GetImageUrl(string isbn)
{
    try
    {
        // Find the pointer to the book cover image.
        // Amazon.com has the most cover images,
        // so go there to look for it.
        // Start with the book details page.
        isbn = isbn.Replace("-", "");
        string bookUrl = "http://www.amazon.com/exec/obidos/ASIN/" + isbn;

        // Now retrieve the HTML content of the book details page.
        string bookHtml = GetWebPageAsString(bookUrl);

        // Search the page for an image tag that has the requested ISBN.
        string imgTagPattern =
          "<img src=\"(http://ec1.images-amazon.com/images/I/[^\"]+)\"";
        Match imgTagMatch = Regex.Match(bookHtml, imgTagPattern);
        return imgTagMatch.Groups[1].Value;
    }
    catch
    {
        return "";
    }
}
```

■ **Note** Using the dedicated Amazon web service would obviously be a more flexible and robust approach, although it wouldn't change this example, which demonstrates the performance enhancements of a little JavaScript. You can get information about Amazon's offerings at http://www.amazon.com/gp/aws/landing.html.

The end result is a page that initially loads with default images, as shown in Figure 29-5. After a short delay, the images will begin to appear, as shown in Figure 29-6.

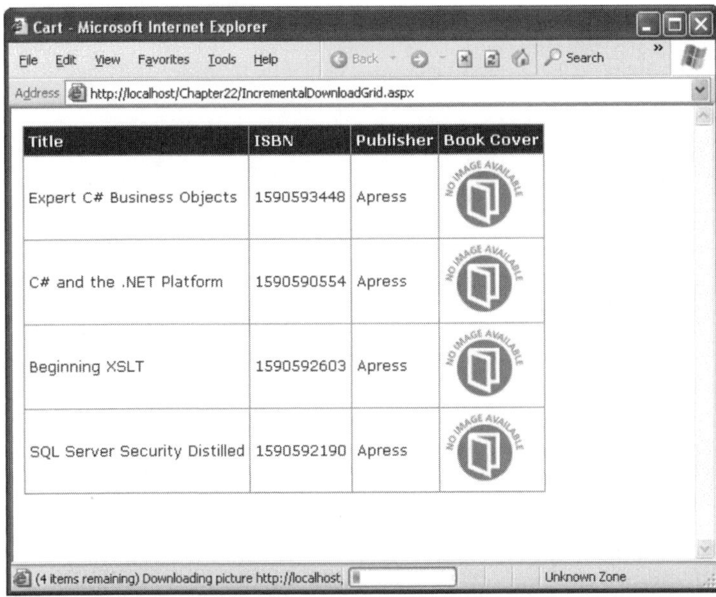

Figure 29-5. The initial view of the page

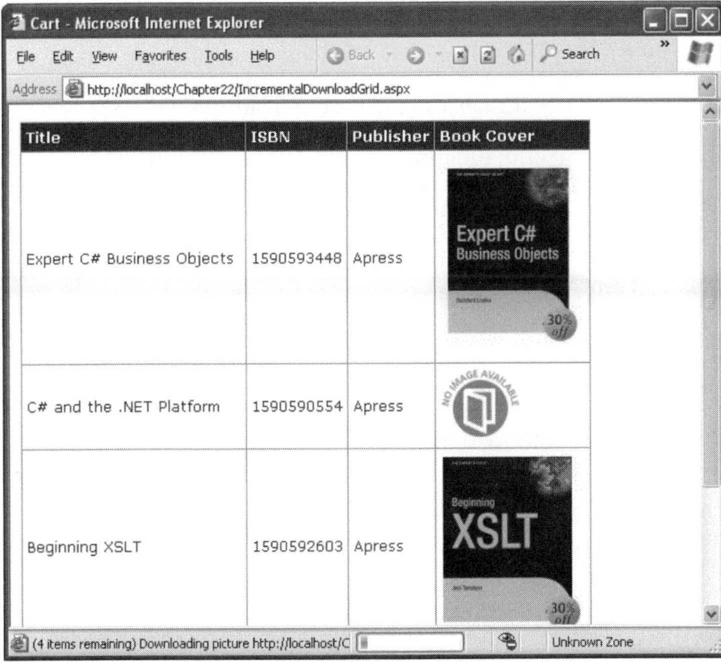

Figure 29-6. The page with image thumbnails

Once loaded, the real book images will load in the background, but the user can begin using the page immediately.

Rendering Script Blocks

So far, the examples you've seen have used static <script> blocks that are inserted directly in the .aspx portion of your page. However, it's often more flexible to render the script using the Page.ClientScript property, which exposes a ClientScriptManager object that provides several useful methods for managing script blocks. Two of the most useful are as follows:

- **RegisterClientScriptBlock():** Writes a script block at the beginning of the web form, right after the <form runat="server"> tag
- **RegisterStartupScript():** Writes a script block at the end of the web form, right before the closing </form> tag

These two methods perform the same task—they take a string input with the <script> block and add it to the rendered HTML. RegisterClientScriptBlock() is designed for functions that are called in response to JavaScript events. You can place these <script> blocks anywhere in the HTML document. Placing them at the beginning of the web form is just a matter of convention and makes them easy to find. The RegisterStartupScript() method is meant to add JavaScript code that will be executed immediately when the page loads. This code might manipulate other controls on the page, so to be safe you should place it at the end of the web form. Otherwise, it might try to access elements that haven't been created yet.

When you use RegisterClientScriptBlock() and RegisterStartupScript(), you also specify a key name for the script block. For example, if your function opens a pop-up window, you might use the key name ShowPopUp. The actual key name isn't important as long as it's unique. The purpose is to ensure that ASP.NET doesn't add the same script function more than once. This scenario is most important when dealing with server controls that render JavaScript. For example, consider the ASP.NET validation controls. Every validation control requires the use of certain validation functions, but it doesn't make sense for each control to add a duplicate <script> block. But because each control uses the same key name when it calls RegisterClientScriptBlock(), ASP.NET realizes they are duplicate definitions, and it renders only a single copy.

For example, the following code registers a JavaScript function named confirmSubmit(). This function displays a confirmation box and, depending on whether the user clicks OK or Cancel, either posts back the page or does nothing. This function is then attached to the form through the onsubmit attribute.

```
protected void Page_Load(object sender, EventArgs e)
{
    string script = @"<script type='text/javascript'>
       function ConfirmSubmit() {
         var msg = 'Are you sure you want to submit this data?';
         return confirm(msg);
       }
    </script>";

    Page.ClientScript.RegisterClientScriptBlock(this.GetType(), "Confirm", script);
    form1.Attributes.Add("onsubmit", "return ConfirmSubmit();");
}
```

■ **Note** To make it easier to define a JavaScript function over multiple lines, you can precede the string with the @ symbol. That way, all the characters are treated as string literals, and you can span multiple lines.

Figure 29-7 shows the result.

Figure 29-7. Using a JavaScript confirmation message

In this example, there's no real benefit from using the RegisterClientScriptBlock() method. However, the ClientScriptManager methods become essential when you're developing a custom control that uses JavaScript. Later in this chapter, you'll see a control that uses RegisterStartupScript() to show a pop-up window.

Script Injection Attacks

Often, developers aren't aware of the security vulnerabilities they introduce in a page. That's because many common dangers—including script injection and SQL injection—are surprisingly easy to stumble into. To minimize these risks, technology vendors such as Microsoft strive to find ways to integrate safety checks into the programming framework itself, thereby insulating application programmers.

One attack to which web pages are commonly vulnerable is a *script injection* attack. A script injection attack occurs when malicious tags or script code are submitted by a user (usually through a simple control such as a TextBox control) and then rendered into an HTML page later. Although this rendering process is intended to *display* the user-supplied data, it actually *executes* the script. A script injection attack can have any of a number of different effects from trivial to significant. If the user-supplied data is stored in a database and inserted later into pages used by other people, the attack may affect the operation of the website for all users.

The basic technique for a script injection attack is for the client to submit content with embedded scripting tags. These scripting tags can include <script>, <object>, <applet>, and <embed>. Although the application can specifically check for these tags and use HTML encoding to replace the tags with harmless HTML entities, that basic validation often isn't performed.

Request Validation

Script injection attacks are a concern of all web developers, whether they are using ASP.NET, ASP, or other web development technologies. ASP.NET includes a feature designed to automatically combat script injection attacks, called *request validation*. Request validation checks the posted form input and raises an error if any potentially malicious tags (such as <script>) are found. In fact, request validation disallows any nonnumeric tags, including HTML tags (such as <b> and <img>), and tags that don't correspond to anything (such as <abcd>).

To test the script validation features, you can create a simple web page like the one shown in Figure 29-8. This simple example contains a text box and a button.

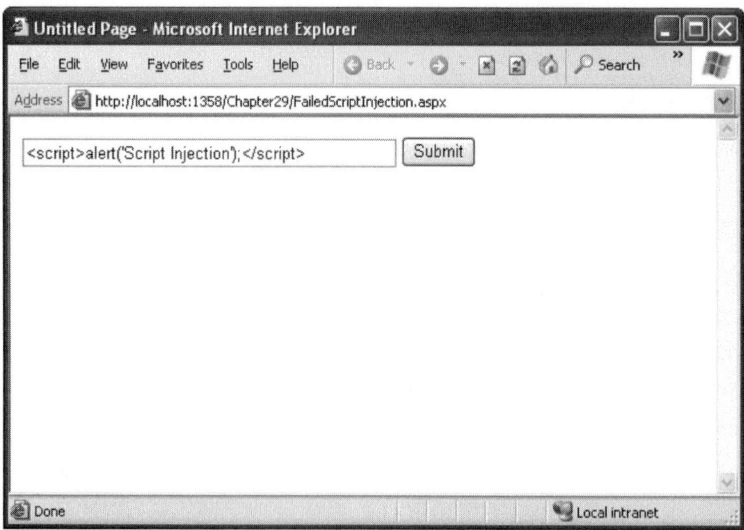

Figure 29-8. *Testing a script injection attack*

Now, try to enter a block of content with a script tag and then click the button. ASP.NET will detect the potentially dangerous value and generate an error. If you're running the code locally, you'll see the rich error page with detailed information, as shown in Figure 29-9. (If you're requesting the page remotely, you'll see only a generic error page.)

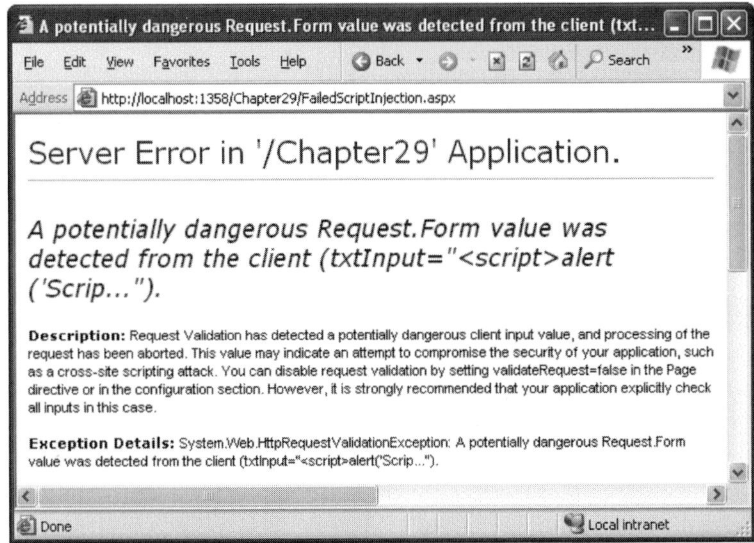

Figure 29-9. *A failed script injection attack*

Disabling Request Validation

In some situations, the request validation rules are just too restrictive. For example, you might have an application where users have a genuine need to specify HTML tags or a block of XML data. (For example, consider a web application that requires that the user submit a block of formatted HTML that represents an auction listing or an advertisement.) In these situations, you can specifically disable script validation by following two steps.

First, you need to set the ValidateRequest property of the Page directive, as shown here:

```
<%@ Page ValidateRequest="false" ...  %>
```

However, this change alone has no effect. That's because ASP.NET 4 changes the way request validation works, by applying it earlier in the page processing lifecycle. The goal of this change is to let request validation work with other, non-ASP.NET file types (which it does). However, the drawback is that request validation always runs, even if you set ValidateRequest to false.

To change this behavior, you can either add custom validation code (as explained in the next section), or you can tell ASP.NET to revert to its pre-version-4 validation behavior. To do that, you need to add the <httpRuntime> element to your web.config file, and set requestValidationMode to 2.0, as shown here:

```
<configuration>
  <system.web>
    <httpRuntime requestValidationMode="2.0" />
    ...
  </system.web>
</configuration>
```

Now, consider what happens if you attempt to display the user-supplied value in a label with this code:

```
protected void cmdSubmit_Click(object sender, EventArgs e)
{
    lblInfo.Text = "You entered: " + txtInput.Text;
}
```

If a malicious user enters the text <script>alert('Script Injection');</script>, the returned web page will execute the script, as shown in Figure 29-10.

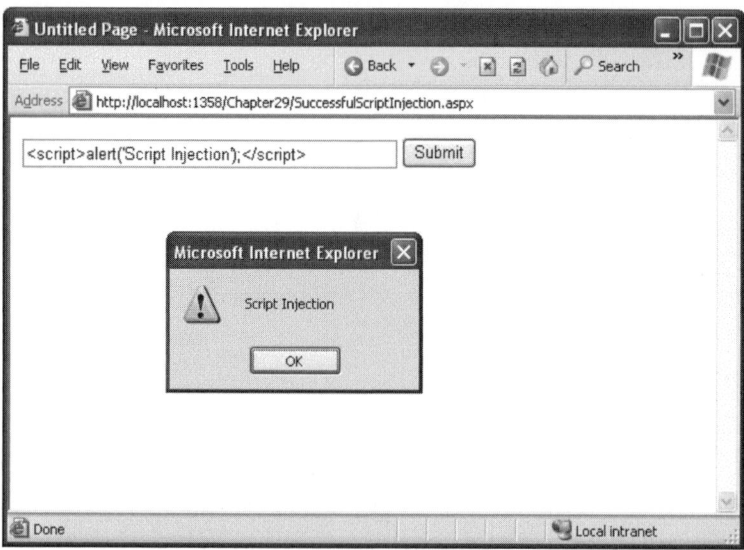

Figure 29-10. *A successful script injection attack*

You can also disable request validation for an entire web application by modifying the web.config file. Add or set the validateRequest attribute of the <pages> element, as shown here:

```
<configuration>
  <system.web>
    <pages validateRequest="false" />
    <httpRuntime requestValidationMode="2.0" />
    ...
  </system.web>
</configuration>
```

Keep in mind that the script in a script injection attack is always executed on the client end. However, this doesn't mean it's limited to a single user. In many situations, user-supplied data is stored in a location such as a database and can be viewed by other users. For example, if a user supplies a script block for a business name when adding a business to a registry, another user who requests a full list of all businesses in the registry will be affected.

To prevent a script injection attack from happening when request validation is turned off, you need to explicitly encode the content before you display it using the Server object, as described earlier in this chapter.

Here's a rewritten version of the Button.Click event handler that isn't susceptible to script injection attacks:

```
protected void cmdSubmit_Click(object sender, EventArgs e)
{
    lblInfo.Text = "You entered: " + Server.HtmlEncode(txtInput.Text);
}
```

Figure 29-11 shows the result of an attempted script injection attack on this page.

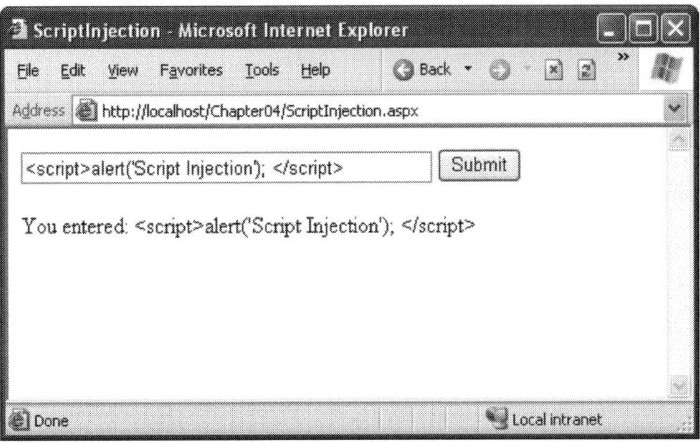

Figure 29-11. A disarmed script injection attack

Extending Request Validation

For the majority of web applications, ASP.NET's standard request validation will work perfectly well. But in situations where you need to selectively allow certain values that are usually denied or deny additional values, you can extend the request validation system with your own custom code.

■ **Note** If you're faced with the choice between disabling request validation completely and adding an exception through code, it's almost always better to add the exception. Otherwise, your application is left open to a wide variety of scripting attacks and other mischief.

To extend the request validation system, you need to create a class that derives from RequestValidator (which is found in the System.Web.Util namespace) and overrides IsValidRequestString:

```
public class CustomRequestValidator : RequestValidator
{
    protected override bool IsValidRequestString(
      HttpContext context, string value,
      RequestValidationSource requestValidationSource,
      string collectionKey, out int validationFailureIndex)
    {
        ...
    }
}
```

The IsValidRequestString() method accepts five arguments:

context: This is the HttpContext for the request, which allows you to access built-in ASP.NET objects like Request, Response, Application, Server, Session, and Cache.

value: This is the string with the text that needs to be validated.

requestValidationSource: This identifies the type of information that's being validated using the RequestValidationSource enumeration. Possible values include Cookies, File, Form, Headers, Path, and QueryString.

collectionKey: If the data source comes from a collection, collectionKey returns the name that's used to index the value. For example, in the case of form data, the collectionKey is the corresponding input control that posted the value.

validationFailureIndex: If the validation runs successfully, validationFailureIndex should be set to 0 and the IsValidRequestString() method should return true. If validation fails, the IsValidRequestString() method should return false and the validationFailureIndex can be set to point to the location in the string where the invalid data begins.

Using this information, it's easy to build a quick-and-dirty validation routine that changes ASP.NET's built-on behavior. In the following example, the validator checks if it's performing form validation. If it isn't, the validator triggers the default implementation, passing the work along. If it is, the validator then searches for <script> tags in the posted input. It rejects values that include this detail, but accepts everything else, making it far more permissive than ASP.NET's usual validation.

```
public class CustomRequestValidator : RequestValidator
{
    protected override bool IsValidRequestString(
      HttpContext context, string value,
      RequestValidationSource requestValidationSource,
      string collectionKey, out int validationFailureIndex)
    {
        if (requestValidationSource == RequestValidationSource.Form)
        {
            int errorIndex = value.ToLower().IndexOf("<script>");
            if (errorIndex != -1)
            {
                validationFailureIndex = errorIndex;
                return false;
            }
            else
            {
                validationFailureIndex = 0;
```

```
                return true;
            }
        }
        else
        {
            return base.IsValidRequestString(context, value,
                requestValidationSource, collectionKey, out validationFailureIndex);
        }
    }
}
```

This example is simply a demonstration that shows how custom validation works. However, it's enough for you to see how you can plug it as much or as little custom validation code as you want.

Tip If you want to *augment* the standard ASP.NET validation, it's a good idea to chain your implementation. After the value passes your checks, you can then call the base IsValidRequestString() implementation to perform the additional built-in checks.

To use the CustomRequestValidator, you simply need to register it in the web.config file with the requestValidationType attribute of the <httpRuntime> element:

```
<configuration>
  <system.web>
    <httpRuntime requestValidationType="CustomRequestValidator" />
    ...
  </system.web>
</configuration>
```

Custom Controls with JavaScript

JavaScript plays an important role in many advanced web controls. In an ideal world, the web-page developer never needs to worry about JavaScript. Instead, web-page developers would program with neat object-oriented controls that render the JavaScript they need to optimize their appearance and their performance. This gives you the best of both worlds—object-oriented programming on the server and the client-side frills of JavaScript.

You can create any number of controls with JavaScript and the HTML document model. Common examples include rich menus, specialized trees, and advanced grids, many of which are available (some for free) at Microsoft's `http://www.asp.net` community site. In the following sections, you'll consider two custom controls that use JavaScript—a pop-up window generator and a rollover button.

Pop-Up Windows

For most people, pop-up windows are one of the Web's most annoying characteristics. Usually, they deliver advertisements, but sometimes they serve the slightly more valid purpose of providing helpful information or inviting the user to participate in a survey or promotional offer. A related variant is the pop-under window, which displays the new window underneath the current window. This way, the advertisement doesn't distract the user until the original browser window is closed.

It's fairly easy to show a pop-up window by using the window.open() function in a JavaScript block. Here's an example:

```
<script type="text/javascript">
  window.open('http://www.apress.com', 'myWindow',
    'toolbar=0, height=500, width=800, resizable=1, scrollbars=1');
  window.focus();
</script>
```

The window.open() function accepts several parameters. They include the link for the new page and the frame name of the window (which is important if you want to load a new document into that frame later, through another link). The third parameter is a comma-separated string of attributes that configure the style and size of the pop-up window. These attributes can include any of the following:

- height and width, which are set to pixel values
- toolbar and menuBar, which can be set to 1 or 0 (or yes or no) depending on whether you want to display these elements
- resizable, which can be set to 1 or 0 depending on whether you want a fixed or resizable window border
- scrollbars, which can be set to 1 or 0 depending on whether you want to show scrollbars in the pop-up window

As with any other JavaScript code, you can add a <script> block that uses the window.open() function, or you can use the window.open() function directly with a JavaScript event attribute.

You may want to use the same pop-up functionality for several pages and tailor the pop-up URL based on user-specific information. For example, you might want to check whether the user has already seen an advertisement before showing it, or you might want to pass the user name to the new window as a query string argument so that it can be incorporated in the pop-up message. In these scenarios, you need some level of programmatic control over the pop-up, so it makes sense to create a component that wraps all these details. The next example develops a PopUp control to fill this role. As with the custom controls you considered in Chapter 27, you can place the code for this control in the App_Code directory, but a more robust approach is to put it in a separate class library assembly (which is the approach you'll find in the sample code).

Here's the definition for the PopUp control:

```
public class PopUp : Control
{ ... }
```

By deriving this component from Control, you gain the ability to add your pop-up to the Toolbox and drop it on a web form at design time.

To ensure that the PopUp control is as reusable as possible, it provides properties such as PopUnder, Url, WindowHeight, WindowWidth, Resizable, and Scrollbars, which allow you to configure the JavaScript that it generates. Here's the code for the PopUp properties:

```
public bool PopUnder
{
    get {return (bool)ViewState["PopUnder"];}
    set {ViewState["PopUnder"] = value;}
}

public string Url
```

```
{
    get {return (string)ViewState["Url"];}
    set {ViewState["Url"] = value;}
}

public int WindowHeight
{
    get {return (int)ViewState["WindowHeight"];}
    set
    {
        if (value < 1)
        throw new ArgumentException("WindowHeight must be greater than 0");
        ViewState["WindowHeight"] = value;
    }
}

public int WindowWidth
{
    get {return (int)ViewState["WindowWidth"];}
    set
    {
        if (value < 1)
        throw new ArgumentException("WindowWidth must be greater than 0");
        ViewState["WindowWidth"] = value;
    }
}

public bool Resizable
{
    get {return (bool)ViewState["Resizable"];}
    set {ViewState["Resizable"] = value;}
}

public bool Scrollbars
{
    get {return (bool)ViewState["Scrollbars"];}
    set {ViewState["Scrollbars"] = value;}
}

// Constructor sets default values.
public PopUp()
{
    PopUnder = true;
    Url = "about:blank";
    WindowHeight = 300;
    WindowWidth = 300;
    Resizable = false;
    Scrollbars = false;
}
```

Now that the control has defined these properties, it's time to put them to work in the Render() method, which writes the JavaScript code to the page. The first step is to make sure the browser supports JavaScript. You can examine the Page.Request.Browser.JavaScript property, which returns true or false, but this approach is considered obsolete (because it doesn't give you the flexibility to distinguish between different levels of JavaScript and HTML DOM support). The recommended solution is to check that the Page.Request.Browser.EcmaScriptVersion is greater than or equal to 1, which implies JavaScript support.

If JavaScript is supported, the code uses a StringBuilder to build the script block. This code is fairly straightforward—the only unusual detail is that the Boolean Scrollbars and Resizable values need to be converted to integers and *then* to strings. That's because the required syntax is scrollbars=1 rather than scrollbars=true (which is the text you end up with if you convert a Boolean value directly to a string).

Here's the complete rendering code:

```
protected override void Render(HtmlTextWriter writer)
{
    if (Page.Request.Browser.EcmaScriptVersion.Major >= 1)
    {
        StringBuilder javaScriptString = new StringBuilder();
        javaScriptString.Append("<script type='text/javascript'>");
        javaScriptString.Append("\n<!-- ");
        javaScriptString.Append("\nwindow.open('");
        javaScriptString.Append(Url + "', '" + ID);
        javaScriptString.Append("','toolbar=0,");
        javaScriptString.Append("height=" + WindowHeight + ",");
        javaScriptString.Append("width=" + WindowWidth + ",");
        javaScriptString.Append("resizable=" +
          Convert.ToInt16(Resizable).ToString() + ",");
        javaScriptString.Append("scrollbars=" +
          Convert.ToInt16(Scrollbars).ToString());
        javaScriptString.Append("');\n");
        if (PopUnder) javaScriptString.Append("window.focus();");
        javaScriptString.Append("\n-->\n");
        javaScriptString.Append("</script>\n");
        writer.Write(javaScriptString.ToString());
    }
    else
    {
        writer.Write( "<!-- This browser does not support JavaScript -->");
    }
}
```

To use the PopUp control, you need to register the control assembly and map it to a control prefix with the Register directive. You can then declare the PopUp control on a page. Here's a sample web page that does this:

```
<%@ Page Language="C#" AutoEventWireup="true" CodeFile="PopUpTest.aspx.cs"
 Inherits="PopUpTest" %>
<%@ Register Assembly="JavaScriptCustomControls"
 Namespace="CustomServerControlsLibrary" TagPrefix="cc1" %>

<html xmlns="http://www.w3.org/1999/xhtml" >
<head runat="server">
  <title>Untitled Page</title>
</head>
<body>
  <form id="form1" runat="server">
    <div>
```

```
      <cc1:popup id="PopUp1" runat="server"
       Url="PopUpAd.aspx" Scrollbars="True" Resizable="True"/>
    </div>
  </form>
```

Figure 29-12 shows the PopUp control in action.

■ **Tip** Usually, custom controls register JavaScript blocks in the OnPreRender() method, rather than writing it directly in the Render() method. However, the PopUp control bypasses this approach and takes direct control of writing the script block. That's because you don't want the usual behavior, which is to create one script block regardless of how many PopUp controls you place on the page. Instead, if you add more than one PopUp control, you want the page to include a separate script block for each control. This gives you the ability to create pages that display multiple pop-up windows.

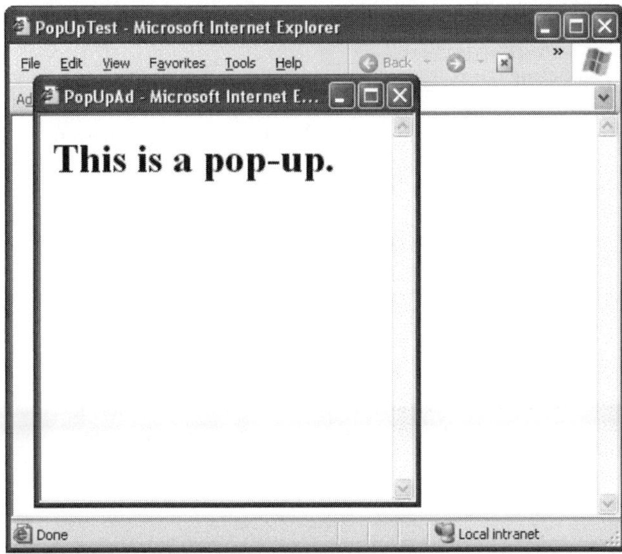

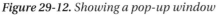

Figure 29-12. Showing a pop-up window

If you want to enhance the PopUp component, you can add more properties. For example, you could add properties that allow you to specify the position where the window will be displayed. Some websites use advertisements that don't appear for several seconds. You could use this technique with this component by adding a JavaScript timer (and wrapping it with a control property that allows you to specify the number of seconds to wait). Once again, the basic idea is to give the page developer a neat object to program with and the ability to use the rendering methods to generate the required JavaScript in the page.

Rollover Buttons

Rollover buttons are another useful JavaScript trick that has no equivalent in the ASP.NET world. A rollover button displays one image when it first appears and another image when the mouse hovers over it (and sometimes a third image when the image is clicked).

To provide the rollover effect, a rollover button usually consists of an <img> tag that handles the onclick, onmouseover, and onmouseout JavaScript events. These events will call a function that swaps images for the current button, like this:

```
<script language='JavaScript'>
  function swapImg(id, url)
  {
    var elm = document.getElementById(id);
    elm.src = url;
  }
</script>
```

A configured <img> tag would then look like this (where RollOverButton1 is the name of the rendered <img> element for the control):

```
<img src="buttonOriginal.jpg"
 onmouseover="swapImg('RollOverButton1', 'buttonMouseOver.jpg');"
 onmouseout="swapImg('RollOverButton1', 'buttonOriginal.jpg');" />
```

Rollover buttons are a mainstay on the Web, and it's fairly easy to fill the gap in ASP.NET with a custom control. The easiest way to create this control is to derive from the WebControl class and use <img> as the base tag. You also need to implement the IPostBackEventHandler to allow the button to trigger a server-side event when clicked.

Here's the declaration for the RollOverButton control class and its constructor:

```
public class RollOverButton : WebControl, IPostBackEventHandler
{
    public RollOverButton() : base(HtmlTextWriterTag.Img)
    { ... }

    // Other code omitted.
}
```

The RollOverButton class provides two properties—one URL for the original image and another URL for the image that should be shown when the user moves the mouse over the button. Here are the property definitions:

```
public string ImageUrl
{
    get {return (string)ViewState["ImageUrl"];}
    set {ViewState["ImageUrl"] = value;}
}

public string MouseOverImageUrl
{
    get {return (string)ViewState["MouseOverImageUrl"];}
    set {ViewState["MouseOverImageUrl"] = value;}
}
```

The next step is to have the control emit the client-side JavaScript that can swap between the two pictures. In this case, it's quite likely that there will be multiple RollOverButton instances on the same page. That means you need to register the script block with a control-specific key so that no matter how many buttons you add there's only a single instance of the function. By convention, this script block is registered by overriding the OnPreRender() method, which is called just before the rendering process starts, as shown here:

```
protected override void OnPreRender(EventArgs e)
{
    if (!Page.ClientScript.IsClientScriptBlockRegistered("swapImg"))
    {
        string script =
          "<script type='text/javascript'> " +
          "function swapImg(id, url) { " +
          "var elm = document.getElementById(id); " +
          "elm.src = url; }" +
          "</script> ";
        Page.ClientScript.RegisterClientScriptBlock(this.GetType(),
          "swapImg", script);
    }
    base.OnPreRender(e);
}
```

This code explicitly checks whether the script block has been registered using the IsClientScriptBlockRegistered() method. You don't actually need to test this property; as long as you use the same key, ASP.NET will render only a single instance of the script block. However, you can use the IsClientScriptBlockRegistered() and IsStartupScriptRegistered() methods to avoid performing potentially time-consuming work. In this example, it saves the minor overhead of constructing the script block string if you don't need it.

■ **Tip** To really streamline your custom control code, put all your JavaScript code into a separate file, embed that file into your compiled control assembly, and then expose it through a URL using the WebResource attribute. This is the approach that ASP.NET uses with its validation controls, for example. To learn more about the WebResource attribute, refer to the "Design-Time Support" chapter that's included on the only book page as part of the Bonus Content for this book.

Remember that because RollOverButton derives from WebControl and uses <img> as the base tag, it already has the rendering smarts to output an <img> tag. The only parts you need to supply are the attributes, such as name and src. Additionally, you need to handle the onclick event (to post back the page) and the onmouseover and onmouseout events to swap the image. You can do this by overriding the AddAttributesToRender() method, as follows:

```
protected override void AddAttributesToRender(HtmlTextWriter output)
{
    output.AddAttribute("id", ClientID);
    output.AddAttribute("src", ImageUrl);
    output.AddAttribute("onclick", Page.ClientScript.GetPostBackEventReference(
```

```
    new PostBackOptions(this)));

  output.AddAttribute("onmouseover",
    "swapImg('" + this.ClientID + "', '" + MouseOverImageUrl + "');");

  output.AddAttribute("onmouseout",
    "swapImg('" + this.ClientID + "', '" + ImageUrl + "');");
}
```

As you learned in Chapter 27, the Page.ClientScript.GetPostBackEventReference() method returns a reference to the client-side __doPostBack() function. Using this detail, you can build a control that triggers a postback. You also need to be sure to specify the id attribute for your control so that the server can identify it as the source of the postback.

The final ingredient is to create the RaisePostBackEvent() method, as required by the IPostBackEventHandler interface, and use it to raise a server-side event, as shown here:

```
public void RaisePostBackEvent(string eventArgument)
{
    OnImageClicked(new EventArgs());
}

public event EventHandler ImageClicked;
protected virtual void OnImageClicked(EventArgs e)
{
    // Check for at least one listener and then raise the event.
    if (ImageClicked != null)
      ImageClicked(this, e);
}
```

Figure 29-13 shows a page with two rollover buttons.

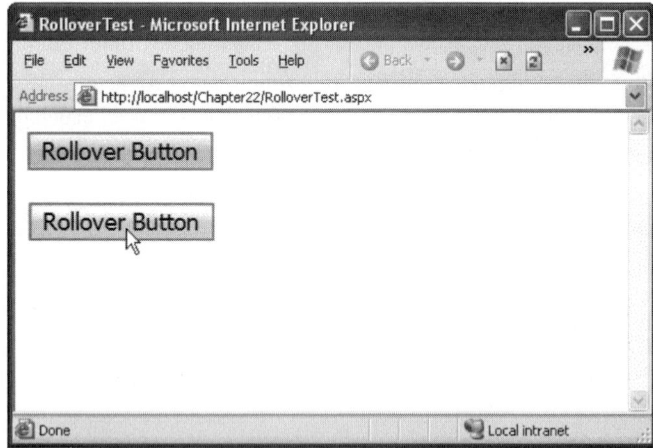

Figure 29-13. *Using a rollover button*

One way to improve this control is to add image preloading, so the rollover image is downloaded when the page is first rendered (rather than when the mouse moves over the image). Without image preloading, you may notice a delay the first time you move your mouse over the button.

The easiest way to perform preloading is to create a script that runs when the page is loaded. This script needs to create a JavaScript Image object and set the Image.src property to the image you want to preload. (If you have several images to preload, you can simply assign the src property to each image, one after the other.) The Image object won't actually be used in your page, but the image files you've preloaded will be automatically stored in the browser's cache. If you use the same URL elsewhere in the page (for example, in the swapImg() function), the cached version will be used.

Here's the code you need to add to the OnPreRender() method to implement image preloading:

```
if (!Page.ClientScript.IsStartupScriptRegistered("preload" + this.ClientID))
{
    string script =
      "<script type='text/javascript'> " +
      "var preloadedImage = new Image(); " +
      "preloadedImage.src = '" + MouseOverImageUrl + "'; " +
      "</script> ";

    Page.ClientScript.RegisterStartupScript(this.GetType(),
      "preload" + this.ClientID, script);
}
```

Frames

Frames allow you to display more than one HTML document in the same browser window. Frames can be used to provide navigational controls (such as a menu with links) that remain visible on every page. Frames also give you the ability to independently scroll the content frame while keeping the navigational controls fixed in place.

In modern day website design, frames are considered outdated. They have a notable list of quirks, including poor support for varying screen sizes and devices (such as mobile phones). The most obvious limitation with frames is the fact that the URL shown in the browser reflects the frame's page, but it doesn't convey any information about what documents are currently loaded in each frame. Thus, bookmarks and the browser history may not capture the current state of a page. Frames are also deprecated in XHTML 1.1.

In ASP.NET development, it's far more common to create multipart pages using the master pages feature discussed in Chapter 16 than to use frames. However, frames may still have some specialized uses, such as when bringing together existing documents from different websites into a single window.

■ **Tip** For more information about frames, refer to the tutorial at http://www.w3schools.com/html/html_frames.asp or the FAQ at http://www.htmlhelp.com/faq/html/frames.html. Frames, like JavaScript, are completely independent of ASP.NET. They are simply a part of the HTML standard.

Frame Navigation

Frames aren't always that easy to integrate into an ASP.NET page. Showing separate frames is easy—you simply need to create an HTML frames page that references the ASP.NET pages you want to show and defines their positioning. However, developers often want an action in one frame to have a result in another frame, and this interaction is not as straightforward. The problem is that each frame loads a different page, and from the point of view of the web server, these pages are completely separate. That means that the only way one frame can interact with another is through the browser, using client-side script. (Another way to solve this problem is to avoid frames altogether, and use the ASP.NET master pages feature instead. That way, the separate pages are combined into one HTML document on the server, rather than simply displayed together on the client.)

For example, consider the following HTML page, which defines a frameset with two frames (a sidebar on the left and a content frame on the right):

```
<html>
  <head>
    <title>Frame Test</title>
  </head>
  <frameset framespacing="1" cols="200,*">
    <frame name="menu" src="Frame1.aspx" scrolling="no" />
    <frame name="content" src="" scrolling="auto" />
    <noframes>
      <body>
        <p>This page uses frames, but your browser doesn't support them.</p>
          </noframes>
  </frameset>
```

The left frame shows the Frame1.aspx page. In this page, you might want to add controls that set the content in the other frame. This is easy to do using static HTML, such as an anchor tag. For example, if a user clicks the following hyperlink, it will automatically load the target NewPage.aspx in the frame on the right, which is named content:

```
<a href="NewPage.aspx" target="content">Click here</a>
```

You can also perform the same feat when a JavaScript event occurs by setting the parent.[FrameName].location property. For example, you could add an <img> tag on the left frame and use it to set the content on the right frame, as shown here:

```
<img src="ImgFile.gif" onclick="parent.content.location='NewPage.aspx'">
```

However, navigation becomes more complicated if you want to perform programmatic frame navigation in response to a server-side event. For example, you might want to log the user's action, examine security credentials, or commit data to a database and then perform the frame navigation. The only way to accomplish frame navigation from the server side is to write a snippet of JavaScript that instructs the browser to change the location of the other frame when the page first loads on the client.

For example, imagine you add a button to the leftmost frame, as shown in Figure 29-14. When this button is clicked, the following server-side code runs. It defines the <script> block and then registers it in the page. When the page is posted back, the script executes and redirects the rightmost frame to the requested page.

```
protected void Button1_Click(object sender, EventArgs e)
{
    string url = "http://www.google.com";
```

```
    string frameScript = "<script type='text/javascript'>" +
      "window.parent.content.location='" + url + "';</script>";
    Page.ClientScript.RegisterStartupScript(this.GetType(),
      "FrameScript", frameScript);
}
```

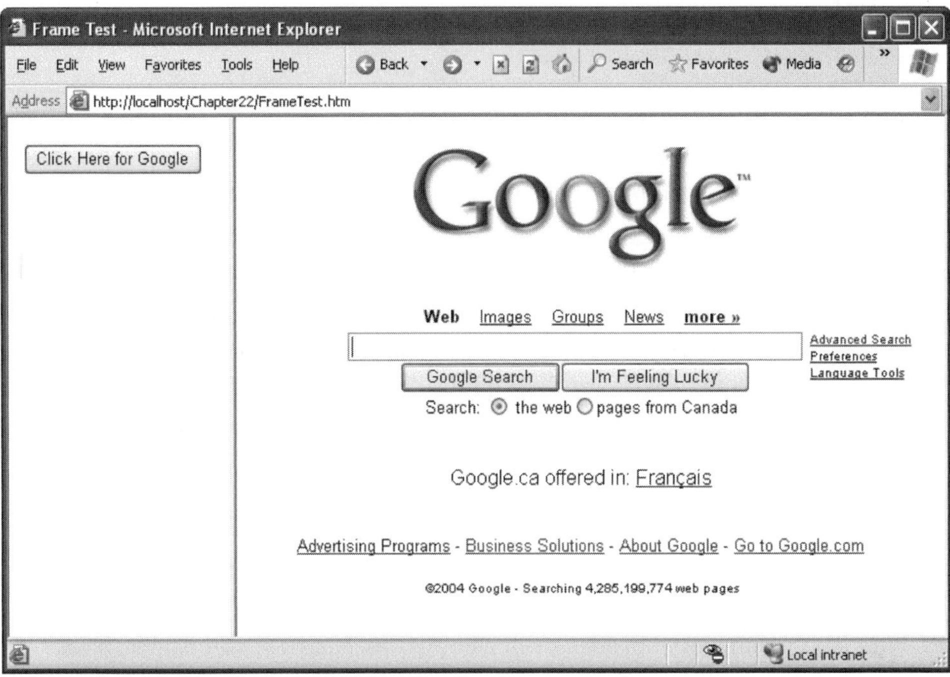

Figure 29-14. Using server-side code to control frame navigation

---

■ **Tip** Oddly enough, in this example the RegisterClientScriptBlock() method probably works slightly better than the RegisterStartupScript() block method. No matter how you implement this approach, you will get a slight delay before the new frame is refreshed. Because the script block doesn't depend on any of the controls on the page, you can render it immediately after the opening <form> tag using RegisterClientScriptBlock(), rather than at the end. This ensures that the JavaScript code that triggers the navigation is executed immediately, rather than after all the other content in the page has been downloaded.

Inline Frames

One solution that combines server-side programming with frame-like functionality is the <iframe> tag (which is defined as part of the HTML 4.0 standard). The <iframe> is an inline, or embedded, frame that you can position anywhere inside an HTML document. Both the main document and the embedded page are treated as complete, separate documents.

Here's an example of an <iframe> tag:

```
<iframe src="page.aspx" width="40%" height="80">
</iframe>
```

The key problem with the <iframe> tag is that support is not universal across all browsers. Internet Explorer has supported it since version 3, but Netscape added it only in version 6. However, you can define static text that will be displayed in browsers that don't recognize the tag, as shown here:

```
<iframe src="page.aspx" width="40%" height="80">
  <p>See the content at <a href="page.aspx">page.aspx</a>.</p>
</iframe>
```

Once you've added an <iframe> to your page, you can define it in the code-behind to access it programmatically by adding the runat="server" attribute and ID attribute. ASP.NET doesn't have a control class that specifically represents the <iframe>, so the <iframe> will be represented as an HtmlGenericControl.

Now you can set the src attribute at any point to redirect the frame:

```
IFrame1.Attributes["src"] = "page.aspx";
```

Of course, you can't actually interact with the page objects of the embedded page. In fact, the page isn't even generated in the same pass. Instead, the browser will request the page referenced by the src attribute separately and then display it in the frame. However, you can use a variety of techniques for passing information between the pages, including session state and the query string.

Figure 29-15 shows a page with two embedded frames, one of which has a border. The topmost <iframe> is using the page processor from earlier in this chapter, which indicates to the user that a part of the page is still being processed.

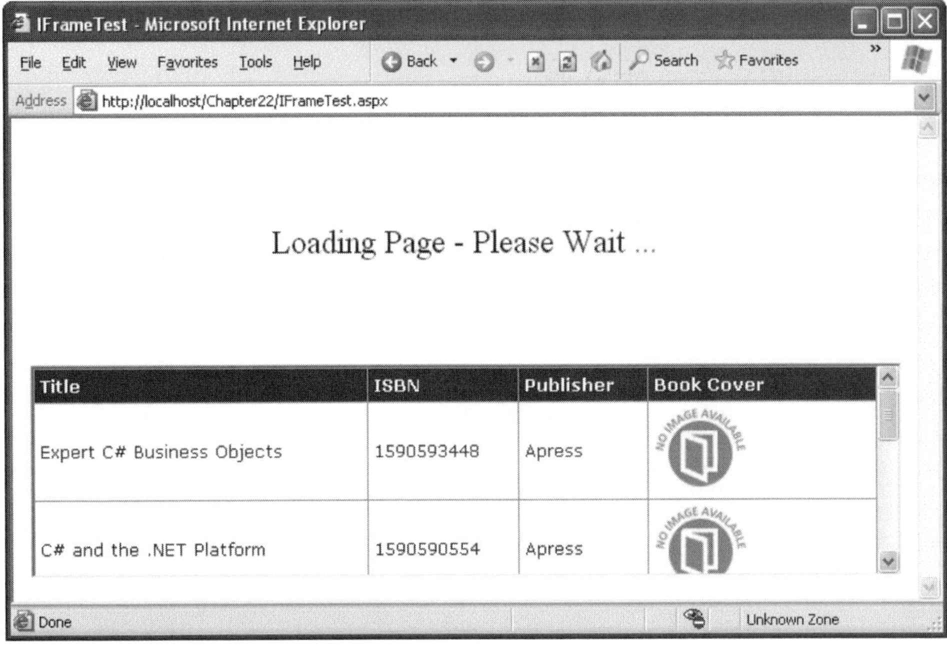

Figure 29-15. Using inline frames

Understanding Ajax

One of the main reasons developers use JavaScript code is to avoid a postback. For example, consider the TreeView control, which lets users expand and collapse nodes at will. When you expand a node, the TreeView uses JavaScript to fetch the child node information from the server, and then it quietly inserts the new nodes. Without JavaScript, the page would need to be posted back so the TreeView could be rebuilt. The user would notice a slightly sluggish delay, and the page would flicker and possibly scroll back to the beginning. On the server side, a considerable amount of effort would be wasted serializing and deserializing the view state information in each pass.

You've already seen how you can avoid this overhead and create smoother, more streamlined pages with a little JavaScript. However, most of the JavaScript examples you've seen so far have been self-contained—in other words, they've implemented a distinct task that doesn't require interaction with the rest of the page model. This approach is great when it suits your needs. For example, if all you need to do is show a pop-up message or a scrolling status display, you don't need to interact with the server-side code. However, what happens if you want to make a truly dynamic page like in the TreeView example, one that can call a server-side method, wait for a response, and insert the new information dynamically, without triggering a full-page postback? To design this solution, you need to think of a way for your client-side script to communicate with your server-side code.

Recently, a new buzzword has appeared in web programming circles. It's *Ajax* (which was originally shorthand for Asynchronous JavaScript and XML), and it's an application of JavaScript that's distinguished by one special characteristic. Namely, Ajax-style pages communicate with the server in the background to request additional information. When the client-side code receives this information (which may be transmitted as an XML package), it carries out additional actions. For example, a page that uses Ajax techniques might grab a live stock quote and refresh a portion of the page, all without triggering a full-page postback. Furthermore, the communication between the client and server happens asynchronously, so the client isn't interrupted. The advantages are greater responsiveness and a seamless browsing experience that's free of page refreshes.

■ **Note** Conceptually, these examples are similar to the asynchronous image-downloading example you saw earlier, which fetched additional information (the images) asynchronously and then updated the page. However, the image grid worked because images are really separate resources, not part of the page. You can't use the same technique to insert dynamic text or arbitrary HTML. Instead, you need to use Ajax techniques.

Programming Ajax pages can be complicated, not because the JavaScript techniques are particularly difficult (they aren't), but because you sometimes need messy workarounds to ensure browser compatibility. In an ideal world, ASP.NET programmers wouldn't need to worry about writing Ajax-style pages at all. Instead, you would use a higher-level framework on the server that could emit the JavaScript code you need. ASP.NET is heading in this direction, but it's moving slowly—after all, Microsoft needs time to carefully consider the different ways these client-side features can be integrated into ASP.NET's server-side model. Later in this chapter, you'll learn about *client callbacks*, which are the first rudimentary example of Ajax in ASP.NET.

■ **Note** In the next chapter, you'll learn about ASP.NET AJAX, which offers a higher-level way to build Ajax-style pages.

The XMLHttpRequest Object

The cornerstone of Ajax is the XMLHttpRequest object. XMLHttpRequest is both incredibly useful and deceptively simple. Essentially, it allows you to send requests to the server asynchronously and retrieve the results as text. It's up to you to decide what you request, how you handle the request on the server side, and what you return to the client.

Although there is wide support for the XMLHttpRequest object in modern browsers, there's a subtle difference in how you access the object. In some browsers, including Internet Explorer 7, Firefox, Safari, and Opera, the XMLHttpRequest object is implemented as a native JavaScript object. In versions of Internet Explorer before version 7, it's implemented as an ActiveX object. Because of these differences, your JavaScript code needs to be intelligent enough to use the correct approach when creating an instance of XMLHttpRequest. Here's the client-side JavaScript code that Microsoft uses to perform this task for the client callback feature you'll consider later in this chapter:

```
var xmlRequest;
try
{
    // This works if XMLHttpRequest is part of JavaScript.
    xmlRequest = new XMLHttpRequest();
}
catch(err)
{
```

```
    // Otherwise, the ActiveX object is required.
    xmlRequest = new ActiveXObject("Microsoft.XMLHTTP");
}
// Either way, by this point xmlRequest should refer to a live instance.
```

■ **Note** This code fails if the browser doesn't provide the native or ActiveX version of the XMLHttpRequest object. This problem occurs with really old browsers, such as Internet Explorer 4 and Safari 1. If you need to support old clients like these, Ajax programming is not suitable. Pages that rely heavily on Ajax also fail if JavaScript is not enabled in the browser. One option is to test for JavaScript support (by examining the Request.Browser.EcmaScriptVersion property) and redirect the user to a simpler version of the page if JavaScript is not supported.

Sending a Request

You'll use two key methods to send a request with the XMLHttpRequest: open() and send().

The open() method sets up your call—it defines the request you want to send to the server. It has two required parameters: the type of HTTP command (GET, POST, or PUT) and the URL. Here's an example:

```
xmlRequest.open("GET" , myURL);
```

Additionally, you can supply a third parameter to indicate whether the request should be performed asynchronously and two more parameters to supply user name and password information for authentication. It's unlikely you'll use the user name and password parameters, because this information can't be safely hard-coded in your JavaScript code. Client-side code is never the right place to implement security.

■ **Note** By default, all requests you make with the XMLHttpRequest object are asynchronous. There is almost never a reason to change this behavior. If you choose to make the call synchronously, you may as well force a postback—after all, the user will be unable to do anything while the page is stalled waiting for a response. If it's not asynchronous, it's not Ajax.

The send() method fires off the request. Assuming your request is asynchronous, it returns immediately.

```
xmlRequest.send(null);
```

Optionally, the send() method takes a single string parameter. You can use this to supply additional information that's sent with the request, like the values that are sent with a POST request.

On Internet Explorer browsers, it's acceptable to leave out the parameter for the send() method. However, in Firefox you must supply a null reference, or the callback will behave erratically. This is one of the many quirks you'll find in cross-browser compatibility when writing client-side script.

Handling the Response

Clearly, one detail is missing here. You've learned how to send a request, but how do you handle the response? The secret is to attach an event handler using the onreadystatechange property. This property points to a client-side JavaScript function that is called when the request is finished and the data is available:

```
xmlRequest.onreadystatechange = UpdatePage;
```

Of course, you need to attach the event handler *before* you call the send() method to start the request.

When the response is returned from the server and your function is triggered, you can extract the information you need from the xmlRequest object using the responseText and responseXML properties. The responseText property gives you all the content in a single long string. The responseXML property returns it as a tree of node objects.

■ **Note** Even though the name Ajax implies XML content, you can also return something else from the server, including plain text. For example, if the server is returning a single piece of data, there's no reason to wrap it up in a complete XML document.

An Ajax Example

Now that you've taken a quick tour of the XMLHttpRequest object, you're ready to use it in a simple page. To build an Ajax-style page in ASP.NET, you need two pieces:

- The Ajax-enabled web page, which includes the client-side code for making the request through the XMLHttpRequest object
- Another page or resource that can handle the requests from the first page and send the appropriate response

The first ingredient is obviously an .aspx web page. The second ingredient could be another .aspx web page, or it could be a custom HTTP handler. The HTTP handler is a more lightweight option, because it doesn't use the full-page model.

■ **Tip** For a quick refresher about custom HTTP handlers, refer to Chapter 5.

The following example implements the server-side functionality as an HTTP handler. The HTTP handler accepts information through the query string (in this case, it checks for two parameters) and then returns two pieces of information. The first piece of information is the sum of the two arguments that were passed in through the query string. The second piece of information is the current time on the web server. The information is *not* a legitimate XML document—instead, the two values are simply separated by a comma.

Here's the complete code for the HTTP handler:

```
public class CalculatorCallbackHandler : IHttpHandler
{
    public void ProcessRequest (HttpContext context)
    {
        HttpResponse response = context.Response;

        // Write ordinary text.
        response.ContentType = "text/plain";

        // Get the query string arguments.
        float value1, value2;
        if (Single.TryParse(context.Request.QueryString["value1"], out value1) &&
            Single.TryParse(context.Request.QueryString["value2"], out value2))
        {
            // Calculate the total.
            response.Write(value1 + value2);
            response.Write(",");

            // Return the current time.
            DateTime now = DateTime.Now;
            response.Write(now.ToLongTimeString());
        }
        else
        {
            // The values weren't supplied or they weren't numbers.
            // Indicate an error.
            response.Write("-");
        }
    }

    public bool IsReusable
    {
        get
        {
            return true;
        }
    }
}
```

■ **Note** In this example, the HTTP handler has an unrealistically easy job. After all, if you were simply interested in adding two numbers, your client-side code could accomplish the task without the Ajax request. This pattern becomes more important when the server-side code needs to do something the client can't, such as look up information in a server-side resource (a file or database), use sensitive information (such as secret numbers), or perform complex operations using classes that are available only in the .NET Framework.

Now that you have the HTTP handler in place, you can call it at any time using the XMLHttpRequest object. Figure 29-16 shows a sample page (named AjaxCalculatorPage.aspx) that fires off a request every time the user presses a key in either text box. The request supplies the values from the two text boxes, and the result is displayed in the shaded box at the bottom of the page. Just to prove that Ajax is at work, an animated GIF appears at the top of the page. You'll notice that the lava lamp keeps flowing without a pause while the callback takes place.

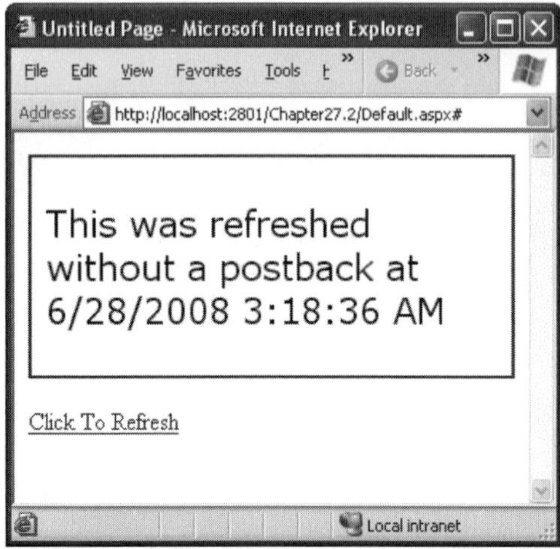

Figure 29-16. *An Ajax-style page*

Here's the basic outline of the page, without the JavaScript code. You'll notice that the page plugs into the client-side JavaScript in two ways. First, the onload event in the <body> tag launches the CreateXMLHttpRequest() function, which creates the XMLHttpRequest object. Second, the two text boxes use the onKeyUp event to trigger the CallServerForUpdate() function.

```
<html xmlns="http://www.w3.org/1999/xhtml">
  <head runat="server">
    <title>Ajax Page</title>
      <script type="text/javascript">
        <!-- JavaScript functions go here. -->
    </script>
  </head>
  <body onload="CreateXMLHttpRequest();">
    <form id="form1" runat="server">
      <div>
        <table style="width: 296px">
                    <td><img src="lava_lamp.gif" alt="Animated Lamp" />
          <td>This animated GIF won't pause, demonstrating that
           your page isn't posting back to the server.

        <br /><br />

        Value 1: 
        <asp:TextBox id="txt1" runat="server"
         onKeyUp="CallServerForUpdate();" /><br />
        Value 2: 
        <asp:TextBox id="txt2" runat="server"
         onKeyUp="CallServerForUpdate();" /><br /><br />
```

```
      <asp:Label id="lblResponse" runat="server" ... />
    </div>
  </form>
```

The CreateXMLHttpRequest() function uses the technique you saw earlier to instantiate the appropriate version of the XMLHttpRequest object:

```
var XmlRequest;

function CreateXMLHttpRequest()
{
    try
    {
        // This works if XMLHttpRequest is part of JavaScript.
        xmlRequest = new XMLHttpRequest();
    }
    catch(err)
    {
        // Otherwise, the ActiveX object is required.
        xmlRequest = new ActiveXObject("Microsoft.XMLHTTP");
    }
}
```

The CallServerForUpdate() function finds the text box objects, grabs their current values, and uses them to build a URL that points to the HTTP handler. The code then sends an asynchronous GET request to the HTTP handler.

```
function CallServerForUpdate()
{
    var txt1 = document.getElementById("txt1");
    var txt2 = document.getElementById("txt2");

    var url = "CalculatorCallbackHandler.ashx?value1=" +
      txt1.value + "&value2=" + txt2.value;
    xmlRequest.open("GET", url);
    xmlRequest.onreadystatechange = ApplyUpdate;
    xmlRequest.send();
}
```

Finally, the ApplyUpdate() function runs when the response is received. Assuming no error occurred, the new information is parsed out of the returned text and used to create a message that's displayed in the label:

```
function ApplyUpdate()
{
    // Check that the response was received successfully.
    if (xmlRequest.readyState == 4)
    {
        if (xmlRequest.status == 200)
        {
            var lbl = document.getElementById("lblResponse");

            var response = xmlRequest.responseText;
            if (response == "-")
```

```
            {
                lbl.innerHTML = "You've entered invalid numbers.";
            }
            else
            {
                var responseStrings = response.split(",");
                lbl.innerHTML = "The server returned the sum: " +
                  responseStrings[0] + " at " + responseStrings[1];
            }
        }
    }
}
```

This code checks the readyState value to ensure that the response has been received. readyState begins at 0 when you create the XMLHttpRequest object, then changes to 1 when you call open(), then changes to 2 when the request is sent, then changes to 3 when the response is being received, and finally changes to 4 when the response has been completely loaded. If readyState is 4, the code then checks the status property, which provides the HTTP response code. A value of 200 indicates the response was received successfully; other codes indicate some sort of error (like a missing page, a busy web server, and so on).

■ **Note** It's worth pointing out that Ajax doesn't save you from any server round-trips, and it rarely reduces the server processing time. The real difference is that round-trips occur silently in the background, which gives the application a more responsive feel.

Using Ajax with Client Callbacks

Using the Ajax approach, you can create impressive, highly responsive web pages. However, writing the client-side script is time-consuming. Visual Studio can't provide the same rich design experience you get when writing server-side code, and it doesn't provide debugging tools to help you track down the inevitable errors that crop up in the loosely typed JavaScript language. And even when you've successfully completed your task, you'll need to test on a wide range of other browsers, unless you're intimately familiar with the minor variations in JavaScript support on different browsers.

For these reasons, many developers don't write their client-side script by hand, even when designing an Ajax-style page. Instead, they prefer to deal with a higher-level component that can generate the script code they need. One example is the free third-party Ajax.NET library, which is available at http://ajax.schwarz-interactive.de/csharpsample. Ajax.NET uses attributes to flag methods, which then become remotely callable through a client callback and a custom HTTP handler. Another example is ASP.NET AJAX, the more comprehensive Ajax toolkit that's discussed in the next chapter.

Although both ASP.NET AJAX and Ajax.NET are good choices, you can perform the most essential Ajax task—sending an asynchronous request to the server—using ASP.NET's more straightforward *client callback* feature. Client callbacks give you a way to refresh a portion of data in a web page without triggering a full postback. Best of all, you don't need the script code that uses the XMLHttpRequest object. However, you *do* still need to write the client-side script that processes the server response.

Creating a Client Callback

To create a client callback in ASP.NET, you first need to plan how the communication will work. Here's the basic model:

1. At some point, a JavaScript event fires, triggering the server callback.
2. At this point, the normal page life cycle occurs, which means all the normal server-side events fire, such as Page.Load.
3. When this process is complete (and the page is properly initialized), ASP.NET executes the server-side callback method. This method must have a fixed signature—it accepts a single string parameter and returns a single string.
4. Once the page receives the response from the server-side method, it uses JavaScript code to modify the web page accordingly.

The ASP.NET architecture is designed to abstract away the communication process, so you can build a page that uses callbacks without worrying about this lower level, in much the same way you can take advantage of view state and the page life cycle.

In the next example, you'll see a page with two drop-down lists boxes. The first list is populated with a list of regions from the Northwind database. This happens when the page first loads. The second list is left empty until the user makes a selection from the first list. At this point, the content for the second list is retrieved by a callback and inserted into the list (see Figure 29-17).

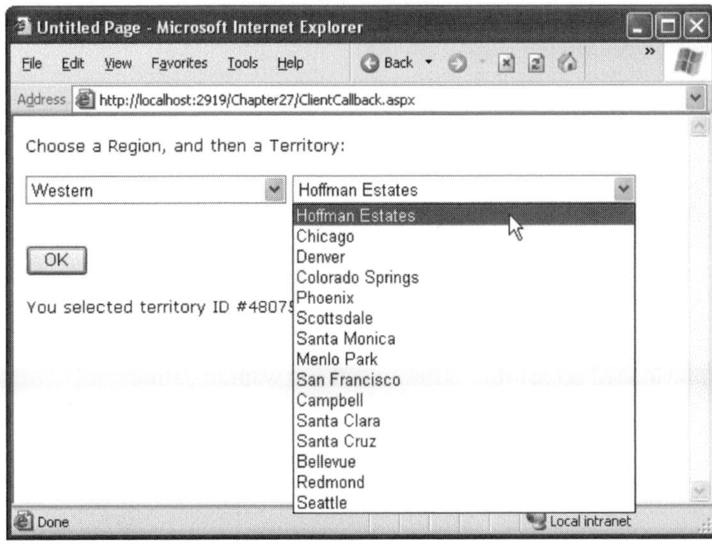

Figure 29-17. *Filling in a list with a callback*

Figure 29-18 diagrams how this process unfolds.

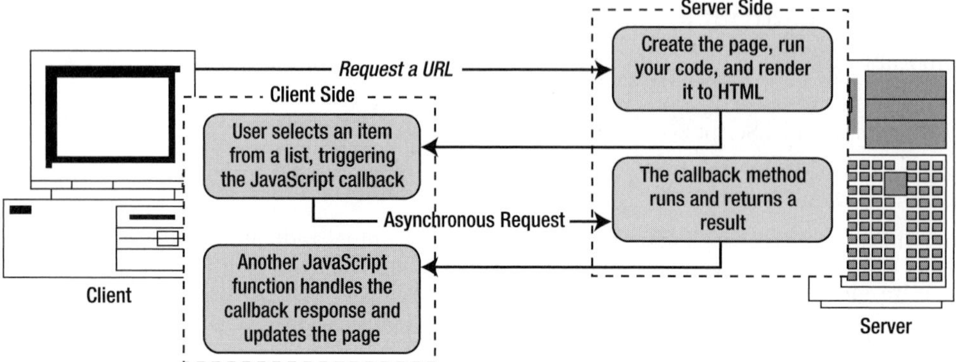

Figure 29-18. The stages of a callback

Building the Basic Page

The first step is to create the basic page, with two lists. It's easy enough to fill the first list—you can tackle this task by binding the list declaratively to a data source control. In this example, the following SqlDataSource is used:

```
<asp:SqlDataSource id="sourceRegions" runat="server"
 ConnectionString="<%$ ConnectionStrings:Northwind %>"
 SelectCommand="SELECT * FROM Region" />
```

And here's the list that binds to the data source:

```
<asp:DropDownList id="lstRegions" Runat="server" DataSourceID="sourceRegions"
 DataTextField="RegionDescription" DataValueField="RegionID"/>
```

Implementing the Callback

To receive a callback, you need a class that implements the ICallbackEventHandler interface. If you know your callback will be used in several pages, it makes sense to create a dedicated class (much like the custom HTTP handler used in the previous Ajax example). However, if you want to define functionality that's intended for a single page, you can implement ICallbackEventHandler in your web page, as shown here:

```
public partial class ClientCallback : System.Web.UI.Page, ICallbackEventHandler
{ ... }
```

The ICallbackEventHandler interface defines two methods. RaiseCallbackEvent() receives event data from the browser as a string parameter. It's triggered first. GetCallbackResult() is triggered next, and it returns the result back to the page.

■ **Note** The key limitation of ASP.NET client callbacks is that they force you to transmit data as single strings. If you need to pass more complex information (such as the result set with territory information, as in this example), you need to design a way to serialize your information into a string and deserialize it on the other side. Depending on the complexity of your task, you may be better off using ASP.NET AJAX, as discussed in Chapter 30.

In this example, the string parameter passed to RaiseCallbackEvent() contains the RegionID for the selected region. Using this information, the GetCallbackResult() method connects to the database and retrieves a list of all the territory records in that region. These results are joined into a single long string separated by the | character.

Here's the complete code:

```
private string eventArgument;

public void RaiseCallbackEvent(string eventArgument)
{
    this.eventArgument = eventArgument;
}

public string GetCallbackResult()
{
    // Create the ADO.NET objects.
    SqlConnection con = new SqlConnection(
      WebConfigurationManager.ConnectionStrings["Northwind"].ConnectionString);
    SqlCommand cmd = new SqlCommand(
      "SELECT * FROM Territories WHERE RegionID=@RegionID", con);
    cmd.Parameters.Add(new SqlParameter("@RegionID", SqlDbType.Int, 4));
    cmd.Parameters["@RegionID"].Value = Int32.Parse(eventArgument);

    // Create a StringBuilder that contains the response string.
    StringBuilder results = new StringBuilder();
    try
    {
        con.Open();
        SqlDataReader reader = cmd.ExecuteReader();
        // Build the response string.
        while (reader.Read())
        {
            results.Append(reader["TerritoryDescription"]);
            results.Append("|");
            results.Append(reader["TerritoryID"]);
            results.Append("||");
        }
        reader.Close();
    }
    finally
    {
        con.Close();
    }
    return results.ToString();
}
```

You can't use declarative data binding in this example, because the callback method can't directly access the controls on the page. Unlike in a postback scenario, when RaiseCallbackEvent() is called, the page isn't in the process of being rebuilt. Instead, the RaiseCallbackEvent() method is called out-of-band to request some additional information. It's up to your callback method to perform all the heavy lifting on its own.

Because the results need to be returned as a single string (and seeing as this string has to be reverse-engineered in JavaScript code), the code is a little awkward. A single pipe (|) separates the TerritoryDescription field from the TerritoryID field. Two pipes in a row (||) denote the start of a new row. For example, if you request RegionID 1, you might get a response like this:

```
Westboro|01581||Bedford|01730||Georgetow|01833|| ...
```

Clearly, this approach is somewhat fragile—if any of the territory records contain the pipe character, this will cause significant problems.

Writing the Client-Side Script

Client-side scripts involve an exchange between the server and the client. Just as the server needs a method to prepare the results, the client needs a function to receive and process them. The JavaScript function that handles the server response can take any name, but it needs to accept two parameters, as shown here:

```
function ClientCallback(result, context)
{ ... }
```

The result parameter has the serialized string. In this example, it's up to the client-side script to parse this string and fill the appropriate list box.

Here's the complete client script code that you need for this task:

```
<script type="text/javascript">
function ClientCallback(result, context)
{
    // Find the list box.
    var lstTerritories = document.getElementById("lstTerritories");

    // Clear out any content in the list.
    lstTerritories.innerHTML= "";

    // Get an array with a list of territory records.
    var rows = result.split("||");

    for (var i = 0; i < rows.length - 1; ++i)
    {
      // Split each record into two fields.
      var fields = rows[i].split("|");
      var territoryDesc = fields[0];
      var territoryID = fields[1];

      // Create the list item.
      var option = document.createElement("option");

      // Store the ID in the value attribute.
      option.value = territoryID;
```

```
        // Show the description in the text of the list item.
        option.innerHTML = territoryDesc;

         // Add the item to the end of the list.
        lstTerritories.appendChild(option);
    }
}
</script>
```

One detail is missing. Although you've defined both sides of the message exchange, you haven't actually hooked it up yet. What you need is a client-side trigger that calls the callback. In this case, you want to react to the onchange event of the region list:

```
protected void Page_Load(object sender, EventArgs e)
{
    lstRegions.Attributes["onchange"] = callbackRef;
    ...
```

The callbackRef is the JavaScript code that calls the callback. But how exactly do you need to write this line of code? Fortunately, ASP.NET gives you a handy GetCallbackEventReference() method that can construct the callback reference you need. Here's how you use it in this example:

```
    ...
    string callbackRef = Page.ClientScript.GetCallbackEventReference(
      this, "document.getElementById('lstRegions').value",
      "ClientCallback", "null", true);
}
```

The first parameter is a reference to the ICallbackEventHandler object that will handle the callback—in this case, the containing page. The second parameter is the information that the client will pass to the server. In this example, a snippet of JavaScript is required to look up the appropriate control (lstRegions) and extract the currently selected value.

■ **Tip** Many client callback samples use the JavaScript collection document.all to retrieve control objects. This is not recommended, because document.all is an extension to JavaScript supported in Internet Explorer but not in other browsers (such as Firefox). Instead, use the document.getElementById() method shown previously.

The third parameter is the name of the client-side JavaScript function that will receive the results from the server callback. The fourth parameter includes any context information that you want to pass to the client-side function. This is helpful if you handle several callbacks with the same JavaScript function and you need to distinguish which response is which. Finally, the last parameter indicates whether you want to perform the callback asynchronously. This should always be true to prevent locking up the page in the event of a network problem.

Disabling Event Validation

In Chapter 7, you considered SQL injection attacks and POST injection attacks. POST injection attacks are attacks in which a malicious user alters the HTTP POST request that's sent to the server so it includes a value that isn't available in the corresponding control. For example, a user might change a posted parameter to indicate a list selection that isn't actually in the list. Left unchecked, this can trick your code into revealing sensitive data.

ASP.NET defends against POST injection attacks using *event validation*. Event validation works by verifying that all posted data makes sense before ASP.NET executes the page life cycle. Unfortunately, event validation often causes problems with Ajax-style pages. In the current example, items are dynamically added to the territory list. When the user chooses a territory and posts back the page, ASP.NET will raise an "Invalid postback or callback argument" error because the selected territory isn't defined in the server-side control.

■ **Note** The event validation feature isn't necessarily a feature of all controls. It's implemented only for control classes that are decorated with the SupportsEventValidation attribute. In ASP.NET, most controls that rely on posted data use this attribute (such as the ListBox, DropDownList, CheckBox, TreeView, Calendar, and so on). The exception is controls that don't restrict allowed values. For example, the TextBox control doesn't use event validation, because the user is allowed to type any value in it.

You can work around the event validation problem in two ways. The safest approach is to explicitly tell ASP.NET about additional values that it should allow in the control. (ASP.NET keeps track of all the allowed values using a hidden input tag named __EVENTVALIDATION.) Unfortunately, this approach is tedious and often impractical.

To use this approach, you must call the Page.ClientScript.RegisterForEventValidation() method for each possible value. You need to perform this task at the rendering stage by overriding the Page.Render() method as shown here. Here's an example that allows the user to select a territory with a TerritoryID of 10 in the lstTerritories control:

```
protected override void Render(HtmlTextWriter writer)
{
    ClientScript.RegisterForEventValidation(lstTerritories.UniqueID, "10");
    base.Render(writer);
}
```

The obvious problem with this approach is that in many cases you won't know all the possible values. They may be generated dynamically or retrieved from another source (such as a web service). In the current example, you'd need to retrieve the full list of possible TerritoryID values from the database, loop through them, and register each one. Not only does this create extra work, but it also introduces problems if more regions are added after the page is served.

Instead, the only realistic approach in this situation is to disable event validation. Unfortunately, you can't disable event validation for a single control, so you must switch it off for the entire page using the EnableEventValidation property of the Page directive:

```
<%@ Page ... EnableEventValidation="false" %>
```

■ **Note** You can also disable event validation for an entire website by setting the enableEventValidation attribute of the pages element to false. However, this isn't recommended because it can introduce security risks to other pages.

To retrieve the selected territory in your code, you can't use the lstTerritories control. That's because the lstTerritories control is the server-side version of the list, so it doesn't contain the dynamically added values. Instead, you need to retrieve the selection directly from the Request.Forms collection:

```
lblInfo.Text = "You selected territory ID #" + Request.Form["lstTerritories"];
```

Once you disable event validation, you need to think carefully about security. In this example, you need to consider whether there is a possibility that a hacker might submit a TerritoryID selection that isn't in the list. If some territories or regions shouldn't be available to all users, you need to make sure your code includes the necessary security checks. Namely, when a user chooses a territory, your code must check to make sure the requesting user is allowed to view that territory before you go any further. This isn't a concern in the current example, because the full list of territories is available to all users. In this example, the only potential problem is the possibility that an attacker will supply a territory ID that doesn't exist and generate an error that you must catch.

■ **Note** Clearly, client callbacks represent a powerful feature that lets you build more seamless, dynamic pages. But remember, client callbacks rely on the XMLHttpRequest functionality, which limits them to modern browsers. Some browsers may support JavaScript but not client callbacks. If in doubt, you can check whether a browser appears to support Ajax callbacks using the Request.Browser.SupportsCallback property.

Client Callbacks "Under the Hood"

It's worth noting that when the callback is performed, the target page actually starts executing a trimmed-down life cycle. Most control events won't execute, but the Page.Load and Page.Init event handlers *will*. The Page.IsPostBack property will return true, but you can distinguish this callback from a genuine postback by testing the Page.IsCallback property, which will also be true. The page rendering process is bypassed completely. View state information is retrieved and made available to your callback method, but any changes you make are not sent back to the page. Figure 29-19 shows the life cycle events.

The only problem with the current implementation of client callbacks is that the programming interface is still fairly primitive, especially in its requirement that you exchange only strings. The current trend in ASP.NET is to use the callback features to build dynamic features into dynamic controls, rather than consuming them directly in the page. You'll see an example of this technique in the next section.

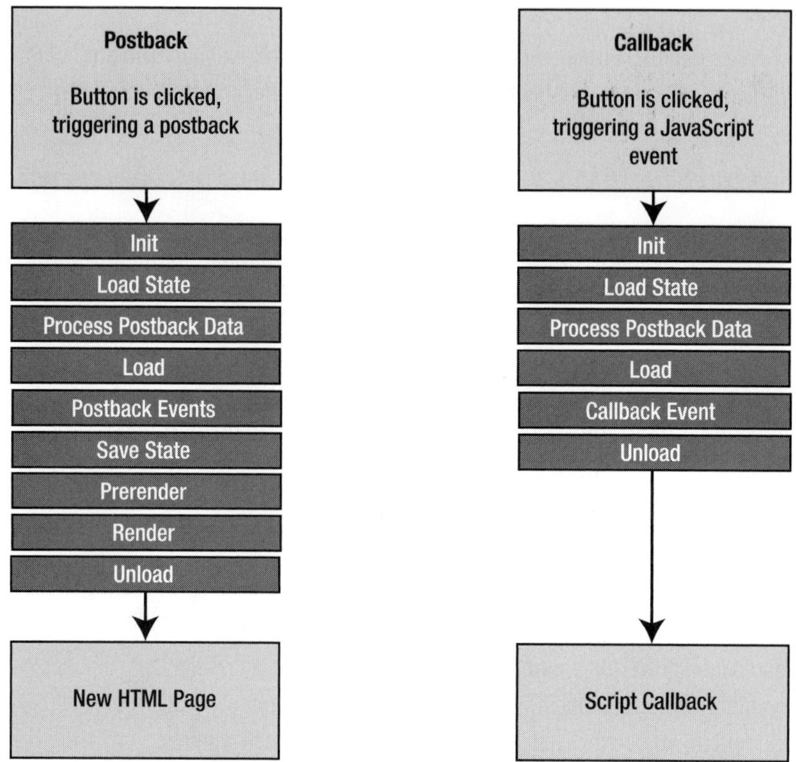

Figure 29-19. *Comparing postbacks and callbacks*

Client Callbacks in Custom Controls

Integrating client callbacks into a page is a fair bit of work. However, a much better option is to use them to build rich controls. You can then use these controls in as many pages as you want. Best of all, you'll get the Windows-style responsiveness without having to delve into the lower-level callback infrastructure.

Although there's no limit to the type of controls you might build with dynamic callbacks, many controls use callbacks to simply refresh a portion of their user interface (such as the TreeView). With a little ingenuity, you can create a container control that provides this functionality for free.

The basic idea is to create a new control that derives from Panel. This panel contains content that you want to refresh. At some point, a client-side JavaScript event will occur that causes the panel to perform a callback. At this point, the panel will fire a server-side event to notify your code. You can handle this event and tweak any of the controls inside the panel. When the event finishes, the panel gets the new HTML for its contents and returns it. A client-side script replaces the current panel contents with the new HTML using a little DHTML.

Figure 29-20 shows the process for a custom control named DynamicPanel.

■ **Note** This control presents a straightforward example of how you can integrate Ajax techniques into a custom control. The end result is also a relatively practical control. However, you probably won't use the DynamicPanel in a real web application. That's because ASP.NET AJAX includes a similar but more powerful version called the UpdatePanel, which you'll learn how to use in Chapter 30.

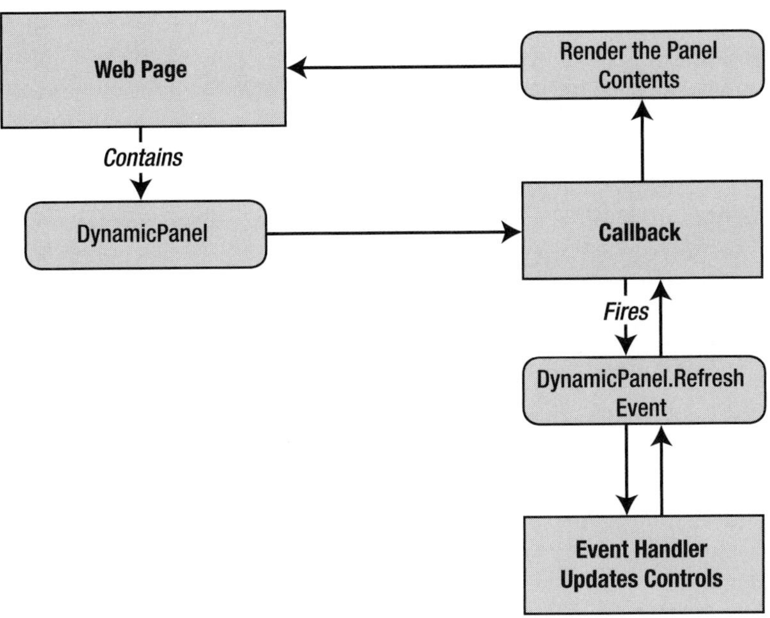

Figure 29-20. Refreshing a portion of the page through a callback

The DynamicPanel

The first step is to derive a class from Panel and implement ICallbackEventHandler:

```
public class DynamicPanel : Panel, ICallbackEventHandler
{ ... }
```

As part of the ICallbackEventHandler, the DynamicPanel needs to implement the Raise_CallbackEvent() and GetCallbackResult() methods. At this point it's a two-step process. First, the DynamicPanel needs to fire an event to notify your page. Your page can handle this event and perform the appropriate modifications. Next, the DynamicPanel needs to render the HTML for its contents. It can then return that information (along with its client ID) to the client-side web page.

```
public event EventHandler Refresh;

public void RaiseCallbackEvent(string eventArgument)
{
    // Fire an event to notify the client a refresh has been requested.
    if (Refresh != null)
    {
        Refresh(this, EventArgs.Empty);
    }
}

public string GetCallbackResult()
{
    // Prepare the text response that will be sent back to the page.
    EnsureChildControls();
    using (StringWriter sw = new StringWriter())
    {
        using (HtmlTextWriter writer = new HtmlTextWriter(sw))
        {
            // Add the ID that identifies this panel.
            writer.Write(this.ClientID + "_");

            // Render just the part of the page inside the panel.
            this.RenderContents(writer);
        }
        return w.ToString();
    }
}
```

Here's the client-side script code that finds the panel on the page and then replaces its content with new HTML:

```
<script type="text/javascript">
  function RefreshPanel(result, context)
  {
    if (result != '')
    {
      // Split the string back into two pieces of information:
      // the panel ID and the HTML content.
      var separator = result.indexOf('_');
      var elementName = result.substr(0, separator);
      // Look up the panel.
      var panel = document.getElementById(elementName);
      // Replace its content.
      panel.innerHTML = result.substr(separator+1);
    }
  }
</script>
```

Rather than hard-code this script into every page in which you use the panel, it makes sense to register it programmatically in the DynamicPanel.OnInit() method:

```
protected override void OnInit(EventArgs e)
{
    base.OnInit(e);
    string script = @"<script type='text/javascript'>...</script>";

    Page.ClientScript.RegisterClientScriptBlock(this.GetType(),
      "RefreshPanel", script);
}
```

This completes the basics of the DynamicPanel. However, this example still has a significant limitation—the page has no way to trigger the callback and cause the panel to refresh. That means it's up to your page code to retrieve the callback reference and insert it into your page.

Fortunately, you can simplify this process by creating other controls that work with the DynamicPanel. For example, you can create a DynamicPanelRefreshLink that, when clicked, automatically triggers a refresh in the associated panel.

The first step in implementing this solution is to revisit the DynamicPanel and implement the ICallbackContainer interface.

```
public class DynamicPanel : Panel, ICallbackEventHandler, ICallbackContainer
{ ... }
```

This interface allows the DynamicPanel to provide the callback reference, rather than forcing you to go through the page.

To implement ICallbackContainer, you need to provide a GetCallbackScript() method that returns the reference. Here the Panel can rely on the page, making sure to specify itself as the callback target, and on RefreshPanel() as the client-side script that will handle the response.

```
public string GetCallbackScript(IButtonControl buttonControl, string argument)
{
    return Page.ClientScript.GetCallbackEventReference(
      this, "", "RefreshPanel", "null", true);
}
```

The DynamicPanelRefreshLink

Now you're ready to implement the much simpler refresh button. This control, named DynamicPanelRefreshLink, derives from LinkButton.

```
public class DynamicPanelRefreshLink : LinkButton
{ ... }
```

You specify the panel that it should work with by setting a PanelID property:

```
public string PanelID
{
    get { return (string)ViewState["DynamicPanelID"]; }
    set { ViewState["DynamicPanelID"] = value; }
}
```

Finally, when it's time to render itself, the DynamicPanelRefreshLink finds the associated DynamicPanel control using FindControl() and then adds the callback script reference to the onclick attribute.

```
protected override void AddAttributesToRender(HtmlTextWriter writer)
{
    DynamicPanel pnl = (DynamicPanel)Page.FindControl(PanelID);
    if (pnl != null)
    {
        writer.AddAttribute("onclick", pnl.GetCallbackScript(this, ""));
    }
}
```

The Client Page

To complete this example, create a simple text page, and add a DynamicPanel and a DynamicPanelRefreshLink underneath it. Set the DynamicPanelRefreshLink.PanelID property to create the link.

Next, place some content and controls in the panel. Finally, add an event handler for the DynamicPanel.Refresh event and use it to change the content or formatting of the controls in the panel.

```
protected void Panel1_Refresh(object sender, EventArgs e)
{
    Label1.Text = "This was refreshed without a postback at " +
      DateTime.Now.ToString();
}
```

Now when you run the page, you'll see that you can click the DynamicPanelRefreshLink to refresh the panel without posting back the page (see Figure 29-21).

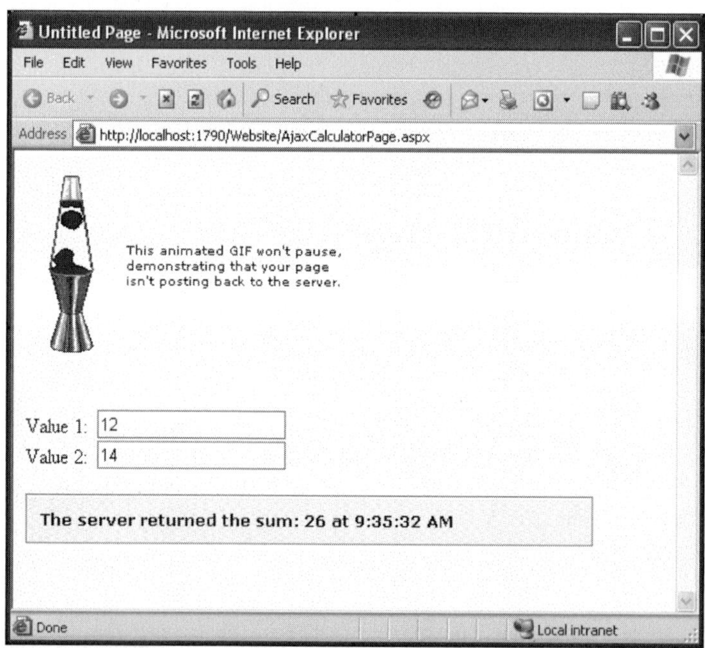

Figure 29-21. The DynamicPanel

Summary

In this chapter, you saw how a bit of carefully chosen JavaScript code can extend your ASP.NET web pages with more responsive interfaces and more dynamic effects. Along the way, you saw how to develop .NET solutions for some traditional HTML and JavaScript techniques, such as page processors, rollover buttons, and frames. You also explored Ajax and the new client callback feature that helps you implement seamless page updates. You can do a lot more by creatively applying a little JavaScript. For more ideas, check out some of the custom controls available at Microsoft's `http://www.asp.net` community website, or continue to the next chapter where you'll dip into ASP.NET AJAX, a server-side programming framework for developing Ajax-style pages.

CHAPTER 30

ASP.NET AJAX

In the previous chapter, you entered the world of client-side programming. You learned a few essential techniques for using JavaScript, and you considered how to create more responsive pages with Ajax techniques, either on your own or through the client callback feature in ASP.NET.

These examples presented a fairly well-rounded foundation that you can use to build a variety of advanced pages. Unfortunately, the programming model leaves a lot to be desired. If you rely on pure JavaScript, it's up to you to bridge the gap between ASP.NET's server-side abstraction and the more limited HTML DOM. Sadly, it's not easy. Without the benefit of Visual Studio's IntelliSense and its debugging tools, it's difficult to write error-free code and diagnose problems. It's also a challenge to create script code that works on all modern browsers, because minor quirks and implementation differences abound.

The ASP.NET client callback feature partially addresses these problems by giving you a server-side model that you can use to generate some of the client-side code you need (namely, the code that performs asynchronous requests using the XMLHttpRequest object). However, the client callback model is far from perfect. The interfaces feel a bit clunky, the integration into the page model is a bit awkward, and data typing is nonexistent. It's up to you to devise a way to serialize the information you need to transmit into a single string, and it's up to you to write the JavaScript code that receives the callback, deserializes the string, and updates the page. All in all, the client callback feature is an excellent tool for building Ajax-enabled controls but a less appealing way to design complete web pages.

ASP.NET developers have another option. They can use the ASP.NET AJAX toolkit, which provides several features that can help you build Ajax-style pages. In this chapter, you'll explore ASP.NET AJAX and learn how to use it to create the next generation of highly interactive, dynamic web pages.

Introducing ASP.NET AJAX

ASP.NET AJAX consists of two key parts: a client-side portion and a server-side portion.

The client-side portion is a set of JavaScript libraries. These libraries aren't tied to ASP.NET in any way—in fact, non-ASP.NET developers can use them in their own web pages. The client libraries don't expose much in the way of *features* (for example, there aren't any prebuilt pieces of functionality you can drop into your web pages). Rather, they establish a basic foundation you can use to develop ASP.NET AJAX pages. This foundation extends the JavaScript language to fill in a few of its gaps (for example, by adding support for inheritance), and provides some basic infrastructure (for example, methods for managing component lifetime, manipulating common data types, and performing reflection).

The server-side portion of ASP.NET AJAX works at a higher level. It includes controls and components that use the client-side JavaScript libraries. For example, a web form that contains the DragPanel component (from the ASP.NET AJAX Control Toolkit) gives users the ability to drag a panel around in the browser window. Behind the scenes, there's some custom JavaScript at work, and that JavaScript uses the client-side ASP.NET AJAX libraries. However, the DragPanel renders all the JavaScript code it needs, saving you the trouble of writing it yourself.

Clearly, ASP.NET AJAX is the start of a new direction in ASP.NET development. Before going any further, it's worth getting an overview of all the features that ASP.NET AJAX provides. Here's a quick rundown:

- **JavaScript language extensions:** These extensions make JavaScript work a little more like a modern object-oriented language, with support for namespaces, inheritance, interfaces, enumerations, and reflection.
- **Remote method calls:** ASP.NET AJAX pages can call web services that you design. This feature allows you to get information from the server without performing a full-page postback. It solves the same problem as the client callback feature you learned about in Chapter 29, but it lets you work with strongly typed methods instead of stuffing all your data into a single string.
- **ASP.NET services:** This feature allows you to call the server to use one of two ASP.NET services—one that uses forms authentication information and one that gets data from the current user profile.
- **Partial page refreshes:** The new UpdatePanel control gives you a way to define a portion of a page that will be updated without requiring a full-page postback. Best of all, you don't need to write any JavaScript code to manage the updating process.
- **Prebuilt controls:** The popular ASP.NET AJAX Control Toolkit is stocked with more than 30 controls and control extenders that use ASP.NET AJAX to great effect. They allow you to make controls collapse and expand, add dynamic animations, and support autocompletion and drag-and-drop. And once again, these classes handle the low-level JavaScript details so you don't need to.

You'll explore all of these features in this chapter.

ASP.NET AJAX on the Client: The Script Libraries

The client-side portion of ASP.NET AJAX relies on a small collection of JavaScript files. There are two ways to deploy the ASP.NET AJAX script files. If you build an ASP.NET 3.5 application, they're available through the System.Web.Extensions.dll assembly and served out on demand. If you're creating a non-ASP.NET application or adding client-side features to an ordinary HTML page, you can download the JavaScript files separately from the ASP.NET AJAX website (http://www.asp.net/ajax/downloads) as part of the Microsoft AJAX Library.

■ **Tip** The Microsoft AJAX Library is also a worthwhile download if you want to take a closer look at the actual JavaScript code. This download includes "debug" versions of each of the three core files, as well as the final production versions. The production versions strip out all whitespace and comments in order to make the file as small as possible. By comparison, the largest file is MicrosoftAjax.js, which is just under 300 KB in its debug version but requires about 90 KB in its production version.

If you download the Microsoft AJAX Library, you'll find that ASP.NET AJAX uses just three core JavaScript files—MicrosoftAjax.js, MicrosoftAjaxWebForms.js, and MicrosoftAjaxTimer.js. Along with these essentials are over 100 very small JavaScript files that store globalization information (for example, data formats that apply to different cultures).

In ASP.NET, you won't find individual JavaScript files for the client libraries. Instead, the client libraries are embedded in the System.Web.Extensions.dll assembly and served up as a *script resource.* Script resources allow you to map a URL to a resource that's embedded in an assembly. For example, here's a sample script block that extracts the ASP.NET AJAX script library:

```
<script src="/YourWebSite/ScriptResource.axd?d=RUSU1mIv69CJ9H5JUAOSw8L4674
LfxGOQg6Nw7HtNHheB3bMiw7Ov16bX1KPG6N1oTYEi65ggRoIP1-hWapSttV3udoNXGrkO95YGEzuXOM1&am
p;t=633127440334523405" type="text/javascript">
</script>
```

ASP.NET includes a script resource handler that response to these requests. It examines the passed-in query string argument and returns the requested script file.

ASP.NET AJAX on the Server: The ScriptManager

Obviously, you wouldn't want to type long URLs that point to script resources on every page that requires ASP.NET AJAX. The solution is to use an ASP.NET control called the ScriptManager.

The ScriptManager is the brains of the server-side ASP.NET AJAX model. It's a web control that doesn't have any visual appearance on the page. However, it performs a key task—it renders the links to the ASP.NET AJAX JavaScript libraries.

To add the ScriptManager to a page, you can drag it from the AJAX Extensions tab of the Toolbox. Here's how the ScriptManager is declared in the .aspx file:

```
<asp:ScriptManager ID="ScriptManager1" runat="server"></asp:ScriptManager>
```

Each page that uses ASP.NET AJAX features requires an instance of the ScriptManager. You can only use one ScriptManager on a page.

Along with rendering the links for the ASP.NET AJAX client libraries, the ScriptManager also performs several other important tasks. It can render references to other script files (often at the request of other ASP.NET AJAX-enabled controls and components), create proxies that allow you to call web services asynchronously from the browser, and manage the way UpdatePanel controls refresh their content. You'll explore all of these topics in this chapter.

■ **Tip** If you're using ASP.NET AJAX features throughout your website, it makes sense to place the ScriptManager in a master page. However, this can occasionally cause problems, because different content pages may want to configure the properties of the ScriptManager differently (for example, adding new scripts and web service references). In this scenario, the solution is to use the ScriptManager in the master page and the ScriptManagerProxy in your content page. Each content page can configure the ScriptManagerProxy control in the same way it would configure the ScriptManager.

Now that you've seen the bare essentials of the ASP.NET AJAX model—the client-side libraries and the server-side ScriptManager control—you're ready to begin building pages that use ASP.NET AJAX features. You'll begin by using ASP.NET AJAX as an alternative to the client callback technique to get information from the server. Next, you'll see how to use ASP.NET AJAX-enabled web controls to get rich

Ajax-style effects (such as drag-and-drop and autocompletion) with little extra effort. Finally, you'll take a deeper look at the ASP.NET AJAX client libraries that support these features and learn how to build your own ASP.NET AJAX component.

Server Callbacks

The first ASP.NET AJAX example you'll consider is a revised version of the client callback page from Chapter 29. This page includes two drop-down list boxes (see Figure 30-1). The first shows a list of regions, and the second displays the territories in the selected region. The trick is that the second list is filled each time the user makes a selection in the first. The process of filling the list box requires a call to the server, which performs the database lookup and supplies the list.

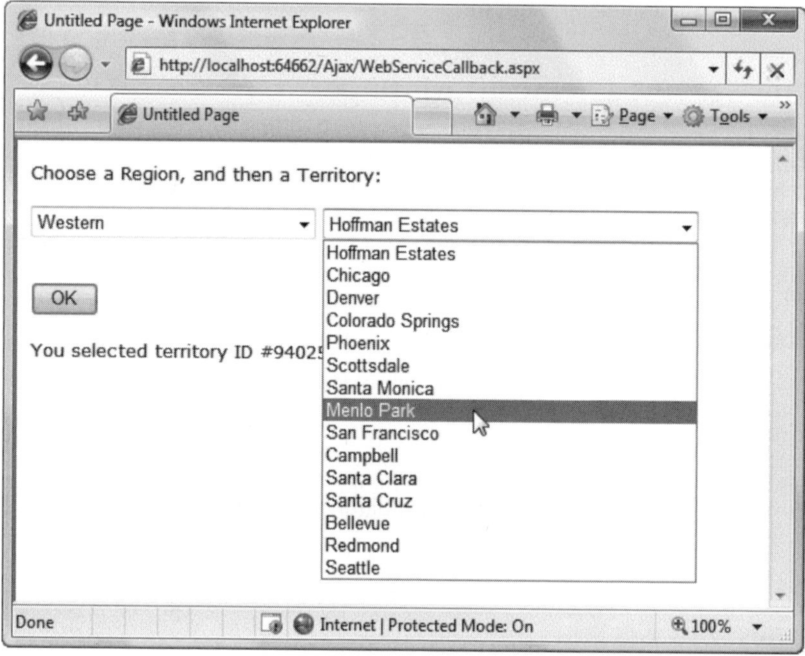

Figure 30-1. *The dynamic list example revisited*

To make this page work using the ASP.NET client callback feature, you need to implement the slightly cumbersome ICallbackEventHandler interface. ASP.NET AJAX uses a different approach. In ASP.NET AJAX, callbacks are always made to a separate server-side method—technically, a *web service*. This design improves the separation of logic, helping you organize your code. More important, it takes care of the serialization work. That means you don't need to devise your own method to send complex data (like the string-splitting system that you saw in Chapter 29, which clumsily separated values with the pipe character).

In the following sections, you'll see how to build the web service you need, and you'll consider several options for consuming it.

Web Services in ASP.NET AJAX

When performing a server callback with ASP.NET AJAX, your client-side JavaScript code calls a method in a server-side web service.

A *web service* is a collection of one or more server-side methods that can be called by remote clients. To call a web service, that client sends a request message over HTTP. This is similar to the process of performing a web-page postback, except the body of the request contains the arguments that are being passed to the method. ASP.NET then creates the web service object, runs the code in the corresponding web method, returns the result, and destroys the web service object. The request and response message format varies—traditionally, it's an XML-based standard called SOAP, but in ASP.NET AJAX, it's a lighter-weight text-based alternative called JSON (JavaScript Object Notation), primarily for browser compatibility reasons.

ASMX and WCF Web Services

.NET has two web service technologies, .asmx and WCF.

In this chapter, you'll see how to use the original ASP.NET web service model, often known as *.asmx* web services, in accordance with its file extension. It's also possible to use a WCF (Windows Communication Foundation) service as the backend for an ASP.NET AJAX page. Conceptually, this approach is the same as using an ordinary .asmx web service. WCF is in many ways the successor to .asmx web services—it's a more comprehensive platform that encompasses a host of scenarios that .asmx web services don't take into account. However, none of these advanced scenarios are usable with ASP.NET AJAX pages. From a practical point of view, both web service technologies give you exactly the same capabilities in an ASP.NET AJAX page.

WCF services require slightly more work to implement because they must be registered correctly in the web.config file. This registration step configures the WCF service to use JSON serialization. (The same configuration step is performed through an attribute with .asmx web services.) The easiest way to create a WCF service that has the required configuration settings is to choose Website ➤ Add New Item from the Visual Studio menu, and then pick the AJAX-Enabled WCF Service template. However, there's nothing wrong with using .asmx services to avoid the web.config configuration hassles, as done with the examples in this chapter.

It's important to realize that although the ASP.NET AJAX callback mechanism uses web services, it's a specialized implementation. If you're familiar with web services, you'll find that ASP.NET AJAX imposes some extra limitations. First, your web page can't call non-ASP.NET AJAX web services (for example, third-party web services created on other platforms). This is because they won't support the stripped-down, simplified JSON model that ASP.NET AJAX uses. Second, your web page can't call web services in different domains (on other web servers). This is because most web browsers prevent cross-domain use of the XMLHttpRequest object to stop potential cross-site scripting attacks.

These limitations don't prevent you from using the ASP.NET AJAX callback feature the way it's intended—as a mechanism for a page to perform server-side application tasks. However, if you've used web services to expose server-side functionality to rich clients, third-party developers, and non-.NET applications, you need to realize that the use of web services in ASP.NET AJAX is less ambitious.

■ **Note** There are ways around these limitations. For example, you could call a web method in your web application, and have that web method call a web method that exists in another domain. This bridging technique works because the web server code doesn't have the same restriction as the browser—it's free to launch cross-domain calls to other web services.

Creating the Web Service

The web services you'll use with ASP.NET AJAX consist of two pieces: an .asmx file that acts as the web service endpoint, and a .cs file that has the actual C# code. You add these files to the website that contains the ASP.NET AJAX page that will use the web service.

The quickest way to create a web service in Visual Studio is to choose Website ➤ Add New Item (or Project ➤ Add New Item for web projects), choose the Web Service template, supply a filename (in the following example it's TerritoriesService), and click Add. If you're creating a projectless website, the .asmx file will be placed in the web application directory, while the matching .cs file is placed in the App_Code folder so that it will be compiled automatically.

■ **Note** You don't need to host your web application in an IIS virtual directory in order to use web services with ASP.NET AJAX. Instead, you can test it using the integrated web server in Visual Studio. This works because the script code that calls your web service automatically uses a relative path. As a result, no matter what port the Visual Studio web server chooses, the web page will be able to construct the right URL.

The .asmx file is unremarkable—if you open it, you'll find a single line with a WebService directive that identifies the language of the code, the location of the code-behind file, and the name of the class:

```
<%@ WebService Language="C#" CodeBehind="./App_Code/TerritoriesService.cs"
  Class="TerritoriesService" %>
```

In this example, a web service named TerritoriesService.asmx was created, with a code-behind file named TerritoriesService.cs. The code-behind class defines a class named TerritoriesService, which looks something like this:

```
[WebService(Namespace = "http://tempuri.org/")]
[WebServiceBinding(ConformsTo = WsiProfiles.BasicProfile1_1)]
[System.Web.Script.Services.ScriptService]
public class TerritoriesService : System.Web.Services.WebService
{...}
```

■ **Note** By default, the ScriptService attribute is commented out. Make sure you remove the comment markers to create a web service that can be called from an ASP.NET AJAX page.

The class derives from System.Web.Services.WebService, which is the traditional base class for web services. However, this is just a convenience, and it isn't necessary. By deriving from WebService, you gain access to certain built-in objects (such as Application, Server, Session, and User) without needing to go through the static HttpContext.Current property.

You'll also notice that the web service class declaration is decorated with three attributes. The first two—WebService (which sets an XML namespace that's used in web service messages) and WebServiceBinding (which indicates the level of standards compliance that the web service supports)—only apply when you're calling the web service using SOAP messages, and aren't relevant in ASP.NET AJAX pages. However, the third attribute—ScriptService—is much more important. It configures the web service to allow JSON calls from JavaScript clients. Without this detail, you won't be able to use your web service in an ASP.NET AJAX page.

Creating the Web Method

With these details in place, you're ready to write the code for your web service. Every web service contains one or more methods that are marked with the WebMethod attribute. The WebMethod attribute makes the method remotely callable. If you add a method that doesn't include the web method attribute, your server-side code will be able to use it, but your client-side JavaScript won't be able to call it directly.

```
[WebService(Namespace = "http://tempuri.org/")]
[WebServiceBinding(ConformsTo = WsiProfiles.BasicProfile1_1)]
[System.Web.Script.Services.ScriptService]
public class TerritoriesService : System.Web.Services.WebService
{
    [WebMethod()]
    public void DoSomething()
    { ... }
}
```

It's not necessary to make the method public (as done here), but it's usually done as a matter of convention and clarity.

Web methods have certain restrictions. The data types you use for parameter values and return values must use one of the data types listed in Table 30-1.

Table 30-1. *Web Service Data Types for Parameters and Return Values*

Data Type	Description
The basics	Basic C# data types such as integers (short, int, long), unsigned integers (ushort, uint, ulong), nonintegral numeric types (float, double, decimal), and a few other miscellaneous types (bool, string, char, byte, DateTime).
Enumerations	Enumeration types (defined in C# with the enum keyword) are supported. However, the web service uses the string name of the enumeration value (not the underlying integer).
Custom objects	You can pass any object you create based on a custom class or structure. The only limitation is that only public data members and properties are transmitted, and all public members and properties must use one of the other supported data types. If you use a class that includes custom methods, these methods will not be transmitted to the client, and they will not be accessible to the client.

Data Type	Description
Arrays and collections	You can use arrays of any supported type. You can also use an ArrayList (which is simply converted into an array), but you can't use more specialized collections such as the Hashtable. You can use generic collections. In all these cases, the objects in the collection must also be serializable.
XmlNode	Objects based on System.Xml.XmlNode are representations of a portion of an XML document. You can use this to send arbitrary XML.
DataSet and DataTable	You can use DataSet and DataTable to return information from a relational database. Other ADO.NET data objects, such as DataColumns and DataRows, aren't supported. When you use a DataSet or DataTable, it's automatically converted to XML in a similar way to using the GetXml() or WriteXml() methods.

Session State in a Web Service

The WebMethod attribute accepts a number of parameters, most of which have little bearing in ASP.NET AJAX pages. One exception is the EnableSession property, which is false by default, thereby rendering session state inaccessible in your web service. This default makes sense in a traditional non-ASP.NET AJAX web service, because there might not be any session information, and the client might not maintain the session cookie at all. But with an ASP.NET AJAX web service, the web service calls are always being made from the context of an ASP.NET web page, which is executing in the context of the current web application user, and that user has a live session and a session cookie that's transmitted automatically along with the web service call.

Here's an example that gives a web method access to the Session object:

```
[WebMethod(EnableSession = true)]
public void DoSomething()
{
    if (Session["myObject"] != null)
    {
        // (Use the object in session state.)
    }
    else
    {
        // (Create a new object and store it in session state.)
    }
}
```

For the drop-down list example, the web service must provide a way to retrieve the regions that fall in a given territory. The following code shows a web service that contains a web method named GetTerritoriesInRegion(), which retrieves the regions:

```
[WebService(Namespace = "http://tempuri.org/")]
[WebServiceBinding(ConformsTo = WsiProfiles.BasicProfile1_1)]
```

```
[System.Web.Script.Services.ScriptService]
public class TerritoriesService : System.Web.Services.WebService
{
    [WebMethod()]
    public List<Territory> GetTerritoriesInRegion(int regionID)
    {
        SqlConnection con = new SqlConnection(
          WebConfigurationManager.ConnectionStrings[
          "Northwind"].ConnectionString);
        SqlCommand cmd = new SqlCommand(
          "SELECT * FROM Territories WHERE RegionID=@RegionID", con);
        cmd.Parameters.Add(new SqlParameter("@RegionID", SqlDbType.Int, 4));
        cmd.Parameters["@RegionID"].Value = regionID;

        List<Territory> territories = new List<Territory>();
        try
        {
            con.Open();
            SqlDataReader reader = cmd.ExecuteReader();

            while (reader.Read())
            {
                territories.Add(new Territory(
                  reader["TerritoryID"].ToString(),
                  reader["TerritoryDescription"].ToString()));
            }
            reader.Close();
        }
        catch (SqlException err)
        {
            // Mask errors.
            throw new ApplicationException("Data error.");
        }
        finally
        {
            con.Close();
        }
        return territories;
    }
}
```

The code in the GetTerritoriesInRegion() method is similar to the code you used in Chapter 29 to serve the client callback. However, this code has a key difference—instead of returning a single long string with the results, the information is returned using a strongly typed list of Territory objects. This is a much tidier approach that prevents casual errors.

The Territory class wraps two pieces of string information. It uses public member variables rather than properties because it's intended solely as a data package that transports information over the wire:

```
public class Territory
{
    public string ID;
    public string Description;

    public Territory(string id, string description)
```

```
    {
        this.ID = id;
        this.Description = description;
    }

    public Territory() { }
}
```

You can place this class definition in the same code file as the web service, or in a separate file in the App_Code directory.

Calling the Web Service

Now that you've created the web service you need, the next step is to configure your page so it knows about TerritoriesService. To do this, you need to add the ScriptManager control to your page. Then, add the <Services> section in the tag for the ScriptManager control. This section lists all the services your page uses and their locations, using ServiceReference elements. Here's how you add a reference for the TerritoriesService.asmx file shown earlier:

```
<asp:ScriptManager ID="ScriptManager1" runat="server">
  <Services>
    <asp:ServiceReference Path="./TerritoriesService.asmx"  />
  </Services>
</asp:ScriptManager>
```

When the page is rendered on the server, the ScriptManager will generate a JavaScript proxy. In your client-side code, you can use this JavaScript proxy to make your calls.

Here are the two lists in the web form:

```
<asp:DropDownList ID="lstRegions" Runat="server" DataSourceID="sourceRegions"
 DataTextField="RegionDescription" DataValueField="RegionID"
 onchange="GetTerritories(this.value);">
</asp:DropDownList>

<asp:DropDownList ID="lstTerritories" Runat="server">
</asp:DropDownList>
```

The first list is filled through ordinary ASP.NET data binding, using a data source control. More interestingly, it uses the onchange attribute to hook up a client-side event handler. This way, when the user picks a new territory, the JavaScript function GetTerritories() is triggered, and the current list value is passed in as an argument.

Technically, you could place all the code from the GetTerritories() function directly in the onchange event attribute and reduce the number of JavaScript functions you need to write. However, separating the code that calls the web service improves the readability of your code and makes it easier to maintain.

Here's the JavaScript code for the GetTerritories() function:

```
function GetTerritories(regionID)
{
    TerritoriesService.GetTerritoriesInRegion(regionID,
      OnRequestComplete, OnError);
}
```

If you've programmed with ASP.NET web services before, you'll notice that the client-side syntax for calling a web service in ASP.NET AJAX is different than the .NET syntax. In a .NET application, you must create the proxy object first, and then call the web service on that object. In an ASP.NET AJAX page, you use a ready-made proxy object that has the same name as your web service class.

Client-side web service calls are asynchronous, so you always need to supply the original web method parameters along with one extra parameter, which identifies the client-side JavaScript function that should be called when the result is received. (In this example, it's the function named OnRequestComplete.) Optionally, you can add another reference that points out the function to use if an error occurs. (In this example, that's the function OnError.)

To complete this example, you need to supply the client-side function that handles the response. In this example, the function is named OnRequestComplete(). It receives the return value through its single parameter and then adds the information to the second drop-down list box on the web page:

```
function OnRequestComplete(result)
{
    var lstTerritories = document.getElementById("lstTerritories");
    lstTerritories.innerHTML = "";

    for (var n = 0; n < result.length; n++)
    {
        var option = document.createElement("option");
        option.value = result[n].ID;
        option.innerHTML = result[n].Description;
        lstTerritories.appendChild(option);
    }
}
```

The remarkable feature of this code is that it's able to work with the result returned from the web method without any extra deserialization work. That's all the more impressive considering that the web method returns a generic list of Territory objects, which obviously has no equivalent in JavaScript code. Instead, ASP.NET AJAX creates a definition for the Territory object and returns the full list in an array. This allows your JavaScript code to loop over the array and examine the ID and Description properties of each item.

■ **Tip** There's one minor tweak that you can introduce here. Instead of using the document.getElementById() method, you can use ASP.NET AJAX's $get alias, which performs the same function and looks like this:

```
var lstTerritories = $get("lstTerritories");
```

This is a common convention in ASP.NET AJAX pages.

Now this example works exactly as the client callback version in Chapter 29. The difference is that this version uses a strongly typed web method, with no messy string serialization code. Also, you don't need to add any server-side code to retrieve the callback reference and insert it dynamically. Instead, you can use a straightforward proxy that provides access to your web service.

As a finishing touch, you can add timeout and error-handling functions, as shown here:

```
function OnError(result)
{
    var lbl = document.getElementById("lblInfo");
    lbl.innerHTML = "<b>" + result.get_message() + "</b>";
}
```

The OnError() function receives an error object, complete with a get_message() method that retrieves the error text and a get_stacktrace() method that returns a detailed call stack showing where the error occurred. Figure 30-2 shows what happens when the web method fails to connect to the database and throws a standard ApplicationException with this code:

```
throw new ApplicationException("Data error.");
```

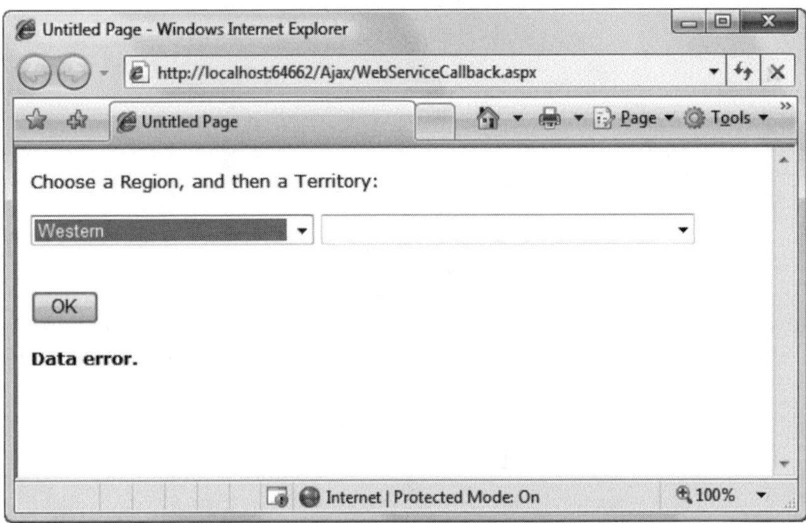

Figure 30-2. *Dealing with server-side errors on the client*

This demonstrates the ASP.NET AJAX version of the client callback model. Although it has the same plumbing as the ASP.NET client callback feature, the ASP.NET AJAX version provides a stronger foundation that's built on web services. However, both approaches have one feature in common—no matter which technique you use, you still need to write your own JavaScript code to update the page.

Placing a Web Method in a Page

In most cases, it makes sense to create a separate web service to handle your ASP.NET AJAX callbacks. This approach generally results in clearer pages and makes it easier to debug and refine your code. However, in some situations you may decide you have one or more web methods that are designed explicitly for use on a single page and that really shouldn't be reused in other parts of the application. In this case, you may choose to create a dedicated web service for each page, or you might choose to move the web service code into the page.

Placing the web method code in the page is easy—in fact, all you need is a simple bit of cut-and-paste. First, copy your web method (complete with the WebMethod attribute) into the code-behind class for your page. Then, change it to a static method, and add the System.Web.Script.Services.ScriptMethod attribute. Here's an example where the web method (named GetTerritoriesInRegion) is placed in a web page named WebServiceCallback_PageMethods:

```
public partial class WebServiceCallback_PageMethods : System.Web.UI.Page
{
    [System.Web.Services.WebMethod()]
    [System.Web.Script.Services.ScriptMethod()]
    public static List<Territory> GetTerritoriesInRegion(int regionID)
    {
        // Farm the work out to the web service class.
        TerritoriesService service = new TerritoriesService();
        return service.GetTerritoriesInRegion(regionID);
    }

    ...
}
```

Next, set the ScriptManager.EnablePageMethods property to true, and remove the reference in the <Services> section of the ScriptManager (assuming you don't want to use any non-page web services):

```
<asp:ScriptManager ID="ScriptManager1" runat="server" EnablePageMethods="true">
</asp:ScriptManager>
```

Finally, change your JavaScript code so it calls the method through the PageMethods object, as shown here:

```
PageMethods.GetTerritoriesInRegion(regionID, OnRequestComplete, OnError);
```

The PageMethods object exposes all the web methods you've added to the current web page.

One advantage of placing a web method in a page is that the method is no longer exposed through an .asmx file. As a result, it's not considered part of a public web service, and it's not as easy for someone else to discover. This is appealing if you're trying to hide your web services from curious users.

Another reason you might choose to code your web methods in the page class is to read values from view state or the controls on the page. When you trigger a page method, a stripped-down version of the page life cycle executes, just like with the ASP.NET client callback feature you saw in Chapter 29. Of course, there's no point in trying to modify page details because the page isn't being rerendered, so any changes you make will simply be discarded.

■ **Note** It makes no difference to the security of your application whether you place your web methods in a page or a dedicated web service. Placing your web method in the page may hide it from casual users, but a real attacker will start by looking at the HTML of your page, which includes a reference to the JavaScript proxy. Malicious users can easily use the JavaScript proxy to make spurious calls to the web method. To defend against threats like these, your web methods should always implement the same security measures you use in your web pages. For example, any input you accept should be validated, your code should refuse to return sensitive information to users who aren't authenticated, and database access should use parameterized commands to prevent SQL injection attacks.

ASP.NET AJAX Application Services

Creating and calling custom web services is clearly a valuable technique in ASP.NET AJAX. You can use web services to return additional data from a server-side database (as in the TerritoriesService example), to trigger a server-side task, to get user-specific session information, and so on. To make your life easier, ASP.NET AJAX also includes built-in services that you can use to access three commonly used features: forms authentication (Chapter 20), membership roles (Chapter 21), and user profiles (Chapter 24). Although you could build similar services of your own, it makes more sense for ASP.NET AJAX to provide a consistent web service model. In the future, it's quite likely that ASP.NET AJAX will provide more built-in services.

Before you can use any of these services, you need to add the <system.web.extensions> section to the web.config file. Inside, you need to add an element for each service you want to use:

```
<?xml version="1.0"?>
<configuration>
  ...
  <system.web.extensions>
    <scripting>
      <webServices>
        <authenticationService ... />
        <profileService ... />
        <roleService ... />
      </webServices>
    </scripting>
  </system.web.extensions>
  ...
</configuration>
```

When using the services in your client-side JavaScript, you call them through the Sys.Services property. For example, Sys.Services.AuthenticationService provides access to the methods of the authentication service.

The following sections show you how to enable and use each of these three services. To see these services in action, you can refer to the downloadable code for this chapter, which includes a sample website that demonstrates all three services.

Authentication Service

The authentication service allows you to use forms authentication by calling a web service. To enable it, you use the <authenticationService> element in the web.config file, as shown here:

```
<authenticationService enabled="true" requireSSL="false" />
```

If requireSSL is set to true, the cookie is only transmitted back to the server when the browser is requesting a page over SSL. Otherwise, the cookie is sent with every request.

■ **Note** One limitation of the authentication service is that it only supports cookie-based authentication.

When using the authentication service, you must also be using forms authentication. Here's a web.config file that supplies these details:

```
<?xml version="1.0"?>
<configuration>
  <configSections>...</configSections>
  <system.codedom>... </system.codedom>

  <system.web>
      <authentication mode="Forms">
        <forms loginUrl="./Login.aspx" />
      </authentication>
      ...
  </system.web>

  <system.web.extensions>
    <scripting>
      <webServices>
        <authenticationService enabled="true" requireSSL ="false" />
      </webServices>
      <scriptResourceHandler enableCompression="true" enableCaching="true" />
    </scripting>
  </system.web.extensions>

  <system.webServer>...</system.webServer>
</configuration>
```

Once you've enabled the authentication service, you can use the members that are listed in Table 30-2 in your client-side JavaScript code.

Table 30-2. *Authentication Service Members*

Member	Description
login()	Tests the supplied user name and password and logs the user in if they are valid. The forms authentication ticket is generated and the authentication cookie is returned, just as when logging in through server-side code on a login page. When calling login(), you can use additional parameters to specify if a persistent cookie should be used, and to provide a URL where the user will be redirected after a successful login. The actual login process is asynchronous, so you must supply callbacks to respond when the login process completes or fails.
logout()	Removes the current user's authentication ticket using an asynchronous call. You can supply callbacks that are triggered when the logout process completes or fails.
get_isLoggedIn()	Returns true if the user is currently logged in, and false otherwise.

■ **Note** You might wonder if the asynchronous login() method is actually useful. After all, a user usually needs to complete the login process before going on to the next task, so there's not much else to do while an asynchronous login request is under way. One minor advantage of the login() control is that it allows users to log in without refreshing the page. (This is particularly significant because the server-side Login control isn't supported by the UpdatePanel control, which you'll learn about later.)

As with all the application services, the authentication service does its work asynchronously. That means your code carries on while the login process is under way. To react when the login has completed, you must supply a redirect URL (in the fourth parameter) or a JavaScript callback (in the sixth parameter).

Here's an example that uses the latter approach and calls the onLoginCompleted() function after the server responds, and onLoginFailed to inform the user when the asynchronous call fails:

```
// Pull the user name and password from two text boxes
// (using the $get shortcut).
var username = $get("txtUserName");
var password = $get("txtPassword");

// Log in using the authentication service.
Sys.Services.AuthenticationService.login(username.value, password.value,
  false, null, null, onLoginCompleted, onLoginFailed, null);
```

The last argument of the login() method accepts any object. It's known as the user context object, and this pattern is preserved in all of the ASP.NET asynchronous AJAX application service calls. Essentially, the user context object is passed to your callbacks. Here's what the login callback functions look like:

```
function onLoginCompleted(validCredentials, userContext, methodName)
{
    // The asynchronous login attempt has finished, but you still need to check
    // the Boolean validCredentials parameter to determine if it succeeded.
    if (validCredentials == false)
    {
        $get("lblStatus").innerHTML = "Login failed.";
    }
    else
    {
        $get("lblStatus").innerHTML = "Currently logged in.";
    }
}

function onLoginFailed(error, userContext, methodName)
{
    alert(error.get_message());
}
```

Notice that a complete login process simply means you've received the server response. It doesn't indicate that the user was successfully logged in. In order to determine if the user was logged in, you must check the validCredentials parameter, as shown in this example.

Role Service

The role service allows you to use role-based authorization (as described in Chapter 23) by calling a web service. To enable it, you use the <roleService> element in the web.config file, as shown here:

```
<roleService enabled="true" />
```

To use the role service, the user must already be authenticated (through forms authentication or Windows authentication). Although you don't need to perform this authentication through the forms authentication service, in many cases you'll choose to implement both the authentication service and role service at the same time.

Here's a web.config that uses forms authentication (with the authentication service) and roles (with the role service):

```
<?xml version="1.0"?>
<configuration>
  <configSections>...</configSections>
  <system.codedom>... </system.codedom>

  <system.web>
      <authentication mode="Forms">
        <forms loginUrl="./Login.aspx" />
      </authentication>
      <roleManager enabled="true"/>
    ...
  </system.web>

  <system.web.extensions>
    <scripting>
      <webServices>
        <authenticationService enabled="true" requireSSL="false" />
        <roleService enabled="true"/>
      </webServices>
      <scriptResourceHandler enableCompression="true" enableCaching="true" />
    </scripting>
  </system.web.extensions>

  <system.webServer>...</system.webServer>
</configuration>
```

Once you've enabled the role service, you can use the members of the Sys.Services.RoleService class, which are listed in Table 30-3, in your client-side JavaScript code.

Table 30-3. Role Service Members

Member	Description
load()	Retrieves the role information for the current user on the client side. You must do this before you call isUserInRole() or get_roles(). The load process is asynchronous, so you must supply callbacks to react when the process completes or fails.
isUserInRole()	Returns true if the user has been assigned the role that you indicate. You must call load() before using this method.
get_roles()	Returns an array of strings, one for each role that's assigned to the current user. You must call load() before using this property procedure.

The first step to using the role service is calling load() and supplying the appropriate callbacks. You can then test the user's role membership when the completed callback fires.

The following code shows the most common way to implement this pattern. It shows a specific <div> (named adminControls) when the current user is an administrator:

```
function pageLoad()
{
    // The page is loading. Get the current user's roles.
    Sys.Services.RoleService.load(onLoadRolesCompleted, onLoadRolesFailed,
      null);
}

function onLoadRolesCompleted(result, userContext, methodName)
{
    // The roles have been retrieved.
    // Test role membership and configure the page.
    if (Sys.Services.RoleService.isUserInRole("Administrator"))
    {
        $get("adminControls").style.display = "block";
    }
}

function onLoadRolesFailed(error, userContext, methodName)
{
    alert(error.get_message());
}
```

■ **Note** As you'll learn later in this chapter, ASP.NET AJAX automatically calls the pageLoad() function (if you've added it) after the page is loaded and the client-side ASP.NET AJAX framework has been initialized. It's similar to handling the JavaScript onload event.

Remember, you should only call RoleService.load() if you know the current user is authenticated. That means you can safely call load() on a secured (non-anonymous) page, or after calling Sys.Services.AuthenticationService.get_isLoggedIn() and verifying it's true. If you call load() and the user isn't authenticated, the operation will appear to complete successfully, but no role information will be returned.

Maintaining Security when Using Application Services

When using forms authentication and role-based authorization, you must keep good security practices in mind. For example, when you enable the role service, you must assume it's possible for end users to discover their role membership (in other words, to determine the exact name of each role they belong to). If this isn't acceptable, you need to limit your role checking to server-side code.

Most importantly, you should never rely on client-side code to hide sensitive information. In the previous example, a <div> is displayed or hidden based on a role test. However, the content of that <div> is easily retrievable in the client-side markup of the page, even if it's not currently displayed. For that reason, this <div> isn't an acceptable place to put sensitive content (such as information that only administrators should be able to see). It *is* a reasonable place to put controls that only apply to administrators (for example, links that will fail with security exceptions for other types of users), provided they don't indirectly provide information that might be useful to a hacker.

Lastly, if you provide a client-callable web method, you must assume it can be called by users in any role (and even anonymous users if it's in an unsecured part of your website). Your client-side code might check role membership before allowing a call to a specific web method, but malicious users can call the same method through other mechanisms. Thus, if you need to create a secure web method, your web method needs to perform its own role checking, as described in Chapter 23.

Profile Service

The profile service allows you to use the profiles feature to retrieve user-specific information that ASP.NET automatically stores in a server-side database (as described in Chapter 24).

To enable the profile service, you use the <profileService> element in the web.config file.

```
<profileService enabled="true" writeAccessProperties="..."
  readAccessProperties="..." />
```

You must supply a comma-separated list of properties that will be made accessible on the client (in the readAccessProperties attribute) and changeable on the client (in the writeAccessProperties attribute). Remember, there are security implications to your choice. If you allow read access, logged-in users can hack the system to read these properties in their profile at any time. If you allow write access, logged-in users can circumvent your client-side code to arbitrarily change these values in their profiles, avoiding any sort of validation or data checking. Neither one of these possibilities is necessarily cause for alarm, but depending on the type of information you store in a profile and the way you act on it, it may introduce a problem in some scenarios. Caution—and a detailed threat analysis—is a good idea if you plan to use these services in a website that has high security requirements.

Here's a web.config file using the profile service (and the forms authentication service to log the user in):

```
<?xml version="1.0"?>
<configuration>
  <configSections>...</configSections>
```

```
  <system.codedom>... </system.codedom>

  <system.web>
      <authentication mode="Forms">
        <forms loginUrl="./Login.aspx" />
      </authentication>
      <profile enabled="true">
        <properties>
          <add name="FirstName" />
          <add name="LastName" />
          <add name="CustomerCode" />
        </properties>
      </profile>
    ...
  </system.web>

  <system.web.extensions>
    <scripting>
      <webServices>
        <authenticationService enabled="true" requireSSL="false" />
        <profileService enabled="true"
          readAccessProperties="FirstName,LastName,CustomerCode"
          writeAccessProperties="FirstName,LastName" />
      </webServices>
      <scriptResourceHandler enableCompression="true" enableCaching="true" />
    </scripting>
  </system.web.extensions>

  <system.webServer>...</system.webServer>
</configuration>
```

Once you've enabled the profile service, you can use the members of the Sys.Services.Profile-Service class, which are listed in Table 30-4, in your client-side JavaScript code.

Table 30-4. *Profile Service Members*

Member	Description
load()	Retrieves the profile properties (that you've listed in the readAccessProperties attribute) for the current user on the client side. You must do this before you can access the profile data through the properties collection. The load process is asynchronous, so you must supply callbacks to react when the process completes or fails.
properties	Provides a collection of profile data that you can read or change. You access individual properties by name, as in Sys.ProfileService.properties.FirstName.
save()	Passes the current values in the properties collection back to the web server, where they will be updated. Values that aren't listed in the writeAccessProperties attribute won't be passed back to the server—they're simply ignored.

Here's a small portion of client-side JavaScript that uses the profile service to display property data in an alert box:

```
function pageLoad()
{
    Sys.Services.ProfileService.load(null,
      onProfileLoadCompleted, onLoadFailed, null);
}

function onProfileLoadCompleted(numProperties, userContext, methodName)
{
    var profile = Sys.Services.ProfileService.properties;
    alert ("Your name is " + profile.FirstName + " " + profile.LastName);
}

function onProfileLoadFailed(error, userContext, methodName)
{
    alert(error.get_message());
}
```

You can modify any value in the properties code and then use a similar call to save the updated profile:

```
Sys.Services.ProfileService.save(null, onSaveCompleted, onSaveFailed, null);
```

This gives you the ability to retrieve and change profile data without triggering a full-page postback.

ASP.NET AJAX Server Controls

The web service features in ASP.NET AJAX give your client-side code a valuable window to the server. However, they force you to shoulder most of the hard work. It's up to you to craft the right web methods, call them at the right times, and update the page appropriately using nothing but JavaScript. In a complex application, this can be quite tedious.

For this reason, ASP.NET provides a higher-level server-side model that provides controls and components you can use in a web form. Using these ingredients, you can work entirely with server-side code. The ASP.NET AJAX controls will emit the ASP.NET AJAX script they need, and they'll use the ASP.NET AJAX script libraries behind the scenes. The potential drawback to this approach is reduced flexibility compared to do-it-yourself JavaScript programming. Although server-side controls are more productive than JavaScript, even with the help of the ASP.NET AJAX client libraries, server-side controls also limit what you're able to do. For example, if you want to have several controls interact with one another on the client side, you'll almost certainly need to write some client-side script.

In the following sections, you'll see how to use the three ASP.NET AJAX controls that are included as part of the core ASP.NET framework. These controls include the remarkably powerful UpdatePanel, the Timer, and the UpdateProgress control. All of these controls support *partial rendering*, which is a key Ajax concept. Using partial rendering, you can seamlessly update content on a page without forcing a full postback.

■ **Note** All the ASP.NET AJAX controls require a ScriptManager. If you place them on a page that doesn't contain a ScriptManager, they won't work and will throw an InvalidOperationException.

Partial Rendering with the UpdatePanel

The UpdatePanel is a handy control that lets you take an ordinary page with server-side logic and make sure it refreshes itself in flicker-free Ajax style.

The basic idea is that you divide your web page into one or more distinct regions, each of which is wrapped inside an invisible UpdatePanel. When an event occurs in an UpdatePanel that would normally trigger a postback, the UpdatePanel intercepts the event and performs an asynchronous callback instead. Here's an example of how it happens:

1. The user clicks a button inside an UpdatePanel.
2. Some client-side JavaScript code (that has been generated by ASP.NET AJAX) intercepts the client-side click event and performs an asynchronous callback to the server.
3. On the server, your normal page life cycle executes, with all the usual events. Finally, the page is rendered to HTML and returned to the browser.
4. The client-side JavaScript code receives the full HTML and updates every UpdatePanel on the page by replacing its current HTML with the new content. (If a change has occurred to content that's not inside an UpdatePanel, it's ignored.)

■ **Note** The ASP.NET AJAX UpdatePanel serves a similar purpose to the DynamicPanel custom control that was developed using ASP.NET's client callback feature in Chapter 29. Both controls use an asynchronous call to fetch new content and update part of the page without a full-page postback. However, the DynamicPanel in Chapter 29 is more limited, because you must use it with the DynamicPanelRefreshLink in order to trigger the asynchronous update. The UpdatePanel can intercept a postback that's triggered by any control inside the panel. Also, UpdatePanels work in concert—by default, every UpdatePanel is updated after every postback, although you can change this behavior.

The UpdatePanel control works in conjunction with the ScriptManager control. When using the UpdatePanel, you must be sure that the ScriptManager.EnablePartialRendering property is set to true (which is the default value). You can then add one or more UpdatePanel controls to your page, after the ScriptManager.

As you drag and drop controls in an UpdatePanel, the content appears in the <ContentTemplate> section. Here's an example of an UpdatePanel that contains a label and a button:

```
<asp:UpdatePanel ID="UpdatePanel1" runat="server">
  <ContentTemplate>
    <asp:Label ID="Label1" runat="server" Text="Label"></asp:Label>
    <asp:Button ID="Button1" runat="server" Text="Button" />
  </ContentTemplate>
</asp:UpdatePanel>
```

The UpdatePanel is a template-based control. When it renders itself, if copies the content from its ContentTemplate into the page. As a result, you can't dynamically add controls to the UpdatePanel using the UpdatePanels.Controls collection. However, you *can* insert controls dynamically using the UpdatePanels.ContentTemplateContainer.Controls collection.

The UpdatePanel doesn't derive from Panel. Instead, it derives directly from Control. The UpdatePanel has one role in life—to serve as a container for content that you want to refresh asynchronously. Unlike the standard ASP.NET Panel, an UpdatePanel has no visual appearance and doesn't support style settings. If you want to display a border around your UpdatePanel or change the background color, you'll need to place an ordinary Panel (or just a static <div> tag) in your UpdatePanel.

■ **Tip** Later in this chapter, you'll learn about the ASP.NET AJAX Control Toolkit, which includes a component called UpdatePanelAnimationExtender. This component extends the UpdatePanel with animated effects that signal when the panel's content is refreshed. For example, one possible animated effect is to fade in the new content over the old content.

On the page, the UpdatePanel renders itself as a <div> tag. However, you can configure the UpdatePanel so it renders itself as an inline element by changing the RenderMode property from Block to Inline. For example, you could take this step when you want to create an UpdatePanel that wraps text inside a paragraph or some other block element.

Figure 30-3 shows a sample web page that consists of three UpdatePanel controls (which have been highlighted using an off-white background color). Each UpdatePanel features the same content: a Label control and a Button control. Every time the page is posted to the server, the Page.Load event fills all three labels with the current time:

```
protected void Page_Load(object sender, EventArgs e)
{
    Label1.Text = DateTime.Now.ToLongTimeString();
    Label2.Text = DateTime.Now.ToLongTimeString();
    Label3.Text = DateTime.Now.ToLongTimeString();
}
```

This page demonstrates the flicker-free refreshing of an asynchronous callback. Click any button, and all three labels will be quietly updated. The one exception is if the client browser doesn't support the XMLHttpRequest object. In this situation, the UpdatePanel will downgrade to using full-page postbacks.

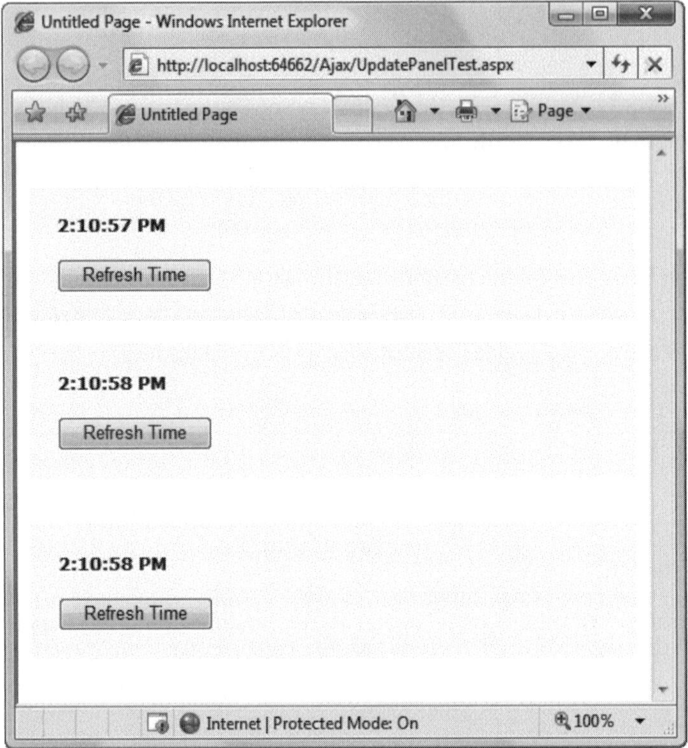

Figure 30-3. Using the UpdatePanel to avoid full-page postbacks

Handling Errors

When the UpdatePanel performs as asynchronous callback, the web-page code runs in exactly the same way as if the page had been posted back. The only difference is the means of communication (the page uses as asynchronous XMLHttpRequest call to get the new data) and the way the received data is dealt with (the UpdatePanel refreshes its inner content, but the remainder of the page is not changed). For that reason, you don't need to make significant changes to your server-side code or deal with new error conditions.

That said, problems can occur when performing an asynchronous postback just as they do when performing a synchronous postback.

You can test this behavior by adding code like this to the event handler for the server-side Page.Load event:

```
if (IsPostBack)
  throw new ApplicationException("This operation failed.");
```

When the web page throws an unhandled exception, the error is caught by the ScriptManager and passed back to the client. The ASP.NET AJAX client libraries then throw a JavaScript error in the page.

What happens next depends on your browser settings. If you've enabled script debugging (as described in Chapter 29), Visual Studio breaks on the line that caused the error. However, because this error is being deliberately thrown by the ASP.NET AJAX infrastructure to notify you about a server-side problem, this behavior isn't much help. You can't correct the server-side problem by changing the client-side code that throws the error. Instead, you'll simply need to stop the application or continue running it and ignore the problem.

If you aren't using script debugging, the browser may or may not notify you that a problem has occurred. Usually, most browsers are configured to quietly suppress JavaScript errors. In Internet Explorer, an "Error on page" message appears in the bottom-left corner of the status bar, indicating the problem. If you double-click this notification icon, a dialog box will appear with the full error details, as shown in Figure 30-4. Alternatively, if you've enabled the Display a Notification About Every Script Error setting in Internet Explorer, you'll see the message shown in Figure 30-4 when the error occurs, and you won't need to double-click the notification icon. (Choose Tools ➤ Internet Options, then click the Advanced tab, and then look in the Browsing section to find this setting.)

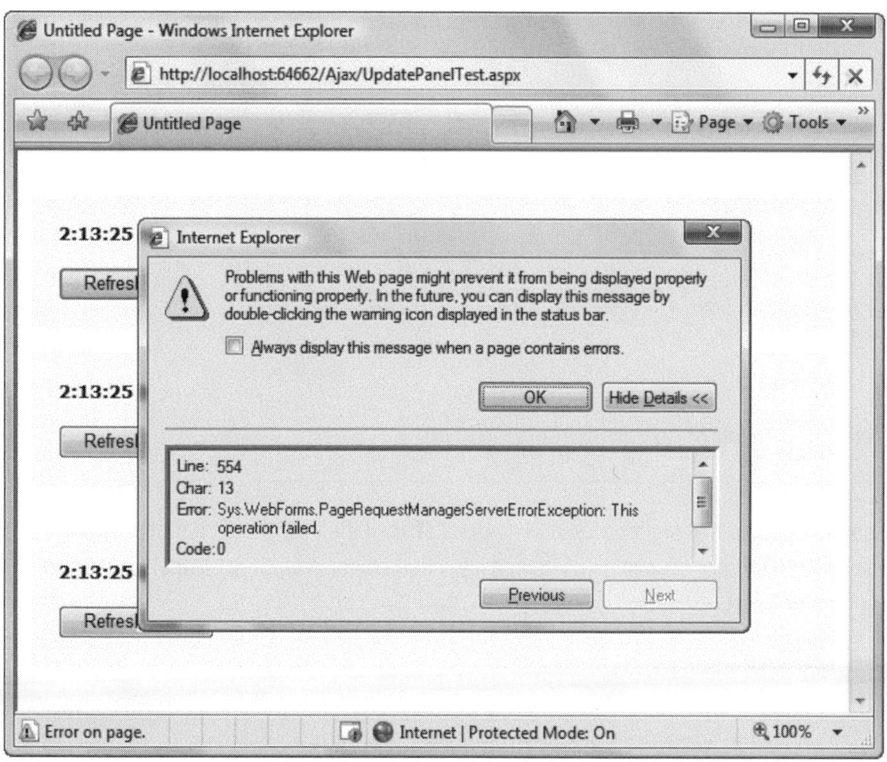

***Figure 30-4.** Displaying a client-side message about a server-side error*

You can change this behavior by handling the error with client-side JavaScript. To do so, you need to register a callback for the endRequest event of the System.Web.PageRequestManager class. (The PageRequestManager is a core part of the application model in ASP.NET AJAX. It manages the refresh process for the UpdatePanel controls and fires client-side events as the page moves through the stages in its lifetime.)

Here's a client-side script block that does exactly that. First, it defines a function that's triggered automatically when the page is first loaded. There's no need to use the onload event here, because ASP.NET AJAX automatically calls the pageLoad() function, if it exists. Similarly, ASP.NET AJAX calls the pageUnload() function when the page is being unloaded. All other events need to be hooked up manually—and that's what this pageLoad() function does. It gets a reference to the current instance of the PageRequestManager, and attaches a second function to the endRequest event:

```
function pageLoad()
{
    var pageManager = Sys.WebForms.PageRequestManager.getInstance();
    pageManager.add_endRequest(endRequest);
}
```

The endRequest event fires at the end of every asynchronous postback. In this example, the endRequest() function checks if an error has occurred. If it has, the error message is displayed in another control, and the set_errorHandled() method is called to suppress the standard ASP.NET AJAX error-handling behavior (the error message box). Alternate steps you could take include hiding or displaying a content region, displaying additional information, disabling controls, prompting the user to try again, and so on.

```
function endRequest(sender, args)
{
    // Handle the error.
    if (args.get_error() != null)
    {
        $get("lblError").innerHTML = args.get_error().message;

        // Suppress the message box.
        args.set_errorHandled(true);
    }
}
```

Figure 30-5 shows the new result of this error-handling code.

■ **Note** ASP.NET includes two controls that can't be used in an UpdatePanel: the FileUpload control and the HtmlInputFile control. However, these controls can be used on a page that contains an UpdatePanel, so long as they aren't actually in the UpdatePanel.

Conditional Updates

If you have more than one UpdatePanel and each is completely self-contained, you can configure the panels to update themselves independently of one another. Simply change the UpdatePanel.UpdateMode property from Always to Conditional. Now, that UpdatePanel will refresh itself when you click a button inside it, but not when you click a button inside another UpdatePanel. If you modify the example shown in Figure 30-3 so that all the UpdatePanel controls are conditional, they'll all work independently. When you click a button, the label in that panel will be updated. The other panels will remain untouched.

There's an interesting quirk here. Technically, when you click the button, all the labels will be updated, but only part of the page will be refreshed on the client side to show that fact. Most of the time, this distinction isn't important. However, it can lead to possible anomalies because the new updated value of each label will be stored in view state. As a result, the next time the page is sent back to the server, the labels will all be set to their most recent values.

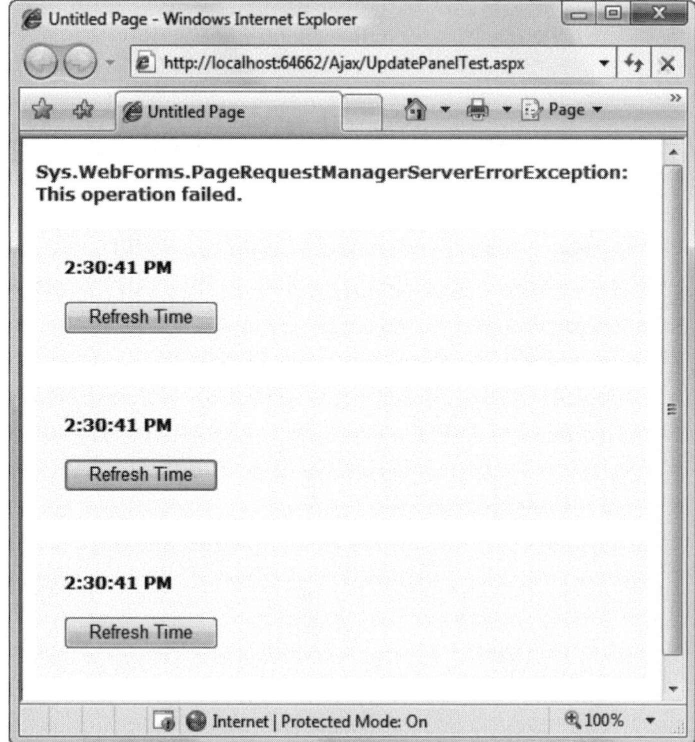

Figure 30-5. *Showing error information in the page*

■ **Tip** For more complex page designs, you can nest one conditional UpdatePanel in another. When the parent panel updates itself, all the contained panels will also update themselves. However, if one of the controls in a child panel triggers an update in that child panel, the rest of the parent panel won't be updated.

Interrupted Updates

There's one caveat with the approach shown in the previous example. If you perform an update that takes a long time, it could be interrupted by another update. As you know, ASP.NET AJAX posts the page back asynchronously, so the user is free to click other buttons while the postback is under way. ASP.NET AJAX doesn't allow concurrent updates, because it needs to ensure that other information—such as the page view state information, the session cookie, and so on—remains consistent. Instead, when a new asynchronous postback is started, the previous asynchronous postback is abandoned.

For the most part, this is the behavior you want. If you want to prevent the user from interrupting an asynchronous postback, you can add JavaScript code that disables controls while the asynchronous postback is under way. To do this, you need to attach an event handler to the beginRequest event, in the same way that you added an event handler to the endRequest event in the error handling example. Another option is to use the UpdateProgress control discussed later in this chapter.

Triggers

When you use conditional update mode, you have a few other options for triggering an update. One option is to use *triggers* to tell an UpdatePanel to render itself when a specific event occurs in a specific control on the page.

Technically, the UpdatePanel always uses triggers. All the controls inside an UpdatePanel automatically become the triggers for the UpdatePanel. In the current example, you've seen how this works with nested buttons—when the Button.Click event occurs, an asynchronous postback takes place. However, it also works with the default event of any web control (as designated by the DefaultEvent attribute in that control's code), provided that event posts back the page. For example, if you place a TextBox inside an UpdatePanel and set the TextBox.AutoPostBack property to true, the TextBox.TextChanged event will trigger an asynchronous postback and the UpdatePanel will be updated.

Triggers allow you to change this behavior in two ways. For one, they allow you to set up triggers to link to controls outside the panel. For example, imagine you have this button elsewhere on your page:

```
<asp:Button ID="cmdOutsideUpdate" runat="server" Text="Update" />
```

Ordinarily, this button would trigger a full postback. But by linking it to an UpdatePanel, you can change it to perform an asynchronous postback. To implement this design, you need to add an AsyncPostBackTrigger to the UpdatePanel that specifies the ID of the control you're monitoring and the event that triggers the refresh:

```
<asp:UpdatePanel ID="UpdatePanel1" runat="server" UpdateMode="Conditional">
  <ContentTemplate>
    <asp:Label ID="Label1" runat="server" Font-Bold="True"></asp:Label>
  </ContentTemplate>
  <Triggers>
    <asp:AsyncPostBackTrigger ControlID="cmdOutsideUpdate" EventName="Click" />
  </Triggers>
</asp:UpdatePanel>
```

The EventName attribute specifies the event you want to monitor. Usually, you don't need to set this because you'll be monitoring the default event, which is used automatically. However, it's a good practice to be explicit.

Now, when you click the cmdOutsideUpdate button, the click will be intercepted on the client side, and the PageRequestManager will perform an asynchronous postback. All the UpdatePanel controls that have UpdateMode set to Always will be refreshed. All the UpdatePanel controls that have UpdateMode set to Conditional *and* have an AsyncPostBackTrigger for cmdOutsideUpdate will also be refreshed.

■ **Note** You can add multiple triggers to the same UpdatePanel, in which case any of those events will trigger an update. You can add the same trigger to several different conditional UpdatePanel controls, in which case that event will update them all. You can also mix and match triggers and nested controls in a conditional UpdatePanel. In this case, both the events in the nested controls and the events in the trigger controls will cause an update.

You can use triggers in one other way. Instead of using them to monitor more controls, you can use them to tell the UpdatePanel to ignore certain controls. For example, imagine you have a button in your UpdatePanel. Ordinarily, clicking that button will trigger an asynchronous request and partial update. If you want it to trigger a full-page postback instead, you simply need to add a PostBackTrigger (instead of an AsyncPostBackTrigger).

For example, here's an UpdatePanel that contains a nested button that triggers a full postback rather than an asynchronous postback:

```
<asp:UpdatePanel ID="UpdatePanel1" runat="server" UpdateMode="Conditional">
  <ContentTemplate>
    <asp:Label ID="Label1" runat="server" Font-Bold="True"></asp:Label>
    <br />
    <br />
    <asp:Button ID="cmdPostback" runat="server" Text="Refresh Full Page" />
  </ContentTemplate>
  <Triggers>
    <asp:PostBackTrigger ControlID="cmdPostback" />
  </Triggers>
</asp:UpdatePanel>
```

This technique isn't as common, but it can be useful if you have several controls in an UpdatePanel that perform limited updates (and so use asynchronous postbacks) and one that performs more significant changes to the whole page (and so uses a full postback).

Optimizing the UpdatePanel

The UpdatePanel sometimes gets a bad reputation for bandwidth. That's because the UpdatePanel almost always transmits more information than you need.

For example, imagine you're creating a page that shows a table from a server-side database. The most efficient option is to implement the page with ASP.NET AJAX and web services. If you take this approach, your page will call a server-side web service to get exactly the information it wants—in this case, the records in the table. The drawback is that you need to write the client-side JavaScript that examines this information and converts it to HTML.

Compare this to a similar solution that uses an UpdatePanel with a rich data control like the GridView. In this scenario, you can avoid writing almost any code. However, the UpdatePanel needs to request much more information to refresh itself. Instead of getting just the raw data, it needs the complete user interface. In this example, that means the web server needs to send the entire rendered content of the GridView, the rendered content for any other controls inside the UpdatePanel, and the complete view state for the page. Clearly, this is far more information than what's required for the do-it-yourself web service approach.

To get the best performance from the UpdatePanel, it helps to understand this sometimes painful reality. You should also keep a few best practices in mind:

- Before introducing an UpdatePanel to your page, strive to reduce the view state as much as possible. Use the EnableViewState property to turn off view state for every control that has variable content but doesn't need to use view state to maintain it.
- Place the least amount of content possible inside each UpdatePanel. In the example described here, that means the UpdatePanel should only include the GridView. Use the triggers feature to place any other controls that may trigger an update outside of the UpdatePanel.

- If you have several updateable areas in your page, place them in separate UpdatePanel controls, and make each one conditional. When the web server answers an UpdatePanel callback, it sends the rendered markup for that UpdatePanel and any other non-conditional UpdatePanel controls on the page. If you only need new content for one panel, there's no need to get it for any others.
- In complex pages with multiple update panels, consider refreshing them manually. To put this technique into practice, make your panels conditional and set the ChildrenAsTriggers property to false. Now, the only way to cause a refresh is to explicitly call the Update() method on one or more UpdatePanel controls during a callback.

And remember, the UpdatePanel approach will never be worse than the postback approach, because the postback approach always posts back the entire page. The UpdatePanel approach only pales in comparison to hands-on ASP.NET AJAX coding.

Timed Refreshes with the Timer

The previous section showed you how to refresh self-contained portions of the page. Of course, in order for this technique to work, the user needs to initiate an action that would ordinarily cause a postback, such as clicking a button.

In some situations, you might want to force a full- or partial-page refresh without waiting for a user action. For example, you might create a page that includes a stock ticker, and you might want to refresh this ticker periodically (say, every 5 minutes) to ensure it doesn't become drastically outdated. ASP.NET AJAX includes a Timer control that can help you implement this design.

The Timer control is refreshingly straightforward. You simply add it to a page and set its Interval property to the maximum number of milliseconds that should elapse before an update. For example, if you set Interval to 60000, the timer will force a postback after one minute elapses.

```
<asp:Timer ID="Timer1" runat="server" Interval="60000" />
```

If the Timer is in an UpdatePanel, it will trigger an asynchronous postback. If it's not, and it's not linked to an UpdatePanel with a trigger, the Timer will trigger an ordinary full-page postback.

■ **Note** Obviously, the timer has the potential to greatly increase the overhead of your web application and reduce its scalability. Think carefully before introducing an automatic postback feature, and make the intervals long rather than short.

The timer raises a server-side Tick event, which you can handle to update your page. However, you don't necessarily need to use the Tick event, because the full-page life cycle executes when the timer fires. This means you can respond to other page and control events, such as Page.Load.

The timer is particularly well suited to pages that use partial rendering, as discussed in the previous section. That's because a refresh in a partially rendered page might just need to change a single portion of the page. Furthermore, partial rendering makes sure your refreshes are much less intrusive. Unlike a full postback, a callback with partial rendering won't cause flicker and won't interrupt the user in the middle of a task.

To use the timer with partial rendering, wrap the updateable portions of the page in UpdatePanel controls with the UpdateMode set to Conditional, and add a trigger that forces an update whenever the timer fires:

```
<asp:UpdatePanel ID="UpdatePanel1" runat="server" UpdateMode="Conditional">
  <ContentTemplate>
    ...
  </ContentTemplate>
  <Triggers>
    <asp:AsyncPostBackTrigger ControlID="Timer1" EventName="Tick" />
  </Triggers>
</asp:UpdatePanel>

<asp:Timer ID="Timer1" runat="server" Interval="60000" OnTick="Timer1_Tick" />
```

All the other portions of the page can be left as is, or you can wrap them in conditional UpdatePanel controls with different triggers if you need to update them in response to other actions.

To stop the timer, you simply need to set the Enabled property to false in server-side code. For example, here's how you could disable the timer after ten updates:

```
protected void Timer1_Tick(object sender, EventArgs e)
{
    // Update the tick count and store it in view state.
    int tickCount = 0;
    if (ViewState["TickCount"] != null)
    {
        tickCount = (int)ViewState["TickCount"];
    }
    tickCount++;
    ViewState["TickCount"] = tickCount;

    // Decide whether to disable the timer.
    if (tickCount > 10)
    {
        Timer1.Enabled = false;
    }
}
```

Time-Consuming Updates with UpdateProgress

ASP.NET AJAX also includes an UpdateProgress control that works in conjunction with partial rendering at the UpdatePanel. Essentially, the UpdateProgress control allows you to show a message while a time-consuming update is under way.

■ **Note** The UpdateProgress control is slightly misnamed. It doesn't actually indicate progress; instead, it provides a wait message that reassures the user that the page is still working and the last request is still being processed. You saw one implementation of this technique with a JavaScript page processor in Chapter 29.

When you add the UpdateProgress control to a page, you get the ability to specify some content that will appear as soon as an asynchronous request is started and disappear as soon as the request is finished. This content can include a fixed message or image. Often, an animated GIF is used to simulate some sort of progress indicator.

Figure 30-6 shows a page that uses the UpdateProgress control at three different points in its life cycle. The top figure shows the page as it first appears, with a straightforward UpdatePanel control containing a button. When the button is clicked, the asynchronous callback process begins. At this point, the contents of the UpdateProgress control appear underneath (as shown in the middle figure). In this example, the UpdateProgress includes a text message, an animated GIF that appears as progress bar, and a cancel button. When the callback is complete, the UpdateProgress disappears and the UpdatePanel is updated, as shown in the bottom image of Figure 30-6.

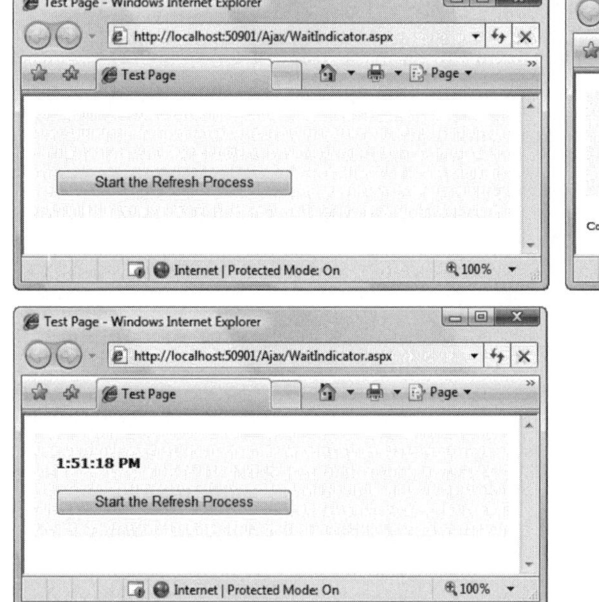

Figure 30-6. A wait indicator

The markup for this page defines an UpdatePanel followed by an UpdateProgress. The UpdateProgress control includes a cancel button, which you'll examine in the next section.

```
<asp:UpdatePanel ID="UpdatePanel1" runat="server">
  <ContentTemplate>
    <div style="background-color:#FFFFE0;padding: 20px">
      <asp:Label ID="lblTime" runat="server" Font-Bold="True"></asp:Label>
      <br /><br />
      <asp:Button ID="cmdRefreshTime" runat="server"
       OnClick="cmdRefreshTime_Click"
       Text="Start the Refresh Process" />
    </div>
  </ContentTemplate>
</asp:UpdatePanel>
<br />

<asp:UpdateProgress runat="server" id="updateProgress1">
```

```
  <ProgressTemplate>
    <div style="font-size: xx-small">
      Contacting Server ... <img src="wait.gif" />
      <input id="cmdCancel" onclick="AbortPostBack()" type="button"
        value="Cancel" />
    </div>
  </ProgressTemplate>
</asp:UpdateProgress>
```

This isn't the only possible arrangement. Depending on the layout you want, you can place your UpdateProgress control somewhere inside your UpdatePanel control.

The code for this page has a slight modification from the earlier examples. Because the UpdateProgress control only shows its content while the asynchronous callback is under way, it only makes sense to use it with an operation that takes time. Otherwise, the UpdateProgress will only show its ProgressTemplate for a few fractions of a second. To simulate a slow process, you can add a line to delay your code 10 seconds, as shown here:

```
protected void cmdRefreshTime_Click(object sender, EventArgs e)
{
    System.Threading.Thread.Sleep(TimeSpan.FromSeconds(10));
    lblTime.Text = DateTime.Now.ToLongTimeString();
}
```

There's no need to explicitly link the UpdateProgress control to your UpdatePanel control. The UpdateProgress automatically shows its ProgressTemplate whenever *any* UpdatePanel begins a callback. However, if you have a complex page with more than one UpdatePanel, you can choose to limit your UpdateProgress to pay attention to just one of them. To do so, simply set the UpdateProgress.AssociatedUpdatePanelID property with the ID of the appropriate UpdatePanel. You can even add multiple UpdateProgress controls to the same page, and link each one to a different UpdatePanel.

Cancellation

The UpdateProgress control supports one other detail: a cancel button. When the user clicks a cancel button, the asynchronous callback will be canceled immediately, the UpdateProgress content will disappear, and the page will revert to its original state.

Adding a cancel button is a two-step process. First, you need to add the JavaScript code that performs the cancellation. Here's the code you need (which you must place after the ScriptManager control):

```
var pageManager = Sys.WebForms.PageRequestManager.getInstance();
pageManager.add_initializeRequest(InitializeRequest);

function InitializeRequest(sender, args)
{
    if (pageManager.get_isInAsyncPostBack())
    {
        args.set_cancel(true);
    }
}

function AbortPostBack()
{
```

```
    if (pageManager.get_isInAsyncPostBack()) {
     pageManager.abortPostBack();
    }
}
```

Once you've added this code, you can use JavaScript code to call the AbortPostBack() function on the page at any time and cancel the callback. Here's the HTML button in the current example that calls the AbortPostBack() function when it's clicked:

```
<input id="cmdCancel" onclick="AbortPostBack()" type="button" value="Cancel" />
```

Typically, you'll place this button (or an element like this) in the ProgressTemplate of the UpdateProgress control, because it only applies while the callback is under way.

■ **Tip** It makes sense to use an abort button for tasks that can be safely canceled because they don't affect external state. For example, users should be able to cancel time-consuming queries. However, it's not a good idea to add cancellation to an update operation, because the server will continue until it finishes the update, even if the client has stopped listening for the response.

Managing Browser History

Every time your page performs a full-page postback, the web browser treats it as a page navigation and adds a new entry to the history list. However, when you use the UpdatePanel to perform an asynchronous callback, the history list isn't touched. This drawback becomes particularly apparent in an ASP.NET AJAX page that performs a complex process with multiple steps. If the user inadvertently clicks the Back button in an attempt to return to a previous step, the browser will jump back to the previous *page*, and all the work the user has done to that point will be lost.

Fortunately, ASP.NET 4 has an elegant solution. Using the ScriptManager, you can take control of the browser's history list. You can add items to the list at will, and react when the user clicks the Back or Forward button to make sure the page state is correctly restored. In fact, this process is so seamless that it works *better* than navigation with an ordinary web form, because the user won't ever be prompted to repost the previous set of values to restore the page. And as with most of the ASP.NET AJAX features, the history support gives you a painless way to get functionality that would be extremely difficult to code on your own without running into quirks and browser compatibility headaches.

To see how the ScriptManager's browser history feature works, you can create a straightforward example with the Wizard control. Here's a stripped-down example that places a three-step wizard inside an UpdatePanel:

```
<asp:UpdatePanel ID="UpdatePanel1" runat="server">
  <ContentTemplate>
    <asp:Wizard ID="Wizard1" runat="server" ...>
      <WizardSteps>
        <asp:WizardStep runat="server" title="Step 1">
          This is Step 1.
        </asp:WizardStep>
        <asp:WizardStep runat="server" title="Step 2">
          This is Step 2.
        </asp:WizardStep>
        <asp:WizardStep runat="server" Title="Step 3">
```

```
        This is Step 3.
      </asp:WizardStep>
    </WizardSteps>
    ...
  </asp:Wizard>
  </ContentTemplate>
</asp:UpdatePanel>
```

As it's currently written, this page gives you the benefits of ASP.NET AJAX. You can click the links in the wizard to move from one step to another seamlessly, without page flicker. However, the history list won't change.

Adding History Points

To solve this problem, you must start by setting the ScriptManager.EnableHistory property to true. This allows you to use the ScriptManager to add history points and react to history navigation.

Next, you need to call the ScriptManager.AddHistoryPoint() method in your server-side code to add an item to the history list. When you call AddHistoryPoint(), you supply three arguments: the state, the key, and the page title. Here's what these values signify:

- **State:** The state is a string that stores some information that relates to your history point. When the user returns to this history point (using the Back or Forward buttons in the browser), you can retrieve the associated state. For example, in the wizard example it makes sense to store the wizard's current step index. That way, when the user returns to a state point, you can switch back to the corresponding step.
- **Key:** The key is a unique string name that's used to store your state information. It allows your page to store multiple state values without a conflict. This is primarily useful if you have multiple controls that use the history list. For example, imagine you have two Wizard controls on the same page. As long as each one uses a different key, they can both store their current step index at the same time.
- **Title:** The page title is displayed at the top of the browser window and recorded in the history list. By choosing a suitable title, you can clearly indicate what each history item represents and make the history list far more practical. Alternatively, you can choose to omit the title argument, in which case the history point will use the current page title.

In the wizard example, it makes sense to add the history point when the control changes to a new step. You can do this by reacting to the wizard's ActiveStepChanged event. Here's the code that does the trick:

```
protected void Wizard1_ActiveStepChanged(object sender, EventArgs e)
{
    // Verify this is an asynchronous postback, and ensure that it's
    // not a navigation attempt.
    if ((ScriptManager1.IsInAsyncPostBack) && (!ScriptManager1.IsNavigating))
    {
        string currentStep = Wizard1.ActiveStepIndex.ToString();

        ScriptManager1.AddHistoryPoint("Wizard1",
          Wizard1.ActiveStepIndex.ToString(),
          "Step " + (Wizard1.ActiveStepIndex + 1).ToString());
    }
}
```

Before adding the history point, the code checks two details. First, the code checks the IsAsyncPostBack property to verify that the step is changing as part of an asynchronous callback operation. This ensures that the history point won't be added when the page is first created and the ActiveStepIndex property is set for this first time, or if the step changes during a regular post back. Second, the code checks the IsNavigating property, which is true when the user clicks the Forward or Back button to move to a new state point in your page. When this happens, you don't need to store state—instead, you need to *restore* it by handling the ScriptManager.Navigate event. (You'll see how to do this shortly.)

When adding the history point, the code uses the index name Wizard1 (to match the name of the Wizard control). It stores the current step index and sets the page title to a descriptive string like "Step 1." You'll notice that the page title adds 1 to the ActiveStepIndex property, because the ActiveStepIndex uses standard zero-based counting.

If you run the page now and move from step to step, you'll see the new items appear in the history list, as shown in Figure 30-7. However, if you click a history item or use the Back or Forward button to return to one of them, nothing happens, because you haven't yet written the code to restore your page state.

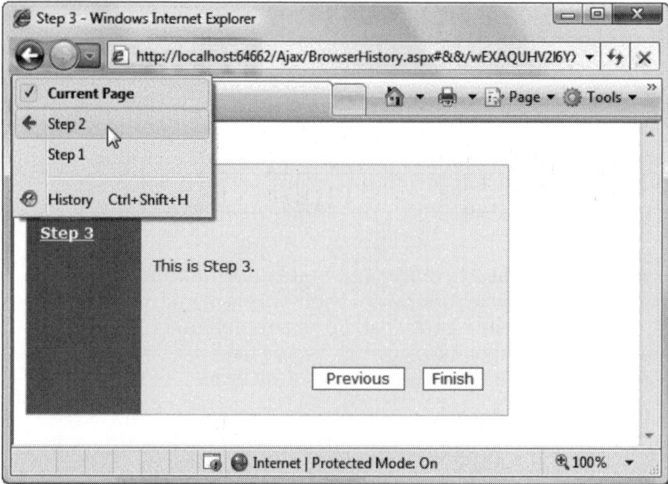

Figure 30-7. *Custom history points*

Restoring Page State

When the user moves forward or back in the history list, the ScriptManager performs an asynchronous callback to refresh the page. At this point, you handle the ScriptManager.Navigate event and modify the page.

When handling the Navigate event, it's up to you to retrieve the state you need using the HistoryEventArgs.State collection and the state key you used when you first added the history point. If you can't find the appropriate state value, the user has probably returned to your page's first bookmark. This means you should return the wizard to its initial state.

Here's the code that the wizard example uses to return the appropriate step:

```
protected void ScriptManager1_Navigate(object sender, HistoryEventArgs e)
{
    if (e.State["Wizard1"] == null)
    {
```

```
        // Restore default state of page (for example, for first page).
        Wizard1.ActiveStepIndex = 0;
    }
    else
    {
        Wizard1.ActiveStepIndex = Int32.Parse(e.State["Wizard1"]);
    }
    Page.Title = "Step " + (Wizard1.ActiveStepIndex + 1).ToString();
}
```

This code also updates the page title to match the history, because the ScriptManager won't perform this step on its own. With this event handler in place, the wizard example now works perfectly.

How State Is Stored in the URL

At this point, you might be wondering where state values are stored. Interestingly, the ScriptManager places them in the page URL. It uses Base64 encoding to obfuscate the value and tacks a hash code on the end for verification.

Here's the sort of URL you'll see in the wizard example:

```
http://localhost:64662/Ajax/BrowserHistory.aspx#&&/wEXAQUHV2l6YXJkMQUBMmLWUszDqKb/+4
7LFQFHDQfzfzoo
```

■ **Note** The state information is placed after the URL fragment marker (#). As a result, the state information won't disturb any query string arguments you might be using, which will appear before the fragment marker.

The history state uses the same encoding mechanism as view state. This means that users can, with minimal effort, retrieve your state values. However, users can't tamper with these values, because they won't be able to generate a proper hash code without the web server's private key.

Unlike with view state, you can't apply encryption to the state values. However, you can remove the encoding and hash code if you want to see them more clearly. Just set the ScriptManager.EnableSecureHistoryState property to false, and your URL will change to something like this:

```
http://localhost:64662/Ajax/BrowserHistory.aspx#&&Wizard1=2
```

Of course, this opens up the possibility that the user might change a state value by modifying the URL.

■ **Note** The URL storage mechanism has interesting ramifications for bookmarking. For example, if a user adds a bookmark for an ASP.NET AJAX page that uses the history list, that bookmark will capture the current page state. However, other details will be lost, like the view state of all the controls on the page. With careless design, this could cause a problem. For example, imagine a wizard that forces users to fill out certain details before allowing them to advance to the final step. If you store the current step as a history item, the user could return to the final step through a bookmark, even though all the controls that belong to earlier steps will be empty.

Deeper into the Client Libraries

So far, you've spent most of your time using the higher-level features that the ASP.NET AJAX framework provides. You began by considering web service support, and then you explored key server controls like the UpdatePanel, Timer, and UpdateProgress. Along the way you've seen a few details of the client-side ASP.NET AJAX model—for example, the $get alias and the events of PageRequestManager. However, you haven't explored the underlying plumbing.

Many developers will prefer this approach. They'll rely most on the server-side features in ASP.NET AJAX and dip into the client model to handle the occasional event. However, there's one task that requires a better understanding of the client-side model: creating custom controls that use ASP.NET AJAX features.

In the following sections, you'll take a tour of the client libraries and learn how to use them. Once you have a solid grasp of these basics, you'll learn about how you can create a basic client-side ASP.NET AJAX control. However, you *won't* learn how to extend this example into a full-blown ASP.NET web control. Custom control development with ASP.NET AJAX is a complex, detailed topic. If you're a business developer, you'll probably prefer to use existing ASP.NET AJAX controls rather than code your own. If you're a component developer, you can continue down the path to custom control development with another book. Two good choices are *ASP.NET AJAX in Action* (Manning, 2010), which illuminates the entire ASP.NET AJAX toolkit in detail, and *Advanced ASP.NET AJAX Server Controls For .NET Framework 3.5* (Addison-Wesley, 2008), which focuses on control design.

Understanding the Client Model

The fundamental building block of ASP.NET AJAX is the client-side JavaScript libraries. They provide the glue that holds all the other features together. Figure 30-8 shows a high-level look at ASP.NET AJAX that shows where the client libraries fit in.

The client libraries add a dash of .NET flavor to the JavaScript world. They consist of three central parts:

- **JavaScript extensions:** These give you a way to use object-oriented techniques with ordinary JavaScript code.
- **Core JavaScript classes:** These establish a stripped-down framework with basic client-side functionality that's required in an Ajax application. The core classes include classes for string manipulation, components, networking, and web services.
- **UI Framework:** This sits on top of the infrastructure established by the core classes. The UI Framework adds the concept of client-side controls and the client-side page.

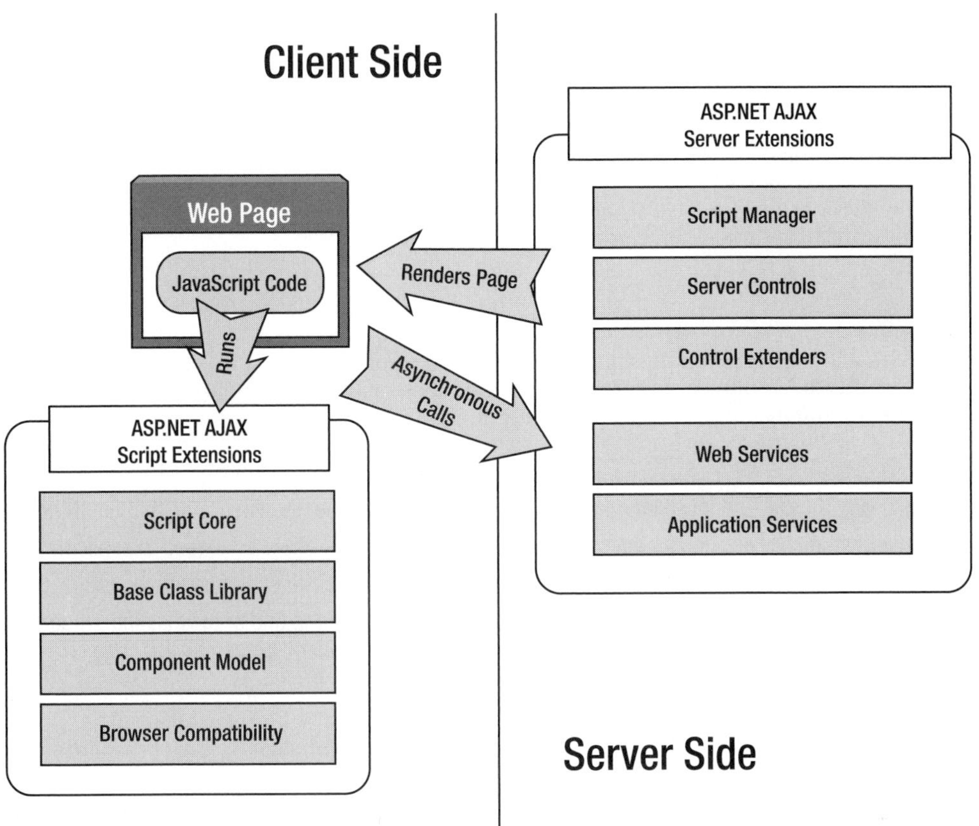

Figure 30-8. *The ASP.NET AJAX architecture*

■ **Note** Altogether, the client libraries are quite compact, requiring the client to download less than 200 KB of script code. When visiting an ASP.NET-powered site, this script code is only downloaded once, and then cached by the browser. In addition, ASP.NET sends a compressed version of the script document if the browser supports it. (ASP.NET only uses compression when receiving requests from Internet Explorer 7 or later. Even though earlier versions of Internet Explorer support compression, there is a bug that causes browser cache settings to sometimes be ignored.)

Object-Oriented Programming in JavaScript

JavaScript is not a true object-oriented language, because it lacks support for core object-oriented features like inheritance and interfaces. However, JavaScript is often described as an *object-based* language, because JavaScript provides built-in objects (representing browser windows, the current HTML document, and so on).

Unfortunately, JavaScript doesn't include the ability to define custom classes. However, there are popular workarounds that developers use to create code constructs that approximate classes.

First, it's easy enough to create a one-off object with any set of properties you choose. You simply need to create an ordinary object (using the var keyword) and then create the properties you want by assigning to them. For example, this code creates an employee object with two attached string variables: FirstName and LastName.

```
var emp = new Object;
emp.FirstName = "Joe";
emp.LastName = "Higgens";
```

The problem with this code is that it doesn't use a class. As a result, there's no way to verify that the object you're using is truly an employee, and there's no way to be sure that two employee objects really expose the same set of members.

■ **Note** JavaScript is a very flexible and loose language. In the preceding example, the FirstName and LastName properties are created automatically as soon as the code assigns values to them—there's no need to explicitly declare the properties first. This trick makes it easy to create objects, but it's also rife with many potential problems. For example, it's easy to accidentally create a new property by referring to one of the existing properties but inadvertently using the wrong name.

To create a more standardized object definition, JavaScript developers usually fall back on one of two tricks: closures or prototypes.

Closures

Essentially, a *closure* is a function that encapsulates a class. You don't actually run a closure function. Instead, you run the nested functions inside it. These functions are effectively the methods (and property procedures) of the class. They have access to any variables defined inside the closure function.

The easiest way to understand the closure model is to consider an example. Here's a closure that effectively defines an Employee class with a first and last name:

```
function Employee(first, last)
{
    // The private section.
    var _firstName = first;
    var _lastName = last;

    // The public section.
    this.set_FirstName = function(first) {
       _firstName = first;
    }
    this.get_FirstName = function() {
       return _firstName;
    }
```

```
    this.set_LastName = function(last) {
       _lastName = last;
    }
    this.get_LastName = function() {
       return _lastName;
    }
}
```

The variables that you define in the closure (in this example, _firstName and _lastName) are local to the Employee() function, and can't be accessed outside the function. On the other hand, the methods (in this example, set_FirstName(), get_FirstName(), and so on) can be called at any time.

To create an employee object, you'd use code like this in the same script block or in a different script block that occurs later on the page:

```
var emp = new Employee("Joe", "Higgens");
var name = emp.get_FirstName() + " " + emp.get_LastName();
alert(name);
```

The first line creates a variable named emp, and sets emp to hold a reference to the Employee() function. In other words, your object instance is really just a function pointer—one that points to the constructor that creates the object. Figure 30-9 shows the result.

Figure 30-9. *Creating a custom object in JavaScript*

Early builds of ASP.NET AJAX used closures for object-oriented programming. However, later builds switched to the prototype system.

■ **Note** Technically, the Employee() function gives itself four new properties: set_FirstName, get_FirstName, set_LastName, and get_LastName. It assigns a function to each property. This allows you to invoke each property as though it were a method. In other words, when you write emp.get_FirstName(), you are accessing the get_FirstName() property, which is actually a function.

This system introduces some possible errors. For example, you might refer to a function when you mean to invoke it (by omitting the parentheses), or inadvertently remove a method from an object (by assigning to the property). Developers must balance the value of objects in client-side script against the extra complexity they entail.

Prototypes

The other approach developers use to define classes in JavaScript is with *prototypes*. For various technical reasons, prototypes are preferred in ASP.NET AJAX. Prototypes offer better performance in some browsers (such as Firefox), and they provide better support for reflection, IntelliSense, and debugging. These differences are because prototypes have their members "baked in," while closures create their members each time an object is instantiated.

To use a prototype, you rely on the public prototype property that every JavaScript object has. This property exposes the public interface for the object. To add publicly callable methods to an object, you assign new properties to the prototype.

Here's a refactoring of the code you saw earlier that defines an Employee object using the prototype:

```
Employee = function(first, last)
{
    // The private section.
    this._firstName = first;
    this._lastName = last;
}

// The public section.
Employee.prototype.set_FirstName = function(first) {
    this._firstName = first;
}
Employee.prototype.get_FirstName = function() {
   return this._firstName;
}
Employee.prototype.set_LastName = function(last) {
   this._lastName = last;
}
Employee.prototype.get_LastName = function() {
   return this._lastName;
}
```

The Employee object itself is actually a reference to a function that plays the role of a constructor. This function initializes all the private members. The public members are defined separately, by adding to the prototype. The code that uses the prototype version of the Employee class remains the same:

```
var emp = new Employee("Joe", "Higgens");
var name = emp.get_FirstName() + " " + emp.get_LastName();
alert(name);
```

There's a subtle difference in the way that closures and prototypes work. Essentially, a closure creates the specialized members for your object (set_FirstName, get_FirstName, and so on) every time a new object is created based on that closure. But with the prototype approach, the prototype object is created and configured once, and then copied into each new object. This is the reason for the performance improvement on some browsers.

Just as importantly, prototypes make certain tasks, such as reflection, easier in ASP.NET AJAX. Thus, the prototype approach is preferred.

Registering Classes with ASP.NET AJAX

Closures and prototypes are already available in the JavaScript language. In the following sections, you'll see three ingredients that ASP.NET AJAX adds for object-oriented development: namespaces, inheritance, and interfaces. But before you can use any of these features, you need to register your JavaScript class with the ASP.NET AJAX framework.

This step is easy. First, make sure your JavaScript code is on a web page that includes the ASP.NET AJAX client libraries. (The easiest way to do this is to add the ScriptManager control to the page, and make sure you script blocks fall after the ScriptManager control.) Once the ASP.NET AJAX client libraries are available, you simply need to call the registerClass() method on your constructor function after you've defined your prototype, as shown here:

```
Employee = function(first, last)
{ ... }

Employee.prototype.set_FirstName = ...
Employee.prototype.get_FirstName = ...
...

Employee.registerClass("Employee");
```

Remember, technically the Employee variable is a reference to the constructor function that you use to create employee objects. You can call the registerClass() method because the ASP.NET AJAX client libraries add methods for registering classes, namespaces, interfaces, and enumerations.

■ **Note** In the rest of this chapter, we'll refer to the code structures you can create with ASP.NET AJAX as classes. These aren't the full-fledged, typesafe classes you see in .NET. More accurately, they are class-like constructs that are registered as classes with the ASP.NET AJAX client libraries.

Even once you've registered the Employee class, you still use the same code to create employee objects. However, ASP.NET AJAX is now aware of your class and provides it with a bit more built-in functionality. One example is reflection, which allows you to get type information from your class using code like this:

```
var emp = new Employee("Joe", "Higgens");
alert(Object.getTypeName(emp));
```

If you use this code with an instance of an unregistered class, you'll see the class name Object. However, if you've registered your Employee class, you'll see the more precise name Employee.

The Object class provides several more members that you can use to get type information from a registered custom class, including implementsInterface (to test if the class implements a specific interface), getInterfaces (to find out all the interfaces a class implements), inheritsFrom (to test if the class inherits from a specific class directly or indirectly), and isInstanceOfType (to test if an object is an instance of a specified class or a class derived from that class).

■ **Tip** When debugging, you can step into the JavaScript for the ASP.NET AJAX client libraries. For example, if you enable client script debugging (as described in Chapter 29) and place a breakpoint on the code statement that invokes registerClass(), you can step into the code for the registerClass() function. Best of all, the ScriptManager is intelligent enough to realize that you're running in debug mode, so it uses the debug version of the JavaScript client libraries, which means you can look at a nicely formatted, commented version of the JavaScript code. Using this trick is a great way to learn more about how ASP.NET AJAX works.

Base Types

The ASP.NET AJAX client libraries extend several core JavaScript types with helper functions. In many cases, these extensions make these types work more a little more like their .NET counterparts.

Table 30-5 lists the JavaScript types that ASP.NET AJAX extends.

Table 30-5. *Extended JavaScript Types in ASP.NET AJAX*

Type	Description
Array	Adds static methods that allow you to add, remove, clear, and search the elements of an array.
Boolean	Adds a parse() method that allows you to convert a string representation of a Boolean into a Boolean.
Date	Adds formatting and parsing methods that allow you to convert a date to and from a string representation, either using an invariant representation or using the appropriate representation for the current locale.
Number	Adds formatting and parsing methods that allow you to convert a number to and from a string representation, either using an invariant representation or using the appropriate representation for the current locale.
String	Adds a very small set of string manipulation methods for trimming strings and comparing the start or end of a string with another string. (The Sys.StringBuilder class adds another way to build strings.)
Error	Adds a number of properties for common error types, which return the appropriate exception objects. For example, Error.argument returns a Sys.ArgumentException object.

Type	Description
Object	Adds a getType() and getTypeName() method, which are the starting points for reflecting on type information (as demonstrated in the previous section).
Function	Adds methods for managing classes, including the methods for defining namespaces, classes, and interfaces, as demonstrated in the following sections.

In the following sections, you'll see how to build smarter classes that live in distinct namespaces, inherit from other classes, and implement interfaces. Then, you'll consider some of the more advanced classes in the ASP.NET AJAX client libraries.

Namespaces

Traditionally, all JavaScript functions exist in the same global namespace. However, ASP.NET AJAX adds the ability to separate the functions that represent classes into separate, logical namespaces. This is particularly useful for preventing any conflict between the built-in ASP.NET AJAX classes and your own.

To register a namespace, you use the Type.registerNamespace() method before you create your class. You then place the type in the namespace using a fully qualified name (as in Business.Employee). Here's an example:

```
Type.registerNamespace("Business");

Business.Employee = function Employee(first, last)
{ ... }

Business.Employee.prototype.set_FirstName = ...
Business.Employee.prototype.get_FirstName = ...
...

Business.Employee.registerClass("Business.Employee");
```

And here's how you create an instance:

```
var emp = new Business.Employee("Joe", "Higgens");
```

If you use the Object.getTypeName() method now, you'll get the fully qualified class name.

The need to put the namespace name before each member makes the code more verbose than it was before. To save some space, it's a common convention to define each method separately and then assign all the methods to the prototype in one step. Here's an example of this technique:

```
Type.registerNamespace("Business");

Business.Employee = function(first, last)
{ ... }

function Business$Employee$set_FirstName(first) {
    this._firstName = first;
}
function Business$Employee$get_FirstName() {
    return this._firstName;
}
function Business$Employee$set_LastName(last) {
```

```
    this._lastName = last;
}
function Business$Employee$get_LastName() {
    return this._lastName;
}

Business.Employee.prototype = {
  set_FirstName: Business$Employee$set_FirstName,
  get_FirstName: Business$Employee$get_FirstName,
  set_LastName: Business$Employee$set_LastName,
  get_LastName: Business$Employee$get_LastName
};

Business.Employee.registerClass("Business.Employee");
```

Both approaches are acceptable, but the one shown in the preceding example is the most common approach, and the one you'll find if you explore the ASP.NET AJAX JavaScript files. Just remember that if you choose to use this two-part approach, the convention is to name each member using the fully qualified namespace and class, but substituting the dollar sign ($) for the dot (.), as in Business$Employee$set_FirstName.

Inheritance

ASP.NET AJAX also provides support for creating classes that inherit from other classes. When you register the derived class, you provide the name of the base class as a second argument. Here's an example that creates a SalesEmployee class that derives from Employee. Note that in order for this to work, the Employee class must be defined earlier in the script block (or in a previous script block):

```
Business.SalesEmployee = function(first, last, salesDepartment)
{
    // Call the base constructor to initialize the parent class data.
    // The base class constructor accepts two parameters,
    // which represent the first and last name.
    Business.SalesEmployee.initializeBase(this, [first, last]);

    // Initialize the derived class data.
    this._salesDepartment = salesDepartment;
}


Business.SalesEmployee.prototype.get_SalesDepartment = function() {
    return this._salesDepartment;
}

Business.SalesEmployee.registerClass("Business.SalesEmployee",
  Business.Employee);
```

The registerClass() call passes in the name of the new class (as a string) and the name of the parent class (as a reference to the parent class function). When you register a class in this way, it gains all of the members in the parent class, along with its own members. Thus, you can set and get the department, first name, and last name information from any SalesEmployee object:

```
var salesEmp = new Business.SalesEmployee("Joe", "Higgens", "Western");
var desc = salesEmp.get_FirstName() + " " + salesEmp.get_LastName() +
  " " + salesEmp.get_SalesDepartment();
alert(desc);
```

If the derived class supplies a member with the same name as the parent class, the version in the parent class is automatically overridden. Unlike the C# language, there's no way to create members that must be overridden or prevent members from being overridden. Furthermore, the derived class has access to all the variables that are defined in the parent class (although you should avoid accessing them directly, and use the property accessor methods instead).

The only magic in the SalesEmployee code is the initializeBase() call, which allows the constructor to call the constructor of the base class so it can initialize the first and last name. The initializeBase() method is one of the members that ASP.NET AJAX adds to the basic function type. Along with initializeBase(), you can callBaseMethod() to trigger a method that's present in the base class but overridden in the derived class.

Interfaces

To define an interface in JavaScript, you use the same prototype pattern you use to create a class. The prototype property exposes the members of the interface. However, you need to go to additional lengths to ensure that your interface can't be used like an object. These rules aren't enforced, so it's up to you to create an interface that behaves properly.

First, the interface constructor should not contain any code, nor should it assign any data. Instead, it should simply throw a NotImplementedException to prevent it from being instantiated. Similarly, the members that are defined in the prototype should not contain any code, and should throw a NotImplementedException when called. This requirement makes JavaScript interface definitions quite a bit longer than C# interface definitions.

The easiest way to understand the ASP.NET AJAX interface model is to look at one of the interfaces defined in ASP.NET AJAX. The Sys.IDisposable interface provides an ASP.NET AJAX equivalent to the .NET System.IDisposable interface, which gives objects a way to release the resources they're using immediately. The Sys.IDisposable interface defines a single method, named dispose().

Here's the full code for the IDisposable interface:

```
Type.registerNamespace("Sys");

Sys.IDisposable = function Sys$IDisposable() {
    throw Error.notImplemented();
}
function Sys$IDisposable$dispose() {
    throw Error.notImplemented();
}

Sys.IDisposable.prototype = {
    dispose: Sys$IDisposable$dispose
}
```

To register an interface, you use the registerInterface() method instead of registerClass():

```
Sys.IDisposable.registerInterface("Sys.IDisposable");
```

To use an interface, you must first ensure that your class includes the members with the required names:

```
Business.SalesEmployee.prototype.dispose = function() {
    alert("Disposed");
}
```

If they do, you can implement the interface by changing the way you register your class. When you call registerClass(), simply supply the interface you want to implement as the third argument.

```
Business.SalesEmployee.registerClass("Business.SalesEmployee",
  Business.Employee, Sys.IDisposable);
```

If you want to implement several namespaces, add as many additional arguments as you need after the third argument—one for each interface.

Here's some code you can use to test the dispose behavior. When the SalesEmployee object is disposed, you'll see the disposal message appear:

```
var salesEmp = new Business.SalesEmployee("Joe", "Higgens", "Western");
salesEmp.dispose();
```

The Web-Page Framework

As you've learned, the ASP.NET AJAX client libraries use a multilayered design. At the lowest level are a set of JavaScript language enhancements that allow object-oriented patterns, and a set of extensions to the core JavaScript data types. ASP.NET AJAX also includes a set of core client-side classes and a client-side page model that's built on top of this infrastructure. This model includes classes for the web service callback feature you considered at the beginning of this chapter, specific classes to support web controls like the UpdatePanel, and control classes that wrap the page and its elements.

The Application Class

The starting point for the web-page model is the Sys.Application class. When an ASP.NET AJAX-enabled web page is loaded in the web browser, an instance of the Sys.Application class is created. The Application object manages the components on the page and loads any external script files that are registered with the ScriptManager. The ScriptManager inserts the code that creates the Application object, and the Application object does all the client-side work for the server-side ScriptManager.

The Application object raises two key events. The load event occurs after the page is first processed on the browser and after every postback, including asynchronous postbacks. The unload event occurs when the user navigates away to a new page. To handle these events, you simply need to add JavaScript functions with the names shown here:

```
<script type="text/JavaScript">
function pageLoad()
{
    alert("Being loaded");
}
function pageUnload()
{
    alert("Being unloaded");
}
</script>
```

Many of the earlier examples in this chapter have used the pageLoad() function—and now you understand how it plugs into the ASP.NET AJAX infrastructure.

The Application class also provides an init event, which fires when all the scripts have been loaded for the page but before its objects have been created. The init event fires once, when the page is first processed. It doesn't fire after asynchronous postbacks. You can attach an event handler to the init event using the Application.add_init() method. ASP.NET AJAX components react to the init event to create client-side controls.

The PageRequestManager Class

Another keenly important class is the PageRequestManager. The PageRequestManager is created if the page supports partial rendering, and uses one or more UpdatePanel controls on the server side.

The PageRequestManager class fires a series of events that you can respond to with client-side JavaScript code. Table 30-6 lists these events. In previous examples in this chapter, you've used the PageRequestManager to handle asynchronous callback errors with the UpdatePanel control (by handing endRequest) and to implement cancellation with the UpdateProgress control (by handling initializeRequest).

Table 30-6. *PageRequestManager Events*

Event	Description
initializeRequest	Occurs before an asynchronous postback begins. At this point, you can cancel the postback using the Cancel property of the Sys.WebForms.InitializeRequestEventArgs object that's passed to the event handler.
beginRequest	Occurs before the asynchronous postback request is sent (but after initializeRequest). At this point, you can initialize wait indicators on the page (for example, start a "please wait" animation). This event provides a Sys.WebForms.BeginRequestEventArgs object, which you can use to determine what element caused the postback.
pageLoading	Occurs after the response is received for an asynchronous callback, but before the page is updated. At this point, you can remove wait indicators. This event provides a Sys.WebForms.PageLoadingEventArgs object that provides information about the panels that will be updated as a result of the asynchronous postback response.
pageLoaded	Occurs after the response is received for an asynchronous callback and the page has been updated. This event provides a Sys.Web-Forms.PageLoadedEventArgs object that details which panels were updated and created.
EndRequest	Occurs after the asynchronous response has been processed (after the pageLoaded event), or during the processing of the response if there is an error. You can check for an error at this point and provide a customized error notification. This event provides a Sys.WebForms.End-RequestEventArgs object that details the error that occurred.

A Client-Side AJAX Control

The full web-page framework is beyond the scope of this chapter. (To learn more about the client-side model, refer to the documentation at http://go.microsoft.com/fwlink/?LinkId=116063.) However, you can learn a lot by considering a quick crash-course example. In this section, you'll explore one of the examples from the ASP.NET AJAX documentation: a client-side button that updates its appearance when the mouse moves over it. For better organization, all the code for this button is placed in a separate JavaScript file named HoverButton.js.

To create this control, you use the prototype pattern shown earlier. You begin by registering the namespace, you define the constructor for the control (with the private data), and then you define the public interface using the prototype property. In this example, the class is named HoverButton, and it exposes events that fire when the button is clicked, when the mouse moves over it, and when the mouse moves away.

Here's the overall structure of the code:

```
Type.registerNamespace("CustomControls");

// Define the constructor.
CustomControls.HoverButton = function(element) {
    CustomControls.HoverButton.initializeBase(this, [element]);

    this._clickDelegate = null;
    this._hoverDelegate = null;
    this._unhoverDelegate = null;
}

CustomControls.HoverButton.prototype = { ... }

CustomControls.HoverButton.registerClass('CustomControls.HoverButton',
  Sys.UI.Control);
```

Notice that custom controls must always begin their constructor with a call to initializeBase(), which triggers the constructor in the base Control class.

The prototype includes methods for getting and setting the button text, and methods for attaching event handlers to the three events. ASP.NET AJAX includes a higher-level event model than pure JavaScript. One of the advantages of this event model is that it deals with browser compatibility issues.

To attach and detach event handlers in JavaScript, you use the addHandler() and removeHandler() methods. Here's the implementation code:

```
CustomControls.HoverButton.prototype = {
    get_text: function() {
        return this.get_element().innerHTML;
    },
    set_text: function(value) {
        this.get_element().innerHTML = value;
    },

    add_click: function(handler) {
        this.get_events().addHandler('click', handler);
    },
    remove_click: function(handler) {
        this.get_events().removeHandler('click', handler);
```

```
    },

    add_hover: function(handler) {
        this.get_events().addHandler('hover', handler);
    },
    remove_hover: function(handler) {
        this.get_events().removeHandler('hover', handler);
    },

    add_unhover: function(handler) {
        this.get_events().addHandler('unhover', handler);
    },
    remove_unhover: function(handler) {
        this.get_events().removeHandler('unhover', handler);
    },

    initialize: function() { ... },
    dispose: function() { ... },

    ...
}
```

There are two more methods in the prototype for the HoverButton class: an initialize() method that's called automatically when a HoverButton object is being created, and a dispose() method that's called when it's being released.

The initialize() method sets up the link between the custom events that are defined in the HoverButton class and the JavaScript events that exist in the page. For example, here's the code that sets up the hover event so it fires when the mouse moves over the button or when focus passes to the button:

```
var element = this.get_element();

if (this._hoverDelegate === null) {
  this._hoverDelegate = Function.createDelegate(this, this._hoverHandler);
}
Sys.UI.DomEvent.addHandler(element, 'mouseover', this._hoverDelegate);
Sys.UI.DomEvent.addHandler(element, 'focus', this._hoverDelegate);
```

This code states that when the mouseover or focus events occur for the client-side element, the _hoverHandler delegate should be triggered.

The _hoverHandler delegate is defined at the end of the prototype. It simply triggers the linked event handler, as shown here:

```
_hoverHandler: function(event) {
    var h = this.get_events().getHandler('hover');
    if (h) h(this, Sys.EventArgs.Empty);
}
```

Finally, the initialize() method calls the base initialize() method in the Control class:

```
CustomControls.HoverButton.callBaseMethod(this, 'initialize');
```

The dispose() method has an easier task. It simply checks if the event handlers exist, and removes them if they do. Here's how it does its work for the hover event:

```
var element = this.get_element();

if (this._hoverDelegate) {
    Sys.UI.DomEvent.removeHandler(element, 'hover', this._hoverDelegate);
    delete this._hoverDelegate;
}
```

It ends by calling the base class implementation of the dispose() method, using this code:

```
CustomControls.HoverButton.callBaseMethod(this, 'dispose');
```

There's one final detail. The script must notify the Application class when it reaches the end of its code. To make this happen, you need to add this code statement to the end of the page:

```
if (typeof(Sys) !== 'undefined') Sys.Application.notifyScriptLoaded();
```

This isn't necessary if your script code is placed in the page or embedded in an assembly. In these cases, the notifyScriptLoaded() method is called automatically. But in this example, the JavaScript code is placed in the HoverButton.js file, so this line is necessary.

■ **Tip** To look at the full script code, you can refer to the downloadable samples for this chapter.

Now that you have the JavaScript code for your client-side component, you're ready to use it in a page. The first step is to register your script with the ScriptManager, as shown here:

```
<asp:ScriptManager runat="server" ID="ScriptManager01">
  <Scripts>
      <asp:ScriptReference Path="HoverButton.js" />
  </Scripts>
</asp:ScriptManager>
```

This ensures that your script will be loaded after the ASP.NET AJAX client libraries, and will have full access to the client-side model.

Next, you need to add the HTML element that will serve as the basis for your client-side control. In this example, it's the modest button shown here:

```
<button type="button" id="Button1" value="Click Me"></button>
```

Lastly, you need to create the client-side control and hook up event handlers. To create the control, you use the ASP.NET AJAX $create alias (which triggers the Sys.UI.Component.create() method) when the page is first loaded. At this point, you supply the fully qualified class name of the control, other properties you want to set (such as the text, style, and event handlers), and a reference to the underlying object in the page (which you can retrieve using the $get alias).

Here's the script code that creates the HoverButton, sets its initial properties, and attaches an event handler to the hover event:

```
function pageLoad(sender, args) {
    $create(CustomControls.HoverButton,
      {text: 'A HoverButton Control',element: {style: {fontWeight: "bold",
```

```
borderWidth: "2px"}}},{hover: doSomethingOnHover },
      null, $get('Button1'));
}
```

Once you've registered a component by calling $create, you can retrieve a reference to it at any later point by using $find. Here's an event handler that changes the text of the button when it's hovered over:

```
function doSomethingOnHover(sender, args) {
    var hoverButton = $find('Button1');
    hoverButton.set_text("In hover mode.");
}
```

It's important to realize the difference between $find and $get. The $get alias retrieves an HTML element from the page (like the <button> element). The $find alias retrieves a full ASP.NET AJAX client component (like the HoverButton object). Clearly, if you want to interact with the properties you've defined in your custom control, you need to use $find to retrieve the control object.

As you can see from this example, creating client-side ASP.NET AJAX components isn't a trivial process. Although there isn't a high level of complexity, there are a lot of details to manage, and the poor error-catching abilities of the loosely typed JavaScript language can make debugging into a serious chore. For this reason, most ASP.NET developers will prefer to use ready-made server-side controls and components that have ASP.NET AJAX plumbing, rather than write their own. In future releases of Visual Studio, there may be better design support for creating client-side ASP.NET AJAX classes.

■ **Note** Custom controls aren't the only type of client-side ASP.NET AJAX ingredient that you can use. You can also create custom components, which have no visual appearance. (For example, the ASP.NET Timer web control uses a client-side component.) Or, you can use *behaviors* (classes that derive from Behavior) that extend the behavior of existing page elements. Behaviors are used by control extenders, which are the topic of the next section.

Control Extenders

At this point, it might occur to you that you could build a custom ASP.NET control that renders client-side JavaScript code that uses the ASP.NET AJAX client libraries. In fact, that's essentially what the ASP.NET AJAX controls you've seen so far (the UpdatePanel, UpdateProgress, and Timer) do. Implementing this design is fairly straightforward. You simply need to add the code that registers your custom JavaScript with the ScriptManager in the page, and render the basic HTML that you need and the JavaScript that creates the control.

Although this approach works, it's tedious and unnecessarily limiting. The problem is that ASP.NET AJAX doesn't just allow you to design new types of controls, it also allows you to design effects that could apply to countless controls. In fact, these multipurpose effects—such as automatic completion, drag-and-drop, animation, resizing, collapsing, masked editing, and so on—represent the most common way to use ASP.NET AJAX.

For that reason, ASP.NET AJAX encourages a different model—one that uses control extenders to add ASP.NET AJAX features to existing controls. Using control extenders, you can add Ajax effects to an existing page without needing to change the control set that it uses.

ASP.NET doesn't include any control extenders. However, the ASP.NET AJAX Control Toolkit does. The ASP.NET AJAX Control Toolkit is a remarkable collection of controls and control extenders that use ASP.NET AJAX features but can be dropped onto your web page like any ordinary server control.

The most remarkable part of the ASP.NET AJAX toolkit is that it's being developed using a collaborative, open-source model that allows community participation. The ASP.NET AJAX Control Toolkit is free and includes full source code, which makes it a great tool for developers looking to outfit their web pages with Ajax effects and developers who want to learn to build their own control extenders.

In the following sections, you'll try out the AutoCompleteExtender from the ASP.NET Control Toolkit, and you'll take a quick look at what else it offers.

Installing the ASP.NET AJAX Control Toolkit

To get the ASP.NET AJAX Control Toolkit, surf to `http://www.asp.net/ajaxlibrary/act.ashx`. You can follow the links to the CodePlex download page, where you'll see several download options, depending on your version of .NET and whether you want the source code. At the time of this writing, the simplest download option is a 6.4 MB ZIP file named AjaxControlToolkit.Binary.NET4.zip, which is designed for ASP.NET 4 and doesn't include the source code. Once you've downloaded this ZIP file, you can extract the files it contains to a more permanent location on your hard drive.

Inside the ZIP file, you'll find a a central assembly named AjaxControlToolkit.dll and a host of smaller satellite assemblies that support localization for different cultures. You'll also see a zipped folder named AjaxControlToolkitSampleSite, which contains a huge sample website that demonstrates all the ASP.NET AJAX Control Toolkit ingredients, and a ReadMe.html file with installation instructions.

To get started developing with the ASP.NET AJAX Control Toolkit, you could simply copy the AjaxControlToolkit.dll assembly (and the culture-specific subfolders) to the Bin folder of your own web application. However, life is much easier if you get Visual Studio to help you out by adding the new components to the Toolbox. Here's how:

1. Make sure the SampleWebSite folder is in a reasonably permanent location on your hard drive. If you move the SampleWebSite folder after you complete this process, Visual Studio won't be able to find the AjaxControlToolkit.dll assembly. As a result, it won't be able to add the necessary assembly reference when you drag the controls onto a web page. (The only way to fix this problem is to remove the controls from the Toolbox and then repeat the process to add them from their new location.)

2. First, you need to create a new Toolbox tab in Visual Studio to hold the controls. Right-click the Toolbox and choose Add Tab. Then, enter a name (like AJAX Toolkit) and press Enter.

3. Now, you need to add the controls to the new tab. Right-click the blank tab you've created and select Choose Items.

4. In the Choose Toolbox Items dialog box, click Browse. Find the AjaxControlToolkit.dll (which is in the SampleWebSite\Bin folder) and click OK.

5. Now, all the components from AjaxControlToolkit.dll will appear in the list, selected and with checkmarks next to each one. To add all the controls to the Toolbox in one step, just click OK.

Figure 30-10 shows some of the controls that will appear in the new Toolbox tab.

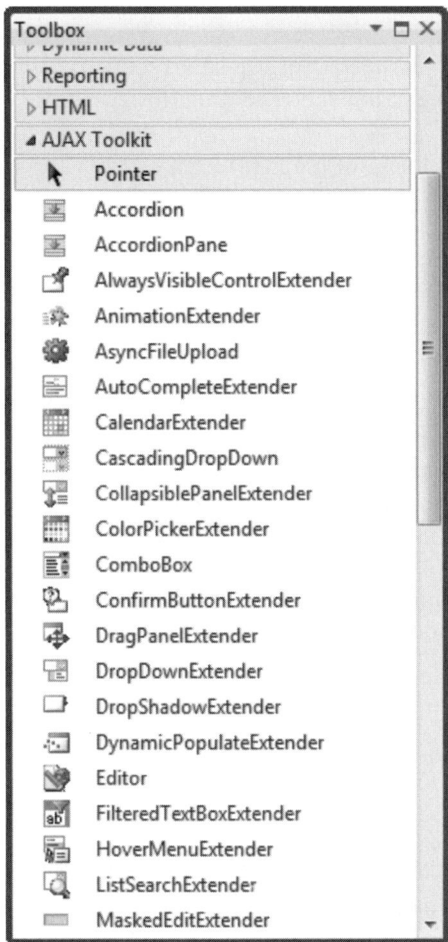

Figure 30-10. *Adding the ASP.NET AJAX Control Toolkit to the Toolbox*

Now you can use the components from the ASP.NET AJAX Control Toolkit in any web page in any website. First, begin by adding the ScriptManager control to the web page. Then, head to the new Toolbox tab you created and drag the ASP.NET AJAX control you want onto your page. The first time you add a component from the ASP.NET AJAX Control Toolkit, Visual Studio will copy the AjaxControlToolkit.dll assembly to the Bin folder of your web application, along with the localization assemblies.

The ASP.NET AJAX Control Toolkit is stuffed full of useful components. In the following sections, you'll get your feet wet by considering the useful AutoCompleteExtender.

The AutoCompleteExtender

The ASP.NET team has been careful to avoid duplicating existing controls with ASP.NET AJAX variants. For example, it might seem tempting to create an AutoCompleteTextBox server control. However, this design introduces several problems:

- You need to replace your existing TextBox controls with AutoCompleteTextBox controls to use this functionality. This is a major (and potentially disruptive) change to make in an established page.
- If you have already extended the TextBox control or are using a third-party component that extends the TextBox control, you need to sacrifice these features.
- If another ASP.NET AJAX feature is implemented in a different TextBox-derived class (say, a NumericOnlyTextBox that discards any key press that isn't a digit), you won't be able to use both features at once.
- If you want to use the autocomplete feature with a different control, you need to wait for someone to create a control that encapsulates that functionality. A significant amount of duplicated work is required to support all text-based controls.
- Developers need to learn two similar but different control models and switch back and forth between them depending on the scenario.

A better solution would allow you to add dynamic features to your website without replacing the controls you're already using. ASP.NET AJAX enables this with another new concept, called control *extenders*. Control extenders are bits of Ajax-style functionality that plug into ordinary server controls. To use a specific feature, you simply need to add the right control extender and attach it to the appropriate control.

One example is the AutoCompleteExtender, which allows you to show a list of suggestions while a user types in another control (such as a text box).

■ **Note** Although the AutoCompleteExtender, like many extender controls, ends with the word "Extender," not all extenders do. In the following section, you'll get an overview that lists all the extenders and all the ordinary controls in the ASP.NET AJAX Control Toolkit.

Figure 30-11 shows the AutoCompleteExtender at work on an ordinary TextBox server control. As the user types, the drop-down list offers suggestions. If the user clicks one of these items in the list, the corresponding text is copied to the text box.

Creating this example is fairly easy. First, you need to add a ScriptManager to the page. Next, you need to add an ordinary text box, like this:

```
Contact Name:<asp:TextBox ID="txtName" runat="server"></asp:TextBox>
```

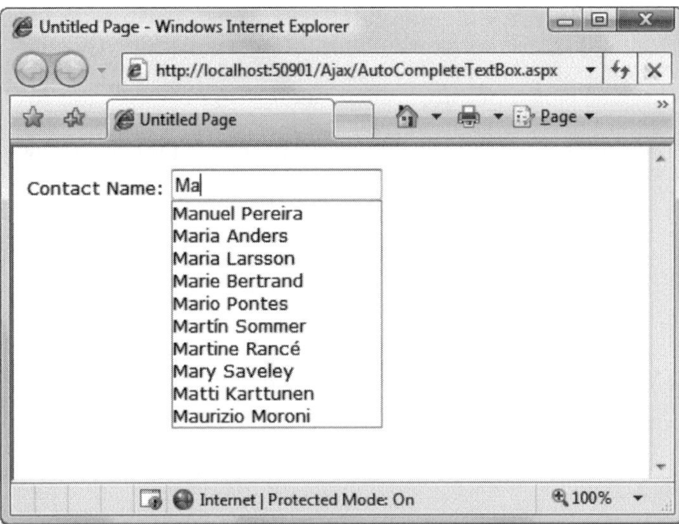

Figure 30-11. *Providing an autocomplete list of names*

Next, you need to add an AutoCompleteExtender control that extends the text box with the autocomplete feature. The trick is that the list of suggestions needs to be retrieved from a web method, which you need to create. Here's an example web service named AutoCompleteService with a method named GetNames() that provides the list of suggestions:

```
[WebService]
[System.Web.Script.Services.ScriptService]
public class AutoCompleteService : System.Web.Services.WebService
{
    [WebMethod()]
    public List<string> GetNames(string prefixText, int count)
    { ... }
}
```

Here's the tag you need to call this service:

```
<ajaxToolkit:AutoCompleteExtender runat="server"
 ID="autoComplete1" TargetControlID="txtName"
 ServicePath="AutoCompleteService.asmx" ServiceMethod="GetNames"
 MinimumPrefixLength="1">
</ajaxToolkit:AutoCompleteExtender>
```

This assumes that the ajaxToolkit namespace is registered at the top of your web form:

```
<%@ Register Assembly="AjaxControlToolkit" Namespace="AjaxControlToolkit"
  TagPrefix="ajaxToolkit " %>
```

The easiest way to add an ingredient from the ASP.NET AJAX Control Toolkit is to drag it from the Toolbox. That adds both the Register directive (if it's not already there) and the control tag.

You'll notice that the AutoCompleteExtender links to the corresponding server control through the AutoCompleteExtender.TargetControlID property. It also uses a MinimumPrefixLength property, which allows you to wait until the user has entered a specific number of letters before using the list of suggestions. This is a handy feature if the list is so long that a single character won't provide a useful list of suggestions.

The most time-consuming part of this example is creating the GetNames() web method. It accepts two parameters, which indicate the text the user has typed so far and the desired number of matches (which is ten by default).

```
[WebMethod]
public List<string> GetNames(string prefixText, int count)
{
    ...
```

Next, the code retrieves the complete list of possible suggestions, which is drawn from the Northwind database. This list is cached for an hour to ensure quick retrieval:

```
    ...
    if (Context.Cache["NameList"] == null)
    {
        Context.Cache.Insert("NameList", QueryNames(), null,
            DateTime.Now.AddMinutes(60), TimeSpan.Zero);
    }
    List<string> names = (List<string>)Context.Cache["NameList"];
    ...
```

With the list in hand, the next step is to cut down the list so it provides only the ten closest suggestions. In this example, the list is already sorted. This means you simply need to find the starting position—the first match that starts with the same letters as the prefix text. Here's the code that does it:

```
    ...
    int index = -1;
    for (int i = 0; i < names.Count; i++)
    {
        if (names[i].StartsWith(prefixText))
        {
            index = i;
            break;
        }

        // Give up if the search has passed to the next letter.
        // (This improves performance.)
        if (String.Compare(names[0], prefixText) == 1) break;
    }

    // Give up if there isn't a match.
    if (index == -1) return new List<string>();
    ...
```

The search code then begins at the index number position and moves through the list in an attempt to get ten matches. However, if it reaches the end of the list or finds a value that doesn't match the prefix, the search stops.

```
    ...
    List<string> wordList = new List<string>();
    for (int i = index; i < (index + count); i++)
    {
        // Stop when the end of the list is reached.
        if (i >= names.Count) break;

        // Stop if the names stop matching.
        if (!names[i].StartsWith(prefixText)) break;

        wordList.Add(names[i]);
    }
    ...
```

Finally, all the matches that were found are returned:

```
    ...
    return wordList;
}
```

The ASP.NET AJAX Control Toolkit

The AutoCompleteExtender is only one of the many components that are included in the ASP.NET AJAX Control Toolkit. Table 30-7 lists the control extenders that are currently available, and Table 30-8 lists the controls.

Table 30-7. *Control Extenders in the ASP.NET AJAX Control Toolkit*

Name	Description
AlwaysVisibleControlExtender	This extender keeps a control fixed in a specific position (such as the top-left corner of the web page) even as you scroll through the content in a page.
AnimationExtender	This powerful and remarkably flexible extender allows you to add animated effects such as resizing, moving, fading, color changing, and many more, on their own or in combination.
AutoCompleteExtender	This extender allows you to supply a list of suggested entries based on partial user input. The list of entries is generated by a web service method, as described in the previous section.
CalendarExtender	This extender shows a pop-up calendar that can be attached to a text box for easier entry of dates. When the user chooses a date, it's inserted in the linked control.
CascadingDropDown	This extender lets you link drop-down lists without coding the solution by hand (as shown in the first example of this chapter).
CollapsiblePanelExtender	This extender lets you collapse and expand panels on your page. The rest of the page content reflows around them automatically.

Name	Description
ColorPickerExtender	This extender shows a pop-up color picker that can be attached to a text box for easy color selection.
ConfirmButtonExtender	This extender intercepts button clicks on a Button, LinkButton, or ImageButton control and displays a confirmation message. The click event is suppressed if the user chooses to cancel the operation in the confirmation dialog box.
DragPanelExtender	This extender allows you to drag a panel around the page.
DropDownExtender	This extender turns almost any control into a drop-down list when the mouse moves over it. For example, you can use the DropDownExtender in conjunction with an ordinary Label control. The user can then move the mouse over it, pick a different item from the list (thereby changing the text in the label), and then move the mouse away (allowing the label to revert to its ordinary appearance).
DropShadowExtender	This extender adds a graphical drop shadow effect around a panel. The drop shadow can be partially transparent, and you can control the size and roundness of its corners.
DynamicPopulateExtender	This simple extender replaces the contents of a control with the result of a web service method call.
FilteredTextBoxExtender	This extender allows you to restrict certain characters from being entered in a text box (such as letters in a text box that contains numeric data). This is meant to supplement validation, not replace it, as malicious users could circumvent the filtering by tampering with the rendered page or disabling JavaScript in the browser.
HoverMenuExtender	This extender allows content to pop up next to a control when the user hovers over it.
ListSearchExtender	This extender allows the user to search for items in a ListBox or DropDownList by typing the first few letters of the item text. The control searches the items and jumps to the first match as the user types.
MaskedEditExtender	This extender restricts the kind of input that can be entered in a text box using a mask. (A *mask* is a string that defines a pattern for fixed-length text, and supplies prompt characters to help the user enter the value. For example, a phone number mask might display (___) ___-____ in the text box. As the user types, the placeholders are replaced with the valid numeric characters, and nonnumeric characters are rejected.) You can use the MaskedEditExtender in conjunction with the MaskedEditValidator to make sure that the user can't circumvent the JavaScript code and enter an invalid value.

Name	Description
ModalPopupExtender	This extender allows you to create the illusion of a modal dialog box by darkening the page, disabling controls, and showing a superimposed panel on top.
MultiHandleSliderExtender	This extender transforms an ordinary TextBox control into a slider. However, this slider has features beyond the standard ASP.NET server-side equivalent. Most notable, it supports multiple thumbs that can be dragged independently along the slider track. This is useful when using a slider to indicate a range of values.
MutuallyExclusiveCheckBox-Extender	This extender allows you to associate a "key" with multiple CheckBox controls. When the user clicks a check box that's extended in this way, any other check box with the same key will be unchecked automatically.
NumericUpDownExtender	This extender attaches to a text box to provide configurable up and down arrow buttons (at the right side). These buttons increment the numeric or date value in the text box.
PagingBulletedListExtender	This extender attaches to a BulletedList and gives it client-side paging capabilities so that it can split a long list into smaller sections.
PasswordStrength	This extender attaches to a text box. As you type, it ranks the cryptographic strength of the text box value (the higher the ranking, the more difficult the password is to crack). It's meant to be used as a guideline for a password-creation box.
PopupControlExtender	This extender provides pop-up content that can be displayed next to any control.
ResizableControlExtender	This extender allows the user to resize a control with a configurable handle that appears in the bottom-right corner.
RoundedCornersExtender	This extender rounds the corners of any control for a clean, professional look.
SliderExtender	This extender converts a text box into a graphical slider that allows the user to choose a numeric value by dragging a thumb to a position on a track.
SlideShowExtender	This extender attaches to an image and causes it to display a sequence of images. The images are supplied using a web service method, and the slide show can loop endlessly or use play, pause, previous, and next buttons that you create.

Name	Description
TextBoxWatermarkExtender	This extender allows you to automatically change the background color and supply specific text when a TextBox control is empty. For example, your text box might include the text *Enter Value* in light gray writing on a pale blue background. This text disappears while the cursor is positioned in the text box or once you've entered a value.
ToggleButtonExtender	This extender turns the ordinary ASP.NET CheckBox into an image check box.
UpdatePanelAnimation-Extender	This extender allows you to use the same animations as the AnimationExtender. However, it's designed to work with an UpdatePanel and perform these animations automatically when an update is in progress or once the panel has been refreshed.
ValidatorCalloutExtender	This extender extends the client-side logic of the ASP.NET validation controls so that they use pop-up validation callouts that point to the control with the invalid input.

Table 30-8. *Controls in the ASP.NET AJAX Control Toolkit*

Name	Description
Accordion	This control stacks several content panels, and allows you to view one at a time. When you click a panel, that panel is expanded and the other panels are collapsed (so that just the header is visible). Additional features include an automatic fading effect and an option to limit the size of the control (in which case large content regions use scrolling when visible).
AsyncFileUpload	This control is similar to the FileUpload web control, except it does its work asynchronously, allowing the user to continue interacting with the page. (Obviously, posting back the page or navigating to a new page will interrupt the asynchronous file transfer.) The AsyncFileUpload control can also be configured to show another control while the upload is taking place. Usually, this second control (which is referenced by the ThrobberID property) shows a simple animation so the user knows that an upload is underway.
ComboBox	This control is inspired by the Windows combo box, which provides a drop-down list (like the ASP.NET DropDownList control) *and* allows the user to type in arbitrary text (like the ASP.NET TextBox control). It adopts much of the programing interface and most of the conventions of its Windows counterpart.
Editor	This remarkably powerful control provides HTML editing, complete with a toolbar of commands. The user can switch between three views: Html (which shows the markup), Design (which shows a correctly rendered preview, like a word processor), and Preview (which is similar to Design, but not editable).

Name	Description
NoBot	This control performs several checks to attempt to detect whether an automated program (a bot) is accessing the page rather than a human. If NoBot determines that a bot is accessing the page, the request will be denied. This technique is used to prevent programs that steal content or submit comment spam to blog postings, although it can obviously be circumvented. For example, NoBot forces the browser to perform a JavaScript calculation that uses the HTML DOM and submit the result, which aims to catch a non-browser application accessing the page. NoBot can also reject requests that post the form back extremely quickly, or post it back a large number of times in a specific time interval. Both behaviors suggest that an automated program is at work rather than a human.
Rating	This control allows users to set a rating by moving the mouse over a series of stars until the desired number of stars are highlighted.
ReorderList	This control creates a scrollable template list that allows the user to rearrange the order of items by dragging and dropping them.
Seadragon	This advanced control allows the user to zoom into a massively magifiable image. Behind the scenes, these images are composed out of a series of much smaller tiles, which are managed on the web server. To create a Seadragon image, you need the free Deep Zoom Composer tool (`http://tinyurl.com/26wjeqt`). It's also worth noting that these zoomable images are a much hyped feature that's built into Silverlight.
TabContainer	This control resembles the tabs shown in a Windows. Each tab has a header, and the user moves from one tab to another by clicking the header.

To use any of these controls or control extenders, you simply need to drop them onto a form, set the appropriate properties, and run your page. Figure 30-12 shows the collapsible panel in both expanded and collapsed states. Figure 30-13 shows a draggable panel, both before and after dragging.

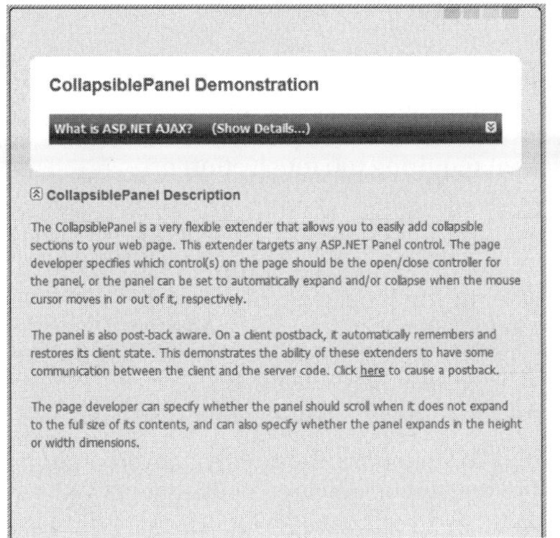

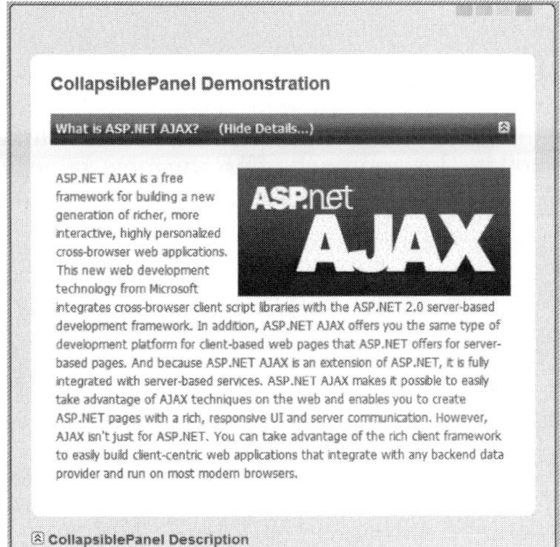

Figure 30-12. *A collapsible panel*

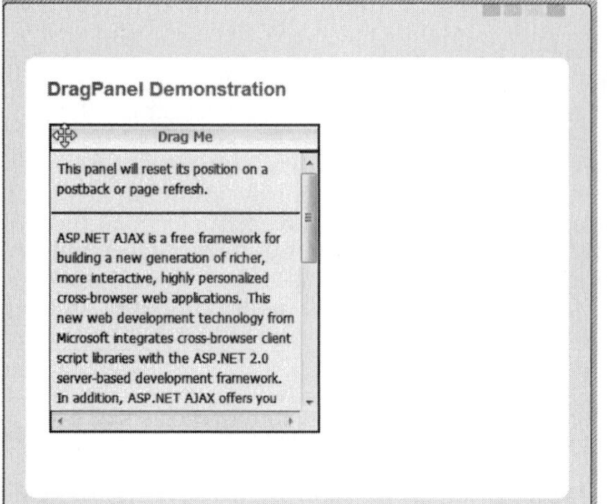

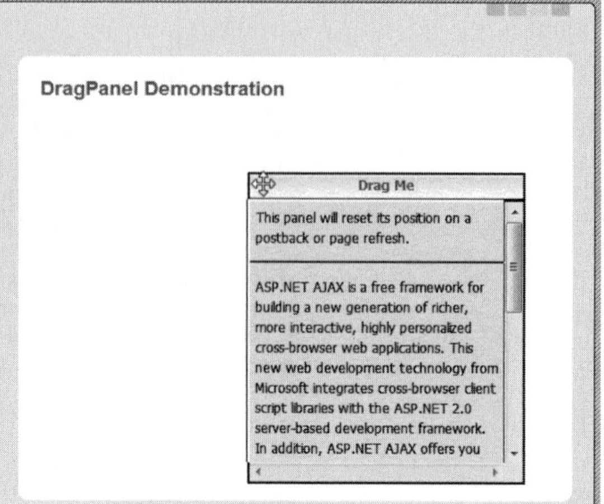

***Figure 30-13.** A draggable panel*

You can test drive all of the ASP.NET AJAX Control Toolkit components online at `http://www.asp.net/ajax/ajaxcontroltoolkit`.

Summary

The most exciting feature of ASP.NET AJAX is that it isn't just another JavaScript library or a simple .NET component that simplifies callbacks. Instead, it's a multilayered platform that allows you to build more responsive and dynamic pages—and, ultimately, an altogether different type of web application.

As you saw in this chapter, you can plug into the ASP.NET AJAX framework on three separate levels:

- You can write your own JavaScript code that calls server-side functionality. In this case, you expose the web methods you need and use automatically generated JSON proxies to call them.
- You can keep using ordinary ASP.NET server controls but extend them with ASP.NET AJAX-fortified ingredients such as the UpdatePanel, or use the snazzy controls and control extenders that are included with the ASP.NET AJAX Control Toolkit. This approach offers the most value without requiring too much effort or introducing too much complexity to your project.
- You can create your own client-side components, controls, and behaviors, and use them independently or in conjunction with a custom ASP.NET server control. This is by far the most complex approach. To truly master it, you'll need a fine-grained understanding of the client-side ASP.NET AJAX model, which is almost a platform of its own. That means you'll need to dig deep into the ASP.NET AJAX documentation, or consider a dedicated book on the subject like *Advanced ASP.NET AJAX Server Controls For .NET Framework 3.5* (Addison-Wesley, 2008).

Remember, the ASP.NET AJAX platform is still evolving rapidly. To keep up with the latest developments, be sure to visit `http://www.asp.net/ajax`. You may also want to consult a dedicated book that delves deeper into more specialized ASP.NET AJAX features.

CHAPTER 31

■ ■ ■

Portals with Web Part Pages

Websites are more sophisticated than ever. Nowadays it's not enough if a website has a great look and feel. It has to be easy to use and must present exactly the information that users want to see. In addition, users want websites to present this information in a specific way—based on their individual preferences. Therefore, personalization and user profiles have become more important in web development.

But users want to be able to customize more than simple profile information. They want to be able to customize the website's user interface to fit their requirements, with the goal of accessing the information they need for their daily business as soon as they are logged in. So, in this chapter, you will learn how you can create modular and dynamically configurable web pages to fulfill these sorts of requirements using the ASP.NET Web Parts Framework and personalization features.

Web Parts vs. ASP.NET AJAX

There is some overlap between the functionality included with the ASP.NET AJAX extensions and Web Parts. For example, the Accordion control (which is included with the ASP.NET Control Toolkit), allows you to minimize and restore parts of your web page, much as you can with web parts. Similarly, the DragPanel control allows you to reposition content regions by dragging them the mouse, also like web parts. Now the question arises: when should you use which functionality?

The answer to that question is simple: web part pages are much more than just a single piece of functionality such as the one provided with the Accordion control or the DragPanel control. The Web Parts Framework is a complete framework for personalization. If you need this complete framework, then you should use the Web Parts Framework. This functionality includes personalization of the appearance of your page for groups of users and single users, personalization with custom settings for each module plugged into your web application, dynamic extensibility with the possibility of adding new modules to your website at runtime and without the need of recompilation, and so on. If you need all this together, then web parts are the right way to go. If you just need a single piece of functionality, such as minimizing and restoring parts of your web page, or functionality such as dragging content around the space of your web page, then the Web Parts Framework is probably too oversized for your application. If that's the case, you'll be better off just using the appropriate ASP.NET AJAX controls. You can combine the two technologies as well, if you need both. You will learn more about ASP.NET AJAX in Chapter 30.

Typical Portal Pages

In a personalized environment, users want specific information stored in a profile, as you learned in Chapter 24. Furthermore, users want to be able to customize most of a website's appearance and the information it displays.

A good example of a personalized website is Microsoft's MSN. As soon as you log into MSN, you can configure the information displayed on your personal home page. For example, MSN allows you to select the types of information items you can see and then displays those pieces of information on your personal home page, as shown in Figure 31-1.

Some of the information items you can select are simple, such as the search item displayed in the upper-right corner of Figure 31-1, and others are more complex, such as the stock quotes listed in the bottom-right corner. Interestingly, you have many more possibilities than just selecting information items. You can specify where the information is displayed on the page by dragging items into different positions on the web page. When you log off and then later return to the page and log in, all the changes you have made will be present—the page design will appear exactly how you left it.

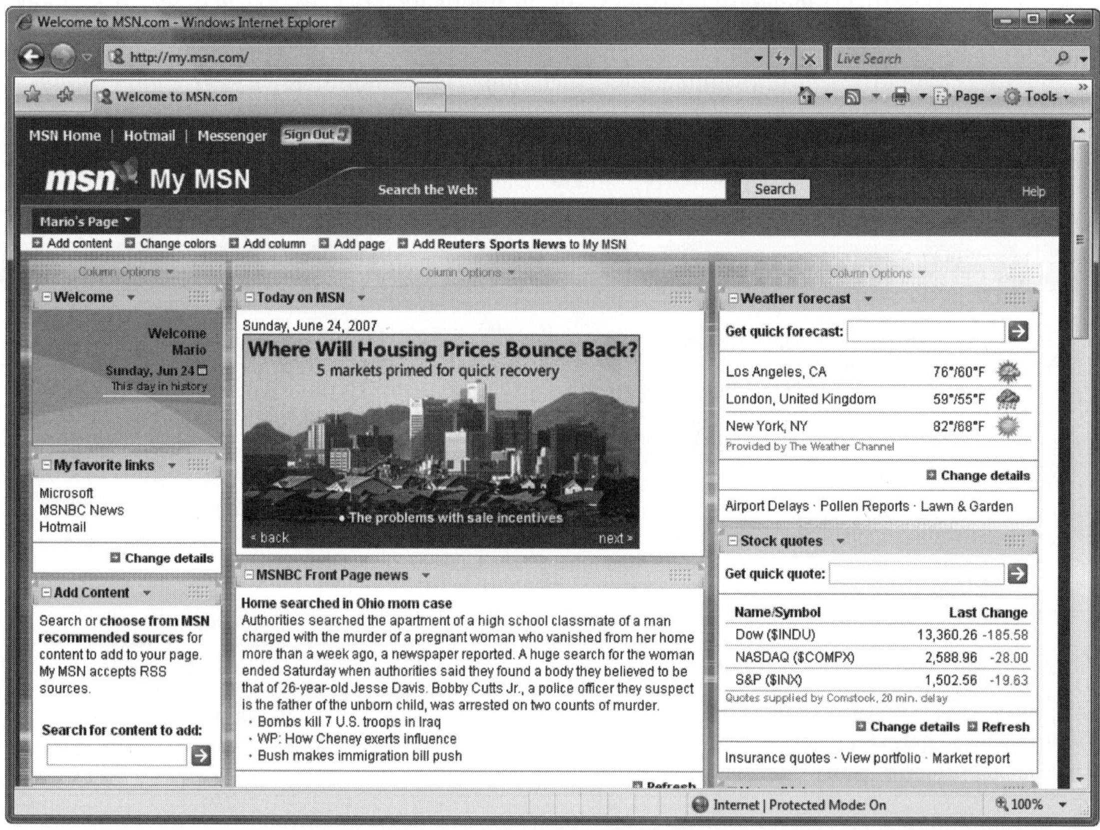

Figure 31-1. *MSN: a good example of a personalized home page*

These types of pages define content areas where the user can add or remove information items. The user can select the information items from a list of available items, which are nothing more than reusable user interface elements (or controls in ASP.NET), and add them to the specified content areas of the web page. In most cases, a portal page defines multiple content areas: a main area in the center of the page for displaying the most important information, a navigational area in the left or right section of the page, and optionally another area (either on the left or right side of the page) for small items (such as a weather item or a quick-links list). Most web pages also include a header and footer (which you can create easily with master pages).

Using the ASP.NET Web Parts Framework, you can create customizable web pages on your own easily. The framework consists of controls and components that perform the following work for you:

Defining customizable sections: The framework allows you to structure your page and specify customizable sections of the page through web part zones.

Offering components for item selection: In addition to customizable sections, the framework ships with special sections that allow you to edit properties for information items displayed on the page, or to add and remove information items to or from the page.

Customizing the web page: As soon as the user is logged into your application, she can customize the web page by dragging and dropping items displayed on the web page onto different customizable sections. The user can even close or minimize content to create more space for other, more interesting content.

Saving the customized appearance: ASP.NET automatically saves the user's personalized appearance of the web page through its personalization infrastructure.

A page that uses this framework is called a web part page, and the information items that can be displayed on the page are called web parts. All the pieces you put together to display on the page are controls, as you will see in the next section. Therefore, to create web part pages, you just need to know how to put all your custom and prebuilt controls together to create a customizable page. You will learn the details of how to do this in this chapter.

Basic Web Part Pages

The first thing you need to know is how to create a basic web part page. In the following sections, you will learn the major steps for creating such a page. After that, you will learn how to create web parts: the information items that go on the web part page.

The steps for creating a web part page are as follows:

1. **Create the page:** Create a simple ASP.NET page as usual with Visual Studio .NET. You don't need any special type of page—this is an .aspx page just like any other page. Before you continue, you can structure the layout of your page using HTML tables to create, for example, a page with a navigation area, a main area, and a side panel for additional information (similar to the MSN page presented in Figure 31-1). This page could be a master page to provide a consistent look and feel across your pages.

2. **Add a WebPartManager control:** Next, you need to add a WebPartManager control to your page. The WebPartManager control is available in the Web Parts toolbox of Visual Studio when you have the visual designer for ASP.NET pages opened. This is an invisible control that knows about all the available web parts on a page and manages personalization. The WebPartManager needs to be the first control created on a web part page, because every other web part-related control depends on it.

3. **Add WebPartZone controls:** Every section on the page that should display your custom web parts is encapsulated in an instance of the WebPartZone control.

Add a WebPartZone control on every section of your page that should contain web parts and be customizable.

4. **Add web parts:** You can use simple user controls, prebuilt user controls, custom server controls, or controls directly inherited from the WebPart base class. You can place all these controls into a web part zone using the Visual Studio designer, by writing the tag code manually or by writing custom code. The ASP.NET infrastructure does the rest automatically.

5. **Add prebuilt zones and parts:** If the user wants to add or remove web parts at runtime or edit properties of web parts, you need to add prebuilt zones to your web page, such as the CatalogZone (which allows the user to add web parts to the page).

After you have completed these steps, your web part page is ready to use. Remember that you need to include authentication (either Windows or forms authentication) to your application so that the framework can store personalized information on a per-user basis. By default, this information is stored in the file-based database ASPNETDB.MDF, which is automatically created in the App_Data directory if you have SQL Server Express installed. Otherwise, you need to create the database in the full version of SQL Server using aspnet_regsql.exe, as described in Chapter 21 (personalization information is stored in the same database as user information). As is the case with any other part of the framework, and as you have learned for the membership and roles APIs, your custom provider can replace the personalization infrastructure without affecting the application itself.

Creating the Page Design

The first step of creating a web part page is to create an .aspx page in your solution. You don't have to add a special item—just add a simple web form to your project. Afterward, you can structure the basic layout of your page as you'd like.

The following example uses a simple HTML table to structure the page with a main center area, a configuration area on the left, and a simple information area on the right:

```
<form id="form1" runat="server">
<div>
<table style="width: 100%">
    <tr valign="middle" style="background: #00ccff">
        <td colspan="2">
            <span style="font-size: 16pt; font-family: Verdana">
                <strong>Welcome to Web Part pages!</strong>
            </span>

       <td style="height: 22px">
            Menu

        <tr valign="top">
        <td style="width: 20%">
        <td style="width: 60%">
        <td style="width: 20%">

</div>
</form>
```

The first table row is just a simple header for the application. Within the second row, the table contains three columns. The left one is used as a column for configuration controls (such as a control for selecting available web parts), the center column is used for displaying the main information, and the right column is used for little web parts with additional information. Notice that the first row includes a second column for a menu; you will use this menu later for switching between the modes of the page (for example, from the Browse mode that merely displays information to the Design mode that allows the user to move web parts from one zone to another). You can see the page layout in Figure 31-2.

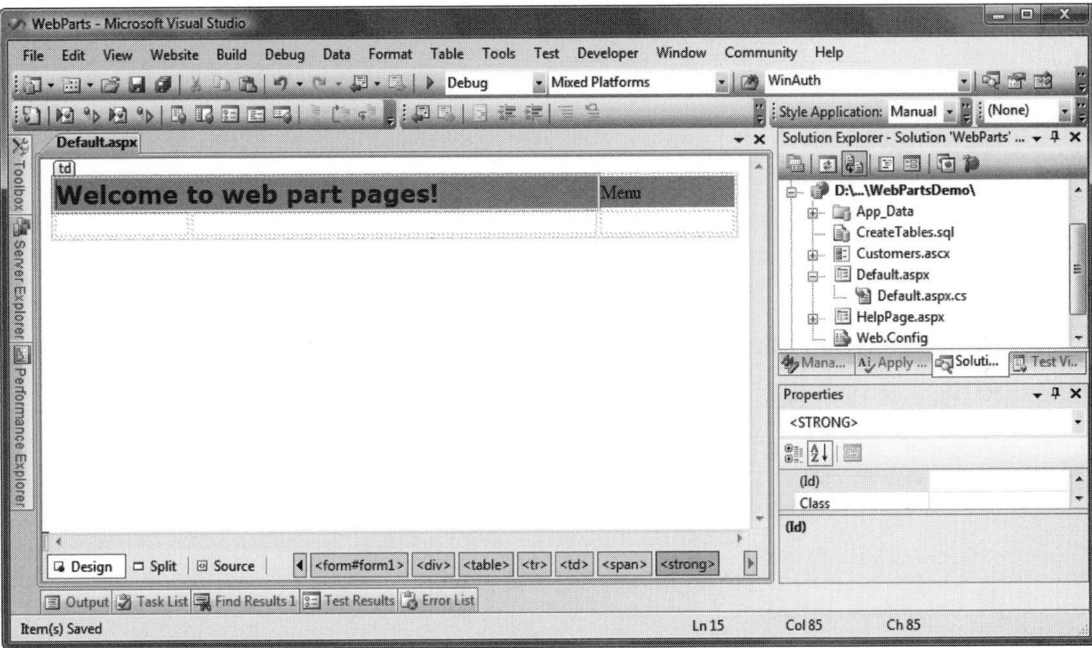

Figure 31-2. The basic layout of the page

WebPartManager and WebPartZone Controls

After you have created the web page's design, you can continue adding the first web part controls to your page. These controls are summarized in the WebParts section of Visual Studio's Toolbox. For this example, the first control to add at the top of your page is the WebPartManager control. The WebPartManager works with all the zones added to the web page and knows about all the web parts available for the page. Furthermore, it manages the personalization and makes sure the web page is customized for the currently logged-on user. The following code snippet shows the modified portion of the page code:

```
<form id="form1" runat="server">
<div>
<asp:WebPartManager runat="server" ID="MyPartManager" />
<table style="width: 100%">
    ...

</div>
</form>
```

The WebPartManager also throws events that you can catch in your application to perform actions when the user adds or deletes a web part or when a web part communicates with another web part. (You will learn more about web part communication later, in the "Connecting Web Parts" section.)

After you have added the WebPartManager to the page, you can add customizable sections to your web part. These sections are called web part zones, and every zone can contain as many web parts as the user wants. With the web part zones added, the complete code looks as follows:

```
<form id="form1" runat="server">
<div>
<asp:WebPartManager runat="server" ID="MyPartManager" />
<table style="width: 100%">
    <tr valign="middle" style="background: #00ccff">
        <td colspan="2">
            <span style="font-size: 16pt; font-family: Verdana">
                <strong>Welcome to Web Part pages!</strong>
            </span>

        <td style="height: 22px">Menu
        <tr valign="top">
        <td style="width: 20%">
            <asp:CatalogZone ID="SimpleCatalog" runat="server">
            </asp:CatalogZone>

        <td style="width: 60%">
            <asp:WebPartZone ID="MainZone" runat="server">
            </asp:WebPartZone>

        <td style="width: 20%">
            <asp:WebPartZone ID="HelpZone" runat="server">
            </asp:WebPartZone>


</div>
</form>
```

As you can see, the page now contains three zones: two zones for adding custom web parts to the page and one special zone. The special zone is a CatalogZone, which displays every web part that is available for the current page. It displays the list of available web parts and allows the user to select web parts from this list and add them to the page. In the designer, the code presented previously looks like Figure 31-3.

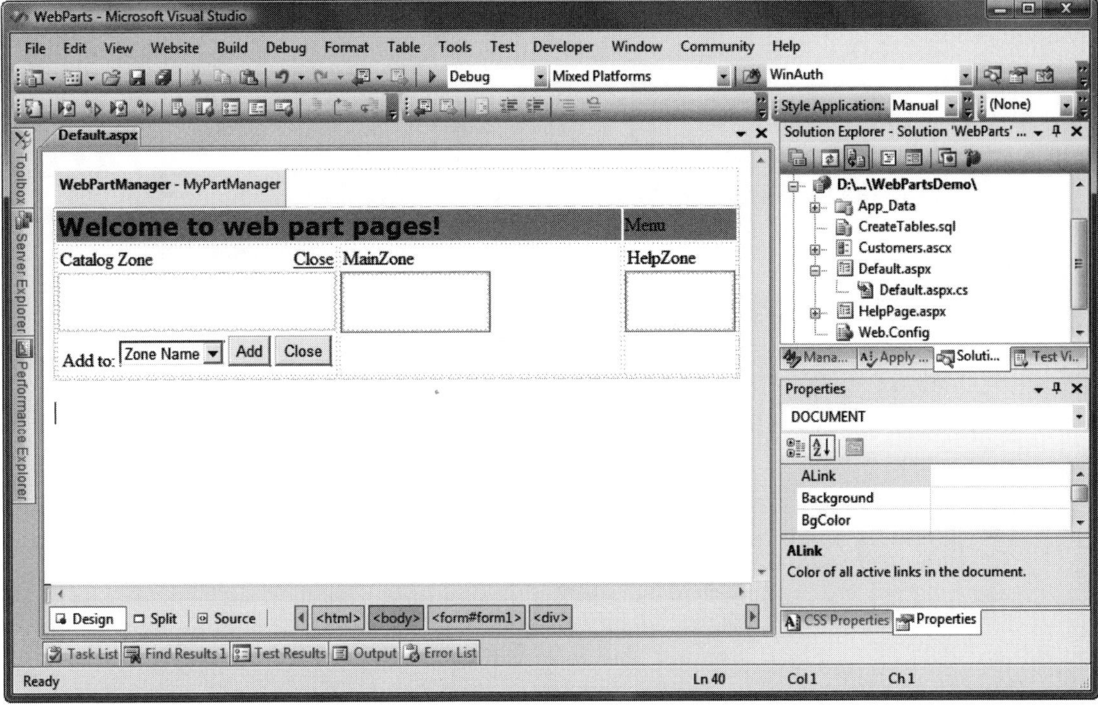

Figure 31-3. *Web part pages in the Visual Studio designer*

Adding Web Parts to the Page

Now you can start adding web parts to the web page. A web part is an ASP.NET control. You can use any type of control as a web part on your web parts page, including existing server controls, existing user controls, and custom server controls you have created on your own. You don't even need to implement any special interfaces if you don't need to interact with the web parts infrastructure or with other web parts on the page. Adding controls to a web part page is as simple as adding controls to a basic page. The only difference is that you add the controls to one of the previously added web part zones instead of to the page directly. For this purpose, web part zones use templates. The concept is the same as with grid controls, where you can specify a template that is created for every row in the grid. The template just defines the appearance of the web part. You can add existing server controls to a zone as follows:

```
<asp:WebPartZone runat="server" ID="HelpZone">
    <ZoneTemplate>
        <asp:Calendar runat="server" ID="MyCalendar" />
        <asp:FileUpload ID="FileUpload1" runat="server" />
    </ZoneTemplate>
</asp:WebPartZone>
```

The previous example shows the web part zone you added earlier in this chapter for the right section of your page. This zone now contains two controls: the standard Calendar control as well as a

FileUpload control. Figure 31-4 shows the page in the Visual Studio designer after you have added this zone template.

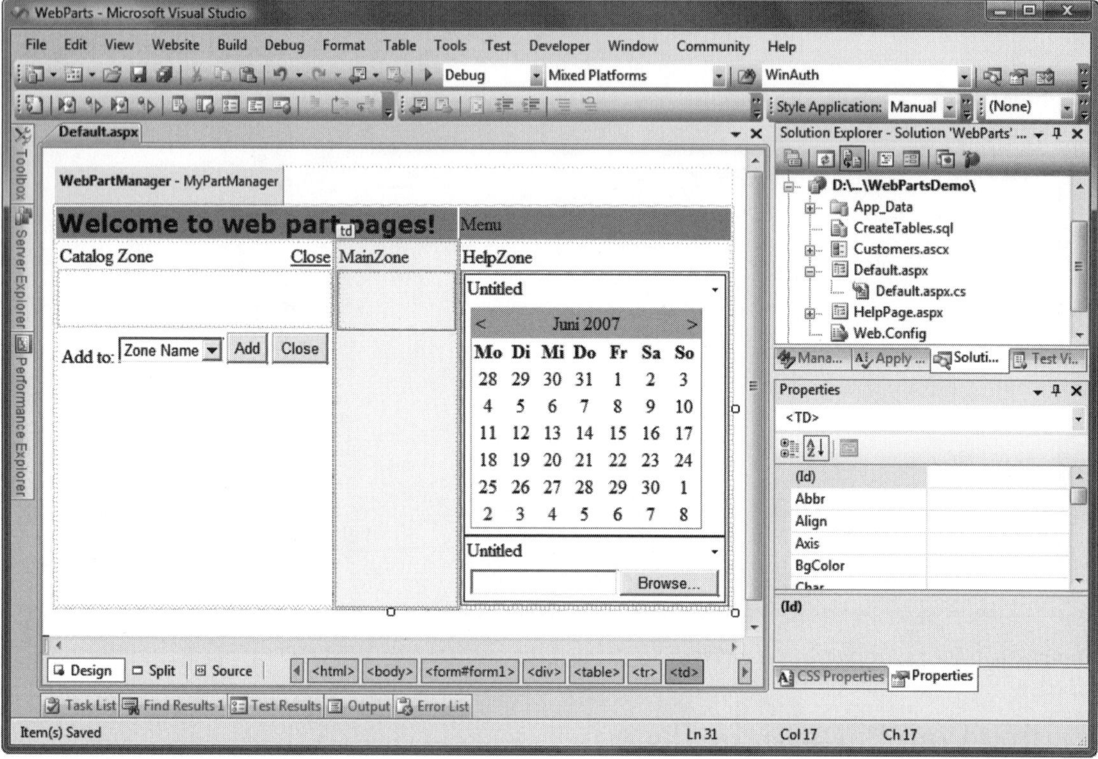

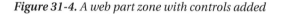

***Figure 31-4.** A web part zone with controls added*

You can create one or more user controls and add them to one of the web part zones. For example, create the database tables shown in Figure 31-5, and fill in some test records so that you can use these records to extend the sample later. The database is included in the book's downloads as a file-based SQL Server Express database as a part of the web part samples in the App_Data ASP.NET directory. You can either use this database as a file-based database for your training or attach it to your SQL Server instance—both approaches are possible.

Based on the Customer table, we will show you how to create your first web part now. Just add a new user control to your solution, open the database in the Server Explorer, and drag and drop the Customer table from the Server Explorer on your ASP.NET user control. The designer automatically creates the data source as well as a GridView that displays the data. (Don't autoformat the GridView; this will happen automatically later, based on the WebPartZone controls.)

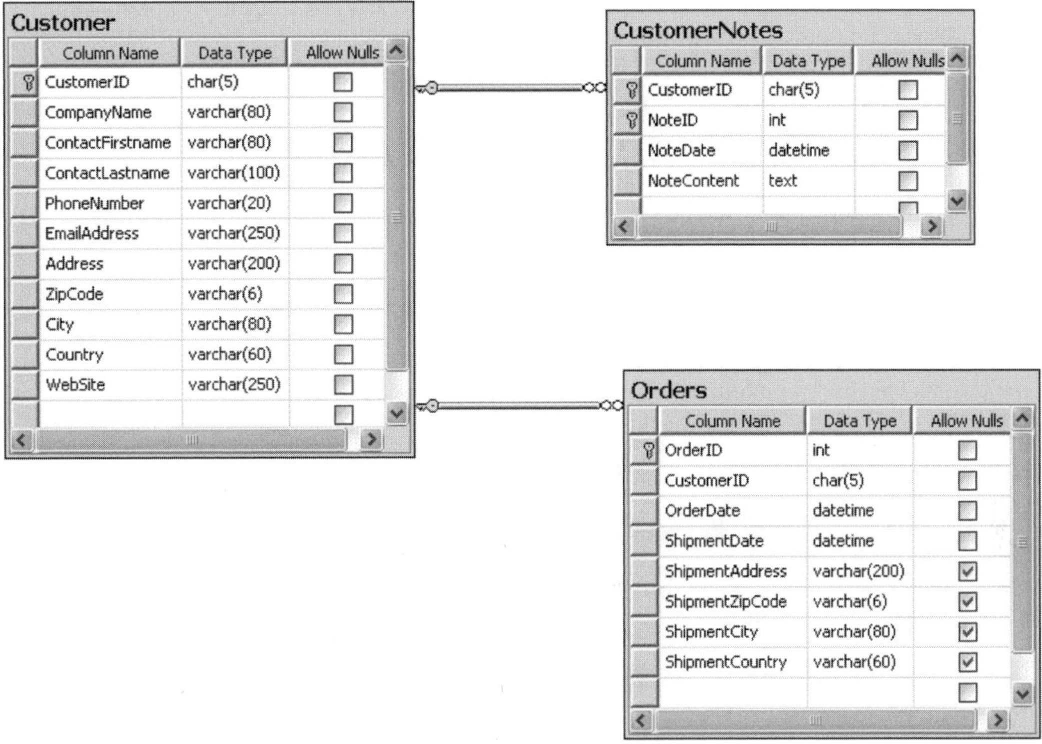

***Figure 31-5.** Database tables for the sample solution*

Now you can add the newly created user control to your main web part zone by dragging it from the Solution Explorer onto the web part zone. The designer creates the necessary entries for registering the control in your page and then adds the control to the web part zone, including adding the <ZoneTemplate> tags containing the content for a web part zone for you, as follows:

```
<asp:WebPartZone runat="server" ID="MainZone">
    <ZoneTemplate>
        <uc1:Customers ID="MyCustomers" runat="server" />
    </ZoneTemplate>
</asp:WebPartZone>
```

Finally, you can add a special web part to the previously added CatalogZone control. Because this zone is used to display catalogs of web parts, you can add only special controls such as the PageCatalogPart to this zone. You add special controls in the same way that you add normal WebPartZone controls—through a ZoneTemplate.

```
<asp:CatalogZone runat="server" ID="SimpleCatalog">
    <ZoneTemplate>
        <asp:PageCatalogPart runat="server" ID="MyCatalog" />
    </ZoneTemplate>
</asp:CatalogZone>
```

Before you start the web application, you can autoformat WebPartZone controls by opening the smart tag for the corresponding zone. Note that in the Visual Studio designer, the buttons for opening the smart tag sometimes overlap a little bit. Therefore, be careful to really select the smart tag of the zone itself and not of its containing web parts. You will see that formatting applies automatically to every control that is placed directly into a zone. Also note that every formatting action you perform on the web part itself overrides the formatting selected on the web part zone. Next, test the application by running your created web part page, and then you can debug the page. When you start the solution for debugging the page, you will see the screen in Figure 31-6 (depending on your autoformat selections).

You may notice that for every web part a title and a box for minimizing, restoring, and closing the web part is displayed with default captions. Later, in the "Customizing the Page" section, you will learn how to customize these captions.

Because you have not configured any authentication method yet, by default the application uses Windows authentication. Therefore, you can customize the web part page in terms of minimizing single parts and closing single parts. Without any additional effort, the same is true when you authenticate your users through forms authentication (either with or without using the membership API introduced in Chapter 21). So far, you cannot move web parts from one zone to another. To do this, you have to switch to a special page mode that you will learn about in the next section. When you close the browser and start another browser session, the page appears in the same layout as when you left it. That's because the WebPartManager stores your changes in the personalization store.

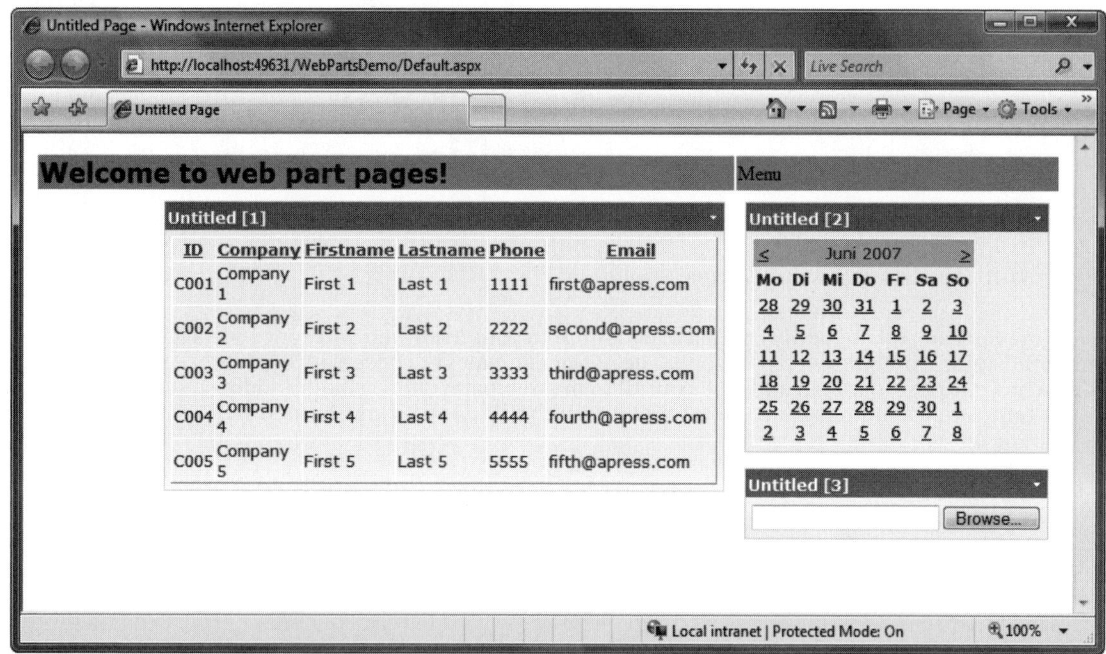

Figure 31-6. The web part page displayed in the browser

Again, by default these settings are stored in the SQL Server Express Edition-based aspnetdb.mdf database that is stored in the App_Data directory if you have not changed any configuration settings. You can change this default behavior by creating a database on the server of your choice using aspnet_regsql.exe. (This tool works with SQL Server only; for other databases, you have to create your own provider.) You can configure the provider with this database in your web.config configuration file as follows:

```
<webParts>
<personalization defaultProvider="MyProvider">
    <providers>
        <add name="MyProvider"
           type="System.Web.UI.WebControls.WebParts.SqlPersonalizationProvider"
           connectionStringName="CustomSqlConnection" />
    </providers>
</personalization>
</webParts>
```

You have to add the connection string (CustomSqlConnection in this example) to the <connectionStrings> section of the configuration file, and it should point to the database created with aspnet_regsql.exe.

Customizing the Page

At this point in the example, you can customize some parts of the web part page, you can minimize and restore web parts, and you can close web parts. However, adding web parts previously closed to the web part page is not possible, as the CatalogZone with the PageCatalogPart does not display automatically. In addition, you are not able to change the position of web parts by simply dragging and dropping them from one zone to another.

The reason for this is that a web part page supports multiple display modes, and you have to be in the correct mode to do this. You can configure these display modes through the WebPartManager's DisplayMode property. Table 31-1 lists the available display modes that are available as static properties of the WebPartManager class.

Table 31-1. *Web Part Page Display Modes*

Mode	Description
BrowseDisplayMode	This is the default mode and is used for displaying contents of a web part page.
DesignDisplayMode	When activating this mode, the user can change the position of web parts by dragging and dropping.
CatalogDisplayMode	If activated, the WebPartManager displays the catalog web part, which allows the user to add web parts to the web part page.
ConnectDisplayMode	When activated, the user can configure connections between connectable web parts (more about this later in this section).
EditDisplayMode	Allows the user to edit properties of web parts. This mode displays web parts of an editor. The EditorZone control is one of the prebuilt web part zones that allow you to display web part editor controls, which allow the user to modify settings for web parts.

Now, add a Menu control to the first row of your layout table, as follows:

```
<table style="width: 100%">
    <tr valign="middle" style="background: #00ccff">
        <td colspan="2">
            <span style="font-size: 16pt; font-family: Verdana">
                <strong>Welcome to Web Part pages!</strong>
            </span>

        <td style="height: 22px">
            <asp:Menu ID="PartsMenu" runat="server"
                      OnMenuItemClick="PartsMenu_MenuItemClick">
            </asp:Menu>

    ...
```

Next, you can create code in your page that populates the menu with all the available display modes for the WebPartManager. To do this, you just need to iterate through the DisplayModes property, which is a collection of WebPartDisplayMode items, and verify whether the mode is enabled. This is necessary because certain modes are available only if personalization is enabled. If personalization is disabled but a mode requires personalization to be enabled, this property returns false and you cannot use the display mode. In addition, you can query the property RequiresPersonalization of a WebPartDisplayMode to see whether a display mode requires personalization to be enabled or not. Finally, if the display mode is enabled, just add it to the menu.

```
protected void Page_Load(object sender, EventArgs e)
{
    if (!this.IsPostBack)
    {
        MenuItem Root = new MenuItem("Select Mode");

        foreach (WebPartDisplayMode mode in MyPartManager.DisplayModes)
        {
            if (mode.IsEnabled(MyPartManager))
            {
                Root.ChildItems.Add(new MenuItem(mode.Name));
            }
        }

        PartsMenu.Items.Add(Root);
    }
}
```

Remember that you need to populate the menu only on the first request, because with view state enabled, it remembers its state and therefore its child menu items. When the user clicks the menu item, you have to switch to the appropriate web part page mode. You can do this by setting the WebPartManager's DisplayMode property to the selected WebPartDisplayMode, as follows:

```
protected void PartsMenu_MenuItemClick(object sender, MenuEventArgs e)
{
    MyPartManager.DisplayMode =
        MyPartManager.DisplayModes[e.Item.Text];
}
```

Now when the user selects the Catalog mode from the menu, the CatalogZone with the PageCatalogPart will be visible, and you can add web parts you closed previously to the web part page again (see Figure 31-7).

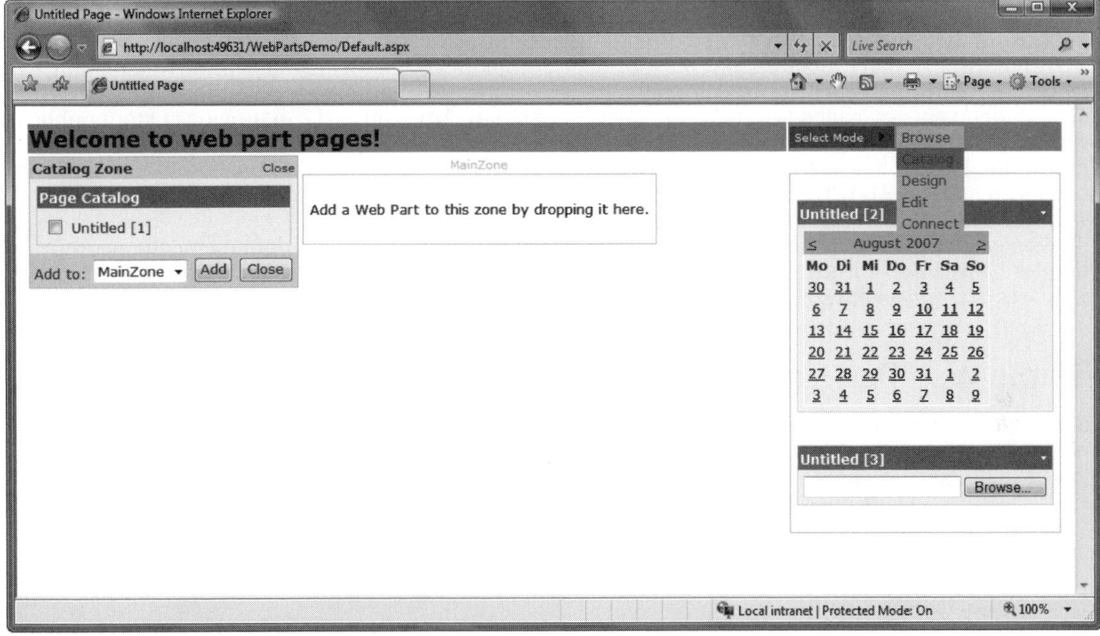

Figure 31-7. The CatalogZone displayed in the Catalog mode

■ **Note** Customizing the page via dragging and dropping uses special DHTML features of Internet Explorer and therefore works only for Internet Explorer. All the other features—such as adding personalization, minimizing and maximizing windows, and adding web parts from the catalog to specific zones—work with any browser of your choice.

All the changes you make will be stored persistently in the personalization store based on the personalization provider. Later, in the "Final Tasks for Personalization" section, you will learn how you can enable and disable personalization at a per-page level. Furthermore, if you are developing a custom web part from scratch, you can define properties on the class that are stored in the personalization store. By doing this, you can specify whether personalization happens on a per-user basis or is shared across authenticated users. You will learn how to do this in the next section.

Creating Web Parts

Now that you know the steps for creating web part pages with ASP.NET, it's time to take a closer look at web part development. As you know, a web part can be any type of ASP.NET control, including user controls, built-in or custom server controls, and ASP.NET controls directly inherited from the WebPart base class of the new namespace System.Web.UI.WebControls.WebParts.

You have seen that every web part on your page automatically gets a default caption and default menus for minimizing and restoring the web part. Now it's time to learn how you can customize this text and add menu entries (called verbs) to your custom web part. Any web part can provide custom public properties that the user can modify through an editor web part, which you can add to a web part called EditorZone. This EditorZone is displayed when the web part page is switched to the Edit mode, as introduced in Table 31-1. To do this, you have to create a separate editor part for your web part and somehow connect them. The next section shows how to do this.

Finally, web parts can communicate with other web parts through a well-defined mechanism. Therefore, these web parts exchange data and display information based on events that happen in other web parts. You will learn how to connect web parts in the "Connecting Web Parts" section.

Simple Web Part Tasks

You have already seen that the simplest way to create custom web parts is to create user controls. The only difference is that you add these controls to the ZoneTemplate section of a web part zone instead of directly to the page. The ASP.NET Web Parts Framework wraps your user control into an instance of GenericWebPart. This GenericWebPart class makes sure your user control gets the frame and the verbs menu for minimizing, restoring, and closing the web part. The same is true for any other server control (either built-in or custom): as long as an ASP.NET control is not inherited from System.Web.UI.WebControls.WebParts.WebPart, the Web Parts Framework wraps this control into an instance of GenericWebPart.

If you want to access the properties and events of the controls you have added as web parts to your page, you can do this as you do usually. For example, if you want to catch the Calendar's SelectionChanged event of your previously created web part page, double-click the Calendar in the visual designer of Visual Studio. You'll see your event procedure and can add some code. The following code shows an example that sets the previously added Calendar control's SelectedDate property on the first request to the page:

```
protected void Page_Load(object sender, EventArgs e)
{
    if (!this.IsPostBack)
    {
        // This is a strange workaround for
        // the calendar... but it's the only way it works
        // whether the calendar is in a Web Part zone or not...
        Calendar helper = new Calendar();
        helper.SelectedDate = DateTime.Now.AddDays(30);
        helper.VisibleDate = DateTime.Now.AddDays(30);

        MyCalendar.SelectedDate = helper.VisibleDate;
        MyCalendar.VisibleDate = helper.VisibleDate;
    }

    ...
}
```

So, you have complete access to the controls added as web parts and don't have to do anything special here. But what if you want to access web part-specific properties such as the title of the web part or web part-specific events? As mentioned, every web part that is not inherited from System.Web.UI.WebControls.WebParts.WebPart is wrapped automatically into an instance of GenericWebPart. If you want to access web part-specific properties, you somehow have to retrieve the web part and then set or get the properties you need. Fortunately, the WebPartManager class includes a WebParts collection property that contains all the web parts available for the page. The advantage of accessing web parts directly through the WebPartManager is that you don't have to know which Web Part zone they have been added to (remember that the user can change this as she wants).

The following example uses the WebPartManager's WebParts collection to iterate through the web part and assign a default title for every web part that has been wrapped into a GenericWebPart class by the framework:

```
protected void Page_Load(object sender, EventArgs e)
{
    if (!this.IsPostBack)
    {
        int i = 1;
        foreach (WebPart part in MyPartManager.WebParts)
        {
            if (part is GenericWebPart)
            {
                part.Title = string.Format("Web Part Nr. {0}", i);
                i++;
            }
        }
    }

    ...
}
```

You can also modify other aspects through the web part properties. Table 31-2 shows some typical examples and gives you an overview of the most important properties of a WebPart control.

Table 31-2. *Important Properties of the WebPart Class*

Property	Description
AllowClose	Specifies whether the user can close the web part. If set to false, the close menu verb is not displayed in the web part's verbs menu.
AllowConnect	Enables or disables connecting functionality of the web part.
AllowEdit	Enables or disables editing properties of the web part through a custom EditorPart.
AllowHide	If set to true, the user can hide the web part on the page.
AllowMinimize	If set to true, the user can minimize the web part through the web part's minimize menu entry.

Property	Description
AllowZoneChange	When the user should be able to change the position of the web part by dragging it from one WebPartZone to another, you have to set this property to true and otherwise to false (the default is true).
CatalogIconImageUrl	As you have seen previously, the PageCatalogPart displays a list of web parts available for a page. If you want to add a special icon to be displayed in the PageCatalogPart in the CatalogZone, you can set the CatalogIconImageUrl to a valid image.
ChromeType	Customizes the appearance. You can specify whether the web part should have a border, a title bar, and the verbs menu that contains the menu actions for minimizing or closing your web part. This property is of type PartChromeType, which supports the values None, BorderOnly, TitleOnly, TitleAndBorder, and Default.
ChromeState	Defines the web part's initial appearance state. This property is of type PartChromeState and can have the values Minimized or Normal so that the web part initially is minimized or displayed.
ConnectErrorMessage	Specifies the error message that is displayed if an error occurs when connecting one web part to another. This could happen if the target web part throws an exception when being connected to another web part.
Controls	This important collection gives you access to all the controls that are contained in the web part. You'll learn more about this immediately following this table.
Description	Specifies a friendly, user-ready description for the web part.
Direction	Specifies the content flow direction (LeftToRight or RightToLeft) within the web part. If left at its default NotSet, it will use the default for the current culture.
DisplayTitle	Gets a string that returns the title that is displayed in the web part. If you haven't set the Title property, it returns either the automatically generated title or the title specified from the containing control.
ExportMode	As you will see later in this chapter, in the "Uploading Web Parts Dynamically" section, you can export and import information and settings from web parts. This property specifies which parts of a web part can be exported or imported.
HasSharedData	Specifies whether the web part contains personalized properties that are persisted for multiple users.
HasUserData	Specifies whether the web part contains personalized properties that are persisted on a per-user bases.

Property	Description
HelpUrl	Through the HelpUrl property, you can specify a URL that returns contents to be displayed as help for the web part. This can point to a static HTML page or to any other type of page, including an .aspx page. As soon as you specify this URL, the web part displays an additional verb menu for opening the help of this web part.
HelpMode	When a HelpUrl is specified, you can determine where the help is displayed. The help can be displayed in a modal or modeless pop-up window, or you can specify to navigate to the help page directly.
Hidden	Gets or sets a value that determines whether the web part is hidden on the page.
IsClosed	Gets or sets a value that determines whether the web part is closed.
IsShared	Gets or sets a value that determines whether the web part is visible for all users or for specific users only. You will learn more about this in the "Authorizing Web Parts" section.
IsStandalone	Determines whether the web part is contained in a WebPartZone (false) or is a stand-alone web part without being a part of a WebPartZone (true).
IsStatic	Gets or sets a value that determines whether the web page is statically added to the web page through the designer (true) or dynamically imported to the web page (which means that the part is added programmatically to the page).
Title	Gets or sets the title to be displayed in the title bar of the web part.
TitleUrl	The title can be displayed as a URL to point to a details page for the web part. If this URL is specified, the web part renders the title as a link that points to this URL instead of static text.
Verbs	Returns the entries in the web part's menu that typically contains the Minimize, Close, or Help verb. You can customize the verbs by modifying this collection.
Zone	Returns a reference to the WebPartZone to which the web part is currently added.
ZoneIndex	Returns the WebPartZone's index to which the web part is currently added.

As mentioned in Table 31-2, the Controls collection of the WebPart control contains all the controls hosted within the web part. When it comes to the GenericWebPart, this collection contains the controls you have added to the WebPartZone. So, you can iterate through the WebPart controls stored in the Controls collection to find your control and do something with it. The following example shows how you can access the controls of the whole ASP.NET page (through the WebPartManager added to the page) to set properties of the web part that contains the Calendar control added earlier in this chapter:

```
foreach (WebPart part in MyPartManager.WebParts)
{
    if (part.Controls.Contains(MyCalendar))
    {
        part.AllowClose = false;
        part.HelpMode = WebPartHelpMode.Modeless;
        part.HelpUrl = "CalendarHelp.htm";
    }
}
```

Controls added to the WebPartZone are available directly from within the page. Therefore, if you want to set any web part-specific properties when loading the page, you can do this the other way around as well. Instead of iterating through the WebPartManager's WebParts and then accessing every web part's Controls collection, it might be faster to catch the control's events and then access the web part's properties through the control's Parent property, as follows:

```
protected void MyCalendar_Load(object sender, EventArgs e)
{
    GenericWebPart part = (GenericWebPart)MyCalendar.Parent;
    part.AllowClose = false;
    part.HelpMode = WebPartHelpMode.Modeless;
    part.HelpUrl = "CalendarHelp.htm";
}
```

This is definitely faster than searching controls in collections of controls as shown previously. The previous example is doing the same initialization work as shown in the other example: it disables the close function for the web part that contains the calendar MyCalendar and then specifies a help page for the calendar that can be displayed in a modeless pop-up browser window. Figure 31-8 shows the result of these modifications. Take a close look at the menu displayed for the web part. Because you have initialized the HelpUrl, it now displays an additional Help menu entry. On the other hand, because you have set the AllowClose property to false, it doesn't contain a Close menu entry anymore.

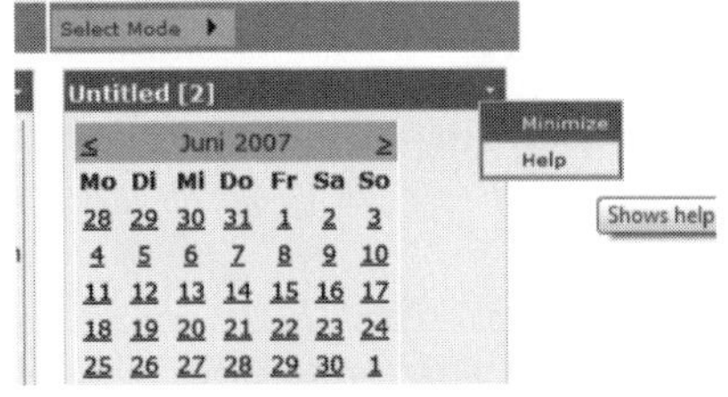

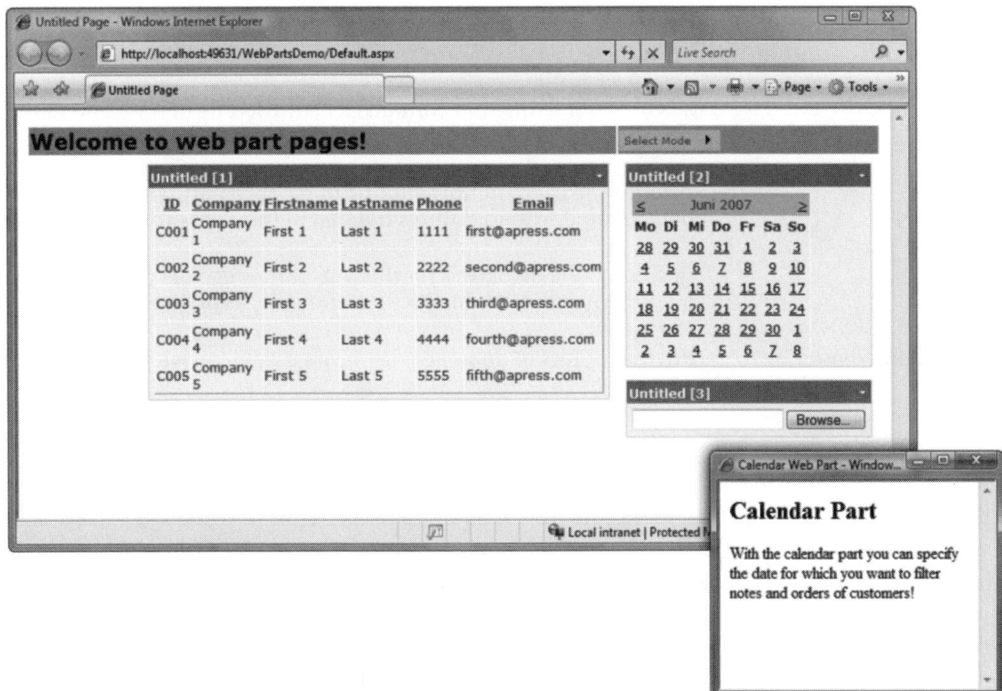

Figure 31-8. The previously made changes in action

Note that the Help window you see in Figure 31-8 is just a simple HTML page displayed in a browser pop-up. You can see that by taking a look at the previous code snippet as well, where you specify CalendarHelp.htm as a help page. The help page could be a dynamic page such as an ASP.NET page, as well, because the Web Parts Framework is doing nothing other than adding necessary client-side script code for opening a pop-up window that just executes an HTTP GET request to the URL configured in the HelpUrl property.

Implementing the IWebPart Interface

Until now you have accessed web parts from the outside only. But when creating a user control that will be used as a web part on a web part page, you can access properties of the web part from inside the user control as well. To a certain degree, you can control the web part's appearance and behavior in a more detailed manner by implementing the IWebPart interface.

The IWebPart interface defines a contract between your control (a server control or user control), which is used by the GenericWebPart wrapper class to communicate with your control for specific things such as automatically retrieving a control's title so that you don't need to set it from outside every page where you are going to use this web part. Table 31-3 lists the members you have to provide in your web part when implementing the IWebPart interface.

Table 31-3. *The Members of the IWebPart Interface*

Member	Description
CatalogIconImageUrl	Gets or sets the URL to an image displayed for the web part in the PageCatalogPart of a CatalogZone.
Description	Gets or sets a string that contains a user-friendly description of the web part.
Subtitle	Specifies the user-friendly subtitle of the web part. This one is concatenated with the title contained in the Title property of the web part.
Title	Specifies a title displayed for the web part. With this property specified, you don't need to set the title from outside, as previously described.
TitleIconImageUrl	URL that points to an image displayed as an icon within the title bar of the web part.
TitleUrl	Specifies the URL to which the browser should navigate when the user clicks the title of the web part. If this URL is set, the title renders as a link; otherwise, the title renders as static text.

As you can see, implementing this interface is not too much work. You can now implement the interface in the previously created Customers user control as follows:

```
public partial class Customers :
                 System.Web.UI.UserControl, IWebPart
{
    private string _CatalogImageUrl;
    public string CatalogIconImageUrl
    {
        get
        {
            return _CatalogImageUrl;
        }
        set
        {
            _CatalogImageUrl = value;
        }
    }

    private string _Description;
    public string Description
    {
```

```
    get
    {
        return _Description;
    }
    set
    {
        _Description = value;
    }
}

public string Subtitle
{
    get { return "Internal Customer List"; }
}

private string _TitleImage;
public string TitleIconImageUrl
{
    get
    {
        if (_TitleImage == null)
            return "CustomersSmall.jpg";
        else
            return _TitleImage;
    }
    set
    {
        _TitleImage = value;
    }
}

private string _TitleUrl;
public string TitleUrl
{
    get
    {
        return _TitleUrl;
    }
    set
    {
        _TitleUrl = value;
    }
}

public string Title
{
    get
    {
        if (ViewState["Title"] == null)
            return string.Empty;
        else
            return (string)ViewState["Title"];
    }
    set
```

```
            {
                ViewState["Title"] = value;
            }
        }
    }
```

When implementing the IWebPart interface, you should think about which property values you want to put into view state and which values are sufficient as private members. To save bytes sent across the wire with the page, you should add as little information as possible to the view state. You should use view state only for information that the user can edit while browsing and that you don't want to lose between page postbacks. In the previous example, you used private members for every property of the web part, but not for the title property, because it might change while browsing (for example, if you want to display the current page of the GridView in the title bar as well). When implementing this interface, the information (which is set from outside) is automatically passed in by the GenericWebPart to your control's implementation. Consider the following code in the code-beside of your Default.aspx page, assuming that you have added an instance of the previously created Customer control and associated the following event-handling procedure to its Load event:

```
protected void MyCustomers_Load(object sender, EventArgs e)
{
    // Some of the properties are set; others like the TitleImageUrl are not!
    GenericWebPart part = (GenericWebPart)MyCustomers.Parent;
    part.Title = "Customers";
    part.TitleUrl = "http://www.apress.com";
    part.Description = "Displays all customers in the database!";
}
```

When someone sets the web part's title this way from outside, the GenericWebPart class passes the value to the interface implementation of the Title property so that you can handle the information. On the other hand, if someone queries information such as the Title or TitleUrl, the GenericWebPart retrieves the information from your control by calling the appropriate property in your IWebPart implementation. This way your control can return default values even for properties that have not been explicitly set. Your implementation of the TitleIconImageUrl is doing this. To reiterate, here is the fragment of the previous IWebPart implementation:

```
...
private string _TitleImage;
public string TitleIconImageUrl
{
    get
    {
        if (_TitleImage == null)
            return "CustomersSmall.jpg";
        else
            return _TitleImage;
    }
    set
    {
        _TitleImage = value;
    }
}
...
```

This property returns a default image URL if no TitleImage has been set. This means even if you don't set this property in the previously shown Load event procedure of your web part page, the web part displays the CustomersSmall.jpg image as a title image (see Figure 31-9). Although you have not set the TitleImageUrl in the MyCustomers_Load event procedure in the web part page, the icon for the title is displayed because of its default value provided through your implementation of IWebPart.

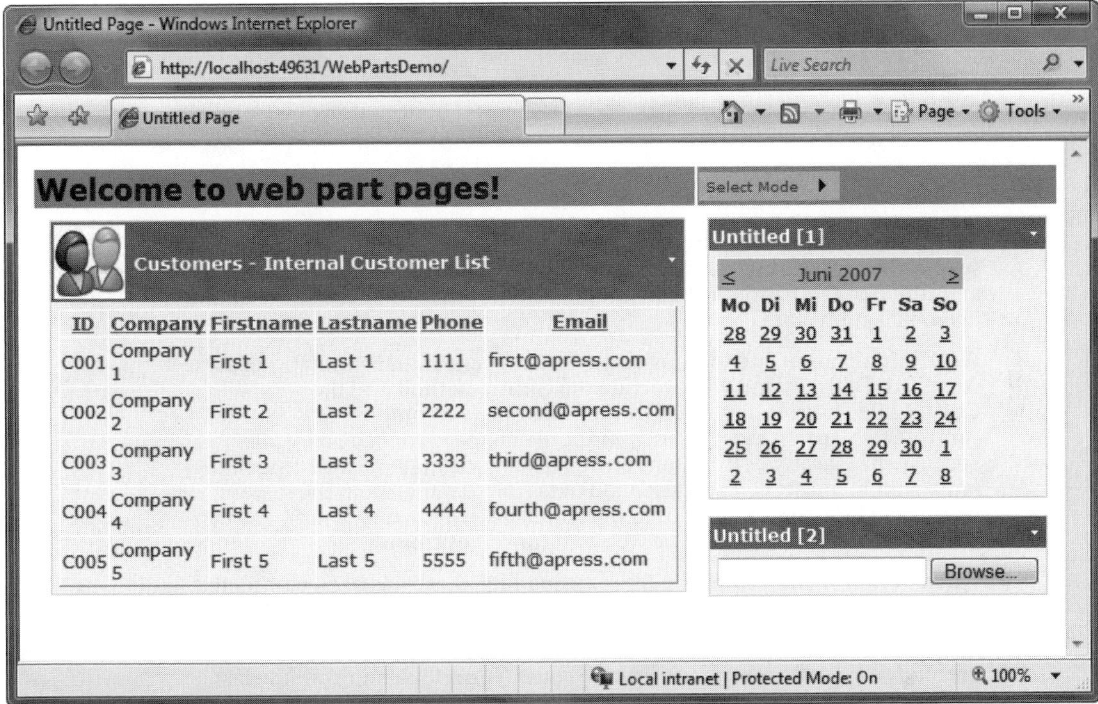

Figure 31-9. Customized Customers web part through the interface implementation

Developing Advanced Web Parts

Implementing web parts through user controls is a fairly easy way to create web parts. But user controls have some disadvantages as well:

Restricted reusability: You cannot add them dynamically to web part pages of other web applications without manually copying the ASCX file to the directories of the other web application. You can encapsulate manually implemented WebPart classes in separate assembly DLLs, and you therefore can reuse them in multiple web applications by referencing them through Add References or by copying the DLL into the target web application's Bin directory.

Restricted personalization: Personalization with user controls is restricted to common properties such as title, title URL, and so on. You cannot have custom properties in the user control that are stored in the personalization store. Only classes that inherit from web part can have this sort of functionality.

Better control over rendering and behavior: When using custom server controls, you have better control over the rendering process and can generate user interfaces more dynamically.

Therefore, sometimes implementing advanced web parts as server controls inherited from System.Web.UI.WebControls.WebParts.WebPart is useful. With the basic know-how for creating custom ASP.NET server controls, you are ready to create this sort of web part. All you have to keep in mind when creating a custom web part this way is that ASP.NET pages and ASP.NET controls are processed by the runtime (which determines the order of control and page events and what to do in each of these events). This makes it much easier, because you always have the steps for the implementation in mind. For more information about creating custom server controls, refer to Chapter 27.

The steps for creating a custom web part are as follows. (These steps will be familiar to you if you keep the ASP.NET page and control life cycle from Chapter 27 in mind.)

1. **Inherit from WebPart:** First you have to create a simple class that inherits from System.Web.UI.WebControls.WebParts.WebPart.
2. **Add custom properties:** Next, add custom properties of your web part and specify through attributes which of those properties can be edited by the user and which of these properties are stored on a per-user or shared basis in the personalization store.
3. **Write initialization and loading code:** Override any initialization procedure you need. Typically you will override the OnInit method and the CreateChildControls method if you want to create a composite control/WebPart. In most cases, you should create composite controls, because that saves you from rendering HTML code manually. During the initialization phase, you can also load data from databases; in the loading phase (catching the Load event or overriding the OnLoad method), you can initialize other properties of the web part (or server control).
4. **Catch events of child controls:** After the loading phase has been completed, controls will raise their events. Next you can add the event handlers for your child controls to your custom web part.
5. **Prerender:** Before the rendering phase starts, you should perform the last tasks, such as setting the properties of your controls and building the control structure based on data sources they are bound to (for example, calling the DataBind method if you don't use the DataSources programming model).
6. **Render the HTML:** Finally, you have to write code to render your web part. This time you don't override the RenderControl method (as is the case for server controls). You have to override the RenderContents method that is called from the base class in between rendering the border, title bar, and title menu with the appropriate verbs.

Keeping these steps in mind, creating a custom web part is easy (although it's not as easy as creating web parts based on user controls). Let's create a simple web part using this technique. The web part allows customers to add notes to the CustomerNotes table presented in Figures 30-5 and 30-10.

Before You Start: Creating Typed DataSets

Before you dig into the details of developing the web part, you have to add special components for easily accessing the data stored in the database. (You also need these components to complete the code samples shown in this chapter.)

In the web parts that you will develop in this chapter, you need to access data from the Customer table and the CustomerNotes table shown in Figure 31-5. You'll create a simple typed DataSet to access both tables (you can find more information about DataSets in Chapter 8), which you'll add to your web application project, as shown in Figure 31-10. To do so, right-click your project, select Add New Item, and then select DataSet from the Add New Item dialog. Name the DataSet CustomerSet. After you have added the DataSet to your project (remember that Visual Studio will add it to the App_Code directory if you're developing a projectless website), you can drag both the Customer table and the CustomerNotes table from the Server Explorer of Visual Studio onto the DataSet surface. (You need to have a connection configured in the Server Explorer for that purpose. Note that if you use the database as a SQL Server Express file-based database, you will find this connection in the Server Explorer automatically. Also note that we provide the required database introduced in Figure 31-5 as a part of the samples download for this chapter.)

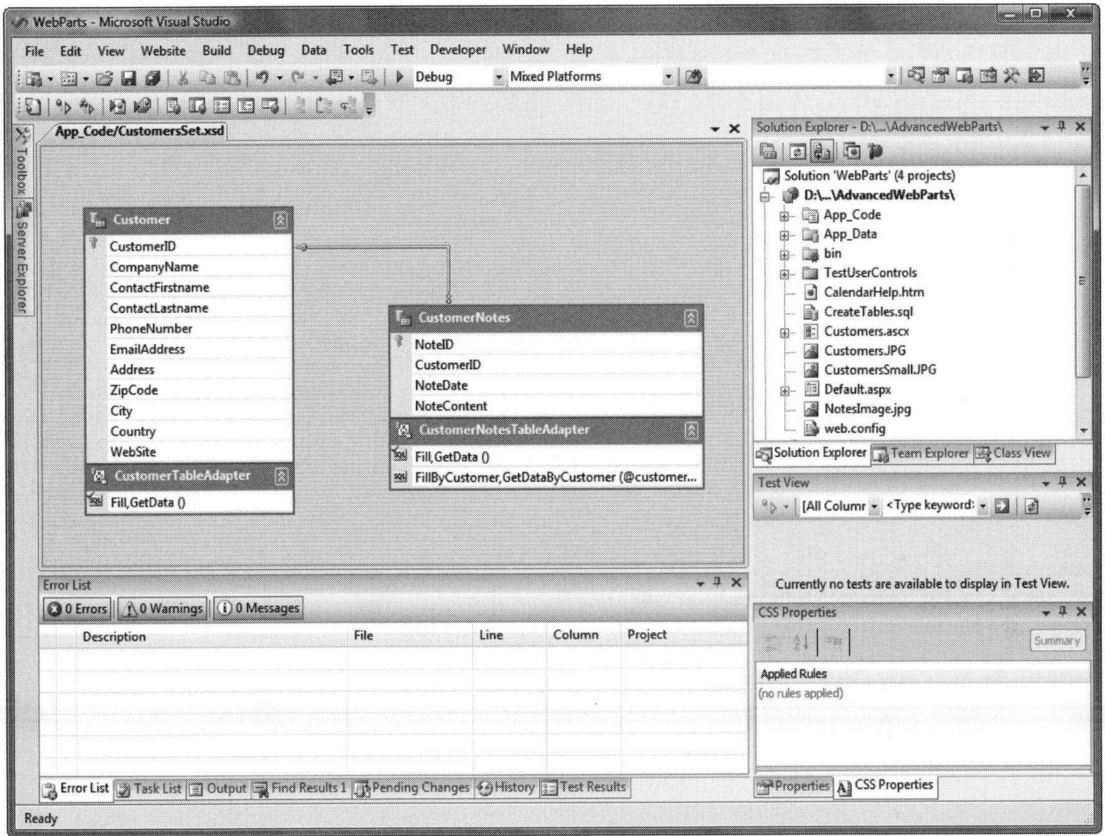

***Figure 31-10.** The typed DataSets necessary for the solution*

The typed DataSet extends the DataSet class and provides typed table adapters that you will use to develop the remaining parts of the web application in this chapter. For the CustomerNotes table, we added a second query to the typed DataSet, as you can see in Figure 31-10 (right-click the DataTable in the designer and select Add ➤ Query). You'll use this later for querying notes that belong to a dedicated customer. Therefore, the query has a parameter called customerId that enables you to pass in the customer's ID for which you want to retrieve notes. Just one last note: in general, you should always create the business layer and data access layer before you start creating the actual user interface components—and web parts are definitely user interface components. Components in the business layer and data access layer are reusable across different applications, just as this typed DataSet is.

The Custom WebPart's Skeleton

First, you have to create a custom class that inherits from WebPart. Also, you need to import the System.Web.UI.WebControls.WebParts namespace so you have easy access to the Web Parts Framework classes.

```
using System;
using System.Web.UI;
using System.Web.UI.WebControls;
using System.Web.UI.WebControls.WebParts;

namespace Apress.WebParts.Samples
{
    public class CustomerNotesPart : WebPart
    {
        public CustomerNotesPart ()
        {

        }
    }
}
```

Next, add some properties to your web part. For every property procedure in your class, you can specify whether the property is personalizable on a per-user or on a shared basis, as well as whether the property is accessible to users. For example, in your CustomerNotesPart, you can include a property that specifies the default customer for which you want to display the notes, as follows:

```
private string _Customer = string.Empty;

[WebBrowsable(true)]
[Personalizable(PersonalizationScope.User)]
public string Customer
{
    get
    {
        return _Customer;
    }
    set
    {
        _Customer = value;
    }
}
```

The WebBrowsable attribute specifies that the property is visible to end users, and the Personalizable attribute specifies that the personalization scope for the property is on a per-user basis.

Initializing the Web Part

To write the initialization code, you can optionally create child controls; you do this just as you would create a composite web part. You can render the web part on your own if you don't want to use prebuilt controls in the RenderContents method; however, using composite controls makes life much easier, because you don't have to worry about the HTML details. To create controls, you have to override the CreateChildControls method as follows. Don't forget to declare instance variables for every control you are going to create in your WebPart class.

```
private TextBox NewNoteText;
private Button InsertNewNote;
private GridView CustomerNotesGrid;

protected override void CreateChildControls()
{
    // Create a text box for adding new notes
    NewNoteText = new TextBox();

    // Create a button for submitting new notes
    InsertNewNote = new Button();
    InsertNewNote.Text = "Insert...";
    InsertNewNote.Click += InsertNewNote_Click;

    // Create the grid for displaying customer notes
    CustomerNotesGrid = new GridView();
    CustomerNotesGrid.HeaderStyle.BackColor = System.Drawing.Color.LightBlue;
    CustomerNotesGrid.RowStyle.BackColor = System.Drawing.Color.LightGreen;
    CustomerNotesGrid.AlternatingRowStyle.BackColor =
                                  System.Drawing.Color.LightGray;
    CustomerNotesGrid.AllowPaging = true;
    CustomerNotesGrid.PageSize = 5;
    CustomerNotesGrid.PageIndexChanging += CustomerNotesGrid_PageIndexChanging;

    // Add all controls to the controls collection
    Controls.Add(NewNoteText);
    Controls.Add(InsertNewNote);
    Controls.Add(CustomerNotesGrid);
}

void CustomerNotesGrid_PageIndexChanging(object sender,
                                         GridViewPageEventArgs e)
{
    // Insert Page Change Logic
    // ...
}

void InsertNewNote_Click(object sender, EventArgs e)
{
    // Insert new note here
    // ...
}
```

Within the CreateChildControls method, all controls used by the custom web part are created. Don't forget to add them to the Controls collection of the web part so that the ASP.NET runtime is aware of these controls and can manage view state and all the other things that happen in the life cycle of the page (as described in Chapter 27). Furthermore, the method sets up the event-handling routines as shown with the InsertNewNote button or the CustomerNotesGrid GridView control.

Loading Data and Processing Events

The next phase in the control's (web part's) life cycle is the loading phase. Here you can connect to your database and load data into your control. To do this, you have to override the OnInit and OnLoad methods or catch the Init and Load events of the web part. Both ways have the same effect. But when overriding the OnLoad method, for example, don't forget to call base.Onload() so that the base class's loading functionality is executed as well. Therefore, it makes sense to set up event handlers once and catch the events of your custom control so that you can't forget this, as follows:

```
public CustomerNotesPart()
{
    this.Init += CustomerNotesPart_Init;
    this.Load += CustomerNotesPart_Load;
    this.PreRender += CustomerNotesPart_PreRender;
}

void CustomerNotesPart_Init(object sender, EventArgs e)
{
    // Load data from the database...
}

void CustomerNotesPart_Load(object sender, EventArgs e)
{
    // Initialize other properties ...
}
```

You will see how to implement the PreRender event later. Now you can write functionality for loading the data from the database. Let's assume that you have already created a typed DataSet for your CustomerNotes table. You can create a helper method for binding the previously created GridView to the data from the database and then call this method in the Load event as follows. For simplicity, the method binds the information directly to the GridView and doesn't use caching for optimizing data access, because you should concentrate on web part creation now. Note that you need to import the CustomersSetTableAdapters namespace created with the previously designed, typed DataSet.

```
void BindGrid()
{
    EnsureChildControls();

    CustomerNotesTableAdapter adapter =
        new CustomerNotesTableAdapter();

    if (Customer.Equals(string.Empty))
        CustomerNotesGrid.DataSource = adapter.GetData ();
    else
        CustomerNotesGrid.DataSource = adapter.GetDataByCustomer(Customer);
}

void CustomerNotesPart_Load(object sender, EventArgs e)
{
    // Initialize web part properties
    this.Title = "Customer Notes";
    this.TitleIconImageUrl = "NotesImage.jpg";
}
```

```
void CustomerNotesPart_Init(object sender, EventArgs e)
{
    // Don't try to load data in Design mode
    if (!this.DesignMode)
    {
        BindGrid();
    }
}
```

Remember the call to EnsureChildControls; as you don't know when ASP.NET really calls CreateChildControls() and therefore creates the child controls (because it creates them as they are needed), you need to make sure controls are available from within this method by calling EnsureChildControls. (You can find more information about this in Chapter 27.)

Now you have loaded the data into the grid. During the next phase of the life cycle, events are processed by the ASP.NET runtime. Your custom web part has to catch the event for the previously added InsertNewNote button that submits a new note to the database and the CustomerNotesGrid that changes the page, as follows:

```
void InsertNewNote_Click(object sender, EventArgs e)
{
    CustomerNotesTableAdapter adapter =
            new CustomerNotesTableAdapter();

    // Note that the NoteID is an identity column in the
    // database and therefore is not required as a parameter
    // in the method generated by the DataSet!
    adapter.Insert(Customer, DateTime.Now, NewNoteText.Text);

    // Refresh the Grid with the new row as well
    BindGrid();
}

void CustomerNotesGrid_PageIndexChanging(object sender,
                                         GridViewPageEventArgs e)
{
    CustomerNotesGrid.PageIndex = e.NewPageIndex;
}
```

Finally, you have to load the data into the GridView in one more place in your code. As soon as someone changes the value for the Customer property, you want your web part to display information associated with the newly selected customer. Therefore, you have to modify the property's code as follows:

```
[WebBrowsable(true)]
[Personalizable(PersonalizationScope.User)]
public string Customer
{
    get
    {
        return _Customer;
    }
    set
    {
```

```
            _Customer = value;

            // Don't try to load data in Design mode
            if (!this.DesignMode)
            {
                EnsureChildControls();
                CustomerNotesGrid.PageIndex = 0;
                CustomerNotesGrid.SelectedIndex = -1;
                BindGrid();
            }
        }
}
```

You should reset the page index in case the new data displayed will not fill as many pages as the previous data source filled.

The Final Rendering

You have now initialized the web part, created controls, wrote code for loading data, and caught control events. So, it's time to render the web part. Immediately before you render the web part, you can set final property values on your controls that affect rendering. For example, you should disable the InsertNewNote button if the user has not initialized the Customer property. And of course the GridView can now create the necessary HTML controls for displaying the data to which it is bound. To do this, you need to call the DataBind method as follows:

```
void CustomerNotesPart_PreRender(object sender, EventArgs e)
{
    if (Customer.Equals(string.Empty))
        InsertNewNote.Enabled = false;
    else
        InsertNewNote.Enabled = true;

    CustomerNotesGrid.DataBind();
}
```

In the RenderContents method, you can create the HTML code to lay out your web part. If you don't override the method, the web part automatically renders the previously added controls in the order they have been inserted into the web part's Controls collection within the CreateChildControls method. Because this layout is simple (just a sequence of the controls), you will now override the RenderContents method to create a better, table-based layout, as follows:

```
protected override void RenderContents(HtmlTextWriter writer)
{
    writer.Write("<table>");

    writer.Write("<tr>");
    writer.Write("<td>");
    NewNoteText.RenderControl(writer);
    InsertNewNote.RenderControl(writer);
    writer.Write("");
    writer.Write("</tr>");
```

```
    writer.Write("<tr>");
    writer.Write("<td>");
    CustomerNotesGrid.RenderControl(writer);
    writer.Write("");
    writer.Write("</tr>");

    writer.Write("");
}
```

This code renders an HTML table through the HtmlTextWriter with two rows and one column. The first row contains the text box and the button, and the second row contains the GridView with the notes. Finally, your RenderControl method uses the RenderControl methods of the child controls to render the text box, button, and grid in a specific position within the table. Therefore, you have easily overridden the default rendering of the WebPart base class.

More Customization Steps

As previously shown, with the IWebPart interface a custom web part implemented this way can override properties such as the title or description. Furthermore, you can specify default values for other properties of the web part by just setting the values for them (which works best in the Load method). You can even override the implementations of default properties and methods from the web part. The following example shows how you can initialize the web part and override web part properties:

```
void CustomerNotesPart_Load(object sender, EventArgs e)
{
    // Initialize web part properties
    this.Title = "Customer Notes";
    this.TitleIconImageUrl = "NotesImage.jpg";
}

public override bool AllowClose
{
    get
    {
        return false;
    }
    set
    {
        // Don't want this to be set
    }
}
```

This code initializes some of the web part's properties in the Load event with default values. It then overrides the AllowClose property to always return false, and it ignores any set operation by just leaving the logic here. This way, you have created a web part where the caller cannot override this behavior by just setting this property from outside. You really have complete customization and control over what can and can't be done with your web part. This is the sort of power you can never get when working with user controls.

Using the Web Part

Now it's time to see how to use the custom web part in your web part page. To do this, register the web part on your web part page using the <%@ Register%> directive at the top of the web page, as follows:

```
<%@ Register TagPrefix="apress" Namespace="Apress.WebParts.Samples" %>
```

Remember that you used the namespace Apress.WebParts.Samples in the class file of the custom web part. The <%@ Register %> directive assigns the prefix Apress to this namespace. Therefore, you can use the web part in one of the previously created WebPartZone controls, as follows:

```
<asp:WebPartZone runat="server" ID="MainZone">
    <ZoneTemplate>
        <uc1:Customers ID="MyCustomers"
                       runat="server" OnLoad="MyCustomers_Load" />
        <apress:CustomerNotesPart ID="MyCustomerNotes" runat="server" />
    </ZoneTemplate>
</asp:WebPartZone>
```

Now you can test your newly created web part by starting your web application. Figure 31-11 shows the results of your work.

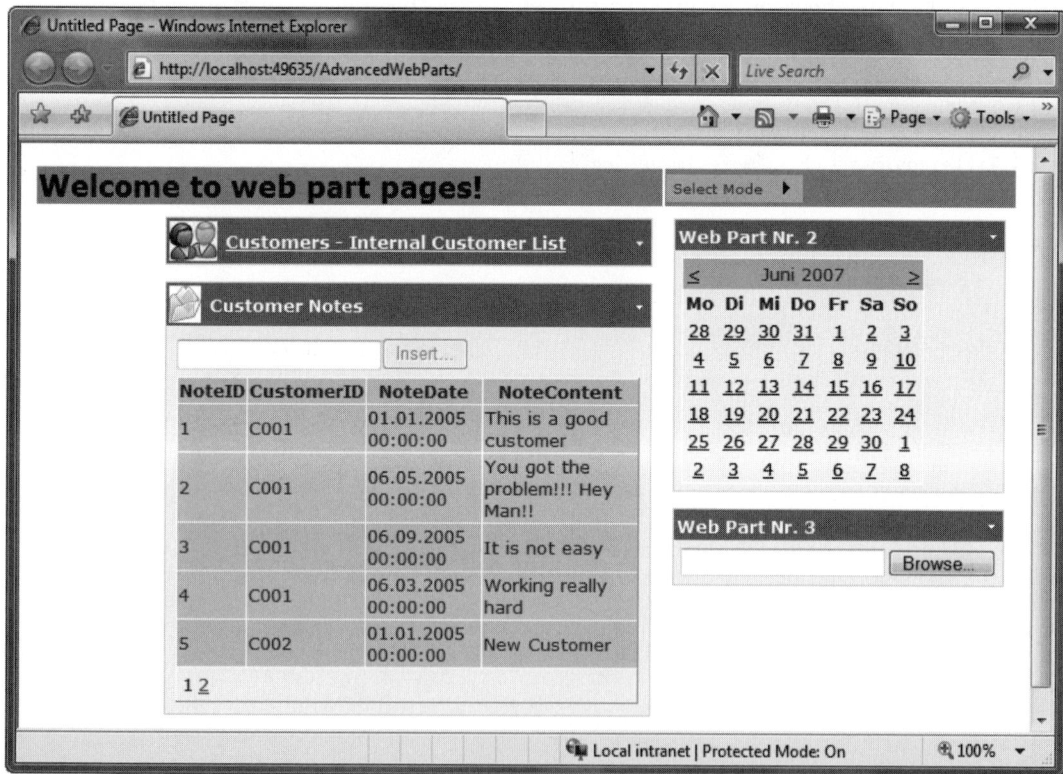

Figure 31-11. The custom web part in action with the other web parts

Web Part Editors

In the previous example, you created a custom web part with a personalizable property called Customer. This property determined whether the content of the GridView in the web part displays information for just one customer or for all customers. You were not able to change this property through the web part page's user interface, so you will now see how you can accomplish this.

The ASP.NET Web Parts Framework provides functionality for editing properties of web parts. As you saw when creating the Menu control for switching the page's DisplayMode, it includes an Edit mode. However, if you try to activate it now, you will get an exception about missing controls on the page. The missing pieces for the Edit mode are the EditorWebZone and some appropriate editor parts. Both are prebuilt; the WebPartZone hosts editor parts. You can use them by adding an EditorZone and one of the prebuilt editor parts to your page, as follows:

```
<asp:EditorZone runat="server" ID="SimpleEditor">
    <ZoneTemplate>
        <asp:AppearanceEditorPart ID="MyMainEditor" runat="server" />
    </ZoneTemplate>
</asp:EditorZone>
```

This code adds an AppearanceEditorPart to the zone, which allows you to configure the appearance of the web part, including its title and chrome settings (see Table 31-2). Now you can switch to the Edit mode on your page; Figure 31-12 shows the steps required for opening an appropriate editor on your page.

Table 31-4 lists the available editor web parts of the framework.

The PropertyGridEditorPart editor part is a suitable way to enable the user to modify the previously implemented Customer property of your web part. Just add the editor part to your page as follows, and edit your custom web part:

```
<asp:EditorZone runat="server" ID="SimpleEditor">
    <ZoneTemplate>
        <asp:PropertyGridEditorPart ID="MyPropertyEditor" runat="server" />
        <asp:AppearanceEditorPart ID="MyMainEditor" runat="server" />
    </ZoneTemplate>
</asp:EditorZone>
```

Table 31-4. *Editor Web Parts Shipping with ASP.NET*

Editor Part	Description
AppearanceEditorPart	Allows you to configure basic properties of the web part, including its title and its ChromeStyle.
BehaviorEditorPart	Includes editors for modifying properties that affect the behavior of the web part. Typical examples of such properties are the AllowClose or AllowMinimize properties, as well as properties such as TitleUrl, HelpMode, and HelpUrl. Every property modifies behavior such as whether the web part can be minimized.
LayoutEditorPart	Allows the user to change the web part's zone as well as its ChromeState. By the way, this editor enables browsers where changing a web part's zone through dragging and dropping doesn't work manually through the controls of this editor part.
PropertyGridEditorPart	Displays a text box for every public property of your custom web part that includes the attribute [WebBrowsable(true)].

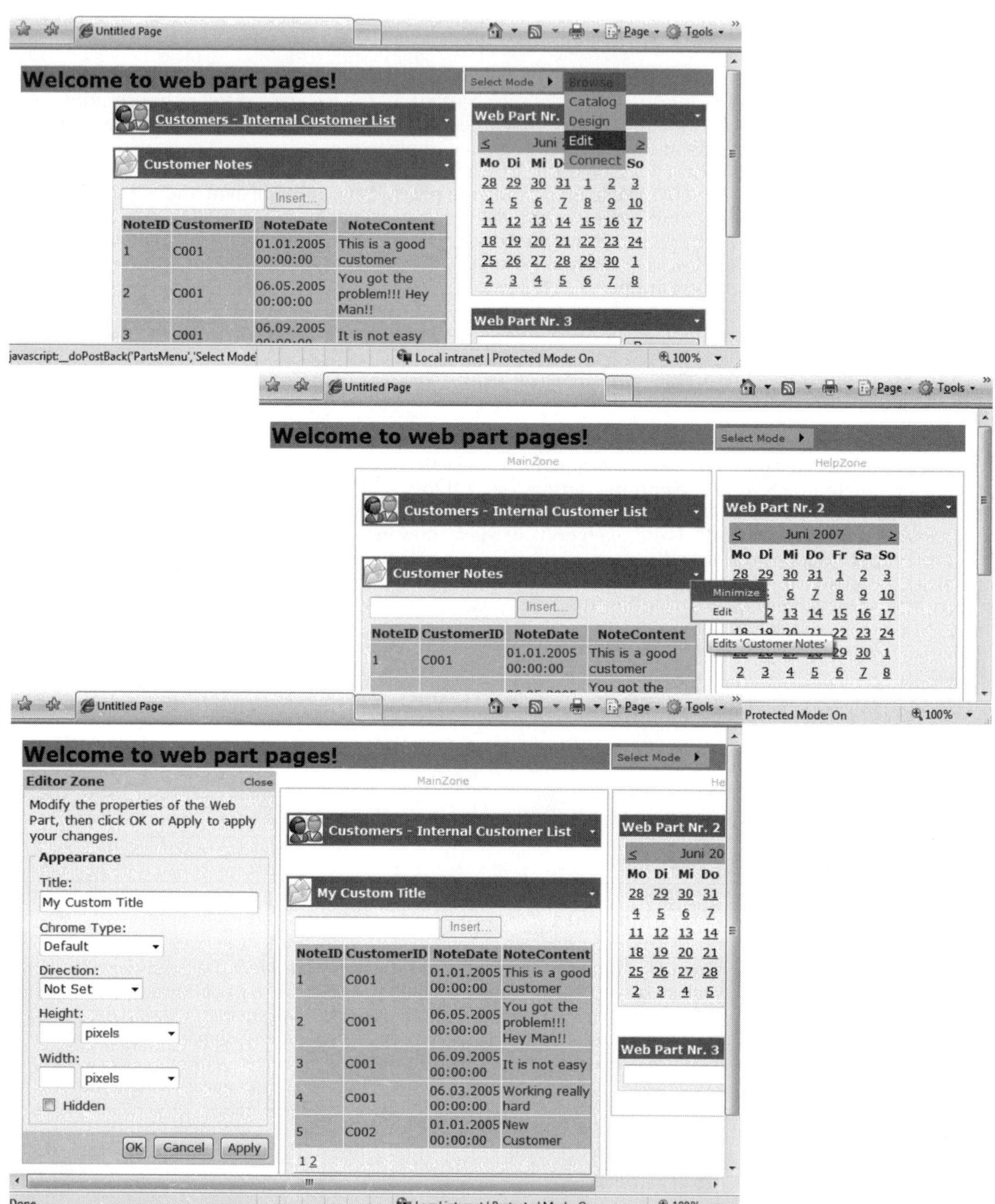

Figure 31-12. Editing properties of your web parts

Figure 31-13 shows the results. As soon as you switch to the Edit mode and edit your custom web part, you can change the value for the Customer property.

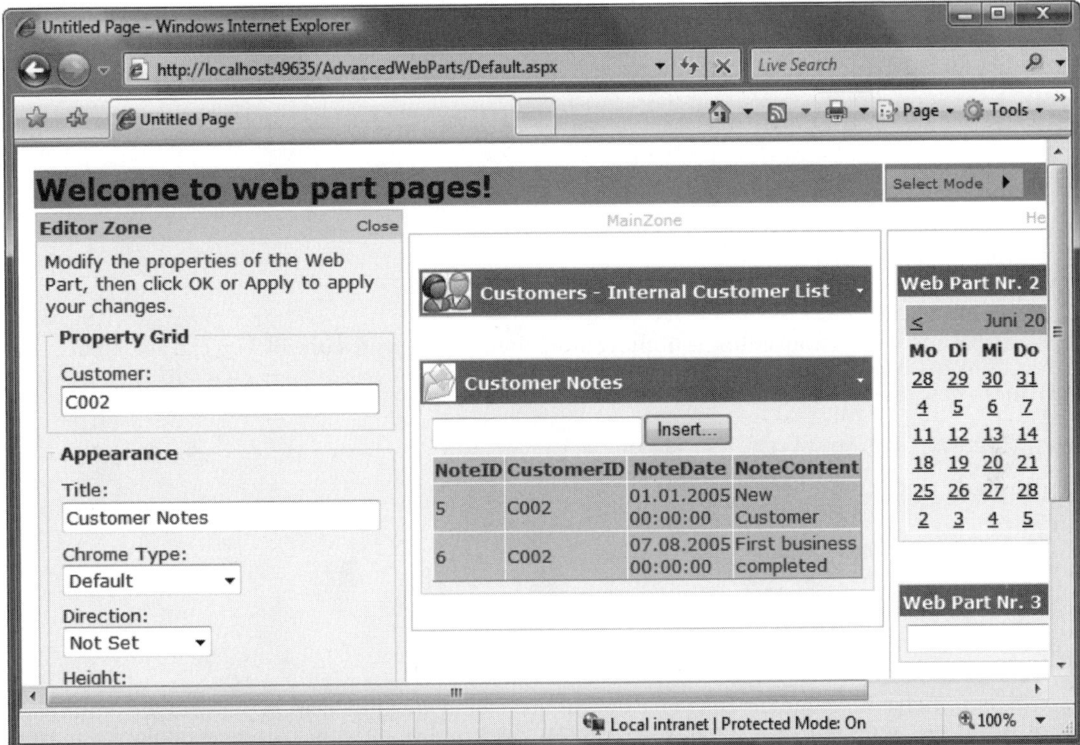

Figure 31-13. The PropertyGridEditorPart in action

Because you have called BindGrid in the property's set method previously, the appearance of the web part changes as soon as you hit the Apply button of the EditorZone. Additionally, if you add a [WebDisplayName] in addition to the [WebBrowsable] attribute to your custom property, you can control the name of the property that the editor will display.

Creating a Custom Editor

Displaying a text box, where the user has to manually enter the customer ID to select a customer, is not a great ergonomic solution. Creating a custom editor that enables the user to select the customer from a list would be more helpful. That's what you'll learn in this section.

Creating a custom editor for a web part page is as easy as creating a custom web part or a custom server control. The only difference is that you need to inherit from EditorPart instead of WebPart or WebControl, as follows:

```
public class CustomerEditor : EditorPart
{
    public CustomerEditor()
    {
```

```
        //
        // TODO: Add constructor logic here
        //
    }

    public override void SyncChanges()
    {
        // Initialize EditorPart with values from WebPart
    }

    public override bool ApplyChanges()
    {
        // Apply changes to the WebPart's properties
    }
}
```

Again, because the custom editor is nothing more than a composite control, you can add child controls by overriding the CreateChildControls method. In this case, you need to create a list for displaying the customers available in the database, as follows:

```
private ListBox CustomersList;

protected override void CreateChildControls()
{
    CustomersList = new ListBox();
    CustomersList.Rows = 4;

    Controls.Add(CustomersList);
}
```

Now that you have created the list, you can load the data in the initialization phase of the EditorPart control. Again, assuming you have already a typed DataSet for working with customers in place, you can catch the Load event and then load the customers, as follows:

```
public CustomerEditor()
{
    this.Init += CustomerEditor_Init;
}

void CustomerEditor_Init(object sender, EventArgs e)
{
    EnsureChildControls();

    // Adapter requires importing the CustomersSetTableAdapters namespace
    CustomerTableAdapter adapter = new CustomerTableAdapter();
    CustomersList.DataSource = adapter.GetData();
    CustomersList.DataTextField = "CompanyName";
    CustomersList.DataValueField = "CustomerID";
    CustomersList.DataBind();

    // Add an "empty" item to the list at the first position
    // so that the user has the option to select "no specific" customer
    // to be displayed in the results list. That means when the user
    // selects this empty entry, all customers should be displayed in
```

```
    // the GridView for the customers
    CustomersList.Items.Insert(0, "");
}
```

Finally, you have to synchronize changes between the EditorPart and the actual web part. First we'll show how to retrieve information from the web part. To do this, you have to add code to your SyncChanges method, which you have to override when inheriting from EditorPart. Within this method, you get access to the web part that will be edited through the base class's WebPartToEdit property. Then you have access to all the properties of your web part as usual.

```
public override void SyncChanges()
{
    // Make sure that all controls are available
    EnsureChildControls();

    // Get the property from the WebPart
    CustomerNotesPart part = (CustomerNotesPart)WebPartToEdit;
    if (part != null)
    {
        CustomersList.SelectedValue = part.Customer;
    }
}
```

When the user updates the value in the editor by clicking Apply, you have to update the web part's property. You can do this in the ApplyChanges method, where again you can access the web part through the base class's WebPartToEdit property, as follows:

```
public override bool ApplyChanges()
{
    // Make sure that all controls are available
    EnsureChildControls();

    // Get the property from the WebPart
    CustomerNotesPart part = (CustomerNotesPart)WebPartToEdit;
    if (part != null)
    {
        if (CustomersList.SelectedIndex >= 0)
            part.Customer = CustomersList.SelectedValue;
        else
            part.Customer = string.Empty;
    }
    else
    {
        return false;
    }

    return true;
}
```

The method returns true if the value has been updated successfully and returns false otherwise. That's it—you have created a custom editor. But how can you use it? Somehow the infrastructure has to know that this editor has to be used with only specific web parts—in this case with the

CustomerNotesPart. To do this, modify the originally created web part. It has to implement the IWebEditable interface as follows:

```
public class CustomerNotesPart : WebPart, IWebEditable
{
    #region IWebEditable Members

    EditorPartCollection IWebEditable.CreateEditorParts()
    {
            // Create editor parts
            List<EditorPart> Editors = new List<EditorPart>();
            CustomerEditor Editor = new CustomerEditor();
            Editor.ID = this.ID + "_CustomerEditor_1";
            Editors.Add(Editor);
            return new EditorPartCollection(Editors);
    }

    object IWebEditable.WebBrowsableObject
    {
        get { return this; }
    }

    #endregion

    // Rest of the implementation
    ...
```

This method works for user controls and server controls. The GenericWebPart that wraps user controls and server controls verifies whether the wrapped control implements the IWebEditable interface. If the control implements the interface, it calls the control's implementation of the interface for providing the custom editors. The CreateEditorParts method just returns a collection of EditorParts to be displayed for this WebPart, and the WebBrowsableObject property returns an instance of a class (typically the editable WebPart control) containing the personalizable properties. Figure 31-14 shows the results.

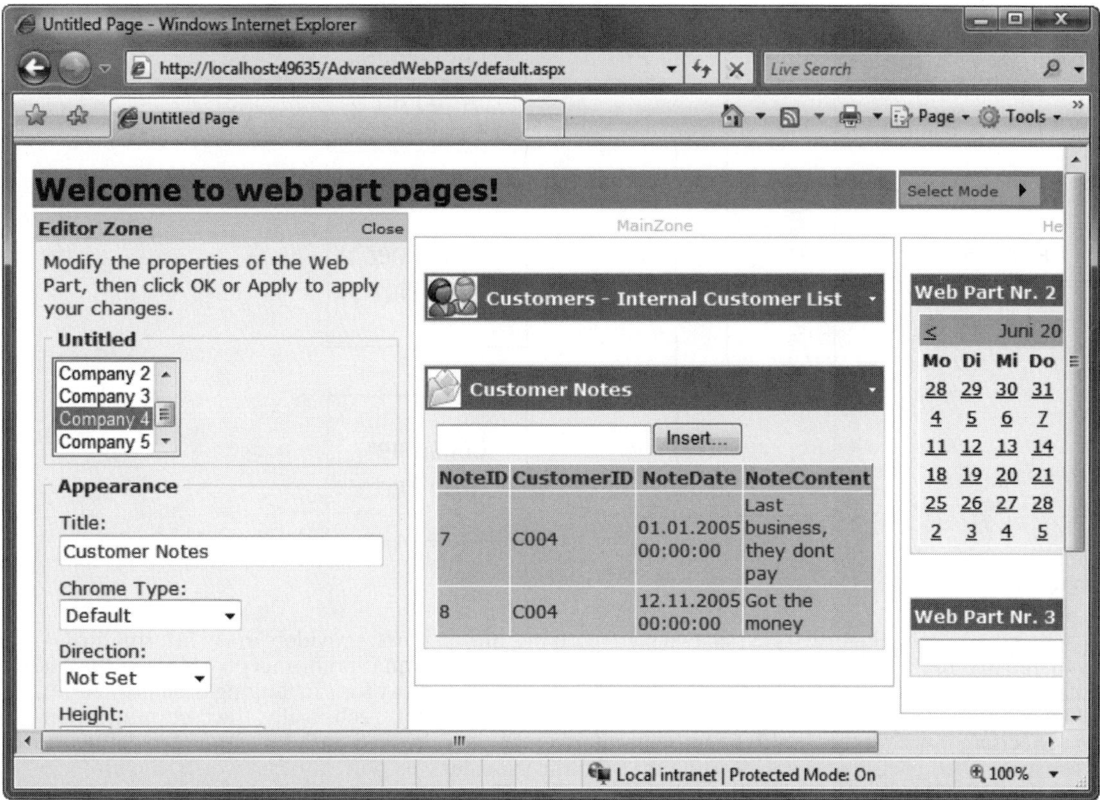

Figure 31-14. The custom editor part in action

Connecting Web Parts

Web parts can also exchange information in a well-defined manner. For example, a web part that displays a list of customers could notify another web part (or many other web parts) if a specific customer has been selected so that the other web part can display information according to the selection in the customer web part. The ASP.NET framework lets you create such “connectable” web parts and offers the possibility of statically or dynamically connecting web parts. For creating connectable web parts, you have to create and combine several pieces. Figure 31-15 shows these pieces and how they relate to one another.

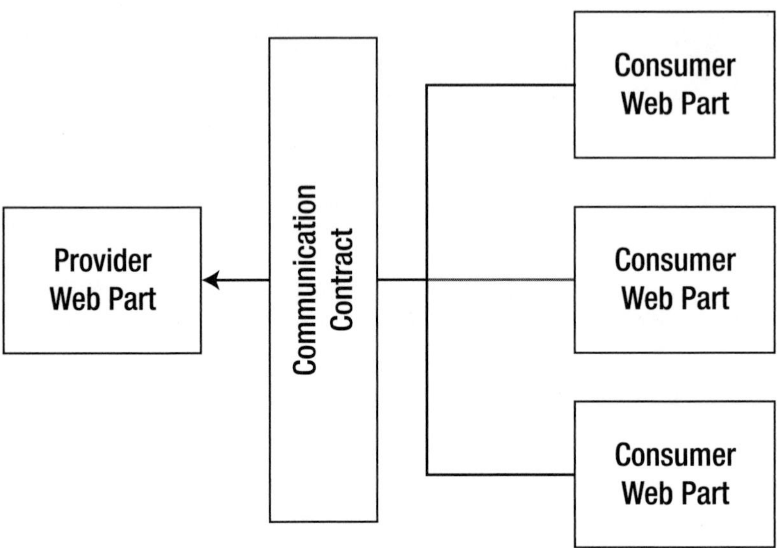

Figure 31-15. *The pieces for creating connectable web parts*

You can see that Figure 31-15 has two primary types of web parts: providers make information available to other web parts, and every web part that requires information from a provider web part is a consumer web part. Finally, you have to establish a standardized way for exchanging the information, which leads to the final missing piece: the communication contract. Technically, the communication contract is an interface that has to be implemented by the provider web part. This interface defines how a consumer web part can access information from the provider web part. In other words, the provider web part makes its data available through this interface. The steps for creating and connecting web parts are as follows:

1. **Create a communication contract:** The first thing you should think about is, which information needs to be exchanged? Based on the response to this question, you can design an interface for data exchange that has to be implemented by the provider web part.

2. **Create a provider web part:** Next you can create the provider web part. This web part has to perform two tasks: it needs to implement the previously defined communication contract interface or know a class implementing this interface, and it needs to provide a method that returns an instance of a class implementing the interface. This method must be marked with the [ConnectionProvider] attribute.

3. **Create a consumer web part:** Next, you can create a consumer web part. The consumer web part does not need to implement any interfaces, but it needs to know how to communicate with the provider. Therefore, it needs to know about the interface (which means if you have the consumer in a separate DLL, it needs to reference an assembly that defines this interface). A consumer web part then needs to implement a method that is marked with the [ConnectionConsumer] attribute. This method accepts a variable as a parameter that implements the previously defined communication contract interface.

4. **Configure the connection:** Finally, you have to configure the connection between the consumer and the provider web part. You can do that statically through the <StaticConnections> section within the <WebPartManager> control tag in your markup code of the .aspx page, or the user can configure connections at runtime. You will learn more details about how to implement both ways later, in the "Static Connections Between WebParts" section.

You can connect only web parts inherited from WebPart; because user controls and custom server controls are wrapped by the GenericWebPart, the framework has no direct access to the methods marked with the [ConnectionProvider] and [ConnectionConsumer] attributes.

Previously you created a web part for displaying customer notes in a grid. Because notes can get long (remember, the column is a text column), it might be nice to have a larger text box for editing the value of this field. To learn about web part connections, in the next sections you will create a simple web part that displays the text for the notes, and then you will modify the old web part to become a provider web part.

Defining the Communication Contract

The first step is to design the communication contract. Because your web part will provide just simple text and date information, the communication contract is fairly simple:

```
namespace Apress.WebParts.Samples
{
    public interface INotesContract
    {
        string Notes { get; set; }
        DateTime SubmittedDate { get; }
    }
}
```

This contract defines two properties: one for retrieving and updating the notes text for a customer and the second for retrieving the date of a submitted entry. Now the provider has to implement this interface, while the consumer needs be aware of the interface only.

Implementing the Provider Web Part

Now you will implement the provider that needs to implement the previously created connection contract. In our example, the provider web part will be the previously created CustomerNotesPart. You need to modify the CustomerNotesPart so it implements the INotesContract communication contract interface and contains a public method with the [ConnectionProvider] attribute. The code is as follows:

```
public class CustomerNotesPart
    : WebPart, IWebEditable, INotesContract
{
    #region INotesContract Members

    public string Notes
    {
        get
        {
            // Get the NoteContent value from the grid's data source
            // ...
        }
```

```
        set
        {
            // Update value to the grid's data source
            // ...
        }
    }

    public DateTime SubmittedDate
    {
        get
        {
            // Get the NoteDate value from the grid's data source
            // ...
        }
    }

    #endregion

// Rest of the implementation
...
```

Within the property procedures, you need to add the appropriate code for retrieving the values from the data source you have bound to the GridView in the web part's original version. Updating the data in the property's set procedure means updating the value in the GridView's data source and then using, for example, a SqlCommand or a SqlDataAdapter for updating the values on the database. Retrieving the SubmittedDate from the GridView's data source might look like this:

```
public DateTime SubmittedDate
{
    get
    {
        EnsureChildControls();

        if (CustomerNotesGrid.SelectedIndex >= 0)
        {
            int RowIndex = CustomerNotesGrid.SelectedRow.DataItemIndex;

            DataTable dt = (DataTable)CustomerNotesGrid.DataSource;
            return (DateTime)dt.Rows[RowIndex]["NoteDate"];
        }
        else
        {
            return DateTime.MinValue;
        }
    }
}
```

You can verify whether an item has been selected in the GridView. (To do this, you need to enable selection on the GridView.) If an item is selected, you retrieve the DataItemIndex, which you then can use as an index for accessing the DataRow of the DataTable, which is bound to the GridView. You can read the value from the DataRow and return it.

The next thing your provider web part has to support is a method marked with the [ConnectionProvider] attribute. This method returns the actual implementation of the communication contract interface, which is the web part in this case. Therefore, you need to implement it as follows:

```
[ConnectionProvider("Notes Text")]
public INotesContract GetNotesCommunicationPoint()
{
    return (INotesContract)this;
}
```

That's it! Your provider web part is ready to use. Next you need to implement the consumer web part, which is much easier.

Creating the Consumer Web Part

The consumer web part retrieves information from the provider web parts for its own purposes. In this example, you just display the text for the currently selected note in the CustomerNotesPart that you have implemented as the provider.

For this purpose, you create a new web part server control from scratch. This control acts as a consumer to your previously created CustomerNotesPart. Just add a new class that inherits from the WebPart base class. The web part uses the CreateChildControls for creating a label that displays the date, a text box that displays the notes text, and a button that updates the notes text.

```
public class CustomerNotesConsumer : WebPart
{
    private Label NotesTextLabel;
    private TextBox NotesContentText;
    private Button UpdateNotesContent;

    protected override void CreateChildControls()
    {
        NotesTextLabel = new Label();
        NotesTextLabel.Text = DateTime.Now.ToString();

        NotesContentText = new TextBox();
        NotesContentText.TextMode = TextBoxMode.MultiLine;
        NotesContentText.Rows = 5;
        NotesContentText.Columns = 20;

        UpdateNotesContent = new Button();
        UpdateNotesContent.Text = "Update";
        UpdateNotesContent.Click += UpdateNotesContent_Click;

        Controls.Add(NotesTextLabel);
        Controls.Add(NotesContentText);
        Controls.Add(UpdateNotesContent);
    }

    void UpdateNotesContent_Click(object sender, EventArgs e)
    {
        // Update code needs to be implemented later
    }
}
```

Next, you have to add a simple method that is called by the ASP.NET Web Parts Framework automatically if the web part is connected to another web part. This method accepts the other connection point (which is the provider) as a parameter and needs to be marked with the [ConnectionConsumer] attribute so that the runtime knows this is the method to be called for passing in the provider.

```
private INotesContract _NotesProvider = null;

[ConnectionConsumer("Customer Notes")]
public void InitializeProvider(INotesContract provider)
{
    _NotesProvider = provider;
}
```

With the provider initialized, the web part can consume information from the provider by just calling properties (or methods) defined in the communication contract. For example, in the PreRender event you can initialize your controls, whereas in the button's event procedure you might think you can directly update the notes content by setting the Notes property appropriately. But it is not that easy: actually you cannot predict when the Web Parts infrastructure is going to initialize your provider, as you don't know in which order web parts are added to the page. You need to be aware of this. Therefore, whenever the user clicks the button, you just set a flag telling your web part that it should not take the data out from the provider and that it should update the provider instead of retrieving the value.

```
private bool UpdateFormTextBox = false;

void UpdateNotesContent_Click(object sender, EventArgs e)
{
    UpdateFormTextBox = true;
}

protected override void OnPreRender(EventArgs e)
{
    // Don't forget to call base implementation
    base.OnPreRender(e);

    // Initialize control
    if (_NotesProvider != null)
    {
        if (UpdateFormTextBox)
            _NotesProvider.Notes = NotesContentText.Text;
        else
            NotesContentText.Text = _NotesProvider.Notes;

        NotesTextLabel.Text =
            _NotesProvider.SubmittedDate.ToShortDateString();
    }
}
```

You have to validate whether the provider has been initialized. If it hasn't been, the web part is not connected with any other web part, and therefore you cannot access any information. However, with this code in place, you are basically finished. You have created a consumer web part and a provider web part, and communication between the two takes place through the communication contract interface. Next, you can connect these web parts either manually or dynamically at runtime.

When testing the previous code, you will probably figure out that the connection provider's user interface might not be updated appropriately when you call the provider in the prerendering phase of the life cycle. Again, you don't know when your prerendering stage and when the provider's prerendering stage will be completed. Therefore, you have to complete the update earlier. Because the infrastructure ensures that connection points will be initialized appropriately before the prerendering stage takes place, you can perform the update in your connection consumer method as follows:

```
[ConnectionConsumer("Customer Notes")]
public void InitializeProvider(INotesContract provider)
{
    _NotesProvider = provider;
    if (UpdateFormTextBox)
        _NotesProvider.Notes = NotesContentText.Text;
}
```

Now that you have created both a connection consumer and a connection provider, you will modify the web part page to support the connections between these two web parts.

Static Connections Between Web Parts

The simple way to connect web parts is through static connections. How can you do that? Well, let's think about the roles of the different controls involved in web part pages again. The WebPartManager knows about all the web parts and manages features such as personalization. WebPartZones are areas on your web page that can contain web parts, while the web parts are independent controls. If you think about it a moment, you will recognize that the WebPartManager might be a good starting point for taking a closer look at connection points. You are right: static connection points are configured through the WebPartManager as follows:

```
<asp:WebPartManager runat="server" ID="MyPartManager">
    <StaticConnections>
        <asp:WebPartConnection ID="SimpleConnection"
                               ProviderID="MyCustomerNotes"
                               ConsumerID="MyNotesConsumer" />
    </StaticConnections>
</asp:WebPartManager>
```

The ID values used for the ProviderID and ConsumerID are just the ID values of the web parts as they have been added to the WebPartZone. You can find these web parts in the zones of your web part page, as you can see in the following code fragment:

```
<table width="100%">
...
    <asp:WebPartZone runat="server" ID="MainZone" >
        <ZoneTemplate>
            <uc1:Customers ID="MyCustomers"
                           runat="server"
                           OnLoad="MyCustomers_Load" />
            <apress:CustomerNotesPart
                           ID="MyCustomerNotes" runat="server" />
        </ZoneTemplate>
    </asp:WebPartZone>
...
    <asp:WebPartZone runat="server" ID="HelpZone">
```

```
        <ZoneTemplate>
            <apress:CustomerNotesConsumer
                    ID="MyNotesConsumer" runat="server" />
            <asp:Calendar runat="server" ID="MyCalendar"
                          OnLoad="MyCalendar_Load" />
            <asp:FileUpload ID="MyUpload" runat="server" />
        </ZoneTemplate>
    </asp:WebPartZone>
...
```

When configuring this connection point, you will recognize that the consumer web part always displays information from the selected entry of the CustomerNotes web part.

Dynamically Configuring Connection Points

If you don't want to connect web parts statically but want the user to have the possibility of connecting web parts at runtime, you cannot use the WebPartManager's StaticConnections configuration. But providing dynamic configuration of connection points is nearly as simple as configuring static connection points. All you need to add to your page is a special zone called ConnectionsZone, as follows:

```
<asp:ConnectionsZone ID="MyConnections" runat="server">
    <ConnectVerb Text="Connect Now..." />
    <CancelVerb Text="Don't connect" />
    <DisconnectVerb Text="Release connection" />
</asp:ConnectionsZone>
```

The child tags of ConnectionsZone are optional and allow you to customize the default user interface created for editing the connections. When having added such a zone onto your web part page, the Web Parts Framework allows you to switch the DisplayMode to the ConnectDisplayMode (which is not possible otherwise). If you want to edit connections for a web part in the running web application at runtime, users need to perform the following tasks to connect web parts:

1. Switch to the Connect mode.
2. Select the consumer web part, and select Connect from the web part's menu.
3. Now the connection editor appears in the previously added ConnectionsZone. Here you can select a provider and click the Connect button.
4. The web parts are connected now. You can release the connection by clicking the Release button.

Figure 31-16 shows ConnectionsZone in action.

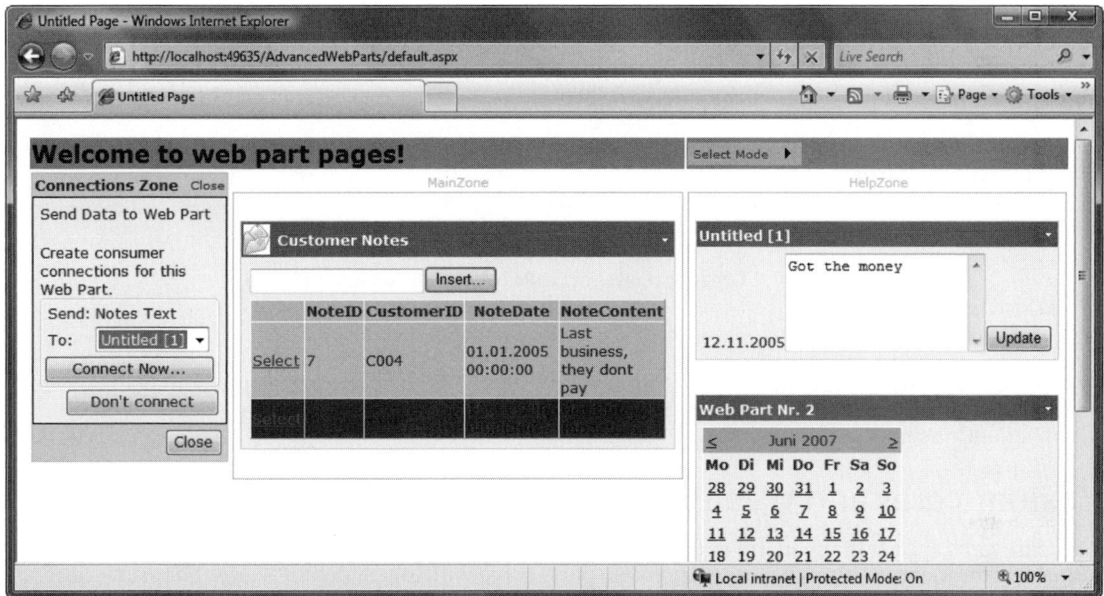

Figure 31-16. ConnectionsZone in action

Multiple Connection Points

A web part provider can make multiple connection points available, while a web part consumer can consume multiple provider connection points. In that case, every connection point requires a unique ID on both the consumer side and the provider side. On the provider side, you specify the connection point ID in the [ConnectionProvider] attribute, as follows. Compared to your previously created provider CustomerNotesPart, you just add a unique ID as a second parameter to the ConnectionProvider attribute construction:

```
[ConnectionProvider("Notes Text", "MyProviderID")]
public INotesContract GetNotesCommunicationPoint()
{
    return (INotesContract)this;
}
```

Similar to the provider, you can specify an ID for consumer endpoints in the same way if a web part is a consumer of multiple providers, as follows (again, compared to the previously created consumer CustomerNotesConsumer, you just add the unique ID as a second parameter of the attribute's constructor):

```
[ConnectionConsumer("Customer Notes", "MyConsumerID")]
public void InitializeProvider(INotesContract provider)
{
    _NotesProvider = provider;
}
```

These IDs have to be unique within the web part. This means other web parts can define connection points with the same ID. When configuring static connections for web parts that support multiple connection points, you have to specify those through additional ProviderConnectionPointID and ConsumerConnectionPointID parameters, as follows:

```
<asp:WebPartManager runat="server" ID="MyPartManager">
    <StaticConnections>
        <asp:WebPartConnection ProviderID="MyCustomerNotes"
                               ProviderConnectionPointID="MyProviderID"
                               ConsumerID="MyCustomerNotesConsumer"
                               ConsumerConnectionPointID="MyConsumerID" />
    </StaticConnections>
</asp:WebPartManager>
```

In the case of dynamic configuration, the user can select the connection point to connect to based on the name specified as the first parameter in the previously used [ConnectionProvider] and [ConnectionConsumer] attributes.

Custom Verbs and Web Parts

Web part verbs appear in the menu of the title bar that each web part supports. You have used verbs frequently throughout this chapter because web parts come with lots of default verbs. For example, if you close or minimize a web part, you have to click a verb in the web part's menu. Fortunately, verbs don't require space on the screen when you don't open the web part's verb menu. You can extend verbs as well—and it's much simpler than you might think.

To extend verbs, you just need to override the Verbs property of your custom web part. Within your overridden version of the Verbs property, you can create and return an array of WebPartVerb objects where each represents one entry in the web part's verb menu. You can catch the click event of each verb in a web part event handler.

The following example is an extension of your previously implemented CustomerNotesConsumer web part and shows how simple extending the verbs menu is:

```
public override WebPartVerbCollection Verbs
{
    get
    {
        WebPartVerb RefreshVerb =
                new WebPartVerb("Refresh",
                        new WebPartEventHandler(RefreshVerb_Click)
                );
        RefreshVerb.Text = "Refresh Now";
        WebPartVerb[] NewVerbs = new WebPartVerb[] { RefreshVerb };

        WebPartVerbCollection vc =
            new WebPartVerbCollection(base.Verbs, NewVerbs);
        return vc;
    }
}

protected void RefreshVerb_Click(object sender, WebPartEventArgs e)
{
    UpdateFormTextBox = true;
}
```

The previous code adds a new verb, Refresh Now, to the previously created CustomerNotesConsumer web part. This verb provides the same update functionality as the button added previously. For every verb you want to display for your web part, you need to create an instance of WebPartVerb. This instance requires you to specify an ID for the verb as well as a delegate reference to the event handler that is called when the user clicks the verb. Finally, you need to create and return an instance of WebPartVerbCollection that contains all the verbs you want to display for your web part. Because you have to make sure standard verbs such as Edit, Minimize, and Close will not get lost, you create a WebPartVerbCollection containing the verbs from the base class implementation as well as an array of new verbs. That's it! When you now launch and test your web part page, you will recognize a new verb in the verbs menu of the CustomerNotesConsumer web part.

User Controls and Advanced Web Parts

You have seen lots of cool features of the ASP.NET Web Parts Framework. But when you want to use built-in functionality such as web part connections or custom editors, you have to deal with one essential drawback: the lack of designer support. The advanced web parts you created in the previous sections have all been from scratch by inheriting from System.Web.UI.WebControls.WebParts.WebPart. In your web part implementation, you have to code all control instantiations as well as the layout of those controls. That's funny for geeks, but honestly, this approach really lacks in terms of productivity, doesn't it? So, the question is, how can you deal with this problem? How can you integrate the design-time support you get from user controls with the powerful infrastructure of the Web Parts Framework with all of its nice features such as web part connections, custom editors, and custom verbs? The answer is much simpler than it seems.

On its own, a user control is just another ASP.NET control that is partially compiled at runtime by the infrastructure. That's why user controls have some limitations. Still, ASP.NET allows you to load user controls dynamically through the Page.LoadControl method. This means all you have to do is create a low-level web part directly inherited from WebPart as before, and in its CreateChildControls method you just need to load the user control of your choice through Page.LoadControl. The following example shows a simple web part that allows you to dynamically select a user control that should be loaded into this web part. The user control needs to be referenced through its relative virtual path within the web application.

```
public class UserControlHostPart : WebPart
{
    private bool _ControlUpdated = false;
    private string _CurrentUserControlPath = string.Empty;

    [WebBrowsable(true)]
    [Personalizable(PersonalizationScope.User)]
    public string CurrentUserControlPath
    {
        get { return _CurrentUserControlPath; }
        set
        {
            if (!_CurrentUserControlPath.Equals(string.Empty))
                _ControlUpdated = true;

            _CurrentUserControlPath = value;
        }
    }

    private Label FallBackLabel = null;
    private Control CurrentControl = null;

    protected override void CreateChildControls()
```

```
    {
        // Label showing a default text if no control is loaded
        FallBackLabel = new Label();
        FallBackLabel.Text = "No control selected";
        FallBackLabel.EnableViewState = false;

        // If a user control is selected, you need to
        // load this control through Page.Load
        LoadSelectedControl();

        // Add the controls to the parent
        Controls.Add(FallBackLabel);
        if (CurrentControl != null)
            Controls.Add(CurrentControl);
    }

    private void LoadSelectedControl()
    {
        if (!_CurrentUserControlPath.Equals(string.Empty))
        {
            try
            {
                CurrentControl =
                  Page.LoadControl(_CurrentUserControlPath);
            }
            catch (Exception ex)
            {
                FallBackLabel.Text =
                  "Unable to load control: " + ex.Message;
            }
        }
    }

    protected override void OnPreRender(EventArgs e)
    {
        base.OnPreRender(e);

        if (_ControlUpdated)
        {
            // Remove the currently loaded control
            Controls.Remove(CurrentControl);
            LoadSelectedControl();
            Controls.Add(CurrentControl);
        }
    }

    public override void RenderControl(HtmlTextWriter writer)
    {
        if (CurrentControl != null)
            CurrentControl.RenderControl(writer);
        else
            FallBackLabel.RenderControl(writer);
    }
}
```

As you can see, loading the user control dynamically is easy. The previous control provides a property that you can modify through an editor web part and that allows the selection of a user control that needs to be loaded. In the CreateChildControls method, the web part checks whether a user control path is provided through the property, and if it is, it calls Page.LoadControl for dynamically loading the user control and adding it to the controls collection. That's it.

However, you do need to know when a control currently loaded into your web part host gets replaced with another control. Think about the life cycle of an ASP.NET server control, for example. When a control is loaded and the page is posted to the server, the control gets created early in the life cycle of a page right before the view state is loaded into the control if there is one (typically on postbacks a view state is available for a control). This means when hitting the Apply button in the editor web part (for example, the property grid editor), CreateChildControls is called early in the processing stage of the postback—eventually before the property CurrentUserControlPath is set in the UserControlHostPart. Therefore, you need to capture this update and reload the newly selected control before the view state and properties get serialized, if the property has been updated by an editor web part. The right time to do this is at the OnPreRender event, which is raised right before ASP.NET starts serializing ViewState and ControlState into the page and before the actual rendering takes place. Figure 31-17 shows the control in action.

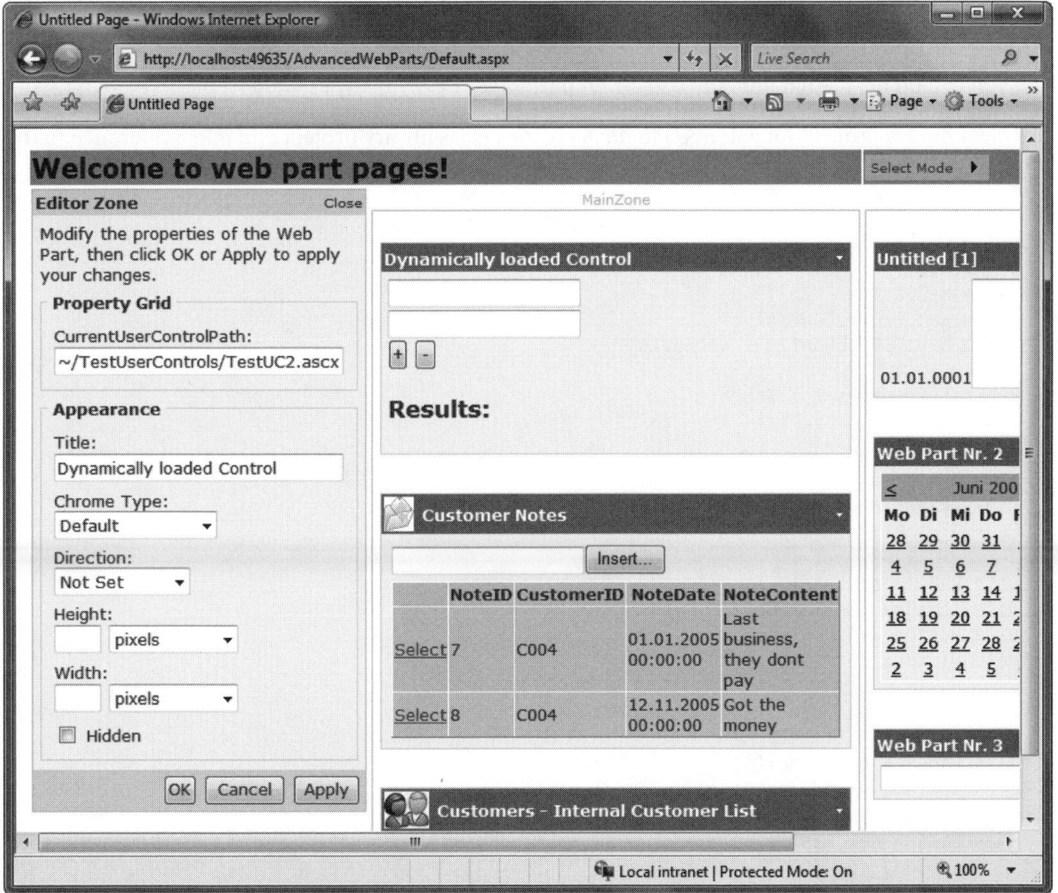

Figure 31-17. The UserControlHost web part in action

This technique provides you with the power of using web part connections, custom editors, or custom verbs offered by the Web Parts infrastructure, which originally are not available for user control-based web parts. For example, if you want to connect a user control loaded into the user control host, the UserControlHostPart just needs to implement the communication contract (if it is a provider) or needs to implement a ConnectionConsumer method as introduced in the "Connecting Web Parts" section. You can establish the communication to the hosted user control either by casting the control to its specific code-beside (or code-behind) type or—in our opinion a better approach—by letting the user control implement an interface that can be used as a communication contract between your UserControlHost web part and the contained user control. Finally, this is really a powerful technique to bring the full power of the Web Parts Framework to user controls and therefore combine this power with the convenience of the user control designer in Visual Studio 2005.

Uploading Web Parts Dynamically

Web part pages are all about personalization. But so far, the web parts you have used in your pages are statically defined. You have added those web parts to ZoneTemplate controls of several WebPartZone controls added to the page. Wouldn't it be nice to have the ability to dynamically upload web part definitions and new web parts onto an existing web part page? If you take a close look at the Toolbox in Visual Studio 2005, you will recognize an ImportCatalogPart web part offered by ASP.NET. That's the key for what you will do next—dynamically add a web part to your previously created web part page.

First you must develop a custom web part—once again. But this time you will encapsulate the web part in a class library project. All you need to do is create a class library project and add a reference to the System.Web.dll assembly. Afterward, you can create a web part like the following one:

```
using System;
using System.Collections.Generic;
using System.Web;
using System.Web.UI;
using System.Web.UI.WebControls;
using System.Web.UI.WebControls.WebParts;

public class ExternalPart : WebPart
{
    public ExternalPart()
    {
        this.ExportMode = WebPartExportMode.All;
    }

    private Label TestLabel;
    private TextBox TestTextBox;
    private Button TestButton;
    private ListBox TestList;

    protected override void CreateChildControls()
    {
        TestLabel = new Label();
        TestTextBox = new TextBox();
        TestButton = new Button();
        TestList = new ListBox();

        Controls.Add(TestLabel);
        Controls.Add(TestTextBox);
```

```
        Controls.Add(TestButton);
        Controls.Add(TestList);

        TestButton.Click += TestButton_Click;
    }

    void TestButton_Click(object sender, EventArgs e)
    {
        TestList.Items.Add(TestTextBox.Text);
    }

    public override void RenderControl(HtmlTextWriter writer)
    {
        TestLabel.Text = "Enter value:";
        TestLabel.RenderControl(writer);
        writer.WriteBreak();
        TestTextBox.RenderControl(writer);
        writer.WriteBreak();
        TestButton.Text = "Add";
        TestButton.RenderControl(writer);
        writer.WriteBreak();
        TestList.RenderControl(writer);
    }
}
```

This is really a simple web part, but it is interesting: take a close look at the constructor. You need to mark web parts as exportable by setting their ExportMode property to an appropriate value. The ExportMode property is of the type WebPartExportMode and can be set to None (meaning no property values will be exported at all), All (meaning all properties will be exported), or NonSensitiveData. (NonSensitiveData means that only properties marked as non-sensitive—by specifying the value false for the isSensitive parameter of the Personalizable attribute's constructor when applied on a property—will be included in the export. The default value of the isSensitive parameter of the Personalizable attribute is false.) Note that export means exporting the metainformation and current property values for a web part into an XML file. In other words, it is not about downloading the binary with all the settings; it's just about downloading the current state of the web part. This means when you import an exported web part on another web part page, you have to deploy the binary to this target website before you can import the web part through the CatalogZone. You'll learn more about that after you have tested the web part and its exportability.

To test the web part, we recommend you create a simple web part page where you add a reference to the web part class library created previously and load the web part into a simple WebPartZone as follows:

```
<%@ Page Language="C#" AutoEventWireup="true"
         CodeFile="Default.aspx.cs" Inherits="_Default" %>
<%@ Register TagPrefix="apress"
             Assembly="ExternalWebPart"
             Namespace="Apress.ExternalWebParts" %>

<html xmlns="http://www.w3.org/1999/xhtml" >
<head runat="server">
    <title>Untitled Page</title>
</head>
<body>
```

```
<form id="form1" runat="server">
<div>
<asp:WebPartManager ID="TestPartManager" runat="server" />
<asp:WebPartZone runat="server" ID="TestZone">
    <ZoneTemplate>
        <apress:ExternalPart runat="server" ID="TestExport" />
    </ZoneTemplate>
</asp:WebPartZone>
</div>
</form>
```

To be able to export the description of the web part, you need to enable export for the web part page in your web.config file as follows:

```
<system.web>
    <compilation debug="true"/>
    <authentication mode="Windows"/>
    <webParts enableExport="true" />
    ...
    <!- other parts of system.web related configuration ->
    ...
</system.web>
```

When you now start the web part page created previously, you will recognize a new menu verb in the title bar of the web part page, as shown in Figure 31-18. When you click this new Export verb in the web part menu, ASP.NET will create an XML description file for your web part, which you need to save on your hard disk as a .WebPart file. This .WebPart file contains all the current property settings of your web part, as well as the basic type description of the web part (namespace and class name), and looks as follows:

```
<?xml version="1.0" encoding="utf-8"?>
<webParts>
  <webPart xmlns="http://schemas.microsoft.com/WebPart/v3">
    <metaData>
      <type name="Apress.ExternalWebParts.ExternalPart" />
      <importErrorMessage>Cannot import this Web Part.</importErrorMessage>
    </metaData>
    <data>
      <properties>
        <property name="AllowClose" type="bool">True</property>
        <property name="Width" type="unit" />
        <property name="AllowMinimize" type="bool">True</property>
        <property name="AllowConnect" type="bool">True</property>
        <property name="ChromeType" type="chrometype">Default</property>
        <property name="TitleIconImageUrl" type="string" />
        <property name="Description" type="string" />
        <property name="Hidden" type="bool">False</property>
        <property name="TitleUrl" type="string" />
        <property name="AllowEdit" type="bool">True</property>
        <property name="Height" type="unit" />
        <property name="HelpUrl" type="string" />
        <property name="Title" type="string" />
        <property name="CatalogIconImageUrl" type="string" />
```

```
        <property name="Direction" type="direction">NotSet</property>
        <property name="ChromeState" type="chromestate">Normal</property>
        <property name="AllowZoneChange" type="bool">True</property>
        <property name="AllowHide" type="bool">True</property>
        <property name="HelpMode" type="helpmode">Navigate</property>
        <!-property name="ExportMode" type="exportmode">All</property->
      </properties>
    </data>
  </webPart>
</webParts>
```

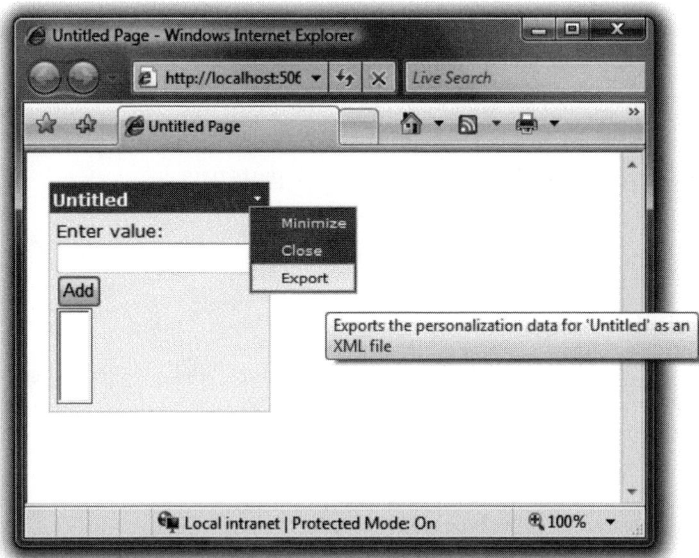

Figure 31-18. Exporting the previously created web part

You use this .WebPart file to import a web part description into an existing portal page. But it is not as easy as just importing the .WebPart file. Before you can import a .WebPart file successfully on the target page, you need to deploy the assembly DLL containing the implementation of the WebPart class into the Bin directory of your web application. Furthermore, you need to modify the .WebPart file so the <type> tag in the <metadata> section contains the assembly name in addition to the namespace name and class name. Furthermore, you have to make sure the properties do not conflict with the settings of the target web part page. With the default properties supported by every web part, the only property you have to take into account for avoiding problems is the ExportMode property. If the target site does not allow exports (which is the default setting if you do not set the enableExport attribute in your web.config file as demonstrated earlier) and the .WebPart file defines All or NonSensitive for the ExportMode property, the import will fail. Therefore, you might need to modify the .WebPart file as follows:

```
<?xml version="1.0" encoding="utf-8"?>
<webParts>
  <webPart xmlns="http://schemas.microsoft.com/WebPart/v3">
    <metaData>
      <type name="Apress.ExternalWebParts.ExternalPart, ExternalWebPart" />
```

```
      <importErrorMessage>Cannot import this Web Part.</importErrorMessage>
    </metaData>
    <data>
      <properties>
        <property name="AllowClose" type="bool">True</property>
        <property name="Width" type="unit" />
        ...
        <property name="HelpMode" type="helpmode">Navigate</property>
        <!-property name="ExportMode" type="exportmode">All</property->
      </properties>
    </data>
  </webPart>
</webParts>
```

Now you are ready to import the web part on your target website. To complete the import, you have to perform the following steps after you have created the web part and exported (or manually created) the web part description introduced earlier:

1. Add a CatalogZone with an ImportCatalogPart to your target web parts page.
2. Deploy the assembly of your web part to the target site's Bin directory.
3. Launch the web part page, switch to the catalog mode, and upload the .WebPart file.
4. Now you can add the web part through the PageCatalogPart to your page.

The easiest part is adding an ImportCatalogPart to the CatalogZone of your web part page as follows:

```
<asp:CatalogZone runat="server" ID="SimpleCatalog">
    <ZoneTemplate>
        <asp:PageCatalogPart runat="server" ID="MyCatalog" />
        <asp:ImportCatalogPart runat="server" ID="MyImport" />
    </ZoneTemplate>
</asp:CatalogZone>
```

Actually, in a real-world scenario, deploying the web part assembly you want to import is the hardest challenge. For this simple example, it is sufficient to copy the class library's assembly DLL containing the implementation of the web part created earlier into the target site's Bin directory. In real-world scenarios, you would need to establish a well-defined process for uploading web parts. You could also dynamically upload web parts, but that can become a huge security risk for your website if you do not establish well-defined reviewing and testing processes up front. You don't ever want to let anyone upload web parts you have not reviewed as the owner of a site. This should always be done by a website administrator or website owner. As soon as you have copied the assembly, you can import the web part by switching to the catalog zone and uploading the .WebPart file to the web part page. If the Web Parts Framework cannot load the type for the web part defined in the .WebPart file, the import will fail. Figure 31-19 shows the ImportCatalogPart in action, and Figure 31-20 shows the imported web part added to the page.

If you take a closer look at the Figures 30-19 and 30-20, you will recognize that ASP.NET supports two types of web part catalogs by default: a page catalog and an imported web part catalog. The first one shows all statically added web parts that are currently closed, and the second catalog shows web parts that have been imported dynamically to the web part page. Before you can import a web part, you need to switch to the imported web part catalog.

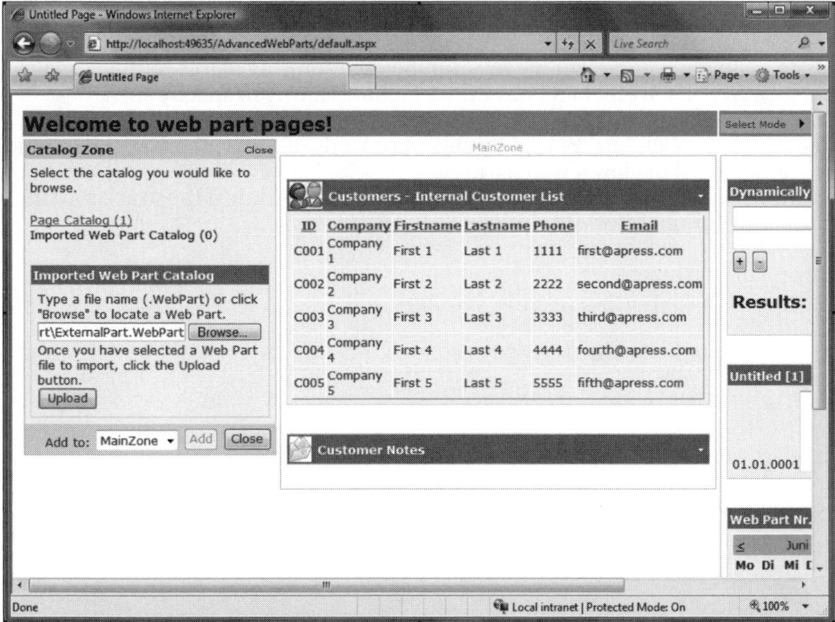

Figure 31-19. *ImportCatalog web part in action*

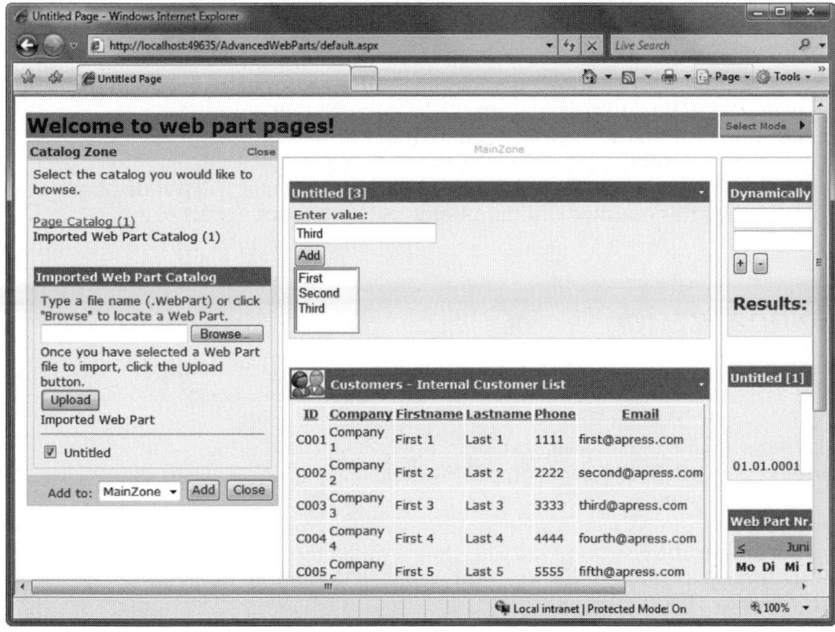

Figure 31-20. *The imported web part in action*

Authorizing Web Parts

When you have all your web parts on your page, you might want to make some available to specific groups of users. Fortunately, the ASP.NET Web Parts Framework includes a way to specify such authorization information for web parts. All you need to do is catch one specific event of the WebPartManager class called AuthorizeWebPart. Within this event procedure, you can encapsulate logic for deciding whether a user is authorized to view a web part.

The following example shows how to display the CustomerNotes web part only if the user browsing to the page is member of the local Administrators group:

```
protected void MyPartManager_AuthorizeWebPart(
                 object sender, WebPartAuthorizationEventArgs e)
{
    // Ignore authorization in Visual Studio Design Mode
    if (this.DesignMode)
        return;

    // Authorize a web part or not
    Type PartType = e.Type;
    if (PartType == typeof(CustomerNotesPart))
    {
        e.IsAuthorized = false;
        if (User.Identity.IsAuthenticated)
        {
            if (User.IsInRole("BUILTIN\\Administrators"))
                e.IsAuthorized = true;
        }
    }
}
```

Because authorization takes place on types of web parts and not on individual instances of web parts, you get the type of the web part to be authorized from the WebPartManager in the event arguments. You then can make authorization decisions based on the type of the web part as demonstrated previously. As soon as you set the IsAuthorized property of the WebPartAuthorizationEventArgs structure passed in to false, the WebPartManager will not display web parts of this type—neither on the page nor in other situations such as a PageCatalogPart of a CatalogZone.

Final Tasks for Personalization

Finally, you should keep in mind a couple of final tasks for personalization. You can configure personalization properties on a per-page level through the WebPartManager, as follows:

```
<asp:WebPartManager runat="server" ID="MyPartManager">
    <Personalization Enabled="true" ProviderName="YourProvider" />
</asp:WebPartManager>
```

If you want to configure personalization settings for the whole application, you have to do that through the <webParts> configuration element of the <system.web> section in the web.config application configuration, as follows:

```
<webParts>
```

```
<personalization defaultProvider="MyProvider">
    <authorization>
        <allow roles="BUILTIN\Administrators"/>
        <deny roles="BUILTIN\Guests" />
    </authorization>
    <providers>
        <add name="MyProvider"
           type="System.Web.UI.WebControls.WebParts.SqlPersonalizationProvider"
           connectionStringName="CustomSqlConnection" />
    </providers>
</personalization>
</webParts>
```

This code also shows that you can even configure the specific users for which personalization is enabled or disabled. You do this through the <authorization> element; this element works the same way as the <authorization> element you learned about in Chapter 23.

Clearing Personalization

How can you delete personalization information from the store? To do this, you can use the Personalization property of the WebPartManager class; this gives you access to the personalization provider, the settings, and the functions for resetting personalization information. You can do this as follows:

```
if (MyPartManager.Personalization.HasPersonalizationState)
    MyPartManager.Personalization.ResetPersonalizationState();
```

You can then include functionality in your application for resetting personalization in this way. This could be an administration page, for example.

Summary

In this chapter, you learned how to create real-world web part pages. Such pages include requirements such as personalization, as well as a modularized structure through web parts that enable the user to select exactly the information that should be displayed. You also learned what WebPartManagers, WebPartZones, and WebParts are and what their tasks are.

Then you learned about important advanced features such as connecting web parts and authorizing web parts. You also learned how to add custom properties to WebParts that will be stored on a per-user or shared basis, and you created custom editors for editing those properties.

The ASP.NET Web Parts Framework provides you with a huge set of functionality. You never have to implement your own portal framework, as it is already included with the framework.

CHAPTER 32

■ ■ ■

MVC

Microsoft has introduced MVC as an alternative to web forms (covered in Chapter 3). MVC is based on ASP.NET, so all the skills you have learned in previous chapters can be applied to an MVC application. MVC is a framework that lets you leverage your ASP.NET knowledge to build applications quickly—much like web forms and much like the dynamic data framework covered in Chapter 33.

MVC stands for Model-View-Controller—the names of the three major components of this style of application development. *Model* refers to a data model, which is something that you can use to perform create, read, update, delete (CRUD) operations on your persistent application data.

We'll be using the Entity Framework to create a data model for a SQL Server database in this chapter, but you could use other database modeling technologies (such as LINQ to SQL or a different kind of storage altogether (such as the file system). The abstraction of functionality is a key theme in MVC. Your model is the only part of the application that interacts with the data store.

A *view* is what is presented to the user; it is an ASP.NET .aspx page. The content of the page will usually be tied to the CRUD operation the user is trying to perform and so will generally contain the details of one or more data items or the means to edit or delete data items. Of course, the content and purpose of a view will depend on your project.

Controllers are C# code files that bridge between views and models. A controller receives a request from a client (such as a request for the default page for the application to view the details of a specific data record) and selects the view that will service the request.

Choosing Between MVC and Web Forms

MVC has a number of advantages over web forms. The separation between the model, view, and controller allows for easier unit testing of each aspect of your application. You can get a lot more control over the fine detail of an MVC application. Most important, it avoids the large amount of state data transfer between the server and client that has made the adoption of web forms outside the Internet so troublesome.

But the web forms framework remains a very strong platform. There are rich libraries of controls that allow you to create powerful applications quickly and simply. It is easier to get a web forms application up and running, and the skills to create web forms applications are widespread and readily available in the marketplace. Web forms aren't going away—the features will continue to be developed and updated.

We expect that web forms will remain dominant for intranet applications but that ASP.NET applications developed for the Internet will (gradually) gravitate toward MVC for the better testing support and increased control it offers.

Creating a Basic MVC Application

We will start by creating a simple MVC application. This allows us to show you the structure of an MVC project and explain how the core elements work together. To start, create a new project in Visual Studio 2010, selecting ASP.NET MVC2 Web Application from the set of project templates. We have named our project BasicMVCApplication—we have included this project and all the other examples from this chapter in the source code download for this book, available for free at Apress.com.

When you create the project, you'll be prompted to create a unit test project. The MVC model is well-suited to unit testing because the model, view, and controller can be tested separately. We won't be covering unit testing in this book, so there is no need to create the unit tests. If you have used our project name, you'll see a project structure like the one shown in Figure 32-1.

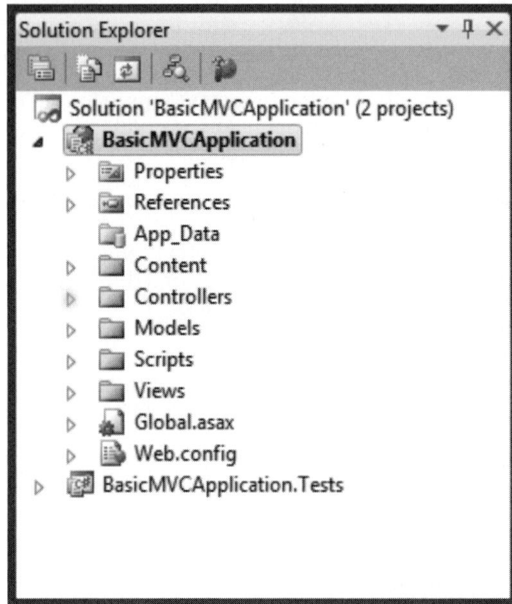

Figure 32-1. *The MVC project structure*

The names of the project folders match their functions. The Content folder contains static items for your application, such as images. Likewise, the Scripts folder is where JavaScript files are stored; the MVC project template creates files for jQuery and some basic validation and Ajax features.

The Controllers folder contains your controller classes. As you'll see when you start to create controllers, there is a specific structure that you should use inside this folder, which Visual Studio 2010 will handle for you.

The Models folder contains the data models you are using; there can be more than one. We will use the Entity Framework to generate a model for our example, and it is in this folder that we will place the type definitions and context classes.

Finally, the Views folder contains the .aspx files that will be used to render content to the user. Like the Controllers folder, there is a specific structure that is used in this folder. The structure of an MVC project is a convention. You don't have to place items in the default folders, but by doing so, you'll be able to take advantage of some of the built-in MVC convenience features.

Creating the Model

The model part of an MVC application can be anything that is able to operate on your application data. Typically, it is either a LINQ to SQL or Entity Framework model, which is what we will use in this chapter. Repeating the theme of abstraction that runs through MVC, separating the model from the other components allows you to change the model with minimum effort—moving from storing data in a series of text files to using SQL Server, for example. The classes that contain the logic to work with your data live in the Models folder.

We will use the Microsoft Northwind sample database and create an Entity Framework model for our sample application. Right-clicking the Models folder and selecting Add New Item allows you to pick the ADO.NET Entity Data Model from the list of templates. From then on, we followed the steps described in Chapter 13 to create the model from the database. We called the data model Northwind.edmx and selected all the database tables for inclusion in the model. Because we created the model in the Models folder, the namespace for our derived context is BasicMVCApplication.Models. You should compile your project once you have created the data model. This makes the model data types available for use when you come to create the controllers and means you can use IntelliSense to complete the class names for you.

Creating the Controller

Controllers process requests and determine which view should be returned to the client. Many of the requests will come from views. For example, a user might request the default page for your MVC application, which the controller will choose to service with a view that lists all the records in a given database table. The HTML generated by the view may contain links that make further requests to the controller—for example, a link that requests a detailed view for a specific table row.

The simplest way to create a controller is to right-click the Controllers folder and select Add and Controller from the pop-up menus. You will be prompted for the name of the new controller, which should follow the naming convention of ending with *Controller*. For example, we are going to create a controller to work with the Products table of the Northwind database, so we used the name ProductController. There is a check box to add action methods for Create, Update, Delete, and Details scenarios. Select this box so that Visual Studio creates the template methods with the right naming conventions. A new file called ProductController.cs has been created in the Controllers folder. Here is the first part of the new file:

```
using System;
using System.Collections.Generic;
using System.Linq;
using System.Web;
using System.Web.Mvc;
using BasicMVCApplication.Models;

namespace BasicMVCApplication.Controllers {
    public class ProductController : Controller {
        //
        // GET: /Product/

        public ActionResult Index() {
            return View();
        }

        //
        // GET: /Product/Details/5
```

```
        public ActionResult Details(int id)
        {
            return View();
        }
```

The comments before each method tell you the format of the request that will lead to a controller method being called. For example, the Index method will be called when the user requests the /Product/ URL.

For our basic application, we want this method to return all the items in the Northwind Products table. That means it is the job of the Index controller method to get the records from the Product table and to select the view that will be used to display them. Here is the completed method:

```
public ActionResult Index() {
    NorthwindEntities db = new NorthwindEntities();
    var data = db.Products;
    return View(data);
}
```

It is a pretty simple method. You create a new instance of the NorthwindEntities context class, get the contents of the table through the Products property, and finish by calling the View method and returning the result. We'll explain the View method in the "Customizing Views" section later in the chapter, but it selects the default view used to display the index of the Products table. You'll complete the remaining controller methods later; next you will create the Index view you just referenced.

Creating the Index View

When you called View from inside the controller Index method, you passed a collection of Product instances as the method argument. This has the effect of telling the MVC framework that the Index view for the Product type should be used to display the data, which is a problem because that view doesn't exist.

To create that view, right-click anywhere in the code for the controller Index method, and select Add View. You will see that the name of the view has been inferred from the controller method name. Select the Create a strongly typed view option, and select the BasicMVCApplication.Models.Product type from the list; this will create a view that uses the members of your data model type. If there are no types available, compile the project and try again. You can see the Add View dialog box in Figure 32-2.

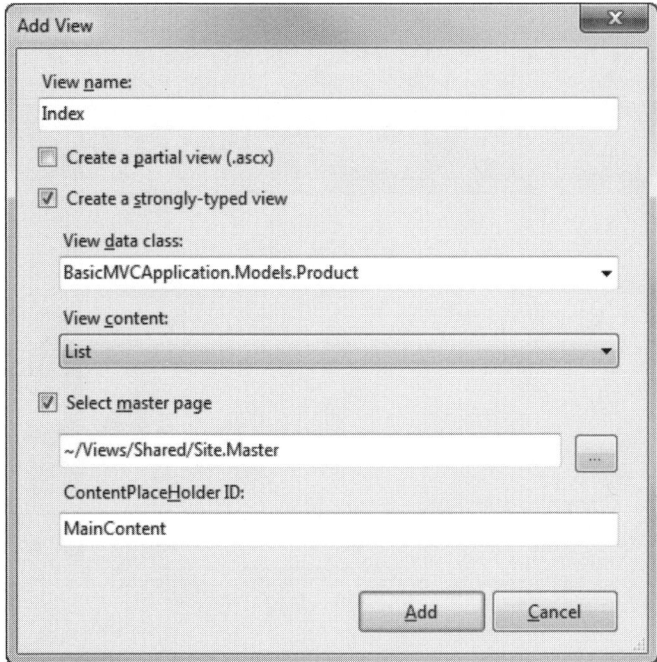

Figure 32-2. *The Add View dialog box*

Select List for the view content, which selects the kind of view that will be created for you. Options exist to match each of the template methods created in the controller class. You'll come back to the other view types when you build the rest of the views in the "Completing the Controller and Views" section that follows. When you click the Add button, Visual Studio creates a Views/Products folder and generates the view as the Index.aspx file. You'll see some new tags in that file, but don't worry about them for the moment; we cover them in the "Customizing Views" section.

Testing the (Incomplete) Application

You have a model, a partially coded controller, and a single view. That's just enough for you to check that everything is working. Select Start Without Debugging from the Debug menu. Your browser will show the default view for the application, which was created by the MVC template when you created the project. You'll change the default view later. To reach the controller, append /Product to the URL that the browser has loaded. For example, the URL is as follows:

```
http://localhost:51895/Product
```

The port number for testing is assigned at random. You will have a different one when you test your project. This will call the Index method of the controller, which will get the product information from the data model and select the Products/Index.aspx view to display them. Figure 32-3 shows the result.

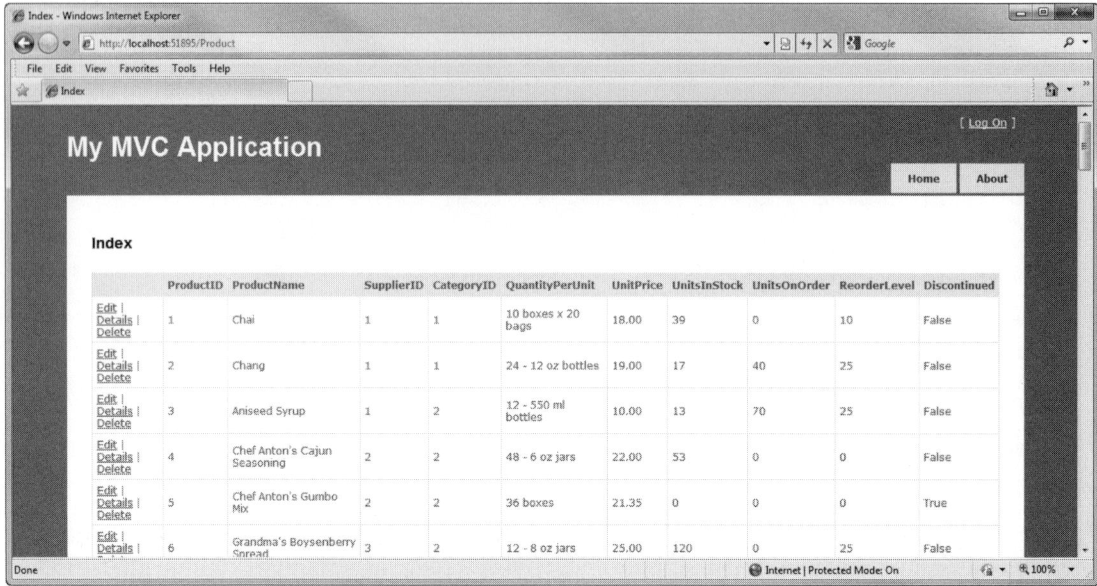

Figure 32-3. Testing the application

You can see that each row is listed and that there are Edit, Delete, and Details links for each one. At the bottom of the screen is a Create New link. If you click any of these links, you will see an error. That's because you have not created the views that support these links or implemented the associated controller methods. You'll do that in the next section.

Completing the Controller and Views

Now that you have the basic framework in place, you can implement the rest of the controller methods and add the views that go with them. Let's start with the controller methods. The pattern for the first few is the same—get the Product data, pass it to the View method, and return the result:

```
using System;
using System.Collections.Generic;
using System.Linq;
using System.Web;
using System.Web.Mvc;
using BasicMVCApplication.Models;

namespace BasicMVCApplication.Controllers {
    public class ProductController : Controller {
        //
        // GET: /Product/

        public ActionResult Index() {
            NorthwindEntities db = new NorthwindEntities();
            var data = db.Products;
            return View(data);
```

```
        }

        //
        // GET: /Product/Details/5

        public ActionResult Details(int id) {
            NorthwindEntities db = new NorthwindEntities();
            var data = db.Products.Where(e => e.ProductID == id).Select(e => e).Single();
            return View(data);
        }

        //
        // GET: /Product/Create

        public ActionResult Create() {
            return View(new Product());
        }
```

For the Details method, you get the ID of the record that is wanted as an argument to the method; you use that in the LINQ query to find the matching product, which you pass to the View method.

There are two Create methods. The first was shown earlier and is called when the user clicks the Create New link on the Index view. Your job is to create a new Product instance and pass it to the View method. The second method is called when the user has filled out the details of the new product and submitted the form. Here is the template method that was created for you:

```
[HttpPost]
public ActionResult Create(FormCollection collection) {
    try {

        return RedirectToAction("Index");
    } catch {
        return View();
    }
}
```

You are going to change the argument to the Create method so that it is an instance of Product. This is a convenience feature of MVC where the attributes in the HTTP POST operation are transformed into the data type that the controller is working with—in our case the Product class from the Northwind data model:

```
[HttpPost]
public ActionResult Create(Product prod) {
    try {
        NorthwindEntities db = new NorthwindEntities();
        db.AddToProducts(prod);
        db.SaveChanges();
        return RedirectToAction("Index");
    } catch {
        return View();
    }
}
```

In the Create method, you add the Product passed in as the argument to the database using the data model and redirect the user to the Index view. We'll explain the different types of ActionResult you can return in a while.

The remaining methods for the Edit and Delete functions come in matched pairs, just like the Create methods. The pattern in each case is the same—one method called when the user wants to start the Edit or Delete process and one method called when the user has finished the process and wants to change the data. Here is the Edit pair:

```
public ActionResult Edit(int id) {
    NorthwindEntities db = new NorthwindEntities();
    var data = db.Products.Where(e => e.ProductID == id).Select(e => e).Single();
    return View(data);
}

[HttpPost]
public ActionResult Edit(int id, FormCollection collection) {
    try {
        NorthwindEntities db = new NorthwindEntities();
        Product prod = db.Products.Where(e => e.ProductID == id).Select(e => e).Single();

        UpdateModel(prod);
        db.SaveChanges();

        return RedirectToAction("Index");
    } catch {
        return View();
    }
}
```

The first Edit method is simple enough. You are passed the ID of the product that the user wants to edit. You get the product data from the model and pass it to the view for display. The second method is more interesting—you are passed the ID of the product that the user has edited and a FormCollection that contains the name/value pairs that describe the product. You obtain the unedited version of the data from the database and then call the UpdateModel method. This is a very useful convenience method that updates the object you obtained from the model using the fields that the user has submitted. You then save the changes in the data model. Lastly, here are the Delete methods—nothing new in these:

```
public ActionResult Delete(int id) {
    NorthwindEntities db = new NorthwindEntities();
    var data = db.Products.Where(e => e.ProductID == id).Select(e => e).Single();
    return View(data);
}

[HttpPost]
public ActionResult Delete(int id, FormCollection collection) {
    try {
        NorthwindEntities db = new NorthwindEntities();
        Product prod = db.Products.Where(e => e.ProductID == id).Select(e => e).Single();
        db.Products.DeleteObject(prod);
        db.SaveChanges();
        return RedirectToAction("Index");
    } catch {
```

```
        return View();
    }
}
```

For each of the controller methods, right-click the code statements, and add the view as you did for the Index view. You need only add a view for the first of the paired methods. You should end up with five views in the Views/Product folder—Create.aspx, Delete.aspx, Details.aspx, Edit.aspx, and Index.aspx.

Now you have a complete, albeit basic, MVC application. If you select Start Without Debugging from the Debug menu, you'll see the list of products, and now that you have implemented the controller methods and created the views, the links to edit products, see the details, and delete products all function.

Modifying the Site.Master File

The final task is to update the Site.Master file in the Views/Shared directory so that it no longer references the HomeController that was created by the Visual Studio MVC project template. Edit the file, and change the first action link so that the last argument in is Product, as follows:

```
<li><%: Html.ActionLink("Home", "Index", "Product")%></li>
```

Delete the second link; it refers to an About action method that you are not going to implement in this chapter.

Extending the Basic MVC Application

The MVC application created in the previous section is basic because, although the core features work, the application has some pretty big holes. We wanted to get the core features up and running to show you how the model, views, and controller work together and to demonstrate how easy it is to get something simple working. In the following sections, you'll build on the basic MVC application to create something more robust and useful.

■ **Note** So that you can see the effect of different features, we have duplicated the project we created in the previous section and called it ExtendedModel. You can get the projects from this chapter and the examples from all the other chapters in the source code download for this book, available for free at Apress.com.

Configuring Routing

To test our MVC application, we have to select Start Without Debugging from the Debug menu and then append /Product to the URL that the browser loads. That's not ideal, especially since the default page doesn't contain anything we are interested in.

The MVC framework maps URL requests to controllers using ASP.NET routing. We explain more about how routing works in Chapter 33, where we cover dynamic data. In the Global.asax file, you will see the RegisterRoutes method, which contains the following statement:

```
routes.MapRoute(
    "Default",
    "{controller}/{action}/{id}",
    new { controller = "Home", action = "Index", id = UrlParameter.Optional }
);
```

This statement calls the MapRoute method to register a route that does two important things for our application. First, it sets the format for requests so that when views are rendered, links back to the MVC application are in the form controller/action/ID. For example, if you wanted to see the details of a product whose ProductID is 7, the URL would be /product/details/7. If you want to change the format of the URLs for your MVC application, this is where you do it.

The second important part of the statement is the last argument to the MapRoute method, which specifies the default values that will be used when they are not supplied as part of the URL. This is why the Index controller method is invoked when you make a request to /product—you have not supplied an action, so the default value Index is used. By specifying id = UrlParameter.Optional, you are saying don't append a record ID if one isn't supplied in the request.

You want the ProductController to be the one that is used by default, so change the MapRoute call as follows:

```
routes.MapRoute(
    "Default",
    "{controller}/{action}/{id}",
    new { controller = "Product", action = "Index", id = UrlParameter.Optional }
);
```

Notice that although the controller class is called ProductController, you specify Product in the route. Save the change, and select Start Without Debugging from the Debug menu. The default URL for the application will be loaded in the browser, and you should see the list of products from the database, as generated by the controller Index method. The previous setting used the HomeController class and the views in the Views/Home folder. You don't need those anymore, so you can delete them from the project. You should also delete the Controllers/HomeControllerTest.cs file from the unit test project.

You can do more with routing. For example, if you want to see the details of a particular product, you use a URL such as /Product/Details/1, which will invoke the Details method in your controller and select the Product/Details.aspx view to display the Product with the ProductID of 1. If you omit the ID, such that you call /Product/Details, you get an exception. You can use routing as one technique to prevent this kind of problem—we'll show you another in the "Validating Data" section. Add the following statement to the Global.asax file:

```
routes.MapRoute(
    "DefaultDetails",
    "{controller}/Details",
    new { controller = "Product", action = "Index", id = UrlParameter.Optional }
);
```

This route, called DefaultDetails, is applied when you receive a request with a URL aimed at any controller, ending with /Details (and therefore omitting the ID). The route maps the URL to our ProductController class and sets the action to Index, which will generate the default list of product records.

This new route must be placed before the Default route that was already present. This is because routes are applied in order until a match is made, and the default route will match any URL received. Now when you call /Product/Details, you don't see the exception—you see the list of product records instead.

Adding Error Handling

You used routing in the previous section to avoid one kind of error, but that technique works for only one kind of problem. You need a general error handling capability, which is what we will demonstrate in this section. MVC supports method filters, which let you annotate controller methods to change the way they behave. One of the most useful filters is HandleError, which specifies how exceptions thrown in a controller method are dealt with. Before you can use the HandleError filter, you must enable custom error handling for your MVC application in web.config. Add the following line in the system.web section:

```
<customErrors mode="On" />
```

Here is the HandleError filter applied to the controller class. This means that any exception that is thrown by any of the action methods in the controller will be handled using the custom error policy.

```
namespace BasicMVCApplication.Controllers {
    [HandleError]
    public class ProductController : Controller {
```

When you apply the HandleError filter with no arguments, you are specifying that any exception thrown by the methods covered by the filter will result in the Views/Shared/Error.aspx view being used. This view simply displays the message "Sorry, an error occurred while processing your request." To test this, try to view the details of a product that doesn't exist, such as with a URL similar to the following (the port number used will differ):

```
http://localhost:51895/Product/Details/100
```

You can be more specific. It is useful to display the generic error view as a backstop, but you might want to give the user more specific information. Create a view in the Views/Shared folder called NoSuchRecordError.aspx with the following content:

```
<%@ Page Language="C#" MasterPageFile="~/Views/Shared/Site.Master"
Inherits="System.Web.Mvc.ViewPage<System.Web.Mvc.HandleErrorInfo>" %>

<asp:Content ID="errorTitle" ContentPlaceHolderID="TitleContent" runat="server">
    Error
</asp:Content>

<asp:Content ID="errorContent" ContentPlaceHolderID="MainContent" runat="server">
    <h2>
        Sorry, you requested a record that doesn't exist.
    </h2>
</asp:Content>
```

This is a variation on the default error view but with a message that is specific to requesting a product that doesn't exist in the database. Now apply the HandleError filter to the Details controller method like this:

```
[HandleError(View="NoSuchRecordError")]
public ActionResult Details(int id) {
```

The filter instructs the MVC framework to use the NoSuchRecordError view for any exception thrown by the Details method. You have to change the backstop filter to be as follows:

```
[HandleError(Order=2)]
public class ProductController : Controller {
```

An Order value of 2 will ensure that the controller-wide filter will be applied only if there isn't a HandleError filter with a higher order available. If you had not set a value for Order, the default error view would have taken precedence.

Now if you try to get the details for a nonexistent product, you will be shown the new error view. If any of the other controller methods throw an exception, then the default error view will be used.

The problem you face now is that the user will be told they requested a nonexistent record even if a different kind of problem arises in the Details method. Not to worry—you can be even more specific. First you create an exception in the ProductController class that you will use when you can't find a record the user has requested:

```
class NoSuchRecordException : Exception {
}
```

You then modify the Details method to explicitly check to see whether a record was returned by the LINQ query and throw the new exception if there isn't one.

```
[HandleError(View="NoSuchRecordError",
    ExceptionType=typeof(NoSuchRecordException))]
public ActionResult Details(int id) {
    NorthwindEntities db = new NorthwindEntities();
    var data = db.Products.Where(e => e.ProductID == id).Select(e => e);
    if (data.Count() == 0) {
        throw new NoSuchRecordException();
    } else {
        Product record = data.Single();
        return View(record);
    }
}
```

You have changed the HandleError filter by adding a value for the ExceptionType property, specifying the type of the exception you want the filter to apply to. Now when you throw a NoSuchRecordException(), the NoSuchRecordError.aspx view will be used, but the more generic Error.aspx will be used for all other types of exception (because you have applied the controller-wide backstop filter).

Adding Authentication

The default MVC project created by the Visual Studio template contains a controller for user authentication—it is the AccountController class. Before you can use this controller, you need to modify it so that it doesn't refer to the HomeController that you removed earlier. To do that, replace each of these three instances:

```
return RedirectToAction("Index", "Home");
```

so that they are as follows:

```
return RedirectToAction("Index", "Product");
```

This change causes the authentication controller to redirect the user to the product controller at the end of each authentication action. The default master page contains links for users to log in, log out, and register a new account.

The Authorize filter allows you to control which users can access your controller methods. Here is the Authorize filter applied to the Delete method in the product controller class:

```
[Authorize]
public ActionResult Delete(int id) {
    NorthwindEntities db = new NorthwindEntities();
    var data = db.Products.Where(e => e.ProductID == id).Select(e => e).Single();
    return View(data);
}
```

When the user clicks a link to delete a product record, the MVC framework is checked. If the user has logged in, then the action will proceed—but if they have not, they will be prompted to provide their username and password or to create a new account.

You can be more restrictive by specifying user names as part of the filter. Here is the Authorize filter applied so that the Delete method is available only to the user John Doe:

```
[Authorize(Users="John Doe")]

public ActionResult Delete(int id) {
```

Now only John Doe can perform delete actions—every other user will be prompted for credentials. The Authorize filter can also be applied to the entire controller class. Here is the Authorize filter applied to the ProductController class, which means that only authenticated users can access the controller actions:

```
[HandleError(Order=2)]
[Authorize]
public class ProductController : Controller {
```

The Authorize filter has an Order property that works just like the HandleError Order property. If you apply the Authorize filter for the entire controller level and for a specific action method, the controller-wide setting will take precedence unless you use the Order property.

Consolidating Data Store Access

Each method in the controller creates a new instance of the data model context and contains its own logic for reading and writing data. You want to consolidate and abstract access to the data model so that you have less code repetition and improve connection performance. To do that, create a class called NorthwindAccessConsolidator that handles the interactions with the model in one central place. Put this class in the ProductController.cs file, as follows:

```
class NorthwindAccessConsolidator {
    private NorthwindEntities db = new NorthwindEntities();

    public IEnumerable<Product> ListProducts() {
        return db.Products;
    }

    public Product GetProduct(int id) {
        IEnumerable<Product> data = db.Products
```

```
            .Where(e => e.ProductID == id)
            .Select(e => e);
        return data.Count() > 0 ? data.Single() : null;
    }

    public void DeleteProduct(int id) {
        Product prod = GetProduct(id);
        if (prod != null) {
            db.Products.DeleteObject(prod);
            SaveChanges();
        }
    }

    public void StoreNewProduct(Product prod) {
        db.Products.AddObject(prod);
        SaveChanges();
    }

    public void SaveChanges() {
        db.SaveChanges();
    }
}
```

The only oddity in this class is that the SaveChanges method is publicly accessible. We have done this to support the model update feature we rely on in the Edit action method. You can refactor the controller class to make use of the new model access consolidator class:

```
public class ProductController : Controller {
    private NorthwindAccessConsolidator nwa
        = new NorthwindAccessConsolidator();

    //
    // GET: /Product/

    public ActionResult Index() {
        return View(nwa.ListProducts());
    }

    //
    // GET: /Product/Details/5

    [HandleError(View = "NoSuchRecordError", ExceptionType = typeof(NoSuchRecordException))]
    public ActionResult Details(int id) {
        Product prod = nwa.GetProduct(id);
        if (prod == null) {
            throw new NoSuchRecordException();
        } else {
            return View(prod);
        }
    }

    //
    // GET: /Product/Create
```

```
public ActionResult Create() {
    return View(new Product());
}

//
// POST: /Product/Create

[HttpPost]
public ActionResult Create(Product prod) {
    try {
        nwa.StoreNewProduct(prod);
        return RedirectToAction("Index");
    } catch {
        return View();
    }
}

//
// GET: /Product/Edit/5

public ActionResult Edit(int id) {
    return View(nwa.GetProduct(id));
}

//
// POST: /Product/Edit/5

[HttpPost]
public ActionResult Edit(int id, FormCollection collection) {
    try {
        Product prod = nwa.GetProduct(id);
        if (prod != null) {
            UpdateModel(prod);
            nwa.SaveChanges();
            return RedirectToAction("Index");
        } else {
            throw new NoSuchRecordException();
        }
    } catch {
        return View();
    }
}

//
// GET: /Product/Delete/5

public ActionResult Delete(int id) {
    return View(nwa.GetProduct(id));
}

//
// POST: /Product/Delete/5

[HttpPost]
```

```
        public ActionResult Delete(int id, FormCollection collection) {
            try {
                nwa.DeleteProduct(id);
                return RedirectToAction("Index");
            } catch (Exception ex) {
                Console.WriteLine(ex);
                return View();
            }
        }
    }
```

The refactored controller creates an instance of the NorthwindAccessConsolidator class and then uses it in each of the action methods.

Adding Support for Foreign Key Constraints

You may have noticed that everything works fine if you create a new product and then delete it but that you get an exception if you try to delete one of the existing product entries. This happens because there is a foreign-key constraint between the Northwind Products and Order_Details tables, such that rows in Order_Details must have valid ProductID values taken from the Products table. To fix this, when you are asked to delete a product, you need to delete any Order_Detail instances that use the ProductID as well. Update the DeleteProduct in the NorthwindAccessConsolidator class like so:

```
public void DeleteProduct(int id) {
    Product prod = GetProduct(id);
    if (prod != null) {
        IEnumerable<Order_Detail> ods =
            db.Order_Details
            .Where(e => e.ProductID == id)
            .Select(e => e);
        foreach (Order_Detail od in ods) {
            db.Order_Details.DeleteObject(od);
        }

        db.Products.DeleteObject(prod);
        SaveChanges();
    }
}
```

Customizing Views

When you created your basic MVC application, you had Visual Studio generate the views for you automatically. This is a useful feature, but the views that you end up with are pretty simplistic and should be tailored to the specifics of your data model types. For example, if you start the MVC application and click the Create New link, you'll see that the view contains a field for the user to enter a ProductID value and field for the Discontinued value. We don't want the user to enter a ProductID—this is the primary key for the Products database table and will be generated automatically for you. And you don't want the user to be able to enter text freely for a Boolean field. In this section, we'll show you how to work with the MVC views so that they work better with the constraints of your data model and better suit your overall application. There are three components that you need to know about in order to master MVC views—they are the model data, the view data, and the HTML helpers.

Modifying the View

Take a look at the Product/Details.aspx view that Visual Studio created for you. The page definition for an MVC view specifies what data model type it will use. Here is the page definition for the Details view, which will be used to display an instance of the Product class in the Entity Framework data model created at the start of the chapter:

```
<%@ Page Title="" Language="C#" MasterPageFile="~/Views/Shared/Site.Master"
Inherits="System.Web.Mvc.ViewPage<BasicMVCApplication.Models.Product>" %>
```

The members of the type that will be displayed are available via the Model reference, which you can see throughout the Details view:

```
<div class="display-label">ProductID</div>
<div class="display-field"><%: Model.ProductID %></div>

<div class="display-label">ProductName</div>
<div class="display-field"><%: Model.ProductName %></div>

<div class="display-label">SupplierID</div>
<div class="display-field"><%: Model.SupplierID %></div>
```

It is through these calls to Model that the Details view is created. For each element of the Product data model type, there is a call to get the value of that type in the Details.aspx file. The first thing you want to do is tidy up the display. Rather than just listing the field names and values, you will display the product details in a table:

```
<%@ Page Title="" Language="C#" MasterPageFile="~/Views/Shared/Site.Master"
Inherits="System.Web.Mvc.ViewPage<BasicMVCApplication.Models.Product>" %>

<asp:Content ID="Content1" ContentPlaceHolderID="TitleContent" runat="server">
    Details
</asp:Content>

<asp:Content ID="Content2" ContentPlaceHolderID="MainContent" runat="server">

    <h2>Details</h2>

    <fieldset>
        <legend>Product Details</legend>
        <table>
                <tr><td>Product Name:</td><td><%: Model.ProductName%></td></tr>
                <tr><td>Supplier ID:</td><td><%: Model.SupplierID%></td></tr>
                <tr><td>Category ID:</td><td><%: Model.CategoryID%></td></tr>
                <tr><td>Quantity per Unit:</td><td><%: Model.QuantityPerUnit%></td></tr>
                <tr><td>Unit Price:</td><td><%: Model.UnitPrice %></td></tr>
                <tr><td>Units in Stock:</td><td><%: Model.UnitsInStock%></td></tr>
                <tr><td>Units on Order:</td><td><%: Model.UnitsOnOrder%></td></tr>
                <tr><td>Reorder Level:</td><td><%: Model.ReorderLevel%></td></tr>
                <tr><td>Discontinued:</td><td><%: Model.Discontinued%></td></tr>
        </table>
    </fieldset>
    <p>
```

```
        <%: Html.ActionLink("Edit", "Edit", new { id=Model.ProductID }) %> |
        <%: Html.ActionLink("Back to List", "Index") %>
    </p>

</asp:Content>
```

You'll notice that you have removed the reference to the primary key. You need this to work with the data model, but you don't need to display it to the user. When you refactored the view, you simply took out the call to Model.ProductID.

The next step is to change the way that some of the fields are displayed. You will start with the UnitPrice field. Change the view so that the markup for the unit price is as follows:

```
<tr>
    <td>Unit Price:</td>
    <td><%= String.Format("{0:F2}", Model.UnitPrice) %></td>
</tr>
```

You can use the standard ASP.NET features in your MVC views. In this case, you call the String.Format method to display the UnitPrice field in a suitable form for a monetary amount. You just pass in the Model.UnitPrice value as the argument to the method call.

One of the nicest features of MVC are the HTML helper methods, which make it easy to generate HTML using the model data. You don't want to display Boolean values as text strings, so you modify the tags for the Discontinued field to be as follows:

```
<tr>
    <td>Discontinued:</td>
    <td><%= Html.CheckBoxFor(e => e.Discontinued, new {disabled="true"})  %></td>
</tr>
```

Here you are using the Html.CheckBoxFor helper method. This method takes a lambda expression that identifies which field the check box relates to and an object that you can use to specify additional HTML attributes. The lambda expression selects the Discontinued field and sets the disabled attribute (because you are displaying static details). When the Details view is rendered, the call to the HTML helper method will generate a fragment of HTML that defines the check box and sets the state to match your model data.

There are HTML helper methods to create most types of HTML inputs, including drop-down lists, password controls, and text areas—you'll use some of these features in the next section. Table 32-1 lists the most commonly used HTML helper methods.

Table 32-1. *MVC HTML Helper Methods*

Helper Method	Description
ActionLink	Creates a link that calls a controller method in the MVC application
BeginForm	Creates a form that will post back to a controller method
CheckBoxFor	Creates a check box for a Boolean value
DropDownListFor	Uses a SelectList to create a drop-down list

Helper Method	Description
ListBoxFor	Creates a list that allows multiple selections
PasswordFor	Creates a text box suitable for entering a password
RadioButtonFor	Creates a radio button
TextAreaFor	Creates a multiline text entry area
TextBoxFor	Creates a single-line text entry box

The helper methods listed in Table 32-1 are known as the *strongly typed* helper methods and were introduced as part of MVC 2. They accept lambda expressions to identify the data field they will generate HTML for and generate compile-time errors if the field does not exist or cannot be rendered into the requested kind of HTML.

The ActionLink helper method, which is used to generate links that call back into the MVC application, is also very useful. The default Details view contains two links at the bottom of the page—one to edit the record being viewed and one to return to the Index view. You can modify the template to add a new link that calls the Delete method in the controller:

```
<%: Html.ActionLink("Edit", "Edit", new { id=Model.ProductID }) %> |
<%: Html.ActionLink("Delete", "Delete", new { id=Model.ProductID }) %> |
<%: Html.ActionLink("Back to List", "Index") %>
```

Now when you view the details page, you have the option to delete the product record without going back to the Index view. The ActionLink method takes care of generating a link that will target the right action in the controller, as defined by the routing set up earlier.

Adding View Data

We still have a couple of issues with the Details view. The SupplierID and CategoryID fields are keys into other tables, and displaying the field values directly doesn't help the user. It would be nice if you could supply the user-friendly values from the other Northwind tables. We will show how to do this using the view data feature, which lets controllers pass information to views alongside the model data.

First, you need to add methods to the NorthwindAccessConsolidator class so that you can get the user-friendly names for the category and supplier:

```
public string GetSupplierName(Product prod) {
    return db.Suppliers
        .Where(e => e.SupplierID == prod.SupplierID)
        .Select(e => e.CompanyName)
        .Single();
}

public string GetCategoryName(Product prod) {
    return db.Categories
        .Where(e => e.CategoryID == prod.CategoryID)
        .Select(e => e.CategoryName)
        .Single();
}
```

You then need to update the controller to get the category and supplier and pass them to the view. Here is the revised Details method:

```
public ActionResult Details(int id) {
    Product prod = nwa.GetProduct(id);
    if (prod == null) {
        throw new NoSuchRecordException();
    } else {
        ViewData["CatName"] = nwa.GetCategoryName(prod);
        ViewData["SupName"] = nwa.GetSupplierName(prod);
        return View(prod);
    }
}
```

You can pass arbitrary data to the view by using the ViewData collection, which you inherit from the default controller class. All you need to do is define a key and a value. In our Details method, we have defined the CatName key to be the category string we want to use and the SupName key to be the supplier name.

To access the data in the view, you access the keys you defined in the controller. Here are the modified tags from the Details.aspx view:

```
<tr>
    <td>Supplier:</td>
    <td><%: ViewData["SupName"] %></td>
</tr>
<tr>
    <td>Category:</td>
    <td><%: ViewData["CatName"] %></td>
</tr>
```

The values that you set in the controller will now be displayed in the view when it is rendered. The SupplierID and CategoryID fields are still available via the model data, but you have just chosen not to use them.

The combination of being able to access the model data fields and easily generate HTML around them means you can tailor views easily. With very little effort you have improved the Details view to remove unwanted elements, format some of the data elements more clearly, and add extra functionality, as shown in Figure 32-4.

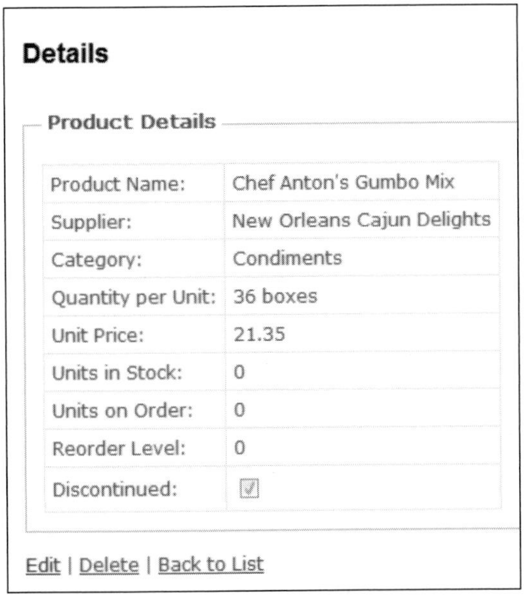

Details

Product Details

Product Name:	Chef Anton's Gumbo Mix
Supplier:	New Orleans Cajun Delights
Category:	Condiments
Quantity per Unit:	36 boxes
Unit Price:	21.35
Units in Stock:	0
Units on Order:	0
Reorder Level:	0
Discontinued:	☑

Edit | Delete | Back to List

Figure 32-4. Customizing the Details MVC view

Adding to the Model

We are going to move on to the Edit view now. Much of what we covered can be applied to this view, but there are a couple of wrinkles that let us demonstrate some other useful MVC features in this section and the next one. Here is the updated Edit.aspx:

```
<%@ Page Title="" Language="C#" MasterPageFile="~/Views/Shared/Site.Master"
Inherits="System.Web.Mvc.ViewPage<ExtendedModel.Models.Product>" %>
<asp:Content ID="Content1" ContentPlaceHolderID="TitleContent" runat="server">
    Edit
</asp:Content>
<asp:Content ID="Content2" ContentPlaceHolderID="MainContent" runat="server">

    <h2>Edit</h2>

    <% using (Html.BeginForm()) {%>

    <fieldset>
        <legend>Edit Product Details</legend>
        <table>
<tr><td>Product Name:</td><td><%: Html.TextBoxFor(model => model.ProductName) %></td></tr>
<tr><td>Supplier:</td><td><%: Html.TextBoxFor(model => model.SupplierID) %></td></tr>
<tr><td>Category:</td><td><%: Html.TextBoxFor(model => model.CategoryID) %></td></tr>
<tr><td>Quantity per Unit:</td>
    <td><%: Html.TextBoxFor(model => model.QuantityPerUnit) %></td></tr>
<tr>
```

```
    <td>Unit Price:</td>
    <td><%: Html.TextBoxFor(model => model.UnitPrice,
        new {Value = String.Format("{0:F2}", Model.UnitPrice)})%></td>
    </tr>
<tr><td>Units in Stock:</td>
    <td><%: Html.TextBoxFor(model => model.UnitsInStock) %></td></tr>
<tr><td>Units on Order:</td>
    <td><%: Html.TextBoxFor(model => model.UnitsOnOrder) %></td></tr>
<tr><td>Reorder Level:</td><td><%: Html.TextBoxFor(model => model.ReorderLevel) %></td></tr>
<tr><td>Discontinued:</td><td><%: Html.CheckBoxFor(model => model.Discontinued) %></td></tr>
        </table>
    </fieldset>
    <p>
        <input type="submit" value="Save" />
    </p>
    <% } %>
    <div>
        <%: Html.ActionLink("Back to List", "Index") %>
    </div>
</asp:Content>
```

There are a couple of differences to mention straightaway. We have used the BeginForm HTML helper method. This generates the HTML required for a form that will post back to our controller with a URL—in this case /Product/Edit/<ProductID>. The second difference is that we have used the TextBoxFor HTML helper method for most of the data fields—this method creates an editable text box that contains the value for the data model field you specify. You supply the formatted UnitPrice value by overriding the value attribute of the text box.

■ **Tip** When using the result of String.Format to set the value for a text box, be sure to specify the HTML attribute as Value (not *value*, with a lowercase *v*). If you do not, the MVC HTML helper method will ignore your formatted string.

If you start the application and click one of the Edit links, you can see how the view is rendered, shown by Figure 32-5.

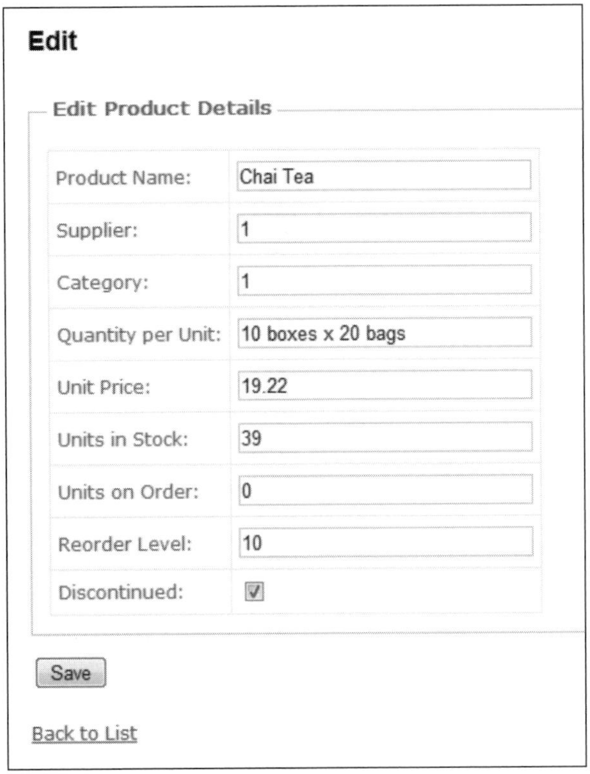

Edit

Edit Product Details

Product Name:	Chai Tea
Supplier:	1
Category:	1
Quantity per Unit:	10 boxes x 20 bags
Unit Price:	19.22
Units in Stock:	39
Units on Order:	0
Reorder Level:	10
Discontinued:	☑

Save

Back to List

Figure 32-5. *The modified Edit view*

There is a problem with the Supplier and Category fields again. The previous solution won't work because the user needs to pick from a list, rather than see a single value. You are going to solve this by extending the data model and using some useful view data and HTML helper methods.

First you must extend your NorthwindAccessConsolidator class to let you get a complete list of supplier and category names and then get a SupplierID or CategoryID from a name string:

```
public IEnumerable<string> GetAllSuppliers() {
    return db.Suppliers.Select(e => e.CompanyName);
}

public int GetSupplierID(string name) {
    return db.Suppliers
        .Where(e => e.CompanyName == name)
        .Select(e => e.SupplierID).Single();
}

public IEnumerable<string> GetAllCategories() {
    return db.Categories.Select(e => e.CategoryName);
}

public int GetCategoryID(string name) {
```

```
    return db.Categories
        .Where(e => e.CategoryName == name)
        .Select(e => e.CategoryID).Single();
}
```

Now you are going to extend the data model by adding a new class in the Models folder called ProductListWrapper. This class is a simple wrapper that encompasses a Product instance and defines two new fields to track the supplier and category names:

```
namespace ExtendedModel.Models {

    public class ProductListWrapper {
        public Product product { get; set; }
        public string SelectedSupplier { get; set; }
        public string SelectedCategory { get; set; }
    }
}
```

You now modify the first Edit method in the controller so that it creates an instance of ProductListWrapper that is returned using the View method. This is the Edit method that is called when the user clicks the Edit link in the Index view. You use the ViewData feature to pass instances of the SelectList class to the view. This is a special MVC type that you can use to send lists of objects for rendering.

```
public ActionResult Edit(int id) {

    ViewData["categories"] = new SelectList(nwa.GetAllCategories());
    ViewData["suppliers"] = new SelectList(nwa.GetAllSuppliers());

    Product prod = nwa.GetProduct(id);

    ProductListWrapper wrap = new ProductListWrapper() {
        product = prod,
        SelectedCategory = prod.Category.CategoryName,
        SelectedSupplier = prod.Supplier.CompanyName,

    };
    return View(wrap);
}
```

Having changed the controller Edit method so that it creates and returns an instance of the wrapper class, you need to update Edit.aspx so that the view knows how to render the new type. You start by changing the page definition so that it refers to the wrapper type, as shown in bold:

```
<%@ Page Title="" Language="C#" MasterPageFile="~/Views/Shared/Site.Master"
Inherits="System.Web.Mvc.ViewPage<ExtendedModel.Models.ProductListWrapper>"
%>
```

The model references in the view need to be updated from model.Fieldname to model.product.Fieldname to reflect the structure of the wrapper type. Here is an example of a modified declaration:

```
<tr><td>Product Name:</td><td>
    <%: Html.TextBoxFor(model => model.product.ProductName) %></td></tr>
<tr>
```

To complete the changes to Edit.aspx, you need to use the SelectList instances that you added to the view data. You do that by using the DropDownListFor HTML helper method, which takes a field from the model data and an instance of SelectList from ViewData (which you have to cast to SelectList explicitly).

```
<tr><td>Supplier:</td>
<td><%: Html.DropDownListFor(model =>
    model.SelectedSupplier, ViewData["suppliers"] as SelectList)  %></td></tr>
<tr><td>Category:</td>
<td><%: Html.DropDownListFor(model =>
    model.SelectedCategory, ViewData["categories"] as SelectList)  %></td></tr>
```

The HTML helper generates a drop-down list with each of the values you supplied in the SelectList and ensures that the values in the SelectedSupplier and SelectedCategory fields are initially selected in the list.

The last step is to modify the controller Edit method that is called when you post back the changes. In this method, you need to unpack the wrapper Product instance, update the SupplierID and CategoryID values so that they match the user selections, and store the Product record via the data model. Here is the new method:

```
[HttpPost]
public ActionResult Edit(int id, FormCollection collection) {
    try {
        Product prod = nwa.GetProduct(id);
        if (prod != null) {
            ProductListWrapper wrapper = new ProductListWrapper() {
                product = prod
            };
            UpdateModel(wrapper);
            prod.SupplierID = nwa.GetSupplierID(wrapper.SelectedSupplier);
            prod.CategoryID = nwa.GetCategoryID(wrapper.SelectedCategory);
            nwa.SaveChanges();
            return RedirectToAction("Index");
        } else {
            throw new NoSuchRecordException();
        }
    } catch {
        return View();
    }
}
```

By creating a simple addition to the data model and updating the controller and view, you have been able to map the numeric foreign-key values into something that the user can understand and change by selecting from a list. You could use this same approach to mix data from two different data models into a single application—creating data types that combine elements from two different data stores, for example. We picked this example because it demonstrates the flexibility of the MVC framework. Small adaptations can create a lot of value for little effort.

Validating Data

Now that you have tidied up the view that the user edits data with, it is time to add support for validating what is entered. You get some validation support from the data model. If the user tries to enter a string value in a field that the database is expecting a numeric value for, then the user will be shown an error screen—either the default ASP.NET stack trace screen or a custom error page if you have enabled custom error handling in your controller and application. Most users won't be able to unpick a stack trace to determine that they entered an unexpected value—and nor should they, which is why there are some solid validation features built into the MVC framework.

Performing Basic Validation

The MVC framework makes it very easy to check for validation errors when data is posted back from the client to the controller. We have changed the signature of the Edit method that receives the user data so that the MVC framework will automatically create an instance of ProductListWrapper from the form values.

To check for validation errors, you call ModelState.IsValid. If there are validation problems, you return from the method early, specifying that the ProductListWrapper instance pass to the Edit method be viewed using the Edit view. Notice that you included the lists of supplier and category names as view data again. This is because Edit.aspx depends on this data to render the display. If you do not include the lists of names, an exception will be thrown when the view is rendered. We have shown the changes to the Edit controller method in bold:

```
public ActionResult Edit(int id, ProductListWrapper pwrap) {
    try {
        if (!ModelState.IsValid) {
            ViewData["categories"] = new SelectList(nwa.GetAllCategories());
            ViewData["suppliers"] = new SelectList(nwa.GetAllSuppliers());
            return View("Edit", pwrap);
        }

        Product prod = nwa.GetProduct(id);
        if (prod != null) {
            ProductListWrapper wrapper = new ProductListWrapper() {
                product = prod
            };
            UpdateModel(wrapper);
            prod.SupplierID = nwa.GetSupplierID(wrapper.SelectedSupplier);
            prod.CategoryID = nwa.GetCategoryID(wrapper.SelectedCategory);
            nwa.SaveChanges();
            return RedirectToAction("Index");
        } else {
            throw new NoSuchRecordException();
        }
    } catch {
        return View();
    }
}
```

In Edit.aspx you need to add a statement to take advantage of the validation support:

```
...
<legend>Edit Product Details</legend>

<%= Html.ValidationSummary("Edit was unsuccessful. Please correct the errors and
    try again.") %>

    <table>
...
```

Now if you submit data that does not match the field types in the data model, you will see the result of the validation check. As an illustration, Figure 32-6 shows the result of entering non-numeric values for the UnitsOnOrder and ReorderLevel fields. You can see that the message you included to the Html.ValidationSummary method is displayed as well as a message for each problem that was encountered. The text boxes for the problem items are highlighted for the user as well. 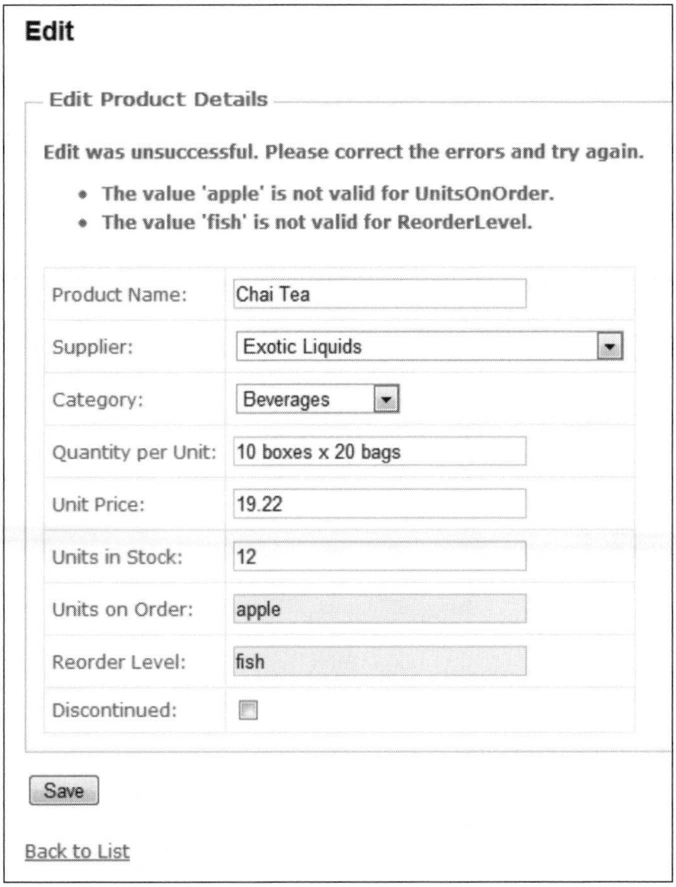

Figure 32-6. *Data validation summary*

If you want to embed validation warnings alongside the data field, you can use the ValidationMessageFor helper method, which will generate a validation warning for a specific data item. For example, here is the helper method applied to the ReorderLevel field:

```
<tr>
    <td>Reorder Level:</td>
    <td>
        <%: Html.TextBoxFor(model => model.product.ReorderLevel)%>
        <%: Html.ValidationMessageFor(model => model.product.ReorderLevel) %>
    </td>
</tr>
```

If you try to submit an edit using a non-numeric value for the reorder level, you see the field-specific error shown in Figure 32-7. The validation helper methods have a number of overrides that let you control the messages that are displayed.

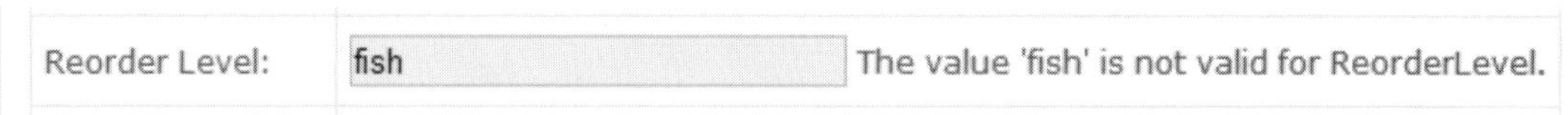

Figure 32-7. *A field-specific validation error*

Adding Validation Annotations

The MVC framework supports metadata annotation for validation, which allows you to use some standard annotations to enforce common validation rules and to define custom constraints. You can use the partial class feature to associate a metadata class with the data model types and then apply C# annotations to it.

To jump right in, here is the metadata class that applies a range validation check to the UnitsInStock property from the Product model data type, which was created in the Models project folder:

```
using System.ComponentModel.DataAnnotations;

namespace ExtendedModel.Models {

    [MetadataType(typeof(ProductMetaData))]
    public partial class Product {

        public class ProductMetaData {
            [Range(1, 50)]
            public object UnitsInStock { get; set; }
        }
    }
}
```

You define the partial class to have the same signature as the Product class generated when you created the Entity Framework data model. We have applied the MetaDataType attribute to our partial class, specifying that the ProductMetaData class will hold the metadata for the Product class (this is indirect, you know, but stay with us—you need to do this only once for each data model type you want to annotate).

In the ProductMetaData class, you define a property with the same name as the field you want to perform validation on. You don't have to match the property type—the metadata system works on the member names. You define a property called UnitsInStock and annotate it with the Range attribute, specifying that the valid ranges for the UnitsInStock field are between 1 and 50.

If you try to edit a record and provide a value for UnitsInStock that is outside the specified range, a validation error is generated, as shown in Figure 32-8.

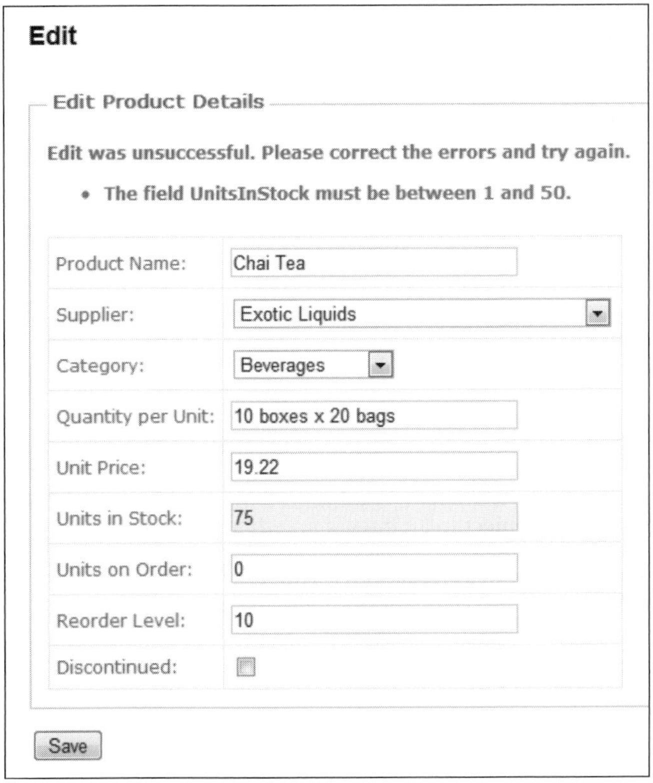

Edit

Edit Product Details

Edit was unsuccessful. Please correct the errors and try again.

- The field UnitsInStock must be between 1 and 50.

Product Name:	Chai Tea
Supplier:	Exotic Liquids
Category:	Beverages
Quantity per Unit:	10 boxes x 20 bags
Unit Price:	19.22
Units in Stock:	75
Units on Order:	0
Reorder Level:	10
Discontinued:	☐

Save

Figure 32-8. *A validation error generated from a Range annotation*

The validation attributes are in the System.ComponentModel.DataAnnotations namespace. We used the RangeAttribute, which allows us to specify a range for a numeric value; there are other attributes that let you specify the length of a string (StringLengthAttribute), match a regular expression (RegularExpressionAttribute), ensure a value is supplied (RequiredAttribute), and specify that a value of a certain type (DataTypeAttribute).

You can also create custom validation attributes by deriving from the ValidationAttribute class. Here is a simple attribute that ensures a numeric value is either odd or even:

```
using System.ComponentModel.DataAnnotations;

namespace ExtendedModel.Models {

    public class OddOrEvenAttribute: ValidationAttribute {
        public Mode mode {get; set;}
```

```
        public OddOrEvenAttribute(Mode m) {
            mode = m;
        }

        public override bool IsValid(object value) {
            try {
                if (int.Parse(value.ToString()) % 2 == 0) {
                    return mode == Mode.Even;
                } else {
                    return mode == Mode.Odd;
                }
            } catch {
                return false;
            }
        }


        public enum Mode {
            Odd,
            Even
        };
    }
}
```

The IsValid method is called by the MVC framework when data is submitted for the data model field to which the attribute has been applied. Try to cast the object to an integer and then check to see whether it is odd or even. If you get an error performing the cast or the number isn't correctly odd or even, you return false, indicating that the value hasn't passed validation. If you return true, you indicate that the value is valid. Here is the custom attribute applied to UnitsInStock via the metadata class:

```
using System.ComponentModel.DataAnnotations;

namespace ExtendedModel.Models {

    [MetadataType(typeof(ProductMetaData))]
    public partial class Product {

        public class ProductMetaData {
            [Range(1, 50)]
            [OddOrEven(OddOrEvenAttribute.Mode.Even,
                ErrorMessage="Units In Stock must be even")]
            public object UnitsInStock { get; set; }
        }
    }
}
```

We have supplied a value for the ErrorMessage property, which will be shown to the user as the validation warning if an unsuitable value is submitted, as shown in Figure 32-9.

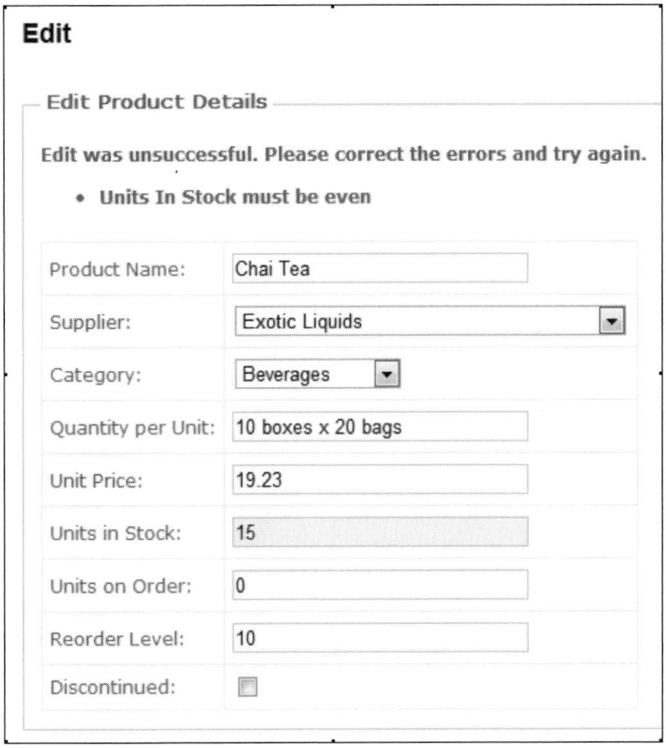

Figure 32-9. A validation message from a custom validation attribute

Using Action Results

In the controller methods, you return the result of the View method or, in one case, the RedirectToRoute method. In this section, we'll explain the significance of these methods and show you how to can use them to control your MVC application.

The MVC framework requires all controller action methods to return an instance of ActionResult—this is how the framework knows what to do—render a view for the user, call another action method, and so on. To make life easier for the MVC programmer, Microsoft has included a number of helper methods that you can use to create instances of subclasses of ActionResult to achieve different effects.

For example, to tell the MVC framework to render a view to the user, you return an instance of ViewResult. This is the subclass of ActionResult that tells MVC that a view is required. The helper method to create a ViewResult is View, which is why we have been using it so liberally. View has a number of overloads. Pass an object to View as the sole argument, and the MVC framework will determine the view to use based on the action method name and use it to display the object you supplied. Other overrides let you specify the master page, the view, and the object to display.

If you want to return the results of another controller method, then you can return the RedirectToRouteResult class, which you can easily create using the RedirectToAction help method. Table 32-2 describes the most useful controller helper methods and the types they return, two of which we demonstrate in the following sections.

Table 32-2. Controller ActionResult Helper Methods

Helper Method	ActionResult Subclass	Description
Views	ViewResult	Renders a view
RedirectToAction	RedirectResult	Returns the result of another controller method
Json	JsonResult	Serializes a data model object using JSON
Javascript	JavaScriptResult	Returns a script to be executed by the client
FileResult	FileResult	Returns the contents of a file

Returning JSON Data

Returning data from the model in JSON format is commonly required when using scripts, including those written using jQuery. You can return data as JSON simply by passing an object to the JSON helper method—although you should be careful when doing this using data model classes created by the Entity Framework or LINQ to SQL wizards. The automatically generated data models contain circular references that make navigation between data from different tables easy but that upset the JSON emitter. We have added a new action method to our controller that writes out details of a product as JSON:

```
public ActionResult JsonDetails(int id) {
    Product prod = nwa.GetProduct(id);
    if (prod == null) {
        throw new NoSuchRecordException();
    } else {
        return Json(new {
            ProductId = prod.ProductID,
            ProductName = prod.ProductName,
            SupplierID = prod.SupplierID,
            CategoryID = prod.CategoryID,
            UnitPrice = prod.UnitPrice,
            UnitsInStock = prod.UnitsInStock,
            UnitsOnOrder = prod.UnitsOnOrder,
            ReorderLevel = prod.ReorderLevel,
            Discontinued = prod.Discontinued
        }, JsonRequestBehavior.AllowGet);
    }
}
```

If you had passed in the Product instance as the argument to the Json method, you would have received an exception reporting the circular dependency. We have avoided this by creating a new anonymous type that contains just the properties we want serialized. You call this method by requesting a URL such as the following:

```
http://localhost:7474/Product/JsonDetails/1
```

You receive the following JSON data as the result:

```
{
    "ProductId":1,
    "ProductName":"Chai Tea",
    "SupplierID":1,
    "CategoryID":1,
    "UnitPrice":19.2256,
    "UnitsInStock":12,
    "UnitsOnOrder":0,
    "ReorderLevel":10,"
    Discontinued":false
}
```

When you called Json in the JsonDetails method, you supplied an additional argument with the AllowGet value from the JsonRequestBehavior enumeration. This is a security measure added to MVC 2 that requires you to explicitly enable returning JSON data for HTTP GET requests.

Calling Another Controller Method

Earlier in the chapter we showed you how to create a custom error view. That was a useful example but would have required a different view to be created for each kind of application exception—fine for a simple example but cumbersome for a real project.

We will revisit error handling to demonstrate the use of the RedirectToAction helper method. Say you want to create a more general error view that displays two strings—one to indicate the kind of problem the user has encountered and one that will be helpful to the programmer in figuring out what happened in the code. You start by creating a new method in your ProductController class:

```
public ActionResult CustomError(string message, string detail) {
    ViewData["ErrorMessage"] = message;
    ViewData["ErrorDetail"] = detail;
    return View("CustomError");
}
```

This is a very simple method—you provide a message string and a detail string that are passed to the view using the view data feature. You then call the View helper method to display a view called CustomError. Here are the contents of Views/Shared/CustomError.aspx:

```
<%@ Page Language="C#" MasterPageFile="~/Views/Shared/Site.Master"
Inherits="System.Web.Mvc.ViewPage<System.Web.Mvc.HandleErrorInfo>" %>

<asp:Content ID="errorTitle" ContentPlaceHolderID="TitleContent" runat="server">
    Error
</asp:Content>

<asp:Content ID="errorContent" ContentPlaceHolderID="MainContent" runat="server">
    <h2>
        Sorry, an error occurred while processing your request.
    </h2>
    <h3><%: ViewData["ErrorMessage"] %>  </h3>
    <h4><%: ViewData["ErrorDetail"]%></h4>
</asp:Content>
```

To demonstrate the use of the new controller method, you will update the Details method so that you use the CustomError view when dealing with a request for a nonexistent record:

```
public ActionResult Details(int id) {
    Product prod = nwa.GetProduct(id);
    if (prod == null) {
        return RedirectToAction("CustomError",
            new {
                message = "You requested an unknown product",
                detail = String.Format("No record for ID of {0}", id)
            });
    } else {
        ViewData["CatName"] = nwa.GetCategoryName(prod);
        ViewData["SupName"] = nwa.GetSupplierName(prod);
        return View(prod);
    }
}
```

When using the RedirectToAction helper method, you must supply the name of the controller method you want to call and provide an object that has properties whose names match the parameters of the target method—in our case, you created properties for message and detail since they are the parameter names for the CustomError controller method. Requesting a record that doesn't exist causes the Details method to call the CustomError method and generate the view shown in Figure 32-10.

My MVC Application
Sorry, an error occurred while processing your request.
You requested an unknown product
No record for ID of 100

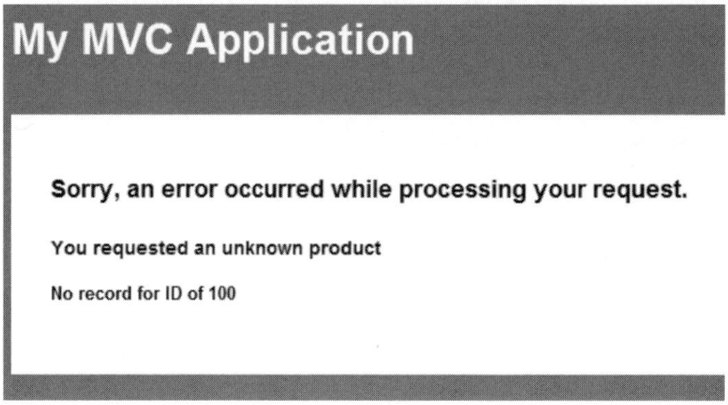

Figure 32-10. *A general-purpose error view*

Summary

In this chapter, we showed how to create a basic MVC application using the Northwind database to generate the model. We explained how to create controller classes and views and how all three components fit together. We showed you how to extend the basic application to include validation and authentication and how to route requests between controller methods—all you need to know to get up and running with MVC.

We like MVC a lot, but when starting a project, you should think carefully about what you are trying to achieve before adopting MVC in preference to web forms. And, if you are building a simple data-centric application, you should read Chapter 33 of this book, where we cover the dynamic data system—yet another alternative that mixes design elements of both MVC and web forms.

CHAPTER 33

■ ■ ■

Dynamic Data

ASP.NET Dynamic Data allows you to build data-centric web applications quickly and with very little effort. Template pages are populated by inferring type information from a data model schema, and little or no coding is required. The amount of functionality you can get with 15 minutes of work can be pretty impressive, and once the basic features have been created for you, there are extensive options for customization.

Creating a Dynamic Data Application

The best place to start with ASP.NET Dynamic Data is to create an example website. Only then can you see how easy it is to get up and running and how much functionality is available out of the box. For the examples in this chapter, we will be using the Microsoft Northwind sample database, which we have included with the source code download for this book. You can get the data and all the sample projects from Apress.com.

At the heart of an ASP.NET Dynamic Data website is a database model. You can generate the model using LINQ to SQL or the Entity Framework, which we described in Chapter 13. We will use LINQ to SQL in this chapter; we demonstrated creating the Entity Framework model in Chapter 13. The basic approach to Dynamic Data remains the same irrespective of which you use for your projects.

Creating the Dynamic Data Site

The first step is to create a new ASP.NET Dynamic Data project. Select File ➤ New ➤ Website in Visual Studio. Select the ASP.NET Dynamic Data Linq to SQL Web Site template, as shown in Figure 33-1. Clicking OK creates the project.

■ **Tip** If you have downloaded the source code to accompany this book from Apress.com, you can find the website created in this section in the Northwind1 directory for this chapter.

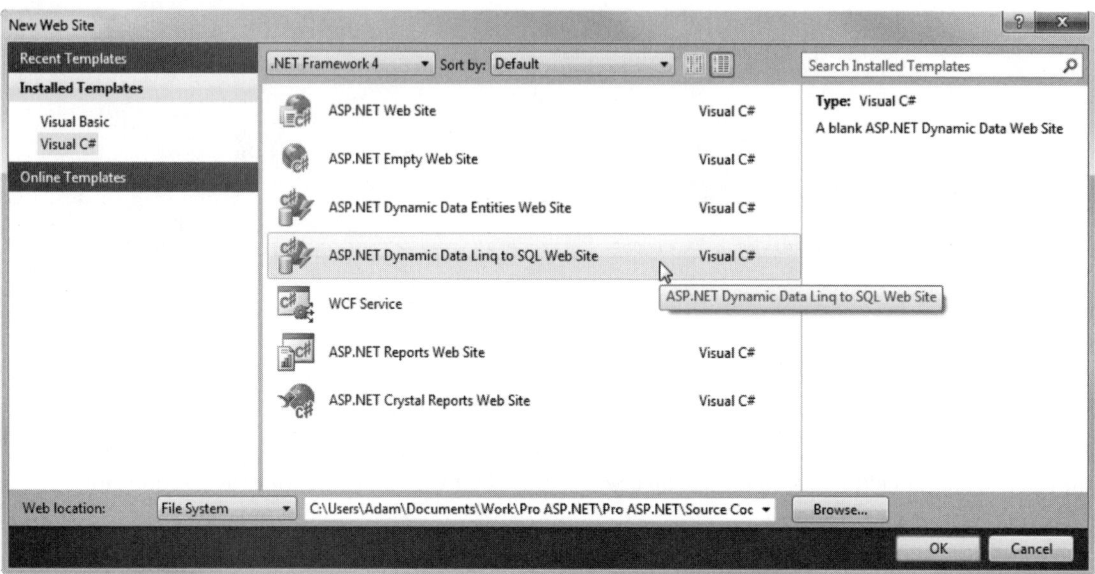

Figure 33-1. *Selecting the ASP.NET Dynamic Data Linq to SQL Web Site template*

Next, you need to import the data. Right-click the App_Data folder in the Solution Explorer, and select the Add Existing Item menu item. Navigate to where you downloaded the sample files, select the Northwind.mdf file, and click the Add button. You will see that a Northwind item will be added to the App_Data folder.

To create the data model that the Dynamic Data system will use, right-click the website icon in the Solution Explorer, select Add New Item, and choose LINQ to SQL Classes from the template list. Since you are using the Northwind database in this example, name the new item Northwind.dbml. You will see a warning dialog box prompting you to put the LINQ to SQL classes in the App_Code folder, as shown in Figure 33-2.

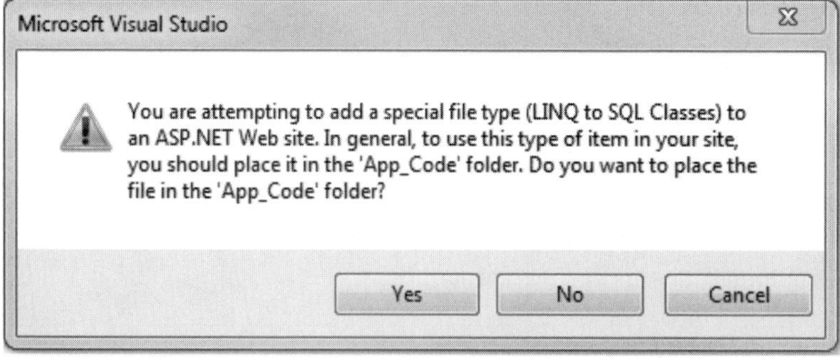

Figure 33-2. *Placing the data model classes in the App_Code folder*

Click the Yes button. The Northwind.dbml file will be created in your project, and the Object Relational Designer window will open. You now need to populate the data model with the tables you want to use from the database. Right-click the Northwind.mdf file you added earlier, and select the Open menu item to open the Server Explorer. Expand the Northwind.mdf Tables item, and drag the Customer, Order, Order_Detail, and Product tables into the designer window. Visual Studio should look like Figure 33-3, showing the tables you have imported into the data model and the foreign-key relationships between them.

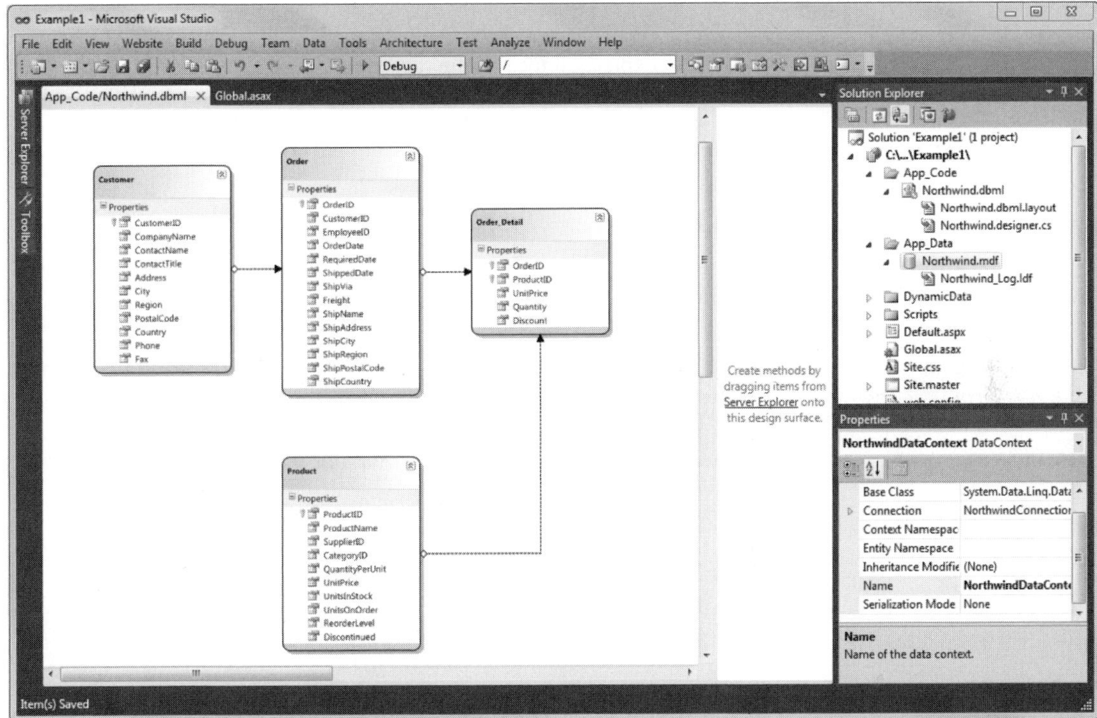

Figure 33-3. The visual representation of the data model

The last step is to register the data model you just created with the ASP.NET Dynamic Data system. Open the Global.asax file, and uncomment the line in the RegisterRoutes method that calls DefaultModel.RegisterContext, shown here:

```
public static void RegisterRoutes(RouteCollection routes) {
    //                    IMPORTANT: DATA MODEL REGISTRATION
    // Uncomment this line to register a LINQ to SQL model for ASP.NET Dynamic Data.
    // Set ScaffoldAllTables = true only if you are sure that you want all tables in the
    // data model to support a scaffold (i.e. templates) view. To control scaffolding for
    // individual tables, create a partial class for the table and apply the
    // [ScaffoldTable(true)] attribute to the partial class.
    // Note: Make sure that you change "YourDataContextType" to the name of the data context
    // class in your application.
    DefaultModel.RegisterContext(typeof(YourDataContextType),
       new ContextConfiguration() { ScaffoldAllTables = false });
```

We have highlighted the two other changes you need to make to this line. Change YouDataContextType to NorthwindDataContext and change false to true so that the uncommented line looks like this:

```
DefaultModel.RegisterContext(typeof(NorthwindDataContext),
            new ContextConfiguration() { ScaffoldAllTables = true});
```

Changing the type registers the data model. Changing the value of the ScaffoldAllTable property asks the ASP.NET Dynamic Data system to expose all four of the tables that you included in the data model to the web application. We'll show you how to be more restrictive about the tables you expose in the "Customizing with Routes" section later in the chapter. And that's it—you've created an ASP.NET Dynamic Data site. In the next section, you'll explore the result.

Exploring the Dynamic Data Site

You can look at what you created by selecting Debug ➤ Start Without Debugging in Visual Studio. A new browser window will open, and the URL for your development web server will be loaded. If you followed the instructions in the previous section, you should see something very similar to Figure 33-4.

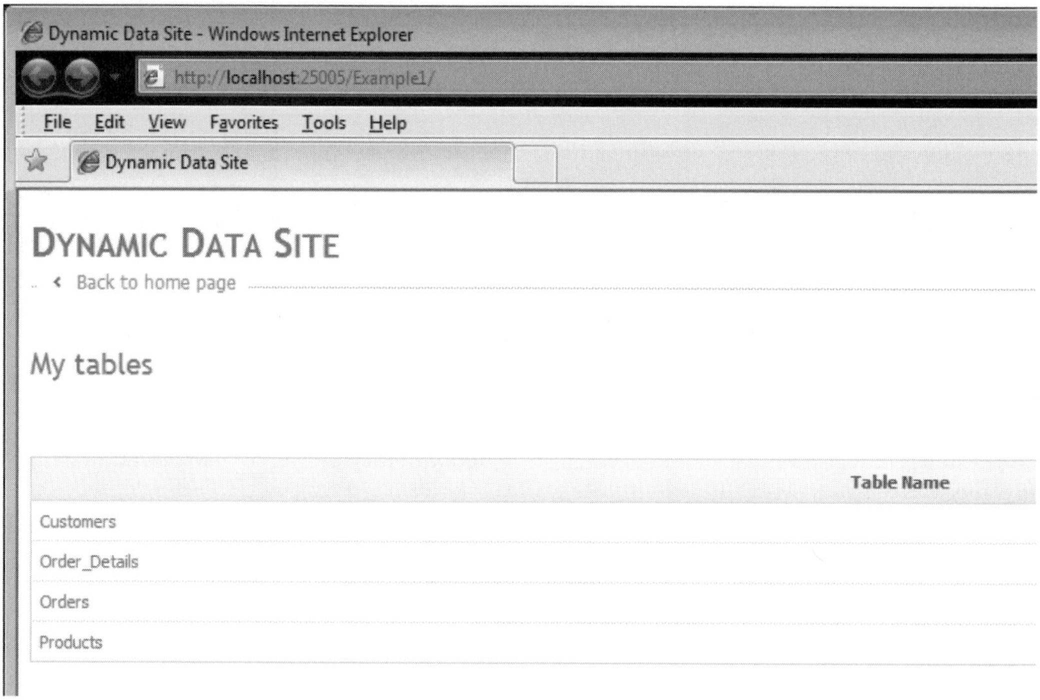

***Figure 33-4.** The home page of the ASP.NET Dynamic Data site*

What you can see is *scaffolding*—the ASP.NET Dynamic Data system has taken the four tables from your data model and built a structure around them. You can see a link for each of the tables in the default page for the site, which is Default.aspx.

Click the Customers link. You will see a page that contains the first ten records from the Northwind Customers table, as shown in Figure 33-5.

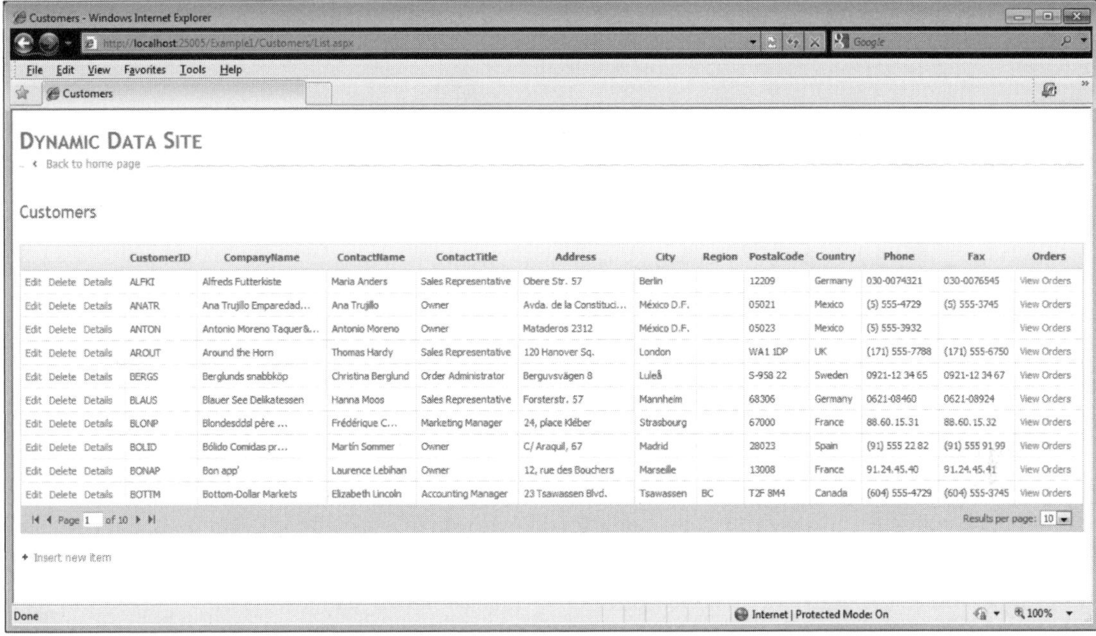

Figure 33-5. The Customers page

The ASP.NET Dynamic Data system has created the table from the data model. You can see that the columns of the table on the web page match the columns of the Customers table in the database.

The scaffolding that has been created for you lets you do some interesting things. At the bottom of the screen, you can change how many records are displayed on a page. You can also move between pages or go to a specific page.

At the left of each row are three links—Edit, Delete, and Details. Clicking Edit opens a new page where you can edit a record (and save the changes by clicking the Update link). The Details link shows you a similar page but without the ability to change the data. Delete, as you might expect, allows you to remove the data from the database. If you click one of the column headers, the data will be sorted using that column as the key.

All well and good—but take a look at the right side of the browser window. The ASP.NET Dynamic Data system has recognized the foreign-key relationship between the Customers table and the Orders table and has automatically added a View Orders link for each record. Click one of those links, and you see a page that contains all the orders for the customer you selected, as shown in Figure 33-6.

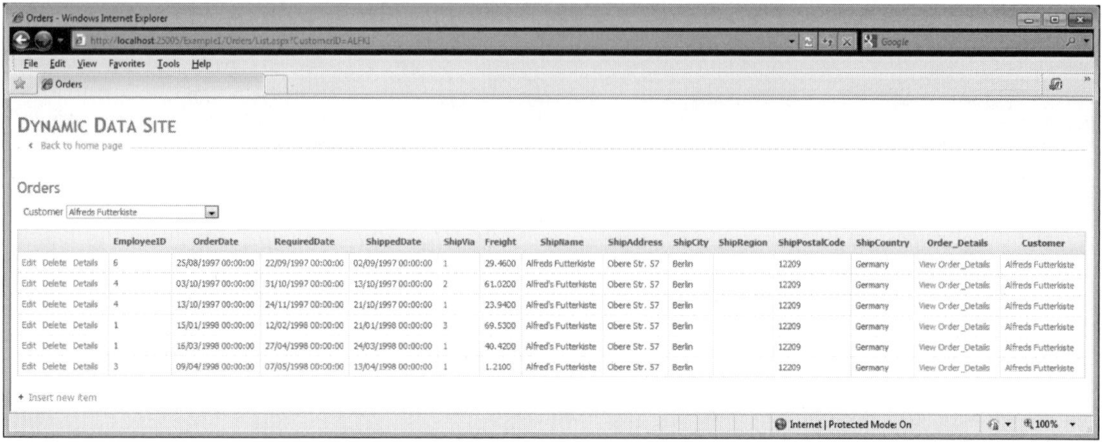

Figure 33-6. The filtered Orders page for a customer

Notice how on the right side of this page, the ASP.NET Dynamic Data system has used the data model to determine that there are two foreign-key relationships in the Orders table—one to Customers, which you used to get to this page and one with Order_Details, which shows the specifics of what a customer has ordered. Clicking an Order_Details link moves you to another page, where each record has a link to a record in the Order table and to a record in the Product table. You get the idea.

Click the Back to home page link= at the top of the page to return to the list of tables, and click the Orders link. Notice that there is a Customer drop-down box, as shown in Figure 33-7.

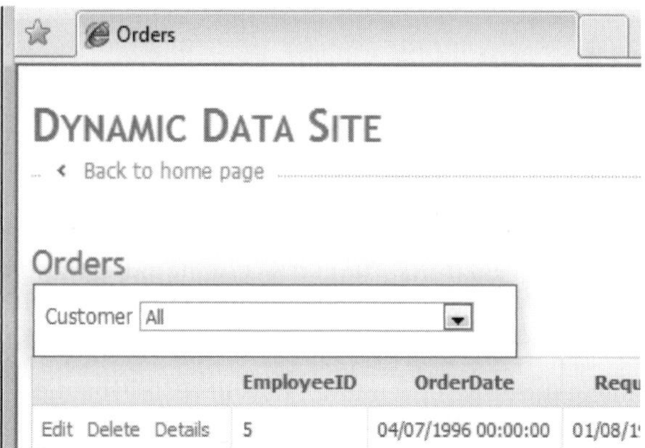

Figure 33-7. The Customer filter on the Orders page

The drop-down list contains the names of all the customers, and selecting a customer filters the data on the page to show only orders from that customer. Last, but not least, at the bottom of the page is the Insert new item link, which opens a page you can use to create new records. Once again, the ASP.NET Dynamic Data system uses the relationships between tables to make the Customer field a drop-down box that contains the names of all the customers in the database.

Understanding the Anatomy of a Dynamic Data Project

By generating a data model and changing a single line of code, you were able to create a web application that exposes tables from a database—and does so in an intelligent and useful way. You got full CRUD support and a clever use of foreign keys to make the interface more usable. We thought this was pretty cool when we first started using ASP.NET Dynamic Data, and we hope you feel the same way.

Now that you have seen what an ASP.NET Dynamic Data application looks like, it is time to take a moment to look at the project to understand the major parts.

The ASP.NET Dynamic Data system is not, as you might expect, a code-generation feature. It is actually a very flexible and configurable template system. If you look at the Visual Studio Solution Explorer window for your project, you can start to see how it works.

The App_Code directory contains the code for the application. There is nothing in there at the moment aside from the data model classes, but you'll add some code as you begin to customize the site in the following sections. The Add_Data folder contains the data source. In the case of the example project, it contains the Northwind data files.

Things start to get interesting with the DynamicData folder. Expand this in the Solution Explorer view, and then open the PageTemplates folder, which is shown in Figure 33-8.

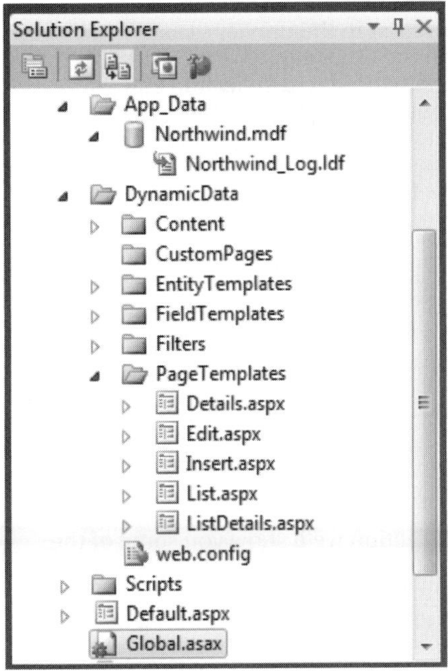

Figure 33-8. *The default page templates directory*

You will see five files. These are the pages that the ASP.NET Dynamic Data system uses to display your data. The List.aspx page is the template used to list the records in a table, the Details.aspx page is used to view the detail of a record, and so on. The one page you have not seen yet is ListDetails.aspx, which you'll use in the "Customizing with Routes" section later in the chapter. Page templates are all user controls built using the rich data controls that we discussed earlier in this book.

If you expand the other folders, you'll get a sense of how the pieces of an ASP.NET Dynamic Data site fit together. The Filters folder contains the control used to filter the rows shown in a list of records. The FieldTemplates folder contains the controls used to display different kinds of data field.

The EntityTemplates folder supports a Dynamic Data feature that is new to ASP.NET 4, called *entity templates*. Entity templates are markup consumed by the DynamicData control to format data elements. We'll show you how to use these in the "Using Entity Templates" section of this chapter.

The CustomPages folder supports one of the mechanisms for customizing an ASP.NET Dynamic Data site. You can place your own page templates in this folder to customize the way that data is displayed. We explain the use of this folder in the "Creating Custom Templates" section.

The final folder, Content, contains the static elements used to render the display as well the control that is used to page through lists of records.

The remaining item of note is the Global.asax file. This file is especially important in an ASP.NET Dynamic Data project because it is used to register the data model, as you saw when you created a site earlier in the chapter. It is also used to register routes, a topic we explore in the "Customizing with Routes" section of this chapter.

Customizing a Dynamic Data Site

We want to make three points by breaking out the project structure in the previous section. The first is that a Dynamic Data application is built on ASP.NET, just like all the other sites you have built in this book. Second, Dynamic Data relies on a series of templates, which are used to display and edit your data. The third point, which is the topic this section, is that just about everything in a Dynamic Data application can be customized. In fact, there are so many different ways of extending, changing, and tailoring a Dynamic Data application that it can be difficult to decide which to use. In the following sections, we'll show you some of the different techniques available to change the appearance and behavior of a Dynamic Data application.

■ **Tip** If you have downloaded the source code to accompany this book from Apress.com, you can find the website we create in this section in the Northwind2 directory for this chapter.

Customizing with Templates

Templates are essential to Dynamic Data applications, and in this section we'll show you some of the different ways that you can use templates to customize the way your data is presented to clients. Some of these techniques modify existing templates, others require new templates, and some use code to extend the behavior of the application. All of these methods help underline the flexibility of the ASP.NET Dynamic Data system, which has been designed to make these tasks (relatively) painless.

Editing the Default Templates

The DynamicData\PageTemplates folder contains the templates that are used by default to display, edit, and create data records. A change to one of these templates affects all the tables in the data model that use the defaults.

As a simple example, open the List.aspx default template, and switch to the Design view. Click the GridView in the middle of the page, and then click the small edit arrow that appears at the right edge of the grid to open the GridView Tasks menu, as shown in Figure 33-9.

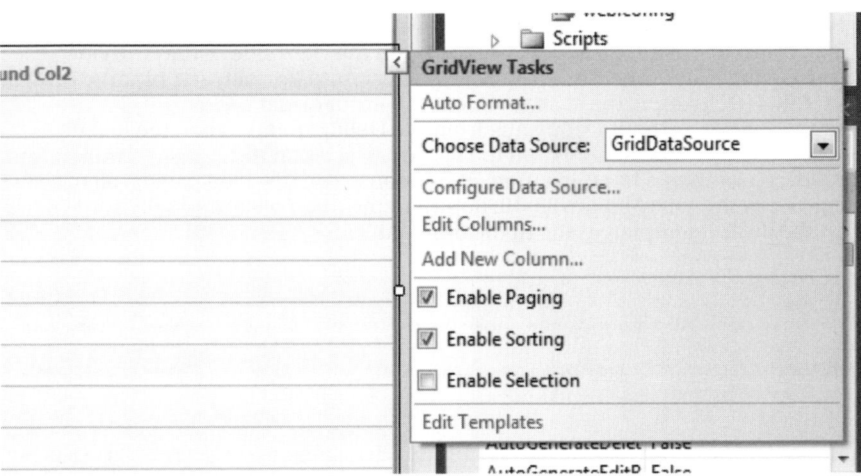

Figure 33-9. The GridView Tasks menu

Using this menu, you can change the basic behavior of the GridView. For example, if you deselect the Enable Paging option, then all the records will be displayed in a long list when you view a table. If you deselect the Enable Sorting option, then you won't be able to sort the rows by clicking a column header.

Let's make a simple but distinctive change by selecting the Auto Format option. This will open the AutoFormat dialog box, which allows you to apply predefined styles to the GridView. Select the Classic style from the list, and click OK. Select Start Without Debugging from the Debug menu, and click any of the table names from the main page when it loads in the browser.

■ **Tip** Before you select Start Without Debugging, right-click the Default.aspx page in the Solution Explorer window, and select Set As Start Page from the menu. If you are editing a template page and start debugging, Visual Studio will try to load the page you are editing, which will usually throw an exception.

If you look at the tables one by one, you will see that the formatting change you applied has affected the list view for all the tables in the data model. This is what you would hope for when you modify a default template. The other views—Edit, Update, and so on—remain unchanged, as does Default.aspx.

Creating a Custom Page Template

Changing the default template is all well and good, but what if you want to customize the way that just one table is handled? One approach is to create a custom page template and place it in the DynamicData\CustomPages folder.

Let's say that you want to use different templates for the Products table. Expand the Solution Explorer so that you can see the DynamicData\CustomPages folder. Right-click CustomPages, select New Folder from the menu, and name the folder Products. Open the PageTemplates folder, copy the List.aspx page, and paste a copy into the newly created Products folder.

Double-click the copy you just made of List.aspx—take care to ensure that you are editing the file you just copied and not the default template. Click the tasks arrow on the right side of the GridView control, and deselect Enable Paging. Click the tasks arrow again, select Auto Format, and pick the Brown Sugar scheme from the list. Click OK to apply the style and close the AutoFormat dialog.

Save the page file, and select Start Without Debugging from the Debug menu. When the default page loads in the browser, select the Products table from the list. You'll see that the custom template you created is applied. The brown color scheme has been used, and because you disabled paging, all the records are shown in a long list, as shown by Figure 33-10. Return to the main page, and select one of the other tables. You'll see that the default template is for all the other tables.

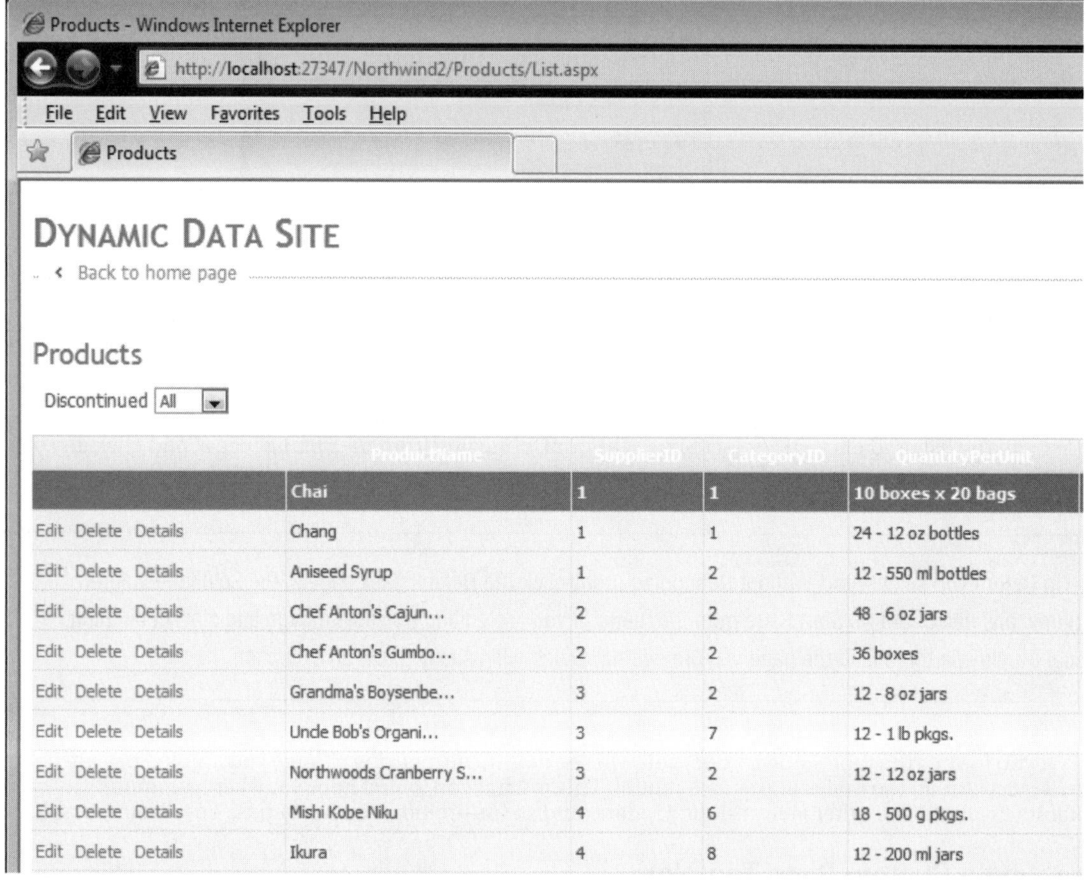

***Figure 33-10.** Applying a custom template*

That's how simple it is to create a custom page template. First, create a folder with the name of the table you want the new template to apply to. Second, copy one of the default templates into the folder and modify it. You can have a custom template to match each of the default templates. For example, if you copied the default Edit.aspx template into the Products folder, you would have created custom templates for the List and Edit actions.

Using Entity Templates

Entity templates are new to ASP.NET 4 and allow you to control the layout of data elements on a page without needing to create an entirely new template.

If you look at the default Edit.aspx, Insert.aspx, and Details.aspx templates, you will see that they use the DynamicEntity control. Figure 33-11 shows the component in the Design view of the Edit.aspx template.

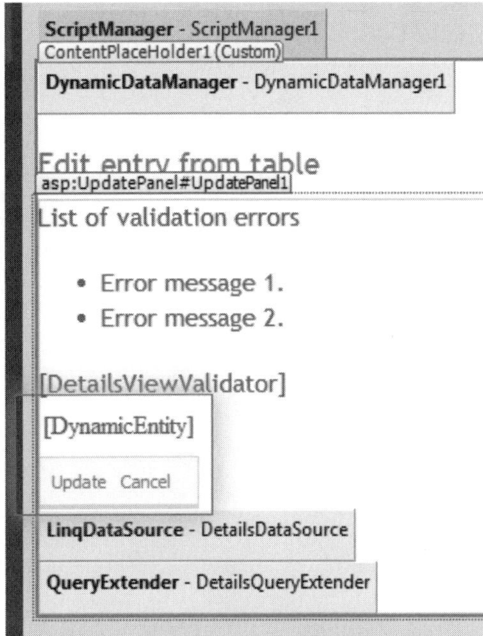

Figure 33-11. The DynamicEntity component in the Edit.aspx template

If you look at the Source view, you will see the following statement:

```
<asp:DynamicEntity runat="server" Mode="Edit" />
```

The DynamicEntity control generates the view for each data element to be displayed. There are three modes (Default, Edit, and Insert), which correspond to the three files in the DynamicData\EntityTemplates folder (Default.ascx, Default_Edit.ascx, Default_Insert.ascx).

Changing one of these control templates changes the way that data elements are displayed for all tables. Take a look at Default.ascx, which you can see here:

```
<%@ Control Language="C#" CodeFile="Default.ascx.cs" Inherits="DefaultEntityTemplate" %>

<asp:EntityTemplate runat="server" ID="EntityTemplate1">
    <ItemTemplate>
        <tr class="td">
            <td class="DDLightHeader">
                <asp:Label runat="server" OnInit="Label_Init" />
            </td>
```

```
            <td>
                <asp:DynamicControl runat="server" OnInit="DynamicControl_Init" />
            </td>
        </tr>
    </ItemTemplate>
</asp:EntityTemplate>
```

In a page template where this entity template is used, each field will be displayed in two columns. The first column will list the name of the field (the database table column name), and the second column will list the value. The Details.aspx page template uses the Default.ascx element template, so when you click the Details link for a row in any of your tables, you get something similar to Figure 33-12.

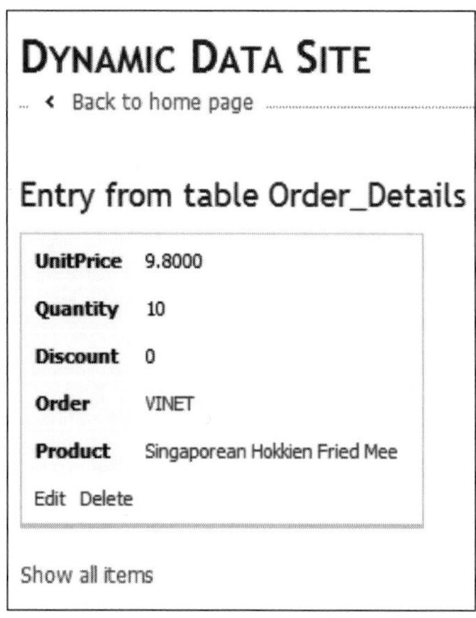

Figure 33-12. *The standard Default.ascx entity template*

If you change this entity template, you will change the appearance of every data element that is rendered in this way. Let's edit the template to add some additional structure, shown here:

```
<%@ Control Language="C#" CodeFile="Default.ascx.cs" Inherits="DefaultEntityTemplate" %>

<asp:EntityTemplate runat="server" ID="EntityTemplate1">
    <ItemTemplate>
        <tr class="td">
            <td class="DDLightHeader">
                <asp:Label runat="server" Text="Field name:" />
            </td>
            <td>
                <asp:Label runat="server" OnInit="Label_Init" />
            </td>
            <td class="DDLightHeader">
                <asp:Label runat="server" Text="Field value:" />
            </td>
```

```
            <td>
                <asp:DynamicControl runat="server" OnInit="DynamicControl_Init" />
            </td>
        </tr>
    </ItemTemplate>
</asp:EntityTemplate>
```

All you have done here is add a Field name and Field value header. If you save these changes and then view the details of a data record, you can see the effect of the changes, as shown in Figure 33-13.

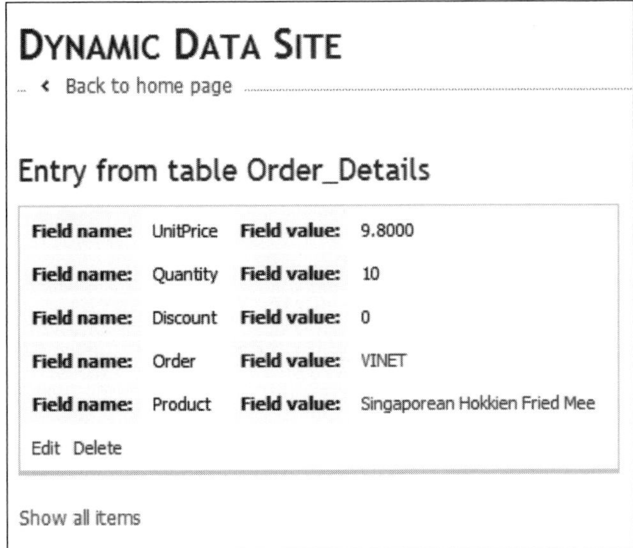

Figure 33-13. *The results of changing the entity template*

If you look at the details view for different tables, you'll see that all of them were affected when you changed the entity template. If you want to change the way data elements are displayed for a single table, then you need to create a new entity template.

When changing a generic entity template, you must be careful to leave the DynamicControl in place. This is because the template will be used with a range of tables, and you don't know in advance what the structure of the table will be. In creating a template for a single table, you can make reference to individual columns of the table and be incredibly specific in what you include or exclude.

Let's create a custom entity template for the Products table. To do this, right-click the EntityTemplates folder, select Add New Item, and pick Web User Control from the templates list. The name of the entity template must match the database table that you want it to apply to, in this case, use Products.ascx.

Copy the following markup into Products.ascx. The listing contains four table rows, each of which contains a named reference to a column in the Products database table, specified using the DataField property of DynamicControl.

```
<%@ Control Language="C#" AutoEventWireup="true" CodeFile="Products.ascx.cs"
Inherits="DynamicData_EntityTemplates_Products" %>

<tr class="td">
    <td class="DDLightHeader">
        <asp:Label ID="Label1" runat="server" Text="Product Name" />
    </td>
    <td>
        <asp:DynamicControl ID="DynamicControl1" runat="server" DataField="ProductName" />
    </td>
</tr>
<tr class="td">
    <td class="DDLightHeader">
        <asp:Label ID="Label2" runat="server" Text="Price per Unit" />
    </td>
    <td>
        <asp:DynamicControl ID="DynamicControl2" runat="server" DataField="UnitPrice" />
    </td>
</tr>
<tr class="td">
    <td class="DDLightHeader">
        <asp:Label ID="Label3" runat="server" Text="Discontinued?" />
    </td>
    <td>
        <asp:DynamicControl ID="DynamicControl3" runat="server" DataField="Discontinued" />
    </td>
</tr>
<tr class="td">
    <td class="DDLightHeader">
        <asp:Label ID="Label4" runat="server" Text="Units in Stock" />
    </td>
    <td>
        <asp:DynamicControl ID="DynamicControl4" runat="server" DataField="UnitsInStock" />
    </td>
</tr>
```

Open the code-behind file Products.ascx.cs, add a using statement for the System.Web.DynamicData namespace, and change the base class to EntityTemplateUserControl, as shown here:

```
using System;
using System.Collections.Generic;
using System.Linq;
using System.Web;
using System.Web.UI;
using System.Web.UI.WebControls;
using System.Web.DynamicData;

public partial class DynamicData_EntityTemplates_Products : EntityTemplateUserControl
{
    protected void Page_Load(object sender, EventArgs e)
    {

    }
}
```

Save all the changes, and select Start Without Debugging from the Debug menu. When the browser has loaded the Default.aspx page, select the Products table from the list, and click Details for one of the records shown. If you have followed along, the custom entity template should be applied, and you should see something very similar to Figure 33-14.

Figure 33-14. *Applying a custom entity template*

■ **Tip** In this case, you created a default entity template for the Products table. If you wanted to create a custom replacement for one of the other defaults, you would have had to follow the naming convention. For example, to create a custom entity template for editing the Products table, you would have had to create a template called Products_Edit.ascx in the EntityTemplates folder.

Customizing Field Templates

If you expand the DynamicData\FieldTemplates folder in the Solution Explorer, you will see the set of default field templates, as shown in Figure 33-15. In the same way that entity templates control the appearance of data rows, field templates control the appearance of individual data types.

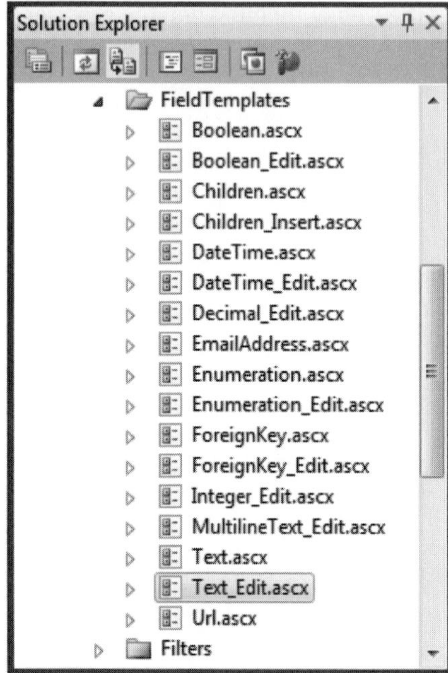

Figure 33-15. *The default field templates*

The Dynamic Data system uses the types in the data model to infer which template should be used to display a field. The best way to understand this is to make a customization. Open the Text_Edit.ascx template, which we have highlighted in Figure 33-15. Change your template so that it matches the following one. We have highlighted the required changes, which set the background color to gray and the foreground color to white.

```
<%@ Control Language="C#" CodeFile="Text_Edit.ascx.cs" Inherits="Text_EditField" %>

<asp:TextBox ID="TextBox1" runat="server" Text='<%# FieldValueEditString %>'
CssClass="DDTextBox" BackColor="Gray" ForeColor="White"></asp:TextBox>

<asp:RequiredFieldValidator runat="server" ID="RequiredFieldValidator1" CssClass="DDControl
DDValidator" ControlToValidate="TextBox1" Display="Static" Enabled="false" />
<asp:RegularExpressionValidator runat="server" ID="RegularExpressionValidator1"
CssClass="DDControl DDValidator" ControlToValidate="TextBox1" Display="Static"
Enabled="false" />
<asp:DynamicValidator runat="server" ID="DynamicValidator1" CssClass="DDControl DDValidator"
ControlToValidate="TextBox1" Display="Static" />
```

Save the changes, and select Start Without Debugging from the Debug menu. When the browser has loaded the project start page, select one of the tables from the list, and click Edit for one of the data rows. You will see something similar to Figure 33-16.

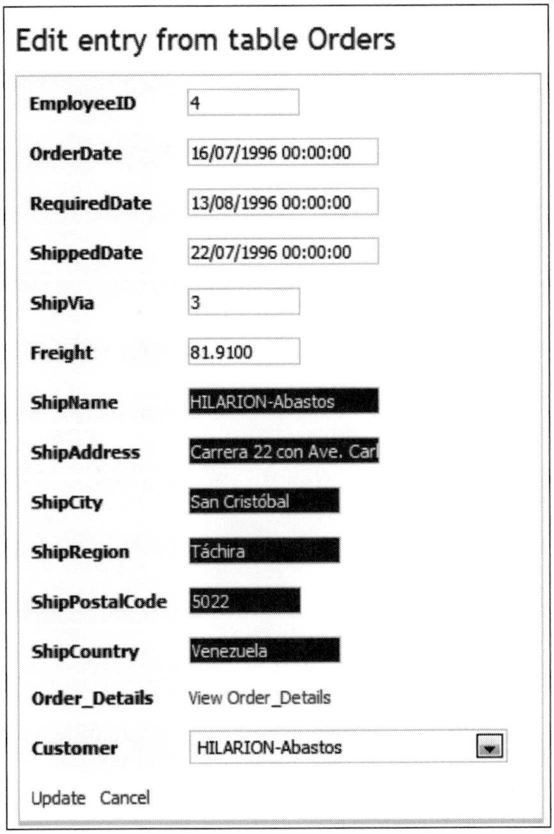

Figure 33-16. *Changing a field template*

You will see that some of the fields have the new color scheme. These are the text fields, which makes sense since you modified the Text_Edit field template. If you had wanted to change all the fields, you would have had to change Decimal_Edit, Integer_Edit, and so on, as well.

By modifying the field templates whose name ends with _Edit, you specify how certain kinds of fields are displayed when you are editing or inserting a record. If you want to change the display for the details view, you need to edit the field templates that don't have an _Edit suffix, such as Text.ascx or Boolean.ascx.

Double-click the Boolean.ascx template, and add a BackColor attribute to the markup so that the content of the file matches the following:

```
<%@ Control Language="C#" CodeFile="Boolean.ascx.cs" Inherits="BooleanField" %>

<asp:CheckBox runat="server" ID="CheckBox1" Enabled="false"  BackColor="Blue"/>
```

Save the changes, and select Start Without Debugging from the Debug menu. Select the Products table from the list when the browser has loaded the start page, and then click the Details link for one of the records in the list. You should see something similar to Figure 33-17, depending on the row you picked.

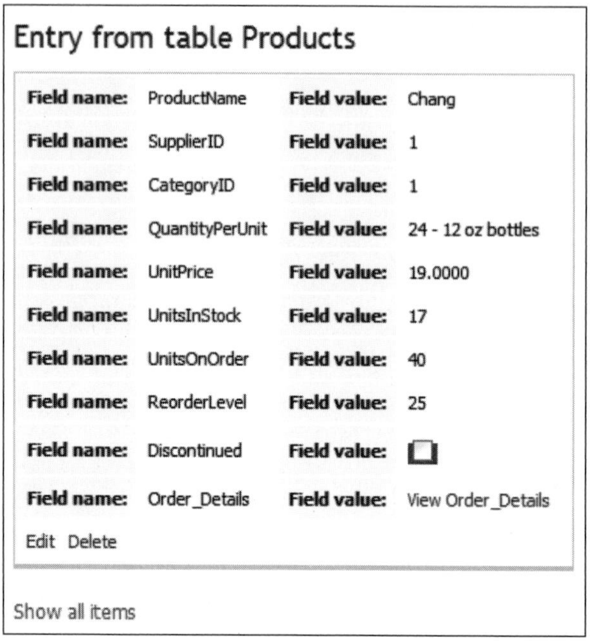

Entry from table Products

Field name:	ProductName	**Field value:**	Chang
Field name:	SupplierID	**Field value:**	1
Field name:	CategoryID	**Field value:**	1
Field name:	QuantityPerUnit	**Field value:**	24 - 12 oz bottles
Field name:	UnitPrice	**Field value:**	19.0000
Field name:	UnitsInStock	**Field value:**	17
Field name:	UnitsOnOrder	**Field value:**	40
Field name:	ReorderLevel	**Field value:**	25
Field name:	Discontinued	**Field value:**	☐
Field name:	Order_Details	**Field value:**	View Order_Details

Edit Delete

Show all items

Figure 33-17. *Modifying a nonediting field template*

You can't create a field template that applies only to a given type in a given table just by creating a new file. You can't create a template that is used only for Booleans in the Products table, for example. But you can achieve this effect by using metadata. See the "Customizing with Metadata" section for details.

Customizing with Routes

The ASP.NET Dynamic Data system uses the ASP.NET routes feature to map requests to page templates. You can use this feature to customize a number of aspects of your data-driven site. Routes can be hard to get your head around. Certainly, it took us some time to get comfortable with them. In the following sections, we'll explain how they work and the kinds of customization you can perform with them.

■ **Tip** If you have downloaded the source code to accompany this book from Apress.com, you can find the website we create in this section in the Northwind3 directory for this chapter.

Understanding Routes

Routes allow you to define the URLs that your Dynamic Data applications will support and the conditions under which they will be used. Here is a sample route:

```
routes.Add(new DynamicDataRoute("AllRows.aspx") {
    Action = PageAction.List,
    ViewName = "List",
    Model = DefaultModel
});
```

Routes are mappings between URLs that clients call and page templates. The constructor argument to the DynamicDataRoute class specifies the client URL that you want to map, relative to the application URL, which in this case is AllRows.aspx. This means that any URL that reaches your Dynamic Data application and ends with AllRows.aspx should use this mapping. The properties you set on the DynamicDataRoute tell ASP.NET what the mapping is for and when it should be applied.

The Action property specifies what the route is for, expressed as a value from the PageAction enumeration. The values in the enumeration are Details, Edit, Insert, and List. By setting the Action property to PageAction.List, you are telling the ASP.NET Dynamic Data system that it can use this URL to list the rows in a table.

The ViewName property is the name of the page template to which you want to map the URL. You have specified the List template, which is mapped to the List.aspx template in the PageTemplates folder or, if you have supplied a table-specific custom template, to the matching List.aspx template in the CustomTemplates folder.

The Model property is the data model to which you want this URL to apply. We are using only one data model in this chapter, although the ASP.NET Dynamic Data system will work with more than one. For all of our examples, you will set this value to DefaultModel.

In an ASP.NET Dynamic Data application, routes are defined in the RegisterRoutes method in the Global.asax file. You call the Add method on the RouteCollection instance that is passed in as an argument to the RegisterRoutes method with the name routes.

When the ASP.NET Dynamic Data system creates the scaffolding for your application, it tries to find a route that can be used for each of the CRUD actions for each of the tables in your data model. If it finds a route, it knows it can enable that CRUD action on that table. No route found means that the action is not available on that table.

The simplest way to explain this is with an example.

Open the Global.asax file, and scroll down until you see the RegisterRoutes method. Comment out the route definition that starts with routes.Add, the one that defines the URL {table}/{action}.aspx. Make sure you comment out all four code lines. Copy the sample route definition shown previously into the RegisterRoutes method so that your method looks exactly the same as the following one. We have highlighted the sections that you need to add or comment out.

```
public static void RegisterRoutes(RouteCollection routes) {
    //                    IMPORTANT: DATA MODEL REGISTRATION
    // Uncomment this line to register a LINQ to SQL model for ASP.NET Dynamic Data.
    // Set ScaffoldAllTables = true only if you are sure that you want all tables in the
    // data model to support a scaffold (i.e. templates) view. To control scaffolding for
    // individual tables, create a partial class for the table and apply the
    // [ScaffoldTable(true)] attribute to the partial class.
    // Note: Make sure that you change "YourDataContextType" to the name of the data context
    // class in your application.
    DefaultModel.RegisterContext(typeof(NorthwindDataContext),
        new ContextConfiguration() { ScaffoldAllTables = true});
```

```
        routes.Add(new DynamicDataRoute("AllRows.aspx") {
            Action = PageAction.List,
            ViewName = "List",
            Model = DefaultModel
        });

        // The following statement supports separate-page mode, where the List, Detail, Insert,
        // and Update tasks are performed by using separate pages. To enable this mode,
        // uncomment the following route definition, and comment out the route definitions in
        // the combined-page mode section that follows.
        //routes.Add(new DynamicDataRoute("{table}/{action}.aspx") {
        //    Constraints = new RouteValueDictionary(new { action = "List|Details|Edit|Insert" }),
        //    Model = DefaultModel,
        //});

        // The following statements support combined-page mode, where the List, Detail, Insert,
        // and Update tasks are performed by using the same page. To enable this mode, uncomment
        // the following routes and comment out the route definition in the separate-page mode
        // section above.
        //routes.Add(new DynamicDataRoute("{table}/ListDetails.aspx") {
        //    Action = PageAction.List,
        //    ViewName = "ListDetails",
        //    Model = DefaultModel
        //});

        //routes.Add(new DynamicDataRoute("{table}/ListDetails.aspx") {
        //    Action = PageAction.Details,
        //    ViewName = "ListDetails",
        //    Model = DefaultModel
        //});
    }
```

Save the changes, and select Run Without Debugging from the Debug menu. Hover the mouse over the names of the tables in the list. You should see that the URL is something like this:

```
http://localhost:27294/Northwind3/AllRows.aspx?Table=Customers
```

This is the URL you mapped with your route in Global.asax. The ASP.NET Dynamic Data system has looked for routes that map URLs with the PageAction.List action and has found the one you defined. Click the link for the Customers table. Although the list display may look familiar, there is a significant change. Try clicking the Edit or Details link for one of the rows. They don't go anywhere, which is because you have not defined any routes that provide access to the page templates for editing or viewing the details of data rows.

Changing the URL Format

One of the customizations you can do with routes is to change the URL format. You can see that the sample route we opened this section with led to the previously shown URL, with the ASP.NET Dynamic Data system supplying the name of the table to work on as a URL parameter. Change the route in Global.asax so that it looks like the following one (we have emphasized the change):

```
routes.Add(new DynamicDataRoute("{table}/{action}/AllRows.aspx") {

    Action = PageAction.List,
    ViewName = "List",
    Model = DefaultModel
});
```

Save the changes, and start the application again. This time, when you hover over the table names in the list, the URL format will be as follows:

```
http://localhost:27294/Northwind3/Products/List/AllRows.aspx
```

The {table} and {action} tags are used to construct the URL. Once the table name has been included in the URL, the ASP.NET Dynamic Data system doesn't need to include it as a parameter. If this all seems odd, it is because the way a route appears in a code listing creates an impression that you are defining an action to go with a URL. In fact, a route defines a URL that can be used to reach one or more templates, and the ASP.NET Dynamic Data system looks through all the routes you have defined to work out which ones have to be called to perform the actions required for the scaffolding.

Constraining a Route

You can also make routes apply to only one table by supplying a value to the Table property of the DynamicDataRoute class. Change the route in Global.asax to match the following:

```
routes.Add(new DynamicDataRoute("AllRows.aspx") {
    Action = PageAction.List,
    ViewName = "List",
    Model = DefaultModel,
    Table = "Products"
});
```

We've highlighted the addition to the route, which now applies only to the Products table. Select Start Without Debugging from the Debug menu, and you should see something similar to Figure 33-18.

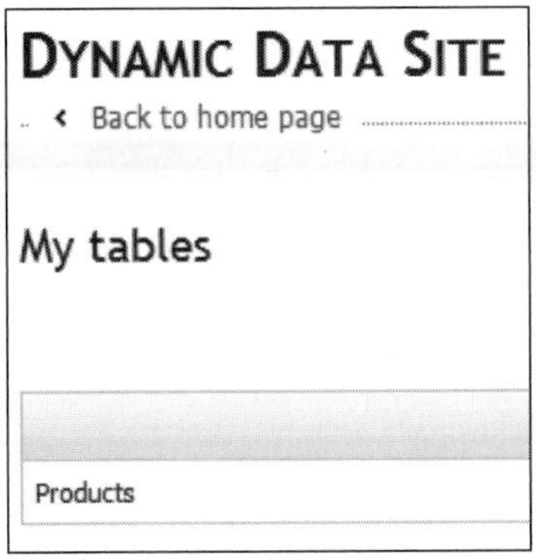

DYNAMIC DATA SITE

‹ Back to home page

My tables

Products

Figure 33-18. *The effect of constraining the single route to a single table*

Only the Products table has been exposed. This is because the only route you have created is now limited to the Products table. Remember, the ASP.NET Dynamic Data system looks for routes for each of the CRUD actions for each of the tables. In this case, it has found a route that supports the List ("read" in CRUD terms) action on the Products table. Since no routes are available for any actions for the other tables, they cannot be exposed.

If you want to create a route that applies to multiple actions or multiple tables, you need to use the DynamicDataRoute.Constraints property, which requires an instance of the RouteValueDictionary class. To make a route work for the List and Details actions for the Products and Orders tables, you would use the Constraints property, as shown here:

```
routes.Add(new DynamicDataRoute("{table}/{action}.aspx") {
    Model = DefaultModel,
    Constraints = new RouteValueDictionary(
        new {
            action = "List|Details",
            table = "Products|Orders"
        })
});
```

You pass a new anonymous type to the constructor for RouteValueDictionary that contains string properties with the names of the DynamicDataRoute properties you want to set. Unlike the DynamicDataRoute properties, you can specify multiple values in the RouteValueDictionary by using the bar sign as a separator. You assign the RouteValueDictionary you have created to the DynamicDataRoute.Constraints property.

This route exposes the List and Details page templates for the Products and Orders tables. Two little tricks make this route work. First, when using constraints like this, you have to use the {table} and {action} tags in the URL format; otherwise, the ASP.NET Dynamic Data system doesn't construct the URLs properly. Second, the template name defaults to the action name if you omit the ViewName property (which specifies the name of the page template to use). So, in this route, the List action is mapped to the List.aspx template, which is exactly the behavior you want.

If you make the route the only one in Global.asax and select Start Without Debugging from the Debug menu, you'll see the new route take effect. You will see that both the Orders and Products tables appear in the main list and that the Details links in the lists of rows work.

You now know enough about routes to understand the default route we had you comment out at the start of this section, which we have repeated here:

```
routes.Add(new DynamicDataRoute("{table}/{action}.aspx") {
    Constraints = new RouteValueDictionary(new { action = "List|Details|Edit|Insert" }),
    Model = DefaultModel,
});
```

This route applies to all tables (because there is no Table property or constraint) and can be used for the List, Details, Edit, and Insert actions. These actions will be mapped to the default page template names, and the URL format that the route supports includes both the action and the name of the table to which it applies.

So, that's how routes work. If you don't quite understand what we've shown you here, don't worry. Carry on reading, and you'll see more examples of how routes can be used, which will help make the way that routes function clearer.

Switching to Single-Page Editing

When you create a new Dynamic Data project, Global.asax contains three routes, two of which are commented out. In this section, you are going to change two of the default routes to change the editing mode of your site. Comment out all the routes in Global.asax except for the two shown here, and save the changes:

```
routes.Add(new DynamicDataRoute("{table}/ListDetails.aspx") {
    Action = PageAction.List,
    ViewName = "ListDetails",
    Model = DefaultModel
});

routes.Add(new DynamicDataRoute("{table}/ListDetails.aspx") {
    Action = PageAction.Details,
    ViewName = "ListDetails",
    Model = DefaultModel
});
```

The first route exposes the ListDetails.asax template for use with the List action for all tables. The second route exposes the same template for use with the Details action, also for all tables. (As a reminder, you know that these routes apply to all tables because there is no value set for the Tables and Constraints properties.)

These routes might seem odd. After all, they point to the same page template but support different actions. And what happened to the other actions? The answer is all in the template. The ListDetails.aspx page template handles all the actions in a single page. Select Start Without Debugging from the Debug menu, and you can take a look.

Click one of the table names, and you'll see the familiar records listing. But click the Edit button, and you'll see the first change. Editing is now done in-line, as opposed to being handled by a different page template. It's the same with the Select link; click Select for a data row, and scroll down the page. You'll see the record details in a box beneath the table rows.

The reason you have two routes using the same page template is because the template has been designed to support multiple actions in-line. The reason that you only need routes for the Details and List actions is that the others are handled by Ajax in the ListDetails page template. This is a good example of how the features of a page template and the Dynamic Data routes can be combined.

Using Different Templates for Tables

When the ASP.NET Dynamic Data system processes routes, it looks at each of the page actions for each of the tables and stops when it finds a match for each one. This means that the first route that supports an action for a table is the one that will be used. You can use this to exert fine-grained control over which templates are used. Edit Global.asax so that the RegisterRoutes method matches the one shown here:

```
public static void RegisterRoutes(RouteCollection routes) {

    DefaultModel.RegisterContext(typeof(NorthwindDataContext),
        new ContextConfiguration() { ScaffoldAllTables = true});

    // route 1
    routes.Add(new DynamicDataRoute("Products/{action}.aspx") {
        Constraints = new RouteValueDictionary(new { action = "List|Details|Edit|Insert" }),
        Model = DefaultModel,
        Table = "Products"
    });
```

```
    // route 2
    routes.Add(new DynamicDataRoute("{table}/ListDetails.aspx") {
        Action = PageAction.List,
        ViewName = "ListDetails",
        Model = DefaultModel
    });

    // route 3
    routes.Add(new DynamicDataRoute("{table}/ListDetails.aspx") {
        Action = PageAction.Details,
        ViewName = "ListDetails",
        Model = DefaultModel
    });
}
```

To understand what effect these routes will have, let's walk through the discovery process that the ASP.NET Dynamic Data system follows, looking for each of the actions for each of the tables in the data model. We have numbered each route in the comments in the listing.

Let's start with the Customers table. Working down the list of routes, can you find a match for the Details, Edit, Insert, and List actions? Route 1 applies only to the Products table, so no match there. Route 2 applies to all tables and supports the List action—that's a match. Route 3 applies to all tables and supports the Details action—that's another match. There are no matches for the Edit and Insert actions.

Repeating the process for the Orders and Order_Details tables gives you the same result. Route 1 doesn't match, but routes 2 and 3 each support one of the actions you are looking for.

For the Products table, you get a different result. Route 1 applies to this table (because of the value of the Table property), and for each of the four actions, you get a match (because of the values in the RouteValueDictionary). Following this through gives you the results shown in Table 33-1.

Table 33-1. *Route Discovery by Table*

Tables	Action	Route	Page Template
Customers, Orders, Order_Details	List	2	ListDetails.aspx
Customers, Orders, Order_Details	Details	3	ListDetails.aspx
Customers, Orders, Order_Details	Edit	No match	
Customers, Orders, Order_Details	Insert	No match	
Products	List	1	List.aspx
Products	Details	1	Details.aspx
Products	Edit	1	Edit.aspx
Products	Insert	1	Insert.aspx

Select Start Without Debugging from the Debug menu, and explore the results. If you click the Products table, you will see that it is displayed using the multipage templates, such that editing or viewing the details of a record takes you to different pages. The other tables use the single-page Ajax-enabled template.

Using routes to match tables to templates is compatible with creating custom page templates. The routes determine the name of the template that will be used, but the CustomTemplates folder is still checked to see whether a custom template exists. To demonstrate this, let's create a custom template for the Orders table.

Right-click the DynamicData\CustomPages folder in the Solution Explorer, select New Folder, and change the name of the folder to Orders. Copy the List.aspx file from the DynamicData\PageTemplates folder, copy the List.aspx file, and paste it into the Orders folder you just created so that your Solution Explorer window looks like the one shown in Figure 33-19.

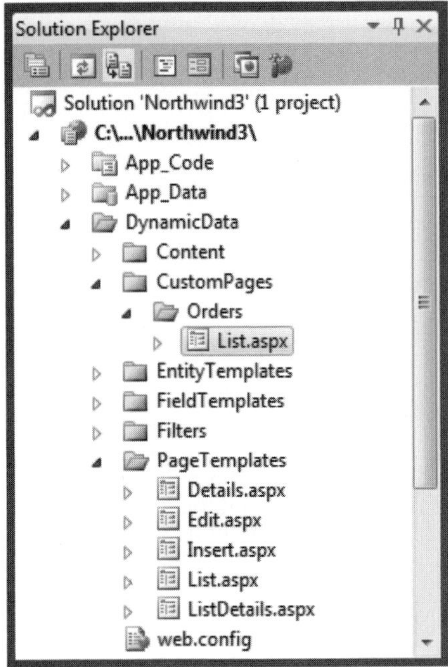

Figure 33-19. *Copying the List.aspx page template*

Edit the newly copied template so that you can tell it is the custom one; we have added a text message, as shown in Figure 33-20.

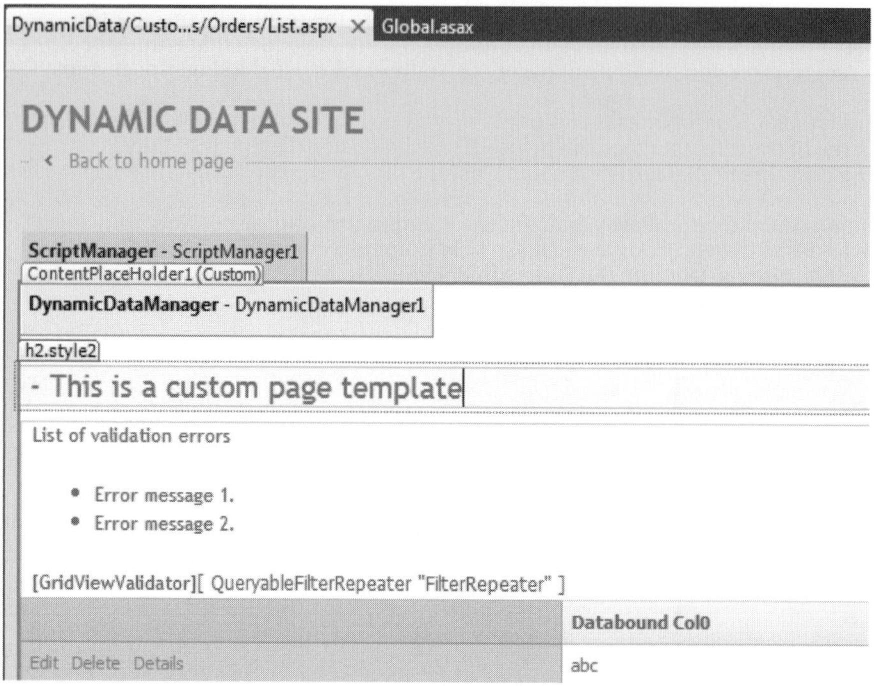

Figure 33-20. Modifying the custom page template

Now that you have your custom template, you can define your routes. Replace the RegisterRoutes method in Global.asax with the following one. We have modified route 1 to support both the Products and Orders tables; this included changing the URL format that the route maps so that the ASP.NET Dynamic Data system can include both the table name and the action without conflicting with the formats mapped by the other routes.

```
public static void RegisterRoutes(RouteCollection routes) {

    DefaultModel.RegisterContext(typeof(NorthwindDataContext),
        new ContextConfiguration() { ScaffoldAllTables = true});

    // route 1
    routes.Add(new DynamicDataRoute("{table}/{action}/Custom.aspx") {
        Constraints = new RouteValueDictionary(new {
            action = "List|Details|Edit|Insert",
            table = "Products|Orders"
            }),
        Model = DefaultModel,
    });

    // route 2
    routes.Add(new DynamicDataRoute("{table}/ListDetails.aspx") {
        Action = PageAction.List,
        ViewName = "ListDetails",
```

```
        Model = DefaultModel
    });

    // route 3
    routes.Add(new DynamicDataRoute("{table}/ListDetails.aspx") {
        Action = PageAction.Details,
        ViewName = "ListDetails",
        Model = DefaultModel
    });
}
```

Select Start Without Debugging from the Debug menu. If you click the Customers or Order_Details table, the single-page ListDetails.aspx template will be used. If you click the Products table, the standard multipage List.aspx template will be used. If you click the Orders table, your newly created custom List.aspx template is used, as you can see in Figure 33-21.

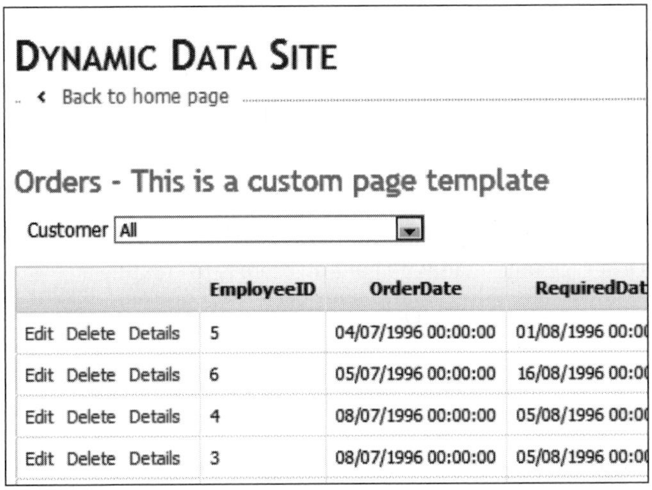

DYNAMIC DATA SITE

‹ Back to home page

Orders - This is a custom page template

Customer All

	EmployeeID	OrderDate	RequiredDat
Edit Delete Details	5	04/07/1996 00:00:00	01/08/1996 00:0
Edit Delete Details	6	05/07/1996 00:00:00	16/08/1996 00:0
Edit Delete Details	4	08/07/1996 00:00:00	05/08/1996 00:0
Edit Delete Details	3	08/07/1996 00:00:00	05/08/1996 00:0

Figure 33-21. *Checking that the custom page template has been used*

Customizing with Metadata

The ASP.NET Dynamic Data system supports defining metadata classes. These customizations are applied at the data model and allow some exceptionally fine-grained control.

■ **Tip** If you have downloaded the source code to accompany this book from Apress.com, you can find the website created in this section in the Northwind4 directory for this chapter.

Creating a Metadata Class

The ASP.NET Dynamic Data system for metadata relies on partial classes. You create a partial class for the data model type you want to customize and a separate class that will be used for metadata, and you associate the two together using an annotation. This is easier to understand through an example.

Right-click the App_Code folder in the Solution Explorer, select Add New Item from the pop-up menu, and click Class in the list of templates. The name you give the class file is not important—we used Metadata.cs. Click the Add button to create the new file. Open the file for editing and remove all the content, replacing it with the following code:

```
using System.ComponentModel;
using System.ComponentModel.DataAnnotations;

[MetadataType(typeof(Order_DetailMetadata))]
public partial class Order_Detail {
}

public class Order_DetailMetadata {
}
```

The using statements reference namespaces that contain the attributes that you will use in the following sections. The interesting part is the Order_Detail class. This is a partial class that extends the Order_Detail class generated in the data model. Notice that we use the singular form; we are referring to the data type, not the table.

You apply the MetadataType attribute to the partial class to indicate that you want to provide metadata for this data type. The argument to this attribute is the type of the class you will use. We have created another class in the same file called Order_DetailMetadata. That's all there is to creating a metadata class. You can define multiple metadata relationships in the same class file. For example, if you wanted to declare metadata for the Products table, you would create a partial Product class, as shown here:

```
using System.ComponentModel;
using System.ComponentModel.DataAnnotations;

[MetadataType(typeof(Order_DetailMetadata))]
public partial class Order_Detail {
}

public class Order_DetailMetadata {
}

[MetadataType(typeof(ProductMetadata))]
public partial class Product {
}

public class ProductMetadata {
}
```

Changing Display Names

Having created the metadata classes, you can start to use them to customize your Dynamic Data application. A good starting point is to change the display name of the Order_Details table—just because the database doesn't allow spaces in table names doesn't mean that your users should have to see the underscore in the name.

You perform customizations with metadata by applying attributes to the class named in the MetadataType attribute—the Order_DetailMetadata type for the Order_Details table in the example. To change the display name of the table, you use the DisplayName attribute, as follows:

```
using System.ComponentModel;
using System.ComponentModel.DataAnnotations;

[MetadataType(typeof(Order_DetailMetadata))]
public partial class Order_Detail {
}

[DisplayName("Order Details")]
public class Order_DetailMetadata {
}

[MetadataType(typeof(ProductMetadata))]
public partial class Product {
}

public class ProductMetadata {
}
```

In the listing, we have specified a display name of Order Details (without the underscore). If you select Start Without Debugging from the Debug menu, you'll see the change on the start page for the application, as shown in Figure 33-22.

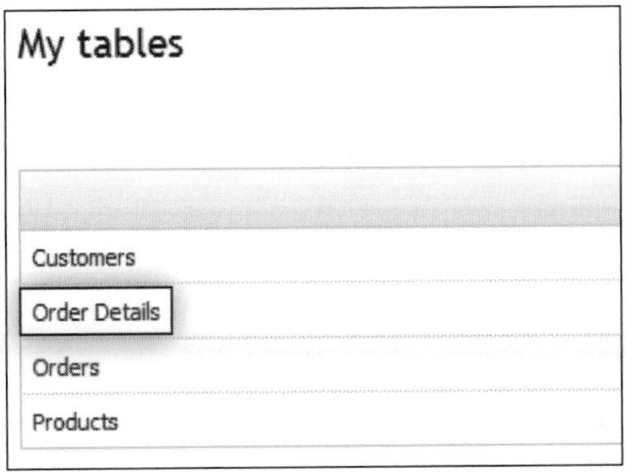

My tables

Customers
Order Details
Orders
Products

Figure 33-22. The modified table display name

And because you have made the modification in the data model, it applies to wherever the table name is used in the page templates. If you click the link for the table in the main page, you'll see that the display name has changed here as well.

You can also change the name of columns in a table. To do this, you need to add properties to your metadata class with the same names as the columns you want to modify. As an example, let's use the UnitsInStock and UnitPrice columns from the Products table, as follows:

```
using System.ComponentModel;
using System.ComponentModel.DataAnnotations;

[MetadataType(typeof(Order_DetailMetadata))]
public partial class Order_Detail {
}

[DisplayName("Order Details")]
public class Order_DetailMetadata {
}

[MetadataType(typeof(ProductMetadata))]
public partial class Product {
}

public class ProductMetadata {

    [DisplayName("In Stock")]
    public object UnitsInStock {get; set;}

    [DisplayName("Price")]
    public object UnitPrice {get; set;}
}
```

You don't need to worry about the type for the properties—we have used object. What is important is that the property name matches the name of the table column. Once you have defined the properties in the metadata class, you can apply the DisplayName attribute, just as you did for the table name.

Save the changes to the Metadata.cs file, and select Start Without Debugging from the Debug menu. Click the link for the Products table in the start page, and note the changes in the column names, as shown in Figure 33-23.

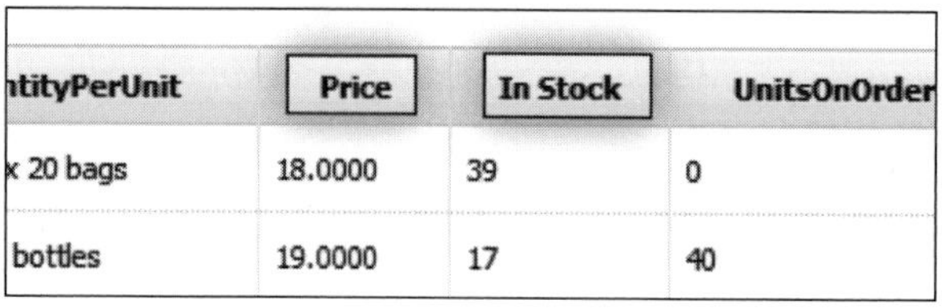

ntityPerUnit	Price	In Stock	UnitsOnOrder
x 20 bags	18.0000	39	0
bottles	19.0000	17	40

Figure 33-23. Changing the display name of columns

Once again, these changes take effect wherever the column names are used. If you click the Details link for one of the records, you'll see that the new Price and In Stock titles are used there as well.

Changing Visibility

You can use attributes to control the visibility of columns and tables in the scaffolding templates. To hide a column, you apply the ScaffoldColumn attribute with a false argument, as follows:

```
using System.ComponentModel;
using System.ComponentModel.DataAnnotations;
```

```
[MetadataType(typeof(Order_DetailMetadata))]
public partial class Order_Detail {
}

[DisplayName("Order Details")]
public class Order_DetailMetadata {
}

[MetadataType(typeof(ProductMetadata))]
public partial class Product {
}

public class ProductMetadata {

    [DisplayName("In Stock")]
    public object UnitsInStock { get; set; }

    [DisplayName("Price")]
    public object UnitPrice {get; set;}

    [ScaffoldColumn(false)]
    public object SupplierID { get; set; }
}
```

You have defined a property for the SupplierID column and applied the ScaffoldColumn attribute. If you start the Dynamic Data application now and select the Products table, you will see that the SupplierID column has disappeared.

You can do the same thing for tables using the ScaffoldTable attribute. The following code defines a metadata class for the Customers table and uses the attribute to hide the entire table:

```
using System.ComponentModel;
using System.ComponentModel.DataAnnotations;

[MetadataType(typeof(Order_DetailMetadata))]
public partial class Order_Detail {
}

[DisplayName("Order Details")]
public class Order_DetailMetadata {
}

[MetadataType(typeof(ProductMetadata))]
public partial class Product {
}

public class ProductMetadata {

    [DisplayName("In Stock")]
    public object UnitsInStock { get; set; }

    [DisplayName("Price")]
    public object UnitPrice {get; set;}
```

```
    [ScaffoldColumn(false)]
    public object SupplierID { get; set; }
}

[MetadataType(typeof(CustomerMetadata))]
public partial class Customer {
}

[ScaffoldTable(false)]
public class CustomerMetadata {
}
```

If you view the home page for the application, you'll see that there is no link for the Customers table. Using this attribute has a different effect than omitting a table using routes. Even though there is no link for the table, the ASP.NET Dynamic Data system still uses the table for foreign-key relationships. Click to view the Orders table, and you'll see that you can still filter by Customer.

Customizing Field Formatting

If you look at the records in the Orders table, you will see that the OrderDate, RequiredDate, and ShippedDate columns all have timestamps that are set to midnight. This is because the default formatting for time stamps includes both the date and time, as shown in Figure 33-24.

Orders

Customer All

	EmployeeID	OrderDate	RequiredDate	ShippedDate
Edit Delete Details	5	04/07/1996 00:00:00	01/08/1996 00:00:00	16/07/1996 00:00:00
Edit Delete Details	6	05/07/1996 00:00:00	16/08/1996 00:00:00	10/07/1996 00:00:00
Edit Delete Details	4	08/07/1996 00:00:00	05/08/1996 00:00:00	12/07/1996 00:00:00
Edit Delete Details	3	08/07/1996 00:00:00	05/08/1996 00:00:00	15/07/1996 00:00:00
Edit Delete Details	4	09/07/1996 00:00:00	06/08/1996 00:00:00	11/07/1996 00:00:00

Figure 33-24. *Unformatted time stamps in the Orders table*

You can change the formatting with the DisplayFormat string, which allows you to supply a standard .NET format string to be used to display the field. The following code shows how we have applied this to the three date fields in the Orders table:

```
[MetadataType(typeof(OrderMetadata))]
public partial class Order {
}

public class OrderMetadata {

    [DisplayFormat(DataFormatString = "{0:yy-MM-dd}")]
```

```
    public object OrderDate { get; set; }

    [DisplayFormat(DataFormatString = "{0:yy-MM-dd}")]
    public object RequiredDate { get; set; }

    [DisplayFormat(DataFormatString = "{0:yy-MM-dd}")]
    public object ShippedDate{ get; set; }
}
```

The format string we have selected shows the date in a compact form and omits the time entirely. If you save these changes to your Metadata.cs code file and select Start Without Debugging from the Debug menu, you'll be able to see the display changes, as shown in Figure 33-25.

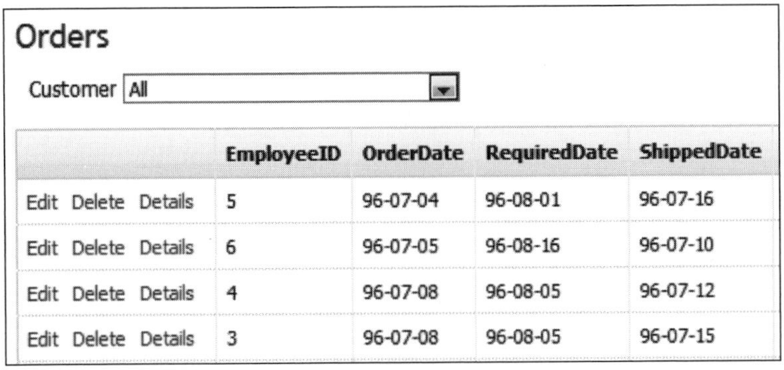

Orders

Customer All

	EmployeeID	OrderDate	RequiredDate	ShippedDate
Edit Delete Details	5	96-07-04	96-08-01	96-07-16
Edit Delete Details	6	96-07-05	96-08-16	96-07-10
Edit Delete Details	4	96-07-08	96-08-05	96-07-12
Edit Delete Details	3	96-07-08	96-08-05	96-07-15

***Figure 33-25.** The formatted date fields*

Using a Custom Field Template

In the "Customizing with Templates" section, we showed you how to change the appearance of all fields of a given type. Using metadata, you can change the appearance of a given data column. First you need to create a new field template. You copy and paste the Text.ascx file in the FieldTemplates folder and rename the copy REDText.ascx. Then change the content to match the following code—a simple label that displays white text on a red background:

```
<%@ Control Language="C#" CodeFile="REDText.ascx.cs" Inherits="TextField" %>

<asp:Label ID="Literal1" runat="server" Text="<%# FieldValueString %>" BackColor="Red"
ForeColor="White"/>
```

You can then use the UIHint attribute to tell the ASP.NET Dynamic Data system that your custom field template should be used to display a column. In the following code, we have used the attribute to apply our REDText template to the ShipName column:

```
public class OrderMetadata {

    [DisplayFormat(DataFormatString = "{0:yy-MM-dd}")]
    public object OrderDate { get; set; }

    [DisplayFormat(DataFormatString = "{0:yy-MM-dd}")]
```

```
    public object RequiredDate { get; set; }

    [DisplayFormat(DataFormatString = "{0:yy-MM-dd}")]
    public object ShippedDate{ get; set; }

    [UIHint("REDText")]
    public object ShipName { get; set; }
}
```

When you start the application and view the Orders table, you see that the ShipName fields are displayed using your template, as shown in Figure 33-26.

ShipVia	Freight	ShipName	ShipAddress
3	32.3800	Vins et alcools Chevalier	59 rue de l'Abbaye
1	11.6100	Toms Spezialitäten	Luisenstr. 48
2	65.8300	Hanari Carnes	Rua do Paço, 67
1	41.3400	Victuailles en stock	2, rue du Commerce

Figure 33-26. *Testing the use of the custom field template*

Customizing Validation

You can use the metadata system to customize validation for data fields. In the following sections, we give you some examples of how to do this.

Requiring a Field Value

The Required attribute indicates that a value must be provided for a given field. The following code shows the application of the Required attribute for the UnitsInStock column from the Metadata.cs code file. We have used the ErrorMessage property to provide a message to be shown to the user if they try to add a record without a UnitsInStock value.

```
[MetadataType(typeof(ProductMetadata))]
public partial class Product {
}

public class ProductMetadata {

    [DisplayName("In Stock")]
    [Required(ErrorMessage = "You must enter how many items we have in stock")]
    public object UnitsInStock { get; set; }

    [DisplayName("Price")]
    public object UnitPrice {get; set;}

    [ScaffoldColumn(false)]
    public object SupplierID { get; set; }
}
```

You'll notice that we have applied this alongside the DisplayName attribute. To test the validation, select Start Without Debugging from the Debug menu, click the link for the Products table, and click the Insert new item link at the bottom of the page. You'll see the Insert page; click Insert without filling any of the fields. The validation errors for the insert are shown on the page, as illustrated by Figure 33-27.

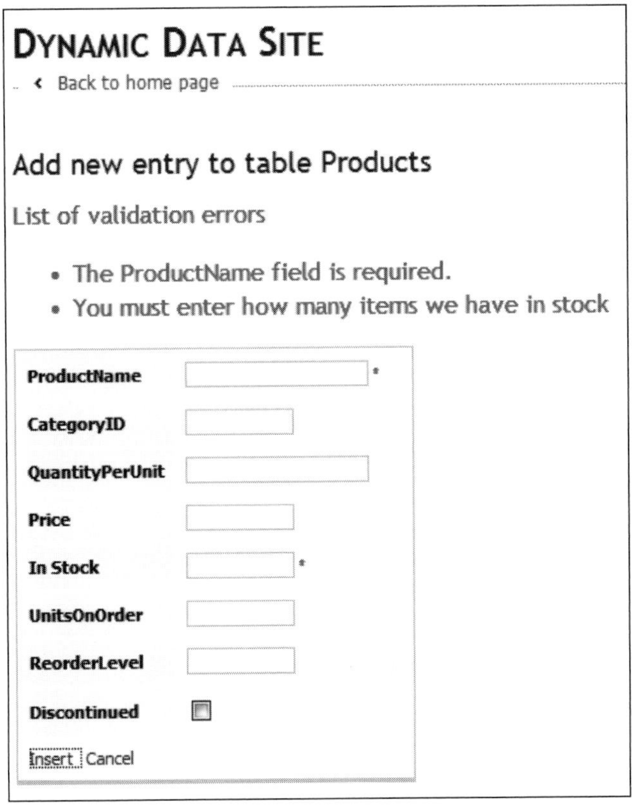

Figure 33-27. *The validation error created by the Required attribute*

You'll see that there are two validation errors. The first has been picked up by the ASP.NET Dynamic Data system from the data model schema: the ProductName column doesn't allow null values. The second error comes from the use of the Required attribute, which has allowed you to supplement the schema constraints without changing the data model or the underlying database.

Specifying a Valid Range

The Range attribute allows the range of valid field values to be specified for numeric types. The following classes show the Range attribute applied to the UnitsInStock column of the Products table:

```
[MetadataType(typeof(ProductMetadata))]
public partial class Product {
}
```

```
public class ProductMetadata {

    [DisplayName("In Stock")]
    [Required(ErrorMessage = "You must enter how many items we have in stock")]
    [Range(0, 100)]
    public object UnitsInStock { get; set; }

    [DisplayName("Price")]
    public object UnitPrice {get; set;}

    [ScaffoldColumn(false)]
    public object SupplierID { get; set; }
}
```

We have specified that only values from 1 to 100 are allowed. If you try to create or edit a record in the Products table and supply a value that is outside the range, a validation error is displayed, as illustrated by Figure 33-28.

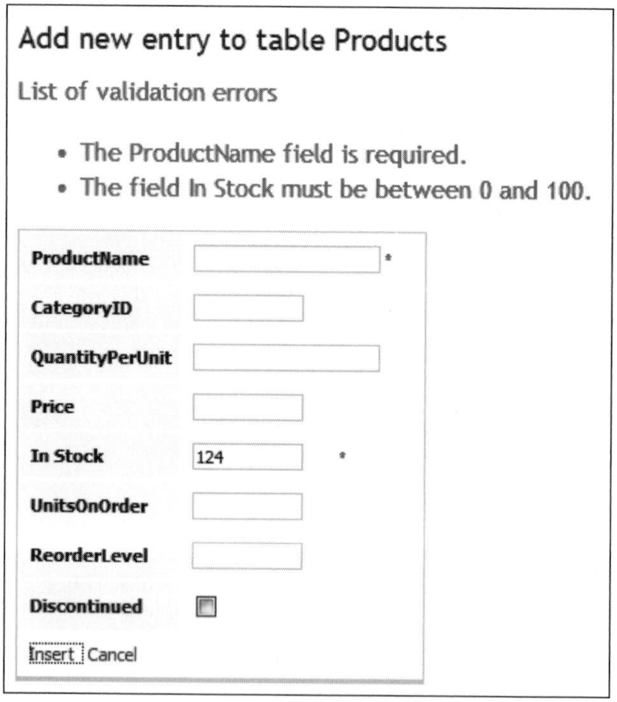

Add new entry to table Products

List of validation errors

- The ProductName field is required.
- The field In Stock must be between 0 and 100.

ProductName *
CategoryID
QuantityPerUnit
Price
In Stock 124 *
UnitsOnOrder
ReorderLevel
Discontinued
Insert Cancel

Figure 33-28. A range-based validation error

Customizing Validation Using Extensibility Methods

If you expand the Northwind.dbml item in the App_Code folder, you will see the Northwind.designer.cs code file. If you open this file, you will see the classes that have been generated by LINQ to SQL. This is the data model that your Dynamic Data application has been driven by. Each type has a region that is labeled Extensibility Method Definitions. You will use these methods to perform custom field validation. Here are the partial methods or the Product type:

```
partial void OnLoaded();
partial void OnValidate(System.Data.Linq.ChangeAction action);
partial void OnCreated();
partial void OnProductIDChanging(int value);
partial void OnProductIDChanged();
partial void OnProductNameChanging(string value);
partial void OnProductNameChanged();
partial void OnSupplierIDChanging(System.Nullable<int> value);
partial void OnSupplierIDChanged();
partial void OnCategoryIDChanging(System.Nullable<int> value);
partial void OnCategoryIDChanged();
partial void OnQuantityPerUnitChanging(string value);
partial void OnQuantityPerUnitChanged();
partial void OnUnitPriceChanging(System.Nullable<decimal> value);
partial void OnUnitPriceChanged();
partial void OnUnitsInStockChanging(System.Nullable<short> value);
partial void OnUnitsInStockChanged();
partial void OnUnitsOnOrderChanging(System.Nullable<short> value);
partial void OnUnitsOnOrderChanged();
partial void OnReorderLevelChanging(System.Nullable<short> value);
partial void OnReorderLevelChanged();
partial void OnDiscontinuedChanging(bool value);
partial void OnDiscontinuedChanged();
```

The methods you are interested in are the ones that have the form On<FieldName>Changing. If you implement these methods in your partial classes, they will be called when the user provides a field value. Let's imagine that you want to complement the use of the Range attribute in the previous example by ensuring that only even numbers can be used in the UnitsInStock field. To do that, you must implement the extensibility method for the field. It is the one with the following signature:

```
partial void OnUnitsInStockChanging(System.Nullable<short> value);
```

To implement this, you add an implementation of this method to the Product class you created in the Metadata.cs code file, as follows:

```
public partial class Product {

    partial void OnUnitsInStockChanging(System.Nullable<short> value) {
        if (value % 2 == 1)
           throw new ValidationException("Stock level must be an even number");
    }
}

public class ProductMetadata {

    [DisplayName("In Stock")]
    [Required(ErrorMessage = "You must enter how many items we have in stock")]
    [Range(0, 100)]
    public object UnitsInStock { get; set; }

    [DisplayName("Price")]
```

```
    public object UnitPrice {get; set;}

    [ScaffoldColumn(false)]
    public object SupplierID { get; set; }
}
```

If you throw an exception in your implementation of the OnUnitsInStockChanging method, then it will be used to present the user with a validation error. Save the additions to the Metadata.cs file, and start the application by selecting Start Without Debugging from the Debug menu.

Click the link for the Products table, and click Edit for one of the data rows. Set the In Stock field value to be an odd number, and click Update. If the value you entered was outside the range you applied in the metadata, then you will see a range validation error. If the value you entered was in range but odd, then you will see the message you passed into the exception you threw in the OnUnitsInStockChanging method, as shown in Figure 33-29.

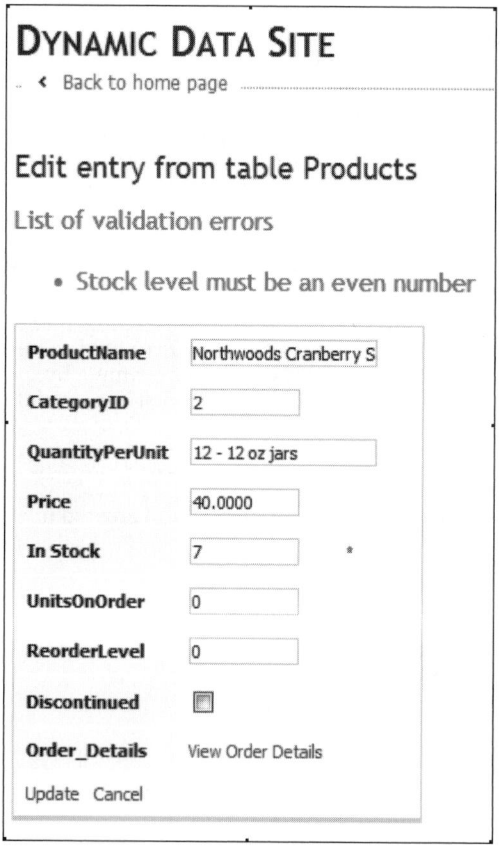

Figure 33-29. *A validation error created via the extensibility methods*

Summary

In this chapter, you learned about ASP.NET Dynamic Data support. We hope you agree that this feature allows you to easily create data-centric applications with a minimum of effort. We showed you how to use LINQ to SQL to generate the data model, but the same approach works equally as well with the Entity Framework.

One of the most striking aspects of Dynamic Data is the way in which it can be customized. Page templates, field templates, metadata, attributes, and extensibility methods can be used to change the appearance, functionality, and validation methods of a Dynamic Data application—often with little or no coding required.

We think that this capability is a useful component of ASP.NET, and we hope that the examples we have demonstrated in this chapter have led you to agree.

CHAPTER 34

■ ■ ■

Silverlight

Although the Web is easily the most popular environment for business software, there are some things that web applications just can't do, or can't do very well. Even if you outfit your ASP.NET web pages with the latest cutting-edge JavaScript and Ajax you won't be able to duplicate many of the capabilities that desktop applications take for granted, such as animation, sound and video playback, and 3D graphics. And although you can use JavaScript to respond on the client to focus changes, mouse movements, and other "real-time" events, you still can't build a complex interface that's anywhere near as responsive as a window in a rich client application. (The saving grace of web programming is that you usually don't need these frills. The benefits you gain—broad compatibility, high security, no deployment cost, and a scalable server-side model—outweigh the loss of a few niceties.)

That said, developers are continuously pushing the limits of the Web. These days, it's not uncommon to watch an animated commercial or play a simple but richly designed game directly in your browser. This capability obviously isn't a part of the ordinary HTML, CSS, and JavaScript standards. Instead, it's enabled by a browser plug-in, sometimes for a Java applet, but most commonly for Flash content.

Microsoft's Silverlight technology is a direct competitor to Flash. Like Flash, Silverlight allows you to create interactive content that runs on the client, with support for dynamic graphics, media, and animation that goes far beyond ordinary HTML. Also like Flash, Silverlight is deployed using a lightweight browser plug-in and supports a wide range of different browsers and operating systems. At the moment, Flash has the edge over Silverlight, because of its widespread adoption and its maturity. However, Silverlight boasts a few architectural features that Flash can't match—most importantly, the fact that it's based on a scaled-down version of .NET's common language runtime (CLR) and thus allows developers to write client-side code using pure C#.

In this chapter, you'll take a detailed tour of Silverlight. You'll learn how it works, what features it supports, and what features aren't quite there yet. You'll also consider how you can use Silverlight to supplement ASP.NET websites.

Silverlight Versions

Silverlight exists in several versions. The first version, Silverlight 1, was a relatively modest technology. It included the 2D drawing features and the media playback features. However, it didn't include the CLR engine or support for .NET languages, so developers were forced to use JavaScript.

The second version, Silverlight 2, added the .NET-powered features that have generated the most developer excitement. It introduced a scaled-down CLR, a subset of .NET Framework classes, and a user interface based on Windows Presentation Foundation (WPF), which desktop developers use to build cutting-edge Windows applications.

The versions that have followed—Silverlight 3 and Silverlight 4—keep the same underlying infrastructure and simply add more features.

This chapter assumes that you're using Silverlight 3, which is the version that's bundled with Visual Studio 2010. However, almost all the material you'll learn in this chapter applies to Silverlight 2 or later. For a more comprehensive look at the full range of Silverlight features, refer to *Pro Silverlight 3 in C# 2010* (Apress, 2009).

Understanding Silverlight

Silverlight uses a familiar technique to go beyond the capabilities of standard web pages—it uses a lightweight browser plug-in.

The advantage of the plug-in model is that the user needs to install just a single component to see content created by a range of different people and companies. Installing the plug-in requires a small download and forces the user to confirm the operation in at least one security dialog box (and usually more). It takes a short but definite amount of time, and it's an inconvenience. However, once the plug-in is installed, the browser can process any content that uses the plug-in seamlessly, with no further prompting.

Figure 34-1 shows two views of a page with Silverlight content. On the top is the page you'll see if you don't have the Silverlight plug-in installed. At this point, you can click the Get Microsoft Silverlight picture to be taken to Microsoft's website (`http://silverlight.net`), where you'll be prompted to install the plug-in and then sent back to the original page. On the bottom is the page you'll see once the Silverlight plug-in is installed.

■ **Note** Silverlight is designed to overcome the limitations of ordinary HTML to allow developers to create more graphical and interactive applications. However, Silverlight isn't a way for developers to break out of the browser's security sandbox. For the most part, Silverlight applications are limited in equivalent ways to ordinary web pages. For example, a Silverlight application is allowed to create and access files, but only those files that are stored in a special walled-off isolated storage area. Conceptually, isolated storage works like the cookies in an ordinary web page. Files are separated by website and the current user, and size is severely limited.

A key point to keep in mind when considering the Silverlight development model is that in most cases you'll use Silverlight to *augment* the existing content of your website (which is still based on HTML, CSS, and JavaScript). For example, you might add Silverlight content that shows an advertisement or allows an enhanced experience for a portion of a website (such as playing a game, completing a survey, interacting with a product, taking a virtual tour, and so on). Your Silverlight pages may present content that's already available in your website in a more engaging way, or they may represent a value-added feature for users who have the Silverlight plug-in.

Although it's easily possible to create a Silverlight-only website, it's unlikely that you'll take that approach. The fact that Silverlight is still relatively new, and the fact that it doesn't support legacy clients (most notably, it has no support for users of Windows ME and Windows 98) mean it doesn't have nearly the same reach as ordinary HTML. Many businesses that are adopting Silverlight are using it to distinguish themselves from other online competitors with cutting-edge content.

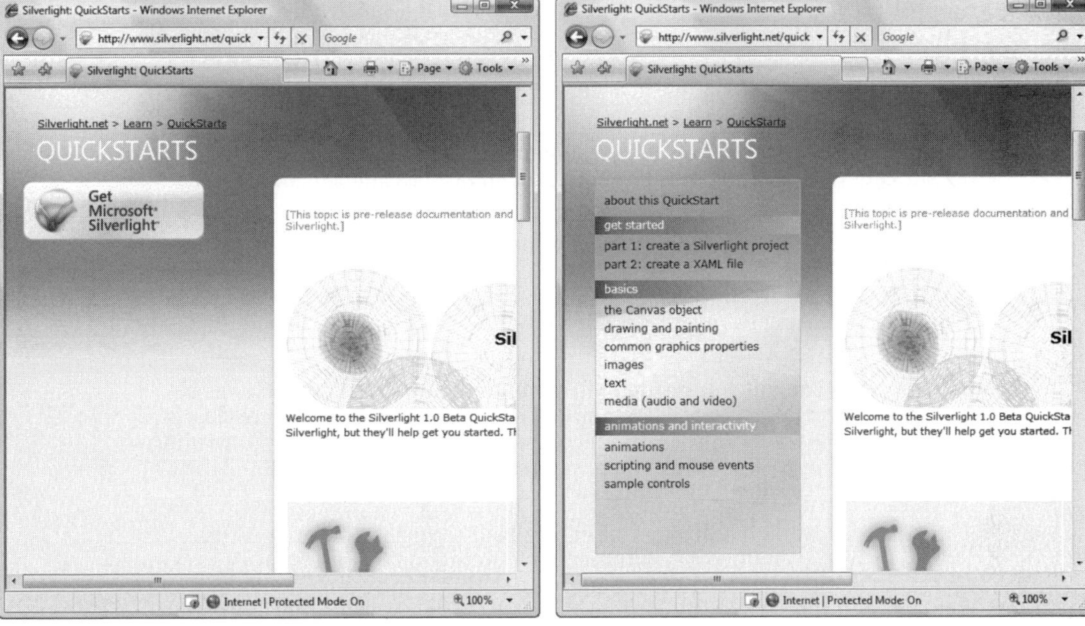

Figure 34-1. *Installing the Silverlight plug-in*

Silverlight vs. Flash

The most successful browser plug-in is Adobe Flash, which is installed on over 90 percent of the world's web browsers. Flash has a long history that spans more than ten years, beginning as a straightforward tool for adding animated graphics and gradually evolving into a platform for developing interactive content.

It's perfectly reasonable for ASP.NET developers to extend their websites using Flash content. However, doing so requires a separate design tool, and a completely different programming language (ActionScript) and programming environment (Flex). Furthermore, there's no straightforward way to generate Flash content using server-side .NET code, which means it's difficult to integrate ASP.NET content and Flash content—instead, they exist in separate islands.

Silverlight aims to give .NET developers a better option for creating rich web content. Silverlight provides a browser plug-in with many similar features to Flash, but one that's designed from the ground up for .NET. Silverlight natively supports the C# language and uses a range of .NET concepts. As a result, developers can write client-side code for Silverlight in the same language they use for server-side code (such as C# and VB), and use many of the same abstractions (including streams, controls, collections, generics, and LINQ).

The Silverlight plug-in has an impressive list of features, some of which are shared in common with Flash, and some which are entirely new and even revolutionary. They include the following:

- **2D Drawing:** Silverlight provides a rich model for 2D drawing. Best of all, the content you draw is defined as shapes and paths, so you can manipulate this content on the client side. You can even respond to events (like a mouse click on a portion of a graphic), which makes it easy to add interactivity to anything you draw.

- **Controls:** Developers don't want to reinvent the wheel, so Silverlight is stocked with the essentials, including buttons, text boxes, lists, and a grid. Best of all, these basic building blocks can be restyled with custom visuals if you want all of the functionality but none of the stock look.
- **Animation:** Silverlight has a time-based animation model that lets you define what should happen and how long it should take. The Silverlight plug-in handles the sticky details, like interpolating intermediary values and calculating the frame rate.
- **Media:** Silverlight provides playback of Windows Media Audio (WMA), Windows Media Video (WMV7-9), MP3 audio, and VC-1 (which supports high-definition). You aren't tied to the Windows Media Player ActiveX control or browser plug-in—instead, you can create any front-end you want, and you can even show video in full-screen mode.
- **The Common Language Runtime:** Most impressively, Silverlight includes a scaled-down version of the CLR, complete with an essential set of core classes, a garbage collector, a JIT (just-in-time) compiler, support for generics, threading, and so on. In many cases, developers can take code written for the full .NET CLR and use it in a Silverlight application with only moderate changes.
- **Networking:** Silverlight applications can call old-style ASP.NET web services (.asmx) or WCF (Windows Communication Foundation) web services. They can also send manually created XML requests over HTTP and even open direct socket connections for fast two-way communication. This gives developers a great way to combine rich client-side code with secure server-side routines.
- **Data binding:** Although it's not as capable as in its big brother (WPF), Silverlight data binding provides a convenient way to display large amounts of data with minimal code. You can pull your data from XML or in-memory objects, giving you the ability to call a web service, receive a collection of objects, and display their data in a web page—often with just a couple of lines of code.

Of course, it's just as important to note what Silverlight doesn't include. Silverlight is a new technology that's evolving rapidly, and it's full of stumbling blocks for developers who are used to relying on .NET's rich libraries of prebuilt functionality. Prominent gaps include lack of database support (there's no ADO.NET), no support for 3D drawing, and fewer rich controls (although many developers and component companies are building their own). All of these features are available in Windows-centric WPF applications, and they may someday migrate to the Silverlight universe—or not.

■ **Note** In essence, Silverlight is a .NET-based Flash competitor. It aims to compete with Flash today, but provide a path to far more features in the future. Unlike the Flash development model, which is limited in several ways due to the way it's evolved over the years, Silverlight is a starting-from-scratch attempt that's thoroughly based on .NET and WPF, and will therefore allow .NET developers to be far more productive. In many ways, Silverlight is the culmination of two trends: the drive to extend web pages to incorporate more and more rich client features, and the drive to give the .NET Framework a broader reach.

Silverlight System Requirements

With any web-centric technology, it's keenly important to have compatibility with the widest possible range of computers and devices. Although Silverlight is still evolving, it already stacks up fairly well in this department:

- **Windows computers:** Silverlight works on PCs with Windows 7, Windows Vista and Windows XP. The minimum browser versions that Silverlight 2 supports are Internet Explorer 6 and Firefox 1.5. Silverlight will also work in Windows 2000, but only with Internet Explorer 6.
- **Mac computers:** Silverlight works on Mac computers with OS X 10.4.8 or later, provided they have Intel hardware (as opposed to the older PowerPC hardware). The minimum browser versions that Silverlight 2 supports are Firefox 1.5 and Safari.
- **Linux computers:** Although Silverlight doesn't currently work on Linux, the Mono team is creating an open-source Linux implementation of Silverlight 1 and Silverlight 2. This project is known as Moonlight, and it's being developed with key support from Microsoft. To learn more, visit `http://www.mono-project.com/Moonlight`.

■ **Note** The system requirements for Silverlight may change as Microsoft releases plug-ins for other browsers. For example, the Opera browser currently works on PCs through an unsupported hack, but better support is planned in the future. To see the latest system requirements, check `http://www.microsoft.com/silverlight/resources/install.aspx`.

Installing Silverlight requires a small-sized setup (about 5 MB) that's easy to download. (You can get it at `http://silverlight.net`.) That allows Silverlight to provide an all-important "frictionless" setup experience, much like Flash, but quite different from Java.

■ **Note** In order to *run* Silverlight applications, you simply need the Silverlight browser plug-in. In order to *create* Silverlight applications (and open the sample project for this book), you need Visual Studio 2010, which includes full support for Silverlight 3. Alternatively, you can use Expression Blend—a graphically oriented design tool—to build and test Silverlight applications. Overall, Expression Blend is intended for graphic designers who spend their time creating serious eye candy, while Visual Studio is ideal for code-heavy application programmers.

Creating a Silverlight Solution

Now that you've installed the Silverlight Tools for Visual Studio, you're ready to create your first Silverlight project. Here's what you need to do:

1. Select File ➤ New ➤ Project in Visual Studio, choose the Visual C# group of project types, and then choose Silverlight subgroup (on the left). Finally, select the Silverlight Application template (in the middle). It's a good idea to use the "Create directory for solution" option, so you can group together the two projects that Visual Studio will create—one for the Silverlight assembly and one for the ASP.NET website.
2. Once you've picked the solution name and project name, click OK to create it.
3. You'll be asked whether you want to create a host website. To create an ASP.NET website for hosting your Silverlight application (rather than a simple HTML file), make sure the setting "Host the Silverlight application in a new Web site" is checked. You'll also need to supply a project name for the ASP.NET website. By default, it's your project name with the added text ".Web" at the end, as shown in Figure 34-2.

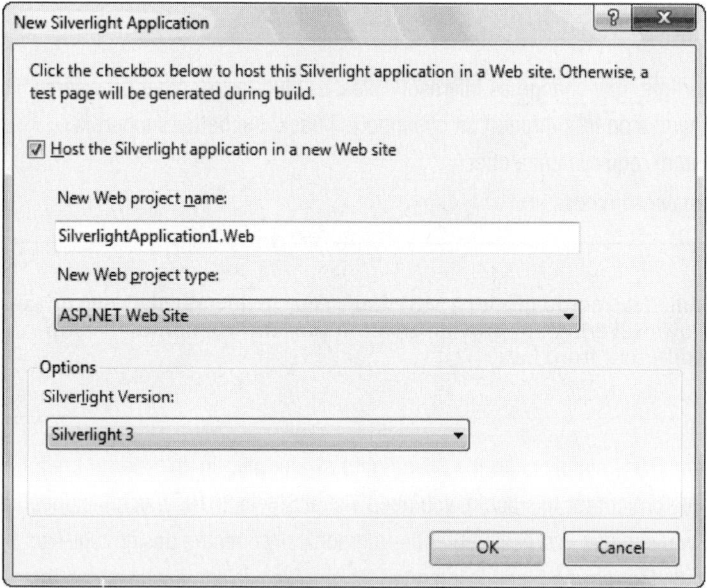

Figure 34-2. *Creating an ASP.NET website to host Silverlight content*

4. You can choose to create a projectless ASP.NET website or an ASP.NET web project by selecting the appropriate option in the Project Type list box. Either approach gives you the same ability to host Silverlight content. Chapter 2 describes the difference.
5. Finally, click OK to create the two projects.

When you follow these steps, you'll end up with a single solution that holds two projects—a familiar ASP.NET website, and a dedicated Silverlight project, as shown in Figure 34-3.

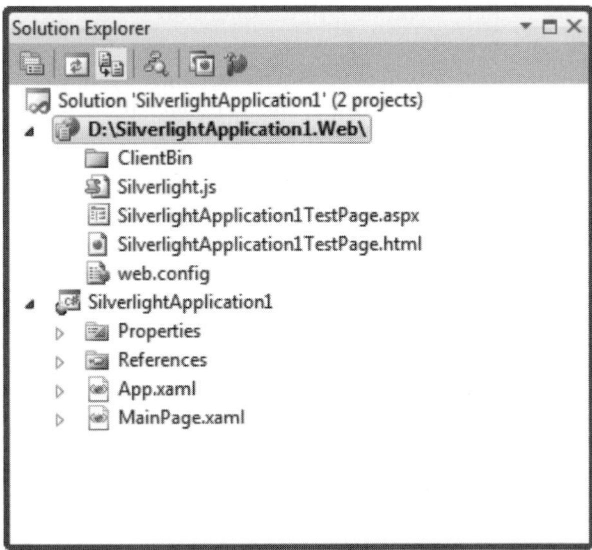

Figure 34-3. Creating an ASP.NET website to host Silverlight content

Silverlight Compilation

When you create a Silverlight solution, Visual Studio generates a new ASP.NET website that can hold ordinary web forms, HTML pages, and web services. However, there's a difference between this website and the ones you've seen throughout this book—namely, it's already set up with the ability to host Silverlight content.

To understand how this works, you need to know a bit more about the Silverlight compilation process. When you compile the solution shown in Figure 34-3, here's what happens:

1. First, the Silverlight project is compiled into a DLL file. For example, if you have a project named SilverlightApplication1, the csc.exe compiler will create the file SilverlightApplication1.dll, with all the code and markup that the Silverlight project contains.

2. Next, the assembly is placed into a special application package called a XAP file. (You'll learn a bit more about XAP files in the following sidebar, "Understanding XAP Files.") The XAP file includes the DLL assembly for your project, any other dependent assemblies you're using (except for the ones that are a part of the core Silverlight runtime), and the application manifest file AppManifest.xml, which lists the files that comprise your application. If you add other content files to your Silverlight project (for example, images), they will be automatically embedded in the XAP file.

3. Finally, Visual Studio copies the XAP file to the ClientBin folder in the ASP.NET website, as shown in Figure 34-4. (This is similar to assembly references—if an ASP.NET website references a private DLL, Visual Studio automatically copies this DLL to the Bin folder.) Once your Silverlight application is in the ClientBin folder, it's accessible to the pages in your ASP.NET website.

These steps ensure that your ASP.NET application always gets the most recent version of your Silverlight project. Technically, you don't need to place the XAP file in the ClientBin folder—it's just a convenient standard that separates the Silverlight content from the rest of your website.

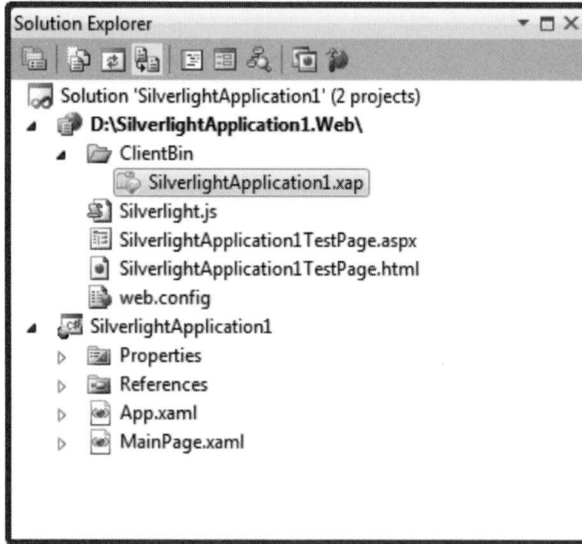

Figure 34-4. *The compiled Silverlight application*

Understanding XAP Files

Technically, the XAP file is a ZIP archive. To verify this, rename a XAP file like SilverlightApplication1.xap to SilverlightApplication1.xap.zip. You can then open the archive and view the files inside.

The XAP file system has two obvious benefits:

- **It compresses your content:** Because this content isn't decompressed until it reaches the client, it reduces the time required to download your application. This is particularly important if your application contains large static resources that can be easily compressed, like XML documents or blocks of text.
- **It simplifies deployment:** When you're ready to take your Silverlight application live, you simply need to copy the XAP file to the web server, along with TestPage.html or a similar HTML file that includes a Silverlight content region. You don't need to worry about keeping track of the assemblies and resources.

However, there's one potential stumbling block. When hosting a Silverlight application, your web server must be configured to allow requests for the XAP file type. This file type is included by default in IIS 7, provided you're using Windows Server 2008, Windows 7, or Windows Vista with Service Pack 1. If you have Windows Vista without Service Pack 1, you have an earlier version of IIS, or you have another type of web server, you'll need to add a file type that maps the .xap extension to the MIME type application/x-silverlight-app. For IIS instructions, see `http://learn.iis.net/page.aspx/262/silverlight`.

The Entry Page

Although the XAP package makes deployment easy, you still need to take an extra step to allow users to run your Silverlight application. That's because users can't run a Silverlight application by directly requesting the XAP file. Instead, they need to surf to an entry page that instantiates the Silverlight plug-in.

In an ASP.NET website, you have two options for your entry page:

- **Create HTML files with Silverlight content:** You place these files in your ASP.NET website folder, just as you would with any other ordinary HTML file. The only limitation of this approach is that your HTML file obviously can't include ASP.NET controls, because it won't be processed on the server.
- **Place Silverlight content inside an ASP.NET web form:** In this case, the <object> element that loads the Silverlight plug-in is inserted into a dynamic .aspx page. You can add other ASP.NET controls to different regions of this page. The only disadvantage to this approach is that the page is always processed on the server. If you aren't actually using any server-side ASP.NET content, this creates an extra bit of overhead that you don't need when the page is first requested.

Of course, you're also free to mingle both of these approaches, and use Silverlight content in dedicated HTML pages and inside ASP.NET web pages in the same site. When you create a Silverlight project with an ASP.NET website in Visual Studio, you'll start with both. For example, if your Silverlight project is named SilverlightApplication1, you can use SilverlightApplication1TestPage.html or SilverlightApplication1TestPage.aspx., as shown in Figure 34-4.

Either way, the Silverlight plug-in is defined in exactly the same way—using an <object> element that's wrapped in a <div> element. You position that <div> element where you want the Silverlight content region to appear on your page.

Here's a shortened version of the the default .aspx entry page, without the styles and the JavaScript error-handling code:

```
<%@ Page Language="C#" AutoEventWireup="true" %>

<!DOCTYPE html PUBLIC "-//W3C//DTD XHTML 1.0 Transitional//EN"
"http://www.w3.org/TR/xhtml1/DTD/xhtml1-transitional.dtd">
<html xmlns="http://www.w3.org/1999/xhtml" >
<head runat="server">
    <title>SilverlightApplication1</title>
    <style type="text/css">...</style>
    <script type="text/javascript" src="Silverlight.js"></script>
    <script type="text/javascript">
        function onSilverlightError(sender, args) { ... }
    </script>
</head>

<body>
    <form id="form1" runat="server" style="height:100%">
```

```
    <div id="silverlightControlHost">
        <object data="data:application/x-silverlight-2," type="application/x-silverlight-2"
         width="100%" height="100%">
            <param name="source" value="ClientBin/SilverlightApplication1.xap"/>
            <param name="onError" value="onSilverlightError" />
            <param name="background" value="white" />
            <param name="minRuntimeVersion" value="3.0.40818.0" />
            <param name="autoUpgrade" value="true" />
           <a href="http://go.microsoft.com/fwlink/?LinkID=149156&v=3.0.40818.0"
            style="text-decoration:none">
               <img src="http://go.microsoft.com/fwlink/?LinkId=161376"
                alt="Get Microsoft Silverlight" style="border-style:none"/>
           </a>
       </object>
      <iframe id="_sl_historyFrame"
       style="visibility:hidden;height:0px;width:0px;border:0px"></iframe>
    </div>
    </form>
</body>
</html>
```

The key detail in this markup is the highlighted <div> element. This element is a placeholder that represents the Silverlight content region. It contains an <object> element that loads the Silverlight plug-in and an <iframe> element that's used to display it in certain browsers. The <object> element includes four key attributes: data (which indentifies it as a Silverlight content region), type (which indicates the required Silverlight version), and height and width (which determine the dimensions of the Silverlight content region).

```
<object data="data:application/x-silverlight-2,"
  type="application/x-silverlight-2" width="100%" height="100%">
    ...
</object>
```

The <object> element also contains a series of <param> elements that specify additional options to the Silverlight plug-in, such as the location of the XAP file that contains the Silverlight application you want to run, the JavaScript routine to run if the plug-in can't be loaded, the background color of the Silverlight region, and the minimum required verson of Silverlight:

```
<param name="source" value="ClientBin/SilverlightApplication1.xap"/>
<param name="onerror" value="onSilverlightError" />
<param name="background" value="white" />
<param name="minRuntimeVersion" value="3.0.40818.0" />
<param name="autoUpgrade" value="true" />
```

Finally, the <object> element has some HTML markup that will be shown if the <object> tag isn't understood or the plug-in isn't available. In the standard test page, this markup consists of a "Get Silverlight" picture, which is wrapped in a hyperlink that, when clicked, takes the user to the Silverlight download page.

```
<a href="http://go.microsoft.com/fwlink/?LinkID=149156&v=3.0.40818.0"
 style="text-decoration:none">
    <img src="http://go.microsoft.com/fwlink/?LinkId=161376"
     alt="Get Microsoft Silverlight" style="border-style:none"/>
</a>
```

■ Note By default, the entry page configures the Silverlight content region to take up the entire space in the web browser window. If you want to display other content in your page, you'll need to tweak the style rules that appear at the top of the entry page.

Here's what happens when this page is requested:

1. The server creates all the server-side objects (in this example, that includes the ScriptManager and Silverlight controls) and begins the ordinary ASP.NET page lifecycle.
2. After all the events have fired (and any event handling code has finished), the server renders the page to ordinary HTML, one web control at a time..
3. When the page is fully rendered, it's sent to the client. The server-side objects are released from memory.
4. When the browser receives the page, it begins processing it. When the browser encounters the <object> element, it initializes the Silverlight plug-in, downloads the XAP file for the Silverlight application, and starts the application.
5. The Silverlight application runs in the client browser. No more server-side web page code will be executed, unless the user navigates to another page or refreshes the current page (both of which will shut down the current Silverlight application and restart the entire process). If the user interacts with an ASP.NET control elsewhere on the page, that control may post back the page (which will effectively end the currently running Silverlight application) or call back to the web server using ASP.NET AJAX (which won't disturb it). As you'll see later in this chapter, the Silverlight application also has the ability to trigger web server code by calling a web service.

You can add a number of parameters to the <object> element that represents the Silverlight content region. Table 34-1 lists the most important.

Table 34-1. *Basic Parameters for the Silverlight Plug-In*

Name	Value
source	A URI that points to the XAP file for your Silverlight application. This parameter is required.
onError	A JavaScript event handler that's triggered when a unhandled error occurs in the Silverlight plug-in or in your code. The onError event handler is also called if the user has Silverlight installed but doesn't meet the minRuntimeVersion parameter.
background	The color that's used to paint the background of the Silverlight content region, behind any content that you display (but in front of any HTML content that occupies the same space). If you set the Background property of a page, it's painted over this background.

Name	Value
minRuntimeVersion	This is the minimum version of Silverlight that the client must have in order to run your application. If you need the features of Silverlight 3, set this to 3.0.40818.0 (as slightly earlier versions may correspond to beta builds). If Silverlight 2 is sufficient, use 2.0.31005.0.
autoUpgrade	A Boolean that specifies whether Silverlight should (if it's installed and has an insufficient version number) attempt to update itself. The default is true.
enableHtmlAccess	A Boolean that specifies whether the Silverlight plug-in has access to the HTML object model. Use true if you want to be able to interact with the HTML elements on the test page through your Silverlight code.
initParams	A string that you can use to pass custom initialization information. This technique is useful if you plan to use the same Silverlight application in different ways on different pages.
splashScreenSource	The location of a XAML splash screen to show while the XAP file is downloading.
windowless	A Boolean that specifies whether the plug-in renders in windowed mode (the default) or windowless mode. If you set this true, the HTML content underneath your Silverlight content region can show through. This is ideal if you're planning to create a shaped Silverlight control that integrates with HTML content.
onSourceDownload-ProgressChanged	A JavaScript event handler that's triggered when a piece of the XAP file has been downloaded. You can use this event handler to build a startup progress bar.
onSourceDownload-Complete	A JavaScript event handler that's triggered when the entire XAP file has been downloaded.
onLoad	A JavaScript event handler that's triggered when the markup in the XAP file has been processed and your first page has been loaded.
onResize	A JavaScript event handler that's triggered when the size of a Silverlight content region has changed.

Hybrid Pages

Ambitious ASP.NET developers might use Silverlight to add new functionality (or just sugarcoat) existing ASP.NET pages. Examples include Silverlight-powered ad content, menu systems, and embedded applets (like calculators or games).

When dealing with this sort of interaction, it's important to understand the lifetime of a Silverlight application. Ordinarily, ASP.NET code runs on the web server, and ASP.NET controls post the page back to the server. The problem is that when the page is posted back, the current Silverlight application ends. The web server code runs, a new version of the page is sent to the browser, and the browser loads this new page, at which point your Silverlight application restarts. Not only does this send the user back to the starting point, it also takes additional time because the Silverlight environment must be initialized all over again.

If you want to avoid this disruption, you can use ASP.NET AJAX techniques. A particularly useful tool is the UpdatePanel that's described in Chapter 30. The basic technique is to wrap the controls that would ordinarily trigger a post back and any other controls that they modify into one or more UpdatePanel controls. Then, when the user clicks a button, an asynchronous request is sent to the web server instead of a full post back. When the browser receives the reply, it updates the corresponding portions of the page, without disrupting the Silverlight content.

Creating a Silverlight Project

Now that you understand how your ASP.NET website can host a Silverlight application, you're ready to start designing that application.

Every Silverlight project starts with a small set of essential files, as shown in Figure 34-5. All the files that end with the extension .xaml use a flexible markup standard called XAML, which you'll dissect in this chapter. All the files that end with the extension .cs hold the C# source code that powers your application.

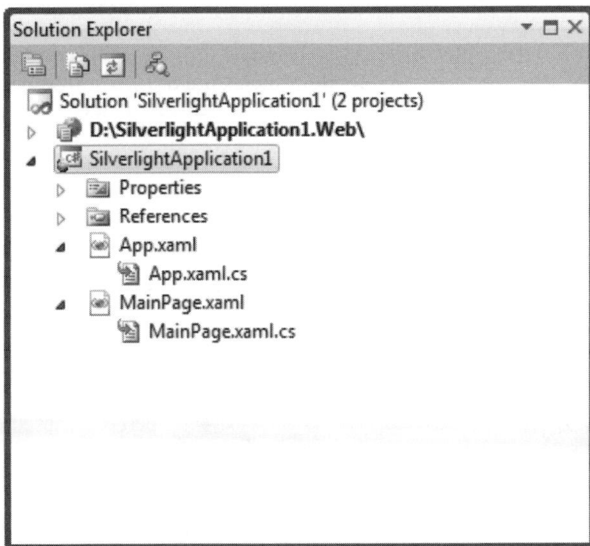

Figure 34-5. *A Silverlight project*

Here's a rundown of the files shown in Figure 34-5:

- **App.xaml and App.xaml.cs:** These files allow you to configure your Silverlight application. They allow you to define resources that will be made available to all the pages in your application, and they allow you react to application events such as startup, shutdown, and error conditions. In a newly generated project, the startup code in the App.xaml.cs file specifies that your application should begin by showing Page.xaml.

- **MainPage.xaml:** This file defines the user interface (the collection of controls, images, and text) that will be shown for your first page. Technically, Silverlight pages are *user controls*—custom classes that derive from UserControl. A Silverlight application can contain as many pages as you need—to add more, simply choose Project ➤ Add New Item, pick the Silverlight User Control template, choose a file name, and click Add.
- **MainPage.xaml.cs:** This file includes the code that underpins your first page, including the event handlers that react to user actions. Like all the code in a Silverlight application, these events run on the client side.

Along with these four essential files, there are a few more ingredients that you'll only find if you dig around. Under the Properties node in the Solution Explorer, you'll find a file named AppManifest.xml, which lists the assemblies that your application uses. You'll also find a file named AssemblyInfo.cs, which contains information about your project (such as its name, version, and publisher) that's embedded into your Silverlight assembly when it's compiled. Neither of these files should be edited by hand—instead, they're modified by Visual Studio when you add references or set projects properties.

Designing a Silverlight Page

Every Silverlight page includes a markup portion that defines the visual appearance (the XAML file) and a source code file that contains event handlers. To customize your first Silverlight application, you simply need to open the Page.xaml file and begin adding markup.

Visual Studio gives you two ways to look at every XAML file—as a visual preview (known as the design surface) or the underlying markup (known as the source view). By default, Visual Studio shows both parts, stacked one on the other. Figure 34-6 shows this view and points out the buttons you can use to change your vantage point.

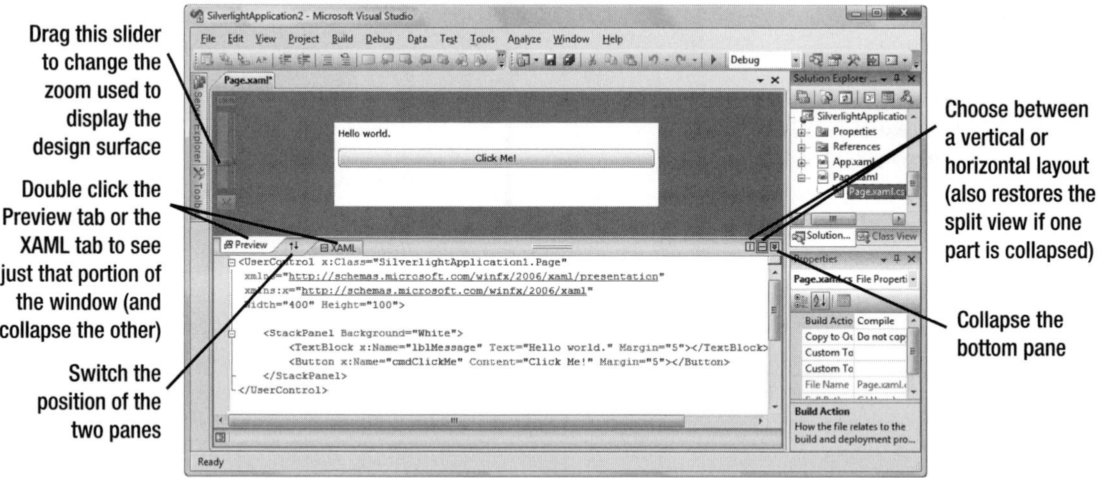

Figure 34-6. Viewing XAML pages

As you've no doubt guessed, you can start designing your XAML page by dragging controls from the Toolbox and dropping them onto the design surface. However, this convenience won't save you from learning the full intricacies of XAML. In order to organize your elements into the right layout containers, change their properties, wire up event handlers, and use Silverlight features like animation, styles, templates, and data binding, you'll need to edit the XAML markup by hand.

To get started, you can try creating the page shown here, which defines a block of text and a button. The portions in bold have been added to the basic page template that Visual Studio generated when you created the project.

```
<UserControl x:Class="SilverlightApplication1.Page"
 xmlns="http://schemas.microsoft.com/winfx/2006/xaml/presentation"
 xmlns:x="http://schemas.microsoft.com/winfx/2006/xaml"
 Width="400" Height="100">

  <StackPanel Background="White">
    <TextBlock x:Name="lblMessage" Text="Hello world." Margin="5"></TextBlock>
    <Button x:Name="cmdClickMe" Content="Click Me!" Margin="5"></Button>
  </StackPanel>
</UserControl>
```

This creates a page that has a stacked arrangement of two elements. On the top is a block of text with a simple message. Underneath it is a button. These three elements are just a sampling of what Silverlight provides—for more, just scan the Visual Studio Toolbox. You'll find the essential graphical widgets that rich client developers rely on, like text boxes, check boxes, list boxes, and buttons. Table 34-2 gives you an at-a-glance look at some of your options, many of which you'll study in this chapter.

■ **Note** In Silverlight terminology, each graphical widget that meets these criteria (appears in a window and is represented by a .NET class) is called an *element*. The term *control* is generally reserved for elements that receive focus and allow user interaction. For example, a TextBox is a control, but the TextBlock is not.

Table 34-2. Basic Silverlight Elements

Class	Description	Type of Element
TextBlock	An all-purpose text display control. If you wish to give different formatting to multiple pieces of inline text, you can nest one or more Run elements inside the TextBlock element.	Text display
Image	An element that displays a supported image file. Silverlight supports JPEG and PNG, but not GIF images.	Image display
Button	The familiar button, complete with a shaded gray background, which the user clicks to launch a task.	Common control
TextBox	The familiar text-entry control.	Common control
PasswordBox	A text box that masks the text the user enters.	Common control

Class	Description	Type of Element
CheckBox	A box that can be checked or unchecked, with optional content displayed next to it.	Common control
RadioButton	A small circle that represents one choice out of a group of options, with optional content displayed next to it.	Common control
ListBox	A list of items, out of which a single one can be selected.	Common control
ComboBox	A drop-down list of items, out of which a single one can be selected.	Common control
HyperlinkButton	A link that directs the user to another web page.	Common control
Slider	An input control that lets the user set a numeric value by dragging a thumb along a track.	Common control
ProgressBar	A colored bar that indicates the percent completion of a given task.	Common control
Calendar*	A one-month-at-a-time calendar view that allows the user to select a single date.	Date control
DatePicker*	A text box for date entry, with a drop-down calendar for easy selection.	Date control
Border	A rectangular or rounded border, which is drawn around the contained element.	Simple container
ScrollViewer	A container that holds another element with large content and provides a scrollable view onto it.	Simple container
TabControl	A container that places items into separate tabs, and allows the user to view just one tab at a time.	Layout container
StackPanel	A layout container that stacks a group of child elements from top to bottom or left to right.	Layout container
Canvas	A layout container that allows you to lay out a group of child elements with precise coordinates.	Layout container
Grid	A layout container that arranges child elements in an invisible grid of cells.	Layout container
GridSplitter*	A resizing bar that allows users to change the height or adjacent rows or the width of adjacent columns in a Grid.	Layout tool
Line	A shape element that draws a line.	Shape primitive

Class	Description	Type of Element
Rectangle	A shape element that draws a rectangle.	Shape primitive
Ellipse	A shape element that draws an ellipse.	Shape primitive
Path	A shape element that draws the shape that's defined by a geometry object.	Shape primitive
MultiScaleImage	An element that supports Silverlight's Deep Zoom feature, and allows the user to zoom into a precise location in a massive image.	Rich control
MediaElement	A media file, such as a sound (which has no visual appearance) or a video window.	Rich control
DataGrid*	A multicolumn, multirow list filled with a collection of data objects.	Rich control

** These elements are not a part of the core Silverlight runtime. When you add them to a page, Visual Studio adds a reference to a separate assembly, which will be deployed in the compiled XAP file with your application.*

Silverlight's Add-On Assemblies

The architects of Silverlight have set out to keep the core framework as small as possible. This design makes the initial Silverlight plug-in small to download and quick to install—an obvious selling point to web surfers everywhere.

To achieve this lean-and-mean goal, the Silverlight designers have removed some functionality from the core Silverlight runtime and placed it in separate add-on assemblies. These assemblies are still considered to be part of the Silverlight platform, but if you want to use them, you'll need to package them with your application. This represents is an obvious trade-off, because it will increase the download size of your application. (The effect is mitigated by Silverlight's built-in compression, which you'll learn about later in this chapter.)

Two commonly used Silverlight assemblies are

- **System.Windows.Controls.dll:** This assembly contains a few new controls, including the Calendar, DatePicker, TabControl, and GridSplitter.
- **System.Windows.Controls.Data.dll:** This assembly has Silverlight's new built-from-scratch DataGrid.

Both of these assemblies add new controls to your Silverlight toolkit. In the near future, Microsoft plans to make many more add-on controls available. Eventually, the number of add-on controls will dwarf the number of core controls.

When you drag a control from an add-on assembly onto a Silverlight page, Visual Studio automatically adds the assembly reference you need. If you select that reference and look in the Properties window, you'll see that the Copy Local property is set to true, which is different from the other assemblies that make up the core Silverlight runtime. As a result, when you compile your application, the assembly will be embedded in the final package. Visual Studio is intelligent enough to recognize assemblies that aren't a part of the core Silverlight runtime—even if you add them by hand, it automatically sets Copy Local to true.

Understanding XAML

To understand the markup that underpins this page, you need to know a bit more about XAML. Conceptually, XAML is a markup language that plays an analogous role to HTML. HTML allows you to define the elements that make up an ordinary web page.

Every element in a XAML document maps to an instance of a Silverlight class. The name of the element matches the name of the class *exactly*. For example, consider the elements that were added in the previous example. The <StackPanel> element instructs Silverlight to create a StackPanel object (which lays out a group of elements in a horizontal or vertical stack, one next to the other). The <TextBlock> element instructs Silverlight to create a TextBlock object (which displays a block of formatted text). As in HTML, the way you nest elements in XAML is important. Because the <TextBlock> element is nested inside the <StackPanel> element, and because the StackPanel is a container control, the TextBlock is rendered inside the StackPanel.

When you use an element like <TextBlock> in a XAML file, the Silverlight parser recognizes that you want to create an instance of the TextBlock class. However, it doesn't necessarily know what TextBlock class to use. After all, even if the Silverlight namespaces only include a single class with that name, there's no guarantee that you won't create a similarly named class of your own. Clearly, you need a way to indicate the Silverlight namespace information in order to use an element.

In Silverlight, classes are resolved by mapping XML namespaces to Silverlight namespaces. In the sample document shown earlier, two namespaces are defined in the root <UserControl> element (followed by the Width and Height attributes that set the dimensions of the Silverlight page):

```
<UserControl x:Class="SilverlightApplication1.Page"
    xmlns="http://schema.microsoft.com/winfx/2006/xaml/presentation"
    xmlns:x="http://schemas.microsoft.com/winfx/2006/xaml"
    Width="400" Height="100">
```

You'll find these two namespaces in every XAML document you create for Silverlight:

- `http://schema.microsoft.com/winfx/2006/xaml/presentation` is the core Silverlight namespace. It encompasses all the Silverlight classes, including the Grid, StackPanel, TextBlock, and Button used in this example. Ordinarily, this namespace is declared without a namespace prefix, so it becomes the default namespace for the entire document. In other words, every element is automatically placed in this namespace unless you specify otherwise.
- `http://schemas.microsoft.com/winfx/2006/xaml` is the XAML namespace. It includes various XAML utility features that allow you to influence how your document is interpreted. This namespace is typically mapped to the prefix x.

These two namespaces give you access to the core library of Silverlight elements.

Mapping Additional Namespaces

In many situations, you'll want to have access to different namespaces in a XAML file. For example, you might create a custom Silverlight control. Or, you might choose to use one of the few Silverlight controls that aren't a part of the core framework (such as the Calendar, DataGrid, or DatePicker). In this case, you need to define a new XML namespace prefix and map it to the right assembly. Here's the syntax you need:

```
<UserControl x:Class="SilverlightApplication1.Page"
  xmlns:w="clr-namespace:Widgets;assembly=Widgets"
  ...
```

The XML namespace declaration sets three pieces of information:

- **The XML namespace prefix:** You'll use the namespace prefix to refer to the namespace in your XAML page. In this example, that's w, although you can choose anything you want that doesn't conflict with another namespace prefix.
- **The .NET namespace:** In this example, the classes are located in the Widgets namespace. If you have classes that you want to use in multiple namespaces, you can map them to different XML namespaces or to the same XML namespace (as long as there aren't any conflicting class names).
- **The assembly:** In this example, the classes are part of the Widgets.dll assembly. Assuming you've added a reference to your Silverlight application that points to the Widgets assembly, it will be automatically included in the final XAP package. This assembly can't be an ordinary .NET assembly—instead, it must be a Silverlight class library assembly (which you can easily create with Visual Studio).

Once you've mapped your .NET namespace to an XML namespace, you can use it anywhere in your XAML document. For example, if the Widgets namespace contains a control named HotButton, you could create an instance like this:

```
<w:HotButton Text="Click Me!" Click="DoSomething"></w:HotButton>
```

Setting Properties

Each element in a XAML document corresponds to a class. Similarly, each attribute you set corresponds to a property or event, just as in ASP.NET. Silverlight uses type converters to convert the string value to the appropriate data type. In many cases, this is an easy task—for example, there's no difficulty in changing a string with a number into a number or a string with a color name into the corresponding color value:

```
<StackPanel Background="Red">
```

However, in other situations you need to set a property using an object that can't be easily represented as a single string. For example, instead of filling the page with a solid color background, you might prefer to create a more advanced brush that can paint a gradient.

In Silverlight, complex properties are handled with a nested element syntax. The nested element takes a two-part name in the form *ClassName.PropertyName*. Inside this element, you can instantiate the object you want with the appropriate element.

For example, the following markup sets the StackPanel.Background property by creating a RadialGradientBrush. It does this using a <StackPanel.Background> element (rather than setting the Background attribute of the <StackPanel> element, as in the previous example). To configure the RadialGradientBrush, you need to supply a center point for the gradient, and the gradient stops (the colors in the gradient). Figure 34-7 shows the result.

```
<UserControl ... >
  <StackPanel>
    <StackPanel.Background>
      <RadialGradientBrush Center="0.5,0.5">
        <GradientStop Offset="0" Color="LightSteelBlue" />
        <GradientStop Offset="1" Color="White" />
      </RadialGradientBrush>
    </StackPanel.Background>
```

```
    <TextBlock x:Name="lblMessage" Text="Hello world." Margin="5"></TextBlock>
    <Button x:Name="cmdClickMe" Content="Click Me!" Margin="5"></Button>
  </StackPanel>
</UserControl>
```

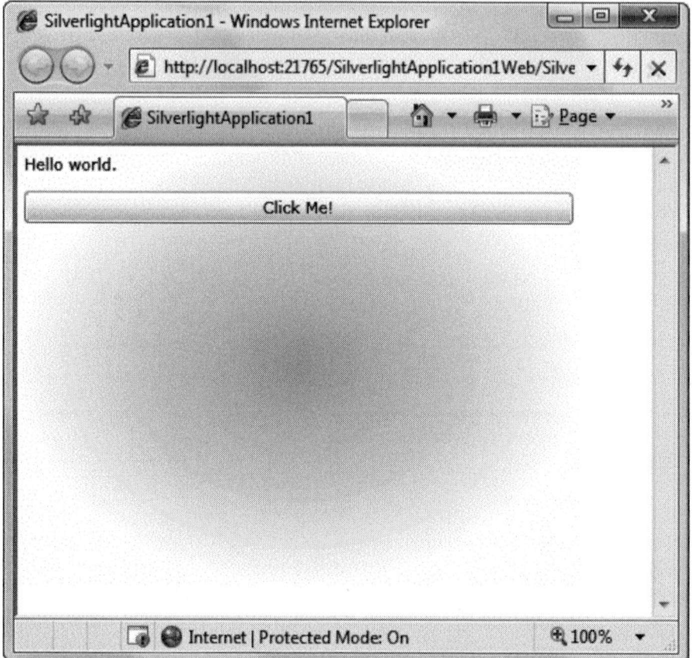

Figure 34-7. *A Silverlight page with a RadialGradientBrush background*

The XAML Code-Behind

XAML allows you to construct a user interface, but in order to make a functioning application, you need a way to connect the event handlers that have your application code. XAML makes this easy using the Class attribute shown here:

```
<UserControl x:Class="SilverlightApplication1.Page"
    xmlns=http://schema.microsoft.com/winfx/2006/xaml/presentation
    xmlns:x="http://schemas.microsoft.com/winfx/2006/xaml"
    Width="400" Height="100">
```

The x namespace prefix places the Class attribute in the XAML namespace, which means the Class attribute is a more general part of the XAML language, not a specific Silverlight ingredient.

In fact, the Class attribute tells the Silverlight parser to generate a new class with the specified name. That class derives from the class that's named by the XML element. In other words, this example creates a new class named SilverlightApplication1.Page, which derives from the base UserControl class. The automatically generated portion of this class is merged with the code you've supplied in the code-behind file.

Usually, every XAML file will have a corresponding code-behind class with client-side C# code. Visual Studio creates a code-behind class for the Page.xaml file named Page.xaml.cs. Here's what you'll see in the Page.xaml.cs file (not including the namespace imports):

```
namespace SilverlightApplication1
{
    public partial class Page : UserControl
    {
        public Page()
        {
            InitializeComponent();
        }
    }
}
```

Currently, the Page class code doesn't include any real functionality. However, it does include one important detail—the default constructor, which calls InitializeComponent() when you create an instance of the class. This parses your markup, creates the corresponding objects, sets their properties, and attaches any event handlers you've defined.

■ **Note** The InitializeComponent() method plays a key role in Silverlight content. For that reason, you should never delete the InitializeComponent() call from the constructor. Similarly, if you add another constructor, make sure it also calls InitializeComponent().

There's one more detail to consider. In your code-behind class, you'll often want to manipulate controls programmatically. For example, you might want to read or change properties or attach and detach event handlers on the fly. To make this possible, the control must include the Name attribute:

```
<TextBlock x:Name="lblMessage" Text="Hello world." Margin="5"></TextBlock>
```

This model is surprisingly like developing an ASP.NET web page. However, the underlying plumbing is completely different. XAML markup is parsed on the client side by the Silverlight engine using a scaled-down version of the CLR. The final content is rendered using a specialized Silverlight control that's embedded in the page. ASP.NET markup is processed by the ASP.NET engine on the server, along with any ordinary HTML that the page contains. The final result is rendered to HTML and then sent to the client.

Handling Events

To attach an event, you use attributes. However, now you need to assign the name of your event handler to the name of the event. This is similar to the approach used in ASP.NET web pages, except for that fact that event attributes do not begin with the word On.

For example, the Button element exposes an event named Click that fires when the button is triggered with the mouse or keyboard. To react to this event, you add the Click attribute to the Button element, and set it to the name of a method in your code:

```
<Button x:Name="cmdClickMe" Click="cmdClickMe_Click" Content="Click Me!"
 Margin="5"></Button>
```

■ **Tip** Although it's not required, it's a common convention to name event handler methods in the form ElementName_EventName. If the element doesn't have a defined name (presumably because you don't need to interact with it in any other place in your code), consider using the name it would have.

This example assumes that you've created an event handling method named cmdClickMe_Click. Here's what it looks like in the Page.xaml.cs file:

```
private void cmdClickMe_Click(object sender, RoutedEventArgs e)
{
    lblMessage.Text = "Goodbye, cruel world.";
}
```

Figure 34-8 shows the previous example at work. When you click the button, the event handling code runs and the text changes. This process happens entirely on the client—there is no need to contact the server or post back the page, as there is in a server-side programming framework like ASP.NET. All the Silverlight code is executed on the client side by the scaled-down version of .NET that's embedded in the Silverlight plug-in.

You'll find that Silverlight elements provide a subset of the full set of events found in rich client platforms like WPF and Windows Forms. You'll find most of the events that you expect, including change events (like TextChanged and SelectionChanged), keyboard events (KeyDown, KeyUp, GotFocus, and LostFocus), mouse events (MouseLeftButtonDown, MouseLeftButtonUp, MouseEnter, MouseLeave, and MouseMove), and initialization events (Loaded).

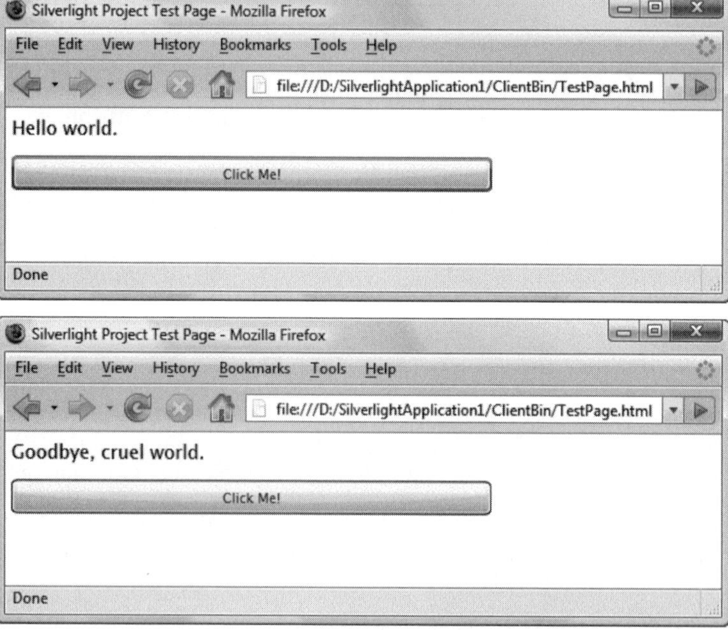

Figure 34-8. *Running a Silverlight application (in Firefox)*

Browsing the Silverlight Class Libraries

In order to write practical code, you need to know quite a bit about the classes you have to work with. That means acquiring a thorough knowledge of the core class libraries that ship with Silverlight.

Silverlight includes a subset of the classes from the full .NET Framework. Although it would be impossible to cram the entire .NET Framework into Silverlight—after all, it's a 5 MB download that needs to support a variety of browsers and operating systems—Silverlight includes a remarkable amount of functionality.

The Silverlight version of the .NET Framework is simplified in two ways. First, it doesn't provide the sheer number of types you'll find in the full .NET Framework. Second, the classes that it does include often don't provide the full complement of constructors, methods, properties, and events. Instead, Silverlight keeps only the most practical members of the most important classes, which leaves it with enough functionality to create surprisingly compelling code.

■ **Note** The Silverlight classes are designed to have public interfaces that resemble their full-fledged counterparts in the .NET Framework. However, the actual plumbing of these classes is quite different. All the Silverlight classes have been rewritten from the ground up to be as streamlined and efficient as possible.

Before you start doing any serious Silverlight programming, you might like to browse the Silverlight version of the .NET Framework. One way to do so is to open a Silverlight project, and then show the Object Browser in Visual Studio (choose View ➤ Object Browser). Along with the assembly for the code in your project, you'll see the following Silverlight assemblies:

- **mscorlib.dll:** This assembly is the Silverlight equivalent of the mscorlib.dll assembly that includes the most fundamental parts of the .NET Framework. The Silverlight version includes core data types, exceptions, and interfaces in the System namespace, ordinary and generic collections, file management classes, and support for globalization, reflection, resources, debugging, and multithreading.
- **System.dll:** This assembly contains additional generic collections, classes for dealing with URIs, and classes for dealing with regular expressions.
- **System.Core.dll:** This assembly contains support for LINQ. The name of the assembly matches the full .NET Framework, which implements features that were added in .NET 3.5 in an assembly named System.Core.dll.
- **System.Net.dll:** This assembly contains classes that support networking, allowing you to download web pages and create socket-based connections.
- **System.Windows.dll:** This assembly includes many of the classes for building Silverlight user interfaces, including basic elements, shapes and brushes, classes that support animation and data binding, and a version of the OpenFileDialog that works with isolated storage.
- **System.Windows.Browser.dll:** This assembly contains classes for interacting with HTML elements.
- **System.Xml.dll:** This assembly includes the bare minimum classes you need for XML processing: XmlReader and XmlWriter.

■ **Note** Some of the members in the Silverlight assemblies are only available to .NET Framework code, and aren't callable from your code. These members are marked with the SecurityCritical attribute. However, this attribute does not appear in the Object Browser, so you won't be able to determine whether a specific feature is usable in a Silverlight application until you try to use it. (If you attempt to use a member that has the SecurityCritical attribute, you'll get a SecurityException.) For example, Silverlight applications are only allowed to access the file system through the isolated storage API or the OpenFileDialog class. For that reason, the constructor for the FileStream class is decorated with the SecurityCritical attribute.

Layout

Silverlight inherits the most important part of WPF's extremely flexible layout model. Using the layout model, you organize your content in a set of different layout containers. Each container has its own layout logic—one stacks elements, another arranges them in a grid of invisible cells, and another uses a hard-coded coordinate system. If you're ambitious, you can even create your own containers with custom layout logic.

This is important, because the top-level UserControl that defines a Silverlight page can hold only a single element. To fit in more than one element and create a more practical user interface, you need to place a container in your page and then add other elements to that container.

Silverlight provides three Panel-derived classes that you can use to arrange layout: StackPanel, Canvas, and Grid. You've already seen the StackPanel, which places items in a top-to-bottom or left-to-right stack (depending on the value of the Orientation property). In the following sections, you'll consider the Canvas and the Grid.

The Canvas

The Canvas is the simplest of Silverlight's three layout containers. It allows you to place elements using exact coordinates, which is a poor choice for designing rich data-driven forms and standard dialogs, but a valuable tool if you need to build something a little different (such as a drawing surface for a diagramming tool). The Canvas is also the most lightweight of the layout containers. That's because it doesn't include any complex layout logic to negotiate the sizing preferences of its children. Instead, it simply lays them all out at the position they specify, with the exact size they want.

To position an element in the Canvas, you use *attached properties*. Attached properties are another concept that's brought over from WPF. Essentially, an attached property is a property that's defined by one class but used by another. Attached properties are a key extensibility mechanism, because they allow classes to interact in flexible ways even without prior planning.

The Canvas provides a good example. To position elements in a Canvas, you need to set three details: the Left coordinate, the Top coordinate, and the ZIndex layer. The simplest possible design, which Silverlight doesn't use, is to define Left, Top, and ZIndex properties in the base FrameworkElement class. Because all elements inherit from FrameworkElement, this would ensure that all elements have the layout properties that the Canvas needs. However, this apparently straightforward solution quickly runs into serious problems. First, it risks cluttering the FrameworkElement with dozens of properties, because different layout containers need to track different details. Confusingly, many of these properties will have no effect unless the element is being used with a specific container. And if you want to devise a new layout container that uses a different layout mechanism, you're out of luck, because you can't revise the FrameworkElement class on your own.

Attached properties offer a solution to this problem. With attached properties, the Left, Top, and ZIndex properties are defined with the element that uses them—the Canvas. However, the elements inside the Canvas can "borrow" these properties to position themselves. This way, elements don't need to be specifically designed to work with the Canvas—they just do. It also makes more sense conceptually for the properties to be "attached" to the Canvas, because it's the Canvas that reads these values and acts on them, not the contained element.

To set an attached property in XAML, you use a two-part syntax with a period. The portion on the left of the period is the name of the class where the property is defined (like Canvas), while the portion on the right of the period is the name of the property (like Top). Here's an example that places a TextBlock in a specific location in a Canvas:

```
<Canvas>
  <TextBlock x:Name="lblMessage" Text="Hello world."
   Canvas.Top="30" Canvas.Left="30"></TextBlock>
</Canvas>
```

Coordinates are measured from the top-left corner, so this places the element 30 pixels from the top and left edges. If you don't set the Top and Left properties, they default to 0, which places the element in the top-left corner.

■ **Note** Because the Canvas uses absolute positioning, there's no need to use properties that can influence other layout containers, such as Margin, Padding, HorizontalAlignment, and VerticalAlignment. These have no effect on the layout logic that the Canvas uses.

If you want to modify an attached property programmatically, you need to use a slightly more convoluted syntax. You must call a method that's named in the form ClassName.SetPropertyName(). In other words, to set the Canvas.Top property you can call Canvas.SetTop(). When calling this method, you must pass in two parameters: the element you want to modify and the new value you want to set. You can call the corresponding Get method (in this case, Canvas.GetTop()) to retrieve the current value of an attached property.

The following line of code uses this technique to change the Canvas.Top property that's applied to the TextBlock to 100:

```
Canvas.SetTop(lblMessage, 100);
```

■ **Note** Confusingly, you can set attached properties on an element even if it's not in the right container. For example, you can set Canvas.Top and Canvas.Left on elements that aren't placed in a Canvas. In this case, the attached property is set, but it has no effect.

Layering Elements in a Canvas

If you have more than one overlapping element, you can set the attached Canvas.ZIndex property to control how they are layered.

Ordinarily, all the elements you add have the same ZIndex: 0. When elements have the same ZIndex, they're displayed in the same order that they're declared in the XAML markup. Elements declared later in the markup are displayed on top of elements that are declared earlier.

However, you can promote any element to a higher level by increasing its ZIndex. That's because higher ZIndex elements always appear over lower ZIndex elements. Here's an example that uses this technique to reverse the layering of two rectangles:

```
<Rectangle Canvas.Left="60" Canvas.Top="80" Canvas.ZIndex="1"
 Fill="Blue" Width="50" Height="50" />
<Rectangle Canvas.Left="70" Canvas.Top="120" Width="100" Height="50"
 Fill="Yellow" />
```

Now the blue rectangle will be superimposed over the yellow rectangle, despite the fact that it's declared earlier in the markup.

■ **Note** The actual values you use for the Canvas.ZIndex property have no meaning. The important detail is how the ZIndex value of one element compares to the ZIndex value of another. You can set the ZIndex using any positive or negative integer.

The ZIndex property is particularly useful if you need to change the position of an element programmatically. Just call the Canvas.SetZIndex() method with the element you want to modify and the new ZIndex value you want to apply. Unfortunately, there is no BringToFront() or SendToBack() method—it's up to you to keep track of the highest and lowest ZIndex values if you want to implement this behavior.

Dragging Circles

You can put these concepts together using a simple example.

Figure 34-9 shows a Silverlight application that allows you to draw and move small circles. Every time you click the Canvas, a red circle appears. To move a circle, you simply click and drag it to a new position. When you click a circle, it changes color from red to green. Finally, when you release your circle, it changes color to orange. There's no practical limit to how many circles you can add or how many times you can move them around your drawing surface.

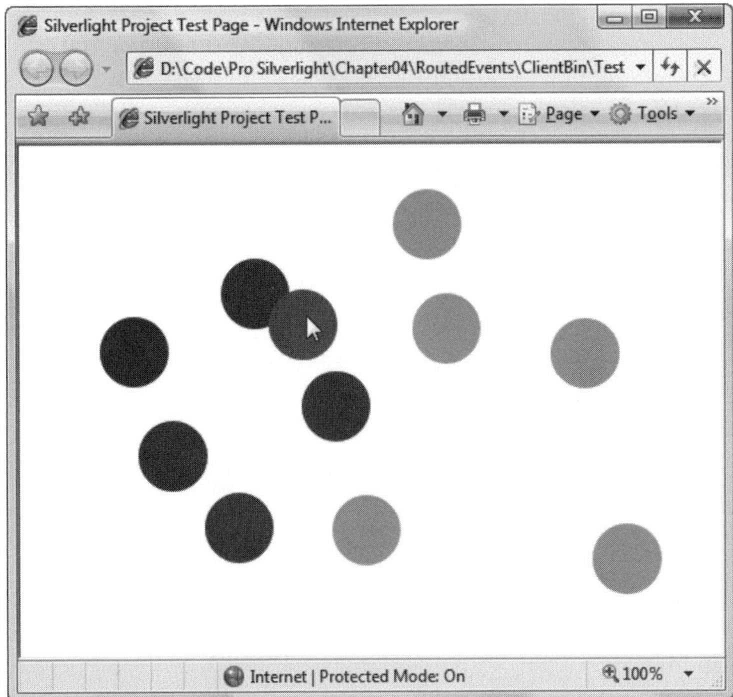

Figure 34-9. Dragging shapes

Each circle is an instance of the Ellipse element, which is simply a colored shape that's a basic ingredient in 2D drawing. Obviously, you can't define all the ellipses you need in your XAML markup. Instead, you need a way to generate the Ellipse objects dynamically each time the user clicks the Canvas.

Creating an Ellipse object isn't terribly difficult—after all, you can instantiate it like any other .NET object, set its properties, and attach event handlers. You can even use the SetValue() method to set attached properties to place it in the correct location in the Canvas. However, there's one more detail to take care of—you need a way to place the Ellipse in the Canvas. This is easy enough, as all layout containers include a Children property that holds a collection of child elements. Once you've added an element to this collection, it will appear in the Canvas.

The XAML page for this example uses a single event handler for the Canvas.MouseLeftButtonDown event. No other elements are defined.

```
<Canvas x:Name="parentCanvas" MouseLeftButtonDown="canvas_Click"
 Background="BlanchedAlmond">

 </Canvas>
```

In the code-behind class, you need two member variables to keep track of whether or not an ellipse-dragging operation is currently taking place:

```
// Keep track of when an ellipse is being dragged.
private bool isDragging = false;
```

```
// When an ellipse is clicked, record the exact position
// where the click is made.
private Point mouseOffset;
```

■ **Note** Unlike ASP.NET, it's perfectly acceptable to use instance variables to retain state in a Silverlight application. That's because a Silverlight application remains in memory for its entire lifetime. This is quite different from the code-behind classes that you create for ASP.NET pages. Here, instance variables are unreliable, because they're dropped from memory every time the page is rendered and they aren't available in subsequent post backs (unless you take additional steps to store them somewhere else).

Here's the event-handling code that creates an ellipse when the Canvas is clicked:

```
private void canvas_Click(object sender, MouseButtonEventArgs e)
{
    // Create an ellipse (unless the user is in the process
    // of dragging another one).
    if (!isDragging)
    {
        // Give the ellipse a 50-pixel diameter and a red fill.
        Ellipse ellipse = new Ellipse();
        ellipse.Fill = new SolidColorBrush(Colors.Red);
        ellipse.Width = 50;
        ellipse.Height = 50;

        // Use the current mouse position for the center of
        // the ellipse.
        Point point = e.GetPosition(this);
        ellipse.SetValue(Canvas.TopProperty, point.Y - ellipse.Height/2);
        ellipse.SetValue(Canvas.LeftProperty, point.X - ellipse.Width/2);

        // Watch for left-button clicks.
        ellipse.MouseLeftButtonDown += ellipse_MouseDown;

        // Add the ellipse to the Canvas.
        parentCanvas.Children.Add(ellipse);
    }
}
```

Not only does this code create the ellipse, it also connects an event handler that responds when the ellipse is clicked. This event handler changes the ellipse color and initiates the ellipse-dragging operation:

```
private void ellipse_MouseDown(object sender, MouseButtonEventArgs e)
{
    // Dragging mode begins.
    isDragging = true;
    Ellipse ellipse = (Ellipse)sender;
```

```
    // Get the position of the click relative to the ellipse
    // so the top-left corner of the ellipse is (0,0).
    mouseOffset = e.GetPosition(ellipse);

    // Change the ellipse color.
    ellipse.Fill = new SolidColorBrush(Colors.Green);

    // Watch this ellipse for more mouse events.
    ellipse.MouseMove += ellipse_MouseMove;
    ellipse.MouseLeftButtonUp += ellipse_MouseUp;

    // Capture the mouse. This way you'll keep receiveing
    // the MouseMove event even if the user jerks the mouse
    // off the ellipse.
    ellipse.CaptureMouse();
}
```

The ellipse isn't actually moved until the MouseMove event occurs. At this point, the Canvas.Left and Canvas.Top attached properties are set on the ellipse to move it to its new position. The coordinates are set based on the current position of the mouse, taking into account the point where the user initially clicked. This ellipse then moves seamlessly with the mouse, until the left mouse button is released.

```
private void ellipse_MouseMove(object sender, MouseEventArgs e)
{
    if (isDragging)
    {
        Ellipse ellipse = (Ellipse)sender;

        // Get the position of the ellipse relative to the Canvas.
        Point point = e.GetPosition(this);

        // Move the ellipse.
        ellipse.SetValue(Canvas.TopProperty, point.Y - mouseOffset.Y);
        ellipse.SetValue(Canvas.LeftProperty, point.X - mouseOffset.X);
    }
}
```

When the left mouse button is released, the code changes the color of the ellipse, releases the mouse capture, and stops listening for the MouseMove and MouseUp events. The user can click the ellipse again to start the whole process over.

```
private void ellipse_MouseUp(object sender, MouseButtonEventArgs e)
{
    if (isDragging)
    {
        Ellipse ellipse = (Ellipse)sender;

        // Change the ellipse color.
        ellipse.Fill = new SolidColorBrush(Colors.Orange);

        // Don't watch the mouse events any longer.
        ellipse.MouseMove -= ellipse_MouseMove;
        ellipse.MouseLeftButtonUp -= ellipse_MouseUp;
```

```
            ellipse.ReleaseMouseCapture();

            isDragging = false;
        }
    }
```

The Grid

The Grid is the most powerful layout container in Silverlight. In fact, the Grid is so useful that when you add a new XAML document for a page in Visual Studio, it automatically adds the Grid tags as the first-level container, nested inside the root UserControl element.

The Grid separates elements into an invisible grid of rows and columns. Although more than one element can be placed in a single cell (in which case they overlap), it generally makes sense to place just a single element per cell. Of course, that element may itself be another layout container that organizes its own group of contained controls.

■ **Tip** Although the Grid is designed to be invisible, you can set the Grid.ShowGridLines property to true to take a closer look. This feature isn't really intended for prettying up a page. Instead, it's a debugging convenience that's designed to help you understand how the Grid has subdivided itself into smaller regions. This feature is important because you have the ability to control exactly how the Grid chooses column widths and row heights.

Creating a Grid-based layout is a two-step process. First, you choose the number of columns and rows that you want. Next, you assign the appropriate row and column to each contained element, thereby placing it in just the right spot.

You create grids and rows by filling the Grid.ColumnDefinitions and Grid.RowDefinitions collections with objects. For example, if you decide you need two rows and three columns, you'd add the following tags:

```
<Grid ShowGridLines="True" Background="White">
  <Grid.RowDefinitions>
    <RowDefinition></RowDefinition>
    <RowDefinition></RowDefinition>
  </Grid.RowDefinitions>
  <Grid.ColumnDefinitions>
    <ColumnDefinition></ColumnDefinition>
    <ColumnDefinition></ColumnDefinition>
    <ColumnDefinition></ColumnDefinition>
  </Grid.ColumnDefinitions>

  ...
</Grid>
```

As this example shows, it's not necessary to supply any information in a RowDefinition or ColumnDefinition element. If you leave them empty (as shown here), the Grid will share the space evenly between all rows and columns. In this example, each cell will be exactly the same size, depending on the size of the containing page.

To place individual elements into a cell, you use the Row and Column attached properties. Both these properties take 0-based index numbers. For example, here's how you could create a partially filled grid of buttons:

```
<Grid ShowGridLines="True" Background="White">
  ...

  <Button Grid.Row="0" Grid.Column="0" Content="Top Left"></Button>
  <Button Grid.Row="0" Grid.Column="1" Content="Middle Left"></Button>
  <Button Grid.Row="1" Grid.Column="2" Content="Bottom Right"></Button>
  <Button Grid.Row="1" Grid.Column="1" Content="Bottom Middle"></Button>
</Grid>
```

Each element must be placed into its cell explicitly. This allows you to place more than one element into a cell (which rarely makes sense) or leave certain cells blank (which is often useful). It also means you can declare your elements out of order, as with the final two buttons in this example. However, it makes for clearer markup if you define your controls row by row, and from right to left in each row.

There is one exception. If you don't specify the Grid.Row property, the Grid assumes that it's 0. The same behavior applies to the Grid.Column property. Thus, you leave both attributes off of an element to place it in the first cell of the Grid.

Figure 34-10 shows how this simple grid appears at two different sizes. Notice that the ShowGridLines property is set to true so that you can see the separation between each column and row.

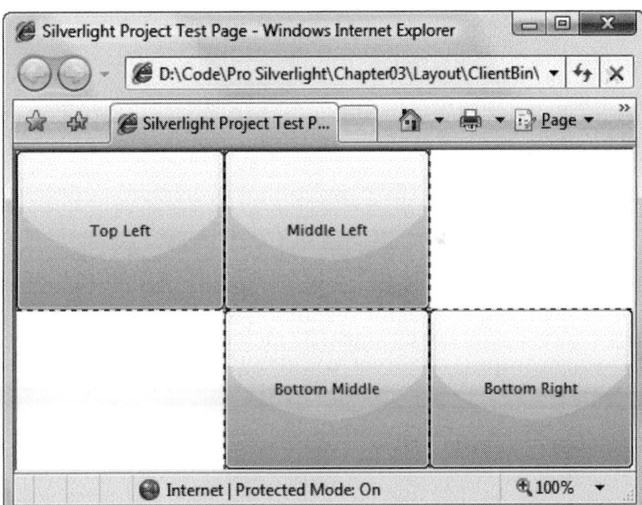

***Figure 34-10.** A simple grid*

■ **Tip** In Figure 34-10, the grid grows to fit the available size in the web page. To use this design, you must remove the Height and Width attributes from the UserControl start tag at the top of your page. That way, the UserControl will use all the available space on the page.

Fine-Tuning Rows and Columns

As you've seen, the Grid gives you the ability to create a proportionately sized collection of rows and columns, which is often quite useful. However, to unlock the full potential of the Grid, you can change the way each row and column is sized.

The Grid supports three sizing strategies:

- **Absolute sizes:** You choose the exact size using pixels. This is the least useful strategy because it's not flexible enough to deal with changing content size, changing container size, or localization.
- **Automatic sizes:** Each row or column is given exactly the amount of space it needs, and no more. This is one of the most useful sizing modes.
- **Proportional sizes:** Space is divided between a group of rows or columns. This is the standard setting for all rows and columns. For example, in Figure 34-10 you can see that all cells increase in size proportionately as the Grid expands.

For maximum flexibility, you can mix and match these different sizing modes. For example, it's often useful to create several automatically sized rows and then let one or two remaining rows get the leftover space through proportional sizing.

You set the sizing mode using the Width property of the ColumnDefinition object or the Height property of the RowDefinition object to a number. For example, here's how you set an absolute width of 100 pixels:

```
<ColumnDefinition Width="100"></ColumnDefinition>
```

To use automatic sizing, you use a value of Auto:

```
<ColumnDefinition Width="Auto"></ColumnDefinition>
```

Finally, to use proportional sizing, you use an asterisk (*):

```
<ColumnDefinition Width="*"></ColumnDefinition>
```

This syntax stems from the world of the Web, where it's used with HTML frames pages. If you use a mix of proportional sizing and other sizing modes, the proportionally sized rows or columns get whatever space is left over.

If you want to divide the remaining space unequally, you can assign a weight, which you must place before the asterisk. For example, if you have two proportionately sized rows and you want the first to be half as high as the second, you could share the remaining space like this:

```
<RowDefinition Height="*"></RowDefinition>
<RowDefinition Height="2*"></RowDefinition>
```

This tells the Grid that the height of the second row should be twice the height of the first row. You can use whatever numbers you like to portion out the extra space.

Nesting Layout Containers

The Grid is impressive on its own, but most realistic user interfaces combine several layout containers. They may use an arrangement with more than one Grid, or mix the Grid with other layout containers like the StackPanel.

The following markup presents a simple example of this principle. It creates a basic dialog box with an OK and Cancel button in the bottom-right corner, and a large content region that's sized to fit its content (the text in a TextBlock). The entire package is centered in the middle of the page by setting the alignment properties on the Grid.

```
<Grid ShowGridLines="True" Background="SteelBlue"
 HorizontalAlignment="Center" VerticalAlignment="Center">
  <Grid.RowDefinitions>
    <RowDefinition Height="*"></RowDefinition>
    <RowDefinition Height="Auto"></RowDefinition>
  </Grid.RowDefinitions>

  <TextBlock Margin="10" Grid.Row="0" Foreground="White"
   Text="This is simply a test of nested containers."></TextBlock>
  <StackPanel Grid.Row="1" HorizontalAlignment="Right" Orientation="Horizontal">
    <Button Margin="10,10,2,10" Padding="3" Content="OK"></Button>
    <Button Margin="2,10,10,10" Padding="3" Content="Cancel"></Button>
  </StackPanel>
</Grid>
```

You'll notice that this Grid doesn't declare any columns. This is a shortcut you can take if your grid uses just one column and that column is proportionately sized (so it fills the entire width of the Grid). Figure 34-11 shows the rather pedestrian dialog box this markup creates.

■ **Note** In this example, the Padding adds some minimum space between the button border and the content inside (the word OK or Cancel). In controls that provide a Padding property, like the Button, it acts as an internal margin between the control borders and the inner content.

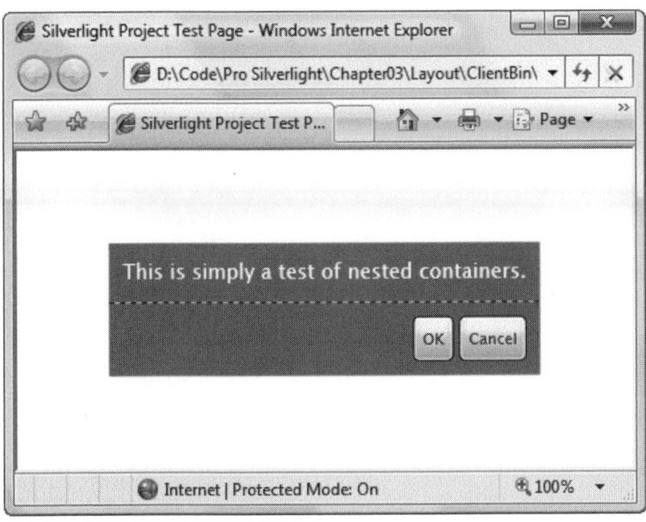

Figure 34-11. A basic dialog box

At first glance, nesting layout containers seems like a fair bit more work than placing controls in precise positions using coordinates. And in many cases, it is. However, the longer setup time is compensated by the ease with which you can change the user interface in the future. For example, if you decide you want the OK and Cancel buttons to be centered at the bottom of the page, you simply need to change the alignment of the StackPanel that contains them:

```
<StackPanel Grid.Row="1" HorizontalAlignment="Center" ... >
```

Similarly, if you need to change the amount of content in the first row, the entire Grid will be enlarged to fit and the buttons will move obligingly out of the way.

Spanning Rows and Columns

You've already seen how you place elements in cells using the Row and Column attached properties. You can also use two more attached properties to make an element stretch over several cells: RowSpan and ColumnSpan. These properties take the number of rows or columns that the element should occupy.

For example, this button will take all the space that's available in the first and second cell of the first row:

```
<Button Grid.Row="0" Grid.Column="0" Grid.RowSpan="2" Content="Span Button">
</Button>
```

And this button will stretch over four cells in total by spanning two columns and two rows:

```
<Button Grid.Row="0" Grid.Column="0" Grid.RowSpan="2" Grid.ColumnSpan="2"
 Content="Span Button"></Button>
```

Row and column spanning can achieve some interesting effects and are particularly handy when you need to fit elements in a tabular structure that's broken up by dividers or longer sections of content.

Using column spanning, you could rewrite the simple dialog box example from Figure 34-11 using just a single Grid. This Grid divides the page into three columns, spreads the text box over all three, and uses the last two columns to align the OK and Cancel buttons.

```
<Grid ShowGridLines="True" Background="SteelBlue"
 HorizontalAlignment="Center" VerticalAlignment="Center">
  <Grid.RowDefinitions>
    <RowDefinition Height="*"></RowDefinition>
    <RowDefinition Height="Auto"></RowDefinition>
  </Grid.RowDefinitions>
  <Grid.ColumnDefinitions>
    <ColumnDefinition Width="*"></ColumnDefinition>
    <ColumnDefinition Width="Auto"></ColumnDefinition>
    <ColumnDefinition Width="Auto"></ColumnDefinition>
  </Grid.ColumnDefinitions>
  <TextBlock Margin="10" Grid.Row="0" Grid.Column="0" Grid.ColumnSpan="3"
   Foreground="White"
   Text="This is simply a test of nested containers."></TextBlock>

  <Button Margin="10,10,2,10" Padding="3"
    Grid.Row="1" Grid.Column="1" Content="OK"></Button>
  <Button Margin="2,10,10,10" Padding="3"
    Grid.Row="1" Grid.Column="2" Content="Cancel"></Button>
</Grid>
```

Most developers will agree that this layout isn't clear or sensible. The column widths are determined by the size of the two buttons at the bottom of the page, which makes it difficult to add new content into the existing Grid structure. If you make even a minor addition to this page, you'll probably be forced to create a new set of columns.

As this shows, when you choose the layout containers for a page, you aren't simply interested in getting the correct layout behavior—you also want to build a layout structure that's easy to maintain and enhance in the future. A good rule of thumb is to use smaller layout containers such as the StackPanel for one-off layout tasks, such as arranging a group of buttons. On the other hand, if you need to apply a consistent structure to more than one area of your page, the Grid is an indispensable tool for standardizing your layout.

Animation

Animation is a key feature in Silverlight, as it provides some visual glitz that a server-based programming framework (like ASP.NET) can't easily emulate. In Silverlight, animation can be used to apply effects—for example, icons that grow when you move over them, logos that spin, text that scrolls into view, and so on—or as a way to design more ambitious commercials and browser-based games.

Animations are a core part of the Silverlight model. That means you don't need to use timers and event-handling code to put them into action. Instead, you can create them declaratively, configure them using one of a handful of classes, and put them into action without writing a single line of C# code.

Animation Basics

Silverlight animation is a scaled-down version of the WPF animation system. In order to understand Silverlight animation, you need to understand the following key rules:

- Silverlight performs time-based animation. Thus, you set the initial state, the final state, and the duration of your animation. Silverlight calculates the frame rate.
- Silverlight uses a property-based animation model. That means a Silverlight animation can do only one thing: modify the value of a property over an interval of time. This sounds like a significant limitation (and in many ways it is), but there's a surprisingly large range of effects you can create by simply modifying properties.
- To animate a property, you need to have an animation class that supports its data type. For example, if you want to change a property that uses the double data type (which is one of the most common scenarios), you must use the DoubleAnimation class. If you want to modify the color that's used to paint the background of your Canvas, you need to use the ColorAnimation class.

Silverlight has relatively few animation classes, so you're limited in the data types you can use. At present, you can use animations to modify properties with the following data types: double, object, Color, and Point.

As a rule of thumb, the property-based animation is a great way to add dynamic effects to an otherwise ordinary application. However, if you need to use animations as part of the core purpose of your application and you want them to continue running over the lifetime of your application, you probably need something more flexible and more powerful. For example, if you're creating a basic arcade game or using complex physics calculations to model collisions, you'll need greater control over the animation. Unfortunately, Silverlight doesn't have an option for frame-based animation, so you'll be forced to create this sort of application the old-fashioned way—using a timer that fires periodically to update your visuals.

Defining an Animation

Creating an animation is a multistep process. You need to create three separate ingredients: an animation object to perform your animation, a storyboard to manage your animation, and an event trigger to start your storyboard. In the following sections, you'll tackle each of these steps.

The Animation Class

There are actually two types of animation classes in Silverlight. Each type of animation uses a different strategy for varying a property value.

- **Linear interpolation:** With linear interpretation, the property value varies gradually over the duration of the animation. Examples include DoubleAnimation, PointAnimation, and ColorAnimation.
- **Key frame animation:** With key frame animation, values can jump abruptly from one value to another, or they can combine jumps and periods of linear interpolation. Examples include ColorAnimationUsingKeyFrames, DoubleAnimationUsingKeyFrames, and PointAnimationUsingKeyFrames.

In this chapter, you'll focus exclusively on the most commonly used animation class: the DoubleAnimation class. The DoubleAnimation class uses linear interpolation to change a double from a starting value to its ending value. Like all animation classes, it's defined in the System.Windows.Media.Animation namespace.

Animations are defined using XAML markup. Although the animation classes aren't elements, they can still be created with the same XAML syntax. For example, here's the markup required to create a DoubleAnimation:

```
<DoubleAnimation From="160" To="300" Duration="0:0:5"></DoubleAnimation>
```

This animation lasts 5 seconds (as indicated by the Duration property, which takes a time value in the format Hours:Minutes:Seconds.FractionalSeconds). While the animation is running, it changes the target value from 160 to 300. If the DoubleAnimation is able to run at Silverlight's default maximum frame rate, it will adjust the value 60 times per second. Each time, it sets a value that's proportionately between the starting and ending values. For example, a fast-paced animation might change 160 to 160.4, then 160.8, then 161.2, and so on, making each change after just a fraction of a second. The overall effect is that the double value will appear to change smoothly and continuously for the entire duration of the animation.

There's one important detail that's missing from this markup. The animation indicates how the property will be changed, but it doesn't indicate what property to use. This detail is supplied by another ingredient, which is represented by the Storyboard class.

The Storyboard Class

The storyboard manages the timeline of your animation. You can use a storyboard to group multiple animations, and it also has the ability to control the playback of animation—pausing it, stopping it, and changing its position. However, the most basic feature provided by the Storyboard class is its ability to point to a specific property and specific element using the TargetProperty and TargetName properties. In other words, the storyboard bridges the gap between your animation and the property you want to animate.

Here's how you might define a storyboard that applies a DoubleAnimation to the Width property of a button named cmdGrow:

```
<Storyboard x:Name="storyboard"
  Storyboard.TargetName="cmdGrow" Storyboard.TargetProperty="Width">
  <DoubleAnimation From="160" To="300" Duration="0:0:5"></DoubleAnimation>
</Storyboard>
```

The Storyboard.TargetProperty property identifies the property you want to change in the target element. (In the previous example, it's Width.) If you don't supply a class name, the storyboard uses the parent element. If you want to set an attached property (for example, Canvas.Left or Canvas.Top), you need to wrap the entire property in brackets, like this:

```
<Storyboard x:Name="storyboard"
  Storyboard.TargetName="cmdGrow" Storyboard.TargetProperty="(Canvas.Left)">
  ...
</Storyboard>
```

Both TargetName and TargetProperty are attached properties. That means you can apply them directly to the animation, as shown here:

```
<Storyboard x:Name="storyboard">
  <DoubleAnimation
   Storyboard.TargetName="cmdGrow" Storyboard.TargetProperty="Width"
   From="160" To="300" Duration="0:0:5"></DoubleAnimation>
</Storyboard>
```

This syntax is more common, because it allows you to put several animations in the same storyboard but allow each animation to act on a different element and property. Although you can't animate the same property at the same time with multiple animations, you can (and often will) animate different properties of the same element at once.

All Silverlight elements provide a Resources property, which holds a collection where you can store miscellaneous objects. The primary purpose of the Resources collection is to allow you to define objects in XAML that aren't elements, and so can't be placed into the visual layout of your content region. Resources can be retrieved in your code or used elsewhere in your markup. The Resources collection is a convenient storage place for the button-growing animation:

```
<UserControl ... >
  <UserControl.Resources>
    <Storyboard x:Name="storyboard">
      <DoubleAnimation
       Storyboard.TargetName="cmdGrow" Storyboard.TargetProperty="Width"
       From="160" To="300" Duration="0:0:5"></DoubleAnimation>
    </Storyboard>
  </UserControl.Resources>

  <Grid>
    <Button x:Name="cmdGrow" Width="160" Height="30"
     Content="This button grows" Click="cmdGrow_Click"></Button>
  </Grid>
</UserControl>
```

Notice that it's now given a name, so you can manipulate it in your code. (You can also add a name to the DoubleAnimation if you want to tweak its properties programmatically before launching the animation.) You'll also notice that you need to explicitly specify the Storyboard.TargetName property to connect it to the right element when you're using this approach.

Now you simply need to call the methods of the Storyboard object in an event handler in your Silverlight code-behind file. The methods you can use include Begin(), Stop(), Pause(), Resume(), and Seek(), all of which are fairly self-explanatory.

```
private void cmdGrow_Click(object sender, RoutedEventArgs e)
{
    storyboard.Begin();
}
```

Now, clicking the button launches the animation, and the button stretches from 160 to 300 pixels, as shown in Figure 34-12.

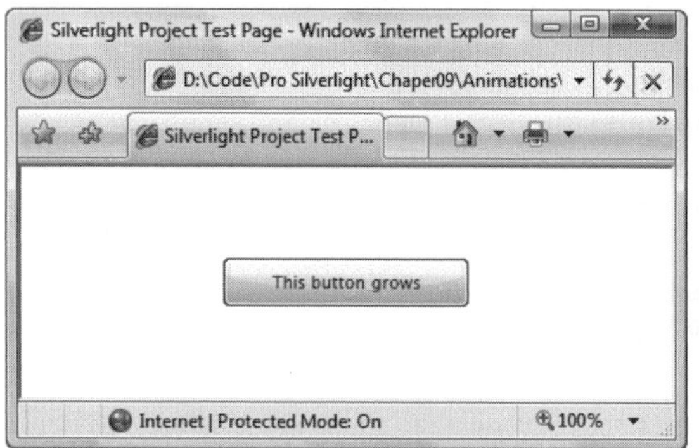

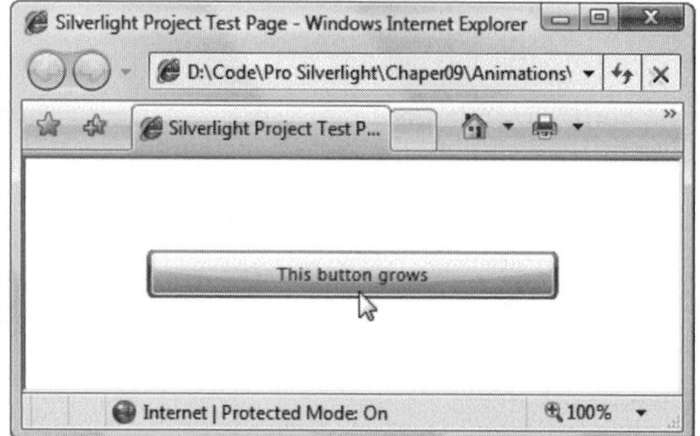

Figure 34-12. *Animating a button's width*

Configuring Animation Properties

To get the most out of your animations, you need to look a little closer at the base Animation class, which defines the properties that are provided by all animation classes. Table 34-3 describes them.

Table 34-3. *Properties of the Animation Class*

Name	Description
From	Sets the starting values for your animation. In many situations, you won't set From. In this case, Silverlight uses the current value of your element. For example, if you didn't set the initial width in the growing rectangle example, it would start at whatever it is currently. This is particularly useful if you're animating a value that might be changed by other code or other animations. In this situation, you want the animation to start from the current value, not jump abruptly to a preset From value.
To	Sets the ending value for your animation. In some situations, you won't set From or To. In this case, the property returns to whatever initial value is set in the XAML markup. For example, you could use this technique to shrink the rectangle in the previous example back to its original size when it's clicked.

Name	Description
By	Instead of using To, you can use By to create a cumulative animation. By sets a number that will be added to the initial value. For example, if you replace the To value in the rectangle-growing example with a By value of 10, the rectangle will grow 10 pixels wider than its current width over the course of the animation. If you run this animation every time the rectangle is clicked, it will continue to grow and grow.
Duration	The length of time the animation runs, from start to finish, as a Duration object.
AutoReverse	If true, the animation will play out in reverse once it's complete, reverting to the original value. This also doubles the time the animation takes.
RepeatBehavior	Allows you to repeat an animation a specific number of times. Or, you can use Forever to repeat the animation endlessly.
BeginTime	Sets a delay that will be added before the animation starts (as a TimeSpan). This delay is added to the total time, so a 5-second animation with a 5-second delay takes 10 seconds. BeginTime is useful when synchronizing different animations that start at the same time but should apply their effects in sequence.
SpeedRatio	Increases or decreases the speed of the animation. Ordinarily, SpeedRatio is 1. If you increase it, the animation completes more quickly (for example, a SpeedRatio of 5 completes five times faster). If you decrease it, the animation is slowed down (for example, a SpeedRatio of 0.5 takes twice as long). You can change the duration of your animation for an equivalent result. The SpeedRatio is not taken into account when applying the BeginTime delay.
FillBehavior	Determines what happens when the animation ends. Usually, it keeps the property fixed at the ending value (FillBehavior.HoldEnd), but you can also choose to return it to its original value (FillBehavior.Stop).

An Interactive Animation Example

Sometimes, you'll need to create every detail of an animation programmatically in code. In fact, this scenario is fairly common. It occurs anytime you have multiple animations to deal with, and you don't know in advance how many animations there will be or how they should be configured. It also occurs if you want to use the same animation in different pages, or you simply want the flexibility to separate all the animation-related details from your markup for easier reuse.

It isn't difficult to create, configure, and launch an animation programmatically. You begin by creating the animation and storyboard objects you need and adding the animations to the storyboard. You should also clean up your animations by reacting to the Storyboard.Completed event that fires when they finish.

The following example demonstrates a slightly more realistic use of animation, which is shown in Figure 34-13. It begins with a content region that's filled with irregularly shaped rectangles. When you click a rectangle, it begins to fall toward the bottom of the Canvas, and simultaneously begins to change color. You can click several rectangles in quick succession to start several simultaneous animations. To make this work, the page uses multiple storyboards, one for each rectangle that's currently falling. The storyboards are created as they're needed using code.

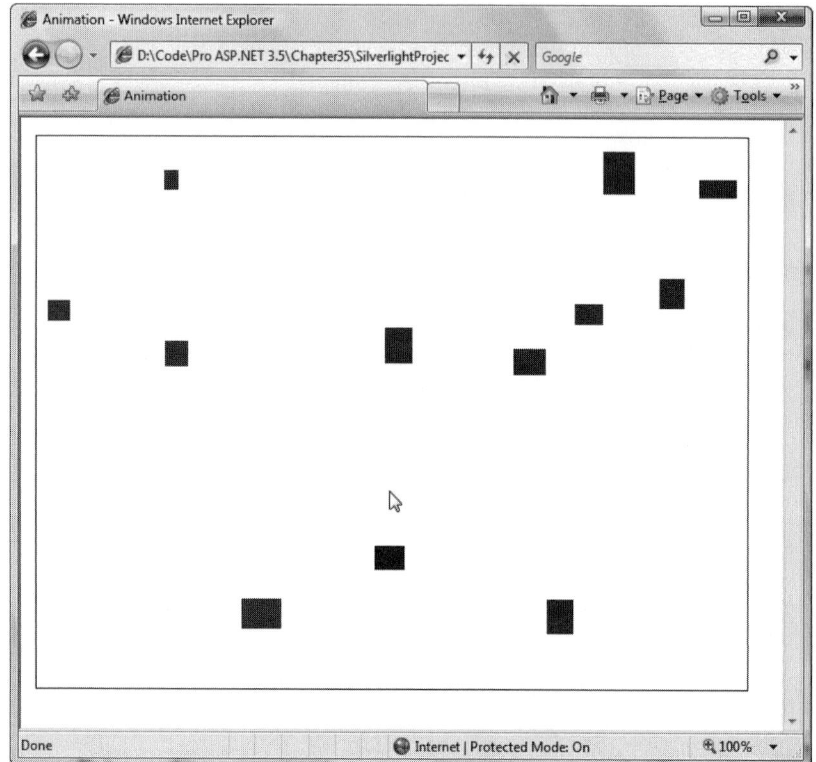

Figure 34-13. Falling rectangles

The markup for this example defines a simple page with a Border and a Canvas inside. The markup doesn't include a storyboard, because that detail needs to be created dynamically when the rectangle is clicked.

```
<UserControl x:Class="SilverlightApplication1.FallingRectangles"
 xmlns="http://schemas.microsoft.com/winfx/2006/xaml/presentation"
 xmlns:x="http://schemas.microsoft.com/winfx/2006/xaml" Loaded="Page_Loaded"
 Width="500" Height="500">
  <Border BorderBrush="SteelBlue" BorderThickness="1">
    <Canvas x:Name="canvas" Background="AliceBlue"></Canvas>
  </Border>
</UserControl>
```

You'll also notice that the Canvas doesn't contain any other elements. That's because this example uses a more flexible approach—it generates the rectangles dynamically. When the Canvas is loaded, it creates 20 rectangles of random size, at random locations. It wires the MouseLeftButtonDown event of each one to the same event handler.

```
public void Page_Loaded(object o, EventArgs e)
{
    // Generate some rectangles.
    Random rand = new Random();
    for (int i = 0; i < 20; i++)
    {
        // Create a new rectangle.
        Rectangle rect = new Rectangle();
        rect.Fill = new SolidColorBrush(Colors.Red);

        // Size and place it randomly.
        rect.Width = rand.Next(10, 40);
        rect.Height = rand.Next(10, 40);
        Canvas.SetTop(rect, rand.Next((int)(this.Height - rect.Height)));
        Canvas.SetLeft(rect, rand.Next((int)(this.Width - rect.Width)));

        // Handle clicks.
        rect.MouseLeftButtonDown += rect_MouseLeftButtonDown;

        // Add it to the Canvas.
        canvas.Children.Add(rect);
    }
}
```

When a rectangle is clicked, the new storyboard needs to be created, along with the appropriate animations. In this case, you need two animations, one for each property you plan to modify. The first animation is a DoubleAnimation that changes the Canvas.Top property to shift the rectangle down the page, while the second animation is a ColorAnimation that blends its color.

This storyboard is added to a collection so you can easily track the currently running storyboards (and the corresponding animated elements). An event handler is hooked up so your code can receive notification when the animation ends. Then the animation is started.

```
// Collection for tracking animations.
private Dictionary<Storyboard, Rectangle> animatedShapes =
  new Dictionary<Storyboard, Rectangle>();

private void rect_MouseLeftButtonDown(object sender, MouseButtonEventArgs e)
{
    Rectangle rect = (Rectangle)sender;

    // Create the storyboard for the rectangle.
    Storyboard storyboard = new Storyboard();

    // Create the animation for moving the rectangle.
    DoubleAnimation fallingAnimation = new DoubleAnimation();
    Storyboard.SetTarget(fallingAnimation, rect);
    Storyboard.SetTargetProperty(fallingAnimation,
      new PropertyPath("(Canvas.Top)"));
    fallingAnimation.To = this.Height - rect.Height;
    fallingAnimation.Duration = TimeSpan.FromSeconds(2);
    storyboard.Children.Add(fallingAnimation);

    // Create the animation for changing the rectangle's color.
```

```
    ColorAnimation colorAnimation = new ColorAnimation();
    Storyboard.SetTarget(colorAnimation, rect.Fill);
    Storyboard.SetTargetProperty(colorAnimation, new PropertyPath("Color"));
    colorAnimation.To = Colors.Blue;
    colorAnimation.Duration = fallingAnimation.Duration;
    storyboard.Children.Add(colorAnimation);

    // Track the rectangle.
    animatedShapes.Add(storyboard, rect);

    // React when the storyboard is finished.
    storyboard.Completed += storyboard_Completed;

    // Start the storyboard.
    storyboard.Begin();
}
```

This storyboard wraps two animations: a DoubleAnimation that moves the rectangle, and a ColorAnimation that changes the color of the associated brush object. The ColorAnimation uses linear interpolation, which means it will progressively blend the color from its initial value (in this example, red) to its final value (blue). The code for setting up the animations is fairly straightforward, once you're used to the attached property syntax (which is used to set Storyboard.Target and Storyboard.TargetProperty) and the PropertyPath object (which is used to provide the string that points to the property you want to animate).

When the storyboard ends, it's time to clean up. Here's the simplest code you could use to accomplish this task:

```
private void storyboard_Completed(object sender, EventArgs e)
{
    // Stop the storyboard.
    Storyboard storyboard = (Storyboard)sender;
    storyboard.Stop();

    // Remove it from the tracking collection.
    animatedShapes.Remove(storyboard);
}
```

However, there's a problem here. Animations don't actually change the underlying value of a property; they simply override it temporarily. But you won't necessarily notice this fact, because completed animations don't actually stop. Instead, when an animation reaches its end, it continues to hold the property at its final animated value. This means that after a storyboard has finished, the animated rectangle remains at the bottom of the page, and is still colored blue.

Here's the problem. When you create storyboards dynamically, you open up the possibility that there could be a significant number of storyboards running at the same time. To ensure good performance, it's important to explicitly stop the storyboard when its animations are finished. The code just shown does exactly that. However, stopping the animation returns your animated properties to their original values. In this example, that means each time you stop the animation of a falling rectangle it will jump back up to its original position and revert to the color red.

The solution is to retrieve the current value of the Canvas.Top property for the rectangle, then stop the animation, and then set the animated value. This last step moves the rectangle to its most recent animated position. The result is that every time a storyboard ends, the rectangle remains in its new position. Here's the code that implements this design:

```
private void storyboard_Completed(object sender, EventArgs e)
{
    // Stop the animation but keep the new position.
    Storyboard storyboard = (Storyboard)sender;
    Rectangle rect = animatedShapes[storyboard];
    double newTop = Canvas.GetTop(rect);
    storyboard.Stop();
    Canvas.SetTop(rect, newTop);

    // Remove it from the tracking collection.
    animatedShapes.Remove(storyboard);
}
```

Although the Canvas.Top property is set manually after the animation is stopped, the color is not. As a result, the rectangle reverts to its initial red color as soon as the storyboard is stopped.

■ **Note** There is one possible exception to the behavior described here. If you set the FillBehavior property of the animation class to FillBehavior.Stop, the storyboard will stop holding values when it ends. In the rectangle-dropping example, that means the rectangle would spring back to its original position and revert to the color red, even if you don't explicitly stop the storyboard.

There's another interesting quirk in this example. The animation always uses the same duration (2 seconds). However, the square you click may be close to the bottom or far from the bottom. As a result, squares closer to the bottom will fall more slowly, and squares farther from the bottom will fall faster.

Transforms

As you've already learned, Silverlight animations work by modifying the value of a property. Elements have several properties that can be usefully changed. For example, you can use Canvas.Left and Canvas.Top to move an element around. Or, you can alter the Opacity setting to make an element fade into or out of view. However, it's not immediately clear how you can perform more exciting alterations, like rotations.

The secret is *transforms*. A transform is an object that alters the way a shape or other element is drawn by shifting the coordinate system it uses. You can use transforms to stretch, rotate, skew, and otherwise manipulate the shapes, images, and text in your Silverlight user interface. Transforms are useful for getting the right shape you want, but they're even more interesting when you're animating. By animating a property in a transform, you can rotate a shape, move it from one place to another, or warp it dynamically.

Table 34-4 lists the transforms that are supported in Silverlight.

Table 34-4. Transform Classes

Name	Description	Important Properties
TranslateTransform	Displaces your coordinate system by some amount. This transform is useful if you want to draw the same shape in different places.	X, Y
RotateTransform	Rotates your coordinate system. The shapes you draw normally are turned around a center point you choose.	Angle, CenterX, CenterY
ScaleTransform	Scales your coordinate system up or down so that your shapes are drawn smaller or larger. You can apply different degrees of scaling in the X and Y dimensions, thereby stretching or compressing your shape.	ScaleX, ScaleY, CenterX, CenterY
SkewTransform	Warps your coordinate system by slanting it a number of degrees. For example, if you draw a square, it becomes a parallelogram.	AngleX, AngleY, CenterX, CenterY
MatrixTransform	Modifies your coordinate system using matrix multiplication with the matrix you supply. This is the most complex option—it requires some mathematical skill.	Matrix
TransformGroup	Combines multiple transforms so they can all be applied at once. The order in which you apply trans-formations is important—it affects the final result. For example, rotating a shape (with RotateTransform) and then moving it (with TranslateTransform) sends the shape off in a different direction than if you move it and *then* rotate it.	N/A

Technically, all transforms use matrix math to alter the coordinates of your shape. However, using prebuilt transforms such as TranslateTransform, RotateTransform, ScaleTransform, and SkewTransform is far simpler than using the MatrixTransform and trying to work out the right matrix for the operation you want to perform. When you perform a series of transforms with TransformGroup, Silverlight fuses your transforms together into a single MatrixTransform, ensuring optimal performance.

Using a Transform

To transform an element, you set its RenderTransform property with the transform object you want to use. Depending on the type of transform you're using, you'll need to fill in different properties to configure it, as detailed in Table 34-4.

For example, if you're rotating an element, you need to use the RotateTransform and supply the angle in degrees. Here's an example that rotates a button clockwise by 25 degrees:

```
<Button Content="A Button">
  <Button.RenderTransform>
    <RotateTransform Angle="25"></RotateTransform>
```

```
  </Button.RenderTransform>
</Button>
```

When you rotate an element in this way, you rotate it about the element's origin (the top-left corner). If you want to rotate a shape around a different point, you can use the handy RenderTransformOrigin property. This property sets the center point using a proportional coordinate system that stretches from 0 to 1 in both dimensions. In other words, the point (0, 0) is designated as the top-left corner, and (1, 1) is the bottom-right corner. (If the shape region isn't square, the coordinate system is stretched accordingly.)

With the help of the RenderTransformOrigin property, you can rotate any element around its center point using markup like this:

```
<Button Content="One" Margin="5" RenderTransformOrigin="0.5,0.5">
  <Button.RenderTransform>
    <RotateTransform Angle="25"></RotateTransform>
  </Button.RenderTransform>
</Button>
```

This works because the point (0.5, 0.5) designates the center of the shape, regardless of its size.

■ **Tip** You can use values greater than 1 or less than 0 when setting the RenderTransformOrigin property to designate a point that appears outside the bounding box of your shape. For example, you can use this technique with a RotateTransform to rotate a shape in a large arc around a very distant point, such as (5, 5).

Animating a Transform

To use a transform in animation, the first step is to define the transform. (An animation can change an existing transform but not create a new one.) For example, imagine you want to allow a button to rotate. This requires the RotateTransform, which you can add like this:

```
<Button x:Name="cmd" Content="A Button" RenderTransformOrigin="0.5,0.5">
  <Button.RenderTransform>
    <RotateTransform x:Name="buttonTransform"></RotateTransform>
  </Button.RenderTransform>
</Button>
```

■ **Tip** You can easily use transforms in combination. In fact, it's easy—you simply need to use the TransformGroup to set the RenderTransform property. You can nest as many transforms as you need inside the TransformGroup. You'll see an example in the bomb game that's shown later in this chapter.

Now here's an animation that makes a button rotate when the mouse moves over it. It acts on the Button.RotateTransform object, and uses the target property Angle. The fact that the RenderTransform property can hold a variety of different transform objects, each with different properties, doesn't cause a problem. As long as you're using a transform that has an angle property, this animation will work.

```
<Storyboard x:Name="rotateStoryboard">
  <DoubleAnimation Storyboard.TargetName="buttonTransform"
   Storyboard.TargetProperty="Angle"
   To="360" Duration="0:0:0.8" RepeatBehavior="Forever"></DoubleAnimation>
</Storyboard>
```

The button rotates one revolution every 0.8 seconds and continues rotating perpetually. While the button is rotating, it's still completely usable—for example, you can click it and handle the Click event.

If you place this animation in the Resources collection of the page, you can trigger it when the user moves the mouse over the button:

```
private void cmd_MouseEnter(object sender, MouseEventArgs e)
{
    rotateStoryboard.Begin();
}
```

To stop the rotation, you can react to the MouseLeave event. At this point, you could stop the storyboard that performs the rotation, but this causes the button to jump back to its original orientation in one step. A better approach is to start a second animation that replaces the first. This animation leaves out the From property, which allows it to seamlessly rotate the button from its current angle to its original orientation in a snappy 0.2 seconds:

```
<Storyboard x:Name="unrotateStoryboard">
  <DoubleAnimation Storyboard.TargetElement="cmd.RenderTransform"
   Storyboard.TargetProperty="Angle" Duration="0:0:0.2"></DoubleAnimation>
</Storyboard>
```

Here's the event handler:

```
private void cmd_MouseLeave(object sender, MouseEventArgs e)
{
    unrotateStoryboard.Begin();
}
```

With a little more work, you can make these two animations and the two event handlers work for a whole stack of rotatable buttons, like the one shown in Figure 34-14. The trick is to handle the events of all the buttons with the same code, and dynamically assign the target of the storyboard to the current button using the Storyboard.SetTarget() method:

```
private void cmd_MouseEnter(object sender, MouseEventArgs e)
{
    rotateStoryboard.Stop();
    Storyboard.SetTarget(rotateStoryboard, ((Button)sender).RenderTransform);
    rotateStoryboard.Begin();
}

private void cmd_MouseLeave(object sender, MouseEventArgs e)
{
```

```
    unrotateStoryboard.Stop();
    Storyboard.SetTarget(unrotateStoryboard, ((Button)sender).RenderTransform);
    unrotateStoryboard.Begin();
}
```

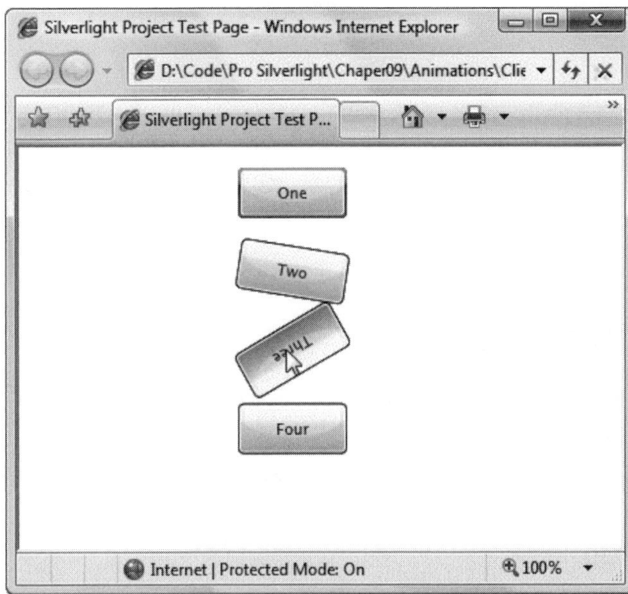

Figure 34-14. Using a render transform

There are two limitations to this approach. First, because the code reuses the same storyboards for all the buttons, there's no way to have two buttons rotating at once. For example, if you quickly slide the mouse over several buttons, the buttons you leave first might not rotate all the way back to their initial position, because the storyboard is commandeered by another button. If this behavior is a problem, you can code around it by creating the storyboards you need dynamically in code, as demonstrated with the falling squares example.

Using Web Services with Silverlight

The examples you've seen in this chapter have focused on the features of the Silverlight platform. The entry pages you've used haven't contained any additional content, and the ASP.NET website has been little more than a thin shell that serves out the real package—the client-side Silverlight application.

Although it's perfectly legitimate to have a website that includes Silverlight-only pages, there are other techniques that allow you to extend the interaction between the client-side Silverlight world and the server-side ASP.NET world.

Without a doubt, the most effective way for a Silverlight application to tap into server-side code is through web services. The basic idea is simple—you include a web service with your ASP.NET website, and your Silverlight application calls the methods in that web service. The web service code can perform server-side tasks, access server-side databases, and so on. With a little extra work, it can even use ASP.NET services like authentication and session state. Best of all, because the page isn't posted back, your Silverlight application continues running without interruption.

Silverlight applications support a variety of web service technologies, including SOAP-based services, simple REST services that return XML or JSON data, and full-featured WCF services that are built with .NET.

In this chapter, you'll concentrate on WCF (Windows Communication Foundation) services, which are the best choice for Silverlight applications. The other networking options are often more work, but they're useful if you need to access third-party web services that are outside your control.

Creating the Web Service

Much like the JavaScript in an ASP.NET AJAX page, Silverlight applications can call WCF services. To create a WCF service for a Silverlight application, right-click your ASP.NET website in the Solution Explorer and choose Add New Item. Choose the "Silverlight-enabled WCF Service" template, enter a file name, and click Add.

■ **Note** A Silverlight-enabled WCF service is a WCF service that supports basic HTTP binding (rather than the more stringent WS-* standards, which Silverlight doesn't support). Silverlight-enabled services can also access the HTTP context for the current request, which provides everything from cookies to caching. To interact with the current HTTP content, use the HttpContext.Current static property.

To add a new web service method, you simply add a new method to the code file, and make sure that it's decorated with the OperationContract attribute. For example, if you want to add a method that returns the current time on the server, you might modify the interface like this:

```
[ServiceContract]
[AspNetCompatibilityRequirements(RequirementsMode =
 AspNetCompatibilityRequirementsMode.Allowed)]
public class TestService
{
    [OperationContract]
    public DateTime GetServerTime()
    {
        return DateTime.Now;
    }
}
```

Adding a Web Reference

You consume a web service in a Silverlight application in much the same way that you consume one in a full-fledged.NET application. The first step is to create a proxy class by adding a Visual Studio web reference.

To add the web reference, follow these steps:

1. Right-click your Silverlight project in the Solution Explorer and choose Add Service Reference. The Add Service Reference dialog box will appear (see Figure 34-15).

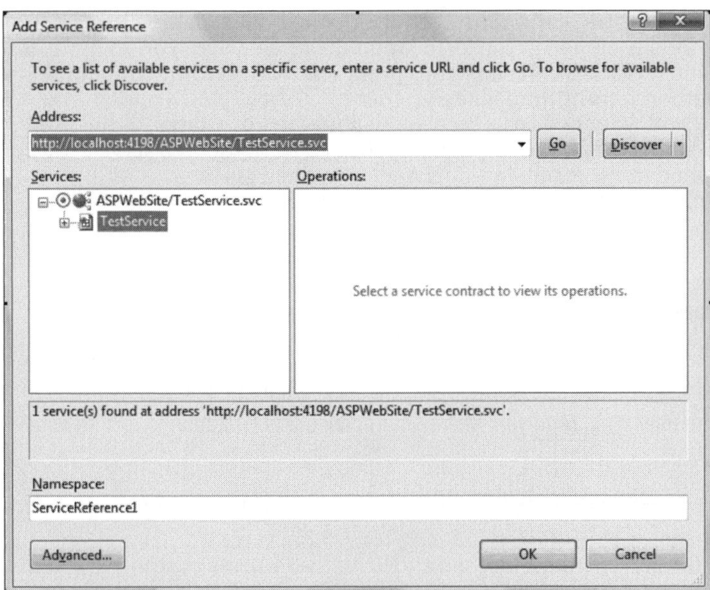

Figure 34-15. Adding a service reference

2. In the Address box, enter the URL that points to the web service and click Go. (Or, just click the Discover button to automatically find all the web services that are in your current solution.)

3. In the Namespace box, enter the C# namespace that Visual Studio should use for the automatically generated classes.

4. Click OK. Visual Studio will create a proxy class—a class that you can interact with to call your web service. The proxy class is named after the original web service class—for example, Visual Studio will create a proxy class named TestServiceClient for the TestService shown earlier. The proxy class contains methods that allow you to trigger the appropriate web service calls, and it takes care of the heavy lifting (creating the request message, sending it in an HTTP request, getting the response, and then notifying your code).

5. To see the file that contains the proxy class code, select the Silverlight project in the Solution Explorer, click the Show All Files button, expand the Service References node, the service reference, and the Reference.svcmap node inside, and open the Reference.cs file.

Calling the Web Service

To use the proxy class in a Silverlight page, open the code-behind file for your XAML page. Then import the namespace that you specified for the service reference in step 3. Assuming you used the namespace MyWebServer and your project is named MySilverlightProject, you'll need this statement:

```
using MySilverlightProject.MyWebServer;
```

In Silverlight, all web service calls must be asynchronous. That means you call a method to start the call (and send off the request). This method is named in the form MethodNameAsync(). For example, if your web service includes a method named GetServerTime(), your proxy class will provide a method named GetServerTimeAsync(). This method returns immediately.

After you call an asynchronous method, your code can carry on to perform other tasks, or the user can continue to interact with the application. When the response is received from the web service, the proxy will trigger an event, which is named in the form MethodNameCompleted (as in GetServerTimeCompleted). You must handle this event to process the results.

■ **Note** This two-part communication process means that it takes a bit more work to handle a web service call then to interact with an ordinary local object. However, it also ensures that developers create responsive Silverlight applications. After all, making an HTTP call to a web service can take as long as one minute (using the default timeout setting), so it's not safe to make the user wait. (And yes, Microsoft imposes this limitation to ensure your code can't give their platform a bad name.)

Here's how to call the TestService.GetServerTime() method shown earlier when a button is clicked:

```
private void cmdGetTime_Click(object sender, RoutedEventArgs e)
{
    // Create the proxy.
    TestServiceClient proxy = new TestServiceClient();

    // Attach an event handler to the completed event.
    proxy.GetServerTimeCompleted += new
      EventHandler<GetServerTimeCompletedEventArgs>(GetServerTimeCompleted);

    // Start the web service call.
    proxy.GetServerTimeAsync();
}
```

To get the results, you need to handle the completed event and examine the corresponding EventArgs object. When generating the proxy class, Visual Studio also creates a different EventArgs class for each method. The only difference is the Result property, which is typed to match the return value of the method. For example, the GetServerTime() method works in conjunction with a GetServerTimeCompletedEventArgs class that provides a DateTime object through its Result property.

When accessing the Result property for the first time, you need to use exception handling code. That's because this is the point where an exception will be thrown if the web service call failed—for example, if the server couldn't be found, the web method returned an error, or the connection timed out.

Here's an event handler that reads the result (the current date and time on the server) and displays it in a TextBlock:

```
private void GetServerTimeCompleted(object sender,
  GetServerTimeCompletedEventArgs e)
{
    try
    {
```

```
        lblTime.Text = e.Result.ToLongTimeString();
    }
    catch (Exception err)
    {
        lblTime.Text = "Error contacting web service";
    }
}
```

■ **Tip** Even though web service calls are performed on a background thread, there's no need to worry about thread marhsalling when the completed event fires. That's because the web service proxy ensures that the completed event fires on the main user interface thread, allowing you to access the controls in your page without worry.

By default, the web service proxy waits for one minute before giving up if it doesn't receive a response. You can configure the timeout length by using code like this before you make the web service call:

```
proxy.InnerChannel.OperationTimeout = TimeSpan.FromSeconds(30);
```

Configuring the Web Service URL

When you add a service reference, the automatically generated code includes the web service URL. As a result, you don't need to specify the URL when you create an instance of the proxy class.

However, this raises a potential problem. All web service URLs are fully qualified—relative paths aren't allowed. If you're using the test web server in Visual Studio, that means you'll run into trouble if you try to run your application at a later point, when the test web server has chosen a different port number. Similarly, you'll need to update the URL when you deploy your final application to a production web server.

You can solve this problem by regenerating the service reference, but it's usually easier to change the address dynamically in your code. To do so, you need to create a new EndpointAddress object with the appropriate URL, and then pass that as a constructor argument when creating an instance of the proxy class.

For example, the following code ensures that the web service call always works, no matter what port number the Visual Studio test web server chooses (assuming the web service is named TestService.svc and is placed in a website with the virtual directory named SilverlightApplication1.Web).

```
// Create the proxy.
TestServiceClient proxy = new TestServiceClient();

// Create a new URL for the TestService.svc service using the current port number.
proxy.Endpoint.Address = new EndpointAddress("http://localhost:" +
  HtmlPage.Document.DocumentUri.Port + "/SilverlightApplication1.Web/TestService.svc");
```

You could use similar code to create a URL based on the current Silverlight page, so that the web service continues to work no matter where you deploy it, so long as you keep the web service and Silverlight application together in the same web folder.

Cross-Domain Web Service Calls

Silverlight allows you to make web service calls to web services that are a part of the same website with no restrictions. Additionally, Silverlight allows you to call web services on other web services if they explicitly allow it with a policy file.

To make this possible, you must create a file named clientaccesspolicy.xml, and place that in the root of your website (for example, in the c:\inetpub\wwwroot directory of an IIS web server). The ClientAccessPolicy.xml file indicates what domains are allowed to access your web service. Here's an example that allows any Silverlight application that's been downloaded from any web server to access your website:

```
<?xml version="1.0" encoding="utf-8"?>
<access-policy>
  <cross-domain-access>
    <policy>
      <allow-from>
        <domain uri="*"/>
      </allow-from>
      <grant-to>
        <resource path="/" include-subpaths="true"/>
      </grant-to>
    </policy>
  </cross-domain-access>
</access-policy>
```

When you take this step, third-party Silverlight applications will be able to call your web services and make arbitrary HTTP requests (for example, download web pages). Ordinarily, neither task would be allowed in a Silverlight application. (Desktop applications and server-side applications face no such restrictions—no matter what policy file you create, they will be able to do everything an ordinary user can do, which means they can download any public content.)

Alternatively, you can limit to access to Silverlight applications that are running on web pages in specific domains. Here's an example that allows requests from Silverlight applications that are hosted at www.sompecompany.com or www.someothercompany.com:

```
<?xml version="1.0" encoding="utf-8"?>
<access-policy>
  <cross-domain-access>
    <policy>
      <allow-from http-request-headers="*">
        <domain uri="http://www.somecompany.com" />
        <domain uri="http://www.someothercompany.com" />
      </allow-from>
      <grant-to>
        <resource path="/" include-subpaths="true"/>
      </grant-to>
    </policy>
  </cross-domain-access>
</access-policy>
```

You can use wildcards in the domain names to allow subdomains. For example, *.somecompany.com allows requests from mail.somecompany.com, admin.somecompany.com, and so on.

Furthermore, you can selectively allow access to part of your website. Here's an example that allows Silverlight applications to access the services folder in your root web domain, which is presumably where you'll place all your cross-domain web services:

```
<?xml version="1.0" encoding="utf-8"?>
<access-policy>
  <cross-domain-access>
    <policy>
      <allow-from>
        <domain uri="*"/>
      </allow-from>
      <grant-to>
        <resource path="/services/" include-subpaths="true"/>
      </grant-to>
    </policy>
  </cross-domain-access>
</access-policy>
```

Custom Controls that use Silverlight

By this point, it may have occurred to you that crafty ASP.NET developers could devise custom ASP.NET controls that render themselves into Silverlight applications. For example, you could build a Silverlight version of the ASP.NET AdRotator control that renders a Silverlight-powered ad bar, suitable for inclusion on an ordinary ASP.NET page.

Unfortunately, this model isn't quite as simple as it seems at first. One challenge is the fact that Silverlight applications depend on separate resources, like XAML files. These files can be embedded in your ASP.NET assembly and retrieved when needed using the ASP.NET web resources model, but this design complicates life. Furthermore, you need a way to customize the Silverlight content based on the properties of the custom control. For example, you may need to examine properties set on the server control and use that to change the details in the embedded XAML. ASP.NET AJAX has possible solutions for this sort of challenge, but they're fairly involved and out of the scope of this chapter.

In the future, developers will get better tools that make this scenario—building custom ASP.NET controls that generate Silverlight content—easier and more practical. In the meantime, cutting-edge developers who are planning to experiment can check out http://msdn.microsoft.com/en-us/magazine/cc135987.aspx for an example that works with Silverlight 1.0.

Summary

In this chapter, you took a thorough look at Silverlight, a programming platform that runs in the browser and is modeled after .NET and WPF.

Silverlight is one of Microsoft's most closely followed new technologies. In fact, the relase of Silverlight 2 inspired more developer interest than virtually any other Microsoft product since .NET 1.0. Subsequent versions of Silverlight continue to build upon this framework and extend it with new features. Increasingly, Microsoft is closing the gap between rich WPF-based desktop applications and Silverlight-powered web content.

■ **Tip** In this chapter, you received a rapid tour that included some of Silverlight's most important features. However, there are entire feature areas that this chapter doesn't have room to cover, including styles, control templates, isolated storage, and data binding. To undertake a more comprehensive exploration of Silverlight, check out *Pro Silverlight 3 in C# 2010* (Apress, 2009).

Index

Special Characters

A

B

■ C

D

E

F

G

H

■ I

J

■ K

■ L

■ M

N

■ O

P

Q

R

S

U

■ V

■ W

X